PROPERTY OF
KEVIN D. RAY

The
Biblical
Expositor

THE BIBLICAL EXPOSITOR

The Living Theme of
The Great Book *with General and
Introductory Essays and Exposition
for each Book of the Bible*

Introduction by
BILLY GRAHAM

Consulting Editor
CARL F. H. HENRY

A. J. HOLMAN COMPANY
DIVISION OF J. B. LIPPINCOTT COMPANY
Philadelphia and New York

© 1960, 1973 by A. J. Holman Company

Published simultaneously in the
United States and Canada

Library of Congress Catalog Card Number: 60-5198

U.S. Library of Congress Cataloging in Publication Data

Main entry under title.

The Biblical expositor.

1. Bible—Commentaries. I. Henry, Carl
Ferdinand Howard, birth date   ed.
BS491.2.B5 1973   220.7   73-599
ISBN-0-87981-020-3

Contents

Contents

Introduction

I am delighted that *The Biblical Expositor* is being reissued in this new and more convenient one-volume format. The previous edition of this outstanding work has justifiably had wide distribution, and has been of inestimable value to thousands of Christians in understanding the Word of God more clearly.

The primary purpose of a Bible commentary should be to illuminate the meaning of the Bible as God's Word for today. This purpose is admirably accomplished by *The Biblical Expositor*. Each book of the Bible is clearly, yet simply, explained by some of the world's leading evangelical scholars. Helpful, also, are the introductory articles dealing with special aspects of the Bible and its application for today. I am especially impressed, however, with the way each contributor seeks to show the practical application of the Biblical text to practical Christian living.

From time to time the Billy Graham Evangelistic Association has reprinted various sections of *The Biblical Expositor* in *Decision Magazine*. Many have indicated that these studies have been very helpful in their personal understanding of the Word of God.

One of the greatest needs of our generation is for Christians to understand the Bible and apply it to everyday life. I pray that *The Biblical Expositor* will be even more widely circulated in this edition, and will thus help many to understand and apply the Bible. This is a valuable tool for every student of the Word of God.

BILLY GRAHAM

Montreat, N. C.
January 1973

The Living Word of God

WILBUR M. SMITH
Fuller Theo. / Moody

WHETHER A CERTAIN BOOK will live for generation after generation, century after century, cannot be predicted at the time the work is written, any more than any father and mother can predict with assurance that their child will live to an advanced age. An author may think and hope that his *magnum opus* has qualities that will assure its survival long after he has gone, but he would not dare announce such a hope.

With the Bible it is different. Over and over again it speaks of itself as a living book. For example, Peter declares that we are "begotten again not of corruptible seed but of incorruptible through the word of God, which liveth and abideth. For, all flesh is as grass, and all the glory thereof as the flower of grass. The grass withereth, and the flower falleth: but the word of the Lord abideth for ever" (I Pet. 1:23-25). The Apostle Paul speaks of "the word of life" (Phil. 2:16); Stephen refers to the Old Testament as "the living oracles" (Acts 7:38); and our Lord said of His own words, "they are spirit and they are life" (Jn. 6:63).

In this prefatory word I would like to consider the qualities and characteristics of the Bible which make it the Living Word, and to note how its influence testifies to the fact that it is in truth the Living Word. If in the phrase of Peter, "the word of God which liveth," the impersonal pronoun *which* is changed to the personal pronoun *who*, we discover the first quality that makes this the Living Word—it is *the word of God Who liveth and abideth forever*. There are great virtues and unique qualities in such classics as Homer's *Iliad*, Plato's *Dialogues*, Augustine's *City of God*, Dante's *Divine Comedy*, Shakes-

xi

peare's *Hamlet,* and Goethe's *Faust,* and many of the problems of our contemporary life, our temptations, and even our sins, are confronted by these works. But whatever inspiration, quickening and enrichment of mind, and stirring of heart some may find in these works, their authors are dead: they were truly contemporary only with their own age. To be specific, let us take the exquisite love letters of Robert Browning and Elizabeth Barrett. They throb with the love that so completely possessed these two noble hearts. But Robert Browning and Elizabeth Barrett are not living today: they cannot address these words to a new generation; they cannot keep their promises, nor do anything to carry out their expressed desires.

God, Whose Word we have in the Bible, is from everlasting to everlasting. The counsels of the Lord stand fast; He is able to bring to pass whatsoever He has foreordained (Is. 46:10, 11). When we open the pages of the Scriptures and read His words, whether of warning or exhortation, of comfort or assurance, of promise or judgment, it is the living God who still speaks. After the decease of his beloved, Robert Browning could not say, "She *loves* me," but the Apostle John could say sixty years after the ascension of the Lord, "He *loveth* me" (Rev. 1:5). Christ can be called *Immanuel,* "God with us," only if He lives forever, for and with His people. No person mentioned within the covers of Holy Writ could ever say, except the Lord Jesus, "Lo, I am with you always even unto the end of the age" (Mt. 28:20). When we open the book of the Word of God, it lives for us as the pages of no other book could ever live, because its Author, and the One of Whom it continually speaks, is the living and everlasting God.

Here is the appropriate place, I think, for recording an incident that occurred when I was in my late teens. To my knowledge, it has never been referred to in print by anyone else present on the occasion. In 1914, Sir William Ramsay came to Chicago to deliver three series of lectures: in the morning at the University of Chicago, in the afternoon at the Central Y.M.C.A., and in the evening, at Moody Bible Institute. As all know, Ramsay was a true believer and a staunch defender of the faith. In his early days he was one of the most brilliant classical scholars in Great Britain. This particular evening, he allowed his classical lore to push aside for a moment a great Pauline truth with which he certainly had been acquainted for years. He casually used the phrase, "the divine spark in every man." When Professor Ramsay had completed his lecture, Dr. James M. Gray, then president of Moody Institute, in his usual, gracious manner, felt compelled to make this statement before pronouncing the benediction: "I am sure our learned guest would not want anyone to leave this auditorium tonight with any false idea in his mind. There is *no* divine spark in every man. We are all dead in trespasses and sins by nature, and remain such until we are quickened and born anew by the Holy Spirit." And so it is. All of classical literature with which Sir William was so well acquainted was powerless to communicate to the men and women of the Mediterranean world deliverance from the dread power of sin, a true love for Almighty God, and the hope of a blessed life to come. These great realities are communicated to the hearts of men only by the touch of the Living Word of the living God.

Secondly, the Bible is the Living Word because from beginning to end *it speaks of and shows the Way of Life,* even life eternal. At the very beginning of the Biblical record of human history, we read of "the tree of life," a tree which reappears after history is concluded and eternity has begun (Gen. 2:9; 3:22, 24; Rev. 2:7; 22:2, 14, 19). Even the profound interpretation of some of the deeper aspects of the law of the Lord, the Book of Deuteronomy, repeatedly emphasizes the fact that the law, the commandments, the ordinances of God, were given that men might *live:* "Ye shall walk in all the ways which the Lord your God hath commanded you, that ye may live, and that it may be well with you, and that ye may prolong your days in the land which ye shall possess" (Deut. 5:33; see also 4:1; 8:1; 30:6, 16, 19).

Our Lord came that we might have *life,* and that we might have it more abundantly (Jn. 10:10). All the Epistles of the New Testament stress the fact that those who embrace with faith the truths concerning Christ as Saviour walk in *newness of life* (Rom. 6:4). The tragic pronouncement which no man has ever been able to contradict, "the wages of sin is death," is accompanied by the promise, "but the gift of God is eternal life through Christ Jesus our Lord" (Rom. 6:23). Thus all who bear witness to this Gospel are spoken of as those who are "holding forth *the word of life*" (Phil. 2:16). Our Lord himself is more significantly called "the Word of life" (I Jn. 1:1), and the Bible declares that it is only as this living Word is imparted to us that we experience life in the fulness with which God intended it. The primary assertion of this truth is made in the familiar words of Deuteronomy, "All the commandments which I command thee this day shall ye observe to do, that ye may live, and multiply, and go in and possess the land. . . . [He] fed thee with manna, which thou knewest not, neither did thy fathers know; that he might make thee know that man doth not live by bread only, but by every word that proceedeth out of the mouth of the Lord doth man live" (8:1-3). These words our Lord himself quoted in the first of the three temptations in the Judaean wilderness (Mt. 4:4).

Moreover, the Bible is the Living Word because *in its pages the deepest problems of life are frankly faced, and the solutions to them clearly presented.* The four basic problems in any serious philosophical consideration of man in relation to this universe in which he lives are (*1*) the certainty and character of God, (*2*) the origin of the universe, (*3*) the deliverance from the power of sin, including reconciliation to a holy God, and (*4*) the ultimate destiny of mankind. A vast library of books has been written by men compelled to face these problems, but none except this Book of Divine Revelation has any final and satisfying answer. All the philosophies of the world have not been able to give us a true knowledge of God, as the Athenians confessed.

When science has completed all of its investigations, it will still have to admit that it knows nothing of the actual origin of this universe, and man must still rest upon that initial revelation of God as the Creator of the world, without Whom "was not anything made that was made." Every major world religion has felt constrained to say something to wretched, hopeless, fear-stricken mankind regarding sin which enslaves men, in which we are born, and from which, humanly, we are never able to escape. But no volume has offered the true solution to this problem except this Living Word of God, which presents the living Lamb of God Who came to take away the sin of the world and Who put away sin by the sacrifice of Himself (Jn. 1:29; Heb. 9:26). We are cleansed from sin by His precious blood, and will ultimately be delivered from all sin and its consequences by His perfect, eternal redemption.

As to the future, where can one turn for real illumination? No man knows what a day will bring forth—never more true than in the days of this generation. How unrewarding is a study of the great writers of the nineteenth century when one is looking for *hope* in an hour such as this in which we live! It is not in Ruskin or Carlyle, Mommsen or Romain Roland; nor in the gloomy pages of Karl Marx, Nietzsche and Bertrand Russell. No man wrote more about the hopes of humanity in the last half century than H. G. Wells, but his last book, a shriek of agony at the dropping of the atomic bomb, is suggestively entitled *Man at the End of His Tether*. When toward the close of their remarkable work, *The Science of Life*, Wells and Julian Huxley felt compelled to say a word about immortality, they acknowledged, "Upon the continuity of any individual consciousness after bodily cessation and disintegration, *The Science of Life* has no word of assurance" (Vol. II, p. 1434).

As long as man yearns for an ultimate triumph of righteousness, deliverance from the fear of death, a life of glory to come, freedom from all the miseries of this life and the completion of an all-embracing redemptive work, he will find his hope alone in the Living Word. In this Word of hope is revealed the Christ Who has defeated sin and overcome death, Who will make all of His enemies His footstool, and Who will reign in righteousness forever. It is as true today for modern man as it was for David three thousand years ago—"In His Word do I hope" (Ps. 119:114).

There are other problems in life, of course, besides these. In all such perplexities, the wrong solution brings misery; and the right solution, joy and freedom. The Holy Scriptures reveal the commandments of God for man's daily experiences, external and internal: guidance for our relationships with one another in the family, in the world of business, in the state, in the church, in all social fellowship. In this Word, all men are equal in the sight of God; redemption is offered without price to male and female, Greek and barbarian, rich and poor, old and young, brown, black, yellow and white. When Bertrand Russell warned a few years ago at Columbia University that the only hope for this world was for men to act according to the principles of Christian love, he confessed—even if unwittingly—that the secret of right living was not found in any of the great philosophical tomes with which he was so thoroughly acquainted, but in this Living Word of God. Our world is undergoing convulsive changes. We are having to create new vocabularies to keep pace with events that are taking place. The boundaries of nations are changing, systems of government are changing, ways of life are changing, but the deep problems of life are the same, and we find their divine, and therefore right, solution in this living revelation of a perfect and ever-living God.

In a number of ways this Word proves itself to be dominated by this attribute of life. Primarily, *the Word communicates life*. Let us return to the passage which we cited at the outset: "Having been begotten again, not of corruptible seed, but of incorruptible, through the word of God which liveth and abideth." The apostle is here but interpreting the words of the Lord Himself, when, in the famous parable of the wheat and tares, He said, "The seed is the Word of God" (Lk. 8:11). The virtue, the mystery, the significance of any seed is that it consists of living substance. It is able to reproduce the plant or animal from which it came: the word here, *sperma*, has entered vitally into our modern scientific nomenclature. As we have our first life from the sperm of our human parents, so we are born the second time by a power containing and communicating divine life, namely, the seed of the Word which proceeds from the living God. This is why the angel of the Lord, opening the prison doors for the apostles, could command them to "go, stand and speak in the temple to the people all the words of this life" (Acts 5:20).

The written Word of God and the incarnate Word of God are intimately related: the written Word reveals the incarnate Word. Through embracing by faith the incarnate Word of God, Christ our Saviour, we are born again, we receive eternal life, and this life is freely offered to us in the written and preached Word of God. From the day of Pentecost to this hour, and until the end of this age, millions upon millions have known and will know what it is to be delivered from the power of death and to possess eternal life, because they have received the seed of this Living Word, and there then begins to be formed in them anew the image of the Son of God.

The Scriptures are the Living Word of God because they have the capacity for *nourishing* the souls of men. How often in the magnificent 119th Psalm David cries out, "My soul cleaveth unto the dust: quicken thou me according to thy word" (vv. 20, 25, 107, 149, 154, 156, 159). When Christ called Himself the bread of life (Jn. 6:35, 45) He meant, of course, that we are to feed upon Him, that, for believers, He is the source of constant nourishment and strength. This is experienced in the Lord's Supper in part, but I believe principally and more constantly in our partaking of the Word of God. A healthy follower of Christ says with the prophet of old, "Thy words were found and I did eat them; and thy words were unto me a joy and the rejoicing of my heart: for I am called by thy name, O Lord, God of hosts" (Jer. 15:16). If we have treasured and read over and over again telegrams and letters from those we dearly love, and have found new life, buoyancy, courage and strength in communications from the heart of another to our heart, how much more essential is it that we, the children of God, should continually nourish our souls in that Living Word which proceeds from the mind and heart of a holy and loving God.

It is possible, we grant, to become moved and stimulated, even temporarily exalted, by reading some of the noblest pages of literature; for example, Milton's description of the inner feelings of Adam and Eve immediately after their fall, as recorded in Paradise Lost. Some of us know what it is to pace the floor in excitement after reading some great page of Ruskin, or to be sent to our knees by a page in the biography of some noble servant of God. But, after all, these authors are dead. Though their voice is heard in these pages, they are not aware of us, they do not know our needs, we cannot communicate with them, and they cannot give us the guidance of their wisdom. In contrast, the moment we open the Word of God, we are assured that God stands behind its promises. By reading, believing, and meditating upon these precious promises, we are "made partakers of the divine nature" (II Pet. 1:4). One may spend a lifetime in the study of Shakespeare, yet not develop the genius of Shakespeare in his own soul; and as for the character of Shakespeare, who would want it? God intended, however, that as we feed upon the Living Word, in which the Incarnate Word is revealed, we shall be growing up into the fulness of manhood in Christ Jesus, knowing that we have been foreordained to be made conformable to His image (Eph. 4:13; Rom. 8:29). This Living Word of God is the indispensable source of nourishment for the new life of God which we have in our souls.

The qualities of continuous life found in the Word of God and its capacity for quickening the lives of men and women in succeeding generations can be demonstrated by the history and influence of almost any page of the Holy Scriptures. From the sixty-six books of the Bible, I have selected for illustration, the Book of Exodus. The event so dramatically unfolded in its opening chapters, the deliverance of the children of Israel from their Egyptian bondage, is referred to as a cause for encouragement and hope, as an incentive to confidence in God, and to holiness of life, more than 140 times in the Old Testament alone! Within his own lifetime, less than forty years after the great event, Moses could exhort this nation about to enter the Promised Land with these words: "Hath God assayed to go and take him a nation from the midst of another nation, by trials, by signs, and by wonders, and by war, and by a mighty hand, and by an outstretched arm, and by great terrors, according to all that Jehovah your God did for you in Egypt before your eyes? . . . And because he loved thy fathers, therefore he chose their seed after them, and brought thee out with his presence, with his great power, out of Egypt. . . . Know therefore this day, and lay it to thy heart, that the Lord He is God in heaven above and upon the earth beneath: there is none else" (Deut. 4:34, 37, 39).

In the sixth chapter of Deuteronomy, which contains the Shema and the exhortation regarding the word of God in the heart of the redeemed, Moses says in conclusion, "When thy son asketh thee in time to come, saying, What mean the testimonies, and the statutes, and the ordinances, which the Lord our God hath commanded you? Then thou shalt say unto thy son, We were Pharaoh's bondmen in Egypt; and the Lord brought us out of Egypt with a mighty hand: and the Lord showed signs and wonders, great and sore, upon Egypt, upon Pharaoh, and upon all his house before our eyes; and he brought us out from thence, that he might bring us in, to give us the land which he sware unto our fathers" (6:20–23). Observe that the exhortation begins, "These words which I command thee this day shall be upon thy heart" (v. 6).

This miraculous deliverance is spoken of again and again by Joshua, by the author of Judges, in the two Books of Samuel and frequently in the Kings and Chronicles. (The references are too numerous to give in complete form; the following are only suggestive: Josh. 5:4–6; 24:5–7; Judg. 6:8, 13; I Sam. 12:6, 8; II Chron. 6:5; 7:22.) In his prophetic prayer uttered at the time of the dedication of the temple, Solomon says, "For they be thy people, and thine inheritance, which thou broughtest forth out of Egypt, from the midst of the furnace of iron; that thine eyes may be open unto the supplication of thy servant, and unto the supplication of thy people Israel, to hearken unto them whensoever they cry unto thee. For thou didst separate them from among all the peoples of the earth, to be thine inheritance, as thou spakest by Moses thy servant, when thou broughtest our fathers out of Egypt, O Lord God" (I Kings 8:51–53). On at least seven different occasions, Jeremiah used the Exodus records of God's delivering His people from Egypt in his unheeded warnings and exhortations; for example, "Thus saith the Lord of Hosts . . . For I spake not unto your fathers nor commanded them in the day that I brought them out of the land of Egypt, concerning burnt-offerings or sacrifices: but this thing I commanded them, saying, Hearken unto my voice, and I will be your God, and ye shall be my people; and walk ye in all the way that I command you, that it may be well with you. But they hearkened not, nor inclined their ear, but walked in their own counsels and in the stubbornness of their evil heart, and went backward, and not forward" (Jer. 7:21–24; see especially the use of Ex. 21:2 in Jer. 34:14–17).

Daniel, in fervent prayer, pled with God as the One who had redeemed Israel: "And now, O Lord our God, that hast brought thy people forth out of the land of Egypt with a mighty hand, and hast gotten thee renown, as at this day; we have sinned, we have done wickedly" (9:15). The priests and the Levites in Jerusalem after the Exile petitioned God as their deliverer from Egypt (Neh. 9:9) and in the same prayer claimed the mercy of God as manifested in the time of the making of the golden calf: "Yea, when they had made them a molten calf, and said, This is thy God that brought thee up out of Egypt, and had wrought great provocations; yet thou in thy manifold mercies forsookest them not in the wilderness: the pillar of cloud departed not from over them by day, to lead them in the way; neither the pillar of fire by night, to show them light, and the way, wherein they should go" (Neh. 9:18, 19).

After "the four hundred silent years," during which no prophetic voice was heard in Israel, the Book of Exodus continued to speak as the time for the advent of our Lord had arrived. Christ Himself, in answering the Sadducees on the vital doctrine of the resurrection, reminds His interrogators that their own Torah, the one portion of the Old Testament which they believed to be truly inspired of God, testified to their error in denying the resurrection: "But as touching the dead, that they are raised; have ye not read in the book of Moses, in the place concerning the bush, how God spake unto him, saying, I am the God of Abraham, and the God of Isaac, and the God of Jacob? He is not the God of the dead, but of the living: ye do greatly err" (Mk. 12:26, 27; from Ex. 3:2–6). More than one-third of Stephen's speech, leading to his martyrdom, is devoted to events described in the Book of Exodus (Acts 7:17–36). The familiar central pronouncement concerning Israel, "Now therefore, if ye will obey my voice indeed, and keep my covenant, then ye shall be mine own possession from among all peoples: for all the earth is mine: and ye shall be unto me a kingdom of priests, and a holy nation" (Ex. 19:5, 6) is applied by the Apostle Peter to the followers of the Lord Jesus (I Pet. 2:5, 9).

To mention only one reference in the New Testament to the Ten Commandments, Paul quotes directly from Exodus 20:12 when giving instructions in the conduct of a true Christian home: "Honor thy father and mother (which is the first commandment with promise), that it may be well with thee, and thou mayest live long on the earth" (Eph. 6:2, 3). The same apostle, in speaking of spiritual gifts, refers to that experience in the life of Moses when, coming down from Mount Sinai, his countenance was radiant with the glory of God (II Cor. 3:7, 13; from Ex. 34:33). The ninth chapter of the Epistle to the Hebrews is hardly more than a Christian consideration of the significance of the objects of, and service in the Tabernacle as recorded in Exodus 24:6–8; 25:8–39; 26:31–33; 30:10; 31:18. The words of the Lord to Moses as he was about to construct the tabernacle (Ex. 25:40) are repeated in Hebrews 8:5; the early experiences of Moses, preceding the Exodus, are summarized with profound spiritual insight in Hebrews 11:23–27, and the exhortations in the Epistle to the Hebrews are sealed with the solemn warning, "Our God is a consuming fire" (12:29; from Ex. 19:16, 19).

This vital, inspiring influence of the Book of Exodus does not cease with the close of the New Testament writings, but continues without interruption century after century. In the writings of the Church Fathers of the first two centuries following the close of the Apostolic Age, *there are over 450 references to the Book of Exodus alone* (passages are quoted from thirty-seven of the forty chapters of Exodus, and Chapter 23, significantly, is referred to thirty-four different times). The use of Exodus in Augustine is even more vital. Let us here confine ourselves to but one verse from Exodus, 22:20, and to one book of Augustine, his epochal *City of God*. In rebuking the Platonists for giving honor to angels, he says, "If any immortal power, then, no matter with what virtue endowed, loves us as himself, he must desire that we find our happiness by submitting ourselves to Him, in submission to whom he himself finds happiness. If he does not worship God, he is wretched, because deprived of God; if he worships God, he cannot wish to be worshipped in God's stead. On the contrary, these higher powers acquiesce heartily in the divine sentence in which it is written, 'He that sacrificeth unto any god, save unto the Lord only, he shall be utterly destroyed' (Ex. 22:20)" (Book X, Chap. 3). "From that heavenly city, in which God's will is the intelligible and unchangeable law, from that heavenly council-chamber—for they sit in counsel regarding us—that holy Scripture, descended to us by the ministry of angels, in which it is written, 'He that sacrificeth unto any god, save unto the Lord only, he shall be utterly destroyed'—this Scripture, this law, these precepts, have been confirmed by such miracles, that it is sufficiently evident to whom these immortal and blessed spirits, who desire us to be like themselves, wish us to sacrifice" (Book X, Chap. 7).

Augustine returns to this passage toward the end of his argument: "He must be an uncommonly stupid, or a shamelessly contentious person, who has read through the foregoing books to this point, and can yet question whether the Romans served wicked and impure demons. But, not to speak of their character, it is written in the law of the true God, 'He that sacrificeth unto any god save unto the Lord only, he shall be utterly destroyed.' He, therefore, who uttered so menacing a commandment decreed that no worship should be given either to good or bad gods" (Book XIX, Chap. 21). "God, whom the Hebrew sages worshipped, forbids sacrifices to be offered even to the holy angels of heaven and divine powers, whom we, in this our pilgrimage, venerate and love as our most blessed fellow-citizens. For in the law which God gave to His Hebrew people He utters this menace, as in a voice of thunder: 'He that sacrificeth unto any god, save unto the Lord only, he shall be utterly destroyed,' " (Book XIX, Chap. 23).

Passing over the Middle Ages and coming down to the Reformation, we can say that Luther not only found the Book of Exodus throbbing with life, but at times he was really overwhelmed with it, as the following words from his *Table Talk* testify: "We must remain scholars here; we cannot sound the depth of one single verse in Scripture; we get hold but of the A.B.C. and that imperfectly. . . . I have many times essayed thoroughly to investigate the ten commandments, but at the very outset, 'I am the Lord thy God,' I stuck fast; that very one word *I* put me to a non-plus. He that has but one word of God before him, and out of that one word cannot make a sermon, can never be a preacher."

While in the period of the Reformation, we must look into that greatest of all theological compendiums of that age, Calvin's *Institutes of the Christian Religion*. To an exposition of the Ten Commandments, Calvin devotes almost one hundred pages (Book II, Chap. VIII. It is most interesting to note that one of the greatest theological works yet published in America, the *Systematic Theology* of Charles Hodge, gives over two hundred pages to this same

portion of the Word of God in the final volume, III, pp. 259-465).
On the subject of idolatry, Calvin again and again quotes from
Exodus, particularly 25:17; 32:1–6; 33:11; 34:6 (Book I, Chaps. X,
XI). Even in discussing the symbolical meaning of the words of
institution of the Lord's Supper, he thoroughly investigates Exodus
4:2–4; 7:10–12 (Book IV, Chap. XVII. 15). Calvin's remarks on
the sovereignty of God in hardening the hearts of men cannot be
improved upon in a discussion of Exodus 8:15 and 11:3 (Book I,
Chap. XVIII. 2; Book II, Chap. IV. 6). These are but a few of the references to Exodus in this epochal work, and for over three centuries
men have been considering these ancient passages because Calvin
found them alive with abiding truths for the Christian.

The Decalogue was given more attention in the great catechisms
of the Reformation and subsequent generations than any other one
theme. In the Shorter Catechism, drawn up by the Westminster
Assembly in the seventeenth century, of 107 questions, 43 are based
upon the Decalogue (Questions 40 to 82). Questions 43 and 44, with
answers, read as follows: "Q. What is the preface to the ten commandments? A. The preface to the ten commandments is in these
words: 'I am the Lord thy God, which have brought thee out of the
land of Egypt, out of the house of bondage.' Q. What doth the preface to the ten commandments teach us? A. The preface to the ten
commandments teacheth us, That because God is the Lord, and our
God, and Redeemer, therefore we are bound to keep all his commandments."

The legal codes of Britain rest upon the Decalogue. King Alfred,
the greatest of all the early kings in Britain, issued a legal code near
the end of the ninth century—the first legal document ever compiled, as far as we know, in that land—arranged in three sections:
the Introduction, the Laws of Alfred Proper, and the Laws of Ine.
The Introduction consists of two parts, the first of which is historical,
based on the Mosaic law. *The Cambridge History of English Literature* comments: "The insertions from the Mosaic law give a universal
character to Alfred's Code. They are rendered somewhat freely, large
portions of the Latin texts being omitted, and other portions added;
thus Exodus 22:7, 8, reads in Alfred's Code, 'If anyone entrusts his
property to his friend: if he shall steal it, let him pay double; if he
know not who has stolen it, let him excuse himself'" (Vol. I, p. 109).
The laws of our own nation relative to kidnapping are based upon

the words, "He that stealeth a man and selleth him, or if he be found in his hand, he shall surely be put to death" (Ex. 21:16).

For over three thousand years, the Jewish people have rigidly and hopefully celebrated the Passover, the details for which are set forth in Exodus 12. For example, in the *American Jewish World* for April 15, 1949, the article by Rabbi Israel Gerstein, "Passover, Festival of Freedom," concludes: "Passover 5709 will be an exhilarating experience to all who enter into its spirit wholeheartedly, for it will commemorate not alone Yetsias Mitsrayim but also Yetsias Europe, the exodus from Europe which is going on under our very eyes. Passover will give us a means to express our joy with which the heart is brimful at the miraculous event which the rebirth of Israel as a nation constitutes, and it will enable us to view it in its true perspective, namely, as another act in the drama which began way back there on that first Passover, for the same God Who redeemed Israel from Egyptian slavery has redeemed it from homelessness today. Passover will also recall to our leaders in Israel that on the way to the Land of the Fathers in ancient days, our people stopped off at Mount Sinai, where it received the Code which was to guide its life on the land. The experience at Sinai was a necessary prerequisite to success in its own homeland, for true freedom can be attained by the Jew only when he patterns his life after the exalted teachings of the Torah."

How many poems and dramas written in all the principal European languages, as well as Hebrew, have taken their inspiration from the momentous events recorded in the Exodus. Every large art gallery in Europe, and in Britain, has more than one painting by a famous artist on a theme from some passage in these forty chapters. Two of William Cowper's influential Olney Hymns were derived from the Book of Exodus, "Jehovah-Rophi," from Chapter 15, and "Jehovah-Nissi" from 17:15.

We turn from these examples of influence upon nations and peoples to instances of the influence of passages from this one book upon individual lives. Writing in the journal of his first voyage under date of September 23, 1492, Columbus said, "Thus the high sea was very necessary to me, such as had not appeared but in the time of the Jews when they went out of Egypt and murmured against Moses, who delivered them out of captivity." The Elizabethan Medal, commemorating the defeat of the Spanish Armada, bore this inscription from Exodus 15:10, "He blew with his wind and they were scattered." On the seal selected for the United States at the time of the

Declaration of Independence, by a committee consisting of Franklin, Adams and Jefferson, the design represented the Egyptians drowning in the Red Sea while Moses was leading the Israelites to freedom, and the motto read, "Rebellion to tyrants is obedience to God."

From the 39th chapter, the account of the erection of the tabernacle, Milton, in his monumental *Paradise Lost*, penetrates to the divine purpose for the building of the tabernacle with the following words:

> Thus laws and rites
> Established, such delight hath God in men
> Obedient to His will that He voutsafes
> Among them to set up His tabernacle—
> The Holy One with mortal men to dwell.
> By His prescript a sanctuary is framed
> Of cedar, overlaid with gold; therein
> An ark, and in the ark His testimony,
> The records of His covenant; over these
> A mercy-seat of gold, between the wings
> Of two bright Cherubim; before Him burn
> Seven lamps, as in a zodiac representing
> The heavenly fires. Over the tent a cloud
> Shall rest by day, a fiery gleam by night,
> Save when they journey; and at length they come,
> Conducted by His Angel, to the land
> Promised to Abraham and his seed.

When Ruskin was a small boy, his mother insisted on his memorizing "every syllable accurately" seventeen chapters of the Bible, in addition to eight Psalms. Of the six chapters of the Old Testament which he memorized, two were from the Book of Exodus, Chapters 15 and 20. Looking back upon those days, Ruskin at fifty-five years of age said that his mother's insistence that he memorize these chapters "established my soul in life. Truly, though I have picked up the elements of a little further knowledge—in mathematics, meterology, and the like in after life—and owe not a little to the teaching of many people, this material installation of my mind in that property of chapters I count very confidently the most precious and on the whole the one essential part of all my education. For the chapters became indeed strictly conclusive and productive to me in all modes of thought" (Fors Clavigera, Letter 42, June, 1874; in Ruskin's *Works*, Vol. XXVIII, pp. 101-102).

In the same generation, another Englishman lived on the other side of the world in striking contrast to the luxury and aristocratic intelligentsia of Ruskin. One of the most consecrated missionaries of the nineteenth century, James Gilmour, alone among the Chinese and Mongolians, subsisting on native food in the meanest quarters, burdened for souls and seeing very few conversions, found comfort in the Book of Exodus. When the London Missionary Society rebuked him for the extremely severe life of self-discipline which he compelled himself to follow, Gilmour said, "I feel called to go through all this sort of thing and feel perfectly secure in God's hands. It is no choosing of mine, but His; and following His lead, I have as much right to expect special provision to be made for me as the Israelites of old had in the matters of the Red Sea, the manna and water in the desert, the crossing of Jordan and the fall of Jericho."

In 1866 when the China Inland Mission was beginning to experience a phenomenal growth, Hudson Taylor found unusual meaning in Exodus 36:6, 7. The overwhelming response to an appeal for two thousand pounds for supplying new missionaries with equipment and passage to China prompted Taylor to write, "We were reminded of the difficulty of Moses and of the proclamation he had to send throughout the Camp to prepare no more for the building of the Tabernacle, as the gifts in hand were more than sufficient. We are convinced that if there were *less* solicitation for money and *more* dependence upon the power of the Holy Ghost and the deepening of spiritual life, the experience would be a common one in every branch of Christian work."

The thrice-elected Governor of Illinois during the time of the Civil War, Richard Golesby, was at one time much discouraged with the progress of the war. When the Union armies were being steadily driven back, he sent a melancholy letter to the White House, in which he told the President that he thought all was lost. When the letter came, Abraham Lincoln sent this startling telegram to Springfield: "Dear Dick: Read Exodus 14:13: 'Fear ye not, stand still and see the salvation of the Lord.'—Abraham Lincoln."

A recent book by Andrew Drummond, *German Protestantism since Luther,* contains the following relevant paragraph: "The relief of poverty was a subject that engaged the sympathetic attention of active Christians in Germany, who had heard of the work of Dr. Chalmers in Glasgow. In 1852 a town councillor of Elberfeld, named Daniel von der Heydt, was reading his Bible; impressed with Jethro's advice that Moses should delegate his authority to assistants, he applied this idea to the problem of poverty. Voluntary helpers were to be assigned the task of visiting a group of poor families and taking an interest in their welfare. Neighbourly supervision, inspired by Christian kindness, was a contrast to impersonal, official routine. This carefully graded method, co-operating with the public authorities, was adopted by many cities and was particularly successful in Elberfeld and Leipzig. Self-respect and good citizenship were thus promoted."

This marvelous Word of God has so quickened men that, by the inspiration it has communicated, the finest art and the most stirring music have been created. By this Word men and women through the ages have been impelled to suffer and even to die for Christ. Around this book, from that Easter Sunday afternoon on the Emmaus road, when the Lord opened the Scriptures to the two disciples, to this hour, millions of men and women, boys and girls, have gathered every Lord's Day, and each week day. As all human beings come to the table day by day to eat and drink for the necessary nourishing of their bodies, because that of which they are partaking is mysteriously transformed in their bodies to all that makes for vigor of life, so also around this Living Word do all true children of God continue to gather, that understanding and believing its revealed truths, they may, in their inner man, go from strength to strength.

I would propose one other testimony to the fact that this Bible is the Living Word, that is, *its inexhaustibleness.* Humanly speaking, there is nothing quite so inexhaustible in the world as the living phenomena of nature. In spite of all the wonderful discoveries in biology in the last century—many of them in our own half-century —such as the chromosome, the whole concept of genes, the molecular structure of the various parts of the body, and the mysteries of the blood that flows in our veins, there are still many more things to be learned from this seemingly unfathomable reservoir of biological lore. I recall once being taken through the Mellon Institute in Pittsburgh by a friend who was himself working on the subject of wheat flour there. He showed me an entire shelf of books on this subject, and then told me that there were two other scientists in that institution engaged in further research into the mysteries of this white powdery substance called wheat flour. As these living phenomena of nature seem to be inexhaustible in their innumerable facets of biological laws and truths, so this Living Word of God is found to be inexhaustible. The more we study it, the more do we realize what fathomless treasures are yet to be uncovered in these pages.

No one has witnessed to this more ably than the learned Augustine, who, in a letter to his son in A.D. 412, wrote, "Such is the depth of the Christian Scriptures, that even if I were attempting to study them and nothing else from early boyhood to decrepit old age, with the utmost leisure, the most unwearied zeal, and talents greater than I have, I would be still daily making progress in discovering their treasures; not that there is so great difficulty in coming through them to know the things necessary to salvation, but when any one has accepted these truths with the faith that is indispensable as the foundation of a life of piety and uprightness, so many things which are veiled under manifold shadows of mystery remain to be inquired into by those who are advancing in the study, and so great is the depth of wisdom not only in the words in which these have been expressed, but also in the things themselves. . . ."

Many phrases in the Book of Exodus have entered into the literature of Europe, and our own English literature. Repeated hundreds of times and used in innumerable ways are such phrases as "making bricks without straw," "the burning bush," "the destroying angel," "the pillar of fire," "the Holy of Holies," and, as in the great oratorio, "Let my people go." The mysterious word *manna* has had such marked influence upon English literature that the *Oxford English Dictionary* is compelled to give more than two full columns to a discussion of its uses from the time of King Alfred in 897 to the close of the nineteenth century. Here we note that the word has been used, in addition to its original meaning, for spiritual nourishment, especially the Holy Eucharist; it has been adopted in the nomenclature of pharmacy, and appears in botanical classifications as a species of grass, generally called Italian millet. So likewise the word *Sinai,* from which derives *Sinaitic,* which has been given more than a geographical connotation in modern literature.

We would be the first to admit that the Bible is not the only great book in world literature to which references are made in famous works of subsequent centuries. Volumes have been written on the influence of the classics, for example, in English, French and German literature. While it is true also that one could find scores, if not hundreds, of references to various passages in the Book of Exodus simply introduced in the literary composition of some notable work, still, in most cases the use of the Scriptures is not merely for embellishment of the composition, as it would be in Dante or Shakespeare. Men are influenced in their lives and guided in their actions by these various passages, faith is sustained, warnings are emphasized, encouragement is given, guidance is supplied and action is inspired by the constant remembrance of and reference to the Word of God. It exercises a living influence in the lives of men.

Tennyson's words are the cry of every human heart:

> 'Tis life, whereof our nerves are scant,
> Oh life, not death, for which we pant;
> More life, and fuller, that I want.

This longing for life is not satisfied by literature itself, but by the divinely inspired record of God's redemptive work through Jesus Christ, by Whom we are born again unto a living hope, and in Whom alone we have eternal life. This is, indeed, as no other volume in the world, the Book of Life.

The
Old
Testament

The Old Testament

FRANCIS R. STEELE

Redemption is the theme of the Bible from the very beginning of Genesis to the last verse of Revelation. Throughout the Bible the great design of God's plan of reconciliation is made clear. Why a plan was required, what it should be and to what end it is directed are the very heart of the history, prophecies, poetry, and drama of the thirty-nine books which comprise the Old Testament.

The Old Testament opens with the simple, familiar, yet always majestic statement of Creation: "In the beginning God created the heaven and the earth . . . and God saw everything that he had made, and, behold, it was very good" (Gen. 1:1, 31). Contrast this statement with the first verse of Revelation 21: "And I saw a new heaven and a new earth: for the first heaven and the first earth were passed away. . . ."

I. Covenant of Redemption

What caused the necessity for a new heaven and a new earth? The ruin of the first by sin. Nothing less than a new creation could satisfy the Creator. Out of the need to save man from ruin, God's redemptive action is born, and to that end He gave to the world a Redeemer and lighted the way with the Old Testament.

Since a testament is a covenant, a contract of special promise, the Old Testament by its very title reveals a God Who is ready to make a vital contract with men. The Bible is the revelation of the personality of God and of His relationship to His creatures. His great

3

concern and carefully designed plans for man, who by creation bore the divine image yet sullied it by the fall, are expressed in a continuing covenant relationship.

God did not simply observe impersonally nor intrude haphazardly in the affairs of men, but He supervised and controlled them to fulfil His plan. He entered into a relationship of promise with chosen men, setting forth conditions of obedience based on promises of His own faithfulness.

The Bible becomes largely meaningless unless we appreciate the significance of the fact that the living God has specially revealed Himself and His purposes in a bilateral covenant, that is, He enters into an agreement involving His promises and man's destiny.

II. *Preparation for the Messiah*

The theme of Redemption is developed in the Old Testament in terms of *preparation for the Messiah*. Its main illustrative symbol, "the blood of the lambs," prefigures and anticipates the central theme of the New Testament *provision of the Messiah*, with its corresponding symbol, "the Lamb of God." The Old Testament is the record of God's outworking of His preordained plan to restore righteousness to a rebel world. This He does by laying the foundation for the twofold appearance of the Messiah: first as sacrifice, later as sovereign.

Just as a great symphony composer develops a theme with varied motifs in several movements, so the Old Testament incorporated salient points that appear again and again. The recurrence of these motifs not only interprets and augments the theme of redemption, but it also provides the unifying design of the Old Testament, *preparation for the Messiah*, and ties together the thirty-nine books written over a period of fourteen hundred years by many authors.

Before we proceed to study the Old Testament in outline form, let us consider three salient points: (1) God's use of chosen human agents, (2) the gradually unfolding symbol of sacrifical "blood," and (3) the preservation of the line of descent of the promised "seed," one day to reach its climax in the birth of the Messiah.

1. Chosen Agents

One remarkable aspect of God's redemptive plan is His decision to work conspicuously through human agents. Far more often than through direct divine action, God has worked through men and women chosen by Him to be His agents. The power to fulfil their mission, of course, is always divinely supplied. God apparently wished to show that in and through men obedient to Him, He could implement a plan to salvage the wreckage wrought by human disobedience. As then, so now, God uses men to accomplish His program in this world.

God began with *Adam* who, through obedient service, was to glorify the Creator who placed him in charge of affairs on earth. But Adam disobeyed, and by this act of flagrant disobedience introduced sin into the human race and human history. But God did not begin all over again. He chose rather through this sinful, rebellious family, despite its obvious defeat and shame, to achieve eventual victory and glory.

The race of Adam grew in number. In time God planned a detailed revelation to mankind of His character and purpose and chose a second man, *Abraham*. As Adam had fast multiplied into a vast population, so Abraham soon became a great nation. But there was this significant difference: God chose to use the family of Abraham—and the nation springing from it—as a particular vehicle for the special revelation of His redemptive plan. While its basic elements had been known before, several new and important stipulations, involving Abraham and his descendants, were added. For example, the promises made to Abraham, and the covenants resulting from them, are more explicit and contain more details than the plan of God recorded earlier in Genesis. These Abrahamic promises deal largely with the establishment of a righteous nation springing from Abraham's descendants. That nation in its time was to be a living testimony to the rest of the world of the supernatural power of God to effect righteous obedience in a world of unrighteous disobedience; and, in the future, this same nation was to provide a world-wide witness to the sovereign authority of God over the earth. The specially chosen people were also to exhibit the character of their God clearly to the world through elaborate rituals and many regulations touching their daily lives.

God later chose *Moses* as His instrument to communicate the religious and civil laws setting forth how God's people were to sanctify or set themselves apart from the world. Only such a distinctive separation of the people could testify to the holiness of God and the deadliness of sin, as well as to the resulting need of special cleansing before anyone or anything tainted with sin could become acceptable to God. Central in this particular revelation, as we shall note later, were the sacrifices.

In times of crisis and for the accomplishment of His special purposes, God rarely intervened directly, but chose a man for His mission: *Joshua* to occupy Canaan; *Saul* to integrate under kingship the scattered tribes of Israel in the face of strong opposition; *David* to deliver them from the Philistines and establish peace, so *Solomon* could build the glorious temple, center of worship. Then one leader after another—*Hezekiah, Josiah, Daniel, Nehemiah*—was raised up to perform God's bidding at His appointed time and by His power.

2. *Blood Sacrifice*

The second motif which plays a prominent part in illuminating the theme of redemption is the symbol of *blood sacrifice for cleansing from sin.* Already in the Garden of Eden, it is introduced by implication when animals are slain that their skins may provide coverings for the disobedient pair, Adam and Eve (Gen. 3:21). Here the principle is already established which is explained in Leviticus 17:11: "for the life of the flesh is in the blood: and I have given it to you upon the altar to make an atonement for your soul for it is the blood that maketh an atonement for the soul." Since the word "atonement" literally means "covering," the eternal principle that "the wages of sin is death" is attested by the fact that the sin of Adam, needing atonement or "covering," required the sacrifice of an innocent substitute whose blood must flow in death. Herein also lay the ground of the acceptability of Abel's sacrifice—firstlings of the flock (Gen. 4:4)—and the anger of Cain that his offering, the fruit of the ground, was rejected. Later, the first act of Noah after leaving the Ark was to offer a sacrifice (Gen. 8:20).

In a poignant way, Abraham learned later the significant element of substitution: *the innocent suffering in place of the guilty.* At God's command, he prepared to offer his son Isaac as a human sacrifice on Mount Moriah—only to have his hand stayed by divine command

and to find a ram provided as a substitute for Isaac (Gen. 22). This scene is a vivid anticipation of the Sinless Substitute on the cross for doomed sinners (Gal. 2:20).

This principle is again dramatized on a scale that includes all Israel with the institution of the Passover (Ex. 12). Here a sacrifical animal suffers death instead of the firstborn males among the Israelites. The shed blood of the slain animal, displayed openly, signifies the obedient trust of those Israelites who performed the sacrifice. This ritual act separated those who performed it unto God and to His leader Moses for the journey to the Promised Land.

On the wilderness journey, further instructions were abundantly given to emphasize the need for constant cleansing from sin. The Israelites were continually reminded that "the soul that sinneth, it shall die" unless a substitute avails. A New Testament writer pointedly summarized the fact that the Old Testament covenant is sealed by blood: "Without shedding of blood is no remission" (Heb. 9:22).

Through the later centuries of Israel's history, temple sacrifices multiplied and not infrequently the people, falling into gross sin, blended their forms of worship with that of pagan cults about them. But after lapses into idolatry, the return of the nation to God was celebrated by thousands of sacrifices indicating repentance and a renewal of their vows to the Lord.

The shed blood, the blood of the innocent substitute, dominates Old Testament symbolism to keep ever before the children of Israel (and the present day reader as well) the fact and guilt of sin, as well as the promise of God to forgive all who turn to Him in faith by the blood of the sacrifice. One day this shadow would receive substance, for all these ritual regulations pointed forward to the Perfect Sacrifice for the sins of guilty mankind (II Cor. 5:21). In place of the countless thousands of animals whose symbolic death had no intrinsic merit or virtue (Heb. 10:4), there would appear the Lamb of God (John 1:29) Whose death would decisively loose the chains of sin from those in bondage.

3. Line of Promise

Perhaps the most important thread binding the Old Testament together is the one which, from Adam onward, preserved from generation to generation the line of the promised "seed." Beginning in the Garden of Eden with God's announcement to the serpent that "the seed of the woman shall bruise thy head" (Gen. 3:15), the line of descent was carefully preserved against every attempt of Satan to destroy it. Abel is murdered; Seth is put in his place (Gen. 4:8, 25). The whole race is contaminated with gross sin and must be destroyed, but Noah is spared. Sarah is barren, so God supernaturally gives Abraham and Sarah a son, Isaac. The family of Jacob are about to be absorbed into the population of Egypt, so God raises up Moses to deliver the Israelites, especially the family of Judah through whom the Messiah would one day come. So it continues; kings, Gentiles and numberless unknowns had a place in the line of descent of the promised seed, the Anointed One (Messiah), for whom the successive generations hopefully watched, most in ignorance of His true function, some in believing faith. This much they knew: He would come of the tribe of Judah, of the line of David, to restore glory to Israel. Over and over, the prophets repeat in the course of Hebrew history, even in times of deepest gloom and faintest hope, the promise: "Yet once again I will restore my glory to Israel."

The plan and promise of God required that the knowledge of His purpose and the line of His "seed" be preserved from physical termination and spiritual contamination despite Satan's attempts to frustrate the program of redemption. God thwarted all counterattacks, demonstrating His ability to perform His will with respect to a particular promise centered in a special person, the Messiah.

III. Structure of the Record

Having examined the three major motifs which run through the thirty-nine books, let us view the Old Testament as a whole to see how the major theme, *preparation for the Messiah*, is developed. This development does not follow a simple, regular pattern, and sometimes it is not easily discernible. Nonetheless, the unifying theme is present throughout the books in varying degree and makes a coherent whole of a sacred literature compiled over more than a millennium and written by two score human authors. The theme constantly appears in successive books, often in a new guise, and cast in varied literary forms since the Old Testament contains not only narrative prose, but also legal text, psalms, proverbs and prophetic writings.

In our English translation, the order of the separate books of the

Old Testament differs from the ancient manuscripts and even from the Modern Hebrew Bible. Originally a simple threefold division prevailed under the headings: the Law, the Prophets and the Others (later called the Writings). The Law, comprising the five books of Moses, the first books in the Bible, has remained uniform in character and position in all collections. Jewish editions include among the Prophets six books we would not ordinarily consider in that category: Joshua, Judges, I and II Samuel, and I and II Kings. But the Jews considered authors of these books, even though anonymous, to be exercising the office of prophet. Moreover, Daniel, Ezra and Nehemiah are not listed as prophecy in the Jewish text, probably because these authors are regarded chiefly as leaders, rather than prophets. The third Jewish category (the Others) contains the five well-known poetical books (Job, Psalms, Proverbs, Ecclesiastes, and Song of Solomon, and Lamentations, plus Ruth and Esther, and the "prophetic" books of Daniel, Ezra and Nehemiah, together with I and II Chronicles. Obviously this division includes the sacred books considered as not properly belonging either to the Law of Moses or the Prophets.

Our English Bible follows an arrangement which is chronological rather than stylistic, and after the Law lists all the books that might be regarded chiefly as historical records. Next follow the Poetical Books; then, the Prophets, four major and twelve minor. The designation "major" and "minor" refers to length of the books and implies no inherent superiority of one over the other.

The prophets of the Old Testament are unique among religious functionaries in world history in every essential characteristic. Their office and responsibility stemmed from the choice and authority of God, not from any outstanding personal qualification. Coming from many different walks of life, they served in the particular capacity and for the specific purpose for which God appointed them. They did not seek, nor often gain, prominence in the eyes of men. Indeed, they were usually scorned, defamed, imprisoned, and sometimes even executed, because of the bitter resentment their message aroused.

Their ministry was not primarily "prophesying" in the commonly accepted meaning of that word, that is, the prediction of coming events, although this element was frequently included in their message. Their chief function was to serve as the "voice" of God to His people, reminding them of His commandments, warning them of punishment which must follow upon disobedience, and exhorting them to trust in the protection and providence of a God faithful to keep His word and to deliver His people from disaster—if they obey and serve Him. Essentially, the contrast between priest and prophet was this: the priest represented the people before God; the prophet represented God to the people.

The alert reader of the Old Testament will note God's frequent use of a pair of men to carry out His purposes: a leader and a prophet. Each leader, good or bad, had a prophet as God's voice to guide or correct him. Thus, Saul had Samuel; David, Nathan; Ahab, Elisha; Hezekiah, Isaiah; Nebuchadrezzar, Daniel; and Herod, John the Baptist. Much of their ministry was predictive, most of it corrective, and all of it instructive and authoritative.

The Old Testament picture of the ministry of God's prophets to His chosen people is significant. Time and again God's people turned from their Lord and wandered into idolatry and the gross and immoral practices of the pagan people among whom they dwelt. Time and again God sent a prophet to rebuke the people for their sin and to warn them of righteous punishment if they persisted in sin. Individuals and nations alike came within the scope of the pronouncement of these men of God. They prefaced their words with "Thus saith the Lord," not by way of figure of speech or hollow formula, but in very truth. In the sovereign grace of God, every warning, no matter how grave, whether addressed to King David, the City of Nineveh or the Kingdom of Judah, carried with it the promise of divine forgiveness conditioned on repentance and faith, as well as the theme of the eventual, glorious restoration of Israel to the eternal praise of God.

The outline following does not divide either evenly or proportionately the time periods or the number of Bible books. Rather, the division follows the main development of the major theme throughout sacred history.

Vast periods of time are passed over silently; while others, which are of relatively minor significance judged only by secular standards, are recorded in detail. The reason for this is that the Bible is not primarily a record of history, even of Israelite history, but a record of God's purpose in redemption, an exposition of man's predicament in sin and a revelation of the only solution to that predicament. Thus God's revelation of His plan as recorded in the Old Testament was dictated by His purpose, and historic periods and events are introduced selectively rather than proportionately to show the sovereign God at work redeeming sinful men who place obedient faith in His Word.

IV. Survey of the Record

1. "In the Beginning"		Genesis and Job,
a. Prelude in Shinar		Two books: unmeasured
(Babylonia)	?–2100 B.C.	time.
b. Patriarchs in Canaan	2100–1850 B.C.	
2. On the March		Exodus through Ruth,
a. Egyptian Bondage	1850–1450 B.C.	7 books: 750 years.
b. Exodus and Conquest	†1450–1100 B.C.	
3. In the Land		I Samuel through II
a. United Israel	1100–931 B.C.	Chronicles;
b. Separate Kingdoms	931–586 B.C.	Psalms through
		Lamentations;
		Hosea through Zephaniah;
		22 books: 500 years.
4. A Remnant Restored		Ezekiel and Daniel;
a. Babylonian Captivity	586–538 B.C.	Ezra, Nehemiah, Esther;
b. Release to Rebuild	538–445 B.C.	Haggai, Zechariah,
		Malachi;
		8 books: 155 years.

† Israel's great deliverance, which stands at the threshold of Hebrew national history, is sometimes assigned an "early" and sometimes a "late" date. Some (most evangelical scholars) support the early date, that is, the day after Passover, the 15th of Nisan (March/April), 1446 B.C.; others (most liberal scholars) adopt a later date, holding Rameses II (1300-1234 B.C.) was Pharaoh of the Exodus (about 1290 B.C.) or that Meneptah (1234-1225 B.C.) was Pharaoh of the Exodus. Difficulties of the late dating are sketched by J. Barton Payne in *An Outline of Hebrew History*. The early date, 1446 B.C., is supported by the following internal and external considerations: I Kings 6:1 asserts that Solomon's temple (founded in 966 B.C.) was begun in "the four hundred and eightieth year after the children of Israel were come out of the land of Egypt." In Judges 11:26, Jephthah (in 1092 B.C.) notes that Israel had taken Heshbon about three hundred years earlier, or about 1400 B.C., after forty years in the wilderness. The archaeologist Garstang dates the fall of Jericho about 1400 B.C., forty years after the Exodus (*Joshua-Judges,* p. 54). The Amarna letters to Amenhetep IV (1380-1362 B.C.) tell of plunder and pillage by the Hebrews already in Canaan. Hence, for historical, archaeological and scriptural reasons, most evangelical scholars support the date of 1446 B.C., viewing Amenhetep II as Pharaoh of the Exodus.—ED.

1. "In the Beginning"

The record opens with a description of beginnings in a majestic style appropriate to the serene wisdom and power of Almighty God in creation.

Prelude in Shinar (?–2100 B.C.). Abruptly, sin and rebellion enter through flagrant disobedience to God's known will, and ruin follows the estrangement of God's highest creation, man. Succinctly given is the explanation of the subsequent course of history, a human predicament wherein evil appears to triumph; life is a long struggle against insuperable odds; pain outweighs pleasure, and inexorably death waits at the end.

The reassuring message of the Old Testament is that God knows this and still controls His creation; that He plans to restore righteousness and blessedness to man and the universe and now makes known His remedy for the sin of mankind. At the very beginning, in the midst of apparent defeat and failure, the promise of deliverance is given and the coming of the Redeemer foretold (Gen. 3:15).

Redeemer Foretold (Gen. 3:15). In spite of this, sin breeds murder (Gen. 4:8) and such widespread rebellion and iniquity (Gen. 6:5) that a cataclysmic, divine judgment overtakes the entire race of man, except Noah and his family. Even after this drastic purging of the human race, the roots of sin once more spring up in Noah and his descendants, the world being populated by a race of men almost totally ignorant of God.

Patriarchs in Canaan (2100–1850 B.C.). Out of such an alien environment of remarkably advanced material culture (the Near East of 2000 B.C.), but rank spiritual wickedness, God chose Abraham. Through this man He would build a nation, Israel, which would (1) testify to the world of His holiness and mercy and (2) supply a channel through which the Messiah at last would come to bless the whole world and bring salvation to countless thousands of men (Gen. 12:1–3). Yet first it was necessary for Abraham himself, because of the temptations of unbelief, to learn lessons of faith and obedience, before the promised son, Isaac, was to be miraculously born.

Little is recorded of what Isaac said or did. His chief significance lies in the fact that he is the son of promise and faith in contrast to Ishmael, the son of unbelief and works. These two men thereafter set the spiritual pattern for all others: either as Isaac, a child of God by faith, or as Ishmael, simply a creation of God outside the spiritual family through unbelief.

In Jacob we meet a man whose personal character was inferior to that of his grandfather, Abraham, yet nonetheless he was a man God chose to use. Jacob lacked patience to wait upon God and determined instead to work things out for himself. Although God had already promised him preferment over his brother Esau (Gen. 25:23), he spent years trying by his own wits to achieve this status. Finally, stripped of all possessions, he had a dramatic encounter with God (Gen. 32:24) which brought him at last into obedience to the divine will. After his reconciliation with the brother he had formerly feared (Gen. 33:4), his name Jacob (usurper) was changed to Israel (prince of God), a name God's chosen people were to bear forever afterwards.

In summary this section discloses the intrusion of sin into God's perfect creation; His promise of redemption to Adam; the judgment of the flood upon man's world-wide rebellion; and the covenant with Abraham and his family that the Messiah, the Redeemer, would come through their descendants. God had set in motion His program to rescue man from sin and to restore righteousness to the universe.

2. On the March

As revealed earlier to Abraham (Gen. 15:13), the sons of Jacob went down to Egypt to escape severe famine in Canaan. Here they were met and provided for by their young brother, Joseph, whom they had sold into slavery some years earlier. Eventually, the whole family was located in the region of Goshen. Little information is preserved for us concerning this period. The biography of Joseph is remarkable in the spotless character it portrays, and Joseph himself is significant as a type of courageous obedience to the will of God. Of far higher caliber than Jacob, more consistently observant of moral and ethical principles even than Abraham, Joseph's life supplies evidence that the child of God can withstand the blandishments of Satan and continue faithful through years of neglect or even imprisonment.

Egyptian Bondage (1850–1450 B.C.). The four-hundred-year sojourn was a wise provision for God's people, since it permitted them to develop, prosper and increase in number in isolation from outside pressures and interference. Then oppression suddenly befell them in order that God might demonstrate both His great power over proud Egypt and the complete dependence of His people upon His mercy for their well-being. As God had preserved His people from extinction by famine through refuge in Egypt, so He preserved them now from absorption into Egypt by a mighty deliverance. The

Hebrew bondage in Egypt, far from frustrating God's plan, advanced it.

Exodus and Conquest (1450–1100 B.C.). The Exodus was for the people of that day one of the most profound experiences in human history and, for people of later ages, one of the most significant of all spiritual lessons. Its center is the Passover. Not only was an oppressed people miraculously delivered from a proud and mighty world power, but a marvelous pageant of salvation was enacted on the borders of Egypt.

First, God selected a leader, Moses, and, deferring to his feeble faith, appointed Aaron as his spokesman. A contest with Pharoah and his counselors involved the signs of the ten plagues, the last of which threatened death to all firstborn males throughout Egypt. This was the background for the institution of the Passover in which the firstborn son of every believing Israelite family was spared by the mark over each door of the sacrificial blood of a lamb. One of the clearest pictures of redemption in the Old Testament, the Passover looks back to Mount Moriah (Gen. 22) and even to the Garden of Eden (Gen. 3:21) and forward to Calvary. Death was visited upon all who were not "under the blood" of the innocent substitute. Salvation was wrought, not by the intrinsic merit of the individual, but through the obedience of faith.

The next day the Israelites marched out of Egypt to the edge of the wilderness only to find themselves caught between the Red Sea and the Egyptian army. Again, instead of trusting God, they complained loudly and bitterly to Him, a practice characteristic of their behavior throughout the wilderness journey. Once again God in mercy miraculously delivered them through the Red Sea in a remarkable picture of personal salvation from sin and separation unto God. But no matter how God manifested His power in their behalf— dividing the waters of the Red Sea, providing manna and quail, causing water to gush from the rock—they still grumbled at the slightest hardship. Even in sight of the sign of His continual presence —the pillar of fire and the cloud—the people murmured against God whenever trouble or trial arose. Yet He remained faithful to His vacillating and thankless people.

Failing through unbelief to enter the Promised Land upon their first approach, after a two-year march through the wilderness (Num. 13), the Hebrews wandered thirty-eight years until the faithless, adult generation perished in the wilderness. Then they crossed the

Jordan dry-shod to occupy the land. The process of settling in a time of confusion and spiritual relapse made it almost appear that God had rescued His people from Egypt only to lose them among the Canaanites, a people whose vile religious practices infected everyone with whom they came in contact. But always a few faithful Hebrews bore a remnant's clear testimony to the truth; if light flickered low, it did not go out.

3. In the Land

The early part of the next period turns primarily upon the lives of four persons: one prophet and three kings: Samuel, Saul, David and Solomon. At the side of each king stood a special prophet as the voice of God. Samuel, raised up of God to replace the evil sons of Eli, admirably and obediently bore out his initial response to the call of God, "Speak; for thy servant heareth" (I Sam. 3:10). It was he who sought out and anointed both Saul and David.

United Israel (1100–931 B.C.). The lives of the three kings dramatically illustrate three different patterns of behavior in response to correction when a servant of God in a place of leadership falls into sin. To offset the pernicious influence of spiritual defection on the part of men occupying higher stations in life, these rulers bore a responsibility to conduct themselves circumspectly as leaders of the children of Israel.

On the surface Saul's sin appears less serious than David's; he simply failed to comply fully with God's command utterly to destroy all the Amalekites and their possessions. Nevertheless for this defection God took the kingdom away from Saul and his family, and Samuel was the bearer of this dire news (I Sam. 15:23).

David's sin combined lust, adultery, and deliberate murder, yet he was forgiven and restored—though not without sore punishment. The reason for the different treatment of these two men lies in an important aspect of God's dealing with sinful men. The lesson of these two lives has long outlived the men themselves: God does not grade sins according to a scale of guilt, for all sin is abomination to Him, and even the "slightest sin" alienates the sinner completely from Him. What does count, however, is the sinner's reaction to the promptings of conviction from the Holy Spirit. Saul, confronted with his failure, lied and tried to excuse himself (I Sam. 15:9, 13, 20–21), so God rejected him and took the throne of Israel from him (vv.

22–23). On the other hand, when the prophet Nathan charged King David with infamous behavior (II Sam. 12:7), he confessed immediately (v. 13, cf. also Ps. 51) and was forgiven. No matter how trivial or grave any sin may appear, immediate and unqualified confession is required, and forgiveness then follows (I Jn. 1:9). David, not Saul, God said, was "a man after mine own heart, which shall fulfil all my will" (Acts 13:22).

Solomon, a man of exceptional talent, living in a time of unprecedented opportunity, made a good beginning in life, but deteriorated in his later years. In some respects, it appears easier to remain true to God in times of adversity than in times of ease; desperation drives a man to God, plenty tempts him to trust himself. The ministry of the prophet Ahijah during the crisis is significant; more than likely, as he had counseled Jeroboam (I Kings 11:29–31) he mediated the Word of God also to Solomon (vv. 9–11).

Thus we see that at the beginning of Israel's history, God chose three men as leaders—Saul, David and Solomon—to whom He spoke through three prophets—Samuel, Nathan and Ahijah. The lessons of these kings may be summarized briefly: power corrupts; repentence restores; wealth allures. Despite these human failures, however, God continued to guide His people on toward fulfilment of His promises in Christ.

Separate Kingdoms (931–586 B.C.). The sin of Solomon's idolatry (I Kings 11:4–8) led to a defection (vv. 11–13, and 29–40) under Jeroboam in which ten of the tribes set up an independent kingdom based upon a deliberate counterfeit of the true worship of God in Jerusalem (I Kings 12:26–33). Thereafter, the interest of God centered in the southern kingdom (Judah) although He did not leave the northern kingdom (Israel) without a witness. Indeed, the major prophetic ministry before the eighth century B.C. was through Elijah and Elisha, and to Israel, rather than Judah.

However, the promise of God to Abraham, reaffirmed and strengthened through David, was not set aside. If ten tribes were given over officially and irrevocably to idolatry, and Judah herself frequently fell into apostasy through evil leadership, nonetheless, God had His hand upon the line of David. He continued to raise up faithful kings and fearless prophets to preserve the knowledge of righteousness from complete disappearance.

From Rehoboam to Zedekiah, only three outstandingly good kings reigned in Judah—Jehoshaphat, Hezekiah, and Josiah. For each one God raised up a prophet—Micaiah, Isaiah and Huldah (prophetess)—to give divine guidance in times of crises. Teaching and hearing the law of God played a significant role in bringing back the people to knowledge of an obedience to the will of God. This always resulted in blessing and protection, and, in some cases, deliverance from the enemy (cf. for Jehoshaphat, II Chron. 17:7–10; for Hezekiah, II Chron. 30:22; and for Josiah, II Chron. 34:29–30). Furthermore, during times of revival the sacrifices of God became specially meaningful. The worship of Baal and Ashtoreth with their orgiastic ritual was crassly materialistic at best and grossly carnal and vile at worst. Only spiritual worship of a spiritual God yielded true satisfaction and peace of soul. At times the end seemed near. Once a young prince (Joash) was hidden by the priest Jehoiada and his wife from those who sought to wipe out the seed royal (II Kings 11). But the line of the royal seed was preserved and the throne remained in the family of David.

Israel to the North proved a source of trouble and temptation to Judah until the Northern Kingdom fell to the onslaught of Assyria and ceased to exist as a political entity. Dishonoring and weakening alliances by treaty, and intermarriage with Israel, brought divine punishment upon Judah. Finally the cumulative wickedness of Judah caused God to bring the Babylonian army upon Jerusalem to destroy city, country and temple. The majority of the population went into a captivity that extended seventy years until Babylonia's fall to Persia. Then, under the gloom of destruction, a note of hope was struck by Jeremiah when, just before Jerusalem fell, he bought a piece of land in Judah to testify that one day God's people would be restored to their promised land (Jer. 32:6–25).

4. A Remnant Restored

The Exile in Babylon, whether primarily punishment or testing, was clearly no accident, but God's will for His people. He expressly commanded them through Jeremiah to surrender to Nebuchadrezzar and live, rather than resist and die. This message proved to be so unpatriotic and unpalatable that Jeremiah eventually found himself in prison.

Babylonian Captivity (586–538 B.C.). The only record of the Exile is contained in the prophecies of Ezekiel and Daniel. The former, a priest of Jerusalem, was taken into exile together with Jehoiakim and lived by the river Chebar in the town of Tell Abib. Ezekiel stressed again and again that "sin must be punished, but God is merciful and after punishment will restore His people." Having warned the Jews in exile that Jerusalem was doomed, Ezekiel changed his message after Jerusalem fell and began to predict the future restoration of capital and nation for the glory of God.

Daniel, in his dual role of statesman and prophet, was probably best known to his contemporaries for the prominent position he held in the government of Babylon. Raised from a royal hostage to third place in the kingdom, where he exercised wise rulership, Daniel never swerved from his determination to serve God with all his heart. By lip and life, he testified to the excellence of the God of Heaven as compared with the pagan deities of the Gentile world. Prediction of the eventual triumph of God over all the nations of the earth was part of that message; but as the years rolled by in Babylon, the Jews became so well adjusted to their new land that they almost forgot Judah and Jerusalem, now in ruin and desolation.

Release to Rebuild (538–445 B.C.). At the stroke of God's time clock, however, deliverance came. As prophesied by Isaiah and Jeremiah (Jer. 25:11, 12) when seventy years expired, God raised up Cyrus (Is. 44:28—45:4) to decree that the Jews might return to rebuild their country. God chose Ezra to rebuild the temple and Nehemiah to rebuild the walls of Jerusalem. This they accomplished despite the opposition of foes, both within and without the camp. The people who remembered the former glory of the temple wept to see the poorly-built restoration.

But many Jews never returned. Some continued under Persian sovereignty; Esther was their protector there when enemies sought to instigate a pogrom to exterminate them. Others were scattered elsewhere in foreign lands. Nevertheless, some did return to the land where they belonged and where they must be to await the coming of the Messiah.

Even under a Roman yoke, Judea was a Jewish land and Bethlehem a Jewish town in the days of Cæsar Augustus when a babe was born in a stable. The *prophets* had long foretold the event; the *seed* of Abraham had been preserved through the line of David; millions of slaughtered *animals* had reminded the pious that "the wages of sin is death," and now the *man*—the Son of Man—is born. At this point the story of Redemption is taken up and carried on in the New Testament. In the Old Testament, however, the Messiah is a figure of promise, the long awaited hope. The sacred writings unite to relate a profound and vivid message: man is now a fallen sinner exposed to the wrath of a holy God; indeed, he cannot save himself from doom; but God promises salvation as a gift centered in the coming Redeemer.

The
Five Books
of Moses

The Five Books of Moses

OSWALD T. ALLIS

THE FIRST FIVE BOOKS of the Bible, the Pentateuch, are commonly called the Five Books of Moses. So far as we know, they have always been grouped together as the Law (Torah). Jesus in describing the witness of the Old Testament Scriptures to Himself summarizes them in terms of "the law of Moses, and the prophets and the psalms" (Lk. 24:44). Thus, at the time of the Lord's earthly ministry, the Jews recognized a threefold division of the Scriptures. The Law came first, as it does in every arrangement of which we have any record.

I. The Unity of the Five Books

The first book, aptly called Genesis (beginning) in the Greek Version, begins with creation and brings the history down in an ever-narrowing stream to the death of Joseph. The name of the author is not stated, but since it so evidently prepares the way for the story of the Exodus and the great events which follow, it is proper to assume that it was written or compiled by Moses.

How much of Genesis is based on trustworthy ancient traditions and records which Moses had knowledge of and how much is a matter of direct revelation, we cannot say. Abraham probably possessed records of events lying in the distant past, and the genealogies in chapters 5 and 11 and the Table of Nations in chapter 10 may go back to a very early date. On the other hand, the account of creation must be a matter of revelation, but whether to Moses or not, we cannot say. The fact that Abraham caused his servant to swear by "the

23

Lord the God of heaven, and the God of the earth" (Gen. 24:3; cf. 14:19, 22) would indicate knowledge of the creation before Moses' time. That Genesis stands in close relationship with the other books of the Pentateuch is confirmed by the fact that even the critics who divide it into three major documents—J, E, and P—find all these documents represented elsewhere in the Pentateuch. [The critics employed J to denote material in which *Yahweh* is used as the name of God; E, the documents in which Elohim is used as the name of God; and P for material by a priestly writer.—Editor.] This indicates that in its literary form Genesis has much in common with the books in which Moses figures so prominently.

All four books which follow Genesis relate to Moses and his times. Exodus deals with the period from the oppression in Egypt and the birth of Moses to the erection of the tabernacle. Leviticus, the manual of the priests, is closely connected with Exodus by the account which it gives of the consecration of Aaron and his sons on the eighth day after the erection of the tabernacle (Lev. 9:1; cf. Ex. 29:35). All the laws it contains are declared to have been given by God through Moses at Sinai (Lev. 7:37, 38; 25:1; 26:46; 27:34).

Numbers deals with the events of the year after the erection of the tabernacle up to the refusal of the people to go up to possess the land and their sentence to perish in the wilderness (Chs. 1—14); the period of wandering is passed over briefly (Chs. 15—19). Then the narrative describes events of the fortieth year and concludes with commandments given by Moses to Israel while encamped in the plains of Moab (Chs. 20—26).

Deuteronomy consists mainly of three addresses delivered by Moses in the plains of Moab and concludes with a brief appendix describing his death. Such a brief survey indicates that these four books record a sequence of events all of which took place during the lifetime of Moses. His name appears constantly in connection with the events described. The laws and instructions of the Lord are all given through him. It is several times stated that he wrote them down (for example, Ex. 24:4; Deut. 31:9, 22; cf. Jn. 5:46). It is eminently proper, therefore, to call these five books "the books of Moses."

II. *The Pentateuch is Theocratic History*

The Pentateuch, like the rest of the Scriptures, is the record of God's acts and words. As such it is pervaded by the supernatural.

The most common names for Deity, "Lord" (*Yahweh*) and "God" (*Elohim*) occur more than two thousand times. The Pentateuch records God's wonders of old. Any attempt to minimize or eliminate the miraculous runs directly counter to the whole spirit of the Pentateuch. It is not ordinary history; it is extraordinary history.

The Pentateuch is Human History. Being the record of God's dealings with man, the Pentateuch gives a most faithful picture of man in the light of God's plan of redemption. It exhibits him at his best and at his worst. With a candor which is at times shocking, it shows the depth to which sinful man can fall. It is the most truthful exposé of the fact that the heart of man is deceitful above all things and desperately wicked.

The Pentateuch is Catastrophic and Redemptive History. The fall is the first catastrophe, the Protevangelion (Gen. 3:15), the first promise of redemption; the history which follows may be summarized in terms of blessing, disobedience, punishment, repentance, forgiveness, restoration, a cycle which repeats itself again and again. It is the reverse of a naturalistic evolution: it is the story of divine mercy combating and overcoming human depravity and sin.

III. The Religion of the Pentateuch

The very first verse of Genesis strikes the keynote of monotheism. "In the beginning God created the heaven and the earth." And this God is represented as sovereign over the creation which He has brought into being. He is the author of life; He is the moral governor of the world. He creates man in His own image and capable of communion with Himself. He demands obedience of the man whom He has created and for the sin of disobedience man is driven out of the garden, the place of communion with God. The terrible consequences of this disobedience are shown by comparing Genesis 1:31, "And God saw everything that he had made, and behold it was very good," with Genesis 6:5, "And God saw that the wickedness of man was great in the earth and that every imagination of the thoughts of his heart was only evil continually." But the keynote of redemption has already been struck in the Protevangelion (Gen. 3:15), first announcement of a Saviour, where perpetual enmity is declared between the seed of the woman and that of the serpent, and the promise is given, "it shall bruise thy head and thou shalt bruise his heel."

This promise of redemption is confirmed in the Covenant made with Noah and then with Abraham. This same God, who styles Himself the God of Abraham, of Isaac, and of Jacob (Ex. 3:6), makes one of the greatest nations of antiquity, Egypt, serve His purposes regarding their descendants. He brings them down into Egypt because of the famine of Canaan; He delivers them from the bondage of Egypt by mighty signs and wonders; He brings them to Sinai and there He makes known unto them His law. This law consists of the Decalogue (Ex. 20), the book of the Covenant (Chs. 21—23) and all the other commandments and statutes and ordinances contained in the Pentateuch which were given Israel to observe and do.

In the Pentateuch we meet, either in express statement or in type or in intimation, the great and essential doctrines of that ethical monotheism which is taught in the Old Testament prophets and in the New Testament. The Decalogue is recorded twice (Ex. 20; Deut. 5) and the summary of it—the two great commandments of which Jesus said, "On these two commandments hang all the law and the prophets" (Mt. 22:40)—is taken from the Pentateuch (Deut. 6:5; Lev. 19:18). Israel is to worship the Lord and Him only. That this is not merely henotheism (the exclusive worship of one among many gods) but monotheism (the recognition of the existence of no other gods) is indicated by Deuteronomy 4:35, which declares, "There is none else beside him" (cf. v. 39; also 32:29).

The unity of God (Deut. 6:3) is set in contrast with the many gods of the nations. His spirituality is emphasized (Deut. 4:15–20). He is holy and His people are to be holy (Lev. 11:44, 45). The word "holy" appears first in connection with Moses' call: "The ground on which thou standest is holy ground" (Ex. 3:5); and the thought of the holiness of God is prominent in the entire law, especially in connection with the tabernacle which is called the sanctuary (Ex. 25:8) and its worship. Because of His holiness, His separation from everything that is sinful, the Lord is to be feared. Abraham's obeying the command to sacrifice Isaac is said to be a proof that he feared God (Gen. 22:14). Moses' triumph song at the Red Sea declares: "Who is like unto thee, O Lord, among the gods? who is like unto thee, glorious in holiness, fearful in praises, doing wonders?" (Ex. 15:11).

At Sinai the manifestation of the presence of the Lord is terrifying (Ex. 19); He is unapproachable; sacrilege will be punished with death. The God of Sinai is invisible, a Spirit; and every form of idolatry is strictly forbidden (Deut. 4:15–24). The people hear only a voice, the voice of God pronouncing the Ten Commandments. But so terrible is the sound that they ask that it be not repeated (Deut. 5:23–27); their prayer is granted and God speaks to them through Moses.

At Sinai the meaning of sacrifice, expiation by blood, is set forth in detail. The Covenant is ratified by blood (Ex. 24). Seven chapters (1—7) in Leviticus are devoted to the subject of ritual sacrifice. Its significance is clearly set forth in Leviticus 17:10–16; and this passage is referred to in Hebrews 9:11–28, where the typical meaning of the Old Testament ritual is expounded in the New Testament light of the Gospel.

The strictness of the law and the severity of the penalties for disobedience have given rise to the claim that the God of the Old Testament is an "angry God," so we need to remind ourselves that the love of God, His mercy and His grace are made abundantly clear already in the Pentateuch. The greatest proof of that love is the deliverance from Egypt which is referred to repeatedly elsewhere in Scripture and is the great type of redemption from the bondage of sin. By delivering the people from Egypt, God claimed them in a peculiar sense as His own. Because of this deliverance, He demanded their obedience and their love (Deut. 6:5; cf. Ex. 20:6). His love for them goes back to the fathers (Deut. 4:37). This love is not only a love of Israel as a nation, although this finds expression in the deliverance from Egypt; it is also an individual and personal relationship. The use of the singular "thou" in every command of the Decalogue applies to every individual Israelite, as well as to the nation as a whole.

While the Mosaic law is formal, ceremonial, external, it is also *spiritual* and *inward*. Faith is demanded in the Pentateuch as elsewhere in the Bible. Abraham "believed God, and it was accounted unto him for righteousness" (Gen. 15:6); and the faith of Abraham is celebrated elsewhere in the Old Testament and also in the New Testament. He is pre-eminent among the heroes of the faith of whom we read later in Hebrews 11, and his faith expressed itself in obedience. The sacrifice of Isaac was an act of obedient faith which is unparalleled, and it is richly rewarded (Gen. 22:15–18; 26:2–5). Paul later reminds us that the promise which preceded the law by 430 years was not abrogated by the law (Gal. 3:17).

The Sinaitic Covenant is made with Israel, and the entire legislation is addressed to and directly concerns Israel as the seed of

Abraham. As Paul expresses it: their "advantage" over the rest of mankind consisted chiefly in this, that "to them were committed the oracles of God" (Rom. 3:2). Consequently, we should not forget, as Israel has been so prone to do, that already in the Abrahamic Covenant the *world-embracing* character of this promise is stressed: "And in thee shall all the families of the earth be blessed" (Gen. 12:3; cf. 18:18; 22:18; 26:4). Such passages as Isaiah 19:23–25, Psalm 72:11 and Psalm 150:6, which include the whole of God's creation by inference or by express statement, are based upon the Abrahamic Covenant, from which Paul argues so strongly for the co-heirship of Gentiles with Jews in the household of faith (for example, Gal. 3:8, 9).

Such in brief summary is the ethical monotheism of the Pentateuch. When we study these "five books of Moses," we are impressed with two things: the lofty conception which it gives us of the God of the patriarchs and of Moses who demands the wholehearted obedience of His people, and the frequent and terrible apostasies which marked the history recorded in the Pentateuch. It is made abundantly plain that this wonderful religion was not of Israel's inventing nor of Israel's choosing, but that it was imposed upon Israel from above and was not at all congenial to the fallen nature of man.

As we study the Pentateuch, we do not wonder that it is referred to so often elsewhere in the Bible, that almost the last word of the last of the Old Testament prophets should be this: "Remember ye the law of Moses my servant, which I commanded unto him in Horeb for all Israel, *with* the statutes and judgments" (Mal. 4:4); that Jesus should have said "Think not that I am come to destroy the law, or the prophets: I am not come to destroy but to fulfil" (Mt. 5:17). Especially significant are Jesus' words to the unbelieving Jews regarding Moses, "For had ye believed Moses, ye would have believed me: for he wrote of me. But if ye believe not his writings, how shall ye believe my words?" (John 5:46, 47). It has been calculated that there are in the New Testament about ninety quotations from the Pentateuch and upward of one hundred references to it.

It is hardly necessary to remind the reader that while the great doctrines of the New Testament have their roots in the Pentateuch, they are not all set forth with equal clearness or fulness. This is notably the case with the doctrine of the future life. Such passages as Genesis 25:8 and 37:35 point clearly to a belief in a future life; and Jesus' application of Exodus 3:6 in Matthew 22:32 indicates the wealth of meaning which is contained in such an Old Testament passage. The faith of Abraham would be incredible without it. The Christian doctrine of the future life rests upon the fact of the resurrection of Christ. But such a statement as John 8:56 indicates that the Old Testament saints may have had a much clearer understanding of God's plan of redemption than we realize.

IV. The Pentateuch and Comparative Religion

The information which the spade has brought to light with regard to the religious beliefs and practices of the ancient Egyptians, Babylonians, and other nations with which Israel came in contact has led to the attempt by students of comparative religion to derive the religious beliefs and practices of Israel from these neighboring peoples. That there are similarities and points of contact we must admit. Man's search after God and God's revelation to man have elements in common (Rom. 2:14, 15). But careful comparison of the religion of the Pentateuch with the ethnic faiths of that period indicates very clearly the unique superiority of the spiritual, ethical monotheism made known to Israel through Moses over the idolatrous, sensuous polytheism of these other nations.

That the religion of Israel has a different source is illustrated by the building of the tabernacle. Moses was undoubtedly familiar with the religious practices of the Egyptians among whom he spent the first forty years of his life. He may have visited some of their magnificent temples. But when he was on Mount Sinai with God he received the command, "According to all that I show thee, after the pattern of the tabernacle, and the pattern of all the instruments thereof, even so shall ye make it" (Ex. 25:9); and in the last two chapters of Exodus the words "as the Lord commanded Moses" sound like a refrain. Whatever points the religion of Israel had in common with the ethnic faiths in matters of detail, it was essentially distinct from them. It claimed to be, and it was, a revelation from God.

In view of the lofty religious teachings of the Pentateuch, it is not surprising that "critical" scholars who aim to fit the Pentateuch into an evolutionary scheme, which traces the origin of the religion of Israel back to the crude and carnal beliefs and practices of Israel's neighbors, have found it necessary to treat the Pentateuch as non-Mosaic and to divide it into "documents," the earliest of which some would now place in the Exilic period. For if the Pentateuch is accepted as dependable history and as Mosaic, the course of Israel's early history cannot be fitted into such a scheme of development. It begins at a higher point than these ethnic faiths ever attained.

V. The Pentateuch and Archaeology

The past century and a half has been pre-eminently the age of archaeological research. Exploration and excavation in the Near East have opened up vistas which were closed for centuries or shrouded in myth and legend. Some of these discoveries have an important bearing upon the Pentateuch. They have been both helpful and disappointing.

On the one hand, they have shown that writing (hieroglyphic and cuneiform) was invented more than a thousand years before the time of Abraham, and that alphabetic writing came into use about the time of Moses or earlier. This supports the references (about forty) to writing in the Pentateuch. It has also been shown that Semitic dialects very similar to Hebrew were spoken in Moses' day and much earlier. Documents, such as the Pyramid Texts, the Code of Hammurabi and the El Amarna Letters, have thrown much light upon the culture, religious and secular, of the nations of antiquity with which the patriarchs and Moses were more or less familiar. In Palestine, great cities such as Gezer, Megiddo, Taanach, Haaor, Gibeon, Shechem, Dothan and Jericho have been excavated more or less extensively. Their elaborate fortifications have proved that the spies sent out by Joshua did not exaggerate when they reported that "the people that dwell in the land are strong and the cities are fortified and very great" (Num. 13:28). These excavations have cast welcome light on conditions in Palestine in the days of Abraham and of Moses.

On the other hand, it is disappointing that the excavations in Palestine have produced so very few literary remains. Recent excavations at Gibeon have yielded a number of jar handles with the name Gibeon written on them. The fact that this has been hailed as a unique discovery shows that for Palestine we are still dependent largely, if not entirely, on "sequence dating" based on the character of the potsherds embedded in the many strata of these ancient cities for the determining of their age and history. Whether or to what extent this dearth of written documents is due to the following of the Egyptian custom of writing on perishable papyrus we do not know;

but the fact is that, apart from the Biblical sources, documentary evidence for the time of Abraham and Moses comes to us from outside Palestine.

Valuable as is the light which archaeology has thrown on the history of ancient Israel it must be recognized that it is meager, fragmentary and often ambiguous. A familiar example of this is the problem of the date of Exodus. Whether Thothmes III or Rameses II was the Pharaoh of the oppression is still vigorously debated by scholars. The identification of Hammurabi with Amraphel (cf. Gen. 14:9) now seems increasingly improbable. The claim that the Habiru of the Amarna Letters are the Hebrews of Joshua's day is doubtful, to say the least. A discovery which solves one problem may raise several others. Sweeping statements are to be avoided.

We cannot say without qualification that archaeology has confirmed the Biblical record. The correctness of the mention of camels in Genesis 24 and of Philistines in Genesis 21 and 26 is challenged by archaeologists. But we may well expect that further research will confirm the Scriptures. In all such cases, the Christian should trust the Scriptures, rather than the inconclusive evidence of archaeology, and, where there is conflict, cherish the hope that further research will end it. Much as we value the evidence which archaeology has produced and eagerly as we look forward to further confirmations of the Pentateuch resulting from such research, it is well to remember that our confidence in the Bible does not rest on such discoveries but on the witness of the Holy Spirit to its claim to be the very Word of God.

Genesis

H. C. LEUPOLD

THE BOOK OF GENESIS is very properly regarded as the book of beginnings. The "creation account" is not merely exalted poetry; it is a divine revelation of the creation of all things. As such, it serves to introduce the entire book.

The Creation Account (1:1—2:3)

The opening declaration of the Bible (1:1) is that God is ultimate and prior to the universe, and that nature and man owe their being and continuance to Him. The "creation account" tells us as much about God as about His creation: He is a personal, sovereign, rational, moral being. The grand fact to which the entire Genesis narrative swiftly points is that the eternal God is also the God of creation, of conscience, of judgment, of human redemption and restoration.

After the basic assertion attributing creation to God alone, the statement, "the earth was," is cast into such form in Hebrew that we may catch its force by some such translation as this: "And the earth lay there" (1:2). How long? We are not told. The statement allows an adjustment with the claims of the geologist who requires vast ages for geologic processes. We understand the opening statement to mean: When God began His creative work, He first made the universe "in the rough." "Heaven and earth" is the Hebrew way of saying "the universe."

The Spirit of God mysteriously moved and worked on this chaotic mass, ordering and preparing it for the great things yet to be brought into being. The six great days of creation exhibit the Spirit's work. In them all things basic to human existence were marvelously made.

Whether the days of Genesis follow a long time period, whether they are six immediately successive literal days (the writer's view) or six days of divine activity separated by long intervals, or whether they are themselves to be understood as ages, are questions that have long troubled expositors. Some facts are plain. The inspired writer of Genesis is more interested in events than in chronology, a characteristic of the Eastern mind. He is not writing with an eye on the harmony of religion and science in some far-off century whose basic interest is in the arrangement of fossils according to complexity of their anatomy or physical structure. While he notes that there are divinely graded "kinds" of life, his emphasis falls on the dependent, moral and spiritual character of the universe ("and God saw that it was good," 1:4, 12, 18, and so forth) and on the towering significance of man as a moral agent.

The first day witnessed the creation of light, that mysterious form of energy whose wonders and marvels the twentieth century scientist has only begun to understand. This light is thought of as merely existing and flooding the universe; we do not know if it was localized anywhere. How it existed apart from the sun, the center from which light was later to emanate, we are not told.

The second day witnessed the inauguration of physical laws summed up in the word "firmament," which is also defined (1:8) as "heaven." It involved chiefly the separation of waters into lower and upper. The firmament gives us such essentials for human existence as surface waters, an intervening air-space, and a heaven with clouds.

On *the third day* solid earth and water, apparently mixed in one conglomerate until then, were separated so that the earth appeared, and continents and seas came into being. That day also vegetation clothed the bare earth.

On *the fourth day* the luminaries were created. Certain of the opaque heavenly bodies, already brought into being in the initial creation, were now made luminous. Light was centered chiefly in the sun, and to a lesser degree, in the moon and the stars.

On *the fifth day* all kinds of sea animals and birds were brought into being.

On *the sixth day* God created the various mammals that move on the ground, and man. The creation of man is very obviously represented as the climax of the work that God wrought in all these days. It is introduced by special planning on God's part, the divine words "Let us" (God speaks in the fulness of His majestic being) intimating the importance of this step. Nor should we overlook the singular dignity with which God invested man. This is indicated chiefly by the parallel phrases "in (God's) image and according to (his) likeness," that is to say, *very much* like God. We are given no definition at this point as to what the image of God involves; yet the high station of man could not be set forth more emphatically than by the statement that man is much like God. Man's dominant position in the realm of created things is mentioned.

When it is said (1:31) that all that God had made was "very good," the idea of perfection is involved. The statement indicates that in each case God achieved what His divine wisdom had intended. This allows for growth and development under God, but it excludes imperfection and sin. The Creator Himself could rejoice over His work of creation.

I. First Story: Heaven and Earth (2:4—4:26)

After the introduction, the Book of Genesis provides headings to mark its own divisions, and these headings may be regarded as an outline of the plan of composition. The Hebrew word *toledoth* (story) is used thus ten times (cf. 5:1; 6:9; 10:1; 11:10, and so forth). The King James Version regularly but inaccurately translates this word as "generations," and the Revised Standard Version employs varying translations.

1. A Supplementary Explanation (2:4-25)

What this second chapter contains must be fitted, in point of time, within the framework of the six days. Its concentration on the activity of the sixth day deepens the impression already given by the opening chapter that the drama of heaven and earth finds its crucial center in man, divinely stationed at the apex of the world of creatures.

Concerning man we are given additional information. His creation involves a lower factor unmentioned in chapter 1; he was formed from the dust in which divine breath was infused. Man is a creature as well as a bearer of God's image. Man was especially favored, moreover, by his assignment to a special place of habitation, "a garden in Eden." Tokens of divine favor surround him on every hand.

Two distinctive trees are set in the garden, the tree of knowledge and the tree of life. Some scholars think (as does the writer) that these trees are best described as sacramental in character, the one providing opportunity to acquire further knowledge as man needed it in this earthly life, and the other having the capacity of imparting indestructible physical life. Other scholars regard their function as symbolic, the one pointing to the requirement of moral obedience to God's command in the discrimination of good and evil, and the other to man's prospect of undying life in Eden on condition of obedience.

It is further shown (2:15–22) in what a fatherly manner God dealt with the first pair. They had a place of habitation; they had an assigned task, a pleasant one; they had permission to eat freely of the fruit of the trees in the garden; they had one simple, clear-cut prohibition: Do not eat of the tree of knowledge. Man was not cumbered by a perplexing array of commandments which might be forgotten or overlooked; he had one single commandment that summarized the will of God for him.

Since the relation of the sexes to each other would always be a matter of concern to mankind, the account also furnishes details of the precise manner of the creation of woman. As a result we can understand her and her destiny better. To prepare man for this divine gift of a life's companion, God assigns a task to man beforehand, the naming of the various creatures that surround him. This may not have been so confusing and complicated a task as we are now inclined to assume. The species may not as yet have been numerous; the major classes alone may have existed. But the immediate purpose behind this assignment was to produce in Adam an awareness that all creatures were living in pairs except him, and that no form of animal life could meet his lack. That prepared him for the gift of a helper to be at his side. That the first pair's nakedness was in no sense a cause of embarrassment for them attests the state of innocence in which they lived.

2. The Great Crisis in the Relation of Heaven and Earth: the Temptation and the Fall (3:1–24)

Sooner or later a test had to come to a free moral being like man. This chapter tells how it came. A factual account of what transpired is offered. While elements of mystery appear, this is not allegory. Since the New Testament, which is the standard for our interpretation of the Old, refers to the Fall as an historical event, we must regard it as such (I Cor. 15:21).

The mystery centers largely in the person of the tempter, referred to only as "the serpent." For reasons not disclosed, no further identification is given. Satan does not appear by name. Yet the sinister figure of this chapter is morally accountable, for after the Fall he is treated as such and his punishment is decreed. When we claim that Satan here tempted Adam and Eve, we are not indulging in vague surmises, for the New Testament confirms this (Jn. 8:44; Rom. 16:20; Rev. 12:9).

The arch-liar begins by calling into question the truth of God's word. He skilfully leads the woman to question the goodness of God. Such questioning is mistrust and doubt, the opposite of faith. The very moment the woman began to mistrust God the Fall took place; the act of taking forbidden fruit was merely evidence that the Fall had occurred. The woman apparently used the same approach upon Adam when "she gave some to her husband, and he ate."

Immediately, evidences of a serious disturbance appear in the character and attitude of the first human pair. Serious moral damage has occurred; from this point, man is afraid of God and shuns him. Man tries to lie himself out of the difficulty, and goes so far as to blame God for what has taken place. Man deteriorates speedily from the being God originally made him to be.

Though punishment has to be laid upon man, there is at the very outset proof of divine grace. A strong promise, rich in hope, is pronounced even as the Lord is addressing the serpent (3:15). This promise, clear evidence of divine grace, is that "the seed of the woman"—a person or persons born of womankind—in the course of time will inflict crushing defeat on the tempter; for a crushed head is fatal. ("Bruise" is not to be taken in the mild sense, because of the contrast of "head" and "heel.") This verse has been with good reason regarded from days of old as the "first gospel" (proto-evangel).

But at the same time various disabilities are laid upon mankind—pain, toil, physical death, and banishment from the garden. In a sense the curse threatened was instantly carried out; and man did die on the day he ate of the forbidden fruit. He set the barrier of sin between himself and God, and such separation, or alienation, from God is death in the most tragic sense of the word. Physical death is a further consequence.

But God in his mercy prevented man from making his miserable lot irremediable. For from the manner in which the case is stated in Genesis 3:22, we are forced to conclude that the eating of the fruit of the tree of life, which had originally been destined to confirm man in his holy estate, now would have been the greatest calamity. It would have prevented him from ever escaping by death this degraded physical existence. For man's own good, God therefore successfully barred our first parents from access to the tree of life, driving them from the garden and placing the cherubim and a flaming sword to guard the garden entrance.

The closed gate to paradise and the complete disbarment of man from his original habitation are the fateful consequences of the Fall. No more tragic story than that of the third chapter could be written in the annals of mankind.

3. Early Developments (4:1-26)

Sin in Vicious Form (4:1-15). Once sin has entered the world and man has fallen, the terrible impetus of evil is made apparent in the narrative that follows. The latent possibilities of sin become tragically apparent to our first parents in the lives of their own sons. Brother slays brother.

When God calls the first murderer to account, Cain uses foolish evasions; he speaks bitterly, as though God were expecting too much of him; he denies his guilt until confronted with it by God. His insolence turns into despair (4:13). For reasons best known to God, Cain's life is spared; he is permitted to live, perhaps in his very unhappiness a warning to those persons who in those early days peopled the earth. God promises him safety against any avenger that might later appear on the scene, by some "sign" (not "mark") that God wrought for Cain's reassurance. Yet the murderer is condemned to the life of "a fugitive and a wanderer on the earth."

The Family of the Cainites (4:16-24). At this point two branches of the human family develop as relatively distinct groups. Cain's descendants are recorded by names and significant achievements through several generations, beginning with Lamech, the bigamist. The spirit of innovation in worldly pursuits was strong, and his children forged ahead in new endeavors. Jabal, the originator of the idea of the movable home, the tent, moved with his flocks when pasturage demanded a change of location, thus becoming the first nomad. Jubal devoted himself to music and invented stringed and wind instruments. Tubal-Cain blazed a trail in metallurgy by making cutting instruments of bronze and iron. Utter absorption in earthly things characterizes and pervades the descendants of Cain.

The Family of the Sethites (4:25, 26). Still another family group is described in contrast to the family of Cain. The brief indications take us into an entirely different setting. When Seth is born, he is at once regarded as a gift from God, given under very special circumstances ("God has appointed me another child," v. 25). The very next verse, which speaks of men beginning "to call upon the name of the Lord," is rightly construed to indicate the beginning of public worship.

II. Second Story: Adam (5:1—6:8)

The development of one of the two branches of the human family is traced in stereotyped statistics, each patriarch being reported in practically the same formula. Unlike the Cainites who were deeply involved in earthly pursuits, the Sethites were not deeply concerned with the things of this earth. This account is called "the story of Adam" because it deals with the type of life that men lived who, like Adam, were conscious of their higher destiny though the stamp of death was upon them.

God's warning that death would be the outcome if man sinned (2:17) was no idle threat. The sin of Adam and Eve caused death to become the lot of man. That the Sethites recognized that this doom was upon them because of sin is implied by the refrain, "and he died," which with dreary monotony runs through this chapter even as it runs through life.

But a clear and positive note is struck in the account of Enoch (5:21–24). Seventh from Adam in the line of Sethites, Enoch had the unique distinction that he "walked with God." Beyond a doubt this means that he did what all these Sethites did, only in a greater degree than they, excelling all in true piety.

The last verse of chapter 5 introduces another Sethite who is also going to play a significant role in the development of God's plan for mankind.

Where chapter 5 had swiftly outlined how the true descendants of Adam (the word *adam* also means "mankind" in Hebrew) moved along as a separate group, chapter 6:1–8 pictures the blending of the two groups which took place at the time when men were beginning to multiply their kind on the face of the earth. The Sethites (called the "sons of God") indiscriminately took wives to themselves, sometimes from their own group, sometimes from among the Cainites (designated as "daughters of men"). In the light of the previous developments, this is all that this passage can mean. There is no reference to fantastic angel-marriages, as is sometimes claimed in our day.

God's decision to destroy mankind, being a decision of major importance, is now announced (6:5–8), with one notable exception indicated, Noah.

III. Third Story: Noah (6:9—9:29)

1. Noah's Walk with God (6:9–22)

Though Noah was outstanding for "righteousness" among his contemporaries, "perfect" (KJV) is too strong a term to use. He did what God wanted all men to do; he trusted in God and walked according to His will. The same fine phrase that was used with reference to Enoch—"he walked with God"—occurs here. To save this true follower of His, God first communicates to Noah His decision to destroy the world. He then indicates briefly by what means He is determined to save this man (6:15–17). Imbedded in the set of divine directives for the ark is the word that indicates God's attitude to Noah: "but I will establish my covenant with you" (v. 18). Apparently this is only a preliminary indication of that which is reported somewhat later in Genesis 9:9–17, the covenant which God established with Noah after the Flood.

2. The Flood (7:1—8:22)

The entrance of Noah into the ark (7:1–16), a momentous occasion, beautifully illustrates God's providential care for His creatures, in spite of the fact that man's sin has made judgment imperative. When the world is destroyed because of man's sin, it is clear how largely the creatures exist for man's sake.

Verse 11 indicates that the promised rains were already falling while the long process of entering the ark was coming to an end. There were two major sources of the flood waters: "fountains of the great deep," subterranean waters that had originally abounded in great measure, and rain from heaven above. To make plain the fact that the heavens poured down torrential rains, the figurative expression is used, "the windows of the heavens were opened," an expression still employed because of its vividness. So vast was the flood that traditions concerning it in ancient times are well nigh universal among nations and tribes of mankind.

The account of the entry into the ark of Noah and his family and the beasts and birds of every kind that accompanied them is then detailed (7:13–16). The flood continued and destroyed all flesh on the earth (vv. 17–24).

The recession of the flood (8:1–14) is signaled by the successive release of birds which effectively portrays the earnest longing for release from captivity on the ark by man and beast. Noah did not venture to undertake the exit from the ark (vv. 15–19) until God specifically commanded him to go forth.

Appropriately, upon his release from the ark, Noah built an altar and offered a sacrifice to the Lord (8:20). Immediately the Lord made a divine pronouncement that such a universal flood should never again take place before the great and final end of all things. To this He added a detailed promise as to what man might hope for as constant factors in his life, not one of which has ever been denied. There will always be, "while the earth remains, seedtime and harvest, cold and heat, summer and winter, day and night" (v. 22).

3. Basic Ordinances for the Post-diluvian World (9:1–17)

Since the flood had come as a result of men's disregard of the will of God in their lives, God provides directions at the very outset. Each order provides basic instruction. The propagation of the human race is to continue, and in the process of its increase, the children of men are to replenish the earth.

At the outset, since they are more prolific than man, it might have seemed that beasts would soon crowd man out and utterly destroy him. A promise of God to the contrary is given: natural dread of man shall be characteristic of the beasts, and man shall have power over them, not they over him (9:2). Henceforth man was also to be permitted to eat animal food (v. 3), though with certain restrictions about the use of blood, which Scripture always regards as a particularly sacred element. In this connection, a special warning is laid upon man's conscience about the taking of human life, a crime often characterizing the violence of the pre-flood days.

The Covenant of the Rainbow (9:8–17). As a seal of His promise,

God appoints the rainbow in the clouds as "the sign of the covenant," sight of which was to call to mind God's significant pledge.

4. *The Future of the Races of Mankind (9:18–29)*

After the drunkenness of Noah, another significant word is given concerning the future development of the three branches of the family of Noah. Concerning Canaan, Ham's son, Noah's words (9:25) are chiefly prediction, which, since it involves disabilities, may be labeled a "curse." Nothing whatever in the Scriptures indicates that this curse consisted in a change of the color of the persons involved, though it is known that the Canaanites were dark-skinned. All that is disclosed is that Canaanites (see 10:15–18) shall be a servile race, never dominant for any length of time, always subjugated in the end.

The blessing on Shem (9:26) is mysterious. That it takes the form of a benediction may be due to the possibility that the thought of the blessings which the Semites would inherit stirred the old patriarch to praise God.

The descendants of Japheth (9:27) would have, as the name in the Hebrew implies, abundant room to expand (enlarge). The Japhethites, now commonly known as the Indo-Europeans, did extend, in days of old, over a vast area reaching from India to Spain.

IV. *Fourth Story: the Sons of Noah (10:1—11:9)*

1. *Table of Nations (10:1–32)*

The unique genealogical account of the descendants of Shem, Ham and Japheth is without parallel; no nation of antiquity has preserved anything like it. In the early story of mankind, nations simply took no interest in other nations except where necessity compelled them. But in Israel, a broad outlook prevailed, and this Table of Nations, which constitutes the first half of the story of the sons of Noah, testifies primarily to the *unity of the human race*.

2. *The Confusion of Tongues (11:1–9)*

Again we have an event which, like the story of the fall of mankind, finds no real parallel in the literature of other nations. The attempt to build the Tower of Babel may have occurred some one hundred years after the flood at a time when, some writers estimate, there were on the earth about thirty thousand people. Up to this time these people all had "one language and one vocabulary"—the translation "few words" (RSV) has little to commend it. One language made unity of purpose and endeavor easier to achieve than it otherwise might have been.

Unity of enterprise centered at this time in the building of a tower. The builders made it clear what motivated this undertaking: they wanted "to make a name" for themselves; that is, achieve fame for generations to come by the very magnitude of the enterprise. Secondly, this tower was to be a rallying point, lest they "be scattered abroad upon the face of the earth." Harmless as this second objective sounds, it was the more dangerous of the two. For this expresses a purpose directly opposed to the clearly expressed will of God, "Fill the earth" (9:1). This project therefore involved direct defiance of God.

God's purpose was not to be thwarted by the arrogant plans of man and retributively He causes the confusion of tongues and scatters the workmen (to be remembered by posterity) over the face of the earth. The Tower of Babel has commemorated, forever afterward, the folly of men in proposing their own way.

V. Fifth Story: the Descendants of Shem (11:10–26)

The genealogy of the family of Shem marks the gradual unfolding of the great family of Semites, out of which Israel and his line are to come. Heretofore there had been no division of Jew and Gentile, but that day is dawning, and the general history of mankind is now ended.

VI. Sixth Story: Abraham (11:27—25:11)

At the very beginning of this account (11:27), the family line of Terah is given, one of whose three sons is Abram. Abram's childlessness is mentioned and the departure from Ur for Haran, five hundred miles northwest of Ur in the land of Mesopotamia, is briefly narrated. Some time after his arrival in Haran, Terah died. Since the original objective of Terah's group was the land of Canaan

(v. 31), the supplementary command in Genesis 12:1–3 does not involve a venture totally without direction on Abram's part.

1. The Call of Abram (12:1–9)

God commands Abram to make a complete break with the past and with all family ties, and promises Abram that on His part, He will make of His faithful follower a great nation, a great name, a blessing on those who bless him, a curse upon those who curse him, and "in thee shall all the families of the earth be blessed." The terminology is even stronger than the Revised Standard Version gives, that these families "will bless themselves." The messianic character of the promise is crystal clear (cf. Gal. 3:15–18), and it appropriately is the climax of the word of God to Abram.

Abram in Canaan (12:4–9). Abram obediently departed, and the route may have led past Damascus. Abram stopped first at Shechem, some thirty miles north of Jerusalem. There the Lord appeared to him, giving him the promise that his descendants should hold this land. Abram responded with a reverent sacrifice, confessing his faith in the word of the Lord and publicly proclaiming his faith in Him. He followed this same procedure at Bethel, some ten miles north of Jerusalem.

2. Trip to Egypt during Famine (12:10–20)

Heroic as he appeared when we first encounter him, Abram did not hold fast and remain in the Promised Land. When a famine occurred, he made his way to Egypt, and there engaged in a stratagem which further dims our picture of him as a completely heroic man. He foolishly has Sarai, his wife, play the part of his sister, and Pharaoh, who takes the supposed sister into his household, is plagued by God until the truth is made known and Sarai is released. Abram by Pharaoh's command is instantly sent away from Egypt with all his family.

3. Separation from Lot (13:1–18)

But deception and cowardice are not characteristic of Abram, and the man of faith so powerfully depicted by the writer of Genesis emerges by the grace of God. The Lord guided Abram step by step and blessed him far beyond what his merits and achievements thus far indicated would appear to predict.

The immediate cause of the separation of Abram from Lot was strife among their shepherds, leading to serious misunderstandings among kinsmen (which would have been offensive even in the sight of the natives [note 13:7]). Abram makes his generous offer; Lot, his selfish choice. Immediately after the separation, Abram dwelt in Canaan while Lot pitched his tent in the area of Sodom, a center of terrible wickedness. The Lord then shows Abram all the land that he and his seed are to have in perpetuity, promises him a great posterity beyond measure. Abram thereafter, as directed, travels throughout the length and breadth of Canaan.

4. Abram's Victory over the Kings (14:1–24)

If chapter 13 emphasized Abram's magnanimity, chapter 14 stresses his valor. Abram was a man of courageous faith. Faith prompted him to venture forth with a comparatively small force against the combined strength of several kings. At the same time, Abram appears in a new light as an important person at ease among kings and their retinues.

When the news of the capture of his nephew reaches him, he promptly arms a band of homeborn slaves, who were no doubt unusually dependable, joins the forces—we have no knowledge how strong these forces were—of Aner, Eshcol, and Mamre (14:24), and starts in pursuit. The enemy, caught in a surprise night-attack near Dan, in northern Gilead (cf. Deut. 34:1), are routed, prisoners and booty being captured. As Abram returns, the hero of the expedition, a memorable meeting with a venerable and mysterious figure takes place just outside Jerusalem. This personage was the priest-king of the city, named Melchizedek, a worshipper of the true God whom Abram reverenced.

Melchizedek, whose name means "king of righteousness," expresses his friendship and perhaps has religious kindship with Abram by offering the most common form of hospitality, "bread and wine" (14:18). In Melchizedek the author of Hebrews, centuries later, sees a type of Christ, inasmuch as Melchizedek combines in himself two offices which were not even combined in the commonwealth of Israel, namely those of priest and king. As such, he is a type of Christ of a higher order even than Aaron (Heb. 7:11–28).

5. God's Covenant with Abram (15:1–21)

As time passes, year after year, the possibility of Abram's ever having a son, so necessary for the realization of God's promises, appears to become remote. Now, for the first time, God makes an explicit promise of a son, always heretofore implied in what was promised. God dramatically points Abram to the innumerable stars as the best measure of the number of his descendants. Given a clear promise, Abram "believed in the Lord, and he reckoned it to him for righteousness" (15:6). One marvels that a writer as early as Moses could have attained such deep insight into the saving power of faith, but the word so plainly recorded is later lifted into prominence by the Apostle Paul in Romans 4:3 and Galatians 3:6. The only factor that counts in Abram's transaction with God is faith, and faith only insofar as it grasps God's promise, not faith as an achievement of man.

God proceeds to honor this justifying faith by establishing a covenant with Abram under striking circumstances. The whole procedure was in the form and nature of a "vision" (15:1). In the vision he has already been invited to step out and look at the stars. God then reminds him how faithfully He has dealt with him ever since He called him forth into the land of Canaan. Still in the vision, Abram falls into a deep sleep in which a strong dread falls upon him. This dread seems to be in anticipation of the bondage Israel will suffer in the land of Egypt, where Abram's descendants are to be for four generations (v. 16), a generation at that time being reckoned as a hundred years.

6. Birth of Ishmael (16:1–16)

Abram's faith must grow by his waiting and learning to depend on God more fully, but in the process his faith falters and, with Sarai's connivance, he resorts to human machinations in an attempt to make the promise come to pass. By Hagar, Ishmael is conceived, and a promise is given to Hagar that this son will be the head of a great line, numbered in multitudes (16:10). A strange promise is added that "he will be a wild man: his hand will be against every man, and every man's hand against him; and he shall dwell in the presence of all his brethren" (v. 12). In the begetting of Ishamel,

Abram demonstrated his doubt and tampered with the covenant God had given him, and in consequence left to generations centuries later a division, full of hate, that must still be calculated as a cause of international conflict.

7. Covenant Sealed by New Names and Circumcision (17:1–27)

Since a covenant was made in Genesis 15:18, we may be puzzled at the multiplicity of covenants, perhaps even regarding 12:1–3 as the equivalent at least of a covenant. It seems simpler to think of this chapter as the sealing of the one covenant of chapter 15, and to call only that a covenant which the Lord so describes. That Abram needs more words from God to build on may well be understood, for at this point he is already ninety-nine years old. It is also appropriate in this chapter that God should be designated as "Almighty God." By His power He can do what man in his weakness can hardly conceive.

At this point Abram becomes Abraham, which could mean "father of a multitude." To the covenant previously agreed upon, a new feature is added, a symbolic outward sign, circumcision—involving all males of the family, the slaves as well as the freemen (17:10). All men who share in the covenant are to bear this mark upon their flesh.

That such a custom was distinctly appointed for so holy a purpose is apt to strike us today as exceedingly strange. Nor can purely utilitarian considerations, such as a sanitary expedient, appeal to us as having been the primary purpose behind the rite; a deeper meaning must be sought. Two considerations require investigation here: first, the rite as such represents a putting away of evil, a kind of purification; in fact, more specifically it points to the necessity of the purification of life at its very source. It is not a sacrament which will supply the needed grace and the desired effect, but it suggests in a symbol what obligations are laid upon those who stand in covenant relation with God, namely, to put away the foreskin of their hearts (Jer. 4:4), to circumcise the heart and "be no longer stiffnecked" (Deut. 10:16). This effect only the Lord's grace can achieve in man and, therefore, man in seeking to accomplish this must seek the Lord. Secondly, this rite is tied up closely with the messianic hope. For if it indicates the purification of life at its source, it points forward to Him through Whom all such purification is to be achieved, Who is Himself also to be born of a woman, the One in Whom for the first time that which circumcision prefigures will be actually realized.

This rite is not, however, a divinely ordained instrumentality for initiation into the people of God, at least not for a native Israelite, who belonged to the company of God's people by virtue of birth. By circumcision he was made aware of his covenant obligations and received a perpetual badge or reminder of them.

Parallel with Abraham's change of name comes Sarah's (no longer Sarai). Since either form of the name seems to mean "princess," the change merely indicates a more dignified relationship (17:15).

Covenant or no covenant, Abraham still aims to simplify matters by settling upon Ishmael as the son of promise. But Ishmael is not the one whom God has had in mind, and furthermore, the true heir is not to be born "after the flesh." God makes it clear that grace is to be the all-controlling consideration and that Sarah's very son is involved and no other (17:19).

When the promise of a son is given, with his name stipulated Isaac (Gen. 17:19), God goes on to promise fruitfulness for Israel. As for Ishmael, "twelve princes shall his line produce, and I appoint him to be a great nation" (v. 20).

8. The Lord's Appearance at Mamre (18:1–33)

In chapter 18 the promises of God reach a climax. On the whole, this is an incident without parallel in the Scriptures. While it is true that God appeared to some individuals to speak to them personally, even under human guise, we have no case on record in which He sat down to eat with them, and spoke at such length, yet gave no visible display of His divine power and majesty. So authoritative is the manner in which the heavenly visitor makes the promise of 17:21 final, the promise concerning the child to be born within a year, that husband and wife are certain, as never before, that it will be fulfilled.

Then Abraham, the friend of God, is informed of the impending overthrow of Sodom and Gomorrah. He and his descendants are to know that what happens to these cities is a divine judgment, not an accident. Now comes the grand passage in which Abraham intercedes for the few righteous persons that might possibly still dwell in the city. Abraham's faith made him broadminded and sympathetic for the dangers of others. The boldness of his prayers, which would have been unpardonable but for the deep humility that accompanied them (cf. v. 27), amazes us.

9. *Wickedness of Sodom and its Overthrow (19:1–38)*

Though strictly speaking this chapter is not a portion of the history of the chosen people, it relates an occurrence that was to teach the chosen people a lesson; for the site of this calamity was upon the borders of the land of promise. The chapter shows also how some of the relatives of Abraham undergo a rather rapid deterioration.

The chapter, furthermore, is a sequel to the preceding one. There is hardly a more horrible account anywhere in the pages of Scripture. Both the degeneracy described and the catastrophic overthrow of the cities are startling in their lurid and gruesome details. Martin Luther confessed that he could not read the chapter without a feeling of deep revulsion.

Prelude to the destruction of Sodom is the arrival in that city toward evening of the two angels, those who had previously visited Abraham. When they come to the home of Lot, he is graciously hospitable and insists that instead of simply staying within the city as they themselves suggested, they come into his dwelling and spend the night. As the night goes on, the men of Sodom, young and old, press about the house to urge upon the visitors the depravity for which the name of the city has become synonymous. This repulsive behavior is just what Lot had feared when he urged the visitors to stay with him. After the men of Sodom are providentially diverted from their purpose, Lot is allowed to convey a warning to his prospective sons-in-law. But they ignore it, because they regard the threatened overthrow as a huge joke.

The next morning Lot temporizes all along the way and finally secures permission to stay in one of the towns nearby, which, because it was small, was not so likely to have enough wickedness in it to call for divine judgment. The angels make this concession. Lot depicts a weak and reluctant saint of God who fails to appreciate the favor he is being shown; yet for Abraham's sake he is spared.

Lot's wife, her heart still clinging to the foul city, disobeyed the injunction of the angels and looked back. But God's warnings cannot be disregarded with impunity. Even Jesus referred to her in a significant word (Lk. 17:32).

10. Abraham and Sarah at the Court of Gerar (Gen. 20:1–18)

Though the hour of the fulfilment of the long-awaited hope is before the door, the recipient of the promise is far from perfect. Sojourning in Gerar, Abraham told Abimelech, king of that country, that Sarah was his sister. If early in his career he was guilty of the same sin (12:10–20), we could excuse it on the ground that he had but recently become a faithful follower of God. The same excuse no longer holds; Abraham had a basic weakness in his character, a touch of cowardice.

It would be foolish to deny the similarity of this episode with other episodes recorded in Gensis 12:10–20 and 26:7–11. It is equally foolish to claim the identity of the incidents on the ground that they merely represent three different forms of the original event, forms assumed while being transmitted by tradition. Critics seem to forget that certain incidents may repeat themselves in the course of one life, or that lives of children often constitute a strange parallel to those of their parents.

There are striking differences between this account and that of 12:10–20. Note six points of difference: two different places are involved—Egypt and Philistia; two different monarchs of quite different character—one, idolatrous, the other, one who fears the true God; different circumstances prevail—famine on the one hand, nomadic migration on the other; different modes of revelation are employed—the one king surmises the truth, the other receives revelation in a dream; Abraham's reaction to the accusation is quite different in the two instances—in the first, silence; in the second instance, a free explanation before a kind of spiritual discernment; lastly, the two conclusions are radically different—in the first, dismissal from the land; in the second, an invitation to stay.

In any event, why should a nation perpetuate several forms of an incident that reflects no honor whatsoever upon its first father?

11. Birth of Isaac, Expulsion of Ishmael (21:1–21)

When Isaac is born, the gift of the child is ascribed to the Lord. The name given is best rendered as "laughter," for with the gladness springing out of hope fulfilled, Sarah sees her own heart made light. Abraham is happy beyond words.

As the child grows up, the relation between him and Ishmael is bitter. That which is involved is hardly covered by the colorless translation which says that Sarah saw the son of Hagar "playing with her son Isaac." Rather, Ishmael was "mocking." This appears to be what the New Testament has in mind when Paul says (Gal. 4:29) he "persecuted" him. Ishmael made light in a painful way of the spiritual destiny of the lad and caused Isaac to feel that all the importance attached to him was unwarranted. Abraham settles the question as God directs him by sending Hagar and Ishmael away.

God's interest and concern for the wayfarers are described as Hagar calls upon God. An angel of God assures the frightened woman that God "will make of him a great nation" (21:18). This recalls the previous promise (16:10–12) and encourages the mother to build her faith on it. The Hebrew says literally: "Make strong thy hand on him." Verses 20 and 21 imply that the promises made to Ishmael by God were being fulfilled. God's providence watches over him as he grows up.

12. *Abraham's Covenant with Abimelech (21:22–34)*

The account of Abraham's covenant with Abimelech at Beersheba demonstrates how influential and prominent a personage Abraham had become under the Lord's blessing. Neighboring kings sought his good will; Abraham was a mighty man of his day.

This story rounds out the picture of his life and is essential to our understanding of Isaac's experiences with the Philistines. As usual, Abraham stands out as a man who acts in harmony with his faith.

When Abraham reproved Abimelech because his well had been seized by his servants, Abimelech assures Abraham that he had not known of this, and it is implied that the well was immediately restored to its rightful owner, Abraham. Thereupon the two make a solemn covenant indicating that the well is Abraham's.

13. *The Sacrifice of Isaac, Burial of Sarah (22:1—23:20)*

The supreme test of faith that Abraham had to face was the sacrifice of Isaac. There was need for the test. Abraham had to be made aware of a danger that threatened his living relation to God. Because Isaac was born late in his father's life and was a son to whom unusual importance was attached, and also dearly beloved, there certainly was danger that the father might succumb to the temptation of loving him overmuch—for that matter, down in the depths of his heart, more than the Lord Himself. This tendency had to be removed before the danger became insurmountable. Viewed thus, the need of a test that makes Abraham aware of the danger and helps him overcome it is readily apparent.

In any case, God Himself proposed the test. The amazing thing was the obedience of the patriarch, even to the point where the father's hand was stretched out to take the knife. By that time the proof was complete that Abraham would not draw back; he was fully committed. For Abraham the experience was summed up in a unique point of view, expressed in the name he gave the place, Jehovah-jireh, "the Lord will provide." In an amazing way, a substitute sacrifice was prepared by the Lord, a provision that Abraham well and immediately understood. God thereupon renewed his promises to Abraham.

This remarkable event, historical and complete in itself with reference to Abraham, has prophetic import. Under God's providence, it becomes a type of the sacrifice on Calvary. God does not expect man to do for Him what He is not ready to do for man. Abraham and all men are expected to give up their dearest possession to God. This willingness on Abraham's part to make this sacrifice prefigures God's act in giving His Son as Redeemer.

In Abraham's case, the type is all the more to the point because Isaac is an only son, even as Christ is the only begotten Son of God. Nor is it merely a case of pious ingenuity when we discover a parallel between these two. Romans 8:32 sanctions this approach in a word that reads like an allusion to this chapter: "He that spared not his own Son but delivered him up for us all. . . ."

Twenty years later Sarah died (23:1–20). Since the test of the sacrifice of Isaac, the family had moved from Beersheba back to the vicinity of Hebron, roughly halfway between Jerusalem and Beersheba. The purchase of a burial plot for Sarah is in itself an act of faith. Believing that God would give this land to his descendants, as He had promised, Abraham wanted to be buried there and wanted his wife to rest in the same ground.

14. The Marriage of Isaac (24:1–67)

This account of Isaac's marriage is a charming romance. Too advanced in age to do all he would have liked to do, Abraham must enlist the help of his steward Eliezer. Abraham recognized the im-

portance of providing a wife for one from whose line the great
blessing for all the world would ultimately come. The choice demanded double caution, since the very idea of taking a wife from
among the unbelieving Canaanites was out of the question. Detailed
instructions are given to Eliezer, who is to make the long journey
back to Mesopotamia. The matter is of such moment that the servant
must even take a solemn oath governing his conduct. By putting his
hand under the thigh of Abraham, Eliezer signified that Abraham's
progeny were involved. In no case is Eliezer to take a wife from the
neighborhood. Should no suitable candidate be found in Haran, the
servant is absolved from his oath.

For Eliezer the sense of responsibility is so great and the relief at
the successful completion of his mission so overwhelming that the
morning after Rebekah has been chosen he cannot even for a moment
consent to a delay. The very next day after she had met Eliezer,
Rebekah, well aware that she may never see her family again, is on
her way, blessed by their good wishes. She is ready to become the
wife of a man whose father sends so unusual a servant.

15. Abraham's Second Marriage and Death (25:1–11)

Abraham's life now draws to a swift conclusion. In Genesis 17:4,
God had promised Abraham that he would be the "father of a multitude of nations." So at this point we learn where the ancestors of
these nations came from: Abraham married a second time.

Keturah did not have quite the same standing as Sarah, and she is
therefore called a concubine (25:6) and put in a class with Hagar.
However, there was nothing dubious about the whole procedure,
and it is not likely that Abraham took her as a secondary wife during
Sarah's lifetime. The descendants involved are the fathers of certain
Arab tribes which were well enough known to the Israelites of old
but cannot readily be identified in our time. Then Abraham, "full of
years," died at the age of 175 years.

VII. Seventh Story: Ishmael (25:12–18)

With the distinctive heading employed ten times in the book of
Genesis—"this is the history of"—this section on Ishmael is opened.
In Scripture the alien elements, the portions that have only inci-
dental connection with the development of God's kingdom, are

always disposed of briefly. The Bible retains the memory of such groups, but it allots them their proper place. What is not a part of the people of God is unimportant. Ishmael's marriage, the names of his sons, their number—twelve—and the length of Ishmael's life, the death of Ishmael and the dwelling place of his descendants are all that is given.

VIII. Eighth Story: Isaac (25:19—35:29)

1. Birth and History of the Two Brothers (25:19–34)

The account is related to that which went before by a brief summary (25:19–20). Strangely, Rebekah is also barren at first, as Sarah was, so Isaac resorts to prayer (25:21) that God's promises may be realized. After his wife conceives, an unusual incident takes place: Rebekah's children—for they were twins—before they are born jostle one another. Feeling that this portends something, Rebekah inquires of God in prayer whether any significance is to be attached to it. She is informed by an oracle, which is preserved for us in poetic form, that again the usual law of nature should not prevail, but that the elder should be subservient to the younger—Esau should be of less importance than, and obedient to, Jacob.

Verses 27–34 give briefly and dramatically the sale of the birthright of Isaac. Esau, unmindful of the importance of birthright, readily sold it to Jacob for the pottage he had cooked. Esau "despised his birthright."

Jacob was a spiritually minded man with appreciation of spiritual values and with distinct spiritual ambitions. He had ambitions especially in the matter of carrying on the line of promise from which the Saviour would come. The aspirations apparently were begotten by the divine word of promise (25:23). The Lord had destined Jacob to pre-eminence. Jacob gladly accepted the choice and aspired to attain to the treasure promised. His eagerness was commendable, but his means in arriving at the desired end were not above reproach. He was not fully confident of God's methods for arriving at the goal and felt the need of occasionally inserting his own assistance. Such an attitude was one of mistrust. But his spiritual aggressiveness was by no means to be despised, nor was it wrong.

2. Scenes from Isaac's Life (26:1–35)

Isaac is not quite as important a character as Abraham was. Chapter 26 records the few incidents wherein he is the outstanding figure.

At Gerar (26:1–11). Like Abraham, Isaac pretends that his wife is his sister when he too goes to dwell in Gerar. Is it likely that a man whose father had twice erred and been corrected in the matter of a wrong line of conduct should go and repeat his father's mistake? Our answer is that the father's weakness often reappears in the life of his son.

His Prosperity (26:12–17). Where Abraham was for the most part a shepherd, Isaac engages extensively in agriculture and leads a settled form of life. Under the blessing of God he even enjoyed phenomenal harvests—"a hundredfold."

Strife over Wells (26:18–22). A further incident grew out of Isaac's contacts with the people of Gerar. Strife over wells springs from the fact that possession of them is extremely important in that land.

The Appearance of the Lord (26:23–25). Already (vv. 3–5) God had appeared to Isaac and renewed to him the promise to Abraham. Now He adds further reassurance.

Covenant with the Philistines (26:26–33). Lest we think too lightly of Isaac, we are here shown that he enjoyed the esteem of neighbors practically in the same measure that his father did.

Esau's Hittite Wives (26:34, 35). Esau married two daughters of Hittites, a cause for grief on the part of his faithful, God-fearing parents.

3. Isaac Blesses Jacob (27:1–45)

This well-known chapter is usually distorted in that Jacob is represented as the man who together with his mother was guilty of evil, whereas Isaac and Esau are represented as grievously wronged. In truth, all four characters appear equally in the wrong; for the basic word of guidance that the family possessed as to the relation of the brothers in days to come is found in 25:23, "the elder shall serve the younger." There is every reason to believe that Isaac knew the word and good ground for holding that the sons were not ignorant of it.

Now Isaac, in preparing to bless Esau (17:4), is openly taking a step to annul this word. He and Esau are working in defiance of it. Though Rebekah and Jacob are using deception, it can at least be claimed that they are doing it in the interest of bringing the promise of God to pass. Jacob cleverly deceives his father and obtains the blessing in Esau's stead. But deception is deception.

When the shock of it hits both Isaac and Esau, there is great consternation, but it is finally agreed that there is no possibility of annuling Jacob's blessing. Father and son seem to feel that the hand of the Lord was in all that transpired. Esau, however, now appreciates, perhaps for the first time, what the blessing of the firstborn, which he had bartered away, might have meant to him, and finally prevails upon his father to give him as much of a blessing as he can.

4. Jacob's Departure to Haran and his First Vision (27:46—28:22)

Because of Esau's anger, Jacob finds it wise to leave home, partly in the interest of finding a wife in Mesopotamia. Here again, a brief interlude appears. Lest we think ill of Esau beyond what he deserves, it is here reported how he made a somewhat crude attempt to please his parents (28:6–9).

Now follows the famous Bethel experience. Overtaken by nightfall in the open field near Bethel, Jacob spends the night there, using a stone for a pillow. A dream comes to him, which, according to its import, must truly have been sent by God and have been the equivalent of a vision, for in it the Lord appeared to him. In the dream a ladder, so set that it appears to reach from earth to heaven, is used by angels, who are ascending and descending it. Above it stands the Lord. From what follows, and from what we otherwise know of angels, it would appear that this part of the dream symbolizes the protection of God's holy angels, who are provided for the necessities of God's saints (Ps. 91:11). Their going up and down symbolizes their bringing, humanly speaking, man's petitions before God, and, on the other hand, delivering help from above (cf. also Jn. 1:51).

Upon awakening in the dead of night, Jacob's reaction is twofold. First, he is amazed that the Lord, the faithful covenant God, should come to meet him, the sinner, and give him rich promises in the land of his wanderings. He may have known of the omnipresence of the Lord in general, but he hardly expected to have it displayed, apart from his father's abode, in the midst of a land of wicked inhabitants. The second reaction of Jacob is a fear of God, such as perhaps he had never felt before. This fear, however, was nothing other than a deeper reverence for God and for the place where He had manifested Himself.

On awaking in the morning, Jacob consecrates the stone that served as his pillow. Everything in this place is holy. The stone itself, having been upended that he might recognize it upon his return, is consecrated by the pouring of oil on it as a sort of marker. The place as such is by him now designated as Bethel, "house of God," for Jacob already had in mind to make a sanctuary here. Jacob then says in effect: If God is about to do all this for me which He has promised, there are two things that I want to do as tokens of my gratitude; one is, this stone shall mark a sanctuary at this place; and I will also give a tithe to the Lord. In any case, Jacob deeply appreciated all of the Lord's rich grace toward him. His vow was not marked by a mercenary attitude.

Jacob's vision is one of great symbolical significance. Bethel, because of its meaning, is an important place in Scripture. For the Christian it signifies God's omnipresence. Since Christ himself alluded to this experience in John 1:51—"Hereafter ye shall see heaven open, and the angels of God ascending and descending upon the Son of man"—it is evident that Christ Himself represents the perfect embodiment of continual communion with the Father in heaven. In terms of dispensational truth, the scene depicts Israel the nation, cast out of the Land of Promise because of sin, but strong in the promise of restoration and blessing (28:15).

5. Jacob's Double Marriage and Family (29:1—30:43)

A love story worthily told! But though the chapter in its own way glorifies true love, it shows how in some deep, mysterious way the God of justice let deeper forces come into play in that Jacob, who had in his time so abundantly deceived others, was now deceived himself.

We find Jacob at Haran at a well outside the city. Flocks are gathering preparatory to the ritual of watering them at evening time. The meeting of Jacob and Rachel has something of the providential in it, even as was the case when Eliezer met Rebekah at the well. It is one of the finest tales in any literature of love at first sight.

Arrangements are quickly made for Jacob's permanent stay. The arrangements include some sort of understanding about their marriage. That the seven years "seemed to him but a few days" is the most eloquent way of saying how much he loved Rachel. Cruel deception is practiced by Laban on the wedding night. Fortunately, an adjustment is reached whereby Rachel need not be eliminated, though seven years more of faithful service are added by way of stipulation.

The Growth of Jacob's Family and of his Wealth (29:31—30:43). But now Jacob is a bigamist. In his defense, he never had any intentions of having more wives than one. After Laban's treachery, there was practically no other course for him, at least in the thinking of men at that time. Although the Scripture voices no censure of Jacob, neither, on the other hand, does it condone or approve what he does. The names of the twelve sons ultimately born to the patriarch are indicative of the internal struggle that went on within this family. Several incidents indicate what jealousy took possession of the two wives under these strained relations. Bringing the handmaids into the picture after the custom of those times, even as the Sarai-Hagar case shows, did not solve the difficulties.

In the course of time, Jacob's stay in Mesopotamia turns out to be less pleasant than it first was, for Laban was not too easy to get along with. A new working agreement is reached at the insistence of Laban. Jacob on his part can point to the fact that Laban's wealth has greatly increased, whereas he, who has been largely instrumental under God in securing this added wealth by his hard work, has been unable to secure anything for himself. Laban, when pressed, consents to turn over all "spotted and speckled" lambs and goats to Jacob.

It would seem that Jacob, in consenting to the arrangement, knew that God was blessing him as He had promised, and was ready to make the whole matter an issue of faith. It is also possible that, when he saw how Laban was resorting to all kinds of scheming and chicanery, Jacob felt inclined to match wits with Laban. Still, throughout this strange contest, Jacob never departed from the policy of fair play.

6. Jacob's Flight from Laban (31:1–55)

Finally, the situation in which Jacob found himself became unbearable, and the Lord Himself sanctioned Jacob's departure. His own family, which basically is still a wholesome unit, fully agrees with Jacob. The daughters of Laban themselves see clearly how cruel advantage has been taken of them by their father's machinations. Jacob is not slow to act; he maneuvers his flocks into a suitable position. Three days' journey separates them in any case.

The whole nomad group departs. Laban, on discovering what has happened, sets out in pursuit, apparently with hostile intent. Only God knows what might have been the outcome. So God Himself intervenes, appearing to Laban in a dream by night, and forbids him to undertake any act of reprisal.

When Laban finally overtakes his son-in-law, he plays at first the part of the outraged father in a hypocritical speech. Finally he comes to the issue: "Why did you steal my goods?" Unaware that Rachel has stolen her father's idols, Jacob threatens death to the guilty one should such a one be found. The tents and all the possessions are searched. Rachel outwits her father by pretending that her sickness does not allow her to get up from the saddle-bags on which she is sitting and in which she has hidden the images. So Laban fails to find the teraphim.

All the while Jacob's indignation has been rising at all the unkind, unjust treatment at the hands of his father-in-law, and his pent-up feelings demand release. Justly angry, Jacob says what he would have long been justified in saying. This blast serves a wholesome purpose in checking Laban and cooling his indignation. Almost cowed, Laban still speaks boastfully, but concedes that nothing can be done about it, and winds up by suggesting a treaty, as between two hostile forces. The spot is usually designated *Mizpah* (watchpost).

Certainly the unkindest word spoken in this connection is the one where Laban invoked the judgment of God and His intervention on the one (meaning Jacob) who might venture to break this covenant. The words "the LORD watch between me and thee when we are absent one from another" (31:49) are words full of mistrust and unkind spirit.

7. Jacob and Esau (32:1—33:20)

Preparations for Meeting Esau (32:1–23). After Jacob and Laban have parted, an unusual vision is granted to Jacob. He sees the angels of God, two bands of them, for that is the meaning of the name (Mahanaim) which he gives to the place. Without doubt this vision was given him to strengthen his faith for the unusual trials ahead.

After sending a friendly message to Esau, Jacob learns that his brother is coming toward him with four hundred men. Jacob does what any godly man would do under the circumstances; he immediately prays. He bases his approach to God for help on the fact that he had not undertaken this journey depending on his own insight, but that God had told him to return. Then follows one of the finest statements that any patriarch ever made. Before Jacob even asks for help, he admits his utter unworthiness of it, "I am not worthy of the least of all the steadfast love and all the faithfulness which thou hast shown to thy servant." Then comes the prayer for divine deliverance, which Jacob bases directly on the promise given him by God, none other than the old promise initially given to Abraham.

Jacob Becomes Israel (32:24–32). After the place of lodging for the night has been reached, Jacob makes ready a great gift of livestock in the hope of softening his brother's anger. Not only now does the full measure of danger strike him with renewed force, but a most alarming and disconcerting thing occurs—a stranger mysteriously appears and grapples with him. He is merely called "a man." As the struggle develops, Jacob discovers the identity of the man and knows that he is God.

Why this unusual procedure was resorted to by God will be difficult to analyze, because there is no event in Scripture quite the equal of the one here described. God appears to have assumed some tangible physical form. But the struggle was more than physical; it was, in essence, the wrestling of prayer. This could well have been done to impress Jacob with the knowledge that, as long as he continued in self-centered ways of living, God was his enemy more than Esau. So he had to fight God first. All this may in the course of that terrible night have dawned, step by step, on Jacob's consciousness. For that matter, does not fervent prayer often involve body and soul? In the end, Jacob secures God's blessing.

Jacob commemorated his experience with God by naming the place Peniel, which means "the face of God." Here he received for his old name, which meant "supplanter," the new name, Israel, "for as a prince hast thou power with God and with men, and hast prevailed" (32:28).

The Brothers' Reconciliation (33:1–20) As morning comes, the much-dreaded meeting takes place; Jacob looks up and sees Esau with his four hundred men. Here is a supreme example how the Lord directs the hearts of men. At the sight of his twin brother, the companion of his youth, all injuries are forgotten and impulsive Esau runs to meet Jacob, falls on his neck and kisses him and both weep as a relief from the tension they have felt; each seems equally glad they have met on amicable terms. After the reconciliation, Jacob journeys to Succoth—location unknown—and presently to Shechem, while Esau goes down into the area far to the south.

8. Jacob's Sons Avenge the Seduction of Dinah (34:1–31)

The record of the seduction of Dinah by Shechem, the son of Hamor, the Hivite, and the vengeful murders committed by two sons of Jacob, Simeon and Levi, reveals to what degree they had departed from the high ideals of godliness exemplified by Abraham and Isaac. The terrible events probably occurred about ten years after Jacob's return to Canaan when Dinah was at least fourteen years old, or possibly fifteen.

The brothers, "pained and very angry that folly had been committed against Israel" (v. 7), took matters into their own hands. Infected by the loose morals in the land of Canaan, they determined a vengeance which Jacob, upbraiding them, could only find a source of deep and lasting trouble.

Not a word can be said to excuse the murderers. The account, as Moses gives it, is strictly objective; it does not commend nor condemn. The author trusts that his readers possess sufficient ethical discernment to judge the deed. Those who regard these accounts as largely legendary should pause at this chapter; for no nation develops legends about events that reflect dishonor upon their nation, particularly, as in this case, upon the tribal father of the priests, Levi.

9. Last Events of Isaac's Life (35:1–29)

God summons Jacob to fulfil the vow he had made years ago at Bethel after his departure from home (28:20–22). Jacob's delay in performing his vow apparently is one of those cases where, under the stress of circumstances, high and holy promises are made, but one waits to fulfil them at a convenient time. Jacob, who needed to be reminded of his vow, now takes the matter in hand with appropriate thoroughness. He knows the serious disorders within his own household, chief of which is idolatry. He therefore calls for all the images of foreign gods in order to dispose of them, and the journey to Bethel begins.

A caravan on the march was easy prey for the Canaanites who were actually in a mood for revenge, but a "terror from God" (35:5) fell upon them and restrained them. Jacob's company, therefore, though very much inferior in numbers, made the trip in safety. Jacob's sons apparently never realized how foolishly they acted in the slaughter of the Shechemites because of Dinah's dishonor.

The building of the altar at Bethel fulfils the vow to establish a house of God on this spot (28:22). By this means, the spot where God had appeared to him was hallowed and the remembrance of the experience preserved. To confirm Jacob's name of Israel (35:10) and reinforce all the blessings of previous experiences (vv. 11, 12), God again appears to Jacob.

As the journey southward continued—for Hebron was now the home where Isaac dwelt—the time for the birth of Rachel's second son drew near in the vicinity of Bethlehem. There, as Rachel breathed her last, she gave her child the tragic name of "son of my sorrow." This name Jacob rightly changed to the more optimistic Benjamin—"son of my right hand."

From this time onward, Jacob enters into the full patriarchal heritage, having at last attained to a spiritual maturity which is analogous to that of the patriarch. Coincident with this is Isaac's receding into the background. Consequently his death is reported, though it does not occur for another twelve or thirteen years.

IX. Ninth Story: Esau (36:1–43)

In harmony with his previous procedure, the author, having concluded the "history of Isaac" and being ready to take up the "history of Jacob," first disposes of the less relevant "history of Esau." In 27:39, 40, Isaac had pronounced a blessing upon Esau, and it is worth noting how it pleased the Lord to bless him and make him to become a nation.

The skeleton history of Esau serves this purpose and bears testimony to a breadth of interest on Moses' part. For though Esau had, indeed, begun to display fully inveterate animosity at Moses' time, Moses believed that it behooved Israel to have a generous interest in this brother-race.

This chapter includes Esau's wives and children and their settlement in Seir (36:1–8); Esau's descendants (vv. 9–14); the Edomitish chiefs (vv. 15–19); the Horite chiefs (vv. 20–30); the Edomitish kings (vv. 31–39); and the Edomitish chiefs—after another classification (vv. 40–43).

X. Tenth Story: Jacob (37:1—50:26)

The last fourteen chapters of Genesis are, without doubt, the most interesting and dramatic of the entire book. A part of the interest of the narrative lies in the great wealth of detail, actually of vast importance since Moses is now writing history that involves the fathers of the twelve tribes. There is much in this history that the tribes themselves should be acquainted with for their comfort and admonition.

It is not the author's skill that renders these chapters dramatic, but the events themselves. The drama involved is practically nothing other than the unusual display of divine providence which shines forth more brilliantly here than perhaps anywhere else in sacred history. God's providence watched over the chosen race as it was about to go, step by step, into the depths of national enslavement. One element of encouragement for these trying days was to be the remembrance of the signal tokens of divine grace experienced just before the years in Egypt.

For all that Joseph is predominant in the entire section, Jacob has still an important role (37:1). In contact with non-Israelites, Joseph surely achieved remarkable prominence, but for the inner spiritual history of the Kingdom of God, he does not come up to the level of his fathers.

However, more distinctly than the others, the life of Joseph stands out as a type of Christ. Abraham exemplifies the Father Who was to give up His only begotten Son. Isaac passively typifies the Son who suffers Himself to be offered up. But in Joseph's case a wealth of suggestive parallels comes to the surface. For as Joseph, a righteous man, is made to suffer for righteousness' sake, but finally triumphs over all iniquity, so the truly Righteous One, the Saviour of man, experiences the same things in heightened degree.

This facet of the story is beautifully supplemented by Pascal (*Pensées*, quoted by Delitzsch): "Jesus Christ is prefigured by Joseph: the beloved of his father, sent by the father to his brethren, the innocent one sold by his brethren for twenty pieces of silver and so made their lord, their saviour, and the saviour of strangers and the saviour of the world; all of which would not have happened if they had not had the purpose to destroy him, if they had not sold and rejected him. In prison Joseph the innocent one between two malefactors—Jesus on the cross between two evildoers; Joseph predicts good fortune to the one and death to the other, though both appear alike—Jesus saves the one and leaves the other in his just condemnation, though both stood charged with the same crime. Joseph begs of the one who is to be delivered to remember him when he is restored to honor, and he whom Jesus saves asks to be remembered when He comes in His kingdom."

The ways of divine providence could hardly be stranger, and God's hand in history is marvelously demonstrated to the eyes of faith.

1. *Joseph and his Brothers (37:2–36)*

In contrast to his brothers, Joseph in every sense had a more solid character than they. He was not involved in the murder of the Shechemites. He kept himself pure over against the things done by Judah (38:1–30) and Reuben (35:22). His father had solid grounds for preferring Joseph, and Joseph may well be thought of as being the only one of the sons with whom the godly father had true spiritual kinship. That does not, however, absolve Joseph from indiscretion. Before his father interpreted his two dreams for him, Joseph told them to his brothers. There may have been a matter of unseemly pride displayed here. Joseph too was doubtless a character that stood in need of cleansing.

This brings us to the matter of the "robe with sleeves" (RSV) rather than "the coat of many colors" (KJV). The first translation is the correct one. Such robes were the distinctive feature of dress of the ruling class, and Jacob, in effect, was indicating by such a gift that he designated Joseph to be the head of the clan after him.

The ill-feelings of the brothers come to head at Dothan. At the sight of Joseph so far from home, the thought of a revenge that they might cleverly cover up entices the brothers to plot murder. They at once devise a plausible explanation for what took place—"a wild beast has devoured him" (37:33). But at least there is a spark of decency and the fear of God left among them: Reuben feels a strong responsibility, not strong enough to make a straightforward approach to the problem, but at least enough to gain a reprieve.

Joseph is stripped of his long-sleeved robe and cast into one of the many cisterns to be found in the land, fortunately dry at the time. Reuben at this point must have left. Judah, saner than the rest, proposes to have Joseph sold at once to a passing band of Ishmaelites, who are Midianites according to their place of residence. Thus Joseph is brought as a slave to the land of Egypt. He was not literally murdered, but the deed by his brothers was hardly less cruel.

2. *Judah and Tamar (38:1–30)*

This story of one of Jacob's sons would seem to indicate that no matter how strongly they believed in the divine destiny of their family, they were running grave danger of being submerged by the Canaanite element, making matrimonial alliances with them and adopting pagan ideals of life. Though the Canaanites were inferior to Israel morally, they were ready to establish close contacts with the descendants of Abraham.

The things that take place in this chapter occurred during the twenty-two years that intervened between the sale of Joseph and the settlement in Egypt. Judah had time to marry, to have a son whom in his seventeenth year he gives in marriage, to have a second son whom in his eighteenth year he gives to the same wife, and two years remain for the rest of the events of this chapter. It is as if the writer were saying: While Joseph was spending dreary years in Egypt, every form of immorality was going on in Canaan. So fast were the children of Jacob becoming like the Canaanites that, had they remained there, they might quickly have lost their racial and spiritual identity. One can readily see why a sojourn in a land like Egypt was a necessity from the Lord's point of view, for the Egyptians of old were noted for their aversion to strangers, especially to shepherds (46:34).

The conclusion of the chapter (38:27–30) records the birth of twin sons to Tamar, Jacob's daughter-in-law, and Judah—a matter of considerable interest to their descendants.

3. *Joseph's Imprisonment and Liberation (39:1—40:23)*

Joseph's lot, certainly a trying one, involved two items of gain for him. As the manager of the affairs of Potiphar, Joseph learned Egyptian ways and business administration, an experience which was later to stand him in good stead. Also, by being humbled, he was to find a sudden rise to honor and dignity less dangerous because in a lowly position he had learned humility. The rapid promotion of Joseph is an indication of the unusual executive ability he must have possessed.

But Joseph stands in need of seasoning of character. The problem centers in the wife of Potiphar, who by this time found Joseph extremely good-looking. Fearing God, Joseph could not yield to her blandishments.

Love spurned turns to hate, and when the woman slanders Joseph, the master in anger has him cast into prison. Joseph seems to face lifelong imprisonment as a result of this unjust treatment, but divine providence is the overruling factor in this life. The Lord has purposes in mind for Joseph and his brothers, and we again read: "The Lord was with Joseph." So Joseph, although still a prisoner, was given a position of trust, and part of the bitterness of his experience was alleviated.

We are justified in saying that the two officials of Pharaoh, the butler and baker, were allowed to dream their dreams primarily because of the bearing they could have on Joseph's future (40:1–23). Joseph's concern for the difficulties of others is demonstrated in his kind inquiries into their dejection. Joseph, experienced in the matter of dreams himself, asserts positively that interpretation of dreams is God's business. In the end he interprets the dreams of both, one favorably, the other unfavorably. On the third day the predicted outcome takes place. The butler is fully restored to service in the immediate presence of Pharaoh. But the story closes on the sad note that the butler did not remember Joseph and the kindness shown him, but promptly forgot.

4. Dreams Interpreted (41:1–57)

But when Pharaoh's two dreams baffle the Egyptian dream-interpreters, the butler remembers Joseph. He confesses his neglect, tells of his experience, and impresses his listeners with the fact that he knows a man who can interpret dreams accurately. One verse (41:14) tells swiftly the preparations that were made to render Joseph presentable at court. It seems as though in a moment Joseph is out of prison and in the royal presence.

The positive tone of Joseph's interpretation is the most amazing thing about it. The "sevens" stand for seven good years and seven bad years; the seven good years in Egypt will be wiped out by the years of blight. God has disclosed what He is about to do.

Briefly, Joseph suggests how to meet the emergency. Pharaoh, recognizing immediately that here is a man with a plan which is far in advance of his own best thinking on the subject, makes Joseph the food administrator on the spot, and defines his authority: only the king shall exceed him in influence. With the beginning of the years of dearth in Egypt come similar years of famine "in all lands." Soon—and it is toward this point the narrative has been moving—people from other lands have to come to the one land where grain is available.

5. Joseph and his Brothers in Egypt (42:1—45:28)

The scene opens in Canaan when the good news first comes that grain is being sold in Egypt. The father and sons have apparently discussed this piece of news before. In perplexity they are looking at one another. With full patriarchal authority, Jacob takes the situation in hand and orders his sons to go to Egypt and buy some. Ten go, but Benjamin is kept home by a father who has become apprehensive for the only child of Rachel he still has.

When the brothers appear before Joseph, he cross-questions them, and one thing after another comes to light. Their attitude has changed, and there seems to be some contrition over the way they have treated their father. In the course of the investigation they give Joseph a rather complete account of what the situation is now after some twenty years.

Finally, lest the family at home suffer, Joseph allows them to depart after further instructions. They may all go home but Simeon, who will be released only if they bring their youngest brother along the next time. The discussion among the ten as a result of this announcement did much to inform Joseph as to their basic attitude on every major issue involved, especially when it becomes evident that they view their selling of Joseph with some measure of remorse.

Both to perplex them and to increase their apprehensiveness, Joseph orders their money to be put back into the mouth of their sacks (42:25). On their arrival home they first give their father a full account of what transpired. Scarcely has the father recovered from this shock, when they go about the business of emptying their sacks of grain, and each man's money is found in the mouth of the sack. To them this appears to seal their doom.

The Second Journey to Egypt with Benjamin (43:1–34). The dreaded day of return arrives. If the family is to stay alive, the trip to Egypt must be made. With deep sincerity Judah pleads that they be allowed to go, taking Benjamin along, and promises that he personally will accept all responsibility (vv. 8, 9). Jacob faces the inevitable, and, seeing no alternative, consents to have Benjamin go.

When they arrive in Egypt, to their surprise they are kindly received and invited to dinner. Hardly has Joseph joined them in his house when they bring their little present. He may have been touched, but treats it lightly, and in a burst of genial friendliness inquires first after their father. Having ascertained that he is well, Joseph turns to examine the new face, that of Benjamin. Carefully he inquires whether this is the youngest. When so assured, he is able to do no more than bless his brother when a rush of feeling overwhelms him so that he is obliged to turn aside for the moment and leave the room, overcome with emotion and tears. Shortly, with every trace of tears removed, the strange Egyptian official comes back and orders the food to be served (43:31–34).

The Successful Outcome of the Last Test (44:1–34). So far everything that Joseph has attempted to do for his brothers has been successful; they are better men than they once were. But one last step is yet to be taken: it must be determined what they will do when they are put in a position where they can postively turn back from their evil way and do what is right in a situation similar to the one when Joseph was sold. Very skilfully Joseph creates a new situation in which the group that once sold him will be tempted in a spirit of selfishness to give up another brother. Benjamin is made to appear as the guilty one. Then it is that Judah, speaking as only a changed man can, makes his unselfish plea. The attitude of the other brothers as they listen to Judah plead convinces Joseph that something of the spirit that now animated Judah lodges also in their breasts.

Joseph Revealed to his Brothers; Family Called to Egypt (45:1–28). The time has come for Joseph to reveal his identity. In utter consternation, the brothers find they have been dealing with Joseph. The situation calls for words from Joseph to alleviate their misgivings. The sale into Egypt is mentioned but passed by quickly, for Joseph understands by this time the deeper purposes of the Lord's providence which had sent him in advance of his family to prepare for the trying times to come. At once, with the clear purpose that marked all his actions, Joseph sets forth his plans for the rest of the family of Israel.

6. *Israel Settled in Egypt (46:1—47:27)*

Jacob's sacrifice at Beersheba, the southern edge of the land, was the equivalent of a prayer for guidance. In a clear vision, the Lord directs the patriarch who wants to do only what meets with divine approval. The story moves over into the land of Goshen, where they are to settle and where Joseph meets Jacob. The meeting is marked by quiet weeping of the two; the issues are too deep for words.

Joseph lets Pharaoh personally confirm the plans that he has for his brothers and their families (47:1-6). Five representatives are set before Pharaoh, rather than all the brothers. When Pharaoh graciously inquires, they answer as they are instructed, and the land of Goshen is made available to them. Then the old patriarch Jacob is presented to Pharaoh and blesses him (vv. 7-10).

7. *Jacob's Preparation for his End (47:28—49:32)*

Though Jacob thought death was near at the time he stood before Pharaoh, he lived seventeen more years near his beloved son in Egypt and reached 147 years of age. As the end approaches, he calls Joseph and asks that he not be buried in Egypt. It is not merely a matter of sentiment that makes him wish to lie with his fathers; it is a matter of faith. Jacob believes God's promises in reference to Israel, the land of Canaan, and the blessing of all nations of the world through the Saviour to come. Jacob wants even his burial to give testimony to his faith. Joseph promises Jacob that his directions will be carried out.

The Blessing of Joseph's Sons (48:1-22). Jacob formally adopts Joseph's sons, who may now have been at least eighteen to twenty years old. His words are, "they shall belong to me," that is, they are to be reckoned as full-fledged sons on a par with his two eldest sons, Reuben and Simeon. Thus Joseph is to be represented among the tribes by two men, each richly blessed.

Jacob's Blessing of his own Sons (49:1-27). The statement in verse 28 by way of summary rightly describes these words of Jacob as a blessing. This term must be taken in its broadest sense, for some of the words spoken were words of censure. However, censure can be a help and blessing to man. As Jacob begins the blessing, he says that he will tell his sons "that which shall befall you in the last days."

Judah gets a unique pre-eminence (49:8–12). "A whelp of a lion" is the symbol of his courage and leadership. Verse 10 clearly refers to the messianic hope and is best translated according to the Hebrew "until Shiloh come." Shiloh means "man of rest." In Him the qualities of Judah will be brought to perfection, for this is clearly a reference to the Messiah, Who is to spring from the tribe of Judah.

In closing, Jacob again charges that he is to be buried with his people and gives explicit directions that he is to be buried in the grave acquired by Abraham. With the giving of the last instruction, he dies, either instantly or within a very few hours.

8. *Burial of Jacob and Death of Joseph (49:33—50:26)*

The entire mourning for Israel by the Egyptians lasted seventy days, which included forty days during which the embalming took place. That the Egyptians mourned is an indication of the high esteem in which he was held, both as a prince in his own right and as the father of Joseph. Martin Luther points out that there is no burial recorded in Scripture quite as honorable as this, or with such wealth of detail.

Joseph requests permission of Pharaoh to go to Canaan to bury his father, and a great cortege is set up to carry out the wishes of Jacob for return of his body to his own country (50:4–10). After the burial Joseph and the entire company return to Egypt.

Thereupon the brethren of Joseph, realizing that their father is gone and fearing that it has been his influence that has softened Joseph's heart toward them, express the fear that now he will turn against them. Their own guilt is causing them to mistrust the brother who befriended them years before. Joseph readily gives them every assurance upon their expression of genuine sorrow and repentance: "Do not be afraid."

Joseph's story is briefly concluded. He lived in Egypt to the end of his days, 110 years, and lived to see his grandchildren.

When he came to die, Joseph, like Jacob, imposed an oath upon the children of Israel that they are ultimately to bring his bones to the Land of Promise. By laying the obligation upon his people, Joseph gave eloquent testimony to his faith in God's promises, and by leaving his body in their midst, he placed them in continual reminder of their promise.

The initial step in the keeping of that promise is recorded. When Joseph dies—the age being repeated in the more solemn style of narrative, as is common in epic poetry also—they embalm him and put him into an *'arón,* a word whose primary significance is "box," used also of the ark of the covenant.

With this scene, which eloquently calls for the continuation provided by Exodus, Genesis comes to a conclusion which indicates that, like the others of the five books of Moses, it is a finished product, designed to be complete in itself, but also to be an integral part of a greater work.

Exodus

MERRILL F. UNGER

EXODUS IS INTIMATELY connected with Genesis and, without a break, carries forward the account of redemptive history there begun.

Although this second book of the Pentateuch covers a long span of years (430 according to Ex. 12:40), the author treats this extended interval with extreme brevity. The entire period, except for the last year, is covered in the first two chapters. That one year in which occurred the climactic event of Israel's deliverance out of Egypt and the inauguration of a new relationship with God occupies the remaining thirty-eight chapters of the book.

The Egyptian sojourn lasted from about 1871 B.C. to about 1441 B.C. (For an analysis of Old Testament chronology from the standpoint of conservative scholarship, see the writer's *Archaeology and the Old Testament*, 1954, pp. 140–152, where the various theories of the date of the Exodus are discussed.) The patriarchal period in Palestine evidently was contemporary with the strong Middle Kingdom in Egypt under the Twelfth Dynasty (2000–1780 B.C.). Joseph became prime minister of, and Jacob stood before, one of the powerful rulers (Amenemes I–IV or Senwosret I–III) of this line of kings. Israel, accordingly, lived in Egypt during the Hyksos Period of foreign domination (1780–1546 B.C.), was oppressed by the great warrior Thutmose III (1482–1450 B.C.) of the Eighteenth Dynasty, and left the country under Amenhotep II (1450–1425 B.C.).

I. Oppression in Egypt (1:1—11:10)

This book of redemption commences where all redemption begins —in need for deliverance. The people became enslaved, and were crushed with cruel burdens. Persecuted and afflicted, they sighed for relief.

1. The Egyptian Servitude (1:1–22)

Joseph died and several centuries passed. A new king, doubtless under the powerful Eighteenth Dynasty, came to the throne. This ruler was unaware of Joseph's past service to the Egyptians, and he oppressed and persecuted the Israelites.

But the oppression of the people is prefaced by a recital of the expansion of the Israelites (1:1–7). From Jacob's modest offspring—seventy persons (v. 5)—his posterity expanded to an amazing extent. They "multiplied and grew exceeding strong . . . so that the land was filled with them" (v. 7). The account of their small beginning serves to emphasize their rapid growth.

This picture of expansion introduces the account of heartless oppression (1:8–14). Jealousy and fear goaded the new monarch to issue harsh decrees intended to reduce the Hebrews and to break their spirit. Taskmasters were appointed over them, and they were demoted to slaves assigned to build the imperial store cities of Pithom (Tel er-Retabeh) and Raamses (Tanis).

But the multiplication of the Israelites was a divine blessing. Their enslavement and unbearable bondage did not deplete their numbers; rather, they increased more and more. The result was that the fear and dread of the Egyptians against the people of Israel were augmented. New burdens, including severe field labor and work in mortar and brick, became the intolerable lot of Jacob's posterity.

The final phase of Israel's affliction by the oppressing Pharaoh assumed the form of planned extinction (1:15–22). The Hebrew midwives, Shiprah and Puah, were instructed to kill all male babies born to Hebrew women. The noble conduct of these women in sparing the male children brought them special divine blessing. Convinced that he could not exterminate the Israelites this way, Pharaoh commanded all his people to drown every male Hebrew baby in the Nile. In this dramatic situation, divine Providence clashed with human perverseness in the struggle of the divine against the diabolical—God supporting His people, and Satan, through the king of Egypt, trying to exterminate them.

2. Preparation of the Deliverer (2:1—4:31)

The intense suffering of the enslaved people accentuated their need for deliverance. The agent of that deliverance was provided in the person of Moses. This section exhibits the first eighty years in the life of one of the greatest men of Old Testament times, a type of Christ as the deliverer. First Moses is presented as a prince in

Egypt (2:1–15). His birth of parents of the house of Levi during the period of great suffering is sheltered by God's providential interest in His chosen people. Beautiful is the story of his mother's three-month concealment of Moses and her later hiding of him in the reeds at the river's bank in a basket of bullrushes, daubed with bitumen (vv. 1–4). Awe-inspiring are the grace and faithfulness of God that causes Pharaoh's daughter to find the child and, her heart touched with pity, to adopt him as her own. Striking is the governance of God, directing the princess, through the infant's sister, to call the child's own mother as a nurse. Not only is the babe spared from death, but he is guarded by Pharaonic power, and his nursing-care is paid for out of the royal treasury (vv. 5–10). He was called Moses, evidently meaning "the child" in Egyptian. But in Hebrew, by a peculiar coincidence of sound and circumstance, the name is connected with the root *mashah* "to draw out," so that the royal princess apparently gave him an Egyptian-Hebrew nickname to fit the circumstances of his being drawn out of the Nile.

Reared in the luxury and intrigue of the Egyptian court, Moses when he was grown up exhibited sterling faith. He refused to be called the son of Pharaoh's daughter, "choosing rather," as a later commentator records, "to bear ill treatment with the people of God than to enjoy the fleeting pleasures of sin. He considered abuse suffered for the Christ greater wealth than the treasures of Egypt, for he looked to the reward" (Heb. 11:24–26).

Despite his great faith, Moses, the Egyptian prince, was not yet ready to serve as deliverer of God's people. His murder in the heat of anger of an Egyptian who was beating a Hebrew, one of his people, mirrored the need of further disciplinary action in his own soul (2:11–14). Forty years as a prince in Egypt were to be followed by forty years as a rustic shepherd in Midian. What he had not learned as heir apparent to the Egyptian throne, he was to learn as a humble keeper of sheep in the quietude of the desert. The voice of God in the solitude of the wilderness, heard above the bleating of the sheep and the soft moan of the wind in the acacia trees, would teach him what was difficult to comprehend in the palace halls at Thebes or Raamses. He must learn to deny the sense of self-importance, to discover his nothingness and God's omnipotence. In Egypt he had learned the wisdom of man; in the desert he was to learn the wisdom of God.

As an exile from Egypt, Moses helped the shepherd daughters of

Reuel (Jethro), the priest of Midian, and gained one of them, Zipporah, as a wife (2:16–22). Meanwhile, as the years passed, there was a change in the occupant of the Egyptian throne. The lot of the enslaved Israelites grew steadily worse. God remembered His covenant with Abraham, Isaac, and Jacob, heard the prayer of His oppressed people (vv. 23–25), and laid His hand upon His chosen deliverer, Moses.

Moses' call and commission are presented in chapter 3. He is given the vision of the burning bush (vv. 1–3). As he looks, a common desert thornbush is aflame with fire, yet it is not consumed. The prickly shrub pictured the sinful, enslaved Israelites, since thorns are the result of the curse of sin (Gen. 3:17, 18). The fire symbolizes their suffering and tribulation. The unscathed bush shows that all the persecution visited upon the people could not annihilate them. As the appearance of the angel of the Lord out of the flaming bush indicates, they are preserved by divine power.

The vision of the burning bush is followed by Moses' call (3:4–10). The One Who calls him reveals Himself as the God of Abraham, Isaac, and Jacob. Moses, who had already removed his sandals because the place on which he was standing was holy ground, now hid his face, for he was afraid to look on God's presence. God's message was one of sovereign grace on behalf of the miserable slaves in Egypt; He saw their helpless condition and was moved to deliver them. The salvation which the Lord was undertaking for His people typified the future incarnation of the Word Who was God (Jn. 1:1, 15) for the redemption of sinful man.

In answering God's call, Moses voices distrust in himself (3:11, 12). "Who am I, that I should go unto Pharaoh and that I should bring forth the children of Israel out of Egypt?" Forty years before in self-confidence he had undertaken the work of deliverance and had run before he was sent. Now the vision and voice of God had revealed his human weakness and taught him humility. God's reply is terse but sufficient: "I will be with you." To bolster faith God gives Moses a sign of His delivering power. Redeemed out of Egypt, the people of Israel would one day serve God upon this very mount where now He revealed Himself to His servant.

To Moses' query—what should he reply when the enslaved people ask him God's name?—God's answer comes, "I am Who I am." This was the disclosure of the eternal God Who by His omnipotence would consummate their redemption from Pharaoh's yoke (3:13–

18). The words "I am Who I am" are evidently intended to be an interpretation not of the name *Yahweh* (Israel's self-revealing, covenant-keeping God) but only of an aspect of the ineffable name— His self-existence and eternally unchanging Being. He is "I *was* Who I was," "I *am* Who I am," "I *shall be* Who I shall be" (all these translations are possible in the original), "the Lord who is and who was and who is to come, the Almighty" of the Apocalyptic seer (cf. Rev. 1:8). To this glorious revelation is appended a glowing promise: not only would the Israelites be rescued from Egyptian bondage, but they would not go out empty-handed (vv. 19–22). They would make their exit laden with jewelry of silver and gold, and clothing. Thus would they despoil the Egyptians.

In chapter 4 Moses offers various objections. He had already pleaded *no ability* (3:11), *no message* (3:13). Now he pleads *no authority* (4:1), *no talent for speaking* (4:10), *no inclination or disposition* (4:13). At every turn, however, God meets his commendable distrust of himself, promising His *Presence* (3:12), the power and efficiency of His *Name*, the faithfulness of His *covenant* (3:14–22), the manifestation of His *omnipotence* (4:2–9), His unfailing *enablement* (4:11, 12), and His *direction* and *instruction* (4:14–16). In the solitude of the desert, as it would be said later of Elijah at Cherith, Ezekiel at Cheber, and Paul in Arabia, Moses came face to face with God. God's preserving Presence (3:1–10) and His eternal Being (3:14) were revelations necessary to the redemption of His people.

By three signs the Lord overruled Moses' objections: the rod which becomes a serpent and is restored to a rod (4:1–5); Moses' hand, which becomes leprous and is healed (vv. 6, 7); water from the Nile, which will become blood upon the dry ground (vv. 8, 9).

In answer to Moses' objection of lack of eloquence, God gave him Aaron to be his spokesman (4:14–17). "He shall speak for you to the people; and he shall be a mouth for you and you shall be to him as God" (v. 16).

Persuaded, at last, Moses takes leave of his father-in-law Jethro and returns to Egypt, buttressed by the Lord's assurance that he could return, since the men who sought his life were dead (4:18–20).

Moses, taking his wife and sons, begins the journey back to Egypt, informed by God of what lies ahead (4:21–23). At a lodging place en route "the Lord met him and sought to kill him" (v. 24). Evidently Moses' wife, objecting to the rite of circumcision, had hindered him from doing what was commanded. His failure to perform a rite so closely connected with the Abrahamic Covenant and the redemption of Israel out of Egypt into Palestine stood in the way of Moses' carrying out his divine commission (vv. 21–23). As deliverer, Moses was in immediate danger of being cut off for his sin. Accordingly, Zipporah circumcised her son, being compelled to do herself what she so much hated, and the reproach was removed. Her words, "Surely a bloody husband art thou to me," show that she had received her husband back as from the dead, being joined to him anew (vv. 24–26).

Moses' meeting with his brother Aaron at the mount of God must have been exceedingly dramatic (4:27, 28). Their joint return to Egypt, their performance of supernatural signs in the sight of the people and the people's reception of them, are links in the progress of God's redemption of His people.

3. *Struggle with the Oppressor (5:1—11:10)*

The persecution of the people (1:1-22) and the preparation of a saviour (2:1—4:31) are followed by the plan and program of redemption (4:29—11:10). In the persecution of the people, Israel is seen in conflict with Pharaoh; in the preparation of a saviour, Moses comes face to face with God. In the progress of the redemptive plan, the God of Israel clashes with Pharaoh (a type of Satan). The drama is designed to disclose the redemptive power of God over His enemies who have enslaved His people. After their appearance before the elders of Israel (4:29-31), God's messengers appear before Pharaoh (5:1-4) and demand in the name of the God of Israel that he let His people go. Pharaoh is defiant. He not only flatly refuses the demand, but also increases the burdens of the people by requiring the same quantity of brick as before with the added obligation that they are to get straw for themselves (vv. 5-19). This discouragement called forth the complaint of the Israelite foremen.

Moses gives himself to prayer (5:22, 23). God reminds Moses of His unfailing promises to Abraham, Isaac, and Jacob, and reveals His name, Jehovah, in its redemptive aspects. Now that He is to deliver the people, no longer is He to deal with them as He dealt with the patriarchs, simply as *El Shaddai*, or "God Almighty" (cf. Ex. 17:1). But as the Lord (*Jehovah*) He is to bring His people out of Egypt, save them from their bondage, redeem them with an outstretched arm and with great acts of judgment, and bring them into the land which by oath He promised to Jacob's descendants.

In this redemptive work, no condition is specified. Their salvation, like ours, is "not of works" but solely by grace. It springs from God's love as its source (Deut. 7:7, 8). The Lord was to demonstrate that deliverance was His work, not theirs. At last they were to know the name of the Lord in a vital salvation experience.

The genealogy that follows records "the heads of their fathers' houses" (6:14–25). As a further indication of divine grace, God calls His enslaved people by name. He is acquainted with their heavy burden and His love not only extends to them as a whole but to each of them.

So severe was their oppression that the people found it difficult to respond to the message of Moses (6:9). To the deliverer himself who needs constant encouragement, and again exhibits hesitancy (vv. 28–30), God gives a renewed commission. The Lord graciously girds Moses with repeated assurances that He will make him "as God" to Pharaoh and Aaron will be his prophet (7:1–9).

In the king's presence, the sign of the rod is employed. Aaron's rod becomes a serpent that swallows up the rods of the Egyptian magicians, who did likewise. Nevertheless Pharaoh's heart was hardened. These miracles by the magicians were scarcely sleight of hand or common jugglery. They were undoubtedly manifestations of evil supernaturalism, similar to demon powers manifest today in spiritism and occultism. Second Timothy 3:8 gives the names of two of these demon-inspired miracle workers, Jannes and Jambres. Similarly, deceiving miracles characterize the rise of Antichrist and the end of this age (II Thess. 9:12).

From chapters 7:14—11:10, nine plagues are visited upon the land of the Nile, climaxed by the tenth, the great judgment upon Egypt. This final disaster is the death of the firstborn and the inauguration of the Passover.

The first plague is announced (7:4–19) when Pharaoh is told that the water of the sacred River Nile will be turned into blood. The execution of the plague (vv. 20–24) is a judgment against the idol river. But Pharaoh's heart remains hardened and the second plague, the overrunning of Egypt with frogs, is invoked. The outcome is the continued hardening of Pharaoh's heart (8:15). The third plague, that of gnats (vv. 16–19), occurs when Aaron stretches out his rod and strikes the dust of the earth causing it to become gnats on man and beast. The Egyptian magicians, who had succeeded in duplicating in part at least the two previous plagues, are unsuccessful at this point and confess to Pharaoh that this is "the finger of God" (8:19).

A second triad of plagues follows. The first involves flies (8:20-32) and makes Pharaoh ready for compromise (vv. 25-28). The king says, "I will let you go to sacrifice to the Lord your God in the wilderness; only you shall not go very far away. Make entreaty for me" (v. 28). But once the flies are removed, Pharaoh again hardens his heart. The plague of the flies is followed by murrain upon all the cattle of the Egyptians; all their cattle die, but the cattle of the Israelites are preserved (9:1-7). When the monarch's heart is rendered impenitent, the plague of boils follows (vv. 8-12). The boils likewise afflict the magicians (v. 11). Again the heart of Pharaoh is hardened.

The last triad of plagues is now executed. The seventh involves hail and fire (9:13-35); the eighth takes the form of locusts (10:1-20). This elicits a compromise from the king that only the men should leave. But with the removal of the locusts, the Lord hardens Pharaoh's heart, and he will not let the Israelites go. Thereupon follows the ninth plague, that of darkness (vv. 21-29). After three days of intense darkness in all the dwellings of the Egyptians, Pharaoh calls Moses and says, "Go, serve the Lord; your children also may go with you; only let your flocks and your herds remain behind" (v. 24). When this is refused by Moses, the Lord further hardens Pharaoh's heart, and the king banishes Moses and Aaron from his presence.

These nine catastrophes prepare the way for the last, the death of the firstborn. These scourges are not only judgments directed against Pharaoh and the satanic power he personifies, but are also attacks against the popular gods of Egypt. The God of the Israelites, at the conclusion of them, triumphs over the demon-inspired idolatry of the Egyptians.

II. Redemption Out of Egypt (12:1—14:31)

Chapter 12 announces the birth of Israel as a nation. The birth pangs are nearly over and the redemption from bondage is about to take place. The first thing announced is a change of the calendar (vv. 1, 2): "This month shall be for you the beginning of months.

It shall be the first month of the year for you." The month which signifies a new beginning is Abib, the month of the "ripening ear," a time when the grain is mature but still soft enough for rubbing in the hand or roasting. A spring month, it corresponds roughly to our April, and after the captivity was called Nisan (Neh. 2:1; Esther 3:7). Redemption then marks a new life and a new beginning. Correspondingly, the moment a soul receives the Lamb of God as Saviour he is regenerated and commences the new life in Christ.

1. Redemption by Blood (12:1–51)

Redemption out of Egypt is to be twofold—by blood (12:1–51) and by power (13:1—14:31). As in all redemption from sin, the truth, "without the shedding of blood there is no forgiveness of sins" (Heb. 9:22), is operative. Before God's power effectually takes the people out of Egypt, it is necessary for the Redeemer-to-come to be typified in His death as a divine-human Saviour. The tenth plague, the death of the firstborn, instituted the Passover with its shedding of the blood of a lamb.

Institution of the Passover (12:1–28). This feast commemorates the rescue out of Egypt. When it was instituted, the Israelites were directed to take a male lamb without blemish, one year old, a lamb for a family, kill it on the fourteenth day of the first month in the evening, and sprinkle its blood with a bunch of hyssop on the two side posts and lintel of the door of the Hebrew houses. When the Lord passed through Egypt on the fateful night and saw the blood on the door post, he would spare the firstborn within. The flesh of the lamb was to be roasted and eaten with unleavened bread and bitter herbs. None was to be left until the morning. The feast was to be eaten with girded loins, fully-shod feet, and staff in hand, in complete readiness to leave Egypt. This memorial feast was to be kept perpetually by Israel (v. 14).

The slain lamb is a type of the Lamb of God Whose blood was to be shed on Calvary, and the hyssop, a common plant of the field, typifies faith. Applying the lamb's blood to the door posts of the Israelite houses in Egypt had the same effect as our applying Christ's shed blood to our hearts by faith. As they were sheltered from the death angel, so the believer is shielded from God's wrath as a result of salvation. "For Christ, our pascal lamb, has been sacrificed" (I Cor. 5:7).

The requirement that the lamb be roasted symbolizes the sufferings of Christ under the wrath of God. The unleavened bread acompanying the roast lamb shows the essential separation of the Israelites from Egypt and their hurried departure from it. The bitter herbs remind the redeemed of their bondage under Pharaoh. Instructions concerning the Passover (12:1–14) are followed by a description of the Feast of Unleavened Bread, inseparably connected with it (vv. 15–20). The lamb was slain on the fourteenth day at sunset, and immediately after sunset, the beginning of the fifteenth day, the Feast of Unleavened Bread began. There was to be no interval between the two feasts, and the Hebrews were to put away all leaven out of their houses. Anyone eating leavened bread during the seven-day period following the Passover was to be cut off from Israel.

As the sacrifice of the pascal lamb is a type of the death of Christ, so the Feast of Unleavened Bread represents the believer's conduct. A holy life and walk should immediately follow the experience of salvation, the "seven days," symbolizing the entire life of a believer after his experience of redemption. In the Bible, leaven typifies evil. Thus the Apostle Paul speaks of leaven as "malice and wickedness," and of unleavened bread as "sincerity and truth" (I Cor. 5:8).

The institution of the Passover and the Feast of Unleavened Bread is appended by a comand given for its celebration by the people about to be delivered (12:21–28).

The Tenth Plague—Death of the Firstborn (12:29–51). Death of the firstborn—from the firstborn of Pharaoh on the throne to the firstborn of the captive in the dungeon—is recounted. As a great cry of distress arises in Egypt, Moses and Aaron are summoned by night and urged to quit the country. Pharaoh even urges them to bless him also (vv. 29–32). The people depart swiftly, richly laden with Egyptian treasure (vv. 31–36) and journey from Raamses to Succoth (vv. 37–39). A great company, approximately 600,000 men, besides women and children, is accompanied by a mixed multitude, as well as their cattle and their possessions. The time of their sojourn is specified as 430 years to the very day (vv. 40–42). The Lord gives further injunctions concerning the Passover as a perpetual ordinance. Only the circumcised shall eat of it; slaves and foreigners are excluded, except when circumcised (vv. 43–50).

2. Redemption by Power (13:1—14:31)

Redemption by blood is followed by redemption by power. The meaning of the shedding of the blood of the pascal lamb in Egypt is realized in the experience of the people by their being removed from Egypt. This has its parallel in the life of the Christian: Cleansed from sin through faith in the blood of Christ, the believer through the power of the Holy Spirit is delivered from sin manifested in the world, the flesh, and the devil.

Consecration of the Firstborn (13:1–16). Since the firstborn of Israel have been delivered in a very special way in Egypt, the Lord commands them to be sanctified unto Him (vv. 1, 2). Holiness is inseparably connected with redemption, for those whom the Lord redeems He claims for Himself. Foundational to such holiness is redemption from Egyptian bondage. This teaches the truth that salvation is unto holiness of life.

As a part of this separation and as an introduction to the setting aside of the firstborn, Moses emphasizes that the seven-day Feast of Unleavened Bread is a ritual to be followed as a perpetual ordinance in connection with the celebration of the Passover (13:1–10). The unleavened bread, as noted in connection with the Passover, typifies holiness and separation of life. The redeemed are to be a holy people. Putting evil away was to be "a sign" on their hand and "as a memorial" between their eyes (v. 9). God meant that the people should diligently observe His commandments concerning separation. Upon Exodus 13:9, 16, as well as Deuteronomy 6:4–9 and 11:13–21, the Jews have built their ordinance of phylacteries. They put upon their hands and forehead at certain times when they pray small leather boxes containing Scripture in an effort to fulfil by ritual what God meant to be performed by practice.

Exodus 13:11–16 formally presents the requirement concerning the sanctification of the firstborn. Every firstborn male, both human and animal, had to be redeemed as a sign of the slaying of the Egyptians and the redemption of the people.

Crossing of the Reed Sea (13:17—14:31). God begins to lead His people and manifest His power in their deliverance as they travel from Succoth to Etham (13:17–22). Moses takes the bones of Joseph with him. The Lord gives the Israelites a pillar of cloud by day and a pillar of fire by night to guide them.

In chapter 14 the pursuit of the Egyptians, the miraculous crossing of the Reed Sea (Heb. *Yam suf,* "Reed Sea"), and the annihilation of the Egyptian army in its waters are graphically narrated. The Lord had told Moses and the people of Israel that Pharaoh's heart would be hardened and he would follow after them (14:1–4). Pharaoh, his chariots and his army made ready, defiantly pursues Israel and overtakes them by the sea at Pihahiroth in front of Baalzephon. The Israelites, stricken with fear, begin to criticize Moses for bringing them out of Egypt to die in the wilderness. Majestically, Moses commands them to be fearless and to trust in the deliverance of God. When Moses leads the people forward at the Lord's instruction, the Presence of God goes behind the Israelites and stands between them and the Egyptians. As Moses stretches out his hand over the sea, a strong east wind divides the waters, and the Israelites go into the sea on dry ground.

God disconcerts the pursuing Egyptians by causing the chariot wheels to drive heavily (vv. 21–25).

The Lord then commands Moses to stretch forth his hand over the sea. The waters return in mighty fury to engulf the armies of Pharaoh, but the redeemed Israelites walk dry-shod through the sea. By perhaps the most dramatic and far-reaching manifestation of power in Old Testament history, God takes His people out of bondage. Faith in the redemptive blood of the pascal lamb is followed by the effective working of the divine power in the experience of the redeemed.

III. Education of the Redeemed in the Wilderness (15:1—18:27)

Being snatched out of bondage with a high hand and an outstretched arm, God's people enter upon training for their holy calling. As God's people, not only do they need to be delivered from their sin, but educated in the ways of righteousness and instructed in godliness.

1. Song of Triumph of the Redeemed (15:1–21)

Filled with the wonder of their deliverance, Moses and the people of Israel sing a song that breathes the spirit of ecstatic praise as divine redemption calls forth worship. In Egypt there was little singing, only weeping and groaning. In Babylon the Israelites would hang up their harps on the willow trees (Ps. 137:2–4). But now they celebrate salvation:

> I will sing to the Lord, for he has triumphed gloriously;
>   the horse and his rider he has thrown into the sea.
> The Lord is my strength and my song,
>   and he has become my salvation;
> this is my God, and I will praise him,
>   my father's God, and I will exalt him.
> The Lord is a man of war;
>   the Lord is his name.
>
> Pharaoh's chariots and his host he cast into the sea;
>   and his picked officers are sunk in the Red Sea.
> The floods cover them;
>   they went down into the depths like a stone.

In this joyful ode, the Lord is acknowledged as Saviour and praised. The great victory wrought is celebrated as His triumph (15:4–10). His power, holiness, and steadfast love are lauded (vv. 11–13). The terrifying effect of this great deliverance on the inhabitants of Philistia, Edom, Moab, and Canaan is described (vv. 14–16), appended with a sure promise that the Redeemer of the Israelites Who brought them out of Egypt would surely bring them into the land of Canaan and plant them on the Lord's mountain (vv. 17, 18).

Following the Song of Moses and the people is the women's chorus, conducted by Miriam, the prophetess, the sister of Aaron (15: 20, 21).

> Sing to the Lord, for he has triumphed gloriously;
>   the horse and his rider he has thrown into the sea.

2. *Testing of the Redeemed (15:22—18:27)*

Israel's triumph is followed by testing; the mountain-top experience, by the valley experience. God redeems His people and blesses them that they may be led on and disciplined to become a blessing to others.

Bitter Trial (15:22–27). The first discipline is the experience at Marah (vv. 22–26), where, after a three-day journey into the wilderness, the people find themselves without water. The waters at Marah are bitter, so the people resume their murmuring against Moses,

"What shall we drink?" (v. 24). When Moses cries to the Lord, the Lord shows him a tree which, when put in the water, sweetens it. The tree is a type of the cross of Christ which sweetens our bitter experience in the world through which we journey as pilgrims. As part of His disciplinary dealing at Marah, God makes a statute and proves His people. If they diligently obey the Lord, He promises He will inflict upon them none of the diseases which He put upon the Egyptians. "For I am the Lord, your healer" (v. 26).

At Elim (15:27) God, as is His custom, gives a respite in the midst of testing, and the people drink from the twelve springs and rest under the seventy palms.

Hunger (16:1–36). Leaving the refreshment at Elim, the congregation comes into the Wilderness of Sin, there to renew their murmuring against Moses and long for the fleshpots of Egypt again (vv. 1–3). God's promise of flesh at twilight and bread in the morning (vv. 4–12) is fulfilled when quail come in the evening and manna appears after the dew of the morning. When the people ask in Hebrew *man-hu,* "What is it?" (vv. 13–15), Moses explains that it is bread from heaven. The quail and manna are both types of Christ, the food of God's people (cf. Jn. 6:33–35). Just as each Israelite gathered according to his need and no more, each individual believer today, whatever his need, finds it met fully in Christ.

The observance of the Sabbath is enjoined in conjunction with the gathering of the manna (16:22–30). The food cannot be hoarded, but must be gathered fresh each day, except for a double portion on the sixth day, to tide God's people over the Sabbath rest. The soul must feed on Christ daily in living faith. As the manna spoiled when it was kept over, except that which was gathered on the sixth day for the Sabbath, so the soul must have a fresh experience with God daily. An *omer* of the manna (about three quarts, sufficient for one person) was also to be gathered and put in a receptacle to be kept before the Testimony (the tablets of the law in the ark) as a memento of God's supernatural feeding of His people during the wilderness years.

Thirst (17:1–7). When the people come to Rephidim, they find fault with Moses because there is no water to drink. Moses cries to the Lord and is directed to take with him some of the elders of the people and the rod with which he had struck the Nile. He is to stand before the rock at Horeb and smite it so that water may come out of it. This Moses does in front of the elders of Israel and calls the place *Massah,* that is, Proof, and *Meribah,* that is, Strife, because the Israelites put the Lord to the proof by their faultfinding, saying "Is the Lord among us or not?" The rock is a type of Christ; the smiting of it symbolizes His death, and the water gushing from it is a type of the Holy Spirit Who was given in consequence of the completed redemptive work of Christ (cf. I Cor. 10:4; Jn. 8:37–39).

Conflict (17:8–16). After the smiting of the rock, the contest with Amalek ensues. The warfare, illustrative of the struggle of the flesh against the spirit in the believer (Gal. 5:17), was precipitated by unbelief which said, "Is the Lord among us or not?" When faith is not exercised in the finished work of Christ and what we are in union with Him, the flesh, exerting itself, wars against the soul (I Pet. 2:12). But walking by the Spirit results in not fulfilling the lusts of the flesh. In the struggle with Amalek, mention is made for the first time of Joshua, a type of our Lord Jesus Christ, the captain of our salvation. Moses on the hilltop represents the risen Christ installed at God's right hand as our priestly advocate. Aaron and Hur at Moses' side support the hands of Moses, but the hands of Christ never falter. He ever lives to make intercession for us, and though the conflict with Amalek will never cease until Christ comes, His intercession assures victory. Moses is instructed to write a memorial of the battle and to record that the remembrance of Amalek shall be utterly blotted out from under heaven. Moses commemorated the victory with an altar named "The Lord is my banner," which indicates not only the perpetual contest with Amalek, but also the certain victory.

3. *Government of the Redeemed (18:1–27)*

Moses' father-in-law, hearing of all that God had done for Israel, comes to visit Moses, with Moses' wife and his two sons, Gershom and Eliezer. This visit is a striking picture of the future Millennial Kingdom. Moses recounts for the Gentiles (Jethro) the way in which the Lord has judged the world (Egypt) in righteousness for Israel's sake and then rehearses the afflictions of Israel and the Lord's deliverance (18:8). Upon this, the Gentiles rejoice because of the Lord's grace to Israel. Thereupon they all worship and visit together (v. 12), followed by Moses, the deliverer, acting in government. During the deliverance of Israel out of Egypt, Zipporah and her sons—Gershom, signifying *a stranger,* and Eliezer, meaning

God my help—were off the scene. Now in a fitting manner they assume their place in this broadly-marked type of the coming Kingdom over Israel (Acts 1:7). Jethro's suggestion (vv. 13–23) that Moses choose able men from all the people as rulers over thousands, over hundreds, over fifties, and over tens, to assist him in administration, indicates God's gracious direction in government.

The entire journey from Egypt to Sinai has two emphases: on one hand, the incorrigible unbelief and sinful murmuring of the redeemed people; and on the other, the resplendent glory of God's gracious faithfulness and patience in dealing with His erring people. In a sixfold manner God has manifested His grace: *redemption* (12:37—13:18); *guidance* (13:19–22); *deliverance* (14:1—15:21); temporal *provision* (15:22—17:7); *victory* in warfare (17:8–16); and governmental *administration* (18:1–24).

IV. Consecration of the Redeemed at Sinai (19:1—34:35)

At Mount Sinai the Israelites are shown that they are a people set apart by God to do a peculiar work. Since they are to be the recipients of divine revelation for the benefit of all mankind, the laws and regulations about to be given to them differ from those of all other nations. Israel is to be a kingdom of priests and a holy nation.

1. Acceptance of the Law (19:1—31:18)

God's mission for Israel is founded upon the idea of a theocracy in which the Lord Himself rules over them as sovereign. In no other way could they be a kingdom of priests and a holy people. God's glorious dealing with them by grace (19:4) is to be appropriated and lived out under the terms of the theocratic covenant (v. 5). Israel's acceptance of the terms of the law and the theocracy is solemnly established.

Israel learns important lessons at Sinai: the holiness of God through the commandments, her own abysmal sinfulness and failure, and the grace of the Lord operating through the provision of priesthood and sacrifice. The holiness of God and the sinfulness of the people are manifested in God's appearing in a thick cloud in unapproachable terribleness. The law, designed to instruct the people in God's holiness and their sinfulness, and by its severe injunctions point them to Christ, is a preparatory discipline until the promised Seed shall come.

The Moral Commandments (20:1–26). Commonly called the Decalogue or Ten Words, the moral prescriptions assume that all duties are owed either to God or to man. The first table (vv. 3–12) deals with religious activity as it concerns "I Am the Lord your God." "You shall have no other gods before me" (v. 3) stresses the unity of God against polytheism. "You shall not make yourselves a graven image . . ." (vv. 4–6) emphasizes the spirituality of God as against idols. "You shall not take the name of the Lord your God in vain" (v. 7) depicts the righteousness of God and issues a command against profanity. "Remember the sabbath day to keep it holy" (vv. 8–11) guards the worship of God against secularism. "Honor your father and your mother" (v. 12), as the representatives of God, warns against irreverence.

The second table (vv. 13–17) concerns duties to fellowmen. "You shall not kill" (v. 13) decrees the sanctity of life and guards against murder. "You shall not commit adultery" (v. 14) protects the sanctity of marriage against violation. "You shall not steal" (v. 15) stresses the sanctity of property against theft. "You shall not bear false witness" (v. 16) upholds the sanctity of character against slander. "You shall not covet" (v. 17) guards the heart against illicit desire.

God graciously speaks to Moses and the people and instructs them in the solemnity of worship, the object of worship, and the altar of worship (20:18–26).

The Social Ordinances (21:1—24:11). These divine precepts concern the rights of persons (21:1–36): the regulation of slavery (vv. 1–11), wrong done to one's fellowman (vv. 12–27), and injuries brought about through neglect or carelessness (vv. 28–36). The rights of persons are followed by the rights of property (22:1–15): they deal with theft (vv. 1–6) and dishonesty (vv. 7–15). Rights of persons and property are followed by the requirements of piety (22:16—23:19): proper conduct (vv. 16–31), the administration of ordinary justice (23:1–9), and the observance of festal seasons (vv. 10–19).

These special laws of the Book of the Covenant were designed to regulate the social and religious life of the people. The promise of the divine Presence with Israel (23:20–23) is made and the glorious prospect before Israel declared, if the people remain true to the Lord (vv. 24–33).

The Religious Regulations (24:12—31:18). Preceding the revelation concerning the tabernacle, priesthood, and offerings, Moses, the priests, Aaron, Nadab, and Abihu, and the seventy elders of Israel go up to Mount Sinai to see God's glory (24:9–11). Afterwards Moses alone is called to ascend higher to glimpse a greater manifestation of God's splendor in a forty-day session during which he receives the tables of the law engraved on stone and the religious regulations (vv. 12–18).

Chief among the religious regulations is the revelation concerning the structure called the *tabernacle* (25:1—27:21). In this building, the center of the worship of Israel, the priesthood is to minister before God in behalf of the people. According to the Epistle to the Hebrews, the tabernacle, as well as the priesthood who officiated and the sacrifices and offerings rendered there, are minutely typical of the person and work of Christ (Heb. 9:1–24; cf. I Cor. 10:1–11).

Concerning the materials for constructing the tabernacle, the Lord directs the people through Moses to take an offering (25:1–9). Materials are to be supplied willingly. Specifications for the construction are to be strictly followed according to divine direction. The ark (vv. 10–22) made of acacia wood (commonly construed as typifying the humanity of Christ) is to be overlaid with pure gold (denoting His deity). The pure gold of the mercy seat speaks of the propitiatory nature of God's throne, for, covered with blood, it becomes a throne of grace instead of judgment to a sinning Israelite. The cherubim (Gen. 3:24), with outstretched wings overspreading the mercy seat (Hebrew, *kapporeth,* "a covering," "an atonement"), guard the holiness of God violated by sin. Above the blood-sprinkled mercy seat, God is to meet with Moses (25:22).

The table for the bread of the Presence (25:23–30), like the ark made of acacia wood overlaid with gold, symbolizes the human-divine Christ. The bread of the Presence portrays our Lord as the nourisher and sustainer of His people. It parallels in spiritual meaning the manna "which comes down from heaven, and gives life to the world" (Jn. 6:33); only the bread of the Presence pictures Christ sustaining His own rather than giving them life. Appropriately, the lampstand of pure gold (25:31–40) typifies Christ as "the light of the world" (Jn. 8:12).

In chapter 26, the divine details of the construction of the tabernacle are specified. The ten curtains of fine linen—white (the color of purity), blue (the color of heaven), purple (the color of royalty), and scarlet (the color of blood)—point to various aspects of our

Lord's person and work. This fact is also true of the tabernacle coverings (vv. 7–14), the boards (vv. 15–30), the veil (vv. 31–35), and the door screen (vv. 36, 37). The veil or curtain separating the holy place from the most holy place is interpreted in Hebrews 10:20 as the "flesh" (the sinless humanity) of our Lord. When Christ died, "the curtain of the temple was torn in two" (Mt. 27:51), and "the new and living way" opened up into God's presence by Christ's death.

The brass (bronze) altar (27:1–8), upon which animal sacrifices are completely burned and which is located in front of the entrance of the tabernacle, pictures Christ's cross. On Calvary, as our whole burnt offering, the divine-human Redeemer offered Himself without spot to God for the sin of the world (Heb. 9:14). The court of the tabernacle is described (vv. 9–15), and the gate of the court (vv. 16–19) is Christ. Accordingly, the colors appear as in the veil (26:31), in contrast to the hangings of the court into which no colors are wrought, barring access to all except those who come through the door of atonement. Oil for the light of the tabernacle (27:20, 21) symbolizes the Holy Spirit, Who enables us to commune and worship as believer-priests in God's presence.

Following the revelation concerning the tabernacle is the divine disclosure concerning the *priesthood* (28:1—29:46). Ideas of priesthood, temple ritual and sacrifices, of course, were not confined to Israel, as history and archaeology demonstrate, but the religious regulations of Israel were unique in their revelation, institution, meaning, and practice. Intended for Jehovah's people, their significance was founded upon God's redemptive program for a sinful race. They belong intrinsically to Exodus as the book of redemption.

The priesthood in Israel was established in Aaron and his sons of the tribe of Levi (28:1–3). Aaron as the high priest (Hebrew, "great priest") is typical of Christ. Our Lord is an eternal, deathless High Priest after the *order* of Melchizedek (Heb. 7), but exercises His office after the Aaronic *pattern* (Heb. 9) which was interrupted by death. The holy garments "for glory and for beauty" with which Israel's high priest was to be clothed (28:3) represent the glory and beauty of Christ as our High Priest. The regalia of the high priesthood, with its colors of gold, blue, purple, scarlet, and the white of fine linen (vv. 5, 6, 15, 33), speaks of the person and the redemptive work of Christ.

The beautifully wrought ephod with the shoulder pieces, each adorned with two onyx stones engraved with the names of Israel's twelve tribes, portrays Christ carrying His people on His shoulders and is the emblem of His supporting strength. The breastplate of judgment, gorgeously embellished with precious stones engraved with the names of Israel's tribes (28:15–29), represents Christ bearing the names of His people upon His heart in God's presence, as Aaron would "bear the names of the sons of Israel in the breastpiece of judgment upon his heart, when he goes into the holy place, to bring them to continual remembrance before the Lord" (v. 29). Closely attached to the breastplate were the enigmatic Urim and Thummim—"Lights and Perfections" (vv. 30, 31), and whether these were precious stones or oracular emblems, they typify the guiding ministry of the Holy Spirit.

The robe of the ephod (28:31–35) was entirely blue, the color of the sky, and characterized the present heavenly priesthood of Christ. The bells and pomegranates adorning the skirts of the robe tell of testimony and fruitfulness in the work of priestly intercession. The gold headplate (vv. 36–38) inscribed with "Holy to the Lord" depicts the glorious beauty of unsullied purity characteristic of the priestly ministry of Christ.

The ordinary attire of the high priest and the regular priests, over which the special high priestly regalia was put (28:39–43), indicates that "the glory and beauty" that characterized Aaron (Christ) characterizes his sons (believer priests in the Church of this age). The linen trousers to cover their naked flesh (v. 42) set forth the righteousness of Christ imputed to the believer, the *sine qua non* of approach to God in a priestly capacity.

The description of priestly regalia is followed by the ritual of their consecration to office (29:1–25). Their cleansing in water (v. 4) symbolizes regeneration (Jn. 3:5, 6; Tit. 3:5). Aaron participates in this rite because as a sinner he needed it. Centuries later Christ (Heb. 7:26–28), Who did not need it as the spotless Lamb of God, nevertheless submitted Himself to John's baptism, to identity Himself with sinners and to fulfil the Aaronic pattern (Mt. 3:13–17). Then the high priest is clothed in his splendid garments (29:5, 6) and anointed (v. 7), symbolic of Christ's enduement with the Holy Spirit (Mt. 3:16; Acts 10:38). The consecration of the priests involves various offerings in which the shedding of blood of various animals takes place (vv. 8–25). Only Aaron, as a striking type of Christ Who was anointed with the Holy Spirit by virtue of what He was in Himself as the God-man Redeemer, was anointed before the blood was shed. The special food of the priests (vv. 26–37) is appropriate to the high calling of those who represent the people before God in daily sacrifice and priestly worship (vv. 38–46).

At this point, the altar of incense of acacia wood overlaid with gold is introduced (30:1–10) in connection with the worship of God in the holy place (vv. 11–38). In this item of tabernacle furniture, Christ is set forth as the believer's intercessor (Jn. 17:1–26; Heb. 7:25) through whom the believer's prayer and praise come before God (Heb. 13:15). The bronze laver (30:18), which was used for washing the priests' hands and feet before entering the holy place, tells of Christ's cleansing the believer from defilement contacted in service in a sinful world (Jn. 13:8–10; I Jn. 1:9). Only the redeemed (30:11–16), the cleansed (vv. 17–21) and the anointed (vv. 22, 23) can truly worship with prayer, praise, and thanksgiving (vv. 34–38), typified by the incense.

The Lord calls, equips, and specifies the workmen who are to construct the tabernacle and its furnishings. Bezaleel of Judah and Aholiab of Dan are named (31:1–11), and the Sabbath as a sign between the Lord and Israel is again enjoined to be kept (vv. 12–18).

2. Infraction of the Law (32:1–35)

The wickedness of the human heart is exposed in chapter 32 as the breaking of the covenant is described. The people so wonderfully redeemed out of Egypt, led supernaturally by the cloud and fire, fed miraculously by manna from heaven, and refreshed by water from the rock, soon manifest their stubborn unbelief and forget the Lord Who had done such great things for them.

The Golden Calf (32:1–14). The wickedness of the people is revealed in their making and worshiping a golden calf. This shocking return to the bull worship of Egypt, in which they copied the idol Apis, brings the wrath of the broken law upon them (vv. 7–10) and only the intercession of Moses saves them from destruction (vv. 11–14).

Broken Tablets (32:15–35). Moses, coming down from the mountain with the tablets of stone engraved with the law of God, surveys the scene of apostasy and debauchery, and angrily throws down the plates and breaks them. Calling for those who are on the Lord's side, the Levites leap up and slay three thousand of the worst offenders. Further confession and intercession of Moses (vv. 30–35) present one of the sublimest pictures found anywhere in the Bible of a man's devotion to the interests of God's people.

3. Restoration of the Law (33:1—34:35)

God's directing hand and His gracious promises are renewed as the divine presence is manifested. Moses, given a new vision for his difficult task (33:1–23), is directed to hew out two other tablets and ascend Sinai once more (34:1–4). There the law and the covenant are renewed, and the sacred festivals and Sabbaths decreed. At Sinai God rewrites the words of the covenant, the Ten Commandments, upon the two stones (vv. 5–28). After a beatific forty-day stay with God, Moses descends with shining countenance to the people (vv. 29–35).

V. Worship of the Redeemed in Tabernacle, Priesthood, and Ritual (35:1—40:38)

The Book of Exodus moves to a climax in the setting up of the tabernacle and the establishment of the official worship of the redeemed nation. When the tabernacle is completed, God's Presence fills it.

1. Gifts and Workmen for the Tabernacle (35:1–35)

A basic tenet of Israel's worship is the seventh day of rest; accordingly, the Sabbath law is restated and re-emphasized (35:1–3). What was enjoined in chapter 25:1–8 concerning giving for the construction of the tabernacle is carried out (vv. 4–29) as the people give willingly and generously. Bezaleel and Aholiab (cf. 31:1–11), the chief artisans, are mentioned again and their divinely-given skill is again described (vv. 30–35).

2. Construction and Appointments of the Tabernacle (36:1—39:43)

Efficient laborers are on hand, and ample material is provided. The people must be restrained from giving (36:1–7). The making of the various parts of the tent of worship is carefully detailed—curtains of finely wrought linen and colored stuff inwrought with cherubim (vv. 8–13), tent coverings (vv. 14–19), frames of acacia wood, bases of silver (vv. 20–30), bars of acacia wood overlaid with gold (vv. 31–34), the inner veil (vv. 35, 36), and the screen for the tent door or outer veil (vv. 36, 38).

In chapter 37, the construction of the ark with the mercy seat (vv. 1–9), the table for the bread of the Presence (vv. 10–16), the golden lampstand (vv. 17–24), and the altar of incense (vv. 25–28) is described, with another mention of the sacred anointing oil and incense (vv. 29; cf. 30:23–38). Chapter 38 gives a similar account of the altar of burnt offering (vv. 1–7), the bronze laver (v. 8), and the court (vv. 9–20), closing with a summary of the skilled workers as well as the amount of gold, silver, and bronze donated and used in the construction of the tabernacle (vv. 21–31). These metals were plentiful in Egypt. The people had left the land of bondage laden with wealth (cf. 12:35, 36), so they had ample resources.

Then follows the account of the manufacture of the priests' garments of blue, purple, and scarlet material (39:1), including the ephod (vv. 2–7), the breastpiece (vv. 8–21), the robe of the ephod (vv. 22–26), the coats (vv. 27–29), and the plate of the holy crown (vv. 30, 31). Blue, purple, and scarlet—the colors of heaven, royalty, and blood—again typify Him Who first came from celestial glory, to be manifested as a king and to die as a criminal in agony and shame for the sin of the world.

The flashing gold of the high priest's crown fastened to his turban and radiating the signet, "Holy to the Lord," brings to a highwater mark the glory of the priesthood in Israel. At the same time, it points to the greater glory of the divine-human High Priest Who, after purchasing the redemption of His own in the world by the sacrifice of Himself at Calvary, was to ascend far above all principality and power to intercede for them in effable majesty.

Against this resplendent scene centering in Israel's high priest, the completion of the work of the tabernacle is announced (39:32–43). Everything is executed strictly "according to all that the Lord had commanded Moses" (v. 32). The repetition of this expression in chapter 39 (vv. 1, 5, 7, 21, 26, 29, 31, 32, 42), as well as in chapter 40 (vv. 19, 21, 23, 25, 27, 28, 32), indicates the importance of the fact that all had been executed according to the divine plan. When the tabernacle in all its parts is presented to Moses and inspected by him, it is found to be exactly what the Lord had directed. Moses accordingly could bless the people because of their obedience in the matter, and did so (39:43).

3. *Erection of the Tabernacle and Filling with the Divine Glory (40:1–38)*

When Moses in turn set up the tabernacle according to God's directions (40:1–15), in perfect obedience (vv. 16–19), brought in the ark (vv. 20, 21), placed the furniture (vv. 22–26), presented the prescribed offerings and ritual (vv. 27–33), and thus "finished the work," God blessed him and the people with His Presence, as Moses had previously blessed the people. The completed tent was filled with the glory of the Lord (vv. 34, 35). So great was the splendor of God's Presence that Moses was not able to enter to minister.

Moreover, the cloud of glory remained over the tabernacle as a permanent guide. As a pillar of cloud by day and a pillar of fire by night, it moved only when the tabernacle (and hence the people) was to move.

Beginning with a mob of miserable slaves in Egypt, Exodus, as the book of redemption, ends with an emancipated nation in fellowship with God, on its way to Canaan with tabernacle, priesthood, and sacrificial system, all pointing to the coming of the Great Redeemer to deliver men from the thralldom of sin and make them sons of God. Keynote of this great book is that He Who is the Deliverer of men's souls can set the destitute drudges of sin and Satan free and transform their groan of oppression into a paean of praise, and the lash of the tyrant's whip into a shout of lilting joy.

Finding Christ as our Redeemer marks indeed our *exodus* from the bondage sin has brought upon the human race. Appropriating the fulness of His redemption is the way to true freedom, which, for the creature, will always consist in separation from sin and fellowship with God in the center of the divine purpose.

Leviticus

J. BARTON PAYNE

LEVI WAS THE THIRD of the twelve sons of the Hebrew patriarch Jacob, or Israel. Jacob died in Egypt about 1859 B.C. "The children of Israel" increased, and by the spring of 1446 B.C., when God rescued them from the Egyptian oppression that had resulted, they had become twelve tribes, totaling well over two million people. The Levites, the tribe of Israel's leader Moses, almost immediately distinguished themselves by their faithfulness to the God Who had redeemed them from bondage (Ex. 32:26). In time they were rewarded with ordination as God's ministers at the sanctuary and became the religious teachers of Israel (Deut. 10:8; 33:8–11).

From Levi, then, comes the name "Leviticus," and appropriately so. For though as a tribe the Levites are mentioned but once in the book (25:32, 33), the functioning of the particular Levitical family of Moses' brother Aaron, the group ordained as God's mediating priests (Ex. 28:1; 40:12–15), is described throughout its pages (cf. 1:5, 7, 8, and elsewhere). Leviticus, correspondingly, stands as the first detailed "book of life" in Scripture, making known in terms of the Levitical priesthood "God's judgments: which if a man do he shall live in them" (18:5). The way of redemption that God opens to mankind constitutes, in fact, the living theme of the entire Bible. On its opening pages, alongside the record of man's sinful estrangement from his Maker, appears the initial pledge of enmity with the evil one, and of man's corresponding life-giving reconciliation with God (Gen. 3:15). God's testament (His covenant, effectuated by death) with Israel subsequently enlarged the truth of the salvation that He bestowed. Like that of the older covenant in general, its theme is God's restoration of men to Himself (Ex. 19:5): "I will take you to me for a people . . . and ye shall know that I am the Lord your God" (Ex. 6:7). The *historical enactment* of Israel's redemption is described in Exodus; but this book concludes with the people's half year of labor preparing the tabernacle ("tent of meeting," ASV), that God might "dwell among them" (Ex. 25:8) and "give commandment unto the children of Israel" (Ex. 25:22).

In the early spring of 1445 B.C., God's people were ready for the written revelation of the *nature* of that redemption. The message God gave is the Book of Leviticus. "And the Lord called unto Moses, and spake unto him out of the tabernacle" (1:1). How Moses recorded God's words is not stated. Most of the writing must have been immediate; but the completion of the Book of Leviticus could not have taken place before events of the fall of 1445 recorded in 16:34b.

The content of Leviticus often concerns Levites, but its message involves all God's people: "Speak unto the children of Israel" (1:2). Christians today often think of Leviticus as a kind of technical manual for priests only; as a result, it has become the least appreciated book in the Pentateuch. But its own introduction teaches otherwise. Its truths were announced in the form of religious laws, but their relevance was by no means limited to a group of professional liturgical experts now extinct. The purpose of Leviticus is to depict God's way of restoring lost men to Himself. The book's message is addressed to the redeemed of all ages, to all men set apart to life with God. The key text, Leviticus 20:26, speaks in universal terms, "Ye [all believers] shall be holy unto me: for I the Lord am holy, and have severed you from other people, that ye should be mine."

Leviticus 20:26 epitomizes two aspects of the way of men's salvation: a redemptive activity on God's part, lifting His people from their lost estate and providing them access to Himself; and a response of appropriation on men's part, demonstrating their commitment to Him by their special way of living, which is "holiness." These two aspects supply the themes, respectively, of the first half (chs. 1–16) and the second half (chs. 17–27) of the Book of Leviticus.

I. The Way of Access to God: Redemption (1:1—16:34)

Jesus Christ said, "I am the way, the truth, and the life: no man cometh unto the Father but by me" (Jn. 14:6). Though Christ's coming to give His life as "a ransom for many" was still fifteen hundred years future, this fact did not deprive believers of the way of salvation in the day of Leviticus. For Christ's death provided satisfaction also for "the transgressions that were under the first testament" (Heb. 9:15). The way of redemption for God's earlier saints anticipated what Christ would yet do. The first sixteen chapters of Leviticus therefore present a series of typical actions that picture the way by which God redeems the lost, separating them from their sin and its consequences. Although the Christian does not observe these ceremonies, depicting in advance what was to be accomplished by the life, death and resurrection of Jesus Christ (Heb. 10:9, 10; Col. 2:16, 17), the truths they present and the great events these predictions designate are of eternal relevance. They describe the only way of salvation possible to sinful men—past, present, or future.

This is not to say that the Israelites in 1445 B.C. necessarily understood the details of what the Christ some day would do. But God did! Were not God the primary author of Leviticus, designing its rituals to anticipate the provision of salvation in history, then much of Leviticus would have to be classed with the magical manipulations of Israel's godless neighbors; and the New Testament's typical interpretations of its ceremonies would have to be rejected as imaginative allegories, foreign to the book's original purpose. Although Moses and the other Levites lacked some comprehension of things that are now clearly revealed, they were consciously aware of the redemptive nature of the message of Leviticus. For them, the sacred activities prescribed by the law served to convey such truths as God's acceptance of substitutionary punishment, and the reality of his subsequent forgiveness. It was this that made any infraction of the Levitical ceremonial so serious (cf. 10:1, 2), for it was, after all, the way of salvation. "Types" are thus to be defined as divine enactments of future redemption; and the standard principle for their identification is that they must have symbolized for their Old Testament contemporaries what they typified for the future. Leviticus (chs. 1–16) presents a series of four such enacted descriptions of the way of access to God: sacrifice, priesthood, cleanness, and the Day of Atonement service.

1. The Propitiation of God's Wrath: Sacrifice (1:1—7:38)

The fundamental means of access to God is this: "Ye shall bring your offering" (1:2), the Hebrew *corbán* meaning something "brought" to God (cf. Mk. 7:11). Though the offerings consisted of food (3:11), they were not brought as if the sacrificial flesh were "needed" by God (cf. Ps. 50:9–13). Neither were they primarily gifts, as if symbols of men's gratitude and devotion to God. Some offerings did reflect thanksgiving on the part of God's people (7:12–

15; see Hannah's offering at the birth of Samuel, I Sam. 1:24–27); but theories venturing to explain sacrifice simply as appreciation, or even as self-dedication, fail to explain the form of the sacrificial ritual in the first seven chapters of Leviticus, and particularly the necessity for the shedding of life-blood. Rather, the basic aim of the offerings was to placate God's righteous wrath against disobedient men and to accomplish the remission of their sins (cf. Heb. 9:22). Leviticus 17:11 describes this goal of propitiation by specifying that the offerings were brought "upon the altar to make atonement for your souls: for it is the blood that maketh atonement by reason of the life" (ASV).

An atonement is, in turn, literally a "covering," a ransom that averts one's punishment (Ex. 30:12; cf. Gen. 20:16). The Hebrew root may even mean a "bribe, to blind the eyes therewith" (I Sam. 12:3; cf. Gen. 32:20). For God has an innate wrath against sin, a wrath satisfied only by loss of life (Num. 25:11–13). But "atonement" furnishes a covering over the sin (Lev. 16:30), provides an intervening sacrifice to bear the punishment that would otherwise fall upon us, should God "see through" to our sin (Deut. 21:6, 9; Num. 16:47–48). Thus the Levitical service provided a substitute "that there be no plague among the children of Israel" (Num. 8:18, 19).

Confessedly Israel's offerings as such were ineffective. Even though their sacrifices were costly, "of the herd and of the flock" (1:2), the most precious possessions of nomadic people, "it is not possible that the blood of bulls and of goats should take away sin" (Heb. 10:4). Their effectiveness lay rather in their typical significance, that is, in their serving, as the New Testament writers put it, as "a figure for the time present, [when] Christ having come a high priest, not through the blood of goats and calves, but through his own blood, once for all, obtained eternal redemption. . . . He offered one sacrifice for sins for ever" (Heb. 9:9–12; 10:12, ASV). As our Lord Himself explains, "This is my blood of the testament, which is shed for many for the remission of sins" (Mt. 26:28). The reality anticipated in the offerings of Leviticus was fulfilled in the interposition of the Lamb of God: "The Lord hath laid on him the iniquity of us all" (Is. 53:6).

Five classifications of sacrifice are then described in the first seven chapters of Leviticus: the *burnt*, the *meal*, the *peace*, the *sin*, and the *trespass* offerings. The forms and purposes of each are given in Leviticus 1—6:7, while supplemental instructions, particularly with reference to the priests, make up 6:8—7:38. The first three classifications are described as "sweet savour" offerings (1:9; 2:2; 3:5), because of their acceptability to God, when lovingly dedicated by the offerer. Such sacrifices, "sensed" with pleasure by God, were anticipations of Christ who "hath loved us and hath given himself for us, an offering to God for a sweet smelling savour" (Eph. 5:2). The other two are styled guilt offerings (4:13; 5:17), because they were occasioned by specific transgressions that left men guilty before God.

All five offerings had much in common, being brought to the central sanctuary (1:3; cf. Deut. 12:6–7) where God revealed Himself (Ex. 20:24), and being burned on the altar as "fire offerings" (1:9). While all reflected the fundamental character of sacrifice as a propitiation of God's wrath, each had certain distinctive features which symbolized, even to the believers of Moses' day, particular aspects of the way of access to God. Each accordingly not only typified in general the sacrificial life of Christ, offered to God in satisfaction for the sins of men, but also such particular aspects of His redemptive work as God chose to reveal. A table summarizing the significances of the five classes is given below on page 129.

With Wholehearted Devotion: Burnt Offerings (1:1–17; 6:8–13). The first of God's messages in Leviticus directs the believer when "his offering be a burnt sacrifice." Indeed, the burnt offering is the earliest class of sacrifice specified in Scripture (Noah's, Gen. 8:20). The ritual by which it was presented involved five steps. These five steps were common to all five Levitical sacrifices, although distinctive features appear for each sacrifice, particularly in the last step. First was the selection of the sacrifice. Burnt offerings could be cattle from the herd (1:3–9), or sheep or goats from the flock (vv. 10–13), or fowl, either doves or pigeons (vv. 14–17). God thus graciously made provision so that even the poorest of His people might have access to Himself. But whatever its size, the animal must be "a male without blemish" (vv. 3, 10), thus typifying Christ. Only one who is perfectly pure can bear the sins of others (I Pet. 1:19). Second step in the ritual was the presentation of the sacrifice at the sanctuary where the offerer laid his hand upon its head and, in faith, appointed it as a substitute to be "accepted for himself, to make atonement for him" (1:4; cf. Num. 27:19–21). By thus assuming the sinner's own position, the victim depicted Christ, Whom God made to be sin for us (II Cor. 5:21) that we might be "accepted in the beloved" (Eph. 1:6). Third, the animal was immediately killed (1:5, 11, 15), its death taking the place of the sinner's (cf. Rom. 6:23). It was punished in his stead, "an atonement for him" (Num. 6:11). The particular symbol of the surrendered life was the blood (cf. Gen. 9:4), also a type of the life of Christ that was yet to be poured out for the propitiation of God toward those with faith in His blood (Rom. 3:25).

Fourth, the life was committed to God by sprinkling of some of the blood and by burning of portions of the flesh (1:5-8, 11, 12, 15); for, once the penalty of death had been paid, the offering became acceptable upon the altar. So Christ, subsequent to His sacrifice upon the cross, could say, "Father, into thy hands I commend my spirit" (Lk. 24:46). Fifth, and last, came a ceremonial indication that fellowship with God was actually restored. The reader will recall that when Israel entered into the older testament at Sinai, Moses took some of the sacrificial blood and sprinkled it over the people. His words, "Behold the blood of the testament which the Lord hath made with you . . ." (Ex. 24:8; Heb. 9:20), explained what they had already experienced, that they were literally "under the blood."

The distinctive feature of the burnt offerings lay in God's accepting them in their *entirety* as a "sweet savour" (1:9, 13). They were therefore designated the "whole burnt sacrifice" (Deut. 33:10); and their very name in Hebrew, *ōlá,* "what goes up," describes how it all ascended in smoke to God. Furthermore, they were presented every morning and evening on the altar of the sanctuary as the "continual burnt offering" (Ex. 29:38–42), whose altar fire "shall never go out" (6:13). The burnt offerings were thus symbolical of the constant, wholehearted devotion that God desires of His people (Rom. 12:1); and they received their typical fulfilment in Christ's self-surrender to the will of God (Heb. 10:5-7). He was obedient, even unto death, for the redemption of His own (Mt. 26:39); and "he ever liveth to make intercession for us" (Heb. 7:25).

With Consecrated Labor: Meal Offerings (2:1–16; 6:14–23). The second revealed category of sacrifice is that of the meal, or cereal, offering. Its King James Version title of "meat" (Old English for "food," not "flesh") offering is now misleading, for it was the one offering not composed of meat. Meal offerings could be selected from fine flour (2:1–3), from baked loaves (vv. 4–11), or from parched "ears of corn" (grain, vv. 12–16). Additional oil and incense emphasized their character as a "sweet savour" to God (v. 2). Then, even as the burnt offerings should have no blemish, so the meal offerings could contain nothing suggesting fermentation or corruption, as leaven or honey (v. 11, except for certain parts used in feasts, cf. 7:13, 14). Salt, however, was present to symbolize the eternally "preserved" nature of God's testament with His people (2:13). While the meal offerings did not in themselves involve bloody flesh, they always accompanied other offerings that did; for example, the continual daily sacrifice (6:20, cf. 23:18, burnt offerings "with their meal offerings"). Even the meal offerings were thus associated with atonement and were never adequate when alone, as is witnessed by the case of Cain's bloodless sacrifice (Gen. 4:3). The officiating priests received the portions that were not burned upon the altar (2:3, 10; 6:16–18), for God's workman is worthy of his hire (I Cor. 9:15, 16).

Man's restoration to God was then brought out in this sacrifice by its designation as a memorial (2:2; 6:15), a "reminder" to God of the reconciled status of Israel (cf. Acts 10:4). Finally, to the people, then and now, this offering symbolizes the consecration to God of our property and the fruits of our labor (Prov. 3:9); in fact, the Hebrew word for meal offering, *minhâ*, could be used for purely human tribute (II Sam. 8:2, 6). But the redemptive event in which the offering found its accomplishment was Christ's life of dedicated righteousness. United with His sacrificial death was His life, lived out in consecrated obedience to fulfil all righteousness for us (Mt. 3:15).

With Reconciled Communion: Peace Offerings (3:1–17; 7:11–34). The third sacrifice, the peace offerings, unlike the burnt offerings, could be either male or female. For though the next three steps in the ritual—the presentation, the slaying, and the commitment to God by blood-sprinkling and by a burning of the richest parts (3:16)—followed the regular pattern, the last step, the ceremonial indication of the restored fellowship with God, consisted of a feast upon the meat of the sacrifice; and for this use the sex of the animal made no difference. Unlike the meal offerings, only a portion of the unburned flesh went to the priests, namely the "wave-breast" and the "heave-thigh" that had been motioned toward God at the presentation (7:30–34). The rest was to be eaten by the offerers (v. 15), and in it the underprivileged and the Levites were likewise to share (Deut. 12:18; 16:11).

Feasting upon the peace offerings took place only at the sanctuary "before the Lord your God" (Deut. 12:18), where men were guests of the divine. The "peace" accordingly lay in their corresponding reconciliation with God, Who had been propitiated through the prior atonement at the altar; and the meal together symbolized their restored fellowship and communion with Him (cf. Ex. 24:11). For the name in Hebrew of the offerings, *sh'lāmim* signifies not only the negative peace of forgiveness, but also the positive peace of soundness, prosperity, and blessing. The *sh'lāmim* therefore included a variety of thank offerings, votive offerings (involving specific requests), and voluntary offerings (out of love for God in general, 7:15, 16).

Ultimately, the peace offerings typified the communion of the saints "in Christ" (Col. 1:27). They closely parallel the sacrament of the Lord's Supper, as we feast on His presence (Jn. 6:51; I Cor. 10:16); and they point forward still to that blessed communion when we shall sit down together in the Kingdom of Heaven (Ps. 22:26; Lk. 14:15; Rev. 19:6–10).

With Substitutionary Punishment: Sin Offerings (4:1—5:13; 6:24–30). The fourth category of sacrifice, which is also the first of the two guilt offerings, is the sin offering. Both it and the trespass offering that follows were occasioned by the offerer's having committed a particular sin and thereby coming under God's corresponding condemnation (4:3). But even as the basic purpose of all Biblical ritual is to provide the man who has broken God's moral law a way of forgiveness through the ceremonial law, so the guilt offerings served particularly as a means for the propitiation of God's wrath against certain sins that a man may have committed. These included unintentional violations (4:2; 5:15, which show that "ignorance of the law is no excuse"), but they were not limited to sins of ignorance, or even to sins that were simply unpremeditated (cf. 5:1, 4). For example, provision was made for crimes of deliberate lying and false swearing (6:2, 3) and of fornication (19:20, 21). Forgiveness was impossible only when the guilty party continued unrepentant, as Scripture puts it, sinning "with a high hand" and thus blaspheming the Holy Spirit (Num. 15:30, ASV; cf. Mt. 12:31, 32).

The value of the sacrifice selected for the sin offering depended upon the seriousness of the offense, and this, in turn, was measured by the status and spiritual responsibility of the guilty party. The most far-reaching sin, one that was committed by God's own minister, the priest (4:1–12), or by the whole people (vv. 13–21), required a bull; sin by a ruler, a male goat (vv. 22–26); and sin by a private citizen, a female goat or lamb (vv. 27–35). God in His graciousness further provided that if, because of poverty, "he be not able to bring a lamb, then he shall bring two doves or pigeons" (5:7), an alternative to which Joseph and Mary were reduced (Lk. 2:24). In fact, that God's forgiveness might be within the reach of everyone, flour could be substituted for pigeons (5:11). This explains the comment in Hebrews, "And *almost* all things are by the law purged with blood" (9:22a).

The second step, presentation, included the offerer's usual laying of his hand upon the head of the victim, that it should take his place in punishment (4:29); but it also involved the distinctive element of a verbal confession of sin (5:5). The root of the Hebrew name for the sin offering, *hattāth,* means to "miss the mark"; and, if God is to forgive, we must humble ourselves and confess our having come short of the glory of God (Rom. 3:23; I Jn. 1:9). But confession alone does not bring forgiveness: there must follow the slaying of the victim, for God's justice can be satisfied only by the infliction of the penalty of death (4:29).

The fourth step, the commitment of the life to God, involved elaborate sprinkling of the blood (4:6, 7). It is this final step, the ceremonial indication of restored fellowship with God, that is the most noteworthy feature of the sin offering. For the truly penitent, the blood had indeed become acceptable upon the altar because the death penalty had been paid; but yet, to indicate that the sin and guilt had been transferred from the people to the sacrificial victim and had been utterly removed, it was prescribed that the victim's body be taken outside the camp and burned (vv. 12, 21). It is true that in the cases of violations that did not involve the priests themselves, the priests, as in the meal offerings, were to eat the unburned portions (6:26), and the blood could be considered holy (v. 27); but even then, the sin transferred to the offerings caused the pots in which they had been boiled to be smashed, or the metal ones scoured (v. 28). So Christ, the only truly effective sin offering (Heb. 10:8, 9), that He "might sanctify the people with his own blood, suffered without the camp," laden with men's reproach and removing their guilt (Heb. 13:11–13). It was because of this fact, that the sin offerings typified His vicarious death, that the writer of Hebrews could conclude, even in reference to the bloodless offerings of the most poor, "and without the shedding of blood is no remission" (9:22b).

With Righteous Reparation: Trespass Offerings (5:14—6:7; 7:1–

10). The fifth and last classification of sacrifice is that of the trespass offering ("guilt" offering, RSV). In many respects, the trespass offering is similar to the sin offering (7:7). But while the stress in the previous classification falls upon the sin and upon the propitiation of God's wrath, this offering, as its very name "trespass" indicates, an "invasion of rights," includes a secondary but still real emphasis upon the harm done and upon the reparations that must be made to the injured party. Whether the sinner had wronged his God (5:15, 16) or his fellow man (6:5), he must first, as a part of the ritual of the trespass offering, make full restitution according to the set estimation, plus twenty per cent for damages. No variation was permitted in selecting the animal to be used in the sacrifice (a ram, 5:15), for compensation necessarily excludes individual considerations. In later days the Hebrew word for the trespass offering, *āshâm*, could actually be used for a payment, without reference to the sacrifice (II Kings 12:16). But the basic atonement is expressly stated to have come in the third and fourth steps, the sacrifice, rather than in the payment (6:7); and indeed a valid *āshâm* could occur without monetary restitution at all (5:17, 18). For salvation is the result of God's grace not of man's righteous efforts. The spirit of repentance, however, that is demonstrated by the restitution, does take precedence over the ceremony (II Sam. 15:22; Prov. 21:3; Eccles. 5:1). Our Lord Himself commanded (Mt. 5:24), "Leave thy gift before the altar, and go thy way; first be reconciled to thy brother, and then come and offer thy gift."

But the ultimate compensation, to which the trespass offering pointed, lay in the activity of Jesus Christ. As the suffering Servant, He became a propitiating sin offering; but Isaiah 53:10 also designates Him as an *āshâm*, a trespass offering. He indeed took our place, made to be sin for us; but at the same time we are granted His place, made to be the righteousness of God in Him (II Cor. 5:21). That is, He made atonement not only by His passive obedience, bearing the penalties for men's sins, but also by His active obedience, redressing every legal claim of God upon the sinner (Gal. 4:4). His life of righteousness is imputed to those who exhibit faith in Him. Each offering thus pointed to a particular aspect of His redemptive work, and one ceremonial situation not infrequently involved several different sacrifices. In the most elaborate, such as the cleansing of a leper, all five of the classes of offerings might be prescribed.

The Significance of the Levitical Offerings

"Sweet savour" Offerings:

Class	Reference	Distinctiveness	Symbolism	Corresponding Typology
Burnt offering	Lev. 1; 6:8–13	Wholly burnt on the altar (1:9)	1. Placating the wrath of God by substituting a victim in death (1:4) 2. Complete and continuous consecration (6:13)	1. Christ's vicarious death for the redemption of sinners (II Cor. 5:21) 2. His entire self-surrender (Ps. 40:8; cf. Lk. 2:49; Mt. 26:39)
Meal offering	Lev. 2; 6:14–23	Non-bloody products, accompanying the bloody offerings (2:1; 23:18)	Consecration of one's life and substance (2:14)	His righteous fulfilling of the law (Mt. 3:15)
Peace offering	Lev. 3; 7:11–34	Most parts eaten before God by the sacrificer (7:15)	1. Placating God's wrath (as above, cf. 3:2) 2. A thanksgiving meal of reconciliation with God (7:12)	1. Vicarious redemption (as above) 2. Communion in Christ (Jn. 6:51) and in the future Kingdom (Rev. 19:6–10)

Guilt Offerings:

Class	Reference	Distinctiveness	Symbolism	Corresponding Typology
Sin offering	Lev. 4—5:13; 6:24–30	For a specific sin (5:1–4); some victims' bodies burned outside the camp (4:12)	1. Placating God's wrath (as above, cf. 4:4) 2. Confession (5:5) and transference of guilt to the animal (4:21)	1. Vicarious redemption (as above) 2. His suffering "without the camp" (Heb. 13:12), the passive bearing of the penalties of men's sins (Is. 53:6)
Trespass offering	Lev. 5:14—6:7; 7:1–10	Same as sin offering, plus repayment of the wronged party (5:15)	1. Placating God's wrath (as above, cf. 5:18) 2. Confession and transferring guilt (as above, cf. 7:7) 3. Social restitution for wrong (5:16)	1. Vicarious redemption (as above) 2. Suffering (as above) (Is. 53:10) 3. His active redressing of every claim of God (Gal. 4:4)

109

2. *The Intercession by God's Ministers: Priesthood (8:1—10:20)*

The way of access to God is one of propitiating sacrifice, but since no man in himself is worthy to approach God and present the sacrifice (Jer. 30:21), there must be a mediating priesthood. The Hebrew word for priest, *kōhĕn*, suggests an "authorized minister" and is therefore occasionally used for a non-religious government official (II Sam. 8:18; cf. ASV footnote). But ordinarily *kōhĕn* is restricted in meaning to God's authorized minister at the altar. The priesthood, moreover, like salvation in general, is a gift from God (Num. 18:7); only God can call the man who is to have access to Himself (8:4, 5; Heb. 5:4).

Actually, the one mediator between God and men is Jesus Christ (I Tim. 2:5); and under the New Testament all Christians have direct access to God through Him without further human mediation (Jer. 31:34; cf. I Pet. 2:9). The priesthood of the older testament, however, existed as a type of the Christ yet to come (Heb. 8:1), the "merciful and faithful high priest in things pertaining to God" Who performed the real "propitiation for the sins of the people" (Heb. 2:17). In the earliest days, His priestly functioning was foreshadowed by the intercessory acts of the patriarchal head of the family (Gen. 8:20; Job 1:5); but at Sinai, God restricted the priesthood to Aaron, the brother of Moses, of the tribe of Levi, and to his descendants (Ex. 28:1; Deut. 18:5). Leviticus, in the only major narrative in the book (8:1—10:20), describes the preparations undergone by Aaron and his sons for their ordination as God's ministers (8:1–36), the inauguration of their ministry at the dedication of the tabernacle (9:1–24), and the disciplinary action that almost immediately had to be taken against Aaron's two older sons, Nadab and Abihu (10:1–20).

Preparing the Ministers: Aaronic Ordination (8:1–36). Ordination of the Aaronic family had been anticipated in Exodus (Ex. 28:1—29:46; 40:12–16) but it was carried out at this later point as the representatives of Israel "gathered together unto the door of the tabernacle of the congregation" (8:4). This consecration of the nation's priests occupied seven days and consisted of four steps that were repeated daily (vv. 33–35). First came their washing (v. 6), a symbol of personal purity. God's ministers are expected to serve as examples of faithfulness to Him (Deut. 33:9); therefore, they must themselves know the cleansing of the new birth in Christ (Tit. 3:5).

Second came their investiture with the priestly garb (Lev. 8:7–9, 13). For Aaron as high priest, this included the "ephod," a sort of surplice on which was hung the breastplate of judgment (Ex. 28:15–30). Its twelve precious stones bore the names of the tribes of Israel "upon his heart before the Lord"; and the urim and thummim, literally "lights and perfections," may refer to these stones, particularly as symbols of the divine guidance that Israel expected God to reveal through His minister (Num. 27:21; I Sam. 28:6). The golden plate on Aaron's mitre had engraved upon it the words that were descriptive of his whole office, "Holiness to the Lord" (Ex. 28:36).

Third came an anointing, with specially consecrated oil, both of the tabernacle, with its equipment, and of the priests (8:10–12, 30). Through this anointing the sanctification of all concerned was accomplished, for the oil symbolized the presence of God's Holy Spirit within the ministry (cf. I Sam. 16:13) and typified the Spirit's measureless enduement of Christ Himself (Lk. 3:22; 4:18; Jn. 3:34).

Fourth came a series of offerings for the new priests (8:14–28; cf. chs. 1–7). Part of the blood of the "consecration" (peace) offering was applied in a unique fashion to the right ear, thumb, and big toe of each candidate (8:23, 24); for true ministers are expected to teach God's word by hearing it, carrying it out, and walking in it devotedly (10:11).

Inaugurating the Ministry: Tabernacle Dedication (9:1–24). Inauguration of the tabernacle service took place immediately after the week of priestly ordination and consisted of a series of sin, burnt, peace, and the accompanying meal offerings, as previously described. Aaron and Moses then pronounced their blessings upon the people (vv. 22, 23). Finally, in public confirmation of God's acceptance of the ministry, the divine glory-cloud appeared to all; and from it there came forth fire that consumed the burnt offering (v. 24; cf. II Chron. 7:1; I Kings 18:38).

Disciplining against Sacrilege: Nadab and Abihu (10:1–20). But fire can likewise bring destruction (cf. Heb. 12:29). The tabernacle was a symbol of God's presence with His redeemed people (Ex. 29:45) and a type of our final communion with Him in heaven (Heb. 9:24); and in God's heaven nothing profane may exist (cf. Rev. 21:27). Thus when Aaron's two older sons, Nadab and Abihu, proceeded to offer incense with "strange fire before the Lord, which he commanded them not," a second flame came forth from the glory-cloud and destroyed them for their sacrilege (10:1, 2). They had failed to "sanctify" Him, that is, to set apart His divine regulations as the only legitimate directives for worship. In this case, apparently, their failure lay in burning the incense before its prescribed evening hour (v. 16; cf. Ex. 30:8). Truly, their intentions may not have been evil; and Nadab and Abihu may be in glory today (cf. the case of Uzzah, II Sam. 6:6, 7). But they acted officially, in their priestly robes (10:5); and their death is a standing warning to ministers against revising the Biblical pattern of church worship to humanly devised forms of "will worship" (Col. 2:23; cf. I Cor. 11:30).

The remainder of Leviticus 10 legislates on three correlative matters. First, Aaron and his surviving sons were ordered, on pain of death, to remain at the tabernacle and exhibit no outward sign of mourning (vv. 6, 7). They had been marked with God's anointing oil, and loyalty to ministerial duty must come before private feelings (cf. Lk. 14:26). Second, and with the same threat, they were directed to abstain from intoxicating beverages in connection with their ministry (10:8–11). The implication seems to be that liquor may have contributed to Nadab and Abihu's failure to distinguish right from wrong. Third, Moses, in reiterating their responsibilities in respect to the sacrifices, discovered that they had not eaten the sin offering, according to Leviticus 6:26 (10:12–20). Aaron, however, legitimately explained that the sin in his own family had rendered their consumption of it impossible, according to 4:3–12 and 6:30. Scripture thus teaches that people must not be disciplined when Scripture itself authorizes the exception.

3. Purification of God's People: Cleanness (11:1—15:33)

Access to God depends upon more than priestly intercession at the altar, for only *"when the days of her purification are fulfilled, shall she bring a lamb for a burnt offering unto the priest, who shall make an atonement for her"* (12:6, 7). Objectively speaking, men's redemption rests upon the finished work of Christ, and upon that alone; salvation, in other words, is an unearned gift from God, in the Old Testament as well as the New (cf. Ex. 19:4). But even a testament may lay down qualifications that must be met by its heirs if they are to receive the promised inheritance. So God's gift of eternal life comes to men in no automatic fashion, but is dependent upon each individual's subjective response of appropriation, commiting himself to God in faith and in repentance (Ex. 19:5; Lk.

13:5). Leviticus in chapters 11 through 15 accordingly lays down a series of "cleanness" prescriptions, standards for the separation of God's people from impurity. These, moreover, go into detail, emphasizing that everything in life must be committed to Him. Four specific categories are considered: animals (ch. 11), birth (ch. 12), leprosy (chs. 13, 14), and human secretions (ch. 15). For each category, various purification rites of washings, sacrifices, and other procedures are outlined.

The reasoning behind the actual prescriptions is summarized in 11:41–47. The basic aim is "to make a distinction between the unclean and the clean" (v. 47, ASV), and uncleanness in turn is seen as stemming from two major causes. On the one hand, uncleanness may be due to inherent character: "They are an abomination" (v. 42). Thus the Biblical regard for bodily hygiene (cf. Deut. 23:12–14) seems to account for prohibitions such as those against animals with unclean habits of eating (11:14, 15), and most of the other forbidden food items appear equally loathsome today (cf. v. 41). Similarly prohibited are all forms of personal injury, such as tattooing (19:28). The Christian's body must be devoted to God as a temple for His Holy Spirit (Rom. 12:1; I Cor. 6:19, 20) and be kept as pure as possible from harm and death. Finally, ethical violations, such as incestuous marriages (18:6), fall within the category of things inherently unclean. The permanently binding nature of such regulations is clear.

On the other hand, some forms of uncleanness seem to have been caused by the negative relationship that God's people sustained toward the religion of Israel. God had said, "I am the Lord that bringeth you up out of the land of Egypt to be your God: ye shall therefore be holy, for I am holy" (11:45); and "holiness" is basically separation (see ch. 17). Thus, even as God was removed from all that was wrong, so His people, out of gratitude to Him for their redemption from bondage, were required to maintain separation from anything that had connotations antagonistic to the faith. In ceremonials, pagan acts such as trimming the corners of the beard (19:27) or boiling a kid in its mother's milk (Ex. 23:19) were forbidden. In matters of conduct too, such acts as the homosexual practice of wearing the clothes of the opposite sex were prohibited (Ex. 23:13). For what had been harmless in itself became "unclean" for holy (separated) people.

Finally, matters that were otherwise legitimate could be excluded because of doctrinal associations. Sexual relations as a whole, while by no means inherently wrong (cf. Gen. 2:28; 9:1), were still symbolical of man's depravity from birth and so kept a man from what was holy (15:2; cf. I Sam. 21:4). Death too, which is the result of sin, had to be avoided in all its aspects (11:39). Even the wearing of garments made of mixed materials, and the sowing of mixed seed, were prohibited (19:19) to symbolize the concept of holiness (separation) itself!

Such regulations are no longer binding upon us in our different age and environment (cf. Acts 15:5). The principles they illustrate, however, remain valid; and in matters involving currently evil associations, God's word still commands, "Abstain from all appearance of evil" (I Thess. 5:22). Often one given act may have involved several of the above reasons for its prohibition as unclean. For example, cutting oneself (19:28) was harmful to one's body, and it also had pagan connotations (cf. I Kings 18:28). No single reason can serve to explain all the Levitical prohibitions; but at least some of the explanations can bring to each Christian today a practical appreciation of their meaning.

From Repulsiveness in Nature: Animals (11:1–47). Knowledge concerning clean and unclean animals dates back to Noah (Gen. 7:2); but the eleventh chapter of Leviticus granted specific instructions on their use as food (vv. 1–23) and on cases of contact with their dead bodies (vv. 24–40). The means for discriminating the clean, and edible, from the unclean are these: For the four-footed beasts (vv. 1–8), to be considered clean, they had to have cloven hoofs and make a cud-chewing motion with their mouths. The first test ruled out the rabbit and the second, the pig; otherwise these standards agree well with acceptable practice. So, too, do the rules for fish, that they have fins and scales (vv. 9–12); for birds, that they be non-predatory (vv. 13–19); and for insects and creeping things, that they be totally excluded, except for certain types of grasshoppers that desert nomads find necessary for food (vv. 20–23; cf. Mt. 3:4). The need for sanitary cooking (cf. vv. 33–35) is emphasized. Such tests were rough; but simplicity was essential, if God's people were to have a practical basis for maintaining hygienic eating habits when scattered among unenlightened pagan neighbors. So we today, while freed from the necessity of exact conformity to these dietary laws (Col. 2:16), must yet conscientiously honor the standards of health (cf. III Jn. 2).

From Congenital Depravity: Birth (12:1–8). The basis for a woman's uncleanness following childbirth may be partially humanitarian, for her days of separation did relieve her of certain normal responsibilities (v. 4). But birth uncleanness is to be explained primarily as a symbol for mankind's innate, congenital depravity. Because of Adam's original sin, we are by nature children of wrath (Gen. 5:3; Rom. 5:18; Eph. 2:3); and thus David confessed, "Behold, I was shapen in iniquity; and in sin did my mother conceive me" (Ps. 51:5). A woman's physical pain in child-bearing is itself part of the curse upon mankind's sin (Gen. 3:16); and her two-week period of uncleanness that followed provided a symbolic demonstration of the presence of sin in all that human life produced (12:5).

Then, however, after a further period of purification, God granted her a way of atonement through sacrifice (v. 7; cf. Lk. 2:24). If her child, moreover, were a male, the period was reduced by one half; for on the eighth day the baby was circumcised (v. 3). This rite, while of hygienic value, primarily symbolized the removal of the child's natural unfitness and impurity (26:41; cf. Ex. 6:12), his inclusion within the saving grace of God's testament (Gen. 17:7, 10), and the regenerate status and imputed righteousness that God's people may claim for their children (Deut. 30:6; Rom. 4:11; I Cor. 7:14). The New Testament then teaches the transmutation of circumcision into our own present initiatory sacrament: "in putting off the body of the sins of the flesh by the circumcision of Christ, buried with him in baptism" (Col. 2:11, 12).

From Bodily Corruption: Leprosy (13:1—14:57). A third matter dealt with in the laws of cleanness is leprosy. The expulsion of its victims from society was a stern measure (13:45, 46), but it reflects the public health requirements that lay behind the legislation. The fact, however, that other more contagious diseases did not involve such a quarantine suggests that the loathsomeness of this illness with its deathlike corruption gave to leprosy an additional symbolic connotation of the uncleanness of sin (cf. Num. 12:9–11). The Hebrew term for leprosy, *sārá'ath,* includes a number of skin diseases, and even types of molds on garments and houses (13:47–59; 14:33–53). But while certain relatively harmless skin irruptions were identified and dismissed (13:12, 13;29–39), the seriousness of the whole discussion points to the presence of true leprosy, Hansen's disease ("raw flesh," v. 10; cf. Num. 12:12 for its advanced stages), hence the need for rules sufficiently broad for general

practical application. The elaborate and cautiously protracted ceremonies for the rare cases of cleansed leprosy (14:1–32; Mk. 5:25,
26) included an anointing of consecration to God (14:14, cf. 8:23)
and the release of a living bird, symbolically carrying away the
former impurity and making atonement (14:7, 53). Thus those
who are Christ's must seek "to be cleansed before the Lord" (v. 5)
through the removal of all corruption, either physical (vv. 8, 9) or
spiritual (vv. 19, 20), both from themselves and from others.

From Sexual Pollution: Secretions (15:1–33). Finally, the fifteenth
chapter of Leviticus relates to sexual pollution associated with various secretions and issues. Certain of these discharges were normal and
unavoidable (for men, vv. 16–18, or women, vv. 19–24). But, just
as in the case of childbirth, they produced uncleannness and were
symbolic of man's depravity from his very inception (see above,
ch. 12). Other abnormal secretions (for men, v. 3, or women, v. 25),
caused by venereal or related diseases (cf. Mt. 9:20), involved a
strict quarantine. But whether sin be inherent or wilful, God's standard is clear: "Separate the children of Israel from their uncleanness,
that they die not in their uncleanness, when they defile my tabernacle that is among them" (15:31).

4. The Accomplishment of Reconciliation: Day of Atonement (16:1–34)

The climactic Old Testament demonstration of the way of access
to God lay in the services to be performed in the fall of each year
on *Yôm Kippurim,* the Day of Atonement. The events of this day
demonstrated the victory over all sins of both priests and people.
In it were summarized the means both of God's objective atonement (16:1–28) and of man's subjective response for receiving the
redemption (vv. 29–34). The fact that its prescriptions were revealed after the death of Nadab and Abihu (v. 1) suggests that
this section, as well as the five preceding chapters, was given to
Moses on the same day as the dedication of the tabernacle. Indeed,
Yôm Kippurim included ceremonial atonement for the tabernacle
itself (defiled by the sinful people vv. 16–21), and its basic ritual
was performed in the most holy place of the tabernacle. On this one
day of the year, Aaron was directed to pass within the veil and
stand before the ark of God's presence, an act which typified Christ's
ascending to heaven to intercede for us (Heb. 9:24).

First, Aaron brought incense, as an act of prayer for mercy "that he die not" (16:13); then, the blood of a bull, to be sprinkled as a sin offering on the "mercy seat" of the ark for himself and for his priestly household (vv. 6, 11, 14); and finally, the blood of a goat, one out of two which had been originally set apart, to be sprinkled in the same way as a sin offering for the people (vv. 9, 15). The mercy seat, Hebrew *kappóreth,* "cover," was a large plate of pure gold on which were mounted two model cherubim (angels), above which God's glory-cloud rested (Ex. 25:17–20). But though it served as the actual cover of the ark, the term *kappóreth* is more exactly rendered the "atoning, or propitiating, cover." For the blood-sprinkled "mercy seat" became an intervening covering between the glory of God above and the plates of the Decalogue below, the "testimony" (16:13; Ex. 25:21), which in turn stood for the moral conditions of the testament, broken by sinful man.

Through this means, God granted men a ceremonial fulfilment that could compensate for their moral deficiency and so make possible His communion with them (v. 22). The effectiveness of the *kappóreth* lay in its being a type of Christ and of the ultimate atonement made as He assumed God's wrath against the guilty. Its translation into Greek, *hilastérion,* the "propitiatory," occurs in Romans 3:23, "God hath set forth Jesus Christ to be the 'atoning cover,' through faith in his blood" (cf. Is. 53:5, 6; I Pet. 2:24). Then after the ceremony, the bodies of the bull and the goat were burned outside the camp (16:27), typical of Christ's death outside the walls of Jerusalem (Heb. 13:12).

The second goat was designated for *azāzél* (16:8). The meaning is not, "for the scapegoat" (KJV), but, as the parallelism with "for the Lord" suggests, for another personality, for Azazel (ASV), that is, for Satan. Specifically, this goat was presented before God to make an atonement "over" it (v. 10 ASV note; not "with" it, KJV, or "for" it, ASV text): it had the sins of the people confessed over it (v. 21), and it was then allowed to escape ("scape" goat) into the God-forsaken wilderness (cf. Lk. 11:24). It must be noted that the goat *is* not Azazel, as though it symbolized either the getting rid of Satan or the laying of men's sins on Satan. Neither is the scapegoat a sin offering, as the first had become (16:9); for men are not to sacrifice to devils (Deut. 32:17). Rather in its substitutionary punishment it symbolized the sending back of sin to its demonic author and thus the breaking of his claims over God's people (cf. Heb. 2:14, 15; I Jn. 3:8).

One of the striking features of the Day of Atonement is its aspect

of recurrence. This applies, in the first place, to the multifold procedures of the day. For the high priest's repeated acts of atonement
were but types that anticipated the work of One Who "needeth not,
like those high priests, to offer up sacrifices, first for his own sins, and
then for the sins of the people" but Who was a high priest "holy,
guileless, undefiled, separated from sinners, and made higher than
the heavens" (Heb. 7:26, 27). In the second place, the necessity for
the annual repetition of the day underlined its intrinsic inability.
So the prophets looked forward to that New Testament in which
God would forever remove the iniquity of the land in one unrepeated
day (Zech. 3:9). The goal of true atonement was finally achieved
by Jesus Christ, whose divine perfection eliminated the necessity
"that he should offer himself often, as the high priest entereth into
the holy place year by year with blood not his own . . . but now once
at the end of the ages hath he been manifested to put away sin by
the sacrifice of himself" (Heb. 9:25, 26).

The Day of Atonement, like the laws of cleanness, stressed the
subjective side of redemption, men's required response if they are
to be included in what God does through Christ. Not only must
Aaron "confess all the iniquities of the children of Israel" (16:16),
each individual must himself bow in humiliation and repentance
before God (v. 29; 23:27–32). The phrase, "Ye shall afflict your souls,"
does not necessarily mean fasting; for regular fasting was nowhere
prescribed in the Old Testament (though it was so taken in later
times; cf. Acts 27:9, "the fast"). But without a submissive faith in
God's way of salvation there can be no access to Him (Heb. 11:6);
"for God resisteth the proud, and giveth grace to the humble" (I
Pet. 5:5).

II. The Way of Living for God: Holiness (17:1—27:34)

"Ye shall be holy unto me: for I the Lord am holy, and have
severed you from other people, that ye should be mine." This key
text of Leviticus (20:26) demonstrates that redemption, the restoration of a man to God, is not an end in itself. Rather, it is but the
first part of God's design, enabling a man to come to His presence,
in order that he may then *be His* and live for His glory (cf. Tit.
2:14). The second half of Leviticus centers about this theme of

holy living and consists of a prescribed "holiness code" (17:1—
26:46) and an appendix on voluntary devotion (27:1–34).

The term "holiness" (Hebrew *qôdhesh*), appears basically as
"separation" (cf. 20:26), the opposite of "profane," not separate
(10:10; Ezek. 22:26). *Qôdhesh* may then assume one of three aspects. First, since God is most separate from His creatures, holy
may be equivalent to "divine." The worship of other gods thus
"profanes" His holy name (20:3), that is, fails to distinguish his
deity. Indeed, holiness is a fearsome thing, for death may follow
upon contact with the divine (Ex. 3:6; 33:20): "Who is able to
stand before Jehovah, this holy God?" (I Sam. 6:20, ASV). But
the almost incredible fact demonstrated by the testament is this:
"Thus saith the high and lofty One; I dwell in the high and holy
place, *with him also that is of a contrite and humble spirit*" (Is.
57:15). For a second aspect of *qôdhesh* is that God shares his holiness with those who are "separated" unto God (20:24; Ex. 19:10,
14). Even inanimate objects, as the tabernacle, and especially its
"holy of holies" (most holy place), may be "sanctified" by His glory
(Ex. 29:43–45). But since holiness means conformity to God, and
since God's purity separates Him from all evil (Hab. 1:13; Amos
4:2), *qôdhesh* may take on a third meaning of morality (20:7, 8).

So in the call of Isaiah, his natural reaction to God's holiness (Is.
6:3) was conviction about his own sin (v. 5); and it resulted in
forgiveness and moral holiness (v. 7). The three main sections of
Leviticus 17–26 then correspond (though not in the same order)
to these three aspects: to divine holiness (chs. 23–25) in terms of
devoted worship; to an object separated in holiness to God (ch.
17) by the ceremonial regard for blood; and to moral holiness (chs.
18–22) in living up to ethical standards. Chapter 26 is a concluding
exhortation.

1. The Ceremonial Standard: Reverence for Blood (17:1–16)

Israel gave evidence of their living for God by showing a ceremonial regard for a substance that He had chosen as holy to Himself, namely, blood. First, they could shed no blood in the slaughter
of animals except at the tabernacle gate (17:1–9). This meant in
practice that meals of meat could be had only as peace offerings
(v. 5). Little hardship, however, was entailed because animals were
so valuable in their nomadic society that only on rare occasions were

they killed and eaten (cf. Gen. 18:7), and when the people did finally settle in Canaan, this law was revoked (Deut. 12:5). Furthermore, this restriction did emphasize the truth that God was the sole author of life and blessing (I Chron. 29:14; Jas. 1:17); and it prevented any isolated practicing of the pagan sacrifices to goats (v. 7 ASV; cf. II Chron. 11:15; not "devils," KJV).

Second, God's people were to eat no blood (17:10-17). Animals that died of themselves might obviously cause poisoning (v. 15); but all blood was treated as "holy," separate, to symbolize a reverence for life in general, but particularly reverence for the atonement that was typified through shed blood (v. 11), until Christ's sacrifice of Himself should fulfil the truth thus taught (Rom. 3:25).

2. The Moral Standard: Ethical Conduct (18:1—22:33)

This central section in the Levitical code of holiness furnishes us with the patterns of life that God requires of His own. If a man today, like the Pharisees of old, takes them as a means for justification, "which if a man do, he shall live in them" (18:5), he can only earn condemnation, for we all fall short (Gal. 3:10-12). But once a man is saved by faith in Christ and hears the reconciled Deity saying, "I am the Lord your God" (18:2), then he "shall *therefore* keep my statutes" (v. 5). Like the saved Israelites of old he must, out of gratitude, dedicate himself to a life that is severed from the immoral patterns of the sinful humanity that surround him (v. 3) and demonstrate his faith by positive obedience, "which if a man do he shall live" (v. 5; cf. Rom. 6:22), for "by their fruits ye shall know them" (Mt. 7:20). Leviticus proceeds to legislate on sexual morals (ch. 18), on ethics in general (ch. 19), on the punishments that are to be exacted for violations (ch. 20), and on the particular standards for God's priestly ministers (chs. 21, 22).

Purity in the Family: Sexual Morals (18:1-30). The standards of family purity to which Israel had been exposed in Egypt were debased (18:3; cf. Gen. 39:7-20), particularly in respect to incest, sexual relations and marriage between close relatives ("to uncover their nakedness," Lev. 18:6). Leviticus (18:7-17) then lists the prohibited degrees of consanguinity (cf. I Cor. 5:1). For even apart from the problems in heredity caused by inbreeding, consanguineous unions disrupt the psychological integrity of the whole family, including that of oneself ("thine *own* nakedness," v. 10).

Verse 18, however, seems to have in view not marriage with two living sisters (forbidden in principle in v. 16), but rather polygamy as a whole; for the passage may well be translated, "Thou shalt not take a wife to another, to vex the other in her life time." The monogamous standard was, in actual fact, often violated in the Old Testament; but it was done to the consistent sorrow of all concerned (cf. I Sam. 1:6). Verse 19 concerns symbolical cleanness (cf. ch. 15); but adultery (18:20), homosexuality (v. 22), and bestiality (v. 23) are classed right along with another practice of the doomed Canaanites, child sacrifice (v. 21), as being equally destructive of the purity of the family. "Commit not any one of these abominable customs!" (v. 30).

Conduct Pleasing to God: General Ethics (19:1–37). Leviticus then presents a variety of ethical prescriptions representative of God's own moral standard. For if morals are to be objectively valid they must be grounded in God: "Ye shall be holy, for I the Lord your God am holy" (v. 2). Motives of social expediency will never insure morality. Ethics become compulsive only upon a heartfelt recognition of the claim that God repeats fourteen times in this one chapter, "I am the Lord."

Reverence for Him will then not only produce a symbolical observance of holiness (separation, v. 19), a respect for God's name (v. 12) and ceremonies (vv. 3b, 5–8, 23–25, 26a, 30), and a corresponding abhorrence for idols (v. 4) with their related practices of magic (v. 26b), bodily disfigurements (vv. 27, 28), and spiritism (v. 31); it will also induce positive practices of love, both toward the immediate family and toward the broader community. In reference to the former, the man who lives for God will honor his parents (v. 3a) and the aged (v. 32), will keep himself from sexual deviation (vv. 20–22), and will keep his children from it as well (v. 29). In reference to the latter, he will protect, not defame, his neighbor (v. 16); he will assist the poor (vv. 9, 10; cf. Ruth 2:15, 16) and the physically handicapped (v. 14) and love the foreigner as himself (vv. 33, 34); and he will insist on complete honesty in property rights (v. 11), within management and labor (v. 13), at court (v. 15), and in commerce (vv. 35, 36).

For the believer is committed to God and to His laws, not just in certain externalities of conduct, but from his innermost spirit. God's love for men becomes his own standard of guidance, first in love toward God, and then toward fellow men: "Thou shalt not hate

thy brother in thine heart but thou shalt love thy neighbor as thyself" (vv. 18, 19). Our Lord said, "On these two commandments
hang all the law and the prophets" (Mt. 22:40), for love is the
fulfilment of the law (Rom. 13:8).

Punishment for Violations: Sanctions (20:1–27). To give sanction
to the above standards, Leviticus proceeds to enumerate certain
prescribed punishments for ethical violations. The death penalty
is invoked against child sacrifice (v. 2), against consulting with
spiritists (vv. 6, 27), against breaking the family unit by cursing
parents (v. 9), and against adultery and other sexual perversions
(vv. 10–16). Modern "merciful" sentiment tends to react against
this divine severity, but surely a higher mercy toward private and
community life demands the removal of that which would destroy
society as a whole (vv. 22, 23). We must be holy, severed from
evil, if we are to be His (vv. 24–26).

Ministry Beyond Reproach: Priestly Standard (21:1—22:33). Finally, Leviticus presents the particular standards that are to be
observed by God's ministers, the Levitical priests. Some of these
precepts involve ceremonial matters that are significant in their
symbolism, but are no longer to be practiced, now that Christ has
fulfilled the concept of priestly mediation (Heb. 7:18, 19). Others,
however, have permanent application, both for Christians in general,
the "universal priesthood" who must serve as examples before the
unbelieving world (I Pet. 2:5, 12), and for the Christian minister,
who is under particular obligation to a life beyond reproach (I Tim.
3:2, ASV), as "a chief man among his people" (Lev. 21:4).

The priest must avoid all personal defilement (21:1–15). Symbolically, he must keep himself from the dead, death being the
mark of sin (v. 1). For the high priest, this duty even superseded
family ties (v. 11, cf. Mt. 10:37), though otherwise a man's natural
affection for the members of his immediate family is recognized
(vv. 2, 3). Morally too the priest must keep himself from a marriage
that would impair his ministry, whether with an evil woman, or
with one simply "profane" (v. 7), for a Christian's marriage must
be only "in the Lord" (I Cor. 7:36; cf. II Cor. 6:14). Further, the
high priest could marry neither a widow nor a divorced woman
(21:14), though such remarriage is otherwise sanctioned (I Cor.
7:39), provided a divorce be on Biblical grounds, (I Cor. 7:15, Mt.
19:9). Physical defects served to bar a priest from service at the
altar (21:16–24), though God yet graciously continued His support

from the offerings that were designated for the priests (v. 22), provided ceremonial cleanness was maintained (22:1–16).

Similar practical matters may today keep a man from the ministry, though the Old Testament ministers served the further typical function of foreshadowing Christ, the perfect priest (Heb. 7:26). For the same typical reason, the sacrificial victims had likewise to be spotless (22:17–25), to be at least a week old when killed, symbolical of self-sustained strength (vv. 26, 27), and to be eaten the same day, thus preventing any possible corruption (vv. 29, 30; cf. I Pet. 1:19). The prohibition of verse 28, however, may have been simply to secure Israel's dissociation from paganism, with its practices of this sort (cf. 21:5; Ex. 23:19).

3. *The Devotional Standard: Regular Worship (23:1—25:55)*

God's own holiness, in the sense of His unique deity, produces by its very nature certain appropriate responses of human devotion from those committed to living for Him. In Leviticus, moreover, God revealed specific directives relative to Israel's regular times of worship (23:1–44), certain arrangements for their sanctuary (24:1–9), the reverence that is due His name (24:10–23), and their observance of periodic sabbatic years (ch. 25).

Disciplined Time for God: Feasts (23:1–44). Israel's set feasts, Hebrew, *mōʿēdh,* an "appointed time" (v. 2), were matters of divine appointment, commemorative of God's past deliverance, symbolic of His present blessing, or typical of His future redemption. Some of the feasts had indeed a secondary correlation with the yearly agricultural cycle; but their origin lay not in any human observation of nature or phases of the moon, but in God's decrees to His supernaturally saved people for their worship and moral living. A table summarizing the significance of the set times is given below on pages 146 and 147.

Heart of the believer's disciplined time for God lies in Sabbath observance (23:3). The Hebrew *shabbâth* means "rest"; and both Israel's experience (Deut. 5:15) and God's own example, that dates back to creation itself (Gen. 2:1–3; Ex. 20:11), teach us of the permanently binding moral obligation that one day in seven "shall be a sabbath of rest; ye shall do no work therein" (23:3). But it is also "the sabbath *of the Lord,*" designed for His service and worship (cf. 24:8; Is. 58:13, 14). It was a symbol of Israel's sanctification to Him (Ex. 31:13) and a type of their future rest, first in Christ (Mt. 11:28) and finally in His heavenly kingdom (Is. 66: 23). The former type is now fulfilled, and Christians no longer keep the Jewish seventh day (Saturday, Col. 2:16, 17); but the latter type is still unfulfilled, and we keep the Christian Sabbath (Sunday, Acts 20:7; I Cor. 16:1–2), which is our Lord's resurrection day (Rev. 1: 10), as an emblem of our eternal rest in Him (Heb. 4:9–11; Phil. 3:21).

The five annual, set feasts of Israel—Passover, Pentecost, Trumpets, the Day of Atonement, and Tabernacles—involved various offerings and included one or two additional "convocation" Sabbaths (cf. 23:7, 8). Passover, Pentecost, and Tabernacles, moreover, were pilgrimage feasts, (Hebrew, *haggim*), dates at which every adult male appeared before God at the central sanctuary (Ex. 23:14–17).

Passover (Lev. 23:5–14), in March or April (depending on Israel's lunar calendar), had been celebrated for the first time a little over one year previously (1446 B.C.), as a symbolic service accompanying the "passing over" of Israel by God's angel that had struck down the firstborn in the land of Egypt (Ex. 12:13). It had been a feast, a heavy meal, to prepare them for the Exodus journey that commenced the next morning (Ex. 12:31–33) and was then made in such haste that their bread-dough did not become leavened (Ex. 12:34). The ceremony centered in their slaying of pascal (Passover) lambs and using their blood to mark the doorways of each house (Ex. 12:6–10). The blood stood as a token (Ex. 12:13) of redemptive substitution (Ex. 13:13); for God's threat had been that *all* the firstborn in the land of Egypt should die (Ex. 11:5). But the death of the lamb served to redeem the firstborn of the Hebrew children who gathered together "under the blood" (Ex. 13:15).

Passover, however, was required to be repeated annually, first, as a historical memorial of Israel's deliverance from Egypt (Ex. 12: 14, 42). Leviticus, then, added a service that anticipated Israel's settlement in Canaan: dedicating to God the first sheaf of spring-time grain, and thus acknowledging Him as the source of all productivity (23:11). But, most significantly, the annual Passover symbolized God's continuing claim over the firstborn and hence men's perpetual need for redemption from their sins, similar to Pharaoh's rebellion (Ex. 13:12, 15). Thus Passover was followed by seven days in which leaven was banned, symbolical of sin put away (Ex. 12:15; Lev. 23:6; I Cor. 5:8). Above all, the lamb that was slain, but of which not a bone was to be broken (Ex. 12:46), typified how "Christ our passover is sacrificed for us" (I Cor. 5:7; cf. Jn. 19:36).

Years later, on the very afternoon the pascal lambs were being prepared, He gave His life that redemption might be accomplished once for all (Jn. 13:1; 18:28). Furthermore, on the evening previous to the regular feast, He with His disciples kept history's last valid Passover (Mt. 26:17) and transformed it into the first Lord's Supper. Both are sacramental seals of our union with Christ (I Cor. 10:16) and with one another in the testament of His blood (I Cor. 10:17; 11:25; cf. Ex. 12:13, 22).

The second of the three annual *haggîm* was the Feast of Weeks (23:15–22). It was later called Pentecost, meaning "fiftieth (day)," for it took place seven weeks and a day after Passover. It thus followed the wheat harvest and became the occasion for the presentation of two loaves as a new meal offering (v. 17). In this symbolic way God was recognized as the source of daily food. A moral lesson was also contained in Pentecost, as foreigners, servants, and the needy were invited to share in the festivities (v. 22; Deut. 16:11).

On the first day of the seventh month (September or October) came the Feast of Trumpets (Lev. 23:23–25). This date may have marked an older new year's day (cf. Ex. 23:16), prior to its shift to the spring at the Exodus (Ex. 12:2; cf. the present *Rôsh Hash-Shānā*, "Jewish New Year's," in the fall). The "memorial of blowing of trumpets" (23:24) appears to have been a symbolical reminder to God; "Ye shall blow an alarm with the trumpets; and ye shall be remembered before the Lord your God, and ye shall be saved from your enemies" (Num. 10:9). Then on the tenth day of the month came *Yôm Kippurîm*, the Day of Atonement (23:26–32; and see above, 16:1–34).

Five days later the third pilgrimage feast began. It was called the Feast of Tabernacles (23:33–43), because Israel was commanded to dwell seven days in temporarily constructed tabernacles or outdoor booths. The practice commemorated the Exodus and the camping in the wilderness (vv. 40–43). It was also call the Feast of Ingathering, for it would mark the termination of the agricultural year (Ex. 23:16). Tabernacles was therefore a time of special rejoicing (23:40) and of sharing with the needy (Deut. 16:14). As the Hebrew Thanksgiving, it came to typify the future ingathering in the Messiah's Kingdom, when all nations shall feast in joy before

The Significance of the Levitical Sacred Times

	Moral Obligation		Historical Symbolism	Spiritual and Sacramental Symbolism		Typology	
	O.T.	Present Form	O.T.*	O.T.	Present Form	O.T.	Present Form
Sabbath (weekly and convocation) (Lev. 23:3)	Rest (Ex. 23:12; cf. creation, 20:11)	Rest (Sunday, changeless moral duty; Rom. 13:10)	Israel's rest from Egypt (Deut. 5:15)	God's sanctifying of Israel (Ex. 31:13)	Sunday preaching and sacraments (Acts 20:7)	Rest in Christ (Mt. 11:28) Heavenly rest (Is. 66:23)	Sunday worship of Christ (Rev. 1:10) Sunday, type of heaven (Heb. 4:11)
Passover (23:5-14)	(No social outreach; exclusive observance Ex. 12:43-44)	—	The Exodus (Ex. 12:14)	Redemption (Ex. 13:15) in common (12:22) Unleavened purity (Ex. 23:18) First sheaf is God's (Lev. 23:11)	Lord's Supper, sacramental communion (I Cor. 10:16) Sincerity and truth (I Cor. 5:8) Church offerings	Christ's substitutionary death (I Cor. 5:7)	Lord's Supper, as a memorial of past atonement (I Cor. 11:24)

126

Festival							
Pentecost (23:15-22)	Social sharing (Deut. 16:11)	Christian compassion	—	Loaves dedicated to God (Lev. 23:17)	Grace at meals	—	—
Trumpets (23:23-25)	—	—	Former New Year? (Ex. 12:2; 23:16)	God to remember Israel (Lev. 23:24)	Regular intercessory prayer	—	—
Day of Atonement (23:26-32)	Humble confession (Lev. 16:28)	Times of penitence	—	Cleansing from sin (Lev. 16:30)	Baptism (Acts 22:16)	Christ's redemption (Heb. 9:12)	Good Friday and Easter services
Tabernacles (23:33-43)	Social sharing (Deut. 16:14)	Christian compassion	Wilderness camping (Lev. 23:43)	Harvest is from God (Lev. 23:39)	Thanksgiving Day	Eschatological ingathering (Zech. 14:16)	Lord's Supper, type of future kingdom (I Cor. 11:26)
Sabbatic Year (25:1-7)	Charity (Ex. 23:11; Deut. 15:2)	Relief offerings	—	God's control of land (Lev. 25:2)	Stewardship of property	—	—
Year of Jubilee (25:8-55)	Liberty; property rights (Lev. 25:10)	Individual rights under God	—	Same (Lev. 25:23)	Same	Eschatological blessing (Is. 61:2-4)	Lord's Supper, type of future kingdom (I Cor. 11:26)

* There are no present day equivalents.

127

Him at His coming again (Zech. 14:16; Lk. 14:15; I Cor. 11:26). Meanwhile, though the moral principles which lie behind the Hebrew feasts maintain permanent validity, the ceremonial observance of the feasts has been abrogated for the Christian Church (Col. 2:16–17), except for the Sabbath and Passover, equalling, respectively, the Lord's Day and the Lord's Supper.

Order in the Sanctuary: Tabernacle Worship (24:1–9). Leviticus legislates concerning two elements of Israel's worship at God's holy dwelling, the tabernacle. First, the burning of pure olive oil in the lamps of the "candlestick" (lamp-stand, v. 4) seems to symbolize the Spirit-nourished witnessing of the Church to a dark world, as this is made possible through the ministry of Christ, the great High Priest (cf. Zech. 4:2, 6; Mt. 5:14–16). Second, the presentation every Sabbath of fresh showbread, the Hebrew for which is literally "bread of (the divine) presence" (24:5–9; cf. Ex. 25:30), pictures the reconciled communion of men with God, around the continuing bounty that results from His presence (cf. Ex. 24:11).

Reverence for God's Name: Blasphemy (24:10–23). The only narrative section in Leviticus, other than chapters 8 through 10 on the priesthood, describes the execution of a Danite half-breed for blaspheming the holy name of God. In Israel a name was more than an arbitrary identification; names had meaning and signified the essence and function of those who bore them (cf. Ex. 6:3, 7). Specifically, God's personal name Jehovah or, more accurately, "Yahweh," means "He is (redemptively) present" (Ex. 3:12–14); and to "blaspheme the name" showed the Danite's contempt for salvation itself. At God's orders, he was stoned to death (24:16, 23). At the same time God revealed legislation on two of the principles concerned: that punishment must be proportionate to the violation, the *lex talionis,* whether death for murder or "an eye for an eye" (vv. 17–21), and that enforcement must be without discrimination relative to the social status of the culprit (v. 22). Such divine standards for judicial procedure are essential to the welfare of society (cf. Rom. 13:4), though to "turn the other cheek" (Mt. 5:39) is equally essential in the area of personal relations.

Extensions of the Sabbath: Sabbatic Years (25:1–55). Leviticus proceeds to combine a holiness in social procedures with a consecrated observance of holy seasons by applying the Sabbath law, not to days, but to cycles of years. That is, upon Israel's entrance into agricultural life in Canaan, every seventh year was to be "a year of rest unto the land" (v. 5). This was not primarily to restore the soil, or even to provide for the poor out of what grew from the untilled fields (v. 6). For though the sabbatic year did involve a humanitarian suspension or cancellation of loans, hence its name "year of release" (vv. 35–38 on the prohibition of usury; cf. Deut. 15:1–15), it was primarily designed for the recognition of God's sovereignty over "the land which I give you" (v. 2; cf. Ps. 24:1). Men's desires must be subordinated to His law (publicly read on the sabbatic year (Deut. 31:10–13), and then God will care for their needs during this and every other year (Lev. 25:18–22).

After seven sabbatic years came the year of jubilee, the fiftieth year (25:8–12), to "proclaim liberty throughout all the land." It added to the features of a sabbatic year the freeing of all Israelite servants and the return of all properties. Supplemental sections explained the sliding scale of values this would entail, depending on the nearness of the year of jubilee (vv. 13–17), the possibilities of redeeming sold property prior to the jubilee (vv. 23–34, 47–55; cf. Ruth 4:3, 4), and the status of those bound to service until the jubilee (vv. 39–46). The sabbatic year and jubilee laws thus taught a concern for those in economic straits (v. 35) and, on religious grounds, opposed social oppression (vv. 17, 43). Slavery is not to exist among God's own, "For they are my servants, which I brought forth out of the land of Egypt: they shall not be sold as bondmen" (v. 42, though cf. vv. 44, 45 on non-believers).

But, though the only properties exempt from the jubilee law were those not economically productive (such as "town houses," 25:30), the legislation must still not be taken as justifying socialism, human possession of productive property on the basis of need (cf. 19:15; Ex. 20:15). Rather, the principle it taught was that of divine possession, "The land is mine, for ye are strangers and sojourners with me" (25:23), and then of the possession by God's stewards of correspondingly permanent property rights. The jubilee was a prophetic type of the blessing that will be granted to the redeemed in the future messianic kingdom (cf. Is. 61:2–4).

4. Concluding Appeal: Exhortation (26:1–46)

The Levitical "code of holiness" concludes with an inspired exhortation. If God's people maintain a holy reverence for Him according to the first table of the Decalogue (vv. 1, 2; cf. Ex.

20:3–11), He on His part will establish the testament (v. 9) to be their God (v. 12), with blessings that will be climaxed in the future kingdom of peace (v. 6; cf. Hos. 2:18–20). But then, in a series of five progressively more severe denunciations (vv. 14, 18, 21, 23, 27), God threatens to avenge violations of the covenant conditions (v. 25) with exile and woe (v. 36; cf. II Chron. 36:16, 17). Restoration, however, may yet follow upon repentance (vv. 40–42); for the Lord our God will never break His testament with those He has redeemed (v. 44; cf. Heb. 9:11–15).

5. *Appendix on Voluntary Devotion: Vows (27:1–34)*

The Book of Leviticus ends with an appendix on vows. Vows, as opposed to the obligatory aspects of holiness that precede, are voluntary obligations which a man may assume before God, generally on condition of some specified blessing (cf. Jacob's vow, Gen. 28:20–22). Often they were vows of abstinence (e.g., a Nazarite's, Num. 6:1–21); but in this chapter they are vows of devotion to God's service of a person (27:2–8), an animal (vv. 9–13), or an object (vv. 14–25). Persons were expected to be redeemed at figures specified in the text, for normally only Levites were to serve in the sanctuary (cf. I Sam. 1:11). For the privilege of redeeming animals and objects, however, an additional twenty per cent payment was required. Moreover, firstborn animals (vv. 26, 27), matters previously "devoted" (placed under the ban, vv. 28, 29; cf. Josh. 6:17, ASV), and tithes (vv. 30–33) could not be devoted at all; they were God's already!

The last of these, the tithe, is particularly significant; for it illustrates the same principle of stewardship that was taught in the jubilee law, though with a universal application (cf. Gen. 14:20; 28:22; Heb. 7:4–14), rather than one limited to the national lands of Israel. Tithing, devoting one-tenth of one's income to God, is required because of the following universal facts: All things come of God (I Chron. 29:14), so if we render Him all we have, we are yet unprofitable servants (Lk. 17:10). But God in His grace decrees a tenth as our token offering, acceptable to Him (Lev. 27:30). Even as Leviticus, the "book of life," commenced with God's provision of a living way to Himself, by redemption through substitution (1:4), so it terminates with man's practice of holy tithing (27:32), a token of our living for Him Who died for us.

Numbers

DAVID W. KERR

REACHING MATURITY is often a painful process, whether in the case of a young child or of a young nation. New freedoms bring new responsibilities. The Book of Numbers is the story of how the Israelites, who had chafed under the imperious rule of Pharaoh, transferred their resentment of authority to Moses, and ultimately to God Himself. The new limits of the divine law were sometimes as irksome as the arbitrary impositions of slavery. The responsibilities of a free people were sometimes more than Israel could fulfil. Yet in it all God was at work, molding a people for His own possession.

I. Preparation for Leaving Mount Sinai (1:1—10:10)

1. Numbering and Arrangement of the People (1:1—2:34)

The census taking is commanded by God, Who communicated with Moses at the tabernacle or, as it is more accurately called, the tent of meeting. This latter expression not only indicates the form of the sanctuary, which like the homes of the Israelites themselves was a tent, but also its purpose, a place where God met with His people through appointed representatives.

The tent of meeting had been completed, according to Exodus 40:17, on the first day of the first month of the second year after leaving Egypt and, therefore, one month earlier than the incidents described in this section. Since the people left the Sinai area just twenty days later and it would have been difficult to count so large a number in that time, it has been suggested that the officers had already been collecting the half shekel required in Exodus 30:13 and that the actual tabulation was made by weighing the money collected, rather than by counting heads. It would seem, however, to be quite within the realm of possibility for the officers to demand reports of the different tribes according to families and fathers' houses. The precise agreement of the accounts in Exodus and Numbers indicates certainly that only one reckoning both of persons and of assessments was made.

The names of those who represent the tribes make use of the older designations of God, namely, as *El*, which was a common Semitic name for Deity, and *Shaddai*, which according to Exodus 6:3 was the name by which the Lord was more familiarly known in patriarchal circles. The antiquity of these lists is suggested by the very fact that several of the names given in Numbers appear to be compounds of Egyptian and Hebrew words.

Since the census is a military one, the final total includes only a part of the men and none of the women, children, or Levites. The figure agrees exactly with that given in Exodus 38:26 and compares reasonably with the later census recorded in Numbers 26. To many modern scholars the number has seemed to be greatly exaggerated since, it is argued, the total population of Israelites must then have been well over two million, which the wilderness area could not possibly sustain. The difficulties involved in the passage of this large group of people are recognized in the Scriptures themselves and the need for special, miraculous provision for their support is clearly stated. Some have tried to reduce the figure materially by understanding the word "thousand" to refer to a family, a clan or military division, rather than a literal number. While there is good Biblical evidence for this argument, another problem is raised by the fact that the numbers here include also hundreds and fifties and that the sum total is based upon the calculation of these. It is best to recognize that the number of Israelites was indeed large and their pilgrimage, which is the theme of this book, was made possible only through divine intervention. With this point of view other passages of Scripture agree (for example, Deut. 29:5; Ps. 78:26-28; I Cor. 10:4).

The people were to be arranged in a camp which was quadrilateral in shape with the sanctuary at its center. Three tribes were assigned to each side with the Levitical families stationed as a kind of buffer between the sanctuary and the rest of the tribes. Obviously, it must not be assumed that the camp of Israel was as orderly as military dispositions of later times. The presence of women and children and the fact that the tents were for domestic, and not military, purposes made a great difference. At the same time, every community must have some orderliness, and He Who is the God of order and not of confusion placed His dwelling in the midst of a neatly-arranged encampment. The symbolism in the plan is obvious: Religion is to be the center and soul of the national life of Israel. Communion with God is to be the privilege of His people; the service of God, their delight.

2. Choosing of the Levites: their Priestly Service (3:1—4:49)

The word "generation" in the heading of these two chapters is more technical than literal and is found earlier in Genesis 5:1, 6:9, and so forth. The description which follows is not that of the descendants of Moses and Aaron. Mention is made only of the immediate family of Aaron while Moses' children are not referred to at all. This is a description rather of the Levitical priesthood as headed by Aaron and designated through Moses. The priestly ministry takes its rise through Aaron as its physical head, and the Levitical organization through Moses as legal founder in the day when the Lord spoke to Moses.

The fact that there were so few priests for so many people made the assistance of large numbers of Levites necessary. Aaron is nowhere called the high priest although he took precedence in office over his two surviving sons. Since he also performed certain rites on the Day of Atonement which later were reserved for the high priest, there is justification for thinking of him as high priest even though such a designation seems to come from a later period when the numbers of priests had increased greatly and the head of the Aaronic family held the title.

The Levites were chosen by way of substitution for Israel's firstborn who were claimed by the Lord. The firstborn of all animate creatures were holy to the Lord and in the case of ceremonially "clean" domestic animals were to be offered in sacrifice. Other domestic animals and human beings were to be redeemed by the payment of five shekels. Luke 2:22–24 indicates that this ritual was performed for our Lord Jesus Christ. The significance of the Levitical substitution is that in theory Israel is a kingdom of priests, as is the Christian Church (cf. Ex. 19:6, I Pet. 2:9) but the actual service is performed by a group of chosen men, in this instance, the Levites.

Some have regarded the Levitical office as one of menial subservience to the priests. Such a conclusion overlooks the fact that the Levites labored in holy things, which was in itself a privilege. They kept the charge of the entire nation, a task as honorable as that of any public servant. Recognition of their standing is revealed in the fact that they were to receive the bulk of the income for religious purposes.

Just as the various tribes were ranged on four sides of a quadrangle, so also the three Levitical families were disposed on three sides of the sanctuary itself, while the immediate families of Moses and Aaron constituted the fourth group and were placed on the east side. As substitutes for the firstborn, the Levites are numbered from one month of age. According to Jewish tradition a child was not thought to be truly living until it reached one month of age, a custom no doubt based upon a high infant mortality rate. Because there was a deficiency in the number of Levites from that of the firstborn, redemption money had to be paid for 273 of the firstborn. Israel was not to take her responsibility to God lightly, but was to render to Him the things that were His.

3. *Cleansing and Blessing of the People (5:1—6:27)*

Removal of Various Defilements (5:1–31). Three classes of people are to be separated from the rest of the camp of Israel: lepers, whose physical defilement was also regarded as symbolic of sin: persons with issues (cf. Lev. 15), whether natural or due to disease: and those who had contact with dead bodies. There is often no clear-cut distinction in the Pentateuchal laws between physical and ritual uncleanness, and the separation is made therefore for both hygienic and ceremonial reasons.

The separated persons must have followed the encampment. Some of them would return to their respective places after one or perhaps several days separation. The lepers, no doubt, scarcely ever resumed normal life although the possibility of recovery is allowed in the law. It is not likely that all segregated persons were grouped together, since the natural revulsion of others would put the lepers by themselves. The attitude of the Levitical law toward dead bodies is in sharp contrast with that of the Egyptians. Similarly, while the Phoenician neighbors of Israel made sex an important aspect of their religious rites, the Israelites were taught that even involuntary sexual issues made them temporarily unholy.

Verses 5 through 10 seem to be a special provision regarding the trespass offering which has already been described in detail in Leviticus 7. When a person commits fraud and has concealed his guilt for some time and later wishes to confess, he must make restitution to the one whom he has wronged, adding an interest penalty of one fifth. If the injured party has died leaving no survivors, the offender is not relieved of his obligation to do justice; payment is to be made to the priest. In addition, since all wrongdoing is an offence against God, compensation must be made to Him in the form of sacrifice. It is interesting that while the priest is usually understood to be man's representative before God, in this instance he is to receive payment on behalf of God.

The ritual described in verses 11 through 31 is the only trial by ordeal mentioned in the Old Testament. This type of trial is known among many ancient peoples and survived in Europe until the Middle Ages. Since the Mosaic law condemns superstitions of the day most vigorously, this process must be something different from heathen practice. It is to be performed before the Lord, pointing to the fact that in this, as in the casting of lots, the decision was expected to be of God. The water to be drunk by the woman, although not sanitary was not poison, as would be the case in a typical trial by ordeal. The expressions which describe the results in the case of guilt probably indicate intense abdominal pain accompanied by swelling of the womb, which would not normally be caused by the indicated dose. These results might, however, be produced in some cases by the emotional disturbance of a guilty one at the time of such a solemn abjuration. According to the Talmud, this practice was discontinued in the early Christian era.

The Law of Nazirite Separation (6:1-21). The law given here apparently regulates an already established practice, for it assumes that such vows are well-known. The idea of separated or holy persons is found in many ancient religions, and it is not surprising to find its parallel in Biblical custom. The Nazirite was a person who was during the time covered by his vow wholly consecrated to the Lord. In token of this separation from the common class of men, he bound himself to abstain (1) from the use of alcoholic drink and even from the grape or its unfermented juice, probably indicating a separation from normal enjoyment; (2) from cutting the hair or beard, which would make for a deviation from normal appearance; (3) from contact with dead bodies, even where the person was a member of the immediate family, pointing perhaps to a separation from the normal affections and emotions of life.

The vows were, no doubt, taken for purposes of self-discipline, but more particularly as an auxiliary to fulfilling some special service to God. By reason of his physical appearance and his abstention from wine, it would be at once apparent to observers that the Nazirite was under oath to God for some reason. It has been suggested that the Nazirite may have been regarded as having almost a priestly character during the period of his vow, since there is a similar abstinence required of the priest during his period of service. This possibility is denied, however, by the part which the priest played in terminating or renewing the Nazirite's vow of consecration.

The Nazirites were not a monastic order, nor were they ever organized as a group of any sort. Both men and women might become Nazirites, although the Biblical record mentions only men as such. The law in Numbers does not envisage a life-long Naziriteship, yet three of the best-known Nazirites—Samson, Samuel and John the Baptist—were such from birth. In their cases, however, it is stated that the parents consecrated the children to this kind of life. The Apostle Paul may have taken a Nazirite vow, since it is stated that in connection with a vow taken at Cenchrea he shaved his head (Acts 18:18).

It is altogether likely that the regulations concerning Nazirites are found in conjunction with the previous legislation because of the rather similar part which the priest plays in ritual.

The Priestly Blessing (6:22–27). A beautiful blessing marks the end of this section which has to do with a cleansed and consecrated people. The blessing, however, is intended not only for those who fulfil the legal requirements given previously, but for all of Israel. In ancient thought the name either of a man or of God stood for his character with all its virtues and powers. The blessing is a three-fold invocation of the Lord's providence, grace and favor, and is described as "putting his name" upon the children of Israel.

In both the Hebrew and the English, the rhetorical structure is poetically beautiful. The first clause asks for material blessings and security from danger; the second seeks the kindness and benevolence of God toward His people, and the third asks for the greatest of all gifts, peace. This last word, a most inclusive one in Biblical thought, embraces not only the absence of strife, but serenity, well-being and abiding happiness. The Risen Christ greeted His disciples with peace and the New Testament writers desired for their readers grace, mercy and peace.

4. *Offerings of the Tribal Chieftains (7:1–89)*

Since the events of this chapter occurred one month earlier than the taking of the census, it is evident that Numbers does not always adhere to chronological order. The equipment for transporting the tabernacle was needed, however, before the actual start on the journey, and so the writer includes at this point the record of items received for this purpose. Although the gifts and offerings are identical for each tribe, the writer is careful to record them in detail. The repetition, monotonous to the modern reader, was characteristic of ancient scribal accounts.

The wagons and oxen to draw them are divided between the families of Gershon and Merari according to their need. The Kohathites receive none of them, because they were appointed to carry on their own shoulders the furnishings which were especially sacred. The total of the offerings is computed (7:84–88).

The relationship of verse 89 to the rest of the chapter is clear if one refers to Exodus 25:21, 22, where instructions are given for making the ark of the covenant. In Numbers 7 the point is reached where the whole of the tabernacle is completed, the altar has been dedicated and the people are getting ready to move from Mount Sinai, where the Lord had been communicating with Moses. Henceforth God will speak to Moses at the sanctuary, His dwelling place. The verb forms used express a continued activity, so that the statement is best understood to mean that from this point onward Moses received the divine messages in the most holy place, at the mercy seat or place of atonement.

5. *The Service of the Lampstand (8:1–4)*

The lampstand had been prepared according to directions and the priests were already charged with its care (See chs. 25, 27 and 37 of Exodus). Care is taken to repeat the command that the wicks of the lamps must be pointing forward, to cast their light across the room and therefore on the table of shewbread. The lighting of the lamps is the next step in formally instituting the tabernacle ritual.

The lampstand is not primarily for practical use, since it was lit at night when no worship was being conducted. Many believe that its chief symbolism lies in the numeral seven which is associated by these interpreters with divine perfection and with the covenant. Others find significance in the oil as symbolic of the Spirit of God. This may be the case, because for the Israelite oil was the principal source of both light and physical energy. Appeal may be made to Zechariah 4:6, which, however, is much later than the Pentateuch. It would seem to be wrong to ignore the emphasis upon the light which must flood the holy place, pointing either to God as the source of light and truth, or to Israel as having been redeemed to bring the light of God to the world.

6. Consecration of the Levites (8:5–26)

Strictly speaking the Levites were "purified" rather than consecrated. Nevertheless, the rites described in this chapter are the formal installation of the Levites to their peculiar office. The purification is both ritual and spiritual. It called first for a sprinkling of water, no doubt from the laver which was used by the priests. Second, all the body hair was to be cut short, though probably not close-shaven. The purpose of this is not clear, though it may very well be a sign of the assuming of a career of devotion to God in somewhat the same manner that the one who assumed a vow shaved his head. Next the clothing was washed, an action required also of both the priests and the people before coming to worship. There is a difference of opinion as to whether there was a fourth requirement, the washing of the entire body. The translation in the King James Version, which seems preferable here, deems that there was not; while the Revised Standard Version seems to favor the idea that there was also the washing of the body.

The outward ritual pointed, of course, to inward purity. To secure the assurance of this, however, the Levites were to offer sin-offerings which would be accompanied by a confession of sin. The symbolism of the whole transaction is impressive. The people through their leaders laid their hands upon the Levites, transferring their responsibilities as a nation of priests to the one group. The Levites then laid their hands upon the sin and burnt offerings, transferring their guilt to them. At the same time the Levites are actually to be presented as a wave-offering, which must have been done by Aaron's leading them in procession before the altar. The wave-offering was apparently initiated at the consecration of Aaron and his sons when Moses waved the breast (of ram) and bread before the Lord (Lev. 8:27).

There is an apparent contradiction between verse 24, which states that the Levites were to begin service in the tabernacle at the age of twenty-five, and 4:3, 4 which sets the minimum age at thirty years. The problem has been resolved either by supposing that for the first five years the Levites were serving a kind of apprenticeship or by supposing that the provisions of chapter 4 refer only to the matter of transporting the tabernacle and that in actual tabernacle service the Levites began their duties at the earlier age.

7. Second Passover (9:1–14)

This is the first anniversary observance of the Passover, kept at the appointed calendar time, just after the offerings of the chieftains. It is, therefore, also earlier than the census of chapter 1. The account is given here, however, because the Passover observance gave rise to a question not faced before and thus to a special provision for a second Passover for the benefit of those who were not able to take part in the first. The special Passover was not to be followed, as far as may be known, by the week of unleavened bread. Here is evidence that the law could be relaxed to make allowance for a conflict in duty. Permission is granted here, as elsewhere in the Old Testament, for the foreigner to participate if he were willing to show humble submission to Israel's God and His law.

8. The Guiding Cloud (9:15–23)

The column of cloud which displayed a fiery appearance at night is mentioned first when the people left Egypt. It continued in sight through the wilderness journey, though it was localized above the tabernacle. It therefore may not have been large in size. It is, however, a distinctly supernatural occurrence. Once again the narrative points back to the time of the completion of the tabernacle when the cloud first settled upon it. Here, however, a stronger emphasis is placed upon the conscientious care which was taken by Moses and the congregation to move or to rest as indicated by the cloud.

It should not be supposed that the divine guidance rendered human forethought and planning unnecessary. Moses very soon asked the help of Hobab, whose experience in desert lore could be so valuable. The spies were sent into Canaan in obedience to God's command. The lesson is clear: Faith in God and obedience to His will call for the best use of human wisdom and effort, while at the same time the best of intention and labor is useless without His sovereign guidance.

That the periods of resting were sometimes lengthy is apparent from the mention of a year during which the cloud remained above the tabernacle. The periods of movement seem to have involved only a few days duration at most. The point, in any case, is that even though the people may have been weary and in need of rest, they moved if God indicated they must. On the other hand, they must often have felt ready to move from certain spots before God allowed them to do so. They submitted to His infinite wisdom in choosing. This paragraph is obviously descriptive of the entire period of the wilderness experience, since it was only a matter of a few weeks before the people reached Kadesh-Barnea and proved themselves unworthy to enter the Promised Land.

9. The Silver Trumpets (10:1–10)

The silver trumpets are to be distinguished from the ram's horn or *shofar* which was used frequently in religious ceremonies and in various combinations of instruments. Use of metal horns or trumpets is depicted in ancient Egyptian and Assyrian remains. They were long tubes with a bell-shaped end and, in several instances, are shown in pairs in the same fashion that is intimated here. Sounds of the metal trumpet may have carried further, and its use would be more effective in signaling or summoning the congregation than the *shofar* would have been. In any event, the silver horns were employed for military and civil purposes. The "alarm" was probably a series of short, staccato blasts.

II. The Wilderness Wanderings (10:11—20:13)

1. Departure from Sinai (10:11–36)

The first stage of the journey from Sinai lasted three days and took the people to the wilderness of Paran. In their traveling the people passed through the wildernesses of Sinai, Paran and Zin. Paran is said to be very desolate although it may not have been as denuded of vegetation then as it is now. Evidently the movement of the people prior to their reaching Sinai had been pretty much that of a disorderly horde. It is now to take on a settled pattern.

In verse 21 it is implied that the Kohathites, who carried the ark, took their prescribed place in the center of the line of march, while in verse 33 the statement appears that the ark of the covenant of the Lord went before the people. It is possible that in this initial step of the journey an actual exception to the general rule was made and that the ark did precede the Israelites, as it did later when they crossed the Jordan (cf. Josh. 3:6). A more satisfactory solution to the problem, however, is that the phrase "went before" means to give leadership, as it does in Deuteronomy 31:3 and I Samuel 18:16, and does not imply physical precedence.

Hobab, Moses' brother-in-law, was asked to act as guide (10:29). He is here called the son of Raguel, though elsewhere his father is called Jethro or Reuel. The spelling *Raguel* in the English version is based upon the Greek and refers, of course, to Reuel. Since Reuel was a patriarchal priest, one of his two names may have been a title. At first Hobab declined Moses' invitation, but he must have accepted it later, for his family entered Canaan with Israel.

The promise to do good to Hobab undoubtedly referred to his inheriting land in Canaan; yet it must also have embraced all that good which Israel could expect of her Lord in the covenant relation with Him. Whatever of grace is contained in the formula, "I will be your God and you shall be my people," is vouchsafed to those who cast their lot with His people.

The prayer which Moses uttered when the ark began to move and when it rested is still used in the Jewish synagogue services when the scroll of the law is removed from its container, the ark (cf. also Ps. 68:1). Moses' words suggest that the movements of the ark had a kind of sacramental character as a pledge of God's presence and leadership and also of the rest He would give to them.

2. A Disobedient and Gainsaying People (11:1—14:45)

The Fire at Taberah (11:1–3). In comparison with the lush verdure of the Nile delta where many of the Israelites had lived, the wilderness of Paran must have been appalling. The privations of the journey before them now began to loom large in the minds of many of the people and complaints were rife. The sinfulness of their attitude lay in their forgetting the great working of God on their behalf thus far and their doubting His kindly providence for the future. The fire at Taberah should be regarded as a merciful warning which went unheeded. It affected only the outlying parts of the camp, and while it caused injury and loss, there is no indication that there were any deaths. The fire of the Lord may have been lightning. Whether there was any effort to extinguish it is not stated. Since the people understood the fire to be caused by God, they asked Moses to intercede and the fire abated. Taberah is not listed later as one of the camping places of the people, and it is likely that this judgment occurred at the same spot as the one which is next described, which greatly overshadowed Taberah in magnitude. *Kibroth Hattaavah* left a deeper impression in the minds of the people.

Moses' Complaint against a People who Prefer Bondage (11:4–30). The mixed multitude mentioned here, described by some translators as "riff-raff," probably consisted of some non-Israelite slaves who had escaped from Egypt. These people are said to have incited the Israelites to a continual discontent. The items of diet listed were staples for the poorer people in Egypt, but they represented a variety which was unobtainable in the wilderness. While the Israelites had cattle and sheep, these were apparently not numerous enough to sustain them in the circumstances then prevailing.

The manna sent by God is described more elaborately here than in Exodus 16 where its appearance is first mentioned. It was not, however, the only item of food as the exaggerated protest of the people had implied, but was a supplement to other kinds of food. In view of the variety of ways in which it could be used and the pleasantness of its taste, their complaint is baseless. It is also evidence of gross ingratitude.

Moses in turn complains to God, though his grievance is justified and is expressed in a prayer of faith rather than in a spirit of rebellion. The implication of the query, "Did I conceive all this people?" (11:12) is that God had, in a manner, done so. In answer to Moses' assertion that the responsibilities of leading so large a multitude were too heavy, the Lord directs the appointment of seventy elders to share in civil administration. This number was later used as authority for the number of members of the Sanhedrin at Jerusalem.

The people's dissatisfaction is regarded as groundless, and the penalty is that they shall receive much more meat than they want. The size of the Israelite encampment is emphasized in the statement that if all the herds and flocks were slain it would feed the people for only a month.

The acceptance of the elders was signified by their receiving the spirit of Moses. Evidence of this was that they prophesied, though as the Revised Standard Version correctly states, they did so no more. The prophesying would consist of declaring the praise of God in an ecstatic or highly excited frame of mind. In the camp itself were two men, Eldad and Medad, who had been called to the sanctuary along with the others but who, for some unknown reason, did not go. These men also received the gift of the spirit and their prophesying caused such a stir that it was reported to Moses. The suggestion was also made that they should be forbidden. Moses pointed out that the working of God's Spirit in others could not possibly detract from his own eminence or usefulness. The greatness of Moses may be seen in the parallel between the incident here and that which is recorded of Jesus and His disciples in Luke 9:51–56.

Graves of Lusting (11:31–35). An amazing fulfilment of the divine threat was brought about by the appearance of vast numbers of quail. These birds, a type of partridge, migrate with the wind and fly about two cubits (one yard) above the ground. The people killed them with ease and accumulated such quantities that they spread them in the sun to dry for future use. The suggestion has been made that the numerous deaths which followed resulted either from over-eating or from poison matter eaten by the quail. While sin often brings its own punishment, the statement must not be overlooked that judgment fell while the people were in the act of eating. It is granted, however, that it was the most greedy among them who died and gave the place its name, *Kibroth Hattaavah,* "graves of lusting."

The Murmuring of Miriam and Aaron (12:1–16). The rumblings of discontent among the people were followed by mutiny in Moses' immediate family. The actual cause was jealousy of Moses' preeminence, natural enough in those who were older than he. The formal occasion was Moses' marriage to a woman who is not named and who may have been an Ethiopian or was possibly a member of a north Arabian tribe. Presumably this was a second marriage. There are intimations that Moses' relations with Zipporah, his first wife, were not always smooth. The intrusion of another woman into the family circle aroused Miriam's resentment. Aaron, who had earlier yielded to the people's desire for a golden calf, now gave in to Miriam's insistence upon the rightfulness of their own claim to equal authority with Moses. The aggressiveness of Miriam in the affair is assumed from the fact that she alone was punished.

This chapter has a twofold purpose: (*1*) It asserts once for all the superiority of Moses as a steward over God's house, the Israelite economy; and (*2*) it points out the difference in the mode of revelation to Moses and that which was given to other prophets. God communicated with the prophets through visions, dreams and dark sayings, or enigmatic speech. This method of revelation should be kept in mind by all interpreters of Biblical prophecy.

As a punishment Miriam was stricken with leprosy. Although she recovered after Moses' intercession, she was required, in accordance with Levitical law, to spend the minimum of seven days in uncleanness and, therefore, in humiliation outside the camp.

The statement that Moses was meek above all men (12:3) is regarded by some as a parenthetical explanation inserted here by a later copyist or editor. Others have suggested that Moses, in recording the incident, was astonished at his own humility in this particular situation. Still others have felt that there is no impropriety in the fact that Moses, who laid bare his own mistakes and failings, should also assert the virtue which enabled him at this time to leave the judgment to God when he and his wife were under attack.

Spies Sent into the Land (13:1–33). The spies were sent at the command of the Lord, which according to Deuteronomy 1:19–25 was an approval of the request of the people themselves. Except for Joshua and Caleb, the names of the men listed here do not appear elsewhere in Scripture. Very likely it was at this time that Moses changed the name Oshea to Joshua, even though the name Joshua is used in the narrative prior to this time.

The spies were to go first to the Negev, ("southward," KJV) which is the southern steppe-land of Canaan, and then on to the "mountain" or highland area. They were to report on the number and type of inhabitants, the strength of their settlements and the fruitfulness of the country. The expedition was apparently made in July or early August at the time of the first ripening of the grapes.

In their report the spies confirmed Moses' promise that Canaan was a land flowing with milk and honey. The statement about the size of the cluster of grapes is no exaggeration; the Hebron district has always been noted for its grapes. There have been records from other countries in more recent times of clusters weighing from twelve to nineteen pounds and borne on a pole for convenience sake. The excuse offered in verse 32 that the land eats up its inhabitants is not a reference to the land as being poor, but rather to the inter-city warfare which was common in this period and tended to diminish the population. The Israelites could expect to be caught in the struggles of these powerful people.

The majority report favored no effort to enter the land. Their view that they could not hope to overcome it was correct, apart from God's help. Contemporary records from Egypt tell of the strength of several of the city-states and also confirm the presence of some of the groups mentioned in the plain and highland areas. The name *Nephilim*, ("giants," KJV), is of uncertain origin, but the context here shows that it refers to people who, in comparison with the Israelites, seemed to be phenomenally tall. No doubt also the spies in their apprehension asserted of all the people what was true only of a few.

The Great Failure: an Unworthy People (14:1–45). Majorities are often wrong, but their opinion usually prevails, and it did in Israel. Reaction against the Exodus experience became general, and a plan was suggested to elect a leader in Moses' place and return to Egypt. Moses and Aaron prostrated themselves in prayer in the sight of the assembled congregation with the result that the glory of the Lord—perhaps as the glowing fire of the pillar of cloud—appeared before the entire group. Meanwhile Joshua and Caleb were pleading with the people to act in faith rather than fear. Admitting that the inhabitants of the land would have to be faced in combat, they pointed out that the Canaanites could be conquered as easily as eating bread, that their defense (literally, shadow or shade) was taken away because the Lord was with His people. In response, the people threatened Joshua and Caleb with stoning.

The Lord's patience is now exhausted. The people have tried God ten times—no doubt a round number; they have forgotten completely His grace and power already shown in so many ways. They have impugned His wisdom and despised His mercy. He is ready to destroy Israel and to fulfil His covenant promises to the patriarchs through Moses.

In his plea for mercy, Moses stresses what might seem to be less than the noblest of motives for sparing Israel. The Egyptians who had been humbled will believe that Israel's God was not omnipotent after all. The Canaanites, who had already heard fearsome reports, will lose their respect for Him too. It is important, however, to realize how closely in ancient times the popular mind tied in the honor of a god with the fortunes of his people (cf. Ex. 12:12; Judg. 16:24; Is. 37:10–12). There would be greater glory to the Lord in sparing His people even though they should be penalized, as they were, by having to remain out of the land which they had been unwilling to enter by faith. Moses' appeal, however, was in the final analysis a dependence upon grace (v. 19) and not just an attempt to persuade the Lord to protect His reputation.

Remorse and repentance may be hard at times to distinguish until they lead to action. Then remorse becomes as self-willed as the action from which it arose, while repentance before God leads to new obedience to Him. The people were sorry for their faithless decision, but they were not yet ready to accept God's will. They were warned that their day of opportunity was gone forever and that any effort to go in to Canaan now would be a further act of disobedience. A foray of considerable size was made into the hill country, only to be repulsed.

3. Additional Laws: Offerings, Sabbath Breaking, the Ribbon of Blue (15:1–41)

Offerings (15:1–31). The offerings mentioned in this chapter have already been delineated in Leviticus. Because the additional provisions here are to apply when the people are settled in the land, they may have been given toward the end of the wilderness wanderings. One commentator, however, suggests that by the clause, "when you come into the land," God is reminding the Israelites that, in spite of their defection, His promises will be fulfilled. According to this view, the laws may have been given immediately after the failure at Kadesh.

The additional prescriptions deal with drink-offerings, the meal-offering (not 'meat-offering' as in the KJV) which should regularly accompany other major sacrifices, and with the sin-offering for those who sin unwittingly. It may be that the offering described here is to cover sins of omission rather than commission: "And if you err and do not observe all these commandments" (15:22). At any rate, the lesson was clearly taught that sin is wrong whether done deliberately or unknowingly. It is also noteworthy that sins done with a high hand, that is, in considered pride and rebellion against God, cannot be atoned for through these offerings. The sinner must bear his punishment.

Sabbath-breaking (15:32–36). The incident of the man who broke the Sabbath law is a case in point. He must have known the law and the severe penalty imposed for breaking it. His attitude may have been a part of the whole complex of insurgence which was expressed on a much larger scale shortly after. Previously the death penalty had been prescribed but not the manner of execution.

The Ribbon of Blue (15:37–41). The exact symbolism of the tassels and the ribbon of blue, which was used to fasten them to the corners of garments, is not clear. The blue may have been a reminder that Israel's law and her relationship to God were of heavenly origin. It is expressly stated that the purpose of the fringe was to remind the children of Israel of their separation unto God and His commandments. In the New Testament our Lord Jesus remarked that the Pharisees, who were the separatist party and proud of their devotion to the law, wore extra large tassels in order to draw public attention.

4. The Rebellion of Korah, Dathan and Abiram (16:1—17:13)

The passage makes it plain that there were actually two movements against Moses and Aaron, the one religious and the other civil. Korah and a group of Levites resented the fact that the priesthood was confined to the family of Aaron. Dathan and Abiram secured a following on the grounds that Moses was playing the part of a prince, insinuating in effect that his rule was as disagreeable as Pharaoh's while the physical circumstances were not at all what they had hoped for.

Moses tried to dissuade Korah by warning him that if he should insist upon intruding into the priestly office, the Lord Himself would show whom He had chosen for priests. He pointed out that the Levitical position is really one of privilege and that Aaron in himself was no better than anyone else. A similar effort to restrain Dathan and Abiram was rebuffed by their refusal to come to talk with Moses. The next day Moses went directly to them.

Korah's persistence was shown by his gathering a group of men with censers to perform a priestly rite at the tabernacle. Curious, perhaps, to see the outcome of the contest, large numbers of people came with them. The glory of the Lord radiated from the cloud. Moses and Aaron in prayer appealed to the justice of God in requesting that only the responsible persons be punished. By going to the dwelling (not the "tabernacle" as in the KJV) of Dathan and Abiram, followed, apparently, by Korah, Moses brought together the chief offenders.

The judgment was possibly brought about by an earthquake of some proportion. The miraculous element is that it occurred as Moses said it would, when and where it did. The men who had expected to offer incense seem to have stayed behind at the tabernacle, and they died by a fire from the Lord. The censers, however, were to be devoted to the divine service and so were gathered up to make a copper plate for the altar of burnt offering. Harsh as the judgment was, the people involved were first given every warning and then challenged as to whether they would choose death with Korah, Dathan and Abiram or life with God's people. The choice was their own.

Many of the people blamed Moses for the disaster. Fundamentally they had not had a change of heart. After another manifestation of the glory of the Lord, a plague broke out among the people. It was brought to an end by Aaron, who made atonement by using the very object which had earlier been involved in death, the censer. It has been pointed out that Aaron in this action did two things which were forbidden in the Levitical law. Though he was high priest, he had contact with dead bodies and he took incense out of the most holy place. The lower law is broken in order to uphold a higher, the sparing of human life. Several times in Numbers there is witnessed the interplay of the goodness and severity of God: severity, as the apostle says, to those who fell, but kindness to those who continued in His mercy (Rom. 11:22).

Further proof of the choice of the tribe of Levi as ministers and of the Aaronites as priests is given in the sign of the blossoming rod. The tribal heads each brought an almond rod on which the name of the tribe was inscribed. The rod for Levi had the name of Aaron as its representative. The rods were left in the tent of meeting over night. In the morning Aaron's rod had not only budded, but it bore some ripe almonds. As a warning against further presumption against the priesthood, Aaron's rod was to be left in the holy of holies beside the ark.

5. *Duties and Revenues of the Priests and Levites (18:1–32)*

Since the people had now been thoroughly impressed with the thought of the sanctity of the tabernacle and its service, a series of regulations was given concerning the relations of the priests, the Levites and the people. The sanctuary was to be in charge of the priests, who were to "bear the iniquity" both of the sanctuary and the priesthood. There is disagreement as to whether this means they were to be responsible for complete performance of every minute regulation and to see that no unauthorized persons transgressed the proper bounds or that they were to make atonement for the sinfulness associated with the sanctuary and the priesthood since all concerned were subject to sin. Perhaps both ideas are involved. The Levites were to minister at the sanctuary, but they were not to touch the sacred vessels and furnishings of the holy place.

Neither the priests nor the Levites were to have any landed inheritance in Israel, so that Israel did not have the same type of wealthy priestly caste as did Egypt or other ancient nations. Yet the priests were to receive a large part of the offerings, such as the portions of the meal, sin and trespass offerings which were not burnt upon the altar; the gifts of the firstfruits and the money paid as redemption for the firstborn; things devoted to God. Some of the food items were to be eaten by the men alone at the sanctuary while others could be used by the priests family at home.

The Levites were to receive a tithe, or tenth, of the produce of the field. Leviticus mentions that a tenth of the herds and flocks was to be holy unto the Lord, but it is likely that these animals would be used in sacrifice and that the Levites did not receive them. The Levites were to give a tithe of their income to the priests. The tithes were to be in lieu of wages for the Levites, "in return for their service." After the people were settled in the land, it would be difficult to collect the tithe if the people wished to neglect it, and injunctions are found in Deuteronomy to be conscientious in this matter.

6. Ordinance of the Red Heifer (19:1–22)

The use of the ashes of an animal in water for purificatory purposes is a very old custom known in religions outside the Bible. It would appear, therefore, that its use in the Mosaic law may represent the dedication of a familiar rite to Israel's peculiar faith. The same could be said of certain other ritual acts prescribed in the Pentateuch.

A female animal is used in several of the offerings, but in this case the distinction is made that the cow must never have borne a yoke. The yoke may have been considered as setting the animal in the class of things for profane use or as causing a blemish. The choice of a red beast is likely due to an association of that color with sin (cf. Is. 1:18). Since the animal was to provide purification for the defiled, it was to be taken outside the camp as a defiled person would be. A rather similar combination of cedar, hyssop and scarlet is involved in the ritual cleansing of a leper (cf. Lev. 14:4–32), though in the ceremony here these items are to be burnt with the body of the heifer.

The most likely reason for the institution of the ordinance at this juncture was that there were a great many persons in the camp at that time who had been defiled by contact with dead bodies. Unlike several of the other ritual laws of Numbers which elaborate or modify provisions found elsewhere in the Pentateuch, this law is unique. Reference to it is made in the Epistle to the Hebrews, where it is one of the 'diverse washings' or baptisms mentioned (Heb. 9:10–14).

7. *Waters of Meribah: Moses' Failure (20:1–13)*

The Israelites came again to Kadesh. Since it is located this time in the wilderness of Zin, rather than Paran, it is suggested that Kadesh was not an oasis or small settlement but a larger area. The arrival of the people was in the first month, that is, about April, and it may be assumed that it was in the fortieth year after leaving Egypt. The statement that the whole congregation of Israel came may imply that the people had been somewhat scattered, but were now together as a unit.

The death and burial of Miriam are given only passing notice. If her death occurred after the regathering at Kadesh, it took place about five months before that of her brother Aaron.

The complaint of the people which aroused Moses' anger was very like those of other times though it may not have been as bitterly expressed. Although Aaron is associated with Moses in the entire incident, his weaknesses have been generally known, so that it is chiefly Moses who is at fault. The sin of Moses has been difficult to explain precisely. It appears, however, that it was twofold. As one who had called often and again for complete obedience to God, Moses should have spoken to the rock as he was told to do, and not have smitten it. In calling the people rebels and saying, "Must *we* bring forth water?" he put himself in the place of God. No doubt his patience was exhausted and one can scarcely blame him from a human point of view, yet he now indicated that the qualities which had fitted him for leadership were fading away. Whatever glory there was in the provision of water, Moses arrogated to himself and "did not sanctify" the Lord in the eyes of the people.

III. Journey into Trans-Jordan (20:14—36:13)

1. Futile Negotiations with Edom (20:14–22)

If Canaan was to be approached from beyond the Jordan rather than from the south, the most direct route from Kadesh lay directly across the territory occupied by the Edomites. These people were descended from Esau, the brother of Israel (Jacob). On the ground of family and thus of racial ties, Moses asked permission to cross on the king's way, which would seem to be a military route. Promise was made to pay for any food or water used and to keep the animals from treading upon the crops. According to Judges 11:16, 17, a similar request was sent in due time to the ruler of Moab who, like the king of Edom, refused.

Scholars differ in their opinions as to whether the Israelites, not willing to have conflict with the Edomites, traveled south of Edom and then to the east of it, passing close to the head of the Gulf of Akabah, or managed by buying from those who lived in the border-lands between Edom and Moab, to cross further north just below the Dead Sea. The narrative in Deuteronomy favors the first of these alternatives.

2. Aaron's Death (20:23–29)

Warning was given prior to the death of Aaron in order that his function as head of the family might be transferred to his son. Why the Lord should have called the trio, Moses, Aaron and Eleazar, to the top of a mountain is not indicated. In Moses' case, it permitted him to view the Promised Land. That can hardly have been true of Aaron. About fifty miles south of the Dead Sea is Jebel Harun, the traditional site of Mount Hor. Moses' removing the various insignia of office from Aaron and putting them on Eleazar must have been a painful task for all concerned.

3. *Victory over Arad, a Canaanite Chieftain (21:1–4)*

The brief account of victory over Arad is apparently not in chronological sequence since Israel was already going away from Canaan at the time of the death of Aaron, but it is placed here, no doubt, because it is the first in a series of victories about to be described. Perhaps Arad's forces attacked about the time the Israelites were breaking camp at Kadesh, after hearing a rumor that Israel would come the way the spies had come. The Israelites vowed to put the kingdom of Arad and its cities "under the ban," that is, to devote them to destruction if the Lord would grant them victory. The Canaanites were defeated and their settlements in the immediate area destroyed, so that it was called Hormah, "devoted." The complete fulfilment of the vow, however, did not take place until the conquest recorded in Judges 1:16, 17.

4. *The Brazen Serpent (21:5–9)*

This incident is one of the few chosen by our Lord Jesus Christ from Old Testament history to illustrate His own person and work. The use of a bronze serpent as a means of healing cannot be associated with the ideas of other ancient people regarding the healing powers of snakes since in this instance it is the bite of the serpent which is to be healed. The essential demand laid upon the people was faith in God's word, since they had only to believe that He would perform what He had promised to those who would gaze at the uplifted serpent. It is this also which is the main point of comparison in Jesus' conversation with Nicodemus, though another element enters also. It is that just as Moses lifted up a likeness of the creature causing death, so Jesus, made in the likeness of sinful flesh, that is, mankind, and for sin, was lifted up for those who believe.

As sometimes happens, that which was only a means of grace was made an object of veneration by later generations and the serpent-image was destroyed on the orders of Hezekiah about 700 B.C.

5. *Journey to Pisgah in Moab (21:10–20)*

The route of march to Pisgah is difficult to trace and some of the stopping points cannot be identified to-day. The book of the wars of the Lord (20:14), apparently a collection of war songs, may have included also the song at the well. Both songs seem to interrupt the narrative, so that some commentators have believed that while the songs themselves come out of the desert experiences, they were not inserted in the narrative by Moses but by a scribe. Others have felt, however, that Moses may have recorded the songs of the wars of the Lord as well. These would then be poetical chants similar to Moses' own triumphal song at the Red Sea (cf. Ex. 15:1–19).

The well, which is the occasion of the one song, was not miraculously provided, but was discovered by digging a few feet below the surface.

6. Conquest of the Amorites under Sihon and Og (21:21–35)

A message asking passage was sent to Sihon, but not to Og. Sihon is called king of the Amorites, a term which is used outside the Bible to describe several of the national groups living in the westlands, that is, from Palestine to the upper Euphrates. The Hebrews, however, distinguished between the Amorites and other people in Canaan. The Babylonian kingdom of Hammurabi which had disintegrated in the eighteenth century B.C. was Amorite, and it may be that the conquerors in Transjordan were some of these people.

According to Deuteronomy, the Israelites were forbidden by God to try to capture Moab and Ammon. They did not hesitate to take those territories which had already been wrested from Moab by the Amorites. Og is not called an Amorite in Numbers, but he is designated as such in Deuteronomy 1:18. The possession of the territories of these kings was the first inheritance of the Israelites in the Promised Land.

The general conception of the relationship of the people of the land to the national deity is seen in the description of the Moabites as the people of Chemosh. Again there is a victory-paean inserted in the narrative. The song, which celebrates the victory of Sihon over Moab, was probably taken over by the Hebrew bards who added the closing lines in commemoration of the Israelite victory.

7. Balaam's Efforts to Curse Israel (22:1—24:25)

The figure of Balaam as well as his actions have posed many problems for interpreters of Scripture. His home seems to have been in the upper Mesopotamian valley, about four hundred miles from Moab. The trips of the embassies as well as Balaam's trip must therefore have taken a few weeks. From the fact that Balaam rode a donkey, which normally was not used for long trips, and the fact that a man named Beor, which is the name of Balaam's father, is mentioned as being an Edomite, some have assumed that Balaam's home was, in fact, much closer to Moab.

Balaam's reputation as a caster of spells was well established. The story must have come to the Hebrews from Balaam himself, perhaps as a kind of confession in a futile attempt to obtain leniency after his capture by the Israelites (31:8). Opinion has differed greatly as to whether Balaam was a prophet of the true God. In general, Jewish interpreters think not, and it is significant that he is condemned in both Old and New Testaments. Some Christians, however, have maintained that Balaam was a believer in God who through covetousness brought about his own undoing. His use of the covenant name "Lord" is no indication of a saving belief in God if the general duplicity of his character is kept in mind. He is described in the Hebrew as a *kosem* or diviner, and such a person is denounced elsewhere in the Bible. Since various groups in the ancient Near East believed in one supreme deity with many lesser deities, Balaam may have acknowledged the existence of Israel's God without being in any sense a true believer.

The incident of the speaking ass has as its only parallel in Scripture the speaking of the serpent in Genesis 3. Both Jewish and Christian interpreters have held that the whole affair occurred in a vision since it seems that those who were with Balaam were unaware of what went on. Others have suggested that the ass brayed in its normal fashion, but that God caused Balaam, who was in a disturbed frame of mind, to understand the message as he did. Some, however, feel that such a view does not do justice to the omnipotence of God who can make even a dumb brute speak.

Balak, the king of Moab, was perhaps a Midianite himself since he consulted with elders from Midian. The Midianites were scattered over various parts of northern Arabia and were marauders who troubled Israel in later times.

The three efforts of Balaam to curse Israel are made from high points, which were often the location of heathen altars; and in this instance it would appear that at least two of the locations were sanctuaries of Baal. The use of seven altars and seven sacrifices accords with the ancient association of that number with deity. The oracles are climactic in order and content. They declare that the electing grace, the protective power and the redeeming purpose of God require the blessing and not the cursing of Israel. When the infuriated Balak refused to pay Balaam, the latter uttered an oracle of doom against Moab, Edom, the Amalekites and the Kenites.

In the midst of this oracle is embedded a prediction of the appearance of a leader who shall be the Star of Jacob and the Sceptre of Israel. He will act as the destroyer of their enemies, Moab and Edom, and give dominion to Israel (24:17, 18). This prophecy was understood by the rabbis to refer to the ideal king or Messiah to come, and it has been applied by many Christians to Jesus. In order to do this, however, it is necessary to translate all the physical terms into spiritual counterparts. It is better to see the fulfilment of this prophecy in David, the king of Israel who did actually crush both Moab and Edom. The ideal can be transferred to the Messiah only in the sense that the throne of David prefigured the rule of Jesus Christ over an infinitely greater kingdom.

8. Phinehas' Campaign against Apostasy (25:1–18)

The statement that Israel began to play the harlot has to be understood in two ways. First, the action of the Israelites involved the worship of a false god, which is often described in the Bible as "whoredom," that is unfaithfulness and therefore spiritual adultery to Israel's husband, the Lord. Second, however, is the fact that the worship of Baal-peor included fertility orgies in which there was actual sexual intercourse in the name of religion. In view of this, the severity of the punishment demanded by God can be understood.

Phinehas did not actually lead the present campaign, which was under the direction of Moses. The leaders in the apostasy were apparently killed first and then hung or impaled in full view of all. A plague also broke out among the people who had accepted the invitation to eat the sacrificial feasts with the Moabites and were then led into immorality. Zimri's arrogance in taking his vestal partner into the very tent of his family and in the sight of Moses displayed a complete disregard for the God of Israel.

Phinehas' act was in contravention of the law which required offenders to be given a trial. In this instance the crime was public, however, and Phinehas acted with a holy zeal to put a stop to any further enticements of this sort. He and his descendants were promised a perpetual priesthood, a promise which was fulfilled except for an interlude in the period of the judges. God's covenant in this connection is called a covenant of peace, that is, one which guaranteed well-being to the house of Phinehas.

9. Second Census of Israel (26:1–51)

A new census was taken after the plague. The size of some of the tribes was altered by the wilderness events. The total number of Israelites was slightly smaller than at the previous census. Mention is made of the fact that among the secular tribes only two men of the previous generation, Joshua and Caleb, had survived. In particular, the tribe of Simeon had decreased sharply, and Ephraim and Naphtali had lost appreciably also. The greatest gains were in the tribe of Manasseh, half of which settled in the Transjordan area.

10. A Fair Method of Dividing the Land (26:52–65)

The second census not only revised the military lists but also provided figures for the division of the land on a more equitable basis. The division would be based upon the drawing of lots to determine the general situation, but not the size, of the inheritance of each tribe. Since the lot was viewed as being decided by God, complaints that human leaders had favored one tribe over another would be eliminated. Again it is emphasized that the Levites as a tribe were not to have a separate inheritance.

11. The Claim of the Daughters of Zelophehad (27:1–11)

Among the Hebrews the line of inheritance was through sons only, except where the father during his life gave part of his estate to a daughter. Zelophehad had died intestate. Since he had not died in the calamity which befell Korah and his rebel friends, his family was entitled to its share with all Israel. His daughters asked that some provision be made for them in their own tribe. Their claim became the occasion of a further elaboration of the inheritance laws, provision being made for the inheritance to pass to the next of kin in the event that a man should die leaving neither sons nor daughters. Chapter 36 adds a further qualification that the daughters who receive the right of inheritance must marry within their own tribe.

12. *Appointment of Moses' Successor (27:12-23)*

The true humility of Moses is seen in his readiness to accept the path to death which God had ordained for him and to be concerned with the securing of an able successor. No doubt Moses was pleased to learn that Joshua, who had been his helper for some time, was judged by God to have the spirit, that is, the powers of mind and personality to qualify for the position. In Moses' prayer, he describes God as the God of the spirits of all flesh; He knows the innermost recesses of man's being and is best able to choose His ministers. It is implied also that it was God who gave the "spirit" to Joshua.

The succession to leadership could have caused great dissension had it not been settled before Moses' death. The laying on of hands did not transfer any of Moses' spirit to Joshua, but rather conferred some of Moses' authority and dignity upon him. It is pointed out that Joshua would not have direct communication with God as Moses did, but that in seeking the divine will he should communicate through the high priest, who would make use of the Urim (cf. Ex. 28:30). The description of the new leader as "going in and out" points to the activities of a shepherd which he is said to be (27:17).

13. *Regulations for Various Offerings (28:1—29:40)*

The relationship of these laws to the preceding section is not clear. Regulations concerning the various periodical feasts are found in Leviticus 23, but the detail of the types of public sacrifices is given here. The offerings involved are those for the daily burnt offering, the Sabbath, new moons, the Passover, the Feast of Weeks, the New Year (Rosh Hoshanah), the Day of Atonement (Yom Kippur) and the Feast of Tabernacles.

The celebration of the new moon as a holy day is not required in the Mosaic law, but it is clear from references in the historical and prophetical books that it was observed from ancient times.

The use of drink offerings antedates the Mosaic period (cf. Gen. 35:14) and was common in the ancient Near East. The Levitical code required drink offerings but did not specify what they should be. Here the amount is indicated in certain cases as well as the fact that they should be of strong wine. The apocryphal work *Ecclesiasticus* (50:15) states that the drink offering was poured out at the foot of the altar.

14. Laws Relating to Vows (30:1-16)

The requirements actually relate to vows made by women, in which men are involved only as the heads of households. Certain exceptions may be made to the general rule that anyone who makes a vow must carry it out. The vow of an unmarried daughter living at home may be annulled by her father as may that of a married woman by her husband. The objection, however, must be stated at the time of the making of the vow; otherwise it is valid and must be fulfilled. If the women does not fulfil it, the man must assume the responsibilty of doing so. Widows and divorcees are under the same solemn obligations to keep their oaths as are men.

15. Vengeance upon Midian (31:1-54)

The war against the Midianites was a holy war led by Phinehas as a priest, rather than by Joshua. Its purpose was the extermination of those who had tried to lead Israel away from her Lord. The ruthlessness of the campaign is characteristic of the times, in which whole towns were often "devoted" (that is, wholly given over to God and therefore not to be used for human advantage. In the case of captives, this usually involved their being put to death. Compare Lev. 27:28, 29 and the explanation of Josh. 5:17). Nevertheless, the annihilation of the Midianites was also carried out at the command of God, against whom the enemy had waged a relentless struggle. Had the Midianite ruse succeeded in turning all Israel to the degrading worship of Baal, the religious history of the world would be a sorry tale. Though Israel later became apostate in the majority, the knowledge of the truth was preserved at this time by the destruction of the forces of evil.

Moses was angry when the victors brought back some of the women as captives, since it was through them that the Hebrews had been seduced. He ordered that only virgins should be spared.

The campaign affected only a segment of the Midianites, since large numbers of them plagued the Israelites a century or so later. The "kings" of Midian who probably were executed after capture were undoubtedly loyal chiefs. The "goodly castles" (KJV) are better described as "encampments" (RSV).

If one may judge by the emphasis in the material, the main point of the chapter is not so much to relate the victory over Midian as to set forth certain principles for conduct after such a victory. For one thing, those who do not go out to battle are to share the spoils equally with those who do. The Levites are to receive one-fiftieth and the priests one five-hundredth of the booty. Ritual uncleanness was incurred by all who had contact with the dead. The only plunder which might be kept was metal objects which could survive fire.

Because the Israelite victory was complete, with no casualties, the soldiers made an oblation as an "atonement." The principle of atonement in the Old Testament is the giving of something in exchange for one's life, so that it is likely that the soldiers made their offering because their lives had been spared in battle.

16. Settlement of Tribes beyond the Jordan (32:1–42)

The excellent grazing lands of Transjordan appealed to the tribes of Reuben and Gad, who were subsequently joined by half the tribe of Manasseh. Their request to be allowed to settle there displeased Moses, since it was likely to discourage the rest of the tribes in reaching their objective. The request was granted, therefore, only when it was explicitly agreed that the fighting men of Reuben, Gad and Manasseh would accompany their brethren to Canaan proper and join in its conquest. The Book of Joshua (22:1–6) states that the promise was kept and that Joshua dismissed the fighters with thanks.

Except for economic reasons, the choice of the two-and-a-half tribes was unwise and proved to be a source of trouble. Isolation from the main body produced misunderstanding among the tribes. It has been pointed out that there were no natural frontiers to the territory, so that it was open to constant attack and was difficult to defend. This was always the first area to be infiltrated by groups from the desert as well as from the north and several times it was lost to Israelite control even before the downfall of the kingdoms.

Apparently Reuben and Gad occupied the lands taken from the Amorites earlier while the Manassites gained their inheritance by further conquest. The statement that these groups "built" certain towns should be understood to mean that they made strongholds of them.

17. *Journey from Egypt Summarized (33:1–49)*

The route which is summarized here agrees for the most part with earlier records in Exodus and Numbers except for a few minor additions. The list of stopping places on the journey from Mount Sinai until the final mustering at Kadesh is, in the main, not found elsewhere. Most of the twenty-one points mentioned in the list cannot be identified today. A few of the happenings on the way are recapitulated in what is otherwise a bare itinerary record made by Moses.

18. *Directions for the Division of Canaan (33:50—34:29)*

Of prime importance to a true possession of Canaan were (1) the driving out of the present inhabitants; (2) the complete annihilation of the cult objects and sanctuaries used by the present inhabitants. It is not said that the people were to be put to death, though in many cases they were. Should the inhabitants remain in the land, there would be social and cultural intercourse which could only result in the religious deterioration of Israel. In that sense the Canaanites would be pricks in their eyes and a thorn in their sides, as indeed they proved to be.

Archeological excavations have revealed the prevalence of altars, figured stones and various religious furnishings at many "high places." The Bible declares that Israel did take over these shrines and dedicate them, supposedly, to the Lord. Idolatrous elements were retained in the worship conducted there and even some fertility rites. The Book of Kings states that worship at the high places was so common that even some of the most pious kings did not attempt to remove it. In the chaotic period of the judges, worship at other places than the tabernacle was sanctioned by Samuel himself, though the heathen elements were expunged from it.

The boundaries of Canaan proper, defined in 34:1–13, do not extend beyond the Jordan, nor do they include the large regions which later were incorporated into the kingdom of David. In general, the limits are the Mediterranean Sea on the west and the Jordan basin from the Sea of Galilee to the southern end of the Dead Sea on the east. The northern and southern lines are drawn roughly parallel across from the termini of the eastern border. The men who were to take charge of the actual division were named before the land was entered. They were to be led by Joshua as civil commander and by Eleazar as religious authority and mediator with God.

19. *The Levitical Cities and Havens of Refuge (35:1–34)*

Although the tribe of Levi could have no permanent section of the land as an inheritance, its members must have places to live. Each tribe, therefore, was to assign certain towns within its regions in order that the Levites might be located throughout Israel. In addition to the residential areas, pasture lands or "suburbs" were to be granted, so that the Levites would have a partial subsistence and a normal occupation when they were not on duty at the sanctuary.

Of the Levitical cities, six were to be havens of refuge for people who were guilty of manslaughter as distinct from murder. Though provision had been made for legal procedures, the traditional law of avenging of blood by a next-of-kin also prevailed, so that one who was not a murderer might easily be killed by an act of vengeance before his case could be heard. Or yet again, the avenger might not accept the judgment of the courts.

Regulations for convicting a murderer require that the accusing evidence must be supplied by two or more witnesses, and it must be shown that the act was done with malicious intent or premeditation. Death as the result of accident or even, apparently, as the result of a sudden flare of temper, is not murder. The killer must, however, spend the remainder of his life in the place of refuge. Of the six cities, three were west of the Jordan and three east.

20. *Laws of Female Inheritance Amended (36:1–13)*

In order to avoid any confusion in the lines of tribal inheritance and thus to avoid occasions of civil strife, further provision was made at the request of the elders of the tribe of Manasseh regarding the inheritance rights of women. Since their marriage to men of another tribe would make them members of that tribe and their property would be transferred to it, the decision was that the daughters of Zelophehad and all other women in their situation should marry within their own tribe.

The concluding verse, 36:13, refers to all the statutes or amendments promulgated by Moses in the section of Numbers which deals with the encampment in the plains of Moab, chapters 27—36.

While some of the historical and legal data of the Book of Numbers has little immediate application beyond its own day and age, nonetheless the eye of faith can see great principles of God's dealing in every part. Even a superficial reading must point to the goodness and severity of God; as Paul would say, on those who fell, severity, but mercy toward those who continue in His mercy. Though two weeks at best would have been enough time to bring Israel from Egypt to Canaan directly, God took forty years. Yet the refining experiences of the wilderness transformed a horde of slaves, imbued with the superstitions of the gods of Egypt, into an army of free men, chastened but ennobled by the law and love of the God of all the earth.

Deuteronomy

HAROLD B. KUHN

ALTHOUGH WRITTEN to serve its own age, the Book of Deuteronomy sets forth truths applicable to men of every age and time. It proclaims that God is one, that fallen man must come to terms with Him, that God's covenant terms involve moral obedience, love and justice, and that an Anointed One is coming to complete the revelation addressed to God's ancient people.

Moses is named as author of the addresses which comprise all but the last chapter of the book. His authorship has been generally accepted until recent times, when some have sought to ascribe the work to an unknown writer in the seventh century B.C. Denials of Mosaic authorship usually rest upon subjective grounds; that is, they rise from previous denials of the antiquity and validity of the message of the book.

We would quote the scholar Haevernick: "If the Pentateuch [and this would include Deuteronomy] is not the work of him who names himself as its author, it is the work of *deception*. The history is then an untrue history: the laws are falsely ascribed to Moses: the predictions have been invented *post eventum*, that is, after the events occurred." We therefore take our place with those who acknowledge Moses as the author.

The addresses or orations which make up the major part of the book were delivered by Moses shortly before his death. They are words of a dying father to his children. In a certain sense, Moses' words mark the close of an epoch, and the beginning of another. They contain a summary of the whole law and wisdom of the people of Israel, particularly with reference to the Lord's choice of them as the people through whom the Hope of all Nations should come. As such, Deuteronomy holds a living message for us today, and stands high among the writings to which Christians may look for spiritual succor. If some have found the book somewhat forbidding, in view of its detailed legislation of the life of the ancient Israelites, they should recall our Lord's frequent quotations from Deuteronomy and its crucial significance in the hour of His temptation.

Deuteronomy has the form and quality of a great sermon in its fluent, rolling style and in its frequent repetition of important ideas for the sake of emphasis. Equally important, it speaks the language of the heart. The language seems almost to sing even its laws to the human heart. They are not set down as mere facts without warmth and emotion. Here divine revelation takes a form that applies truth to the heart with astonishing force.

I. Preface and Historical Statement (1:1–5)

The speaker is introduced, and the locale of the message is fixed as "on this side of the Jordan in the wilderness." The time of delivery is also given, dating from the Exodus, which for ancient Israel was a dividing line for history. The source of the materials to be given is also stated (1:3b); the Lord had commanded reiteration of the law. Moreover, several decisive victories had just given Israel opportunity to pause a bit. Sihon and Og were no longer troubling them (v. 4), for the Lord had granted deliverance. The occasion called for recognition of divine assistance. At this significant time, Moses began to "declare this law" (v. 5). The stage is set for the first of the three addresses comprising the major part of Deuteronomy.

II. First Address of Moses (1:6—4:40)

This shortest of the three orations is more directly historical than the other two. It begins with Israel at the Mount of the Law, traces the failure to advance to the Land of Promise, recounts briefly the period of wandering in the desert, and brings the historical record up-to-date by giving the account of recent events which brought the people to their station east of the Jordan. The address ends with an exhortation to advance.

1. The Lord's Command to Proceed from Sinai (1:6–8)

The law had been given at Sinai, and the camp of Israel had been set in order in accord with the Lord's command. The thrilling events of the Exodus were still vivid in the memories of the people. Now came the word of the Lord, "Ye have dwelt long enough in this mount" (1:6).

The precise course to be taken is given to Israel; the road is to bring the chosen people "to the land of the Canaanites" (1:7), and into the land promised by oath unto their fathers by the Lord, Who had covenanted to give it "unto them and to their seed after them" (v. 8). Israel's possession of Palestine was the grand objective of the Exodus—an objective which could not be fulfilled by remaining in the wilderness, however long the Lord could conceivably sustain His people there.

2. Assistant Administrators for Moses Appointed (1:9–15)

The place of Moses as divinely appointed leader and judge was taken for granted by Israel, yet the task was clearly too great for a single individual. Seeing that Moses was overburdened by details and the demands of his position, his father-in-law, Jethro, wisely suggested a division of labor. The wisdom of this counsel prevailed. Moses told the people, "I am not able to bear you myself alone" (1:9). To this the people agreed (v. 14), and Moses appointed captains and officers, to whom he committed the care of specific groups, some being placed "over thousands," others "over hundreds," others "over fifties" and "over tens" (v. 15). The division of labor, and commissioning of helpers according to ability, took place.

3. The Command of Justice and Equity (1:16–18)

These leaders were not set to work without orders. Moses' address recalled his charge to them to listen with patience to "the causes between your brethren" (1:16) and to make decisions with strict justice and without partiality. They were reminded that "the judgment is God's" (v. 17); that is, that the Lord ultimately will have the final word, and that men who act as judges are under solemn obligation to act justly. In case of situations too difficult for the assistants, Moses promised his own guidance.

It is impossible to emphasize this section of Deuteronomy too strongly. The command to impartiality and to strict justice is the cornerstone, not only of Israel's administrative life, but of Christian integrity as well. Now, as then, God has no patience with injustice, with the degrading of justice in sordid hope of personal gain or personal advantage. The words "the judgment is God's" could well be read today at the installation of every judge, the empaneling of every jury, and the opening of every legal trial.

It is significant that the principle of division of labor was invoked also in the days of the early Church when the apostles were so burdened that they could not carry all administrative details and still perform their major task. At this time, deacons were appointed and charged with the administration of funds for the needy, so that the apostles might freely devote their entire attention to the ministry of the Word and to prayer.

4. Israel's Unbelief and Failure to Possess Canaan (1:19–39)

Moses now recounts a tragic period in the life of Israel. The nation had departed from Horeb (or Sinai), and had been providentially brought through the bleak wilderness which lay between them and Kadesh-barnea (1:19). "The mountain of the Amorites" was at the very frontier of Canaan. Speaking as the Lord's mouthpiece, Moses gave the word, "Go up and possess it" (v. 20). Israel was at the crossroads.

Moses briefly reviews the events described in greater detail in Numbers 13 and 14. He agreed to the sending of scouts to view the landscape, and twelve were appointed and sent. The fuller account in Numbers notes that two of the twelve—Joshua and Caleb— sensed the difficulties, but were convinced that the Lord's leadership would bring the people into possession of the land. The other ten, while agreeing that "it is a good land which the Lord our God doth give us" (1:25), were doubtful that Israel could overcome the obstacles to possession. Moses' words are almost severe, "Ye would not go up, but rebelled against the commandment of the Lord your God" (v. 26). Instead of moving ahead in faith, the leaders of Israel remained in their tents, sulking at God.

No encouragement or exhortation from Moses could move the captains to action. They blamed the spies, saying "our brethren have discouraged our heart" (1:28). Moses' words, "Dread not, neither be afraid of them" (v. 29), fell upon deaf ears; unbelief carried the day (v. 32), and the Lord was displeased. His sentence is solemn: "Surely there shall not one of these men of this evil generation see that good land" (v. 35); only Joshua and Caleb of all the adult and voting population would live to enter Canaan. Even Moses, as we are to learn later, experienced a "dimming of the vision glorious," and, in consequence of disobedience in speech (resulting from extreme provocation at the perversity of Israel), was permitted to see the Land of Promise only from afar.

5. Israel's Presumption and Retreat (1:40–46)

When the captains and elders heard the Lord's pronouncement of judgment, they and the people took a "long second thought" and began to repent with the words, "We have sinned against the Lord; we will go up . . ." (1:41). But such forced repentance amounted only to fear of disaster; it indicated no real change of heart. Proof of this is found in the manner in which Israel sought to defy the Lord. In a presumptuous gesture lacking real faith, the army started ahead on its own. Against Moses' stern warning, "Go not up" (v. 42), they "went presumptuously up into the hill" (v. 43). The language describing their defeat is graphic: like a group of boys who had inadvertently stirred up a nest of hornets, they retreated. Seir and Hormah became Israel's Waterloo.

What follows this serious defeat is tragic. When the tattered remnants of the army drag back to the camp, the people try to repent and to escape the promised judgment. It was too late. "The Lord would not hearken to your voice, nor give ear unto you" (1:45), said Moses. Could the truth be set forth more plainly, that there is a time and season for repentance? The writer of the Epistle to the Hebrews grasps the spiritual significance of this event and writes, "Let us therefore fear, lest a promise being left us of entering into his rest, any of you should seem to come short of it" (Heb. 4:1). When advance ground is indicated, the children of God can fail to possess it only with grave consequences.

6. Thirty-eight Years of Wandering (2:1–15)

This is a melancholy record of Israel's monotonous and pointless wanderings. A vast nation spends thirty-eight years milling around in the wilderness. Moses speaks of these years with restraint: "we compassed mount Seir many days" (2:1). He spells out what he means by "many days" in the remark, "The space in which we came from Kadesh-barnea, until we were come over the brook Zered, was thirty and eight years" (v. 14); solemnly he adds, "until all the

generation of the men of war were wasted out from among the host"
(v. 14b). Men of all ages must note the meticulous manner in which
the word of the Lord was fulfilled. Marking time in a wilderness
where raw nature was king, the nation was kept by divine providence
until all the men responsible for the decision at Kadesh-barnea had
perished. Of the adult population, only Caleb and Joshua remained.

7. A New Period of Faith and Advance (2:16—3:17)

The thirty-eight years of wandering must have been dismal.
During this long funeral march, an average of several dozen persons
per day died. Just how many times Israel broke camp during this
time of wandering is not known. Twelve places are mentioned; there
may have been many more.

But now, all things ready, the nation is to move northward toward
Canaan in God's plan. They are to pass "through Ar, the coast of
Moab" (2:18) and when they come to Ammon they are not to make
trouble for the "children of Lot" (v. 19) who live there. They are
to fight against "Sihon the Amorite, king of Heshbon, and his land"
(v. 24). To facilitate their journey, the Lord promises to make the
nations afraid of the Israelites (v. 25). Israel, however, is not to
make a second attempt to enter Canaan from the south, but is to
travel east of Mount Seir and come to the Jordan Valley opposite
Jericho.

Moses reminds the people that "Sihon king of Hesbon would not
let us pass by him" (2:30), with the consequence that Israel was
compelled to engage in battle—the first major skirmish of the conquest. She came into possession of the territory between the brook
Arnon and Gilead (v. 36), thus clearing away hostile resistance to
the rear. Enroute to Bashan, "Og the king of Bashan came out against
us . . . to battle us at Edrei" (3:1). Providentially, the Lord enabled
the Israelite hosts to overcome Og, so that the territory from Gilead
north to Mount Hermon was firmly in their hands. Tactically both
the conquests (that is, of Sihon and of Og) were necessary. The
territory east of the Jordan had to be secured prior to the invasion
of Canaan itself, to eliminate the possibility of a surprise attack from
hostile forces when the fighting men were across the Jordan.

The account of the battles against Sihon and Og is a grim one.
Losses among the peoples of these kings were heavy, and the plunder
seized was extensive. These accounts convey one overpowering

impression: *the Lord is the God of peoples and nations.* National boundaries are under His control. It is He Who determines the destiny of nations. When a people harden in opposing His will and His plans for them, He uses instruments to chastise, and at times even to destroy them utterly. Israel was thus taught, in graphic fashion, that the Lord is sovereign. Moses in this address makes clear his view of God's government. While some of His dealings may seem mysterious to us, He nonetheless cares for His own. Even through imperfect human affairs, His will can and will be accomplished.

The lands taken by conquest were divided among the tribes of Gad, Reuben and the half-tribe of Manasseh. Verses 12 and 13 of chapter 3 indicate how the land was allotted. The entire area "from Chinnereth [Sea of Galilee] even unto . . . the salt sea" (v. 17) was distributed among the two-and-one-half tribes who chose their portion to the east of the Jordan.

8. *Israel at the Boundary of the Promised Land (3:18–29)*

Much of the Land of Promise was not yet in the hands of the Israelites. Note Moses' words, "The Lord your God hath given you this land to possess it" (3:18). The conquests to this point gave promise that the major part of Palestine, that is, the part west of the Jordan, would soon be theirs also. This does not mean that no great struggles lay in the future. It does mean that the Lord's faithfulness, shown in the battles thus far, would continue to be their strength. "Thine eyes have seen all that the Lord your God hath done unto these two kings: so shall the Lord do unto all the kingdoms whither thou passest" (v. 21). Moses here sought to awaken in the people a new spirit of faith and of obedience. God had shown Himself to be their captain. Whatever obstacles they might encounter in the future, they could depend upon Him; as He had led them thus far, so also He would bring them to full possession of their inheritance.

To be so near to the Land of Promise must have stirred up excitement and anticipation. Moses tells the people how it has been with himself: he had said to the Lord, "I pray thee, let me go over and see the good land that is beyond Jordan" (3:25). Now he reminds them that even he, who had been the Lord's administrator for so many years, must be refused this privilege. He had transgressed in his speech—under extreme provocation with the people, to be sure

—but it was enough to cause the Lord to refuse his petition. We are reminded that God is no respecter of persons; He administers His will without regard for the countenance of man. This incident stands as a perennial reminder that disobedience to God's will does not go unpunished.

The greatness of Moses appears again in his statement (made without bitterness) that another should receive his privilege. He quotes God's statement, "But charge Joshua, and encourage him and strengthen him: for he shall go over before this people, and he shall cause them to inherit the land" (3:28). Moses was to see the land from afar, and another was to take the place of leadership in its conquest.

How shall we think of Canaan, in relation to the Christian life? Some identify it with the Kingdom of Heaven. If this be correct, a profound spiritual lesson is to be learned from the fact that Moses, who is rightly associated with the law, could not bring the people into the land. It is Joshua (whose name is the Hebrew equivalent of *Jesus*) who is to bring the people into the land God had provided. It is Jesus Christ alone Who can bring His people into their eternal home.

9. *Moses' Exhortation to Obedience to the Lord (4:1–40)*

Moses solemnly exhorts Israel to trust the Lord completely. The history given up to this point has been recounted as a basis for this appeal. The Lord has dealt with Israel in a twofold way: He has punished disobedience and lack of faith; and He has shown mercy and providential aid in response to obedience. Verse 1 sounds the keynote of this exhortation: "Now therefore hearken, O Israel, unto the statutes and unto the judgments, which I teach you, for to do them, that ye may live, and go in and possess the land which the Lord God of your fathers giveth you." God's statutes were to be the guiding light of the nation. None should add nor take from these laws and statutes (v. 2), nor should Israel have or serve other gods.

The very place upon which they stood was an object lesson: "Your eyes have seen what the Lord did because of Baal-peor: for all the men that followed Baal-peor, the Lord thy God hath destroyed them from among you" (v. 3). It was not to be so with Israel: already they had experienced great mercy, and they have in possession the "statutes and judgments" (v. 5) which are to be their guides to obedience.

Israel is promised that if she obeys the Lord, she shall become a standard among the nations, who shall come to say, "Surely this great nation is a wise and understanding people" (4:6). It was not long before all nations recognized the quality of Israel's moral code, and had borrowed from her civil laws, at least. Note Moses' eloquent words in verse 7 "For what nation is there so great, who hath God so nigh unto them, as the Lord our God is in all things that we call upon him for?"

But Israel's heritage was not one automatically kept and conserved. Moses said, "Only take heed to thyself, and keep thy soul diligently, lest thou forget the things which thine eyes have seen ... but teach them to thy sons, and thy sons' sons" (4:9). This message remains as vital and as up-to-date as tomorrow's newspaper. God's revelation is soon lost from sight unless care is taken to observe it and to transmit it to the young.

The Lord's mercies to Israel centered in the gift of His covenant to them. Its very giving was impressive. "The mountain burned with fire" (4:11). While God spoke out of the fire, He gave no visible image or form to the law. The obvious lesson is that the Lord is not to be worshipped under any form or image. Moses said, "Ye saw no manner of similitude on the day that the Lord spake unto you in Horeb out of the midst of the fire" (v. 15). Verses 16 to 19 contain the earnest prohibition of idolatry in every form. Sometimes we in our day wonder why such an exhortation was necessary. But God knows the power of bad example and the pull of the visible. Israel was to be projected into the midst of idolatrous peoples, and she must be placed on her guard lest she imitate their practices.

Verses 20 to 24 of chapter 4 sum up the solemn teaching that "the Lord thy God is a consuming fire, even a jealous God." One thing is made certain: He will not share His glory with another; He demands full and unconditioned loyalty; it is not in His nature to co-exist with other gods! Covenant relationship meant that Israel's God was to be her strength. But if Israel should "make a graven image, or the likeness of any thing, and shall do evil in the sight of the Lord" (v. 25), then she would be scattered among the nations, and perforce serve "gods, the work of men's hands, wood and stone, which neither see, nor hear, nor eat, nor smell" (v. 28). Here is a warning picture of a people carried off by force and compelled by grim circumstance to serve foreign deities.

In the most vivid fashion, the Lord was teaching not only Israel, but mankind everywhere, that idolatry is an abomination to Him, and that He demands the total loyalty of men. Israel had been elected as a special "laboratory sample"; through her history the Lord would demonstrate both His pleasure at obedience and His wrath at idolatry.

Again, Israel was to be a proving-ground for the Lord's mercy and forgiveness. Verse 29 of Chapter 4 begins with the words, "But if . . ." and thereupon describes a provision of mercy and of grace should Israel fall into idolatry and consequent judgment. The picture is of a nation scattered and taken captive: "But if from thence thou shalt seek the Lord thy God, thou shalt find him, if thou seek him with all thy heart and with all thy soul" (v. 29). This is a word of comfort to men of all time. "For the Lord thy God is a merciful God" (v. 31) is a promise which every Christian needs. Today, no less than in the days of Moses, sincere penitence and sincere turning to the Lord will result in pardon and restoration.

This passage makes it clear that Israel has been a people of special privilege: "Did ever people hear the voice of God speaking out of the midst of the fire, as thou hast heard, and live?" (4:33). Because God has dealt with them as with no other nation, and in view of His mighty works in their behalf, Moses pleads with them, "Know therefore this day . . . that the Lord he is God in heaven above and upon the earth beneath: there is none else" (v. 39). This knowledge of His goodness should bind them to the Lord in solemn and continuous obedience. Moses concludes this address with words of promise: "Thou shalt keep . . . his commandments . . . that it may go well with thee, and with thy children after thee, and that thou mayest prolong thy days upon the earth, which the Lord thy God giveth thee, for ever" (v. 40).

How full of meaning has been this first address of Moses! He has laid the groundwork for much of the Christian faith by his emphasis upon the unity of God, upon His sovereignty, upon the demands of His holy law, upon His desire for our complete loyalty and full love. The Lord's attitude toward evil, the unfailing rigor of His judgments, and the boundless character of His mercy are abundantly clear. In reality, the unfolding of this phase of Israel's history is actually a dramatic presentation of much that is basic to our faith. God is here revealed in history. A large portion of this survey has been devoted to a fraction of Deuteronomy, because this portion is fundamental to the entire book; the remainder elaborates and underscores what has been laid before us. If we grasp chapters 1 through 4, the rest of the book will easily come to life before our eyes.

III. Historical and Transitional Statement (4:41–49)

These nine verses summarize what has been said, and set the stage for the second address of Moses.

1. Cities of Refuge Appointed (4:41–49)

Verses 41 to 43 of Chapter 4 indicate Moses' quick obedience to a divine command (Num. 35:14) to appoint cities of refuge, to which those who had inadvertently and without malicious intent killed another might flee for safety. There were to be six of these in all, and Moses immediately set up three of them—Bezer, Ramoth and Golan —in the land which had already been conquered. These three cities were available to the inhabitants of the two-and-one-half tribes, and served to prevent rash executions of the patriarchal law. If the law, that in case of a murder the nearest of kin might avenge the death of the slain relative, seems harsh in our day, we must bear in mind that it was a great modification of the practices common among other ancient peoples, and that the provision of cities of refuge greatly softened its application.

2. Introduction to the Second Address (4:44–49)

Verses 44 and 45 summarize the address we have just studied. Note the words, "This is the law which Moses set before the children of Israel: These are the testimonies, and the statutes, and the judgments, which Moses spake unto the children of Israel after they came forth out of Egypt." Thus the law is subdivided into testimonies, statutes and judgments: the *testimonies* declare the will of the Lord; the *statutes* express moral obligations; the *judgments* indicate the measures required to secure social justice. Once more the specifically Mosaic authorship of this material is declared, while the location of its deliverance is clearly given: "On this side Jordan, in the valley over against Beth-peor" (v. 46). This was the place of Israel's first triumphs, which placed in her hands the lands "from Aroer, which is by the bank of the river Arnon, even unto mount Sion which is Hermon" (v. 48).

We take our leave of this scene with the observation that already the conquest has been spectacular: the entire area known today as Transjordan, extending from the middle of the Dead Sea to Mount

Hermon, and from the Jordan and the Sea of Galilee to the desert, was in Israel's hands. No power remained which could effectively challenge her possession of this territory. The forces might with safety push over Jordan and capture the heartland of Palestine without fear of attack from the rear; all was ready for the final push of conquest. But it must be borne in mind that this conquest was not primarily a human situation; its success hinged upon Israel's obedience to the Word of the Lord: both that which Moses has already proclaimed, and that which is to follow.

IV. The Second Address of Moses (5:1—26:19)

Moses' first address laid the groundwork for Israel's understanding of the nature of God, and of His requirements from His people. The second proceeds to elaborate and to spell out in detail the moral law. While the first address has been, in considerable part, historical, the second begins with Moses' emphasis upon the contemporary nature of the covenant between Israel and the Lord. "The Lord made not this covenant with our fathers, but with us, even us, who are all of us here alive this day" (5:3). The covenant under consideration was thus not an agreement confined to those who were personally at Sinai; rather, it was binding upon Israel as a nation forever.

1. A Series of Exhortations (5:1—11:32)

Moses proceeds to the recounting of the greatest feature in the life of Israel, the Exodus. Over and over again, we read in the Pentateuch, "I am the Lord thy God, which brought thee out of the land of Egypt, from the house of bondage" (5:6). This was a living point of departure for the message to which Moses turns his attention (5:1-21).

The Ten Commandments (5:1-21). Moses now recapitulates the Ten Commandments (Ex. 20:1-17), which are basic to the covenant between the Lord and Israel, as well as to all enlightened legislation since the time of Moses. These commandments, which summarize man's duties to God and to his fellows, are not an artificial creation, given to limit man's normal activities. Rather, they reflect the kind of regulation which makes human life bearable. Without them, society as we know it would not exist.

The question arises, Did Moses originate these Ten Commandments? The answer is that it was through Moses that the Lord gave them to mankind. Let it be remembered that they have not been outmoded nor repealed, and that basically they had been known in some form and in sketchy fashion long before. He who presumes to "write his own ten commandments" will eventually and certainly come to grief.

The moral law as expressed in the Ten Commandments is shown to be grounded in the will of the Lord. Moral obligation is thus focused in man's relation to Him, and in Israel's case is rooted specifically in gratitude for mercies shown to her as a nation.

The *first commandment* prohibits the worship of any other gods "before" the Lord (5:7). This not only forbids idolatry, but also warns men against any division of allegiance or any sharing of worship with the deities of nations round about. The Lord must have first and final loyalty.

The *second* prohibits the making of images of the Lord, and turns the thought of men away from the worship of material objects and material forces (to which men have always been tempted), toward the One Who is creator of heaven and earth. Things "in heaven above" or "in the earth beneath" are His handiwork, and not the proper objects of veneration (5:8).

The *third* forbids the irreverent or thoughtless naming of the Lord, whether in jest, in provocation, or in connection with judicial oaths. It is a definite prohibition of both blasphemy and perjury. Any flippancy or dissimulation at this point will lead to guilt (5:11). Its whole thrust is that the name signifies the person, and that the Lord is intensely concerned with the honor accorded Him.

The *fourth* sets apart as sacred one day in seven and indicates that this day is to be hallowed by a cessation of labor. In recognition of the need of men and animals for rest, this commandment grows out of the creature's requirement. In Exodus 20:11, the appeal is based on divine precedent, the Lord's cessation from His creative work on the seventh day. The Hebrews uniformly kept the seventh day; Christians have acknowledged the day of our Lord's resurrection as the day to be honored in terms of the fourth commandment.

The *fifth* emphasizes the duty of children to hold their parents in regard. This commandment, which St. Paul calls "the first commandment with promise" (Eph. 6:2, 3), is responsible, in very large part, for the compactness and stability which characterize family life among the Jewish people even today.

The *sixth, seventh* and *eighth commandments* have specific reference to man's dealings with his fellows. Human life, the sanctity of the husband-wife relationship, and the right of private property are specifically safeguarded. Killing is the final act by which one man breaks fellowship with a brother; adultery is the supreme act of dishonoring both self and the offended party; theft cuts the very roots of trust between men and men.

The *ninth* has special reference to the bearing of false testimony against another in the courts of law and also forbids all forms of deception and false reporting against another.

The *tenth* switches the emphasis from the outer act (expressed by theft or adultery) to the motives which underlie it. It reaches into the depths of human life to probe thoughts and intentions. Our Lord, in the Sermon on the Mount, appeals to this same dimension. Mark 10:19 renders this commandment in terms of "defraud not."

This majestic document correctly sees man's obligations as twofold, reaching first toward God and second toward his fellows. It places the ground for obedience where it belongs: in man's obligation to his Maker. Its driving force is derived from the fact of a gracious relationship, for although Israel was primarily the people of the covenant, Christians have also been admitted to it. The Decalogue is treated with the utmost regard in the New Testament, and the Sermon on the Mount emphasizes its deep meaning. Our Lord in no case abolishes these Ten Commandments; He presses them upon us in terms of their highest reach and urges us toward their spiritual fulfilment.

Events at Sinai and their Meaning (5:22—6:3). Moses spares no pains to impress upon the minds of his hearers the meaning and significance of the events at Sinai. He recalls the fire, the cloud and the darkness (v. 22) and above all, the voice (v. 23). The people were deeply moved (v. 27), and the Lord, wishing that they might always be of the same mind (v. 29), again emphasized the law to Moses, and laid upon him the responsibility of impressing it upon Israel (v. 31).

Obedience is the major theme of the appeal in chapter 6:1–3, which combines exhortation and promise. Long life (v. 2) and continued residence in Canaan (v. 3) are temporal promises, but the Christian has no difficulty in interpreting their spiritual meaning. While we do not obey God simply to secure temporal blessings, there is a relation between the life which holds God always in remembrance and a life of general well-being.

The Shema, or "Hear, O Israel," and its Imperative (6:4–25). From the days of Moses until now, devout Jews have thrilled to the words of verse 4, which is usually rendered by them in the words, "Hear, O Israel, The Lord our God, the Lord is One." These words express Jewish monotheism, but they go much further, for they are followed immediately by the majestic command, "And thou shalt love the Lord thy God with all thine heart, and with all thy soul, and with all thy might" (v. 5). Verses 4 and 5 are, in effect, the text for a sermon which follows: Israel is urged to hold this "great commandment" "in thine heart" (v. 6); these words are to be taught to the children (v. 7), and are to be kept before all Israelites in written form (vv. 8, 9).

A warning against the temptations which growing prosperity brings (6:10–12) and through which Israel will be tempted to forget the source of her blessing, is given. Moses reminds them, and us as well, that an increase of goods will cause men to "forget the Lord." Idolatry is to be strictly shunned (v. 14); men are forbidden to "tempt" God by doubting His mercy and goodness (v. 16), and the glories of the Exodus are to be kept in the minds of the young (vv. 20–23) in perpetual remembrance. As a capstone, obedience should be Israel's "righteousness," that is, it should be the token of their gratitude to Him, and the source of the fear and love through which their service to Him should be rendered.

Practical Commands, Promises, and Warnings (7:1—11:32). Chapter 7 deals with the great question raised by the second commandment. Israel was shortly to be exposed, in a new way, to peoples whose worship was corrupt and whose idolatry was notorious in the world of that time. God saw correctly, that when the first fine zeal of the people cooled, Israel would find herself greatly tempted to imitate her neighbors.

The Lord commanded Israel to root out thoroughly the inhabitants of Canaan (7:2). However harsh this may seem, we must remember that God's ways are higher than our ways, and that only He, in His wisdom, can know when a people has sinned beyond the point of redemption. "The cup of iniquity of the Amorites" being full, the trappings of idolatrous worship were to be destroyed without mercy (v. 5). Throughout this exhortation, the emphasis falls upon the greatness of the Lord's mercies to Israel. "The Lord did not set his love upon you, nor choose you, because ye were more in number than any people: for ye were the fewest of all people: But because the Lord loved you" (vv. 7, 8). This is an eloquent statement of the gift of grace, given nationally then and bestowed so freely upon us personally during the Christian age.

The Lord was to be the strength of Israel in her task of subjugating Canaan (7:18). Nothing was to be left in the land which would subsequently snare the chosen people into idolatry (v. 25). In all of this exhortation, the Lord was concerned that Israel should develop an attitude of utter abhorrence of all things idolatrous and be kept as a people exclusively for His name.

Chapter 8 is a detailed record of the Lord's mercies to Israel during the years in the wilderness. He "humbled" His people (v. 2); He fed them supernaturally (v. 3); He clothed them (v. 4). Above all, He sought to teach them that "man doth not live by bread alone, but by every word that proceedeth out of the mouth of the Lord doth man live" (v. 3), words our Lord later quoted in His encounter with the tempter (Mt. 4:4).

In the desert, physical needs had of necessity been supplied supernaturally, in view of the multitude and the barrenness of the surroundings; but now Israel was to enter a new phase of living, in which the land should bring forth abundantly the things needed to maintain life. Canaan, a land of plenty (8:9) abounded in agricultural and mineral resources, but it was precisely this plenty which would be a temptation to God's people. Not without reason He urged them to "bless the Lord thy God" (v. 10) in the time of plenty, so that they should not forget Him. Throughout this section, the emphasis is continually upon the Lord's visible and abundant mercies during the Exodus and the wandering, and the people are constantly warned against forgetting them in the time of prosperity.

Moses reminds the people of the events surrounding the giving of the law, and of their lapse into idolatry during the very moments in which the Lord was delivering the Decalogue at Sinai (9:1–29). He recounts the prayer of intercession which he uttered at the time, and in reply to which the nation was spared. Moses again emphasizes the greatness of God's grace, and warns against spiritual pride upon the part of Israel. Far from having any merit themselves, they have been rebellious and stiffnecked; only the God of grace could have borne with them.

Chapter 10 deals first with the new tables of stone which replace those Moses broke in his provocation at the sight of Israel's idolatrous worship of the golden calf, and second with the making of the ark of the covenant. The death of Aaron (v. 6) and the separation of the tribe of Levi to the office of the priesthood (vv. 8, 9) are described. The verses which follow underscore the need for obedience upon the part of Israel, and draw attention to the Lord's concern for the fatherless, the widow and the stranger (vv. 18, 19). In the words, "Love ye therefore the stranger: for ye were strangers in the land of Egypt," we find the basis for a strongly humanitarian concern in the life of Israel.

Chapter 11 returns our thought to the Exodus, and reminds Israel that they were a nation snatched from the very jaws of death as the charioteers of Egypt pursued them (v. 4). Mention is also made of the rebellion of Korah (cf. Num. 16), in which Dathan and Abiram, leaders of the civil rebellion, figured prominently (11:6). The remembrance of these "mighty acts" Moses uses to underscore his repeated commands to obedience. "Keep the commandments," he cries (v. 8). In the land to which they were going, the Lord should directly provide for the watering of the crops. Upon Him they should be immediately dependent, since no possibility for irrigation existed in Palestine, such as they had known in Egypt (vv. 10, 11). If they are obedient, the Lord will give rain (v. 14), but if Israel rebels and turns to idols, rain will be withheld (v. 17). These serious words touched the very life of Israel in years to come.

Israel's dependence upon the Lord becomes the basis for a new exhortation to take all of His words to heart (11:18). If Israel will do so, she will stand as a marvel to her neighbors (v. 25); none shall be able to stand before her. But Israel must choose: "Behold, I set before you this day a blessing and a curse" (v. 26). Later, the blessing and the curse will be spelled out in detail and recited respectively from Mount Gerizim and Mount Ebal (cf. 27:1–26).

2. A Series of Laws and Statutes (12:1—21:23)

The next chapters of the narrative deal with Israel's worship and her national life. Chapter 12 opens with a repetition of the command to Israel to root out utterly the idolatrous inhabitants which she shall shortly find in Canaan. No vestige of the vile forms of worship then prevalent among the Canaanitish inhabitants could indeed be left if Israel were to preserve the purity of the worship the Lord had revealed to her. The order of worship which had been common in the wilderness was to be modified as the people adopted a more settled mode of living (12:8–12).

There should be in Palestine one national sanctuary (12:11), to serve as a center of the nation's religious life. This provision was not completely fulfilled until the times of David and Solomon; and the absence of such a central sanctuary during the intervening period led to the frequent worship at the old "high places."

Laws Concerning Idolatry (12:1–4). This section serves as basic legislation for Israel's dealing with the pagan peoples into whose midst she should shortly be thrust, and stands as a continual reminder of the Lord's hatred of idolatry. The same idea is emphasized later in the chapter (vv. 30, 31).

Laws Regulating Israel's Worship (12:5—16:17). To the provision for a central national sanctuary is added in detail a series of injunctions concerning the conduct of worship: The blood of any animal is not to be eaten (12:6). The tithe is sacred to the Lord and not to be eaten (vv. 17–19). False prophets are to be shunned (13:1–5) and those who would secretly bring in idolatrous practices should be summarily dealt with (vv. 6–15).

Israelites are not to disfigure themselves in practices connected with mourning (14: 1, 2); some animals and fowls are clean and suitable for food; others are not (vv. 3–21). This choice of food may, at first sight, seem arbitrary to us; but it must be remembered that there was no refrigeration in those days, and there must have been practical reasons underlying the division of animals into "clean" and "unclean." But beyond all that is the significant purpose of God; He was instilling into the Hebrew consciousness the fact that there *is* a difference between cleanness and uncleanness, between good and evil, which is basic to the Hebrew-Christian revelation.

Special care was made for the tribe of Levi, from whom the priesthood came, and to whom no allotment of land was to be made (14: 27–29); and along with the Levite, the Lord commands care for the stranger, the orphan, and the widow. In Chapter 15, there is detailed instruction given concerning the year of release. Every seventh year those persons who through misfortune or bad management had fallen into debt and into consequent servitude were to be set free. Not only that, but such persons were to be given something with which to begin life again (v. 8). The provision for those who chose permanent servitude is especially interesting: they were permitted to do so, and that state was indicated by the driving of an awl through the ear-lobe to the doorpost of the chosen master (vv. 16–18).

Chapter 16 contains detailed legislation concerning the keeping of the Passover or the Feast of Unleavened Bread as a perpetual memorial of the deliverance of Israel from Egyptian bondage (vv. 1–8). Following this comes legislation concerning the Feast of Weeks (vv. 8–12) and the Feast of Tabernacles (vv. 13–15). On these three solemn occasions thank-offerings were to be presented to the Lord (vv. 16, 17).

Basic Law of Justice (16:18–22). Moses here lays down the fundamental principles which shall govern the administration of civil law in Israel. Judges are to be selected whose basic concern is justice, not personal gain (vv. 18, 19). Such incorruptible men, men whose eyes will not be affected at the prospect of bribes, are to have jurisdiction in both civil and religious matters. In connection with their appointment, the planting of groves and the building of any image are strictly forbidden.

General Civil Legislation (17:1—21:23). This section deals with a wide variety of topics: the treatment of an idolatrous person is set forth in rigid detail (17:1–7); the matter of the appeal of a difficult case is treated (vv. 8–13); and the selection of a king (if such be done in the future) is to follow certain principles (vv. 14–20). Note that the major qualification for kingship is a qualification of character, not of power or wealth. Chapter 18:1–8 makes further and detailed provision for the Levites. Abominations of every sort, including idolatry, witchcraft and spiritualism, are to be forbidden (vv. 9–14).

This brings us to one of the greatest sections of Deuteronomy, that in which the promise of *a Prophet* is given. "The Lord thy God will raise up unto thee a Prophet from the midst of thee, of thy brethren, like unto me" (18:15). Now, of course, this passage (vv. 15–22) refers to the prophetic office as a whole, and is partly fulfilled by the long line of Old Testament prophets whom the Lord ordained; but it received its ultimate fulfilment when the Son of God came among men. It was so understood in Acts 3:22. Thus, the vision of Israel was turned to the future, to a day in which God would in decisive fashion visit His people, to turn them away from sin, and to redeem out of all nations a people for His Name.

In Chapter 19, provision is made for three further cities of refuge on the west side of the Jordan (vv. 1–13). Laws against fraud and against false witnesses follow (vv. 14–21), after which come regulations concerning battle and the siege of cities (20:1–20). These applied especially to the conquest of Palestine, and made humane provisions for those who surrendered peaceably.

Chapter 21 deals, in series, with the care of the body of one found dead (vv. 1–9), the taking of captive wives (vv. 10–14), family inheritance and family discipline (vv. 15–21), and the treatment of victims of hanging for crime (vv. 22, 23). Capital punishment was permitted, but the body was not to hang all night upon the tree (v. 23). This verse in the New Testament underscores the manner in which Christ was made a curse for us; His body was not permitted to remain on the cross beyond sundown. The major point, coming down through the ages, is expressed in Paul's words: "Cursed is every one that hangeth on a tree" (Gal. 3:13).

3. A Series of Laws Governing Israel's Social Living (22:1—26:19)

This section is devoted to the details of life in Israelite society as it developed in the new land of Canaan. The provisions which it sets forth are not only bare laws; they express the social conscience and concern which should be a part of Israel's life.

Law of the Brother's Property (22:1–4). This has to do particularly with property which has strayed or become lost, a situation in which the finder is to act out of a sense of fairness and equity.

Laws Concerning Distinctions (22:5–12). Persons of one sex were not to masquerade as members of the other. Maternal life was to be held in regard, even among birds. Diverse seeds were not to be sown together, nor diverse threads made into a single garment. Like animals were to be hitched together, and the roofs of houses were to be provided with banisters.

Laws Concerning Personal and Family Morality (22:13—24:5). This section deals with several matters: chastity and the sacredness of marriage, punishment for adultery, the exclusion of persons who had been mutilated in accordance with pagan customs, personal cleanliness, the sanitation of the camp, usury or interest, vows, and divorce.

Laws Concerning Economic and Social Justice (24:6—25:19). In these two chapters, provision is made for punishment of theft, for the treatment of articles left as security for debt, and for proper wages for labor. Bills of attainder are forbidden (24:16), and gleanings are to be left for the poor. Punishments are limited by statute

(25:1–3), and provision is made for the protection of widows through the custom of Levirate marriage, in which the brother of the deceased is to marry his widow. Weights and measures were to be strictly honest (vv. 13–15), and stringent honesty was to mark personal dealings.

Laws Concerning Stewardship (26:1–19). The giving of offerings to the Lord has been noted before; but here two special forms are laid down. The first has to do with the presentation of the firstfruits, which were to be given as a thank-offering, and whose presentation was to be accompanied by a special form of confession (vv. 5–10). The second offering was that of the special tithe, given on the third and sixth years of the cycle of seven (reckoned in relation to the year of release), and devoted especially to the Levite, the stranger, the orphan and the widow.

So comes to an end Moses's second address, with the exhortation that all that has been pronounced should be kept wholeheartedly (26:16). In return, Israel should be God's special people, conspicuous among the other nations for their righteousness and for the signal blessing of God.

V. The Third Address of Moses (27:1—30:20)

1. Command to Publish the Law (27:1–10)

In this address, Moses, the man of God, brings to focus all that he has been saying. The law was to be given prominence and publicity; it was to be written upon stone monuments, in letters to be read by all.

2. Sanctions of the Law (27:11–26)

Here is commanded an impressive ceremony, in which half of the tribes should gather on Mount Ebal, near Jacob's Well, and hear the Levites pronounce the "curses" which shall follow the neglect or violation of God's legislation. In reply, the people are to say "Amen"; in other words, to agree solemnly to the keeping of the divine commands.

3. Blessings upon Obedience (28:1–14)

As a counterpart to the pronouncement of the curses on Mount Ebal, there is a series of blessings pronounced upon obedience. In the previous chapter (27:12) half of the tribes were ranged on Mount Gerizim to pronounce blessings; chapter 28 recounts these blessings, which are always contingent upon obedience and which stand as a perpetual reminder to Israel of her covenant with the Lord.

4. Dire Consequences of Disobedience (28:15–68)

This section sums up much of the legislation which has gone before and pronounces the penalties which shall follow upon disobedience. It is a solemn and gripping section, which finally found dramatic and tragic fulfilment in the captivity of Israel in Babylon.

5. Renewal of the Covenant with the Lord (29:1–18)

By every means at his disposal, Moses seeks to guide his people into the way of perpetual obedience. He reasons with them, urging them with all of the vigor he could summon to keep the covenant, made at Sinai and now rehearsed and brought up-to-date.

6. Moses' Final Exhortation to Obedience (29:19—30:14)

The ancient lawgiver pours out his soul in a final appeal. While he foresees the hard hand of judgment upon his people, he also envisions restoration, and the glorious day of the Gospel, in which "the Lord thy God will circumcise thine heart, and the heart of thy seed, to love the Lord thy God with all thine heart, and with all thy soul, that thou mayest live" (30:6). Messianic and predictive, this prophecy points to the day when the Hope of Israel shall come.

7. Two Ways Set before Israel (30:15–20)

In a dramatic closing to his third address, Moses puts his people at the crossroads: they may choose life and good *or* death and evil. The alternatives have been made crystal-clear; the choice now lies with them. Heaven and earth are called upon to witness Moses' faithfulness in presenting the issues (30:19). The venerable man of God has poured out his soul for the people. "Therefore," says he, "choose life, that both thou and thy seed may live: . . . that thou mayest dwell in the land which the Lord sware unto thy fathers."

VI. Moses' Closing Days and Activities (31:1—34:12)

1. A Call to Faith (31:1–6)

Here is a shining example of the method of "line upon line." Moses recalls the victories over Og and Sihon as proof of the Lord's faithfulness, and challenges Israel to courage in the face of her coming tasks.

2. Moses Turns over Command (31:7–30)

One of the marks of greatness is to be able to transfer one's tasks to another with grace when the time comes. Here Moses commits to Joshua his work, and to the priests the law. Joshua was charged with almost unbelievable responsibilities, but with the charge was the promise that the Lord would bring him and the people into their land. Behind him was to stand the law of the Lord, Whose precepts he was to maintain among the people, as Moses had maintained them.

3. Song of Moses (32:1–52)

This touching ode would, if space permitted, deserve detailed analysis. Pitched in the key of Deuteronomy, it deals with the great themes of God's covenant with Israel, His mercies to them, their failures, the penalties which follow disobedience, and the final deliverance. Its theme is that Israel should always prove obedient and live.

4. Moses' Final Blessing upon Israel (33:1–29)

At the end of chapter 32, Moses' lonely death is predicted; but before his passing, he gives a benediction, much like the blessing in chapter 32 and strikingly similar to the blessing of Jacob upon his sons in Genesis 49. The benediction combines crucial historical events in Israel's recent past with the pronouncement of blessing. As Moses nears the end of the benediction, he pronounces words which have been the comfort of millions, both in the days of Judaism and through the centuries of Christianity: "The eternal God is thy refuge, and underneath are the everlasting arms" (33:27). This "exceeding great and precious promise" reminded Israel of the greatness of the One to whom they were bound in covenant.

5. Death and Burial of Moses (34:1–8)

In this record, which is given with the utmost restraint, lie both triumph and pathos. The triumph appears in the firm tread with which Moses, the man of God, climbs the slopes of Mount Nebo, where he knew that the moment of death awaited him. As he reached the summit of the mountain, he looked into the land toward which he had led his people. The pathos of the occasion lay in the fact that he was not to set foot upon it.

The Lord cared for the last rites of Moses (34:6), and his resting place remains unknown to us. This was a wise provision, for it might have become a shrine to the detriment of Israel. So, this mighty man passes from view, and the next glimpse of him comes on the Mount of Transfiguration. There he was permitted to see the One of Whom he prophesied and to partake of the glory of the high moment of the Transfiguration.

6. Final Summary (34:9–12)

Understandably, Israel mourned the loss of Moses (34:8); but the strength of Moses' impression upon God's people was proved by the fact that they immediately rallied to the support of Joshua and prepared to move ahead (v. 9). So ends a great record, a chronicle of the mighty acts of the Lord, leaving a peerless example in the man Moses, whose like Israel never knew again until the greater Prophet came among them.

The
Historical
Books

The Historical Books

FRANCIS I. ANDERSEN

THE LIVING THEME of the entire Bible is Christ. This is obvious in the New Testament, but the Historical Books of the Old Testament also deliver their main message when they speak of Him. In the pointed words of Article VII of the Church of England: "The Old Testament is not contrary to the New: for both in the Old and New Testament everlasting life is offered to mankind by Christ." The New Testament gives this testimony to Jesus Christ in the form of a direct account of His life and teaching; the Old Testament, including its historical sections, in the form of figures and promises, which are still invaluable although their testimony is indirect. The purpose of God in inspiring and preserving the historical books of the Old Testament is therefore to set forth the Gospel of His grace.

I. Theme: Salvation in Prospect

The function of the Book of Joshua, then, in speaking of Christ, is different, say, from that of John's Gospel, though, properly understood, both tell the same good news. Even the identity of the name of the hero of the one with that of the Saviour in the other is a reminder that Joshua is a type of Jesus. Although but a sketch and an outline, Joshua is also a picture in prospect of what God would do; John is a picture in restrospect of what God has done, in His Son. Both books relate how God works out the salvation of man. This is why faith could discern the truth of the cross and resurrection before Jesus was born, and know the salvation of that faith.

A hand cannot perform the same function as an eye; but if each is

191

a member of the same living body, they find their proper function in coordination, in ministering to each other, in working together to some common goal. All the books of the Bible are parts of the same organism. While each has its own peculiarities and distinctive themes, these are not isolated or independent, but make an integral contribution to the total Biblical portrait of Christ. Among other things, the Old Testament historical books set the perspective of the whole history of redemption, just as that which is painted at the edges of the canvas matters so much in making the picture perfect. In the Bible the focus of the portrait is the Lord Himself.

The English Bible presents twelve historical books from Joshua through Esther. This may obscure the fact that the Old Testament contains but two major and extended historical compositions. The first great body of writing in ancient Israel traces the history of God's dealings with mankind from the beginning of the world (in Genesis 1) through the historical sections of the Pentateuch, continuing with Joshua, Judges, Samuel and Kings. It ends with the destruction of the kingdom of Judah by the Babylonians.

II. Building a Covenant People

1. Patriarchal Beginnings

The great theme of this history is the forging by the Lord of a covenant people, and their training to be the birth-cradle of Messiah. The founding of that covenant with Abraham makes the patriarchal stories important, while the redemption of the tribes from Egypt and their settlement in the promised land developed the national scope of the agreement. After the occupation of Canaan under the leadership of Joshua sometime in the thirteenth century B.C., there was a period of turmoil and disunity in which local and national heroes (judges) were raised up by God to defend the tribes from many enemies. This was the background of the more peaceful story of Ruth. The period ended with the establishment of a united monarchy under Saul, but Israel had no real security until David drove back the Philistines and extended his borders in all directions.

2. Israel's Rise and Fall

In the tenth century, under David and Solomon, Israel rose to her greatest glory. This glory was short-lived, however, for after Solomon the nation fell apart and continued as two separate kingdoms until each was destroyed in its turn. At first the rivals fought each other, but finally Israel, as the northern kingdom is now called, became strong under Omri and Ahab. These kings made advantageous alliances with the Phoenicians, helped to arrest the Assyrian advance, and sealed a partnership with Judah by the usual dynastic marriage. But Judah seemed to play the minor role.

With the collapse of the house of Omri, hostilities were renewed, but soon the threat of Assyria overshadowed all local and lesser dangers. Despite a temporary political and economic revival under Jeroboam II of Israel (mid-eighth century) the northern kingdom fell into chaos and finally capitulated entirely to Assyria. Samaria fell in 721 B.C. Judah escaped miraculously and under Hezekiah enjoyed a revival of the old faith. Continuity with the past was shown in their steady loyalty to the house of David, but even this line of kings, with some notable exceptions, fell into apostasy for which finally there was no remedy. Josiah was the last great and good king, but God delivered his sons into the power of Egypt and then Babylon. After Jerusalem fell in 587 B.C. the nation suffered total eclipse.

3. The Parallel History

The other history is found in the books of Chronicles, Ezra and Nehemiah. It covers the same ground as the first work, but differs in several ways. The early part from Adam to David has been compressed into genealogies, precious records which remind us that history is a succession of persons, and not just a series of events. In the period of kings, it pays almost exclusive attention to the history of Judah under the line of David. The place of the temple in the nation's life is emphasized. This literature also continues the history beyond the destruction of Jerusalem. With the deportation of the leaders and most of the upper classes from Judah, the nation seemed at an end. But the faithful ones among the exiles kept the covenant hope alive and finally succeeded in organizing under the Persians a return to Jerusalem. Prophets reappeared and the temple was rebuilt. Later Ezra and Nehemiah achieved other reforms. Esther is a separate story set in the Persian period.

The struggle of the Jews for national independence followed. Political liberty was won when the Greeks were ruling, and lost again when the Romans came, but this story is not recorded in any inspired book.

III. Classification of Books

Here we cannot discuss the complex question of the origin of these books. There is no reason to doubt that the entire substance consists of accurate contemporary records carefully preserved. How and when the collections were made is another matter; they must have grown with the advancing experience of the nation, but except for the decisive roles of Moses in composing the Pentateuch, and the likelihood that Ezra was the author of Chronicles, little is known about the editing of the historical books.

One distinction is commonly made, though it should not be exaggerated: The stream of story from Genesis through Kings reflects the outlook of the prophets, among whom, in fact, Abraham and Moses were already numbered. The succession of prophets may have been largely responsible for the composition of the court chronicles and other material and for the transmission of the whole. The English Bible happily places the book of Ruth at a suitable place in this history, with which it has close affinities. The work of the Chronicler is sometimes called "priestly," but it is misleading to point up this contrast as though the two works were in opposition.

Following the Greek version, the English Bible has the great merit of bringing all the histories into the same section. The listing is quite different in the Hebrew Bible, and the traditional rabbinic division also has something in its favor. It erects no special class of historical books, but groups Joshua, Judges, Samuel and Kings with the prophets. This feature draws attention to the special nature of Biblical history-writing. The Jews called these four histories "former prophets," and they do properly belong with the four "later prophets," Isaiah, Jeremiah, Ezekiel and the Book of the Twelve (Minor Prophets).

There is good reason for believing that the rest of the Old Testament, not only histories like Ruth and Esther and the apocalypse of

Daniel but also the poetical Psalms, Job, Proverbs, and so on, received the general name "prophets." The formula "the Law and the Prophets" is used almost universally in the New Testament (as in the Dead Sea Scrolls) to refer to the whole of the Old Testament and reflects the early system. Later the rabbis made a threefold division which seems to be based on the liturgical use of the books. They distinguished "prophets" from other writings and grouped the five small books together.

No matter how the books are classified, they are unified by a common prophetic theme, and that theme is Jesus (Lk. 24:27; Acts 8:35). Even in an outward and formal way, the prophecies resemble the histories. Books like Isaiah and Jeremiah contain the same forms of composition as the book of Kings, some parts being even word for word the same (cf. Is. 36 with II Kings 18; Jer. 52 with II Kings 24). It might be better to call them all prophetic histories (for the history is written from a prophetic point of view and is itself a prophecy) and historical prophecies (for the prophecies are concerned with history and are woven into its fabric).

IV. Three Kinds of Writing

As literature all these works contain three kinds of writing.

1. National History

The great framework of the whole is the history of Israel as a nation and as the covenant people of the Lord. While the political history of the nations, both internal and international, is narrated, this is instrumental to the analysis of the moral and religious factors in which the prophets find the key to the national fortunes and misfortunes. Even as history, then, the Bible is distinct and unique: it gives not so much an account of the domestic affairs of Israel and of its interaction with its neighbors as a record and an exposition of God's dealings with His people. But the latter is not a super-history, that is, a discernment by mystical intuition of a metaphysical realm beyond history; rather, the experiences of Israel are precisely grounded in historical acts of God in judgment and redemption. As any history is not just a list of events but the grouping of events into meaningful patterns, so in the Bible the meaning is supplied by God Himself declaring His purpose in history as a whole and in particular events. The purpose of God with Israel was to reveal Himself and to offer salvation to all mankind; so Biblical history is not only the history of Israel, it is also the history of revelation and redemption.

To represent the prophets of Israel simply as religious geniuses with a remarkable insight into the significance of life destroys Biblical history. It is but a human activity, however profound, to select events and arrange them with a commentary rooted in some theoretical theology; but the Bible is not such a search for meaning in history, the imposition of meaning on otherwise insignificant incidents. This history is given by God; the events were shaped by His sovereign will and the record is His own explanation of what He is doing. The events do not simply illustrate certain abstract truths; they are the acts of God in history which culminate in the greatest and final act, the coming of our Lord Jesus Christ.

The narrative history of God and His people is found in histories and prophecies alike. Information about invasions and monarchs, and so on, appears in them all and is treated in the same way.

2. Personal Experience

While the Bible has a majestic sense of the grand currents of human history, it is also interested in people, in individuals. While it tells about Israel and the Church as the covenant community, and about Adam and Aaron and David as representative persons, much space is given to incidents in the lives of kings, prophets and private citizens. God has a comprehensive purpose for the race, but at its heart His concern is a burning love for this one and that, for Abraham, Jeremiah, Peter, you and me. Many of the histories of the kings are more concerned about their private character, their faith or their apostasy, than about their public achievements—out of interest for the man himself and for his pivotal significance in the history of redemption.

The attention given to David's great sin and his repentance is a disclosure of weakness in the life of a popular monarch without parallel in ancient records. This could happen only in Israel where the prophets were independently candid in speaking the word of the Lord. And here there is more than concern for David as king and as typical ancestor of Messiah, though this is also present. The incident is a perfect revelation of that free grace which justifies a guilty man by faith alone, without works, and so discloses the love of God for David the sinner.

These Biblical stories about real people have all the artful simplicity of truth, and give the historical books their chief charm as well as their great power. And what a lot of them there are, perfect gems of literary art and clear spiritual channels through which God finds us again and again! Because of them certain characters, Saul, David, Jeremiah and others, are more perfectly and fully known to us as flesh and blood human beings than any other personages of the ancient world before the time of the Greeks and Romans.

Stories of kings and stories of prophets are found in both histories and prophecies. Isaiah tells about Ahaz and Hezekiah, Kings tells about Elijah and Elisha. In many cases the personal circumstances of the prophet were intimately interwoven with the history of Israel. This gave meaning to his message and was sometimes indispensable for the understanding of it.

3. Prophetic Message

The Old Testament throughout is a prophetic account of the history of Israel. This feature is especially evident in the distinct oracles that the prophets delivered from time to time. These are found in the historical as well as in the prophetic books. They came as messages from God bearing on the contemporary situation, so that they were immediately meaningful to their first hearers; but they have a wider reference and function so that their significance endures for all time. They frequently took the form of an exposure of some national evil or personal sin, a warning about the certainty of judgment and an invitation to repent and make amends. The prophecies were thus essentially a preaching of the Gospel even though the grounds for justly pardoning the repentant and trusting sinner established by the atoning death of our Lord were as yet only set forth as a promise. In the light of the Cross, these messages were seen to contain deeper meaning that before had been only dimly discerned.

V. Their Relevance Today

1. The Word of God for All Time

These three strands—national history, personal experience, prophetic message—are woven into the fabric of the prophetic and historical books. The histories are prophetic, in a narrow sense, because they report the acts and words of the prophets. In a wider sense, the selection and arrangement of all the material were the work of prophets and served to set forth their vital teachings at large. Since the Word of God stands for all time, it was just as important for the prophets to write as to speak. Bringing the Word of the Lord to bear on the vast spectacle of the rise and fall of nations, the work of the prophets was completed, and needed no augmentation from the New Testament. The latter concentrates on bringing to perfection the application of the Word of God to the individual; and with the creation of the Church as the covenant-body, no longer a political entity, many institutional features of the Old Testament cease to apply. But prophecy continues; preachers of the Gospel are called "prophets," and the disclosure of the future begun by the Old Testament is continued by the Lord Jesus, and completed by the Spirit through Paul, Peter and John. The Revelation which describes the final grand consummation is also the crown and consummation of all Biblical history and prophecy.

While the historical setting of the original oracles displays their contemporary relevance, we should not suppose that their present value is exhausted by the fact that they are part of the record of by-gone days. God spoke through the prophets to their own day and generation. The Spirit within them was also "testifying beforehand of the sufferings of Christ and the glory that should follow" (I Pet. 1:11). The early Christians insisted that their message was exactly the same as the one the prophets had always declared (Acts 26:22). And through these same words the Spirit has never ceased to speak.

2. Preaching and Predicting

Biblical history-and-prophecy (for we have seen they are one thing) is "fore-telling" as well as "forth-telling." It is a mistake to set these two features in contrast or to make one subservient to the other. There is an intimate agreement between the Old and New Testaments, and this is specially clear when the latter recognizes the two-fold significance of the former. Time and again in the New Testament it is stated that a verse in the Old has found its proper fulfilment. Some people neglect the original history as serious history, treating it as an artificial device to set forth predictions of a distant future. Others belittle the fulfilments of prophecy, regarding them as accidental coincidences exaggerated by later interpretation. Both are mistaken. They fail equally to do justice to the organic unity of the whole Bible, which brings the original events in the Old Testament and their ultimate prophetic fulfilment in Christ into living connection. If Isaiah's portrait of the suffering Servant had historical roots, this does not weaken its force as a God-given prediction of the agony of His Son. If Old Testament references to the Messiah applied first to David, this does not exhaust their meaning; and we do not need to deny the Davidic reference in order to secure their application to Jesus.

From the call of Abraham and especially after the enlargement of the understanding of God that came with the revelations made to Moses at Sinai, the Israelites had a distinct sense of their identity as the chosen object of the Lord's covenant, and of their place in His purposes. There is a spiritual as well as a historical continuity in the unfolding of that purpose. Israel was not only a type of the Church; they were actually the Church in the wilderness (Acts 7:38). It is seated on the throne of David that Jesus exercises His kingly power (Lk. 1:32).

3. Redemptive Meaning of History

No other ancient people had such a sense of historical continuity and progress. It was no accident, but a direct result of the ethical monotheism of the patriarchs and Moses, that true history writing was first achieved by this nation, for only by reference to the will of the sovereign Lord who ordered history and who drives it on to His appointed goal do events have a meaning beyond the immediate effect of incidental circumstances. For Israel that meaning was redemptive. They recognized the insufficiency of human power to overcome evil and the need for divine intervention if they were to be delivered from personal impotence or national disaster. Belief that God would act in this way was well founded in the experience of the Exodus and received constant renewal in the exploits of the Judges, in the achievement of David and in the later deliverances from foreign aggression. These were not simply pictures of redemption; they were real acts of redemption, at once actual and prophetic of Christ. Israel was also made deeply aware of the justice of God's punishments which fell on them constantly, from the wilderness wanderings to the final disaster under Zedekiah. These were at once real judgments and prophecies of the Final Judgment.

The prophetic faith of Israel was also inherently eschatological, that is, prophetic of the end-time. In their experience the purpose of God for His people was never fully achieved in any historical situation. Yet they could not believe that historical circumstances could frustrate its final perfect achievement. That consummation remained a burning hope for the future. It was to be a consummation in history, yet with the transformation of history. As the outgrowth and climax of the historical process, its pattern had already been set. The fall of Samaria was a true Day of the Lord, and also a picture of the Day of Jesus Christ.

This is the deep perspective of the historical books; each particular incident is to be viewed for its place in the great drama of universal judgment and redemption.

Joshua

CHARLES F. PFEIFFER

CANAAN WAS THE LAND of Abraham's sojourn. The patriarchs of Israel, however, never occupied it in any permanent way. They are described as pilgrims and sojourners, seeking "a city which hath foundations, whose builder and maker is God" (Heb. 11:10). In Canaan, Abraham possessed no place even to bury Sarah; the only real estate he ever owned was the burial plot he purchased from Ephron the Hittite (Gen. 23:4–20).

201

God made it clear to Abraham, however, that his "seed" or descendants would one day occupy the land of Canaan (Gen. 13:14–17). After bondage in Egypt (Gen. 15:13), the descendants of Abraham were to be brought back to Canaan where they would dispossess the aboriginal inhabitants and occupy the land.

These promises exhibit the justice of the divine government. God was not yet ready to turn the land over to Abraham during the lifetime of the patriarch because "the iniquity of the Amorites is not yet full" (Gen. 15:16). The inhabitants of Canaan were to be expelled from the land because of their sins. Sacred prostitution, associated with the Baal fertility cult, and infant sacrifice to Molech were among the abominations of Canaanite worship. When the inhabitants of Canaan proved incorrigible, Abraham's descendants at last received their commission to take possession of Canaan by force.

I. Preparing for the Conquest (1:1—5:15)

The death of Moses appeared to be a major catastrophe. Through the wilderness he had brought his people from Egypt to the borders of the Land of Promise. He was the only leader known to the generation born in the wilderness. As lawgiver, judge, and commander-in-chief, he was beloved by the men of his generation. Yet, paradoxically, as long as Moses lived, Israel was destined to wander in the wilderness. When Moses sinned by angrily striking the rock twice to provide water for his murmuring people, God declared, "Because ye believed me not to sanctify me in the eyes of the children of Israel, therefore ye shall not bring this congregation into the land which I have given them" (Num. 20:12).

1. Joshua Commissioned as Moses' Successor (1:1–9)

Soon after the Exodus from Egypt, Joshua distinguished himself as the servant or "minister" of Moses. He was leader of the band of men who repulsed the Amalekites (Ex. 17:9–16). When Moses received the Law, Joshua served as his attendant (Ex. 24:13, cf. 33:11; Num. 11:27–30). As one of the twelve spies sent to survey Canaan, Joshua vainly sought with Caleb to counteract the defeatist attitude of the other ten. Of the adults who left Egypt, Caleb and Joshua alone lived to enter the Promised Land (Num. 14:6–9, 22–24).

The Lord gave solemn directions for Joshua's appointment even before Moses died (Num. 27:15–23). Even though Joshua might appear to have every qualification for the office, being recognized as both an able military leader and a man in the spiritual succession of Moses, yet Moses dared not act on his own impulse. The command of God made it clear that Joshua was the Lord's own choice as successor to Moses.

After Moses' death, Joshua received his specific commission to enter the land of Canaan and possess it. As God had enabled Moses to lead Israel out of Egypt, so He promised to enable Joshua to bring Israel into Canaan. In each case the stress falls on God's power and purpose; the vessel God uses is of secondary importance. The Apostle Paul testified, "I have planted, Apollos watered; but God gave the increase. So then neither is he that planteth any thing, neither he that watereth; but God that giveth the increase" (I Cor. 3:6, 7). Yet the vessel must be clean; God's law must be honored by His servant. Joshua may rely on God's promises, yet he must be faithful to God's Word.

2. Preparation for Crossing the Jordan (1:10—2:24)

Both spiritual and temporal preparation were needed for the invasion of Canaan. A Spirit-prepared leader had been appointed, assured that God would bless faithfulness to His law. Temporally, the army of Israel had to be provisioned while reconnaissance of the enemy's power was effected. The tribes of Reuben, Gad, and the half-tribe of Manasseh were reminded of their obligation to help in the conquest of western Palestine before they could settle down in their transjordanian territory.

The sending of spies to Jericho was a proper military preparation for the battle ahead. The Scriptures do not teach that faith in God precludes the use of means. The builder, the watchman, and the spy in Jericho may be enabled by God to accomplish His purpose for His people. Yet the Psalmist later reminds us: "Except the Lord build the house, they labor in vain that build it: except the Lord keep the city, the watchman waketh but in vain" (Ps. 127:1). Without God's blessing, the use of human means is useless.

The steps of the spies were clearly ordered of the Lord. They came to the house of Rahab, a woman of ill repute who had heard reports of the victories of Israel over Sihon, the Amorite king, and Og, king of Bashan. She had also heard reports of the miraculous opening of the Red Sea and of other evidences of the power of Israel's God. The acts of God on behalf of Israel convinced Rahab that Jericho would soon be taken. At the risk of her life she hid the spies, misdirecting the messengers of the king of Jericho. The Israelite spies promised to spare Rahab's household at the time of the invasion. A line of scarlet thread, placed in Rahab's window, was to enable the Israelites to distinguish her house from those of the other inhabitants of Jericho. After receiving this assurance of safety, Rahab helped the spies to escape.

A woman sinful in life, and of heathen background, Rahab believed the God of Israel and entered the household of faith. The Epistle to the Hebrews tells us that "By faith the harlot Rahab perished not with them that believed not, when she had received the spies with peace" (11:31). Matthew 1:5 lists Rahab as an ancestress of the Messiah. Although the line of God's blessing in the Old Testament was almost exclusively limited to Abraham's seed, the faith of a Rahab did not go unhonored.

3. Crossing the Jordan (3:1—4:25)

Having received a favorable report from the spies, Joshua ordered his armies to break camp at Shittim and advance to the banks of the Jordan. Three days later specific directions were given for the actual crossing of the river. The priests were to carry the ark of the covenant ahead of the camp, and the remaining Israelites were to follow about one thousand yards behind the priests. Thus the priests, bearing the ark, would lead the remainder of the congregation. This was of practical value, for the Israelites did not know the terrain into which they were entering. It served also to remind them that God was the true leader of Israel, since the ark of the covenant of the Lord stood before the camp.

Each Israelite had a responsibility, however. Joshua addressed the people with the words, "Sanctify yourselves; for tomorrow the Lord will do wonders among you" (3:5). At all times God's people are to recognize their spiritual relationship to Him. There are occasions when a special "setting apart" or "sanctification" is appropriate. Before God gave the law to Moses the people were to be sanctified (Ex. 19:10). This involved ceremonial purification, including the washing of their garments, and separation from the normal responsibilities of life (Ex. 19:14, 15). Israel was to be an "holy nation" (Ex. 19:6), and God was to be given the place of pre-eminence. The same language is used later of the Church of Jesus Christ (I Pet. 2:9).

Joshua had a word of encouragement as well as a command for obedience. The priests were to come to the brink of the Jordan and stand still in the waters of the river. God was about to perform a miracle. Crossing the Jordan would be a great encouragement to Israel. If God could open the waters to enable Israel to enter the Land of Promise, He could readily drive out the Canaanites and the other inhabitants of the land. God's miracles were designed for the spiritual and physical well-being of His people. God had directed Moses to lead Israel by the way of the Red Sea, instead of the more direct "way of the land of the Philistines" because His people were not yet ready for war (Ex. 13:17, 18). The opening of the waters of the Red Sea at the beginning of the wilderness wandering, and of the Jordan River at its close, met an immediate practical need and provided the encouragement required for the days of trial ahead.

As the feet of the priests touched the water, the Jordan was cut off so that the people were able to go over on dry ground. The miracle is all the more remarkable when we remember that it took place at the time of the barley harvest in the month of Nisan (March-April), at a season when the Jordan was in flood stage, overflowing its banks. At Jericho the Jordan valley is about fourteen miles wide. The river itself is from ninety to one hundred feet broad, with a depth of from three feet to ten or twelve.

The means God used to accomplish this miracle are not specified. The waters of the Red Sea were held back "by a strong east wind" (Ex. 14:21). Here, at the Jordan, the holding back of the waters appears to be by means of a landslide, possibly the result of an earthquake. We are told that the waters were held as in a heap "a great way off from Adam, the city that is beside Zarethan." Sixteen miles north of the ford opposite Jericho is a hill known as Tel-ed-Damieh, which may be the Adam of our text. Zarethan was evidently located on the west side of the Jordan, opposite Adam.

An Arabic chronicler, Nowairi, tells how, in December 1267, the Jordan was dammed for several hours in this neighborhood by a landslide. Earthquakes are common in the Jordan Valley. That

God may use what we term natural phenomena to accomplish His purposes does not make them less miraculous. The fact that the waters were cut off at the moment the priests bearing the ark entered the water, and that they remained so until the entire company of Israelites had safely crossed, cannot be explained by natural means. If God used a landslide to accomplish His purpose, it was a miracle of timing, nevertheless. This may be compared with the "strong east wind" which held back the waters of the Red Sea at precisely the time when Israel, pursued by Pharaoh's armies, was in need of deliverance. The Scriptures present God as the sovereign of nature; the winds and the waves obey His command.

The Scriptures make clear that God desires a remembrance of His mighty acts in delivering His people. The Passover was an annual memorial of the deliverance from Egypt. In response to God's command, Joshua ordered twelve men, one from each of the tribes, to pick up large stones from the Jordan River bed and carry them to Gilgal. There a cairn, or stone heap, erected to commemorate the crossing of the Jordan, was to serve as a means of teaching the young. When they would ask concerning the meaning of the stones, the pious Israelite would recount the miraculous intervention of God in the history of His people.

Joshua also set up a monument of twelve stones in the midst of the Jordan at the place of crossing (4:9). There is no overt reference to a command from God for the monument in the Jordan. The monument at Gilgal would raise questions concerning the place of crossing which the monument in the Jordan would answer.

At the time the Book of Joshua was written, the monument in the Jordan was still pointed out (4:9). Jewish tradition suggests that the stones were still identifiable after the destruction of Jerusalem by Titus (A.D. 70). Three rabbis are said to have stood on the stones. Such references should not be taken too seriously, inasmuch as the life of the Jews in Palestine was seriously disrupted through Nebuchadrezzar's destruction of Jerusalem (587 B.C.) and subsequent destruction by the Romans (A.D. 70). It is interesting, however, to note that in spite of those calamities the sacred tradition persisted.

The waters of the Jordan returned after the priests ascended the west bank of the river, as they had been held back the moment the feet of the priests entered the water. The priests entered the water first, and left last. As they stood in the river-bed, the remainder of the people of Israel crossed over. Mention is specifically made of the men of Reuben, Gad, and the half-tribe of Manasseh (4:12, 13). Their inheritance was on the east side of the Jordan, but they had agreed to cross with their brethren and assist in the conquest of western Palestine before returning to enjoy their allotted portion.

The crossing took place on the tenth day of Abib (or Nisan), four days before the Passover. The first encampment was at Gilgal, not far from Jericho, where the monument to God's faithfulness in bringing His people across the Jordan was erected.

4. The Encampment at Gilgal (5:1–15)

The miracle of the Jordan had a profound effect on the neighboring nations, Amorites and Canaanites. The knowledge of the crossing of the Red Sea and of the defeat of Sihon and Og had earlier impressed Rahab (2:10, 11). The deliverance of Israel served as a warning to the enemy.

The ordinance of circumcision, practiced from patriarchal times, had not been observed during the period of the wilderness wanderings. The generation which had been circumcised "the first time" (cf. 5:2) in Egypt, except for Caleb and Joshua, was now dead. As a result of sin, Israel in the wilderness was marking time until the death of those who lacked faith to enter Canaan. Although God had promised to bring the new generation into Canaan, the generation born in the wilderness was not given the rite of circumcision, the sign of God's covenant with His people. The covenant was, as it were, held in abeyance until the rebellious generation should die.

With the entrance of the new generation into Canaan, the rite of circumcision again became meaningful. God would have His people set apart to Himself. In Egypt, God's people had been circumcised. In the wilderness, they had separated themselves from Him. Now, in Canaan, they are again circumcised. The name *Gibeath-ha-araloth,* "Hill of Foreskins," was given to the spot where the circumcision took place.

Following the circumcision of the new generation, God said, "This day have I rolled away the reproach of Egypt from off you" (5:9). This doubtless refers to the thoughts and words of the Egyptians. During the time of Israel's vagabond life in the wilderness, the Egyptians could say, "The Lord brought Israel out of Egypt to destroy them in the wilderness" (cf. Ex. 32:12; Num.

13:14–16; Deut. 9:28). With the circumcision of the people at Gilgal, this reproach was rolled away. God was again in covenant relation with His people, and had promised that Canaan would be theirs.

With the nation back in covenant with God, the Passover was observed on the fourteenth of the month Nisan. The first Passover had been observed in Egypt (Ex. 12:1–51), and the second at Mount Sinai (Num. 9:1–14). During the wilderness wandering, the Passover was evidently not observed. Out of fellowship with God, neither Passover nor circumcision had any meaning. In Canaan, Israel, conscious of God's presence, has a new beginning.

As an earnest of the coming possession of Canaan, the manna ceased, and Israel became wholly dependent on the produce of the land, following this Passover observance. There is throughout Scripture an economy of the miraculous. Normally it is God's purpose that His people labor with their hands to produce the necessities of life. The life in the wilderness was abnormal, however. There was no possibility of sustenance apart from a miracle, and God fed His people with manna from heaven (Ex. 16:4–31, 35, 36). Now, however, in Canaan, they will "eat of the fruit of the land" (5:12).

Joshua doubtless felt the responsibility of leadership resting on his shoulders. He was in western Palestine. He would soon be fighting the inhabitants within its walled cities with his untrained forces, but a few days removed from the desert. Final preparation for the battle involved a visible manifestation of God. Reconnoitering the city of Jericho, Joshua was alarmed when he saw a man with drawn sword. Joshua had one question in this moment of crisis: "Art thou for us, or for our adversaries?" (5:13). The stranger did not identify himself as friend or foe. He was not an ally, but a commander— "Captain of the host of the Lord!"

Joshua humbled himself before the stranger. He asked for orders and received them: "Loose thy shoe from off thy foot; for the place whereon thou standest is holy" (5:15). With like words, God had spoken to Moses at the burning bush (Ex. 3:5).

Joshua was the divinely appointed leader of Israel, but Joshua must be led. He is subject to the divine captain. God is not simply the protector of His people, He is their guide. Canaan will not fall to Israel because of the prowess of Joshua, but through the leadership of the captain of the Lord's host. Joshua is not less important, but God is more important.

II. The Conquest of Canaan (6:1—12:24)

Militarily the conquest of Canaan was in three phases, with pockets of resistance continuing until the time of David. Strategically, Joshua divided western Palestine by attacking from the east. The fall of strongly fortified Jericho was a blow to the inhabitants of Canaan. A coalition of southern kings challenged Joshua, bringing on their defeat at Beth Horon. Joshua's conquests ended with the defeat of a northern coalition under the king of Hazor.

1. The Capture of Jericho (5:13—6:27)

As excavations at Jericho indicate, its fortified walls would prove a barrier to the Israelite advance unless the city was to fall. Just as God had brought His people out from Egypt, it was His purpose to bring them into Canaan. Directions were given for the capture of Jericho. Seven priests, bearing seven trumpets, followed by the ark of the covenant, were to march in solemn procession around the city for six days, followed by the army of Israel. Each night the Israelites returned to camp at Gilgal. On the seventh day the city was compassed seven times and then, with the blast of the trumpets and the shout of the people, the walls of the city fell and Israel entered and took Jericho.

The events at Jericho were designed to impress upon Israel the need of confidence in the sure deliverances of God. Archaeologists suggest that God used an earthquake in bringing about the destruction of Jericho. This may well have been the secondary cause, but the Scripture makes clear that the primary cause was the will of God. The Epistle to the Hebrews states, "By faith the walls of Jericho fell down after they had been encircled for seven days" (11:30). The miracle of Jericho may be thought of as both a test of faith and a means of strengthening faith. Israel must know that Canaan was occupied by divine power rather than by human resourcefulness. Moses had warned against the presumption of saying, "My power and the might of my hand hath gotten me this wealth" (Deut. 8:17). The God Who caused the walls of Jericho to fall could be trusted to meet each need in the lives of His people.

Except for Rahab and her household, the entire city of Jericho was to be devoted to the Lord (6:17). The term *herem*, used to describe this act of dedication, is rendered "accursed" in the King James Version of the Bible. The term refers to that which is absolutely and irrevocably consecrated to God. Leviticus 27:28 states the law of *herem*: "No devoted thing shall be sold or redeemed; every devoted thing is most holy unto the Lord." In practice this meant the utter destruction of Jericho (cf. Deut. 13:16). The people and animals were slain; indestructible materials such as metals were consecrated to God and not used for secular purposes.

As the flood constituted God's judgment on Noah's generation, so the conquest of Canaan, of which the destruction of Jericho was the first step, was God's judgment on Canaanite civilization which, with its ritual prostitution and infant sacrifice, formed a cancerous growth on the human race. Canaan had abused God's grace which had been extended from Abraham's time to Joshua's (cf. Gen. 15:16).

Not only was Jericho destroyed, but a curse was pronounced on anyone who would rebuild it. In the days of Ahab, five hundred years later, Hiel the Bethelite disregarded this prohibition at the cost of the lives of two of his sons (I Kings 16:34).

2. Achan's Sin and Israel's Defeat (7:1–26)

The mound of Ai is located west of Jericho, near Bethel. The miraculous fall of Jericho gave rise to confidence that Ai would quickly fall to a small detachment of Israelite soldiers. Instead, thirty-six Israelites were killed and the remainder of the battalion fled toward Shebarim ("the stone quarries").

Defeat did not come because of the size of the Israelite fighting force. It was the result of the sin of Achan who had "acted faithlessly" in stealing, from the spoils of Jericho, silver, gold, and a Babylonian garment.

Joshua feared that the defeat of Israel would bring renewed grounds for confidence on the part of the Canaanites. Sensing that God had turned His back upon them, Israel was disheartened. Actually, at the risk of being accused of impotence by the victorious Canaanites, God was teaching His people an important lesson, the certain consequence of sin. Bearing the name of Israel's God was never a guarantee of divine protection. If the heart was far from God, His blessing must not be presupposed.

The unity of God's people was another important lesson at Ai:

Man does not live to himself. The sin was committed by one man—Achan—yet the whole camp of Israel suffered.

The early Church, in the person of Ananias and Sapphira, had a situation analagous to that of Achan. God's holiness was vindicated in the death of those who would compromise the high morality which God demands of all who bear His name. In neither the case of Achan nor that of Ananias and Sapphira is the question of the salvation of a soul before us. In both instances, physical death is the result of treating lightly the claims of God upon His people.

The text of Joshua 8 leaves it uncertain whether or not the family of Achan died with him in the Valley of Achor. If the text is interpreted to mean that Achan's wife and children died with him, they must be regarded as accomplices in the crime, for Deuteronomy 24:16 forbids the execution of children for their parents' sins: "The fathers shall not be put to death for the children, nor shall the children be put to death for the fathers; every man shall be put to death for his own sin."

3. Victory at Ai (8:1-29)

After the death of Achan, the Israelites again attempted to take the city of Ai, and this time, by making use of a ruse to fool the enemy, they succeeded. An ambush of five thousand men was placed to the west, between Bethel and Ai. Then the main Israelite army, under Joshua, approached the city from the north, whereupon the forces of Ai left the city in order to battle the invaders. The ambush was thus unchecked when it entered and burned the city, before joining forces with the remainder of Joshua's army to bring about the destruction of the army of Ai.

We read in verse 28 that "Joshua burnt Ai, and made it a heap for ever, even a desolation, unto this day." The ruins of et-Tell, identified as Ai by most archaeologists, were excavated in 1933-35 by Mme. Judith Marquet-Krause. The diggings indicate that the site was occupied as early as 3000 B.C., but that it was not occupied during the period between 2200 B.C. and 1200 B.C. Since this includes the period of Joshua, it poses an historical problem. L. H. Vincent suggests that Ai was actually an outpost of Bethel which was of such modest proportions that it left no remains. It is, of course, possible that et-Tell is not really Ai, and that subsequent excavations will unearth the Ai of Joshua's conquest.

4. *Altar Erected at Mount Ebal (8:30–35)*

Accepting the victories at Jericho and Ai as evidences of the faithfulness of God, the nation made a solemn pilgrimage to Shechem, in the heart of enemy territory, to renew their covenant with the Lord. This was an act of obedience to the command of Moses (Deut. 27:2–8).

The valley in which Shechem is located, bounded on the south by the range of Gerizim and on the north by that of Ebal, is frequently described as the most beautiful spot in central Palestine.

An altar of undressed stones was erected on Mount Ebal (Deut. 27:6–8), on which burnt offerings and peace offerings were made. Memorial stones were then set up and plastered. On these stones the law was written, probably inscribed with a stylus while the cement was soft. Otherwise it would have been written with pigment after the plaster had hardened (Deut. 27:2, 4). The law was then read aloud to the vast multitude. As the blessings were read, the six tribes assembled on Mount Gerizim said, "Amen." As the curses were pronounced, the six tribes on Mount Ebal responded, "Amen."

This law, copied on stones and read to the people, could not have been the entire Pentateuch with its narrative portions. It must, however, have included more than the Ten Commandments. Some writers suggest the Book of Deuteronomy, others the "blessings and curses" or a compilation of the laws contained in the Pentateuch, 613 in number according to Jewish tradition. The practice of inscribing law codes on stone goes back to ancient Sumerian and Babylonian times. For example, the famous Code of Hammurabi contains 282 sections, with a prologue and an epilogue.

The scene at Mount Ebal had both a backward and a forward look. Backward, it recognized the faithfulness of God to the covenant which He made with Israel at Mount Sinai. Forward, it recognized the initial victories as an earnest of the greater victories ahead. There were sore trials in Canaan, as there had been in the wilderness, but God had shown His great power, and Israel was prepared to accept His law and pledge faithfulness to the God Who had thus revealed Himself.

5. Deceit of the Gibeonites (9:1–27)

The Israelite victories produced a twofold reaction on the aboriginal inhabitants of Canaan. In the first instance, the kings of southern Palestine determined to fight the Israelite invaders. The three districts of southern Palestine are mentioned: the "hill country" or the Judean mountain terrain, including Jerusalem and Hebron; the "lowland," or, more specifically, the region of low hills south of Aijalon known as the *Shephelah;* and the Philistine Plain, here called "the shore of the Great Sea," that is, the Mediterranean.

A group of Hivites (9:7), however, determined to gain safety for themselves by diplomacy rather than by warfare. Little is known of the Hivites, although they appear as an ethnic group in Palestine during the patriarchal age. It is evident from Genesis 34 that they did not normally practice the rite of circumcision. Many scholars suggest that they form a sub-section of the Horites, or Hurians, a people who scattered over most of the Middle East by the second millennium before Christ. From the sixteenth to the fourteenth centuries B.C., the Hurrian kingdom of Mitanni held the balance of power between the Hittite Empire and Egypt. Mitanni was located in upper Mesopotamia, including the area around Haran.

The city of Gibeon, recently identified with *el-Jib,* was located five or six miles northwest of Jerusalem. It was apparently the chief or capital city of the region including the cities of Chephirah, Beeroth, and Kirjathjearim (9:17).

The Gibeonites sent to Joshua at Gilgal envoys who pretended they were ambassadors from a distant land. They declared that they had heard of the mighty acts of the God of Israel in Egypt and in the conquest of Sihon and Og. Studiously avoiding the mention of Jericho and Ai, the Gibeonites further stated that they represented the elders and people of their land in seeking an alliance with Israel. The ruse succeeded. Without seeking divine guidance, Joshua "made peace with them, to let them live."

The record indicates that Joshua did wrong in making an alliance with the enemy. Although he might not be blameworthy for believing the story of the Gibeonites, who had so convincingly disguised themselves, such a momentous decision should not have been made without seeking the mind of the Lord.

When Joshua learned that the Gibeonites were actually inhabitants of the land of Canaan, he did not go back on his word. Although there was murmuring in the Israelite camp, the leaders insisted that their word, given in the name of the Lord, must be respected. The Gibeonites were, however, reduced to the status of slaves, "hewers of wood and drawers of water."

6. Conquest of Southern Canaan (10:1–43)

From the standpoint of the other inhabitants of southern Palestine, the defection of the Gibeonites was a catastrophe. Joshua, who had gained an important foothold in the area, could be expected to follow up his victories at Jericho and Ai.

Adoni-zedek of Jerusalem took the initiative in seeking to form a confederacy to punish Gibeon and resist the encroachments of Israel. The kings of Hebron, Jarmuth, Lachish, and Eglon responded and marched northward to attack Gibeon.

When the Gibeonites realized their danger, they sent to Gilgal to ask help of Joshua. The treaty evidently included provisions for defensive alliance. Joshua responded promptly. With the promise of God's blessing, he set out from Gilgal to Gibeon by night and defeated the Southern Confederacy at Gibeon. Joshua pursued the enemy northwestward to the upper Beth-horon, then on to Azekah and Makkedah. From lower Beth-horon to Azekah, the armies of the south sustained further casualties in a storm in which the hailstones killed more men than did the swords of the Israelites.

Following the account of this victory, the Book of Joshua preserves for us a quotation from an ancient book of poetry known as the Book of Jasher. The Book of Jasher has not been preserved, although a modern forgery bearing that name is in circulation. It is quoted here, and in II Samuel 1:18, David's lament over the death of Saul and Jonathan. Both of these are in the form of Hebrew poetry, which leads us to suspect that the entire book was poetic. Most peoples of antiquity preserved their histories and legends in poetic form which could be memorized and passed on from generation to generation. No such literature of the Jews has survived, but the quotations from the Book of Jasher and the Book of the Wars of Yahweh (Num. 21:14) suggest that such literature, perhaps first in oral form, did exist among the ancient Israelites. Lacking divine inspiration, it was not preserved, but the inspired writers drew upon it where it served their purposes, as in Joshua 10:12, 13.

The clear teaching of the Scripture is that God miraculously intervened in order to bring about a decisive victory for the forces of Joshua against the Southern Confederacy. The nature of the miracle is not scientifically described. Some have suggested that the prolongation of the daylight came about as a result of refraction of the sun. The record here suggests an intense cold, which produced the hailstones, in a normally hot climate. Refraction of the sun occurs in times of intense cold, and travelers in the Polar regions tell how the sun may be seen for several days when they know that the orb is one degree below the horizon. If this is the explanation of "Joshua's long day," then the miracle occurred late in the afternoon, giving more daylight for further battle.

Others suggest that Joshua did not ask for a prolongation of the daylight, but of the darkness. Joshua, according to this view, did not ask the sun to stand still, but to be silent, that is, to keep from shining. The storm which produced the hailstones which had so devastating an effect on the southern armies, is thought to have refreshed the armies of Joshua, making it possible for them to bring the battle to a successful close.

The five kings of the south took refuge in a cave at Makkedah, but Joshua gave orders for the cave to be guarded and ordered his army to pursue the enemy. At the close of the campaign, the five men were brought out of the cave, slain, and later buried in the cave in which they attempted to hide.

A series of campaigns brought about the subjugation of all of southern Palestine—from Kadesh-barnea to Gaza, all the country of Goshen (in Judah, not the Egyptian district of that name) as far as Gibeon. Campaigns are mentioned at Makkedah, Libnah, Lachish, Eglon, Hebron, and Debir. The rout of their armies and the death of their kings so weakened them that resistance was light. When Joshua marched back to his encampment at Gilgal, he was master of southern Palestine.

7. The Conquest of Northern Canaan (11:1-15)

With southern Canaan in Israelite hands, Jabin, the king of the strongly fortified northern city of Hazor, organized a new confederacy against Joshua. The armies of the north gathered at the waters of Merom, northwest of the Sea of Galilee.

God appeared to Joshua with a promise and a command. The

Lord was about to give another victory to Israel. Joshua, on his part, was commanded to hamstring the horses of the enemy, and burn their chariots. Israel was to trust in God, not in horses, for deliverance. By cutting the tendon of the joint in the hind leg, a horse would be rendered unfit for military use but usable in domestic occupations.

Joshua again attacked suddenly, pursuing the defeated foe as far as Sidon on the Phoenician coast of the Mediterranean. The important city of Hazor, "the head of all those kingdoms," was burned. The smaller cities that "stood on mounds" (11:13, RSV) were not destroyed. With Israel in control of the land, it is possible that Joshua would wish to use these cities for his own purposes.

8. Review of the Conquest (11:16—12:24)

Following the defeat of the Northern Confederacy at Merom, organized resistance to Israel was broken. Important pockets of resistance would continue to plague Israel through the period of the Judges, but with the close of the northern campaign, we can speak of the conquest as successfully accomplished.

The sacred historian here pauses to review the victories of both Moses and Joshua. The victories in Transjordan are reviewed because the tribes of Reuben, Gad, and half the tribe of Manasseh were to be settled there following the conquest of western Palestine.

Thirty-one kings of the city-states of western Palestine, defeated by Joshua, are listed as a kind of appendix to the record of his conquests. Each of these kings was an independent ruler of a city with its environs.

Armies of men are engaged in this struggle, but God participates actively through Joshua who is subject to Him. God has willed to bring His people back to the land covenanted to their fathers. Thus the inhabitants of Canaan are not just Israel's enemies; they are also God's enemies. There is still another factor involved, their own sins, and for these the Canaanites are to be dispossessed. God will not tolerate sin, Israel's or that of any other nation. However, Israel because of Her greater light has greater responsibility than the nations who oppose her. In the Biblical philosophy of history, nothing happens by accident. Victories and defeats exhibit God's power and holiness and His providential control of the destinies of men and nations. He is not a God afar off, but One in Whom we live and move and have our being. His word may be trusted and His faithfulness should be an incentive to human perseverence in well doing. "If God be for us, who can be against us?"

III. Dividing the Territory (13:1—21:45)

Although there was "much land to be possessed," the advancing years of Joshua dictated that the division of the land among the tribes should not be delayed. As in the matter of warfare, so in the distribution of the land among the tribes, divine direction, rather than human reason, was the decisive factor.

1. Unconquered Portions of Canaan (13:1-7)

The Canaanites were still strong in the Philistine territory on the Mediterranean coast of southern Palestine and in the Phoenician territory to the north. Nevertheless, the land was to be allotted to the nine and one-half tribes who were to settle in western Palestine. It would then be their responsibility, trusting in God and assisting one another, to occupy the territory assigned to them. The Philistines were a source of trouble down to the time of David, and the Phoenician coastal cities were never incorporated into Israel. David and Solomon maintained friendly relations with Hiram of Tyre, who was of help in Israelite building operations, including the temple at Jerusalem.

2. The Eastern Tribes (13:8-33)

The tribes of Reuben, Gad, and the half tribe of Manasseh had been granted permission by Moses to settle in the territory east of the Jordan. Here tribal lines were fixed. The southern section was assigned to Reuben, which was bounded on the south by Moab and on the east by Ammon. It extended from the River Arnon, about half way up the eastern shore of the Dead Sea to the junction of the Jordan with the Dead Sea. North of Reuben lay Gad covering the territory east of the Jordan toward the Sea of Galilee. The half tribe of Manasseh occupied the land of Bashan. The boundary between Gad and Manasseh cannot be drawn with any degree of certainty.

3. *The Western Tribes (14:1—19:51)*

Before dividing the territory of western Palestine, the rights of Caleb to territory as promised by Moses were heard and acted upon. Caleb had been a man of faith, and Moses had promised that the land on which his foot had trodden would be his (Deut. 1:36). Joshua assigned to Caleb the city of Hebron as his inheritance.

The tribe of Judah, of which Caleb was a member, was assigned a large area in southern Canaan, portions of which were later designated as the possession of Simeon (19:1). All of the territory east of the Dead Sea was assigned to Judah, whose southern border reached to the land of Edom. Although many important cities were located in this territory and occupied by Judah, Jerusalem remained in Jebusite hands until the time of David (II Sam. 4:5–10).

A fruitful tract of central Palestine, south of the Mount Carmel ridge was assigned to Manasseh and Ephraim. The half of Manasseh which had not settled to the east of the Jordan took the northern part of this allotment, and Ephraim took the southern section, including the area around Shechem.

Although inheritance is normally reckoned through the male members of the family, the daughters of Zelophehad, of the tribe of Manasseh, had earlier pleaded their unusual case before Moses (Num. 27:1–11). Since their father had died without male heir, they desired that provision be made for the inheritance to pass through the daughters in the absence of sons in the household. When the land was apportioned among the families of Manasseh, the daughters of Zelophehad received their rightful share.

Representatives of "the children of Joseph" (the tribes of Ephraim and Manasseh) complained that their territory was not large enough because the Canaanites who dwelt in the valley had "chariots of iron" (17:14–16). Not until the time of David were the Israelites able to use iron. It had earlier been a monopoly, first of the Hittites and subsequently of the Philistines. Joshua assured the Joseph tribes that they would be able to drive out the Canaanites "though they have chariots of iron, and though they be strong" (17:18).

Moving the tabernacle to Shiloh from Gilgal (18:1), Joshua proceeded with the division of the land among the remaining seven tribes. Benjamin was given a portion of territory between Judah and Ephraim (18:11–28), and Simeon was given a part of the portion originally assigned to Judah (19:1–9). Simeon was early absorbed into Judah, losing its tribal identity (cf. Gen. 49:7).

North of Manasseh, bordering the Jordan, was Issachar. Northwest of Issachar, also bordering Manasseh, was Zebulun. Along the Mediterranean from Mount Carmel to Tyre was the land of Asher, with Naphtali occupying the territory north of Issachar and Zebulun and east of Asher.

A small territory, west of Benjamin, between Judah and Ephraim was assigned to Dan. This territory was too small for the Danites (19:47) in view of the fact that the Philistines occupied the most productive part of the country (cf. Judg. 1:34). The majority of the tribe migrated northward where they took the city of Laish—or Leshem (cf. Judg. 18). This became the northernmost city of Israel, named Dan, made familiar from those passages which speak of the extent of Israel "from Dan to Beer-sheba."

4. Cities of Refuge (20:1–9)

According to the Mosaic law (Num. 35:1–34), six cities of refuge were to be established upon the entrance of Israel into the Promised Land. The city of refuge was a sanctuary for one who had committed unintentional homicide. The fugitive had to justify his claim to protection by convincing the elders of the city of refuge that he did not have murderous intent. If he persuaded them of his innocence, he stayed in the city of refuge until his trial in his own city. If acquitted there, he was permitted to return to the city of refuge where he would be safe until the death of the high priest, at which time he might safely return home.

The institution of the city of refuge was a check on the very ancient custom of blood revenge, according to which the avenging of the victim was assumed by the kinsmen of the slain man. No distinction was made between wilful murder and accidental homicide. The cities of refuge, however, did recognize a difference, and provided protection for those innocent of murderous intent. Joshua and Eleazar appointed three such cities in western Palestine which, with the three previously designated in the east, provided easy access from all parts of the land. The "stranger" as well as the native Israelite might flee to these cities.

5. Cities for Priests and Levites (21:1–45)

The tribe of Levi did not receive a portion of land as its inheritance. Although true in a sense of all the tribes, in a fuller sense it could be said of Levi that God was their inheritance (cf. Num. 18:30; Deut. 10:9).

Because of their spiritual calling as ministers and attendants at the sanctuary, members of the tribe of Levi were disbursed among forty-eight cities in all of the tribes. The three branches of the Levites received their names from Levi's three grandsons—the Kohathites, the Gershonites, and the Merarites. The priests, Aaron's sons, were numbered among the Kohathites.

In each case, the city with its pasture land is mentioned. The purpose of this provision is stated in Numbers 35:3: "And the cities shall they have to dwell in, and the pasture grounds ["suburbs"] of them shall be for their cattle, and for their goods, and for all their beasts." All the cities of refuge were among the cities assigned to the Levites.

IV. Concluding Events (22:1—24:33)

With the division of Canaan among the tribes, the life work of Joshua reaches its climax. The tribes which had chosen their inheritance in the east Jordan territory could now be dismissed. Joshua's career closed with a farewell address, followed quickly by his death.

1. Return of the Eastern Tribes (22:1–34)

Joshua warmly commended the eastern tribes for their help in the conquest of Canaan. Their geographical separation from their brethren left them open to temptation, however, and Joshua solemnly warned them of the danger of apostasy. The path of safety is the path of love to the Lord and obedience to His Word. The Christian who must live in a godless environment is subjected to temptation, but he can live a life there in the fulness of the blessing of the Gospel. He must, however, "put on the whole armor of God" (Eph. 6:11).

When the warriors of the eastern tribes returned to their "tents" (that is, "dwelling places," since the term "tent" continued in use long after the Israelites settled in more permanent dwellings), they were commanded to "divide the spoil" with those who had stayed behind to guard the women and children. Moses had given a similar command concerning the division of the spoil of the Midianites (Num. 31:27), and later David enunciated the principle: "As his share is who goes down into the battle, so shall his share be who stays by the baggage; they shall share alike" (I Sam. 30:24). The people of God were one, whether serving at home or on the field of battle, there was no privileged class, and no group prospered at the expense of others. Similarly in the Church, there are different spiritual gifts ministered by the Holy Spirit for the edification of the body of Christ (I Cor. 12). No man has all the gifts, and no man is totally devoid of spiritual gifts. Each is expected to labor faithfully in the place and under the circumstances of God's appointment.

On their way from the camp at Gilgal to their east Jordan homes, the men of the eastern tribes built a memorial altar on the bank of the Jordan. The altar seems to have been built on the Canaan, or west, bank of the Jordan. Large enough to be seen from the east bank, it was designed to serve as a memorial of the link between the tribes on the two sides of the Jordan.

When the western tribes heard of this altar, they assumed that the altar would become a rival sanctuary used for idolatrous worship. This would constitute rebellion against the God of Israel (cf. Deut. 13:13–15). Ten princes, appointed to investigate the matter, pointed out the danger of rebellion against God, and offered the eastern tribes territory in western Palestine (22:19) if this would solve the problem.

The eastern tribes explained that they had no intention of erecting a shrine that would be a rival to the tabernacle worship at Shiloh. The altar was a memorial, not a place of sacrifice. Instead of forming a breach between east and west, it was designed to unite the two by reminding those geographically distant of their kinship in race and, more important, in the worship of the Lord.

The explanation was received by the deputation representing the western tribes. A sense of God's presence was felt throughout the camp of Israel. That which had almost precipitated civil war was now seen as evidence of the fact that God was truly working among the tribes of Israel. How easy—and how dangerous—it is to misunderstand the motives of others. Had the western tribes attacked their brethren instead of sending a delegation to investigate the report, bloodshed and strife would have been the result. Because they acted cautiously, all had opportunity to thank and praise God for His manifest presence in their midst.

2. *Joshua's Farewell Address and Death (23:1—24:33)*

As the Book of Joshua begins with an account of his call to leadership over Israel, so the book closes with his farewell addresses to the people he had led into the land of promise.

In his first address, Joshua rehearsed the evidences of God's love to Israel. Because God had been faithful to His promises, God's people should respond in loving obedience to Him. Victory had come because God had fought for Israel.

Although one phase of the conquest was complete, the enemy still occupied many areas of Palestine. Joshua warned that a spirit of compromise on the part of Israel would result in weakness, and this later took place during the time of the Judges when Israel was oppressed by a series of nations—both within and outside the land. God's sovereign choice of Israel did not give Israel a license to sin. If Israel followed the customs of the Canaanites who were dispossessed, Joshua warned that they would "perish quickly from off the good land which He hath given unto you." At the time of the Babylonian Exile, this literally took place.

Joshua's final address, which contains a resume of the history of Israel from the call of Abraham to his own time, emphasizes the saving acts of God. The Biblical faith is firmly rooted in history. The Bible is not a collection of speculations about God. Nor is it a "theology" in the comprehensive modern sense of the term, although it is the basis for all sound theology. Although a book of great variety, much of the Bible is an account of the acts of God, leading up to the culminating point in the New Testament—the death and resurrection of the Son of God. The recitation of these divine acts which took place in days long past is designed to inspire faith in God's power which will meet our needs in the present and in the future. James urges his readers to a faithful prayer life on the grounds that "Elijah was a man of like nature with ourselves, and he prayed fervently that it might not rain, and for three years and six months it did not rain on the earth. Then he prayed again and the heaven gave rain and the earth brought forth its fruit" (Jas. 5:17, 18).

God's grace is magnified in Joshua's address. Abraham had come from a background of idolatry (24:2). Every step in the history of Israel exhibited God's grace and power. It was He who brought His people out of Egypt and into Canaan. He sent "the hornet" ahead to drive out the enemy, so Israel could not boast in the prowess of the arms of their mighty warriors. Most interpreters think of "the hornet" as a figure of speech for the terror which God caused to fall upon the land of Canaan at the time of Joshua's invasion. Others, following the archaelogist Garstang, regard the hornet as an allusion to the power of the Egyptian Pharaohs, one of whose symbols was a bee or hornet. Garstang thinks that repeated campaigns of the Egyptians in Canaan weakened the land and rendered it ripe for Joshua's conquest.

On the basis of God's faithfulness, Joshua urges the necessity of making a choice between Him and the idols so popular in contemporary Canaan. The people responded with the assurance that they, like Joshua, would serve the Lord. Joshua protested that the Lord is a holy God Who demands holiness of His worshippers, and a jealous God Who can permit no compromise. Israel insisted that they would be true to Him alone: "The Lord our God will we serve, and unto his voice will we hearken." Thereupon the covenant which God had first made with Israel at Mount Sinai was solemnly renewed and a large stone was placed under the oak beside the sanctuary at Shechem as a memorial of the covenant.

At the age of 110 years, Joshua died. In the first verse of the book, Moses is called "the servant of the Lord" and Joshua has the title "Moses' minister." Through a life of faithfulness, Joshua has now earned the title "the servant of the Lord" (24:29). His teaching and example were not in vain, for "Israel served the Lord all the days of Joshua, and all the days of the elders that outlived Joshua, and had known all the work of the Lord, that he had wrought for Israel" (24:31).

The bones of Joseph, which had been brought up out of Egypt at the time of the Exodus, in accordance with his dying request (Gen. 50:24), were buried in Shechem (24:32, 33). Joseph had faith in the promise of God that His people would be delivered from Egypt and restored to the land which God had promised to Abraham, Isaac, and Jacob. The account of the burial of Joseph's bones in Shechem illustrates again God's faithfulness.

Judges

FRED E. YOUNG

THE BOOK OF JUDGES recounts the history of Israel under thirteen men whom God raised up during Israel's decline and disunion after the death of Joshua. It is the tragic account of seven periods of apostasy, seven periods of servitude to heathen nations, and seven notable deliverances. For four hundred years, God's people with incredible faithlessness pursued their own course of action without reference to God's discipline: "Every man did that which was right in his own eyes" (17:6).

That this selfish and shortsighted principle of action led to chaotic conditions was inevitable. Drastic measures had to be taken if the people were to escape utter defeat, and God called out judges to meet the critical need of these centuries. The word "judge" as we know it does not describe these men of Israel, for they had fairly dictatorial powers and their duties were more than judicial. Of the thirteen named in the book several were outstanding: Othniel, Ehud, Deborah, Barak, Gideon, Jephthah and Samson.

I. Invasion of Canaan (1:1—2:5)

The book opens with the mopping-up campaigns undertaken by individual tribes which followed the conquest of Canaan recorded in the Book of Joshua. Total victory apparently was not the goal of the Israelite leaders, though nothing less than that met God's requirement and their need. They settled for less, and this incomplete victory set the stage for dreary years of defeat and made some kind of dictatorial government their lot.

1. Victories of Judah and Simeon (1:1–21)

In the 8th verse of chapter 1, the full measure of Judah's victory over Jerusalem is recorded; yet the city (v. 21) remained in the possession of the Jebusites. There is no contradiction here, for it is true that the men of Judah took the southern part of the city, but the fortress, as well as the northern part, remained in the possession of the Jebusites until the time of David.

Other notable cities were invaded and captured: Hebron (1:20), the burial site of three patriarchs—Abraham, Isaac, and Jacob—and a city of refuge, was given to Caleb (Josh. 20:7); and Bethel (v. 22), a stopping place for nomadic Abraham and for fleeing Jacob, was taken by the house of Joseph.

2. Victories of Other Tribes (1:22–36)

Victory after victory is recounted, but the quality of the victory was modified drastically again and again by being partial. "Mission uncompleted" was, in a manner of speaking, written at the end of each episode, for the tribes failed to complete their task of driving out the inhabitants (1:19, 21, 27, 30, 32, 33). The tribes yielded to the temptation to compromise, forced labor contracts upon the native population, and let matters take their course.

3. Sacrifice at Bochim (2:1–5)

The Israelites were reminded that they had been warned of their mission—total conquest—for "an angel of the Lord came up from Gilgal to Bochim, and said . . . ye shall make no league with the inhabitants of this land; ye shall throw down their altars: but ye have not obeyed my voice." The Jewish commentators generally suppose that "the angel of the Lord" (2:1) refers to Phineas, the high priest. Others look upon him as a divine messenger sent in human form to warn Israel of her lapse of faith in not completely destroying the Canaanite forms of worship. Certainly the Israelites are now told in clear terms that there is a penalty for this disobedience, that the Lord will not do what they have failed to do, and "their gods shall be a snare unto you." The years that lay ahead were to prove how great and well nigh fatal an influence the remaining population had upon the religious life and thought of Israel.

II. Reign of the Judges (2:6—16:31)

1. Introduction to the Story of the Judges (2:6—3:6)

Death of Joshua (2:6–10). These verses supplement Joshua 24:28–31. While Joshua and the elders who had served with him were alive, the people served the Lord. But Joshua appears not to have trained a successor as he himself was trained by Moses. Thus Israel was spiritually bankrupt shortly after the death of Joshua and his cabinet (v. 10). Timnath-heres, Joshua's burial place, is about fifteen miles southwest of Shechem.

Israel's Apostasy (2:11–19). As other generations rose up, it is recorded that "they knew not the Lord, nor yet the works which he had done for Israel" (v. 11). The failure of Israel was to be rooted in this blind ignorance, and they were to be led swiftly and surely into pagan faith and practice: "And they forsook the Lord, and served Baal and Ashtaroth" (v. 13).

Israel and Her Neighbors (2:20—3:6). Now the gods of their neighbors proved enticing. Baal was the great Canaanite god of fertility, while Ashtaroth, the plural of Astarte, was the Canaanite fertility and war goddess known from Mesopotamia to Egypt by various names. Because these idols were agricultural deities and the Hebrews were semi-nomadic, there was a constant temptation to amalgamate these deities with the religion of the Hebrews.

But the anger of God was matched by His mercy, and He "raised up judges which delivered them out of the hand of those that spoiled them" (2:16). God made certain tribesmen their national and religious reformers in a time of decline. Thirteen judges ruled, some possibly simultaneously in different parts of the land, from the death of Joshua to the time of Eli and Samuel.

2. *Othniel, the First Judge (3:7–11)*

Opression by Cushan-rishathaim (3:7, 8). The first great apostasy of Israel was not without its retribution, and the failure to remain separate from pagan tribes brought them into bondage. They were enslaved by Cushan-rishathaim, king of Mesopotamia, for eight years.

Deliverance by Othniel (3:9–11). It was then the Lord raised up Othniel. In verse 10 the method of Othniel's appointment as judge is made clear: "And the Spirit of the Lord came upon him, and he judged Israel, and went to war." This one verse with utmost clarity describes the character of the judge and the nature of his work: possession of the Spirit of the Lord, justice in Israel, and military leadership. The success of Othniel's undertaking was complete, and the land under this younger brother of Caleb, the colleague of Joshua, knew peace until his death forty years later.

The career that had begun so promisingly (1:11–13) with the conquering of Kirjathsepher, continued to be a life of victory and brought Othniel years later triumph in Mesopotamia.

3. *Ehud, the Second Judge (3:12–30)*

Oppression by Moab (3:12–14). After Othniel's death, the children of Israel again turned to evil. Retribution followed when the Lord permitted Eglon, king of Moab, to win allies and proceed to subjugate the children of Israel. With the aid of the Ammonites, the descendants of Lot who lived on the east side of Jordan between the Jabbok and Arnon rivers, and the Amalekites, descendants of Esau and therefore perennial enemies of Israel, Eglon "smote Israel" and entered the city of palm trees, that is, Jericho (3:13). Thus began a period of eighteen years of servitude for the children of Israel.

Deliverance by Ehud (3:15–30). When deliverance came, it was achieved by Ehud, son of Gera and a Benjamite. When the children of Israel sent tribute to Eglon's court (v. 18), it was Ehud who presented it. Later he dismissed the caravan near Gilgal, retraced his steps to the court, and through the ruse of having a secret communication to make to the king, Ehud was invited to the rooftop apartment of Eglon. This was a single-room compartment built on the top of the flat roof of a house with windows on every side for the free passage of air. Once Ehud had Eglon alone, he assassinated him and escaped while the servants of the king waited for the master to finish his siesta. By the time they discovered Eglon dead, Ehud was far from the scene (v. 26).

Ehud then gathered the Israelites from the hill country of Ephraim (3:27, 28) and overwhelmingly defeated the Moabites in a battle near the Jordan. This victory established a reign of peace that lasted eighty years (v. 30).

4. Shamgar, the Third Judge (3:31)

Shamgar, the son of Anath, was a man of tremendous physical power, since he was able to slay six hundred Philistines with an ox goad (a metal-tipped instrument). Before his deliverance of Israel, it had been unsafe to use the major highways, and travelers took to the byroads (5:6).

5. A Co-regency, Deborah and Barak, the Fourth and Fifth Judges (4:1—5:31)

Oppression by the Canaanites (4:1–3). For the third time, the children of Israel revert to evil. Again the Lord disciplines them, and it is by His will that they are enslaved by Jabin, king of Canaan, and held under the cruel domination of his general, Sisera, a tyrant with nine hundred chariots of iron.

Deliverance by Deborah and Barak (4:7–24). The revolt against Sisera, directed by God and handled by Deborah and Barak, constitutes one of the great victories God permitted the children of Israel. Deborah, a judge and prophetess in Israel, summons Barak to tell him that the Lord God has commanded him to take ten thousand men of the tribes of Naphtali and of Zebulun and go toward Mount Tabor. Barak goes on the condition that Deborah accompanies him. When she agrees to do this, she points out that this victory they are to gain is not to be for Barak's glory, for it will be the Lord's doing, and Sisera will be betrayed by a woman.

The circumstances of the defeat of Sisera (4:7–24) are now described. Sisera had started out from Harosheth with his chariots, but when he tried to get back, he found himself in desperate straits. On the left were the hills of Samaria, now in enemy hands; on the right was the swollen river. At this point where the valley narrows until it is only a few rods wide, the horses and chariots became mired in terrible confusion and the overflowing river washed away thousands.

Sisera managed to leave his chariot and flee on foot. He escaped to the tent of Jael whom he assumed to be friendly because of the amicable relationship between her husband and Sisera's king, Jabin. She invited him in, gave him milk and stood in the doorway at his command. No sooner had he fallen asleep than Jael killed him by driving a tent peg through his head.

The fifth chapter of Judges, the song of Deborah, recounts the triumph of God on this day in which Sisera was defeated and Jabin, the king of Canaan, destroyed. The song of Deborah and Barak names the tribes that participated, nine of the twelve, and gives the details of battle.

One of the most notable things about these chapters is that which is most obvious: the leadership of Deborah. The Lord did not limit His revelations to men, but chose a woman as a channel of communication. What Paul was to say later was proved true in early and perilous times: "Not many mighty, not many noble are called . . . and God hath chosen the weak things of the world to confound the things that are mighty." Thus He chose Deborah in a time when women held no great place, and Barak is certainly not depicted as a fearless and distinguished leader. "Not many mighty," so Deborah was chosen. "Not many noble"—Barak filled that place! But God confounded "the things that are mighty" and brought victory to those who were enslaved and despairing.

6. Gideon, the Sixth Judge (6:1—9:57)

Oppression by Midian (6:1–6). At the conclusion of Deborah's song, we learn that the victory of the prophetess and Barak brought peace to Israel for forty years. Lulled by the security of this extended period of rest, the children of Israel again "did evil in the sight of the Lord" (v. 1). This fourth apostasy brought them into servitude to the Midianites who conquered the children of Israel. When they were totally impoverished, the Israelites cried out to God in anguish (v. 6) and a prophet was sent to them to remind them that they had been faithless and had foolishly followed pagan gods (vv. 8–10).

The Midianites were members of a nomadic tribe related to Israel (Gen. 25:1–6) who lived east and southeast of the Dead Sea and beyond the limits of Moab and Edom.

Deliverance by Gideon (6:7—8:35). In Ophrah, a city of Manasseh, about sixteen miles north of Jericho, lived Gideon, whom the Lord had chosen to lead His oppressed people. When the angel of the Lord appeared to make this announcement, Gideon was about his business, threshing corn by beating it with a small stick in a rock-hewn trough used ordinarily for wine pressing. In talking with the angel, Gideon questioned the validity of the stories he had heard about the power and presence of God in the experience of his ancestors (6:13). He hesitated to accept the offer of leadership the divine messenger made. When Gideon was assured of God's assistance in overcoming the Midianites, he still hesitated and described his family as the poorest in the tribe of Manasseh (v. 15) and himself as "the least in my father's house." He doubted his ability to rally his own family to his cause, let alone to gather all Israel under one banner, and asked for concrete evidence that God was behind all that the divine messenger was telling him (vv. 17, 37, 39).

At the direction of the angel of God, Gideon put a kid and unleavened cakes on a rock. When the angel touched it with his staff, a fire arose and consumed the cakes. Granted such evidence of power, Gideon recognized the Lord and feared that he might die. But the Lord Himself reassured him, and Gideon executed the direction to build an altar unto God and cut down the altar to Baal on his father's property (6:27).

When the townspeople threatened to put Gideon to death, his father came to his rescue. Gideon's obedience to God, his personal courage, had not caused him to stand alone when the Midianites and Amalekites mobilized in the valley of Jezreel (6:33). With the Spirit of the Lord guiding him, Gideon rallied his forces throughout Manasseh to meet the Midianite invasion and sent messengers to other tribes asking them to come and meet him and be his allies. He was also assured by the sign of the fleece (vv. 36–40) that the Lord was with him.

Thousands of men gathered for battle, but it was not numerical superiority that the Lord desired lest the Israelites regard this as the heart of the victory. Israel is going to win this battle with only three hundred men, a victory promised by the Lord Himself (7:7). Israel won most of her battles with smaller armies than those of her opponents. "It is not by might, nor by power, but by my spirit." Today this is just as true: the effective force of Christianity is often produced by small groups with Gideon-like faith and courage.

Gideon's band of three hundred, divided into three companies, armed with trumpets, empty pitchers and lamps, won a famous victory (7:15—8:21). They followed with exactness the directions of Gideon, and as they encompassed the camp of the enemy and blew on signal and broke the pitchers, they seemed like a multitude to their oppressors who fled thinking themselves pursued by a host.

The flight of the Midianites across the Jordan (7:22) presented Gideon with the problem of supplying rations for his weary warriors. The men of Succoth (8:5, 6) and of Penuel (v. 8) doubted the ability of Gideon's peasant army to capture the camel-riding Midianites before they escaped into the hinterlands. They taunted Gideon, "Are Zebah and Zalmunna already in your hand?" (v. 6). In modern parlance they would say, "Are you so sure of your quarry that you can add a notch to your gun?" Later Gideon had his revenge for their skepticism and failure to help him (vv. 16, 17).

In verse 14, we have evidence of the antiquity of writing in Canaan. Gideon secured the names of the elders of Succoth from a boy who wrote out their names. This evidence of writing on the part of commoners is plentiful in this period.

Gideon's refusal to become a king (8:22, 23) accentuates the prevailing view that a theocratic government was to be preferred to an hereditary monarch. Gideon's decision reflected his appreciation of the divinely endowed nature of Israel's leaders during the period of the judges. God was working through chosen men, not through families. It was a matter of special grace and not heredity. God endowed men for special missions.

Gideon's mistake in making an ephod (8:27) is difficult to understand. Nor is it easy to determine the nature of the ephod. In Exodus 28, it was a decorated vestment, apparently something like an apron. But the amount of material used in making it, the fact that it was placed in Gideon's city, and that his fellow men "played the harlot after it" (v. 27) suggest that it was an idol. The seed of later apostasy after Gideon's death was planted in this act of idolatry.

The Abortive Reign of Abimelech (9:1–57). Gideon had seventy sons by his many wives, and he also had a son, Abimelech ("my father is king") by a concubine in Shechem. Concubinage was in no way unusual or irregular during this time, and Gideon's marriage to the Shechemite was a type well-known among the early Arabians. In this relationship the wife did not become the property of her husband, but was known as his *sadika* or "female friend." She remained with her own clan and was visited by her husband from time to time. In such a marriage, the children of the union belonged to the wife's clan. This point has an important bearing on the story of Abimelech's attempt at kingship (9:1–57).

To achieve kingship, Abimelech ran on a clever platform to win his election (9:3). Kingship was the favorite form of rule in Canaan, and Abimelech was the son of the person who had been offered the kingship. Abimelech, related to the Shechemites through his mother, asked them, "If you prefer kingship, is it better to be ruled by the seventy sons of an Israelite or by a king who is related to you by blood?" The Shechemites saw an opportunity to restore the family of Hamor, the original Shechemite dynasty (Gen. 33) to power and agreed to finance the campaign of Abimelech from the treasury of the temple of Baal-berith (9:4). This term, "Baal-berith," indicates that the Shechemites were a part to the old tribal association mentioned in Joshua 24:32. By the slaying of an ass (*hamor*) they satisfied the treaty and were therefore called "sons of Hamor" or "sons of the treaty."

Abimelech, desiring a confederation of tribes with Shechem as the capital and himself as king, hired worthless and reckless followers (9:4)—vagabonds, men with nothing to lose and much to gain in the revolutionary movement. Having slain the seventy sons of Gideon, all the men of Shechem and Beth-millo (v. 6) came to acclaim Abimelech king "by the oak of the pillar at Shechem" (v. 6). This historic spot may be the one mentioned in Joshua 24:26, "And he [Joshua] took a great stone and set it up there under the oak of the sanctuary of the Lord."

Jotham, the sole survivor of the family of Gideon's seventy sons, climbed the hill of Gerizim to a vantage point of the city and propounded the famous story of the trees (9:7–21). The point of the story lies in its conclusion. The refusal of the olive tree, the fig tree, and the vine signified the refusal of worthy candidates—Gideon and men like him—to accept the office of kingship. It was natural to use the olive, the fig and the vine as figures in the story because they were staple products of Canaan and upon them depended the agricultural wealth and prosperity of the land. The bramble stood for Abimelech, a worthless fellow, who, although he was unable to fulfil an empty boast, was capable of kindling a fire that could wipe out those who acclaimed him king and their neighbors as well. Verse 16 takes up the argument and hints that good relations between the Shechemites and Abimelech may not last for long. After his speech, Jotham fled to Beer, location unknown.

The Shechemites began to deal treacherously with Abimelech (9:22–25). They set armed bands in the mountains to rob passing caravans and thereby enriched themselves at the cost to Abimelech either by injuring his trade or by interfering with the tolls exacted from caravans for safe conduct through the territory.

Gaal, the son of Ebed, won the confidence of the men of Shechem by an address given at a festival in the temple (9:28). He argued that there was really little kinship between Abimelech and them, and that the Shechemites served the real dynasty of Shechem (Hamor) prior to the insurrection. Since Abimelech was a halfbreed, he had no right to their loyalty, Gaal reasoned. Thus one outsider challenged the right of another outsider to rule. The Shechemites, weary of Abimelech's unfulfilled promises, apparently gave Gaal the opportunity to rid Shechem of Abimelech (v. 31). But Zebul, the lieutenant of Abimelech, maneuvered Gaal into a fatal position before the gates of the city, thus forcing a showdown between Abimelech and Gaal. In the ensuing battle, Gaal was worsted and Zebul remained in charge of the city.

Abimelech was victorious in several succeeding campaigns (9:45, 49). In one case, he sowed a city with salt (v. 45) and relegated it to perpetual desolation.

Abimelech came to Thebez, about twelve miles northeast of Shechem. Having taken the outer city (9:50), Abimelech advanced to the tower fortifications within the city proper (vv. 51, 52). "A certain woman threw an upper millsone upon Abimelech's head" (v. 53). Critically injured, Abimelech begged his armor-bearers to put him to death that he might be spared the disgrace of suffering death at the hands of a woman. Thus the very people who assisted Abimelech in his drive to power were responsible for his death, and the story of Jotham was fulfilled.

Abimelech's life demonstrates the futility of a man's trying to govern without possessing the Spirit of the Lord. Rightful rulers under the leadership of the Spirit have special guidance as they face difficult problems and critical decisions, but evil men, living by the power of the sword, are struck down by the very instrument they trust.

7. *Tola, the Seventh Judge (10:1, 2)*

There is no record of achievement credited to this judge, only certain biographical details: the names of Tola's father and grandfather, and the fact that Tola dwelt and was buried in Shamir in the hill country of Ephraim, where he judged Israel for twenty-three years. Shamir may be Samaria. In Genesis 46:13, Tola and Puah were the sons of Issachar. "Tola" is a red commercial dye derived from an insect common in Israel.

8. *Jair, the Eighth Judge (10:3–5)*

Jair, the Gileadite, had thirty sons who were apparently the heads of thirty villages, which were called Havoth-jair, ("the tent villages of Jair"). Riding on ass colts (10:4) indicated a high estate. Jair continued to rule for twenty-two years.

9. *Jephthah, the Ninth Judge (10:6—12:7)*

Oppression of the Philistines and the Ammonites (10:6–18). After the death of Jair, the children of Israel again "did evil in the sight of the Lord" and served other gods. With the wrath of God upon them, they fell into the hands of the Philistines and Ammonites, and only after eighteen oppressive years did they again cry unto the Lord. Confessing their sins, they pled for deliverance, turned from the strange gods and began to serve the Lord again. And as the Ammonites gathered together against them in Gilead, they sought for a man to lead them against the enemy.

Deliverance by Jephthah (11:1—12:7). Jephthah, a Gileadite without property owing to the circumstances of his birth, became an outlaw and took up residence in the land of Tob, where he gathered to himself a band of desperadoes, and gained fame as a freebooter. The men who aligned themselves with Jephthah were called "worthless fellows." "Worthless" is hardly a satisfactory rendering, since this term implies a lack of moral quality. While they may have been lacking in this respect, the Hebrew word merely implies that they were "empty," that is, without property or material goods and in need (cf. the men who joined David's group, I Sam. 22:2).

Jephthah drove a hard bargain with the Gileadites (vv. 9, 10).

He proposed not only temporary leadership in the campaign against Ammon but also permanent leadership over the clans of Gilead. For the Gileadites to accept the services of a freebooter was one thing, but to nominate as the head of their clan a man whose illegitimate birth drove him into exile was another. The need of the hour dictated the terms of the contract. Jephthah insisted that the compact (11:10) be ratified and witnessed at the local sanctuary of Mizpeh in the presence of the Lord.

The source of contention between Ammon and Gilead was the former's demand that the territory between the Arnon and the Jabbok Rivers be returned to Ammon. The Arnon River runs into the Dead Sea from the east, about twenty-two miles from its northern end, while the Jabbok is a principal tributary of the Jordan. The distance between the Arnon and the Jabbok is fifty miles, and the width of the territory, thought to be demanded as returned, is approximately sixteen miles.

Ammon argued that the land now inhabited by the Israelites was at one time in the hands of Ammon and Moab, brothers from the family of Lot. Sihon, the king of the Amorites, had driven a wedge between Ammon and Moab and occupied the land. Israel answered that Israel had taken the land, not from Ammon and Moab, but from the Amorite, Sihon. Jephthah also reminded the Ammonites that it was customary to take the land which one's god gave them and appealed to their practice of accepting the gifts of their god, Chemosh (11:24). He asks further, "You have had three hundred years to ask for the land to be returned. No one before your time has demanded it. Why do you demand it back after all these years?" (vv. 25–28).

Jephthah vowed to the Lord that if the children of Ammon were conquered, he would offer up for a "burnt offering whoever comes forth from the doors of my house to meet me" (11:31). His only child met him upon his return (v. 34) after his victory over the Ammonites. She urged him to fulfil his vow (v. 36), once she had been given the opportunity to bewail her virginity (v. 37). And this Jephthah did "according to his vow which he had made" (v. 39).

The earliest Jewish interpreters and the Christian Fathers explained the passage in its natural sense. Kimchi, in the Middle Ages, taught that Jephthah built a house for his daughter, in which she lived a virgin, isolated from all the world. He believed that the daughters of Israel visited her annually to bewail her fate. If Jephthah carried out his vow, the following questions need to be considered: (*a*)

Where did he offer her? Shiloh was in Ephraimite territory and Jephthah was not on friendly terms with the Ephraimites. (*b*) What Levitical priest would have offered the sacrifice? (*c*) If Jephthah offered his daughter, would he not incur serious penalty for assuming a priestly function, offering a burnt offering in an unacceptable place, and presenting for a burnt offering something abhorrent to the law and the character of God? The usual interpretation is that Jephthah's daughter remained a virgin and that each year during her lifetime the women of the Gileadite district lamented with her the sad circumstances of her life brought about by her father's rash vow.

War between Jephthah and the Ephraimites arose as the result of tribal pride. The Ephraimites complained that they were not invited to participate in the war against the Ammonites (12:1). Since Ephraim claimed leadership among the northern tribes and the Transjordan area, the men of that tribe felt their honor and status had been insulted in the singlehanded victory of Jephthah's small army. The Ephraimites taunted the men of Gilead by calling them renegade Ephraimite fugitives who, without territorial status, existed by sufferance in the territory of Ephraim and Manasseh.

A battle followed near the fords of the Jordan. The Gileadite password was *shibboleth* (12:6). When the victory was going to the Gileadites and they controlled the passages of the Jordan, the Ephraimites sought to get back to their forces by denying that they were Ephraimites. To detect whether or not this was true, the Gileadites had a quick test: they simply asked each Ephraimite to pronounce *shibboleth*. If he could not pronounce the initial "sh," he was slain. In this conflict, Ephraim lost forty-two thousand men.

The tragedy of this conflict was the internal bickering among the Israelite factions. Instead of uniting for an all-out push against the enemy, they quarreled over status, neglected honor and indulged in personal jealousy. The time was not yet ripe for God to mold them into a united nation. Every man still did that which was right in his own sight.

Jephthah judged Israel for six years, and upon his death was buried in one of the cities of Gilead.

10. Ibzan, the Tenth Judge (12:8-10)

A man of Bethlehem, Ibzan judged Israel for seven years. He and his two successors, Elon and Abdon, were minor judges. Ibzan was born about two miles north of Megiddo in the tribal territory of Zebulon. The biographical note includes the fact that he had thirty sons and thirty daughters and that he took in thirty daughters from abroad for his sons.

11. Elon, the Eleventh Judge (12:11, 12)

Elon, also a Zebulonite, served as a judge ten years. He was buried in Aijalon.

12. Abdon, the Twelfth Judge (12:13–15)

Abdon lived near Shechem and judged Israel for eight years. Forty sons and thirty nephews who each rode on seventy ass colts suggest extensive family relationships as well as wealth and standing. The mention of Amalekites in the territory of Ephraim sounds strange, but perhaps there was an Amalekite family there. Boundaries were not yet fixed so strictly as they later were.

13. Samson, the Thirteenth Judge (13:1—16:31)

Birth of Samson (13:1–24). The narratives surrounding the life of Samson are extensive in comparison with those of the first twelve judges. The account opens with the visit of the angel of the Lord to the wife of Manoah near Zorah. Modern Zorah is fourteen miles west of Jerusalem in the Shephelah, upon an elevation on the northern side of the wadi. (Today the Jaffa-Jerusalem railway runs through this valley.) The angel said the son to be born should be a Nazarite, the word signifying "dedicated" or "consecrated" to the service of the Lord.

The law regulating the Nazarite vow, which could be taken for a given period or for life, is given fully in Numbers 6:1–21. The Nazarite was bound to observe these rules: (1) He must abstain from wine and all other products of the grape, including the fresh and dried fruit; (2) he must allow the hair of his head to grow, and must not touch it with a razor during the period of the vow; (3) he must not touch a dead body. Failure to observe these rules involved the abrogation of the vow. Completion of the vow without defilement was signalized by the shaving of the head and the burning of the hair on the altar, with appropriate sacrifice and ritual.

Manoah asked the name of the angel who informed him of the

impending birth, but the angel refused to give this information (13:17, 18). Angels were not named in the early days of Old Testament history in order to discourage the worship of them.

Woman of Timnah (14:1—15:8). Samson's career began in the aura of a romance (14:1–4) when he met a woman among the Philistines whom he wished to marry. The free movement of Samson in Philistine territory indicates that as yet there was no concerted hostility between the Israelites and the Philistines. Archaeological remains support the belief that for a time Philistine and Israelite societies lived side by side without too much friction. Although his father disapproved of Samson's marriage to a Philistine (v. 3), he helped to arrange it.

The preliminaries of marriage, such as the settlement of a purchase price, were arranged between the fathers of the bride and groom. Ordinarily, the bride was brought to the home of the groom, where a feast preceded the marriage rites. The friends of the groom would be taken from among his acquaintances.

At Samson's wedding, thirty Philistine youth were invited. The details of the wedding seem to imply that this was not an ordinary Hebrew procedure. The riddle proposed by Samson (14:12–14) to the wedding party was solved through the deceit of his bride from fear of the threat of personal injury to her and her father's house (v. 15). Samson, the giant in strength, betrayed early his weakness for the opposite sex, a weakness that followed his career and hindered the full flow of God's Spirit in his life. A lack of maturity also appeared in his hasty and angry retreat from the marriage feast (v. 19). The best man married the bride!

Samson's Arrest and Retaliation (15:9–20). Chapter 15 portrays the courage of Samson in fighting the Philistines. The men of Judah were willing to arrest Samson and turn him over to the Philistine police force, but they would not support Samson's efforts to free Israel from the injustices of the Philistines. Samson's victory over the Philistines at Lehi was accomplished by the might of the Spirit upon him and the superhuman strength by which he wielded to good advantage an unusual weapon, the jawbone of an ass (v. 15).

The Harlot of Gaza (16:1–3). Samson's second love affair, with a harlot in Gaza (v. 1), landed him in custody for part of one night (vv. 2, 3).

Delilah (16:4–22). After this episode, he fell in love with a woman in the Valley of Sorek. But whether the woman was a Philistine or an Israelite in the pay of the Philistines we are not told; her name is Semitic in form. She was offered 1100 shekels of silver to betray Samson from each of the lords of the Philistines (probably five), an amount totalling more than $3000! The price on Samson's head was enormous and from Delilah's point of view outweighed all considerations of love. After several attempts to learn the source of Samson's strength, and subsequent failures, Samson revealed the secret of his power (v. 17). Whether it was a lapse of strength or a wearing down by constant beseeching, we do not know. Once Delilah had the secret of his power, she proceeded to deprive Samson of it by having his hair cut off. Surrounded by the Philistines, he "did not know that the Lord had left him" (v. 20), a tragedy often repeated in the experiences of men who are not aware that the spiritual force is gone from their ministry.

The Philistines easily took Samson, put out his eyes, brought him to Gaza bound in fetters of iron. There he spent his life grinding in the prison house (v. 21). It was probably not the ordinary hand mill, but such as is turned by an ox or an ass.

Death of Samson (16:23–31). The lords of the Philistines sponsored a festival to Dagon to commemorate the capture of Samson. Dagon, the father of Baal, was a Mesopotamian deity worshipped as early as the twenty-fifth century B.C. Originally a grain god, Dagon was the chief deity of Ashdod, had a temple at Gaza, and was adored as far north as Ugarit.

"When their hearts were merry" (16:25), they asked for Samson to put on an act. Led by the attendant to the pillars on which the roof of the house rested, he prayed for the power that once adorned his life to come back and pleaded to die rather than live a sightless life. In a final surge of strength, he demonstrated God's power in a broken vessel and bowed out. His family claimed his body and buried him in the family plot between Zorah and Eshtaol.

The career of Samson had many strange twists. Many things in his life were unworthy of emulation, but potential strength was always present. God uses strange people to perform His wonders. It is truly not by human might nor ingenuity, but by His Spirit that God's will is carried out.

III. Appendices (17:1—21:25)

1. Relocation of the Danites (17:1—18:31)

Micah and the Levites (17:1–13). The story of the relocation of the Danites begins with the story of Micah. When he returned money stolen from his mother (vv. 2, 3a), she used two hundred pieces of it to make several images. Micah had a shrine in which he kept an ephod and teraphim, and he consecrated one of his sons to serve as priest until a Levitical priest arrived from the south (vv. 7, 8). The new arrival told Micah that he was a sojourner (v. 9). (A sojourner was a stranger who took up residence for a time with a family or tribe and was extended certain protective rights.) Micah offered the Levite wages, clothing, and food (v. 10).

The Danite Removal (18:1–31). The Danites in their removal to the north literally stole Micah's shrine, including the priest (vv. 16–20). The priest did not object, because it meant a larger congregation to serve and an increased travel allowance! Micah objected both to the loss of the images and of the services of the priest (vv. 22–25), but his efforts to recover his losses were fruitless (v. 16).

2. The Gibeah Offense (19:1—21:25)

This family argument led to separation. The concubine, in the heat of anger, returned to her home in Judah. After four months, the husband, a Levite, went to the home of the concubine to bring her back. He took provisions and a servant with him (19:3). After several days of feasting with his father-in-law, the Levite and his concubine started home. Arriving at Jerusalem, a six-mile trip from Bethlehem, at nightfall, the servant urged that they spend the night there. The Levite refused to stay because it was a city of foreigners, so the night was spent in Gibeah, a city about four miles from Jerusalem, in the hospitality of another Ephraimite (v. 16).

The demand of the men of the city for the Levite for sexual purposes was met by the offer of the virgin daughter of the host and the concubine of the guest (19:23, 24). This agrees with the procedure in the story of Lot and the base fellows of Sodom (Gen. 19:1–14). The next morning the Levite, on finding his concubine dead, sent a report of the infamous deed throughout Israel.

The chiefs of Israel gathered together to Mizpeh to discuss what action to take (20:1-7), and decided to locate the guilty parties and put them to death (vv. 12, 13). Because the Benjamites refused to turn over the guilty persons and prepared to defend them by force, if necessary, a tragic civil war began and thousands perished.

The Benjamites' failure to recognize the need of correcting evil at its source led to a terrible decimation of their forces. Since the Israelites had vowed not to permit an Israelite to marry a Benjamite and the possibility of the loss of one tribe became a real threat, a plan was formed whereby the Benjamites might be provided with wives from Jabesh-Gilead (21:8-22).

The Book of Judges ends with the verse which characterizes the actions of its many actors, "In those days there was no king in Israel: every man did that which was right in his own eyes." Wherever the person was filled with the Spirit of the Lord, his course of action was inspired and right; but wherever the Spirit was missing, the tragedy of blunder and failure swept over the unorganized tribes. God was preparing the nation, little by little, for the period of the kings.

Ruth

P. A. VERHOEF

THE BOOK OF RUTH is honored on all sides as a literary work of art. In contrast to the stories of the tumult of war and military violence in the Books of Judges and Samuel, it describes the life and adventures of a family in Israel, probably towards the end of the era of the judges (1:1). Opinions differ widely concerning the aim and purport of this book. Evangelical Christians recognize it as an integral part of the whole message of the Scriptures. The guidance of God in the individual experiences of this family is a phase of His high plan of salvation for His people and the world. The book supplies a foregleam of the history of Christmas and the event of Pentecost in that the genealogy with which it ends culminates in the theocratic king David. To his generation the promise of the advent of the Messiah is linked. The inclusion of a Moabite ancestress accentuates the universal meaning of the Messiah: He is not only the Saviour of Israel but of the human race.

I. Grievous Visitations (1:1–5)

The family of Elimelech of Bethlehem in Judah (distinguish from Bethlehem in Zebulon, Josh. 19:15) was grievously afflicted. They lived in the days when the judges "judged," hence in a time when almost everyone did simply as he thought right, a time of religious apostasy, political disorganization, and social chaos (cf. Judg. 2:6—3:4). Under stress of famine they had to migrate out of the Land of Promise, and from Bethlehem, the bread-house of this land, to Moab.

Behind this simple story lies a world of struggle. The providential guidance of God had to be reconciled with the fact that some of His people in the Promised Land died of hunger. The Book of Judges contains no direct indication of such a prolonged famine. Famine was, however, a well-known phenomenon in Palestine, the result both of natural causes and of enemy invasion (cf. Judg. 6:3–6; 10:6, 7).

The possibility of an Israelite family sojourning in otherwise hostile Moab is due probably to the fact that enmity between the two nations did not exclude the friendly intercourse of individuals, or perchance there was a friendly relationship between the two nations at this time. Here Elimelech died, and Mahlon and Chilion took to themselves Moabite wives. Marriage with a Moabite wife was not definitely forbidden in Israel, although union with the women of Canaan was (Deut. 7:3, 4). Such marriage, however, was contrary to the spirit of the law because the Moabites were idolators and were not allowed in the congregation of the Lord (Deut. 23:3; cf. I Cor. 7:12–16; 10:12; II Cor. 6:14–18). The family lived there about ten years, and in this time the two sons also died. The name and inheritance of Elimelech hung in the balance. No affliction was more grievous to an Israelite family than this, for the name of a generation in the Promised Land stood in the service of the advent of the Kingdom of God!

II. Far-Reaching Decisions (1:6–22)

In Moab, Naomi learned that God had once again visited (graciously, cf. Gen. 50:24; Ex. 4:31) His people and given them "food" (RSV, cf. Lev. 3:11, 16; Num. 28:24), as the year had been prosperous in the Promised Land and the harvest plentiful. Thereupon

Naomi decided to leave Moab and its graves, and return to Canaan and to God. The far-reaching implication of this decision was that it formed a ring in the chain which linked the Paradise promise and Christmas.

The daughters-in-law also had to choose. For those whose hearts were given solely to the things of this world, the journey to Canaan was too arduous; the realization of this fact is seen in Naomi's singular insistence that they should return to Moab. The choice which the daughters-in-law had to make was of grave importance; it was a choice between "rest" (KJV) in Moab, that is, a "home" (RSV), and the risk of life by faith alone: between the longings of the natural heart and the exalted desire for God and His service, between Moab and Canaan, between the world and the Church. Naomi based her persistent urging of Orpah and Ruth to return on the fact of her own advanced age. According to tradition (Gen. 38), or as stipulated in the law (Deut. 25:5–10; cf. Mt. 22:23–28) a levirate marriage was no longer possible (1:11–13).

Facing this decision, Orpah gave ear to the whisperings of her natural heart and returned "to her people and to her gods." But Ruth "clung" (RSV) to her mother-in-law, and testified in poetic language that spiritually she had become united with the people and God of Naomi (1:16, 17). This decision of Ruth is a prelude to Pentecost, the first inclusion of a heathen in the people of God; and in her touching words we have a pentecostal confession of a union with God and His people, with the Lord and His Church.

The arrival of Naomi and Ruth in Bethlehem caused a commotion. The painful experiences of the preceding ten years had so changed Naomi that she was hardly recognizable (1:19). She could not reconcile herself to the guidance of God in her life and therefore asked the women rather to call her Mara, that is, Bitter, "for the Almighty [cf. Ex. 6:2; Job 27:2] has dealt very bitterly with me." She had set forth from Bethlehem blessed with a woman's most precious possessions, a husband and sons, but the Lord willed that she return empty. Through His judgment the Lord has "testified against" (KJV) her (cf. Job 10:17), and the Almighty has brought calamity upon (RSV) her (v. 21). Naomi is here the prey of the "theology" of her time which asserted that the measure of one's misfortune stands in close proportion to the personal offense committed (cf. Lk. 13:1–5). At this point she reaches depths of despair, feeling that even God has deserted her.

The dark cloud of affliction, nevertheless, had a silver lining:

Naomi did not return utterly empty. With her was Ruth, the Moabitess, who is characterized as she who returned from the country of
Moab, with this confidence: to the only true God. Furthermore, they
arrived in Bethlehem at the "beginning of the barley harvest" (cf.
II Sam. 21:9). Consequently, this time there would be no shortage
of bread. The same God who brought calamity upon Naomi had thus
provided for the maintenance both of life and of the generation and
inheritance of Elimelech.

III. *A Surprising Encounter (2:1–23)*

For literary beauty, the story of the meeting of Ruth and Boaz is
among the most striking in the Bible. The man who was to play such
an important role in the future history, is introduced as "kinsman"
(*Moda'*, Hebrew) of the family of Elimelech, a man who, in spite
of the prolonged famine, was still master of considerable possessions,
territory and servants (2:1). Ruth is, however, still unknown to this
man. In accordance with the ordinance in the law of Israel (cf. Lev.
19:9, 10; 23:22; Deut. 24:19–22) providing for the needy, she proposes to glean among the ears of grain. Ruth, not wanting to take
"the right of the poor" for granted, declares that she will only glean
ears where she is favorably received (cf. 2:7). Possibly one of the
evils in the time of the judges was that the landowners took no notice
of the stipulation in this law, not understanding its dual meaning:
that the owners are merely stewards of the land and harvest, and that
the crops as a gift from God are destined for all God's children, including foreigners. Ruth goes to gather ears of corn with Naomi's
permission.

Unintentionally she "happened to come" (cf. I Sam. 6:9; Lk.
10:31) to the part of the field belonging to Boaz. The events that
follow make it obvious that God has guided her. Later that same
day (2:4) Boaz appears on the land. The way he and his servants
greet each other reflects the friendly relationship between this employer and his employees (cf. Judg. 6:12; Ps. 129:8). Despite the differences between them, they belong together as children of the same
family, the family of God; and in this, something is seen of the relationships in the renewed community as the result of the atonement
of Christ and the work of the Holy Spirit.

In answer to Boaz's question "Whose maiden is this?" a sympathetic and complete account is given (2:6, 7). Here Boaz meets the woman of whom he has heard favorable tidings (v. 11). He addresses her kindly in a manner that bespeaks a considerable difference in age (cf. 3:10) and having already given further orders in her interest (2:9), admonishes her not to go to another harvest field. Overwhelmed by this kindness, she falls on her face, bowing to the ground, the usual sign of obeisance (cf. Gen. 33:3; I Sam. 24:9; 25: 23; II Kings 4:37). She cannot understand why Boaz takes notice of her, a foreigner (v. 10). Boaz, in his answer, expresses his appreciation for what she has done for Naomi, and voices his acceptance of her as a spiritual daughter of Abraham (vv. 11, 12). It was no trivial matter to leave father, mother, and land of birth. Boaz likens Ruth's "venture of love" to Abraham's "venture of faith" (Gen. 12:1).

The words of verse 12a recall the blessing of Abraham (Gen. 15:1; cf. Ps. 19:12; 119:1, 2; Mt. 5:12). Ruth called herself a foreigner, but the fact is that she had come to take refuge under the wings of the God of Israel (cf. Ex. 19:4; Deut. 32:11; Ps. 17:8; 36:8; 57:2; 63:8; 91:4; Mt. 23:37) as an indication of her wholehearted dedication. Many interpreters regard this verse as the key verse of the whole book.

Ruth was touched and comforted by the kind words of Boaz even though she dared not hope to share the privileges of the humblest of his maidservants (2:13). Her participation in the meal was also evidence of the special place she occupied in the growing love and respect of Boaz. She could partake of the meal, and as dessert Boaz handed her so much of the parched grain (cf. I Sam. 17:17) that she ate until she was satisfied and still had some left over (v. 14; cf. v. 18). Ruth felt herself to be lower than the humblest maidservant (v. 13), but Boaz treated her as a lady of honor (cf. Ps. 113:7, 8), while his gracious gifts (vv. 15, 16) eased her task considerably. When she beat out that which she had gleaned during the day, she had a quantity of twenty-seven pounds, more or less (v. 17).

This striking description of the love of the wealthy Boaz, who raised Ruth from humiliation and loaded her with precious gifts, is a figure of the grace of God in Christ Who lifts the unworthy sinner out of the depths of sin and enriches his life with spiritual and temporal blessings (cf. Rom. 8:32; II Cor. 8:9). With her barley and surplus parched grain (2:14), Ruth returned to the city (v. 18). Naomi was greatly surprised; her question and blessing expressed the realization that something exceptional had happened. Her joy increased, however, and her words became more fervent, when she learned that Ruth had worked in the fields of Boaz. She clearly noticed the hand of God in this, for Boaz was "one of our nearest kin" (RSV, Hebrew, "redeemers"), thus a man pointed out by law and tradition to see that justice was done to his impoverished and lonely relations (cf. Lev. 25:25–34, 47–49). Naomi realized in a flash that the "kindness" (Hebrew, *chesed*) of the Lord had not forsaken the "living or the dead" (RSV, vv. 19, 20). Meanwhile, Ruth went on gleaning until the end of the barley and wheat harvests, which lasted from April until June (v. 23). In this simple information lies a world of expectation, patience, and faith that the meeting had not been in vain. Naomi and Ruth had also to learn that the fulfilment of God's plan often includes long periods of waiting.

IV. Wholehearted Dedication (3:1–18)

After the long period of expectation from the beginning to the end of the harvest, Naomi took the initiative (a confirmation of the fact that the position of women in the Old Testament was not as unfavorable as that of the women of nearby countries) and devised a daring plan which conformed to the stipulations in the law and to the ways established by tradition. She aimed at a "place of rest" (cf. 1:9) for Ruth, in the sense of a marital union, and linked the duty of a kinsman and the levirate in an unusual manner. The person concerned had to buy the land to ease the financial strain and at the same time had to marry Ruth (instead of Naomi, as the latter was too old to bear children) to preserve the lineage of the deceased (cf. 4:3–5). Although Naomi's proposition was very unusual, the sequel proves that it was not to be regarded as incongruous (cf. 3:10–14; 4:5).

The drama now shifts to the threshing floor, a hard, level floor on which the threshed grain was thrown to be winnowed by the evening breeze (cf. Job 21:18; Ps. 1:4; Mt. 3:12). Ruth has to wash and anoint herself as for a marriage feast (Ezek. 16:8–14) or religious ceremony (Ex. 30:17, 18), as a sign that her mourning was over (cf. II Sam. 12:20; Mt. 6:17). Further, she had to go later in the night and lie at Boaz's feet unobserved, waiting to do as he said. By this action Ruth, so to speak, entreated Boaz to marry her. Considering the possibility of the request not being granted, this action had to take place in secret to prevent later embarrassment (3:3, 4; cf. v. 14). Ruth's self-surrender to this plan in which her future and her honor were at stake is complete (vv. 5, 6). Consciously following a well recognized ritual, by which such a claim was customarily made, Ruth's action implied no immodesty. When Boaz in consternation discovered a woman at his feet (v. 8), Ruth shyly made known who she was and asked him to spread his "skirt," literally "wing," over her. The Targum (or Aramaic paraphrase) recognizes this as in itself a claim to espousal, because "wing" also implies the corner of the blanket (cf. Deut. 22:30; 27:20; Ezra 16:8). The expression can, however, also mean that Boaz put her under his protection (cf. 2:12). Her request is founded upon the fact that he is a redeemer (3:9), one that has the right to redeem (KJV, marginal note). The wider interpretation of the term "redeemer" is probably connected with the deeper idea of the redeeming power of God of which that of a mortal is a foreshadowing (cf. Ex. 6:6; Ps. 74:2; Is. 43:1; 44:23; 28:20; Job 19:25).

Boaz's answer is to bless and praise Ruth for her obedience to the voice of piety above that of nature. Her first kindness (*chesed*) she showed in following Naomi to Bethlehem (2:11) and the last in her willingness, through her love for her late husband and her mother-in-law, to become the wife of the man pointed out according to the law of Israel (3:10). In this delicate situation Boaz reacted with sensitivity and piety. The call of his natural heart is sublimated in obedience to the demand of the law and the fear of the Lord. Boaz put her at her ease with the assurance that he would do everything she desired because "all my fellow townsmen" (RSV, literally, "the whole gate of my people") knew that she was a "virtuous woman" (KJV, cf. Prov. 12:4; 31:10).

There was, however, a kinsman nearer than himself, one who had therefore a prior claim to fulfil the duties of a redeemer (3:12). If he did not fulfil his duty, Boaz would, "as true as the Lord lives" (cf. Judg. 8:19; I Sam. 14:39, 45). Being thus assured, Ruth tarried on the threshing floor till the next morning, when very early and unobserved she returned home with some barley (vv. 14, 15). The purity of the awakening love between Boaz and Ruth foreshadows the new man, his desires of heart and body in complete accord with God's holiness and purity. On arrival, Ruth informed her mother-in-law of all that Boaz had said and done, and showed her the barley which he had given her as token of solicitude for Naomi (vv. 16, 17).

Naomi was assured that Boaz would not rest before the matter was accomplished (v. 18). Ruth's complete devotion was bearing fruit.

V. Complete Redemption (4:1–17)

The final day of redemption arrived for the family from Bethlehem. Early that morning Boaz went up to the gate, because he expected to find the nearer kinsman there, and because the city gate was the place where agreements were made and lawsuits settled (Gen. 23:10, 18; Deut. 25:7; Job 5:4; Prov. 22:22; Is. 29:21; Amos 5:12, 15). When the kinsman came by, Boaz addressed him as (literally) "Mr. so and so" (cf. I Sam. 21:3; II Kings 6:8; Mt. 26:18) and requested him to sit down (4:1). When both sides were represented, the lawsuit began. The judges and witnesses were the elders of the city, that is, the heads of the most important families who controlled the city's affairs (cf. Deut. 21:2; 25:7, 8; I Kings 21:8) and usually gathered at the gate for such proceedings (v. 2). When everyone was seated, Boaz explained the situation in the fashion of the East. A piece of land which Naomi wanted to sell belonged to Elimelech. The kinsman's duty in this instance was to take the responsibility of caring for the impoverished family. The kinsman concerned was willing to redeem (v. 4). Then Boaz played his trump and pointed out the singularity of this instance, that is, that the land was encumbered by the levirate: the one who bought the land had to buy Ruth also (cf. RSV, marginal note, "in order to restore the name of the dead to his inheritance," v. 5). The first kinsman found the servitude too great; Josephus and the Targum suggest that he was already married. In any event, he could mar his own inheritance by spending money on land belonging not to himself but to any issue Ruth might have. The kinsman refused to take any risks, the law not explicitly demanding that he should redeem. His chief motive in "fulfilling" the law was, as with so many others, merely a matter of calculated self-interest.

To interpret the action in 4:8 based on a custom which had become obsolete, an explanation is given in verse 7. Many connect the removal of the shoe with the rule in Deuteronomy 25:8–10 (cf. RSV, marginal note). There is, however, a difference in purpose. In the Deuteronomy passage, the action serves to humiliate those who refuse to accept the levirate. In the passage here, there is no word of humiliation and no reference to the levirate; it concerns the right of property. The taking off of the shoe lends the force of law to the matter concerning the redemption and exchanging. The shoe symbolized the right of the owner to set foot upon the land (cf. Ps. 8:7; 60:10). The nearer kinsman ceded his rights to Boaz and confirmed this by the symbolical act described in verse 7 (v. 8). With an appeal to the witnesses present, Boaz assumed the responsibilities connected with the redemption in this singular instance. The land became his property (v. 9) and Ruth instead of Naomi became his wife, to perpetuate the name of the dead (that of Mahlon and/or Elimelech) in his inheritance (v. 10).

In this action of Boaz, we have an illustration of the fact that the law is fulfilled in and by love. The far-reaching responsibilities of this particular case called for a man of integrity, who would not try to fulfil the law with as little exertion as possible, but who would do as much as he could to abound in the service of God. Boaz in this respect was a type of Christ who was completely willing and able to fulfil the demand of God through love. He gave Himself in a special sense to free His Church, His bride, and to enrich her with His wealth in her poverty. As through Boaz, the redeemer, the name and inheritance of Elimelech and his generation were saved, so Christ saves the name of all who belong to Him and gives them an eternal inheritance.

Those present confirmed the fact that they had witnessed the transaction thus settled. They gave a blessing which recalls Genesis 24:60, a blessing of many children and a large, glorious posterity. Ruth the Moabitess was officially accepted in Israel by the representatives of the city and was given a place of honor with the other great ancestresses of the house of Israel (4:11; cf. Gen. 29 and 30). The comparison with the house of Peres, the son of Judah by Tamar (Gen. 38), is made because Peres was one of Boaz's forefathers and was also born out of a levirate union.

God sanctioned the deed of redemption (4:9, 10) in the fertility of Ruth (v. 13). Only then was the deed fully accomplished, for in a wider sense this little boy (cf. 2:20; 3:9) could also be called "redeemer" (v. 14) as the name and inheritance of Elimelech would continue independently in him. The fact that in all the genealogies he is called the son of Boaz is not contradictory, especially if we accept the fact that he was the only son of his parents and thus represented both generations, that of Elimelech as well as that of Boaz.

The favor of God, which, according to Naomi, had left her (1:21), now returned. The boy would strengthen her soul (cf. Ps. 23:3; Lam. 1:11), for, although he had been born to Ruth, he would learn to love Naomi (4:15). Naomi answered to the blessings of the women by regarding the child as her own (cf. Gen. 30:3). In choosing his name, the women took into consideration the fact that the child actually belonged to Naomi in her old age (cf. v. 15). His calling and destiny would be to serve, to perpetuate the generation which otherwise would have died out. In God's plan, however, he was predestined to be of higher service, that is, to be the grandfather of David, the famous king of Israel, and thus also the forefather of Jesus Christ (cf. Mt. 1:5; Lk. 3:32; 22:27; Mk. 10:45).

VI. Significant Genealogy (4:18–22)

The story ends in a genealogy in which the connection between Peres and David is seen, that is, between the forefather of the royal family of Judah (cf. Gen. 49:8, 10) and the man in whom the ideal of the true theocratic kingship was embodied. The genealogy consists of ten names with the omission of others for reasons unknown to us (cf. I Chron. 2:5; 9:15; Mt. 1:3–6). The reader's attention is here turned to the larger significance of the story, namely, the genealogy of the Messiah, Who every Israelite knew was to spring from David.

In this genealogy, the plan of God in the lives of this family is crowned and ended. But the narrative also reveals the golden threads woven through the lives and adventures of these people. Here a commonplace life with its usual experiences, with its seemingly unanswerable questions, its afflictions and blessings, its weal and woe, is put to use by God in preparing for the advent of His Son and His Kingdom. This living theme God wishes to apply through the Book of Ruth to the history of His Church and the life of a Christian, that "all things work together for good to them that love God, to them who are the called according to his purpose" (Rom. 8:28).

I Samuel

WILLIAM J. MARTIN

THE BOOKS OF SAMUEL, treated in the Hebrew text as one book and placed among the prophetical writings, were probably assigned this title because of the initial and central role played by Samuel in an era second in importance only to that of the Exodus. The authorship of the books is not ascribed to Samuel, but it is explicitly stated that he was engaged in scribal activities (I Sam. 10:25). The statement in I Chronicles 29:29—"And the matters of David the king, the first and the last, they are written in the records of Samuel the seer, and of Nathan the prophet, and of Gad the prophet-seer"—would seem to imply that Samuel was joint author with Nathan and Gad. The events recorded cover a period of about one hundred years, probably from about 1050–950 B.C.

Hebrew writing of history is not the mere pegging out of events on the line of time. Acts, not dates, are the stuff of which it is made. Not the *time* of the event, but the *event* itself as the realization of a wilful act, divine or human, alone has significance and must be assigned its proper place in the scale of true values.

The Books of Samuel contain some of the finest historical writing in all literature. There is here no party, class, or personal bias to distort the picture, no spotlighting of the good or shading of the bad, no calculated juxtaposing of statements to blunt the truth. Here is laid bare the universal frailty of human nature; here stands naked the sinner beneath the royal garment; here is revealed the hidden cause behind the visible effect; here truth suffers neither from the malignity of cunning foe nor the menace of ignorant friend. This history differs not only in degree, but also in kind, from all other history of the ancient East. The records of Assyria and Egypt tell us much that is invaluable about their civilizations, their religions, the activities of their kings. About the characters of the kings themselves, alas, we learn but little. Were they good men or bad? Were they truly upright or wicked? What value did they place on truth? To such questions as these, the copious documents supply no answers.

It is not so with the men and kings who come to life in the pages of the Books of Samuel. Not even a royal robe can screen the heart of its wearer. No royal status can procure for him preferential treatment; no royal privacy can insure the secrecy of his thoughts and motives. Royal apparel is accounted here only as the trappings of the stage, and the man beneath the stage-costume stands exposed as one of ourselves, the victim of petty jealousies, petty hates, and petty pride. His sad lot, like ours, is to be beset with a seeming dual personality; within his breast dwells a sinning, scheming Jacob and a heavenly-minded Israel, now the one in command, now the other; kindness prevailing today, tomorrow cruelty; demanding in others the standards of an Israel, defenseless against the Jacob in his own heart; the sovereign of all, himself the subject and slave of his own sinful passions. Surely, one of the greatest of academic follies must be that which professes to see in all this only two separate and contradictory traditions. When scholarship jettisons common sense, the rocks are not far ahead.

The Books of Samuel may be divided into three main divisions, each corresponding roughly to the life and acts of Samuel, of Saul, and of David. There is inevitably considerable overlapping, and some of the subsections might well be treated as main divisions. Nevertheless, it will probably be found that the contents can be more easily mastered if the broad threefold division is kept in mind.

While Samuel is rightly placed at the head of the prophetic succession (Acts 3:24), he also acted as a judge (in the sense of chief administrator of state affairs) and was in fact the last and greatest of these "judges" (I Sam. 4:18; 7:15; Acts 13:20). He officiated as a priest (I Sam. 13:18 implies that it was his sole perogative to offer sacrifices.) He belonged to a section of the Levites which had been settled in Ephraim (Josh. 21:20 and I Chron. 6:33), but he was not of the Aaronic line, which went back to Kohath's firstborn, Amran, while his came from the second son (Ex. 6:18 and I Chron. 6:22). The replacement of Eli by Samuel was thus the rejection of the Aaronic priesthood. Upon him, too, was thrust the role of "kingmaker," anointing Saul, the first (I Sam. 10:1), and David, the greatest of Israel's kings (16:13). The fate of Israel in one of the most critical epochs in her history—the transition from a theocracy to a monarchy—was in his hands.

In the Books of Samuel, stress begins to be laid on the distinction between the external, representative nature of ritual acts and the inner, primary importance of the state of heart. One of Israel's most inveterate failings was to confuse the visible rites with the inner life of faith, of which they were the outward expression, and without which they were but empty symbols (I Sam. 15:22). It was an age of materialism and ruthlessness, inimical to the true faith, and we must not expect to find the standards of men with centuries of evangelical tradition behind them. Besides, it is never the purpose of the record to vindicate human character; it simply depicts it as it really is. Yet Samuel's faith remaind unimpaired, a testimony to his own and succeeding generations, and it gained for him a place among the heroes of the faith praised in the eleventh chapter of Hebrews (v. 32). There his name is linked with that of David, about whose life and motives we here learn so much that deepens our understanding of many of the psalms of this shepherd king. Saul's attempt to make contact with the dead Samuel provides unambiguous proof of the largely tacit belief of the Israelites in a life beyond the grave.

The Books of Samuel form an indispensable chapter in the divine revelation of God's dealings with His people, individually and nationally, and in divine instruction in the meaning of the spiritual realities behind the visible forms of worship. Moreover, they provide us with the record of the steps taken by God to preserve Israel for her twofold purpose: to be the recipients of the oracles of God, and to bring forth, in accordance with the foretold pattern, the Messiah.

A better understanding of conditions in the ancient Semitic East and of Hebrew usage now enables us to give reasonable and sensible explanations of the alleged discrepancies and contradictions which some scholars profess to have found in the narratives. In this commentary, the answers are generally indicated at the appropriate place in the discussion, but the problems themselves are not usually explicitly mentioned.

I. Samuel, Last of the Judges, First of the Prophets (1:1—8:22)

1. Family Background: Birth and Dedication (1:1—2:11)

Samuel's family were Zophites or Zuphites, a section of the Rama-thites (reading Ramathites not as a geographical name but as a plural, with Zophites in apposition, thus, "the Ramathites, Zophites," or in other words, "Zophite Ramathites." The sentence [1:1] would then read: "Now there was a certain man from the Zophite Rama-thites." This construction is much used in Hebrew, especially after personal names; for example, Shimei, the Ramathite, I Chron. 27:27). Ramah was the chief town of his home province and, as was customary in the ancient Semitic East, it gave its name to the sur-rounding populated district (cf. 19:18 where the village or town of Naioth is stated to be in Ramah, and 22:6 where a place Gibeah is, according to the Hebrew, in Ramah). It lay some twenty miles northwest of Jerusalem, in the highlands of Ephraim.

Samuel's father, Elkanah, was a God-fearing man, the husband of two wives, Hannah and Peninnah, between whom relations were strained by Peninnah's arrogance towards the childless Hannah. Hannah's misfortune, however, did not decrease her husband's affection for her (1:8); indeed, she was often the object of special favors. Verse 5 is difficult. Perhaps it should be translated, "but he used to give to Hannah as a portion one of the baked things." There is some indication that things baked were especially esteemed (cf. Gen. 40:17 and Lev. 7:9).

The book opens with the household attending a yearly feast, possibly the Passover, at Shiloh. Even here Peninnah's attacks con-tinue, and Hannah is driven to pray fervently for a son. As she prays inaudibly, she is seen by Eli, the priest, who assumes that she is drunk—a sad commentary on the then low state of true religion. God answers her prayer and she names her child Samuel, that is, the name of God. The name is probably best explained as the resid-ual, significant words of the sentence spoken by Hannah, in full, perhaps, "From the Lord I asked him for *the name* (or honor) *of God*" or "From the Lord I asked for him a *godly name*" (cf. the name of Seth, where only one word is taken from the sentence, Gen. 4:25; or that of Noah, meaning "rest," where the operative word is not repeated: "this—namely 'rest'—will comfort us," and so forth Gen. 5:29).

Hannah, when Samuel is weaned, takes him to Eli at Shiloh and formally dedicates him to life-service in the temple (1:24–28). Then follows her great paean of triumph, the outpouring of the heart of a gifted woman. She praises God for her portion: joy, strength, victory (2:1); for the person of God: unique in holiness, in being, and in saving power (v. 2); He knows and assesses the proud talkers and the arrogant boasters (v. 3); for the wonders of victory: material might is ineffective, the weak are strong, the rich impoverished and the hungry fed, the barren are fruitful and the fertile feeble. Life belongs to God: He fills and empties the grave (v. 5); He is the Lord of all human destinies (vv. 7–9); for the ultimate victory and final judgment are His; He will exalt the kingly Messiah (v. 10). Little wonder that at the birth of the promised Messiah, His mother's song of praise reminds us of Hannah's hymn (Lk. 1:46–55).

2. Failure of Eli, the High Priest (2:12—3:21)

His Sons' Apostasy and the Penalty (2:12–36) The wicked practices of Eli's sons had brought religion into contempt. Eli remonstrates with them, but it is too late. A man of God is sent to warn him: the priestly privileges (Ex. 27:21) had been forfeited and judgment is at hand. The house of Aaron will be all but exterminated, his own house will be reduced to beggary, but from elsewhere God will find a faithful priest.

First Revelation to Samuel (3:1–21). God's first communication with Samuel was a confirmation of the warning to Eli: imminent punishment for his sons' inquity and for his own lack of discipline. Samuel reluctantly discloses the contents of the message to Eli, who receives it humbly without a trace of resentment. Samuel's prophetic status is recognized by all Israel.

3. War with the Philistines (4:1—7:14)

Loss of the Ark of the Covenant (4:1–22). Israel defeated turns for help, as so often in her history, to the externals of religion, in this instance to her most sacred object, the ark of the covenant. Disaster follows, thousands are slain, including Eli's sons, and the ark falls into the hands of the Philistines.

Disastrous Presence of the Ark (5:1—6:1). The ark is placed in the temple of Dagon, whose image next morning is on the ground. Righted by the Philistines, it is found on the second morning shattered (the damage seems to indicate that the image was in an attitude of blessing with his hands raised above his head). Next follows an epidemic of tumors. The association of these tumors with mice, more probably a species of rats, strongly suggests the bubonic plague.

Return of the Ark (6:2—7:2). Its presence having become unbearable, the ark is returned with a guilt offering in the form of five golden tumors and five golden mice (or rats). The cows drawing the cart, although deprived of their young, made straight for Beth-shemesh. Here profane curiosity causes a disaster (it is probably best to read: He slew seventy men, there being fifty thousand men), and the ark passes to Kiriath-jearim.

Defeat of the Philistines (7:3–14). The negative and the positive aspects of repentance are clear: turn from idols, turn to God (I Thess. 1:9). The result is victory over the Philistines and a prolonged peace, commemorated by the erection of a memorial stone, Ebenezer.

4. Judgeship of Samuel and Demand for a King (7:15—8:22)

The pattern of Samuel's judgeship was that of a circuit judge at Bethel, Gilgal, and Mizpah, but his permanent home was in his native place of Ramah. The conduct of his worldly sons is given as a reason for demanding a king, though the real reason may well have been the desire for conformity with other nations (8:20). God bids Samuel acquiesce; he does so, but not without a final rebuke to the people. The price of the monarchy will be conscription, taxation, and serfdom.

II. Saul, Israel's First King (9:1—15:35)

1. Saul's Early Success as King (9:1—12:25)

His Anointing and Presentation (9:1—10:27). An informative sidelight on the activity of Samuel shows him away from secular duties. He entertains guests, no doubt for a spiritual purpose, and maintains an intensive religious life with his own private altar, a pattern that has been repeated in innumerable men of God in the history of the Church, men who were so outstanding in public life that it was assumed by most people that this was the only side to their lives, whereas they maintained in private life a vital participation in spiritual work. Many of Michael Faraday's scientific contemporaries, for instance, might have been amazed to find him engaged on Sundays in pastoral work in a small non-conformist chapel. Saul, obviously with little knowledge of or interest in religious affairs, expected to find a mercenary seer. (In 9:9 we have for the first time a note being made of the fact that words change meaning.)

When Saul appears before Samuel, the Lord reveals to him that this is the future king. Saul is privately anointed and is told to expect confirmatory signs. Later Samuel convenes a public assembly and Saul, in accordance with custom, is taken by lot and is given a public acclamation. Samuel draws up in writing the royal constitution (10:25).

Victory Vindicates Samuel's Choice (11:1–15). Saul rouses Israel against the Ammonites and delivers Jabesh-gilead. Later, Saul's election is ratified by all the people.

Samuel's Retirement (12:1–25). Samuel makes a vindicatory speech and proceeds to a recapitulation of God's great deeds and the many misdeeds of the people. God, he reminds them, has acquiesced in their demand for a king, but He remains their supreme head. Samuel promises his continued intercession and instruction.

2. Consolidation of Saul's Kingship (13:1—14:52)

Saul Intrudes in Priestly Domain (13:1–15). Saul creates a standing army and puts part of it under Jonathan, his son. A victorious skirmish with a Philistine garrison brings about a general mobilization of the Philistines. Saul, in fear and impatient at Samuel's non-arrival, offers sacrifices. Samuel thereupon arrives and severely rebukes him. His foolish act of disobedience has lost for him the kingdom.

Clash with the Philistines: Jonathan's Success (13:16—14:23). Israel, weakened by long subjugation to the Philistines and by disarmament (13:19–23), has now to meet them in the hour of crisis with a depleted army. Jonathan with his armor-bearer in a surprise attack throws the Philistines into panic and confusion. Israel launches a general attack and is victorious.

Jonathan's Unwitting Violation of Saul's Order (14:24–45). Thereafter Jonathan unwittingly violates Saul's order for a fast upon the day of battle. But the people determine that Jonathan shall not die, and he is saved despite Saul's decree.

Other Victories (14:46–48, 52). Saul wages war not only on the Philistines, but also on his enemies on every side, and wins many victories. But despite these victories, Israel was never to know peace in Saul's time.

Genealogical Note (14:49–51). This brief listing of Saul's sons and daughters, as well as other members of his house, would be of greater interest had Saul's line continued in the kingship.

3. Punitive Campaign against the Amalekites (15:1–35)

Saul mobilizes all available forces. The Kenites, who had befriended the Israelites in the past (Judg. 1:16) and who had settled among the Amalekites, are forewarned and depart.

Saul's Partial Obedience (15:1–31). The Amalekites are exterminated, but Saul spares their king, Agag, and the best of their flocks and herds. Saul's lapse is revealed to Samuel by the Lord, and on his way to Saul he is told of his conceit (v. 12). When they meet, Saul's self-laudatory speech is interrupted by the telltale bleating of the sheep (v. 14). His excuse—animals spared to provide a sacrifice for *your* God—does not ring true. Samuel severely censures him and reminds him that obedience is the first and greatest service to God. No right ritual can take the place of a right heart. Saul shows contrition but shrinks from an open breach with Samuel. Samuel finally consents to join him in public worship, but this proves to be their last formal meeting.

Execution of Agag (15:32, 33). Samuel orders Agag to be brought in and, after giving a reason for his sentence, executes him or has him executed. The word used occurs only here, and the traditional meaning of "hewed in pieces" rests on no reliable etymology. It may be related to a somewhat similar word meaning "sweep away".

Rejection of Saul (15:34, 35). At this point, Samuel and Saul separate. Samuel's departure signalizes God's rejection of Israel's first king.

III. Rise of David (16:1—31:13)

1. Selection of David (16:1–23)

Samuel, grieving because of Saul's failure, departs, but God rebukes him for his grief and commissions him to go to the house of Jesse at Bethlehem and to anoint one of his sons as the future king. The anxious inquiry and apprehension of the elders as to the purpose of Samuel's visit indicate the greatness of the authority he wielded among the people. Samuel reassures them that his visit is of a religious nature, and invites them and Jesse and his sons to sacrifice. None of the sons present is chosen, but when the absent David is brought from the sheep, he is recognized as God's choice and is anointed. Samuel offers no explanation of this act to the company. It was probably assumed that David was being dedicated for special divine service. Soon after David is taken to Saul's court to play the lyre to Saul, now afflicted with an evil spirit, in an attempt to restore him. The treatment was, at least temporarily, successful.

Saul likes David and makes him one of his armor-bearers. The fact that we was made *an* armor-bearer (so the Hebrew) may indicate that is was only an honorary title. Verse 21 very probably amplifies verse 19 which states only the bald fact that David's presence was demanded; verse 21 would explain that the request was made graciously. If this is so, then we should read in verse 21 "Now Saul *had* sent unto Jesse saying, let David stand before me, for he has found favour in my eyes." The expression "to stand before" never means "to remain."

2. David and Goliath (17:1–54)

The Philistines had mobilized, and the Israelites took up battle positions. In the space between the two armies, a Philistine champion, Goliath, appeared, challenging the Israelites to produce a representative to fight with him and thus to decide the issue by single combat. This seems to have been a fairly common practice in ancient warfare: Manlius Torquatus, a Roman, for example, according to tradition killed in single combat a giant Gaul in 361 B.C. Goliath was well over nine feet tall and wore scale armor, the weight of which was about 125 pounds. All his equipment was in keeping with his gigantic proportions. (Men of the size of Goliath are not unknown: John Middleton, about A.D. 1600, whose grave is at Hale outside Liverpool, was nine feet, three inches.) Goliath's appearance struck terror into the hearts of the Israelites.

David's three brothers had been called up and David acted as their supplier of rations. The statement (17:15) that David was going back and forth to Saul, does not mean personal visits to Saul, but merely to Saul's army. (Names or titles are often used in this extensive manner; for example, 15:7, "Saul smote the Amalekites," that is, the army of Saul smote them. Moreover the compound preposition found here indicates that his home was his starting-point, not Saul's camp. If the latter had been the case, the preposition "unto" would have been used.) David's first visit to Saul would terminate with an improvement in Saul's condition, and a considerable period may have elapsed before the events recorded here took place. Saul's failure to recognize David is understandable in the light of his mental illness, and there are a number of possible reasons why others did not know him. In the interval, David's appearance may have changed, for instance, the growth of a beard could have made him unrecognizable; or, again, at the court there would be hundreds of young men coming and going, all equally important to their contemporaries. The spotlight of history had not yet for them— as it has for us—rested upon David.

On one particular visit by David, Goliath appeared again, as he had been doing for the past forty days. When David asked what would be done for the man who successfully challenged this Philistine (17:26), he was told that the king would reward the victor with much wealth and give him his daughter to wife. (Verse 26 could be read: "For David had said," and so forth.) Knowing only too well that the men may be fooling him, he turns to others to seek confirmation of this story. His remarks in consequence reach the ears of Saul, who thereupon sends for him. When Saul sees his youthful appearance, he tells him that he could not fight a professional warrior like Goliath. When David recounts to Saul his success against predatory lions and bears (v. 34), Saul agrees to his going and dresses David in his armor.

David, having had no experience of armor, finds it too unwieldy and puts it off. He goes forth with only his staff, his sling and five smooth stones (men early recognized the value of streamlining). Each stone may have weighed about one pound and, as a stone would leave the sling at a speed of between 100 to 150 miles per hour, a direct hit on a normal skull would have killed a man outright. David would have practiced slinging from his childhood. If the men of Gibeah could sling at a hair and not miss (Judg. 20:16), we may be sure that David was little less skilful. One stone accurately was all that he required to slay the Philistine. The defeat of their champion on the terms that had been laid down, doubtless as agreed beforehand with his commanders, signalized a general defeat and subjugation (17:9). They, therefore, sought to save themselves by flight. The Israelites pursued them right up to the gates of Gath and Ekron and then returned to pillage their camp (vv. 51–53).

3. *David's Relationship with Saul (17:55—20:42)*

David is now brought before Saul. The shepherd youth, who previously was merely one of the vast numbers of similar youths entrusted with the carrying of supplies to the camp, now suddenly emerges as a national hero, and his identity, before a matter of indifference, must now be established. This is the obvious explanation for Saul's inquiring about his parentage. As a secondary motive, there was the fact that Saul now viewed him as a future son-in-law. The general statement in 18:5 records Saul's treatment of David as viewed publicly. He set him "over" or "among" the warriors—the preposition could have either meaning.

Friendship with Jonathan (18:1–7). An even greater achievement on this memorable day than the slaying of Goliath was the winning of the friendship of Jonathan. The acquisition of a friend is always more difficult than the defeat of a foe. It would not have been surprising if Jonathan had begrudged David his success and had fallen a victim to jealously. Instead, this is one of the loveliest friendships recorded in the pages of history.

Saul's Open Hostility (18:8—19:17). As Saul heard the women of Israel, at the great public reception accorded to him and David, praising the exploits of David more highly than his own, the seed of jealousy was planted in his heart. This brings on his old trouble. He or his courtiers would have learned from David that he was the one whose services had been enlisted in the past to play to the afflicted king, so David is naturally sent to try by his playing to soothe Saul. Twice Saul throws his spear at David, but no one apparently attributes his action to jealousy; it was probably put down to the nervous strain of the battle, what would now be called "war neurosis." The attacks were obviously intermittent and no hint of them would reach the public. In his periods of sanity he would discharge his duties as if nothing were amiss. In one of these periods, he makes David a commander and offers to give him his daughter Merab as wife. With a fickleness that was probably a sympton of his disorder he gives her instead to another. When he learns that his daughter, Michal, loves David, he offers her to him on condition that he slay one hundred Philistines, hoping that David would lose his own life in the attempt. David slays double this number and Saul's fear of him and hostility to him increase.

As a last resort, Saul tries to enlist the help of Jonathan and his servants against David (as the matter under discussion is an assassination, the servants referred to here would be his personal guard). Jonathan defends David, and Saul relents and receives David as before. In another fit, he again tries to spear David. This time David realizes that this is not simply the irresponsible act of a crazy king but is deliberate, and flees. Saul sends messengers to his house, but his wife Michal helps him to escape. When the messengers arrive, she informs them that David is ill. When they return to remove David, they find that what appeared to be a body in the bed is an image. (The word for "image" is *teraphim* and this passage seems to indicate that it denoted a single object—verse 13 speaks of *its* headrest—of about human size. On the other hand, the well-known passage in Gen. 31:34 refers to a number of small images.) The possession of the image probably did not have the approval of David, if he was even aware of its existence, and certainly it would have been condemned by the religious authorities. It was some kind of pagan survival, which had persisted, just as numerous pagan customs and superstitions still survive in many Roman Catholic countries in Europe.

David's Flight (19:18–24). David seeks refuge with Samuel, the spiritual head of the people, at Naioth, either a village or town in the province of Ramah, where a company of prophets had gathered round Samuel, constituting probably a kind of prophetical academy with Samuel as its head. Similar institutions for the training of scribes and archivists had existed in the ancient Semitic East from time immemorial. David fled here, knowing full well that it was the only place where Saul dare not send a military force against him, as he certainly would have done if he had fled to his native place.

All Saul can do is to send messengers. The first lot are overpowered with the spirit of prophecy, and when he sends two other groups, the same thing in turn happens to them.

Finally Saul goes himself, only to find that he, too, yields to an irresistible urge to prophesy. At the sight, people spontaneously took up a saying that had already become proverbial: "Is Saul also among the prophets?" (I Sam. 10:12). The part of the verb used here, "they were saying" (19:24), implies that it was being repeated on all sides, thus there could be no question of its originating on this occasion, and there is here no reference whatever to its becoming a proverb as in 10:12. The fact that Saul meets Samuel here does not contradict the statement in 15:35 ("and Samuel did not continue to see Saul"). The verb "to see" is used there, as it is in a number of other places, in the meaning of "to visit" (cf. II Sam. 13:5, 6; II Kings 8:29). What 15:35 tells us is that Samuel paid no more visits, formal or otherwise, to Saul.

Jonathan's Intervention for David (20:1–42). David seeks out Jonathan and asks him to find out the cause of his father's hatred and what his intentions towards him really are. David is not prepared to risk another appearance at court and suggests that Jonathan should tell his father, if he inquires as to the cause of David's absence, that he has gone on family business to Bethlehem. Saul's reaction to this, David feels, will indicate his true state of mind. Jonathan, believing firmly in David's ultimate success, and seeing in the present fugitive his future saviour, extracts from him a promise to save his house from extinction. He then arranges with David the sign he will use to inform him of Saul's attitude. Saul, when he discovers that David has absented himself, is enraged and abuses Jonathan and even throws his spear at him. When Jonathan meets David, after giving the sign that confirms his father's displeasure, he confines himself to reminding David of the covenant between them.

4. David's Exile (21:1—25:44)

David Obtains the High Priest's Aid (21:1–15. Ahimelech, surprised at David traveling alone, is told by David that he is on the king's business. To David's request for bread, he gives him the consecrated bread (cf. Mt. 12:4 and Mk. 2:26). In Mark, the reference to "in the time of Abiathar, instead of Ahimelech," would make it easier for people to know the approximate time of the event, for it actually happened in his lifetime, and his fame completely overshadowed that of his ill-fated father. Then again the mention of Ahimelech might have been a little confusing as there were two of that name. Our Lord refers to this to show that the apparatus of ritual is not an end in itself, but merely the cipher of which the moral law is the reality. David assures him that the men and their equipment are ritually clean. He points out that in any case "the bread is being sanctified now by the (sacred) vessel," referring apparently to one of the vessels on the special table for the consecrated bread (cf. the account of the construction of this table in Ex. 37:16, where certain objects for it are referred to as "vessels"). The incident very probably happened on a Sabbath day, otherwise ordinary bread could have been easily prepared. David's next request is for weapons, and he is given the sword of Goliath. Having received food and arms, David departs to Achish, the king of Gath, where he finds that his reputation has preceded him. He feigns madness so successfully that the exasperated Achish made a remark far from complimentary to his courtiers: "Am I short of fools?" (v. 15).

Men Won to David's Cause (22:1–5). David's headquarters at Adullam became the rallying point for fugitives and discontents. The nature of the Palestinian terrain makes it easily possible that the cave by its situation was also a "stronghold" (v. 4). David, in view of his precarious position, leaves his parents with the king of Moab. On the advice of Gad, the prophet, he himself moves into Judah.

Saul's Vengeance on Ahimelech (22:6–23). Doeg, the Edomite, had witnessed the scene between David and Ahimelech at Nob, and in response to Saul's appeal for information, discloses what happened. Ahimelech, and all who were with him at Nob, are summoned before Saul, who accuses them of conspiracy and condemns them to death. Only Doeg the Edomite is found ready to carry out the sentence. Ahimelech's son, Abiathar, alone escapes and informs David. David expresses his sense of responsibility for the tragedy and pledges himself to protect Abiathar.

David's Deliverance of the Men of Keilah (23:1–14). Abiathar had brought with him an ephod, and David's first use of it was to obtain guidance in the matter of attacking the Philistines, who were raiding Keilah. The answer is favorable, so he proceeds against them, defeats them and delivers Keilah. When David hears that Saul is plotting to besiege him in Keilah, he consults the ephod again and learns that the men of Keilah will have no compunction in handing him, their saviour, over to his mortal enemy, Saul.

Saul's Life Spared by David (23:15–24:22). Jonathan visits David in the wilderness of Ziph (wilderness was a term used to describe the uncultivated land lying outside the populated areas that surrounded the cities). He encourages David and predicts his accession to the throne, and the two of them enter into a covenant.

The Ziphites reveal David's whereabouts to Saul and offer to hand him over. Saul sets out to capture David, but the report from home of a projected attack by the Philistines compels him to abandon the chase.

Saul, having repulsed the Philistines, returns with a force of army proportions to continue the pursuit. Saul unwittingly enters a cave in the wilderness of Engedi occupied by David and his men. David's men urge him to take advantage of the situation, but he merely cuts off the hem of Saul's garment. After Saul leaves the cave and goes on his way, David comes out and holds up the severed hem. He calls upon Saul to witness his restraint as proof of his innocency. Saul professes repentance and praises David's action. Since David and his men return to the stronghold, it would seem that David doubted the sincerity of his words and attached no importance to Saul's remarks about his becoming king.

Death of Samuel (25:1). The death of Samuel was an occasion for public mourning. He was buried near his home in the province of Ramah. The phrase "in his house" implies "in his estate." Burial within a house would have been inconsistent with the laws of ritual purity (Num. 19:14–22).

David and Nabal (25:2–44). When Nabal, a rich, mean farmer, is having a sheep-shearing, David sends messengers with greetings and reminds Nabal that the safety his shepherds enjoy is due to the presence of his men. Nabal, refusing to give a material expression of gratitude, insults David's servants and proceeds with his carousal. David's planned revenge for this insolent treatment is prevented by the action of Abigail, Nabal's wife, who meets him on the way with gifts of food for his men. When Abigail next morning tells the sobering Nabal of his narrow escape from death, the shock is so great that it brings on a stroke, which some ten days later results in his death. When David hears the news of Nabal's death, he sends servants—doubtless after a suitable lapse of time—with a proposal of marriage to Abigail. She accepts and, though we hear little of her thereafter, we may be certain that this sagacious woman exercised a beneficial restraint on the impetuous David.

5. Gradual Eclipse of Saul (26:1—30:31)

Second Reprieve of Saul's Life (26:1–25). Although this account is different in almost every detail from that in 24:1–22, there are scholars who would see in them only two versions of the same incident. This treatment of the sources, which does violence alike to historical methods and common experience, may be partly due to an indiscriminative lumping together of the account of Saul's interrupted preliminary pursuit and that of the incident in the cave. But in the one, David is in Horesh in the hills (the word is most probably a collective) of Hachilah; in another he is in the wilderness of Engedi, while in still a third he is in the wilderness of Ziph. In fact, the only thing the Engedi incident and the Ziph have in common is the persons of the informers, and for that a very good reason can be given: the Ziphites, having betrayed David once, knew that the only thing that would save them from his vengeance was his capture by Saul, hence their pertinacity to bring about his apprehension. Recurring situations are part and parcel of any sustained pursuit, and the verb "to chase," like the Hebrew "to pursue," denotes primarily a frequentative and not a terminative action. No terrain anywhere could be more favorable to a fugitive than that of Palestine, and here pursuer and quarry might well play their game of hide-and-seek indefinitely. Those who are familiar with this part of Palestine (west of the Dead Sea) should have no difficulty in believing that Saul and David had many a brush and that even the elusive David could not always maintain a safe distance between them, but must often during these years have escaped only by the skin of his teeth.

Leaving aside the account of the preliminary pursuit in 23:19–28, when David was in the wilderness of Maon, the accounts of the other two incidents differ in the following details. The scene of the first is in Engedi (24:1) where David, with Saul's men within a hairbreadth of him, is hiding in a cave. In the second, David is in open country in the hills of Hachilah opposite (not east of) Jeshimmon in the wilderness of Ziph (26:1, 2). In the first, David cuts off the hem of Saul's garment (24:4); in the second, he removes his spear and water jar (26:11). On the first occasion David in addressing Saul adopts a deferential attitude (24:8); on the second, his air is one of mischievous defiance (26:14). In the first, David, still imbued with a spirit of loyalty and a sense of the inherent right of authority, stresses his belief in the inviolability of the person of Saul, the embodiment of this authority (24:10); in the second, his theme is his outrageous treatment at the hands of Saul.

Saul, in the first, expresses repentence and praises the merciful restraint of David (24:16, 17), and takes an oath from David (24:21); in the second, there is only a curt confession of his own wicked folly (26:21) and no appeal to David. The contrast in the sequence is significant: In the first, David by his return to the stronghold, shows that his spirit is unbroken and that his determination to remain free is undiminished (24:22); in the second, his behavior is that of a weary and despondent man who has lost his faith. It must have taken many years to bring about such a change in a man of David's courage (27:1). There must be many cases in history where like incidents were repeated—Bruce on two separate occasions almost captured Edward II. A theory as flimsy as the one that would identify the two collisions of David and Saul could easily bring a whole discipline into disrepute.

David Settles in Ziklag (27:1-12). David as an extreme measure asks Achish, the Philistine king of Gath, to grant him asylum. Achish complies and provides him with accommodation in the town of Ziklag in his territory (Gath, like Ramah, was the name of both the chief town and the surrounding territory, which together made up Achish's kingdom.) From here David carried out raids against people hostile to Israel, but in his reports to Achish he misled him into believing that his attacks were against districts associated with Israel.

Saul Seeks Samuel's Aid through the Witch of Endor (28:1-25). Saul, threatened by a Philistine onslaught, determines to get in touch with the dead Samuel. In the preamble to this incident, three facts necessary for a full appreciation of the situation are referred to: that Samuel, the mouthpiece of God, was dead; that the agents of the unlawful methods of inquiry, namely, the mediums and wizards, had been suppressed by Saul himself; and that Saul had already invoked God in the prescribed ways, but all in vain. Hence it is only in desperation that Saul in disguise enlists the forbidden help of a medium. He asks her to bring up Samuel. The woman reminds him of the ban, but Saul assures her that she has nothing to fear. Much to her surprise and consternation, she succeeds in bringing up Samuel. She attributes her success, apparently, not so much to her own powers as to the importance of the person of her visitor, and concludes that he can be no less a person than the king himself. Samuel predicts defeat at the hands of the Philistines, and the death of Saul and his sons. The mentally and physically exhausted Saul collapses at this dire prediction. The medium insists on his taking food. Afterwards he departs, as he had come, in the night.

In verse 6 we have one of the rare references to *urim*, elliptical for *urim* and *thummim* (cf. Ex. 28:30; Lev. 8:8; Num. 27:21; Ezra 2:63; Neh. 7:65). They were used as a means of ascertaining the will of God. If the addition in the Greek version to I Samuel 14:41 is authentic, then they were used as lots (RSV). They were kept in the pouched breastpiece of the highpriest. Although the words have a plural form they well may have denoted single objects. The words are often taken to mean "lights and perfections"; it may be, however, that the word *urim* is from a root "to curse." If this is so, then they may have been used in the usual form of drawing lots,

Philistines Refuse to Trust David (29:1–11). The Philistine commanders, enroute with their divisions ("with," not "by," hundreds and thousands) to take up battle positions, object to the presence of David. Possibly Achish with his personal affection for David could not view the situation as objectively as his colleagues and officers. There was only one way to allay their suspicion; David had to turn back.

Sacking of Ziklag and David's Pursuit (30:1–31). On his return, David finds Ziklag, the town assigned to him by Achish, sacked and the inhabitants carried off. David calls for the ephod (to which would be attached the breastpiece containing the *urim* and *thummim*) to seek God's guidance. On receiving an encouraging answer, he sets out in pursuit. He finds an Egyptian slave abandoned because of illness by his Amalekite master, and from him he learns the details of the raid. He overtakes the raiders and attacks and destroys them. David recovers his two wives and great quantities of spoil. David decrees that those left behind (v. 21) because of exhaustion will share equally with the combatants. The spoil is so great that he is also able to send portions to the elders of Judah who had befriended him in those places where he had roamed as a fugitive (vv. 26–31). Verse 20 is difficult. A possible translation might be: "And David captured all the flocks and herds, which they [the Amalekites] had carried off at the head of those possessions [referred to in v. 18] and they [the Amalekites] had said, 'This is the spoil of David,'" if we take the last as an objective genitive. In view of David's raiding activities against them, the robbing of David in particular would be to them the sweetest revenge.

Defeat and Death of Saul and Jonathan (31:1–13). The battle on Mount Gilboa goes against Israel and in the slaughter that follows, three sons of Saul, including Jonathan, are slain. Saul, seeing all is lost, chooses death rather than captivity. His armor-bearer refuses to kill him, and Saul is compelled to fall on his own sword. The armor-bearer also kills himself (v. 5 might also be read "When the armour-bearer saw that Saul was dying." This would make it possible to reconcile the Amalekite's version in II Sam. 1:9 with the account here. In other words, Saul's attempt on his life might not have been immediately fatal, although the armor-bearer assumed it was.). The magnitude of the disaster is shown by the fact that whole cities were abandoned (v. 7). When the Philistines came next day to strip the corpses, they find the bodies of Saul and his sons. They take them for exhibition to Bethshan, but the men of Jabesh-gilead recover them by night and bury the remains in Jabesh.

II Samuel

WILLIAM J. MARTIN

THE BOOKS OF SAMUEL, speaking broadly, stress the national aspects of Israel's history and, in spiritual matters, the relation of the individual to God. The Books of Chronicles describe the public aspect of religion and the visible apparatus of worship. Parts of Samuel are incorporated in I Chronicles. The sections substantially the same are as follows:

I Sam. 31	I Chron. 10:1–12
II Sam. 5:1–3, 6–10	I Chron. 11:1–9
II Sam. 5:11–25	I Chron. 14
II Sam. 6:1–11	I Chron. 13
II Sam. 6:12–23	I Chron. 15, 16 (in part only)
II Sam. 7:8, 10	I Chron. 17, 18, 19
II Sam. 11:1; 12:26–31	I Chron. 20:1–3
II Sam. 21:18–22	I Chron. 20:4–8
II Sam. 23:8–39	I Chron. 11:10–41
II Sam. 24	I Chron. 21

As a revelation of character, II Samuel has never been excelled. In it David occupies the stage. With this superimposed unity, the work is largely free from those digressions which sometimes seem to interrupt the continuity of a story.

I. David's Activities After Saul's Death (1:1—4:12)

1. Amalekite Messenger's Account of Saul's Death (1:1–10)

David had been back two days in Ziklag from his successful expedition against the Amalekite raiders who had pillaged it, when a messenger came with news of the outcome of the battle between the Israelites and the Philistines at Gilboa (I Sam. 31:1–6). This man was an Amalekite who claimed to be the son of a resident alien in Israel. His manner is reminiscent of that of the messenger from the battlefield of Aphek who brought the tragic news of the disaster to Eli the priest (I Sam. 4:12–18). Doubtless there was a recognized pattern of procedure and formalized expressions for such solemn occasions. Babylonian and Assyrian letters provide ample evidence of the existence and perpetuation of stereotyped phrases. Long after the introduction of written messages, the phraseology of the days of verbal messages was retained, as for instance in a common introductory formula "To so-and-so say."

If it is felt that the divergences between this account and the one in I Samuel 31:3–6 admit of no explanation, then that in I Samuel, which is put forward as the considered record of the author, must be viewed as authentic. On the other hand, any discrepancy in the account in II Samuel reflects not on the narrative, but on the character of the messenger. It is quite possible that the account given by the Amalekite of Saul's death was the fabrication of an unscrupulous camp-follower out to obtain a reward or to ingratiate himself with David. It is true that this is what he said, whether or not what he said was true (cf. the false account first given to David about the death of all his sons, II Sam. 13:30). As we know nothing of this man's antecedents and character, we can make no final judgment. We might infer, from David's reaction resulting from personal observation of the man, that he was an unprincipled rascal. If, however, we think it unlikely that anyone, honest or dishonest, would deliberately concoct such a story, then we can only assume that Saul did not die immediately from his self-inflicted wound. The phrase "leaning upon his spear" (v. 6) is hardly the wording one would expect to find as the equivalent of "he fell upon his sword" (I Sam. 31:4).

David's treatment of the Amalekite was, of course, largely dictated by his view of the inviolability of the person of the one in authority. In this he was undoubtedly right; his own position and very existence as leader depended on the observance of this principle. Approval of the action of a man who had made no attempt to save the life of the king would have made it impossible for him to deal with disloyalty, if it had arisen among his own followers. David's allegiance to Saul, despite Saul's open hostility to him, was a mark of true statesmanship as well as a proof of his nobility of character. Another factor that may well have weighed with David was the man's ethnic background, in view of his people's treatment of Israel in the remote past (Num. 14:45) and of himself in the immediate past (I Sam. 30:1–10).

2. David's Lament for Saul and Jonathan (1:11–27)

In the lament for Saul and Jonathan, David expresses his deep sense of loss and his pure affection for Jonathan in words that testify to the high quality of his poetic gift. He begins with the foe: the greatness of their rejoicing will be commensurate with the greatness of the loss (v. 20). Then he speaks of the scene of the tragedy (v. 21). He praises the prowess of Jonathan and Saul (v. 22); their shared death was symbolic of the loveliness of their unity in life (v. 23). As great as is the rejoicing in the camp of the foe, so great will be the mourning of the daughters of Israel (v. 24). And finally, David expresses his oppressive sense of loss at the death of Jonathan and his testimony to his amazing and matchless love (v. 26).

The meaning of the heading to this lament (1:18) has never been satisfactorily explained. Perhaps it refers to the section of the Book of Jashar in which it was recorded. With our typographical aids, we indicate that it is a parenthesis; but in the absence of these, Hebrew must depend on the intelligence of the reader. We should probably put it like this: And he said (it is under "For teaching the sons of Judah archery," as found written in the Book of Jashar). Its assignment to a section on archery might be on account of the decisive role played by the Philistine archers in the battle of Gilboa (I Sam. 31:3). There is also an explicit reference in the lament itself to the effectiveness of Jonathan's bow (v. 22). The phrase "for teaching" occurs also in the title to Psalm 60, but there it is used without an object.

The phrase in verse 21, "fields of offerings," is also difficult. The word used, "heave offering," is a term for a variety of offerings including firstfruits (Num. 18:12–14). Perhaps this was in David's mind; Saul, as Israel's first king, and Jonathan, as Israel's first crown prince and royal heir, were the firstfruits of the royal line. With a slight change in the division of the letters (words were not separated in early Hebrew manuscripts) and in the shape of one letter, it would be possible to read it as "the fields of silence" or "the fields of the realms of the dead" (cf. Ps. 115:17).

3. David in Hebron as King of Judah (2:1–11)

David is divinely guided to leave Ziklag and to settle in Hebron. Here he is anointed by the men of Judah as king over Judah. One of his first acts is to commend the men of Jabesh-gilead for procuring a decent burial for Saul's body. It was an action that showed the abiding gratitude of their hearts, for Saul's first great feat as king was their deliverance from the Ammonites (I Sam. 11:1–11).

Abner, the commander of Saul's army, brought Ish-bosheth, a son of Saul, to Mahanaim and made him king over Israel. One gets the impression that Abner was something of a despot and that his crowning of Ish-bosheth was an autocratic act. David's elevation to the throne, on the other hand, seems to have been on democratic lines. Ish-bosheth clearly was only a puppet king.

4. Fateful Meeting of Abner and Joab (2:12—3:1)

Abner, with the men of Ish-bosheth and Joab, David's nephew, meet at Gibeon with David's men. We are not told whether the meeting was by arrangement or by accident. At Abner's suggestion, twelve of his men met twelve of Joab's men in what was intended to be a trial of strength, but it ended in mutual slaughter. This started a general combat, in which Joab's brother, Asahel, tries to engage Abner. Abner, apparently wishing to avoid the rise of the inevitable blood-feud between him and Joab, repeatedly warns Asahel to desist. He ignores the warnings and finally Abner is forced to slay him. Joab and his other brother, Abishai, now turn in pursuit of Abner. He retreats, but is able to rally his men and make a stand on a hill top. Rather than prolong the battle, Abner appeals to Joab for a cessation of the fighting on the ground that they are brethren.

Abner returns to Mahanaim and Joab to Hebron. In the conflict Joab lost twenty men, and Abner, 360.

Our first introduction indicates that Joab was a cruel, ruthless tyrant and his reprehensible crimes must have left a legacy of blood in Israel. Even David feared to withstand him, and he maintained his position until the time of Solomon, who brought him to justice in accordance with the request of the dying David. He was no credit to David or to Israel, but that did not prevent his portrait from being included in the Biblical record. His character will repay close study.

A Note on David's family (3:2–5)

David now has altogether six wives and concubines. This state of affairs indicates a general relaxation of tension during his seven and a half years in Hebron (2:11). Polygamy brought with it great domestic dangers in the form of jealousies and rivalries. Of the six sons, whose births are recorded here, three—Ammon, Absalom and Adonijah—brought disgrace and great sorrow to David.

6. Abner's Quarrel with Ish-bosheth; His Overtures to David (3:6–21)

Abner had the audacity to take one of the late king's concubines, and Ish-bosheth demanded an explanation of his conduct. The matter at issue was probably not so much a question of morality as the implied threat to the constitution. Any offspring from a union with a wife or concubine of the former king might easily one day give rise to claims of royal descent and become a menace to the ruling house. Abner resents this rebuke and threatens to transfer his loyalty and support to David. As soon as convenient he enters into negotiations with David. David agrees to collaborate on condition that Abner arrange for the return of Michal, Saul's daughter and his first wife. This is done by Abner, although it involves a distressing scene with her present husband (v. 16). Abner then sets about the task of winning the support of the elders of Israel and presumably also of the elders of Benjamin (v. 19), and communicates the successful results of his efforts to David. At a feast given by David in his honor, Abner already addresses David as "my lord the king." Abner sets out to make final preparations for the acknowledgment of David as king of all Israel.

7. *Joab's Assassination of Abner; David's Condemnation (3:22–39)*

Joab returns from a raid and learns of David's friendly reception of Abner and of the peaceful outcome of their discussions. Joab goes to David and expresses his disapproval and falsely and unfairly accuses Abner of planning treachery against David. Then without David's knowledge he sends men in pursuit of Abner to bring him back to Hebron. Joab was presumably waiting for him at the city gate, and slew him there. The expression, "to the middle of the gate," probably means the inner part where there would be the least light. It was an act of revenge for the slaying of his brother Asahel (2:23). When David hears of the crime, he publicly disowns all responsibility, and calls down judgment on the house of Joab for this despicable murder. David's anxiety to disassociate himself from the crime, is prompted by his knowledge that if it were allowed to go uncondemned, it would jeopardize the success of his attempts at reconciliation with Israel. He proclaims a state of public mourning, and he himself follows Abner to his grave, and composes a lament for him. By word and by action, his disapproval is apparent to all, but he is powerless to call Joab to account. His confession of weakness in this respect (v. 39) must only have increased Joab's arrogant confidence. Verse 38 should probably be read, "For David had said . . ." and so forth.

8. *Punishment of Ish-bosheth's Murderers (4:1–12)*

In verse 2 the preposition "to" (in the Hebrew) seems to have dropped out before "son of Saul." "To the son of Saul two men" is the Hebrew for "the son of Saul had two men." The two men mentioned seem to have been employed by Ish-bosheth as the leaders of organized raids, by whom murder was probably taken for granted as part of their lawless activities carried out with the king's consent. They would have no difficulty in gaining admission to the king's house. Verse 6, as it stands, is not easy to explain. The Septuagint refers to a female guard. It is very unlikely that the safety of the king's person would be entrusted to a woman. A literal translation of the verse would read: "And there came here takers of wheat unto the midst of the house."

We may suppose that the two brothers came with a body of their followers, among whom were those responsible for the removal of wheat during raids. Verse 6 is the concise account of the episode; verse 7 goes into more detail. This is brought out best by using a pluperfect tense: "Now they had entered the house," and so forth. After the murder they take the head of Ish-bosheth to David, expecting his approbation. He treats them as he treated the Amalekite who reported the death of Saul. Theirs was the worse crime. In verse 11, the emphasis is on "in his own house," in contrast to the death of Saul which took place on the battlefield. For their deed David punishes them with death. The note in verse 4 is inserted lest we should conclude from what we are about to be told, that this spelled the extinction of the house of Saul.

II. David, King of Israel and Judah (5:1—15:6)

1. David Becomes King of Israel (5:1-25)

Invitation to be King (5:1-5). The Israelites come to Hebron and recall that even in the days of Saul, David was their outstanding leader. David enters into a covenant with the elders of Israel and is anointed king. An important chronological note tells us that he was thirty years of age when he began to reign (that is, in Hebron) and reigned over Judah in Hebron seven and a half years, and over Israel and Judah thirty-three years (5:4, 5).

Capture of Jerusalem (5:6-10). As Hebron by its geographical position probably proved unsuitable for a centralized administration, David sought a new capital. He probably deliberately chose Jerusalem, a neutral place, so as not to give offense either to Israel or Judah. The fact that the Jebusite inhabitants considered it almost impregnable made it all the more desirable as a royal city. The reference in verse 6 to the blind and the lame turning him back seems to indicate the ease with which this natural fortress could be defended. In verse 8, we probably should translate "For David had said, anyone attacking the Jebusites, let him approach the lame and the blind by the water course, these who hate the soul of David, therefore the blind and the lame are saying: he will not come inside." The city or the fortress is already referred to as Jerusalem in the Amarna letters of the fourteenth century.

Friendly Assistance of King of Tyre (5:11, 12). Hiram, the king of Tyre, supplied David's house with the finest of all building timber, cedar trees from the Lebanon. Israel had had no opportunity of developing the skills of a settled community, and Hiram also made good this deficiency by sending skilled workmen.

David's Domestic Affairs (5:13–16). The security and the prosperity that he enjoys is indicated by the fact that he adds to his harem. The number of his children also keeps on increasing.

Philistine Hostility (5:17–25). The growing might of David could not be ignored by the hereditary enemies of Israel. The Philistines decided to attack David, but David defeated them. A second attempt also ended in disaster and general defeat.

2. The Ark Brought to Jerusalem (6:1–23)

The tragic death of Uzzah, who touched the ark in an attempt to steady it, so perturbed David, that he postponed the entry to Jerusalem for three months. The ark was left with Obed-edom, and when its presence brought only blessing, David had it removed to Jerusalem.

Michal, his wife, is offended by David's enthusiastic participation in the celebrations upon the ark's being brought to Jerusalem (6:16–23). When David returns from the ceremony, Michal rebukes him for what she considered to be his undignified behavior. David, obviously annoyed, reminds her that the Lord chose him in preference to her father. As a result of this quarrel David no longer treats her as his wife.

3. David Desires to Build a House for God (7:1–29)

God's Covenant with David (7:1–17). The Lord reveals to Nathan that David will not have the privilege of building a temple, but that his son will do it. The promise was fulfilled in Solomon, but the ultimate fulfilment, that of a throne to be established forever, awaits the coming of "great David's greater Son."

David's Response (7:18–29). He returns thanks for God's great goodness to himself and to his people, and prays for the continual blessing of God on his house. With simple faith he accepts the veracity of the words of God and the certainty of the fulfilment of the promise.

4. David's Military Successes (8:1–18)

Not only did David subdue the Philistines, but he also made Moab a vassal state. He defeated the Aramaeans of Jobah, with territory somewhere north of Damascus, and when the Aramaeans of the province of Damascus came to their help, he routed them and occupied their territory. The king of the territory of Hamath, seeing David's invincible progress, hastened to send him rich presents. The Edomites suffered a heavy defeat, and their subjugation was made permanent by the presence of Israelite garrisons.

A list of David's chief officers in this period of unprecedented progress and power is added.

5. David's Kindness to Jonathan's Son (9:1–13)

David recalls his covenant with Jonathan (I Sam. 20:15–17) and seeks to implement it. He learns from one of Saul's former servants that one son of Jonathan survives—Mephibosheth. In I Chronicles 8:34 he is called Merib-baal, that is, "the contender of Baal." It is often assumed that as *Baal* became more and more associated with a pagan deity, the name was avoided and for it was substituted the word "*bosheth*," shame. There is, however, no reason why Mephibosheth should not have had two names. Mephibosheth, as we have already been told (4:4), was a cripple. David restores to him the family estates and gives him the status of one of his own sons. Ziba, Saul's servant, who supplied the information about Mephibosheth, is put in charge of his property. The story is an appropriate illustration of grace in operation.

6. David's Victory over the Ammonites (10:1–19)

David on some occasion had been treated kindly by Nahash, the Ammonite, and because of this decided to treat his son, Hanun, as a friend. Hanun took David's envoys and treated them shamefully. When the Ammonites realized that David would not let such treatment go unpunished, they hired the Aramaeans to come to their aid. Joab, who was in charge of David's forces, divided his men, one section to meet the Aramaeans, and the other, the Ammonites. His intention seems to have been that one section would merely undertake a holding action, ready to send help if the other found itself in difficulties. His own section attacked the hired Aramaeans first, probably since they were fighting with no real incentive. When they were routed, the Ammonites without further resistance took to flight.

The Syrians, probably feeling that they now had incurred David's displeasure, formed a coalition and mobilized all available forces. In the ensuing battle, David's forces were again victorious, and the members of the coalition became tributary states.

7. *David's Great Sin (11:1—12:25)*

David's Infatuation for Bathsheba (11:1-27). David, now sufficiently strong and well-organized, was no longer compelled to take an active part in the campaigns. With inactivity came self-indulgence, and David had time to be tempted. The sight of Bathsheba, a beautiful woman, bathing aroused his passions, and he succumbed. The outcome of the liaison was inevitable, and David's great problem was how to prevent her husband, Uriah, one of David's most faithful officers, from discovering the state of affairs.

In an attempt to deceive Uriah, David recalled him from the army in the field, and suggested that he should spend some time at home. Uriah, however, does not go, and when questioned later by David, gives as his reason that he cannot indulge himself when he is on active military service. David now writes to Joab and orders him to put Uriah in the most vulnerable position. Joab obeys the king and Uriah is slain. After a little time, David marries Bathsheba.

Nathan's Parable and God's Condemnation (12:1-14). Nathan comes and relates a parable to David. Its purpose, like that of most parables, is to elicit from David a disinterested judgment in a case which does not concern him, but which he later perceives is an exact parallel with his own. This parable of the rich man's appropriation of the poor man's lamb is probably the best known of all Old Testament parables. David is incensed at such conduct, and condemns the perpetration of such a pitiless crime. Nathan shows David that he has passed judgment on himself. He, with his great harem, had deprived a faithful servant of his wife, and had killed him in the bargain. It was actually David who was responsible for Uriah's death, even though he died at the hands of the Ammonites.

Death of Bathsheba's Child and Birth of Solomon (12:15-25). The child born of the illicit union between David and Bathsheba fell ill, and David was in great emotional distress. The seven days its sickness lasted, David gave himself to uninterrupted intercession, but all in vain. When he learned of the child's death, he returned to his normal routine, much to the surprise of his servants. To their demand for an explanation of his change of attitude, his reply was to the effect that while the child lived, he did not know God's will in the matter; now that he was dead, no change could be effected. There was now left only the hope that David would go to him (v. 23), a statement that shows David's faith in a life beyond the grave.

8. Joab's Self-Abnegation at Rabbah (12:26–31)

Joab had defeated the Ammonites on their own territory and only the city of Rabbah (the modern Amman in Jordan) was holding out. Joab refrained from taking it, so that David might have that honor. The inhabitants were forced to perform the hardest forms of toil. (In the record of this episode in I Chron. 20:1–3, part of the final letter of the verb "to put" is missing, with the result that it looks like the final letter of the verb "to saw." It was clearly a case of hard labor, and not torture.)

9. Amnon's Seduction of Tamar (13:1–19)

Amnon becomes infatuated with Tamar, his half sister and, under pretense of being ill, has her sent to nurse him. Here he forces her, and then despises her. She goes away and makes her complaint public. Her brother, Absalom, takes Tamar to his house and awaits an opportunity for retaliation. When Amnon accepts an invitation to a sheep-shearing feast, Absalom has him murdered. Absalom flees to his grandfather in Geshur. It was probably during this exile that Absalom first thought of open rebellion.

10. David's Reconciliation with Absalom (14:1—15:6)

Joab's Ruse (14:1–20). Joab attempts by means of a ruse to effect a reconciliation between David and Absalom. Joab enlists the help of a wise woman who pretends that the life of her only remaining son is threatened by the avenger of blood (Num. 35:19–28). She persuades the king to revoke the law in this instance. Having gained her point, she proceeds to apply David's judgment to the case of

Absalom. David becomes suspicious and cross-examines her and discovers that Joab was the author of the stratagem. Nevertheless, having given his word, David abides by it and gives his permission for Absalom's return. For two years after Absalom's return, he has no contact with the king. Growing restive, he tries to bring pressure to bear on Joab to arrange an interview. When Joab delays, he sets his barley on fire. Joab sees the king, and David receives Absalom.

Absalom's Self-Aggrandizement (15:1–6). Absalom acquires a chariot and runners. He tries to sow the seeds of discontent among the people, and hints that he could improve their condition.

III. *Absalom's Rebellion (15:7—18:5)*

1. *Absalom's Insurrection (15:7-12)*

Absalom gets the king's permission to visit Hebron. By a trick he takes with him two hundred leading men from Jerusalem, knowing that when he proclaims his rebellion, these guests would immediately come under suspicion and be unable to return to Jerusalem. He acquires the services of the wisest of David's counselors, Ahithophel.

2. *David's Fight from Jerusalem (15:13—16:14)*

Few events in ancient history are so fully recorded as the flight of David from Jerusalem. The whole spectacle as he ascends and descends the Mount of Olives is made to pass before our eyes. All property has to be abandoned, and all that he can do is to leave behind ten members of his harem with, in all probability, a skeleton staff, to care for the house. Besides the contents, there would be the livestock, which could not be abandoned. The procession stops at the last house, and David then allows the company to pass on ahead of him. Even in this crisis, David has time to think of his men. He tries to persuade Ittai, who had returned with him from Gath, to return now to his native place. But the bond between them is too strong to break under stress and Ittai continues on with David towards the wilderness. He next sends the priests back with the ark into the city, but requests that they through their two sons will keep him informed.

The news of the defection of Ahithophel is a heavy blow. Hushai, another counselor, appears at the summit of the Mount of Olives, but he is advised to return and secretly to serve the cause of David. Over the summit, Ziba, Mephibosheth's servant, meets him with provisions. (The phrase "yoke of asses" should probably be taken as a collective, that is, "pairs of asses"; cf. I Sam. 25:18 where for a similar load asses were required. A pair of asses would hardly have contributed much to the transport of the "king's household.") On being told by Ziba that Mephibosheth has remained in Jerusalem expecting to see the restoration of Saul's house, David makes Ziba a present of Mephibosheth's estate.

Shimei, a Benjamite, and probably related to Saul, comes to hurl insults at David. When Abishai offers to deal with him, David refuses to allow him to intervene. This restraint probably required more strength of character on David's part than any other single act in his hazardous life.

3. Hushai Frustrates the Counsel of Ahithophel (16:15—17:23)

Hushai wins the confidence of Absalom and acts as one of his counselors. Ahitophel advocates the elimination of David, rightly perceiving that it is he who gives cohesion to his followers. He himself is ready to carry out the task. Hushai in a speech abounding in flowery generalities advises Absalom himself to lead the attack against David. Probably this appeal to his egotism caused Absalom to follow the counsel of Hushai. Hushai, using the sons of the priests as his agents, keeps David informed. On one occasion, only the quick action of a woman in hiding them in a well and concealing the well with a heap of grain prevents their capture (17:15–20). Ahithophel, when he sees his counsel rejected, is so mortified that he commits suicide (v. 23).

4. David in Mahanaim (17:24–29)

David arrives at Mahanaim, where Ish-bosheth's capital had been (II Sam. 2:8). Here three rulers from the territory east of Jordan bring him supplies.

5. David's Organization of His Forces (18:1–5)

David sends out his army in three divisions, one under Joab, one under his brother Abishai, and the third under Ittai, the man from

Gath. His leaders dissuade him from accompanying them, knowing that he is indispensable to the morale of the people. His final request is for them to treat Absalom gently for his sake.

IV. *Overthrow of Absalom and Return of David* (18:6—24:25)

1. *Defeat of Israel and Death of Absalom (18:6—19:8)*

Gain and Loss (18:6–18). The battle between David's forces and Absalom's was fought near the forest of Ephraim, and the forces of Absalom, on being routed, tried to escape in the forest. Absalom sought to flee on his mule, but was caught in a branch and left suspended in midair. Joab hears of this and kills him in defiance of David's express wish. The man who had first found Absalom reminds Joab of the king's request, as his reason for leaving Absalom unharmed. He accuses Joab also of being capable of betraying a colleague. This interchange reveals how despicable the character of Joab really was (vv. 10–15). Joab calls off the pursuit and unceremoniously disposes of Absalom's body in a pit.

David's Reception of the News (18:19–33). Ahimaaz, who had been Hushai's agent, asks to be allowed to take the news to David. Joab refuses and sends a Cushite servant. Later he relents, and Ahimaaz follows the Cushite, but chooses a faster route. When he reaches the city, David's first question is about Absalom. Ahimaaz either cannot or will not give him a straight answer. When the Cushite arrives, again the first question is about Absalom. David, when he hears the news, is crushed by grief and loudly laments his loss. Even in his great sorrow, his poetic gift is not quenched. A great authority on language cites this passage as an example of a "masterpiece of rhythm."

Joab Rebukes Mourning David (19:1–8). Joab reproves the king for his mourning and warns him that he is in danger of disheartening the people and losing their support. To remedy this, he must make a public appearance and address the people. David agrees and goes out to the gate. The public appearances were probably made at the outer side of the gate, so that the people could assemble beyond the precincts of the city in an area unobstructed by houses.

2. *David's Return to Jerusalem (19:9–43)*

After the defeat of Absalom, the people are rent by dissension and discord. The prevalent opinion is that David, who saved them in the past, should be brought back. David, hearing of their wish, asks the priests at Jerusalem to foster a similar desire in the people there. As an incentive he offers to replace Joab by Amasa, Absalom's commander (17:25). Evidently Joab was most unpopular, and now his part in the death of Absalom would make him obnoxious to the king. David is sent for and on his return is met at Jordan by all the people.

Among those who meet him is the now remorseful Shimei (16: 5–14). David again refuses to allow him to be harmed. Mephibosheth is also there, ready to explain his conduct: Ziba had left him in his lameness without transport. David has no wish to go into the rights and wrongs of the case. He is still obliged by his oath to Jonathan to provide for his offspring, and this he does by allowing him to regain half his estate, the other half remaining in Ziba's hands (16:4). Mephibosheth's comment at this announcement leaves the impression that his protestations of loyalty were genuine.

In the company of David was Barzillai, who had helped to supply him with necessities on his flight. David offers him a place with him in Jerusalem, but Barzillai declines on the ground of old age.

3. *Sheba's Rebellion (20:1–26)*

When the companies meet, the men of Israel accuse the men of Judah of removing the king. A controversy ensues, and a mischief-maker, Sheba, exploits the situation to instigate another rebellion. Amasa is authorized to deal with the situation. When Amasa takes longer than is expected to muster his forces, David sends Abishai to suppress the rebellion. Joab accompanies him. On their way they meet Amasa at Gibeon, and as Amasa goes forward to meet Joab, Joab treacherously slays him. One of Joab's men stands by the dead body and recruits men for David in Joab's name. Joab besieges Sheba in Abel. A wise woman uses her influence to have Sheba beheaded and the head cast over the wall to Joab. Joab then raises the siege and returns to Jerusalem.

A note is added on the administrative setup: Joab is again commander-in-chief.

4. Famine on Account of Saul's Crime (21:1–14)

Joshua had been inveigled into making a covenant with the Gibeonites, and it was still binding. Saul on some occasion had failed to observe it, probably by attacking and slaughtering some of their people. When David learns the cause of the famine, he offers to pay a ransom. The Gibeonites refuse and demand the death of seven of Saul's sons. ("Son," in Hebrew, may mean any male descendant.) David spares Mephibosheth, but hands over two sons of Saul's concubine, Rizpah, whom Abner had taken (II Sam. 3:6–11), and five sons of Saul's daughter, Merab. The Gibeonites hang them on a mountain. Rizpah maintains an unbroken vigil by the bodies of her sons. When David hears of her devotion, he sends and collects all the bodies, as well as the bones of Saul and Jonathan, and has them buried in the family burial-place.

5. Finale of the Goliath Feud (21:15–22)

This is no mere note in passing, no stray remark by the writer; it is an integral part of the drama recorded in the pages of Samuel. Had it been omitted every Semitic reader would have found the gap intolerable. Ever since reading the story of David's triumph over Goliath, he has been waiting for this. It is a masterly touch, added just before the curtain falls. Death does not end a quarrel in the Semitic East, neither then or now. It is the beginning of a deathless obsession with revenge, kept alive from brother to brother and from father to son. The avenger of blood neither slumbers nor sleeps. Death must pay for death, and the cry of the kinsman's blood is never silent. The pages of sacred and secular history alike reek with the blood shed by the avenger. Could it be possible for some mysterious reason that this inflexible code was allowed in this instance to lapse? The thing is utterly unthinkable. The mind craves to know in what forms the blood-feud manifested itself.

Here we have the indispensable epilogue to the story of Goliath. It is probably only a selection of the attempts made by Goliath's kin to avenge the ignominious death of Gath's mightiest son. That among the aspirants for this honor one of them might have borne the name of Goliath (leaving aside the question of the possible omission of the word "brother," cf. I Chron. 20:5), is not surprising.

It would have been more surprising if there had been no child in the connection named after the most famous of the clan. The naivete that assumes that the Israelites never repeated names, would postulate an intolerable strain on the nomenclative ingenuity of any people. Of course, they repeated names; there are no fewer than eighteen Shimeis mentioned in the Old Testament. Neither is it surprising that this Goliath should ape his revered namesake even in his equipment, the product probably of the same armorer's workshop. Imbedded in the earlier narratives, dealing with matters of national importance, this story would have been out of place, for a death-feud was ever a private affair.

6. David's Song of Deliverance (22:1–51)

This song has been included in the Psalter (Ps. 18). There are small differences in the two copies, some of which may be merely transcriptional errors. Others may be due to a slight revision done by David himself in adapting it for choral purposes.

For all practical purposes, the commentary on Psalm 18 holds good for this passage.

7. Last Words of David (23:1–7)

Use of the word translated "oracle" (RSV) designates these sayings as a prophetic utterance. Verse 1 speaks of his humble status, "the son of Jesse," and his high exaltation. The second half of the verse, although usually taken as applying to David, could be translated "concerning the anointed of the God of Jacob and the beloved of the songs of Israel." In justification of this interpretation, one could point to the messianic character of the poem.

In verses 2 and 3 David claims to be speaking by inspiration of God. In the second part of verse 3, we have the portrait of the ideal king, a righteous one, whose righteousness has its source in God. His coming will be as the sun on a cloudless morning. From the radiance and the rain, the earth shall be clothed with vegetation. Verse 5 is probably an emphatic question: "Is my house not thus with God? For He has granted me an eternal covenant." All is arranged and in safe keeping. Shall he not cause to come forth all my salvation and delight? But worthless men are as thorns, totally rejected, for no one will touch them. Anyone who will touch them will take an iron weapon (in his hand) and a shaft of a spear. They shall be utterly burned up in fire where they lie (literally, "at the sitting").

8. *List of the Chiefs of David's Mighty Men (23:8–39)*

A somewhat similar list is given in I Chronicles 11:11–41, but it may be drawn from a different period in David's career. This list is divided into two groups of three and thirty. The names and exploits of the three are given in verses 8–12.

In verses 13–17 we have the account of a famous feat performed by three of the thirty—the fetching of the water from the well at Bethlehem, under the very noses of the Philistines. When the water was brought, David refused to drink it, regarding it as having been obtained virtually by the blood of the heroic men. Verse 17 provides a good example of the symbolic use of language in referring to the water: "Is it the blood of the men?" David treats it as if it were the blood of forfeited lives by pouring it out before God (cf. Jn. 6:53–56, where our Lord uses language in this symbolic manner).

There follow the names of Abishai and Benaiah with a reference to outstanding feats.

The next list is headed by Asahel whom Abner slew. This seems to indicate that this is the list from the early period of David's reign. There are thirty-one names mentioned, and the total is said to be thirty-seven. Either there were three in the second group, although only two are mentioned, or a name may have been omitted before "son of the Maachathite" (perhaps Hepher, cf. I Chron. 11:36). The number "thirty" probably came to be used as the title of the group, and not in a strict numerical sense.

9. *Taking of the Census and God's Chastisement (24:1–15)*

Possibly the purpose of the census was to enable David to estimate his military resources, believing that military strength would ensure victory. We are not told when this happened, but there must have been a great sense of security on the part of David at the time, otherwise he would not have allowed his commander-in-chief to embark on a task that was to occupy ten months of the time. On learning that he had 800,000 men at his disposal, David must have felt confident in his own strength. He confesses his sin to God.

Through Gad, the prophet-seer, God offers David a choice of three forms of punishment: famine, fleeing for three months before his enemies, or a pestilence. David chooses the pestilence, as being the form of punishment most directly under the control of God.

10. God's Intervention and David's Intercession (24:16–25)

God orders the destroying messenger to cease and spares Jerusalem. David asks for the punishment to fall upon him as the guilty one. He is commanded by Gad to erect an altar at the place where he saw the divine messenger—the threshing floor of Araunah. When David approaches Araunah with a view to buying the land, he offers to give it to him. David's reply shows his deep spiritual understanding: "I shall not offer to the Lord my God offerings that cost nothing." In the account in I Chronicles 21:18–25 David is even more explicit, when he adds: "I will not lift up [an offering] to the Lord of what is thine." From II Chronicles 3:1 we learn that the threshing floor was on the site of Mount Moriah, and that here Solomon built his temple. Thus David became the link between Abraham, the father of his people, and that great succession of kings and priests who thronged the temple. And the site on which this great temple was to stand was forever associated with the spot where "God himself provided a lamb for the offering" in place of Isaac (Gen. 22:8, 13). And near this spot the true paschal Lamb "was once offered to bear the sins of many" (Heb. 9:28).

I and II Kings

J. A. THOMPSON

293

IT WILL QUICKLY become evident to the reader that the Books of Kings deal with history written from a particular standpoint. The books are written with a religious vision and a practical aim. The subject is not merely history, but the *lessons* of history. The writer's (or writers') concern is to demonstrate how far the nation Israel—its kings, priests, prophets and people—fulfilled the obligations of the covenant made several centuries earlier at Sinai.

Official records were searched for information about the reign of each individual king of Israel and Judah in order to carry out a piece of honest self-judgment. Each king was assessed in terms of his attitude towards the covenant that Israel's fathers had made with God. Two points of comparison lay ready to hand, one in the character of David who "did that which was right in the sight of the Lord," and the other in the character of Jeroboam I "who made Israel to sin." Each king was measured against these two, of whom David represented a king who was faithful to the covenant, and Jeroboam a king who rejected the covenant.

We gather that from his records the compiler of Kings selected facts that would help him to establish his assessment. Many facts were neglected as irrelevant to the purpose at hand. These were again and again covered by a general note at the end of a king's biography. For example, in the case of Solomon, this is the note: "And the rest of the acts of Solomon, and all that he did, and his wisdom, are they not written in the book of the acts of Solomon?" (I Kings 11:41). And again of Joash, for example: "And the rest of the acts of Joash, and all that he did, are they not written in the book of the chronicles of the kings of Judah?" (II Kings 12:19).

Thanks to modern archaeological and historical research, we are able to supplement Biblical records in many places and thus to gain a fuller picture of the political achievements of several of the kings of Israel. But this additional information only serves to confirm the picture in these two books. For in many cases, all that a king had to commend him either to men or to God was a list of political achievements. When, however, these were won at the cost of compromising the covenant obligations to God, the achievement was regarded as of little worth. We shall need to keep this fact in mind when we read the Books of Kings, and to keep on asking ourselves the question: Did this king fulfil the obligations laid upon the people of Israel in the covenant made at Sinai (Ex. 19:4–8; 24:3–8)?

A second feature of the two Books of Kings is that many references are found to the prophets and to the men of God whose chief business was to guard the sovereign rule of God over Israel from the encroachments of kings, priests or people. Indeed, it is in large measure as guardians of the theocracy that we must regard the prophets. We meet them in the Books of Kings rebuking all and sundry. Even kings came under their condemnation. Often they were in king's courts watching the interests of the God of Israel. It was of course precisely in the days covered by the Books of Kings that the pre-Exilic prophets were active. Only some of these are mentioned in the Books of Kings, although a study of the prophets will reveal the mention of numbers of these kings. It was quite normal at the opening of a prophetic book to place a short historical note about the time when the prophet was preaching and formally to state the kings during whose reigns he preached.

How did the people and the rulers of Israel offend God? There were several ways. Any alliance with other gods or other nations was tantamount to a rejection of the covenant made by Moses and the fathers with the God of Israel (Ex. 34:12–17 and so forth). Treaties with other nations in a time of national crisis might displace or weaken faith in God. Apostasy from God as shown in the worship of the gods of the heathen was a clear evidence of departure from the covenant. In particular, worship associated with high places, which we now think may have been connected with some cult of the dead, was held to be a mark of apostasy. Those kings who permitted it were condemned, while those like Hezekiah and Josiah, who destroyed the high places, were praised.

God intended Israel to be separated unto Himself as a holy people, a different people, a loyal and obedient people, a people who showed love one toward another and who would be a light to the Gentiles. Any defection from these standards would merit the condemnation of the prophets, because it would merit the condemnation of God Himself. Acts of oppression in national life, such as the oppression of the poor, the widows and the orphans, the denial of a man's inheritance rights by purchasing his fields in time of need, extravagance by some while others lacked the necessities of life, all pointed to a rejection of the covenant. In an attempt to disclose all these defects, the compiler of the Books of Kings selected material from the official records. When, in due course, the two kingdoms broke up and went into exile, the compiler of this story was at no loss to explain the reason for it, as we shall see in such passages as II Kings 17. Humanly speaking, it seems strange that such a piece of self-judgment should have survived. It did, however, and remains today as a lesson concerning God's discipline of His people when they forsook their covenant obligations.

I. The Reign of Solomon (I Kings 1:1—11:43)

Our story commences at the point where all Israel's foes had been subdued by David, and when the nation, now organized after the days of anarchy which marked the period of the judges, was already in possession of the careful system of administration that David had set in motion. Moreover, the scattered priests, Levites, temple singers and attendants had been organized. Some steps had already been taken towards the building of the temple. All of this was due to the great King David who in so many ways had observed the obligations of the covenant. Even so, his last days were not without difficulty, and plots to seize the throne disturbed the peace of the land.

1. David's Death; Solomon's Anointing (1:1—2:11)

The first Book of Kings opens with David's death and Solomon's anointing. Already too old to be able to care for his affairs, David seemed oblivious to the possibility of plots. We need not read anything sexual into the incident of I Kings 1:1–4, but rather see an illustration of the current belief that a young life with warm blood flowing in her veins might give warmth and life to the failing king.

The plot of Adonijah, David's son by Haggith, was kept secret from David's trusted officers, Nathan the prophet, Zadok the priest, and the others (1:8). Adonijah ingratiated himself with rebels, but eventually the plot was discovered, and David was urged to declare his intention about his successor (vv. 15–40). He declared for Solomon, who was then crowned king (v. 39). Adonijah feared Solomon and sheltered at the altar (v. 50). He was spared for a season, only to meet his death at Solomon's hands on the death of David (2:23–25).

The charge of David to his son Solomon was a plea for him to be true to the covenant obligations of Israel and to keep the commandments of God (2:1–4). Only thus would God's promise to David be established. namely, that the throne of Israel would not be vacant. Possibly David's advice to Solomon in regard to some of the troublesome people in the kingdom was given with a view to preserving the true spirit of the theocracy in the land (vv. 5–9).

Probably we can detect the author's intention at the outset of I Kings as he shows first of all some of the weaknesses in Israel and then records David's statement concerning the only source of strength for any king (2:2, 3).

2. Solomon Eliminates his Opponents (2:12–46)

Immediately after accession to the throne, Solomon proceeded to eliminate those who in David's closing years showed a tendency to rebel against the Lord's anointed. They would only prove a hindrance to the theocracy. In place of Joab, Benaiah was appointed as leader of the army, and Zadok was appointed as priest in place of Abiathar (2:35). Finally Shimei was executed (vv. 36–46).

3. Solomon's Prayer for Wisdom; his First Wise Decision (3:1–28)

In the first days of his reign, there seemed to be some hope that Solomon would follow the steps of his father David. When God appeared to him in a dream, his prayer was that he might rule wisely. His subsequent careful decision in the matter of the two women and the child gave good hope that Israel would have a strong leader in obedience to the covenant obligations. But it was not to be so.

4. The Administration of the Kingdom (4:1–34)

We have a glimpse into the administrative arrangements of Solomon in this chapter. Twelve areas were mapped out in Israel, and governors were appointed over each. These divisions were responsible, each in its month, to support the king's program financially (4:7). The daily consumption of food (vv. 22–25) was considerable. But Solomon was wise (vv. 29–34), and he had a strong army to assist him. He added a chariot wing to his army and built special chariot cities in strategic places (9:19; 10:26). One of these has been found at Megiddo where excavation has revealed separate stable units, each housing thirty horses.

5. Planning and Building of the Temple (5:1—7:51)

Further evidence of the good intentions of Solomon is seen in these chapters. A trade agreement with the Phoenicians (5:1–11), in which Solomon bought cedar and fir in exchange for wheat and oil (vv. 10, 11), the hiring of Phoenician stone masons (vv. 17, 18), the employment of Phoenician bronze workers (7:13, 14), made possible the erection of a beautiful temple. Archaeological discovery has made it clear that the artistic patterns in the cedar and in the bronze, depicting palm trees, pomegranates, open flowers, wreathed work, and animals of various kinds, are typical of the work of Phoenician artists. Perhaps the writer of I Kings is here informing us that already in Solomon's day those dangerous Canaanite-Phoenician influences were at work which were ultimately to be the ruin of Israel.

6. The Temple Dedicated. God's Promise to Solomon (8:1—9:9)

Finally the temple was completed and the ark of God brought out of its temporary home and lodged in the temple (8:4–11). The prayer of Solomon on that occasion was worthy of any man who adhered to the covenant. There was a clear recognition of the peril involved in departure from the ways of God. The possibility of Israel's departing from the way is mentioned, and the possibility of divine forgiveness upon confession of sin is also set forth. Solomon was clearly aware that God had separated His people to be His inheritance (vv. 51–53). Then in an address to the people, Solomon invoked the blessing of God to be upon them to incline their hearts to keep His commandments so that "all the peoples of the earth may know that the Lord is God" (vv. 56–60). The appeal to Israel to "let your heart be perfect with the Lord our God, to walk in his statutes and to keep his commandments" is a stirring appeal to Israel to acknowledge the rule of God in the nation (v. 61).

The account of the second appearance of God to Solomon (9:1–9) may well have been inserted by the author to show the attitude of God toward Solomon's prayer. God's reply gave strong warnings as well as gracious promises. In the observance of the covenant obligations the kings of Israel were to find blessing; departure from them would only result in tragic ruin (vv. 6, 7).

7. Solomon's Trading and Building Program (9:10–28; 10:14–29)

In pursuance of the picture of Solomon's great prosperity, we now have a section devoted to his trading ventures and building program. The port he built on the Red Sea at Ezion Geber (9:26–28; 10:22), excavated in recent years, has produced strong evidence of trade with Egypt and Southern Arabia (Sheba), as well as a remarkable copper refining plant. A search in the country to the north has revealed that there was considerable mining activity in the days of Solomon. We are almost certain now that Solomon took copper from this area for his temple and used the excess for trading purposes. There was also caravan trade with the Arabs (10:15), and an important trade in horses with Egypt and with Asia Minor, if we follow the most recent translation of 10:28, "And Solomon's import of horses was from Egypt and Kue" (RSV, 10:28). The Hebrew text allows this, and ancient records refer often to the land of Kue in Asia Minor.

The extensive building program (9:15–24) caused great concern among the Israelites, for the king made use of what must be regarded as forced labor (5:13–16). This was a factor in the final collapse of the united kingdom after Solomon's death.

8. Visit of the Queen of Sheba (10:1–13)

This visit, described in some detail in the Bible, is now greatly illuminated by the discovery of the extent of the Arab kingdoms in southern Arabia at the time of Solomon. In recent times, important excavations have taken place in the areas behind Aden. Also, the excavation at Ezion Geber shows evidence of trade with southern Arabia. The story of the Queen of Sheba is one more bright gem in the earthly crown of Solomon.

9. *End of Solomon's Reign (11:1–43)*

As the writer reached the close of Solomon's reign, he proceeded to assess the worth of a king who had enjoyed such remarkable opportunities for success. There are hints in the earlier chapters of possible failure, but the final picture given here is that Solomon, who had married many strange women and taken both them and their ways into his court life, compromised his own position with God. He allowed his wives "to turn away his heart after other gods" (11:4). Not only did he build a temple for God, but he built shrines for all his wives (v. 8). He himself "went after" these gods and "did evil in the sight of the Lord." "His heart was not perfect with the Lord his God as was the heart of David his father."

Here then was a king with every opportunity to fulfil the obligations of Israel's covenant with God. He had the splendid example of his father, who, although he did err in a measure, yet knew how to confess and put matters right. He had a kingdom free from external danger, already well organized internally. In short, he had every hope of success. His earliest actions pointed that way, but alas, the sins of pride and compromise ate into his soul, and at the last, we are told that, far from his earning the approval of God, "the Lord was angry with Solomon because his heart was turned from the Lord God of Israel which had appeared to him twice and had commanded him concerning this thing that he should not go after other gods" (vv. 9, 10). So the first of the kings dealt with in these books is assessed and set aside as a failure.

The closing days of Solomon's reign witnessed the activity of the prophet Ahijah. One day he met one of Solomon's governors, Jeroboam, and tearing up his own new garment into twelve strips, gave ten to Jeroboam as a symbolic prophecy of the coming division of the kingdom, after which he would be ruler over ten of the tribes (11:26–40). The prophet indicated that this would happen because the people had forsaken the Lord and worshipped other gods. In other words, they had not been loyal to their covenant with God and had not kept His commandments as had David, Israel's greatest king (v. 33).

II. The Divided Kingdom (I Kings 12:1—II Kings 17:41)

1. The First Period of Antagonism between Judah and Israel (I Kings 12:1—16:28)

On the death of Solomon, the judgment of God fell. When his son Rehoboam came to Shechem to be made king, the people sought for a relief from their burdens. They had many grievances, such as forced labor (5:13–16), extravagance in building (9:15–19), foreign women in the court, religious apostasy (11:1–8), and heavy taxation.

The Revolt under Jeroboam I. First Dynasty of Israel (12:1— 14:20). Rehoboam was asked to give relief, but after consulting the elders and the young men (12:6–15), he decided to follow the advice of the young men who urged him to reply as follows: "My father made your yoke heavy, and I will add to your yoke: my father also chastised you with whips, but I will chastise you with scorpions" (v. 14). It was the sign for revolt. From that day there were two kingdoms in the land, Judah and Israel. This meant that there were two kings, two capitals, two administrations, two systems of priesthood, two armies, in short, duplication of every department of national life.

Jeroboam, having set up a capital at first in Shechem, then at Penuel (12:25), decided that it was necessary to provide for the religious needs of the people. He set about creating centers of worship at Bethel and Dan and provided symbolic representations of the presence of God in the form of golden calves, a system of priests, feast days and indeed the whole range of religious activity that the people would require (vv. 26–33). This was to prevent any possibility of the people going south to worship in Judah (v. 26).

The political change did not in any way absolve Jeroboam from his obligation to be true to the covenant that the people of Israel had made with the Lord. Then ten tribes were just as much a part of the people of God as were the two. Hence the action of Jeroboam was subject to divine assessment. God sent a prophet to condemn the whole thing, to pronounce a curse on the false priests and to warn Jeroboam. It was of no avail, for Jeroboam ignored the warning of the withered hand and the rent altar (13:4–6), and "returned not from his evil way but made again of the lowest of the people priests of the high places" (v. 33).

When his child Abijah became ill, the king sent his wife suitably disguised to visit the prophet in order to inquire about the welfare of the child. Ahijah recognized the wife and spoke of the death of the child (14:12). At the same time, he reviewed the actions of Jeroboam in the light of God's requirements. The wife was instructed to tell her husband that because he had "done evil above all that were before him," despite the fact that God had raised him up and made him a prince over Israel, his house would be rejected (14:7–16). So Jeroboam's reign was assessed as one of failure. The sacred historian makes the comment "And the rest of the acts of Jeroboam, how he warred, and how he reigned, behold they are written in the book of the chronicles of the kings of Israel" (14:19). There were evidently other achievements, but these were not regarded as significant in the mind of the writer. The one significant thing was the failure of Jeroboam to keep the covenant of God Who had placed him on the throne of Israel. Ever after, his example provided a kind of standard of reference for future kings and more than once in the subsequent story, the condemnation of a king is that he walked in the ways of Jeroboam, the son of Nebat (for example, I Kings 16:31). Jeroboam provided a pattern of wickedness and of rejection of the covenant. His reign lasted for twenty-two years, and he was succeeded by his son Nadab (14:20).

Rehoboam of Judah (14:21–31). The compiler of these records endeavored to keep the two lines of kings in focus all the time. His method was to recount the story of one line, to assess the worth of its king in terms of his attitude to the laws and the covenant of God, then return to the king of the other Israelite kingdom in order to record relevant material about him and to assess his value by the same standards. An attempt is made to provide a synchronism between the two lines of kings. At this point in the record, therefore, the writer took up the corresponding king in Judah.

The story in Judah was little better than that in Israel, despite the fact that here was Jerusalem, "the city which the Lord did choose out of all the tribes of Israel to put his name there" (14:21). Under Rehoboam, Judah too did evil in the sight of the Lord. The people built high places, and pillars and Asherim (probably figures of the Canaanite goddess Asherah), on every high hill and under every green tree. Worst of all, they tolerated the presence of sacred male prostitutes (sodomites, v. 24), one of the foulest of the Canaanite practices. Rehoboam was continually at war with Jeroboam of Israel (v. 30), and, moreover, had to suffer at the hands of the Egyptian king Shishak (vv. 25, 26). This invasion is referred to by the writer of II Chronicles (12:2–4), but is described in greater detail in the records of Shishak himself in Egypt. Actually the invasion extended also to Israel, but Judah suffered as a result of the invasion and had to surrender a good deal of her wealth. Rehoboam was a failure according to divine standards.

Abijah (Abijam) and Asa of Judah (15:1–24). Abijam likewise failed to keep the obligations of the covenant and walked in all the sins of his father (v. 3). Only because of the promise made to David was he given a successor on the throne. He fought with Jeroboam of Israel and after approximately three years he died. Whatever else there was about him was ignored by the writer of Kings, although his story could be read in the official chronicles of the land (v. 7).

Asa, the son of Abijam, was one of Judah's best kings and he earned a word of approval from the historian. He "did that which was right in the eyes of the Lord as did David his father" (v. 11). Important religious reforms were carried out which involved the putting away of the sacred prostitutes, the displacement of the queen mother who had made an image for Asherah (v. 13), and the removal of other offensive items. The reform was not complete and the writer of Kings mentions that the high places were allowed to remain. However, in his personal life Asa was "perfect with the Lord all his days" (v. 14). He evidently kept the covenant and the commandments of God well enough to earn the approval of the writer.

Reference is made to his war with Israel (15:16–22). Some of the features of this account have archaeological support. Ben-hadad, son of Tabrimmon, king of Syria, to whom Asa appealed for help, is now attested in Aramaic documents. Also, the rebuilding of Geba (or Gibeah) at this time, on the ruins of the village destroyed at the time of the judges (Judg. 20:36—40), has been demonstrated by excavation. So Asa slept with his fathers having lived a life worthy of his profession as king of God's covenant people. He, at least, was true, even if many in Judah failed.

Nadab of Israel, Son of Jeroboam I (15:25–32). Nadab, the son of Jeroboam I of Israel, was the second and last king of Israel's first dynasty. He reigned but two years before he was slain by a conspirator (vv. 25–28). The assessment of the writer of Kings was that "he did evil in the sight of the Lord, and walked in the way of his father and in his sin wherewith he made Israel to sin" (v. 26). His full story is to be found in "the book of the chronicles of the kings of Israel" (v. 31). So ended the first dynasty of Israel. This sad start, marked by rejection of the ways of God, illustrated very clearly what would be the fate of those kings who rejected the sovereignty of God and failed to recognize His covenant with His people. Alas, it was to be repeated many times over in Israel. The writer of the Book of Kings kept on making his point, as we shall see.

Baasha and Elah, Second Dynasty of Israel (15:33—16:14) Baasha, of the tribe of Issachar, assassinated Nadab, the son of Jeroboam. He was the first of many assassins in the story of Israel. Whatever his other achievements, he did not observe the obligations of the covenant that the people of Israel had once made with their God. "He did that which was evil in the sight of the Lord and walked in the way of Jeroboam and in his sin wherewith he made Israel to sin" (15:34). What a black record was that of the first Jeroboam who thus set the pattern for all future comparison! Yet even Baasha had been exalted by God. The prophet Jehu pointed out to him that he was king in Israel owing to the fact that God allowed it. This would have required that he too should be true to the covenant. His failure could only mean that his house likewise would be swept away (16:2–4, 7). His war with Asa of Judah is noted in 15:16–22, where it seems Asa had the better of the case.

It was during Baasha's time that the capital of Israel was removed to Tirzah. There was to be one more move to Samaria in the days of Omri (16:24). Baasha died after a reign of twenty-four years and was succeeded by his son Elah (v. 6).

Elah was a drunkard and probably a poor ruler from the secular point of view. Be that as it may, one of his army captains, Zimri, slew him one day as he was drinking in Tirzah (v. 9). Zimri proceeded at once to exterminate all the house of Baasha, thus fulfilling the words of the prophet Jehu (16:3, 4). Elah is assessed in much the same fashion as his father. Zimri destroyed the house "for all the sins of Baasha and the sins of Elah his son by which they sinned and by which they made Israel to sin in provoking the Lord God of Israel to anger with their vanities" (v. 13). When a king sinned, the repercussions of his sin were nation-wide; this made his sin all the more grievous. Thus the second dynasty of Israel ended in bloodshed.

Zimri, the Only King of Israel's Third Dynasty (16:15–22). We would hardly expect that a king who gained the throne by bloodshed would prove to be a loyal supporter of the covenant. Nor did Zimri prove to be so. Indeed, he reigned but one week and hardly had time to prove himself (v. 15). Omri, a fellow officer of the king's army, received the support of Israel, and proceeded to Tirzah to besiege it. Zimri saw the writing on the wall and burned himself to death in the palace (v. 18). Yet even here where the reign was so brief we conclude that the editor of I Kings had additional information, for he noted that Zimri died "for his sins which he had sinned in doing that which was evil in the sight of the Lord, in walking in the way of Jeroboam and in his sin which he did to make Israel to sin" (v. 19). The roots of evil were in Zimri even though he did not rule more than a week, for even as an ordinary individual he did not keep the covenant of God. His death saw the end of the third ruling house in Israel.

Omri of Israel, Founder of the Fourth Dynasty (16:23–28). One would gather from the fact that only six verses are given to this king in the sacred record that he was of very little importance. The only facts given about him apart from the account of his usurpation of the throne are first, that he bought a hill from a certain Shemer and built on it a permanent capital for Israel, the town of Samaria, and second, that he was a very evil man. Indeed he "did worse than all that were before him" (v. 25). There were evidently other facts about him, for the writer does hint at his "might" (v. 27); but these are to be found in the ordinary secular records of the day.

Modern research has shown that this Omri was a man of much greater proportions, politically at least, than we would judge from the Bible. Even in a day when news traveled slowly the royal house of Israel came to be known as the "house of Omri" by the great Assyrian empire which lay several hundred miles away to the east. This name, once used, persisted for a long time. That the king of a small state to the west should be so well-known and so well remembered by the Assyrians argues for his prominence in the east. Quite regularly on the Assyrian monuments this designation for the kings of Israel, namely "house of Omri," appears in written records which refer to lands and peoples to the west of Assyria.

We have further information about Omri from another area altogether. The ancient land of Moab to the east of the Dead Sea has given us the famous Moabite Stone which was discovered by a missionary, F. A. Klein, in 1868. The inscription with its thirty-four lines of writing tells the story of Mesha, king of Moab (II Kings 3:4), and his success in throwing off the yoke of Israel many years after Moab had been conquered by Omri, king of Israel.

It is thus evident that Omri was of greater political significance than the Bible indicates. But the very brief reference to him in the Book of Kings serves only to emphasize the attitude of the writer. In God's sight, this king had nothing more to commend himself than military and political exploits which, compared with his great sin, were insignificant. Human achievement and international reputation were no substitute for keeping the covenant of God and walking in His ways. So the Biblical historian, assessing the spiritual and moral worth of Omri, dismisses him in a few verses.

2. The Period of Friendship between Judah and Israel (I Kings 16:29—II Kings 9:37)

Following the period of antagonism between the two Israelite kingdoms, there was a period when the two were friendly and actually cooperated in some common ventures. During the reign of Ahab, that friendship was renewed. Jehoshaphat, king of Judah, visited Ahab and assisted him in a campaign against the Syrians, and Ahab's daughter was married to the son of Jehoshaphat (II Kings 8:16–18). This state of affairs was to last until the time of Jehu, the usurper of the throne of Israel, who caused the death of the king of Judah on the same day as he slew the king of Israel (II Kings 9:27). The period of friendship was fairly brief, lasting barely thirty years and covering the period of the fifth dynasty of Israel. In the Bible, these years are described in considerable detail.

The Biblical narrative is taken up with the story of Ahab, Elijah and Elisha and occupies about fifteen of the forty-seven chapters of the two Books of Kings. It is not entirely clear why so much space should be devoted to these times unless it be that Elijah held special significance for the purpose that the compiler had in mind. We can probably find in Ahab the clearest pattern of a king who departed from the covenant, and the continual striving of Elijah to rebuke and to restore the king may have been taken as a pattern of the work of all the great prophets. Elisha's ministry does not seem to have laid special stress on the failure of the king and the people to keep the covenant, although in a day of national apostasy his miracles may have done something to show the people that the God of Israel still had the power to act on the behalf of those who were loyal to Him.

It is not easy, moreover, to discover why the writer of Kings devoted so much space to Elisha.

Ahab, Second Ruler of the Fifth Dynasty of Israel (16:29—22:40). The story of Ahab's reign is a striking illustration of the consequences of the espousal of false religion and of cultivation of the friendship of those who worship false gods. The widespread repercussions covered both personal and national life. A series of incidents is selected to show Ahab's apostasy and his rejection of covenant obligations.

As a young man Ahab married Jezebel the daughter of Ethbaal, king of the Zidonians (16:31). That in itself was risky and, in any case, it was disobedience to the divine injunction that God's people should not marry Canaanites (Ex. 34:12–16). Not only did Ahab marry this pagan woman, but he "went and served Baal and worshipped him and he reared up an altar for Baal in the house of Baal which he had built in Samaria and he made an Asherah" (16:31–33). It is clear from this that Ahab defied one of the vital obligations of the covenant. The writer of Kings comes early to the conclusion that "Ahab did more to provoke the Lord God of Israel to anger than all the kings of Israel that were before him" (16:33). The vindication of this pronouncement follows in chapters 17 to 22.

Evidently under the influence of Jezebel, the people went over in large numbers to the worship of Baal and other Canaanite gods like Asherah (16:33; 18:19, in both of which passages in the KJV, "groves" should be translated Asherah, the name of a Canaanite goddess).

Modern discovery has made the character of the god Baal clear to us. The god of fertility, he had charge of everything connected with the reproduction and the growth of flocks and crops. One of his spheres was the weather, which has important bearing on the flocks and the crops. In Canaanite mythology, Baal was slain each summer and had to be brought back from the realm of death by a goddess.

Elijah, acting under the direction of God, was to expose the emptiness of these claims. A drought settled on the land and Elijah told the king that there would be no rain till he spoke again (17:1). The drought was severe. Elijah was cared for in miraculous ways, and food was supplied both by the ravens (vv. 2–7, or possibly the "Arabs" since the Hebrew consonants will allow this translation, although the atmosphere of the narrative is that of miracle) and by a widow (vv. 8–24). During the long drought, there was a great shortage of water in the land and even the king felt the stress. He and his servant Obadiah searched the brooks for water (18:3–6). This Obadiah had once sheltered a hundred prophets in caves when the irate Jezebel sought their lives (vv. 3, 4). Elijah's own life was in danger, and the king sought him in many lands at this time (v. 10). Then Elijah met Obadiah and told him to inform his master, King Ahab, that he would now come to meet him. Elijah was acting under divine command. Very soon the rain would come from the God of Israel, and the emptiness of Baal's claims would be revealed.

When Elijah and Ahab met, Elijah commanded the gathering of the 450 prophets of Baal and the 400 prophets of Asherah on Mount Carmel. It was on that day that the great demonstration of the power of God occurred. The people were asked "How long will you go limping with two different opinions? If the Lord is God, follow him; but if Baal, follow him" (RSV, 18:21).

Altars were erected and sacrifices laid. The Canaanite prophets first called on Baal. The cry went on all day. The agreement was that the god that burned his sacrifice with fire was to be God. When Elijah's turn came, he drenched his sacrifice with water (18:31–36). Then in answer to the prayer of Elijah, God sent down fire from heaven. The test was complete. The Lord was God, and to this the people gave assent (vv. 38, 39). The prophet then followed an ancient injunction that false prophets were to be slain (Deut. 18:20), and the prophets of Baal were put to death. To make the vindication of God complete, in answer to the prayer of Elijah, the rain, withheld for about three years, now fell in abundance, appearing first as a small cloud out over the Mediterranean Sea, and then coming down in torrents (vv. 42–46).

In the setting of the times, this should have been sufficient reason for Ahab to return to the God of Israel. Was he not an Israelite? Should he not obey the covenant? True, he had a difficult wife, but that was no reason to foresake the covenant. Pressing his point, the writer goes on to tell how the evil Jezebel, being informed of the slaughter of the false prophets, took steps to take Elijah's life. He fled out of Israel to the far south of Judah. While he was there in deep despair, God spoke to him. To Elijah it seemed that none in Israel had kept the covenant of God but that all had forsaken the Lord. God told of the "seven thousand in Israel, all the knees which have not bowed unto Baal" (19:18). There were yet other tasks for God's servant to do in that apostate land. Jehu was to be anointed as king over Israel to succeed the line of Ahab in due course (v. 16).

Then right outside Israel, God had some plans to reveal in Damascus, where Hazael had to be anointed in readiness to become king there (v. 15). So Elijah returned at the command of God, and on the way indicated to a young man ploughing in a field that he would be his successor in due course (vv. 19–21). This young man was to become the great prophet Elisha.

Two other evidences of Ahab's rejection of the theocracy or rule of God, and of his own departure from the covenant, are yet to be given: the seizing of Naboth's vineyard (ch. 21), and the attitude of Ahab to the false prophets and his rejection of the prophet Micaiah (ch. 22).

In the matter of Naboth's vineyard, we need to understand that in ancient Israel it was the right of every man to possess his piece of land and, as a child of Abraham, to have a share in the Promised Land. Not even kings could usurp inheritance rights. It was otherwise in Canaan where kings and gods took what they desired, for might was right. When Naboth showed an unwillingness to part with his land (21:3), the matter should have ended there, and a man who kept the covenant of God would have gone no further. But Jezebel, whose religion taught her differently, thought otherwise, and asked Ahab, "Dost thou now govern Israel?" (v. 7), by which she implied that it was the king's right to take land. A quickly conceived plot was arranged to trap Naboth. It depended on two false witnesses who would swear that they had heard Naboth blaspheme God and the king and had thus broken an ancient law (Lev. 24:10–16). For this crime the penalty was stoning. The sentence was duly carried out, and Naboth's vineyard became the property of the king. Perhaps there was a certain fear in the heart even of Jezebel in this matter, for she arranged to seize the property in a "legal'" way. In any case, the story shows a further instance of Ahab's rejection of the laws of God. He stood condemned by God, and the prophet Elijah pronounced doom on both him and his house (21:19–24). In fear, Ahab made a show of repentance, but it was of little worth. The commentator remarks "There was none like unto Ahab which did sell himself to work wickedness in the sight of the Lord, whom Jezebel his wife stirred up" (v. 25).

The other evidence of his rejection of the rule of God in his life and in his kingdom was that he refused to consult Micaiah the prophet of God even though he knew who he was, preferring rather to regard the pleasant words of the false prophets. At the close of his life, when war with the Syrians was renewed, he was able to obtain the assistance of Jehoshaphat, king of Judah. Before the battle the king of Judah wished to know the mind of the Lord (22:5) and Ahab called his four hundred false prophets who gave the word of "Adonai" rather than the word of the Lord. The use of this word "Adonai" instead of the Lord in verse 6 suggests someone other than the God of Israel. Probably they spoke in the name of Baal. Jehoshaphat was unhappy and asked for a prophet of the Lord to be called. Ahab had hesitated to call him before, because on other occasions this prophet, Micaiah, had come and given unfavorable prophecies (v. 8).

After the false prophets had performed a symbolic act which portrayed the victory of Ahab (22:11, 12), Micaiah first gave an ironical approval to these words (v. 15), but, being pressed, gave the true word of the Lord (vv. 17–22). He told of a vision in which he saw a false spirit being allowed by God to enter the false prophets and thus deceive the king. It was the desire of Ahab to receive the words of deceivers, rather than the true word of God. God's word was that the day would be an ill one for Ahab (v. 17) and Ahab commanded that he be cast into prison (vv. 26–28).

Finally the two kings went to battle, Ahab being disguised. But a stray arrow lodged in his body and he fell, mortally wounded, and died at the close of the day (22:35). His body was brought to this capital where his blood-stained chariot was washed at the "pool of Samaria." The dogs licked up the blood according to the prophecy of Elijah (21:19).

There were other notable things about Ahab which the historian did not mention. One of these was the magnificent royal palace he built, which we now know (from similar palaces excavated in the East) to have been a palace ornamented with a great deal of ivory. Archaeological research tells us also that he was known to the Assyrians and that in 853 b.c. he sent two thousand chariots and ten thousand foot soldiers to help in a great battle against them at Karkar. It is evident, however, that the compiler of these records had no interest in giving such items as these, for his conclusion was that Ahab was finally unworthy of God's approval and nothing could therefore be gained by recounting the exploits of such a king.

Jehoshaphat of Judah (22:41–50). The first Book of Kings concludes with a brief account of Jehoshaphat of Judah. He was a king who "turned not aside from doing that which was right in the eyes of the Lord" (v. 43). He made some attempt to reform Judah (II Chron. 17:6–9; 19:1–11), although his success was evidently only partial. Yet he himself personally was a worthy king, true to the covenant. Reference is made to his agreement with the king of Israel (v. 44) and to his attempt to open up the port on the Red Sea (vv. 48, 49) which we now know was destroyed after Solomon's time, probably by the Egyptian Pharaoh Shishak.

Ahaziah of Israel, Third King of the Fourth Dynasty (I Kings 22:51—II Kings 1:18). Ahaziah, the third king of the fourth dynasty of Israel, is next passed in review. No good can be recorded about him, for "he did evil in the sight of the Lord and walked in the ways of his father and in the way of his mother and in the way of Jeroboam the son of Nebat who made Israel to sin" (I Kings 22:52). The writer thus had several ways of describing the wickedness of Ahaziah. Finally he is quite specific, and refers to his serving Baal and worshipping him (v. 53).

It was in his day that the Moabites finally threw off the yoke of Israel. The discovery of the famous Mesha stone at Dibon in ancient Moab in 1868 told the story of this rebellion of Moab from the Moabite angle. This account appears to conflict with the Bible story. But the two versions can easily be reconciled if we allow that in fact the Moabites were virtually free at the close of Ahab's life, when he was too busy with wars to be able to bring rebel Moabites under his control. They probably refused to pay his tribute and claimed to be free. But as far as Israel was concerned, the freedom of Moab was not recognized until the failure of the punitive war described in chapter 3.

After reigning only two years, Ahaziah fell through a lattice and was seriously injured. He sent messengers to Ekron to the pagan priests of the Philistines in order to inquire of the god Baal-zebub (II Kings 1:2). For this action he was severely rebuked by Elijah who foretold his death. It was a rejection of the covenant obligations of the kings of Israel to descend to this type of consultation (Deut. 18). The death of the king was a judgment on him for his sin (v. 16). He left no son and his brother succeeded to the throne (v. 17).

Jehoram of Israel, the Last King of the Fourth Dynasty (II Kings 3:1–27; 8:16–24). At this point in the narrative, the simple systematic setting forth of the kings of Judah and Israel is disturbed. It was necessary for the compiler to introduce into his narrative somewhere the important material that he had collected referring to the prophet

Elisha. It did not fit into the usual framework used by the author, but it was added at this point. Some of the stories belonged to the days of Ahaziah, some to the days of Jehoram and some still later. We shall attempt to discover the place of Elisha in maintaining and guarding the theocracy after we have outlined the reign of Jehoram. But we should observe that the story of Jehoram is commenced at II Kings 3:1, some details are given in chapter 3, then the material about Elisha is inserted and it is not until chapter 8 that Jehoram's story is completed.

Jehoram was not by any means a perfect king, but judged in terms of his adherence to the covenant, the writer notes that "he wrought evil in the sight of the Lord; but not like his father and like his mother; for he put away the image of Baal that his father had made." This was an improvement. However he clave to the sins of Jeroboam and so at last was condemned (3:3).

The most important item about him was that he organized a military campaign against Moab. He was assisted in this by Jehoshaphat of Judah and the king of Edom (3:4–9). Elisha approved the alliance and gave some encouragement (vv. 10–20). In the campaign that followed, the territory of Moab was devastated and the Moabites fled from their capital. But Mesha, king of Moab, was not subdued (v. 27) and later he freed his land from Israel's dominion.

Although Jehoram reigned for some ten years, there is little in the way of detailed record. The last we hear of him is that he and the king of Judah had agreed to go to battle against the Syrians (8:28). In the battle, Joram was wounded and went to Jezreel to recuperate. It was while he was there that he was assassinated by the army captain Jehu who inaugurated the fifth dynasty of Israel. His death brought to an end the period of friendship between Israel and Judah.

Stories of Elisha (4:1—8:15). The stories of these chapters are difficult to arrange chronologically. In several places the king is not named, but is designated merely as "the king." However, it was important to refer to the work of this prophet, for in a day when the kings of the land had departed from the ways of God, there were those who were true to Him. Men like Elijah and Elisha had the task of guarding the theocracy and of building up the simple people in the things of God, even if kings were apostate. The kings of Israel themselves only merited the rejection of God. Indeed, Elisha on one occasion told Jehoram that were it not for the presence of Jehoshaphat of Judah, a man of some piety, the cause of Jehoram would be lost at once (3:14).

Some attempts have been made to arrange the material in these sections chronologically. Thus incidents where Gehazi the servant of Elisha is able to move freely about must be placed before the time when he contracted leprosy, and thus 8:3–6 must precede 5:1–27. Again there are chapters in which the prophet appears to be on friendly terms with the king of the time. He was not particularly friendly with Jehoram (3:10–14) and was to become involved in the anointing of the new king, Jehu (9:1–13). Hence stories which suggest friendly relations between Elisha and the king would appear to be later than the time of Jehoram, say in the days of Jehu or his successors. We therefore place such chapters as 6:8–23 somewhat later. The account of Naaman the leper would suggest that he believed that Elisha was attached to the court, and the action of Elisha in coming to the king's aid in the time of his distress showed that he was not far away. Hence we place this narrative later than Jehoram. Since Gehazi is prominent in this story, it must be linked with other stories about him at a time when he was still healthy.

A further line of evidence which helps us to establish the chronological order concerns the Syrian kings. Events connected with Ben-hadad must precede those connected with Hazael who succeeded him. Thus 6:24—7:20 correctly precedes 8:7–15. It is probably impossible to piece the story together in the correct order. This hardly matters, since in any case the character and the work of Elisha are not at all dependent on the correct order of narration of the events.

The writer of II Kings outlined the work of Elisha under two main headings: (1) as a man of political influence, and (2) as a worker of miracles. Politically he is seen first in the description of the invasion of Moab (ch. 3). Then he is involved in the contacts between Israel and Syria (6:8–23; 6:24—7:15; 8:7–15). Finally he is closely associated with the choice of a new king for Israel (9:1–10).

As a miracle worker he plays a notable part in the Bible narrative. He stands out as an honored and respected servant of God who used his powers to relieve suffering and distress. He assisted the widow (4:1–7), helped the lady of Shunem (4:8–37; 8:1–6), cleansed a vessel of food and fed one hundred men (4:38–44), helped a band of prophets in distress (6:1–7), and healed Naaman the Syrian (5:1–27).

Elisha lived during the reigns of five or six kings and died in the days of King Joash (13:14–20). He was of real significance in days of carelessness and apostasy, maintaining the school of the prophets who were a witness to the true God in those days, so that both in speech and perhaps also in writing they continued to press the claims of the covenant God of Israel upon His people, who had turned aside. He will always be remembered as a strong influence for good and for God, seeking to guard the theocracy at a time when regard for the rule of God was at a minimum in Israel.

Jehoram and Ahaziah of Judah (8:16–29). Confusion may arise at this point because two kings with the same name appear as rulers in the two kingdoms of Israel and Judah. In chapter 8:16, the king of Israel is called Joram to distinguish him from the king of Judah, Jehoram.

Jehoram of Judah was not held in high esteem by the writer of Kings for "he walked in the way of the kings of Israel and did as the house of Ahab; for the daughter of Ahab was his wife" (8:18). His reign of eight years was remembered for the troubles on his southern frontier. Up to the days of Jehoshaphat, the land of Edom was in the hands of Judah, but in the days of Jehoram (Joram), the Edomites were able to throw off the yoke of Judah (vv. 20–23). There is archaeological evidence that the old port of Ezion Geber was destroyed about this time. The Books of Chronicles inform us (II Chron. 21:2–4) that he massacred his brothers in an attempt to make his throne secure. This kind of behavior combined with his religious apostasy would earn the contempt of the writer of Kings.

Joram of Israel was still on the throne when Jehoram of Judah died and was succeeded by his son, Ahaziah. He was the son of Athaliah, the daughter of Omri, or more correctly the grand-daughter of Omri. Hebrew usage allows the use of "daughter" for such relationships as these (8:26; cf. 8:18). The compiler of these records did not have a high opinion of Ahaziah, for he is described as walking "in the way of the house of Ahab." Indeed he conducted himself in much the same way as the house of Ahab "for he was the son-in-law of the house of Ahab" (v. 27). Little is told about him, either in the Book of Kings, or in its counterpart, the Book of Chronicles. The one feature of his story that is mentioned is that he went to assist Joram, the king of Israel, in a war against the Syrians. The friendship of the two royal houses is clear from the marriage alliances and from the manner in which Judah went to help Israel in her wars. It was soon to change.

The death of Ahaziah is deferred to chapter 9 of II Kings, until the writer is able to explain the revolution of Jehu, for Ahaziah met his death as a result of this change. Actually, he was slain by the men of Jehu who usurped the throne of Israel (9:27–29). After this murder, Israel and Judah were at enmity and never really became allies again. The last years of Israel's independence were years of hostility to Judah.

3. The Period of Renewed Antagonism between Israel and Judah (II Kings 9:1—17:41)

There was evidently considerable dissatisfaction in Israel with the last kings of the Omri dynasty. The Syrians, having overrun the area to the east of Jordan, had penetrated even to the west of the river, if we allow that some of the incidents in chapters 5 to 7 refer to these days. The prophets were dissatisfied with the state of affairs, for even Elijah had already been shown that Jehu should replace the present king (I Kings 19:15, 16), and Elisha took active steps to insure that Jehu would become king by sending one of the prophets to anoint him in the camp (II Kings 9:1–13). We may conclude that conservative groups like the Rechabites were also sympathetic to the change from the incident in 10:15–18. We turn then to the founding of the fifth dynasty of Israel, and thereafter we shall study the fortunes of Israel and Judah during the second period of antagonism between the two kingdoms.

Jehu of Israel, Founder of the Fifth Dynasty (II Kings 9:1—10:36). When Jehoram of Israel went to war against Hazael of Syria at Ramoth-Gilead, he was wounded in the battle and retired to Jezreel (8:28, 29). He was visited here by Ahaziah of Judah. Presumably the army was left in Transjordan, for when the messenger of Elisha went to anoint Jehu, the text says that he went to Ramoth-Gilead. Calling Jehu out privately, the prophet's representative anointed him in the name of the Lord, to be king over Israel (9:6). He was instructed to "smite the house of Ahab" in order to avenge the blood of God's servants, the prophets, who had suffered at the hands of this wicked house. The house of Ahab was to be eliminated (vv. 8–11). When the fellow officers of Jehu learned what had happened, they received him as king (vv. 12–13).

Jehu proceeded at once to Jezreel where the wounded Joram was recuperating. Riding at a great speed in a chariot, his approach was detected. Joram and Ahaziah of Judah went out to meet Jehu, asking whether he came in peace (9:21–22). There was to be no peace for Jehu while such evil kings lived, and drawing his bow he slew Joram, whose body was cast into the field of Naboth (vv. 22–26). Ahaziah of Judah fled in the direction of Beth-haggan (literal Hebrew), and the men of Joram gave chase and wounded him. He died at Megiddo later in the day (vv. 27–29).

The final act of the day came when Jehu commanded that the evil Jezebel be cast out of the palace window. The dogs ate up her flesh leaving only a few small pieces (vv. 30–37). The parallel account of the death of Ahaziah in II Chronicles 22:9 is difficult to reconcile with the story in II Kings, and we must await more light on the question.

The bloody activities of Jehu did not stop there. He rounded up all the descendants of Ahab, some of whom were still minors, and massacred them. In this action he went far beyond anything commanded by the prophets, and for this he was later condemned by the prophet Hosea (1:4). The massacre went further still. Some of Ahaziah's kindred were found, and these were also slain (10:13–14). Finally, there was a tremendous massacre of the worshippers of Baal, accompanied by a destruction of their images and shrines (vv. 19–29). It was a bloody beginning to the reign of Jehu and alienated not merely the remaining supporters of the dead king of Israel, but also the royal houses of Judah and Phoenicia. When within a short period Jehu again felt the pressure of the Syrians, he had little support and lost the whole of Transjordan, it would seem (vv. 32–33).

The compiler of II Kings is careful to commend the desire of Jehu to remove the offending religion of Baal. The commendation in verse 30, however, must not be taken as a contradiction of the condemnation in Hosea 1:4 of Jehu's large scale massacres. Ultimate judgment was pronounced on the house of Jehu (v. 30, cf. 15:11–12). In fact, the final summary of the compiler is that "Jehu took no heed to walk in the law of the Lord God of Israel with all his heart: for he departed not from the sins of Jeroboam" (v. 31).

External evidence tells us that Jehu actually came under the power of the Assyrians about 841 B.C. The great Assyrian king, Shalmaneser III, has left a picture of Jehu on his large obelisk which was discovered nearly a century ago at Nimrud. It is the only picture of a Bible king that has come down from the ancient world.

The lands lost to the Syrians were not recovered until the days of Jeroboam II. So Jehu slept with his fathers and was succeeded by his son, Jehoahaz. It is evident that the reign of Jehu did not witness a clear acceptance by Israel of the rule of God over the nation. Covenant obligations were neglected, and although Israel claimed to be the people of God, they were far from being so in fact. The external demonstrations of Jehu in which he exterminated the Baal worshippers were of little worth, for in his heart he showed no disposition to keep the law of the Lord his God. The compiler of Kings thus concludes again that, in the case of Jehu, we find a king who was not true to his covenant obligations.

Athaliah, Queen of Judah (11:1–21). Athaliah was the only woman to rule ovei either of these little kingdoms. Like Jehu, she was a usurper. She was a daughter of Ahab, and the mother of Ahaziah, so recently slain by the men of Jehu. Hearing of the death of her son, she seized the opportunity to usurp the throne. In a desperate action, she slew all the royal seed except the boy Joash who was smuggled away by the sister of the dead king (vv. 1–3). For six years this woman reigned over Judah, giving special place to her Baal-worshipping friends, and installing a priest of Baal, Mattan by name, to officiate at her false altars (v. 18).

Eventually a plot was formed to overthrow Athaliah. Reference to the Book of Chronicles shows that the Levites were associated with this plot (II Chron. 22:10—23:21). It was Jehoida, the priest, the husband of the woman who had hidden the boy Joash (II Chron. 22:11), who led the revolt. He had the support of the army (v. 4), the priests, and probably the bulk of the citizens of Judah. At a time when there was a double company of Levites in the temple (II Chron. 23:8), and when those who were to go off duty on the Sabbath were still about, the youth was presented and proclaimed as king. Athaliah was caught off her guard and bravely enough came out to the people (compare Jezebel as she faced Jehu in 9:30, 31). She was seized and slain (v. 16). Subsequently, the false priest was captured and likewise slain.

A vital point for the writer of Kings was a renewal of the covenant between the Lord, the king and the people "that they should be the Lord's people" (11:17–20). A further covenant was made between the king and the people. Actually, if the king ruled according to his covenant obligations, both he and the people would be bound to God in a perfectly natural bond, all the people acknowledging God as supreme ruler over all, with the king as his anointed ruler here on earth. The nature of the covenant when correctly understood and applied would cover all contingencies. In the observance of a covenant relationship to the Lord, Judah and Israel would fulfil their true destiny. It seemed on the death of Athaliah that a new day might have dawned.

Joash of Judah (12:1–21). The boy king showed the promise of success in his early days. "He did that which was right in the sight of the Lord all his days wherein Jehoida the priest instructed him" (v. 2). He did not, however, take steps to remove the high places, which we now think were connected with some kind of cult of the dead. That Jehoash (Joash for short) did later show infidelity to the covenant seems evident. The parallel account in II Chronicles is quite clear on the point (24:18–22), and shows that when the prophet Zechariah protested that the king and the nation were departing from the commandments of God, he was stoned to death.

There was, however, something of good in the reign of Joash, for it was in his days that the temple was repaired. Joash commanded the use of the temple dues and offerings for the repair of the temple (12:4). Because the priests were slow in the execution of the task Joash took it over himself (v. 7) and appropriated the temple revenues (vv. 7–8). In due course, the work was completed. This was naturally of significance for the compiler of Kings, since it was quite in keeping with covenant obligations to preserve the worship of God at the temple, and to insure that it was done in a proper manner.

The closing remarks about Joash are given in 12:17–21. The Syrians passed through Israel and made their way down to the Philistine coast (v. 17). We should refer here to the account of Syria's invasions of Israel in 10:32–34 and 13:3–7. Hazael, by his capture of Gath, was able to command the trade route to Egypt, and now had Jerusalem at his mercy. In those circumstances, Joash bought off the Syrians by giving up some of the sacred objects in the temple (v. 18), as well as part of the temple treasures. Finally, Joash was assassinated following a conspiracy. Details of the conspiracy are not given in Kings, but perhaps it may be connected in some way with the fact that Joash had departed from the policy of those who had put him on the throne some years before. His son Amaziah succeeded him (v. 21).

Thus a reign that commenced with some promise of a faithful adherence to God's covenant with Israel, ended in dismal failure.

Once again the writer of Kings has made his point. Whenever the king or nation departs from the covenant of God and follows evil ways, calamity of some kind occurs and the final result is failure even if there were some elements of good in the reign of the king. Departure from the rule of God can only result in some form of judgment. Sooner or later this kind of behavior brings about the downfall of the nation.

Jehoahaz and Jehoash of Israel, Kings of the Fifth Dynasty (13:1-25). Jehoahaz, son of Jehu, had the unenviable task of ruling Israel at a time when his kingdom was at the mercy of the Syrians. We have seen that Hazael overran the lands to the east of Jordan in his father's day (10:32-33), and had later moved down into Judah. The pressure of the Syrians continued all the days of Hazael and into the time of his successor, Ben-hadad (13:3-7). These kings of Syria reduced Israel to a servile state; their army was now numbered at only ten thousand footmen and ten chariots, a striking contrast with the army of Ahab described on the obelisk of the Assyrian king, Shalmaneser III, who spoke of Ahab's two thousand chariots and ten thousand foot-soldiers, Israel's contribution to the coalition that fought against the Assyrians in 853 B.C.

The Bible here makes a reference to a "saviour" whom God sent to help. This may refer to a new Assyrian king who was soon to weaken the Syrians, or it may refer to the great Jeroboam II who was to deliver Israel in a very short time. In any case, there was no easing of the state of affairs in the days of Jehoahaz. If we ask about the character of this king, we learn that he too "did evil in the sight of the Lord and followed the sins of Jeroboam the son of Nebat" (13:2). Another note in verse 6 tells us that the Asherah (translated as "grove" in KJV) was left in Samaria. Evidently, therefore, the great purge of Jehu did not eliminate these evils, and we may judge that the worship of the Lord was thoroughly Canaanized.

Jehoash (or Joash, in the shortened form of the name), the son of Jehoahaz, succeeded his father just about the turn of the century. For a brief time, his contemporary in Judah was also named Joash. Our chapter distinguishes the two in verse 10 by referring to Joash of Judah and Jehoash of Israel, although the writer reverts to the short form of the name in verses 12 to 19, but returns to the long form of the name in verse 25, concluding the chapter with the short form, Joash.

External history tells us that in about 805 B.C., the Assyrians reduced the Syrians to subjection. Then, soon after 800 B.C., the Syrians fell to fighting one another as we learn from an important inscription found in Syria in recent years. This gave Jehoash the opportunity to recover the lands that had been lost to his enemies in Transjordan (13:24–25).

It was at this time that Elisha died (13:14–21). One of his last acts was to invite Joash, who had come to visit him, to fire arrows out of the window. The number of arrows fired was to represent the number of victories he would win over his enemies, the Syrians. There was a strange unwillingness on the part of Joash to fire more than three times. He probably knew the meaning of the actions, and like Ahab, wished to keep the Syrians reasonably strong as a protection against the Assyrians (vv. 14–19).

Politically it was a new day for Israel with a change in her fortunes, but the writer of Kings is not greatly impressed by this. For him the important fact was that Joash "did that which was evil in the sight of the Lord" (13:11). He concluded his account of Jehoash by referring to his war with Judah in the days of Amaziah. We shall take this up again in the account of Ahaziah of Judah. Once again, however, a king of Israel, who should have been faithful to the covenant, failed to honor his obligations and to recognize that the theocracy was the correct rule for Israel.

Amaziah of Judah (14:1–22). Amaziah began to reign in Judah just as the eighth century was opening, about 800 B.C. After a reign of twenty-nine years he was succeeded by the famous Uzziah. Amaziah seems to have earned the praise of the writer of Kings to a degree, "for he did that which was right in the sight of the Lord." However, he was not like David in the completeness of his obedience, but followed the pattern of his father Joash (14:3). Further, the high places were not taken away and the people sacrificed and burnt incense at these places (v. 4). As soon as Amaziah felt secure, he moved against the murderers of his father. Unlike many others of his time, he confined his vengeance to the murderers themselves, and spared the children (v. 6). Here he followed a law of Deuteronomy 24:16. He had some success against the Edomites and probably prepared the way for his son to reoccupy this land for Judah (vv. 21, 22). Evidently he was puffed up by his success and made some show against the king of Israel who came out to meet him and defeated him in battle. It seems that we may interpret the Bible text to mean that Judah became a sort of vassal of Israel at this time and had to pay a big indemnity (v. 14).

The reign of Amaziah ended in a conspiracy. Possibly the course of events was that the people decided to depose him and appoint his son king in his place (24:21). When he resisted, the people turned against him and he fled to Lachish. He was pursued and slain (v. 19). The account in II Chronicles 25:14–16 indicates that Amazian went after the gods of the Edomites after he had defeated them in battle. In the end Amaziah was a failure. The writer of Kings gives but faint praise to him and adds sufficient defamatory material to make it clear that he, too, largely departed from the covenant obligations he had with the God of Israel.

Jeroboam II of Israel, Fifth Dynasty (14:23–29). The second Jeroboam was surely one of Israel's greatest kings, politically speaking. He had a long reign during which he was able to restore the fortunes of Israel. He reconquered the whole of traditional Israelite territory from Galilee to the Dead Sea (v. 25) and brought Damascus and Hamath under Israel, probably as tributaries (v. 28). These were lands that formerly belonged to David and Solomon who were probably regarded as kings of Judah by the chroniclers of Israel.

The books of the prophets—Amos, Hosea and Isaiah—give us some picture of the remarkable prosperity of those days. This is borne out by excavations in which the fine palaces of Megiddo and Tirzah have been brought to light. Receipts discovered in Samaria, written on broken pieces of pottery, witness to widespread trade. All this prosperity, however, only created social corruption. At the same time there was severe apostasy in religion. Evidently the compiler of Kings did not regard the prosperity of sufficient importance to recount the exploits of Jeroboam, for in a telling way, he showed his disapproval of this politically great king, by dismissing him in seven verses. A study of the three prophets referred to above will show just how far the people of the day departed from the covenant relationship to their God. Jeroboam II, despite his achievements in other ways, stands condemned in a most effective manner.

Uzziah (Azariah) of Judah (15:1–7). The compiler of Kings gives no better treatment to the contemporary king of Judah. He too had a long and prosperous reign, though we would learn little of this from II Kings. There is a better account in II Chronicles 26:3–23, but we gain a picture of the great prosperity of those days from the prophets Amos, Hosea and Isaiah. Archaeological work supplements this impression by the discovery of many settlements in southern Judah at the time. The old port of Ezion Geber was occupied, and there was building in many areas to judge from the archaeological survey of the areas to the far south of Jerusalem. But the writer of Kings is interested in the king, not the prosperity of his regime: "He did that which was right in the sight of the Lord, but only according to all that his father Amaziah had done" (v. 3). The high places were not removed, and the people sacrificed and burnt incense there. Later in his reign, Uzziah interfered in the office of the priests according to II Chronicles 26:16–21, and the leprosy which he contracted was seen as a judgment for this effrontery. In large measure, Uzziah failed to be true to the covenant.

Days of Chaos in Israel, Sixth, Seventh and Eighth Dynasties (15:8–31). Things were moving swiftly to a climax in Israel. Jeroboam II died in 746 B.C. By 722 B.C. the kingdom of Israel had come to its end. In those last twenty-four years, calamity after calamity occurred. Of the six kings who reigned, four were murdered, one taken captive; only one died naturally. There were five ruling houses.

Zechariah, the son of Jeroboam II and the last king of the fifth dynasty (15:8–12), reigned but six months and was murdered by an army captain, Shallum. Thus ended the line of Jehu and the word of the Lord was fulfilled (v. 12). Zechariah followed the evil ways of his father (v. 9).

Shallum (15:13–16) the murderer, the only king of the sixth dynasty, reigned but one month, being assassinated by Menahem, who may have been the military governor in Tirzah. No account of the character of Shallum is given, but we may guess it with some assurance.

Menahem, founder of the seventh dynasty (15:17–22), began his rule in a brutal fashion with the massacre of the inhabitants of the town of Tiphsah which did not open its doors to him. Women and children suffered (v. 16). It was in his days that the first of the Assyrian invasions was met. Pul or Pulu, an Assyrian general who had usurped the throne of Assyria in 745 B.C. and had adopted the name of Tiglath Pileser, a former great ruler in Assyria, turned his attention to the west and soon made contact with Israel. Menahem became his vassal and paid dearly in silver. The assessment, at fifty shekels per head, shows that the Israelites were regarded as slaves who had to buy themselves back from slavery, for Assyrian documents give the average price of a slave at about fifty shekels. Menahem appears in the records of Tiglath Pileser. In the eyes of the writer of Kings, he too forsook the covenant and "did that which was evil in the sight of the Lord" (v. 18).

Pekahiah, the son of Menahem (15:23–26), reigned but two years and followed the evil path of his father. He was presently slain by an army captain, Pekah (v. 25), the only ruler of the eighth dynasty. His successor Pekah (vv. 27–31) is likewise classed as having done evil in the sight of the Lord (v. 28). In his time Assyrian pressure assumed startling proportions, for Tiglath Pileser invaded the area of Galilee and took captive many of the Israelites of that area (v. 29). Pekah's reign was important also for its repercussions on Judah. Indeed, the Assyrian attack on the Galilee area is probably a direct result of the attempt of Pekah to build up an anti-Assyrian coalition. Pekah combined with Rezin of Damascus and invaded Judah, as we learn from chapter 16 (cf. II Chron. 28:5–15; Is. 7:1, 2). Pekah's end came when he was slain by a certain Hoshea. The Assyrian records speak of Pekah and Hoshea and claim that Pekah was deposed by Tiglath Pileser. We may suspect that Hoshea had Assyrian support.

Jotham and Ahaz of Judah (15:32—16:20). The historian returns at this point to pick up the story of Judah with the reign of Jotham, a contemporary of Menahem, Pekahiah and Pekah. This king had been co-regent with his father for a time, owing to the leprosy of his father Uzziah (II Chron. 26:21). The writer of Kings suggests that he paid some kind of respect to his covenant relationship with God and that "he did that which was right" (15:34). In the nation itself, however, there were faults, and where people sacrificed and burnt incense, the high places remained (v. 36). At the close of Jotham's life, the invasion of Judah by Pekah of Israel and Rezin of Damascus began (v. 37), although it was left to his son Ahaz to face this problem.

Ahaz was the reigning king of Judah when the kingdom of Israel came to its end. The compiler of the records in Kings hastens to tell us that this king was a dismal failure. He "did not that which was right in the sight of the Lord his God like David his father but he walked in the way of the kings of Israel, yea, and he made his son to pass through the fire according to the abominations of the heathen—and he sacrificed and burnt incense in the high places and on hills and under every green tree" (16:2–4). The nature of some of the practices of verses 3 and 4 are now partly understood from archaeological discovery. This gross apostasy was bound to bring the judgment of God on the nation. Isaiah, the prophet, was active at the time, and we learn from his prophecy that he had dealings with Ahaz (Is. 7). It was to this king that Isaiah gave the famous Immanuel prophecy of Isaiah 7:14.

In the days of Ahaz, who incidentally is known on Assyrian inscriptions as "Jehoahaz," Pekah, king of Israel, tried to form an anti-Assyrian coalition with Rezin of Damascus. Possibly Pekah sought the support of Ahaz and, on his refusal, he and Rezin his companion invaded Judah. Ahaz was reassured by Isaiah (Is. 7:1-16), but he was unwilling to trust God, and called on the Assyrian king, Tiglath Pileser, to come to his aid (16:7). This cost a good deal in silver and gold (v. 8), but it brought about an attack on Damascus which led to the fall of this city (v. 9), and at the same time led to an invasion of Israel described in II Kings 15:29.

Ahaz was compelled to surrender to Assyria and from the practices of the Assyrians known from their records, we may suggest that one of the prices he had to pay was to set up in his temple one of the symbols of Assyrian authority in the shape of an Assyrian altar (16:9-18). Perhaps the official sacrifices of the God of Israel were still carried on, but the presence of an Assyrian altar in the temple was a mark of subservience. The fact that the king offered sacrifices himself suggests something irregular, and the fact that he "enquired" (v. 15) at the brazen altar, looks as if he introduced some Babylonian ideas into the worship of the temple. It was a sad day for Judah, and the writer of Kings rightly assesses the final worth of Ahaz at very low value. He was still ruling in Judah when the kingdom of Israel came to its end in 722/1 B.C.

Hoshea of Israel, Ninth Dynasty. Final Collapse of Israel (17:1-41). Chapter 17 of II Kings is a most important chapter for understanding the purpose of the two Books of Kings, for it sets out in some detail the basis on which the compiler of these records assesses the value of the various kings. The chapter commences with a brief account of the last days of Israel. Hoshea had been approved as king by Tiglath Pileser (15:30). He reigned nine years in all, but with a change in the ruler of Assyria and with the accession of Shalmaneser V, we suspect that Hoshea in some way gave offense, for the new Assyrian king paid a visit to Israel and Hoshea was brought to heel (17:3). A little while after, Hoshea began intrigues with the king of Egypt and failed to pay his tribute ("he brought no present") to Assyria. Shalmaneser then invaded Israel and captured Hoshea.

Samaria however closed its gates and a siege began. Before the city was taken, the king died and was succeeded by King Sargon (Is. 20:1) who finally took it after a siege of three years (17:5). Many of the Israelites in the area of Samaria went into captivity (v. 6) and were replaced by other peoples from further east (vv. 24–41). There follows in the text in Kings a lengthy discussion of the sins of Israel (vv. 7–23). The emphasis in these verses is on the failure of Israel to walk in the ways of the Lord and to keep His covenant, and the writer shows the consequence of this attitude which led to apostasy of all kinds. If religious apostasy was the basic sin, we judge that the social and personal sins spoken of by the prophets were the natural outcome of such a departure from the ways of God. It was in terms of this insight into the true basis for all healthy living that the compiler of Kings assessed the value of all of Israel's kings.

The new peoples naturally brought into the land their own form of worship, including the shameful practice of passing children through the fire (17:31). Their gods, Adrammelech and Anammelech, were manifestations of the god Moloch, about whom archaeological discovery has told us a good deal. These new dwellers in Israel were, however, fearful that they might offend the local gods and asked for a priest to tell them "the manner of the god of the land" (v. 26). One of the priests who had been carried away captive came and dwelt in Bethel and taught them "how they should fear the Lord" (v. 28). But the move was purely utilitarian, for "they feared the Lord and served their own gods" (v. 33). This mixture of religious outlooks may have contributed to the later confusion between the worship of the Jews and that of the Samaritans (Jn. 4).

What assessment then did the writer of Kings make of Hoshea? "He did that which was evil in the sight of the Lord, but not as the kings of Israel that were before him" (v. 2). Were there some favorable features? We do not know, but there is a passing hint that he may have had something to commend him.

III. The Single Kingdom—Judah after the Collapse of Israel (II Kings 18:1—25:30)

With the collapse of Samaria, Judah was left alone as an independent Israelite kingdom. She kept her independence from 722/1 until 586 B.C. when she too fell before the Babylonians, who, by then, had replaced the Assyrians as masters of the East.

1. Hezekiah of Judah (18:1—20:21)

Hezekiah, one of Judah's best kings, followed the Lord wholeheartedly. He was evidently imbued with the idea of the covenant and remained true to the theocratic ideal. The writer describes him thus: "He did that which was right in the sight of the Lord according to all that David his father did" (18:3). In illustration we are told that he undertook wide reforms, including the breaking down of the images and the Asherim and the destruction of the serpent of brass that had been kept since the days of Moses. "He trusted in the Lord God of Israel so that after him was none like him among all the kings of Judah nor any that were before him" (v. 5). We judge that Hezekiah must have been co-regent with his father for we learn in verse 9 that it was in the seventh year of Hezekiah that Samaria fell. This occurred in 722/1 B.C., before Hezekiah became king alone. The reference in verse 13 must be to his own independent period of rule, for the date is 701 B.C., which would be the fourteenth year of his reign if he began to rule in 715 B.C.

Probably at some time before this, the visit of the Chaldaean Berodach-baladan took place. This man wished to stir up trouble in the west in his overall plan to overthrow the Assyrians. On the occasion of the visit of his messengers, Hezekiah showed them the treasures of the house of the Lord and was severely rebuked for this by Isaiah (20:12–19).

The main features of the reign of Hezekiah, which the writer chose to illustrate his point, were his reforms and his attitude on the occasion of the Assyrian invasion.

The reformation of this king is described in considerable detail in II Chronicles 29:1—31:21, from which it appears that his reforms extended to the former territory of Israel. This suggests either some weakening of Assyrian power or some sort of religious freedom which the Assyrians allowed. Hezekiah's rebellion against Assyria is described in Kings in considerable detail. It would seem that Hezekiah was in a desperate plight and begged for terms (18:13, 14). Then for some reason Sennacherib, the Assyrian king, either changed his mind or found some occasion to attack Jerusalem owing to some hesitancy in Hezekiah. The Assyrians demonstrated against Jerusalem with serious threats and openly scorned the possibility that the God of the Jews could deliver the people. Had not all other gods failed (v. 34)? In his hour of need, Hezekiah sought the Lord and asked the advice of Isaiah, who promised that the Lord would turn aside the Assyrians. This He did (19:1-7).

Some commentators think that the account in 19:8-13 refers to a second invasion of the Assyrians at a time when Tirhaka was king of Egypt, 688-670 B.C., but the point is not clear. In any case the attitude of Hezekiah was to call on the Lord and to "spread it before the Lord" (v. 14). Once again God answered and delivered Judah (vv. 14-37).

Further evidence of the character of this king is given in the discussion of his illness (20:1-11). Isaiah spoke of his death (v. 1), but after a prayer asking for mercy and the confession that he had walked "in truth and with a whole (KJV, 'perfect') heart," Isaiah was able to promise a further period of life (vv. 4-6). It was on that occasion that a remarkable sign was given to the king (vv. 8-11).

As usual in Kings, there is a brief summary at the conclusion of the narrative. It is here that we learn of the conduit that Hezekiah built to bring water into the city. This seems to be the tunnel in which the now famous Siloam inscription was discovered.

2. Manasseh and Amon of Judah (21:1-26)

This king, known on Assyrian inscriptions as one who paid tribute to the Assyrians, came under the strongest condemnation of the writer of Kings, for he returned to all the evils that had been destroyed by his father. The list of pagan practices (21:3-7) clearly depicts the depths to which the people of Judah were capable of descending. Manasseh "seduced them to do more evil than did the nations whom the Lord destroyed before the children of Israel" (v. 9). The prophets protested and promised judgment (vv. 10-15). Even the work of the good King Josiah did not suffice to prevent this final collapse of Judah and the falling of divine judgment on the land. Add to this apostasy the fact of the shedding of innocent blood of those who opposed the king, and we are led to the conclusion that this king must have been further from the ideal of the theocracy than almost any other king of Judah.

Amon, his son, reigned only two years, but he too was infected by the spirit of his father and was finally slain in a conspiracy (21:19–26). A conspiracy of the "people of the land," it seems to have been a popular uprising in protest against the policy of these two kings. Perhaps the boy Josiah was already being prepared for his reign by a suitable education.

3. *Josiah of Judah* (22:1—23:30)

It is remarkable that right at the close of the independence of Judah there should be two such kings as Hezekiah and Josiah. It would seem as if God was giving Judah a chance to repent. The writer of Kings approved of these two kings most warmly. Concerning Josiah the report was "he did that which was right in the sight of the Lord and walked in the ways of David his father and turned not aside to the right hand or to the left" (22:2).

The importance of Josiah in the eyes of the compiler lies in his religious activities. In the first instance, it was as a boy of sixteen (II Chron. 34:3), that he began to seek after the God of David, his father. In the eighteenth year of his reign, he undertook the repair of the temple of God (22:3–7). This was a commendable action.

While these repairs to the temple were going on the "book of the law" was discovered. When this was read to the king, he was distressed and sought the advice of the prophetess Huldah (22:11–20) who foretold the judgment of God upon the people. The effect of the finding of the book was to intensify the reformation which had already begun before the book was found. The words of this "book of the covenant" were read in the ears of the people, and the king made a public declaration that he would keep the covenant of the Lord, to which the people gave approval (23:1–3).

The reformation continued with the destruction of all the paraphernalia of the false cults. Idolatrous priests were "put down," priests who functioned at the high places in the country were forbidden to practice the rites of their cult (23:8, 9). In Jerusalem itself every evidence of false worship was destroyed (vv. 11–14). It is of interest to us to find that the reforms extended to Bethel which was really in the former kingdom of Israel, by now in the hands of the Assyrians. But the fact of Josiah's reforms seems to indicate either that the Assyrians had lost their control there or else that they allowed Josiah some freedom in religious matters.

Among other things Josiah was able to keep the Passover according to the prescriptions of the covenant (23:21). The writer of Kings noted that "there was not holden such a passover from the days of the judges that judged Israel nor of the kings of Judah" (v. 22). This Passover is described in some detail in II Chronicles 35:1–19.

The death of Josiah came about in a tragic way. In an attempt to prevent the Pharaoh Nechoh going to the help of the Assyrians, Josiah was slain in battle (23:29) at Megiddo.

4. The Last Days of Judah (23:31—25:21)

On the death of Josiah in 609 B.C., Judah's course had just over twenty years to run. Jehoahaz, the son of Josiah, succeeded him in Jerusalem, but after three months Pharaoh Nechoh, who now ruled Palestine, deposed him and replaced him by his brother Eliakim whose name was changed to Jehoiakim. At the same time the land was "put to tribute" (23:31–34). Jehoahaz is described in the usual terms (v. 32) and we conclude that he offended against the covenant of God.

Jehoiakim, who reigned eleven years, commenced his reign by paying tribute to Pharaoh. In terms of character he must have been one of Judah's worst kings. The prophecy of Jeremiah paints him in a very bad light (Jer. 22:13–15, 17–19; 26:20–23; 36:21–26). Indeed Jeremiah prophesied that he would have the burial of an ass (Jer. 22:9). II Chronicles says that Nebuchadrezzar "bound him in fetters to take him to Babylon" (36:6). Possibly he was wounded in a battle and taken captive, but died of his wounds and was cast away. The reference in II Kings 24:1–3 is not easy to place historically. Verse 1 may refer to the first visit of the king of Babylon, and verses 2 and 3 to some raid conducted by auxiliaries of Nebuchadrezzar. Be that as it may, Jehoiakim, whose reign was marked by the shedding of "innocent blood" (v. 4), came to his end and was succeeded by his son, Jehoiachin. Jehoiakim "did that which was evil in the sight of the Lord according to all that his fathers had done" (23:37).

The reign of Jehoiachin lasted but three months. Nebuchadrezzar invaded the land and took Jehoiachin captive with his wife and family and the skilled craftsmen and tradesmen (24:11–16). The reason for the invasion is not clear although it may have been the aftermath of some offense of his father. At this time the king of

Babylon did not destroy Jerusalem, but only sought to paralyze the people by removing all the artisans. The king's uncle, Mattaniah, was appointed king and his name was changed to Zedekiah (v. 17). After a reign of eleven years he, too, became involved in intrigue with Egypt and felt the full weight of the Babylonian attack. This time the operations of Nebuchadrezzar were carried on for eighteen months and devastated the whole of Judah, as we learn from archaeological surveys. Finally, the walls of Jerusalem were broken down and the temple razed. Zedekiah was caught trying to escape and his sons were slain before his eyes. He was then blinded and taken in chains to Babylon (25:4–7).

The compiler of Kings compares Zedekiah with Jehoiakim and says that he "did evil in the sight of the Lord according to all that Jehoiakim had done" (24:19). So the last king of Judah followed many of the others and failed to be obedient to the covenant of God.

5. Gedaliah (25:22–26)

There were still people left in Judah even if they were "the poor of the land" (25:12). A certain Gedaliah was left as governor (v. 22). Very soon after, a conspiracy arose and this man was slain with the Babylonian garrison. Many of the remaining people then fled to Egypt, including the prophet Jeremiah (Jer. 40:7—43:7). No comment is made about the worth of Gedaliah, the governor, perhaps because he was not a king.

6. A Final Note (25:27–30)

The remaining comment in these books tells us that after a time Jehoiachin was released by the Chaldaean king, Evil-merodach (561–560 B.C.). Modern excavations have uncovered baked clay tablets in the ruins of Babylon dating to 592 B.C., bearing the name of Jehoiachin and his five sons. The fact that the release of Jehoiachin is mentioned in the Book of Kings is a clue to the final compilation of the Book which must therefore have been after the date of this release. There is no reason, of course, why a good deal of material may not have been already collected before the final compilation was made.

I and II Chronicles

A. M. RENWICK

Reign of Uzziah: Great Success: Presumption 26:1–23
Jotham's Reign: Great Builder: Defeats Ammonites 27:1–9
Reign of Ahaz: Idolatry: Calamities 28:1–27
Hezekiah's Good Reign: the Temple: Passover: Reforms 29:1—31:21
Miraculous Deliverance from Sennacherib: Hezekiah's Acts 32:1–32
Manasseh and Ammon: Impious and Idolatrous 33:1–25
Josiah's Good Reign: Reforms: Honor Moses' Law 34:1—35:27
Last Kings of Judah 36:1–23

I. The Genealogies (I Chron. 1:1—9:44)

AT FIRST GLANCE, reading of these genealogies seems fruitless. The divinely inspired writers, however, had a definite purpose in recording them. The Israelite had a place in the covenant of God and the genealogy proved his descent from Abraham (Ezra 2:61–63; Neh. 7:63–65). Furthermore, since the Messiah was to come out of the tribe of Judah and the house of David, these genealogies make it possible to prove, when the Messiah comes, that he fulfils the prophecies. The Israelite was debtor to many generations, and the moral stature of eminent progenitors inspired him. There was no room for personal vanity; each was a link in a chain. Each person had the obligation to hand on his heritage untarnished.

The writer of Chronicles assumes that his readers know the earlier Books of the Bible and spends little time on explanations.

1. Genealogies of the Human Race (1:1—2:2)

The first genealogies are inclusive and show the descendants of Adam in many lands. Very often the lands bear the names of important men, for example, Madai (the Medes), Javan (the Ionian Isles), Kittim (Cyprus) in I Chronicles 1:5–7. The genealogy (vv. 1–54) shows the *unity* of the human race, in accord with Paul's later statement that all nations are of "one blood" (Acts 17:26). The name *Adam* means "man," a fitting name for our progenitor. We all sinned and fell in him, and Chronicles carries forward the story as to how God is preparing to send the Saviour promised in Genesis 3:15. Later genealogies are confined to Israel from whom salvation would arise.

Much attention, however, is given to descendants of Abraham who were not Israelites, such as Ishmael, Midian, Sheba, Esau and the

Dukes of Edom (1:28–54). The Dukes of Edom were the progenitors of the Arabs who to this very day maintain a bitter antagonism with Israel that has lasted through the centuries.

The genealogies of the Bible do not show every link in the chain of descent; sometimes there are large gaps.

2. Genealogies of Judah (2:3—4:23)

Judah's genealogy is placed first in Israel because of his pre-eminence (Gen. 49:8). Some names are drawn from outside the sacred Scriptures. Others awaken painful memories, such as Tamar (Gen. 38:13–30); and Achan or Achar, "the troubler of Israel" (Josh. 6:18; 7:25). Hezron, son of Pharez, is very important in the genealogy, because the royal house of David is traced to him and the powerful families of Jerahmeel and Caleb (not the son of Jephunneh, for whom see Num. 32:12; Josh. 14:6). David is placed seventh among Jesse's sons (2:13–15), not eighth as in I Samuel 17:12. Possibly one son had died early and dropped out of the genealogy. Zeruiah (mother of the famous Joab) and Abigail seem to be half-sisters of David (2:16, 17). Many names of persons are also names of towns founded by them, such as Hebron, Maon, Ziph, and Tappuah (2:42–45). David's six sons born in Hebron (3:1–4) and thirteen born in Jerusalem (3:5–9) are recorded. Daniel is the same as Chileab (II Sam. 3:2–5). Bathsheba (mother of Solomon) is also called Bathshua.

As to the lineage of the royal house (3:10–24), we notice the faithfulness of God in fulfilling His promise to David that his house and his kingdom would be established forever (II Sam. 7:12–16). For seventeen generations this was literally fulfilled until Judah ceased to be a kingdom in 586 B.C. The promise is finally fulfilled in Christ, the King, "David's greater son," who came of the lineage of Salathiel and the noble Zerubabel who led back the returning exiles in 536 B.C. (3:17–24). The genealogical list was known to Matthew, who shows that Christ came of the lineage of David (Mt. 1:12–16) in accordance with prophecy. The chronicler's special interest in Judah is shown, for he returns to Judean families in 4:1–23. Among these the most honorable is Jabez, a relative of Achan (vv. 9, 10), who in spite of obstacles flourished spiritually.

3. Genealogies of Simeon, Reuben, Gad, and Manasseh (4:24—5:26)

Simeon (4:24–33). The territory of Simeon, Jacob's second son, was carved out of Judah. The tribe was not numerous (cf. Num. 1:23 and 26:14). Its cities had changed much between the time of Joshua and the time of the chronicler (cf. Josh. 19:2–7 with I Chron. 4:24–33). Thirteen families of Simeon increased greatly (4:34–37) and were notable for establishing prosperous colonies in Gedor (south of Judah) and in Mount Seir far to the east (4:39–43).

Reuben (5:1–10). Deprived of his birthright as the firstborn because of his lustfulness (cf. Gen. 49:3, 4 and Deut. 21:17), Reuben's special rights were divided between Joseph, Judah and Levi. His territory was east of the Dead Sea, north of the River Arnon. The tribe penetrated eastwards towards the Euphrates (5:9, 10).

Gad (5:11–17) was also east of Jordan with excellent pasture lands in Gilead and the Hauran, a district of Syria east of the Jordan. Members of this tribe had pushed northwards since the first settlement (Deut. 3:10–13; Josh. 13:25–30).

Half Tribe of Manasseh (5:23, 24). Manasseh and Ephraim, sons of Joseph, received the double portion from the forfeited birthright of Reuben. Half Manasseh received a large and fertile territory between Gad and the Hermon range, here called by its Amorite name "Senir." Valiant tribes east of Jordan captured valuable territories (vv. 18–22), but they had special temptations on the frontiers and fell into idolatry and vice. As a punishment for sin, they were the first to be carried captive to Assyria (vv. 25, 26; cf. II Kings 15:15–20, 29).

4. Genealogies of Levi: their Dwellings (6:1–81)

The tribe of Levi was specially dedicated to priestly duties, and the divine service in the tabernacle and temple. The genealogical list contains such great names as Moses, Aaron, and Samuel. Three great divisions of the Levites corresponded to Gershom, Kohath, and Merari, sons of Levi.

Kohath provided the high priestly lines descended from Eleazar and Ithamar, the sons of Aaron; the high priest was sometimes of one line, sometimes of the other (6:1–15). The list contains good and faithful men like Zadok (cf. I Chron. 12:28; I Kings 1:7, 8; II

Sam. 15:24, 29, 35) and Hilkiah, foremost in the reformation under King Josiah (II Kings 22:14–20). The Kohathites receive additional attention in 6:22–28 and 6:33–38, where the lists are almost identical. Amminadab in verse 22 is the same as Izhar in verse 38. The important genealogy of Samuel (6:27–28, 33, 34) is traced from the son of the fourth Elkanah mentioned.

The Kohathites also had charge of the service of song. The great musical families were the descendants of Heman, grandson of Samuel the prophet (6:33); descendants of Asaph, son of Gershom, who himself wrote Psalms (vv. 39–43 and II Chron. 29:30); and the family of Merari (vv. 44–47). There were representatives of these families for many centuries (cf. II Chron. 35:13; Neh. 11:17, 18). The high priestly functions of Aaron and his family are given (6:49–53). Their line is traced to Ahimaaz in David's time (v. 53).

Cities for the Priests and Levites (6:54–81). Each tribe gave a number of cities for the priests and Levites. The Kohathite priests received thirteen cities, while their non-priest Levites received ten; Merari received twelve. The Levitical cities, given by name (vv. 64–81), are much the same as in Joshua's day, allowing for changes brought about by lapse of time.

5. Genealogies of Issachar, Benjamin, Naphtali, West Manasseh, Ephraim, and Asher (7:1–40)

We notice here only the genealogy of Joshua (or Jehoshua) the son of Non (or Nun), in 7:23-27, of the tribe of Ephraim. Issachar and Naphtali were in the extreme north; Zebulun was slightly south of them. There is no genealogy for Zebulun, unless the scholars are right who insist that the genealogy for Benjamin (vv. 6–12) is really for Zebulun in light of the fact that there is another genealogy for Benjamin. The chronicler has not distinguished clearly between western and eastern Manasseh (vv. 14–19), the eastern having already been dealt with. We note alliances of Manasseh men with non-Israelitish women contrary to custom (7:14, 15). Asher's arms-bearing men, in the far north, had decreased to 26,000. At the settlement they had 53,400 (Num. 26:44–47).

6. Further Genealogies of Benjamin including Saul (8:1—9:44)

Special attention is given to these genealogies because Saul was a Benjamite. His own genealogy is in 8:33–40 and 9:35–44. Many authorities suggest that Benjamin in 8:1 was a grandson of Jacob and son of Bilhan (7:10), and that Ehud (8:6) was another son of Bilhan. This view eliminates many discrepancies. Some of the names in I Chronicles 8:9, 10 suggest Moabite affinity through intermarriage, for example, Mesha, Malcham.

According to 8:28 many Benjamites lived in Jerusalem before the Exile. This was natural, since a large part of that city was in Benjamite territory.

Most modern authorities agree that the inhabitants of Jerusalem mentioned in 9:1–34 resided there after the Captivity, not before. A study of Nehemiah 11:1–36 shows it refers to the same people and proves that not only representatives from Judah and Benjamin returned to Jerusalem, but also some from Ephraim and Manasseh (v. 3), carried away captive many years earlier. Elsewhere, we see that Simeon and Asher were associated with Judah.

The arrangements for carrying on the Lord's work were based upon the plans made by Samuel and David (9:10–16). There were 212 porters or gatekeepers (v. 22), and over them were four chief men (v. 26). Like all the Levites, they served one week at a time in rotation (v. 25).

There was great variety in the service of God—priests, singers, gatekeepers, and also men caring for the treasury, money offerings, sacred utensils, vestments, preparation of sacrifices, and sacred bread. All service was honorable because it was God's service (cf. 9:10–34).

II. The Reign of David I (I Chron. 10:1—29:30)

1. The Fall of Saul's House (10:1–14)

The first nine chapters of I Chronicles, summarized from material already written in Old Testament books, together with some brief additional data, form an introduction to the story of David and his house. Saul had been appointed by God as the first king. The chronicler had to explain his downfall as an introduction to David's history and to point the significant moral. The narrative of Saul's defeat and tragic death (10:1–14) is almost identical with I Samuel 31:1–13. Samuel and Chronicles are based on another and fuller historical document; the chronicler chooses what best serves his purpose. He characteristically adds two verses (13 and 14) to point the moral of Saul's fall for (*1*) disobedience to God, (*2*) necromancy, and (*3*) failure to seek the counsel from God (cf. I Sam. 15:1–9, 11; 28:18). Then follows the tragedy of Gilboa, when "the beauty of Israel was slain upon its high places," and the warrior king died a suicide (cf. II Sam. 1:17–27).

2. *David and his Valiant Men (11:1—12:40)*

David's attractiveness and inspired leadership aroused tremendous enthusiasm in all Israel. The chronicler passes by the years in Hebron, the fratricidal war with the house of Saul, and the deadly feud between Abner (Saul's general) and Joab (cf. II Sam. 1—4). He tells at once the beautiful story of God's selection of David as king many years before (I Sam. 16:12, 13).

David first expelled the Jebusites from their stronghold on Mount Zion (cf. II Sam. 5:6–10) because of its great strategic importance. Joab, with great heroism, entered the city by a water tunnel ("gutter," KJV). The Millo, often referred to, was a great embankment with a tower in the lower city.

David's "mighty men" (11:15–26) were a heroic band, whether we think of men like the three chiefs who, at peril of their lives, brought water for David through the Philistine ranks from the well of Bethlehem, or of the exploits of others like Jehoiada who "slew a lion in a pit on a snowy day."

The stories of the Benjamites from Saul's own tribe who came to David in his adversity (12:1–7), and of the brave Gadites who faced the perils of Jordan to come to David's help in Adullam are very impressive (12:8–15). The contributions in men of arms from each tribe is striking, especially 50,000 (v. 33) seasoned warriors from the small tribe of Zebulun, and 120,000 from the two and a half tribes beyond Jordan (12:37).

3. *Uzza Smitten on Touching the Ark (13:1–14)*

The ark of the covenant should have been the center of Israel's religious life, but for forty-eight years it was well-nigh forgotten (I Sam. 4:11, 22; 6:1–7:2). The proposal to bring it back from Kirjath-Jearim to Jerusalem was a sign of reformation. Because it typified the presence of God, its removal to Jerusalem was a holy ceremony. Carrying it on a *new cart* indicated the need for purity.

God's law was clear that to touch the ark was to incur death, and only the Kohathites could carry it and even then on staves (Num. 4:15). For his sin of irreverence in touching the ark, Uzza paid an awful penalty. The shocked king ordered the removal of the ark to the house of Obed-edom, a Levite qualified to attend it. God blessed his house greatly (13:9–14; cf. 15:18).

4. David's House, Family, and Victories (14:1–17)

Hiram's friendly action in sending cedar and craftsmen was an acknowledgment of David's character and strong position.

The ever-watchful Philistines attacked David as soon as he became king of Israel, and raided the valley of Rephaim. David sought counsel from God and gained a great victory at "Baal-perazim," thus named because God "broke through" on the enemy (14:8–12). Later, in the same place, God miraculously routed the Philistines when they heard "the sound of marching in the tops of the balsam trees" (14:13–17). The unseen forces of God won the day.

5. The Ark Removed to Jerusalem: Arrangements for Worship (15:1—16:43)

After three months David took every precaution to see that the ark of the covenant was carried according to God's law (15:12–15)— by duly sanctified Levites only (Num. 1:50), and carried on staves on their shoulders (Num. 4:1–15). The representatives of the great Levitical families were carefully instructed beforehand (15:4–10). Under the leadership of the three masters of song (vv. 16–24) the musical service was elaborate. Penitence and confession of sin were markedly present with appropriate sacrifices. David wore a robe of fine linen. It was a day of great rejoicing. The only jarring note came from Michal, David's wife, a great sufferer whom we must not judge too severely. Psalm 68 composed for the removal of the ark foretold the ascension of Christ which the procession foreshadowed (Eph. 4:7, 8).

On depositing the ark in the tent where an altar was erected, burnt offerings for atonement, and peace offerings for communion with God and with one another, were offered. The king gave gifts to all (16:1–3), typifying Christ's ascension when He "received gifts for men" (Eph. 4:8). The great choirs of Levites took an important part in the worship. Asaph was made chief master of song (16:4–6).

A special hymn was delivered to him and his assistants. Thus, public worship was inaugurated in Jerusalem before the ark with Abiathar as high priest, while Zadok was high priest in the tabernacle, still at Gibeon. These temporary arrangements prevailed until the temple was built.

6. *David's Purpose to Build God a House (17:1–27)*

David felt it was wrong to dwell in a comfortable and spacious house while the ark of God dwelt in a tent. However, God rejected his plan to build a temple (v. 4), because David had been a man of war and had shed much blood (I Chron. 22:8; 28:3). David's son Solomon, a man of peace, must build it. God speaks graciously to David, reminding him of his marvelous career from the sheepcotes to the throne. God promised David that his throne would be "established for ever" (17:12–14). This was partly fulfilled in David's descendants, but completely fulfilled in Christ, the King, Who is of David's lineage (Lk. 2:4). God also taught David that He had never asked for "a house of cedar." He dwells in the humble and contrite heart, rather than temples of stone. In his prayer of thanksgiving, David rose to great spiritual heights (17:16–27) and accepted all as from God's sovereign grace.

7. *David Engages in Many Wars (18:1—20:8)*

Chronologically these wars belong before the events of chapter 17. God prospered David (18:1–12). The surrounding nations were vanquished one by one; vast quantities of gold and silver captured from these enemies were dedicated to the Lord's service. David, however, like his contemporaries, was guilty of cruelty to chariot horses (18:4). Chapter 20:3 is correct in the Revised Standard Version, "and set them to labor with saws and iron picks and axes," but not in the King James Version. The gracious message to Hanun reflected great credit on David, but the contemptible response of Hanun led to war involving Israel, Ammon, Mesopotamia, Maacah and Zobah. Through the heroism of Joab, all these enemies were routed in spite of their great military power (19:18, 19). Defeated in the country, the Ammonites fortified themselves in their capital, Rabbah. In the spring, Joab defeated them and destroyed their city. David received the Ammonite crown which weighed a talent (114 pounds) of gold.

8. *The Sin of Numbering the People (21:1–30)*

Israel, as a whole, had incurred the divine displeasure. David, too, sinned in that his victories made him proud. At this point, God permitted Satan to tempt him to number the people and so bring punishment on both king and nation. The fact that he was tempted did not free David from personal responsibility. The web of human motives and actions is exceedingly complex, but the great God overrules all in the end. Since it was well known that the people must not be numbered except by command of God (Num. 1:1–3; 26:1–4), David was clearly guilty. Even Joab had strongly opposed the king's design. The census gave 1,100,000 in Israel fit for military service, and 470,000 in Judah. These figures are not quite the same as in II Samuel 24, but they can be reconciled.

When Israel was smitten, David's conscience was thoroughly aroused. He again became the tenderhearted, God-fearing king who loved his people. Given the choice of one of three punishments, he resolved "to fall into the hand of God," and the Lord sent pestilence on Israel (21:9–14).

When seventy thousand had fallen and the destroying angel, near the threshing floor of Ornan the Jebusite, stretched out his sword over Jerusalem to destroy it, David and the elders fell on their faces, and the king prayed that *he* might be punished and the people spared. Clearly David was still a child of grace.

The Lord accepted the entreaty, and ordered David to offer sacrifice on the threshing floor of Ornan, who was of the old Canaanite race. David refused to avail himself of the generous offer of Ornan and paid the full price; he would not offer God what cost him nothing (21:14–25). There, where Abraham once offered his sacrifice, David gave burnt offering (for propitiation) and peace offerings for communion after pardon. God consumed the sacrifice by fire from heaven, giving clear proof that He turned from His anger (vv. 25–27). David declared "This is the house of the Lord God," and there the temple was built.

9. *David Prepares for Building the Temple (22:1–19)*

After his wonderful deliverance, David eagerly pushed preparations for building God's house. Vast quantities of most precious materials were collected (22:3, 4). The amount of gold and silver (v. 14) has been reckoned at £800,000,000 or $2,248,000,000 in gold currency. David made every preparation possible and gave young Solomon special building instructions (vv. 5, 6). His call to his son and the princes is deeply moving (vv. 11–19).

10. Arrangements for the Services of the Levites (23:1—26:32)

Owing to the revolt of Adonijah, David, in his old age, made Solomon king (23:1; cf. I Kings 1:11–53), and made detailed ecclesiastical arrangements before he died. There were 38,000 Levites: (1) 24,000 in charge of temple services; (2) 6,000 officers (superintendents) and judges in civil and ecclesiastical cases; (3) 4,000 porters or doorkeepers; (4) 4,000 choristers (cf. I Cor. 23:1–5).

These were divided according to the great families: (a) Gershomites, (b)Kohathites, (c) Merarites (23:7–23). Solomon scrupulously observed these arrangements (II Chron. 8:14; 29:25).

The functions of the priest in I Chronicles 23:13 should be studied. The duties of the Levites (vv. 24–32) are also most interesting and worthy of study. They are now fully discharged by Christ our "great high priest."

Twenty-four Classes of Priests and Levites Listed (24:1–31). The priests were descended from Eleazar and Ithamar, the sons of Aaron. They were divided into twenty-four "courses," each of which served a week by rotation. The chief men were appointed in the proportion of sixteen from Eleazar to eight from Ithamar (v. 4). The selection was made very formally before the king and high priests (v. 6). Names of the chief men are given in verses 7–19.

The Temple Choristers (25:1–31). Of these choristers, 288 were specially trained and led the rest. Like the priests, they served by rotation in twenty-four "courses." The chiefs were of the families of Asaph, Jeduthun, and Heman. They *"prophesied,"* that is, uttered the divine mind, in song (v. 1).

The Porters or Gatekeepers Named (26:1–19). These men attended to the entrances to the temple, especially the gates, and guarded the precincts. Strong men were required (cf. vv. 8, 11). They were of the families of the Korhites and Merarites (vv. 1, 10, 19). Obed-edom, who was blessed for caring for the ark, had many descendants among the chief gatekeepers (vv. 4–8). There were, in all, ninety-three leaders among the four thousand gatekeepers.

Their duties and place were as usual determined by lot (vv. 13–18). The storehouse ("Asuppim") was allotted to Obed-edom (v. 15). The "causeway of the going up" ascended from the Tyropean valley to the temple area (v. 16). Parbar (v. 18) may mean "suburban part."

Treasures (26:20–28). One treasury was for the support of the services in God's house; another received gifts dedicated for building the temple. Even Samuel, Saul, Abner, and Joab had dedicated wealth for building the future temple (v. 28).

Officers and Judges (26:29–32). The officers (sometimes they were called scribes) attended to civil and religious business and collected tithes and taxes. The judges administered the law. Of the officers and judges, 4,400 were from the family of Hebron, 1,600 from that of Izhar (26:29–32).

11. Officers of State: David's Last Acts (27:1—29:30)

The disposable force of the army was divided into twelve divisions of twenty-four thousand each. Some of the commanders were men of great prowess, such as *Jashobeam* (11:11; cf. II Sam. 23:8), *Dodai* (11:12), *Benaiah* (27:6; cf. II Sam. 23:20, 22, 23).

The Princes of the Tribes (27:16–24). Civil rulers of ten of the tribes are listed, among them Zadok, the high priest, and Elihu (Eliab), brother of David (cf. I Sam. 16:6; 17:13, 28).

Stewards of the King's Property (27:25–31). Some property belonged to David personally and some officially as king. His possessions included much precious metal, immense stores of produce, vineyards and wine cellars, olive and sycamore plantations as well as great herds, including camels, pastured by Arab herdsmen.

David's Last Address to the People and Solomon (28:1–10). The aged ruler, full of years and honor, addresses the great national assembly of leaders (princes) for the last time. He "stood," in spite of infirmity, in honor of the nation to give an address that is affectionate and deeply moving. He dwells on God's sovereignty in choosing first Judah, then his father's house, then himself, the youngest. God chose Solomon to build the temple but forbade David. God does according to His will. If Solomon keeps God's command, his throne will be established for ever, but the promise is conditional. David solemnly tells the people their possession of the land depends on loyalty to God. He appeals affectionately to Solomon to "know the God of his father," that is, to know Him in personal experience and from doing His will (v. 9). There is no deceiving God for "He searcheth all hearts," therefore must He be sought with a perfect (or undivided) heart.

As God gave Moses the pattern of the tabernacle in detail (Ex. 25:40; 26:30), so David received by inspiration from God the plan of the temple (28:11–12), which he handed to Solomon. God ordered Moses to "make all things according to the pattern" shown him in the Mount (Heb. 8:5). God is architect of His house whether in the soul of man or in the Church, and it is His plan we must follow.

Every detail in the arrangements of the temple pointed to the atoning work of Christ "in the fulness of time"; the sacrifices pointed to Calvary. The scheme for the courses of priests and Levites, that for the services of the temple, and the minutest details as to the amount of gold and silver to be put in temple utensils, were all given to Solomon to be put into effect (28:13–18). If Solomon were faithful, he could depend on God's help.

The Last Acts of David (29:1–30). David then announced to the assembly that besides the vast provision made from the royal treasuries for the building of the temple, he personally was giving the equivalent of £19,000,000 or $53,390,000 (vv. 4, 5). This elicited a magnificent response from the assembly, and the amount given by the people was enormous. That it was given "willingly" (vv. 6–10) revealed religious unity and enthusism. They were doing great things to perpetuate true religion in the world.

Finally, the king voiced one of the most sublime prayers ever offered. It contained adoration, thanksgiving, humiliation, and confession of unworthiness (29:10–13). He prayed fervently that God would keep Solomon and the nation in the way of uprightness, and enable them to keep His statutes and testimonies (vv. 17–19). Then all the people fell on their faces in adoration of God, and honored the king (v. 20). Next day the actions of the assembly were ratified by sacrifices on a vast scale. They made atonement for sin (vv. 21–22) and ate and drank in happy fellowship in accordance with Leviticus 7:11-18.

Solomon was now made king publicly before all the people. He took his seat on the throne; the long reign of David was at an end.

III. The Reign of Solomon (II Chron. 1:1—9:31)

The Second Book of Chronicles is a continuation of the first.

1. Solomon Confirmed in the Kingdom: Builds the Temple (1:1—4:22)

In the second year of his reign as king, Solomon and the national assembly went to Gibeon to the tabernacle of the Lord (I Chron. 21:29). The ark had remained at Jerusalem since its removal from Kirjath-Jearim (I Chron. 15:25–29). At Gibeon a holocaust of one thousand burnt offerings was made on the altar erected by Bezaleel (Ex. 27:1–2). All Israel knew the need for atonement. The idea was central in the worship of tabernacle and temple. When God asked Solomon that night what He should give him, Solomon asked for wisdom and knowledge to rule his people (1:10). Because the request was so unselfish, the Lord promised him also great riches and honors (vv. 7-12). He sought the kingdom of God and more was added (cf. Mt. 6:33).

Soon Solomon showed the love for horses and chariots which later became a snare to him. He bought them in Egypt and sold them to the Phoenicians and Hittites and became fabulously rich (1:14–17).

Solomon's Treaty with Huram of Tyre (2:1–16). Solomon organized one hundred and fifty thousand serfs (descendants of Canaanites) under thirty-six hundred overseers, to prepare for building the temple (vv. 1, 17, 18). He secured from Huram, the friendly king of Tyre, a skilful master craftsman (also called Huram) to superintend the work (v. 7). Solomon also contracted to buy valuable timber (vv. 8–10). King Huram acknowledged the God of Israel (vv. 11, 12). Chapter 2:13 should read as follows: "I have sent a skilled man, endued with understanding, Huram my trusted adviser."

Building of the Temple (3:1–17). It was built on Mount Moriah as David appointed (vv. 1, 2). The measurements for every part are minutely given (vv. 3–15), and all was carried out according to plan. In verse 4, read "twenty" instead of "one hundred and twenty." We notice the use of cedar, fir, gold, and jewels throughout the house (3:5–10). The "Holy of Holies" was overlaid with gold worth 600 talents (3,750,000 pounds sterling or $10,537,500). The cherubim were also overlaid. The "vail of blue" was a curtain that separated the Holy Place and the Most Holy, symbolizing the separation of God from man. When Christ died on the cross, this curtain in the temple was miraculously rent in twain to signify that He had opened the way to God. In the Epistle to the Hebrews (9:7–12), the interpretation of symbol and fulfilment is clearly given.

The Furnishings of the Temple (4:1–22). God's house was considered worthy of the best of everything. Every object had spiritual significance; for example, the great altar of brass (v. 1) testified to the need for atonement for sin (cf. Ex. 17:1–5; I Kings 8:64). The molten sea, containing 13,500 gallons of water, showed that even priests needed purifying from sin. All must come to "the fountain opened" in Christ. The ten lavers were for washing the sacrifices; everything offered to God must be pure. The candlesticks symbolized the Light given by God (v. 7). The tables for the shewbread (the bread of the Presence) spoke of Christ, the living Bread.

2. The Ark Removed to the Temple: Solomon's Address and Prayer (5:1—7:22)

The actual building of the temple took seven years (cf. I Kings 6:1–38), the fitting and furnishing took thirteen more (I Kings 7:1–51; 8:1–11). In the twenty-fourth year of his reign, Solomon brought up the ark to the temple. Innumerable sheep and oxen were sacrificed (5:6). After the dedication Solomon offered 120,000 sheep, and 22,000 oxen, most of them used to feed the multitudes. The vast throng must have been impressive with thousands of priests and Levites, the great choir, and the fanfares as the priests and Levites bore the ark to the Holy of Holies (cf. I Kings 8:4; 5:4). In 5:9 we should read, "the staves projected from the ark, so that their ends were seen in the holy place." The most impressive event of all was the descent of the glorious Shekinah cloud, the manifestation of the divine presence, signifying that God had come to His temple (vv. 13, 14).

Solomon's Address and Prayer (6:1–42). Speaking from a brazen platform in the open court, Solomon said that the cloud showed the temple was God's house for ever (vv. 1, 2). God had fulfilled His promises to David (vv. 4–11). Solomon is at his best as he humbly kneels before the Most High (v. 18), confessing that God surpasses all kings as the heavens are higher than earth. The seven petitions

(vv. 22–31) should be specially studied as showing the kind of cases which would be brought before God in His house. There is an ominous forecast of the coming Captivity because of sin (vv. 36–38).

God Answers Solomon's Prayer (7:1–22). That God heard is shown by the fire from heaven which consumed the burnt-offering, and the Shekinah cloud again became intensified in glory (vv. 1–3). (The Church is always dead without the fire of God.) For seven days the people offered their peace offerings on a vast scale, enjoying communion with God, glad in heart, conscious of the divine presence in an eminent degree (vv. 8–11). God promised Solomon even greater things than he had asked. God had sanctified the house that He might remain there forever (v. 16). God's "heart" would be there. He would fulfill His promise to David about his descendants if they kept God's statutes. If they turned to idolatry, they would become a byword (vv. 17–22; cf. I Kings 9:6). These ominous threats were fulfilled in later ages.

3. Acts of Solomon and his Glory (8:1—9:31)

After this, Solomon embarked on great building projects. He rebuilt the twenty cities in Galilee returned to him by Huram (8:1–3; cf. I Kings 9:10–28). He built Tadmor in the wilderness (Palmyra), the ruins of which in the Syrian desert are still impressive. The two Beth-horons, all the store cities, forts in Lebanon, and other cities were built or restored (8:2–6: cf. I Kings 4:26; 9:19; 9:15). Descendants of the old Canaanites were made serfs and employed in the great building operations (8:7-9; cf. I Kings 9:20–23).

The chronicler assumes that his readers know from I Kings of Solomon's marriage to Pharaoh's daughter (I Kings 3:1; 7:8). Her idolatrous tendencies must have led to her removal from the sacred precincts of Mount Zion (8:11). Solomon's marriage to her was a disaster (cf. I Kings 11:31), but he scrupulously observed David's dispositions for divine service (8:14–16). Huram sent Solomon trained sailors (v. 18) to help found a navy at Ezion-geber, on the Gulf of Akaba, the present Elath (cf. I Kings 9:26–28). The Israelites were never great seamen.

The Glory of Solomon (9:1–31). The impression made on the Queen of Sheba, from southern Arabia, reveals Solomon's wisdom and magnificence. Her own splendor and lavishness were great, but Solomon far excelled her (9:1–12). She was impressed by "the ascent by which he went up . . ." (v. 4)—probably a wonderful arched viaduct crossing the valley. Solomon's gold, precious stones, targets (large shields) of gold, his glorious throne, wealth in horses, and extensive territories reaching from Egypt to Euphrates left a great impression (vv. 13-28; cf. I Kings 11:14–29). Nevertheless, his materialism, luxuries, pagan concubines, and crushing taxation had disastrous effects on the nation (cf. I Kings 11:1–3). His one great work for God was the building of the temple.

IV. The Kingdom of Judah (II Chron. 10:1—36:23)

1. Rehoboam and the Revolt of the Ten Tribes (10:1—11:23)

God had told Solomon (I Kings 11:4–13) that because of his idolatries and immoralities He would rend the kingdom and give it to Jeroboam, one of the king's administrators (I Kings 11:28). God promised through the prophet Ahijah that Jeroboam would be king of the northern tribes and have enduring blessings *if he walked* in God's ways (I Kings 11:26–40). Solomon tried to kill Jeroboam, but he fled.

When Rehoboam became king in 975 B.C., upon Solomon's death, the tribes met him at Shechem. Through Jeroboam they demanded some relief from the crushing taxation and servitude of Solomon's day. The older counselors advised him to concede this reasonable demand and win the people, but the younger men counseled brutal severity—"Scourge the people with scorpions." Rehoboam foolishly accepted this mad advice of the younger courtiers. Thus, God brought to fulfilment His promise to Jeroboam. The cry went up, "To your tents, O Israel." The nation was split into the ten northern tribes (Israel), and Judah and Benjamin in the south, under Rehoboam. From now onward, the chronicler traces the history of Judah, not Israel.

Doings of Rehoboam (11:1–23). Rehoboam raised in Judah and Benjamin 184,000 men to fight Israel, but desisted at God's command (vv. 1–4). He then fortified many towns against Egypt, but in vain (vv. 5–12; 12:9). In spite of his father's bitter experience in that respect, he took many wives and concubines, contrary to Deuteronomy 17:17.

Jeroboam, in Israel, appointed priests to serve at pagan altars and minister to "the devils," that is, demons (11:13–17; cf. Lev. 17:7). Many priests and Levites in the northern kingdom refused to sacrifice to the golden calves set up by Jeroboam. They therefore abandoned their "suburbs" (in this case, pastures) and their livings as priests and Levites to come to live in Judah and Jerusalem that they might enjoy the worship of the true God in the temple.

2. Invasion by Shishak: Rehoboam Humbles Himself (12:1–16)

The priests and Levites from the north influenced Rehoboam for three years (11:13, 17). Then he led Judah into unspeakable abominations—pagan high places, graven images, and sodomy, always a terrible sign of moral decline (cf. I Kings 14:22–24). God sent Shishak of Egypt to punish Rehoboam; his fortified cities collapsed (12:5–12). Thereupon, because Rehoboam humbled himself before God, God did not utterly destroy him. Shishak, however, entered the temple and took away its treasures, including the great shields of gold Solomon had made (vv. 1–11).

The final verdict on Rehoboam was that "he did evil, because he prepared not his heart to seek the Lord" (12:14).

3. Abijah at War with Jeroboam (13:1–22)

Abijah (or Abijam), the heir of Rehoboam, reigned from 958 to 955 B.C. With 400,000 men, he prosecuted a war with great success against Jeroboam who led 800,000. From a mountain, Abijah addressed the army of Israel in a speech that was a masterpiece of propaganda. He effectively showed up Israel's moral weakness. Judah had maintained the worship of the Lord in perfect form. Israel could not prosper if they fought against the God of their fathers (13:4–12). In spite of laying a clever ambush, Israel was defeated crushingly, with the loss of half a million men, and Judah captured various towns of Ephraim (vv. 13–20).

4. Asa Opposes Idolatry: Institutes Religious Reforms (14:1— 15:19)

Asa, one of the best of Judah's kings (955–914 B.C.), removed the altars to "strange gods" and cut down the Asherim ("groves"), *tree* trunks dedicated to Ashtoreth (14:2–5). His father's victories secured peace for ten years. While Asa strongly fortified his cities, his real defense lay in the fact that he "sought the Lord" (vv. 6, 7; cf. Ps. 127:1). When Zerah, king of Kush (Ethiopia) invaded Judah with a million men, Asa prayed to God—"it is nothing with thee to help whether with many or with them that have no power" (v. 11)—and gained a crushing victory (vv. 9–15).

Principles of Divine Government (15:1–7). The prophet Azariah expounded these principles to Asa. Those who seek God find Him; those who forsake Him are forsaken by Him (vv. 1–7). Asa put away the "abominable idols" in his dominions and repaired the altar of burnt-offering in Jerusalem. Many from the northern kingdom joined with the people of God in the true worship at Jerusalem, and made a solemn covenant to serve the Lord (vv. 8–15), and "God gave them rest round about."

5. *Asa's Conflict with Baasha: Rebuked (16:1–14)*

From the twenty-sixth year of his reign, Asa's faith declined sadly. He took sacrilegiously the temple treasures to bribe Ben-hadad of Syria to break his alliance with Baasha of Israel, who was threatening Judah (16:1–6).

Asa was severely rebuked by the prophet Hanani for relying on man, rather than on God. Hanani reminded him how the Lord had saved him from the Ethiopians because of his faith. Henceforth Asa would have wars. In spite of a serious disease, he did not seek the Lord, in sad contrast to his early days (16:7–12; cf. I Kings 15:9–24).

6. *Jehoshaphat Prospers but Makes a Disastrous Alliance with Ahab (17:1—18:34)*

Jehoshaphat reigned 914–889 B.C., and like his father Asa, did well in his earlier years, removing the false gods and the high places. God blessed him; neighboring lands feared him (17:1–6, 10, 11). He had the Pentateuch taught in all the cities (vv. 7–9). His prosperity increased and his military might consisted of a citizen army of 1,160,000 valiant men (vv. 12–19).

Alliance with Ahab (18:1–34). The marriage of Jehoshaphat's son Joram (or Jehoram) to the daughter of Ahab was a disastrous mistake (cf. I Kings 22:1–35). Another mistake Jehoshaphat made was to join Ahab in a war against the Syrians, an error that nearly cost him his life. The false prophets prophesied to Ahab only what he wanted to hear as to the advisability of going to the war. Although Jehoshaphat doubted their truthfulness, and heard a real message from God through Micaiah foretelling coming disaster, he went with Ahab to the disastrous siege of Ramoth-Gilead. The rugged, honest prophet Micaiah declared that God had allowed a lying spirit to enter Ahab's prophets to lure him to destruction, and this is what actually happened (18:29–34). The chronicler omits the dramatic detail that in fulfilment of the prophecy of Elijah (I Kings 21:19) on Ahab's body being brought to Samaria (cf. I Kings 22:30–38), the dogs licked Ahab's blood from the chariot in the same spot where they had licked the blood of his victim, Naboth.

7. Jehoshaphat Starts Reforms and is Blessed (19:1—20:37)

Returning from Ramoth-Gilead, Jehoshaphat was rebuked by the prophet Jehu: "Shouldest thou help the ungodly, and love them that hate the Lord?" But the prophet commended him for removing the groves (called *Asherim* because they were devoted to the worship of Ashtoreth, a pagan goddess), and Jehoshaphat prepared his heart to seek God, with good results for the nation (19:1–4). In the administration of justice, he reminded the judges they were judging for God Who was no respecter of persons. The judges were also to warn the people not to trespass against the Lord and bring down God's wrath (vv. 5–11).

God's Help to Jehoshaphat (20:1–37). The great spiritual change in the king is seen in his living faith in God when the Ammonites, Moabites, and Edomites invaded Judah. ("Syria" in v. 2 should read "Edom.") His deeply moving prayer (20:5–12) revealed great confidence in God and thankfulness for past deliverances. God responded by telling the people to "*stand still,* and see the salvation of the Lord" (v. 17), for God was with them. With devout adoration and praise, the king and his people sought the Lord, and He produced such confusion and terror in the enemy that they, in a frenzy, turned their arms upon one another and decimated their vast army. It was the doing of the Lord (vv. 20–30).

Once again, Jehoshaphat foolishly allied himself with the wicked king of Israel, Ahaziah, in a naval expedition which proved a complete failure, but he finally ended his days with the favor of God upon him (20:31, 32; cf. I Kings 22:49).

8. *Jehoram Chastised Because of Sins (21:1–20)*

The marriage of Jehoram, son of Jehoshaphat, to Athaliah, the daughter of Ahab and Jezebel, proved his undoing, for he followed their evil ways. God, however, spared the dynasty because of His covenant with David (21:6, 7; cf. II Sam. 7).

When Jehoram wickedly murdered his brothers, retribution fell upon him. The tributary states revolted, entered Jerusalem, sacked the king's house and carried away his wives. He embraced the religion of Baal and sought to uproot that of the Lord. He was cursed with a terrible disease in the bowels and ended his days in misery. He is remembered as a king who sought to destroy the good work of his father (21:8–20).

9. *Ahaziah's Evil Reign: Usurpation of Athaliah (22:1–12)*

Athaliah, daughter of Ahab, led her son, Ahaziah, into wickedness, as she had her husband Jehoram (22:1–3). Following the ways of the house of Ahab, he came to speedy destruction in 885 B.C., the year of his accession. When he joined his uncle in a war on Syria, the uncle was wounded, and went to Jezreel to recuperate. Visited there by Ahaziah, Jehu, son of Nimshi, raised up of God to punish the wicked house of Ahab, slew them both. Athaliah, mother of Ahaziah, then usurped the throne and murdered all the members of the royal house of Judah she could find, but Joash (aged six) was hidden by his aunt Jehoshabeath, wife of Jehoiada, the high priest (cf. II Kings 11:1–3; II Chron. 22:5–12).

10. *Jehoiada Makes Joash King (23:1–21)*

After six years of misrule by Athaliah, the faithful Jehoiada, with certain trusty officers, skilfully arranged to place the boy Joash (or Jehoash) on the throne (23:3–11). When Athaliah intervened, she was taken outside "the ranges" (the precincts) and slain. The young king and people covenanted "to be the Lord's." The altars of Baal were destroyed (23:16–21), and the services of the temple were arranged as in David's time (v. 18).

11. The Reign of Joash: Good and Bad (24:1–27)

The reign of Joash in 878–839 B.C. is a warning beacon to those who begin well and end badly. While his godly benefactor, Jehoiada, lived, Joash did magnificently—raised much money voluntarily to repair the Lord's house (24:4–11), and set it up "in its old proportions" (v. 13). With the surplus costly vessels were bought for the temple service.

On the death of the good Jehoiada, Joash became an idolater, despised the prophets, and killed Zechariah, the son of Jehoiada, who remonstrated with him (24:17–22).

The wrath of God fell upon Joash. The Syrians defeated him, entered Jerusalem, and carried off much spoil. Great diseases fell on him, and he was finally slain by his servants (24:20–26).

12. Amaziah's Reign: Wars with Edom and Israel: Idolatry (25:1–28)

Amaziah (839–810 B.C.), like his father, began well, ended badly, and was slain. In the war with Edom, he hearkened to the man of God who urged him to send back a hundred thousand hired Israelite soldiers because "the Lord was not with Israel" (25:5–10). According to promise (v. 9), God granted a great victory over Edom ("Seir," vv. 11, 12). His brutality to prisoners was impious (v. 12). Incredibly enough, he brought home the gods of Seir and worshipped them. A prophet pertinently asked "Why hast thou sought after the gods of the people, which could not deliver their own people out of thine hand?" (v. 15). A curse fell on Amaziah.

In crazy pride, he challenged Joash, king of Israel, saying "Come, let us see one another in the face," a polite way of asking him to fight (25:17). Joash propounded the clever parable of the thistle and the cedar, to expose Amaziah's foolish pretensions. In the ensuing war, Amaziah was thoroughly defeated. The men of Joash entered Jerusalem, and carried the treasures of the temple to Samaria (vv. 17–28).

13. Reign of Uzziah: Great Success: Presumption (26:1–23)

Uzziah (otherwise Azariah) reigned with great ability from 810 to 758 B.C. He made Judah prosperous, greatly extended its borders, and made the Edomites, Philistines, Arabs, and Ammonites pay tribute. He promoted irrigation and built great defenses. Not since Solomon had the nation been so strong. Like his father and grandfather, he showed respect to God's cause at first, then degenerated. When he become strong, "his heart was lifted up to his destruction" (26:15, 16) and he presumed to offer incense in the holy place, where only the priests could enter. He wrathfully resisted the high priest, and God smote him with leprosy, necessitating a life of isolation till his death—a sad end for one whose reign had promised so much (vv. 16–23). Hosea and Amos prophesied in this reign and deplored the demoralizing effects of luxury.

14. Jotham's Reign: Great Builder: Defeats Ammonites (27:1–9)

Jotham (758–742 B.C.) had the virtues of his father and none of his defects (27:2). According to Isaiah (chs. 1 and 5), the people were corrupt at that time; devotion to outward rites cloaked much wickedness. With God's blessing, Jotham "became mighty." He built much in Jerusalem and in the remote districts for defense. When the Ammonites revolted, he defeated them and increased their tribute (v. 5). Jotham is an exception to most of the kings; no sin is laid to him.

15. Reign of Ahaz: Idolatry: Calamities (28:1–27)

Ahaz (742–726 B.C.) is one of the worst monarchs of Judah. In a relatively short reign, he piled iniquity upon iniquity—images for Baal (28:2), sons burned to the god Moloch (v. 3), pagan rites in the high places, and sacrifices to the gods of Damascus (v. 23). He rifled the treasures of the temple to pay tribute to Assyria (v. 21), put a replica of a pagan altar of Damascus in the Holy Place, and then closed the temple altogether (v. 24; cf. II Kings 16:1-20). God sent dire punishment upon him by means of Syria, Israel, Edom and the Philistines (vv. 5–21). God's forbearance had no effect upon him (cf. Is. 7:1–8:). Ahaz was buried without honor. But the outlook was not wholly dark, for on the appeal of a prophet, the northern kingdom, even in such evil times, returned to Judah two hundred thousand women and children whom Israel had taken in the war.

16. Hezekiah's Good Reign: the Temple: Passover: Reforms (29:1—31:21)

Hezekiah (726–698 B.C.), a noble, god-fearing king, remedied the dreadful situation left by his wicked father; he opened the temple, reinstated the Levites and priests, and cleansed the filthiness left by the idolaters. He acknowledged God's chastisements for past evil doing (29:3–11). The Levites delivered God's house from pollution and restored and sanctified the vessels broken and cast away by Ahaz (vv. 12-19). In the great sacrifices, everything was offered according to the ceremonial law. For example, the sprinkling of the blood on the altar (v. 22) denoting expiation for sin, and the laying of the hands on the sin offering (v. 23) indicating the laying of sins on the typical substitute, pointed forward to Christ's atonement (vv. 20–24). The crowning point was reached when the burnt offering for sin was made (vv. 25–30). Sacred song was a significant part of the ceremony.

The Passover (30:1–27). The king and assembly sent invitations throughout the northern kingdom, inviting even the scoffers in the north to come from there to join their brethren in Jerusalem in the greatest Passover for centuries (30:11, 18). Hezekiah's appeal to those of Israel to return to the God of Abraham was touching. He associated the deportations to Assyria with their sin in departing from God (30:6, 9). In Jerusalem they began by destroying the pagan altars erected by Ahaz. Those who "prepared their hearts," although unable to observe all the ceremonial rules, were allowed to partake of the Passover (vv. 18, 19). The seven-day feast was extended for another seven days, so great was their joy in its celebration (vv. 23–27). There had been nothing like this since the days of Solomon.

Hezekiah's Reforms (31:1–21). After the Passover, the multitude in their enthusiasm sallied forth and broke down the idolatrous images not only in Judah and Benjamin, but in Ephraim and Manasseh in Israel (v. 1). Hezekiah then arranged the services of the priests and Levites according to the model left by David. When he invited the people to make contributions for the services of the temple, the response was so generous that the priests and Levites had more than enough. Special storehouses had to be arranged for the great heaps of offerings which remained as surplus. Generous provision was made for the wives and families of Levites (vv. 11–19). Hezekiah was sincere and did "what was good and right before the Lord" (vv. 20, 21). He was greatly helped by the prophets Isaiah and Micah (cf. Is. 10:5—39:8, and Mic. 6:1—7:20).

17. *Miraculous Deliverance from Sennacherib: Hezekiah's Acts (32:1–32)*

Immediately after these happy events, Sennacherib of Assyria appeared before Jerusalem. In 722, the Assyrians had conquered Israel and carried away the principal people (cf. II Kings 17:5–10; 18:9–12). Hezekiah showed enormous energy, covering up wells so that the enemy would find no water, and building forts (32:1–5). In a stirring speech, he exhorted the people to be strong and courageous because they trusted in God (vv. 6–8). Sennacherib's servants made propaganda speeches to those defending the walls of Jerusalem to depress their morale (vv. 9–19). Hezekiah and the prophet Isaiah betook themselves to prayer. Then followed the destruction of the Assyrian army by an angel of the Lord, referred to by the chronicler with remarkable brevity. No less than 185,000 Assyrians perished, and, upon his return to the city of Nineveh, Sennacherib was murdered by his sons (vv. 20–23). The chronicler in one verse reports the grave illness of Hezekiah and the miraculous prolongation of his life, but II Kings 20:1–11 tells in detail the answer to Hezekiah's prayer for healing which prolongs his life.

When Merodach-Baladan of Babylon sent ambassadors to Hezekiah, in pride he showed them all his treasures. He was severely rebuked by Isaiah, who said that all these treasures would yet be carried to Babylon, and Hezekiah's descendants as well. This was literally fulfilled (cf. II Kings 20:12–19; Is. 39). God's wrath was roused against Hezekiah for his pride, but he was forgiven (32:25–33).

18. *Manasseh and Amon: Impious and Idolatrous (33:1–25)*

Manasseh (698–643 B.C.) surpassed all his predecessors in wicked idolatry by rearing pagan altars even in God's house (33:5, 7), and worshipping the stars (v. 3, cf. II Kings 21:11–16). On being carried captive to Babylon, he repented. God moved Esarhaddon to send him back to Jerusalem, where he strove earnestly to serve the

Lord and eradicate the paganism he had formerly fostered (vv. 12–17). He himself was pardoned on repenting, but his former evil deeds wrought havoc in the nation (cf. II Kings 23:26; 24: 3, 4). His son Amon, who ruled only two years, did evil, did not repent, and was murdered (vv. 21–24).

19. *Josiah's Good Reign: Reforms: Honors Moses' Law (34:1— 35:27)*

Josiah (641–610 B.C.) is called "the good King Josiah." At sixteen he became interested in the true religion, and at twenty he attacked idolatry of every kind (34:1–4). He destroyed the rites of Moloch, shut the house of the sodomites, and slew pagan priests on their own altar, burning human bones thereon (vv. 1–7; II Kings 23:16, 20). At twenty-six he had the temple repaired and cleansed (vv. 8–13). The discovery of the book of the law (the Pentateuch) in the temple (where it was lost sight of) greatly affected the king when he realized how far their fathers had departed from its teaching. Huldah, the prophetess, declared that all the curses in the book would fall on the land because of idolatry. Josiah, because of his penitence, would not see these evils personally (34:14–28). Josiah solemnly read the book to a great gathering in Jerusalem and renewed the covenant between God and the nation (cf. II Kings 23:4–20). The work of Josiah was effectual in his lifetime, but the reformation merely slowed down the rush to disaster.

The Great Passover (35:1–19). This celebration exceeded even the great Passover in Hezekiah's day. Everything was done according to the laws laid down by David (cf. I Chron. 23:1—26:32; II Chron. 35:2–19). The ark, which had been removed, was restored to its place. Priests and people had been duly sanctified, and all were in their appointed places (35:11–17). There must have been half a million communicants.

The influence of Josiah reached even to the north of the neighboring kingdom of Israel (cf. II Chron. 34:6).

Thirteen years after the great Passover, Pharaoh-nechoh attacked the dominions of Nabopolassar of Babylon (II Kings 23:29). Josiah foolishly opposed him, for Nechoh had no quarrel with him, but Josiah refused to desist and was mortally wounded at Megiddo (35:20–24). With the death of Josiah ended the hope of reformation. The death of no king of Judah was so sincerely lamented as his.

20. *Last Kings of Judah (36:1–23)*

Jehoahaz (otherwise Shallum), the third son, succeeded Josiah in 610 B.C. In three months he was deposed and carried to Egypt by Pharaoh-nechoh (36:1–4; cf. Jer. 22:10–12; II Kings 23:30–34).

Eliakim (called Jehoiakim), Josiah's second son, was then made king (609–598 B.C.). He was an evil ruler (36:5). Urijah, a prophet was put to death for telling him the truth (Jer. 26:20–23). Jeremiah found him unrighteous and hardened in sin (Jer. 22:13–19). He burned in the fire the roll written by Baruch, and Jeremiah foretold a miserable end for him (Jer. 36:1–31). Nebuchadrezzar of Babylon defeated the Egyptians and made Jehoiakim a vassal in 606 B.C. Daniel and others were carried to Babylon. Jehoiakim rebelled in 598 B.C., and was defeated and executed by Nebuchadrezzar, getting "the burial of an ass" (cf. Jer. 22:19). The sacred vessels of the temple were carried to Babylon (36:7). Jehoiachin, the son of Jehoiakim, ruled only one hundred days. Ten thousand captives, including Ezekiel, were carried to Babylon (Ezek. 1:12), along with Jehoiachin (also called Jeconiah, and Coniah).

Zedekiah, fourth son of Josiah, succeeded his nephew (597–586 B.C.). "Brother" in verse 10 should read "uncle." He also was an evil man. (See chapters 8 and 22 of Ezekiel for an account of the conditions in Jerusalem.) Zedekiah was a vassal of Nebuchadrezzar. Jeremiah counseled submission as the only hope. The king secretly honored Jeremiah, but put him in prison for fear of the nobles. When Zedekiah rebelled against Babylon, Nebuchadrezzar besieged Jerusalem eighteen months (II Kings 24:20) and the city was broken up. Zedekiah and part of his army fled. After he was captured, his sons were killed before his eyes, and then his eyes were put out. He was carried in chains to Babylon (Jer. 52:4–15; II Kings 25:1–21). The walls, the temple, and palaces were broken down. The people were taken captive (36:14–21). The Captivity was reckoned from the first deportation in 606 B.C., and lasted seventy years, fulfilling Jeremiah's prophecy (36:21). It ended in 536 B.C., when Cyrus of Persia (then king of Babylon) gave his decree permitting the return (cf. Jer. 25:11; 29:10). To give the returned exiles instruction, warning, and inspiration as to the past of their people, the Books of Chronicles were written.

Ezra

J. STAFFORD WRIGHT

THE BOOK OF EZRA is deliberately written as a continuation of Chronicles, as the opening verses show; these are identical with the closing verses of II Chronicles. Where Chronicles has traced the downfall of the nation, and shown the Exile in Babylon as a period of punishment, Ezra begins the story of the rebirth of the Jewish people. Jeremiah and other prophets had foretold that the Exile would be followed by renewal. In fact this appears clearly in 1:1, which points out the fulfilment of Jeremiah 25:12. Jeremiah, prophesying in 605 B.C., says that the Babylonian power will be broken in seventy years, and Cyrus of Persia captured Babylon in 538 B.C.

The author, or compiler, is unknown, but may have been Ezra himself. He made use of existing documents for events not witnessed personally. Two sections of the book are in Aramaic (4:8—6:18 and 7:12–26). This Semitic language was in common use throughout the Near East at this time.

358

I. Return of the Exiles from Babylon to Jerusalem (1:1–11)

We know from his inscriptions that when Cyrus, king of Persia, conquered Babylon in 538 B.C., he allowed captive peoples of all nations to return to their own countries and that he recognized their gods. His public decree is worded in a way that would appeal to the Jews (1:1–4). While to Cyrus, the words of verse 2 were only a formality, it is a fact that all the gods of wood and stone that were then in Babylon have long since vanished, while the Lord remains the God of heaven and earth. God has remembered His people, and now sends them out in a second Exodus, with sufficient wealth and with full permission, to rebuild their ruined temple.

We know that Cyrus returned the images of their gods and goddesses to all the peoples, but the Jews had no idols. Cyrus therefore gives them the vessels of the temple to take back with them (1:7), while the returning exiles bring their own wealth, and those who stay behind make their contributions (vv. 4, 6). It is clear that many of the Jews had prospered in captivity, where they were not living under prison conditions, but in townships and villages (Jer. 29:5,6). Now that the opportunity to return had come, they preferred to help others to go, rather than go themselves. Life in Judea was likely to be difficult and dangerous, whereas they were assured of reasonable comfort in Babylonia. A similar choice repeatedly confronts us as Christians (cf. Heb. 11:8–27), and may form a test between nominal and real believers. God does not always call us to security.

The returned exiles were not given a king, but a governor. Sheshbazzar may be the same as Shenazar of I Chronicles 3:18, in which case, like Zerubbabel, he was of the royal line of David. He is unlikely to be the same person as Zerubbabel, since in Ezra 5:14 he is referred to as though he were then dead (that is, in 520 B.C.), while Zerubbabel was still living. It was not God's purpose that the Jews should have another king until the coming of the Messiah.

II. The Register of Those Who Returned (2:1–70)

The list may be divided as follows:

(1) The chief men who returned with Zerubbabel (2:2). God provides adequate leaders when He calls to some work.

(2) Families and clans (vv. 3–19).

(3) The inhabitants of various towns and villages (vv. 20–35). Comparatively few settled in Jerusalem itself until after Nehemiah had built the walls (Neh. 7:4).

(4) The priests (vv. 36–39).

(5) The threefold division of Levites (vv. 40–42). The number of Levites is far less than that of the priests. Were the Levites slow to return because they knew that they would be given a more humble position? (cf. also 8:15). The more spectacular work does not rank higher in God's sight, but He looks for faithfulness in the position where He places us, whether high or low.

(6) The Nethinim (vv. 43–54). Their name means *given*, that is, given to help the Levites in their service (8:20). They may have been descendants of the Gibeonites of Joshua 9:27.

(7) Those known as Solomon's servants (2:55–58). Apparently they were similar to the Nethinim.

(8) Those whose genealogy was uncertain (2:59–63).

The restored community moved cautiously. History had shown that the infiltration of paganism led to corruption of the nation, and now it was important that only true Israelites should be given full rights of citizenship. It was specially important for the priesthood to be uncontaminated, since in the past there had been many failures here; so, if a claimant to the priesthood could not prove his descent, he was set aside. The Tirshatha (or governor) left it open for him to be restored if the lost Urim and Thummim should be found. These were the two jewels in the high priest's breastplate (Ex. 28:30), and were used to find out the will of the Lord on certain solemn occasions (I Sam. 28:6). Evidently they had been lost at the destruction of Jerusalem.

III. Building of the Altar and the Temple Foundations (3:1–13)

Sheshbazzar was the nominal head, but Zerubbabel, of the line of David, and Jeshua (or Joshua), the high priest, were the active leaders. It is possible to hold office without having the keenness that should go with the office. They met their fear of the suspicious peoples round about by putting devotion to God first, and rebuilding the altar of burnt-offering in the ruined temple (3:3). Then they began to observe the regular requirements of the law of Moses. The top priority for the people of God is being right in His sight, and living in fellowship with Him.

The altar was not enough. Cyrus had authorized a grant of money for the rebuilding of the temple. So now all the people turn to this work. The foundations are solemnly laid; both the earthly and the living temple need firm foundations (Eph. 2:20–22). The suggestion of verses 10 and 11 is that they sang Psalm 136, as at the dedication of Solomon's temple (II Chron. 5:13; 7:3). Some shouted for joy, others wept, partly through joy, and partly because the new foundations seemed so small compared with the glories of Solomon's temple (Hag. 2:3). Foundations always seem small, but great buildings arise from them. It is not good to be sighing for "the good old days" of the past.

IV. Cessation of the Work Through Opposition (4:1–24)

The peoples who lived round about Jerusalem were not anxious to see the city revive. Many of them were descendants of the foreigners who had been placed in the land by the Assyrian kings after the captivity of the northern kingdom of Israel (II Kings 17:24–41). They now had a form of worship that included the worship of the Lord with the worship of other gods and goddesses. This type of mixed worship had been fatal in the years before the Exile, and, if these people had been allowed to help in the rebuilding of the temple, they would have claimed the right to say how the worship should be conducted. This would have been far too high a price for the world's help.

Unfortunately the Jews did not continue as they had begun, but allowed their enemies to wear them down by irritating opposition, even though they had the authorization of God and of Cyrus to proceed with the building. Their motives were questioned, and they were misrepresented to the authorities, though at first no violence was used against them. Such frustration has more than once proved effective against those who are engaged in God's work, and has led them to adopt some easier course. Haggai 1:4, written at the end of this period of stagnation, shows that the Jews turned to building and decorating luxurious houses for themselves.

It is possible that the Artaxerxes of 4:7 is the Persian king in whose reign Ezra and Nehemiah came to Jerusalem. If so, the compiler of this book has here brought together several examples of similar opposition from the enemies of Judah.

V. Renewal of the Work, and Completion of the Temple (5:1—6:22)

About sixteen years have elapsed since the time when the foundations of the temple were laid, but hardly anything has been done towards the erection of the building. Haggai and Zechariah are spoken of (5:1) as two of the prophets responsible for the revival of spiritual and practical enthusiasm, and some of their prophecies on this occasion are in the books of the Bible that bear their names. Haggai 1 especially should be read at this point to see the attitude of the people. The Word of God, pressed home through the Spirit of God, is always the source of new life. Note that genuine revival must express itself in a practical form.

Once again there was opposition, but this time it was less violent, though none the less dangerous. It took the form of an approach by the local governor who was responsible to the Persian government for the maintenance of order. He asked for the Jewish authority for the building. Unfortunately the Jews could not produce any written document, but they asserted that they had been authorized by King Cyrus, and asked that a search should be made at the Persian capital to discover the actual form of authorization. Meanwhile they had faith in God that He would meet their need, and went quietly on with the building.

Although the copy of the decree was not in Babylon, it was eventually found in Ecbatana in Media. That its form of wording is different from the decree in chapter 1 is easily accounted for. Chapter 1 contains the public proclamation, couched in terms that would specially appeal to the Jews. The copy that was filed in the official records was more precise and formal. There was no need to mention the name of the Lord, but it was necessary to lay down certain specifications for the maximum dimensions of the temple, since Cyrus was making a grant for the total expenses. King Darius not only reaffirmed the decree, but added to it. At this point Zechariah 4:6–10 is worth reading, as it speaks of the great mountain of opposition that led some of the pessimists to think that Zerubbabel would never be able to complete the work that he had begun. God, by the power of His Spirit, had overruled the opposition without the need of earthly might and powerful armies.

King Darius asked for the prayers of the Jews (6:10). In this we are reminded of Paul's later words about prayer for rulers in I Timothy 2:1, 2.

So the work was finished, the temple was dedicated, and a great Passover service was kept. To this were admitted not only the returned exiles, but Jews and Israelites who had not gone into exile at all, provided that they made a clean break with the pagan worship into which some of them had evidently fallen (6:21). Verse 22 naturally emphasized the joy which was shown on this occasion, joy in seeing the climax of the finished work carried out under the clear leading of God.

VI. The Mission of Ezra (7:1–28)

The Bible gives no account of the state of the Jews between the completion of the temple in 516 B.C. and the coming of Ezra in 457 B.C., though it is likely that Zechariah 9—14 and Malachi come into this period. The renewed enthusiasm had once again died away, as so often happens after times of revival and individual renewal. The test of a man or woman of God is not the peaks of spiritual excitement, but the steady maintenance of high standards of godliness.

Ezra was a great student of the law of Moses, and may have held a post under the Persian Empire comparable to Secretary of State for Jewish Affairs. Artaxerxes, king of Persia, was anxious to promote peace among all his subjects, and sent Ezra to examine the state of religion among the Jews in Judea. Moreover, he encouraged other Jews to return with Ezra and settle in their own country. Here is yet another example of how God can use a Gentile ruler, without any human prompting, to bring about a fresh stage in His purposes for His people. Artaxerxes himself made gifts for the temple, and authorized further grants from the local governors in Palestine. He gave Ezra the fullest possible authority in the religious sphere, though he did not make him governor of Jerusalem. The magistrates and judges (7:25) were those who would enforce the Jewish law.

Like Daniel and Nehemiah, Ezra had clearly commended himself to his master by his consistent life, and now his opportunity came to help his people more directly. How important it is for believers today to be equally faithful in positions of responsibility, whether in national, civic, or business life! One notices here how Ezra sees the hand of God Himself in the decree of the king, and how he turns to God in thankfulness and praise (7:27, 28).

VII. Ezra's Journey (8:1-36)

It was eighty years since the original return, and the present generation of exiles had never faced the call of God to go back to Jerusalem. Now Ezra challenges them afresh, and finds a company to join him. Strangely enough, Levites are absent (8:15). Presumably they thought that, if they went back now, there would be only junior positions for them in the temple service, since the best positions would be held by the descendants of those who had come back with the first return. No doubt they held positions of influence as teachers in Babylonia. Christ's words concerning service (Lk. 22:24-27) speak to the servant's desire for prominence.

Ezra shows himself to be a man of faith and of practical wisdom. He refuses an escort of soldiers, relying wholly upon God's protection (8:22), but he is careful not to give any occasion for scandal over the treasures that he handles (vv. 25, 33). This carefulness in the handling of money is as important to Christians today as it was to the witness of God in Ezra's time.

VIII. The Problem of Mixed Marriages (9:1—10:44)

This problem is always near at hand, since sex attraction is such a powerful force. During the history of Israel, intermarriage with pagans repeatedly corrupted the true faith; at best, there was a blending of cults; at worst, the Jewish partner drifted into the easier religion of the other. Christians, facing the same problem today, must solve it by refusal to enter into any marriage unless it be "in the Lord" (I Cor. 7:39; II Cor. 6:14).

In Ezra's day the secular and religious leaders were guilty, as well as the ordinary members of the community (9:1, 2). Knowledge and education by themselves do not give power over sin. Ezra is appalled when he hears what has been happening, and, like Daniel, Nehemiah, and others, he pours out his heart to God in a national confession (vv. 6-15; cf. Neh. 1:5-11; Dan. 9:4-19). Notice that the prayer contains confession, praise, and petition in faith. Can one who has been truly forgiven and blessed turn again to known sin, and remain unmoved in it?

Ezra's example of horror moves others who had previously been indifferent, and they agree upon positive steps to put away the evil and to make a fresh covenant with God for the future (10:3). They are not prepared to let their leader carry the burden single-handed; the matter concerns the whole people of God, as church matters do today. The story shows that they were not content with a hurried decision, but were determined to take the necessary time for a thorough investigation (vv. 13, 14). Yet feelings ran high, and the Revised Standard Version in verse 15 is probably correct in translating "opposed" in place of "were employed about." Presumably other lesser people supported these rebels, and Ezra must have become unpopular with a number of Jews and with their pagan neighbors. But popularity should never be the standard for judging the desirability of a policy, and if church leaders are undergirded by prayer, they will not be unwisely swayed by opposition.

Nehemiah

J. STAFFORD WRIGHT

IT IS USUALLY thought that Ezra and Nehemiah were originally one book. The compiler here made use of personal memoirs of Nehemiah, as well as other material. If Ezra, who must have died before 400 B.C., was the compiler, as many evangelical scholars believe, some names may have been added after his death, since Jaddua, mentioned in 12:22, was living in 330 B.C. However, some scholars think, in view of the frequent recurrence of Hebrew names, the name Jaddua belonged in this instance to grandfather and grandson.

366

I. Nehemiah's Prayer Over Jerusalem's Distress (1:1–11)

Nehemiah held an honored position as cup-bearer to the King of Persia. He might well have thought that the struggles of Jerusalem did not concern him; but when the struggles were brought to his notice, he turned to constant prayer. He knew that the sufferings of his people had come through their sins, but he knew that such Scriptures as Deuteronomy 30:1–5 had promised full restoration in answer to repentance and faith. So in his prayer he began by identifying himself with the nation, confessing its sins, and claiming the promises of God.

It is possible that, when he began to pray, he had no thoughts other than the challenge to pray. But it is clear that, after he had prayed earnestly for several days, God made it clear to him that he was called not only to pray, but to go (1:11). Prayer, in this instance, placed a burden on the petitioner as well as on God.

II. Nehemiah's Return to Jerusalem as Governor (2:1–11)

The king's cup-bearer was more than an ordinary servant; he was chosen for outstanding qualities and held in high regard by the king. Yet Oriental kings were notoriously changeable, and Nehemiah knew that his master might either take no notice of his request, or have him sentenced to death. Yet God prepared the king's heart, and he not only allowed him to return to Jerusalem, but appointed him as governor. Although Nehemiah had already prayed for so long, he sent up an "arrow-prayer" when the critical moment came (2:4). The one sort of prayer is no substitute for the other, but both are needed.

God leads people in different ways. Whereas Nehemiah accepted the king's escort (2:9), Ezra refused such help (Ezra 8:22). In decisions of this kind, only the person directly involved can determine the proper action.

When he reached Jerusalem, Nehemiah met the intense suspicion of the leaders of the enemies of the Jews. Such animosity was probably generated by the jealousy of Sanballat, Governor of Samaria (2:10) who probably hoped to be made governor of Judah as well.

III. Plans to Rebuild the City Wall (2:12–20)

Nehemiah's silence is significant. Sent by God to undertake a great task, he approached it quietly. Nehemiah first explored everything as thoroughly as he could, so that he had a true measure of the extent of his mission. He went out by the southwestern gate, turned east, and went around the walls, examining the ruins. Having estimated all the difficulties, he inspired the people to begin the work.

At first the enemies sneered at them, and suggested that they were planning to rebel against the king of Persia; but Nehemiah boldly declared that they were staking everything on God (2:19, 20).

IV. The Builders of the Wall (3:1–32)

Planned organization has its place in the work of God, and the work was allocated to groups of builders. These included the high priest, Eliashib, who was not afraid of practical service (3:1, contrast 3:5), and Malchijah (v. 11), who was one of those who had been guilty of marrying a heathen wife (Ezra 10:31). God restores and uses the truly penitent.

V. Threats to the Building (4:1—7:4)

In the sections that follow we read of ways in which God's people are constantly attacked when they aim to go forward.

1. Discouraging Sarcasm (4:1–6)

Their enemies keep pointing out the enormity of the work they are attempting. Even if they do erect a wall, it will not be strong enough to keep anyone out. Nehemiah meets this opposition by continued prayer, which asserts the principle of "with what measure ye mete, it shall be measured to you again" (Mt. 7:2).

2. Enemy Attacks (4:7–23)

The campaign of sarcasm had an effect on some of the builders, who began to feel that the work was too much for them (4:10).

They were ready to give up when those who came in daily from the villages brought reports of planned enemy attacks (v. 12). Nehemiah met this new threat by prayer, faith, and practical steps for defense.

3. Disunity Within (5:1–19)

God's work can be hindered by inconsistencies in the Church as much as by direct attack from outside. The poorer people were in desperate need through the heavy interest they were paying on loans from their richer brethren. Nehemiah enforced the law of Moses on usury (Deut. 23:19, 20). The King James Version today gives the impression in several instances that usury was approved, but this is due to the fact that the term had not then acquired its special modern connotation of *exorbitant* interest. Christians should be ready to lend money to each other without asking for interest. Nehemiah personally set a great example in money matters by refusing to take the taxes that were due him as governor (5:14, 15). His private income was evidently sufficient, and he had learned the difficult lesson on being content with an adequate income, and refused to strive after more and more.

4. False Accusations (6:1–14)

The enemies saw that their only hope now was to remove or discredit Nehemiah. They suggested a conference, but Nehemiah put the work of God before talk (6:1–4). They sent an open letter that others could read, accusing Nehemiah of wanting to make himself king, but Nehemiah's life and character were such that he could dismiss the rumor (vv. 5–9). They tried to make him put personal safety first, and hide in the temple from some fancied plot to kill him; to gain their ends they even bribed prophets to persuade him in the name of the Lord. Nebhemiah gave the answer of a humble man of God.

VI. The Completion of the Wall (6:15—7:4)

In spite of all the setbacks, the wall was finished in fifty-two days, a clear demonstration of God's good hand upon the builders (6:15, 16). Yet God's people must never be off their guard, even in a time of success. Infiltration of enemy-inspired ideas might yet spoil the work and bring in pagan standards of life and religion (vv. 17–19). Now it was important to build up the Jewish population of the city. So long as there were no walls to protect them, the people had no wish to settle in the city, but preferred to live in the villages round about (7:4).

VII. The Register of the Returned Exiles (7:5–73)

This register is almost identical with that of Ezra 2. The slight variations in numbers could be due to faulty copying of manuscripts, or Ezra 2 might be the list that was drawn up before the departure from Babylon; and Nehemiah 7, the final list deposited in the temple.

VIII. The Reading and Exposition of the Law (8:1–18)

Since the beginning of the Book of Nehemiah, we have heard nothing of Ezra. It may be that he had returned to the king of Persia to make a report of his work. We cannot blame him for not building the walls, since he had not been authorized to do this, nor did he hold the position of governor. Nehemiah was called of God to rebuild the walls and the city, while Ezra was the priest whose task was to teach the law. God calls each man to his own work, and equips him for this.

Now that the walls are complete, the time has come to re-examine the life of the nation in the light of God's Word. A fine building is no substitute for true teaching. So a day is fixed, a platform is erected for a pulpit, and Ezra is summoned to read the law. Before he does so, the people bow down and worship the Lord. It was important that everyone should understand what they heard, and chosen Levites helped in this. The word "distinctly" in 8:8 (KJV) could bear several meanings, including "with interpretation" (RSV margin), or "with a translation." It may well be that at this time some of the people understood Aramaic better than Hebrew (see the introduction to Ezra), or even were more familiar with the dialects of the neighboring peoples (13:23, 24).

The Word of God first condemned, and the people wept when they realized how far the nation had departed from God's standards (8:9). Yet God does not intend us to remain in a state of condemnation, but means to forgive and renew. So from sorrow the people pass to joy, and arrange to keep the Feast of Tabernacles, which was now due. This feast commemorated the wanderings after coming out of Egypt; once again they were settled in a strong city. The feast was celebrated from the 15th to the 22nd of the seventh month (Lev. 23:39), so they had plenty of time to prepare for it, and kept the feast on a greater scale than it had been kept since Joshua's day (8:17).

IX. *A Prayer of Repentance and Covenant of Obedience (9:1—10:39)*

Now that the people have heard the Word of God and celebrated their new deliverance, the time has come for practical action. From time to time, the Old Testament tells of the renewal of the covenant between God and the people, and this is what happens now.

First, the Levites, representing the people, lead in public prayer to God. They rehearse the mighty acts of God, praising Him for His work in creation (9:6), for His calling out of Abraham (vv. 7, 8), for His deliverance from Egypt (vv. 9–12), and for His giving of the law (vv. 13–15). He forgave the sins of His people again and again (vv. 16–19), taught them by His Holy Spirit (v. 20), and brought them into the Promised Land (vv. 21–25). Their history since then had been marked by rebellion, restoration, and rebellion again, until at last God sent the punishment of the Exile, after giving full warning through the prophets (vv. 26–30). Yet punishment was not total destruction, and the people now are determined to turn from their present sins, and set their seal to a renewed covenant with God (vv. 31–38). It is a good thing to review God's goodness to us, and to examine our lives in the light of this.

Nehemiah, the Tirshatha (that is, Governor), is the first to set his seal to the covenant. The rest follow, with full understanding of what is involved (10:28, 29). Certain points are selected for special mention (vv. 29, 30), and these are mostly summaries of the law, with particular application to the needs of the time. These summaries concern the following: *(1)* Separation from the pagan population: mixed marriages are always unwise (vv. 29–30). *(2)* Respect for the Sabbath and for the seventh year when debts were remitted (v. 31. Deut. 15:1–3). *(3)* Definite giving for the worship in the temple (vv. 32, 33). This was less than the half shekel which was paid in New Testament times and was based on Exodus 30:13, but was probably as much as the general poverty of the people at this time allowed without hardship. *(4)* All were prepared for the manual labor involved in the supply of fuel for the altar (v. 34). Similar work is needed today for our places of worship. (5) The people accept the responsibility for supplying the needs of those who minister in holy things (vv. 35–39), a principle stated again in I Corinthians 9:14.

The consecrated life is a practical life. Just as obedience followed upon repentance in the revival of Nehemiah's day, so we must when we give ourselves wholly to the Lord translate that devotion into practical action.

X. Register of the Inhabitants of Jerusalem and the Villages (11:1—12:26)

Strange as it may seem, it was a real sacrifice for some people to come and build a house and settle in Jerusalem. Some were drawn by lot, while others offered themselves willingly (11:1, 2). During all the years that the city had been defenseless without any walls, most of the returned exiles had preferred to live in farms and homesteads in the villages round about. It was not easy to give up their houses, and settle in a city that might at any time be attacked by the enemies. These enemies did not so much object to the Jews being dispersed over the countryside, but a strong city meant a stronger national sense. Today some prefer the country, others prefer city life, and while it is often possible to have the one that we prefer, we must remember that the service of God overrides any special locality.

There are six lists here: (1) Those living in Jerusalem (11:4–24); leading laymen (vv. 3–9), priests (vv. 10–14), Levites (vv. 15–18), and porters (v. 19), with notes about them in verses 20–24. (2) Occupied towns and villages in the territory formerly assigned to Judah and Benjamin (vv. 25–36). (3) Priests and Levites who came in the original party with Zerubbabel and Joshua nearly one hundred years before (12:1–9). (4) A genealogy of the high priests from Joshua to Jaddua (vv. 10, 11). (5) Priests in the days of Joiakim, who was high priest shortly before Nehemiah came to Jerusalem (vv. 12–21). (6) Heads of Levitical families in the days of Joiakim (vv. 22–26). Lists of this kind show how carefully the Jews preserved formal records, probably in many cases in the temple registry.

XI. *Dedication of the Walls and Arrangements for Worship (12:27–47)*

This section introduces again the personal memoirs of Nehemiah, and gives a picture of the ceremony at the dedication of the city walls. It is a reminder that everything is to be holy to the Lord, and not only the temple. There were two great processions, starting probably in the southwest of Jerusalem. One moved around the city in a counter-clockwise direction, led by Ezra (12:31–37); the other, led by Nehemiah, started northwards and went around the walls in a clockwise direction (vv. 38, 39). How different from the time when Nehemiah had gone around the ruined walls and had had the greatest difficulty in making progress (2:13, 14)!

God, who inspired the beginning of the work, had enabled the people to complete it, and now, as the two processions met, they joined to give thanks to Him (12:40–42). Also they offered sacrifices (v. 43) either as part of the ritual of purification (v. 30), since even our best works are tainted with self and sin, or as an outward expression of dedication. Whatever the outward symbolism here, the result was great joy, and the songs of praise rang out over the countryside as a testimony to the enemies that God was the God of power and fulfilment.

Then full provision was made for the maintenance of the temple worship (12:44–47). Certain men were set aside to keep a check on what was stored in the storage rooms in the temple, both for the actual offerings and for the needs of those who served in the temple. God's servants, who had no opportunity of earning their own living, were to be provided for; everything was to be done decently and in order.

XII. *Nehemiah's Reforms (13:1–31)*

Verses 6 and 7 show that most, if not all, of this chapter took place some years after the events of the previous chapter. After twelve years as governor of Jerusalem, Nehemiah returned to Persia for a time. When he was allowed to return to Jerusalem, he found the people as a whole no longer keeping the terms of the covenant they had made with God. This is the sort of thing that has happened repeatedly, not only in Old Testament times but in the Christian

Church. Revival, enthusiasm, and dedication are followed by depression and carelessness. Often a fresh reformer is raised up, but this time the reformer was Nehemiah himself. We note what needed to be done:

1. Separation (13:1–3)

This incident may have occurred at the time of the dedication of the wall, though the introductory words of 13:4 suggest that it happened later. In accordance with Deuteronomy 23:3–5, the Jews deprived Moabites and Ammonites of any rights that they might have assumed in Israel, often through intermarriage. This was not a matter of persecution, but of citizen rights in a theocratic society. Tobiah (13:7) was an Ammonite (2:19).

2. Cleansing of the Temple; Provision for the Levites (13:4–14)

Ties of kinship had warped the judgment of the high priest, Eliashib, and he had allowed a foreigner to have some of the best apartments in the temple. This meant that there was not enough room for storing the offerings for the Levites and others; and as a result the Levites could no longer afford to live in the temple, but had to return to agriculture. Then the people ceased to bring the offerings, since there was no proper place to store them, and fewer Levites to need them. Thus a vicious circle was set up, only to be broken when Nehemiah turned Tobiah and his furniture out of the temple. Once again the people brought their tithes and offerings, the Levites returned, and proper provision was made for them to have their needs supplied. Eliashib is not the only servant of God to be turned from the true path through family sentiment or pressure.

3. Sanctity of the Sabbath Day (13:15–22)

The Sabbath was set aside by God as a day of rest and worship. Infringement of its sanctity was one of the sins of Judah in pre-Exilic times (Jer. 17:21–27). Now the same sin had arisen among those who had solemnly dedicated themselves to keep it holy (10:31). The habits of the heathen had proved too much for them, and those who had goods to sell were determined to get more and more opportunities of making money, even though it meant working seven days a week. Minds occupied with business cares on God's day of rest are in no fit state to worship Him. Experience shows that the hedging round of the day is necessary for spiritual well-being. For the people's good, Nehemiah took steps to remove temptation from them. So long as there were chances of buying, there would always be weaker people to wander out of the city to the shops. We note that there was no question of necessity involved, since trading was possible on every other day of the week. Only greed, self-indulgence, improvidence, or laziness led people to break the Sabbath in this way. Nehemiah's action with the pagans is relevant when one considers the duty of the Christian Church to influence the legislation of their country as they may have opportunity.

4. Mixed Marriages (13:23–31)

It was about twenty-five years since Ezra had followed through his marriage reforms. Sex and marriage are powerful emotional urges, and often the heart leads the head. Some of the Jews had looked for wives among the pagans, and their children were brought up strongly under their mother's influence. Often they could not understand Hebrew at all, with the result that they could not understand the Scriptures nor the temple services. The implication is that, like Solomon, these Jewish fathers tolerated, and even encouraged, their wives to retain their pagan gods. Pagan faiths are often more glamorous than the revealed truth of God, and are easier to follow because they make less demands on the conscience and on the life. The great tragedy here is that even a possible successor to the office of high priest had married the daughter of Sanballat, the great enemy of Nehemiah. But Sanballat at this time was probably the governor of Samaria, and marriage into his family gave some status, while the weakness of Eliashib, his grandfather (13:7), set a bad example to the young man. Although it is not specifically stated that Nehemiah compelled the Jews to put away their heathen wives, it would be strange if he did not do so, after his strong words and actions. Divorce in these circumstances and under Old Testament regulations cannot be automatically applied to the Christian era, for which the words of Jesus Christ in Matthew 19:3–9 and of Paul in I Corinthians 7 are applicable.

A godly life such as Nehemiah's is begun, continued and rounded off in prayer. Throughout the book prayers have been offered, sometimes committing a fresh situation to God and sometimes, as in this concluding prayer, commending Nehemiah and his work to God.

Esther

WICK BROOMALL

THE VERY BEGINNING of the Book of Esther centers its story in the midst of historical realities. This story is not fiction, the creation of some author's imagination. It is history—plain and simple; names, places, dates and customs are all related on the historical level. Unless we begin with this premise, the story will have little meaning for us.

I. Vashti Demoted (1:1–22)

The story begins with a royal feast that ended in domestic tragedy. In fact, three feasts are mentioned: first, for the royal group (1:1–4); second, for the commoners of Shushan, that is, Susa (1:5–8); third, for the women (1:9–12).

Things went quite well until the seventh day (1:10), when King Ahasuerus, perhaps intoxicated, ordered his queen to display her beauty before the assembled people (vv. 10, 11). Vashti's refusal brought trouble to the royal household. Her refusal must have been due to one or more factors: (1) The woman's innate sense of modesty;

376

(2) the indecorousness of a queen's appearing before a crowd of commoners; (3) the feeling on the queen's part that her husband, by his drunken debauchery, had abdicated his authority over her.

If Esther came to the kingdom for a specific purpose (4:14), surely we can say that Vashti's noble example of womanly modesty will not easily be forgotten. Our modern world needs more women like Vashti, reluctant to expose their half-dressed bodies to the gaze of a multitude.

Ahasuerus, naturally enraged at Vashti's obstinancy (1:12), consults his "wise men" (v. 13) and propounds to them the question of her fate (v. 15). Memucan, one of "the seven princes of Persia and Media" (vv. 14, 15), insinuates that Vashti's rebellion has sinister implications for all husbands. Apparently, because of their obviously cringing nature, the "wise men" make no attempt to justify or extenuate the queen's act. To them it is an act of simple defiance that must be crushed at once before it spreads throughout the empire (v. 18). Memucan, therefore, subtly suggests that the king write a "royal commandment"—inexorable and inflexible—and divorce the queen for her insubordination, putting "another that is better than she" in her place (v. 19). This "Supreme Court" of seven "wise men" —with "Chief Justice" Memucan at the head—"inspired" an edict designed (1) to make men rulers in their own houses, and (2) to make the language of the husband the language of the household (v. 22).

The story does not tell us how this edict was received, but it is hardly likely that the women of the empire received it with great joy. Troops with swords would have been required in every household to see that the order was observed. The king's edict, dealing with the intimate association of husband and wife, could hardly have lasted long. The New Testament deals with this same problem on a much higher level (cf. Eph. 5:22–33).

II. Esther Promoted (2:1–23)

Human nature is just about the same among kings as among commoners. Ahasuerus, his wrath now pacified (2:1), wants his deposed queen to return. But certain "servants" of the king, perhaps fearing the queen's vengeance, concoct a plan which would put another woman in the king's affection. This plan calls for a gathering of all the beauties of the empire at Shushan. Among them surely one could be found that could take the place of Vashti (vv. 2–4).

The story broadens at this point. If the king's new wife is to be selected in a "national beauty contest," it follows that governmental officials (2:3, 8) would bring many beautiful girls to Shushan as competitors for the queenship. One official spied Esther (that is, *Hadassah*) and brought her (v. 8).

But Esther was a cousin of Mordecai, a man whose great-grandfather Kish, a Benjamite, had been carried captive by the great Nebuchadrezzar, king of Babylon (2:5, 6). Moreover, Mordecai had reared Esther from the time of the death of her parents (v. 7). It is probable that at this time Mordecai was about thirty years of age; Esther was perhaps around twenty.

This young woman's features made her the inevitable choice of the king and of all others (2:15–17). Not only was she attractive and pretty (v. 7), but she also possessed noble characteristics. She was obedient to Mordecai (vv. 11, 20) and to the eunuch Hegai, who was in charge of the girls being prepared to meet the king (v. 15). In fact, Hegai seems to have preferred Esther above the others (vv. 8, 9). It is not unlikely that some word from Mordecai might have encouraged Hegai to give Esther more attention (vv. 8, 11). Even though Mordecai's race was apparently known (v. 5; cf. 3:4), Esther was under strict orders from her cousin not to reveal her race (v. 10).

The story does not inform us why Mordecai was so secretive about his cousin's nationality. Perhaps, because of his closeness to the palace (2:5), he had heard that Haman, an avowed hater of the Jews, was currying favor with the king and would soon be in a position to harm the Jews. It was expedient, therefore, for Mordecai to keep a watchful eye on Esther and also on Haman.

Twelve months were given to the preparation of the girls for the king (2:12). At the proper time, each girl presented herself to the king and then returned to the custody of Shaashgas (v. 13). No girl could return to the king unless he took special delight in her (v. 14). It should be noted that all these girls were ostensibly "young virgins" who had never had sexual relations with men.

Esther, it appears, is ready to follow Hegai in all the preparation needful for the king's presence (2:15). Perhaps he knew more than the girls thought he knew about the king's likes and dislikes. Anyway, Esther won the heart of the king and took the place of Vashti in his affection (v. 17). A great feast celebrated the nuptial event (v. 18).

The author of the story is very careful here to date this important event. Esther became queen in the tenth month (December–January) of the seventh year of the reign of Ahasuerus (479 B.C., or four years after the celebration in chapter 1 that resulted in Vashti's divorce). It is believed that between these events Ahasuerus (Xerxes) had made his ill-fated expedition to Greece. Thus he returned from the inglorious defeat at Salamis (480 B.C.) and found comfort in Esther's embrace.

A second gathering of the beauties was held (2:19, 20). Esther, though now queen, is still obedient to Mordecai. Two men, Bigthan and Teresh, who guarded the entrance to the king's sleeping apartment, probably took advantage of the turmoil in the city to attempt to assassinate the king. Josephus tells us that a slave of one of the conspirators revealed the plot to Mordecai. Esther, giving Mordecai the credit, tells the king, who, finding that the story is true, has the would-be assassin crucified (vv. 21–23). The fact that this incident was duly recorded should be kept in mind, for, though perhaps somewhat insignificant at the time, it will yet have an important bearing on the outcome of the story.

III. Haman's Rage (3:1–15)

This chapter may be divided into the following parts: Haman's promotion (3:1); Haman's prejudice (vv. 2–6); Haman's plot (vv. 7–9); the plot promulgated (vv. 12–15a); Haman pacified (v. 15b). However, let us deal rather with the contents of this chapter by asking and answering several questions.

Who was Haman? He is called "the Agagite," but that description in no wise connects him with Agag, the Amalekite king (I Sam. 15:8, 33). He is a Jew-hater (3:10) and a wicked man (7:6). In him we have the same spirit that reappeared in Antiochus Epiphanes, in Nero, and in Hitler. It required a royal edict to get the people to bow down before him (3:2).

Why did Mordecai refuse to bow? Haman's henchmen noticed Mordecai's refusal to prostrate himself before Haman (3:2–4). Mordecai excused himself from noncompliance on the ground that he was a Jew. Undoubtedly he saw in Haman's demand a sinister religious implication. He may even have had in his mind similar situations in the Book of Daniel (chs. 3, 6).

Why did Haman hate the Jews? It is quite evident that he held all Jews guilty of Mordecai's insubordination (3:5, 6). A day was selected by lot (that is, Pur) for the extermination of this hated race (vv. 7–15). Haman is the agent of Satan. The Jews, who hold the messianic seed, must be destroyed (cf. Gen. 3:15). The king agrees with Haman and gives his whim official sanction (vv. 12–15).

IV. Esther's Stage (4:1—5:8)

This chapter is just about the mid-point of the story. Events soon take place rapidly. Let us note some of them.

Mordecai *laments* (4:1–3). His behavior here is reminiscent of Jonah's action at Nineveh.

Esther *resents* (4:4–6). The behavior of her cousin grieved the queen. In her secluded world, she had not yet heard the news of Haman's wanton plans.

Mordecai *presents* (4:7, 8) a plan for petition. By means of Hatach, Mordecai gets a copy of the official decree into Esther's hands and urges her to plead for her people before the king.

Esther *dissents* (4:9–12). She returns word to Mordecai that she has not been in the king's presence for thirty days. To go unbidden would mean her death.

Mordecai *prophesies* (4:13, 14) that Esther will also be a victim of Haman's plot. These verses are the center of the story. Esther will perish if she refuses to take up Mordecai's challenge. Mordecai must have emphasized to his cousin that she had come to her important place for such a crisis as the present one. She must not fail her people.

Esther *consents* (4:15–17) to plead for her people. A need higher than her own life now faces the beautiful queen. She sees her place in the plans of Providence and humbly submits: "if I perish, I perish" (v. 16).

Esther *presents* (5:1–8) herself to the king. She begins to carry out the part assigned to her by approaching the king and inviting him and Haman to her banquet. For some unknown reason she does not tell the king at this point the nature of her request, but she does invite him and Haman to still another banquet on the next day.

V. Haman Liquidated (5:9—7:10)

The steps in Haman's swift downfall can now be progressively enumerated.

Haman's *prejudice* (5:9, 10) is deep; the very sight of Mordecai caused Haman to seethe with rage, but he restrained himself.

Haman's *pride* (5:10–12) is evident. He recounts to his wife and friends his power, progeny, promotion and preferment. His little heart was puffed up; only he had been invited to be at Esther's banquet with the king. Little did he realize what is in store for him.

Haman's *passion* (5:13, 14) is great. Nothing could satisfy him as long as that fly, Mordecai, was in his ointment! Zeresh, his wife, satisfied his rage by suggesting that on the next day he get kingly sanction for Mordecai's crucifixion.

Providence *plans* a countermove (6:1–3). During a restless and sleepless night the official records were read to the king. The king learns that the man who saved his life has never been properly honored. It is impossible, of course, to say whether Haman had anything to do with this suppression of honors for Mordecai.

Haman's *presumption* (6:4–9) is frustrated. At the very moment Ahasuerus is considering the honor that should be bestowed upon Mordecai, his saviour, Haman, appears in the court. Haman, with inveterate pride, falls an easy prey to the query as to what should be done for a man who is to be honored by the king. Haman, believing that only he can be the object of such adoration, elaborately outlines all the honors (vv. 7–9). Pride surely goes before a fall: witness Haman (vv. 10–12). He himself must perform the honors for and upon Mordecai which he presumptuously took to be his own. No man was ever more chagrined than Haman.

Haman's *portent* (6:13) is dark. Zeresh is now no comfort to her husband. She, with a presentiment of coming doom, utters words that soon find their fulfilment.

Haman's *punishment* (7:1–10) follows. It appears that Haman went unwillingly (6:14) to the banquet which he had anticipated with so much delight (5:9, 12). Esther is now ready to present to the king her petition for her people (vv. 2–4). The reference to "my people" brought to the king's attention that his own wife was included in Haman's nefarious plot. Esther, without mincing words, tells her husband that "this wicked Haman" is at the root of all the trouble (vv. 5–7). The king, perhaps to cool his wrath or else to seek a more private place for meditation, goes into the palace garden (v. 7). Haman, realizing the desperateness of his situation, makes the fatal mistake of falling on the queen's couch—an act which the enraged king, now returned to the banquet place, interprets apparently as an assault upon his wife (vv. 7, 8). Haman's doom is so obvious that Harbonah, a eunuch, suggests that Haman could be appropriately executed on the very gallows which he had prepared for Mordecai (vv. 9, 10).

VI. Mordecai (and Esther) Elevated (8:1—10:3)

The remaining part of the story is a contrast, either explicit or implicit, between two prime ministers—Haman, now deceased, and Mordecai, now triumphant.

Haman's authority is transferred to Mordecai (8:1, 2). The king has now a prime minister who once saved his life and is a close relative of his wife.

Haman's decree is nullified by an opposite decree by Mordecai, which, in the king's name, allows the Jews to defend themselves on the fateful day (vv. 8:3–14).

Haman's power and prestige now become Mordecai's (8:15–17). Many people, sensing the power behind Mordecai's name, become Jews. It now appears to be good business to be on the side of the Jews when the fateful day approaches (9:1–3). Even the officials who originally were authorized to excute Haman's decree (3:12–15) now help the Jews (9:3).

Haman's elevation and sinister plan to destroy the Jews now become Mordecai's elevation and triumph over Haman's followers (9:4–16). "The Day" had arrived. Instead of suffering annihilation, as planned by Haman, the Jews are victorious over their enemies. For some reason unknown to us, Esther requests the king for another day to carry out the bloody massacre (vv. 12–16). It is not necessary for us to justify Esther's request. The Bible simply states the facts, as it does in the case of other notable persons (like David) who have committed deeds that some consider unworthy.

Haman's planned Pur (cf. 3:7, a form of divination) becomes Mordecai's Days of Purim (9:17–32). Mordecai straightens out the difference in celebration between the Jews in Shushan (where two days were allowed for slaughter) and the Jews in the provinces (where only one day was allowed). Esther sets her seal to Mordecai's decisions (vv. 29–32).

Haman's greatness as prime minister is far surpassed by Mordecai's greatness as prime minister (10:1–3). Mordecai rose to a higher place than Daniel in the Babylonian empire (cf. Dan. 5:29). He was well liked by all his people and had their interests in his heart.

The
Poetical
Books

The Poetical Books

ANDREW W. BLACKWOOD

In OUR ENGLISH BIBLE, five books have become known as poetical. All such labels must be arbitrary, and not accurate. The Revised Standard Version and other recent translations, such as Moffatt's, rightly print as poetry large portions of the prophetical books, and smaller passages elsewhere.

Bible poetry differs from English verse. A Bible poet does not employ rhyme and does not keep his lines uniform in length. He gives a large place to visual imagery: God is "a sun and shield." The godly man is like a tree; ungodly folk are like chaff. There is also a majestic sense of rhythm, which, in part, carries over into the English Bible, especially in the King James Version. To catch the ebb and the flow, like tides on an ocean beach, read Bible poetry aloud, and deliberately.

Hebrew bards also use parallelism. Often two successive lines, or verses, seem as much alike as an oldtime team of matched bay horses. These "and-parallels" (synonymous) abound in Proverbs 16—22. "But-parallels" (antithetic) appear repeatedly in Proverbs 10—15. Truth thus appears in contrasting forms, as in a team with a white horse and a black one. Other forms of parallelism, more complicated, are less common and need not detain us here.

An understanding of parallelism aids in grasping the meaning of many an unfamiliar passage. In a penitentiary, a visiting minister spoke to a prisoner. Reaching out through the bars, the criminal asked the meaning of a verse in Proverbs. The clergyman had never noticed the passage, but he explained that Bible writers often say the same thing twice, for emphasis, as "Pride goes before destruction, and a haughty spirit before a fall" (Prov. 16:18).

385

I. Approaching the Book of Job

The Book of Job belongs to Hebrew Wisdom literature, which also includes Proverbs, Ecclesiastes, and two books of the Apocrypha (or writings not part of the Hebrew Bible), Ecclesiasticus (Ecclus.) and the Wisdom of Solomon. In addition to prophets, who also wrote books of history, and priests, who led in sacrificial worship, God raised up wise men, or sages. The noblest of them all wrote the Book of Job.

Here we shall deal only with practical concerns, and leave to experts all matters relating to authorship, date, and so forth. We shall approach the Book of Job as an inspired poetic discussion of an age-long question: "Why must a saint of God suffer more than other men not saintly?" Some writers prefer to see here a dramatic treatment of the subject: "The Possibility of Disinterested Goodness." "Doth Job serve God for naught?" Either approach is proper, but if we are to get an unblurred picture of this difficult book, we must keep the camera fixed in one spot.

The first two chapters serve as the Prologue to a dramatic poem. This first part is in prose, full of facts. The inspired author presents Job as a person in history from two points of view. First, he is a good man, a good father, a good friend—perhaps the best man of his day. Second, he suffers greatly. In quick succession this wealthy stockman loses his herds and flocks; his seven grown sons; his health and his hope of old age; his wife's sympathetic understanding; and his friends' respect. All this, the record shows, Job endured at the hands of Satan, the same Devil we know today.

The resulting problem has to do with God, more than Job or the Devil. Does God not rule? Has He not a plan for Job? If He has, why does He permit Satan to drive this saint almost to the grave, "unwept, unhonored, and unsung"? Why does He let wicked men, apparently, live free from pain and loss? This is the hardest question many a believer faces today: "My God, my God, why?" To this question the book gives five answers.

The first appears, indirectly, in the Prologue. These prose chapters (chs. 1 and 2) show that suffering is a test of character. In the end, Job stands this test triumphantly. The second answer calls for fuller treatment. It appears poetically in the main body of the book (chs. 3—11). Here three friends from afar strive to convince Job that he suffers greatly because he has sinned grievously. In three different ways, often eloquently, these able men press their charges, each of them speaking two times and all but one a third time. Job's replies deserve still closer study, notably when he exclaims, "I know that my Redeemer lives!" (19:23–27).

While reading these chapters aloud, single out each speaker. Note his principal line of thought and way of speaking. Also weigh the solution, which the three hold in common: "A man like Job suffers greatly because he has sinned grievously." This holds true of countless mortals, but are there no exceptions? Job rightly claims that he is one. To us Christ is the supreme Sufferer, yet He never sinned. If you were sitting as a judge, you would vote for Job's side of this joint debate.

The third proposal comes from a younger man, Elihu (chs. 32–37). He shows how not to speak. He is not clear, he finds fault with his elders, and he loses his temper. But he is grasping after a vital truth: "Suffering is a means of discipline." As a test of character, suffering may leave a man unchanged. But as God's means of discipline, or teaching, pain and loss make a good man better, more like God.

The fourth solution comes through some of the most majestic poetry in all the Bible (38:1–42:6). God Himself is speaking, out of a storm. He does not refer to Job or his woes. God's majestic words have to do with His sovereignty. No mortal can appraise His wisdom or power. There is nothing for a man to do with God but to trust Him. Here is as close as our book comes to the final solution: "Suffering is a call for faith in God."

The Epilogue (42:7–17) brings forth another solution. This part is in prose, which seems anticlimactic; but not if we quit thinking about sheep and oxen and fix attention on, Job and His God. Let the stress fall, not on Job's returning prosperity, but on his answered prayer (v. 10). Because of what he has learned through suffering, God's man prays for those who have done him deadly wrongs. At the beginning of the book, a saintly farmer prays every day for his grown sons. Now he intercedes for his assailants. Here is the fifth solution: "Suffering is an encouragement to prayer."

A survey of these proposed solutions shows that four hold true today: Suffering is a test of character, a means of discipline, a call for faith in God, and an encouragement to prayer. What about that second proposal? Is suffering always a direct punishment of a man's sins? No, not with a saint like Job. All five together do not give the final answer to our question. For the last word on the subject we must look forward to Job's Redeemer on the cross, "the Lamb of God who takes away the sin of the world." Today if any saint suffers extremely, one reason may be that he resembles Christ.

II. Enjoying the Book of Psalms

The Book of Psalms is the hymnbook of the Hebrew Church. In the original, as in recent versions, the Psalms appear in five books, perhaps chronological. The first (1—41) and the second (42—72) consist of inspired songs, mainly personal. The third (73—89) and the fourth (90—106) have psalms largely social, as about the nation (85). The fifth (107—150) has songs more liturgical; that is, intended for "congregational singing."

The reader ought to know these original divisions. He will also find it useful to make his own classification, according to his spiritual needs today. First, he may single out Praise Psalms, numbering perhaps thirty. Most of them, such as Psalm 103, voice the feelings of a single heart full of adoration, praise, or thanksgiving. Others, such as Psalms 95—100, express the praises of a group, or throng, with hearts full of "wonder, love, and praise."

The largest group consists of Prayer Psalms, which number approximately sixty-five. Some are in the plural (Ps. 85), but many a Prayer Psalm, like a favorite hymn, voices the aspirations of a person alone with his God. For example, take Psalm 51, or 22 which is more difficult. This messianic prayer has in its heart a dramatic turn. Through twenty-one verses the suppliant seems to remain unheard and to feel forsaken. But from verse 22 onward he is heard. As on the day of the cross, the shadows lift. Would that we might tarry to study other Messianic Psalms, such as 45, 72, and 110!

The Prayer Psalms, when assembled, constitute our noblest book of prayers. A much smaller group consists of Teaching Psalms, numbering five or six. Unless we include Psalm 2, which is plural, and somewhat didactic, the Teaching Psalms are in the singular. The best known is Psalm 119, with 176 verses, in twenty-two strophes, corresponding with the twenty-two letters in the Hebrew alphabet. In the older versions, not in the Revised Standard Version, a Hebrew letter appears at the head of each section. Originally each of the eight verses started with this same letter. A mnemonic (memorizing) device!

When John Ruskin was a lad, his mother required him to commit to memory long passages full of Bible beauty, including Psalm 119. After he became a master of consummate English prose, Ruskin declared that among all the passages he had memorized in youth this one had later helped him most. Why? Perhaps because almost every verse here tells about some aspect of God's Written Word.

Another group consists of Testimony Psalms, numbering about thirty. Among them are practically all of the present writer's favorites, except Psalm 103. Some of these testimonies, such as Psalm 46, come from a throng. As in Psalm 107, they share the impulse to "Let the redeemed of the Lord say so!" Many another Testimony Psalm, such as 23, 27, 32, 91, 121, or 122, wells up from one heart. If anyone makes a collection of these Witnessing Psalms, he will have a "treasury of devotion," like the Matterhorn, "unmatched in all the world."

Who can wonder that in public worship the churches of Chistendom use the Psalms more than any other three or four books in the Bible, and that many a believer finds here the best devotional manual? Would that we knew how to read the Psalms more wisely and more lovingly!

III. Appreciating the Book of Proverbs

In the Bible, the Book of Proverbs is the only considerable part intended especially for a young person. Instead of writing vaguely about "Youth," this wise man addresses a young man "old enough to vote," or perhaps a teen-age lad. Contrary to current impressions, the book does not contain prudential maxims like those in Benjamin Franklin; for example, "It is hard for an empty sack to stand upright." It is almost equally hard to find much about God in some commentaries about Proverbs! The book itself has at first a proposition or key sentence (1:7) about God, and the closing poem sounds the same high note (31:10).

This book has two main parts, widely different. The first nine chapters consist of poetry full of beauty and uplift. The inspired bard sings about Wisdom. For us the same Wisdom speaks through Christ. In fact, to a discerning reader this book, more than any other in the Old Testament, sets forth the spirit and teachings of Jesus in Galilee.

These nine golden chapters set forth a practical philosophy for any lad or lass today. For instance, more than any other part of the Bible, they tell about purity. As poetry, the remaining chapters (10—31) move on a lower level. They show the practical workings of the Bible philosophy undergirding a young man's religion. Since the subject changes almost as often as in a pocket dictionary, it is not easy to read most of the book by chapters. In a group of young people, it would be better to have each of them read and understand the first nine chapters, and then deal with the remaining portions differently. Young folk like novel ways.

Encourage each of them to make a collection of proverbs about a variety of topics. Have them study the book to see what subjects it treats. One list runs this way: anger, charity (giving), education, family (duty to parent, and so forth), the fool, friendship, justice, kindness, laziness, liquor, marriage, poverty, thrift, the tongue, wealth, wine, woman, and work. If a young man has at hand a cluster of proverbs about each subject, he can easily prepare to speak on any occasion where he addresses other young folk.

When a thoughtful young fellow starts putting together the various parts of this practical book, he finds that ideally a man's religion consists in being right with God; right with others, one by one; and right with himself. Is there no need for such ethical teaching today, when juvenile delinquency abounds? Yet in the average home or church school, a young person learns little about the one Bible book that God intends for the guidance and restraint of a young man who daily meets temptations.

The book closes with an acrostic poem which a Hebrew lad would commit to memory. It afforded a word picture of the one he should marry: a good woman, a good wife, a good mother, all because she has a good God. As in a mirror, a Hebrew girl could here see what she ought to become through the blessing of God. This word picture shows a good woman like Martha, whom Jesus loved. Thus the poem sums up the practical counsels of the only Bible book especially for a young believer.

IV. Understanding the Book of Ecclesiastes

The Book of Ecclesiastes also belongs with the Wisdom literature. Approximately one half is poetry and one half is prose. More than any other Bible book, in proportion to its length, Ecclesiastes has given English literature memorable sayings. Examples appear in any book of familiar quotations, as by John Bartlett or Burton Stevenson. One of these sayings Phillips Brooks borrowed to warn against horseplay in the pulpit: "As the crackling of thorns under a pot, so is the laughter of a fool" (7:6). More broadly, in *Pilgrim's Progress*, Bunyan got from Ecclesiastes his name for "Vanity Fair," an idea that Thackeray later put into his well-known novel.

"'Vanity of vanities!' says the Preacher, 'vanity of vanities; all is vanity'" (1:2). This key verse introduces a book that perplexes many readers. It seems to consist of chronic, confused complaints by a confirmed skeptic, much like Schopenhauer. Why do these carpings appear in the Sacred Canon? The answer must depend on a study of the book. It purports to be from Solomon. Without entering now into matters about authorship, let us think of such a king when elderly. He is telling others, especially a young man, the essence of an old man's philosophy.

The resulting book differs from Proverbs. That work teaches, deductively. This one explores, inductively. Beginning with human experiences, many of them dark, the inspired author takes up various answers to the agelong question, "What is the *summum bonum*?" Since the discussion follows no discernible order, we may map out our own trail. According to I Kings 3:11, young Solomon once chose as his highest good, not long life, riches, or power—each of them dear to a Hebrew heart—but wisdom. In like manner, this book takes up, weighs in the balance, and finds wanting, various other claimants for distinction as the *summum bonum* here on earth.

From this book the reader can draw up a list of such goals, and then consider each of them, pro and con. They include work, fame, pleasure, learning (or culture), and formal religion. All of these sound strangely modern, but so does Ecclesiastes. About each goal the author says two things, often scintillatingly: first, as a means to an end higher than itself, each of these goals is worthy; second, as an end in itself, any such goal is vanity. As a believer in Christ, and not at all pessimistic, the present writer holds to this philosophy of Ecclesiastes. So does many another elderly man.

Working inductively and uniquely, the sacred writer leads up climactically to the end of chapter 11, where he asks the young reader to look on all such concerns in the light of God's holy judgment. Then follows chapter 12, with its unparalleled word pictures of old age and its increasing decrepitude, amid the deepening shadows of death. At the end comes the message for which we have been waiting, in substance the same message as in I Kings 3:11, 12: "In God's world the *summum bonum* is Wisdom."

From this point of view, Ecclesiastes voices much the same religious philosophy as Proverbs. While far more difficult, Ecclesiastes is almost equally practical. So let us thank God for this portion of His inspired Wisdom literature.

V. Interpreting the Song of Solomon

The Song of Solomon will likewise reward intelligent reading. It consists of lyric poetry; that is, words of beauty intended to be sung as solos. This Bible poetry is "the gift of God to the imagination." The eight chapters sing about "the way of a man with a maid," a subject of perennial interest and utmost concern. The book assumes that there need be nothing unholy or unclean about any part of a young woman's body, all of which comes from God. It would seem strange if there were not in the Bible at least one book about the beauty of love welling up in two young hearts that the Lord has made for each other.

The book seems to contain a succession of more or less related love songs for use at the festivities attending a Syrian marriage. Often such a gala time would continue for a week, and serve as the chief event of the year, or of a lifetime. For such times of community rejoicing, these songs would serve admirably. Even today, where can one find such moving lyrics about the love of "a man for a maid" as the mightiest force in the human heart (cf. 8:6, 7); and also about the triumph of love over lust?

Certain scholars look on these poems as successive stages in a thrilling drama. This interpretation fits many of the facts, but scarcely any two learned interpreters agree about the pattern of this sacred "scenario," or about the meaning of many details. Still other interpreters, especially in former times, have seen here a succession of likenesses to the love that binds the heart of the Church to the Lord Jesus as the heavenly Bridegroom. Many of us grew to manhood in congregations where gifted ministers turned to the Canticles for the texts of exalted message leading up to the Holy Communion. For instance,

I am my beloved's and my beloved is mine;
He pastures his flock among the lilies (6:3).

"Where the Spirit of the Lord is, there is freedom" (II Cor. 3:17) —freedom of reverent interpretation. In their allegorical preaching, the fathers were not always so foolish as we often suppose. From the first two chapters of the Canticles, and one verse of the third, the mightiest preacher between Chrysostom and Luther delivered eighty-six sermons about the Incarnate Christ. Was Bernard of Clairvaux deluded when he saw in these love songs beautiful symbols of the ties that bind the Church to the heart of the Redeemer? And yet many of us prefer to read the Canticles as a succession of love songs for use at a Syrian wedding.

As "the Beauty of the Bible," these five books will richly repay careful reading and diligent study. Instead of approaching them with some mechanical schoolroom method of fitting Bible books into a prefabricated form, first ascertain the purpose and the character of each book. All of this will appear in the chapters of commentary that follow in this volume. With each book adopt a method that suits the facts in the case. Since all of these books deal with God's outdoors, the best time to read them is in summer. One season, work with the Psalms. The next year, with Proverbs. The third summer, with Job. The fourth, with Ecclesiastes and the Song of Solomon. In each of these gardens, learn to love variegated beauty and splendor.

Why not deal with the Bible the way it was written, book by book? Within the book, excepting most of Proverbs, the unit is the paragraph. Instead of following some hop-skip-and-jump way of reading the Bible, here a little and there a little, plan to live with each book long enough to know it as a whole and in its various parts. After some such home course during four summers, you will love these five books as a "golden treasury" filled with heavenly riches for everyday use here on earth.

Job

ROBERT B. LAURIN

ONE OF THE inescapable facts of life is that mankind suffers. Whether religious or not, whether Christian or not, men and women are afflicted by sickness and sorrow. And for century upon century man has sought to discover why. Why has a God of love and power permitted human beings to suffer? Why, in particular, does pain strike the innocent along with the guilty, the religiously devout along with the ungodly? These are theological shoals upon which the faith of countless men and women has gone shipwreck.

The Book of Job was written to solve this problem. The author uses the sufferings of a man named Job to teach the lesson of the meaning of faith. He is intent on showing that faith finds its security in the intellectual and spiritual encounter with an all-powerful, all-wise God. The ways of divine providence transcend the finite speculations of human reason, and so man must rest in the wisdom of a greater intelligence.

I. Prologue (1:1—2:13)

Two opening chapters of the book set the scene, and describe the real reason for Job's sufferings. This answer was never disclosed to Job. But it forms part of the total solution to the problem of suffering and the meaning of faith.

1. The Character of Job (1:1-5)

In the land of Uz, probably a district of Edom to the southeast of the Dead Sea, lived a tribal chief named Job, a man of outstanding piety and integrity. He was one who "feared God and turned away from evil" (1:1). He had both faith and faithfulness, both reverence for God and abhorrence of evil. As a reward for his righteousness, Job had been blessed with a large family and an abundance of other possessions (cf. Ps. 127:3–5; 128:3). All this combined to make him "the greatest of all the people of the east" (v. 3). In the midst of all this however, calamity falls.

2. The Misfortune of Job (1:6—2:11)

One day when the angels and Satan (literally, "the adversary") are standing before God, the character of Job is pointed out to the group by the Lord. But Satan sneers, and attributes Job's piety to selfishness. "Does Job serve God for nought?" he says (1:9). When all is going well, when God has protected and prospered him, there is no reason why he should not serve God. It pays him to keep on good terms with the Lord. Job's life and ritual correctness do not mean that he serves God from his heart. So Satan says that if he be put to the test, and all his possessions taken away, he will curse God to His face (v. 11). The Lord accepts the challenge and allows Satan to strip Job of his goods and his children. But in spite of the fact that Job is left a childless beggar, he justifies God's trust in him. He observes all the signs of mourning, and says, "The Lord gave, and the Lord has taken away; blessed be the name of the Lord" (vv. 20, 21; cf. Jer. 7:29; Mic. 1:16).

After some time the day again arrives when the servants of the Lord come to report to Him. Satan is once more asked about Job, and he replies that he is still not satisfied. "Skin for skin," he says, "all that a man has he will give for his life" (2:4). The origin of this saying is uncertain, but the meaning is probably that a man will give up everything he has to save his neck. Jewish writings seem to relate the words "skin for skin" to the "eye for an eye, limb for a limb" idea in the Mosaic law. Job thus gave up the "skin" of his family for his own "skin." Satan says that the test has not been severe enough. Take away Job's health, and his true loyalties will be shown: "He will curse thee to thy face" (v. 5). Once again the Lord agrees, so long as Satan spares Job's life.

Satan goes out and strikes Job with "loathsome sores," generally identified as elephantiasis or leprosy, so that he is covered from head to foot. Job has now lost everything—his family, his wealth, his health. Even his wife fails him, for as he sits scratching himself with a bit of broken pottery, she comes and says, "Do you still hold fast your integrity? Curse God and die" (2:9). She has the common point of view that it is worth while being good only for what a person can get out of it. But once again Job accepts the will of God, and says, "Shall we receive good at the hand of God, and shall we not receive evil?" (v. 10). Thus Satan is foiled and disappears from the story; a real lesson on the victory of endurance in temptation.

3. The Three Friends of Job (2:11–13)

Three friends come from different parts of Edom to console Job. He is so disfigured by the disease that at first they fail to recognize him. When they do, they break into weeping, and throw dust on their heads in token of distress (cf. Josh. 7:6; I Sam. 4:12; II Sam. 13:19; Lam. 2:10). In fact they mourn for him as for one already dead, for it was customary to mourn seven days for the dead (cf. Gen. 50:10; I Sam. 31:13).

II. The Three Friends' Solution (3:1—31:40)

The stage is now set for the three cycles of speeches. When Job was first struck by his troubles, he gave no indication of rebellion against the will of God. But months have probably passed (cf. 2:11–13), and his suffering has continued unrelieved. So in chapter 3 a change has taken place in Job. He no longer submits unquestioningly to God's will; rather, all he can ponder is the reason for his trouble. He never really curses God, although in later chapters he comes very close to it; he only wonders why. It is the "why" that the three friends seek to explain.

1. First Cycle of Speeches (3:1—14:22)

Job (3:1–26). Job begins by raising three questions: (1) Why was I ever born? (vv. 3–10), or (2) being born, why did I ever live? (vv. 11–19), or (3) having lived, why can I not die? (vv. 20–26). In verses 3 through 10, Job questions any reason for his birth by cursing the day he was born. If his suffering is a condition of his existence, why was he ever born at all? So he says, "Let the day perish wherein I was born" (3:3). He wishes to have his birthday blotted out of existence in the cycle of days and years. According to ancient belief, a curse was not only an expression of a person's wrath, but it also had a certain power to get itself realized. The cause of his misery is the day of his birth, so he wishes revenge upon it. Or at least if it cannot be torn from the calendar, he wants it to be a day of abnormal darkness and terror, a day in which children are no longer born.

Moving on from this, Job asks the second question (vv. 11–19). If he had to be born, why could he not have died at once, instead of being taken on the nurse's knees, and nourished at his mother's breasts? (v. 12; cf. Gen. 30:3; 50:23). At least, if he had died at birth, he would now be in Sheol where "the weary are at rest" (v. 17).

Finally Job asks his third question (vv. 20–26). If for some reason he had to live, why can he not die now, instead of lingering in this terrible state? But death will not come. The thought of suicide does not enter his mind. But by this question Job raises for the first time the wider problem of God's responsibility in allowing the continuance of suffering among men in general. He speaks in the plural of "the bitter ones" (v. 20) and "those who long for death" (v. 21). He knows that it is God who is the cause (v. 23), although he does not directly charge Him with injustice.

Eliphaz (4:1—5:27). The three friends had been silent for a whole week. Now Eliphaz, probably the oldest of the group, finally speaks. However, no kindly comforter is he. Although he begins apologetically (4:2), he goes on to condemn Job for not recognizing that the real reason for his suffering is his sinful life. "You have instructed many," he says, "but now it has come to you, and you are impatient" (vv. 3, 5). Eliphaz here asserts the traditional doctrine—although he claims to have received it in a vision (vv. 12–16)—regarding the connection between sin and suffering. According to this popular belief, one's outward circumstances were an infallible sign of one's inward condition. Since God was just, He rewarded the good and punished the wicked in this life (cf. Ex. 20:5, 6; Ps. 5:5, 6; 7:10–12; Prov. 10:6, 7). If a man did wrong, retribution was inevitable, and the only way to relieve it was to admit the sin and try to live according to God's will. Although on occasion the wicked seemed to prosper, this was only for a brief duration (cf. Ps. 37:1, 2). This is what Eliphaz means when he says, "Think now, who that was innocent ever perished?" (4:7). He then moves on to intimate that Job's suffering is due to his sin. So great and perfect is God, he says, that even the best of His servants—the angels—are not exempt from impurity. Therefore if the angels have imperfections, how much more do human beings? It is as natural for man to experience trouble as it is for sparks to fly skyward (5:7). Thus, Eliphaz concludes, "I would seek God, and to God would I commit my cause" (v. 8). If Job would repent, God would pour out His blessings upon him.

Job (6:1—7:21). The counsel of Eliphaz has fallen on unyielding ears. Job refuses to admit that he is a sinner, and he cannot understand his friend's failure to respond to his cries with pity. His words have been wild, Job admits, but he has good reason: "For the arrows of the Almighty are in me" (vv. 3, 4). Job here for the first time explicitly names God as the author of his suffering. It is this awareness that causes him anguish, not merely his bodily pain as such. Eliphaz sees only the outward cry, but the problem is far deeper. Job believes he is innocent, yet he is being punished by God. So he moves on to denounce God in one of the most pathetic and blasphemous passages in the Old Testament. He has lost all hope of staying alive, of being relieved of his sufferings, and so he loses all fear. Before he dies he is going to tell God in bitterness what he thinks of Him (7:11–21). With cutting irony he poses certain questions of God, concluding with the query: even if he has sinned inadvertently, why does not God pardon him now before he dies and it is too late? After death, vindication would not mean anything to Job, since Job shared the popular Hebrew belief that death is the end of communion between God and His people. In Sheol, the abode of the dead, there were no punishments or rewards. Everyone without distinction went to Sheol (cf. 3:11–26; 30:23; Ruth 1:17; II Sam. 12:23; Jer. 31:15; Eccles. 9:2), but once they got there all moral connotations were supposedly gone. The righteous did not receive rewards and bliss; the wicked were not tormented. Death was an entrance into an eternal nothingness, into a land of forgetfulness (10:21; Ps. 88:13), dust (Dan. 12:2), and darkness (38:17), where there was "no work or thought or knowledge or wisdom" (Eccles. 9:10). Sheol was man's eternal home (Eccles. 12:5) where he slept forever (14:12). A progression in revelation is seen in Daniel 12:2, where Sheol is the intermediate dwelling-place of certain wicked and righteous (the "many"), while still remaining the eternal abode for the rest. But this was after Job's day, so he did not understand this. Thus to the Hebrew, if wrong was to be righted, it must be rectified while man was still alive.

Bildad (8:1–22). Unmoved by Job's cries or his logic, the second friend lashes back at Job. "How long will you say these things, and the words of your mouth be a great wind?" (v. 2). The passionate words of Job have left on Bildad's mind one terrible impression— God has been slandered. It is this particular thing that is Bildad's concern. In spite of Job's violent claims, God is not unjust. Although Job's children died, they perished because they were wicked (vv. 3, 4). And if Job will only repent, he will save himself and be rewarded with even more than his former happiness (vv. 6, 7).

Job (9:1—10:22). With great irony Job admits the principle that his friends have stated. "Truly I know that it is so"; that is, that God is not unjust, and that God blesses the righteous. But the questions remain: What is justice? what is righteousness? He gives the principle a different twist than do his friends. Justice and righteousness seem to be what God wants at any time; they change with the circumstances. Job fervently believes that he is righteous, at least according to past dealings with God, yet God seems to insist on holding him guilty of something. Therefore no other conclusion remains than that God must have altered His standard of justness. "Though I am innocent," says Job, "I cannot answer him" (9:15). The old standard is no longer in effect; one need only look about to see that this is true: "The earth is given into the hand of the wicked" (v. 24). There is no escape from the conclusion that God is responsible for this condition, for "if it is not he, who then is it?" (v. 24). So in seeking a *rationale* of his sufferings, he asks God one awful question after another (10:3–12), and comes to the conclusion that "this was thy purpose" (v. 13). From the very first Job's sufferings were planned by God. Thus Job thinks himself right after all in his belief that God is capricious, or at least that justice does not mean the same thing to God as it does to Job. "If I sin, thou dost mark me. . . . If I am righteous I cannot lift up my head" (vv. 14, 15). No matter how he acts the result is always the same—God punishes him. For some reason God is determined to make him miserable. Job thus reaches the depths of despair.

Zophar (11:1–20). One hears in Zophar's speech the dull thud of exactly what Eliphaz and Bildad had already said. He reiterates the traditional point of view, continuing the theme of his friends. Job must have sinned, or else God would not be afflicting him. To Zophar it is unthinkable that there can be anything but finality in faith, that one's faith might still carry any problems. Faith is cut and dried; only the impious question it. "Oh, that God would speak, and open his lips to you" (v. 5), says Zophar, for you would discover that "God exacts of you less than your guilt deserves" (v. 6). If all Job's sins were punished, he says, his sufferings would be still greater! Thus the solution is to repent, put away sin, and then God will prosper him (vv. 13–20).

Job (12:1—14:22). Job returns here to his real problem—the seeming inconsistency of God. He draws a series of scenes in which disaster overtakes both the wise and the great, and the deceived and the deceiver (12:13–25). By this he implies doubt that God's power, which he does not deny, is just or righteous in the sense in which justice and righteousness are generally understood. Job's friends have resolutely shut their eyes to the obvious facts of life (13:4).

Realizing that he cannot get anywhere with his friends, he tells them to keep silence while he pleads his case with God. So convinced is he of his innocence that he will brave the awful presence of

God. He will chance meeting Him face to face, although it will be perilous, in the hope of obtaining justice as he knows it (13:13–19).

In this passage is found one of the best known verses in the Old Testament, and yet one of the most misunderstood. In the King James Version, 13:15, one reads, "Though he slay me, yet will I trust in him," and many have seen here a great expression of Job's faith in God. But quite the opposite is the case. The text says literally, "Behold, he will slay me; I have no hope," as the Revised Standard Version indicates. A variant reading allows the possible translation, 'Behold, he will slay me; I wait for him." But in either case there is no sense of trust in God. As in verse 14, Job is so convinced of his innocence that he is going to take his life in his hands and plead his case before God. For opposing Him so audaciously, God may slay him ("Behold, He will slay me" perhaps; "I have no hope" that such will not be the case), yet in spite of this he will defend his way to His face. It is not an expression of absolute trust in God, but rather of absolute trust in himself. If God determines to slay him, He will only be shedding innocent blood.

For the rest of Job's speech he outlines his case against God. He feels that God is punishing him unjustly (13:23–28), and since he believes he is going to die, any future justification would be unknown to him, because there is nothing after death (14:1–22). "For there is hope for a tree," he says, "if it be cut down, that it will sprout again" (14:7). But "man lies down and rises not again; till the heavens are no more he will not awake" (v. 12). This is tremendously unjust. If a tree can have a second life, why should it be impossible for man? And for a while he plays with this idea. If God would hide him in Sheol until His wrath was past, and then call him back to life again to the old fellowship and happiness he once knew, how patiently he would wait (vv. 13–17). "If a man die, shall he live again?" (v. 14)—a wonderful dream. But this is all it is. He only raises the question to reject it, for "the mountain falls and crumbles away . . . so thou destroyest the hope of man" (vv. 18, 19). As inexorable as the laws of nature, so certain is it that there is nothing after death. Instead of any hope, all Job knows is that God "prevailest forever against him," God remains unforgiving to the end (v. 20). Whatever happens on earth after death is unknown to man. All he feels is "the pain of his own body" (v. 22), a reference to the pangs of decay as the body lies in the grave. This is not an expression of punishment after death, but rather only of a lingering vitality and quasi-consciousness until the body totally returns to dust.

2. *Second Cycle of Speeches (15:1—21:34)*

Eliphaz (15:1–35). In the second round of speeches, the friends become progressively more vehement and condemnatory of Job, while Job himself becomes all the more obdurate. The pattern is set by Eliphaz. In his first speech he had regarded Job as an essentially religious and reverent man, for there he had said, "Is not your fear of God your confidence?" (4:6). But here he views him as one who is not only abandoning his religion ("But you are doing away with the fear of God," 15:4), but also positively rebelling from God ("you turn your spirit against God," v. 13). In the first speech Eliphaz spoke of the universality of sin as due to the frailty of mankind (4:17–19), but here he implies more pointedly that Job is a sinner because he "drinks iniquity like water" (15:16). At first Eliphaz had sought to persuade Job to repent by describing the ultimate happiness of the man who humbly accepts God's chastenings (4:17–27), but here he seeks to pressure him into repentance by detailing the troubled conscience and inevitable destruction of the wicked (15:17–35). To silence Job, Eliphaz reiterates the conventional argument regarding the inevitability of reward for the righteous and punishment for the wicked. As in many religious debates, the emotional ivy of old age and tradition is wound about the subject in an attempt to remove it from all discussion or even thinking. Eliphaz paints a vivid picture of the life of a wicked man. He is hounded in prosperity by a terrifying conscience (vv. 20–24), and ultimately, with his family and his wealth, is cut down in the midst of life.

Job (16:1—17:16). The awful realization that both his friends (16:1–5) and God (vv. 6–17) have turned against him weighs heavily upon Job. He is sick of hearing the "windy words" of false comfort that his friends have given him. They obviously do not understand the real problem. He is not concerned with alleviating his pain, for he feels that his life is near its end (16:22, 17:1, 11). Rather he longs to prove his innocence to his mocking friends (16:18—17:5). With his face streaked with tears, his battered body clothed with sackcloth, he pleads with God to vindicate him before he goes to the inevitable grave. At least he longs to have a pledge from God that after his death his honor will be vindicated (17:3–16). If he goes to the grave with no word from God, then all hope is gone, for in Sheol "who will see my hope?" (v. 15). He expresses in these words the traditional understanding that all settling of accounts has to take place in the sphere of this life, for once death comes, man goes to the land whence he never returns (16:22), and whence all controversy ceases (17:15, 16.)

Bildad (18:1–21). With the self-righteous, complacent attitude of having solved all of life's problems, Bildad answers Job by monotonously reiterating the old theme of the certainty of early destruction for the wicked in this life. The rigidity and ruthlessness of Bildad's words are typical of a kind of religion that has sometimes infested orthodoxy. Freedom of thought or action is impossible; only blind obedience to the Church is permissible. As Inspector Javert says in *Les Miserables*, "The public functionary cannot make a mistake; the magistrates are never wrong." Regardless of what Job says, the fact remains that the wicked do not prosper; thus the implication is that Job is wicked. So Bildad describes at length the fate of the man "who knows not God." He speaks of the traps that beset him, the terrors that badger him, the diseases that consume him. His possessions are destroyed or taken by others, his descendants are obliterated, and only his evil reputation remains (vv. 5–21).

Job (19:1–29). The ruthless words of Eliphaz and Bildad have impressed Job more than ever with the tragic realization that both God and men are his enemies. He has not a single friend. God has stripped him of his wealth and honor, persecuted him unmercifully, turned his kinsfolk, his close friends, his servants, his wife, and even young children against him (vv. 5–20). And so, pathetically, he looks to the future when perhaps men shall be more understanding. He wants to be able to leave a written record of the facts of the matter, of his innocence, so that in the coming generations his honor will be vindicated. He is so convinced of the injustice of his sufferings, and of the obviousness of this fact, that he is certain that sometime someone must see the situation as it really is. All men cannot be as insensible as his friends, all men cannot be as blinded by tradition. It is at this point, however, that, in a flash of insight, he rises for the moment to a higher truth. He shall have something greater than posthumous vindication; he shall be there himself!

Interpretation of 19:25–27 is perhaps the most difficult task in the entire Old Testament, for the Hebrew text has been very badly preserved. All versions and commentators have had trouble with it. On one point they all agree—the text makes no sense as it stands, and has to be changed. But agreement is lacking over the changes to be made. The traditional view, given impetus by the King James Version rendering of the passage, sees here a belief in the resurrection of the body. If this be correct, then Job has gained an insight into the truth which he never attains again, for he continues in the remaining part of the book along the same lines as before (cf. 21:23–26; 24:21–25; 30:23; 31:1–6).

It is important to keep in mind that the word "Redeemer" is not to be prematurely weighted with Christian connotations. It is better translated "Vindicator," for in the Old Testament it is used of the deliverer or vindicator of a man's honor or debt. The *Goel* ("Vindicator") was the nearest blood-relation who by law was duty-bound to redeem his kinsman from bondage, or his property from debt (Lev. 25:48, 49), or to avenge the death of his relative who had been unjustly killed (Deut. 19:6, 12). It is a term often used by Isaiah to describe God as the One Who delivers Israel from bondage, and thus vindicates the nation's honor (cf. Is. 41:14; 43:14; 44:24; 48:17).

Some feel that Job is making only conditional statements here, that is, he does not assert that he will see God, but that were he to do so, he would find Him friendly. In other words, it appears to Job that he is going to die without the chance to plead his case with God, but if he had opportunity, he knows that God would vindicate him. Others think that this passage must be intimately linked with verses 23 and 24, and to Job's desire for a written record. The "Redeemer" would be some future human being who, having read the account and seen the inequity of the situation, would arise to plead Job's case before God. He would perhaps be related to the "umpire" of 9:33.

The exact meaning of the original cannot be determined for sure, but one thing is clear—Job expects somehow to be vindicated before God, whether in the body or not, we cannot be certain. In light of the fact that in chapter 14 Job raises the question of "something after death," and since throughout the book, especially in chapters 16 and 17, he never really loses all hope that God will eventually maintain his honor, it could well be that in 19:25–27 Job reaches a high point of understanding and hope. He expresses here his conviction that not only will he be cleared of guilt, but that his greatest longing also will be realized in that some day he will meet God face to face, will be brought back from the grave to be present at his own vindication. The "Redeemer" then is the living

God Who holds the answer to Job's situation. Some day He will stand over Job's grave (the "dust"; 19:25), call him to life again (perhaps only momentarily like Samuel in I Sam. 28 or Rachel in Jer. 31:15), and vindicate him in the eyes of the world. Further than this Job does not go, but it is the goal of his faith, and the anticipation of it overcomes him, so that he exclaims, "My heart faints within me" (19:27). Job's words are proof again that God's trust in him (cf. 1:8; 2:3) is justified; he is indeed a man of true faith.

Zophar (20:1–29). Job's tremendous expression of faith in God falls on deaf ears. Zophar's extreme partisanship and injured pride have closed his mind, and so he blazes forth to denounce Job's continuance in sin. He assumes the authority of a religious zealot; he has had a "spiritual experience" which has given him the truth.

In line with the attack of the other friend, Zophar does not attempt to entice Job into repentance by soothing promises of the result of repentance. Bluntly he describes the results of God's inexorable law regarding the wicked's swift destruction. He calls it "the heritage decreed for him by God" (20:29). He speaks of the wicked as greedy, ruthless, oppressive, and all the time implies that this is a picture of Job. He describes Job as receiving a just punishment because "he has crushed and abandoned the poor . . . because his greed knew no rest" (vv. 19, 20). He envisions for Job a future of terror, pain, loss, and destruction, for "this is the wicked man's portion from God" (vv. 23–29). There is no God of love and mercy in Zophar's words, only an impatient, angry judge intent on bringing premature death to the evildoer.

Job (21:1–34). The three friends have steadfastly maintained throughout their speeches that wickedness invariably brings a short, unhappy life, while righteousness insures a long and prosperous existence. It is to this specific argument that Job addresses himself in this speech. He wants his friends to face the facts of life (vv. 1–3, 29–34).

Contrary to what his friends have told him, Job claims that experience shows that the ungodly do reach old age in prosperity and honor, they are blessed with numerous offspring and possessions, they are not bothered by a bedeviling conscience, they do live off the fat of the land, and they do die in peace (vv. 4–13, 17, 18). Zophar had given a lurid description of the evils that befall the wicked; Job responds by a lengthy description of their prosperity. Even the argument about the punishment of the father coming upon his children does not satisfy the justice of Job. He demands that the evildoer himself receive his own punishment (vv. 19–21; cf. Jer. 31:29, 30; Ezek. 18:1–32).

The thing that really brings Job to despair is that in spite of the fact that the wicked arrogantly reject God, still He appears to prosper them. This only compounds the problem, for if men prosper, even though they say to God, "Depart from us" (21:14), then naturally they are led to conclude that they would not gain anything by serving Him. They come to believe that their prosperity rests in their own abilities (vv. 14–16). Job has raised the issue faced by many preachers in the suburban church, who find it difficult to preach about the perils of sin in the midst of obvious prosperity without God.

3. Third Cycle of Speeches (22:1—31:40)

Eliphaz (22:1–30). The turn has come again for Eliphaz to speak, and once more he sets the pattern of the speeches. His words clearly betray his misunderstanding of the nature of God. He conceives of Him as a stern, cold, impassive being, unaffected by the creatures He controls, concerned only with meting out rewards and punishments in automatic "letter of the law" fashion.

With naive logic Eliphaz tries to prove that since it cannot be any advantage to God if a man is righteous, nor can it be any loss to Him if the opposite is the case, therefore the reason for life's punishments and rewards must lie in man himself (22:2, 3). Since God has an inexorable law, Eliphaz asks sarcastically, "Is it for your fear of him that he reproves you?" (v. 4). God automatically and immediately rewards good and punishes wickedness; since Job is suffering, therefore Job must be wicked. The logic of this argument is unassailable if one shuts his eyes to experience and admits the starting premise. But it fails to reckon with the reality that righteousness does not guarantee physical comfort. And furthermore, it denies the revelation of a God who "loves the people of Israel, though they turn to other gods and love cakes of raisins" (Hos. 3:1), a God who is "merciful and gracious, slow to anger, and abounding in steadfast love and faithfulness" (Ex. 34:6). The God of Israel is not a distant, unconcerned being.

Job (23:1—24:25). With a touch of sarcasm directed at his friends' blind acceptance of tradition—as if all questioning of the workings of God were sin—Job begins, "Today also my complaint is rebellious" (23:2). To Job religion is not resignation, as it is with Islam, nor does it exclude the use of intelligence. He refuses to apply the "yours not to reason why, yours but to do or die" attitude to his relationship to God. He takes his stand with Christ's words, "My God, my God, why has thou forsaken me?" (Mt. 27:46).

Job's words are significant, for the fact that though God's "hand is heavy in spite of my groaning" (23:2), though he reaches the depths of physical and mental suffering, he loses neither his faith nor his practice. His heart's desire is for a meeting with God so that he can lay his case before Him, because he is confident that "he would give heed to me" (v. 6). And although he has not been able to find God in this manner, though he has been searching for Him, although he may doubt the justice of God, still his "foot has held fast to his steps" (v. 11). Regardless of the problems of life, one thing he can never question is that it is better to be good than evil, better to be true than false, better to be brave than cowardly.

In chapter 23 Job is perplexed by the fact that what his heart wants to believe about the goodness of God is denied by his own suffering. God seems to be unmoved by his difficulty; He is resolved to destroy him (vv. 13–17). It is this arbitrary, paradoxical God that distresses Job, not his calamities, nor his impending death.

In chapter 24 he shifts his gaze to the wider realm of the world, and again he sees only an inconsistent God. He raises the question, "Why are not times of judgment kept by the Almighty, and why do those who know him never see his days?" (v. 1). Men live by certain laws which they believe have been ordained by God; why then does not God operate according to the same rules? Job has been taught that righteousness should be rewarded. Why does this seldom happen? It is this same question that the Jewish authorities later raised in mockery when Christ hung on the cross. If you are really the Messiah, they said, "come down now from the cross that we may see and believe" (Mk. 15:32).

Bildad (25:1–6). As far as Bildad is concerned, he is content in his speech to reiterate the basic argument of Eliphaz in 4:17–21 and 15:14–16. If God is all-powerful, he claims, if He is purer and more majestic than even the stars, how much wiser and purer must He be than mere man "who is a maggot . . . a worm?" (v. 6). He is attempting to picture Job as tremendously arrogant by placing his wisdom and purity in contrast with the omnipotent God. Indeed in those words he unwittingly approaches the ultimate answer given by God in chapters 38 through 42.

Job (26:1—27:6). Bildad had spoken of the greatness of God, and to this Job answers with biting sarcasm, "How you have counseled him who has no wisdom?" (26:3). Job has never denied God's omnipotence; this very ability has been the crux of the problem. In a vivid picture of the power of God, he emphasizes the fact that this is nothing new to him (vv. 5–14). But the thing that has made the whole situation almost intolerable is that in spite of this, God has been content to punish an innocent man (27:1–6). This is the basic paradox which has faced him throughout all the discussion. "As God lives, who has taken away my right," says Job, "my heart does not reproach me for any of my days." Regardless of what has happened, Job must be honest with himself. He will maintain his innocence to the very end, and he will continue to live what he considers to be a righteous life.

Zophar (27:7—28:28). Blindly, resolutely the answer comes back to Job, probably from Zophar. The tone of these words is contrary to what Job says both before and after. It may well be that Zophar is the speaker in this section, notice of this somehow becoming lost in the process of transmission. This would then give the normal round of speeches. Regardless of what Job has said, the wicked are cast off by God, their wealth does turn to dust, their houses are overrun, and they are cut off in a moment (27:7–23). The mind of this true religious zealot has been unaffected by the facts of life; he has seen only what he wants to see. Furthermore, says Zophar, wisdom is not with man (28:13), it cannot be purchased (v. 15) for only God can give it (vv. 12, 23). So Zophar concludes with a warning to Job, "Behold, the fear of the Lord, that is wisdom; and to depart from evil is understanding" (v. 28). He is still unconvinced of Job's innocence.

Job (29:1—31:40). The whole problem in Job's mind is summed up in these chapters as he compares the former days with those of the present. Rather than an address to his friends, this section is basically a monologue, in which Job dwells pensively on the happy days of the past and contrasts them with the inscrutable present. It is as if one were reading Job's mind. The basic thought is this: in the good old days righteousness was rewarded and wickedness was kept in check (29:1–25), but now ungodliness is rampant and suffering is the reward of righteousness (30:1—31:40). It is again the problem of an apparently capricious God.

Then Job concludes with a last, audacious challenge to God to meet him and answer the force of his logic. He is so confident of his innocence that any indictment God might bring against him he would wear "as a crown" upon his head. He is so certain that he can refute any charge God might level that he is willing to show it to the whole world. So ready is he to tell the story of his life that he will come into God's presence with the confidence of a prince (31:35–37).

The three friends' contention that suffering comes as a punishment for sin certainly cannot be denied. One of the basic principles of the Bible is that God is essentially just, and that He punishes sin and rewards righteousness (cf. Deut. 11:26–28). But what the friends did not realize is that although suffering does often come in this life as a result of sin, this does not explain the whole of suffering. It did not with Job. Thus he was right in opposing his friends' point of view.

III. Elihu's Solution (32:1—37:24)

The friends have either been silenced by Job or have given up trying to convince him of their point of view. At this stage a new figure enters the debate—Elihu, the young thinker and representative of the oncoming generation. He is disgusted with Job, because he tried to justify himself rather than God (32:2). But Elihu is also upset with Job's friends, because they failed to defend God, and by their silence have admitted that Job was right (vv. 3, 11–16). Although he had modestly held back during the course of the arguments, thinking that perhaps his judgment was immature, now he speaks forth because he realizes that old age has not solved the problem (vv. 6–10).

The essence of what Elihu has to say is this: affliction is sent by a God of love in order to discipline and purify. Out of the goodness of God's heart, He sends suffering to the sinner in order to save him from premature death. He does not contradict the doctrine of the friends that the sufferer is always a sinner; but he gives an added emphasis, or at least he approaches the problem from a different point of view. The friends pictured God as an unsmiling judge; Elihu sees Him as a loving father. The friends saw only the negative side of suffering; Elihu emphasizes the positive.

Job had asserted that God refused to answer his questions (33:14–33). This claim on Job's part arises from the fact that he does not realize the many ways that God speaks to men (v. 14). He not only speaks through visions (vv. 15–18), but also through suffering (vv. 19–28). If man will only take the warning in suffering, and ask God for pardon, then he will be restored to health and prosperity. Thus to Elihu when God speaks it is with the purpose of rescuing men from sin and from the suffering which it brings (vv. 29–33).

Job had claimed to be righteous, and because he was suffering, God must be unjust (34:5, 6, 9). But lashing forth at this, Elihu speaks of Job as one "who drinks up scoffing like water, who goes in company with evildoers" (vv. 7, 8). It is impossible that God could be unjust, for He is beyond question, omnipotent, unfailing in His punishment of evil (34:10–33). "God will not do wickedly, and the Almighty will not pervert justice" (v. 12). Therefore, says Elihu, Job is wicked to question God, to speak the way he does (vv. 34–37). The only attitude that a suffering man should take is blind submission to the will of God.

In 35:1–16 Eliphaz admits the fact that there is much oppression of the innocent (v. 9). But he claims that God does not do anything about their cries because they do not pray in the right spirit. It is "because of the pride of evil men" (v. 12). They do not honor God, nor are they really seeking him when they pray; they merely want God to get them well. Thus Elihu still cannot divorce himself from the traditional view that all suffering is proportionately the result of personal sin. Even those who appear to be suffering undeservedly are in truth deserving of their lot. The silence of God to their selfish cries shows this to be true. Elihu, along with the three friends, has resolutely shut his eyes to the experiences of life. Although the vast majority of men pray to God for what they can get out of Him, and not out of pure motives of devotion, still this does not solve the problem that Job has raised. The world is still full of innocent suffering, and only the blind deny it.

In Elihu's final words (36:1—37:24) he continues his emphasis on the educational purpose of suffering. He reiterates his belief that when chastisement comes, it is for the moral welfare of men (36:1–15). If they respond to the persuasions of God, they "spend their days in prosperity and their years in pleasures" (v. 11). If they refuse to listen, they "perish by the sword," they "die without knowledge" (v. 12). It can never be right to question God (36:24—37:24). Man must always "magnify his work" (36:24).

In his last words, Elihu anticipates the answer of God in the following chapters, for he draws a contrast between the weakness of man and the power of God, the ignorance of man and the wisdom of the Almighty. "Behold God is great, and we know him not, neither can the number of his years be unsearchable" (36:26). Elihu speaks of God's control over the rain, the wind, the thunder, the snow, the clouds, and then sarcastically asks Job, "Teach us what we shall say to Him" (37:19). If the physical things are so mysterious to men, it is not likely that men shall solve the mysteries of God's moral order.

Elihu's contribution has real merit. Suffering may be a discipline of love. As Proverbs 3:12 says, "the Lord reproves him whom he loves, as a father the son in whom he delights." Suffering may be a warning that our lives are not right, that we are treading on paths that we should not be travelling (cf. II Cor. 7:10). But although this may explain some suffering, it cannot be applied to all situations. It was not so with Job; he was blameless (1:8). And who can say but such is the case with a spastic child, or with the one born insane? And although Elihu came close to the truth that men must always trust God, even when life seems to go wrong, still he missed the full meaning of faith. It is not wrong to inquire of God with honest doubt; it is only wrong to let doubt cause faith to grow cold.

IV. The Lord's Solution (38:1—42:6)

The great debate has now come to a close. But the participants have reached no agreement; the problem is still unsolved. Although Job has vindicated God's trust in him, yet his mind is in turmoil. He is baffled still by God's seeming silence; he is profoundly convinced still that God is unjust. And thus in order that Job's faith might find its certainty, God speaks to him out of the whirlwind. He comes to him in the majesty and terror of the universe. And His words are remarkable, not only for what they say, but for what they leave unsaid. He makes no reference to Job's suffering, He ignores the accusations of Job's friends, He overlooks the passionate words of Job himself. He scarcely touches the problem which brought on the whole round of debate. His purpose is to show Job the meaning of faith, and so He moves in the realm of the spirit, and not on the level of speculative debate.

1. The First Speech (38:1—40:2)

In the first of God's two speeches to Job, He utters a series of questions designed to show Job that human wisdom must always fail in comprehending divine purpose. Job had been right in maintaining that his suffering was not due to sin; he had been wrong in assuming that his knowledge extended to the actions of God. This point is summed up in the words by which the speech opens— "Who is this that darkens counsel by words without knowledge?" (38:2). Then God asks a series of ironical questions, each of which allows only one answer—God's work in nature is too vast for unaided human intelligence to grasp. If this be so, the implication that God wants Job to draw is that providence must also be beyond the unspiritual man's comprehension.

2. Job's Response (40:3-5)

Job's defenses are gone; he admits his incompetence to judge God. "Behold, I am of small account; what shall I answer thee?" So he intends to give up his critical role and trust in the hand of God. He is beginning to realize that his suffering may have another cause than the wrath of God.

3. The Second Speech (40:6—41:34)

Speaking to Job again out of the whirlwind, the Lord this time considers Job's claim of His injustice in the rule of the world, "Will you even put me in the wrong?" (40:8). With a touch of irony, the Lord invites Job to put on the attributes of deity, if he can, and rule the world for himself. He is attempting to show that Job's inability to rule the vast universe makes him unable to judge God's actions. Therefore Job has no right to ascribe injustice to God. "Deck yourself with majesty and dignity. . . . Look on every one that is proud, and bring him low. . . . Then will I also acknowledge to you that your own right hand can give you victory" (vv. 10–14). If Job only knew what it was to be God, if he only understood the complexity of the universe, if he could only see the end from the beginning, he would realize that God was right. This is the implication in God's words. Job does not even have the strength and the wisdom to cope with the hippopotamus (vv. 15–24) or the crocodile (41:1–34). How much less ability then with the whole creation!

4. Job's Response (42:1–6)

With deep expression of humility and faith Job responds "I know that thou canst do all things. . . . Therefore I have uttered what I did not understand. . . . I despise myself and repent in dust and ashes." Through his vision of God, Job has learned the folly of judging only from hearsay (42:5). The Lord has not said a word about Job's suffering. All He has done is to present Himself as omnipotent and omniscient, but this is enough for Job. In his face-to-face encounter with God he has learned that the all-powerful, all-wise One is a friend, and not an enemy. He has come to know that there are reasons for life outside the understanding of man. Man may be beset in life by problems and doubts, but once he has met God, though the problems may remain, the doubts can but vanish.

V. Epilogue (42:7–17)

Job's reputation is restored in the sight of his friends (vv. 7–9), and he is given double the prosperity that he had previously experienced (vv. 10–17).

1. The Lord's Rebuke of the Three Friends (42:7–9)

Job is commanded to pray for his three friends, after they have offered a burnt-offering, in order that the Lord might not punish them. This is because, according to the Lord, the friends "have not spoken of me what is right." This does not mean that everything the friends said about God was wrong, for it is obvious that they uttered many truths about Him. Nor does it mean that Job was never at fault. If this were so, there would have been no need of Job's repentance (vv. 2–6), nor of the Lord's condemnation (40:2). What God is talking about is the central question in debate between the friends and Job—the connection between sin and suffering. The friends had lied in claiming that God was punishing Job for sin.

This was undoubtedly done in ignorance, but still it was sin. Job was right in maintaining his innocence. It is in this connection that the Lord speaks as He does.

2. *The Lord's Restoration of Job (42:10–17)*

To Job came the greatest approbation that could come to any man in those ancient days—"Job died, an old man, and full of days" (42:17). God restored to him a double prosperity to that of the past. He was given a wife, children in the right proportion, material abundance, and friends. He died with the hand of God upon him.

Thus the book of Job supplies a twofold answer to the meaning of faith in the midst of suffering. (1) Suffering may be a mystery of Providence. In the counsel of the all-wise, all-powerful, all-loving God lies a reason for life's difficulties, and in this we can rest our faith. Above our lives is One Who knows and cares, Who has a purpose behind life's seeming accidents. For if God is so concerned about the wind, and the rain, and the animals, how much more for man? If God is able to control the universe around us, how much more can He direct the lives of men? Thus suffering can befall an innocent man and have a purpose behind it all. For tragedy is not due to any moral imperfection in God, but to a divine purpose which passes beyond our understanding.

(2) Suffering may be a test of reality. This is the answer of the prologue, unknown as it was to Job. Suffering may be a time when the reality of religious profession is being proved to angels, to the world, and to friends. God may be trying to show through difficulty that a man holds to God, not for what He gives, but for Himself. As Paul wrote, "I think that God has exhibited us apostles as last of all, like men sentenced to death, because we have become a spectacle to the world, to angels, and to men" (I Cor. 4:9). Suffering may be the occasion to discover whether faith has been built on words and ritual, or on a true, vital experience with the Lord of the world. We often speak of putting our trust in God, and indeed we must. But there is also a truth in the thought that God may be trusting us; trusting us with His own reputation. He may be allowing us to prove to the world that men can and do serve God, not because they do not suffer, but because they have been gripped by the fact that God loves them, that God has saved them in Jesus Christ, and that God has given them the privilege of carrying this good news to the world.

Psalms

R. LAIRD HARRIS

An outline of the Psalter must be general, since the individual psalms were apparently not collected with particular regard to subject or author. Possibly musical considerations partly determined the present arrangement. The Psalter is divided into five books, each marked at the end by a doxology. Of more significance than a general outline in the study of the Psalms is their classification according to subject matter.

BOOK I, CHIEFLY PRAYERS OF FAITH IN ADVERSITY 1—41
  (Exceptions: Praise Psalms, 8, 24, 29, 33; Royal, 2, 21; Psalms of Righteousness, 1, 15; Penitential, 32; Revelation, 19)
BOOK II, CHIEFLY PRAYERS OF FAITH IN ADVERSITY 42—72
  (Exceptions: Praise Psalms, 47, 48, 50, 65—68; Royal, 45, 72; Penitential, 51; Imprecation, 58, 59)
BOOK III, PSALMS OF TRUST, ESPECIALLY IN NATIONAL DISTRESS 73—89
  (Exceptions: Praise Psalms, 75, 76; Historical, 78, 81; Love for Zion or for Temple, 84, 87; Rebuke to Wicked, 82)
BOOK IV, PSALMS OF PRAISE 90—106
  (Exceptions: Faith in Adversity, 90, 91, 94, 102; Historical, 105, 106; Psalm of Righteousness, 101)
BOOK V, MINGLED PSALMS, CHIEFLY PRAISE AND TRUST IN TROUBLE 107—150
  (Exceptions: Royal Psalms, 110, 132; National Distress, 129, 137; Psalms of Righteousness, 112, 116; Revelation, 119; Love for Zion, 122)
  (Special Categories in Book V: Songs of Degrees, 120—134; Hallel Psalms of Praise, 113—118, 136, and 146—150)

THE CLEARER PICTURE of ancient Israel acquired in recent years as a result of archaeological study fully supports the Biblical picture of David as the fountainhead of psalmody. There was poetry earlier, to mention only Moses' songs in Exodus 15, Deuteronomy 32, and so forth; indeed a nation's earliest literature is often poetic. But David was used of God greatly to advance the art. Gifted as a musician and equipped as a man of deep emotion and great ability, he was providentially taken through extremes of hardship, success, failure, sin, and deep repentance. Several of the psalms of David refer to these incidents—not written "on the spot," but composed in later years with these experiences in mind.

David lived about 1000 B.C. His work revolved mainly about Jerusalem. As Jerusalem has not been excavated, no archaeological light has been shed directly upon David. Indirectly, however, much information on David's kingdom has been made available. Indeed, it is now generally agreed, even by scholars of critical background, that the narrative in II Samuel is the work of a reliable contemporary historian. Gibeah of Saul has been excavated by W. F. Albright and Saul's rude castle exposed to view. In it were the first agricultural implements made of iron that have been found in Israel. The Philistines had brought the iron age. Excavations at Megiddo, northwest of Jerusalem, and Ezion Geber on the coast south of the Dead Sea have revealed the excellence of Solomon's government buildings, horse stables, fortifications, and his amazing copper foundry which was doubtless an important source of his great wealth. Between the rude beginnings of Saul and the advanced culture of Solomon lay the strong hand and wise administration of David, Israel's first real king and, in many ways, her greatest. He unified the realm and brought under his administration the diverse provinces of Transjordan, Phoenicia, and Syria. Under him the armies of Israel prospered. In the period of expansion, wealth increased and the arts prospered. There is no good reason why we should not credit David as the greatest man in this great century of Israel's history.

A previous generation of critical scholars was prone to deny that many or any of the psalms were by David. Two discoveries particularly have dealt a telling blow to this extreme criticism. First, in 1929, French excavators at Ras Shamra (ancient Ugarit) in Syria discovered a large number of tablets written in a dialect akin to Hebrew—ancient Canaanite, it may be called. They come from around 1400 B.C. Similarities with the language and style of the poetry of the Bible are so striking that no longer can one hold that the style of Biblical poetry is late. Unusual words and forms appearing in the Psalms are now regarded as a tie between Biblical poetry and the ancient Ugaritic literature. In theology and concept, the Ugaritic literature is, of course, pagan and far removed from the

Biblical psalms; but in grammar and poetic style it is quite close, and the parallels are very instructive.

The other discovery of moment is the finding of the famous scrolls in caves near the northwest shore of the Dead Sea at the base of the Judean hills. These remarkable scrolls include fragments of all the Old Testament books, except, perhaps, Esther, and range in date from 225 to about 50 B.C. Also considerable non-Biblical literature was found, some of which quotes extensively from the Old Testament, and especially from the Psalms. These quotations indicate the high estimate placed upon our Old Testament canonical books in the second century B.C. They were regarded as truly inspired of God. Handwriting studies show that fragments now known come from about a dozen copies of the Psalter. The quotations show that it was regarded as the work of the Holy Spirit along with the Law of Moses and the other Old Testament books. This evidence is not early enough to demonstrate the Davidic authorship of a majority of the psalms. It is early enough, however, positively to disprove an extreme criticism which had said that most of the psalms were post-Exilic and many reflected the national hopes of the Maccabees who fought so heroically to deliver Israel from Syrian oppression in 165-140 B.C. The early dating makes a real difference in the interpretation of certain of the psalms. The time-honored conservative datings are quite in line with the new evidence.

Hebrew Poetry. Hebrew poetry, like Canaanite poetry in general, is not characterized by rhyme. Rather, there is a balance of parallel members expressing the same thought or a contrasting one in other words, thus: "The heavens declare the glory of God; and the firmament showeth his handywork" (Ps. 19:1). Again, "For who is God save the Lord? or who is a rock save our God?" (18:31). Examples could by multiplied, as everyone who has read the Psalter knows. There are varying types of parallelism, of which we need not speak in detail. Some give a contrast of thought (especially in the Book of Proverbs). In some types, the second line builds upon the first in climactic arrangement: "Give unto the Lord, O ye kindreds of the people, give unto the Lord glory and strength" (96:7). Very often, the parallel member uses unusual words to repeat the thought given in common words in the first member. Observation of this parallelism is obviously a great help to interpretation. Interestingly, many of these "common word—rare word" pairs used in the Psalms are found in the same pairs and positions in Ugaritic literature.

There is a beauty of emphasis in this repetition in Hebrew poetry, but the power of the Psalms is not to be found merely in its literary style. The Psalms, like other great poetry, owe their effect rather to the grandeur of thought, illustration, and concept expressed by the authors under the influence of the Holy Spirit. For instance, in prose one may say that Israel believed in a holy God; the psalmist expressed it with intensity of feeling, "Thy righteousness is like the great mountains, thy judgments are a great deep; O Lord, thou preservest man and beast" (36:6). Poetry has been defined by Wordsworth as "the overflow of spontaneous emotion recollected in tranquillity" (Preface to *Lyrical Ballads,* 2nd Edition). The Psalms are all of this. They speak to the heart. And not only is the vehicle of poetry adapted to that purpose; they were prompted by the Spirit of God, and adapted to all the needs of the soul of man. Blessed is the man who hides these songs of Zion deep in his heart. They are both songs of comfort in the night and songs of praise for use when joy cometh in the morning.

There is doubtless a lesson for us in that God placed this book of poetry in the sacred Canon. We often pride ourselves on our intellectualism, but the fact remains that our emotions are equally as vital as our intellects, and if we would move men to pious trust and godly action, we must shoot our arrows at the heart. The sinner is as often won by a demonstration of God's love as by a demonstration of the accuracy of the gospel narratives. This is not to disparage the significance of Christian evidences. The apostles used argument and testimony to establish the facts of the Gospel. But the reason a sinner disbelieves against abundant evidence is often, perhaps usually, a moral and emotional factor in his make-up. Sin is rooted deeply in the heart. And it is the deep recesses of the heart that are cleansed by the Holy Spirit and filled with God's praises.

The First Person in the Psalms. It is an interesting question as to how far the psalms actually express the thoughts and emotions of David himself. A great many psalms are written in the first person, and it is natural to think of them as expressions of the feeling of the authors. This conclusion, however, does not follow. Great poets have often written poems in the first person expressing the common thoughts of men. Shelley's poem *The Cloud* traces the experiences of a cloud personified, all in the first person. Burns, Poe, Shakespeare, and others speak of all kinds of love and tragedy in the first person. It is quite possible that the first person of the psalmists is a literary device used to express more vividly the common feelings of men. The psalmists had these emotions, but wrote for the rest of us too. Several of the psalms are ascribed to incidents in David's life. It is noteworthy that these psalms are in agreement with the situations mentioned, but they are usually quite general and seldom single out particular events in the incident. For instance, Psalm 56 is ascribed to the time when the Philistines took David in Gath. It expresses trust in time of trouble, but the Philistines, or Gath, or David's capture are not explicitly mentioned. The psalm very likely was written years after the event as David thought upon those desperate days. But he did not write just for the pleasure of writing about his experiences. By the Spirit of God, he was moved to write a general psalm that would also be helpful to us when we are captured by our Philistines in the twentieth century.

This thought is of some importance in the interpretation of the Messianic Psalms. Most of these are in the first person. Do they therefore express the hopes and feelings of their authors? Or are they of broader application and written to express our thoughts too? Or do they present in prophecy the experiences and situations of the desire of nations, the Messiah of Israel? There is no good reason why we should think that the complaint, "My God, my God, why hast thou forsaken me?" was the complaint of David, the author of Psalm 22. It may just as well be supposed that David wrote those words by the Spirit of God to express the experience of the Messiah in His sufferings. Against the background of his own deep sufferings, David could portray the feelings of the One Who suffered the ultimate pain. Against the background of his kingship, David was used to write of the triumphs of the King of kings. Actually, whether a particular psalm speaks directly of the Messiah or not, is not to be decided by observing whether or not it is written in the first person. The psalms should be studied carefully to see what the experiences described are. Did they refer to David or some other author? Could they refer to Christ? Could they refer to any other but Christ? Are they applied to Christ in the New Testament, and if so, how? These questions we shall consider in the interpretation of the rather numerous Messianic Psalms.

Theology of the Psalter. The Psalms touch on most of the important subjects of theology. There is much of the greatness of God, His creatorship, providence, His attributes, and especially His relationship with His children. When these poems are contrasted with the heathen poetry of Ras Shamra of 1400 B.C., one cannot but ascribe to the Holy Spirit the lofty ideals and theology of the Psalms. They assign great value to men as children of God. At the same time, they humble mankind as of little consequence beside the greatness of the Almighty. They give comfort to man in his sorrow, yet severely rebuke his sin. Most wonderful of all, they celebrate his redemption by the mercy of God. Though the Psalms do not give details about the temple ritual, they refer many times to the temple and its sacrifices. Their deep devotional piety teaches us that the temple worship of Israel was not a mere formalism, but was symbolic of a deep faith in God's provision for man's salvation. Salvation by works or by ritual was not part of Israel's creed, and the Psalms show this as truly as do the writings of the prophets.

Divisions of the Psalter. The Psalter was already divided in antiquity into five books: Psalms 1—41; 42—72; 73—89; 90—106; 107—150. The basis of this division is not apparent. It is likely that the Law of Moses was divided into five books for convenience of writing upon scrolls. The books of the Psalms, however, are of quite unequal length. Each book ends in a doxology, a verse or two like Psalm 89:52, "Blessed be the Lord for evermore. Amen and Amen." These doxologies are found in the Septuagint, so they are older than 200 B.C. They may refer to liturgical use of the psalms in temple worship. Their origin and meaning may therefore be forever beyond us. The five books do not correspond to five stages in the composition or canonization of the Psalter, for some of the allegedly latest psalms are in Book III and thirteen psalms in Book V are ascribed by title to David. The reason for the arrangement is uncertain, but fortunately, it makes no difference in our understanding or appreciation of these great songs. The first book is composed of psalms by David exclusively, except that Psalms 1, 2, 10, and 33 have no title. The second book is mainly by David and the Sons of Korah. The third book is largely by Asaph and the Sons of Korah. The fourth book is anonymous except for Psalm 90 by Moses. The last book has thirteen psalms by David and one by Solomon; the rest are anonymous. More important that the division into books is the classification of the psalms according to subject matter. We have very little idea of the type of music which was used to accompany them. Only the instruments are known; the melodies and arrangements are entirely lost to us, as the psalmists had no method of writing music in antiquity.

Classification of the Psalms. It is difficult to classify the psalms because they vary widely in content and one psalm may touch on several different themes. One should not expect exalted lyric poetry to move with the precision of a geometrical demonstration. Some major classes stand out, however.

(1) Just about half of the psalms are prayers or poems expressing the troubled situation of the author—almost always with a note of triumphant faith and trust. These are the prayers which gave the book one of its characteristic Hebrew names: *Tephiloth,* prayers. Interestingly, over fifty of these are Davidic. They may be called poems of trouble and trust or prayers of faith in adversity. The presence of these psalms is probably one reason why the Psalter has been so precious a part of the worship of Israel and the Church. The world is full of trouble. And the only real answer for the troubles of earth is a robust faith in the God Who bows the heavens (Ps. 18:9) and comes down for the relief of His people. The Psalms express this confidence for us, and encourage us in it.

It might be worth while to look briefly at some great and representative psalms of this type. Psalm 18 is a good sample. This psalm is full of bold figures of speech, but the kernel of it is God's deliverance of David. The title ascribes it to the time when "the Lord delivered him from all his enemies and from the hand of Saul," that is, when David gained the throne after Saul's death. The psalm fits this time beautifully, but, again, there are no specific allusions. Verses 1–16 tell of the author's troubles and of God's coming to help. The trouble is briefly described as "the sorrows of death" and "the floods of ungodly men." When David cried to the Lord, He heard out of His holy temple. This probably refers to heaven, though there was an earthly place of worship at Gibeon and possibly elsewhere in those days. In highly poetic language, God is said to come to help. "The earth shook and trembled," does not describe an earthquake. "Fire out of his mouth devoured," does not refer to some oriental dragon deity! "The foundations of the world were discovered at thy rebuke, O Lord, at the blast of the breath of thy nostrils," does not mean that the Hebrews conceived of the wind as the result of God's blowing His breath! All these figures are heaped up expressions to teach that the God Who controls the very forces of nature and is immensely superior to them, has a personal regard for His children and delivers them in time of trouble. The following verses tell of the psalmist's triumph and victory through this same God. But God is not brought nigh by magic as in the Babylonian stories. Rather, the

Lord is a righteous Lord and beholds the upright, and so through His blessing God established David and his kingdom. Psalm 18 is a beautiful example of David's trust in the one supreme, holy God and his recognition of the ethical demands of God's law. The psalm is also given in a second copy, as a specimen of David's writing, in II Samuel 22. We shall say a word about that in considering other parallel psalms.

Another psalm of this nature is the all-time favorite, the Twenty-third, which in tender and poetic language expresses the great truth that God loves and cares for us. A similar thought is expressed in prose in the first part of the famous verse, John 3:16. Under the pastoral figure of a shepherd and his sheep, the eternal care of God is portrayed in never-to-be-forgotten beauty. The figure was most suitable for David, the author, who was taken from following the flock and who doubtless many a time upon his throne remembered his happy boyhood days with his sheep and perhaps a harp and a sling to play with among the hills of Judea. The figure is used else-where in the Old Testament (Ezek. 34:23, 31) and Christ Himself used it to draw attention to His work and His deity (Jn. 10:11).

(2) By far the next largest classification of the Psalter is the cate-gory of Psalms of Praise, of which there are about forty. Very few of these (only seven) are by David, and the majority come in the latter part of the book, after Psalm 91. Here, too, the saints of the ages have adopted these songs as their own. Another Jewish name for the whole Book of Psalms is *Tehillim*, praises. One is reminded of the couplet of Bishop Taylor Smith, "Prayer and praises go in pairs; they have praises who have prayers." The heathen really have very little for which to praise their deities. It is the glory of our faith that we have a God Who is "worthy to be praised." Psalm 148 is an example of a poem which runs the gamut of all creation in extoling the praises of God. But, characteristically, the ultimate reason for praise even here is God's goodness to the redeemed, "a people near unto him, Praise ye the Lord" (148:14).

Certain of these psalms were sung by the Jews of Christ's time at the Passover supper and, indeed, are so used today. Before the meal, Psalms 113 and 114 were sung, and 115–118 afterward. Psalm 136 was called the Great Hallel, and another group of Hallels con-sists of the doxologies of Psalms 146–150. *Hallel* is the Hebrew verb "to praise." *Hallelujah* means "Praise ye the Lord." The Greek form is *Alleluia*. All but one of the above Hallels have the first words (as a title), "Praise ye the Lord," either in the Hebrew or the Septuagint. It is wonderful to recall that the hymns Christ sang with His disciples on the night before His Passion were hymns of praise to God. How much more should we, the recipients of His grace, praise Him Whose name alone is excellent, Who only doeth wondrous things!

Two examples of such songs of praise may be singled out for study: first, the beloved 103rd Psalm. This psalm, one of our favorites for memorization, calls upon us to bless the Lord with all our hearts for all His wonderful works to the children of men. First, the goodness of God to His children is mentioned: He forgives, heals, supplies, and satisfies. Then, the character and attributes of God are celebrated. Here the psalmist dips into past history—the deliverance from Egypt under Moses. He quotes the great verse in which God revealed His name to Moses on Mount Sinai (Ex. 34:6). This memorable verse finds many echoes in the Psalms and other Old Testament books (Num. 14:18; Ps. 86:15, 111:4; 145:8; Joel 2:13; and Neh. 9:17, as well as partial quotations elsewhere). Psalm 103 continues by declaring that God's mercy is higher than the skies, greater than the distance from East to West, more tender than a father's love, more enduring than all time, this is the mercy of God to His children—not to all mankind indiscriminately, but to those who trust in the Lord. So wonderful is the psalmist's thought that he calls on the angels above and to all God's works in all places of His dominion to join in blessing the name of the Lord.

A second Psalm of Praise we may consider is number 148 which has already been briefly mentioned. It is in two halves, verses 1–6 and 7–14. The titles, "Praise ye the Lord," at the beginning and end are outside the structure of the poem and may therefore properly be called titles. The first part begins, "Praise ye the Lord from the heavens." The second part begins, "Praise ye the Lord from the earth" (v. 7). The distinction between heaven and earth is not drawn as we might draw it. At various periods the ancients evidently distinguished the heaven of clouds and birds (our atmosphere), from the heaven of the sun, moon, and stars, and from the heaven where God dwells. Thus, in II Corinthians 12:2, Paul speaks of the latter as the "third heaven." The psalmist includes the fire, hail, snow, and storms with the earth. He includes the "waters above the heavens" as above this lower stratum. In this heavenly sphere, he includes the celestial heavens and also the abode of God and angels. He does not claim to give us a detailed cosmology, but we cannot escape the grandeur of the sweep of his thought that all belongs to the Lord and all should praise Him.

Yet we may add a word here about the Biblical cosmology, because it is frequently misunderstood. We tend to think that the Bible must have shared certain medieval concepts of the earth and sky. Actually, men believed the world was round long before Columbus. The Greeks in surveying large triangles concluded that the measurements they observed showed that the triangles lay upon the surface of a sphere and not on a flat surface. They had even calculated the circumference of the earth with a good degree of accuracy. When the Bible speaks of the "ends of the earth," it likely means no more than we do by referring to the four points of the compass. "Earth" and "land" are identical in Hebrew. The "ends of the earth" simply meant extreme distances in adjacent lands.

Also the phrase, "waters under the earth," in the second commandment, does not refer to some subterranean lake. It means that as no images of the birds and stars above should be made, nor of animals and men upon the earth's surface, so no images of fish which live below shore level in lakes, rivers, and seas should be made and worshipped.

Some have thought that because the Genesis account of Noah's flood says that "the windows of heaven were opened," the Hebrews conceived of a watery mass above a rigid dome. But the same expression is used in Malachi 3:10 as a figure for the storehouse of all God's blessings. It was not meant literally any more than is our expression, "raining cats and dogs"; by that phrase we do not really mean to give the source of household pets. Nor did the Hebrews mean to say that the heavens had windows that opened and shut. To begin with, the Hebrews had windows which were only openings in the wall; they did not have movable glazed sashes that could be opened and shut. The fact is that the Bible does not give any detailed cosmology. Expressions such as the "foundations of the earth" (Ps. 102:25) are to be compared with the remark that God "hangeth the earth upon nothing" (Job 26:7). These are figurative expressions to show the greatness of God, the creator, and emphasize His control over it all.

Of course, the author of Psalm 148 did not know how vast the creation is. But there is a tendency today to feel that our enlarged conception of the size of the universe forbids us to think of a God in the Biblical sense. It must be remembered that even in David's world, man was pretty small. And David did not think of God as just a little bigger than man. To the prophets God was so great that the nations were to Him but as a speck of dust on a balance. Why must the idea of an enlarged universe destroy men's faith? Is it that man by comparison is now seen to be so insignificant as to be worthless? If this be the argument, we might well ask if value is really to be computed by size? Does a rancher with a hundred-thousand-acre farm think less of his tiny baby than does a city dweller on a fifty-foot lot? Psalm 148 declares that God cares more for people than He does for real estate! The psalmist calls on skies, storms, mountains, trees, beasts, and birds to praise God. But the chief item of praise is that God has brought Israel near unto Him. What auxiliary purposes God may have had in establishing the far reaches of this vast universe we may not know. We do know that the same laws of matter and energy apply in distant Sirius that apply in our backyards. May not the same spiritual laws of personality, value, love, and praise apply in God's heaven as in our poor little hearts, only on a grander scale? An old poem for children summed up the argument of the psalmist on the importance of the individual: "I am more than the world, though I am such a dot; I can love and think, and the world cannot." We are not the physical center of the universe. The Bible nowhere says we are. Does it follow that we are not peculiar subjects of the spiritual Kingdom of the Almighty? The psalmist says that we are "a people near unto him. Praise ye the Lord."

(3) There are five psalms which may be called Psalms of the Righteous Man. Psalm 1 illustrates them all by contrasting the way of the righteous man and his blessings with the sinner and his penalties. In these psalms, the author does not claim prefection. Indeed, the psalms as a whole are replete with confessions of sin. Rather, these psalms, like I John 3:6, set in absolute contrast the man whose life is given over to God and led by the Spirit, and the worldling who may have a relative decency without a God-oriented life. Other psalms that may be classified thus are: 15, 101, 112, and 133. Psalm 1 is of special interest in that its figure of a tree planted by the water is found also in Jeremiah 17:7, 8. It can hardly be established, however, which came first. Is Jeremiah a reference to Psalm 1 or vice versa? The First Psalm has no title and may serve somewhat as an introduction to the whole book. We can not be sure whether it was written before or after Jeremiah—or even by Jeremiah himself.

(4) There are about six Royal Psalms: 2, 21, 45, 72, 110, 132, and perhaps 89. Several of these are also messianic, in virtue of the close

connection in prophecy and type between the house of David and the Messiah Who is called, among other titles, the "rod out of the stem of Jesse." Interestingly, only two of these Royal Psalms (21 and 110) are ascribed to David. The Davidic covenant of II Samuel 7 was evidently well known in Israel and was the theme of much prophecy. Psalm 89 is the poetic reflex of II Samuel 7. The hope of the Messiah of David's line is expressed in the prophets in Isaiah 9:7; 11:1, 10; Micah 5:2; Amos 9:11; Jeremiah 23:6; Ezekiel 34:24; Zechariah 12:8, and so forth. It is carried through to the literature of the Dead Sea community and the Jews of Jesus' day (Mt. 22:42). David was a great king, but Israel was not just another nation with another ordinary king and no purpose in the world except to expand. Israel was a theocracy, and its purpose was to testify to the true faith in a sinful world. Its king also did not reign for himself, but as God's representative in a peculiar way. It was not a difficult thing for God to reveal to Israel that David and his successors were a type of the messianic King. We shall study these Royal Psalms later.

(5) Two psalms especially claim the name Penitential: 32 and 51. Other psalms with a penitential note are 38, 130, and 143. Psalm 51 is ascribed by its title to the incident of David's great sin. Psalm 32 would also fit that experience. Not many have fallen as David did from such a height; but surely, few have matched him in his exercises of godly sorrow for his sin. Psalm 51 is a model of penitence, especially because it sees with real spiritual insight that sin is primarily against God. David mourned not just the consequences of sin, but the sin itself. "Against thee, thee only have sinned," he mourns. And yet he also confesses his particular sin of the murder of Uriah (v. 14). His murder of Uriah had been indirect, yet David accepts the rebuke of Nathan, "thou hast slain him with the sword of the children of Ammon" (II Sam. 12:9).

David confesses, however, more than his own particular sin. And because he generalizes, the psalm fits the experience of us all, "Behold I was shapen in iniquity and in sin did my mother conceive me" (51:5). Of course, David is not blaming his parents, but is confessing that from the moment he began to be, he was a sinner. The secret springs of human thought and life are clouded throughout by sinful passion. This we know, and in our better moments we confess it. When we acknowledge our depravity with humble contrition, this is penitence.

The comparison is interesting between Nathan and John the

Baptist, both of whom rebuked kings for adultery. Herod beheaded John the Baptist. If Nathan had faced a lesser king than David, or a king not after God's own heart, he too may well have been executed. But David's ready repentance is indeed a model for us all. "I have sinned," said the king; "Cast me not away from thy presence and take not thy Holy Spirit from me." Some have thought that this verse means that David feared the loss of his salvation and that it should not be used in prayer by a Christian. Another view—and a preferable one—is that David realized that any sin jeopardizes communion and service. He had seen the sad case of Saul. When Saul had sinned and been rejected from being king, the Spirit had left Saul and come upon David. David had apparently been regenerated long before this, but the Spirit had come upon him at his anointing to kingship (I Sam. 16:13). David feared that, for his deep sin, the Spirit would possibly reject him and his house from the kingship, as Saul had been rejected. He prayed that he might not be "put on the shelf," or made a castaway, as Paul expresses it (I Cor. 9:27). Psalm 51 concludes, as all penitence should, with a note of consecration. When David is restored, he will worship and testify aright. Doubtless in his time of impenitence, David had sacrificed to no account, and had prayed prayers that never went "above the ceiling." Now David will offer "sacrifices of righteousness," or, according to a Hebrew idiom, "righteous sacrifices," and with these God will be well pleased.

(6) Objections have often been taken to certain psalms, called the Imprecatory Psalms, which pray God's judgment upon the psalmist's enemies. Psalms 69, 109, 137, and portions of 35, 55, and 58, are usually mentioned as of this type. It probably is an emasculated faith which takes most serious objection to these verses, assuming that sin is not so serious after all. But the Bible has many imprecations (cf. Jer. 11:20; 18:21–23; Neh. 4:4–5), several from the lips of Jesus Himself (cf. Mt. 23:32–36). In Revelation 6:10, the redeemed saints in heaven pray for God's judgment to be made manifest and for sinners to be destroyed. If they, with the holiest of motives, can so pray, it would seem that there are circumstances in which imprecatory prayer can be justified. It should be noted that the imprecations of Psalms 69 and 109 are applied in the New Testament to the impenitent Judas. The psalmist identifies himself with God's cause or with the Messiah Himself and prays for the destruction of all that hinders the triumph of God's Kingdom.

It is not that the Old Testament allows personal vengeance

whereas the New Testament has given us a higher stage of religion. The New Testament does indeed forbid personal vengeance, and so does the Old. On this subject, Paul in Romans 12:19, 20, quotes from the Old Testament (Deut. 32:35) to prove his point. Christ in Matthew 5:38, 39 was not contradicting the Old Testament when He forbade personal vengeance. Rather He was contradicting the tradition of the elders who misquoted the directions God had given for Israel's courts (Ex. 21:24) and applied them wrongly so as to allow personal vengeance. Those directions were quite proper in Exodus 21:24 (also in similar contexts in Lev. 24:20 and Deut. 19:21). An eye for an eye and a tooth for a tooth was not meant to be taken literally in Israel and was never to our knowledge so taken. It was the principle of justice that the punishment should fit the crime without fear or favor. But the Pharisees had taken these verses out of context and had taught that the Scriptures approved of personal revenge. Actually, the Old Testament as well as the New is in full agreement with Jesus' teaching. Proverbs 20:22 is explicit: "Say not thou, I will recompense evil; but wait on the LORD and he shall save thee." The Imprecatory Psalms ask, properly enough, for God's judgments to be manifest on the earth. David is really one of the best examples of a man who would not seek revenge on Saul or Saul's successors despite ample opportunity and apparent justification.

(7) There are verses in the Psalms which at first sight seem to deny the teaching of immortality (Ps. 6:5; 30:9; 39:13; 115:17). If denial of the afterlife be gathered from these verses, the psalmist's thought was unique in the ancient world! The Egyptians, Babylonians, Canaanites, and members of other early cultures all believed in the continuation of conscious existence, as their literature and burial customs show. Also, the psalms themselves give clear teaching on immortality and resurrection (16:8–11; 17:14, 15; 73:23–26 and especially 49:15). The contrary verses, referred to above, do not deny immortality. In their context, they are prayers for deliverance from fatal sickness or danger. They possibly contrast the situation of the living who join in the visible worship and service of God here, with those in the grave whose earthly tongues are stilled and whose work is over. That the dead do enjoy the blessing of being in conscious fellowship with Christ is clear from such verses as II Corinthians 5:8. The negative of these verses in the Psalms may be what is called a negative of comparison. "In death there is no remembrance of

thee," that is, no worship such as there is in this life. The psalmist prays for continuance of life even as Paul did in Philippians 1:21–23 even though he knew that "to die is gain." There are certain other verses in Ecclesiastes and Job which have probably colored the interpretation of these verses in the Psalms. Job in the depths of his despair does say that he will "go whence I shall not return, even to the land of darkness . . . without any order and where the light is as darkness" (Job 10:21, 22). He also rises later to triumphant faith (Job 14:15; 19:25–27; 23:10). Ecclesiastes also considers the philosophy of materialism and pessimism in 3:19 to 4:2, but considers it only to reject it in favor of the worship of God (Eccles. 12:13, 14).

(8) There are four psalms and parts of others which recount the history of Israel (78, 81, 105, and 106). Psalm 105 carries the history from Abraham to the Exodus. Psalm 106 goes on to the period of the judges. Psalm 78, the next to longest psalm in the book, goes from the time in Egypt to the kingdom of David. Psalm 81 refers briefly to the wilderness wanderings, quoting Exodus 20:2. These histories are, of course, poetic and schematic; there is no attempt in them to be detailed or complete. They are histories from the moral and theological point of view. An example of this interpretation of history is Psalm 106:34–38. Israel disobeyed God and failed to exterminate the Canaanites. As a result, they were mingled with them and all too soon were sacrificing their own children to idols. They had spared the guilty in disobedience to God and the result was that they sacrificed the innocent. It is fashionable these days to object to God's stern command to slaughter the Canaanites as being brutal and far from the picture of the loving Jesus; this view denied the propriety of punitive justice. The Israelites also gave way to misplaced mercy. The result of their false clemency was to make the innocent suffer instead of the guilty.

In a very real sense all the Old Testament histories are interpretive histories. The prophets of Israel were not mere archivists recording all events of economic, military, scientific, and social importance. For instance, we now learn that Ahab was an important and powerful military figure of ancient times, but the Bible gives him brief and unfavorable mention, for the Bible was concerned to point out other aspects of Ahab's reign than his conquests. Actually, all history is interpretative. Modern historians tend to emphasize the economic; former students doubtless overemphasized the military. The Biblical historians have written candidly, telling the sins of their heroes as well as their successes. And they have written more accurately than all the secular historians, for they have seen that there is a divine hand moving through all the affairs of men setting up one kingdom and putting down another. History is not meaningless; it is the out-working of God's providence and purposes and in this working of God in history, the psalmist finds real basis for praise.

It is of some interest that the historical allusions of the psalms do not go beyond the times of David, except for the anonymous Psalm of the Captivity, Psalm 137. Several psalms refer in general terms to times of captivity and hardship and to periods of desolation of the temple (for example, 74, 79, 80, 83, 85, 89, 129, and 137). These are quite general poetic descriptions, however, and we must remember that Jerusalem was sacked more than once. David himself suffered two palace revolts. None of the above psalms is ascribed to David, though some of them could be of his days or soon thereafter. Critical scholars have confidently dated many of these to the Maccabean era, but no clear historical allusion occurs in them to those days. Others have noted that the psalms are totally lacking in any reference to the use of elephants, a prominent feature of the Maccabean battles. As noted above, a Maccabean date for any of the psalms is now made impossible by evidence from the Dead Sea Scrolls. And if most of the psalms were written late, as higher criticism has affirmed, it is strange indeed that no psalms detail the later history of the divided kingdom. Several do, however, glorify the nation of Israel, or Zion, its capital, or the temple, its center (84, 37, 122).

(9) There are two famous Psalms of Revelation, 19 and 119. Psalm 19 covers both natural and special revelation in well-defined sections. Verses 1–6 glorify the revelation of God in nature. This has been beautifully set to music in Joseph Addison's hymn, "The Spacious Firmament on High." The heavens are pictured as a tent from which the sun comes forth like a bridegroom for an oriental wedding procession or like a runner for a race. As the sun's circuit is universal, so is the witness of nature to nature's God. We may remark briefly on verse 4 which is quoted in Romans 10:18. The argument is that no man, specifically no Jew, is excusable for his unbelief in the one true God. But in Romans the words are "their sound went into all the earth." In Psalm 19:4 it says "their line is gone out through all the earth." The New Testament words are quoted verbatim from the Septuagint translation. The Hebrew words for "voice" and "line" differ only in one letter. It seems quite likely that the original word

of the psalm was "their voice" and that this has been correctly preserved in the Septuagint and the New Testament, but that in later
years a letter dropped or became confused in our Hebrew manuscripts. The Revised Standard Version quite properly adopts this
reading of the Septuagint. The Hebrew Scrolls from the Dead Sea
area have shown us lately that just this has happened in several cases,
and the Septuagint and New Testament have preserved the correct
reading. There is also another possibility that in Psalm 19:4 "their
line" is an idiomatic expression in Hebrew meaning "their sound,"
but this cannot be proved from other usage.

The second Psalm of Revelation is the long 119th. As is well
known, this is an alphabetic poem with the first eight verses starting
with the Hebrew Aleph, the next eight with Beth, and so on. As
there are twenty-two letters in the Hebrew alphabet, there are 176
verses in the psalm. By design the emphasis is upon God's special
revelation. Eight words are used over and over again to refer to this
revelation: law, testimonies, precepts, statutes, commandments,
judgments, word, and way. It has been called "a holy alphabet for
Zion's scholars!" It is not clear that the poem refers by the word
"law" and its synonyms to the Pentateuch. From the usage of II
Kings 14:6 and other places, the Pentateuch would be called the "law
of Moses," a phrase which Psalm 119 does not use. More likely,
Psalm 119 refers to all of God's special revelation, but verses 97, 99,
and others, seem to indicate that it was a written law.

There are other Alphabetic Psalms: 25, 34, 37, 111, 112, and 145.
The artificiality of these arrangements does not seem greatly to have
hindered the poets from expressing thoughts of real power. It is the
mark of genius that an author uses the style to help in expressing his
thought rather than letting the style cramp his expression. Psalms 9
and 10 are also thought by some to be one poem with an alphabetic
arrangement, though somewhat irregular, running through the combined work. The Septuagint unites these two psalms into one as it
probably was in the original. All of these alphabetic poems are now
illuminated by the discovery in 1950 of a tablet from Ras Shamra
bearing the letters of the alphabet in their later Hebrew order. The
tablet comes from about 1400 B.C. (cf. the *Biblical Archaeologist*,
XII [1950] p. 80). Proverbs 31:10–31 and Lamentations chapters 1
to 4 are also alphabetical poems.

(10) Another special feature is of some interest—the Parallel
Psalms and the refrains. Two psalms are widely known to be parallel,

14 and 53. They differ only in the phrases just before the last verse
and in the names used for God. Psalm 53 uses *God* exclusively; Psalm
14 uses both *God, Lord* (Hebrew, *Adhonay*) and LORD (Hebrew
Yhwh, rendered *Jehovah* in the RSV). Psalm 18 is found as an example of David's poetry in II Samuel 22. The differences through the
whole long poem are very slight. Psalm 108 is a composite psalm
made up of parts of 57 and 60, and again, the differences are slight.
Psalm 70 is parallel to Psalm 40:13–19. The main differences are in
the divine names. LORD (Jehovah) of Psalm 40 is *God* in Psalm 70
twice, the reverse is true once, and it is unchanged once. LORD
(*Adhonay*) is once changed to *God*. First Chronicles 16:8–36 is a
composite poem made up of Psalm 105:1–15; 96:2–13; and 106:1, 47,
48. Again, the differences are slight. It is not clear why these doub-
lets appear or why there are slight differences. Some of the differences observable in the English are mere variations in translation.
A few differences are doubtless due to the insignificant corruptions
that have crept into the Hebrew text through the many years of
copying. That there are so few of these and of such slight significance is a witness to the marvelous faithfulness with which our
Biblical text has been copied from the beginning. Some of the
differences and the fact that there are parallels at all are quite
possibly due to the tunes and practices used in the temple worship. For instance, we have two arrangements of our hymn, "Stand
Up, Stand Up for Jesus," one of which adds a refrain after each
verse. One of our arrangements of "There Is a Green Hill Far Away"
differs from the others by taking verse 5 and making it into a refrain
used after each verse. What slight variations in wording of the
psalms were brought about by adapting them to different tunes
is totally beyond our knowledge. It may be added that the poems
which occur both in the psalms and in the historical books of Samuel
and Chronicles probably appear in the one place merely as poems
and in the other place as hymns to be sung.

Refrains are found within certain psalms. Most famous is that of
Psalm 136 which uses the refrain or response "for his mercy endureth
forever" in every verse. Psalm 8 uses the refrain "O Lord, our Lord,
how excellent is they name in all the earth," at both the beginning
and the end. Psalm 24 repeats a verse (7 and 9) because the answering verses (8 and 10) advance to a climax. Psalm 80 has an instructive triple refrain. In the first instance, it begins "Turn us again, O
God" (v. 3); the second time, it begins, "Turn us again, O God of

hosts" (v. 7); and the third time it completes the climax, "Turn us again, O Lord God of hosts" (v. 19). The variation in the divine names is obviously purposive to secure the emphasis of climax.

In Psalm 49, verses 12 and 20 are very similar and probably were identical originally; the Septuagint still has them the same. The force of the refrain is that men who set such store by riches should recognize that they, like the animals of the field, are bound to die, but the confidence of the psalmist is that he will go to be with God (v. 15). Psalms 42 and 43 have one verse repeated three times. Psalm 42:11 is identical with 43:5. Psalm 42:5 would also be the same in the Hebrew if the first phrase of verse 6, "O my God," were attached to the end of verse 5. This was doubtless the original form, and the Septuagint so reads it. The later Hebrew copyists apparently made a slight mistake in word and verse division. Because there are a few—very few—examples of such mistakes in word division in our Hebrew copies, some critical scholars have argued that the words in old Hebrew writings were run together as is true in certain old Greek manuscripts. Our evidence from early Hebrew manuscripts and inscriptions is against this. We have several old Hebrew inscriptions and now an abundant literature from the Dead Sea community, and in all of these writings, the words are carefully divided by spaces or dots or strokes. The copying was accurate, and we are fully justified in our belief that the originals, being divinely inspired, were copied carefully and providentially preserved from serious error. Westcott and Hort have concluded that the transmission of the New Testament was so good that only one-tenth of one percent is in any doubt. Some similar figure could fairly be alleged for the Old Testament.

Many other refrains will be observed by the student. Psalm 107 repeats verses 6 and 8 three other times, thus dividing the psalm into five sections. Psalm 56 repeats verse 4 in verses 10 and 11 with a variation of the divine names, resulting in a climax. Psalm 46:7 and 11 have the well-known refrain, "The Lord of hosts is with us; the God of Jacob is our refuge." In Psalm 57, verses 5 and 11 are identical. This is of special interest, for verse 11 is part of the last half of the psalm which is used to make part of Psalm 108. It would seem that Psalm 108 was secondary and borrowed from Psalm 57, not vice versa. Psalm 67:3 is the same as verse 5. In Psalm 116, verses 14 and 18 are alike. Psalm 96:7, 8 is identical with Psalm 29:1, 2. And there are others. These refrains and verses which recur in various psalms need not surprise us at all. David may well have used set phrases of prayer and praise again and again. Later authors would be expected to use phrases from the works of David. All these were sung, doubtless many of them to several tunes, as the godly ones of Israel gathered year after year in times of victory and in times of sorrow to praise their God and pour out their hearts in prayer. The literary styles and phrases of the psalms, which recur in the songs of praise composed by the Dead Sea community in the second and first centuries B.C., have penetrated our language and forms of worship. They give a richness we surely should cultivate as we also come into His courts with thanksgiving and into His gates with praise.

(11) Of great importance are the Messianic Psalms. Opinions differ as to the number of psalms that should be so classed. The major ones which seem to speak directly of the Messiah are: 2, 16, 22, 40, 45, 69, 72, 89, and 110. If we include all to which the New Testament refers in the life of Christ, we shall include a larger number, adding: 8, 41, 68, 102, 109, and 118. Some of these are quite explicitly applied to Christ. With others, the application is more indefinite. Each one should be studied on its merits to determine the nature of the prediction involved and this we shall attempt to do.

We may notice to begin with, that these psalms are found in several of the categories given above. Psalms 2, 45, 72, and 110 are Royal Psalms celebrating God's King and His rule in Zion. Psalms 8, 68, and 118 are Psalms of Praise. Prayers for help in trouble are 16, 22, 40, 41, 69, 102, and 109. Psalm 89 is like these, but recalls the Davidic Covenant of II Samuel 7 as a promise for the people in a time of national distress. The Messianic Psalms, thus, are of varied content. They have rather close analogies in many non-messianic psalms. Some students have therefore concluded that these psalms refer primarily to their author and only secondarily to Christ, the antitype. This view must be given due consideration.

It is also possible, however, that the Spirit of God used the experiences through which a prophet like David was passing as a background for the expression of similar but deeper experiences of the Messiah. Thus David was providentially fitted through his great trouble to portray the sufferings of Him Who loved His own unto the end. The kingship likewise was known to be typical of the higher kingship of Christ. The question is, ao the expressions in the Messianic Psalms transcend the experiences of mortal men? If so, they were predictions by men who reflected on their own experiences and foresaw the greater sufferings and triumphs of the Captain of their salvation. If not, these psalms may well have referred to the experiences of their authors which were in turn typical of Christ. It is not impossible that some Messianic Psalms are of one category, others of another. Naturalistic critics will insist that the meaning of a psalm is exhausted in the reference to the author's day, but that it may be referred to Christ by analogy. This hardly suits the New Testament use of these psalms and it makes their reference to Christ no more wonderful than the reference of non-messianic psalms to all of the rest of us in our varied experiences. It robs David of his predictions and Christ of the Psalter's witness.

It may be convenient to start with the Royal Messianic Psalms, one of the most notable of which is Psalm 110. Fortunately, the translation of the vital phrases is not in dispute. The Revised Standard Version agrees with the King James except that the Lord addressed in verse 1 is written with a small "l" and the eternal priest-king of verse 4 is addressed with the human "you" instead of the "thou" reserved by the Revised Standard Version for deity. The implication of the Revised Standard Version is that the subject of the psalm is a mere man, not the Messiah, yet the translation is essentially that of the King James Version. Now to whom does the psalm refer? Much depends on the authorship. If it is by David, it refers to his Lord; David had no human lord above him. If it is by some lesser individual, it might refer to that individual's king—except that in verse 4 it is said to refer to a priest-king.

Many critics have taken the psalm to be one of the latest and to refer to the Maccabean priest-kings of about 140 B.C. Abundant use of the psalms in the Dead Sea literature rules out so late a date as this. It must then refer to a Melchizedek priest-kingship of a different sort. But there was no priest-king in ancient Israel. Both Saul and Azariah were condemned for intruding into the priest's office. The priests were of Levi; the kings were of Judah. Neither David nor his successors could be priest-kings. Of whom then did the author speak? Christ assures us (as does the title) that David spoke this psalm by the Holy Spirit (Mk. 12:36). Christ also draws the obvious conclusion that it refers to Him Who was both David's Lord and David's son, the Messiah. Thus, the psalm cannot refer to David at all nor to his ordinary successors on the throne. To say so is to violate the title and Christ's interpretation. It would also violate the meaning of verse 4 on which Hebrews (chs. 5 and 7) builds so heavily. It cannot refer to the Maccabean priest-kings, as was once thought, both because it is too early and also because they were, after all, priests of Aaron's line. Actually it is a direct prediction of the Messiah. It probably is a basis for the prediction of the Messiah in Zechariah 6:12–15, where Joshua, the high priest, is symbolically crowned, called the Branch, and said to rule upon a throne. The crown, however, was removed from his head and stored in the temple as a symbol for future days. This supports the idea that the Jews because of their prophecies looked forward to a priest-king to come.

Another Royal Psalm is 45 which obviously celebrates a royal wedding. Is it a wedding of Solomon or one of his successors? Or does it celebrate the victory and marriage supper of the Lamb? Here there is a question of translation of the vital verse 6. The Revised Standard Version translates it, "Your divine throne endures for ever and ever." A footnote suggests "your throne is a throne of God, or your throne, O God." The King James Version reads, "Thy throne, O God, is for ever and ever." This reading is the translation of all the old versions (the Greek Septuagint, the Syriac, and the Latin), except the Jewish Targum, which inserts a word into the Hebrew text so that the messianic reference is avoided. The Hebrew plainly says, "Thy throne, God, is for ever and ever." The form of the sentence with the second person of address in verses 5 and 7 makes the vocative "thy throne, O God" necessary. The form of the sentence is quite like Lamentations 5:19, "Thou, O Lord, dost dwell forever, thy throne is for ever and ever" (literal translation). There is no reason to depart from the King James Version translation of Psalm 45:6. And there is surely no justification for the translation "your divine throne." Be it noted, also, that the translation of the Septuagint, "Thy throne, O God, is for ever and ever," is used in Hebrews 1:8. Not only does the New Testament apply this verse to Christ, but it also approves the natural literal translation. The Revised Standard Version translates the Hebrews passage in the same way as does the King James Version, but it offers a footnote, "or, God is thy throne." This rendering would not be suitable for grammar or sense; a throne is not God. It may be gold or ivory, but God is not an adjective. If an adjectival sense were intended, the Greek could have used the adjective *theios*, divine. The adjectival sense in Hebrew would likely have been expressed by the frequent adjectival genitive construction, "a throne of God is to thee," that is, "your throne is divine." But neither of these constructions is used in the Hebrew or Greek. The King James Version translation is clearly to be preferred.

Numerous commentators, however, argue that it is impossible. The impossibility arises from the dogmatic objection that the king addressed in Psalm 45 cannot properly be called God. The answer is plain. Christ is called God both here, in John 20:28, and elsewhere. If Psalm 45 calls the king God, it simply argues that the king addressed is not Solomon, but King Messiah. We should note that, although the word *Elohim* usually translated "God" is occasionally used elsewhere for "judges" or "angels," it is in those places treated as a plural noun which it is according to its Hebrew form. In Psalm 45:6, however, and always when Deity is addressed, the word is conceived of as a plural of majesty and construed as a singular noun agreeing with singular pronouns and verbs. We must conclude that the author of this psalm was not writing of a Davidic king, but of King Messiah.

There is, therefore, no reason to depart from the King James Version, "worship him," of verse 11. There the Revised Standard Version says, "bow to him." The Jewish Publication Society Version says "do thou homage to him." Its translation of verse 6 is "Thy throne *which is of* God *shall stand* for ever and ever" (the italics are theirs, to indicate that they have supplied these words). Such translations import ideas into the Hebrew text which are not there. The most natural translation of Psalm 45, supported in Hebrews 1:8, indicates that the psalm is addressed to the Messiah and not to Solomon or any earthly king.

Psalm 2 is a bit more general, and perhaps we should not be dogmatic about its interpretation. It tells of one who is called the Lord's anointed against whom the kings of the earth rebel. The Lord, however, establishes His throne and bids all to kiss Him in submission. Could this be merely an exalted hyperbolic description of the reign of David or of one of his successors? It surely seems to be a description of a world-wide dominion such as David never enjoyed. Also, in the last three verses, the kings of the earth are admonished to serve the Lord and kiss the son. The son could possibly be the theocratic king of Judah. But the last phrase seems to give the son a superhuman prerogative, "Blessed are all they that put their trust in him." Most naturally interpreted, this would require a direct messianic reference. There is a problem, however, as to the translation of this 12th verse. The word *son* is the Aramaic form *bar* (cf. the New Testament form Bar Jonah, Bartimaeus, and others) rather than the usual Hebrew form *ben* which is already used in verse 7. Aramaic and Hebrew were parallel languages, and David's kingdom included Aramaic peoples to the north. There seems to be no good reason why the author of Psalm 2 could not use an Aramaism. Proverbs 31:1 also uses this word three times. Several have remarked that the Hebrew *ben* might have been avoided because of the following word *pen*, meaning *lest*. *Ben pen* might have sounded harsh. At least, there seems to be no good reason to depart from the old translation, implying as it does that the Son is the object of worship and saving trust. Strangest of all is the treatment of the Revised Standard Version, which changes the text in an extreme manner. It takes the Hebrew consonants, GL BR'D NSHQ BR ("rejoice with trembling, kiss the son"), and transposes the first two letters to the last word so as to make it a combination of the preposition B and the noun RGL ("feet"), to read thus: BR'D NSHQ BRGL ("with trembling, kiss his feet"). There is no evidence for this transposition of the letters either in ancient manuscripts or translations. It can hardly be commended, and seems to be a *tour de force* to avoid the reference to the Son.

The New Testament refers this psalm to Christ in Acts 4:25, 26; 13:33; Hebrews 1:5; and Revelation 19:15 and it appears to refer directly to Him. We may add that the phrase, "this day I have begotten thee" (2:7), is of special interest. The Hebrew word "beget" is used in two main forms: the causative conjugation is used of a father begetting a child; the simple conjugation is used of a mother bearing a child and also of general relationships. The first form, for example, is used in the genealogy of Genesis 11. The latter form is used in Genesis 10:15, 16, and elsewhere, in such situations as: "Canaan begat . . . the Jebusite and the Amorite." This does not mean that the Amorite was a man, for the ending clearly shows that it was a nation. The verse means that the Amorite was a nation within the geographical area of Canaan or in some other relationship. Now, the simple conjugation is used in Psalm 2:7. The reference is not to Jesus' birth, but to the eternal relationship of love between the Father and the Son. There is here no thought of any time of origination of the Son. Acts 13:33 seems to refer to Christ's resurrection as proof of this eternal relationship.

Psalm 72 is somewhat different. It speaks in large terms of the reign of the king, the king's son. His reign shall be wide, righteous, prosperous, and happy. His name shall remain and men shall fear him throughout all generations. Yet there is little here that could not be applied to Solomon as hyperbolic language. The psalm is not applied to Christ in the New Testament.

In all likelihood, the psalm should be compared with 89. This psalm is the poetic counterpart of the Davidic covenant of II Samuel 7. There an eternal throne is promised to David, and it is said that his seed should endure forever. Apparently David understood this covenant to have its eventual fulfilment in the Messiah (Acts 2:30). The prophets understood that the Davidic kingship was prophetic and typical of Christ to come (Is. 11:1; Jer. 23:5; Ezek. 37:24, 25, and so forth). Psalms 72 and 89 may therefore be classed as typico-Messianic because this was involved in the Davidic Covenant. There is mention of the expected sin of David's successors (Ps. 89:30–32), yet God will secure for David an unending throne (vv. 36, 37). The prophecy is fulfilled in David's line which culminated in Jesus Christ according to the line of kings listed in Matthew 1. The New Testament reference is in Luke 1:32.

The Messianic Psalms of Suffering belong to a larger category. One of the clearest of these is Psalm 16 which speaks of the resurrection of Christ, touching only lightly on His suffering. The psalmist begins with a declaration of the Lord's goodness and closeness to him. He rejects the idolatry of the heathen and blesses the Lord Who is ever before him. The crucial verses praise God who "wilt not leave my soul in hell; neither wilt thou suffer thine Holy One to see corruption"; rather, God will take him into His very presence in eternal joy. "Of whom speaketh the prophet this? of himself or of some other man?" we may echo with the Ethiopian eunuch. The real question is one of translation and interpretation. If the words refer to a resurrection, then David was not speaking of himself, as Peter argued pointedly in Acts 2:25–31. If these words refer to recovery from danger, they may have referred to David or to anyone. Likewise, if they refer to immortality, they could refer to anyone.

The vital words are "hell" and "corruption" in verse 10. The first word is the common word *sheol* which is translated "grave" in the King James Version thirty-one times out of sixty-four. It is questionable if it should be always interpreted as the place of departed spirits, as many do today. In Genesis 44:29, Numbers 16:33, Job 14:13, Psalm 49:14, and elsewhere, it is just as likely that the meaning "grave" is more suitable. Indeed, that *sheol* means the place of departed spirits cannot often be proved. But in the later prophets, the word seems to have become used to mean the abode of the wicked dead (cf. Ezek. 32:21). That the righteous (like Jacob) go down to the grave, is obvious. But it cannot be proved that *sheol* is used to describe a state of conscious existence of righteous men after death. It may rather have been a name for the grave which was specialized as time went on to refer to the state or place of conscious existence of the wicked dead. The derivation of the word is very uncertain.

In Psalm 16:10, the word "soul" is the word used often in the Old Testament for the person. Many times it is simply a reflexive pronoun. In Deuteronomy 12:20, "thy soul longeth to eat flesh," simply means, "you crave flesh" (so translated in the RSV). So here, Psalm 16:10 may well be translated, "Thou wilt not abandon me to the grave." The translation of this clause in Psalm 16:10 and Acts 2:27, King James Version, is very unfortunate. It leaves the reader with the impression that Christ after His death went to hell, but was rescued from there. It may even be that the reading was chosen by those in the English church who thought that in some sense Christ went to the underworld (or purgatory?) after His death. Luke 23:43 speaks quite definitely to the contrary. The application of the psalm which Peter makes in Acts 2:31 fits much better the view that this clause merely refers to Christ's arising from the grave. The King James Version should be modified, it would seem, at this point.

In the last clause, the Revised Standard Version translates "or let thy godly one see the Pit." This word "pit" (Hebrew *shachath*), is translated by the Revised Standard Version twelve times with a capital "P" and eleven times without the capital. Sometimes it clearly means a hole that has been dug. Etymologically it may come from *shuach*, to "bow down," or from *shachath*, to "corrupt." Indeed, there may be two words here, one "pit" and the other "corruption." In the same way, the Hebrew word *nachath* has two meanings, depending on whether it comes from *nuach* or *nachath*.

It is highly doubtful if *schachath* should ever be translated "Pit" with a capital. Some critical commentators hold that the "Pit" is the "dungeon of Sheol." This is importing a great deal into the word. Half of the time it cannot mean any more than a hole in the earth. The other instances where it does mean "pit," it probably refers only to the grave (Job 33:18, 22, 24, 28, 30, and elsewhere). On the other hand, in Job 17:14, "corruption" seems to be the necessary translation as it is parallel to the "worm." We may actually suspect that the two meanings became confused, and the word was most suitable for the corruption of the grave. It is translated this way repeatedly in the Septuagint. There is therefore no good reason why the words cannot be translated substantially as in the King James Version, "Thou wilt not abandon me to the grave, thou wilt not permit thy holy one to see corruption."

In line with this is the context. The next verse does not say that David was rescued from danger; it speaks of eternal bliss at God's right hand. Some critical scholars concede that this might imply resurrection "if the psalm were late enough," but feel rather that it refers to belief in eternal life. It is gratifying that these critics admit the doctrine of immortality in Israel at a fairly early date, in view of the psalmist's confidence that he would not go to sheol or the dungeon of sheol, but would go to heaven. But this does not reckon with verse 10. Verse 10 deals with deliverance from the grave and the corruption of the grave. The parallel in Psalm 30:3, 9 is instructive. David there is confident of being rescued from death. His hope, therefore, is for restoration to normal life on earth. Psalm 16, however, anticipates heaven after deliverance from the grave.

To sum up, verse 10 could mean rescue from death or resurrection. Verse 11 could mean resurrection or immortality. The two verses together speak of a death which issues in resurrection glory. If this be the true interpretation, the psalm can only refer to Christ, and thus it is used in the New Testament. Peter accepted this translation and appealed to these verses to prove the resurrection of Christ (Acts 2:25–31). He is emphatic that David, being a prophet, spoke of Christ and that the verses were inapplicable to David whose tomb was just outside of Jerusalem. Christ's tomb, however, was empty and His flesh saw no corruption, Peter argues. Paul's argument in Acts 13:34–37 is identical. In this case, we may say that David is not a type of Christ, but that Christ's resurrection is a type of David's and of ours for it has happened already. The verses refer directly to Christ.

Psalm 22 is another which has always been referred by Christians to the sufferings of Christ. It is quoted in the New Testament on five occasions and is referred to Christ. In itself, the first part of the psalm describing the suffering could apply to many people. But it could not apply to David who is the author. The psalmist's description of the sufferings of Christ on the cross is in some respects more vivid than that of the authors of the Gospels. The psalm abounds in figures of speech. The enemies are clearly wicked men who scorn the righteous sufferer, and they are called bulls of Bashan, dogs, lions. The suffering is intense, physical, prolonged, shameful, public, and accompanied with the scorn of the bystanders. If we give verse 15 its full weight, it was fatal. David in his varied experiences never suffered like this. Jeremiah has been suggested as the author, but it is unlike the tone of Jeremiah or Lamentations. It fits no Jewish method of execution. Also, the title attributes it to David.

Verse 1 was quoted by Christ in His cry from the cross. Incidentally, the better texts of Matthew and Mark agree that the words were *Eloi, Eloi, lama sabachthani,* which is the expected Aramaic form. Much discussion has revolved around this cry. Some earnest Christians have interpreted it to mean that the Father and the Son were separated in this hour of the Son's atonement. It would be unthinkable, however, for the unity of the Godhead to have been broken even for an instant. The poetic parallel in Psalm 22:1 gives the clue to the real meaning. The Father so loved the world that He abandoned the Son to the judgment of the cross and did not deliver Him from His agony. "Why art thou so far from helping me?" is the explanatory parallel.

The contrast is clearly drawn between the wicked mockers who gather around and the careless men who divide the sufferer's garments. The combination of physical and mental agony is precisely given. Both are suffered to the bitter extreme. It seems from the description that the ordeal must end in death even if verse 15 did not say so explicitly. We must also remember the very striking similarity of this holy chapter with Isaiah 53 which plainly affirms the death and burial of the sufferer.

Unfortunately, the exact meaning of verse 16 is uncertain. For the last phrase the Hebrew has, "like a lion my hands and my feet," which hardly makes sense. All the ancient versions take the word "like a lion" as a verb, but this verb does not occur elsewhere. What we have, perhaps, is a rare verb expressing some sort of wounding of the hands and feet of the sufferer done by his wicked antagonists. It marvelously fits the action of crucifixion, though this detail is not quoted in the New Testament.

Not only is the suffering inapplicable to David and precisely suited to Christ, but the consequent triumph is applicable only to Him. The ends of the earth shall hear and worship. Future generations shall declare His righteousness. The sufferer, marvelously delivered, shall tell the praises of the Lord in the congregation (Heb. 2:12). We can only conclude that this psalm was written by David, the prophet, who foresaw the sufferings of Christ and the glory that would follow.

Psalm 40 is a psalm of suffering of special interest since it mentions the sacrifice of Christ. The psalmist is and has been in deep affliction, yet his trust in the Lord is steadfast. Verses 6–8, quoted in Hebrews

10:5–7, refer to Christ's sacrifice for our sins. Verse 12, however (both in the KJV and RSV), includes a seeming confession of sin in the key verses (6, 7, 8) where the subject affirms his purpose to do the will of God to the utmost. As quoted in Hebrews, it is more specific, "Sacrifice and offering thou wouldest not, but a body hast thou prepared me: In burnt offerings and sacrifices for sin thou hast had no pleasure. Then said I, Lo, I come (in the volume of the book it is written of me,) to do thy will, O God." Hebrews remarks that the declaration, "Lo, I come," signifies the end of the Levitical sacrifices by the coming of Christ, and this was accomplished specifically by His offering of His own body once for all.

The problem here is that whereas the psalm says "mine ear's hast thou opened," Hebrews says, "a body hast thou prepared me." This is not just a free variation given by the New Testament; it is a word-for-word quotation from the Septuagint, which here differs from the Hebrew. It is possible that the Septuagint has here made an idiomatic and correct translation. Thus our idiom, "keep your eyes glued to the road" means "pay attention to your driving." On this view, the Hebrew really meant and was understood to mean by the Jews, "a body has thou prepared for me." Some think the Hebrew idiom referred to the piercing of the ears of a perpetual slave, but this is unsure. Different words are used for piercing in Exodus 21:6.

It is also possible that the Septuagint preserves the correct reading, and our Hebrew text has suffered some in transmission since about 200 B.C. Other instances of this have been noted above, supported by evidence from the Dead Sea Scrolls. In this case, the Hebrew text lying back of the Septuagint would differ from our regular text only in two words. Some of the other early versions support the Septuagint in part.

At all events, it seems justifiable to accept the Hebrews 10:5 reading as giving the true sense of the original, and in that case the psalm speaks of the entrance into the world for a special purpose of one who had prepared for him a body for sacrifice. It is this one who cries to God in Psalm 40 for His mercy and preserving truth. If this be granted, the psalm does not speak of David or any other mortal whose body is of no more avail as a sacrifice than was the blood of bulls and goats slain on Jewish altars. Only Christ, who came to fulfil the Levitical types, can be the subject of this psalm. Only He could work redemption.

The mention of iniquities in verse 12, however, has been a problem to many. Some have referred this word to our sins imputed to Christ.

However, if we observe the poetic parallel, "innumerable evils have compassed me about," and also the declaration of righteousness in the context, we shall see that the force of verse 12 is to seek relief from enemies. The sense required is, "troubles have encompassed me, my sufferings have taken hold upon me." Now in the Hebrew, the word "iniquity" is capable of just this double meaning. The word is translated "punishments" or the like in Genesis 4:13, I Samuel 28:10, Psalm 69:27 (RSV) and several other places. If this suggestion be adopted, the psalm concerns the Messiah. David suffered for his own sins. This one came to offer His body a perfect sacrifice. Attacked by sinners and acquainted with grief, He yet made God His trust and fulfilled to the utmost His perfect will for man's redemption.

Psalms 41, 69, and 109 can be considered together. They arise out of deep trouble and affirm an equally great trust in the Lord. The enemies who surround the sufferer are like those who attacked Christ on several occasions. At the same time, Psalms 41 and 69 include clear confessions of sin on the part of the subject. All three are prayers of David. Psalms 69 and 109 are also classed among the Imprecatory Psalms.

A clue to the interpretation of these psalms is found in Psalm 69:25, "Let their habitation be desolate, and let none dwell in their tents." Peter in Acts 1:20 quotes these words and applies them to Judas Iscariot. But Peter changes the quotation to the singular so as to make the personal application to Judas, "Let his habitation be desolate and let no man dwell therein." Apparently Peter was taking the general description of the enemies of the righteous sufferer and applying it to Judas, the enemy of Christ.

Other statements of this psalm are similarly applied. Christ Himself quotes the fourth verse, "they hated me without a cause," as fulfilled in His own situation. This same thought is found in Psalm 109:3 and Psalm 35:7. It is the recurrent affliction of the righteous, most poignantly exhibited in Christ. Similarly, verse 9 is applied in John 2:17 to Christ's first cleansing of the temple which was indeed a notable example of Christ's zeal for His Father's house, but was in a measure applicable to many prophets and reformers in Israel. The last half of this verse is quoted of Christ by Paul in Romans 15:3, "The reproaches of them that reproached thee fell on me." Christ is, of course, the world's greatest example of suffering for righteousness' sake. In this, however, Paul refers to Christ as an example for us that we also might bear the infirmities of others. Verse 22 which mentions the sufferer's gall for food, and vinegar for drink, finds a parallel in the experience of Christ on the cross. Yet none of the Gospels, in reporting the vinegar given to Christ, refers to this psalm. Verses 23 and 24 are cited by Paul in Romans 11:9, 10 and applied to impenitent Israel of his day. The application is certainly broader than to Judas and the enemies of Christ at the crucifixion. Apparently, Paul finds in Psalm 69 a reference to the enemies of the righteous in general. The next verse but one is the verse applied by Peter to Judas after changing the pronouns to the singular, as we mentioned above. These citations are all that the New Testament has from Psalm 69. It would seem that they confirm the view that Psalm 69 is a general psalm depicting the unjust sufferings of the righteous. Christ is, of course, the best historical example of this, but there is nothing in the psalm that cannot be applied to other righteous sufferers, and verse 5 precludes its direct application to Christ. It is typico-messianic.

Psalm 41 is another of this nature. A prayer of David out of deep distress, it concerns a righteous man in trouble who, after verse 3, is spoken of in the first person. He is referred to in verses 3 and 8 as being sick. He confesses in verse 4 that he has sinned against the Lord. There is nothing in all this that could not apply to David or any child of God in trouble. The confession of sin cannot apply to Christ. It seems most logical, therefore, to consider verse 9 as cited by Christ in John 13:18 as a general complaint specifically applied by Christ to Himself because it emphasized in a peculiar way the indignity He suffered at the hands of the traitor. This psalm speaks of treachery, and Judas was the traitor par excellence.

The main difficulty with this view is that it appears to question the force of words like those of Jesus in John 13:18. These words are to be interpreted, however, according to their usage. The New Testament evidently cites as "having been fulfilled," not only direct messianic predictions such as we have noted, but also those typical messianic passages which refer in general to a righteous sufferer and are quite properly applied to Christ. It may be noted that this usage is more frequent in Matthew and John. There may be a hint here of an Aramaic usage. Still, the "Letter of the Churches of Vienne and Lyons," written about A.D. 170, shows this usage ("And thus was fulfilled that which was spoken by our Lord," quoting John 16:2). The word *fulfilled* does not mean that the Lord predicted this particular event, but that this and other similar events agree with Christ's words.

The Greek word "fulfilled" is used, after all, in a variety of senses in the New Testament. It is used of filling up a space or object, of the heart being filled with grief or joy, of God's commands being obeyed, of the arrival of a determined time, of the completion of a speech, and of Scripture being fulfilled. This last usage is illustrated by several passages which speak of true fulfilments of predictions, but also by such a verse as James 2:23, "And the scripture was fulfilled which saith, Abraham believed God and it was imputed unto him for righteousness." This does not speak of a prediction at all, but only brings out the meaning of an Old Testament passage. This, apparently, is all that is intended in several New Testament citations. The incident of Judas' betrayal illustrates and agrees with the portrayal in the Psalms of how righteous people suffer by treachery. But this is not to deny that the prophets specifically predicted Christ in numerous Old Testament passages, which are cited in the New Testament as specifically fulfilled in Him. This is not always expressed, however, by the introductory formula, "that it might be fulfilled."

One more Psalm of Suffering remains, number 109. This is sometimes not classed as a Messianic Psalm, but apparently it should be, for verse 8 is clearly applied in Acts 1:20 to Judas. The psalm as a whole is classed as an Imprecatory Psalm because of the intense curses pronounced upon the sufferer's enemy. Commentators have noted that the psalm also singles out one from among his enemies for especial rebuke (vv. 6–19), and that there seems to be a progress in imprecations from Psalm 35 and 69 to 109, this latter being sharpest of all. Also, there is nothing in this psalm that cannot apply directly to Christ. Accused without a cause, He is rewarded by hatred for His love. His extreme affliction is from the Lord Who will vindicate Him at last. The psalm could be directly messianic; and yet, perhaps, we need not be dogmatic, for there is nothing in the psalm that could not also apply to David. Since the suffering is expressed in general terms, it could, on the other hand, be typico-messianic.

There remain for our consideration three Messianic Psalms of Praise, 8, 68, and 118, and one Psalm of Trust, 102. Here, again, the Messianic Psalms are somewhat similar in subject matter to other Psalms of Praise and Trust. Once more, we may say that the psalmist in his exercises of holy praise was moved by the Spirit of God to advance to the summit of all praise and address the Messiah to come. Psalms 8 and 68 are by David; 118 has no title.

It is a question, however, to what extent Psalm 8 refers to Christ. It is a Psalm of Praise to God for His work of creation. In such vastness, man appears to be inconsequential, but God made man as the head of creation and gave him a dominion over nature which he is still exploiting. It is obvious today that man's position as a thinking, moral, religious being marks him off from all the rest of creation as made in God's image, as little lower than the angels, crowned with glory and honor. We should not be classed with mere animals, as unbelieving biologists are prone to do. Our bodies are indeed of the creature world, but as children of God, we are citizens of an eternal sphere. The question is, to what extent does verse 5 speak of Christ? Ephesians 1:22 refers to Christ as having all things under Him. First Corinthians 15:27 uses similar language, but, from the context, is probably referring to the conquest of His enemies by Christ as described in Psalm 110. The essential passage for us is Hebrews 2:6–8, which refers to Christ's dominion. The meaning of the Hebrews passage, however, is not altogether clear. Some have held that it refers directly to Christ. More likely the argument is that God made man to have dominion; because of the Fall, man lost that dominion; but we see Jesus Who became man that He might suffer, exalted in His resurrection to dominion and glory. According to this interpretation, the psalm celebrates God's works of creation including the creation of man, and Jesus is the fulfilment of the psalm in that He became man and restores man to that estate from whence he fell. The psalm, then, is not directly messianic. The second verse, quoted by Christ in Matthew 21:16, also does not directly predict His triumphal entry, but was quoted to illustrate how God often accepts and arranges for praise from the humble of the earth more than from the great and noble.

In Psalm 68 we have another general Psalm of Praise. It begins with reference to God's works for Israel in olden time. Verse 1 is quoted from Numbers 10:35. Verses 7 and 8 refer to God's going before the people of Israel in the wilderness and are quoted from Judges 5:4, 5, which mentions the same event. Verses 11–18 refer poetically either to some actual victory of God's people, or figuratively to God's power and spiritual conquests. The picture is of God going out before His armies. Verse 11a is better translated in the Revised Standard Version, "The Lord gave the command." The last part is better understood of the heralds who pass on the command. The word is used only here and in Isaiah 40:9, where it probably refers to the herald of Zion, the herald of Jerusalem. The general picture is of the armies of the Lord in victory.

Psalm 68:18 is quoted in Ephesians 4:8, where Paul proceeds to interpret the verse and apply it to Christ. Some have taken Ephesians 4:8 to refer to an imagined descent of Christ to Hades (or even to purgatory). Rather, Paul is arguing that the ascent of God after victory which is celebrated in the psalm, is truly applicable to Christ's ascent before Pentecost when He gave the gift of the Spirit. (In Psalm 68:18, the gifts are poetically represented as the spoils of war which a conquering hero distributes upon his return home.) The One who ascended, Paul says, should be understood as the One Who descended, that is, descended from heaven to earth (not to the lower parts of the earth as KJV and RSV). This one was Christ Who has triumphed gloriously and given the Church the gifts of the ministry of the Spirit. He had come down from heaven and returned on high in victory. Paul, apparently, is applying the general picture of the triumph of God in the psalm, specifically to the work of Christ. The psalm is not directly messianic, but it is instructive to note how readily the New Testament authors applied to Christ what the Old Testament says of God Himself. The New Testament is imbued with the doctrine that Jesus was in every way on a par with the Lord God of the Old Testament. From this angle, we could say that every psalm was messianic, for every one speaks of our trust in and praise for God.

Here we may consider Psalm 102, a Psalm of Trust, which is another example of thus applying Old Testament verses to Christ. As "A Prayer of the Afflicted," it contrasts the brevity of the sufferer's life with the eternity of God and expresses a deep trust in God Who will yet favor Zion and rescue the oppressed. It ends with praise to the God of creation Who has done and will do all these wonders, Who is, indeed, eternal. These verses are quoted in Hebrews 1:10–12 and are applied to Christ. Hebrews inserts the word "Lord" in verse 10 to make clear the application, but shows no hesitancy in applying to Christ what is said of God in the Old Testament. The psalm is not, however, directly messianic.

Our last Messianic Psalm is 118. This apparently was an early psalm celebrating a royal procession to the temple accompanied by worshippers joining in responsive singing. Surely this was the interpretation of the Jews of Jesus' day. The crowds who followed Him at His triumphal entry said, "Blessed is the king of Israel that cometh in the name of the Lord" (Jn. 12:13). Israel's king was always to be of the Davidic house, so the crowd sang, "Hosanna to the son of David; Blessed is he that cometh in the name of the Lord" (Mt.

21:9). That Christ understood this psalm to be a royal recessional is seen from two facts. First, He declared that Israel would suffer until they accepted Himself as the fulfilment of this psalm—their messianic King (Mt. 23:39 and parallels). Secondly, on His triumphal entry, He deliberately carried out the ritual of a royal procession, entering Jerusalem on an unbroken colt, riding through the eastern gate, proceeding directly to the temple in line with ancient custom and prophecy (I Kings 1:28–40; Zech. 9:9). The stone which the builders refused was David and, as the antitype, Christ Himself.

A final remark is in order on verse 25. The Hebrew verb "to save" is *yasha'*, the root of the name *"Jesus."* The imperative, *save now I beseech thee*, is *Hoshi'anna'*, which is reproduced in the New Testament as "Hosanna." The multitudes at Christ's triumphal entry cried to Him, "Hosanna to the son of David" (Mt. 21:9, 15). The Pharisees were doubly scandalized by this, because first, the cry denominated Jesus as the messianic King, and secondly, it ascribed to Him the Hosanna, the cry that Psalm 118:25 addresses to Jehovah Himself! No wonder they were "sore displeased," and said, "Master, rebuke thy disciples" (Lk. 19:39). Jesus, however, accepted this divine homage from the crowd, declaring that if they refused it, nature itself would own Him as its Lord and God (Lk. 19:40). With such a climax in its reference to Christ and so gloriously used by Christ before He suffered, this psalm is indeed a fitting conclusion to the study of the subject. It is the last specifically Messianic Psalm.

Some attention should perhaps be given to a new approach to the interpretation of the Messianic Psalms being fostered today, especially by some Swedish and Norwegian scholars. Studies in Babylonian religion have shown that in Mesopotamia much was made of the New Year festival in the fall. The Jews used the Babylonian calendar just as we use the Roman system, and to this day the Jewish New Year is celebrated in September. At the Babylonian New Year festival, the ceremonies concerned the king especially. The king was supposed to represent his land before the gods, and each year he had to bear punishment for the faults of the nation during the preceding time. He took off his crown, was slapped in the face by the priest and wore garments of mourning. In some cases, at least, a substitute king was crowned for a day and then killed in place of the regular king. The regular king was then crowned again amid general rejoicing and expectations of good luck for the year. The theory of the Swedish school is that this is what we find in Israel. The Royal Psalms are said to celebrate the annual coronation. The songs of suffering, such as Psalm 22 or Isaiah 53, are said to celebrate the humiliation of the king who vicariously bears the sins of the people. These passages were written, they say, only for the annual celebration, but are appropriately applied to Christ by the Church.

We must insist that the Swedish view rests on very little evidence and contradicts what we know of Israelite religion. There is admittedly no evidence whatever for the celebration of the Babylonian New Year festival in Israel. In the fall, the first day of the seventh month, Tishri, there was a holy convocation marked by a Sabbath and the blowing of trumpets and special offerings. It was followed by the Day of Atonement on the tenth of the month. At this time, the sins of the people were dealt with by the priest, not the king, and through the sin offering goat and scapegoat, not the death of a substitute king (Lev. 16; 23:26–44). Nor is there any hint elsewhere in the records of the Old Testament that the king was humbled or left his throne or was re-crowned, or bore the sins of the people.

On the contrary, the religion of Israel was as different from that of Babylon as is day from night. Babylon had a degraded polytheism; Israel, an ethical monotheism. In early Mesopotamia, the people had the concept that the gods in assembly or by their leaders each year decreed the fate of the world and men (and gods) for the ensuing year; hence the importance of the New Year festival. In Israel, however, they understood that the Lord God ruled the world alone and brought to pass His perfect will from eternity unto eternity. It is perverse to compare the two New Years when we know that the deities worshipped were so different.

Finally, we must briefly re-emphasize that the Messianic Psalms, fairly interpreted, do not fit a Babylonian New Year festival. If Psalm 16 predicts a resurrection, it fits no substitute king any better than David! Psalm 40 tells of one entering the world to present his body a sacrifice. No mortal ever entered this world for such a purpose as Christ did in fulfilment of Psalm 40. Also, neither Psalms 22, 16, 40, or Isaiah 53 say anything about the subject being a king.

It is easy to affirm that Psalm 45:6, "Thy throne, O God, is forever and ever," could well have been addressed to a deified king in Jerusalem. It is harder to prove it. True, it is gratifying to have our translation of this verse supported by this recent study, but who may suppose that the prophets of Israel deified their kings? David himself is not spared the detailed recital of his sins. Nowhere in the whole Old

Testament is any man ever deified. How then can we lightly accept Psalm 45:6 as an address to the reigning king as divine?

Psalm 110 is no easier for their view. The subject there addressed is not David, but David's Lord. And it is not true that the kings of Israel were priest-kings in any sense, as Psalm 110:4 calls the Messiah. It is alleged that Solomon and David offered sacrifices before the Lord. Indeed, they did, but all the congregation of Israel did so too. The point is that David and Solomon *gave* the sacrifices; the priests did the ministering. There is one verse that calls David's sons priests (II Sam. 8:18) and naturally the Swedish school cites it with considerable confidence. Comparison with the parallel history in I Chronicles 18:17 shows only that they were chief men. The king James Version translates II Samuel 8:18 that way, also departing from the Hebrew. The Hebrew text literally reads, "and Benaiah the son of Jehoiada and the Cherethites and the Pelethites and the sons of David were priests." This reading would raise many problems. It is better to do as the King James Version has done and follow the reading of the Septuagint, all the ancient versions and the parallel passage in Chronicles. After all, both Saul and King Uzziah were severely judged for acting as priests. It is going in the face of the facts to say that the men of the Davidic dynasty were priest-kings in Jerusalem. Psalm 110 can only refer to Christ. The Swedish school has as little basis for its denial of the predictive character of these psalms as did older critical interpreters.

The Psalms were given by the Spirit of God Who knows the end from the beginning. It was the taunt of Isaiah to the heathen idols of his day that they could not foretell the future whereas the Lord both knew the future and actually caused His purposes to come to pass (Is. 41:22–25). If God has spoken in very fact in the Bible, then supernatural prophetic prediction is not only possible, but expected. It cannot be ruled out for one who believes in the words of Christ and His apostles.

But in the Psalms, there is much more than prediction, as we have seen. The Spirit also searches all things—the depths of the human heart and the breadth of God's ways and counsels. Earnest study of the inspired songs of Zion will lead us into a deeper understanding of God and His glory. It will also evoke in our hearts a more active communion with the Lord of hosts and a sweeter experience of dwelling under the shadow of His wings. "O taste and see that the Lord is good: blessed is the man that trusteth in him (KJV, 34:8)."

Proverbs

KENNETH A. KITCHEN

THE GENERAL TITLE (1:1, 2) names Solomon as author of the major portion of Proverbs. Two-thirds of the book are directly ascribed to him (10:1, and 25:1 *via* Hezekiah's copyists). The first group of "words of the wise [men]" (22:17—24:22) he has incorporated with his own ("my knowledge," 22:17). Perhaps he also added the second group (24:23–34), or this was added in Hezekiah's day along with Solomon's second series of proverbs (chs. 25—29).

Literary Backgrounds. The great fourteen fold discourse (1:8—9:18) on the worth of wisdom and the evils attending its absence or neglect—culminating in the portrait of, and appeal by, Wisdom—contains no direct mention of its author. However, it would be entirely fitting that Solomon should open the book with elevated discourse before the proverbs proper. The ancient Near East supplied a venerable precedent for this, as witness the Egyptian wisdom-books like those of Ptahhotep (2400/2000 B.C.), or Amenemope (?1100/800 B.C.), which preface their counsels with an introduction. Thus, there is no internal reason why Proverbs 1—29 should not have become one work in Hezekiah's reign. The dates of Agur, Lemuel, and of the author of the Good Wife poem (chs. 30, 31) are quite unknown. They too could have been added by Hezekiah's men to round off the book, although they may be later. All of Proverbs *could* have assumed its present form as early as nearly 700 B.C., containing much Solomonic from the tenth century B.C. External data from the ancient Orient allow and support a tenth to seventh century date.

Proverbial literature in written form is very ancient. Between 2700 and 2400 B.C. is the traditional date of the "Teachings" of Imhotep, (Kairos?) to Kagemni, Hardidief and Ptahhotep, with some surviving manuscripts going back to about 2000 B.C. Those of Aniy and Amenemope may date from 1200–1100 B.C., or the latter, perhaps, nearer 800 B.C. From Mesopotamia, Sumerian proverbs exist in copies of roughly 1800 B.C. but were older, and Babylonian collections occur from 1800/1600 B.C. onward. In the fourteenth century B.C., Canaanite princes even quote odd proverbs in their letters to the Pharaohs (*El Amarna Letters*).

The antiquity of Proverbs in style and content is now supported by phraseology and poetic patterns in North-Canaanitic (Ugaritic) literature of the fourteenth century B.C. Occasional Aramaisms hint at an early—not late—date, as they occur in Semitic words in Egyptian as early as the fifteenth century B.C. Personification (as of Wisdom in chs. 1, 8, 9) is ancient in the Near East, in Egyptian, Mesopotamian, and Hittite sources, and comparison with later Greek sources is thus pointless.

The question of dependence of Proverbs 22:17—24:22 upon the

Egyptian Wisdom of Amenemope has been much debated. Solomon's use of Words of the Wise in this passage is datable, at latest, to about 930 B.C. If Amenemope wrote and was known, say, before 950 B.C., he could be among the Wise to whom Solomon alludes. But if Amenemope's work appeared after 930 B.C., then Amenemope must have drawn either on Proverbs or, even likelier, from the same range of current sayings of sages from which Solomon had earlier drawn lessons. In any case, the total disagreement in order of topics and clear theological differences between Proverbs 22:1—24:22 and Amenemope preclude direct copying either way. Finally, the word *shlshm* (KJV, "excellent things"; RSV, "thirty [sayings]") in 22:20 is often considered to be inspired by the "thirty chapters" of Amenemope; however, the term can as easily be an ellipsis for *(ethmol)-shilshom,* "already." In any case, 22:17—24:22 contain not thirty but thirty-three admonitions.

This rich back cloth of the antiquity of proverbial writings as a class, and of language and idioms, serves to emphasize the fitness of Solomon's being divinely impelled to reach the hearts of men by this means.

Proverbs records the distilled wisdom of centuries verified in personal experience. The Words of the Wise perhaps were a variety of sayings current in Israel and beyond in the tenth century B.C., rather than a fixed collection. In Proverbs, wisdom is the attitude of heart which puts God first as man's rightful guide and master. The centrality of God as a person and the theology stemming from this are taken for granted. To the stipulations of the Law and the clarion-call of the Prophets, Proverbs adds principles for right living and observations on life as lived with and without godly wisdom in many spheres.

The wise (who put God first), the upright (who live by God's standards), and the righteous (right with God and with their fellows) are equated; whether faithful Jew then or real Christian now, their conscious trust in and obedience to God personally issues in just and loving conduct toward others. The Book of Proverbs does not hesitate to link good and bad with reward and penalty, because God embodies in Himself both love and justice; He loves to give good gifts of all kinds to His people, and must restrain and obviate evil.

Much can be learned by testing personal conduct against the positive and negative standards and warnings in Proverbs. Christ counseled His followers to be "wise as serpents and harmless as doves" (Mt. 10:16). "Wisdom from above" (Jas. 3:17) finds practical application in the exhortations on conduct which stud the New Testament letters and to which Proverbs is the Old Testament pendant. This is so both in the fourteen fold discourse and in the vast series of pithy instructions and observations which fill most of the book like a chestful of gems.

I. The Title and Prologue (1:1–7)

Once Solomon, Israel's wise king (I Kings 4:29–34), has been named as main author (1:1), the purpose of the book is unfolded: namely, to impart instruction in real wisdom and in upright conduct (vv. 2, 3). The basis for this true wisdom is set forth: men must start with God; fools they be if they neglect or reject this essential foundation (v. 7). All may profit here—the youthful and the simple may learn much, and the already wise may advance yet further (vv. 4–6).

II. Fourteen Words of Exhortation (1:8—9:18)

1. Wealth by Violence and Wisdom's Warning (1:8–33)

After emphasizing the need to heed parental words, the sage denounces those who seek self-enrichment by the downfall of others and by leading men astray (1:8–16). They but guarantee their own eventual fall (vv. 17–19; cf. Mt. 16:26). Wisdom personified then utters her call and warning. She appears virtually as a prophet declaring her message in the prominent and public places in a city— in streets and open squares (v. 20), from the parapets of the city walls and at the city gate, the place of counsel and business (v. 21, RSV). She warns all who disdain, reject or scorn the offered good counsel that, when their folly catches up with them, it will then be too late to turn to her (vv. 22–30; cf. Is. 55:6; Mt. 23:37, 38), for it is none other than God that they spurn (v. 29), to their great loss (vv. 30–32). But since this sad prospect is not Wisdom's preferred plan for men, she earnestly beseeches their attention here and now (vv. 23, 33) to higher and better ways (cf. Ezek. 33:11; II Cor. 6:2).

2. *Treasure the Wisdom from God to Discern Good and Evil Ways (2:1–22)*

To tread resolutely the path of true wisdom brings one to its source (2:1–5), God Who bestows it. God blesses the God-fearing with protection, with enlightenment that brings joy (vv. 6–10), with deliverance from the crooked and their ways and from the lustful, with strength to lead a wholesome life with a confidence denied to the wrongdoer (vv. 11–20). A promise to the righteous and a warning to the wicked follow (vv. 21, 22).

3. *God Honors Those Who Honor Him (3:1–10)*

As God is the fountainhead of all real wisdom, it is man's privilege and duty to draw upon the limitless divine wisdom as opposed to his own poor store (3:5–7; cf. Jas. 1:5), and to manifest his faith by obeying God's practical commands—tithes to the temple then (cf. Mal. 3:10); nowadays, active support for the needs of the Gospel (II Cor. 9). God is truly no man's debtor (vv. 2, 4, 6, 8, 10).

4. *A Discipline Precious Beyond Riches (3:11–20)*

Sometimes God's discipline in the circumstances of life seems hard to bear, but He is acting for good in accordance with His peerless wisdom (3:11, 12; cf. Heb. 12:1–11), a wisdom which, because it carries a rich reward, is worthy to be sought at all costs. The sage stimulates faith by declaring God's supreme power as creator and sustainer of the universe—much as God does for Job (chs. 38—41).

5. *The Sure Way and Loving One's Neighbor (3:21–35)*

Practice of heavenly wisdom that works, based on a real trust in the Lord, first brings assurance of divine control of one's personal situation in daytime activity and the hours of rest alike. Second, it directs one to obey the second great commandment (Lev. 19:18; Mt. 22:39) to help, not hinder, one's fellows and shun evildoers' habits. God's grace is upon the humble, His scorn upon the scornful (3:34; Jas. 4:6; I Pet. 5:5).

6. Wisdom as a Family Treasure (4:1–9)

The sage again stresses the great worth of wisdom. He himself has been taught to treasure it in earlier days by his own father; he is thus teaching his children from personal experience.

7. Wisdom and the Two Ways (4:10–19)

The sage has both taught and guided his son along right ways; this godly wisdom affords a path through life's problems, and obstacles can thereby be overcome (4:11–13). Arrant wrongdoing must be entirely avoided. In glaring contrast to the darkness to which the godless condemn themselves, the way for the righteous is like the dawning day. At first the outlook may seem shadowed and pale gray, but it becomes clearer and sharper as one grows in the attainment and practice of real wisdom (vv. 18, 19; cf. Eph. 4:13). The personal example of the godly is—or should be—a beacon to the world around.

8. The Need for Right Purpose and Worthy Conduct (4:20–27)

God-centered wisdom should condition one's aims and one's means of attaining them. The inmost desires of the will require scrutiny, for they govern one's aims and influence one's behavior (4:23). One should be clear about one's aims and pursue them with forethought and persistence, resolutely refusing to be sidetracked into deceit and wrongdoing (vv. 24–27).

9. Beware of Lust (5:1–6)

Wise precepts are a warning against, and so a sobering antidote for, seductive invitations to bodily lust. What at first may seem pleasure will bring forth its real fruit—utter misery and ultimately the shades of death.

10. Lust Versus Love (5:7–23)

Enslavement to lust and to those who exploit its victims ruins a life. Better far to learn discipline and faithfulness to one true partner with naught to fear, for God sees all.

11. *Beware of Surety, Idleness and Deceit (6:1–19)*

Surety in the Old Testament involves being responsible for some-one, usually on behalf of a third party, for their safety (as in Gen. 43:9; 44:32) or financially (as here, and 11:15; 17:18; 20:16; 27:13). To go surety with someone of whose credentials one knows nothing at all is as rash and foolish as giving a blank check to a total stranger would be today. The sage has no patience with laziness; poverty is all that laziness can justly expect. He points to the busy, orderly ant as an example of productive activity. Deceit, innuendo, and mis-chief-making bring their own reward. For arrogance, lying, murder, plotting of and collusion in evil schemes, perjury and mischief-making, God has no place.

12. *Crass Folly of Adultery (6:20–35)*

Harlotry is vile, but to commit adultery is here clearly labeled as not only utterly wrong, but also as senseless, self-destructive, and disgraceful. It inevitably brings punishment and forever turns the innocent party into a bitter enemy (6:34, 35).

13. *A Parable on Chastity (7:1–27)*

The sage again commends close knowledge of and obedience to the dictates of godly wisdom as an antidote for the blandishments of illicit sex (7:1-5; cf. 5:1-6). This lesson he enforces with the parable of the foolish youth who falls for the wily seductions of the honey-tongued harlot and thereby sets himself squarely on the path to death.

14. *Wisdom Portrayed (8:1—9:18)*

Wisdom's First Address. Here, as in 1:20–33, the sage allows Wisdom again to speak forth personally to men. Again in prominent places—on high places by the road, amid paths, by the entry of the city gates—she addresses men in the name of truth and right, and offers wisdom beyond price (8:1–11). Wisdom stands with the Lord in repudiating all kinds of wrongdoing, but offers rich reward, be-yond the worth of money, to those who so seek. She is the power of rulers; she loves them that love her; and whoever seeks her faithfully will find her (vv. 12, 17, 21; cf. Mt. 7:7, 8). Her pedigree is the finest possible; Wisdom was associated with God before anything else existed, and participated in His work of creation at the beginning of time (vv. 22–31; cf. Gen. 1; Ps. 33:6, 9; Prov. 3:19). Against this impressive testimony she repeats her call—he who finds her, finds life; he who misses her (RSV), ill-serves himself; and he who hates her, loves death.

This graphic picture of the Wisdom of God found its counterpart and fulfilment centuries later in the person of Christ, "the wisdom of God" (I Cor. 1:24). He too proclaims truth (8:7–9; cf. Jn. 1:17; 8:14–19, 31, 32, 45–47; 10; Heb. 2:3). He also enjoins one to seek first God's kingdom before comfort or wealth (vv. 10, 11, 19; 9:10; cf. Mt. 6:33), yet fulfils all one's need (vv. 18, 20, 21; cf. Rom. 8:32; Phil. 4:19). He, as the Word, the *Logos*, is likewise pre-existent (vv. 22–26; cf. Jn. 8:58; 17:24; Eph. 1:4) and associated vitally with the creation (vv. 27–31; cf. Jn. 1:1–3, 10; I Cor. 8:6; Col. 1:16; Heb. 1:2). Finally, as divine Wisdom is shown as the life of men (v. 35), so in fact is Christ (Jn. 1:4; 8:12; 10:10; 11:25; 14:6, and so forth). He is wisdom and the source of real life (I Cor. 1:30), and through none other may eternal life be received (Acts 4:12; I Cor. 3:11).

Wisdom's Second Address. This time Wisdom is a hostess summoning her guests to a feast. When reproof is given to scoffers and to the godly wise, their responses are as different as their respective natures; for "the fear of the Lord is the beginning of wisdom, and the knowledge of the holy [one] is understanding" (9:10). This great and familiar statement underlies the whole attitude to wisdom throughout Proverbs. Again, Wisdom proclaims her high value, and closes with the warning of Folly pictured as a harlot or false prophet inciting men to the knowledge of evil—and to death (vv. 11–18).

III. The Proverbs of Solomon and Words of the Wise (10:1—29:27)

The topics in chapters 10 through 29 are grouped as follows:

God, Man, Wisdom

God and Religion
Wisdom, Instruction and Reproof
Integrity and Perversity
Two Classes, Ways and Ends

Personal Conduct

Diligence and Laziness
Speech, Discretion and Silence
Pride and Humility
The Emotions

Society

Family Life
Kings and Rulers
The Community and One's Fellows
Money Wealth and Poverty.

1. *God, Man, Wisdom*

God and Religion. God is not indifferent to the attitudes His creatures adopt toward Him. Man's proper attitude, for which he was designed, is one of trust in, obedience to, and cooperation with, his Maker, Sustainer and Redeemer. The man who spurns God is ultimately a failure and a contradiction. Hence the terms in which Proverbs states God's attitudes to the "righteous, wise, godly" and the "wicked, foolish, godless" (cf. 14:2); the tension of godly and godless is not glossed over (cf. 28:4).

Thus, the Lord looks after His people's hunger and is their safe stronghold; He loves the earnest seeker after righteousness and delights in pure speech. The godless find lack and trouble; their ways and thoughts He detests (10:3, 29; 11:20; 15:9, 26; 18:10; 29:25). He is omniscient of world and spirit alike (15:3, 11; 22:12), while we know only in part (20:24). As well as being "the beginning of wisdom" (9:10), the fear of the Lord is also "instruction in wisdom" (15:33), averts evil and envy (16:6; 23:17, 18; 24:21, 22) and leads to a life of security and blessing (10:27; 14:26, 27; 19:23; cf. Jn. 10:10; 22:4; Mt. 6:33; 28:14). Even so, men blame God for things when the fault lies in themselves (19:3).

In religion, God heeds and delights in the prayers of faith, but detests the hypocritical "religion" of the wicked (15:8, 29; 21:27). Heeding the Word and trusting personally its Lord assures one's true welfare (16:20); failure to heed is folly (28:9; 29:18). Wrongdoing should be confessed, not concealed, and actively repented. Forgiveness is then assured (28:13), for none are sinless (20:9, 11). Faith must issue in right living (21:3) and rash vows are to be avoided (20:25).

God as utter sovereign has the last word and directs His people's ways (16:1, 2, 4, 9, 33; 17:3; 19:21). Because He grants unmixed blessings (10:22) and real peace (16:7), one should always submit hopes and plans to Him Who leads aright (16:3; cf. 3:5–8). In society God desires justice (12:2, 22; 17:15; 28:5; 29:26) including practical honesty in giving right value and weight in business (11:1; 16:11; 20:10, 23; 23:10, 1). The Almighty Lord and Creator (20:12; 21:30) identifies Himself with the cause of the poor and down-trodden, loving their helpers and judging their oppressors (14:31; 17:5; 19:17; 22:22, 23).

Wealth should not be over-valued or despised. While it is as nothing compared to the fear of the Lord and often coupled with sorrow (15:16), wealth can also be a gift from God (28:25), a trust to be used for others' benefit. Before God, all are but men alike, regardless of external possessions (22:2; 29:13; cf. Mt. 5:45). He sways the hearts even of kings and rulers (21:1) and alone determines who shall have the victory (21:31). Rank arrogance and selfish pride incur His disapproval (15:25; 16:5; 24:17, 18). The Lord is a God of judgment, penetrating the conscience (20:27) and weighing men's hearts (21:2), requiting the evildoer (cf. 22:14) and assessing all men's deeds (24:12).

Wisdom, Instruction and Reproof. Real wisdom, which is doing God's will in a manner consistent with that will, is beyond compare and to be sought at all costs (16:16; 20:15), a source of life (16:22), not bought like so much goods (17:16). Such wisdom should be the goal of a discerning person (17:24), and seeking it is to seek one's own best welfare (19:8). True wisdom applied helps one to be alert against dangers (25:12) and saves one from troubles (28:26). Through the Words of the Wise, Solomon thus appeals to men "to buy truth, wisdom . . . and sell it not" (23:23) in the sense of making a real effort to learn and apply wisdom, and to hold it fast. This wisdom strengthens and enriches (24:3, 4) and is sweet to responsive souls (24:13, 14).

Instruction in the right way and reproof to restore one to that way when straying are to be heeded and treasured; they are fools who ignore sound teaching and reject well-meant rebuke (10:17; 12:1; 13:1; 15:5; 18:15; 19:2, 16, 20, 27). Discernment must be applied to what one learns in order to sift knowledge from folly (14:18). Because fools be self-opinionated (18:2), and scoffers disdain reproof and wise counsel (15:12), they seal their own fate (15:10; 21:16).

Mistakes can be made valuable, overruled, if one is ready to learn what went wrong and willing to be put on the right road. Hence the emphasis in Proverbs on friendly reproof and constructive rebuke. Reproof, like instruction, is to be profited by, not neglected (13:18; 17:10; 25:12). Open rebuke can help directly (27:5); it is severity for kindness' sake (cf. 20:30); such honesty earns a gratitude denied to empty flattery (28:23). Reproof thus benefits the godly wise directly, while to rebuke the scornful can help to bring home timely lessons to the unwary (19:25; 21:11). Persistent refusal of needful correction can be costly (29:1), and at times words may not suffice (29:19).

The truly wise thus feed on and give out positive, helpful counsel. They obey the divine will (10:8). They seek out and acquire knowledge, and that readily (10:14; 14:6; 15:14). Unlike the arrogant, the wise gladly hear and weigh advice (12:15), watch the way they are going (14:8, 15; 21:29), and are modest about their God-given knowledge. They are not like those who proclaim themselves the fools they are (12:23); fools and prudence do not mix (14:7). A discerning mind can sound out deeply-buried intentions of the heart (20:5), for in minds rightly attuned, wisdom makes her abode (14:33). The lips of wise men serve to share knowledge (15:7) and help to draw up sound schemes (cf. 15:22); applied wisdom can defeat and overcome hostile brute force (20:18; 21:22; 24:5, 6). Finally, to neglect the benefit of wise admonition is to despise oneself (15:31, 32).

Integrity and Perversity. The worth and deserts of undying faithfulness and shifty selfishness are set forth in no uncertain terms. Integrity's way is basically sound, bringing its own commendation and opening the path to deliverance from difficulty. Perverse dealings will be exposed, are despised and bring their penalty (10:9; 12:8; 13:15; 14:22; 28:18). Those who follow after and practice good shall reap it, sometimes in high places (12:20; 21:21; 22:11). He who serves faithfully also gives joy, but the untrustworthy servant breeds trouble (13:17; 25:13).

The perverse, the shifty, the schemers, faithful only to self at the expense of others, are known by their evil, and ultimately reap a painful reward (16:30; 17:20; 22:5). Such people are unreliable (25:19).

The value of integrity and of those who show it far outshines material wealth and should be treasured accordingly (19:1, 22; 20:6, 7). Rather a good name than morally and spiritually powerless wealth (22:1)! How different is the quiet support of a staunch friend from the outward "show" of one whose love is less than skin-deep (27:6)!

Two Classes, Ways and Ends. Throughout Proverbs, the view is set forth that all men fall into two basic classes only: those trusting God, living by His rule, and those "without God in the world" and marked only too often by disordered lives. Again the terms of reference are "righteous," "wise," "wicked," "foolish," and so forth.

The upright is known by his fruits (11:30), and his path leads upward to life (15:24), and away from evil (16:17). For him to yield to wrong ways is out of place (25:26). An honored old age is a fitting climax to a righteous life-course (16:31). The upright should not be misused (17:26).

The wrongdoer is likewise known by his deeds (10:10; 13:5); the disloyalty of such will be requited (17:11), and evildoing is like an infection (18:3). Evildoers also find their deeds climaxed by the outcome of later consequences (19:29; 20:17; 21:7; 22:8; 26:27). Such people are neither to be envied nor imitated; their ways stand condemned (24:1, 2, 8, 9, 15, 17, 19, 20).

"Fools" come in for special study. The crass obduracy of fools is a marvel (17:12; 27:3, 22), but is rivaled by conceit and the quick tongue. Indeed, 26:1–12 and 29:8–11 are devoted to fools. They are heedless of, or hostile to, wisdom and the wise; they are unreliable, inflame a community, and give way to anger; they are to be answered to reprove their false pride, but not to one's own undoing.

Usually, however, the righteous and wicked are contrasted in clear colors in single antithetic verses. Their renown after death (10:7), their chosen ways in this life (10:23; 13:16; 14:16), their thoughts and intents (12:5), their influence on companions (13:20), powers for good and ill (14:1) particularly in society (12:10, 26; 28:12, 28; 29:2, 16)—in all this they are different as chalk is from cheese.

So too are the implications and consequences of their contrasting habits of daily life, in which kindness and unkindness each bring a response in numberless little ways as well as in big issues. The righteous avoid much of the trouble in which miscreants land themselves (11:5, 6, 8, 17, 18, 27; 12:21; 13:6, 21, 25; 14:22, 32; 17:13; 21:18; 28:10). Fearing God, they need fear naught else and can face all things with a light heart, while the wicked are pursued by conscience and dire consequences (28:1; 29:6). Between the two classes, the two ways of life, there is ever a basic mutual tension which shows up in every aspect of life (21:8; 29:27).

The same contrast attends the end of the godly and godless. To the former, endurance is promised, though its glorious issue was not to be fully revealed until New Testament times. To the latter comes warning of the destruction they risk bringing upon themselves (10:25, 30; 11:19, 21, 31; 12:3, 7, 28; 13:9; 14:11, 12; 16:25; 21:12). In Proverbs, the two classes, ways and ends, are clearly etched; in the New Testament comes confirmation of this "great divide" along with the Key to safe passage from one state to the other.

2. Personal Conduct

Diligence and Laziness. In the view of Proverbs, a productive life is an asset to be commended as the way for the upright, while laziness is a liability to be despised. Diligence in satisfying life's primary physical needs may bring legitimate wealth and prosperity, while laziness, which leads to poverty and want, is a senseless path to drift along (10:4; 12:11, 27; 13:4; 14:23; 20:13; 21:5; 28:19). Slothfulness creates problems which energetic, godfearing men bypass (15:19). In society at large, not only is diligence prudent and sloth shameful (10:5), but the former may lead to promotion and the latter to a life of hard labor utterly repugnant to a lazy nature (12:24).

Hard work and skill bring satisfaction and recognition (12:14; 22:29; 27:18); and one's very needs spur activity (16:26). Hence, Solomon enjoins his hearers to honest zeal in business, agriculture being his example (27:23–27), reinforcing by the Words of the Wise (24:27) the need to put first things first.

Laziness leads not only to want (19:15; 20:4; see parable, 24:30–34), but also to frustration of those desires which laziness prevents satisfying (21:25). To others the sluggard is an irritant (10:26) and brother to the destructive (18:9). Then 26:13–16 follows up the portrait of the fool (26:1–12) with a sketch of the lazy man. In a few quick strokes are etched the lazy man's readiness to excuse himself from activity (22:13; 26:13), his idleness (19:24; 26:14, 15), and his conceit (26:16).

Speech, Discretion and Silence. The gift of speech, like so many other things, is good or bad only in its use or misuse. Thus, Proverbs often contrasts the use of speech by the just and the wicked, the wise and the fool. As their nature is, so they speak; the one takes care in what he says, the other pours forth poisoned words; the one is of enduring worth, the other is a bane that will pass away (10:32; 12:19; 14:3; 15:28). At law, the true and false witness are distinguished by honesty and by lies respectively (12:17; 14:5), the one saves lives and will endure, while the other is a betrayer who mocks justice, yet will not go unpunished (14:25; 19:5, 9, 28; 21:28). In general, the words of the righteous man are positive and helpful, those of the godless, negative and destructive. The former delivers men, and is himself delivered, from trouble, while the latter seeks others' hurt and is himself harmed (12:6, 13). Gracious speech, which soothes and heals, is a veritable "tree of life" (cf. Gen. 3:22; Rev. 22:2), while illspoken words are as sharp as swords, stinging to anger, a veritable heartbreak (12:18; 15:1, 4). The tongue is a potent power for good and ill and their consequences (13:2; 18:21; cf. Mt. 12:37; Jas. 3, especially vv. 5, 8–12).

Words of the righteous are precious as silver (10:20); they feed others with wisdom (10:21, 31; 15:2; 18:4), and relieve a heart burdened with anxiety (12:25). A graciously helpful word at the right moment can be a real tonic and strength (15:23; 16:23, 24; 18:20; 25:11). Praise should come from lips other than one's own (27:2; cf. Rom. 12:3). And the wise counsel against casting pearls before swine (23:9).

However, there is a kind of fair speech that masks inward deceitfulness and hostility, and Proverbs does not hesitate either to declare this of fools or to warn against it (10:6, 11, 18; 26:23–28).

There is also outright evil talk whose nature and fruits are characteristic and unworthy. All too often such talk sparks anger and hurt with the tinder of malicious gossip (16:27, 28; 17:9; 18:8; 25:23; 26:20, 22). False promises and cruel deception also inflict deep wounds (25:14; 26:18, 19). Evil words which encourage evildoing (17:4; 18:6) do not go unrequited (18:7).

Discreetness and even silence are often golden, keeping one from sin (10:19) and gossip (11:13; 20:19), and preserving one from endless and needless trouble (13:3; 17:27; 21:23). Hasty words are crassest folly (29:20), but even a fool may pass as wise by maintaining an august silence (17:28).

Pride and Humility. Pride stands contrasted to humility and unassuming conduct in Proverbs. Arrogant pride is bluntly labeled as a characteristic of "the wicked" and as sin, the proud incurring God's displeasure (15:25; 21:4). The haughty man is plainly called a "scoffer" (21:24).

Pride and humility are contrasted not only as godless and godly by nature, but also in their outcome, soon or late. Pride brings low, leads to disgrace, precedes a fall or even worse, whereas wisdom is with the humble who are open to advice and whose humility may be a prelude to honor (11:2; 13:10; 15:33; 16:18; 18:12; 29:23). To tackle humble circumstances realistically by honest hard work is far better than putting on an outward show which one cannot in fact live up to (12:9), but even so it is better to share an unassuming character with the poor than become one of the arrogant (16:19). The sheer conceit of delivering an opinion on something before one has even obtained the facts brings its own humiliating embarrassment (18:13).

In public life, arrant pushfulness—pride—will invite humiliation, and be outstripped by self-restraint as by humility (25:6, 7; cf. Lk. 14:7–11). Presumption upon the future is discouraged (27:1; cf. Jas. 4:13–15), and true modesty enjoined (27:2; Rom. 12:3; Phil. 2:3).

The Emotions: Love and Hate. Proverbs has little to say about love directly, but what is said is significant. Unlike strife-stirring hatred, "love covers a multitude of sins" (cf. 10:12), a fact reasserted in the New Testament (Jas. 5:20: I Pet. 4:8) and perfectly consummated in Christ's death and resurrection for the eternal good of erring mankind. Material plenty at the price of discord cannot be compared to the joy possible in humble circumstances where love reigns (15:17). The godly are not to envy or fret over wrongdoers and their apparent prosperity: their outlook is a short-term one—and so is their destiny (24:1, 19, 20; cf. Ps. 73). Furthermore, jealousy is a menace more deadly than even outright anger (27:4).

Anger, particularly a quarrelsome temper, crops up often as a subject in Proverbs. The anger to be avoided is the sort that springs from a sharp temper. Thus it is prudent and honorable to ignore insults and not return evil (12:16; 19:11; cf. Mt. 5:39). The threat of a quarrel should be cut short before it is too late (17:14); and quarrelling is to be left to fools (20:3), especially when the dispute has nothing to do with oneself (26:17). Thoughtless anger leads to wrong, hasty acts and strife, whereas slowness to anger and self-restraint show wisdom and spread healing calm (14:17, 29, 30; 15:18). The conquest of unruly self, a greater prize by far than the capture of a city, is contrasted with strife (16:32; 17:1) and foolish self-will (18:1). Strife and sin go together (17:19); at times only a common appeal to a third party can bring peace (18:18; on a lot cast, cf. 16:33). The trigger-tempered quarreler is always getting into trouble (19:19; 26:21; 29:22) and should thus be avoided (22:24, 25). Scoffers and strife are closely linked (22:10).

Joy and Sorrow are deeply personal things (14:10). In this somber world, joy of itself is fragile (14:13), unless its roots go deep (Hab. 3:17, 18, and the joy in Christ, cf. Phil. 4:4). A cheerful, buoyant nature is an antidote for life's storms; sorrow within saps the will to persist and colors life's outlook darkly (15:13, 15; 17:22). Of the way in which men and women have borne up nobly under illness of every kind, many can bear witness; but a soul plunged in despair can be even harder to help (18:14). Superficial comforters, who do not really feel deeply with the sad of heart, merely intensify a person's gloom, edging it with resentment (25:20). But as a welcome sight stimulates, so does good news give joy (15:30). A great source of joy is a wise friend rich in intimate counsel (27:9).

Hopes and Fears. Here again the godly and godless tread opposite paths. The wishes of the righteous, so far as they conform with God's will, are often fulfilled and issue in good and in gladness. The "expectation of the wicked," which tends to be at variance with God's will, often founders and perishes with them (10:24, 28; 11:7, 23; cf. Jas. 4:3). The pressure of anxiety can be relieved by a helping word (12:25). Frustration is wearisome indeed, but the fulfilment of a legitimate desire can be a great encouragement; however, to restrain fools from evil infuriates them (13:12, 19).

But men and women are never satisfied (27:20), and the enjoyment of a desire attained can be ruined by greed and lack of self-control (25:16, 28).

3. Society

Family Life. The heart and natural unit of society is the family. Hence, Proverbs includes comments on wives, sons, the discipline of children, and other aspects of home life.

The worth of a good wife cannot be overstressed; she is the crown of her husband, a mark of God's good favor, and indeed a gift from God Himself (12:4; 18:22; 19:14). But a wife who makes one ashamed or who quarrels is a continuing source of suffering (12:4;

19:13). As for a woman who is forever squabbling—better to live singly and quietly at the top of the house or in the wilderness than with her (21:9, 19; 25:24; 27:15, 16)! The beauty who cannot control her tongue is a living incongruity (11:22), undeserving of honor accorded the gracious (11:16).

That children need real training and discipline for their own good is made clear (22:15) and so applicable to our day that parents could use Proverbs as a handbook. To direct a child upon the right way, even with stern discipline, is an act of practical love. Conversely, to withhold such correction when it is needed, hinders the child and may even set him on the path leading to destruction (13:24; 19:18; 23:13, 14). Good training in childhood is a firm foundation for adult life (22:6) and sound discipline results in wisdom and sterling character in maturity (29:15, 17).

Sons receive repeated comment. Several times the wise son who is a source of joy to his parents is contrasted with the foolish son who is their sorrow and shame (10:1; 15:20; 28:7; 29:3). Foolish sons—those who grieve their parents, bring loss, shame, and reproach on them, and defraud them—get particular mention (17:21, 25; 19:13, 26; 28:24). Such forfeit their patrimony and bring judgment on themselves (17:2; 20:20). Wise sons should be a strength to their fathers (27:11); fathers, the pride of their sons; and grandchildren the crown of the aged (17:6)—lessons reinforced by the exhortations of the Wise (23:22, 24, 25).

In family affairs, the trouble-maker trips himself up (11:29), and to grasp prematurely at one's inheritance is unwise (20:21; cf. Lk. 15:11–32, especially vv. 12–17). A man who deserts home goes astray in more ways than one (27:8). In times of stress, close brothers and friends can be a tower of strength, and distant ones of little help (17:17; 18:24; 27:10). A brother offended is hard to reconcile (18:19); a servant pampered may supplant one (29:21); and a hypocrite is known and detested (27:14).

Kings and Rulers. Heavy responsibilities rest upon, and high standards are expected from, kings, rulers, and all who wield authority.

Because a ruler depends ultimately on the support and loyalty of a people (14:28; 20:28), it is his duty and in his interest to promote justice (29:14). He should be a source of just dealing, sifting out and accounting for wrongdoers, and endorsing upright speech and conduct (14:35; 16:10, 12, 13; 20:26; 22:11; 25:4, 5).

In line with this, the executive power of rulers puts a sharp edge on their displeasure and can make their favor a rich blessing (16:14, 15; 19:12; 20:2). Loyalty to God and to the ruling powers is enjoined (24:21, 22; cf. Rom. 13:1–5; I Tim. 2:1–4; I Pet. 2:13–17). Modesty, not aggressiveness, is desirable in the company of a ruler (25:6, 7) and likewise in the social graces (23:1–3).

Evil in a land multiplies its rulers; but men of integrity, its prosperity (28:2). Neither false words nor corrupt practice befit a ruler (17:7; 29:4); bad rulers may bring much harm; and when corrupt, the rottenness infects their subordinates (28:15, 16; 29:12).

Themselves often inscrutable, rulers are often inquiring people (25:2, 3) who can be persuaded by dint of persistence and patience. Their hearts, like everyone else's, are within the Lord's control (25:15; 21:1; cf. as examples, Neh. 1:11—2:8; Esther 4:10—5:3).

The Community and One's Fellows. Living wisely is not only living right with God, but also with one's fellow men and women in the daily round, a fact enforced by the lessons in Proverbs.

Nation and City: For the welfare and honor of a nation or city, sufficient wise leaders are needed to guide its affairs, but the people at large may rise or fall in their support of right, or lapse into evil ways (11:14; 14:34). In a town or city, the blessing and bane of the righteous and wicked respectively are felt and appreciated or detested accordingly (11:10, 11).

Neighbors: To be a bad neighbor is emphatically condemned in Proverbs, a point worth noting today. It is sinful, senseless, and ungodly to despise or to seek to harm one's neighbor (11:9, 12; 14:21; 16:29; 21:10; 29:5). Neighbors should not unduly make free of each other's houses (25:17). However, it is one's duty as a godly person to warn others of the consequences of their ways when these lead toward destruction (24:11, 12). It is one thing to have many acquaintances, but a real friend who "sticketh closer than a brother" is the most precious of all (18:24; Christ fulfils this role perfectly).

Suretyship: To make oneself responsible personally or financially for someone of whose character one may know nothing is senseless in the extreme, and is to be avoided (11:15; 17:18; 20:16; 22:26, 27; 27:13; cf. the Eleventh Word of Exhortation, 6:1–5).

Litigation: Justice should be faithfully rendered and partiality and false witness shunned, both sides being heard (18:5, 17; 21:5; 24:23–26; 25:18). Perversion of justice by bribery stands condemned, even though it may penetrate widely into high circles (17:8, 23;

18:16; 21:14). One should not go to law lightly to solve disputes (penalties can be heavy) but seek a private settlement first (25:7b–10; cf. Mt. 5:25, 26; I Cor. 6:1–8).

Crime: Unchastity is a snare and destroyer of the soul (23:26–28), a fact widely ignored in our day. Murderers bring upon themselves the hostility of wronged society (28:17). Partnership in theft destroys one's integrity and turns one's life into a lie (29:24).

Business: The principle of harnessing resources to achieve results is exemplified agriculturally in 14:4. The cunning of commerce is summed up in 20:14. The Wise expressly condemn the filching of others' property, especially from the needy, and invoke God as stout defender of the oppressed (22:28; 23:10, 11).

Personal Issues: Vengeance should not be exacted evil for evil, but committed into the Lord's hand; evil is to be overcome with good (20:22; 24:28, 29; 25:21, 22; cf. Rom. 12:17–21; Mt. 5:44, 45).

The folly of eating and drinking to excess brings poverty; and the unpleasant and harmful aftermath is only too well known (20:1; 23:19–21, 29–35). The Wise also warn one against accepting hospitality which is begrudged by the miserly, and of the embarrassment which may be involved (23:6–8).

In general, all ages have their place and pride—the young have strength to be used for good or ill; the gray hair of the old marks a lifetime of experience (20:29).

Money, Wealth and Poverty. Wealth of itself is neither good nor evil; it is men's use or misuse of it that turns wealth into a blessing or a curse (cf. 10:16). The same considerations apply, broadly, to poverty.

Wealth is a source of power, giving economic mastery (13:8; 22:7), while poverty very easily leaves one at the mercy of every upheaval (10:15). Wealth rightly used is a great blessing, for example, in generosity toward those in real need and in times of crisis (11:24–26; 22:9). Kindness should be shown to the poor, and their common human rights duly respected (14:21; 29:7); the Lord will repay it (19:17; cf. Mt. 25:34–40). To ignore the needs of one's fellows is wicked (21:13; 28:27; cf. I Jn. 3:17); miserliness is despicable (21:26; cf. Gal. 6:10), and it is wrong to make wealth the principal goal of life (23:4, 5; 28:20–22, 25; cf. Mt. 6:24).

Wealth has distinct limitations. It attracts "friends" like flies, while the poor man suffers, conversely, from a dearth of friends (14:20; 19:4, 6, 7). Overabundance can spoil one's sense of values, while poverty may blunt it (27:7). Despite the temptation to think otherwise, one cannot base his life-confidence primarily on physical wealth; it is utterly powerless against divine judgment (11:4, 28; 18:11). Wealth and wisdom are not to be confused; the discerning mind does not weigh a man by the amount of his wealth (28:11).

When men set their hearts on wealth, they too easily wrong others and sin to achieve their shortsighted object (11:16; 13:11; 21:6; 22:16). Better far to remain upright in humble circumstances than to gain wealth by wrongdoing, for greed reaps its own harvest (15:27; 16:8; 28:6).

Arrogance, oppression of the poor by the rich, and bullying of the poor by a poor man are condemned, for the Lord is the guardian of the oppressed, as the Wise point out (18:23; 22:22, 23; 28:3). Before God, rich and poor alike are mere men (22:2).

Legitimate wealth can result from diligence, and poverty from laziness (see Diligence and Laziness, 10:4). Righteous or wicked ways affect estate, and a passion for pleasure and luxury soon empties a purse (15:6; 21:17). In God's providence, a godly man's wealth gives blessing after he has gone, and even the spoils of the greedy may be later channeled to good purposes (13:22; 28:8). Secrecy over poverty or wealth may stem from motives of either pride or humility (cf. 13:7).

IV. The Words of Agur (30:1–33)

Agur appears only in Proverbs. The term *massa* (RSV) may be rendered "oracle," "prophecy" (KJV, RSV), or as the proper name "(of) Massa" (RSV, cf. Gen. 25:14). Agur's utterances are striking in both form and content. Each of the four main sections, two "topical" and two "numerical," is followed by an odd verse or so directed against a specific sin. The use of climactic numerals ("three, yea four," and so on) is an old poetical device in the ancient Near East.

1. God's Might, Truth, and Centrality—and Against Slander (30:1–10)

The might of God as all-wise controller of the world (30:1–4) so completely overwhelms Agur that he declares himself utterly ignorant, even humanly; compare Job 42:1–6 as sequel to God's might in chapters 40 and 41.

The truth of God's Word is tested and tried, and He Himself is a shield and protector of those who turn to Him—but His revealed Word is not to be tampered with (30:5, 6; cf. Deut. 4:2; Mt. 15:6; Rev. 22:18, 19).

The centrality of God in his life is Agur's next concern (30:7–9). He would be free of a lying tongue; he would wish neither wealth (with its pride) nor poverty (in its desperation) to come between him and his God, but simply to have sufficiency for his needs (cf. Deut. 8:10–14; Mt. 6:10, 11, 31–33).

Slander against another's employee may—and justifiably does—rebound on oneself (30:10).

2. Rogues and Devourers—and Against Disobedience to Parents (30:11–17)

To expose rogues, Agur simply lets their characters speak for themselves. Thus he exhibits those disrespectful of parents, the self-righteous who have no ground for their pride, the arrogant, and the blatant oppressors of the poor (30:11–14). The off-spring of the "leach" (exact nature uncertain) introduce four things with "never satisfied" as the common denominator—death, desire for children, and the appetite of parched earth for water and fire for fuel (vv. 15, 16). Then Agur again denounces disobedience to parents (v. 17; cf. Rom. 1:30).

3. Four Wonders—and Against the Adulteress (30:18–20)

Four things beyond his understanding excite Agur's wonder: the flight of the eagle, the glide of a snake, the sailing of a ship, and the intimate companionship of man and woman (30:18, 19). Then by contrast, Agur brands the shameless adulteress as sinner and as a liar for denying her sin (v. 20; cf. I Jn. 1:8).

4. Four Unbearable, Four Wise, Four Dignified Things—and Against Strife (30:21–33)

Four things are unbearable in Agur's view, all of them people whose good fortune goes to their heads: a servant who takes advantage of high office, a senseless man who stuffs himself, a love-hungry woman who finally pins down a husband, and a serving-maid who fancies herself in society (30:21–23).

Four others, small but very wise, can each teach a lesson: the little ants which prudently provide for future needs; the humble badgers which make safe homes amid the rocks; the rulerless locusts which illustrate order and purpose in their march; and the puny lizard, which, readily picked up (RSV), can penetrate even royal palaces (30:24-28).

Four more exemplify dignity: the fearless lion, king of beasts; the "greyhound" (obscure phrase; read as "band of jackals"?); the he-goat; and the king supreme (30:29-31).

Then Agur warns finally against being a source of friction and so of needless and distressing strife (30:32, 33).

V. The Words of Lemuel (31:1-9)

Lemuel, also, occurs only in Proverbs; again *massa* (RSV) is ambiguous, perhaps a name here—"king of Massa" (cf. Gen. 25:14). The words of Lemuel are a twofold exhortation taught him by his mother (31:1). As a king with heavy responsibilities, Lemuel is enjoined to keep clear of mistresses and to leave strong drink for those foolish enough to drown their sorrows by ruining their faculties in this way (vv. 2-7). Secondly, he is exhorted positively to judge his people justly, heeding the rights of those in dire need (vv. 8, 9). Both injunctions are as modern as today, with the traffic in vice that goes on unabated.

VI. The Good Wife (31:10-31)

This noble concluding poem of Proverbs is an acrostic (each verse begins with a new letter of the Hebrew alphabet), which may be a part of Lemuel's words or a separate composition.

The good wife, one whom her husband may trust implicitly, is worth more than precious gems. She is devoted to his welfare and interests, giving him also that intangible personal encouragement that enables him better to face the affairs of outside life (31:10-12, 23). Diligent and tireless in providing for her household's needs, she can face all circumstances with confidence (vv. 17, 25, 27). Thus, her family and herself are well-clothed (vv. 13, 19, 21, 22) and well-fed (vv. 14, 15). She is diligent in business (vv. 16, 18, 24).

This good wife is also generous to the needy, and she is a veritable fountain of helpful and homely wisdom (31:20, 26). So gracious a person deserves the gratitude and praise of husband and children alike (vv. 28, 29) and should be given the recognition that is her due (vv. 30, 31). Mere charm or glamor is not the source of all this. She is "a woman who fears the Lord." From Him come the good wife and her goodness.

Ecclesiastes

W. GORDON BROWN

IN A PHRASE that has become part of our literature, the Preacher gives out his text (1:1, 2). He will repeat "All is vanity" again and again in varied form until its final recitation (12:8). The whole of things is a puff of wind, transitory, futile, vain. In twelve chapters he proves this. But he does so in order to lead man under the sun, that is, man in his common life, to the fear of God in final judgment.

I. The Weary Round (1:3—2:26)

The first point is the weary round of nature (a poem in 1:3-8, though some think almost all the book is Hebrew poetry): sunrise, sunset: south wind, north wind: freshets running one season, freshets running the next. The wearisome round is never satisfying. So life's future is its past; nothing is new. As former things are forgotten, so future things will also be dropped from remembrance (1:9-11).

Having described his observation of the world of nature, the Preacher now gives his personal experience (1:12-18). He makes clear at once that his kingship is a mask by saying that in the past he was king of Israel. Solomon could not say he had been king, for he reigned until death (I Kings 11:42, 43). Other considerations will show that, while lessons may be drawn from Solomon's life, our Preacher really writes at a much later time. His eager mind explores only to find that God has set men under the sky (many mansuscripts read "under the sun") to labor at a bad affair. When it is all viewed, it is just a puff of breath, a pursuit of wind (or a feeding on wind, like Ephraim in Hos. 12:1). The case is as hopeless as straightening the crooked or numbering the lacking. Remembering the acme of Solomon's wisdom (I Kings 4:30, 31) over all others ("all that were before" seems to have this set meaning), the Preacher yet concludes that such knowledge is nothing but wind; for the greater the wisdom the greater the grief; and the more the knowledge, the more the pain.

Now the sage considers whether pleasures are good for man's brief life (2:1–11), only to find them vain: wine in moderation, buildings, vineyards, orchards, groves with pools, slaves, flocks and herds, royal treasurers, musicians, and men's delight in mistresses (the Hebrew word rendered "musical instrument" in KJV we now know to have Ugaritic equivalent meaning "lady"). More than others he has indulged in all he can wisely take to cheer him; but when he considers pleasure, that too is pursuit of wind.

What about the future (2:12–23)? Introduced now when the Preacher wonders about the king's successor, this problem arises again and again. Why, this successor will repeat the predecessor, though wisdom far excels folly, for the wise man uses his head. (Verse 14a is a proverb as were verses 15 and 18 in chapter 1; many more proverbs will follow.) But the same event which comes to wise and foolish is forgotten in common death. This makes life bad, vain, until one despairs that he has used ability to accumulate an inheritance for an heir who may be a fool. What then his reward for all his painful work day and night? All is vanity!

So it is best for a man (2:24–26) to enjoy his work to the full. That is God's gift, "for who eats and who enjoys apart from him?" (The third person singular pronoun is the better reading here.) The good God turns the scale for the good man and makes even the sinner, much to the sinner's disgust, benefit him. Far from being a pietist interpolation, this last paragraph is a step of faith toward the final judgment announced at the end of the book.

II. Time and Eternity (3:1–22)

What shall we say of time and eternity (3:1–15)? Every interest of human life has its proper time and its opposite has its own time, whether in life physical, economic, social or political. (The extended list takes away any idea of fatalism one might draw from v. 2a.) But what does man gain? God made him busy with this and that fine thing in its time, but God put eternity in man's mind without which man cannot grasp His purpose throughout time. So man had better enjoy himself as God grants. God's work is eternal and therefore permanent. So fear God. The past repeats itself in the future; but the God Who knows all seeks from men even what they have driven into the past.

The next paragraph (3:16–22) shows faith in coming judgment, though meanwhile death seems a dark end. If wickedness fills the place of justice, the God Who takes account of time must judge the just and the wicked. So the Preacher thinks, and he thinks also that God makes clear that before Him men are like so many cattle. That is specially clear in death (the word "fate" in RSV is an unnecessarily harsh rendering for a noun that comes from a root meaning "to meet"), for death is the lot of both man and beast, and the breath leaves both. Is a dead man no better than a dead cow? The whole thing is a puff of wind. Death levels in dust. Remember Genesis 3:19. But what about the spirit? Does man go up, and does the beast go down? (The versions must have incorporated the Hebrew vowel points to fix the text in the form of two questions.) Who knows? So man had better rejoice in his present work (as was said in 2:24 and 3:12, and will be said again as in 8:15), since no one can give him a vision of his future.

The thought here seems very negative toward immortality. Note, of course, that the Preacher believed that the God of perfection will judge (3:17). The end of the book declares judgment in the world to come (12:14). We must always remember that it was Christ Who shed light on immortality (II Tim. 1:10).

III. Political Economy (4:1–16)

Our Preacher has seen injustice, now he sees oppression (4:1–6) so hopelessly unrelieved that men already dead are commendable beyond the living, and better than both is the man who never was born to see so great evil. These are hardly the words of so efficient a civil administrator as King Solomon (cf. I Kings 4:20)! And it all springs from jealousy, so it is a damp breath, a longing for wind! With folded hands, the fool eats his heart out with envy of the successful man; so one handful with rest is better than two hands full with toil and vanity.

The advantages of companionship now appear (4:7–12). Another vain thing in daily life is to see a man who has no family responsibility, yet is never satisfied with all he can amass. Two are better than one in business; if one fails, the other will set him up. Two keep each other warm in bed. While someone may overpower a single man, two will successfully resist. So one or two, now three—"a cord of three strands is not quickly torn apart." Remember David's three mighty men (II Sam. 23:9, 16, 18, 19, 23), and the three Hebrew children (Dan. 3).

A promising palace revolution may fizzle out (4:13–16). The wise youth (not "child" as KJV, but "youth," as in I Kings 12:8 and else-where)is better than an old king who can no longer take admonition. Though the lad comes to the throne from prison, the vast crowds are with him. But wait! Later they will lose their joy in him—another instance of life's futility. (Any definite political reference here is now no longer clear.)

IV. Religion and Life (5:1—6:12)

Much of the discussion has been of common life. Now the Preacher sees worship must be performed in the fear of God (5:1–7). One must be careful when he goes to the temple. It is a good place to listen. The sacrifice brought by fools adds to their evil. Avoid rash statement before God. A mere man really needs to say little before God in heaven. He is a fool who talks too much, just as too much business brings dreams. (Verse 2 is another proverb.) The vow once made must be made good; God cannot stand fools (the third time we have had this word in four verses). Do not let your word make yourself sin when you say before the priest ("angel" or "messenger" is used of a priest in Mal. 2:7) that your rash vow was a mere slip, for God may in wrath ruin your work. So omit vain terms and fear God.

Now another comment about justice (5:8, 9): Do not be astounded at injustice to the poor. An official is watching, and there are higher ones above him. Above all is the king.

What about prosperity (5:10–17)? To the owner's disgust, money and goods do not satisfy. The more goods, the more mouths to feed! (Did Malthus, formulating his law, "population breeds up to the point of sustenance," study this saying?) The laborer sleeps well, but the surfeited rich man cannot. It is sickening to see a rich man keep his money to his own injury, or venture and lose it just when he needs it to educate a son. When you die, "you can't take it with you." Days consumed for wind! How sickening and vexing!

And so again contentment with one's daily portion is the best way (5:18–20). The good and the fair is to enjoy the good of one's toil as the gift of God.

A man must enjoy good things in life, or it is all vain (6:1–6). An-other bad experience of everyday life the Preacher now relates: God has enabled a man to gain everything he could desire, but he does not live to enjoy it, and leaves it to a stranger. (Did Jesus have this passage in mind when He told the parable of the rich farmer who died suddenly [Lk. 12: 16–18]?) A man may have a very large family and a long life, but if he does not really have full satisfaction from the good things of life and does not have a proper burial, he would have been better off an abortion without meaning, covered with darkness, knowing nothing. To live two thousand years without seeing good! The only comfort would be the common lot of all in death.

Now three proverbs on appetite (6:7–9): A man works to eat and appetite keeps him working. Both the wise and the fool eat. Sight is better than desire. But this, too, is vexing.

Man is known, but what is good for him (6:10-12)? The best is the present, and man, being human, cannot enter into judgment with the Almighty. Much talk increases vanity to no profit. Man's brief life is a sort of dream. What is good for him? What will come after him?

V. Wise Words (7:1–29)

Already our wise Preacher has given a proverb here and there, but now he gives us a dozen or more (7:1–12). The first six concern the advantage of sadness: deathday is better than birthday, mourning makes a man think, vexation improves the mind, wise minds dwell on mourning, a wise man's rebuke is preferable, fools' flattery is empty, oppression turns the mind, endurance wins, and he is a fool who is angry. It is unwise to say "things used to be much better." Wisdom with an inheritance makes for advantage; knowledge is the defense of its possessors.

Now follow several brief paragraphs: When God puts a crimp in a thing, no one can straighten it out; and God puts bad times with good so that no one may find out the future (7:13, 14). The golden mean (vv. 15–18): a man may perish in the right and a wicked man continue in his evil; so do not be too righteous or too wise, nor too wicked or foolish, but understand both sides, for the reverent man will be quit of them all. In wisdom is strength (v. 19). There is none righteous (v. 20). Have a deaf ear for much that is said (vv. 21, 22).

Wisdom's despair of man now follows (7:23–29). Trying to be wise, the Preacher found it too difficult and too deep. (Solomon could hardly have written these lines!) His mind sought to discover the sum of things and to know wicked folly. An ensnaring woman catches the sinner. By careful reckoning, the Preacher found one man in a thousand but among them all not a woman. (Hold on, another and better side of this depressing picture comes in 9:9.)

For such general perversity, God is not to be blamed: He made man upright at the first, but man deliberately thought out many calculations against His will.

VI. Kings and the King (8:1–17)

Another proverb in praise of wisdom, which may improve even a man's appearance (8:1), is followed by advice to take what the king says, whether you like it or not, since he is absolute (vv. 2–4). (The new version takes the beginning of verse 3, "be not dismayed," with the last of verse 2, "on the matter of the oath of God." It must be remembered that punctuation, verse division, and so forth, are matters of human opinion, later inserted, rather than original inspiration.)

But there is nothing absolute about the future (8:5–9). Loyalty? Yes, the wise man knows propriety, but no one knows what will be, nor how. Death—no one has authority to keep the spirit from it, not even wickedness. Study of human life, where one man dominates another, shows no more.

Faith says, "It is well with the pious"; sight says, "The wicked prosper" (8:10–15). The Preacher saw wicked men buried who had gone to the temple and then in the city boasted about it ("boasted" is a change in the Hebrew of one letter to a closely similar one from the meaning "were forgotten," and this change is supported by many manuscripts and most versions), and he thought this vanity. Delay in justice makes for more crime. Certainly a sinner may do wrong a hundred times, yet there is this assurance: it will be well for the reverent, but not for the wicked. This is the knowledge of faith, though on earth one may find this vanity, that righteous men get the reward of the wicked and vice versa. The practical thing, then, is to enjoy oneself with one's labor on earth.

Wisdom cannot reach the ultimate (8:16, 17). No matter how diligently the wise man may search for the answer, even through sleepless days and nights, he cannot find what God is doing in the world, and the man who says he has found the answer really has not.

VII. The Last Enemy (9:1–16)

Dark death silences all (9:1–6). Our author believed that the works of men right and wise are in God's power, whether for love or hate. But all before men is vain. (Some versions read the first word of verse 2, meaning "the whole thing," as "vanity" with a very slight change in the middle one of the three Hebrew consonants.) The same thing happens to the righteous as to the wicked, to the one who follows the ceremonial law and to the one who does not, to the one who breaks his oath or to the one who keeps it. What a pity this is! The mind of men in life is full of foolish evil, and then comes death. "While there is life, there is hope," so an ignoble life is better than a noble death; for the dead do not know a thing, nor have they reward when their memory is forgotten with their love and hate and zeal in the natural life.

Shall we not say that here again we have the viewpoint found simply "in all that is done under the sun," that is, the viewpoint of nature and the natural man? It is not "the word of faith which we preach." The inspiration of such passages extends only to the accurate recording of the human point of view.

So the thing to do is enjoy thoroughly the life God gave you (9:7–10). Eat, drink, for God has provided. Be well dressed and well groomed. Life with its toil may be vain indeed, but enjoy the love of your wife. What you do, do thoroughly, for in the abode of the dead to which you go, there is nothing, nothing.

If we cannot know about life beyond, is there a principle of suitable reward for work in this life (9:11, 12)? Neither necessities ("bread") nor luxuries ("riches") are assured to those who deserve them. What comes is chance, and men are often suddenly cut off at a bad time.

Yet wisdom is better than might (9:13–16). So had the observer concluded from the story of the small city besieged by a great king and saved from destruction by a poor wise man in it, though the wise man's sad reward was to be forgotten instead of heard. The nearest Biblical incident is the wise woman who saved the old city Abel from destruction over the rebel Sheba (II Sam. 20:16–22).

VIII. More Wise Words (9:17—11:7)

A string of proverbs now begins (9:17, 18), which carries through the next chapter: quiet listening to wisdom is better than the outcry of one who leads fools; it takes only one sinner to ruin a great deal of good.

Chapter 10 contains the longest string of proverbs in the book, loosely connected. We suggest their points: A little folly ruins much wisdom (v. 1). Wisdom is always ready (v. 2). The fool cannot conceal what he is (v. 3). Do not resign the king's employ in a hurry (v. 4). The Preacher has observed this error, folly with great influence and the rich set low, slaves riding and princes walking.

Now comes a list of occupational hazards of the times (10:8–10), for success against which wisdom is recommended.

The point of the next list of proverbs is, do not talk too much (10:11–15). The first means that when a snake has bitten without being charmed, there is no advantage in having a charmer (literally "the lord of the tongue," which the KJV interprets as "babbler"). Why talk so much when you cannot tell the future (v. 15)? Blindness to the future constantly oppresses our writer.

The labor of the fool (some manuscripts read the singular) wearies him, although he does not know so simple a thing as the way to go to town (10:15).

Happy the land that has a good king (10:16, 17). Better that he not be a mere boy nor have princes given to banqueting.

With work a house must be kept in repair (10:18). "Silver meets all demands" (v. 19). Even in secret do not curse an important person, for a little bird may tell (v. 20).

Chapter 11, most or all of it in Hebrew poetic form, gives more maxims or sound advice or pleasant observations, but soon reverts to the two things that trouble the Preacher most: We do not know what God is doing now; we see no real light beyond the grave. The usual moral follows—enjoy life while you have it. But the chapter does not close without a note of judgment to come, which leads to the climax of the book in the next chapter.

"Bread upon the waters" may be business by sea (11:1), but "do not put all your eggs in one basket," use seven or eight (v. 2)! Clouds give rain, trees stay where they fall (v. 3). "Ideal conditions for action are rarely realized" (v. 4). God directs the wind, God builds the foetus, but how, we do not know (v. 5). The combination here of wind and birth reminds one of John 3:8, though there it is the second birth with a play on the word wind (as also here), since the one term in both Hebrew and Greek may mean either wind or spirit. In sowing grain, work early and late, for you do not know which part of the field will be best (v. 6). Sunlight is sweet (v. 7)!

IX. *Old Age (11:8—12:7)*

Even the old man should be glad he is alive, for the darkness ahead is long, and all that comes is futility (11:8). Let the youth be glad within and without, but let him rest assured all his conduct will be judged before God (v. 9). So banish moroseness and evil, for even the dawn of life is futility (v. 10).

Youth must remember God before old age comes (12:1-7). The last two verses of chapter 11 appeal to youth; 12:1 continues the appeal: Remember God in youth, or you will not remember Him in later years. Then follows a classic description of old age. This passage, however, must be taken as a whole, for scholars are not agreed on the meaning of all details. Clear are persistent gloom (v. 2), feeble strength (v. 3), little activity (v. 4), fearful forebodings (v. 5a), loss of appetite (v. 5b). (Locusts were eaten, and the word which occurs here only, and is translated "desire," could mean "caperberry," which was used as an appetizer.) Death itself is now described as a mournful going to eternal rest (v. 5c), the snapping (so the versions, though the Hebrew text that has come down to us reads "removed far away") of a cord or crushing of a bowl. At death may the material part of man come to the ground from which it came, and may the immaterial go back to its origin in God (v. 7, reversing Gen. 2:7)! In saying this last, even though the repeated Hebrew verb the rabbis pointed as a wish rather than as a statement of the future, the Preacher is advancing beyond the gloom that has pervaded his comment on the world beyond, and is preparing for the grand climax of his book.

X. *The Text and the Preacher (12:8–12)*

The sermon being almost finished, the Preacher repeats the text (1:2), though with two words less, that the whole business is a passing breath.

Then some addenda about our Preacher (12:9–11): He belonged to the class of wise men whose business was to teach, especially by the use of proverbs that pleasantly expressed the truth at the same time they goaded men to activity and assured them of the approval of the good Shepherd.

XI. Practical Piety in View of Judgment (12:13, 14)

Here then is instruction, though it may weary one to take it.

The conclusion leads to a height which our book anticipates here and there. The change is like an organist concluding a hymn in the minor key by changing chords in the "amen" from the minor to the major. Now all is heard, so "fear God and keep his commandments, for this is the whole duty of man," namely, practical piety (cf. Mt. 5:48). The great incentive to it is the fear of God's judgment, even of everything secret, good or bad.

Christ and His apostles took up this note of final judgment with frequency and with force (for example, Mt. 7:22, 23; Acts 17:31; Rom. 2:5–11; II Cor. 5:10; Rev. 20:11–15). Here must be the answer to the apparent skepticism which comes to the "man under the sun," who views life only to find it all vanity.

The Song of Solomon

JOHANNES G. VOS

THIS BOOK DESCRIBES the love and marriage of Solomon, called "the beloved," and a country maiden, called "the Shulamite." It consists entirely of speeches, chiefly by the Shulamite and Solomon, King of Israel about 973-933 B.C. Because it is ancient oriental poetry, it differs widely from the way the same basic ideas might be presented by a devout present-day writer. It presents the beauty of a pure love between man and woman, which ripens into an undying mutual devotion. The basic message is the beauty, purity and sacredness of love and marriage—a message much needed in our day of loose thinking on the sanctity of sex, broken marriage vows and easy divorces.

At the same time the Song reminds us that back of all pure human love is the greatest, deepest love of all—the love of God Who gave His Son to redeem sinners, and the love of the Son of God Who suffered and died for His bride, the Church. The Song is not an allegory nor a type, though it has often been treated as one or the other. Rather, it is a parable of the divine love which is the background and source of all true human love.

The interpretation which is given here accepts the traditional view that the Song has two main characters—Solomon and the Shulamite. An alternative interpretation, called "the shepherd hypothesis," holds that there are three main characters—Solomon, the Shulamite and her betrothed shepherd lover to whom she remains true in spite of all Solomon's efforts to win her love for himself. This theory requires taking a great deal for granted for which there is no basis in the Song, and it presents Solomon in an extremely unfavorable light. While the great king had some serious faults, nothing in Scripture suggests that he was such a monster of wickedness as "the shepherd hypothesis" implies. It is much simpler and more satisfactory to regard "the beloved" as Solomon throughout the Song. Of course, the Song in no way condones Solomon's notorious polygamy, which is sufficiently condemned elsewhere in the Bible.

I. Title of the Book (1:1)

"The Songs of Songs" is a Hebrew superlative meaning "the best song" or "the greatest song." "Which is Solomon's" may mean that the Song is about Solomon, but it probably means that Solomon was the author. This accords well with the content of the book, especially its description of nature. No convincing case has been presented against Solomon's authorship.

II. The Shulamite and her Beloved Delight in Each Other (1:—2:7)

The place is perhaps Solomon's garden or woodland park.

1. The Shulamite Longs for her Beloved (1:2, 3)

The Song opens with the Shulamite expressing intense longing for Solomon. The Revised Standard Version has the pronouns "you" and "your" in verse 2a, but in the Hebrew "he" and "his" are used.

2. They Meet and Converse, Expressing Mutual Love (1:4—2:6)

The Shulamite and Solomon meet, and she voices her love for him (1:4). She explains her dark appearance to the women of the palace as due to sunburn; her brothers had made her keeper of the vineyards, but she had not taken care of her own vineyard, that is, her complexion (vv. 5, 6). She expresses her desire for Solomon's companionship, figuratively speaking of him as a shepherd (v. 7). Verse 8 is probably spoken by her female companions. Solomon in figurative language praises her loveliness (vv. 9–11). She replies similarly, praising the king as her beloved (vv. 12–14). He assures her of his delight in her loveliness (v. 15); she replies, expressing delight in him and their surroundings—apparently a woodland bower (vv. 16, 17). Solomon compares himself and the Shulamite to lovely flowers (2:1, 2); with intense feeling she expresses satisfaction in his companionship (vv. 3–6).

3. Refrain Addressed to Daughters of Jerusalem (2:7)

This refrain recurs in 3:5 and partly again in 8:4. Roes (or gazelles) and hinds of the field are timid creatures used as poetic symbols of womanly beauty and modesty. As translated in the Revised Standard Version (". . . stir not up nor awaken love until it please"), the verse is a warning against trying to hasten the process of falling in love. As given in the King James Version (". . . stir not up, nor awake *my* love, till he please"), it is a plea that Solomon be not disturbed, but left quietly alone with the Shulamite.

III. Deepening Love of the Shulamite and her Beloved (2:8—3:5)

Here the Shulamite is apparently alone, recalling past experiences.

1. She is Delighted by his Visit and Invitation (2:8–17)

Here she recalls with delight Solomon's recent visit to her. In verses 10 through 15 she quotes what he had said, including his invitation: "Arise, my love, my fair one, and come away" (2:10). They are filled with such happiness that all nature seems transformed by the beauty of springtime. "The little foxes" (v. 15) may mean cares or annoyances which interfere with the serenity of their love for each other. This section of the Song ranks high in poetic beauty.

2. The Shulamite's First Dream (3:1–4)

In these verses she relates a dream, in which she had gone out through the city streets seeking her beloved, and after finally finding him had led him to her mother's rural home. The dream shows the depth of her desire for her beloved.

3. Refrain Addressed to Daughters of Jerusalem (3:5, see comment on 2:7)

IV. Solemnization of Their Marriage (3:6—5:1)

The place is evidently Jerusalem. The bridal procession approaches. The marriage is followed by a royal banquet. Note that in this section the beloved is repeatedly identified as Solomon (3:7, 9, 11) while the Shulamite is six times (4:8, 9, 10, 11, 12; 5:1) spoken of as his spouse (KJV) or his bride (RSV). Therefore it seems clear that in this section actual marriage, as distinguished from mere betrothal, takes place.

1. Description of the Bridal Procession (3:6–11)

In verse 6 "Who is this" (KJV) should be "What is that" (RSV), as the Hebrew indicates that the question refers to the bed or litter mentioned in verse 7. Solomon is pictured as bringing the Shulamite from her rural home to Jerusalem for the marriage. The "chariot" (KJV) or "palanquin" (RSV) of verse 9 may be identical with the bed or litter of verse 7, though the Hebrew word is a different one. Everything about the bridal procession is beautiful, stately and costly —the palanquin, the perfumes, the guard of sixty brave men, the crown placed on Solomon's head. In verse 11, the word translated "espousals" (KJV) may also be translated "wedding" (RSV).

2. The Bridegroom Sings the Praises of the Bride (4:1–15)

The emphasis on the bride's physical charms may seem strange to us. It must be remembered that this is ancient oriental poetry. The bridegroom sings a song praising the bride's beauty, as is still customary at weddings in Syria. With beautiful figures of speech drawn from the world of nature, he extols the matchless loveliness of the bride. Gilead (v. 1) was a mountain range east of the Jordan River; Amana and Lebanon (v. 8) were two parallel ranges of very high mountains just north of Palestine. Shenir (KJV) or Senir (RSV) and Hermon (v. 8) were two names for the same mountain—a lofty snow-capped peak 9,166 feet high, located at the northern limit of Palestine.

3. Anticipation of the Delights of Married Love (4:16—5:1)

In verse 16 the Shulamite who is now Solomon's bride responds to his lavish praises by a highly poetical invitation to her beloved to enjoy the delights of married love. She speaks of herself figuratively as a garden in which her beloved is to eat delicious fruits. She calls upon the cool north wind and the warm south wind to blow upon her garden that it may be fragrant like spices; that is, that she may be desirable in the eyes of the bridegroom. In 5:1 the bridegroom responds, speaking by anticipation of his enjoyment of the "garden" of married love. The last clause may be taken as the bridegroom's invitation to the guests at the marriage to eat and drink, or it may be taken as the guests' wish of joy for the newly married pair. Of course, we must not judge the words of the bridegroom and bride in this ancient wedding by the conventions of modern society. It is perhaps social convention, rather than real moral purity, that forbids any suggestion of the sexual aspect of marriage in connection with a wedding at the present day.

V. Temporary Absence Followed by Happy Reunion (5:2—8:4)

The place at the opening of this section is probably the royal palace.

1. The Shulamite's Second Dream (5:2–8)

The opening words of verse 2 suggest that what follows is a dream. In the dream the bridegroom knocked at her door, but when she opened the door to admit him, he was not there. She wandered about the city in search of him, and was harmed, rather than helped, by the watchmen on the walls. The fact that when awake (6:2) she knows where her beloved has gone indicates 5:2–8 is a dream.

2. Praising Him to Others, She Claims Him as her Own (5:9— 6:3)

In response to her plea in 5:8, the daughters of Jerusalem ask what is so wonderful about her beloved (v. 9). She replies, praising him highly in poetic language (vv. 10–16). They in turn ask where her beloved has gone, offering to help find him (6:1). She answers that he has gone to his garden (v. 2), adding that she and her beloved belong to each other (v. 3), thus implying that his love is for her alone.

3. The Bridegroom Praises the Bride's Loveliness (6:4–10)

With beautiful, poetic similes, he describes her superlative loveliness. Tirzah (6:4) was a city in northern Palestine. Verse 8 alludes to Solomon's polygamy, but the numbers have no special significance. Solomon's relationship to the Shulamite is something very different from his relationship to the women referred to. The former alone was fit to serve as a parable of the love of Christ for His Church.

4. The Shulamite's Experience in the Nut Orchard (6:11–13)

Here she recalls an emotional experience. She had gone to the nut orchard to look at the flowers and fruits, when suddenly she felt strangely uplifted. The King James Version translates: ". . . my soul made me *like* the chariots of Amminadib." The Revised Standard Version reads: ". . . my fancy set me in a chariot beside my prince," but states in a footnote that this is a conjecture as the meaning of the Hebrew is uncertain. It is possible that Amminadib (6:12, KJV) may mean "princely people." In verse 13, the bride is called Shulamite. This is a feminine noun and probably means an inhabitant of Shunem, a town in northern Palestine; the letters "n" and "l" could sometimes be interchanged in Palestinian place names. Some scholars have thought that the Shulamite was Abishag of Shunem, the beautiful maiden who cared for David in his extreme old age (1 Kings 1:3, 15). The reference to "two armies" (v. 13) is obscure; perhaps it is meant as a description of the Shulamite's dazzling beauty and purity.

5. He Praises her Beauty; She Voices Passionate Devotion (7:1—8:3)

Here again the uninhibited frankness of the bridegroom's description of the bride's physical charms (7:1-9) may seem strange to modern Western tastes. It must be remembered that this is poetry and that it comes from an ancient eastern culture. Modern sophisticated literature tolerates much subtly impure suggestiveness while guarding against explicit mention of the details of bodily beauty; the Song of Solomon mentions these details openly with a clean-minded purity and without any offensive suggestiveness.

In her response to the bridegroom's praise, the bride expresses her passionate devotion to him (7:10—8:3) and invites him to accompany her to the rustic scenes of her childhood. The mention of mandrakes (v. 13) indicates that it was the month of May. The Shulamite expresses the desire that Solomon's love for her might be freely acknowledged in her parental home (8:1, 2). She adds a fervent desire for intimate fellowship with her beloved (v. 3).

6. Refrain Addressed to Daughters of Jerusalem (8:4, see comment on 2:7)

VI. Bridegroom and Bride Converse of their Unquenchable Love (8:5–14)

In this section the place is the Shulamite's rustic home where Solomon has accompanied her in response to her request.

1. Invincible Power of Love (8:5–7)

Verse 5a pictures the arrival at the Shulamite's home. Verse 5b is difficult because the pronouns "thee," "thy" (KJV) or "you," "your" (RSV) are masculine in the Hebrew. This would make the Shulamite the speaker, and Solomon the one spoken to. But that was not

Solomon's birthplace, so he must be the speaker and she the one addressed. Verses 6 and 7 are perhaps the most eloquent description of the power of love ever written. The speaker seems to be the Shulamite. Love is of God; money cannot buy it, nor can any earthly power break it.

2. Recalling her Brothers' Words, She Asserts her Virtue (8:8–12)

These verses seem to recall words spoken long before by the Shulamite's brothers. The language is highly figurative. Chastity is called "a wall;" moral looseness, "a door." The meaning seems to be that if the sister was virtuous, the brothers would arrange a marriage for her; if not virtuous, they would use sterner measures to guard her chastity. The Shulamite herself declares that "a wall" is the figure that fits her conduct. She asserts her maturity ("my breasts," v. 10) over against her brothers' former denial of it ("no breasts," v. 8). The connection of verses 11 and 12 with the context is not fully clear. The speaker is still the bride. Baal-hamon has not been identified, but the name means "place of a multitude." The Shulamite's small vineyard is contrasted with Solomon's extensive one.

3. Mutual Farewells in Hope of Speedy Reunion (8:13, 14)

Verse 13 is spoken by Solomon, verse 14 by the Shulamite. He is ready to depart, but first desires to hear her voice. She replies, expressing the wish that his return may be quick like "a gazelle or a young stag" (RSV), "a roe or a young hart" (KJV), bounding over the mountains.

It is a remarkable fact that the Song of Solomon is nowhere quoted in the New Testament, though it was undoubtedly regarded as inspired, canonical Scripture in the time of Christ. The lack of reference to it in the New Testament is an objection to allegorical interpretations which find many details of Christian doctrine and experience in the Song. While interpreting it literally, we must certainly regard it as also a parable of the divine love which provides salvation for sinners and makes them the bride of Christ. In addition to leading us to a higher view of the beauty, purity and power of the love between man and woman in the sacred bond of marriage, it should stir us up to a higher appreciation of the divine love, and a deeper response of love on our part to the Lord Who first loved us.

The
Prophetic
Books

The Prophetic Books

J. KENNETH GRIDER

OUTSIDE ISRAEL there were prophets of a sort, windbags who prattled for their own dismal deities. Even within Israel a few false prophets had been given nothing to say and went ahead and said it. Jeremiah lamented them and the Lord abhorred them (Jer. 23:9–32).

But among the Hebrews there were also real seers of the most high God. Inspired personalities they were; mighty, creative personalities, men who took to prophesying in soul-deep earnest. These were not set aside to their office by any act of human ordination but by divine designation. They were admitted into the Righteous One's privy council chambers and went out—were sent out—to announce His proposals for the people.

They were straight-from-the-shoulder men, those stout and devout hearts who in their times stood up and stood out in solitary grandeur. Chins up, faith up, they minced no words. If the dancing, drinking society women of Bethel were like "fat cows," that is what they were called (Amos 4:1). Natural men then, as now, preferred a gospel of "sweetness and light," but that is not what they got. These pre-Protestants, like Luther later, took their stand for righteousness against all the rot of their times. Kings and commoners, wise men and empty fellows, the rich and the poor, priests and pagans—they all came under the requirements of these hard-hitting preachers.

Not like the philosophers who speculate about the world and its ills from comfortable armchairs, not like the medievalists who took shelter in monasteries, these men went to the people, to the masses and the classes. Not all heeded, but the prophets went to them.

Know-it-alls, sufficient to themselves, heady and haughty, the Israelites of pre-Exilic times "refused to hearken," "turned a stubborn shoulder" (RSV) as oxen did to prevent a yoke's being put on them; even "stopped their ears" and made their hearts "an adamant stone" (Zech. 7:11, 12). As late as Malachi's day, their words were "stout against . . . the Lord" (Mal. 3:13). But under God's call the prophets gave this work their all. They seldom earned money at prophesying. Their lives were frequently endangered. Yet they had to disturb sinful men, else there would have been in their hearts a burning fire shut up in their bones (Jer. 20:9). With the ruggedness of the deserts that often produced them, they dispensed God's word as responsibly as has any group of men the world has known.

A motley group, actually, the prophets! No tears for Amos, but floods of them for Hosea and Jeremiah. Isaiah was likely of a royal family whereas Amos was from the farm. Malachi had a lot of steel in him while Jonah was like the most human of men; for that fumbling, grumbling fellow, sulking "in proud isolation" outside Nineveh, jealous that heathen as well as Hebrews had a place in the Lord's love, was surely about as human as a man can be.

These men were greater than kings, for you cannot select, say, four Israelite kings so influential upon the world as were Amos, Hosea, Isaiah, and Jeremiah. In their day, too, they were consorts to kings, advisers on policy. Whether the king was a saint like Hezekiah or a sinner like Ahab, the prophets were God's spokesmen in palaces.

While some, like Ezekiel and Zechariah, were priests as well, the prophets were nearer to God than the priests. Was not Moses, the first of them, closer to God than Aaron? (Peter considers Samuel to have been the first prophet as such [Acts 3.24]. But Moses is called a prophet in Hos. 12:13, Deut. 18:15, and so forth. Actually, Abraham who lived some five hundred years before Moses, is called a prophet [Gen. 20:7, 17], but that is rather loose usage of the term.) The priests sought to present men to God, and the prophets presented God to men. To do that the prophets had to be in closer converse with Him. This conferring "not with flesh and blood," but with the Lord Himself, is what enabled them to see into the center of things —present and future. This is why they could foretell Israel's doom, herald her dawn, and announce the coming of her Dayspring from on high!

There was not just a handful of these holy men back there. The schools of the prophets produced many who would divine for the

Lord. Four hundred gathered about King Ahab (I Kings 22:6). Only a few, among the entire number, are known to us by name.

The earlier ones did not write down their messages. We call them the pre-literary prophets. Major men among them were Samuel, Elijah, and Elisha. Of relatively minor importance in their number were Nathan, Gad, Ahijah, and Micaiah.

There were some sixteen prophets—we call them the literary or writing prophets—who wrote down at least a part of their message. They are also called "canonical," because what they wrote became a part of that literature in which men heard the voice of God authentically and which was gathered into what we call the Old Testament Canon. Three of them—Isaiah, Ezekiel, and Jeremiah—are called Major Prophets, because their writings are much more lengthy than the others. Daniel is often called one of them. Besides these, there are the twelve so-called Minor Prophets, whose writings range in length from the twenty-one verses in Obadiah to the fourteen chapters in Zechariah.

Except for Hosea, Amos, and Jonah, who ministered to the northern kingdom, both the Major and Minor Prophets exercised their gifts in the southern kingdom, Judah and Benjamin. Thus in the pre-Exilic period, while Hosea, Amos and Jonah preached in the north, Joel, Obadiah, Isaiah, Micah and Nahum labored in the southern kingdom. During the period of the Babylonian Exile, Ezekiel and Daniel ministered to the Captivity, while Jeremiah, Habakkuk, and Zephaniah struggled to get God's message to the people of Judah before its fall in 587 B.C. The prophets of the restoration in Jerusalem were Haggai, Zechariah, and Malachi. This essay purposes to introduce the reader to these sixteen Old Testament prophetic books.

I. Large and Noble Words

Although many a Jew thought of Gentiles as "the spittle that falleth from a man's mouth," or as the "lesser breeds without the law," the Gospel according to the prophets included them in the Lord's loving care. The Book of Jonah, for example, is a roomy four chapters with a wide-hearted outlook on God's readiness to spare all who will repent. For Gentile Nineveh, sometime capital of the Assyrian Empire, oppressor of the Hebrews, humbled itself in sackcloth and ashes, turned from its wickedness, and the Lord saw and delighted Himself, saw and delivered it.

Isaiah also spoke large and noble words about the wideness of God's tender concern; he too saw that the One high and lifted up has a map of the whole world in His hands. There was hope even for that man whose sins were as scarlet: the hearts of men in all nations could be made as white as snow (Is. 1:18). The sovereign dominion of the thrice-holy Lord of hosts certainly included Egypt and Assyria. Zechariah, that prophet of the placid who dreamed his dreams during the "rebuilding" days, told a people full of hope—and it is thrilling —that "ten men, from nations of every language, shall lay hold of him that is a Jew, saying, 'Let us go with you; for we have heard that God is with you' " (8:23, Moffat). One is sure that that prophet of peace would never have minded if even Edom, the proud one, feuder with Judah for centuries (see Obadiah), were to be among those who would companion the Jew and go with his God. (Malachi, God's messenger on world missions of a still later time, went so far as to admit that some Gentiles were rendering a more acceptable worship to the Lord than were the Jews themselves [1:10, 11, RSV].) There is something of the Apostle Paul in these big-hearted Hebrews, something even of Jesus Himself.

II. Insight and Foresight

No one has to be told that the prophets were primarily forthtellers, and that the foretelling of events was largely bound up with the fact that they told forth God's will and purposes. Evangelical Christians will approve the view that the "prefix 'pro' in the word 'prophet' does not mean 'beforehand,' as in such words as 'progress' and 'procession,' but 'instead of,' as in the word 'pronoun.' " Certainly the prophets spoke in the Lord's stead. They were His mouthpieces, deputized to disperse His word. Aaron was thus Moses' "prophet" (Ex. 7:1) in going before Pharoah. But just as their minds were not sense-bound, neither were they time-bound. Included in the telling forth of the prophets, therefore, was the foretelling of numerous events and circumstances. Like miracles, such predictions have always been looked upon by conservative Christians as helping to verify the divine inspiration of their utterances and writings.

It is no problem to us who believe the Bible that some predictions, such as those relating to a judgment to come upon a city or nation, were never fulfilled. Such predictions were actually warnings and were often made—and that publicly—so that they would not come to pass; for when men called on God, He would call off the impending doom. Predictions such as these were conditional just as many of the promises are. *Conditional*

III. Their Master Light

The coming of a king used to be announced at various points along a route of travel by one who went ahead of the entourage. King Jesus' coming was also heralded by a forerunner. Malachi speaks of this advance messenger (3:1), and Jesus Himself states that that prediction was fulfilled by John the Baptist, greatest of all the prophets (Mt. 11:9–11). But not just the Baptist prepared the way for Christ. Old Testament personages as a whole did that, particularly the writing prophets.

Christ was to the prophets the glory of Israel, the light of the Gentiles, indeed, the "desire of all nations" (Hag. 2:7). He was "the Master light of all their seeing." They knew that one day—it would be man's "finest hour"—the "Sun of righteousness [would] arise with healing in his wings" (Mal. 4:2). One scholar says that, summed up, it was "the function of prophecy to prepare for Him." They rose to their loftiest heights "when they pointed men's weary eyes to the Redeemer," in Andrew Blackwood's words, who sees their distilled essence when he says, "The great reason, after all, why we should study the prophets is because they prepared the way for the coming of Christ." Even a liberal, who wanted to minimize prediction as much as possible, says of the pre-Exilic prophets: "These men were not merely preachers of repentance. They were heralds of the coming kingdom of God." In the New Testament itself we read, "To him all the prophets witness, that through his name whosoever believeth in him shall receive remission of sins" (Acts 10:43). And Jesus—He knew they had talked of Him. For "beginning from Moses and from all the prophets he interpreted to them in all the scriptures the things concerning himself" (Lk. 24:27). Not just Christ and Christians think the prophets are shot through with the messianic, but many Jews do also. Their Talmud states that "all the prophets have only prophesied concerning the days of the Messiah" (*Sanhedrin*, xxxiv, col. 2).

Not only the broad outlines of Christ's coming were seen by the

time – Daniel
place – Micah
virgin – Isaiah

death – Isaiah
resurrection – Isaiah
triumph – Zechariah
betrayal – Zechariah

refiner – Malachi
fuller – "

502 *The Biblical Expositor*

prophets. There would indeed appear in the lineage of David "a righteous Branch" (Jer. 23:5). But the very time of this appearance is told by Daniel (9:24–26). The place is foretold by Micah (5:2): "But thou, Bethlehem Ephratah, though thou be little among the thousands of Judah, yet out of thee shall he come forth unto me that is to be ruler of Israel; whose goings forth have been from of old, from everlasting." That the birth was to be by a virgin mother was seen by Isaiah (7:14), who saw more perhaps than any of those who lived beforehand (chs. 7, 9, 11, and 53). Isaiah also reported details of Christ's death (cf. Acts 8:32–35); for example, that He would be "numbered with the transgressors" (53:12). However vague in the prophet's own understanding, he talked also of the resurrection of Christ when, after mention of the "righteous servant's" death, and of His "grave" (53:9), the prophet continues: "When thou shalt make his soul an offering for sin, he shall see his seed, he shall prolong his days . . ." (v. 10).

And take Zechariah. That prophet saw ahead with a concreteness not given to many of his fellows. He entered into Jesus' high triumph when he exclaimed, "Rejoice greatly, O daughter of Zion . . . behold, thy King cometh unto thee: he is just, and having salvation; lowly, and riding upon an ass, and upon a colt the foal of an ass" (9:9; cf. Mt. 21:5–9). In a reference to Judas' betrayal of Christ he writes, "So they weighed for my price thirty pieces of silver. . . . And I took the thirty pieces of silver, and cast them to the potter in the house of the Lord" (11:12, 13; cf. Mt. 26:15; 27:5).

It never dies—that dream of the prophets about the coming Deliverer. It never even fades. Malachi, the last of them, is as full of hope as any. He looked for a refiner (3:2) who with fire would purify presumptuous men; for a fuller (3:2) who would clothe men with garments washed in His own blood.

And finally He appeared, He "of whom Moses in the law, and the prophets, did write, Jesus of Nazareth" (Jn. 1:45). The prophets had foretold Him, their characters had foreshadowed His; and their teachings, learned by "mouth to mouth" converse with the speaking God, had prepared the way for what He would say.

IV. They Left a Legacy

If you want to find luster in language, turn in your Bible to these Old Testament seers and have a look at their eloquence. They were wizards with words, stylists whose prose often soars to poetic heights. Read again Isaiah, chapters 35 and 53, or a hundred other passages from the prophets, and see.

Remember too as you read these revelations of God's character and purposes that those in that "goodly fellowship" were the main driving force in the religion of Israel. Call to mind that what they said, always in sympathy with Sinai as it was, has gone into the very warp and woof of Western civilization's moral code. Note also the contemporaneity of what they said and saw so long ago; for example, Zechariah's vision of a Jerusalem "without walls" (2:4). In this mid-twentieth century we know that walls or "curtains" can be divisive, that "high walls lead to high explosives"; and we can see the importance of rebuilding cities and nations without them.

It will be seen that, like John Milton, the Hebrew seers wrote "to justify the ways of God with man." But they were no optimists, no men to say with Alexander Pope: "Whatever is, is right," or with Robert Browning, "God's in his heaven—All's right with the world!" Nor were they the sour sort, speakers only of doom. They were realists, robust realists, who looked upon the status quo with a penetrating scrutiny and who sought to put God into it in its every phase. They were no mere dreamers, as Plato was, for whom the world is a shadowland only, a rough copy of the real one, but men who saw that it is a real place with flesh-and-blood troubles in it, with destiny-determining events happening, where men in their ultimate concerns grope for the living God.

These men were stoned, some of them—stoned to death. Some were sawed in two, others slain with the sword. But they had not set out to save their own skins. Theirs was a far view, and they counted not their lives here in this "spoilt and fallen world" dear to themselves. They left a world unworthy of them such a legacy that it stands to this day deeply—very deeply—in their debt.

Isaiah

GLEASON L. ARCHER, JR.

THE VERY FIRST chapter of Isaiah supplies the foundation upon which all of Isaiah's subsequent teaching is built. Here are suggested all the major themes of doctrine which are to be developed throughout the remainder of his preaching ministry. Of especial importance is the first appearance of the phrase, "the Holy One of Israel," which occurs in verse 4 and keeps recurring throughout the entire sixty-six chapters. It signifies that He Who is holy (that is, separate from, and exalted above, all creation both in transcendent majesty and moral purity) has given Himself to His covenant nation, Israel, and claimed her as His own precious possession (Ex. 19:5). He has chosen her as the channel through which He will make known His redeeming message to all mankind, in preparation for His coming to earth in Jesus Christ. In this title, the Holy One of Israel, God's purity displays itself as an active principle which vindicates itself, both in the chastening of Israel when disobedient and in delivering her from her foes when she meets the conditions of repentance and faith. In every passage where this title appears, this basic principle is in operation. Outside the Book of Isaiah, the phrase occurs but five times in the Old Testament; but in these sixty-six chapters, it occurs no less than twenty-six times and attests in a striking way the unity of the authorship of the entire book attributed to Isaiah.

I. The Volume of Rebuke and Promise (1:1—6:13)

1. First Sermon: Rebellion Confronted with Judgment and Grace (1:1–31)

Introduction (1:1). The first verse indicates the historical setting in which these prophecies were given. King Uzziah (790–739 B.C.) had started off well as a God-fearing, Scripture-believing king to whom the Lord granted military and economic success. But at the height of his power, pride had led him to pre-empt the prerogative of priest and offer incense within the Holy Place of the temple in Jerusalem. He dragged out the remaining eleven years of his life quarantined as a leper.

His son Jotham (751–736 B.C.) had carried on very creditably as his father's successor, although his reign lacked the glamour and glory of Uzziah's. He too tried to foster godliness and obedience to the precepts of Scripture. His gravest mistake was in early associating his son, Ahaz (743–725 B.C.), with him in the government, although Ahaz may perhaps have concealed his idolatrous proclivities until his father's death. The first twelve chapters of Isaiah were largely composed in his reign, and dealt with the issues to which he gave rise by his worldly-mindedness and idolatrous heresy.

Hezekiah (728–696 B.C.) proved to be a noble and virtuous son of this reprobate father, and in matters of religion and morals his policies were such that Isaiah's influence attained its maximal power. Yet in matters of politics, Hezekiah neglected the prophet's message, to the great detriment of the nation, despite the last-minute deliverance of Jerusalem from the Assyrian army. Not mentioned in this verse was Hezekiah's degenerate son, Manasseh, in whose reign Isaiah composed chapters 40 through 66, and under whose tyrannous oppression the prophet suffered martyrdom.

Indictment: Israel Guilty of Ungrateful Rebellion (1:2-9). The heavens and the earth are summoned as witnesses to God's holy remonstrance of His disobedient people. All creation, both angels and men, are bidden to behold how God will deal with these covenant-breaking Jews, so as to uphold the demands of His holy law, yet further His age-long plan of redemption. Because of the covenant relationship, first established with Abraham in Genesis 12, later confirmed with the nation gathered at the base of Mount Sinai (Ex. 19), and ratified by the establishment of a God-fearing and triumphant monarchy in King David, God describes this posterity of Abraham as His "children." They properly belong in His household, bound to Him by tender ties of filial love; they bear His name as "the people of the Lord"—for so they are known to all the heathen—and all their material and spiritual needs are supplied by His fatherly bounty. He took them when they were a demoralized, hopeless pack of slaves, groaning under the lash of their taskmasters in Egypt, and He brought them safely through the howling wilderness to the Land of Promise. They owed everything to Him, and yet, after seven centuries of experiencing His goodness to them as a nation, they had welcomed the corrupt leadership of their new king, Ahaz, and had *rebelled* against their lawful Sovereign and violated their vows of fidelity to their divine Father. Even the brute beasts show thankfulness and loyalty to their owners who feed and care for them, but Israel has sunk below even such elementary gratitude as this.

The firstfruits of their sin have been the sorrows of foreign invasion (1:5-9). God has warned and admonished them through the chastisement of suffering, yet they seem to be past repentance. Like a human body afflicted with wounds and disease from head to toe, they have been ravaged and plundered by their enemies (as God promised they would be, in Deut. 28:35); their cities have been depopulated and burned by the Edomites, the Philistines, the Syrians under Rezin, and the North Israelites under Pekah (details in II Chron. 28:5-18). Under the blundering incompetence of Ahaz, Judah has been left open to every invader and stripped of all possible defense; she lies helplessly ringed about with armed foes like a city under siege. If it were not for a remnant of true believers (and the hope of Israel lies with this little minority which remains faithful to God) the whole nation would have been destroyed root and branch as Sodom and Gomorrha were of old. But a remnant there is, and for their sake the Lord will deal as mercifully with the nation as a whole, as is consistent with His holy love. Upon the faithfulness of this small group, He will build His Kingdom through the centuries to come— a hopeful promise embodied in the very name of Isaiah's elder son, Shear-jashub ("A Remnant Shall Return"), mentioned in chapter 7.

The Sentence of Grace (1:10–31). In verses 10 through 15 the prophet denounces the sinful subterfuge of hypocritical worship. Spiritually these inhabitants of Jerusalem, the holy city, are no better than the degenerates of Sodom, for they have to a like degree turned their back upon the light of revelation granted them (natural revelation in the case of the Sodomites, and special revelation in the case of the Jews). They have impudently attempted to appease the Lord and buy His favor upon their unholy lives by lavish and regular sacrifices according to the letter of the Mosaic law. But God will not be bribed by those who make their own will and their personal happiness and pleasure the highest rule for their lives. Sacrifices are intended to give expression to a loving heart and a yielded soul, but these hypocrites only mock the Lord with their forms of worship and their hollow observance of holy days. Their worship and prayer are utterly despised and rejected by God, since they are only intended to cover up unrepented sin and bloody oppression of the weak and defenseless. Verses 11–14 cannot possibly be interpreted as prophetic disapproval of the blood-sacrifice as such, for the same rejection would then be directed against prayer as well, in verse 15. No one supposes that the Hebrew prophets ever took a stand against prayer!

Verses 16–20 contain a solemn summons to choose between two alternatives: forgiveness or destruction. Those who validly approach God must do so as repentant sinners. But repentance involves (1) the putting away of all wrongdoing with a sincere purpose never to do it again ("Put away the evil of your doings from before mine eyes"); (2) the claiming of God's forgiveness on the basis of His covenant promise to cleanse the believer who presents blood-sacrifice ("Wash you, make you clean"); and (3) an amendment of life towards a genuine obedience to God's revealed will ("Seek justice, relieve the oppressed," and so forth).

Verse 18 contains the well-known gospel invitation in which God summons guilty sinners to reason with Him before the bar of justice, for the word rendered "reason together" has a courtroom connotation in Hebrew. There they must confess that they are guilty as charged: their sins are as scarlet, the color of the bloodshed they have committed. But no sooner do they feel overwhelmed with their sense of guilt than God interposes in His marvelous grace to assure them that He is ready to cleanse away their stains of wickedness and shameful sin—so completely that the account against them shall be discharged in full, leaving them as free from offense as innocent babes. Yet this gracious forgiveness (1:19) can only be granted upon the condition of a yielded heart and a sincere purpose to put God's will first in their lives. For a repentant nation, the promise is prosperity and protection; but for those who spurn God's gracious offer of reconciliation, there can be no alternative but death and slaughter at the hands of their foes.

Verses 21–23 give expression to the Lord's sorrow at the moral downfall of His people. Their ancient loyalty and love have now given way to a base lust after false gods and the satanic values of this world. Like a chaste bride who later becomes a filthy adulteress, so Israel has violated her covenant of loyalty and obedience and shamed the name of her heavenly Husband. This process of degeneration is like the adulteration of precious silver with base alloy, or like wine which has been fraudulently mixed with water in order to cheat the customer in the market place. All the classes of government, all the leaders of society, have proven unfaithful to their trust. The very ones entrusted with the protection of society and the enforcement of the laws have conspired to set the Torah at nought, conniving with professional gangsters for a share of the spoil, and awarding the decision in the law court to the litigant able to pay the judges the largest bribe. If bribes are not pressed upon them, these rapacious magistrates pursue monetary rewards with shameless zeal.

Verses 24–31 present a contrasting portrait of the Israel that is yet to be, after divine chastisement has wrought its salutary work and a repentant remnant turns to the Lord in true submission. The omnipotent Sovereign of the universe Who has claimed Israel as His own ("the Lord of hosts, the Mighty One of Israel") will not permit His holiness to be trampled on and His revelation flouted by this rebellious generation. He will at last give vent to His holy wrath and bring upon them the condemnation they have challenged Him to enforce. He will so deal with them in catastrophic judgment and calamity that they shall be purified like ore in the smelting furnace: the worthless slag will be removed and cast away, while the good, pure metal will be drawn off and taken up out of the heat of the furnace. Once again a theocracy will be established in the earth on the basis of God's law (1:26) and their rulers and officials will show the same earnest attention to God's will as characterized the generation of Joshua ("as at the beginning" of the theocracy). Then shall God's ideal for Israel be realized, and there shall be a holy city which will be faithful and true to their Lord.

Zion shall be bought back out of slavery ("redeemed")—first, in the restoration from Babylon; second, in the deliverance through Calvary; third, in the establishment of God's latter-day people as a Millennial Kingdom. But this restoration will involve no setting aside of the holy demands of God's law; judgment will be visited upon the disobedient and unrepentant of Israel, and a righteous penalty shall fall upon all of their ungodly foes as well. None who join in rebellion ("transgressors") against God's word shall have any part in this coming Kingdom, nor those "sinners" who miss the true purpose of their life and live for self and this world. Catastrophic judgments upon the arena of history shall utterly crush their pretensions and power, and they shall at last be "ashamed" of their idols. That is to say, they shall be overwhelmed with humiliation at the consequences of their folly in rejecting the one true God, and substituting for Him imaginary and powerless gods—the idols of sexual defilement (worshiped under "sacred" oak trees or temple gardens in ritual prostitution). Like withering plants and trees in time of drought, their pagan or paganized society and culture will shrivel up and waste away to nothingness, and their guilty souls shall be cast along with their shameful works into the fires of God's eternal judgment ("none shall quench them").

2. Second Sermon: Present Chastisement for Future Glory (2:1—4:6)

Theme: God's Provision for the Repentant will be Millennial Bliss (2:1–4). To encourage the faithful few of Isaiah's generation, God reveals His ultimate purpose to bless His people with a restored Paradise, thus inspire them to keep true to their trust and endure with the steadfastness of those who are certain of ultimate victory. God's gracious purpose for Israel will not ultimately be thwarted, despite her present intransigeance. The "mountain of the Lord's house," that is, the Kingdom of God, shall some day be established in supremacy over all the governments of this earth. All the survivors of the Gentile nations will turn to the holy city for their worship and inspiration (the plain implication being that a temple will once again crown the hill of Moriah in the final age) and look to God's instruction and His Holy Scripture as the rule for their life. When this takes place, the Lord will enforce His holy requirements upon all mankind and they shall live in peace, in a warless society, in willing submission to the absolute authority to their divine ruler.

Solution: Only Divine Judgment can Cleanse and Equip Israel for her Mission (2:5—4:6). Judah is a nation ripe for judgment (2:5–11). Her only salvation is to repent of her sins of idolatry and pride. There will come a Day of the Lord to crush her pride and strip her of material resources (vv. 12–17). Then, at last, Judah shall have to abjure false gods and discard them (vv. 18–22). All classes of Jewish society are to be humbled and punished for their guilt (3:1–12), for the divine judge has pronounced His verdict against them (3:13—4:1).

The promise is made that Israel will be revived and experience ultimate blessedness under the Messiah (4:2–6). God's ultimate plan for a holy people will be realized when Christ, the Branch, blesses Mount Zion with His glorious presence.

3. Third Sermon: Judgment and Exile for the Stubborn, Unfaithful Nation (5:1–30)

Parable of the Vineyard (5:1–7). God is disappointed with His unfaithful, carnally minded people.

God's Indictment of the Wild Grapes (5:8–23). Six woes are pronounced upon Israel for greedy selfishness, for vicious dissipation, for cynical materialism, for perversion of the standards of morality, for proud self-sufficiency, for alcoholic self-indulgence, and for selling justice and integrity for silver.

God's Judgment (5:24–30). The penalty will be expulsion from Palestine and utter destruction of their culture and material achievements.

4. Fourth Sermon: The Prophet Cleansed and Commissioned by God (6:1–13)

The Vision of God's Holiness (6:1–4). Uzziah's death (739 B.C.) was symbolic of the passing of a golden age when God had favored a Scripture-honoring king and nation with manifold blessings. Already Uzziah's ungodly grandson, Ahaz, was becoming a dominant force in the government, and Isaiah was filled with foreboding. Kneeling at the gate of the Holy Place of the temple, he was granted a vision of the omnipotent God of Israel in His unapproachable holiness and sovereign majesty. The radiant six-winged seraphim symbolized the hosts of angelic beings who surrounded God's throne with adoration and praise, ascribing infinite holiness to the Almighty Creator, the Lord of Israel, the triune Sovereign of the universe. No wonder that material creation trembled and quaked before this awesome visitation from the court of heaven!

Confession of Sin and the Cleansing of Sanctification (6:5–7). In the face of this display of God's holiness, Isaiah realized more deeply than ever before the hopeless depravity of his nation and even of himself as a member of that nation. Sin-stained and impure of soul, they had no justifying goodness to present before God; in His presence they were "undone"—convicted, condemned, without excuse. How could their defiled lips speak forth acceptably the praises of God like these glorious angels of heaven? But at this very moment of self-condemnation, Isaiah experienced also the redeeming grace of God. The angel seized with priestly tongs a glowing coal from the altar of incense, a coal taken from the altar of sacrifice outside of the Holy Place, and applied it to the prophet's mouth. Because the unblemished victim had been offered upon the altar and the sacrifice had been accepted by God in fire, provision had been made for the believer's sin. His guilt was atoned for, and his lips—representative of his body committed to a life of witness—were purged of impurity, fitted for both praise and intercession, and also for the proclamation to men of the word of God.

Response and Commission (6:8–13). The sinner is not redeemed and regenerated for his own benefit only; he holds his salvation in trust for his Saviour. Every born-again believer is to be a witness for the Lord. No sooner was Isaiah assured of his cleansing than he was called to serve as the Lord's mouthpiece to others. He was invited, not compelled, for it was he who had to respond of his own free will. But once he had presented himself for his orders, he was given a difficult, almost heartbreaking commission. No career of conquest and glory stretched out before him, but an almost vain and fruitless ministry of warning and remonstrance to a gainsaying and stiff-necked generation. Since the people were already determined in their hearts not to heed the Lord, the preaching of His prophet would only harden them the more, rendering them altogether insensible to spiritual truth by a process of judicial blinding (cf. Rom. 1:21, 28). God's grace would persist in directing the most earnest warning and remonstrance to their unwilling ears, but it would not compel them to believe against their will, nor would it set aside the fundamental law of the moral universe: "From him that hath not shall be taken away even that which he hath."

How long would this spiritual deterioration go on in Israel, the prophet inquired. Would it mean the utter extinguishment of the lamp of Israel's testimony to the one true God? No, came the answer, it would endure until the complete devastation of the Holy Land and the removal of its populace to foreign exile (that is, to Babylon in the days of Nebuchadrezzar). But thereafter a remnant or tenth part would *return* from the Exile (following the most plain and obvious rendering of the verb, rather than the adverbial construction of the ASV) to the Land of Promise. Even this tenth part of the nation, the remnant of loyal believers, would experience decimation and calamity over the centuries; yet a "holy seed" or residue of true followers of God would survive, and in them would be the ultimate hope of Israel. In them would the covenant promises be fulfilled.

II. The Volume of Immanuel (7:1—12:6)

1. First Sermon: Immanuel Rejected by Worldly Wisdom (7:1-25)

Background and Historical Situation (7:1, 2). To the north, the kingdom of Israel under King Pekah (752–740–732 B.C.), semi-independent ruler of Gilead, 750–732 B.C., and of the Northern Kingdom, 740–732 B.C., had formed an alliance with the kingdom of Damascus under King Rezin (about 740–732 B.C.) to curb the growing power of Assyria, which was steadily pushing its empire westward to the Mediterranean. Eager to line up all the western kingdoms in this alliance, they had tried to compel Ahaz of Judah to join them. When he refused, they declared war on Judah and sent expeditions to subjugate the land and add its army and resources to their own. Their announced purpose was to set a certain "son of Tabeel" upon the throne as a puppet ruler. With good reason the hearts of the Jews were filled with apprehension. Where should they find help against this formidable coalition? In Assyria itself or in God? This was the issue which faced Judah in 735 B.C.

The Issue of Faith (7:3–9). God's answer to their perplexity came through His faithful prophet, who had in faith named his son Shear-jashub, "A Remnant Shall Return." The Lord had decreed the destruction of these ungodly allies, who had reckoned without His sovereign power and thought to trample upon His people. Rezin and his capital, Damascus, are soon to be smitten; and as for Ephraim, Pekah's apostate kingdom, it shall within sixty-five years be so destroyed as to lose permanently its national identity—a fate realized after the fall of Samaria in 722 B.C. and the later immigration of foreigners under the Assyrian resettlement policy (II Kings 17:24). Facing King Ahaz with this divine promise, Isaiah was bidden to offer him one last opportunity to repent of his sinful life and put his trust in God. If he would trust the Lord's promise and desist from his unholy alliance with Assyria, Ahaz would benefit by this blow of judgment against his northern foes. Otherwise their defeat would bring him no personal deliverance, only disaster.

The Sign of Immanuel (7:10–25). Although the king should have needed no confirmation to trust in God's promise, the Lord graciously offered to corroborate Isaiah's message by any miraculous sign Ahaz might name. But like so many others who are really intent upon their own will and way alone, the king closed his mind to any and all evidence, clothing his obduracy with a pious pretext: he would not presume to put the Lord to any test, a most impudent rejoinder after God had just summoned him to test Him. From this time on, Ahaz hardened his heart completely against God's truth in order to pursue his own policy of clever statesmanship. He robbed the treasures dedicated to God in the temple, in order to bribe the Assyrians to do what they were planning to do anyway—invade Syria and Ephraim (II Kings 16:8). He even destroyed many of the holy vessels of the Lord and shut up the temple against all who would worship God. In every part of Jerusalem, he had shrines and altars erected to the idols of the heathen; likewise in the other principal cities of his kingdom (II Chron. 28:24, 25).

Since Ahaz refused to name a sign, the Lord granted a miraculous seal of His promises to the entire house of David, namely, the sign of the virgin-born Immanuel. The ultimate and principal reference of verse 14 was to Jesus Christ (Mt. 1:23), Who alone could grant a permanent and complete deliverance to God's people. But there was a more immediate need to be met at that critical juncture in Hebrew history: the deliverance of Judah from the powerful coalition of Israel and Damascus.

In the campaigns which took place in the next two years, the Syrians crushed the army of Ahaz and carried many off into captivity (II Chron. 28:5). The Israelite army under the leadership of Zichri completely defeated a second Jewish army, slaying 120,000 of them and carrying off 200,000 more as captives (II Chron. 28:8). Jerusalem itself was brought under siege, and the kingdom would have been utterly overwhelmed had God not intervened. The Lord therefore granted a type of Immanuel, who was to serve as a time-indicator for the fulfilment of the divine promise that both Samaria and Damascus would be crushed and removed as threats to the survival of Judah. This infant, who was to be born within the year, would not attain the age of moral accountability (that is, twelve or thirteen years of age) before both Damascus and Samaria would be devastated and forsaken. This promise was given most probably in 735 B.C.; the baby boy who was to serve as the type of Immanuel was doubtless born in the following year, 734. By the time he was twelve, Damascus had been overthrown by Tiglath-Pileser in 732 and Samaria fell to the armies of Sargon II in 722 B.C. Judah itself was to be so ravaged by the Assyrian hordes that its land in large measure would revert to pasturage, and the young lad's diet was therefore to consist of "butter" (the Hebrew word really means "curdled milk," a favorite drink of shepherds) and honey, rather than the more usual food of city-dwellers (7:15). The ploughed fields and fruitful vineyards would be destroyed and revert to scrub and forest (vv. 23–25) because of the Assyrian depredations.

2. Second Sermon: Speedy Deliverance Foreshadowing the Coming Deliverer (8:1—9:7)

The Fall of Syria and Samaria Foretold (8:1–4). Who was this type of Immanuel to be? God does not leave us long in doubt. He promises to Isaiah a son, who is to bear the prophetic name of Maher-shalal-hash-baz, "Swift is the booty, speedy is the prey"—indicating the desperate flight of the Samaritan and Syrian armies before their conquerers. Who was to be his mother? The prophetess mentioned in verse 3, to whom Isaiah was already engaged at the time of his encounter with Ahaz, and who would at that time have been a virgin.

This promised baby boy was to serve as God's time-indicator; before he reached the age of two years old and able to talk, both Damascus and Samaria would have been smitten by the Assyrians.

And it came to pass, for not only was Damascus stormed in 732 B.C., but also Samaria had to capitulate to the conqueror and cede the northern provinces of its kingdom to the Assyrian Empire (II Kings 15:29). In the antitypical fulfilment, of course, the mother of Immanuel was to be a virgin not only at the time she conceived in the womb, but also thereafter until her son Jesus was born in Bethlehem—a miracle hinted at by the peculiar wording of 7:14, but not consummated until Christmas Eve.

The Foolish Choice Made by Worldly Wisdom (8:5–8). God's inspiration and guidance were symbolized by the gentle, healing waters of the Pool of Shiloah (the Siloam of the gospel record). Rejecting the Lord's guidance, the disobedient Jews were to be overwhelmed by the flood-waters of the Euphrates, symbolizing the invading hosts of Assyria. Yet the fact that Judah is spoken of as the land of Immanuel suggests that for the Messiah's sake, the Hebrew kingdom will not be utterly annihilated by this terrible flood.

The Ultimate Triumph of Grace (8:9–15). God challenges the heathen nations to do their worst in extinguishing the light of Israel. They shall only be smashed against the rock of judgment, because "God is with us" (Immanuel), that is, with His covenant people, the true believers of Judah. Isaiah and his faithful followers were not to be intimidated by the charge of "conspiracy" or "treason" (rather than "confederacy," in v. 12), even though they took a stand against the popular alliance with Assyria against the northern coalition. They were to put all their trust in the Lord Himself, and "sanctify" Him (testify to His holy omnipotence) before their countrymen, esteeming Him their impregnable refuge. Yet He would also be a stumbling stone and a rock of judgment to destroy and remove from Israel all those like Ahaz who refused to believe and obey.

A Summons to Trust in God Alone (8:16–22). This "law" or "revelational instruction" (*tōrah*) is to be sealed up, as a prophecy before the event, in order that when it comes to pass, the prophet's message may be objectively verified as that of the Lord of history. The believing remnant of true disciples will confidently await the fulfilment of all God's promises, taking their stand upon the revealed and inscripturated Word of God. Isaiah and his two symbolically named sons, A-Remnant-Shall-Return (Shear-jashub), and Swift-the-Booty-

Speedy-the-Prey (Maher-shalal-hash-baz), stand as testimonies to what God has solemnly sworn to do to Israel and on behalf of Israel. They join in affirming to a Bible-ignoring generation that any cult or religious group which claims inspiration or authority contrary to the Holy Scripture shall be deprived of any light or dawn of salvation, but shall know only the unutterable and unending misery of those who have been cut off eternally from the love and fellowship of God. Men's notions and philosophies may change; more "modern" and "up-to-date" viewpoints may supplant the old; yet the revealed Word of God shall never be altered and shall forever vindicate itself as true, triumphing over all who deny it.

Light Will Come from God the Redeemer (9:1–7). The portion of the Twelve Tribes which first fell under the foreigner's yoke was the region of Zebulun and Naphtali, the area known as Galilee. It was ravaged by the armies of Tiglath-Pileser and annexed to the Assyrian Empire in 732 B.C., when it was "brought into contempt" and plunged into "gloom." (The RSV rendering of 9:1 is to be preferred to the KJV here.) Yet, in the marvelous providence of God, it was precisely this very region which was in later times to be visited by the radiant light of Jesus, the Messiah (cf. Mt. 4:13–17), Who made His headquarters in Galilee. The prophet by inspiration foresees how God is going to multiply the small nation of those who return from the Babylonian Exile into a great and mighty people, achieving (under the Maccabees) notable victories on the battlefield. But over and above these temporary and limited successes, the scope of the prophecy extends to the multiplication of Christ's disciples from a little band of 120 to a host of many millions, victoriously extending the frontiers of Christ's spiritual empire over all the earth. Ultimately the final triumph of Armageddon is in view.

This glorious future is assured to God's people because of the Messiah Who is yet to come. Verse six tells us (1) that He will be born as a human child, rather than appearing full-grown as a heavenly conqueror; (2) that He will be a son or heir of the house of Israel—a Jew; (3) that He will be the ultimate ruler of the earth; (4) that He will be a wonder or marvel as a counselor, imparting the counsel which alone can save man from eternal doom; (5) that He will be God Himself, and specifically God in His aspect as champion in battle; (6) that as God he will be the Eternal One—both the possessor of eternity and the author of eternal life (lit.: "father of eternity"); (7) the Prince or Ruler of peace—bestowing well-being (*shālōm*) of soul, and, in the Millennial Kingdom, prosperity and warlessness to the whole world in the age to come. He shall exercise this royal authority upon the throne of David, as his descendant and lawful heir (according to the promise of II Sam. 7:16); yet He will far surpass the glory of David both in extent and in duration("there shall be no end"). The perfect righteousness of God shall be enforced in His benevolent administration and shall prevail in the eternal Kingdom of Heaven itself. This glorious consummation will be brought to pass by the zeal of the Father on behalf of His beloved Son. To this promise we, equally with the generation of Isaiah, look forward with eager anticipation; for us too it is "the blessed hope" of Christ's appearing.

3. Third Sermon: The Inexorable Doom of Exile for Proud Samaria (9:8—10:4)

The boasting of Samaria is vain (9:8–12). Samaria is incorrigible (9:13–17). Sin results in self-destruction (vv. 18–21): the ravages of fire and civil war await her. Captivity impends for the ruling classes (10:1–4) who ruthlessly exploit their subjects.

4. Fourth Sermon: The False Empire Vanquished; the Glorious Empire to Come (10:5—12:6)

God's Instrument for Judgment Shall in Turn be Judged (10:5–34). Assyria is God's tool for vengenance (vv. 5, 6) despite the fact that she is guilty of arrogant pride of power (vv. 7–11). Her doom will be utter destruction (vv. 12–19). But the chastened remnant of Israel shall ultimately triumph (vv. 20–23). Hence Assyria is not to be feared by those who trust in God alone (vv. 24–34).

The Spirit-Empowered Messiah to Restore and Reign (11:1–16). In fulfilment of God's promise to David, the son of Jesse (II Sam. 7:13), Immanuel is to appear as his lineal descendant, a "rod" (or Branch) out of his "stem" or "stump," as it should preferably be rendered (11:1–3). This suggests that the noble tree of David's line would first be felled (as took place in 587 B.C.), and then a shoot would spring out of the lopped-off stump as Messiah, the King. He was to be a fruit-bearing branch (the term here is *nēzer*, cryptically suggesting Nazareth, a feminine form of this same noun, Mt. 2:23), producing the fruit of the Spirit in all His perfection, and also the fruitage of the Vine in its living branches (Jn. 15:1–8).

His equipment is to consist in the sevenfold Spirit of God. This number seven reappears in connection with the symbolic stone of Zechariah 3:9 and the seven spirits before God's throne in Revelation 4:5. This number signifying divine completeness indicates the perfection of Messiah's enduement for the task of redemption: wisdom, spiritual understanding, good counsel, power for conquest, knowledge of the Lord, and a godly reverence for Him. Unlike the children of Adam, this Holy One shall have a delight in doing the Father's will which is free from all taint of self-interest.

He will furnish complete and final vindication of God's holy law as against the challenge of Satan-following mankind, who have been permitted down through the ages to contaminate the atmosphere of the world with rebellion and sin (11:3–5). But Christ is to put an end to man's arrogance and disobedience, correcting all wrongdoers and compelling every knee to bow to the sovereignty of God. His judgment will be based on the true facts, not according to specious appearances ("after the sight of His eyes") or the spoken testimony of men. The godly believers, "the meek of the earth," who have humbly put their trust in God and who have suffered from the ruthless oppression of worldlings, shall find their wrongs avenged and every injustice made right. The execution of His verdict shall be accomplished by the "rod" or shepherd's staff (the Hebrew term can also mean a king's scepter) of His mouth; that is, His spoken utterance shall convey with it divine and efficacious power (similarly "the sword of his mouth" in Rev. 19:15).

All aggression will cease in Immanuel's holy Kingdom, for all men everywhere will know God as their Lord, and His will shall be the most important thing in their lives (11:6–9). So complete shall the transformation be that non-human creation will, according to the teaching of Romans 8:19–22, share in the glorious liberation from vanity and evil. As a symptom and reflection of the spiritual change in mankind, even the predatory beasts and noxious serpents dwelling in the Lord's holy "mountain" (or Kingdom) will live in gentle harmony with those upon whom they formerly preyed. Thus the restoration to the peaceful conditions of the Garden of Eden will be complete during the Millennium.

On the threshold of His Kingdom, the Messiah is to appear as a standard or ensign, to rally together to His cause all the people of

God. These are specified as comprising the nations (or *gōyim*) as well as converted Jews (11:10–16). It is significant that the ingathering of the Gentiles is mentioned first (perhaps with reference to the present New Testament age); but then it is made as clear as Hebrew can express it that the Lord will "a second time" (in contrast to the first restoration after the fall of Babylon) regather the Hebrew people from every geographical region (north, south, east and west) to which they have been scattered, so as to assemble them in the Land of Promise. When this takes place, there will no longer be any hostility between the Ten Tribes and the Two (an enmity which had cursed Israel for centuries up until Isaiah's generation)—a condition made possible of fulfilment when the Second Commonwealth was set up, eventually to become the unified Jewish realm of Maccabean times. In the later course of history, even the hybrid and paganized element of the Ten Tribes which found expression in Samaritan hostility was completely eliminated from the scene.

The last three verses foretell the complete conquest by God's people (Jewish and Gentile) over the unbelieving world, and over all those aspects and phases of heathen depravity and opposition anciently exemplified by Philistia and Moab. With this conquest shall come the removal of every geographical or spiritual barrier between east and west, Assyria and Egypt, for a perfect harmony and mutual understanding shall govern all the surviving nations of mankind.

How strange that He Who was spoken of as the rod or shoot of Jesse in verse 1 of chapter 11 should a little later (v. 10) be called the root of Jesse! How can the one and same person be both root and branch at the same time? Of no mere human messiah could this ever be true. But understanding Immanuel to be Jesus Christ, it becomes apparent how both statements could be true. As lineal descendant of David's family, He was indeed the rod or Branch. But could there have been such a thing as the covenant of grace, had it not been for Christ's atonement, on the basis of which it was possible to bestow forgiveness of sins and to extend the gracious promises of redemption to Abraham, to Moses and to David? Truly the Lamb of God, slain "from the foundation of the world" (I Pet. 1:19, 20) furnished the ground for the very existence of a chosen people and a chosen royal line. In that sense He was indeed "the root of Jesse."

The Song of Thanksgiving and Triumph (12:1–6). This song beautifully expresses the joy of Christ's redeemed as He comes again to rule over Zion and reign supreme over all the nations of earth.

III. God's Judgment-Burdens upon the Nations (13:1—23:18)

1. Burden upon Babylon (13:1—14:27)

Babylon, which is to fall to the Medes and Persians, will ultimately become an uninhabited wilderness (14:1–22). The song of triumph sounds over the king of Babylon and his satanic patron as he is brought down to Hades (14:1–20). His doom is utter and irrevocable destruction (vv. 21–27).

2. Burden upon Philistia (14:28–32)

Philistia will be crushed (by Assyria under Sargon and Sennacherib), but the Lord will be the refuge of His people.

3. Burden upon Moab (15:1—16:14)

Moab is to be the scene of pitiable desolation (15:1—16:9). Her arrogant pride will be punished with Assyrian devastation (16:10–14).

4. Burden upon Damascus and Samaria (17:1–14)

Damascus and Ephraim (northern Israel) shall be ruined (17:1–3), but some day Samaria will produce a remnant of true believers who abhor idolatry (vv. 3–8). Chastening must come first, however (vv. 9–11). The horrors of the coming Assyrian invasion are foretold (vv. 12–14.)

5. Burden upon Ethiopia (18:1–7)

The prophet answers the Ethiopian envoys that their carcasses shall rot on the field of battle. Yet some day Ethiopia will bring to God the tribute of faith.

6. Burden upon Egypt (19:1—20:6)

Egypt shall be plagued with civil war and Assyrian bondage and suffer from drought and devastation (19:1–10). These woes result from the folly of pride and worldly wisdom (vv. 11–14). Eventually God's people will triumph over Egypt (vv. 15–18), and she shall be converted and delivered, to share with Israel in God's favor (vv. 19–25). Yet the immediate future holds conquest and captivity by Assyria (King Essarhaddon) (20:1–6).

7. *Second Burden upon Babylon (21:1–10)*

Babylon shall be conquered by Medo-Persia and her idols shall perish.

8. *Burden upon Dumah (or Edom)(21:11, 12)*

Dumah, which means "silence," is an anagram for Edom. The prophet may be signifying by symbol the silence of decay which will cover the land. The query in verse 11, "Watchman, what of the night?" is interpreted by some expositors to mean, "How much of the night has already passed?" The cryptic answer in verse 12 suggests that day or night, light or darkness, depend upon Edom's choice.

9. *Burden upon Arabia (21:13–17)*

The northern tribes of Dedan and Kedar shall be driven into flight (by conquering Assyrians and Chaldeans).

10. *Burden upon Jerusalem, the Valley of Vision (22:1–25)*

This gay, careless city shall be stormed by the enemy, for it trusted only in its munitions, not in God (22:1–14). Shebna, a representative of crass materialism, shall be replaced by God-fearing Eliakim in public office (vv. 15–25).

11. *Burden upon Tyre (23:1–18)*

An amazing downfall awaits this commercial center of the world (23:1–7). God has decreed this calamity because of her pride (vv. 8–12). After seventy years of desolation, she shall serve in ignominious slavery (vv. 13–18).

IV. First Volume of General Judgment and Promise (24:1—27:13)

1. First Sermon: Universal Judgment to Follow Universal Sin (24:1–23)

An all-consuming destruction shall come upon all classes of society (24:1–13), but the believing remnant shall survive to glorify God (vv. 14–16a). For the present, the cause of wickedness prevails (vv. 16b–23).

2. Second Sermon: Praise to the Lord as Deliverer, Victor, and Comforter (25:1–12)

God is adored as a wise and righteous judge and avenger (25:1–3) Who faithfully delivers those who trust in Him (vv. 4–8). Isaiah predicts the joy of those who have waited for Him and seen His triumph over godless nations like Moab (vv. 9–12).

3. Third Sermon: A Song of Rejoicing in Judah's Consolation (26:1–21)

The Lord is praised as the defender of Israel (26:1–3). Fiery destruction awaits stubborn infidels, but peace and enlargement will be the lot of true believers (vv. 10–15). After sore tribulation comes new life and peace (vv. 16–19). Trust in Him Who shall bring this wicked world into judgment (vv. 20, 21).

4. Fourth Sermon: Punishment for Oppressors and Preservation for God's People (27:1–13)

The prosperity of the Israelite vine after the Day of the Lord is promised (27:1–6). Israel shall be purged and preserved, but God-rejecting heathen shall be destroyed (vv. 7–11). Israel shall be regathered to her land (vv. 12, 13).

V. The Volume of Woes upon the Unbelievers of Israel (28:1—33:24)

1. First Sermon: God's Dealings with Drunkards and Scoffers in Israel (28:1-29)

Woe to the Drunkards of Ephraim (28:1-8). This message, delivered while the northern kingdom was heading for its tragic fall under the reign of Hoshea, was intended as a warning to the worldly-minded sophisticates of the southern kingdom also, who were influencing Judah to the same slippery, downward path. Proud of the beauty of their vine-clad, orchard-crowned countryside and of their fashionable, well-built cities, the boastful leaders of Ephraim, the elite of Samaria, were confidently resolved to repair completely the devastations resulting from the previous Assyrian invasion. But they were reckoning without the covenant God whom they had forsaken, and Who had determind their permanent destruction through the power of the Assyrians, even the fall of Samaria and the deportation of its population—a melancholy fate which overtook them in 722 B.C.

Instead of heeding the voice of God's prophets, Hosea, Isaiah and Micah, these self-sufficient materialists staggered irrevocably down the highway of destruction, looking with bleary and self-deluded eyes upon the menacing signs of impending doom. This intoxication of soul found expression in the crassest alcoholism and orgiastic self-indulgence, which left its polluting stain upon the very spiritual and moral leaders of the nation, the prophets and the clergy. Having forsaken their God and their Scriptures, these idol-worshiping church leaders had abandoned even their pretense at enlightened ethics to justify their heresy, and had fallen into the inevitable degradation of the laity whom they had so long misled. Having inculcated in them the more modern and enlightened views of religious philosophy, convincing them that there was good in all religions, the leaders finally found themselves groveling in the bestialities of the crassest nature-religion and Baalism.

Judah's Scoff at God's Teaching Answered by the Lord's Retribution (28:9-22). The scoffers who rule at Jerusalem (v. 14) now utter their words of scorn at Isaiah's stern, old-fashioned message, saying (vv. 9, 10): "Who does Isaiah think we are, gullible children in kindergarten? We have no time for his monotonous, unvarying message of outmoded piousness, always viewing with alarm and painting a black picture of the future, always harping on the same theme day in and day out." But this contemptuous rejection of God's message is straightway answered: Since these heedless free-thinkers refuse to hear God's summons to repent, coming to them from prophets speaking to them in their native Hebrew, they shall have to learn of His righteous judgment from Assyrian-speaking foreigners, who shall inflict appropriate punishment upon them. They have turned a deaf ear to the Lord's invitation to trust in Him alone and renew their strength in Him; therefore they shall have to learn the hard way that He keeps His word and punishes disobedience. Line upon line and precept upon precept, this grim lesson shall be dinned into their ears until their ungodly self-will is crushed by blow after blow of calamity and disaster.

But for those who will trust in God's promise and yield their heart to Him, there is a glorious assurance. The king and governmental leaders have made a covenant with death and the powers of Hades, for they have made an alliance with the ruthless and God-despising Assyrians, in the hope that their invading armies (or "overflowing scourge," 28:15) would pass Judah by as loyal allies. But the conquering hordes from the East will crush and devastate the southern kingdom and bring all their defenses and false hopes tumbling down about their ears. With inexorable pressure their brutal exactions shall be imposed upon them day after day and year after year without let-up. The prophetic perspective extends past the depredations of Sargon II to the fearful devastation by Sennacherib's hosts in 701 B.C., when every walled city but Jerusalem itself was stormed and laid waste.

Yet in the midst of these murky clouds of doom, there flashes forth a radiant burst of sunlight for the remnant of the faithful (28:16). The present government of Zion under King Ahaz has failed miserably; but some day God Himself shall set up in Zion a firm foundation-stone for the spiritual temple of God. That stone will be Christ Jesus (I Pet. 2:6, 7), Who will appear in the meeting-place appointed between God and man in the holy city, at the place of the effectually atoning blood-sacrifice. He will be a "tried stone," containing no faults or cleavages, and able to withstand the craftiest temptations and heaviest pressure that Satan could bring against Him. He will be a "precious cornerstone," outweighing in value all that the world can offer, and by His atoning merit making all the difference between eternal heaven and eternal hell. He will provide a basis for the salvation of sinners so firm and sure that it will not require any contributory work of man; He will furnish a revelation of unchangeable truth, upon which sinners may safely stake their immortal souls. The true believer who trusts this promise of God will not "be in haste," that is, become excited and alarmed; nor will he ever (as the New Testament paraphrases it) be "ashamed" for having entrusted his soul to a false refuge.

An Analogy from Agriculture (28:23–29). The farmer does not plow just for the sake of plowing, but only as the preparation for sowing seed and planting the crops he intends in each specified section of his field. Observe the law of cause and effect illustrated hereby. The farmer receives from God the intelligence to prepare and carry out his plan in a methodical way, using the finer threshing instruments for more delicate types of crop, and the heavier and harsher for the tougher species. Even so (is the implication) God knows how to administer appropriate discipline according to the need of each sinner. He avoids chastening too severely the man who might repent and get right with Him once more; the harsher penalties are reserved for the incorrigible.

2. Second Sermon: Judgment upon Blind Souls who Try to Deceive God (29:1–24)

Careless Jerusalem is Ariel ("hearth of God"), where fires of destruction shall burn (29:1–4). Sudden destruction shall also befall the foes of God's people (vv. 5–8). It is wretched folly to try to deceive Him with a sham faith (vv. 9–16). True Israel shall some day be cured of blindness (vv. 17–24).

3. Third Sermon: Confidence in Man versus Confidence in God (30:1–33)

Disaster impends for Jews who seek deliverance with the help of Egypt rather than of God (30:1–5). The diplomatic mission to Egypt will prove futile (vv. 6, 7). Self-willed Judah shall be crushed by calamity (vv. 8–17). Destruction is decreed for heathen powers who oppress Israel (vv. 27–33).

4. Fourth Sermon: Deliverance through God's Gracious Intervention (31:1—32:20)

Woe to those who rely on Egyptian allies (31:1-3)! God will defend Judah without human aid (vv. 4-9). Israel will ultimately be delivered by her messianic King (32:1-8). After her chastisement and restoration, the Spirit shall be poured out upon her (vv. 9-20).

5. Fifth Sermon: Punishment of Treacherous Deceivers and the Triumph of Christ (33:1-24)

Treacherous Gentiles (like Sennacherib) will be crushed by God (33:1-6). The scene of woe as covenant-breaking Assyria invades is depicted (vv. 7-9). But retribution shall lay the heathen waste and punish the hypocrites of Israel (vv. 10-16). The safety and joy of the faithful under the reign of Christ are assured (vv. 17-24).

VI. Second Volume of General Judgment and Promise (34:1—35:10)

1. First Sermon: Destruction of the Gentile World-Power (34:1-17)

The Day of the Lord shall overtake all nations (34:1-3). It will crush both satanic powers and heathen foes like Edom (vv. 4-7). Desolation shall follow upon this destruction (vv. 8-15). God's guarantee to fulfil the promise made to Israel of permanent possession of the land is given (vv. 16, 17).

2. Second Sermon: The Ultimate Bliss of God's Redeemed (35:1-10)

Zion shall be glorified by the presence of the Lord (35:1, 2). His strength and abundance shall replace His people's weakness and poverty (vv. 3-7). The blessed security of the redeemed on the highway of holiness is assured (vv. 8-10).

VII. The Volume of Hezekiah (36:1—39:8)

1. Destruction of Judah Averted (36:1—37:38)

Scene I: The World-power Challenges the Lord (36:1-22). The arrogant conqueror orders Judah to submit unconditionally (vv. 1-10). The people are directly summoned to surrender to Assyria (vv. 11-22).

Scene II: God's Answer to the Challenge (37:1-38). Hezekiah repentantly appeals to God (37:1-4) and receives a first assurance of divine deliverance (vv. 5-7). The world-power of Assyria renews its defiance (vv. 8-13), and Hezekiah appeals to God in the temple (vv. 14-20). God grants a second assurance: the boastful pagan shall be crushed (vv. 21-35). The promise is miraculously fulfilled (vv. 36-38).

2. Destruction of Judah's King is Averted (38:1—39:8)

Scene I: Hezekiah's Deliverance from Deadly Sickness (38:1-22). He offers up a prayer of faith in the face of apparently fatal illness (vv. 1-3). God graciously answers and confirms His action by a sign (vv. 4-8). Hezekiah utters an eloquent psalm of praise (vv. 10-20). The medical report is given (v. 21).

Scene II: Hezekiah's Foolish Pride (39:1-8). Because he displays his wealth to the envoys (39:1, 2), God condemns his pride and imposes a sentence of national exile upon Babylon (vv. 3-7). Hezekiah repentantly submits to God's sentence (v. 8).

VIII. The Volume of Comfort (40:1—66:24)

1. The Purpose of Peace (40:1—48:22)

The Majesty of the Lord, the Comforter (40:1-31). Comfort is proclaimed to the chastened Israel of the future (vv. 1-11). The greatness and wisdom of the Creator are infinite (vv. 12-17). The contrast is drawn between the Lord and false gods (vv. 18-26). The love of the true and living God can be trusted all the way (vv. 27-31).

The Challenge of the God of Providence to Unbelievers (41:1–29). His providence is based on His omnipotence (vv. 1–7). Israel is an instrument of Providence (vv. 8–10). The chosen people will overcome their heathen foes (vv. 11–16) and God will deliver them in their need and prosper them (vv. 17–20). God's foretelling the future proves His omniscience (vv. 21–29).

The Servant of the Lord, Individual and National (42:1–25). The messianic Servant is presented as the tender Prophet (vv. 1–4). He is the promised Saviour of both Jew and Gentile (vv. 5–9). The Gentiles praise God for His justice and grace (vv. 10–13). God will come to punish idolators and restore backslidden believers (vv. 14–17). Israel's strange blindness will draw chastening upon them (vv. 18–25).

Redemption by Grace (43:1—44:5). God's love will support, redeem and restore His people (43:1–7) who are His witness to the world (vv. 8–13). God's sovereignty will be demonstrated by the crushing of the Chaldeans and restoring their captives (vv. 14–21). Israel's punishment is only the result of ingratitude (vv. 22–28). The servant-nation shall yet be converted (44:1–5).

Dead Idols or the Living God (44:6–23)? Monotheism challenges the idol-worshiping world (vv. 6–8). Polytheism blinds the heathen to manifest truth (vv. 9–20) The witness of Israel is to be vindicated in the future (vv. 21–23).

The Sovereign God Employing and Converting the Heathen (44: 24—45:25). The Lord decrees restoration through the Persian Cyrus (44:24–28). He promises irresistible victory to Cyrus, as a type of Messiah (45:1–6). God's sovereignty is vindicated against human critics (vv. 7–13). The Gentiles are to be converted (vv. 14–19). They are invited to be saved by faith in the Lord (vv. 20–25).

Lessons Taught by Babylon's Downfall and Israel's Preservation (46:1—47:15). The helplessness of idols is contrasted with the omnipotence of the one true God (46:1–13). Enslavement awaits Babylon for undue cruelty to Israel (47:1–7). Doom impends the godless culture and philosophy of this world (vv. 8–11). Human sorcery and astrology are powerless to avert God's judgment (vv. 12–15).

Judgment upon Faithless, Hypocritical Israel (48:1–22). God presents false Jews with evidence of fulfilled prophecy (vv. 1–8). God's glory is to be upheld by Israel's chastening (vv. 9–11). The Almighty will send a Gentile deliverer against Babylon (v. 16). The chastened Jews are to flee out of Babylon and return home (vv. 17–22).

2. The Prince of Peace (49:1—57:21)

Messiah-Servant Will Bring Restoration to Israel and Light to Gentiles (49:1-26). Messiah will proclaim restoration to Israel and salvation to the heathen (vv. 1-7). God graciously delivers and succors His redeemed (vv. 8-13). Disheartened Israel is reassured of God's loving care (vv. 14-26).

Sinfulness of Israel Contrasted with the Obedience of the Servant (50:1-11). Sin separates the Lord from His wife Israel (vv. 1-3). Christ as the true Israel responds obediently to God's will (vv. 4-9). Believers are invited to submission and faith, while rebellious unbelievers are warned of judgment to come (vv. 10, 11).

Encouragement to Trust in God Alone, Not Fearing Men (51:1-16). God's mercy to Abraham endures even today (vv. 1-3). The spiritual sons of Abraham, who eagerly follow after God's righteousness, are living stones (I Pet. 2:5) hewn from the same bedrock of God's covenant faithfulness as was Abraham himself. If God fulfilled for him the more difficult promise of a numerous posterity, even though Isaac was not born until Abraham had reached a hundred, God can also transform the spiritual wilderness of Zion into a Garden of Eden and put a song of unquenchable joy into the mouth of His redeemed.

Israel is summoned to trust in God alone (51:4-8). Pay careful heed, O Israel, to the Lord's promise: He will issue a new "law" or "revelational instruction" (that is, the Gospel of Christ), which will manifest His holy justice (as Christ fulfils for sinners all the requirements of the law), and yet impart His salvation to believers of even the remotest nations ("the isles"). It is absurd to doubt God's ability to deliver Israel and judge heathen, for the Almighty has power to destroy and cast aside the present heaven and earth as worn-out garments, and establish a new order transcending the transiency and decay of this present age. And so God's true believers (here defined as those in whose heart the law is written—see Jer. 31:33) need never cringe before the power of mortal men (those who "kill the body, and after that have no more that they can do," Lk. 12:4). However fearsome their threats, they have in their body the seeds of decay and in their unregenerate soul the sentence of death. The only permanent value in this life is the covenant faithfulness of the Lord God Almighty.

The believers pray that God may perform these promises (51:9–

11). God always requires a response of faith on the part of those to whom His promise is given, and so here the believing remnant recall how their Lord in Moses' time smote the raging dragon of Egypt and gave their fathers a dry path through the midst of the Red Sea. They are confident that He will retrieve their children from the coming disaster and bring them back in joy from Exile to the holy city as He has promised.

God assures His people that the omnipotent Creator is faithful (51:12-16). How unreasonable and illogical it is for a believer to tremble before the foes of Almighty God! Whether it be the cruel henchmen of King Manasseh, or the fury of the Chaldeans under Nebuchadrezzar a hundred years hence, they shake their puny fists in vain against the Lord of heaven and earth or against His redeemed people! Translating verse 14a as "He that is bent down shall speedily be loosed," we see that the godly who are bound in oppression by their persecutors, both present and future, will be the only ones to survive as a nation, and their needs shall be unfailingly supplied by the Lord. To the restless sea of ungodly mankind, God will apportion disquietude and ceaseless turmoil ("stirreth up the sea"). But the people of God have only to keep faithful in proclaiming His message ("I have put my words in thy mouth"), and He will specially preserve them from the malice of Satan. In all their persecutions, they shall be more than conquerors, and God will fashion His new heaven and earth to be a holy kingdom for them.

Israel Summoned to Awaken and Return to Gods' Favor (51:17—52:12). The penalty of captivity will be sufficient (51:17-23). Israel is pictured as bloodied from her wounds and fallen to the ground in a drunken stupor—having drunk of the wine of God's wrath. Her sons or inhabitants have all been either slain or carried off in captivity, as a condign punishment for the egregious apostasy of the nation ("who shall bemoan thee?"). But now at last (and the prophetic viewpoint here is 538 B.C., after the fall of Babylon) a new day has dawned, bringing forgiveness and restoration to captive Israel and righteous retribution to her foes. The Lord is "pleading" the cause, or vindicating the rights, of His chastened people as against the merciless Chaldeans who made them grovel in the dust.

The Lord restores Israel for His own glory (52:1-6). God's holy nation is bidden to arise from the dust of mourning and degradation and lay hold by faith upon the benefits of God's marvelous grace. He has appointed for her strength to prevail against Satan and all his works and provided beautiful garments predictive of the imputed righteousness of Jesus Christ Whose holy perfection covers the shameful nakedness of the helpless sinner. Believers constitute a City of God which is holy because God has invested them with His atoning and sanctifying grace and has claimed them as His own peculiar possession. From this verse (52:1) came that significant phrase, "Jerusalem the Holy," which the Christ-rejecting Jews of the First Revolt (A.D. 67–70) vainly inscribed upon their coins, but which has remained as a precious title of the Church of God ever since.

God watches over His people with even-handed justice towards their Gentile foes. In the shameful years before the fall of Jerusalem (587 B.C.), the Jews as a nation had bartered away their status as God's holy people for the worthless, empty allurements of idolatry and self-will. Correspondingly, when their captivity comes to an end with the overthrow of Babylon, King Cyrus of Persia will set them free without any bribe or material inducement of any kind, and he will crush the arrogance of the God-deriding Chaldeans.

The redeemed respond to the glad tidings of salvation (52:7–12). The heralds of God's deliverance are pictured as descending from the surrounding hills to proclaim their good tidings to the ruined city of Jerusalem. Their feet are called beautiful because they bear the best message human ears can hear. God is at hand to bestow peace and well-being (*shālōm*) upon His repentant people; He lavishes His goodness and benevolence upon them ("tidings of good") and grants a full deliverance ("salvation") from bondage, sin and fear. Israel's watchmen, those prophets and godly witnesses who man her spiritual ramparts for the transmission of God's warnings, shall sing aloud with joy as they see the Lord's ransomed return from Babylonian bondage and take up life anew as the commonwealth of the Lord. Most of all, they glory in the demonstration God has given of His power to rescue His people even from the most powerful potentates of earth, and to preserve them from the apparently unavoidable fate of permanent dispersion and absorption into the Gentile peoples.

But the prophetic watchmen have one urgent caution for their countrymen: they are to leave Babylon completely behind and take none of it with them. As the family of Lot was to flee from Sodom without looking back, and as Israel was to leave the smoking ruins of Jericho without touching any of its spoil, so the returning exiles were to abandon the unholy, flesh-worshiping culture of Babylon physically and mentally. They were to come back to the Land of Promise in godly simplicity and erect their new commonwealth upon no other basis than Holy Scripture and its perfect rule for their lives. Nor were they to be apprehensive that they would be in any way handicapped or put to disadvantage by this complete abandonment of Babylon and all it stood for; the Lord Himself would grant His safe-conduct to the defenseless band of returning settlers, warding off all possible foes from in front and from the rear, without need of any men-at-arms. (Compare Ezra's later rejection of an escort of Persian troops as he made his journey to Jerusalem in 457 B.C., Ezra 8:22.)

The Divine Servant Triumphs through Vicarious Suffering (52:13—53:12). His amazing triumph through humiliation is foretold (52:13–15). Despite the improper chapter division in our Bible, these three verses belong to chapter 53 and have no connection with what precedes. Here we have the highwater mark in Old Testament revelation. Nowhere in all Hebrew Scriptures is there to be found a more profound treatment of the person and work of our Redeemer, and indeed even the New Testament can show no fuller discussion of the meaning of the cross.

Redeemed Zion is here presented with her God-man Redeemer, the most wonderful person Who has ever lived, one Whose sacred person, combining within Himself a complete divine nature and a complete human nature, exceeds all mortal comprehension. It is said of Him that He shall "deal wisely"—a word implying that by prudent and intelligent action He shall succeed in His mission—and that He shall attain a triumph and exaltation far beyond all other men. The surpassing nature of this exaltation is brought out by the three successive verbs of sublimation: "shall be exalted and lifted up" (the same as were used in Is. 6:1 of the enthronement of God) "and shall be very high." Thus we read in Philippians 2:9: "Wherefore God highly exalted him and gave unto him the name which is above every name." Yet this remarkable exaltation is to be attained only through an equally remarkable humiliation of the Servant: "As many were astonished at thee . . . so shall he sprinkle many nations . . ." (52:14). Just as His degradation is to be of the most surpassing nature, so also His impact upon the world and its rulers will be of the most surprising intensity. All observers of His Good Friday sufferings shall be dumbfounded by the disfiguring torments and maltreatments inflicted upon Him above and beyond that experienced by other men. But as they witness the stupendous results of His resurrection victory, they shall find themselves absolutely speechless as they are confronted by His spotless purity and self-sacrificing love. They shall be powerless to utter a word of self-justification as they behold the dread indictment of their sin presented by the spectacle of God dying upon a cross for the sins of guilty man. As they feel the impact of His holiness and of His unfathomable love, they shall experience the cleansing power of His atonement through the sacrament of baptism and all that which it spiritually represents: "He shall sprinkle many nations." (There is very slender evidence for translating: "He shall startle many nations"; the verb *hizzeh* occurs often in Scripture, but elsewhere always means "sprinkle," and is used of applying the blood of atonement or the water of purification.)

The Servant as viewed by man is rejected and despised (53:1–3). The prophet, as spokesman for repentant Israel, suggests by his query, "Who hath believed?" the amazing unbelief of the Jewish nation and, by implication, of mankind in general. "He came unto his own, and his own [people] received him not" (Jn. 1:12). Through Him God revealed His mighty "arm," that arm through which He had performed the redeeming miracles of Moses' day (cf. Deut. 4:34, "by a mighty hand and an outstretched arm"), accomplishing even mightier wonders through His messianic Servant, even to the raising of the dead (cf. Jn. 12:37, 38, where this verse from Isaiah is said to be fulfilled). But Israel refused to give heed. Christ did not conform to their notions of what the Messiah should be like: a conquering hero clad in celestial glory and crushing on the battlefield all the heathen foes of Jewry. Instead, He was destined to come as a "tender plant" (or "suckling babe," as the word may also be rendered), a root (cf. 11:10) out of an unglamorous and unpromising environment ("a dry ground"). In appearance he would lack the ostentatious pomp of a world conqueror and present only the humble demeanor of the gentle Prophet from Galilee. After an initial phase of popularity in which His true redemptive mission would be totally misunderstood, He would be finally rejected by His own nation, disillusioned because they could not use Him as a tool for their nationalistic aspirations. What a travesty of a Messiah, what a sorry figure He would cut before the jeering rabble, as they cried in disillusionment: "Away with him; crucify him!"

The Servant as viewed by God, is the vicariously suffering Redeemer (53:4–6). Strangely enough, the suffering and contempt the Messiah would have to bear would be endured not because of His own iniquity or unworthiness (as are other men's), but for the sake of the very people who rejected Him. They had penal judgments to bear, but He would suffer them in their place! Even though they refused to acknowledge Him as their Saviour or sin-bearer, He would undergo the humiliation and maltreatment of Jewish and Roman soldiery, He would suffer the frightful agony of the cross, as their substitute at the place of judgment. The broken law required the penalty of death; that penalty He would pay in the sinner's place. He would endure "the chastisement of our peace," that is, the infliction of the punishment for sin, which, by being paid in full, would lead to "peace" between a holy God and unholy mankind. Note how explicitly it is stated here that Christ would suffer, not simply as a consequence of men's sins (for the innocent often suffer as a consequence of the sins of others), but as a remedy for their guilt—a remedy so efficacious that God might preserve His own righteousness and still forgive the sins of the ungodly who believe and receive His gift of eternal life (Rom. 3:26). This repentance, faith and forgiveness on the basis of Christ's vicarious atonement bring about "peace" between God and His people.

The substitutionary character of Christ's penal death could not be more clearly stated by human speech than it is in 53:6. This plainly affirms that all men are guilty sinners in need of a saviour; that the root and basis of their sin consists in their turning away from God's will to follow their own, exalting self to the place of supremacy that belongs only to God; and that the Lord caused all of these sins of ours to light upon His Servant. Even as the blood-avenger of the Mosaic ordinance (Num. 35:19 uses the same verb as here: *pāga'*) "met" the offender in the way in order to slay him, so the avenging wrath of the law met our sin-bearer and representative on Golgotha to put Him to death. It should be clearly understood that this doctrine of vicarious, substitutionary atonement is the only doctrine of atonement taught in Scripture. Thus also Peter, mindful of this verse, declared: "Who his own self bore our sins in his own body on the tree" (I Pet. 2:24). Note also that the benefit of the atonement potentially extends to all who have need of a Saviour: "the iniquity of us all."

The Passion, as viewed by man, is tragic persecution of the innocent (53:7-9). Not a word would He speak in His own defense, it is here predicted. Unresistingly He would stand before His persecutors and let them inflict their malice upon Him. How nonplussed were all His judges at the various mock-trials to which He was subjected on Good Friday! Caiaphas, Herod and Pilate were all baffled and vexed by His absolute silence before His accusers. Only when He was asked of His Messiahship and royal status did He deign to open His mouth, for to have remained silent then would have been unfaithfulness to His heavenly mission.

"By oppression and judgment," that is, by an act of judicial murder devoid of any genuine legality, He would be taken away—a travesty of justice in which no witnesses would be allowed for the defense and where the judge himself would act as His prosecutor. "And as for his generation" (this translation is preferable to "who shall declare his generation?"), that is, of the circle of His contemporaries, "who was considering that he was cut off out of the land of the living because of the transgression of my people to whom the stroke was due?" At the time of His death no mortal man would appreciate the real cause of the Saviour's death, that He was dying for the sins of Israel (as well as the larger Israel of the Christian Church). Now follows a very strange and detailed prediction concerning the place of His death and burial. How could a man be apportioned a death with guilty criminals ("the wicked"), and yet actually be interred with a man of wealth? Only of Jesus was this so. He was crucified between two thieves, yet buried in the tomb of Joseph of Arimathea. Of whom else would it ever be true that He would be the Sinless One? "He had done no wrong, neither was any deceitfulness in his mouth." And yet, despite this sinlessness, He would be consigned to death with guilty felons.

The Passion, as viewed by God, provides redemption for sinners and victory over sin (53:10-12). What lay behind this tragic miscarriage of justice? Was the Father helpless to deliver His Son? On the contrary, the crucifixion was altogether according to His sovereign good pleasure ("it pleased the Lord to bruise him"); He thereby accomplished the redemption of His elect. Turning directly to the Lord, the prophet affirms, "If thou appointest his soul [or life] a trespass-offering, he shall see his posterity." Not just an ordinary "offering for sin" is specified here, but a "trespass-offering" (*āshām*), which under the Mosaic law required an actual restitution for sin to be made, along with the blood sacrifice itself—a restitution amounting to six-fifths of the damages involved. May this not be understood as implying that the atoning death of Christ offers more than enough satisfaction for the sins of guilty mankind? At any rate, it will be by this atonement, states Isaiah, that the physically childless Christ will engender a spiritual progeny, upon whom He shall look with deep satisfaction as His own children, and through whom (as His mystical body) He shall prolong His life's work here upon earth. And how will these spiritual children of His be engendered? Through a personal knowledge of Christ as their Lord and Saviour: "By the knowledge of himself shall a righteous one, my servant, justify many." He is called a "righteous one" in order to distinguish Him as generically different from all other men, "for there is none righteous, no not one." How shall He justify those who know Him, causing them to be accepted as righteous in God's sight? By bearing the penalty of their transgressions.

Verse 12 acclaims His glorious triumph and exaltation. Because of His redeeming work on Calvary, God will appoint to Christ a portion *consisting of* (rather than *with*) the "great." Who out of all mankind are greater in heaven's eyes than God's elect? In and of themselves they are guilty, lost sinners, fit only for perdition, but because of divine grace they have been elevated to the sublime status of sonship. Upon them depends the destiny of men and nations; they hold the keys of the Kingdom, for by their preaching of the Gospel they alone can unlock the gateway to heaven. Christ's spoil of victory, then, shall consist in His redeemed people, and with them He shall divide the blessed spoil of the converts whom they win for the Lord by their intercession and testimony. "He that reapeth receiveth wages and gathereth fruit unto life eternal: that both he that soweth and he that reapeth may rejoice together" (Jn. 4:36).

Consequent Blessing to Israel and the Church (54:1–17). Captive Israel will some day be multiplied and enlarged (vv. 1–3). The exiled wife will be graciously restored (vv. 4–8). God promises His unchanging favor (vv. 9, 10). The radiant beauty of the future Church and Millennial Israel is described in glowing colors (vv. 11–17).

Grace for All Sinners who Trust in Christ (55:1–13). Blessing shall be bestowed upon meritless penitents (vv. 1–5). There is a sure refuge in God's unfathomable grace (vv. 6–11). The Word of God is sure and efficacious (vv. 9, 10). Receiving His Word by faith, the captive Jews are released and joyfully return to Zion (vv. 12, 13).

Inclusion of the Gentiles in the Blessing of Israel (56:1–8). Israel is admonished to maintain a godly witness (vv. 1, 2). Permanent blessing is promised even to childless believers (vv. 3–5). Believing Gentiles will be included among God's covenant people (vv. 6–8).

Condemnation of the Wicked Rulers of Israel (56:9—57:21). Israel's prophets are venal professionalists (56:9–12). Heavenly reward awaits persecuted believers (57:1, 2). Ungrateful Jews shall be forsaken by their trusted idols (vv. 11–13). Compassion will be granted to the repentant, but there can be no peace for the wicked (vv. 14–21).

3. The Program of Peace (58:1—66:24)

Contrast Between False Worship and True (58:1–14). Israel's hypocrisy is exposed and contrasted with service from a yielded heart (vv. 1–7). Protection and blessing are promised those who turn to a godly life (vv. 8–12). There is a reward for hallowing God's holy Sabbath (vv. 13, 14).

Confessing Her Depravity, Israel is Rescued by God's Intervention (59:1–21). Sin prevents the manifestation of God's redeeming love (vv. 1–8. Utter degeneracy and hopelessness result from self-centered life (vv. 9–15a). God intervenes to deliver helpless sinners (vv. 15b–21).

Glorious Prosperity and Peace of the Redeemed (60:1–22). The darkness of the world is to be overcome by the Divine Light of Israel (vv. 1–3). Because the Lord has intervened to rescue His people from their own depravity, and has interposed His own righteousness in their behalf, they are miserable captives no longer. He bids them to rise from the dust and enter fully into the glorious new life which is theirs as witnesses to redeeming grace. The source of their bright testimony to the benighted world is not found in their own excellence or superiority: "His glory shall be seen upon thee." They are to reflect His radiance by their dedicated lives, and as they remain true to this mission, they shall in the end prevail over the wisdom and power of this world. To them shall worldlings be drawn, disillusioned by the blackness of ignorance, sin and despair which has enveloped their souls in misery.

The darkened world is attracted by the light of the Gospel (60:4–10). From all quarters of the globe converts shall be attracted to the Church of Christ, because He shall be exalted in her midst. As the New Testament Israel, these glowing prospects shall be fulfilled for her in the world-wide outreach of the Gospel; in a spiritual sense, the heathen are drawn to Zion when they become adopted into the family of faith. Yet the language of these assurances goes beyond the fulfilment which history has already witnessed. "Thy daughters shall be carried in the arms" (v. 4) and "the ships of Tarshish . . . bring thy sons from far" (v. 9) suggest a continuing racial distinction between Jew and Gentile (although, of course, only Christians are involved in each group). "Foreigners shall build up thy walls" (v. 10) reinforces this same distinction (although perhaps they might be said to build the spiritual walls of Christ's temple by offering themselves as "living stones"). A very sharp distinction is implied by the statement in verse 12: "That kingdom and nation that will not serve thee shall perish." Although this too might simply be referred to the destruction of world powers at Armageddon, the general tone of this passage seems to imply a regathering of Christian Jews with the enthusiastic support and assistance of Gentile believers. At any rate, one point is incontestable: a most astonishing triumph shall be gained by the Hebrew-Christian religion over all the proud world religions and philosophies that men have always substituted for the truth of God. All the deceptive glories of Gentile empires and cultural achievements shall crumble to the dust before the power of Christ, "the ruler of the kings of the earth" (Rev. 1:5). All the wealth and economic resources of earth shall be brought forward as tribute to lay at the Master's feet; the tribes of the Arabian peninsula are first particularly mentioned, but then there are other hosts of willing subjects who come by ship from the extreme West (Tarshish) to lay their treasures before Him.

The glory and peace of Millennial Zion are described (60:11–14). That the gates of Jerusalem, a city once so downtrodden and despised by the Gentiles (v. 11), shall remain forever open once Messiah sits upon the throne suggests a warless society. Nor shall there be any independent government, for all political opposition shall be utterly crushed (v. 12). Verse 13 clearly suggests that the historical site of the temple will be once again gloriously adorned, and that literal Jerusalem shall be the focal point of the adoring worship of the millennial world. To apply all this spiritually to the Church of today would be a difficult *tour de force;* Mount Zion is often called the footstool of God's throne, but never the Church.

The characteristics of the Millennial Kingdom are contrasted with the former theocracy (60:15–22). After the ages of devastation and ignominy meted out to Israel for her unfaithfulness, there shall be glory and triumph. Instead of wretched poverty, there shall be fulness of wealth to which all the erstwhile proud nations of earth shall bountifully contribute. War shall be banished; no invader shall set foot upon the sacred soil of Israel. Observe how unsuited these terms are to a description of heaven; for example, verse 18: "Violence shall no more be heard in thy land." Heaven has never been a place of wrongdoing or oppression; this can only apply to literal Palestine. The complete fulfilment of God's redemptive program involves nothing less than the earthly vindication of the Son of God, so that in the very spot where He was once despised and rejected as king, He shall reign supreme over a world-wide domain compelled to obey His will and conform perfectly to the righteous standards of the Holy One. Then shall converted Israel and all the rest of surviving mankind know from personal experience that the Lord God keeps His covenant promises to the letter, and that He is the Saviour from sin, Who redeems His people from bondage, the Holy One of Israel Who by His mighty power enforces His righteous standards upon the earth. This is the glorious future in store for the people of God; they shall share in the joys of the Millennium upon earth as a prelude to the eternal joys of heaven.

Indeed, the ultimate vista of this scene extends even to heaven itself. The transition seems to take place at verses 19 and 20, for these are substantially repeated in Revelation 21:22–24 and are there applied to the New Jerusalem, the City of God which descends "out of heaven from God" (Rev. 21:10). As the Lord's vineyard or good olive tree (60:21), the people of God shall have an eternal portion in heavenly Canaan, that blessed land where there shall be no night, and where sorrow and tears shall be banished away.

The Spirit-filled Christ by Whom the Kingdom Comes, Rejoicing the Redeemed (61:1–11). In the empowering of the Messiah by the Spirit to preach a life-transforming Gospel (vv. 1–3), we have the ordination-charge of the Father to the Son, as Jesus made clear by His application of this passage to Himself in His sermon at Nazareth (Lk. 4:18–21). He has been anointed (and it is from this verb "anoint," *māshah,* that the title "Messiah" or "Anointed One" is derived) to preach the Gospel to the meek—to those who are bowed over in repentance for sin and humble recognition of their need of a Saviour. This gospel message will effectively (*1*) comfort those who are broken-hearted over their sin and wretchedness by assuring them of God's forgiveness and love; (*2*) deliver sinners from bondage to Satan, sin, and the fear of death; (*3*) announce the arrival of the Kingdom of God, bestowing grace upon repentant believers and condemnation and wrath upon all who reject the true faith; (*4*) bestow a life-transforming joy upon those who mourn over sin and the sorrows of life; (5) make them new creatures, "trees of righteousness, the planting of the Lord," showing forth an entirely new principle of life, partaking of the divine nature as born-again children of God; and (6) glorify the Triune God as perfect in holiness, righteousness, and love.

The glory of the new life which replaces the old (61:4-9) is such that those who are saved by faith in this Gospel shall rebuild their whole life upon a new foundation, even as restored Israel was to rebuild its ruined cities after the return from Babylon in 537 B.C. This reconstruction was to be no mere end in itself, but typically prophetic of the rebuilding of the Israelite theocracy as the New Testament Church, for Gentile converts are to be intimately associated with them in the Lord's work (v. 5). Converts to the Gospel shall all be elevated to the lofty status of priesthood; it shall no longer be restricted to the tribe of Levi (v. 6). Nowhere is this new order described more clearly than in I Peter 2:5: "Ye also as living stones are built up as a spiritual house, as a holy priesthood, in order to offer up spiritual sacrifices acceptable to God through Jesus Christ." God's people will enjoy the wealth of the Gentile nations, as they by missionary activity gather into the Church the precious jewels of God's elect, and together partake of the glory of the Bride, Christ's holy spouse. The shame of enslavement and bondage to Babylon and to Satan shall be wiped out, and the disgrace of the Exile and Dispersion shall be doubly compensated for by an eternal portion in God's heavenly Kingdom. The language here also suggests the glories and felicities of Christ's thousand-year rule upon earth, although not as explicitly as in some other passages.

The regenerate believer joyfully embraces these promises (61:10, 11). He centers his whole attention upon his Divine Redeemer, and rejoices in the unimaginable bounties of His sovereign grace. Covered with the white garments of Christ's imputed righteousness, the believer finds himself adorned with the Saviour's grace and perfection, and exults as a bride at her wedding. Through His adoring Church, the strong Son of God reproduces His own holy nature, causing His divine love to spring forth from the transformed souls of born-again Christians, constrained by His indwelling Spirit to praise God with joyous lips and Christ-centered lives.

Zion Restored and Glorified (62:1—63:6). God promises to acknowledge Israel as His beloved spouse (62:1-5). Zion shall become a glorious metropolis untroubled by invaders (vv. 6–9). God's favor will rest upon His holy people (vv. 10–12). Final doom of Zion's heathen foes is pronounced (63:1–6).

Remembering God's Former Mercies, Repentant Israel Pleads for Deliverance (63:7—64:12). The prophet recalls the Lord's tender care during the Exodus (63:7–9). He recounts God's patient discipline of rebellious Israel (vv. 10–14). Chastened Judah now appeals to the Father's love (vv. 15–19). God is besought to assert His power over the heathen (64:1–4). Believing Israel confesses her unworthiness and depravity (vv. 5–7) and appeals to the Lord for restoration and pardon (vv. 8–12).

God's Mercy is Reserved for Spiritual Israel Alone (65:1–25). Ungodly, idolatrous, hypocritical Israelites will incur a sure retribution (vv. 1–7), but the believing remnant shall enjoy the inheritance, while the faithless reap calamity (vv. 8–12). In the end time, blessing shall be meted out to the obedient and unceasing torment to the disobedient (vv. 13–16). The ultimate bliss of Israel in the sin-purged earth is anticipated (vv. 17–25).

Externalism in Worship Replaced by Heart-Sincerity (66:1–24). God's judgment shall overtake unrepentant worshipers (vv. 1–4). Marvelous deliverance is reserved for the repentant (vv. 5–9). Unparalleled prosperity awaits true Israel during the Millennium (vv. 10–14). Idol-loving infidels shall be consigned to hell (vv. 15–17). God's glory shall be revealed to spiritual Israel and their Gentile converts (vv. 18–21). Eternal heaven shall be the portion of the redeemed, eternal hell that of the damned (vv. 22–24).

Doctrinal Summary

The Book of Isaiah bears the same relationship to the Old Testament as the Epistle to the Romans bears to the New Testament. It serves as a compendium of almost all the major doctrines revealed by God during the pre-Christian age, with extended treatment of the doctrine of God in His omnipotence, His omniscience, and His redemptive love. As over against the imaginary gods of the polytheistic heathen, He reveals Himself as the one true God, ordaining all the events of history according to His master plan and demonstrating the authority of His revealed Word through the test of fulfilled prophecy. Above all, He is the Holy One of Israel, Who requires that His covenant people manifest a living faith by a godly life, and brings to bear upon their conscience both the forces of prophetic warning and appeal and the pressures of adversity and suffering where repentance is stubbornly withheld. But as the Holy One Who has bound Himself by the gracious promises of the covenant, He also displays Himself as the defender and deliverer of His people, Israel, ready to rescue them from the arrogant Gentile oppressor whenever they forswear their trust in pagan alliances or mere carnal weapons and turn to Him in full repentance and faith.

Yet in the last analysis, even the custodians of the Old Testament revelation, despite their training in godliness and their privileges of access to God, are only guilty, fallen sinners in need of a Saviour. This Saviour is revealed to be the coming Messiah, the King Who shall realize on earth the fulfilment of divine justice, goodness, and truth, yet also the divine-human Servant of the Lord Who presents His body as a vicarious atonement for the sins of God's people. Through the suffering of His unmerited humiliation, He will attain the glory of exaltation to absolute supremacy over the world and absolute victory over His foes. He shall bring deliverance not only to the true believers of national Israel, but shall also conquer the hearts of many Gentiles; they shall be gathered unto Him in repentance and faith from every quarter of the globe. The final act in the drama of history will be the establishment of His rule upon earth and the banishment of sin, warfare, suffering, and poverty. All the surviving race of mankind shall rejoice to own Him as Lord and Saviour.

Jeremiah

J. G. S. S. THOMSON

THE LIVING THEMES that emerge from the pages of this great book are notable not for their great variety and diversity, but for their abiding relevancy. The grace of God, the theology of covenant, the deadly nature of sin, the shining qualities that make a man a great prophet, the importance of faith, the eternal nature of the Word of God, the necessity of divine judgment upon a fallen moral society—from these Jeremiah formed the central theme of his great symphony in theology.

Jeremiah's long ministry of over forty years stretched from 625 B.C. until a few years after Judah ceased to be a state in 586 B.C. After some fifty years of religious apostasy under Manasseh, religious reform was inaugurated under Josiah (621–607 B.C.). Jeremiah enthusiastically supported the reform until he realized that it was not changing the people's hearts. Two years after Josiah's death, the battle of Carchemish (605 B.C.) established Babylonian control over western Asia. From that time Jeremiah unsuccessfully advocated submission to Babylon. Under the last four kings of Judah, twenty-one years of religious apostasy and political weakness made the fall of Jerusalem in 586 B.C., and exile, inevitable.

The distressing cirumstances in which Jeremiah worked, and the extraordinary extent to which idolatry had replaced revealed religion in Judah, are fully exposed in Jeremiah's prophecies. Jeremiah's spiritual anguish which this apostasy occasioned is accurately mirrored. Yet he was no pessimist. He was essentially God's warrior, but a warrior who was also watchman and witness.

In Jeremiah's oracles, God, the moral governor of the world, is Israel's covenant God. Through Israel He sought to achieve moral purposes. Alas, the northern kingdom's adulteries with Baalim compelled God to divorce (that is, exile) her. Judah, the southern kingdom, failed to learn from Israel's experience. She outdid Israel in sexual impurities, yet Judah repudiated the charges of religious infidelity. Therefore God must judge her.

No principle is discernible in the arrangement of Jeremiah's prophecies. Oracles under Judah's last five kings do not follow chronological sequence. The chapter sequence in Hebrew differs from the order in the Septuagint, and the latter shows considerable though unimportant omissions. This suggests a different recension. Jeremiah dictated his prophecies and Baruch wrote them down (36:1-8, 32). The disorderly arrangement might be evidence of primitiveness.

I. Jeremiah, God's Warrior (1:1—33:26)

1. The Summons: Jeremiah's Call and Commission (1:1-19)

Divine Inauguration (1:1-3). Divine encounter is the starting point of all true service for God. In our encounter with God is born the conviction that God has purposes to fulfil through us. In such a moment of divine initiative "the word of the Lord" came to Jeremiah. The word was to be central in his ministry (1:9; 5:14; 15:16; 20:9; 23:29, 30; cf. also Is. 55:10, 11; Heb. 4:12-14). It was self-authenticating, inescapable, the word of God to be spoken in God's name.

Divine Election (1:4, 5). The Lord "knew" (chose, v. 5; cf. Amos 3:2; Hos. 13:5) and "sanctified" (consecrated) Jeremiah before his conception (cf. Is. 49:15; Lk. 1:15-17; Gal. 1:15). And Jeremiah was "ordained" (appointed) "a prophet unto the nations." God appointed him primarily to his native Judah, but because she was involved in the maelstrom of international politics, Jeremiah was a prophet to the great heathen powers also (25:15-29; chs. 45—51). Even as the Gospel is for all (Jn. 3:16), so also Hebrew prophecy is universal and timeless.

Divine Commission (1:6-10). Jeremiah hesitated (v. 6), but God brushed aside pleas of immaturity and inexperience (cf. Ex. 3:11, 12; 4:10-17). The messenger's limitations are unimportant when God elects the messenger (v. 5), directs the mission (v. 7b), and communicates the message (v. 7c). The promise of the protecting presence, the touch of the empowering hand, the plenitude of divine grace and inspiration enable Jeremiah to commit himself to his destructive-constructive mission (vv. 8–10): destructive in that it announced judgment upon sin; constructive in that it could lead to repentance. God had authorized him; he could do no other.

Divine Intention (1:11–16). The moment of high ecstasy was the moment of vision. *(1)* The almond tree (*shākēdh*, Heb.) in blossom is the first harbinger of nature's awakening from winter sleep; so God is awake (*shōkēdh*) to empower the prophetic word, execute His judgments and save alive the remnant. Amid spiritual and moral deadness, God is always awake and active. (*2*) A seething pot, over flames fanned by the north wind, boils over; so God is about to cause judgment to boil over from the north southward upon Judah for her idolatry. God's first word to sinful Judah is of judgment (cf. I Pet. 4:17).

Divine Injunction (1:17–19). The injunction in verse 17a is a common figure in Scripture (cf. II Kings 4:29; Lk. 12:35). As Jeremiah did his part (v. 17), God would do His (vv. 18, 19). Divinely imbued with courage and resolution, Jeremiah faced his Herculean task. In the fiercest conflicts, he knew his most powerful antagonists could not finally prevail.

2. Judah's Situation (2:1—13:27)

Judah's Sickness (2:1—6:30). Jeremiah's earliest discourses are principally a condemnation of Judah's spiritual apostasy, and a plea for repentance while judgment tarries.

(1) God's Original Purpose (2:1–3). God chose Israel to be His bride (v. 2; cf. Hos. 2; 2–20; Is. 54:5), the Sinaitic Covenant being the marriage bond (Ezek. 16:8). She responded with all the ardor of her first love (Ex. 24:8). Being "holiness unto the Lord," she clung to her protector and provider (v. 3). Like the firstfruits (Ex. 23:19; Deut. 18:4; 26:2–11), Israel was consecrated to the Lord. An unhallowed person who ate the consecrated firstfruits "offended," so did those who "devour" Israel, the Lord's firstfruits.

(2) The Purpose Defeated (2:4–28). Defeat came early in Israel's history (v. 20). Base ingratitude explains Israel's apostasy. Pursuing illusory gods, she pursued illusory hopes and purposes (vv. 5, 11, 13). Jeremiah's generation committed the same folly (v. 9). Pagans do not abandon their false ancestral worship, yet Israel had forsaken her true ancient faith (vv. 10, 11). Thus she exchanged reality for illusion (vv. 12, 13) and lost national independence, resources,

religion and ideals (vv. 14–18). Sin pays its own wages (v. 19). Israel, the choice vine, became a degenerate vine (v. 21). Throwing off all restraint, she plunged into obscene idolatry (vv. 20, 23–24) until her sins became ineradicable (v. 22), her bondage unbreakable (v. 25), her penalty inescapable (v. 26), her situation untenable (vv. 27, 28).

(3) Judah's Spiritual Insensibility (2:29–37). Her spiritual failure is revealed in her "pleading" (complaining or expostulating) with God (v. 29), her inability to learn from God's corrective dealings (v. 30), her senseless forsaking of her faithful God (vv. 31, 32), her ability to teach experts in immorality (v. 33), and her wanton cruelty (v. 34; cf. II Kings 21:16). Yet Judah protests her innocence and presumes upon God's clemency (v. 35)! The clear-sighted Jeremiah was not duped. National calamities warned of worse to follow. Alliances with pagan nations would be futile (cf. 37:5) in an inexorable day of doom (vv. 36, 37).

(4) Judah's Spiritual Adultery (3:1–5). To describe apostate Judah as a prostitute (vv. 1–3) was no exaggeration. Canaanite religion involved the worshipers in foul sexual impurities, and when Judah indulged in these revolting practices, she became a harlot. A Hebrew could not take back his wife whom he had divorced (v. 1; cf. Deut. 24:1–4); so Judah, still undivorced yet living in adulterous unions "with many lovers," could not return to the Lord. In both instances, the "woman" is defiled for the former "husband." Punishment (v. 3c) had induced only sham repentance (v. 3b), endearing language (v. 4) without a change of heart (v. 5). God treats sin with deadly seriousness.

(5) Israel's Bill of Divorcement (3:6—4:4). The adulterous conduct (v. 6) of the unrepentant (vv. 7, 9) northern kingdom (Israel) had compelled the Lord to divorce her (v. 8), that is, send her into exile (722 B.C.). But the southern kingdom (Judah) persisted in her harlotry (v. 8). Hers had been a make-believe repentance (v. 10) during Josiah's Reform, which had been entirely superficial and basically false. Judah's wilfulness, and her longer warning, made Israel more righteous than she (v. 11). Sincere repentance (Is. 11:12–14; Hos. 1:11; Ezek. 37:16–28), a return to God, and confession (vv. 12, 13), alone can effect reconciliation (v. 14). Given a change of heart, a reunited nation (v. 14), under wise shepherds (kings) who teach wisdom (v. 15), will then worship the Lord in Jerusalem (vv. 16, 17a), and will walk before

Him in humility (v. 17b). Visible symbols of the divine presence will then be unnecessary (v. 16). Verses 19 and 20 glance back to verses 1–5.

Meantime, in the north a ray of hope! Some confess paganism's impotency to satisfy (v. 23). In response to God's call (v. 22), they repent with bitter weeping "upon the bare heights," thus turning the place of prostitution into the place of penitence (v. 21), and cast themselves upon the Lord's grace (vv. 24, 25). God will not compromise on the necessity for repentance (4:1). It is the pathway to blessing (v. 2), the cutter that breaks fallow ground, the lance that circumcises the hearts (vv. 3, 4).

(6) Judah's Bill of Divorcement (4:5–18). Alas, of such repentance there was no evidence in Judah. Realizing that the Lord must inevitably hand her, too, a bill of divorcement, Jeremiah announces her doom. She is urged to take refuge (vv. 5, 6a) from the beast of prey the Lord is sending to ravage the land (vv. 6b, 7); and the heart of prince, priest, and false prophet alike melts (v. 9). If we read "they" for "I" (v. 10), we can ascribe the verse to the false prophets, their predictions of good belied by Judah's doom. Like a destructive burning desert wind (vv. 11, 12), and with the speed of vultures, the foe swoops (v. 13). Reference to Dan in the far north, then to Ephraim nearer home, means the foe is fast approaching (vv. 15–17). Judah must now repent (v. 14) or perish (v. 18).

(7) Jeremiah's Anguished Cry (4:19–31). The Hebrews spoke of the emotions as located in the bowels. Jeremiah's references to them and to the walls of his heart reveal the thrill of horror that electrified him as he anticipated the approaching calamity. His willingness to think himself into his nation's woes (vv. 19, 20) bespeaks the authentic prophet of the Lord, in whom love, devotion, fidelity, and patriotism burn like a consuming fire. The heralds of the Cross need a heart like Jeremiah's. The prophet's question (v. 21) is answered by the Lord (v. 22). In what is acknowledged to be one of the greatest passages in all prophetic literature, Jeremiah announces the words of doom which the Lord gives him. Judah's moral impotency and spiritual degeneracy (v. 22) are matched by the desolation prevailing in Judah's land reminiscent of the primeval chaos in Genesis 1:2 (vv. 23–28). The most seductive blandishments (v, 30) or poignant appeals (v. 31) of Jerusalem will fail to move her former paramours, now turned enemies.

(8) None Righteous in Judah (5:1–9). Jeremiah searches for one righteous person in Jerusalem (cf. Gen. 18:23–33); but the social

virtues of honor, integrity, and honesty have gone (v. 1). Men swear by the Lord's name (cf. 4:2; Deut. 10:20), the most solemn form of oath, only to perjure themselves (v. 2; cf. Is. 48:2). Yet the Lord demands integrity from His people (v. 3a), a demand resisted even when He corrected them (v. 3b). Is it because they are poor, untutored in their religion (v. 4)? Sin would then be due to poverty, lack of education. No, it was the Jerusalem intelligentsia, the wealthy, influential, and educated, who had thrown off the restraints involved in allegiance to the Lord and obedience to His law (v. 5), only to wear stronger fetters, submit to shameful bondage, and prostitute God's goodness to unholy ends (vv. 7–9).

(9) Doom Advances (5:10–19). The questions in verse 9 are now answered affirmatively. Reading "vine-rows" for "walls" (v. 10), Judah is a vine (cf. 12:10; Is. 5:1–7) which the enemy is to devastate. The nation's treachery against the Lord (v. 11) is denial of His power, indifference to sin's consequences, and contempt for the Lord's prophets (vv. 12, 13). But the prophetic word, lampooned as "wind," is in fact a consuming fire (v. 14). The devouring instrument of doom is described in verses 15–17. This doom is not due to God's arbitrariness, whim, or caprice. He controls the calamity (v. 18), and makes the ensuing exile which is here prophesied serve disciplinary and, therefore, moral purposes (v. 19).

(10) People, Prophet, and Priest Guilty (5:20–31). As the issue of Judah's doom is moral, so is its cause. The people are sottish (v. 21), recalcitrant (v. 22), rebellious (v. 23), hardened (v. 24). This iniquitous behavior compelled God to correct them (v. 25), but evil men continued in sin (vv. 26–28). But sin against man is sin against God Who expresses His horror of it (v. 30). But spiritual as well as secular leaders were involved in national guilt (v. 31). False prophets claiming to speak God's word, and priests acting in conjunction with that word, contributed to the national corruption. "An appalling and horrible thing" (v. 30) had indeed come to pass, and the tragedy was that "my people loved to have it so" (v. 31).

(11) The Alarm Sounds (6:1–8). A warning is given to flee the doom hanging over Jerusalem (vv. 1, 2). Under the figure of shepherds and flocks, the devastating power of the enemy is described (v. 3). The favorable midday hour of siesta slips by (v. 4), so a night attack is planned (v. 5) by a determined, ruthless enemy (v. 6). Jerusalem merits destruction. As a cistern keeps its water cool, so the city keeps her sins fresh and in full vigor (v. 7). A last minute appeal to submit to the Lord's moral discipline is made to prevent

her separation from her God, which her sinfulness will effect unless she repents (cf. Is. 59:1, 2; Rom. 8:35–39).

(12) The Deaf Ear (6:9–15). Jerusalem will soon resemble a stripped vine (v. 9). She is now so morally insensible that she cannot hear. Her inner ear is uncircumcised, its covering prevents the word from penetrating to the heart (v. 10). Jeremiah, filled with God's wrath, is ordered to pour it out upon the city (v. 11) that has derided His word, and become so hardened in selfishness, double-dealing, and incurable frivolity that she is incapable of blushing for shame (vv. 13–15).

(13) The Disobedient Heart (6:16–21). God's repeated entreaties to walk the ways of prosperity, tranquility, and security had been disobeyed (v. 16). His watchmen (prophets, Ezek. 3:17) had warned Judah in vain (v. 17). Such disobedience of word and law merits punishment (vv. 18, 19) the costliest sacrifice cannot avert (vv. 20, 21). There is no known substitute for obedience (I Sam. 15:22; Hos. 6:6).

(14) The Refining Fire (6:22–30). The pitiless invader (vv. 23, 24) and the emotions which news of his advance stirs within Jerusalem's breast (v. 24) are now described. Bitter mourning will be required (vv. 25, 26). In this hopeless situation, Jeremiah realizes God has sent him to test (RV, margin) Judah by fire. But all his efforts to smelt and refine her have failed; only dross remains. She has no precious metal within her. Judah's sin is ineradicable (vv. 27–30), and she is incapable of reform.

Judah's Folly (7:1—8:3). Probably the oracles in this section were delivered on the occasion described in chapter 26:1-7, that is, soon after Josiah's Reform. Neither ritual nor temple can charm away God's judgment upon sin.

(1) The Remedy Prescribed (7:1–11). False confidence in the temple at Jerusalem and its ritual cannot save, but amendment of life, obedience to God, social morality, social justice, forsaking idolatry, will (vv. 3–7). Those guilty of social sins, immorality, perjury, and idolatry (vv. 8, 9) are not made secure by standing in God's house (v. 10), otherwise it would become "a den of robbers" (v. 11; cf. Mt. 21:13). A change of heart and conduct was the remedy.

(2) The Remedy Repudiated (7:12–15). After the repudiation (v. 13), what then? The Jerusalem temple will perish as the Shiloh tabernacle with the ark (I Sam. 1—3) perished (v. 14; Ps. 78:60).

That is to say, the Lord's destroying the temple must be in the interests of true religion. True religion will not disappear when the temple disappears and exile takes place (v. 15), just as it did not vanish when tabernacle and ark disappeared.

(3) The Remedy Annulled (7:16–20). Since Judah is so incurably sin-sick that intercession for her is useless (v. 16), Jeremiah's intercession for her was rejected (14:7). Her chronic ailment was rooted in her idolatrous cult worship performed to spite the Lord (vv. 17, 18)! But the studied insult recoils upon her own head (v. 19) by setting alight God's moral indignation (v. 20)!

(4) Substitute Remedies Futile (7:21–26). Verse 21 is spoken in ironic contempt. How Judah sacrifices is unimportant, so utterly futile are her sacrifices. Verse 22 does not mean that there was neither ritual nor code claiming divine authority, otherwise the Mosaic origin of Deuteronomic laws, and of those in the Book of the Covenant, is denied. Jeremiah is saying nothing so pointless. He is urging the supremacy of the moral demand over ritual in Israel's revealed religion (v. 23). The law of obedience supersedes the law of sacrifice. When that demand was spurned, incurable sickness resulted (vv. 24–26).

(5) Sick unto Death (7:27–31). Jeremiah's attempts to stir Judah's conscience only revealed her inability to hear (v. 27). She did not, because she could not, respond (v. 28). She was spiritually dead. The Lord's rejection of her was inevitable (v. 29), as was also her increasing expertness in devising idolatrous abominations (vv. 30, 31).

(6) Judgment Certain (7:32—8:3). So appalling will be the Lord's judgment be that where His people sacrificed their children (v. 31) they themselves will be slaughtered, and in such numbers that many will remain unburied (vv. 32, 33). The sound of laughter will cease in the land (v. 34), the corpses of those who have been buried will be desecrated (8:1, 2), and the miserable survivors will long for death (v. 3).

Judah's Blindness (8:4—9:1). (1) Spiritual Blindness (8:4–7). Judah's spiritual blindness is, of course, unnatural and incorrigible. A man who falls picks himself up; when he strays, he searches the right road (v. 4). Not so, spiritually blind and backslidden Judah, now hardened in sin (v. 5). The Lord waits in vain for her to repent. She is blind even to her sin (v. 6), and plunges ever deeper into the morass. The spiritual light has gone out within her (cf. Mt. 6:22, 23).

Migratory birds discern unerringly seasons and directions, so natural man by conscience distinguishes right from wrong. How much more, then, should God's people; but alas, they have ignored the light until spiritual sight has gone (v. 7).

(2) Religious Blindness (8:8–11). The wisdom claimed by Judah was not innate but was developed in the form of a written religious code which, says Jeremiah, religious leaders have falsified (v. 8). In issuing directions (Deut. 24:8; Hag. 2:11–13), the priests may have claimed divine sanction or approval for what was their own invention, or they may have insisted that Judah could sin with impunity. This falsification was equivalent to rejecting God's word, and for this the Lord would humiliate them (v. 9) by despoiling and exposing them (vv. 10, 11).

(3) Moral Blindness (8:12–17). The expectation is that the leaders will manifest a sense of shame, but of this they are incapable (v. 12). Religious blindness produces moral blindness. To reject God's word is to reject the light at noonday. Finally doom comes (v. 13): news of the invader's lightning advance stupefies Judah, and the day of God's visitation dispels idle daydreams (v. 14). No mercy can be expected from such a ruthless foe (vv. 15–17).

(4) Prophetic Despair (8:18—9:1). This poignant lament over Judah's calamity mirrors Jeremiah's emotions. His sorrow makes him feel "heavy" (v. 18, sick, Heb.) as he foresees his people exiled and abandoned by God because of Israel's idolatry (v. 19). If harvest fails, summer fruits are still a possibility; but if both fail, famine is inevitable. This parable of Judah's spiritual, religious, and moral condition reveals the utter hopelessness of her situation (v. 20). This leaves Jeremiah broken with grief (v. 21). Since there is now no sovereign remedy for Judah's wounds (v. 22), Jeremiah laments until, in a paroxysm of grief, he bursts into tears (9:1).

Judah's Treachery (9:2–22). (1) Treachery Unmasked (9:2–9). Viewing Jerusalem's inhabitants as faithless adulterers, the prophet longs to escape as from a midnight mist (v. 2). Since treachery is causing society to disintegrate, an inn where travelers meet by chance and owe each other no loyalties would be preferable. Social confidence is so worm-eaten that neighbor slanders neighbor, every blood brother plays the part of Jacob (v. 4; cf. Gen. 27:36). Barbed slanders fly everywhere, and power indeed corrupts (v. 3). Lying becomes natural to the tongue, progress in sin becomes automatic (v. 5), and the lamp of knowledge, knowledge of God Who is holiness and truth, is blown out (v. 6). The Lord has tried to refine His people from this dross in the crucible of suffering (v. 7) but the smelting processes have failed (v. 8). Judah's outrage upon the Lord's holiness must be "avenged" (v. 9).

(2) Treachery "Avenged" (9:10–22). In this fresh lament, Jeremiah is not describing the calamities that have befallen Judah's rural (v. 10) and urban (v. 11) life; he is explaining them (v. 12; cf. Hos. 14:9). Thinking men can see beyond Judah's tragedy, recognize the cause and take heed; but "will he to whom the mouth of the Lord has spoken" (the false prophets)? Israel's long record of disobedience to God's revealed will in the law (v. 13), of stubborn persistence in idolatry (v. 14) makes it unlikely. Bitter affliction (v. 15), exile, and a pursuing sword (v. 16) are inevitable. Professional mourners (v. 17) who excite spectators to grief (v. 18) are summoned, but the agonized cry of departing exiles (v. 19) makes conventional dirges pointless. The Lord Himself must compose the lament (v. 20a) which will never be forgotten (vv. 20b–22).

Judah's Idolatry (9:23—10:25). (1) Knowledge of God is Man's Glory (9:23–26). Two detached oracles are here taken together and related to their present context. Wisdom, power, or wealth not dedicated to God are never ground for praise (v. 23). Ultimately they are folly, impotency, and poverty. Knowledge of and obedience to the Lord Who is gracious, just, and righteous are the sole ground for a man's glory, because he who knows, trusts, and obeys the Lord himself becomes gracious, just, and righteous (v. 24). By that criterion, the uncircumcised Gentile and the Jew circumcised in flesh, but not in heart, will be judged alike (vv. 25, 26). The outward rite without the inward spirit which it symbolizes is useless (cf. Rom. 2:28, 29).

(2) Worship of Idols Man's Shame (10:1–5). Probably verses 1–16 were addressed to Jews living in exile. They are not to imitate the pagan idolator nor permit celestial phenomena to frighten them (v. 2). Idolatry, like astrology, is an absurdity (vv. 3–5a). Jeremiah emphasizes the *vanity* of idolatry and the *impotency* of idols (mere "scarecrows," so "pillars," v. 5). Since they can neither bless nor molest, let them not intimidate.

(3) God and Idols Contrasted (10:6–16). The Lord's omnipotence makes Him supreme (v 6). This King of nations (v. 7a) and King of kings (v. 7b) is, therefore, to be feared. "They" (v. 8, idolatrous nations) become, like the idols they worship, moral and spiritual bankrupts. Idols are nonentities, lifeless and powerless: the Lord is the everlasting fountain of truth, life, power, and justice

(v. 10). This ethical monotheism of Israel's revealed religion was idolatry's death knell (v. 11). When this omnipotent, omniscient Creator (v. 12) manifests His power (v. 13) in the universe He created, the idol-maker is stupefied (v. 14), his idol's unreality is unmasked (v. 15), and God, Who is "Jacob's portion" still, is all and in all (v. 16).

(*4*) Idolatrous Judah Warned (10:17–25). The Exile, for which Judah is to prepare herself (v. 17), will be engineered by God (v. 18). The thought fills Jeremiah with pain and nausea (v. 19). The "tent" (land) is ruined, and there is none to restore it (v. 20). "The shepherds" (leaders) have lived without God and are responsible (v. 21) for the oncoming disaster (v. 22). Jeremiah then voices Judah's feelings. She now sees that man, morally weak, cannot determine his own destiny (v. 23). Her sins deserve chastisement but she pleads for chastisement tempered with mercy (Ps. 78:38, 39), and not more chastisement than the heathen nations through whom the Lord punishes her (v. 25). Unless her punishment is mitigated, she will be "diminished" (Heb.), and God's purposes for and through her will fail (v. 24).

Judah's Faithlessness (11:1—12:17). (*1*) The Covenant Ratified (11:1–5). The covenant referred to here is the original covenant established at Horeb (vv. 3–5), not the covenant of Josiah's Reform (II Kings 22:3—23:24). The Lord commands Jeremiah to remind Judah (vv. 1, 2) of the consequences of disobeying this covenant (v. 3). When he established this covenant at the Exodus, He chose Israel to be His peculiar people. Israel voluntarily responded and pledged obedience to the Lord her God and the Lord pledged fidelity to His promises (vv. 4, 5).

(*2*) The Covenant Violated (11:6–14). In his preaching ministry (v. 6), Jeremiah based his plea for obedience on several considerations:

(*a*) Past disobedience (vv. 7, 8). The Lord's earnest and incessant protestations to "hearken" had failed, and upon "the stubbornness of their evil heart," God had implemented His penalties (Deut. 8:19; 28:15–68).

(*b*) Present disobedience (vv. 9–14). The return of Jeremiah's generation to the ancient covenant at Josiah's Reform had yielded no permanent results. The reformation had not taken hold of the heart. A nation-wide conspiracy (v. 9) to resume their sinful ways, and renounce allegience to the Lord (v. 10), will mean punishment

(v. 11) and humiliation (v. 12). Every Judean town has its idol, every Jerusalem street its altar to Baal (v. 13). In such a situation, intercession is futile (v. 14). Contrition, confession, repentance, obedience alone can move God, not a meaningless cry for mercy.

(3) The Covenant Perverted (11:15–17). Yet faithless Judah ("my beloved") still frequents the temple! But her presence there is only an intrusion. Vows and sacrifices without obedience and social morality, she assumes, will meet her covenant obligations, placate her covenant God, procure forgiveness and prevent disaster (v. 15). This perversion would soon be exposed. Judah, God's flourishing olive tree, was about to be struck by lightning in the approaching hurricane, and disfigured (vv. 16, 17).

(4) The Preacher of Covenant Menaced (11:18–23). The truth of Jeremiah's commission (1:7–10) now emerges. Greatest opposition came from his own townsfolk (v. 21; cf. 1:1) who plot his death. Jeremiah was thunderstruck (v. 18). The unsuspecting lamb, led to the slaughter by those it trusts, is a parable of Jeremiah's trusting attitude (v. 19a) toward those who secretly plot to cut him off in his prime (v. 19b). In extremity he prays to God Who tests the reins (seat of emotions), and heart (seat of intentions), and knows who is in the right (v. 20). God's purposes will triumph. Those who cooperate with them will finally prevail; those who oppose them must ultimately perish (vv. 21–23).

(5) The Preacher of Covenant Perplexed (12:1–6). Jeremiah's problem is, how to reconcile God's righteousness with the wicked's prosperity (v. 1; cf. Ps. 37, 39, 49, 73; Job 21–7, 8). Evil men resist God with impunity; they oppose His servants and prosper, yet His justice is axiomatic! Indeed, their stability and prosperity are of God (v. 2a), yet they are religious humbugs (v. 2b)! Conversely, Jeremiah has been tested by the Lord and found not wanting (v. 3a), yet evil men malign him with impunity. The Lord rebukes Jeremiah's intolerant solution (v. 3b, 4), and leaves his problem unsolved, because it has no solution! If, in comparative calm, he runs for shelter ("secure," RV), what will he do in the tornado (v. 5)? "Pride" is a jungle, swampy after floods, and difficult to walk in. Jeremiah is to gird himself for severer tests!

(6) The Covenant God's Aversion (12:7–13). This section and the following (vv. 14–17) have no connection with their context, but they illumine the Lord's dealings with His covenant people. He has cast them off (v. 7), and they have turned upon Him like a

savage beast, provoking Him still further to wrath (v. 8). His questions (v. 9a) express His hurt surprise at having to incite invading nations ("beasts," v. 9b) against Judah whom they devastate (vv. 10–13). Yet this was "my [the Lord's] sorrow," and because of Judah's reckless indifference (v. 11) and His own sword (v. 12). Failing harvests, the expression of divine anger, humiliate Judah still further (v. 13).

(7) The Covenant God's Intention (12:14–17). Attacker and attacked will both be exiled (v. 14). But in grace God will restore both (v. 15). Then, if the erstwhile hostile neighbor (Edom, Moab, and others) learn true religion from His covenant people, and swear allegiance to Him (Deut. 6:13), He will establish them to live in fellowship and peace with Judah (v. 16). But disobedience will involve utter destruction (v. 17).

Judah's Obduracy (13:1–27). (1) The Stubborn Heart (13:1–11). This acted parable of the loincloth (vv. 1–7) made of linen, a material worn by priests (Ex. 28:39) and symbolizing Israel's purity in fellowship with God (cf. v. 11), signifies Judah's corruption and degeneracy. The rotting of the loincloth denotes that Israel, chosen to serve God, will be humiliated and ruined (v. 10b). The cause of this tragedy is the Lord's rejection of Judah because of her stubbornness and persistence in idolatry (v. 10a). God's intention was a united, loyal Israel bringing Him fame and renown, but disobedience frustrated the intention (v. 11).

(2) Mental Paralysis (13:12–14). This parable of the wine jars, which symbolize Judah, signifies that the Lord will fill the degenerate and headstrong prince, priest, prophet, and people with stupefaction and bewilderment (v. 13) as the jars with wine (v. 12) which denotes God's wrath. In a state of mental stupor, they will collide with each other and fall helpless to the ground to rise no more (v. 14).

(3) Twilight (13:15–19). The sands in God's hourglass have almost run out. Hence, a last plea for humility, confession, obedience (v. 15). The sun is setting behind "the mountains of twilight," and Judah will stumble on, lost in the encompassing murk, unless she makes for the kindly light of the Lord, her true home (v. 16). Hardened in her pride, Judah spurns God's appeal, and in the presence of his nation's suicide, Jeremiah breaks down (v. 17). He laments especially the fate of Jehoiachin and Nehushta, the queen-mother (v. 18; 22:26), who had great influence in Judah. The magnitude of this disaster in 597 B.C. is expressed in verse 19.

(4) Midnight (13:20-27). Jerusalem is here addressed. The foe from the north advances, and the city's flock is scattered (v. 20). Lovers whom she courted now tyrannize her (v. 21). Adulterous Jerusalem receives the adulteress' punishment (cf. v. 26; Hos. 2:10) for her sin (v. 22). Through established habit, her sinfulness is now so ingrained that she is incapable of goodness and repentance (v. 23). She has lived without God (v. 25), and the whirlwind (v. 24) will expose her person (v. 26). Long established habits in lewdness (v. 27a) make cleansing "impossible" (v. 27b), but not to God for Whom nothing is too hard (v. 27c, RV). Where sin abounds, grace superabounds.

3. Jeremiah's Encounter (14:1—33:26)

Tenderness for Judah (14:1—15:9). (1) He Describes Judah's Distress (14:1-6). Judah's persistence in sin renders Jeremiah's intercession futile. Because of a drought (v. 1), the whole land is in deep distress (v. 2). Efforts to find water fail and cause disappointment ("shame") and grief (v. 2; cf. II Sam. 15:30). Ploughmen are dismayed (v. 4); the hind, most affectionate of animals, abandons her newly born calf, and other beasts pant exhausted and blinded by heat, hunger, and thirst (vv. 5, 6).

(2) He Confesses Judah's Sins (14:7-9). In his confession, Jeremiah identifies himself with his nation's sins and urges the Lord to act, if not for Judah's sake, then for His honor's sake among idolatrous people (cf. Josh. 7:9) or for His covenant's sake (Ex. 34:5-7), since Judah's only hope is grace. But God seems as indifferent to Judah's distress as would be the aloof, casual traveler (v. 8). He resembles "a man surprised" (Septuagint: "fast asleep"; cf. Ps. 44:22-26), yet Judah is His possession since His name has been called over her (v. 9).

(3) He Pleads Judah's Cause (14:10-18). The Lord's apparent aloofness (vv. 8, 9) is only commensurate ("thus") with Judah's desertion and sinfulness (v. 10); Jeremiah's intercession (v. 11) and Judah's fastings and offerings are futile. They cannot defer God's judgments (v. 12). Jeremiah argues that the faithless prophets have duped the people by their false promises (v. 13). Jeremiah's accusations against the former (v. 14) suggest that some were deliberate deceivers, others were time-servers and adulterers, still others falsely patriotic. Whatever their motives, the disasters they denied would overtake both them (v. 15) and their dupes (v. 16). Again the

tenderhearted Jeremiah is moved to tears over the slain and the hungry, and the approaching exile of prophet and priest (vv. 17, 18).

(4) He Acknowledges Judah's Impotency (14:19—15:1). Jeremiah's persistence in interceding for Judah in spite of discouragement shows that this was an important prophetic duty (cf. Amos 7:2, 5). Standing in God's counsels and possessing God's Spirit, Jeremiah could interpret God's mind and pray effectively, but not after the Lord had determined on a course of action (15:1). In his prayer Jeremiah confesses Judah's sins (v. 20), pleads the glory of God's name, of His throne over the ark, of His covenant, of His reputation among the heathen, and the humiliation of His people who now wait for mercy (vv. 21, 22). The Lord replies that even if a Moses (cf. Ex. 17:11; 32:11–14, 30–32; Num. 14:13–24; Deut. 9:18–20, 25–29) or a Samuel (I Sam. 7:8, 9; 12:19–23; Ps. 99:6–8) should now intercede, it would avail nothing (15:1).

(5) He Announces Judah's Fate (15:2–9). Jeremiah's answer to Judah's question, "whither?" if there be no forgiveness, is a melancholy enumeration of four kinds of disaster, and four modes of punishment (vv. 2, 3), the cause of which was Manasseh's sin (cf. II Kings 21:11–15; 23:26, 27; 24:3, 4). The tenses in verses 6–9 should be future throughout. When disaster ultimately overtakes Judah, all pity, human (v. 5) and divine (v. 6), will be exhausted. In God's winnowing processes, Judah will be blown into exile like chaff (v. 7). Motherhood will again be crucified. Nameless horrors were the lot of defenseless women in those cruel days (vv. 8, 9).

Jeremiah's Bitterness Because of Judah (15:10–21) (1) He Laments His Fate (15:10–18). Jeremiah's faithful exposure of Judah's sins and false presumptions, and his proclamation of Judah's fate, only led to a worsening of the situation. Obedience to God's call only made him an object of nation-wide rancor. The moneylender and defaulting debtor fared better than he (v. 10). Verse 11 may mean that the Lord will strengthen Jeremiah and cause his opponents to urge him to intercede for them (cf. 21:1, 2; 37:3; 42:2), or he would have said "amen" to his opponents' curses (v. 10) if he had not prayed for them. Verse 12 seems to mean: Can anything defy the northern foe (Babylonians)? For verses 13 and 14, see 17:3 and 4. Verse 15 resumes the dialogue begun in verse 10. Jeremiah pleads his faithfulness and claims protection (v. 15), confesses that the word revealing God's nature and purpose, bitter though it was to proclaim, was a joy to him (v. 16a), and that he is wholly dedicated to the Lord (vv. 16b, 17). "Thy hand" means God's guidance and inspiration (cf. Is. 8:11; Ezek. 1:3; 37:1). Yet the Lord has let him down as an unreliable brook does the thirsty wayfarer (v. 18)! Thus Jeremiah gives vent to bitter feelings engendered by the ineffectiveness of his message—feelings which he has been bottling up for months.

(2) God Offers Release (15:19-21). After the passionate outbursts, the still small voice (v. 19), which neither commiserates nor commends but condemns! Jeremiah's renunciation of God's service, implicit in this outburst (v. 18), calls for God's rebuke and Jeremiah's repentance and eventual restoration to service. For "stand before me" (v. 19), see I Kings 10:8, Numbers 16:8, 9, Deuteronomy 17:12, and II Kings 5:16. Upon God's servants the perpetual demand is obedience (cf. Ex. 4:16; 7:1) and the reward is more service! Only the most precious in Jeremiah's character, purified from all sinful alloys, will satisfy the Lord. To His servants the promise is secure (v. 20a): the power that prevails (v. 20b), the presence that protects, and peace on the battlefield (v. 20c). In the face of opposition or indifference (v. 21), the message must be delivered.

Loneliness in Judah (16:1-21). (1) Jeremiah's Isolation (16:1-9). Jeremiah is forbidden to marry (v. 2). In the approaching catastrophe, the children whom the prophet might beget (v. 3) would simply die "deaths of sicknesses" (v. 4, Heb.). Nor is he to share his people's common griefs (v. 5) and joys (v. 8). Death will be so common that the dead will be unburied, unlamented, unmourned (v. 6), and the living unsolaced (v. 7). The self-denying Jeremiah was to persist in asceticism even to the point of isolating himself from Judah's domestic joys (vv. 8, 9).

(2) Judah's Suicide (16:10-13). The oncoming disaster that was to engulf a generation still mystified by Jeremiah's threats of calamity (v. 10a) is now explained. There was a tragic lack of the sense of sin (v. 10b) in a people noted for its sinfulness (cf. 5:19; 13:22). Judah's blindness must have grieved and puzzled Jeremiah. How thoroughly the false prophets had done their work! Their fathers' sins (v. 11) paled into insignificance in the light of their own apostasy (v. 12); therefore, theirs would be the greater condemnation. Exiled far from God's land, the processes of spiritual suicide would proceed apace (v. 13) because they would conceive that the covenant bond had been severed and God's favor taken away.

(3) God's Promise (16:14-21). Verses 14 and 15 are found sub-

stantially in 37:7 and 8, where the context is better. Here it is a word of hope within a message of doom. This is common in Jeremiah (3:14; 4:27; 5:10, 18; 27:22; 30:3; 32:37). The hope here is of a restoration from exile that will vie with the redemption from Egypt (vv. 14, 15). Meantime, the Lord's lynx-eyed fishers and hunters (Judah's enemies) will miss none (v. 16). God, Who sees Judah's sins (v. 17), must first administer double punishment (cf. Is. 40:2) for their pollution of the land with idols (v. 18; cf. Lev. 26:30). Meantime, in his loneliness, the Lord is Jeremiah's strength and security (v. 19a). Jeremiah "sees" the day when Jew and Gentile, having seen the utter futility of idols, shall acknowledge one God, Lord of heaven and earth (vv. 19, 20). When this *necessary consequence* of Jeremiah's work emerges, God will again begin to reveal Himself in His omnipotent greatness, and teach men His sacred name (v. 21).

Witness to Judah (17:1–27). (1) Her Guilt is Indelible (17:1–4). The metaphor of engraving characters into rock (v. 1) expresses both the indelible quality of Judah's sin and the hardness of her heart. Not that her sin was ineradicable, but her *guilt* was. Her sin is inveterate because it is cut into her very "heart" and religion ("horns of your altars," v. 1), and is reappearing in her offspring (v. 2). Asherim ("groves," v. 2) were symbols in pagan religion. As a consequence of sin, "my mountain in the field" (v. 3, Jerusalem? cf. 21:13) will be despoiled; or read "the" for "my" and relate the phrase to verse 2.

(2) To Trust is to be Blessed (17:5–8). The principle stated here explains Judah's punishment. Judah had trusted "in man," for example, in Egypt (cf. Is. 31:3), but natural and moral weakness ("flesh") had disappointed (v. 5). Having forsaken God, her helper, she, now barren and profitless, resembles a twisted, shrivelled-up tree (v. 6). By contrast, to trust in God, the fountain of living waters (v. 7), is to be like a tree which, fed by waters that never run dry, remains ever green in drought. Confidence in God produces vitality, stability, serenity, and harmony of character (v. 8).

(3) The Heart is Deceitful (17:9–11). If, as many scholars surmise, verses 9 and 10 should immediately precede verse 14, then Jeremiah is here confessing the evil of his own heart. God has been exposing the sinfulness of a heart which Jeremiah thought belonged wholly to God. If he was unconscious of his heart's

incurable sickness, then who can know it (v. 9)? "I," answers the Lord. He searches the heart's abyss where evil lurks (Ps. 139:1). If the issues of life are settled there (Prov. 4:23), Jeremiah needs "a clean heart" (Ps. 51), and so prays for healing (v. 14). A bird who hatches another's eggs and is then forsaken by the brood symbolizes the loss of ill-gotten gain by a man in his prime who then degenerates into moral and spiritual folly (v. 11).

(4) God Vindicates the Righteous (17:12–18). The temple was conceived to be the throne of God's glory (v. 12), the hope of Israel. To forsake Him brings shame and destruction; to abide by the perennial spring (v. 13) brings healing and salvation (v. 14). Perhaps it was his imprecations upon his jeering opponents (v. 15) that exposed the deceitfulness of his heart to Jeremiah (cf. v. 9). He protests that he never planned to renounce his calling (v. 16a), nor were his prophecies of doom vindictive (v. 16b), God is his witness (v. 16c); and he prays that his fidelity should not occasion him shame (v. 17). Verse 18 seems to contradict verse 16 and 17, but perhaps he now prays in this fashion realizing Judah was incorrigible.

(5) The Sabbath is to be Hallowed (17:19–27; cf. Ex. 20:8–11; Deut. 5:12–15). The whole people is addressed (vv. 19, 20). Burdens (merchandise and produce) are not to be borne on the Sabbath (vv. 21, 22; cf. Neh. 13:15–22). If the people, unlike their forefathers (v. 23), hallow the Sabbath (v. 24), Jerusalem, under David's line, will become again the nation's shrine (vv. 25, 26). But disobedience will bring destruction (v. 27; cf. Ex. 31:12–17).

Visit to the Potter's House (18:1–23). (1) The Divine Potter (18:1–10). The parable illustrates the providential rule of the world. Jeremiah notices "the wheels" (v. 3), the lower worked by the feet, and the upper which rotated with the lower, on which the clay rested. Several attempts to make a vessel failed (v. 4). So is Israel in the hands of the divine potter (vv. 5, 6). After repeated failure, the Lord still refuses to abandon the clay and tries to reshape it. It is the vessel that is essential, not the shape. The potter's intention is conditioned by the people's obedience or recalcitrance, according to which He punishes or blesses (vv. 7–10), but His designs will ultimately be achieved. He is always in sovereign control, but the nation (or individual, 17:10) He is forming for His own designs is responsible for a proper response. That response determines how He will treat them.

(2) The Purpose Delayed (18:11-17). Actually the divine potter is "framing" (molding) "evil" against Judah which moral amendment alone can avert (v. 11). But Judah is so much the helpless victim of her own passions that her case is hopeless (v. 12). Yet she once was the Lord's betrothed virgin (v. 13). The *sense* of verse 14 is that Israel's forsaking God, her rock, is unnatural (8:7). Lebanon's snows never fail, but how inconstant is Israel! Through idolatry she has stumbled in old paths (v. 15) with inevitable results (vv. 16, 17).

(3) The Plot against Jeremiah (18:18). If people believe Jeremiah's predictions, the authority of the spiritual leaders is nullified. He must therefore be silenced. The state, they insist, will not come to an end; there will always be available those who reveal God's will (cf. Ezek. 7:26) in moral and ethical matters. The plan, therefore, was to slander Jeremiah by giving heed to his pronouncements and, using them to brand him as a traitor, have him put out of the way.

(4) Jeremiah's Prayer (18:19-23). This imprecatory prayer is directed against Jeremiah's opponents, not the nation. It accords ill with the prophet's loving concern for his people, but he was a man of like passions as we are. Not having a clear hope of future existence, he emphasized the vindication of God's honor in this life. He who has stood in the breach between his enemies and God (v. 20) now prays for their destruction (vv. 21-23). It is as if in despair, realizing the inevitability of his opponents' self-destruction, he exclaims "So be it!" He prays only that the Lord should do what He has already threatened to do. In fact, the parable in the following chapter illustrates God's answer to Jeremiah's prayer.

Shattering of the Earthen Vessel (19:1-15). (1) The Earthen Vessel Bought (19:1-9). The vessel marred in the potter's hands was refashioned (18:4); this one is destroyed. The significance of the command (v. 1) is not revealed immediately (v. 2). After buying the vessel, Jeremiah assembles the nation's leaders and conducts them to the Potsherd Gate and proclaims a word that sets the ears atingling (vv. 1-3; cf. I Sam. 3:11). Because of judicial murder (II Kings 21:16; 24:4) and idolatry, the Lord's dwelling place is no longer "home" (v. 4). Baal worship, so far removed from God's mind (v. 5), will receive dreadful retribution (v. 6) by the sword (vv. 7, 8) and the siege (v. 9).

(2) The Earthen Vessel Broken (19:10-15). The significance of

the command (v. 1) is now clear (v. 10). Jeremiah's smashing the vessel symbolizes God's manner of dealing with Judah (vv. 11, 12). So complete would be Judah's breaking that unclean Topheth (v. 13; cf. II Kings 23:10) would have to be used as a cemetery. Sacrificing on roof tops was quite common (v. 13; 32:29; II Kings 23:12; Zeph. 1:5). Jeremiah then repeats the message in the temple (vv. 14, 15).

Meeting with Pashhur (20:1–18). (1) Jeremiah Answers his Adversary (20:1–6). For similar encounters see Amos 7:10–17 and Isaiah 22:15–19. Pashhur had oversight ("chief officer," RV) of the temple (v. 1; 29:26). Only a person in authority would have dared so to demean Jeremiah (v. 2). While protesting the unjustified humiliation and acute discomfort of the stocks, Jeremiah calls Pashhur "Terror on every side" (v. 3; cf. RV, v. 10; 6:25; 46:5; 49:29; Lam. 2:22), symbolizing the Babylonian terror that would submerge Judah. Pashhur belonged to the pro-Egyptian party whose policy would yet occasion terror and consternation for Pashhur and Judah (vv. 4–6) when it failed. Some interpreters suggest Pashhur was a priest who silenced true prophets and allowed false prophets to spread their lies (v. 6b; cf. 14:14–16)—clearly a ruinous policy!

(2) Jeremiah Accuses God (20:7–13). This section and the following are among the most important in the whole of the prophetic literature. Perhaps those words came to Jeremiah while in the stocks. "Enticed" by God, against his better judgment, to become God's prophet, he had met only mockery, isolation, disappointment (v. 7). His God-inspired message had brought only reproach and violence (v. 8). Yet every resolution not to utter God's word lights a searing fire within him which he cannot endure (v. 9). And a perpetual whispering campaign among familiar friends to boot! "He's a terror! Let's denounce him! Let's be alert for the false move, the rash word." Once incriminated, Jeremiah would face charges of treason arising from his policy of surrender, and give the pro-Egyptian party their revenge (v. 10). But trusting in God, his strong Deliverer, Jeremiah's mood of despair passes. God is with him, his adversaries cannot prevail (v. 11; 1:19). God knows his inmost motives, secret thoughts, singleness of aim (v. 12). Deliverance is sure, and in that conviction, faith sings its triumph song to the great Deliverer (v. 13).

(3) Jeremiah Anathematizes his Birth (20:14–18; cf. Job 3:3–12). To the ancient Hebrew, blessing and cursing did really result in corresponding effects. In a fresh mood of despair, Jeremiah wishes he

had never been born, and curses the day of his birth and the messenger who announced it, but not his parents (vv. 14, 15). The messenger was usually rewarded; instead, Jeremiah offers a curse commensurate with that of Sodom and Gomorrah (v. 16) because he slew him not *in embryo* (v. 17). His question (v. 18) expresses well his sense of overpowering anguish at the bitterness of life.

Counsel of Surrender (21:1–14). (1) The King's Inquiry (21:1, 2). This incident belongs to the early stages of the siege of Jerusalem begun in 588 B.C. In chapters 1 through 20 Jehoikim reigned; now it is Zedekiah. Pashhur (v. 1) is not identical with his namesake in 20:1. The latter would go into exile (20:6) with Jehoiachin. Nebuchadrezzar was attacking Judah, and Zedekiah requests Jeremiah to pray ("inquire") for him. Perhaps Zedekiah still hoped that God would intervene for Judah (v. 2; cf. II Kings 19:35).

(2) The Prophet's Reply (21:3–10). The skirmishes with the Babylonians outside the walls of Jerusalem are futile; the city will fall (v. 4). The Lord Himself will fight against Jerusalem (v. 5), weaken her defenders, and deliver the survivors to the enemy (vv. 6, 7). There is yet one alternative to this "way of death" (v. 8; cf. Deut. 11:26; 30:15–20). "The way of life" was surrender to Babylon. He who would "fall away" (desert) would escape alive (v. 9; cf. 38:2; 39:18; 45:5; Job 2:4). But Jerusalem's fate was sealed (v. 10; 38:3). Why did Jeremiah counsel surrender and thus invite misunderstanding (37:13, 14; 38:24–27)? (a) When Babylon defeated Egypt at Carchemish twenty years earlier (608 B.C.), Jeremiah realized that God would accomplish His purposes upon Judah and the world through Babylon; (b) he realized that though God would effect Judah's judgment through Babylon, yet beyond judgment lay redemption which only God Himself could accomplish; (c) these convictions were based, not on the insights of a shrewd man of public affairs, but on God's revelation to him as His prophet.

(3) The Lord's Controversy (21:11–14). These verses consist of two detached fragments that are taken together. In verse 11 either omit "and" or insert "thou shalt say" after "Judah." "The house of David" (king and princes) failed to administer justice, hence the controversy between it and the prophets of the God of righteousness. The Lord's constant demand was for social morality and social justice as well as organized religion, and when that demand

was denied, a controversy was inevitable (v. 12). The geographical features (v. 13) are inapplicable to Jerusalem, but she is being addressed. Her false confidence (v. 13b) will disappear in the conflagration (v. 14).

Demand for Justice (22:1—23:8). (1) The Plea for Righteousness (22:1–12). This section contains two oracles. (a) Verses 1–9 concern the reigning monarch. Jeremiah is to challenge the court (vv. 1, 2) to execute justice (cf. II Sam. 8:15; I Kings 10:9) in behalf of those who have no advocate (v. 3), for example, "the stranger" (cf. II Sam. 12:1–15). Use of power to protect the powerless would yet avert disaster (v. 4), but God will punish its misuse (v. 5) with desolating destruction (vv. 6–9). (b) Verses 10–12 concern Shallum (Jehoahaz; I Chron. 3:15; II Kings 23:31–35). "The dead" was Josiah, killed at Megiddo (II Kings 23:29). His was a happier fate than Shallum's, whom Pharaoh Necho deposed and removed to Egypt, a land of no return (vv. 10–12).

(2) The Punishment of Unrighteousness (22:13–19). The subject here is the unjust Jehoiakim (II Kings 23:36—24:7). This irreligious king (36:1) built for selfish reasons and with unjust methods, as with forced labor (vv. 13, 14). Ostentatious cedar palaces are no proof of true kingship (v. 15a). Josiah, his father, lived a full-orbed life without neglecting "judgment and justice," but then he knew God (vv. 15b, 16). Because of his covetousness, and his crimes to gratify it (v. 17), the unrighteous Jehoiakim would die unwept by relative or subject (v. 18). After burial, his corpse would be dishonored. "The burial of an ass" was no burial; its carcass was left for the vultures.

(3) The Prophet's Lament (22:20–30). Judah's destitution—without allies ("lovers"), with a reputation for disobedience, without competent rulers ("shepherds"), living in a false security—may be the consequences of Jehoiakim's reign. It is used to introduce Jeremiah's lament for Jehoiachin, his successor (II Kings 24:8–16; 25:27–30), also called Jeconiah (24:1) and Coniah (37:1). Though he were as dear to the Lord as a ring to its owner, yet will He fling him away (vv. 24, 25), and his mother (II Kings 24:12, 15) Nehushta (II Kings 24:8), and both shall die in exile (vv. 26, 27; 52:31, 32). As a broken image or vessel is tossed away, so is Coniah (vv. 28, 29), never to have a successor (v. 30).

(4) The Lord our Righteousness (23:1–8). Judah's "shepherds" (rulers, 22:22), forgetting that "power means opportunity for serv-

ice," have scattered the Lord's flock (cf. Ezek. 34:31) and must be punished (vv. 1, 2). But the Shepherd of Israel will gather a remnant and appoint true shepherds over them (vv. 3, 4). Jeremiah then prophesies Messiah's coming, King David's greater Son, "a righteous shoot" (v. 5; cf. Zech. 3:8; 6:12). Messiah will "deal wisely" (also said of the Servant of the Lord, Is. 52:13), rule over a united Israel, and be called "the Lord our Righteousness" (vv. 5, 6). Both King and subjects will be righteous. When Jesus the Messiah appeared, He came not as the Prophet, Priest and King of Psalm 2, Deuteronomy 18, and Psalm 110, but as the suffering Servant of Isaiah 53, thus fulfilling all righteousness (Mt. 3:15) *and,* in His own divine fashion, these other preceding Old Testament prophecies. In the hour of humiliation, the exiles are promised restoration that will eclipse the redemption from Egypt (vv. 7, 8), but the promise is conditional (18:7–10).

Denunciation of the False Prophets (23:9–40). (*1*) Their Character (23:9–15). Along with the court, the false prophets had contributed to Judah's plight. First, let us take a glance through another window of Jeremiah's soul (v. 9). He is heartbroken, unstrung, dazed, as he muses over the judgment he must utter. The false prophets' abuse of power had profaned land and temple (vv. 10, 11). In the falling darkness (13:16), or in their judicial blindness, they will miss the smooth path along which they glide under a momentum that will carry them on to ruin (v. 12; Ps. 35:6). Worse than prophesying by Baal (v. 13) is their immorality, their falsehood. Because it encourages evildoers, it smacks of Sodom (v. 14), and must be punished (v. 15).

(*2*) Their Claims (23:16–22). They insisted their message originated with God, but their violation of basic moral standards and their hypocrisy (v. 14) proved the claim fallacious. Their messages originated in their diseased imaginations, from whence come vain hopes (v. 16). Smooth talk to the irreligious and refractory (v. 17), devoid of demand for repentance, cannot possibly emanate from prophets who have been admitted to the divine "council" to hear God's word (v. 18). Contrary to their smooth prophecies, the whirlwind of divine fury is being whipped up (v. 19) to execute the Lord's purposes (v. 20). The claims of the false prophets to be God-sent, God-inspired messengers (v. 21) are put to the test (see II Tim. 3:16–18, where the test of inspired Scripture is laid down). If they were true prophets, would they not have urged Judah to forsake her sins (v. 22)? This is precisely what they did not do (vv. 11, 14).

(3) Their Communications (23:23-32). They cannot escape the Day of the Lord: omnipotent, omnipresent, and omniscient (vv. 23, 24). The "revelations" they claim to receive through dreams (v. 25; cf. Num. 12:6, and elsewhere) are foolish fancies (v. 26) which they preach to make men forget God's name, that is, all that God is in Himself (v. 27a). Earlier prophets did this when they reduced the Lord to the level of a Baal, so that men could not distinguish the one from the other (v. 27b). Let the dreamer tell his dreams, and let the receiver of God's word declare that word, but do not confuse the two (v. 28). The effect of each makes it easy to distinguish them. The one has dynamic power, a divine energy that burns and blasts and converts (v. 29; cf. 5:14; 20:9); the other is a soothing syrup that lulls the conscience. The Lord is against all misuse of genuine prophecies (v. 30), the parrot-like repetition of words to which "thus saith the Lord" is tacked on (v. 31), the hawking about of dreams, a frivolity that deludes and damns (v. 32).

(3) The Prophetic "Burden" (23:33-40). The Hebrew *massa* means "burden," but figuratively what is taken up on the lips, hence prophetic utterance (II Kings 9:25, RV margin; Is. 13:1). In the future, when people ask facetiously "What is the burden?" Jeremiah is to say, "You are the burden." Whereas the Lord used to bear this "burden" (that is, Israel; cf. Is. 46:3, 4), he now tosses it aside (v. 33). To eliminate the sarcastic use of *massa* (vv. 34-36), two substitute phrases are provided (v. 37). Those who persist in the use of *massa* will receive dire punishment (vv. 38-40).

The Two Baskets of Figs (24:1-10). (1) The Edible Figs (vv. 1-7). This chapter contrasts the Jews now in exile with Jechoniah (22:20-30) since 597 B.C., with those left behind in Judah. The latter claimed that their deliverance implied their superiority over the former. The two baskets of figs (vv. 1-3) may have been brought to the temple as firstfruits. Through the first-crop figs, a delicacy (Is. 28:4), God told Jeremiah that He looked upon the exiles with favor and would restore them to Judah (vv. 4-6). Not because they were the cream of the nation (II Kings 24:14-16)—God is no respecter of persons (Acts 10:34)—but their experiential knowledge of God (given them in the sorrow of the Exile?) had produced repentance toward God in their hearts (v. 7).

(2) The Overripe Figs (24:8-10). These represent Zedekiah and the Jews left in Jerusalem in 597 B.C. They believed that temple, priesthood, and sacrifice kept them close to the Lord, and on the other hand, their exiled brethren in Babylon, now cut off from these

religious institutions, were *ipso facto* cut off from the Lord. Jeremiah later exposed the fallacy of this theory which made temple and ritual essential to fellowship with God (29:7), and the very people who now held it were to learn in exile that God's grace was available in an unclean land. Meantime, they were soon to realize, through the judgment that was overtaking them (vv. 8–10), that they were inferior to their brethren already in exile.

The Cup of God's Fury (25:1–38). (1) The Moral Principle in Judgment (vv. 1–7). The year 604 B.C. was a momentous one (v. 1). In it Jeremiah wrote down his prophecies (36:1–3); and the battle of Carchemish decided the suzerainty of Babylon over Egypt, Judah, and all western Asia. Jeremiah now pronounces judgment upon the nations over whom God had set him (1:10). To all Judah (v. 2) he had for twenty-three years (626–604 B.C., cf. 1:2) preached God's word (v. 3), as had the prophets before him (v. 4). It had been a word of repentance, promise (v. 5), and appeal (v. 6). Alas, idolatrous Judah obstinately disobeyed the word and provoked the Lord Who gave it. Judgment became inevitable (v. 7) because God takes sin seriously.

(2) The Moral Purpose in Judgment (25:8–14). The God of grace now pronounces judgment (v. 8) upon recalcitrant Judah and the surrounding nations. His unwitting instrument ("servant," v. 9; cf. Is. 45:1) of judgment is the pagan Nebuchadrezzar (v. 9). The cessation of merrymaking and marriage, the silent millstones, the unlit cottage lamps—such deathly stillness and darkness are the measure of Judah's utter desolation (vv. 10. 11). Verses 12–14, which in turn announce sinful Babylon's humiliation and destruction in fulfilment of the Lord's intentions, seem to interrupt the sequence of the chapter. The reference to Jeremiah in the third person is also difficult. But the whole section teaches that God's judgments upon the nations are not arbitrary or capricious, but moral in purpose. The purpose is to recompense them according to their deeds (v. 14).

(3) The Symbolic Description of Judgment (25:15–29). The wine cup, symbol of judgment (49:12; Is. 51:17, 21–23), contains "the wine of this fury," that is, God's fury (v. 15). The fury, in the form of war ("the sword") and calamity (13:13, 14), will induce frantic bewilderment, shock, and dismay (v. 16). Jeremiah then gives this symbolic cup to the nations (v. 17). He begins with Judah (v. 18), then continues with Egypt in the south (v. 19), Uz, east of Edom, and Philistia in the west (v. 20), the countries east of Jordan (v. 21),

Phoenicia in the northeast (v. 25) and north (v. 26) including "Sheshach" (cypher for Babel or Babylon). All shall be compelled to drink the wine of God's fury (vv. 27, 28), but judgment begins at the house of God, Judah, over whom the Lord has pronounced His name in token of ownership (v. 29).

(4) The Divine Activity in Judgment (25:30–38). The Lord is the God of this sinful world, and being righteous His self-manifestation involves the world in judgment. He treads down the nations (v. 30) with whom He has a controversy and contends with them in judgment (v. 31). It is He Who raises the tempest of judgment (v. 32), therefore "that day" is the Day of the Lord (v. 33). Rulers ("shepherds") and ruled ("the flock") will be scattered (v. 34). There is no escaping this divine destroyer when in fierce anger He goes forth like a devouring lion (vv. 35–38).

Conflict of Faith (26:1—29:32). (1) Conflict with Enemies (26:1–24). (a) Occasion of the conflict (26:1–6). Probably we have here the circumstances in which the temple address (ch. 7) was delivered in 608 B.C. (v. 1). Josiah is dead, Egypt is strong, Necho has deposed Jehoahaz in Jehoiakim's favor (II Kings 23:29, 30). Temple, state, Davidic dynasty still function in Judah, but a blind faith in the temple (7:4) has created a false sense of security (7:10). Jeremiah must now announce that if Judah does not repent (vv. 2–5), temple and city will be so utterly ruined that in their curses men will say, "May such and such become like Jerusalem" (v. 6).

(b) The accusation against Jeremiah (26:7–11). Jeremiah's immense courage and fidelity in the face of certain death (v. 9), and the erroneous attitude of priest, false prophet, and people toward the temple (vv. 7, 9), are vividly protrayed. Jeremiah is free to preach repentance and punishment (v. 3), denounce sin and disobedience (v. 4), but to predict in God's name the ruin of the temple was blasphemy which neither priest nor false prophet would tolerate (v. 9). He was worthy of death (cf. Mt. 26:61; Acts 6:11–14; 7:54). Happily, the last word was not with "pestilent prelates," but with princes and people (vv. 10, 11).

(c) The answer of Jeremiah (26:12–15). He resolutely reaffirms the divine inspiration of the offending words. His plea is not that his enemies have misrepresented him, but that he is the prophet of the Lord speaking an authentic, authoritative word from the Lord (v. 12). He can therefore only reiterate his message (v. 13), submit to a legally constituted court (v. 14), protest his innocence, and attest anew that, having been sent by God, his mission and message were in origin and inspiration divine (v. 15).

(*d*) The acquittal of Jeremiah (26:16–24). Convinced that Jeremiah's claims were true, the court conceded his right to speak (v. 16). A man who would die rather than withhold unpalatable truth must be sincere. Had not Micah (Mic. 1:1) proclaimed a similar message (Mic. 3:12) without detriment? What Jeremiah was saying (18:7, 8) had been true in Micah's day, so why slay God's prophet (v. 19)? The killing of one of Jeremiah's contemporaries (vv. 20–23) proves his life was endangered, but God delivered him (v. 24; cf. 39:14; II Kings 22:12–20).

(2) Conflict with False Prophets (27:1–22). (*a*) Occasion of the second conflict (vv. 1–4). Early in the reign of Zedekiah (v. 1, not Jehoiakim), Jeremiah was commanded to make a yoke (symbol of submission) of bars and thongs, and to don it (v. 2). By the hand of certain foreign envoys then in Jerusalem (v. 3), perhaps to persuade Zedekiah to join a rebellion against Babylon, Jeremiah sends a warning message from the Lord (v. 4). The significance of Carchemish had not yet been grasped in Jeremiah's generation.

(*b*) Jeremiah appeals to five kings (27:5–11). The kings (v. 3) are told that Israel's God, having created all things by His omnipotent power, has the disposition of them (v. 5). In His wisdom, He has placed the kings in Nebuchadrezzar's hand (v. 6) for a limited period (v. 7). They should therefore submit to this divine providence. Since Nebuchadrezzar is God's "servant," rebellion against Babylon is rebellion against God and can issue only in disaster (v. 8). To prophesy otherwise is to prophesy a lie (vv. 9, 10). Exile is the only alternative to submission (v. 11).

(*c*) Jeremiah appeals to Zedekiah (27:12–15). Jeremiah has a similar message for Zedekiah. In His inscrutable wisdom, God has purposed to deliver Jerusalem to Nebuchadrezzar who will also despoil His temple. Zedekiah then should submit to God's providence by submitting to Babylon (v. 12). Surrender will bring salvation (v. 13). The prophets who advise otherwise are liars (v. 14); they do not speak in God's name, and to believe them is to perish (v. 15).

(*d*) Jeremiah appeals to Judah (27:16–22). Because the priests were a force in Judah's politics, Jeremiah's appeal to them might conceivably influence "all this people." Alas, the false prophets' assurance that the temple vessels now in Babylon (II Kings 24:13) would soon be returned (v. 16) captivated the priestly imagination and rallied them to support rebellion against Babylon, now being mooted in Jerusalem. Jeremiah challenges the false prophets to produce one of the prophet's credentials—intercession for their people (v. 18). Not only would the temple vessels now in Babylon not be returned (cf. v. 16), but those now in the temple would also be carried off to Babylon (vv. 19–22).

(3) Conflict with Hananiah (28:1–17). (a) Occasion for the third conflict (vv. 1–4). The dates of this and the previous conflicts are identical. Hananiah was one of the false prophets who were devoid of two main essentials of prophecy—revelation and mission. Their religion was probably a blend of semi-heathenism and obsolete eighth century prophetic ideals, such as the indestructibility of Jerusalem. They lacked the high morality of God's prophets, exaggerated the importance of ritual, condoned the easy morals of the people, prophesied the speedy end of Babylonian suzerainty and the return of the temple vessels. Such was Hananiah who now confronts Jeremiah in the temple (v. 1), claims divine inspiration (v. 2a), and prophesies the return of the temple vessels and of the exiles of 597 B.C. (vv. 2b–4; cf. 22:24–27; II Kings 24:11–16).

(b) Jeremiah's first answer to Hananiah (28:5–11). God gave Jeremiah no *specific* word to add to what he had already proclaimed. Hananiah's "prophesy" coincides with Jeremiah's natural wishes (v. 6) but does not correspond to the Lord's intention. Jeremiah's own ministry had failed to convince the false prophets, so he will appeal to the great prophets of the past. These prophets of doom required no confirmation (v. 8), their willingness to proclaim doom being sufficient. The prophets of success did require confirmation in the shape of fulfilment (vv. 6, 9). Agreement between a prophet's message and Israel's traditional faith was required (Deut. 18:1–5); but Jeremiah's appeal to tradition failed to convince Hananiah, who then graphically reaffirmed his own conviction (vv. 10, 11).

(c) Jeremiah's second answer to Hananiah (28:12–17). "Jeremiah went his way" (v. 11), either in despair, or to reflect on the issues involved. While he reflected, the message for Hananiah was received (vv. 12, 13). Resistance to Nebuchadrezzar, God's instrument of judgment (v. 14), will bind a heavier yoke on Judah's neck. Hananiah therefore was a false prophet, inducing people to pin their hopes on pure illusions, and perverting ("taught rebellion against") God's word (vv. 15, 16). God's verdict came swiftly. Hananiah's "prophecy" (v. 3) was discredited by history; Jeremiah's (v. 16) was fulfilled in two months (cf. vv. 1, 17).

(4) Conflict with Shemaiah (29:1–32). (a) Occasion of the

fourth conflict (vv. 1–3). Shemaiah was also one of the false prophets. Jeremiah, probably about 596 B.C., sent a letter to those exiled to Babylon in 597 (cf. II Kings 24:11–16). Zedekiah's "diplomatic mission" carrying the letter was perhaps going to Babylon in connection with the revolt hinted at in chapter 27, or with the yearly tribute levied upon Judah by Babylon. Disappointed hopes of a speedy return to Judah, and the false notion that the exiles were cut off from God's grace, led Jeremiah to write his now famous letter.

(*b*) Jeremiah's letter to the exiles (29:4–23). In it he says exile is the will of God. The exiles must therefore maintain a strong family life, and work for, not against, Babylon's welfare (vv. 4–7). This implied a lengthy exile and gave the lie to promises of a speedy return (vv. 8, 9). But the Lord had not forgotten them. Their future was as bright as His promises if they maintained themselves in His grace (vv. 10–15). Conversely, unrepentant Jerusalem would be sent into permanent exile (vv. 16–19). The lying prophecies, immorality, and false claims of the false prophets in Babylon mark them off for judgment (vv. 20–23).

(*c*) Shemaiah's letter to Jerusalem (29:24–28). Jeremiah's assertions—that God can be worshipped apart from temple and ritual, that a Jew can be loyal to Jerusalem and Babylon (witness Daniel and his friends), that the return is still many years off—roused a storm of protest which found expression in Shemaiah's letter. He insists that the Jerusalem priests should have prevented the mad Jerusalem prophet (Jeremiah) from writing to the exiles in Babylon, and undermining the prestige of those who claimed to be prophets among them (vv. 26–28).

(*d*) Jeremiah's reply to Shemaiah (29:29–32). After Jeremiah had listened to the reading of Shemaiah's letter, the word of the Lord came to him. Because of false claims and false prophecies (v. 31), Shemaiah will have no descendants among the exiles who will return to Judah (v. 32).

The Substance of Faith (30:1—31:40). (1) The Promises of God (30:1–4). Seen against its dark background of disaster, this little "Book of Consolation" (30:1—31:40) illustrates perfectly the definition of faith in Hebrews 11:1. "The words" (v. 2), in the form of divine promises, would console and inspire the exiles whom the Lord would restore many years later (29:10) to Palestine (v. 3).

(*2*) The Promise of Deliverance (30:5–11). The Day of the Lord (v. 7; cf. Joel 2:1, 2) will be a day of acute distress (vv. 5, 6). But through judgment comes salvation (v. 7b), and liberty (v. 8) to Church and state to serve God and Messiah (v. 9; Ezek. 37:24–28). The exiles, then, need not despair; they have not passed beyond the Lord's reach (v. 10; cf. Is. 40:27). He is with them, correcting them justly for their sins (cf. 10:24), and the heathen nations too (v. 11).

(3) The Promise of Healing (30:12–17). God's judgment of exiled Judah is severe indeed. Humanly speaking, she is incurably ill (vv. 12, 13) from the wounds God is inflicting. Allies ("lovers") have forsaken her (cf. 4:30); her sorry plight is due to her sins (vv. 14, 15). But the Lord Who judges both Judah and her enemies (v. 16) will become her physician and her friend (v. 17).

(4) The Promise of Restoration (30:18–24). There is consolation also for northern Israel. When she is restored to the old fatherland (v. 18), Israel, once weak and despised, will increase in strength and honor and live under the Lord's protection (vv. 19, 20). One of their number (cf. Deut. 17:15) will rule them as prince on the throne and serve them as priest at the altar, by God's appointment (v. 21; cf. Heb. 5: 4, 5). They will truly be the Lord's people, but the wicked will perish in judgment (vv. 22–24).

(5) The Promise of Grace (31:1–6). The tenses here are in the prophetic past, that is, the future is viewed as already accomplished. The Lord redeemed Israel from Egypt in grace and sustained her in the wilderness by grace; He will do so again in the wilderness of present exile (v. 2). From far off Zion, the Lord will come in grace to redeem the chastened exiles from Babylon, and reunite them in joy and prosperity (vv. 4, 5) and worship (v. 6).

(6) The Promise of Gladness (31:7–14). The reunited Israel will magnify God in Zion for His saving acts toward her (v. 7). Under the leadership of her Father-God (vv. 8, 9) she will return penitently and prayerfully. Her judge will become her Redeemer (vv. 10, 11). His bounty and consolation will be the theme of the song of her people (vv. 12, 13) and the motive of their sacrifices (v. 14).

(7) The Promise of Consolation (31:15–17). In 3:21, 22, the children themselves weep because of their sins; here Rachel their mother weeps over them from her grave. Her grief is inconsolable (v. 15) because in return for her "work" on her children's behalf, she has received only blighted hopes. But the Lord's consolation and promise of restoration (v. 16) bring hope for the future (v. 17).

(8) The Promise of Transformation (31:18–30). Confession, humility and repentance based upon "knowledge" (experience) will

mark the returning exiles (vv. 18, 19; cf. 3:21—4:4). The Lord responds in grace to once wayward Ephraim (v. 20) who becomes again an instrument in His hands (vv. 21, 22). Judah too will return transformed to dwell in righteousness, holiness, and prosperity (vv. 23–25). From this sweet reverie, Jeremiah awakes (v. 26). Within this transformed society prospering under the Lord's protection (vv. 27, 28), men would realize that they suffer both for their fathers' sins and their own. Both views are true, but a stricter justice in retribution would be maintained in the reconstituted society (vv. 29, 30).

(9) The Promise of the New Covenant (31:31–34; cf. Heb. 8:8–12; 10:16, 17; Rom. 11:27). Faith and forgiveness and true instruction, which had been present in the Old Covenant, would predominate in the New. The New Covenant would be permanent (vv. 31, 32), written on the heart, not on stone. It did not introduce a new Decalogue, but its power insured obedience of the old. It did not impose a new legalism or ceremonial ritual, but it brought moral regeneration (cf. 4:4; 24:7), and thus it insured its own fulfilment (v. 33). It also imparted new insights into the character of God, which was to bear fruit in the lives of the members of the New Covenant, but divine grace and forgiveness remained paramount (v. 34).

(10) The Pledge of God (31:35–40). Sun, moon and stars obey laws which insure a unified universe. It is as impossible for God to destroy Israel as it is for the heavenly bodies to disobey these laws (vv. 35, 36), or for a man to measure the expanse of the universe or the earth's depths (v. 37). This indestructible people shall inhabit a reconstructed Zion (vv. 38, 39) that will be holy unto the Lord and stand forever (v. 40).

The Action of Faith (32:1–44). (1) Circumstances of the Action (vv. 1–5). The siege of Jerusalem had been going on for a year (cf. v. 1 with 39:1), and the end of the temple and state was now inevitable. Jeremiah, arrested after the temporary raising of the siege (37:5, 11–15), was in prison (v. 2; 38:28) because of his policy of surrender (vv. 3–5). Yet, though all seemed lost, Jeremiah had faith in Judah's future, faith which expressed itself in a most significant action.

(2) Details of the Action (32:6–12). The Lord revealed to Jeremiah that his cousin was coming to ask him to exercise the duties of next-of-kin by purchasing a parcel of land belonging to the family in

Anathoth. The property would thus remain in the family (vv. 6–8b). This request was to Jeremiah not a coincidence but a divine revelation, God's promise and pledge (v. 8c). Hence the meticulous care in preparing and preserving legal title deeds (vv. 9–12, 14).

(3) Significance of the Action (32:13–15). Since the cousin's request implied the Lord's promise, Jeremiah's assent implied faith in the promise. The title deeds will be laid up "many days" (v. 14) but they will be needed some day (v. 15)! This ruinous investment was to faith perfectly safe. The promise of God covered every exigency. The future of revealed religion and of God's people was guaranteed by His power and grace.

(4) Faith Falters (32:16–25). The specter of doubt suddenly appears before this man of faith, and he takes refuge in prayer (v. 16). There is nothing too difficult (cf. Gen. 18:14) for an omnipotent God (v. 17), perfect in love, justice, and glory (v. 18), the omniscient and righteous judge of all men (v. 19). He Who in grace delivered Israel (vv. 20–22) now judges her (vv. 23, 24). But the Lord's promise and Jerusalem's doom (v. 25) create a dilemma before which faith falters.

(5) Faith Upheld (32:26–44). The Lord answers faith in its own language (cf. vv. 17, 27). Nothing is too wonderful or difficult for Him. The present catastrophe (vv. 28, 29) and the reasons for it (vv. 30–35) are set forth; but so also are the Lord's promises and purposes for His chastened people (vv. 36–43). And Jeremiah believes that what he has just done (vv. 9–14) will some day become a daily occurrence in Judah (v. 44).

The Vision of Faith (33:1–26). (1) A Vision of God (vv. 1–3). Jeremiah is confined in the guard-court (v. 1; 32:2, RV), but his faith soars to new heights of vision. God, Who is all and in all, in providential grace is actively present in the world He created (v. 2). To Him men pray and He reveals "difficult" things, things that are inaccessible to or hidden from the minds of men (v. 3; cf. v. 18a; 48:6b–8a). He Himself cannot be grasped by men's minds (Job 11:7) but He has revealed Himself in His name Jahweh (Ex. 3:13, 14).

(2) A Vision of Restoration (33:4–9). The text of verses 4 and 5 is extremely difficult, but its subject is the siege. Healing for Judah's "incurable" wounds is promised, and peace with stability or faithfulness, that is, God's faithfulness to His promises (v. 6). Israel will be restored to her original unity (v. 7) and be cleansed from

sin (v. 8; Ezek. 36:25) to become again a praise to her God and a source of dread to the heathen nations (v. 9; cf. 32:20, 21).

(3) A Vision of Prosperity (33:10–13). In Judah, now wasted and uninhabited (v. 10), the signs and sounds and sights of prosperity will gladden men's hearts again. But her prosperity will also be religious. The best sound of all will come from a restored temple where the Lord will be praised and magnified again (v. 11; cf. Ps. 118) by a restored people. But economic prosperity will also return to the now devastated Judah (vv. 12, 13).

(4) A Vision of Messiah (33:14–26). This section is not in the Septuagint. Verses 15 and 16 largely repeat 23:5 and 6. There righteousness is applied to Messiah, here to Zion. Both King and people will manifest it. Messiah will maintain the permanence of David's house (v. 17), and of sacrificial priesthood, worship, and offering (v. 18); a prophecy fulfilled in Christ, great David's greater Son. God's covenant with David (II Sam. 7:16; I Kings 2:4) and the priestly family is infallible (vv. 19–22). Naturally, a permanent messianic kingship and priesthood necessitate a permanent Israel and Judah ("the two families," vv. 23, 24; Ezek. 35:10), and the pledge of the nation's indestructibility (vv. 25, 26) is identical with the pledge in verses 20 and 21.

We pause to recapitulate the living themes of this first section: (1) Behind everything is the everlasting love of the covenant God for Israel, His covenant people. It is the covenant grace of God over against Israel's lamentable failure in this experiment in divine-human covenant relations that explains the nation's history in general and the Lord's dealings with Jeremiah's generation in particular. (2) The deadly seriousness with which God treats the sinfulness of His covenant people is also prominent. (3) Sin is dynamic not static, active not passive; and it works itself out under many different and terrible manifestations. (4) Jeremiah's response of obedience to God's call to service made the most searching demands upon him in the region of his love, his faith, and in the elemental depths of his personality.

II. Jeremiah, God's Watchman: Hastening the Word (34:1—45:5)

The living themes in this section are: (1) The strange behavior of men grown so hard in sinful rebellion against God that their senseless hearts become darkened. (2) The power of God's Word, and Jeremiah's determination to preserve that Word for generations yet unborn. (3) The religious aspect of true patriotism personified in Gedaliah and Jeremiah.

1. The Released Slaves (34:1–22)

Jerusalem's Fall Inevitable (34:1–7). Jeremiah is not in prison (v. 2) so this incident probably falls within the siege's first phase. The Lord commanded him to announce Jerusalem's destruction and Zedekiah's capture, but the king will die in peace in Babylon (vv. 3–5). Doubtless Jeremiah's words conveyed a tacit appeal for surrender as the sole means of escaping punishment for rebellion against Nebuchadrezzar who was then besieging other cities in Judah.

The Covenant to Free the Slaves (34:8–10). At the instigation of Zedekiah, slave-owners covenanted under solemn oath (vv. 18, 19) to liberate their Hebrew slaves (vv. 8–10; cf. Deut. 15:12). Slaves were at least assured of food, hence their great numbers in Jerusalem at this time. Perhaps Zedekiah hoped to strengthen the city's will to resist by liberating the slaves.

The Covenant Broken (34:11). The Babylonians raised the siege to fight the Egyptians coming to Judah's help (v. 21b; 21:2; 37:5, 11). Assuming that Jerusalem had been delivered, the slave-owners broke their covenant. This act was both cynical and perfidious. Their perjury implied contempt of the religious sanctities involved in their oath (v. 15), and contempt of human personality. They were in fact insulting the Lord, profaning His name (v. 16).

What a Broken Covenant Signified (34:12–16). A liability during the siege, the slaves were liberated; a necessity when the siege was raised, they were re-enslaved. No wonder Jeremiah's prophetic indignation blazed forth. He quotes God's covenant with the nation's forefathers (v. 13), and the law arising therefrom (v. 14; Deut. 15:12). In covenanting to obey that law in the temple, they did right (v. 15); in breaking their covenant and perjuring their oath, they profaned the holy name of the Lord (v. 16).

The Breaking of the Covenant Punished (34:17–22). When the slave-owners proclaimed the slaves' release, the Lord proclaimed their liberty; they will now come under the yoke of the returning Babylonians for having compelled their slaves to return to slavery (vv. 17–20). They had transgressed their covenant (vv. 8, 10,

13–15). The severity of the punishment (v. 20) is the measure of the heinousness of a breach of faith in the eyes of the covenant God of Israel.

2. The Rechabites (35:1–19)

The Rechabites' Loyalty to Jonadab (35:1–11). The Rechabites traced their ancestry and religious ideals back to Jonadab (II Kings 10:15), who had helped Jehu to exterminate the contaminating influences of the Canaanite fertility cult of Baal (II Kings 10:15–23). Jonadab's descendants were to avoid the settled life of field and vineyard (vv. 6, 7) in order to preserve the worship of the Lord in pristine purity. Now, two centuries later, armed invasion (II Kings 24:1, 2) compelled the Rechabites to abandon their tent life and come to Jerusalem (v. 11). The Lord commands Jeremiah to bring the Rechabites to the temple and to set wine before them (vv. 1–5), but they reaffirm their undeviating loyalty to Jonadab's precepts and ideals (vv. 6–11).

Judah's Disloyalty to the Lord (35:12–15). Through their unswerving fidelity, God's word came to Jeremiah concerning Judah (vv. 12, 13). To Jonadab's words (v. 14a) and restricted ideal (v. 14b), the Rechabites had been faithful for nearly two and a half centuries. What a rebuke (v. 13b) to Judah's faithlessness to the Lord, and disobedience to His commandments (v. 14c). Let it be a call to repentance, amendment of life, abandonment of idolatry (v. 15).

The Lord's Verdict (35:16–19). He commends the Rechabites and condemns Judah (v. 16). Judah's faithlessness must therefore be punished (v. 17) and the Rechabites' faithfulness acknowledged. Jonadab's name will never die out in Israel (v. 18), and from among his posterity someone will always "stand before" the Lord (v. 19) to fulfil the prophetic or the priestly ministry (see note on 15:19).

3. The Word of God Transcribed (36:1–32)

The Proclaimed Word Recorded (36:1–4). This important passage (dated 604 B.C., v. 1; cf. 25:1) shows how Jeremiah's prophecies were first written down. It witnesses to the authenticity of the whole book. The prophecies cover a prophetic ministry of twenty-three years (v. 2b; cf. 25:3). "Concerning Israel," Jeremiah had proclaimed hope (for example, 31:2–22); "concerning Judah" and "the nations"

(v. 2a), judgment (for example, 25:1–38). The prophecies were written in the hope that Judah might yet repent and be forgiven (v. 3). Baruch, who wrote as Jeremiah dictated (v. 4), was a faithful friend (32:12, 13; 43:3, 6; 45:1).

The Written Word Read (36:5–8). Jeremiah was not yet imprisoned (v. 19) but he was forbidden the temple (v. 5), probably by the priests (cf. 29:24–27) ever since the encounter with Pashhur (20:1–6). Baruch therefore must read the written word. The choice of a fast day insured a large sympathetic audience (v. 6). If they pray penitently, the Lord may accept them (v. 7a) and avert their doom. It was "the words of the Lord" that Baruch read (v. 8).

Consternation of the Princes (36:9–20). The summary statement in verse 8 is now expanded. An unexplained year's delay followed (cf. v. 1 with v. 9a). The desired circumstances (v. 6) eventually materialized (v. 9b) and Baruch read God's word. Jeremiah's friends were present (v. 10). At the princes' request, Baruch reread God's word (vv. 11–15), which alarmed them exceedingly (v. 16). Verse 29 explains their consternation. Having discovered the origin of the treasonable words (vv. 17, 18) they insure the safety of the scroll and its producers (cf. 26:20–23) and report to Jehoiakim (vv. 19, 20).

Contempt of the King (36:21–26). The offending words were then read to Jehoiakim. When Jehudi read three or four columns, the king cut them out of the scroll and tossed them into the fire until the scroll was destroyed (v. 23; cf. II Kings 22:8–13). The princes concurred with the king's contempt for God's word (v. 24). The arrest of the servants of God's word was foiled because the Lord Who watches over both word and servant "hid them" (v. 26).

Concern of the Prophet (36:27–32). God overruled Jehoiakim's sacrilege. He watches over His Word both to perform it and preserve it. Jeremiah's concern was to rewrite his prophecies (v. 27, 28). The contemptuous king and people were condemned (vv. 29–31). God further overruled by adding to the contents of the original scroll (v. 32). In that dark age some treasured God's word (cf. 26:16–19; 36:25), and under God saved it for posterity.

4. The Word of God Communicated (37:1—38:28a)

Zedekiah's First Request for the Word (37:1–10). Jeremiah communicated the word of God to Zedekiah during the siege. An introductory note (vv. 1, 2) describes Zedekiah's accession and subsequent disobedience to the word of God. Zedekiah's request for prayer (v. 3; cf. 21:1; Is. 37:2–5) came after the Babylonians' raising of the siege (v. 5; cf. ch. 34). He probably wanted guidance from God in the new circumstances, or sought assurance that Egypt would defeat Babylon. The word given (v. 6) brought no such assurance (v. 7). But God's directive was clear (vv. 8–10): He purposed to destroy Jerusalem, even if Egypt defeated Babylon.

The Servant of the Word (37:11–16). Having communicated God's word, Jeremiah, taking advantage of the raising of the siege (v. 11), attempted to go to his native Benjamin (v. 12). His purpose is not clear. "To take his portion" may have some connection with 32:6–44, but that belongs to the second stage of the siege. He was arrested as a deserter (v. 13). Probably because he had advocated surrender (for example, 21:8, 9), his protestations of innocence went unheeded (v. 14), and he was beaten and imprisoned (vv. 15, 16). The friendly princes of Jehoiakim's reign (26:10–24; 36:19) had been in exile since 597 B.C. (cf. 24:1–7); the princes in Zedekiah's reign (v. 15), the "bad figs" (24:8–10), had felt the lash of Jeremiah's tongue (34:8–22), and hated him.

Zedekiah's Second Request for the Word (37:17–21). During the "many days" of verse 16, the siege was resumed. Zedekiah's second request for a word from God (v. 17a) proves he believed Jeremiah was God's prophet. Alas, fear (38:5, 24–28) rendered the word ineffective (cf. Mt. 13:20, 21). Jeremiah's dignified "there is" (v. 17b) signifies that God's word, and his faith in it, are with him still, persecution notwithstanding. Jeremiah's protestations (v. 18), expostulations (v. 19; cf. 28:2–4), and supplications (v. 20) moved Zedekiah to act for his welfare (v. 21).

The Servant of the Word (38:1–13). Jeremiah, the servant of the word, continued to mediate the word (v. 1b). At this late hour, the word given is identical with previous announcements (cf. vv. 2 and 3 with 21:9 and 10). The charge against Jeremiah (v. 4) was well-founded. In the circumstances, Judah's leaders were bound to silence this seditious agitator. Only if the latter's action springs from "profound conviction" can it be excused. Jeremiah, the servant of the word, knew Jerusalem would fall, and knew why it would fall. Hence, his "treasonable" advice, and the leaders' "patriotic" action (vv. 5, 6). The story of Jeremiah's deliverance is well-known (vv. 7–13).

Zedekiah's Third Request for the Word (38:14–23). Before granting Zedekiah's request (v. 14), Jeremiah asks for royal protection and predicts royal disobedience (v. 15). Zedekiah swears a solemn oath (v. 16) and hears again the uncompromising word (cf. 21:9, 10). Surrender means safety, rebellion means retribution (vv. 17, 18). The king explains why he will not comply (v. 19). The importunate Jeremiah (v. 20) then "sees" (v. 21b) the royal women submitting themselves to the Babylonian princes (v. 22a), taunting the irresolute Zedekiah as they go. False friends have led the king into a quagmire (v. 22b; cf. v. 6), but by rejecting the word, Zedekiah had asked from God, he is responsible for Jerusalem's doom and his own (v. 23).

The Servant of the Word (38:24–28a). Having refused God's word, Zedekiah swears Jeremiah to secrecy, otherwise the princes will kill him (vv. 24, 25; cf. v. 5). Jeremiah agrees to Zedekiah's expediency (vv. 25, 26) and eventually satisfies the princes, shields the king, and saves himself (vv. 27, 28).

5. The Word of God Fulfilled (38:28b—39:18)

Its Significance for Babylon (38:28b—39:3). Unconsciously the Babylonians were now fulfilling God's word. Nebuchadrezzar was His "servant" (25:9; 27:6; 43:10). This, however, did not save the Babylonians in their day of doom. (See the standard commentaries here concerning the state of the Hebrew text.) The resumé in 39:1 and 2 is paralleled by 52:4 through 6. When Jerusalem fell, the Babylonian princes sat in judgment over her inhabitants (v. 3).

Its Significance for Jerusalem (39:4–10). This section is not in the Septuagint. Realizing that Jeremiah's prophecies of doom were about to be fulfilled, Zedekiah and the army attempt in vain to escape (v. 4). In Riblah, Nebuchadrezzar condemned Zedekiah's rebellion (v. 5), and pronounced sentence (vv. 6, 7), but his life was spared as Jeremiah predicted (34:2–5). Jerusalem was destroyed and her inhabitants exiled (vv. 8, 9). Thus sinful Judah discovered that the Lord's word cannot fail. Only the poorest people were spared (v. 10).

Its Significance for Jeremiah (39:11–18). We can only faintly imagine Jeremiah's feelings as he witnessed the fulfilment of God's word. Probably Nebuchadrezzar had heard of Jeremiah's advocacy of surrender from deserters, and this led him to attend to his welfare

(vv. 11–14). Before Jerusalem fell (cf. v. 15 with 38:13, 28) Ebed-melech, the Ethiopian (v. 16), who because of his trust in God (v. 18b) risked his life to save Jeremiah (38:7–13), received a promise from God (vv. 17a, 18a). God's promise of good, like His decree of doom, stands fast.

6. Gedaliah's Governorship (40:1—41:18)

Jeremiah's Patriotism (40:1–6). Chapter 40 continues Judah's story. The Babylonian official's remarks (vv. 2, 3) would be based upon what the deserters from Jerusalem had said on reaching enemy camp during the siege. Jeremiah was liberated at Ramah (v. 1), and left to choose Babylon or Judah as his place of domicile (v. 4). He elected to remain in Judah, and his immediate needs were provided for (v. 5). Jeremiah's place is with Gedaliah and the remnant. God had said the exiles would return; he must therefore prepare for their return by assisting Gedaliah to build "the nucleus of the new Isreal."

Gedaliah's Policy (40:7–12). The Jewish soldiery who had eluded the Babylonians rallied to Gedaliah the governor (vv. 7, 8). His first task was to restore confidence. He adjured the people not to fear the Babylonian officials left behind to police Judah (v. 9). He would represent their interests with the Babylonians (v. 10a) who had not denuded the land completely (v. 10b). With the return of confidence, embers of hope began to glow again (vv. 11, 12).

Gedaliah's Generosity (40:13–16). The cup of Judah's affliction was not yet full, however. Ishmael, at the instigation of the king of Ammon, plotted Gedaliah's assassination (vv. 13, 14), but Gedaliah refused to believe the report. The plot was too irrational, unpatriotic, and treasonable. Gedaliah was to learn too late that jealousy and resentment drive men to senseless violence. Johanan appreciated the appalling consequences latent in Ishmael's intention and was prepared to kill him (v. 15), but Gedaliah refused to sanction secret murder (v. 16).

Gedaliah's Assassination (41:1–10). Ishmael, who belonged to the house of David (v. 1), probably adhered to the anti-Babylonian or pro-Egyptian party who treated Jeremiah and his friends (hence Gedaliah) as traitors. The date in verse 1a still marks the fast of Gedaliah. Ishmael's despicable deed brought death to others besides Gedaliah.

Johanan's Intervention (41:11–18). Johanan's pursuit was so swift that he overtook Ishmael at Gibeon, one mile north of Mizpah. To escape vengeance, Ishmael had to abandon his captives and flee eastward to Ammon (vv. 11–15). Johanan and the refugees traveled southward, intending to migrate to Egypt, fearing Nebuchadrezzar would take reprisals against them for Gedaliah's death (vv. 16–18).

7. Jeremiah's Final Word in Judah (42:1—43:7)

The Word Desired (42:1–6). If we assume that Jeremiah and Baruch were also carried off by Ishmael (cf. 40:6 with 41:10), they too went south to Bethlehem (41:17). The refugees now ask Jeremiah to pray for them (42:1, 2). They wanted guidance from God (v. 3). Jeremiah stood in the councils of the Lord and had power in prayer. Note the significant changes in the possessive pronouns used with "God" in verses 2–6. The people's request (v. 3) and the oath (v. 5) suggest sincerity, but they assumed that their preconceived intention to move to Egypt, and God's guidance, would coincide! Jeremiah's words (v. 4) hint that the assumption was ill-founded. He also surmised their rejection of God's word which did not confirm their decision, oaths and protestations notwithstanding (vv. 5, 6).

The Word Declared (42:7–22). The period of ten days (v. 7) is significant. Jeremiah wanted to be sure that he was announcing God's will, not his own. Nor did he flinch from declaring the offending word (vv. 8, 9). If they abide in Judah, they will become the nucleus of the new Israel which God was about to construct. The Lord's "repenting" concerned His conduct, not His purposes (v. 10). Judah might seem insecure and inhospitable, Egypt safe and attractive (vv. 13, 14), but the future lay with Judah! To choose the false security of Egypt would mean further judgment (vv. 15–18). In the face of mounting opposition, Jeremiah adds a final appeal (v. 19a), rebuke (vv. 19b–21), and warning (v. 22).

The Word Disobeyed (43:1–7). After Jeremiah had declared God's word (v. 1) he was charged with what he had so carefully avoided (v. 2; cf. 42:7)! The accusation in verse 3 does not merit refutation, so Jeremiah remains silent. Jeremiah's companions decided to abide by their own counsel (v. 4), placed themselves under Johanan's leadership and went down to Egypt, taking Jeremiah and Baruch with them (vv. 5, 6). They finally arrived at Tahpanhes (cf. 2:16), a town on the Palestinian-Egyptian frontier (v. 7).

8. Jeremiah's Final Word in Egypt (43:8—44:30)

Egypt's Conquest Foretold (43:8–13). God's first revelation to Jeremiah in Egypt concerned Nebuchadrezzar's conquest of that land. Jeremiah's prophetic action and word (vv. 8–10) must have sobered the fugitive Jews looking on. Eighteen years later (568 B.C.), when perhaps Jeremiah would be dead, the destructive power of Babylon (v. 11) would overtake them and Egypt (v. 12). "Cleopatra's Needle" was one of the pillars mentioned in verse 13. They were erected in 1500 B.C. by Thotmes III.

Judah's Judgment Recalled (44:1–6). Jeremiah's second prophetic word concerned the widely scattered Jewish refugees in Egypt (v. 1). They had quickly established themselves in idolatrous ways in Egypt (cf. vv. 15–19), but a reminder of God's judgments might wean them from these heathen practices. Jeremiah then recalls idolatrous Judah's devastation (vv. 2, 3), the vanity of pleading with her (vv. 4, 5; cf. 7:25; 25:4), and the inevitability of her doom (v. 6).

Jewish Fugitives in Egypt Warned (44:7–14). Jeremiah then pleads with the refugees from Judah to learn from history. To persist in idolatry was to sin against themselves (v. 7), and God would afflict them in Egypt (v. 8), as He had afflicted their fathers in Jerusalem (vv. 8–10). Indeed, God's decree has already gone forth (v. 11). They had disobeyed God in coming to Egypt, and their idolatry was a betrayal of the first principle of revealed religion—that the Lord their God is one Lord. They must therefore perish (vv. 12–14).

The Warning Rejected (44:15–23). Jeremiah's prophecy of inevitable doom (vv. 11–14) was soon justified. The Jews in Egypt rejected the prophet's plea (vv. 15, 16), and vowed to continue the cult of Ishtar (v. 17; 7:18). Fidelity to her cult, they argued, brought prosperity (v. 17c), abandonment of it (cf. II Kings 23:4–8) resulted in Josiah's death (II Kings 23:29), Egyptian domination (II Kings 23:31–35), the first exile (II Kings 24:8–16), Jerusalem's destruction (II Kings 25:1–22), Gedaliah's assassination (II Kings 25:23–25), and flight to Egypt (II Kings 25:26). Jeremiah's counter arguments (44:20–23) achieved nothing.

The Warning Reiterated (44:24–30). Verse 25 was spoken in irony.

So widespread will be the destruction of Egyptian Jewry that the Lord will no longer be named in the land (vv. 26, 27). The few casual survivors will then know that God's word is sure (v. 28). The sign heralding its fulfilment would be Pharaoh Hophra's untimely death in 570 B.C. (vv. 29, 30). Two years later Nebuchadrezzar invaded Egypt and fulfilled the word of Jeremiah's prophesy (vv. 26–28).

9. *Jeremiah Admonishes Baruch (45:1–5)*

Fight Discouragement (45:1–4). The "book" (v. 1) is identical with the one mentioned in 36:1–4, while "these words" (v. 1) are the words referred to in 36:4. Both passages bear the same date. Chapter 45 is then a supplement to 36:8. It owes its present position to Baruch's unwillingness to introduce a personal reference into Jeremiah's story and so interrupt it. Jeremiah's prophecies of doom against Judah occasioned Baruch acute anxiety concerning his own fate (v. 3). The Lord countered Baruch's sorrow by urging him to consider the divine sorrow which was infinitely greater. A powerful antidote to personal despair! The Lord is demolishing what He had constructed, uprooting what He had planted (v. 4; 1:10; cf. 25:15–38). Could Baruch's sorrow begin to compare then with God's sorrow? The more so since no alternative to judgment remained.

Flee Self-Aggrandizement (45:5). Baruch then must discipline himself to accept God's will. In the midst of this divine destruction it was unseemly for Baruch "to seek great things" for himself (v. 5a). Whereas the Lord was "compelled" to pluck up Judah, the choice vine He had planted, Baruch's life was being spared. He must therefore use that redeemed life to serve God's purposes, not to further his own ends. Baruch's personal ambitions are not disclosed, but God's will for his life is plain—to give to the world the Word of God which had been given to Jeremiah. And Baruch's life, spared in Judah's dreadful debacle, was dedicated to the successful accomplishment of that divine purpose.

The themes in this section are, in very truth, living themes. *(1)* Establishment in habits of sinful rebellion against God still leads to fearful spiritual insensibility. Men who will not see degenerate into men who cannot see. (2) Yet God continues to speak His revelatory Word because even in such a situation He refuses to leave Himself without a witness. (3) But servants of the Word are required to witness to that Word and interpret it, preserve it and suffer for it, love and reverence it. (4) God's children should be true patriots. The religious patriot is not blind to the sins of his native land, but in recognizing them and witnessing against them, he still loves and suffers for the land of his birth, more especially when its calamities are God's judgments upon its sins.

III. Jeremiah, God's Witness to the Nations: The Lord God Omnipotent Reigneth (46:1—52:34)

This closing section also teaches important themes: (1) God is on the throne of the universe and is in absolute control of it. (2) This is a moral world, and the important things in it are not power and riches, but character and morality. (3) This sinful world is under the judgment of God.

1. Jeremiah's Wider Mission (46:1)

Jeremiah's primary mission was to Judah, but it is clear from the account of his call that he had a wider mission to fulfil (1:5b, 10a, 15; cf. 25:15–29; 28:8). Judah's geographical position made that inevitable. It lay between Babylon and Egypt, and was immediately surrounded by some half dozen smaller nations. Her destiny therefore was inextricably bound up with theirs, and by the same token Jeremiah's call to prophesy against Judah made him "the prophet unto the nations." Hence, God's word to him "concerning the nations" (46:1).

2. Egypt (46:2–28)

Occasion of the Prophecy (46:2). In 609 B.C., Pharaoh Necho was Judah's overlord (II Kings 23:29–35). But in 605 B.C. he was defeated by Nebuchadrezzar at Carchemish on the Euphrates. This battle ended Egyptian, and established Babylonian, suzerainty in western Asia. Hence Jeremiah's insistence on Judah's surrender to Babylon (21:1–10; 27:5–12). It was also in 605 B.C. that Jeremiah commanded the nations to drink the goblet of God's fury (25:1, 15–28).

Egypt Discomfited (46:3–12). The pride of Egyptian military might is set in array at Carchemish (vv. 3, 4), but in ironical astonishment Jeremiah describes Egypt's utter rout (vv. 5, 6). Her vaunted strength, powerful as the Nile in flood (vv. 7, 8), and her numerous allies (v. 9), cannot weather this fateful day of God's vengeance (v. 10) for Megiddo (II Kings 23:29). The wounds inflicted upon Egypt by Babylon are incurable (v. 11), and the noise of her panic reverberates throughout the earth (v. 12).

Egypt Invaded (46:13-24). Foreseeing Nebuchadrezzar's invasion of Egypt (v. 13), Jeremiah calls upon her to defend herself (v. 14). But God smites her "strong one" (Apis, the sacred bull), and troops and traders panic (vv. 15, 16). Pharaoh has procrastinated, his name becomes a synonym of disaster (v. 17). Towering like Tabor, Nebuchadrezzar will dominate Egypt and exile her people (vv. 18, 19). The Babylonian gadfly will sting Egypt (v. 20), expose her military weakness (vv. 21, 22), cut down her cities like trees and put her to shame (vv. 23, 24).

Egypt Humiliated (46:25-28). Amon and those who trust in him, including Judah, will be humiliated by the Lord at the hand of Nebuchadrezzar (vv. 25, 26). For Judah, however, this is not the final word. The Lord will bring her again to her own land, chastened and purified (vv. 27, 28).

3. Philistia (47:1-7)

Occasion of the Prophecy (47:1). It was occasioned by an otherwise unknown attack by Egypt upon the Philistine city of Gaza (v. 1). Herodotus (II. 159) seems to suggest that Pharaoh Necho attacked Gaza on his return from Megiddo. Jeremiah may refer to this here.

Devastation of Philistia (47:2-4). The advancing army from the north (that is, Babylon) is a raging torrent which submerges Philistia (v. 2). The stamping of horses and rumbling of chariots cause panic-stricken fathers to abandon their children (v. 3). In addition, Philistia's allies are spoiled, as are also the Philistine remnant in Caphtor (probably Crete), the original home of the Philistines (cf. Amos 9:7; Deut. 2:23; and note the name Cherethites in Ezek. 25:15, 16; Zeph. 2:4, 5).

Lamentation of Philistia (47:5-7). "Baldness" (v. 5) symbolized mourning (16:6; Deut. 14:1; Mic. 1:6). The Anakim (cf. Num. 13:22, 28, 33, and elsewhere) were related to the Philistines (Josh.

11:22). Cutting oneself was also a mark of mourning (16:6; cf. Lev. 19:28; Deut. 14:1). In their mourning the Philistines plead that the destroying sword should cease from destruction (v. 6). But Jeremiah answers (v. 7) that this is impossible, since the sword is the Lord's, and it must continue until it has accomplished His judgments.

4. Moab (48:1–47)

Moab's Territory Invaded (48:1–6). The Moabites occupied a high fertile plain east of the Dead Sea. The place names listed are mentioned elsewhere in the Old Testament, except Misgab (v. 1), which probably signified "high fort," and Madmen (v. 2). It is chiefly the sense of shame that possessses Moab (vv. 1, 2a) in her hour of destruction (vv. 2b–4). The grief-stricken fugitives will find safety only in flight, so destitute is their land (vv. 5, 6).

Moab's Self-Confidence Exposed (48:7–10). It is her insolence that has wrought Moab's destruction (v. 7). She is suddenly stripped of her deeds, her treasures, and her national deity, Chemosh (mentioned on the Moabite Stone) on which she relied, and is left forlorn (vv. 8, 9). Her desolation is the Lord's doing and must be accomplished with energy (v. 10).

Moab's Self-Indulgence Exposed (48:11–25). Moab has never known exile. In her undisturbed existence, she has grown haughty and indulgent, but now she is being disturbed (vv. 11, 12). Chemosh in whom she trusted was pure illusion, as Bethel was to Israel (v. 13; Amos 5:5). Her own might will also be illusory (v. 14) in battle (v. 15). Moab's neighbors are called upon to lament her calamity (vv. 17–19), described in verses 20–25.

Moab's Self-Conceit Exposed (48:26–28). Moab had dared to match herself against God (v. 26a), and mock at God's people (v. 27). But she is now an object of revulsion and derision (v. 26b), a hunted fugitive among her mountain fastnesses (v. 28).

Moab's Self-Glorification Exposed (48:29–39). Moab's insufferable insolence was notorious (v. 29). Her choleric bombast and inveterate falsehood were known also to the Lord (v. 30). But boasting would change to wailing in her day of doom (vv. 31–34), wailing in which Jeremiah shared (vv. 31, 32a, 36). Religion will die out in Moab (v. 35), the whole land will mourn the national shame and dishonor (vv. 37–39).

Moab's Utter Destruction (48:40–47). Like an eagle Nebuchadrezzar would swoop upon this people (vv. 40, 41) who had defied the Lord in His face (v. 42). There would be no escape from divine justice (vv. 43, 44), nor from the devouring flame (v. 45). Yet in the moment of doom a word of consolation is spoken to the stricken Moabites. The Lord will yet turn back their captivity (vv. 46, 47).

5. Ammon (49:1–6)

Occasion of the Prophecy (49:1). Ammon lay north of Moab and east of the country of Gad. Milkom (for Milkam "their king," v. 1), Ammon's national deity (I Kings 11:5, 33), here symbolizing the nation, had treacherously seized the territory of the Israelite tribe of Gad, probably in the deportation of 734 B.C. (II Kings 15:29). Jeremiah remarks that Gad's brother Israelites could have taken over the territory.

Ammon's Humiliation and Restoration (49:2–6). For Ammon's treachery, Rabbah, her capital, will be destroyed and she will go into exile (vv. 2, 3). She will be dispossessed of all that she gloried in, and will discover she has been living in a false security (vv. 4, 5). But in spite of the mean advantage she took of the stricken Gad, Ammon, like Moab (48:47), Judah, and Israel, will be brought back from exile (v. 6).

6. Edom (49:7–22)

The Certainty of Edom's Fate (49:7–15). Verses 7, 9, 10a and 14–16 correspond to Obadiah 8, 5 and 6, and 1–4, respectively. Teman was in northern Edom. In the day of wrath, Edom's proverbial wisdom fails her (v. 7), and the neighboring Dedanites are urged to flee to inaccessible places until the day of vengeance is past (v. 8). The Lord will make a clean sweep of Edom (vv. 9, 10), but will care for the grief-stricken widows and orphans (v. 11). If those not originally destined to drink the cup of God's fury (that is, Israel) shall drink it, how much more Edom (v. 12; cf. 25:15, 25). Her doom is certain (v. 13) as is also the manner of effecting it (vv. 14, 15).

The Completeness of Edom's Fate (49:16–22). Edom's pride, as she exults in her inaccessible fastnesses, will be changed to trembling (v. 16). Her overthrow will appall passersby (vv. 17, 18).

Edom's foe will be as destructive as a pitiless lion let loose on a flock (vv. 19, 20), or as an eagle that swoops on its prey (vv. 21, 22).

7. Damascus (49:23–27)

Jeremiah describes the paralysis that seizes the inhabitants of the chief cities as the "evil tidings" of Nebuchadrezzar's advance reaches them (vv. 23, 24). He conquered the country in 605 B.C. Above the din of the capital's terror, one of the citizens is appalled by the renowned city's downfall (v. 25). Her army will be humiliated, and the proud palaces of Ben-hadad (the king of Damascus; cf. I Kings 15:18; II Kings 12:3, and elsewhere) destroyed by fire (vv. 26, 27).

8. Kedar (49:28, 29)

Kedar was a powerful Arab tribe (Is. 60:7). Nebuchadrezzar's conquest of Kedar is to be performed at God's behest (v. 28). This nomadic tribe will discover that the isolation of the desert in which they wander does not secure them against the Babylonian terror (v. 29).

9. Hazor (49:30–33)

The Counsel against Hazor (49:30, 31). The phrase "kingdom of Hazor" (v. 28) may denote that Hazor was a confederacy of Arab tribes. The Lord commands them to seek refuge in solitary places, because Nebuchadrezzar has determined to include them in his plans of conquest (v. 30). Then God commands the Babylonians to accomplish their designs against Hazor, whose prosperity and remote seclusion have engendered a sense of false security (v. 31).

The Calamity of Hazor (49:32, 33). The Babylonians will strip Hazor of her possessions, but it is the Lord Who is their real enemy (v. 32). Their settlements will become a desolate wilderness (v. 33).

10. Elam (49:34–39)

The Design against Elam (49:34–36). Elam was the hilly country east and northeast of Babylon. The Tigris flowed between them. This prophecy is dated seven or eight years after those immediately preceding (cf. v. 34 with 46:1, 2). God will break Elam's archery (cf. Is. 22:6), her main weapon of defense. He plans to attack her from every side, making escape impossible (v. 35).

The Dismay of Elam (49:37–39). The Lord's wrath and His swift sword will fill Elam with consternation, and when He sits in judgment upon her, destruction will be let loose (vv. 37, 38). But as ever God's judgments are tempered with mercy (v. 39).

11. Babylon (50:1—51:64)

Two features of this long prophecy distinguish it from those in chapters 46 through 49. Jerusalem has already fallen, and Jewish exiles have been living in Babylon for some time. Again, the prophecy betrays a vindictiveness towards Babylon that is absent from the rest of the Book of Jeremiah (cf. 29:4–7 with 50:15, 29; 51:11). But the former feature is not incompatible with a high view of Hebrew prophecy, while inconsistency is not necessarily involved in the second.

Babylon's Fall Inevitable (50:1–3). Babylon's fall (v. 2a) brings her deities into disrepute (v. 2b) because it unmasks their powerlessness. Babylon's foe "out of the north" (v. 3a) was the Medo-Persian armies under Cyrus; Judah's northern foe had been first the Scythians and then the Babylonians.

Its Significance for Israel (50:4–8). Babylon's fall will bring Judah's exile to an end, reunite Israel and Judah (v. 4a), and engender within them penitence for sin (v. 4b). The reunion will be primarily spiritual, because both will "join themselves" to the Lord in an everlasting covenant (v. 5) in a restored temple. Cured of idolatry and rid of unfaithful shepherds, they shall wander off into apostasy no more (v. 6). The plea in verse 7a (cf. 2:3) will be no longer valid. In divine justice will reside Israel's hope (v. 7b) as she, resembling the he-goat that pushes its way to the front of the flock, marches out of captivity to freedom in the vanguard of the liberated nations (v. 8).

Its Explanation (50:9–20). The Lord incites the nations (see 51:27, 28) to fight against Babylon, none of whom will return from the attack empty-handed (vv. 9, 10). Babylon's arrogance and wanton cruelty (v. 11) will be punished when the Lord's wrath burns against her (vv. 12, 13). She has sinned against God, so He now takes terrible vengeance upon her (vv. 14–16). Assyria had exiled Israel, and Babylon, Judah (v. 17), but vengeance is finally accomplished (v. 18), and a united and pardoned Israel will dwell satisfied and secure in Palestine (vv. 19, 20).

Its Description (50:21—51:14). The Lord commands the foe to destroy Babylon (vv. 21, 22), the former hammerer of nations (v. 23). He brings all his weapons forth from His armory (vv. 24, 25), that is, from the attacking nations, and Babylon's wealth is seized (v. 26), her young warriors perish (v. 27), captives escape (v. 28), and she falls in her arrogance (vv. 29–33). By contrast the Lord is Israel's *goël* (redeemer, v. 34; cf. Prov. 23: 11; Is. 43:14). Upon all that Babylon trusted has come the sword (vv. 35–37) and her overthrow is complete (vv. 38–40). The ruthless foe advances against her (vv. 41–44; cf. 6:22–24) to fulfil the Lord's designs (vv. 45, 46). While the Lord fights against Babylon (51:1–4), he protects Israel (vv. 5, 6). Luxurious Babylon, the former terror of nations (v. 7), is now fatally wounded by the Lord (vv. 8, 9), Who thereby vindicates Israel (v. 10). Babylon's foes are incited against her afresh (vv. 11, 12) and her doom is reiterated (vv. 13, 14).

Babylon's Divine Antagonist (51:15–26). For verses 15–19, see 10:12–16. The Lord's address to Babylon in verses 13 and 14 is continued in verse 20 where the present tense denotes continuous action in the past. Babylon has been God's war-club (cf. 50:23). With it He executed His judgments (vv. 21–23). But now Babylon's day of doom has dawned in which the Lord will recompense her oppression of Zion (v. 24). Babylon, like a destroying mountain in her pride, will be destroyed by the Lord (vv. 25, 26).

Babylon's Final End (51:27–58). The nations rally to Babylon's destruction (vv. 27, 28), but it is God's designs they fulfil (v. 29). As the city burns, messengers of doom run in quick succession to inform the king (vv. 30–32), and foes reap a rich harvest (v. 33). Israel then recounts the wrongs Babylon wrought upon her, invokes vengeance upon her enemy; to which the Lord responds with promises of retaliation (vv. 34–37). Whereas the Babylonians used to growl like a lion over his prey (cf. Amos 2:4), they will be filled with stupefaction (vv. 38, 39), their city devastated and their god humiliated (vv. 40–44). In the turmoil, Israel will be safe (vv. 45–47). While the whole earth exults over Babylon's fall (vv. 48, 49), the Jewish exiles remember God and Jerusalem and prepare to return (v. 50). They also bewail their ignomony and the temple's desecration (v. 51) by the Babylonians, but at the last God judges the idols of the Babylonians, destroys their city, humiliates their mighty men, and writes over their history, "vanity of vanities" (vv. 52–58).

Babylon's Herald of Doom (51:59–64). Why should Zedekiah visit Nebuchadrezzar in the fourth year of his reign (v. 59)? To convince him that he (Zedekiah) was not implicated in revolt (cf. chs. 27 and 28). "With Zedekiah" (v. 59; but cf. RV margin) went Seriah, Baruch's brother (cf. 32:12), to whom Jeremiah gave certain instructions (vv. 60–64). In this dramatic fashion, Jeremiah attests that his prophecies of Babylon's triumph over Judah (for example, 21:1–10) do not mean that Babylon will stand forever and Judah perish forever. Implicit in these instructions is Jeremiah's conviction that, despite appearances, the future lies with exiled Judah! The reading of the oracle (v. 61) would, in the circumstances, be of a semi-private nature. But after the potent prophetic word has been sent forth on its triumphant missionary career from the lips it will then, in written form, be sunk in Babylon's river, Euphrates (v. 63), and be conveyed, so to speak, into every phase of Babylon's life to effect that city's irreparable doom (v. 64). Compare 13:1; 19:1; 27:2; 43:9, for other examples of prophetic symbolic action.

12. Judah (52:1–34)

Jerusalem Taken (52:1–11). Compare this passage with II Kings 24:18–25, 21:27–30, and Jeremiah 39:1–10. Zedekiah began to reign in 597 B.C. Eleven years of unfaithfulness to God (v. 2) and of shilly-shally in politics terminated in disaster in 586 B.C. The connection between man's sin and God's displeasure manifested in judgment is unmistakable (v. 3). The date in verse 4 is still a Jewish day of mourning (cf. Zech. 8:19). So also is the date in verse 6 which now commemorates the capture of Jerusalem by Titus in A.D. 70. Compare Lamentations 2:19, 20, 4:4, 8–10, 5:10, for famine conditions in Jerusalem.

Jerusalem Spoiled (52:12–30). The ninth of the month (cf. v. 12) has been observed as a day of mourning since Titus desecrated the second temple in A.D. 70. The nineteenth year of Nebuchadrezzar (v. 12) was 586 B.C. Temple and palace were stripped of their treasures (v. 13). What Jeremiah's thoughts were as he witnessed the fulfilment of his predictions (vv. 14–30) are more easily imagined than described. The pillars of brass (v. 17), too heavy to transport to Babylon, were broken. The vessels enumerated (vv. 19,

20) were of gold (I Kings 7:50; cf. Ex. 25:29) and dedicated to the service of the Lord. The pots and shovels (Ex. 27:3) and the basins were used in connection with the altar. A cubit was eighteen inches (cf. v. 21). A "chapter" (v. 22a) was the ornamental work around the top of a pillar, while "pomegranates" (vv. 22, 23) were a favorite decorative motif. Potential leaders in whom revolt might have found its focal point were slain (vv. 24–27a). Of the three deportations (vv. 28–30), the third is not mentioned elsewhere in the Old Testament (but cf. Josephus' *Antiquities* X. ix. 7). Read "seventeenth" for "seventh" in verse 28. "Seventh" would refer to the deportation of 597 B.C., but statistics given here (v. 28) and in II Kings 24:14–16 conflict.

Jehoiachin Elevated (52:31–34). Nebuchadrezzar had carried Jehoiachin of the house of David captive to Babylon in 597 B.C. (II Kings 24:8–16). Now his successor Evil-merodach treats the royal exile with favor and admits him to the royal table (vv. 33, 34). In this way the Lord is with David (II Sam. 7:8–17), and in the midst of judgment continues to prepare the coming of great David's greater Son in Whose life, death, and resurrection God was to visit and redeem His people. Thus Jeremiah's prophecies of judgment close, implicitly at least, with a prophecy of redemption.

The living themes of this final section will have become plain. (1) Preachers of God's Word must still proclaim the necessity and the inevitability of divine judgment, a judgment that is not arbitrary, but righteous and moral. (2) The modern Nebuchadrezzars will have their brief day and pass away into oblivion like those of the past. (3) As the covenant community was constantly under the judgment of their covenant God, so the Church of Jesus Christ is under judgment. Judgment must still begin at the house of God. (4) God is on the side of truth and justice in this moral world. His righteous judgments must be established. The vision of the new heavens and the new earth wherein dwelleth righteousness is certain of fulfilment.

Lamentations

J. G. S. S. THOMSON

ONE THEME pervades Lamentations: the sufferings of Jerusalem consequent upon the capture of the city by Nebuchadrezzar.

I. The Meaning of Jerusalem's Afflictions (1:1–22)

These sufferings, however, have a special significance. They are traceable to God's wrath awakened by Judah's sins. They are not, therefore, representative of sufferings in general. They represent one

597

aspect of suffering. This aspect is elucidated in chapter 1 and developed in the remainder of the book.

1. The Description of Jerusalem's Afflictions (1:1-7)

Several elements enter into the city's sufferings. There is loneliness (v. 1). So deserted are her once crowded thoroughfares that Jerusalem is as a widow lonely and forlorn. There is also bitterness (v. 2a). At nightfall when men sleep serenely, Jerusalem sobs bitterly. From among her once trusted friends none is left to console her. There is also disappointment (v. 2b). Jerusalem's "lovers" (political allies) have proved fickle and treacherous. Even her own children who survived the destruction have proved faithless (v. 3). Again, Jerusalem is denied the consolation of her religion. She is bereft of the inspiration of solemn assemblies, temple services, and sacrifices (v. 4). There is also her humiliation. Enemies bully her (v. 5a), God afflicts her (v. 5b), children forsake her (v. 5c), rulers disappoint her (v. 6), memory mocks her. (v. 7). Truly she is desolate like a widow in weeds.

2. The Explanation of Jerusalem's Afflictions (1:8-18)

The explanation, which has already been alluded to (v. 5b), is twofold: God's judgments and Judah's sinfulness. This is the theological core of Lamentations.

Jerusalem has sinned (1:8-11). Her manifold transgressions have rendered her ceremonially unclean; men shun her as they would a leper, and she instinctively shrinks away (v. 8). Now that her uncleanness is "in her skirts," that is, exposed, she recalls her past negligence and breaks out into bitter wailing (v. 9). In addition, the Lord's hitherto inviolate holy of holies has been desecrated and plundered by the heathen (v. 10), the sanctuary which the high priest alone could enter—and only once a year! This sacrilege evokes renewed distress, and a confession of vileness (v. 11b).

Jerusalem's iniquity has aroused the Lord's indignation (1:12-18). She describes as incomparable the anguish with which God has afflicted her in His anger (v. 12). His fire has scorched her (v. 13). It was His hands that fashioned a yoke out of her transgressions and laid it upon her (v. 14). It was His feet that trampled her in the winepress of His wrath (v. 15). Tears and entreaties avail nothing (vv. 16, 17a), the divine decree against her stands (v. 17b). She can only acknowledge that God's judgments are justified. She has sinned, but she appeals for compassion (v. 18).

3. The Effect of Jerusalem's Afflictions (1:19–22)

Jerusalem's bitter affliction has discredited the allies in whom she trusted (1:19a). Her testimony is, "Vain is the help of man" (cf. v. 2). In her present extremity, even her own religious and secular leaders are unable to succor or console (v. 19b). Betrayed by faithless friends, she turns to God in prayer. Thus early the Lord's judgments are beginning to bear fruit. Her prayer, largely a repetition of her troubles, is nevertheless offered at the place of penitence, confession, and self-abasement. Emotionally ("my bowels") she is deeply distressed; mentally ("mine heart") she is greatly agitated; and morally she is profoundly disturbed as she confesses, "I have grievously repelled" (v. 20). She is humiliated too by enemies whose jeers emphasize that it was her covenant God Who has afflicted her. Her own studied indifference to the prophetic warnings of judgment has also insured their fulfilment against her (v. 21). This prayer of confession and self-abasement ends with a cry for vengeance upon her enemies. This appeal has moral motivation. They have been as guilty as she; therefore they merit the same punishment (v. 22).

II. The Actualities of Jerusalem's Afflictions (2:1–22)

The stark reality of Jerusalem's affliction is now exposed. Jeremiah does not deal in generalities, because he was an eyewitness of what he describes. The theological reflection present in chapter 1, that Jerusalem's sufferings were due to divine judgment upon her sinfulness (1:5, 8, 14, 20, 22), is prominent also in chapter 2.

1. Jerusalem's Adversary (2:1–8)

In almost every line of this part of the poem it is reiterated that the Lord afflicted the city. The phrase "the beauty of Israel" probably refers to the temple (cf. Is. 64:11), while "footstool" may refer either to the temple (cf. Ezek. 43:7; Ps. 132:7; Is. 60:13) or to the ark (I Chron. 28:2). Its destruction had been the work of the Lord (1:1)! So also the destruction of homesteads and fortresses, and the desecration of kingdom (cf. Ex. 19:6) and king (v. 2). He had humbled Israel's pride and power ("horn") and intensified her groaning (vv. 3–5). But the cruelest stroke of divine judgment was the demolition of the temple, and the cessation of solemn feasts, sabbaths, sacrifices, and temple services (vv. 6, 7). So fearful a disaster as the cessation of religion must have been the consequence of a carefully planned and thoroughly executed work of God (v. 8).

2. Jerusalem's Agony (2:9–16)

Further evidence of the Lord's activity in judgment is now given in the descriptive details of the city's anguish. Her very gates have gone, her statehood has disintegrated, the whole system of legal administration has collapsed (cf. Jer. 18:18; Ezek. 7:26; Mal. 2:7), and God withholds His word from the prophets (cf. Mic. 3:5, 6). This spiritual deprivation, so movingly described in verse 9, struck Jerusalem dumb with despair. Signs of anguished mourning are everywhere (v. 10), but the anguish penetrated to the inner recesses of mind and heart. Note how Jeremiah again thinks himself into his people's sorrows until they become his own (vv. 11, 12; cf. Jer. 4:19; 9:1). The unparalleled nature of Jerusalem's anguish exposes the inadequacy of Jeremiah's consolations (v. 13). The lying prophets, who had "whitewashed" Judah's sins and lulled her into a false security instead of insisting on amendment of life, must share the blame for her affliction (v. 14; cf. Jer. 27:10, 15). She is become the butt of cruel men whose taunts cut deep (vv. 15, 16). The truth already emphasized is reiterated: Jerusalem's affliction is a judgment from God. But in devising it He has only fulfilled His word (v. 17; cf. Lev. 26:14–20; Deut. 28:15, 16).

3. Jerusalem's Entreaty (2:17–22)

Having acknowledged that Jerusalem's desolation was God's just judgment upon her sins, Jerusalem must now cast herself upon God's grace and invoke His aid in prayer. This she is now exhorted to do. Here the sincerity (v. 18a), continuity ((vv. 18b, 19a), intensity (v. 19b), and urgency (v. 19c), of prayer are emphasized. The apple of the eye was the pupil, denoting an object requiring special care (cf. Deut. 32:10; Ps. 17:8). The Jews divided the night into three watches of four hours each (Ex. 14:24; Ps. 63:6); the Romans observed four watches (cf. Mt. 14:25). Jerusalem's prayerful entreaty in response to Jeremiah's exhortation (vv. 18, 19) is in verses 20–22. The former passage illumines the prophet's own devotional life (cf. Jer. 7:16; 11:14; 14:11; 15:15–18, and elsewhere). In her entreaty, Jerusalem remonstrates with the Lord. The severity of His judgments (v. 20a) produces outrages upon natural instincts (v. 20b) and religious sanctities (v. 20c). Young and old, male and female suffer alike (v. 21). Terrors which now surround on every side (cf. Jer. 6:25; 20:3)—war, disease, and famine—have been summoned by the Lord as if to a festival of destruction and death (v. 22). No victim escapes from this festival of carnage which God has convoked.

III. Some Factors in Jerusalem's Afflictions (3:1–66)

1. The Rod of God's Wrath (3:1–20)

The first person singular may signify that Jeremiah's sufferings are representative of the nation's. The rod of God's wrath has afflicted (3:1), therefore these verses acknowledge repeatedly that it is the Lord Who has engineered the long succession of sorrows now enumerated: darkness (v. 2), disease (v. 4), bitterness (v. 5), restrictions (vv. 6–10), pain (vv. 11–13), humiliation (vv. 14–17), until unrelieved despair has quenched all hope (v. 18). From the depths of his misery Jeremiah finally appeals to the Lord to remember his anguish (v. 19), because he himself holds them in remembrance, and they fill him with a sense of shame (v. 20).

2. The Multitude of God's Mercies (3:21–39)

"This" (3:21) may refer to the lovely words of consolation that follow, in which case Jeremiah's "hope" (v. 21) is inspired by the Lord's mercies. However, the structure of the poem demands that it be taken with verse 20; consequently, it becomes the sense of shame (v. 20b) deriving from sin that ministers comfort to his broken spirit, knowing that "a broken and a contrite heart" God will not despise (Ps. 51:17). He dares to hope, therefore, that even for his case there is pardoning grace. He has not yet exhausted divine mercy. It is unfailing, as each returning day proves (vv. 22, 23).

Naturally, then, the Lord is the sum of all Jeremiah's desires (v. 24; Ps. 16:5; 73:26; 119:57; 142:5; cf. Num. 18:20). He will submit himself to the Lord and await His help (v. 25).

God's goodness makes such submission man's highest good (3:26), and the time of undisciplined youth (v. 27) is when submission should be established. Discipline will then become increasingly habitual, while its moral value will become increasingly apparent. The characteristics of spiritual discipline are then described: willingness to be solitary and silent in suffering, recognition that it is from God (v. 28), manifesting absolute submission to chastisement (vv. 29, 30). And the ground for such disciplined submission to God's will is the conviction that chastisement is not forever (v. 31). God will finally incline to compassion (v. 32) because His chastisement is motivated not by caprice, but by moral purpose (v. 33). God is also aware of injustices (vv. 34–36), but He permits them in order to serve His own purposes (v. 37). He permits both good and evil (v. 38), but no man should complain of the latter because it is a consequence of sin (v. 39). Let a man therefore complain not of suffering or chastisement, but of his sins.

3. The Justice of God's Judgments (3:40–54)

If suffering then is due to sin, the afflicted believer will search his heart to find out wherein he has sinned (3:40a). He will repent (v. 40b), seek pardon in prayer (v. 41), penitently confess and humbly acknowledge that when God chastises (v. 42), His judgments are just. These judgments are then described (vv. 43–54), but note also their effects: God is separated from His people; prayer can no longer get through to Him (v. 44); His people are humiliated (vv. 45–47); and Jeremiah is pained beyond measure by Jerusalem's distress (vv. 48–54). Verses 52–55 may refer to Jeremiah's experiences (Jer. 38:6).

4. The Prayer of God's People (3:55–66)

In the midst of his misery, Jeremiah begins to pray (3:55). He recalls God's past intervention in answer to prayer (vv. 56, 57a), communicating assurance to him (v. 57b) and acting as his advocate against his enemies (v. 58). He now prays God to intervene again by delivering him from his present distresses (v. 59), and by requiting his enemies (vv. 64–66) for the wrongs they have committed against him (vv. 60–63). The imprecations in Jeremiah's prayers (vv. 64–66; cf. Jer. 18:23) were directed against the nation's enemies, not the prophet's personal antagonists! They reflect the sterner spirit of the Old Covenant, and they reveal an eagerness for the vindication of God's glory and for vengeance upon Judah's enemies in this life.

IV. Some Lessons From Jerusalem's Afflictions (4:1–22)

1. The Vanity of Human Glory (4:1–12)

"Gold," "fine gold," and "holy [that is, precious] stones" (4:1) are figures of speech. The fine gold is "the precious sons of Zion" (v. 2). The poet is comparing Judah's former glory with her present miseries. Zion's sons used to be fine gold, but by some strange process the precious metal is now esteemed as worthless as a potter's earthen vessel (v. 2b). Judah's glory has departed. Under pressure of famine conditions, even maternal instincts have disappeared (v. 3). This is true also of children reared in opulent circumstances (vv. 4, 5). The vanishing of Judah's glory is ascribed to Judah's sins, which must have been greater than those of Sodom, because Judah's sufferings have been greater in that they have been more prolonged (v. 6). The former glory is again contrasted with present miseries (vv. 7, 8). The living are more unfortunate than the dead (vv. 9, 10). All this is due to God's anger, though many believed He would never allow the heathen to enter His dwelling place (vv. 11, 12).

2. The Vanity of Human Leadership (4:13–16)

The responsibility for Judah's fate is placed firmly on the shoulders of her religious leaders (4:13; cf. Jer. 5:31; 6:13; 23:11). Their iniquities (cf. Jer. 26:8), especially their oppression of innocent men, prove they were unfaithful and unworthy of their high office. After Jerusalem fell, they staggered about in utter perplexity. Their old senseless confidence disappeared as their world tumbled in ruins about them. The dupes of their false leadership shun them for fear of contracting ceremonial uncleanness from their bloodstained garments (v. 14), and urge them to flee the city as if they were lepers (v. 15; cf. Lev. 13:45). These leaders, once vain and unscrupulous, can find no refuge even in foreign lands (v. 15b), and thus draw upon themselves Cain's curse (Gen. 4:12, 14). It is God Himself Who has scattered them in His wrath (v. 16a) because of their ruthless behavior (v. 16b).

3. The Vanity of Human Resources (4:17–20)

Doubtless Judah's reliance upon Egypt (4:17; cf. Jer. 37:5–10) is the subject here. As disaster became more certain and the situation more hopeless, Judah's confidence in the vaunted resources of Egypt became more futile and pathetic. She watched and waited in vain for Egypt's promised aid. As the siege dragged on, the dangers for the defenders of the doomed city increased because, from certain vantage points, the besiegers were able to shoot at them (v. 18). When Jerusalem finally fell, the besiegers relentlessly hunted out the defenders who were attempting to evade capture (v. 19). The reference to King Zedekiah (v. 20) also illustrates the vanity of human resources. He was "the breath of our nostrils" in the sense that upon him rested Judah's hopes for continued existence as a nation in Moab or Ammon (cf. Jer. 40:11). This fond hope also proved vain when the Babylonians trapped Zedekiah near Jericho (Jer. 52:8, 9).

4. The Vanity of Human Pride (4:21, 22)

Human pride is personified in Edom. Edom's arrogance toward Judah stemmed from her alliance with Babylon. Because Edom refused to ally herself with Egypt and Judah against Babylon, Nebuchadrezzar gave her control of certain neighboring rural districts (cf. Ezek. 25:12–14; 35:5; Obad. 10–15). But she overreached herself by annexing some of the territory of the now stricken Judah (cf. Ezek. 35:10–12). This arrogant act aroused Judah's bitterest hatred (cf. Is. 34; 63:1–6; Ps. 137:7). Edom is assured that the vanity of her pride will soon become manifest. Judah has already received punishment for her sins (v. 22a; cf. Is. 40:1), but Edom will soon be drinking the same bitter draught from the cup of God's fury (v. 21b). The opening words of verse 21 are spoken in irony. Judah's messianic hope promises forgiveness and security (v. 22a); Edom's future will bring upon her arrogant pride divine punishment and shameful humiliation (v. 22b).

V. The Issues of Jerusalem's Afflictions (5:1–22)

1. Jerusalem Invokes God's Grace (5:1–18)

This chapter differs from the others in that, strictly speaking, it is a prayer, not a lament. It does describe Judah's afflictions, but these are a necessary part of the prayer. They become the ground for the invocation of divine grace. This prayer is concerned with the miseries of the residue left behind in Judah and does, therefore, illustrate the result which God's disciplinary dealings are designed to achieve, that of bringing those whom He disciplines to the place of humility and confession. There they cast themselves unreservedly upon God's compassion and power. This is well expressed in verse 1, which sums up the theme of this last chapter. The verses that follow describe Judah's reproach. She is a stranger in her own land (vv. 2, 3); she is impoverished and humiliated (vv. 4–6); upon her has fallen the punishment of her own sins (cf. v. 16) and those of her forefathers (v. 7). Under the rule of upstart governors (v. 8) life is hard and cruel (vv. 9, 10). Nor can she erase the memory of the dreadful atrocities committed upon her by the Babylonian soldiery (vv. 11–14). Joy (v. 15) and honor (v. 16) have gone, and the will to survive seems to be dying within her as she views her desolation (v. 18). But the Lord's stern discipline has awakened within Judah a sense of her own sinfulness, worthlessness, and helplessness. And finally, out of the depths of the bitterness occasioned by divine chastisement, she invokes God's grace and compassion.

2. Jerusalem Invokes God's Glory (5:19–22)

Judah's awakened sense of worthlessness and powerlessness achieves something else, however. It restores her faith in God's glory and power as well as in His grace and pity. Zion, God's throne on earth, has gone, but He still reigns in omnipotence and everlasting righteousness from His throne on high (5:19; Ps. 45:6). As she invokes the eternal glory of her God of grace, Judah dares to believe that her covenant God will neither forget her nor forsake her permanently (v. 20). But this hope will become experience only as He effects within her the grace of repentance and the miracle of moral conversion (v. 21; cf. II Cor. 3:5). The prayer of disciplined Judah closes (v. 22) then, not in hopeless despair as the King James and Revised Versions suggest, but in the conviction that all is not lost, as the marginal readings propose. God's anger is not forever, therefore the present rejection and alienation are only temporary. The final word of this God of grace and glory to His sinning but repentant people is not one of contempt and wrath, but of hope founded upon promised grace. Divine discipline will eventually bring forth "the peaceable fruit of righteousness" unto Judah who has been so sorely exercised thereby (cf. Heb. 12:5–13).

Ezekiel

WALTER R. ROEHRS

 T HE OPENING WORDS of the Book of Ezekiel "I saw visions of God" (1:1) usher us at once into the majesty and grandeur of the revelation that characterizes the whole book. The glory of the Lord appears to Ezekiel in such unearthly splendor and such cosmic proportions that he is at a loss to describe adequately what he sees.

In spite of bizarre features and bewildering details these visions nevertheless made unmistakably clear to Ezekiel and his hearers what they needed to know. He falls upon his face as a result of the first appearance of the vision, fully recognizing the unlimited power of the God whose messenger he is to be. When he sees the same glory of the Lord leaving the temple and the city of Jerusalem, there can be no doubt that the doom of destruction upon Israel's rebellion is at hand. But the vision returns to bring an unequivocal message of hope and restoration to exiled and penitent Israel. Ezekiel sees the glory of the Lord returning so that "the name of the city from that day shall be 'The Lord is there'" (48:35).

I. Israel, a Rebellious House, Will Fall (1:1—24:27)

1. God Sends Ezekiel as His Spokesman to the Rebellious House (1:1—3:27)

The Glory of the Lord Appears to Ezekiel (1:1-28). As Ezekiel "was among the captives by the River Chebar" (1:1) in Babylonia, the world of his day seemed full to the brim with the defeat and ignominy of the God of Israel. His gracious purposes appeared to be frustrated. How could His chosen people be the means of salvation to the ends of the earth if they were helplessly in the grip of the Bablyonian conqueror? How could the promises come true that all the nations of the earth should flow to Jerusalem and the house of the Lord if, within a few years, the city and temple would be leveled to the ground?

Ezekiel himself was a symbol of this frustration. In his thirtieth year he, "the priest, the son of Buzi" should now be ministering at the altar in Jerusalem.

But the introductory verses of his book (1:1–3) indicate how God proceeded to tell Ezekiel that He had not lost control of the world. "In the land of the Chaldeans," who boasted that their god Marduk now ruled the four quarters of the earth, "the heavens were opened" and the glory of the Lord burst in upon His confused world. In "visions of God" he was to learn and tell others that the Lord God Omnipotent reigns and by His mighty acts of judgment and mercy is achieving His purposes.

It was "in the fifth year of King Jehoiachin's captivity" (593-2 B.C) when all this began to happen, and Ezekiel notes even the day of this great turning point in his life.

The remaining verses of the first chapter are devoted to a rather detailed account of what Ezekiel saw in this opening vision (1:4–28). Each feature that he mentions and describes no doubt served a double purpose. The God of Israel was identifying Himself to the captives in far off Babylonia by the same means of revelation by which He had previously made Himself known to His people. At the same time, the exiles are to understand that the heathen gods whom they saw and heard described with similar features were a lie and deception.

As Ezekiel looked, he saw a fiery storm cloud coming out of the north (1:4). The heathen gods were personifications of the forces of nature whose original home was located in the mysterious north. Ezekiel is to remind Israel again of Him whose "way is in the whirl-wind and the storm, and the clouds are the dust of his feet" (Nahum 1:3). He alone is to be feared for "the light of Israel will become a fire and his Holy One a flame; and it will burn and devour" (Is. 10:17). There is no brightness in the Babylonian sun-god, for the God Who of old led Israel in a pillar of light "covers himself with light as with a garment" (Ps. 104:1, 2). He comes now in visitation upon His people from the north (cf. Jer. 1:14; 4:6).

Next Ezekiel describes four living creatures that he saw emerge from the cloud (1:5–14). In their retinue the Babylonian gods had many-headed and composite creatures, part human and part animal. The captives could see them depicted in sculpture and hear them described in myth and hymn. Israel should know, however, that not only the inanimate forces of nature but all "living creatures" are in the service and at the disposal of Him Who "commanded and they were created" (Ps. 148:5). They exist individually: man, lion, ox, eagle. But whatever their individual faces, appearance, or endowments, they are but one in their ultimate purpose: they stand at attention, as it were, ready at the beck and call of Him Who fashioned them. They looked strange indeed. Human eyes were not accustomed to seeing the diversity of the "living creatures" in the single perspective of divine authority and power. No single word seemed adequate to describe this many-faced totality. In general, however, they resembled the cherubim, those heavenly messengers and executors of divine missions with whom the Israelites were well acquainted (cf. ch. 10; Gen. 3:24; I Kings 6:27–29; Is. 37:16; Ps. 80:1; 99:1).

Ezekiel's attention is now drawn to a wheel upon the earth at the side of each of the living creatures (1:15–21). Like the living creatures, these wheels were ready to move in any direction without turning, for "their construction was as it were a wheel within a wheel." The captives no doubt saw the image of the Babylonian god Marduk drawn about the streets on an ornamented chariot. But in the land of Marduk, Israel is to hear once again from the lips of Ezekiel of Him Who has a chariot of fire at His command (cf. II Kings 2:11).

As Ezekiel's eyes moved upward, he saw the living creatures bearing aloft what appeared to be shining firmament upon which rested the likeness of a throne, as the appearance of a sapphire stone. Here was enthroned the "appearance of the likeness of the glory of the Lord" in the "likeness as the appearance of man" (1:22–28a). Ezekiel and his hearers were to know that the Lord, Whose dwelling place was "between the cherubim" in the temple, was not confined to any place nor limited in the exercise of His dominion. He rules supreme also in the land of Israel's captors. In spite of all appearances to the contrary, He is even now carrying out His purpose of setting "his glory among the nations" (39:21).

Overwhelmed by what he had seen, Ezekiel fell upon his face and heard "a voice of one that spoke" (1:28b).

God Commissions Ezekiel (2:1—3:27). Ezekiel was not to spend time in private meditation of the vision but was to go to the children as a messenger of the Lord of Whose glory he had been given a glimpse. Therefore God at once prepares him for this mission in an extended briefing session. He begins the instruction by calling him "Son of man" (2:1), a form of address that Ezekiel is to hear some ninety times more in the course of his ministry. Ezekiel is always to be aware of the signal honor that is his as the spokesman of Him

Who made man from the dust of the ground and Whose word, even on human lips, still has creative power.

As God's emissary to His creatures and particularly the chosen people, Ezekiel might expect a good reception for his message. But God does not send him out under the false pretense of an easy success. From the very outset he prepares him for bitter opposition from the children of Israel, "a rebellious house," "impudent children and stiff-hearted." In the end, however, they will have to concede "that there hath been a prophet among them" (2:2–7).

The next lesson in Ezekiel's orientation course for his ministry comes to him in another visionary experience and assures him of a deep inner satisfaction in the performance of his prophetic duty in spite of its distasteful aspect. A scroll inscribed with "lamentation and woe and mourning" appeared. As he ate it at the explicit command of the Lord, it was in his mouth "as honey for sweetness" (2:8—3:3).

Before God lets Ezekiel begin his task, He impresses upon him once more that he will be confronting an "impudent and hard-hearted" people. But He also assures him that in His employ, his weakness will be transformed into strength equal to the task (3:4–11).

How badly Ezekiel needed all this instruction and encouragement! When the glory of the Lord departed, borne aloft by the creatures, he went in "bitterness, in the heat of my spirit" (3:12, 13).

After an interlude of seven days, during which Ezekiel "sat astonished" among the captives at Tel-abib, "the word of the Lord came" to him again to complete his training course (3:14–16). The Lord now points out to him that He is entrusting him with a fearful responsibility. The ultimate destiny of each individual among his hearers is in his hands because his position is that of a "watchman unto the house of Israel." His own life will be forfeit if he fails to sound the alarm so clearly that each person should be able to recognize the danger that threatens his relationship to God. But for Ezekiel's comfort God also informs him that his responsibility ends when he has faithfully spoken the word of warning (vv. 17–21).

Ezekiel needed encouragement to assume these frightening responsibilities. The Lord therefore grants him another vision of his glory, "as the glory which I saw by the river Chebar" (3:22, 23).

But where, how, when, how often is he to speak his terrifying message? In a final word of instruction, God gives him an explicit answer also to these questions (3:22–27). For the time being, he is to reprove the hardness of his hearers only as God permits him to use his tongue at all and as they gather in his house to hear his words. No other words are to pass his lips. God's word, for a time, has exclusive right to his speaking.

2. First Series of Symbolic Actions (4:1—7:27)

Ezekiel inaugurates his ministry by "acting out" his message in accordance with the Lord's definite instructions. These symbolic acts were a visual portrayal of the impending judgment upon the people of Jerusalem.

Siege of the City (4:1–3). On a tile of soft clay, Ezekiel is to portray Jerusalem and a siege of that city. He is to use an iron pan, "and set it for a wall of iron" between himself, as God's representative, and the city. The purpose of this "charade" is to indicate that God will shut Himself off from the claims and cries of the people and be on the side of those who press the siege.

Exile (4:4–8). The second action of the prophet consists in lying on his left side and then on his right side for a specified number of days. In this way he was to demonstrate that both Israel, the Northern Kingdom, and Judah will "bear their iniquity" for many years. In both instances each day represented a year; their totals, 390 and 40 respectively, evidently were also symbolic of the long period of time that each part of the chosen nation would suffer the judgment of the Exile in foreign lands.

Famine (4:9–17). In a third symbolic act, Ezekiel portrays the sufferings that his people will endure in the siege and fall of Jerusalem as well as in the Exile. During the siege, the inhabitants will suffer a lack of bread and water to supply their physical needs (4:11, 16, 17; cf. Lam. 1:11; 2:11, 12, and so forth). During the siege as well as the Exile, they will not be able to observe the dietary laws regarding clean and unclean food. They will be deprived of the very means in which they have trusted vainly for their safety, the careful performance of a ritual (cf. Lev. 19:19; Deut. 22:9–11; Hos. 9:3, 4).

Death by Pestilence, Famine and Sword (5:1–17). But catastrophe of still greater proportions is in store for the rebellious nation. To symbolize it, Ezekiel is directed to shave his head and beard and to divide the hair into three parts. Then he is to burn a third, smite a third with a knife, and scatter a third in the wind. In doing so, he signifies that the greater part of the inhabitants will die by pestilence, famine and sword in the siege and fall of Jerusalem. The remaining third will be forced to go into exile and even there God will "draw out a sword after them."

The symbolic acts no doubt had attracted a circle of curious spectators. Ezekiel explains to them the meaning of what he had done. It is not Babylon and its fall that he has portrayed, but the well-deserved and irrevocable judgment upon unholy Jerusalem. Instead of being the center from which salvation might radiate to all nations, it has outdone the heathen in wickedness. Therefore God will no longer spare or have pity. Its punishment will be so severe because it has trodden under foot the greatest gifts of God's favor.

Prophecy against the Mountains of Israel (6:1–14). His theme announced, Ezekiel enlarges upon it and addresses the country under the figure of "the mountains of Israel." It is a message of doom, but not judgment for judgment's sake. God's ultimate purpose is to cleanse and restore a purified and penitent people. It is summed up in the recurring refrain: "Ye shall know that I am the Lord" (6:7, 10, 13, 14, and about sixty times elsewhere).

Evidence of Israel's guilt can be found on all mountain tops and under every green tree. There, as in pagan countries, were the paraphernalia for the worship of nature instead of the Creator. The punishment will fit the crime; the idol-worshipers will perish in the ruins of the idol altars.

A Dirge upon Fallen Israel (7:1–27). Israel's doom is not a vague and distant possibility. Its day of judgment is at hand. In poetic language Ezekiel mourns the fall of the city in a form resembling a dirge with the refrain: "The end has come" (7:1–13). Also in a highly dramatic manner, he then describes the fall as if its terrors had already struck (vv. 14–27).

3. Vision of Israel's Doom (8:1—11:25)

Idolaters in the Temple (8:1–19). Some fourteen months after his call Ezekiel sees again the glory of the Lord as it had appeared to him in the very beginning (1:27). Transported "in a vision by the Spirit of God" to Jerusalem, he sees it standing in a court of the temple. In the dazzling light of that glory, Ezekiel sees the darkest recesses of his people's unfaithfulness. Wherever he is directed to look, he beholds the perversity of the human heart which, to this very day, so easily exchanges "the glory of the immortal God for images resembling mortal man or birds or animals or reptiles" (Rom. 1:23). The glory of God, standing in the court, shows up the folly of all idol worship (8:1–4).

The temple itself is desecrated by unholy things and heathen worship. Northward at the gate of the altar Ezekiel is shown the "image of jealousy" that provokes to jealousy (8:5, 6). Its appearance is not described, but it demonstrates in a concrete way that Israel has "stirred me [God] to jealousy with what is not god; they have provoked me with their idols" (Deut. 32:21; cf. Ex. 20:4, 5; Deut. 4:23, 24).

But the terrible tour is far from complete, for in his vision Ezekiel next sees seventy elders worshiping creeping things and loathsome beasts (8:7–12). They thought they could escape detection, but the Lord penetrates all chambers of darkness. In spite of trappings of pretense and decency, idols are, in reality, creeping things and loathsome beasts. Incense to whatever popular idol remains a stench of iniquity.

The women weeping for a Babylonian deity are the next to come under the Lord's condemnation (8:13, 14). No longer do they acknowledge the Lord. They weep for Tammuz, the popular god of vegetation and fertility. Part of the ceremony devoted to insuring a return of the growing season consisted in mourning over Tammuz, who in the barren time of year was said to have died. In their folly, the women serve a pagan god instead of the living God.

Ezekiel finally sees twenty-five men worshiping the sun (8:15–18). The idolatry with which Israel is charged is not merely an outward deviation in form or the result of popular ignorance. It is a deliberate and complete turning from God as if the entire priesthood with the high priest at their head (I Chron. 24:5–19; II Chron. 36:14) stood with their backs to the Holy of Holies and gave their full devotion to the heathen sun god. This is precisely what Ezekiel sees in the vision.

Judgment upon Jerusalem (9:1—11:25). The abominations that Ezekiel had seen will not go unpunished. Years before it actually happened and in the symbolic imagery of the vision, Ezekiel sees the destroying weapon of God's justice in the hands of the appointed executioners smiting the wicked inhabitants of the city (Ex. 12:23; II Sam. 24; II Kings 19).

But there are also those in the city who have not bowed the knee before Baal and who "sigh and cry for all the abominations that be done in the midst thereof." A man clothed in linen has placed a mark on their forehead before the slaughter begins. They may be in the same outward circumstances with the wicked; they may suffer because of the wicked; but they will not share their ultimate and final fate. God knows them that are His; they will not be destroyed (9:1–11; cf. Ex. 12; Rev. 7:3; 14:1).

Out of a vision of the glory of the Lord on the river Chebar came the voice that commissioned Ezekiel to be a prophet (1:1–28). Now from the same glory of the Lord, as it appears to Ezekiel in a vision in Jerusalem, there issues the command to destroy the desecrated and unholy city. At the Lord's direction coals of fire are taken from the cherubim and scattered over Jerusalem (10:1–7). When the burning of Jerusalem and the massacre of its inhabitants took place years later (586 B.C.), it appeared to be the natural result of Babylonian military superiority. But this vision was to make clear that the Lord Who is enthroned above the cherubim is executing His judgment in history through these Babylonians.

As the command of the Lord is carried out, His glory and particularly the executors of His judgment are again described (10:8–22). Essentially they have the same features as the living creatures except that they are now more closely defined as cherubim. In the temple at Jerusalem, the Lord, Whom heaven and earth cannot contain, had condescended to dwell among the cherubim in a temple built by hands. How good the Lord had been to Israel! Of all the nations of the earth He had chosen them as His particular people; in their behalf He had done mighty deeds of deliverance; He had been longsuffering with their weaknesses, forgiving iniquity and pardoning sin. But the Lord is not only mighty to save, He also has the power to destroy those who persist in sinning against His undeserved goodness.

When Ezekiel saw the glory of the Lord for the first time (1:1–28), it had meaning particularly for his own person. Now Israel is concerned directly. They should know that they stand condemned before the Lord who will not tolerate the spurning of His mercy and Who, to punish such base ingratitude, has at His command all power in heaven and earth. Will the rebellious house repent when Ezekiel tells them of his vision?

Prophecy reveals that they will not. The gracious presence of God withdraws from the temple (10:18–22). This is the ultimate catastrophe—a people without God. No human eyes can see God move, nor does He need the wings of cherubim to transport Him, but what Ezekiel sees is real nevertheless.

In the visions we are not given a documentary film with episode upon episode in historical sequence. Rather, like a transparency held against the light of holiness, the visions reveal in true perspective the black guilt of Israel and its dire consequence.

The steadfast refusal of the princes of Israel to recognize the truth of what the prophets said is graphically demonstrated in the vision of the twenty-five men. The hard forehead of impenitence has not been softened by the first blows of adversity (cf. Amos 4:6–13). From the capture of Jerusalem six years previously under Jehoiachin and the exile of some of its inhabitants, the leaders of the people in Jerusalem (twenty-five in number as in the group in 8:16) have not learned anything. It did not shatter their self-righteousness nor their fanatic belief in the indestructibility of their city (11:3). The exiles, they say, may in some way have deserved what befell them and their going was good riddance. But they themselves are safe within its walls as meat is protected from fire in a cauldron. Ezekiel, God's spokesman, is called upon to set matters straight. Jerusalem is a cauldron only in the sense that it is filled with the slain. It will not be a hiding place to protect them from the invader. Dragged from its walls, the leaders will meet their judgment far from their homes (cf. II Kings 25:18–21).

Two of the leaders are mentioned by name, Jaazaniah and Pelatiah. The latter, perhaps the representative of the entire twenty-five, falls dead as the result of Ezekiel's prophesying. It is a part of the vision of things to come, just as the dead that "fill the courts of the temple" (9:7) were not slain until several years later (11:1–13; cf. Jer. 28:17).

At this point, the Lord lets Ezekiel see beyond the devastated city and the Exile into the remote horizons of His ultimate purpose. He answers the desperate query of Ezekiel: "Ah Lord God! wilt thou make a full end of the remnant of Israel?" (11:13). The Lord reveals that there will be a remnant. As righteous and inevitable as are His judgments, so sure and unceasing are His tender mercies. While scattered in exile from Jerusalem, the Lord will remain to those who seek Him "as a little sanctuary in the countries where they shall come" (v. 16).

When the hammer blows of His justice have broken the stony

heart of a wicked people, God will gather a remnant from "among the nations" and bring them back to the Land of Promise. He will give them a "heart of flesh" (11:20) that they may again be the bearers of His promise. A temple will again be built as the place of His habitation until He will dwell among them in that Temple not made with hands and the seed of Abraham, regardless of race, will serve Him in singleness of purpose and pure devotion (vv. 15–21; cf. Jer. 31:33; Rom. 11:25; Rev. 21:22).

But it is still the day of God's fire and brimstone upon the rebellious house of Israel. He will not pity or spare. And so the vision ends in a climax of doom: "The glory of the Lord went up from the midst of the city." When God leaves, the end has begun (11:22, 23).

After the vision Ezekiel faithfully performs his watchman duty. The prophet-watchman sounds the alarm. He tells the exiles all the things the Lord had showed him.

4. A Second Series of Symbolic Actions and Words of Doom (12:1—14:23)

King and People in Exile (12:1–20). The symbolic actions and the added explanations in chapters 4 through 7 did not shatter the unholy pride of Israel. Because they were the chosen people and the kings of the house of David were their rulers, they thought that they were unconquerable. By acting out the part of a refugee setting out from his own house, Ezekiel portrays the rebellious house with the prince at its head leaving all behind but "an exile's baggage" and setting out into the night of exile. The king will not even see where he is going. Blinded, he will die in the unseen land of his captors (12:1–16). (For the fulfilment of this prophecy cf. Jer. 39:4–7; 52:4–11; II Kings 25:1–7.)

In 4:16, 17 Ezekiel had demonstrated the lack of food and water during the siege. Now he stresses that these rations of scarcity will be consumed with the fearful awareness of the desolation all about them (12:17–20).

This doom will come true in spite of a popular proverb of unbelief (12:21–28). Ezekiel's message of warning, God told him, would meet with determined resistance. There are those who say that prophets like Ezekiel have for a long time cried "Wolf! Wolf!" but nothing happened. They shrug off the warning by quoting a clever, flippant saying about prophets' bad dreams never coming true for a long time, if ever. But God's judgment will not be deflected by popular slogans. Mistake not His long and tireless warnings as evidence of weakness; His patience is at an end. "The day of the Lord" will be in "their day."

Message to False Prophets (13:1–23). The popular defiance of the word of God is the direct result of false promises made by lying prophets. Ezekiel denounces them because they have misled the people by crying "Peace, and there was no peace" (13:10). Those who heard them should have known that "they have uttered delusions and seen lies." That the Lord had not sent them, as they claim, is clear, for instead of exposing as sin what God condemned, they curry favor by "daubing with whitewash" the nation's defiance of God. They have not repaired the breaches in the wall of righteousness that alone is a people's protection, but have helped to undermine it. The wall of lies they have erected, behind which the people now take refuge, is a painted delusion. It will not ward off the storm of divine wrath. When God shatters the wall, its builders will fall with it (vv. 1–16; cf. Jer. 23:9–12; Mt. 23:27; Acts 23:3).

The same kind of falsehood characterizes women who pose as prophetesses (13:17–23). Ezekiel describes their techniques of sorcery, their lying divinations. Just what they were and how they worked, we can no longer tell precisely, but it is clear that they plied their evil trade as a means of a livelihood. But their fraud will be unmasked, and their imaginary control over the destinies of men will be exposed in the same judgment that overtakes the lying prophets.

Visit of the Elders of Israel (14:1–11). God's judgment will likewise not be averted because the people give lip service to His Word. Ezekiel has occasion to point this out when elders of the people come to him apparently to be instructed by him. They may sit at the feet of God's spokesman, but it is all a pose; their hearts, which they have made a shrine of idols, are far from Him. This idolatrous disposition of the heart is as well known to the Lord as the abominations that stood openly in the temple in Jerusalem (8:1–11:25). A false prophet whom the Lord has given over to his own delusion may tell his flock what they want to hear, but from God's spokesman these hypocrites will get the true verdict: "They shall bear their punishment." Only when they have been purged from God's people will He again dwell among them.

Rationale of Retribution (14:12–23). God is about to unleash on

His treacherous and faithless people the four destroyers: hunger, wild beasts, sword, and pestilence (cf. Lev. 26). Some of the people may think that God could not go through with it because He would become involved in a conflict between His goodness and His justice. Suppose that there were only three righteous persons among them—such as Noah, Daniel, and Job—will not God have to rescind His sentence for their sakes if He is to remain just? Such reasoning is false. God's judgment will be just in all respects; no one will be punished for what he has not done; nor will anyone save those from punishment who deserve it. A "remnant that shall be brought forth" will understand that God has "not done without cause" all that He has done.

5. *Parables of Doom (15:1—19:14)*

Ezekiel now turns to parables and allegories to make clear to his people the guilt and impending doom of the rebellious house.

The Burning Vine (15:1-8). If the branches of a vine do not bear fruit, they are worthless. Because they cannot be used for other purposes, especially if they are already charred by fire, nothing remains but to burn them completely (cf. Is. 5:1-7; Jer. 2:21; Hos. 10:1). God has looked in vain for the fruits of His goodness and mercy in Israel and therefore Israel deserves to be burned as rubbish. In herself and as a nation among others, she is of no value and has no claim to God's favor. Charred by the flames of God's previous judgments, total destruction awaits her.

A Faithless Wife (16:1-63). In the parable of the burning vine Ezekiel had established the fact that Israel did not fulfil her purpose as God's chosen nation. To show that God had every reason to expect Israel to respond to His goodness, he now tells the parable of a faithless and lewd wife. Because she defiled herself, her sin is outrageous and her punishment is well deserved. It is not a pretty picture that Ezekiel draws. Only the ugly picture of whoredom can give us some inkling of how black, putrid, and offensive sin is to God.

In her beginnings, Israel had no natural endowments to entitle her to her position as God's chosen nation (16:1-14). By nature and disposition she had a close kinship with her neighbors, the heathen Amorites and Hittites. She had no beauty to commend her, no innate strength even to exist. But God stooped down to lift her from ignoble extinction, adorned her with beauty and strength, and made her the object of His special concern. She became renowned for her "beauty and splendor" which He "had bestowed upon" her. In such a way does Ezekiel recall to the rebellious house her lowly origin in Canaan, her precarious existence in Egypt, her deliverance from shameful bondage, her intimate relationship with God by His covenant at Sinai, her gift of a land flowing with milk and honey, her prosperity in the days of David and Solomon.

The purpose of the parable is to "make known to Jerusalem her abominations" (16:2). The stark realism of Scripture reveals the tragic course of Israel's iniquity. Exalted above all nations, Israel plunged into depths of depravity and prostituted every goodness of God to her base desires. At the root of it all was her trust in her own beauty. She wanted to be free and independent of God, but she became the victim of mad folly, the slave of her own passions, and the mockery of cruel masters. In describing her base ingratitude to God and her wanton madness, the picture language of the parable gives way at times to a recital of events in history: Israel's trust in foreign alliance for safety rather than in God and the degrading worship of her heathen neighbors (vv. 15–34).

Ezekiel had not minced words in describing Israel's crime, nor does he do so now as he announces her punishment in the same shocking terms (16:35–43). Hers will be the tragic terrible fate of a harlot, stripped, humiliated and destroyed by those to whom she had in folly given herself. But clear and straight though his message was, it still sounded stranger than fiction to Ezekiel's hearers. But to Ezekiel the destruction of Jerusalem was already an accomplished fact. When it actually came as an event of history, the irony of human folly became manifest: God destroys the pride of men by the very idols of their desires.

To underscore once more how utterly without excuse the chosen nation is and how God, if He is to remain true to Himself, cannot but give them over to destruction, Ezekiel introduces two sister nations as supporting characters in the drama of his parable (16:44–52). Of the same spiritual parentage, they too are animated by a spirit of idolatry. The only difference is that Israel's guilt is greater because sin is measured in direct ratio to grace that it spurns. Apostate Samaria and heathen Sodom were swept away in God's fury. Can Jerusalem's day of judgment be long in coming?

The two sisters, Samaria and Sodom, enter the story to reveal Jerusalem's sin in its proper perspective of blackest guilt and to add luster to God's mercy (16:53–63). Where sin has abounded, no matter whether it be the sin of apostasy (Samaria) or of pride (Sodom) or of unfaithfulness (Jerusalem), "the grace of God doth much more abound," even as Christianity's great apostle in later centuries reminds his readers (Rom. 5:20). After the judgment of God has served its purpose, He stands ready to restore to fellowship with Him every sinner who feels the shame of his sin (Rom. 11:32). He will remember His covenant with Israel and carry forward His plan of salvation in a new and everlasting covenant (Jer. 31; Heb. 8:6–13). In the fulness of time, He will establish it in Israel (Jn. 4:22) and thereby all her sisters in sin can become daughters by adoption into God's household of faith (Eph. 1:3–13; 2:11–22).

The Eagles and the Vine (17:1–24). But the rebellious house refused to be warned. She was sure that the Babylonian threat could be averted by playing the game of international power politics. She would be saved by breaking her agreement with the Babylonian king Nebuchadrezzar, and allying herself with Egypt which was challenging Babylonian world supremacy. By means of another parable, Ezekiel portrays the delusion of such a false hope and then points, in the same imagery, to the sure promises of God to be realized in the root or stump of Jesse which would bring the restoration of the house of David.

Both the Babylonian ruler and the Egyptian Pharaoh are represented as eagles (17:1–21; cf. Jer. 48:40; 49:22). Jehoiachin, king of Judah, is the top of the cedar (Jer. 22:23) that is cropped off by the first eagle (Nebuchadrezzar) and brought to the city of merchants (Babylon). Jerusalem is permitted to have in Zedekiah a ruler from its own midst ("seed of the land," 17:5) although by comparison with the independent kings before him his powers were limited ("a low spreading vine"). Nevertheless the kingdom could continue ("planted in fertile soil"), but Zedekiah will treacherously break his agreement and look for support to the other eagle (Egypt, v. 15). Because this help will not be forthcoming, his kingdom will be destroyed and scattered, and he himself will die in Babylonia. Great will be the fall of the house of David! (cf. II Kings 24, 25).

In terms of the same imagery, Ezekiel again shows that God's gracious purpose will not be thwarted (17:22–24). Men may break their promises and bring about the fall of the kingdom of Israel, but God's covenant will stand. From the line of David ("the high cedar") will come the ruler of God's kingdom (cf. II Sam. 7:12–17).

Humble and meek ("a tender one"), this Son of David will neverthe-less dwarf all other powers ("the trees of the field"). Under His scepter, all men will be safe and find their needs supplied (cf. Is. 11; Lk. 2:67–75).

Israel's Responsibility (18:1–32). Ezekiel now attacks the self-righteous attitude of the rebellious house. They argued that they did not deserve the dire judgments that God was threatening to in-flict upon them and expressed this idea in a cynical proverb: "The fathers have eaten sour grapes, and the children's teeth are set on edge" (v. 2). If the present generation is going to suffer, they mean to imply, it can only be because they will unjustly suffer the consequence of the sins of their forefathers.

In unmasking the hypocritical self-righteousness that was hiding behind this proverb, Ezekiel does not enter into a discussion of all the mysteries of God's providence and His dealing with men. He does not presume to solve the problem of why God, Who lets His sun rise on the good and the evil, permits the good to be affected by His judgments upon the evil. God has His gracious purposes for the good even then, mysterious and unseen though they be. But one thing Ezekiel is permitted to assert without qualification: in the ultimate issues of life and death, God deals justly with man. The just man will live (18:5–9); a wicked son will not live because he has a righteous father (vv. 10–13); a wicked father will die but his righteous son will live (vv. 14–20); the wicked will live if he turns to God, and the righteous will live only if he perseveres in his righteousness (vv. 21–29). But God's mercy is ever ready to forgive: "Have I any pleasure at all that the wicked should die? saith the Lord God: and not that he should return from his ways, and live?" (v. 23). The way to life is still open: "Wherefore turn yourselves, and live ye" (v. 32).

Dirge for Israel (19:1–14). In performing his duty as a watchman, Ezekiel seizes upon every form of rhetoric to impress upon his hearers that the just God will carry out His threat. In a beautifully poetic and allegorical dirge, he now mourns the downfall of the kingdom of Israel as an accomplished fact (19:1–9). Israel is repre-sented as a bereaved lioness. The captivity of Jehoahaz, the first young lion (cf. II Kings 23:31–33), and of Jehoiachin, the second young lion (cf. II Kings 24:8–16), were not accidents of history. These calamities were the result of Israel's surrender of her God-appointed and unique character in a foolish desire to be like other nations.

Ezekiel changes the picture to show that the captivity will not be restricted to the princes (19:10–14). All Israel, a vine planted in God's grace, will be uprooted to languish in the Exile. Because of King Zedekiah's unfaithfulness, "the strong rod," the fire of God's wrath, is kindled.

6. A Third Series of Rebukes and Threats (20:1—22:31)

Israel's Apostasy (20:1–32). The elders of Israel, who have been entertained rather than instructed by Ezekiel's parables and allegories, still think that they are entitled to God's favor as His chosen people without removing the idols from their heart. In a passage parallel to that in chapter 16, Ezekiel rehearses the great moments of Israel's history. Her record of deliberate refusal to accept her obligations and responsibilities as God's instruments of salvation shows her obstinate from the very beginning in Egypt. Callous to God's mercy and judgment during the wandering in the desert, she defiled herself by every abomination of idols upon the entry into Canaan to this very day. Therefore God will not defer pouring out His wrath upon them.

Israel's Return (20:33–44). God has spared Israel in the past "for his name's sake." His ultimate plan of salvation, likewise to the glory of His name, will not be defeated, however great Israel's unfaithfulness. The very judgment He is about to inflict on Israel will remove the obstructions to His good and gracious will. Then God will bring them again "into the bond of the covenant" (v. 37), as once He did their forefathers under Moses. As in the first Exodus, He will bring them out of the lands of their captivity, plead with them, purge out the rebels among them, lead them into the land promised to their fathers, and accept the services of their new devotion. So Israel after the flesh will again become the bearer of God's promises of grace to all people.

Fire and Sword (20:45—21:32). Ezekiel again takes up the theme of the certainty of the judgment by which God will begin to achieve His purpose. Destruction will come upon "the south" (the land of Judah) like an unquenchable fire. The rebellious house refuses to believe it and expresses its skepticism by saying: "Doth he not speak parables [riddles]?" (20:45–49).

Changing the metaphor, Ezekiel goes on to say that the kingdom of Judah will be devoured by the sword (21:1–32). God has already drawn it from the scabbard. Ezekiel is to sigh "with a breaking heart and bitter grief" to impress upon his hearers that it will cut down all inhabitants (vv. 1–7).

In the Song of the Sword (21:8–17), the prophet continues to describe the slaughter that nothing can resist. It is God's sword, put into the hands of the Babylonians as His executioners (vv. 18–27). Nebuchadrezzar, the king of Babylon, is even now on the march to bring his war machines against the walls of Jerusalem. He may trust in his own power and rely on superstitions for direction, but he is God's appointed avenger nevertheless. Finding the omens favorable, he will make Jerusalem his first objective and destroy the kingdom of David "until he [David's greater Son] come whose right it is; and I will give it him" (v. 27; cf. Gen. 49:10).

The heathen nation of the Ammonites will also be cut down by the sword of the Lord in the hand of the Babylonians (21:28–32). Ezekiel here touches on the judgment of God on the enemies of Israel that he develops fully later (25:1—32:33). Any nation that attempts to obstruct the promises given by God to His chosen nation will become "fuel for fire."

Jerusalem Arraigned (22:1–31). Jerusalem is not guilty of minor lapses and an unintentional lack of good judgment, but of dreadful sin, a total depravity that has undermined "church and state." God has been debased into an idol, and His "holy things" have been despised. In consequence, man is also degraded. Every crime against society stalks about brazenly in bloody cruelty; every decency is flaunted (22:1–16). Israel is therefore no longer silver that can be refined; it is a lump of worthless dross to be melted in the furnace of God's wrath (vv. 17–22).

Nor is Israel's sin restricted to certain groups (22:23–31). All classes of society stand indicted: princes, prophets, priests, and people. Because of this total corruption God's mercy is at an end. Ezekiel sees the fire of His wrath poured out upon these evildoers.

7. Two Final Parables and the Last Symbolic Action of Doom (23:1—24:24)

The rejection of God by His chosen people is again portrayed as a breaking of the sacred ties of wedlock. As in chapter 16, the vileness of Israel's sin is not obscured by squeamish considerations of nice language. Much may be lost by failure to use the right word for the black sin of adultery through labeling it instead with inoffensive terms such as "indiscretion" or "wild oats."

Allegory of the Two Sisters (23:1–49). Again these are two sisters in crime: Aholah, who represents the larger Northern Kingdom of Samaria, and Aholibah, who represents Jerusalem, the capital of Judah. The names are similar to indicate their close relationship as sisters. Aholah means "her tent (or tabernacle)" and Aholibah, "my tent (or tabernacle) in her." The difference in their names seems to reflect the fact that when the northern tribes seceded at Solomon's death they established their own tent or sanctuary, but that the true sanctuary or temple was in Jerusalem (23:1–4).

Although similar in its general features to the story of the two lewd sisters in chapter 16, this allegory is designed to stress the truth that the judgment upon the depravity of Israel is inevitable. Samaria has been destroyed; Jerusalem cannot hope to escape.

Samaria played the harlot to Assyria and Egypt by rejecting the promises of God and seeking security in the armed strength and the false gods of her neighbors. In consequence, she had been destroyed by the Assyrians more than one hundred years earlier (23:5–10).

Aholibah, also a harlot, will share her sister's fate (23:11–35). Knowledge of Samaria's punishment has not deterred the Southern Kingdom from becoming guilty of the same infidelity: she "doted upon" the Assyrians and the Egyptians. Their power became the god in whom they trusted; they bowed down to their idols of stone and wood. History will repeat itself and Jerusalem will drink the "sister's cup, a cup of horror and desolation" (v. 33). There is no horror or desolation Jerusalem will not suffer "because thou hast forgotten me and cast me behind your back" (v. 35).

The sin and past punishment of Samaria and the iniquity and still impending judgment of Jerusalem now merge into a single picture of guilt and punishment (23:36–49). In the perspective of the unchanging justice of God, what will happen has already happened; and what has happened must happen again. The wages of sin are paid the sisters in full: not only shall they be stoned and slain, but also their sons and daughters shall die and their habitations be destroyed (v. 47).

The story of Aholah and Aholibah delineates the tragic irony of man's sin. Just as Samaria's and Jerusalem's paramours are their executioners, so sin has within it the sting of death.

The Rusty Cauldron (24:1–14). When the next word of the Lord comes to Ezekiel, the hour of Jerusalem's judgment has already struck. That very day the king of Babylon opens the siege of Jerusalem. Nor is there any doubt that Nebuchadrezzar will finish what he has begun. Jerusalem, says Ezekiel in a new allegory, is like a cauldron under which a huge fire is kindled. All the inhabitants—none is excluded—suffer the hot terrors of the siege only to face a worse lot when the victors drag them out of the city. Then the cauldron itself is set on fire. It must be destroyed because its spots of rust will not yield to cleansing (24:12, 13). "Woe to the bloody city!" (v. 9). The blood of its innocent victims has cried to God for vengeance (Gen. 4:10). God has been patient and longsuffering. Now He comes to judge and He will not go back, spare, nor repent (v. 14).

Death of Ezekiel's Wife (24:15-24). As God's watchman, Ezekiel is a sad and lonely figure, his personal life almost completely submerged in the performance of his unappreciated task. As herald of national calamity, he tells us almost nothing about himself. The one glimpse of his private life is stark tragedy, the death of his wife, "the delight of his eyes" (v. 16). No doubt it would have gone unmentioned except that this tragic loss also plays a part in his public ministry. As a "sign" to his fellow exiles, he is to refrain from the customary mourning rites. His people, too, will be overcome by grief to "pine away and groan to one another" when God takes from them Jerusalem, "the desire of their eyes" (KJV, v. 21).

8. News of the Fall of the Rebellious House (24:25-27)

The news of the fall of the rebellious house will be brought to Ezekiel by a refugee and mark a turning point in his ministry. His mouth will be opened and he will be no longer dumb.

II. Foreign Nations Guilty of Crimes Against God and His People Will be Destroyed (25:1—32:32)

The siege of Jerusalem, foretold by Ezekiel, has begun. Before we hear of its fall, we come upon a long interlude outlining the fate of other nations. In the mystery of His electing love, God had chosen Israel from among all the peoples of the earth (Rom. 9:1-33), but Israel could enjoy this privileged position only as long as she served the purpose of her election. She could not presume to rely on God's favor without doing His will. Once she repudiated the covenant of grace, she came, like all nations, under God's judgment over sin. That was the burden of Ezekiel's message to this point.

In rejecting God, Israel had in her folly turned to other nations for assurance of her own security. But when Israel leaned upon them, they broke like reeds (29:6, 7). The collapse of these nations, however, is not an unexplainable accident of history. Israel is not autonomous, nor are the other nations; they, too, are within the control and the rule of God. Israel could not sin with impunity, nor can other nations escape the wrath of God. They, too, will come under the rod of His justice and know that He is the Lord.

There is a great corollary to this principle of God's providence: the purposes of God's mercy will not be defeated by the enemies of His chosen people. His plan of salvation will not be thwarted. There will be a restoration of God's people and every promise to Israel will be encompassed and fulfilled in a new covenant of grace. Should the faithful in Israel be tempted in the fire of judgment to despair and to think that the power of men was stronger than God's promises of salvation, let them hear how God shapes the destiny of all nations. None of them will be able to oppose His good and gracious will. The stronger and the mightier, the greater will be their fall. The prophecy at this point does not explicitly mention the participation of the heathen nations in the blessings of God's people, although it may be implied in the recurring phrase: "They shall know that I am the Lord."

These oracles of judgment, pronounced at various times upon the heathen nations, are grouped under the nation's name to which they apply. In one of them is the latest date recorded in the book, the twenty-seventh year of the Captivity (29:17). By their position in the book, these oracles concerning foreign nations are not only an interlude in the prophecies of Ezekiel to his own people, they are also a prelude to his later glorious picture of the future of God's Kingdom.

Conspicuous by its absence among the nations mentioned is Babylon (cf. Is. 13 and Jer. 49:1—51:64). It is possible that a prophecy of its destruction would only have fed the false hopes that both Jeremiah and Ezekiel had to deflate. The rebellious house was convinced that the Babylonian Exile would end shortly. But the time of deliverance was not at hand.

Seven nations are indicted and condemned. Five—Ammon, Moab, Edom, Philistia, Sidon—are dealt with summarily. Three full chapters are devoted to Tyre and the oracle against Egypt is the most elaborate.

1. The Word of the Lord concerning Six Palestinian Neighbors of Israel (25:1—28:26)

Ammon, Moab, Edom, Philistia (25:1–17). These nations, the immediate neighbors of Israel, were hostile to Israel from the very beginning. They are indicted for the part they played during the siege and after the fall of Jerusalem. Ammon gave expression to unholy glee over the destruction of the temple (25:1–7); Moab arrogantly rejoiced that Israel received no special consideration as God's chosen nation (vv. 8–11); Edom committed acts of vengeance (vv. 12–14); and Philistia likewise took vengeance "with malice of heart" (vv. 15–17). Each indictment is as terse as the sentence of doom to match it. Whatever its form, the punishment will be recognized as the Lord's doing.

Tyre and Sidon (26:1—28:26). Two great commercial cities of the world, Tyre and Sidon, are arraigned next. Their rejection of God expressed itself in rank materialism. Although trust in things may appear to men to be less reprehensible than violent deeds against God's people, the prophet demonstrates in three full chapters devoted to the indictment and sentencing of Tyre and Sidon that this type of godlessness is the sin of hell itself.

Never a great military power, Tyre had not waged aggressive wars against Israel. Still she rejoiced over Jerusalem's fall as did the other nations, because she thought Tyre's position would be enhanced. Already the undisputed metropolis of trade by sea, Tyre hoped to rise to new heights of prosperity by extending her commercial ventures to the ends of the earth. If wealth was her god, its bulging warehouses were her temples.

God will shatter this false security (26:1–21). He will "bring up many nations" against Tyre and reduce her to a barren rock and a village of fishermen (v. 14). Nebuchadrezzar, king of Babylon, is specifically mentioned among the instruments of God's wrath (v. 7). Tyre had trusted in its merchant marine to acquire her riches. In poetic allegory, Ezekiel now describes Tyre as a magnificent luxury liner that will be wrecked by the wind and the seas and sink into oblivion (27:1–36). The finality of its destruction finds expression in a lament over its former glory.

The arrogance and self-conceit of Tyre are epitomized in the description of her prince. Like Adam, and indeed like Satan, he wanted to be like God and thereby brought down upon himself the sentence of death. The hands of foreigners will slay him.In the lament over him, Ezekiel continues to compare his fall to Adam's in the garden of Eden. Given a paradise, he made it a den of violence and iniquity. Nothing will remain of his domain but ashes (28:1-19).

Sidon, closely associated with Tyre, will not escape punishment for her sins (28:20-23).

All these nations will vanish, but Israel will be restored (28:24-26).

2. Seven Words of the Lord Concerning the Seventh Nation (29:1—32:32)

No nation on earth will be able to prevent God's plan of salvation from going into effect, but only seven are specifically mentioned by Ezekiel. This number no doubt is significant, for, as so often in Scripture, seven is used to denote completeness, and here it would express the absolute and unlimited extent of God's control of world events (Deut. 7:1). This universality of God's control is underscored further by the arrangement of the next four chapters of the book. They contain seven oracles against this seventh nation, Egypt, which Ezekiel received from the tenth to the twenty-seventh year of the Captivity. Each oracle is introduced by the phrase, "The word of the Lord came to me . . . ."

There are doubtless other reasons why the denunciation of this seventh nation is more elaborate than even the one against Tyre. Unlike all other nations mentioned, Egypt had been a world empire. Indeed, at this point in history, she challenged the Babylonian supremacy. Recent archaeological discoveries confirm the fact that the outcome of the contest between these two giants hung in the balance at this time. Unbelieving Israelites at home and in exile hoped to escape God's rod of retribution which He had placed into the hands of the Babylonians by the timely intervention of the armies of Egypt. Without equivocation, with a certainty beyond the guesses of political sagacity, Ezekiel makes it plain that this battle for world dominion would end in disaster for Egypt. The power of the Pharaoh cannot prevent the destruction of Jerusalem nor halt the scattering of Israel among the nations.

Jerusalem's trust in power politics, rather than in God, is utterly unrealistic for still another reason. Egypt, the prophet says, would only exploit a possible victory for her own selfish purposes and Jerusalem would, therefore, merely exchange one yoke for another, domination of the Babylonians for oppression by the Egyptians. But this shall not be, says Ezekiel. In her role as the executor of God's vengeance upon Israel, Babylonia will also initiate God's judgment upon Egypt (29:3). When a chastened Israel returns from the Babylonian Captivity, not even "the great dragon" of the Nile, as a representative of all world powers, will be in a position to interfere with Israel in her role as the bearer of God's promise.

Fall of Egypt (29:1–16). The first oracle speaks in general terms of the judgment that awaits Egypt because of her sinful trust in herself. In the opening verses Pharaoh, a great dragon (cf. Is. 51:9; 27:1; Ps. 74:13), is accused of ascribing to himself the power of the Creator. This monster of arrogance, together with his people, will be subdued by God and left to perish. The poetic description of the breaking of Egypt's power is then explained: Egypt will suffer the ravages of war, and her people will be dispersed. Israel will no longer be tempted to place her hope of survival upon this broken reed of marsh grass. Although partially restored after the severest blows of God's judgment, Egypt will "never again rule over the nations" (vv. 15, 16).

Nebuchadrezzar's Wages (29:17–21). In the last dated prophecy of his book (the twenty-seventh year of the captivity, 571 B.C.), Ezekiel specifies that as the bearer of God's sword of vengeance Nebuchadrezzar will despoil the wealth of Egypt to repay him for the destruction of Tyre which brought him no substantial booty. It appears that the people of Tyre succeeded in removing their treasures beyond his reach before her downfall. Nebuchadrezzar will reduce Egypt to a "lowly kingdom" which will crumple like a reed. A "horn" of strength, however, will spring forth in Israel (29:21). In establishing His kingdom of grace among men, God will use a chastened and weakened Israel. This kingdom will remain strong to proclaim His name among men.

Woe to Egypt (30:1–19). In an undated oracle, Ezekiel continues to describe the judgment on Egypt in terms of God's day of wrath (cf. Joel 1:15; 2:1, 2; Zeph. 1:14–18). Woe and dark calamity will be the lot of the land of Egypt and its allies. Nebuchadrezzar is again mentioned as the executor of God's wrath. His fire will destroy all on which the Egyptians had based their security: their idols, their princes, their strong cities.

Judgment upon Pharaoh (30:20–26). Dated as from the eleventh year of the Exile, the next oracle emphasizes that the military reverses, already suffered by Egypt, will continue until Nebuchadrezzar has completely vanquished Pharaoh and scattered his people.

The Great Cedar (31:1–18). Egypt is depicted as a cedar that crashes to the ground. By reason of her lofty position of influence among the nations and her abundance of resources, Egypt is like a cedar of Lebanon, which has no rival among the trees of Eden (31:2–9). But height can be weakness, and her towering strength is the very source of her downfall. Egypt's "heart was proud of its height . . . foreigners, the most terrible of the nations, will cut it down and leave it" (vv. 10, 12). Nations will be shaken at the sound of her fall, and she will vanish from the scene as completely as men, cut down by death from whence there is no return (vv. 16, 18).

Lament for Pharaoh and Egypt (32:1–32). The judgment upon Egypt concludes with lamentations over her fall. Ezekiel, who sees the end as an accomplished fact, attends, as it were, the funeral of Egypt and utters dirges in keeping with the prevailing customs of mourning for the dead.

In the first dirge (32:1–16) he resumes the comparison of Pharaoh with a dragon (29:1–8), whose depredations will cease when left on the ground after capture to be devoured by the birds of the air (vv. 1–4). The dark Day of the Lord, the symbol of God's universal judgment upon a wicked world, dawns for Pharaoh and his people (cf. 30:1–26; Is. 13:9–11). Once the king of Babylon has put down the turbulence of Egypt, she will no longer be able to trouble the waters of God's gracious purposes (vv. 13, 14).

In the same year Ezekiel is directed to compose another funeral ode over Egypt (32:17–32). Ezekiel is to point out that when God speaks His word of judgment, the mightiest nations are brought down from their proud heights in a destruction that is as complete, inevitable, and permanent as death itself. Egypt will be no exception. The irrevocable sentence of death that God pronounces on all nations that oppose Him will seal Egypt's fate.

The prophecies against Israel's enemies close with unmistakable assurance that at no time does the opposition against God's people get beyond His control. The Day of the Lord has come in history, and it will come to end history.

III. Chastened Israel will be Restored and God's Kingdom will Flourish (33:1—48:35)

The foreign nations, the enemies of God's people, lie buried forever, but Israel shall rise from the grave of the Exile. Israel after the flesh remains the undeserving and often unwilling instrument through which God's plan of mercy is carried forward to its final goal: the salvation for all men. So Ezekiel is permitted to see and portray the glorious Kingdom of grace to the end of time.

To achieve His purposes, God will begin, as it were, where He had left off. The chosen people will be reconstituted as a national group in the Holy Land under the special care of God. But vital as Israel after the flesh is in the unfolding of God's plan of salvation, it is nevertheless only a means to the end. The promises of His grace are given in terms of the provisions of the Old Covenant, but the New Covenant will exceed the framework of the Old. God's people will be gathered from all nations and tongues. By the grace and power, supplied by the Mediator of the New Covenant, the new Israel will worship and serve God in wholehearted devotion. As the old Israel enjoyed the special protection of God, so will the new Israel. The onslaughts of the mightiest foes will not prevail against His chosen people.

All this is seen in the perspective of prophetic vision. The more distant scene and the immediate future merge into a single view of God's accomplished salvation. What God did for His people of old and what He will do in the fulness of time and at the very end of time, constitute the lines of one and the same picture.

1. The Prophet of Restoration and the Basis of His Message (33:1–20)

Before the news of the fall of Jerusalem arrives, God prepares Ezekiel for the proclamation of deliverance and restoration that is now to dominate his message. In his new role, he is to remain a watchman whose duty is to warn against dangers. There is a good reason why, in effect, Ezekiel is newly commissioned as a watchman when he begins his task as the messenger of God's mercy (33:7–9; cf. 3:17–19). Neither the grace of God nor His wrath operates mechanically. The ultimate issues of life and death confront each individual, and there is no group insurance against God's judgment. God indeed "has no pleasure in the death of the wicked" and His grace is full and free. But the sentence of death remains over each individual unless he turns from his wickedness, yields the fruits of repentance, and perseveres to the end (vv. 10–20; cf. 18:1–32).

2. *News Arrives of the Fall of Jerusalem (33:21–33)*

Although Ezekiel is to remain a watchman, there will be an outward change in the performance of his duty: he will no longer be restricted in the use of his mouth. His dumbness has served its purpose as a sign (cf. 33:21, 22; 3:25–27; 24:25–27). News of the fall of Jerusalem thus marks the great turning point in the ministry of Ezekiel. No longer primarily a preacher of doom, he is now to have full use of his tongue to proclaim God's message of salvation.

But a warning against a false understanding of God's goodness is still very much in place at this point (33:23–29). Jerusalem lies in ruins, the Holy Land is desolate, yet there are still people in whom even this catastrophe of God has not produced repentance and who therefore are not ready for, nor entitled to, a message of mercy. In Palestine "the inhabitants of the waste places," those who have escaped death in the fall of Jerusalem, cling perversely to the false notion that their descent from Abraham gives them license for every abomination and automatically guarantees their eventual possession of the Promised Land. For them the warning is needed: they cannot expect to, nor will they, receive any promise of life.

In Babylonia when the exiles realize Ezekiel's word of doom has come true, he is "the talk of the town" (33:30–33). Curious crowds gather about him. Warnings are still needed so that they will not misunderstand the good things that Ezekiel is now saying. They find them pleasant, even entertaining, but their hearts, unchanged by his words of judgment, remain untouched by the message of grace.

3. *The Promises of God (34:1—39:29)*

After the principles of the blessing of God have been laid down and the responsibility of Ezekiel in announcing it has been made clear, the promises themselves are presented in beauty and power. Already a few rays of hope have been flashed through the lowering gloom of judgment (cf. 11:16–21; 16:60; 20:40–44; 26:20; 28:25, 26;

29:21). They gave blessed assurance that the threatened punishment was not an end in itself and that God's good and gracious will to save will prevail. Now the light of these promises breaks forth in full splendor and almost blinding brilliance.

Restoration under an Eternal King (34:1–31). The rapacious rulers of Israel were false shepherds who ruled "with force and cruelty." Because they exploited the sheep instead of feeding them, "My flock was scattered . . . My sheep became a prey." Therefore the Lord will depose them and deliver His flock from their mouth (34:1–10).

In their stead God will supply His flock with a good shepherd, under whose rule there will be peace and security for all. Representing and establishing God's own dominion, this shepherd-king will unite under his scepter his people scattered far and wide among the nations. The resources of his Kingdom are sufficient to provide every want; the weakest member will find refuge and will be protected from every violence. Appointed of God like David of old, yet greater and more glorious, he will put into lasting effect the peace of a New Covenant of God with men (34:23–31; cf. Jer. 23:1–8).

This picture of the future seems to be as bizarre and involved as a surrealist painting. The lines of the past, the present, and the future are woven into the one pattern; the colors of symbol and reality blend. The Old Covenant merges into the New Covenant only to reappear. Nevertheless, its meaning in broad outline is not unintelligible if we let the light of the whole of God's revealed truth fall upon it.

The fulfilment of these promises began with the gathering of ancient Israel, scattered upon the hills like sheep without a shepherd, and her return to Palestine. Under the gracious rule of God, greater blessings are to come. In the fulness of time, great David's greater Son will establish God's eternal and universal Kingdom of grace on earth. In it all the promises of the Old Covenant will be fulfilled. Its subjects will be "a chosen generation, a peculiar people, a royal priesthood," assembled under its spiritual sway from every nation under the sun. Drawing upon the unlimited resources of grace the King supplies, even the weakest will want nothing to attain the fulfilment of life's highest purposes. Finally, all injustice inflicted by their fellowmen will be swept away when the King will say, "Come, ye blessed of my Father, inherit the kingdom prepared for you from the foundation of the world" (Mt. 25:34; cf. Jn. 10:1–18; Heb. 13:20; I Pet. 2:25; 5:4).

Restoration on the Hills of Israel (35:1—36:15). The next word of the Lord that comes to Ezekiel stresses the restoration of the land of Israel. Like the preceding prophecy, it contains a negative and a positive aspect. First, His people are assured that no hostile power will be able to interfere with God's plans for them. Edom (Mount Seir), already mentioned in the judgment against Israel's neighbors (25:12–14), is the representative of all hostility to God's kingdom. Although not one of the great world powers of the ancient world, Edom epitomized the antagonism to God because it "cherished perpetual hatred" against Israel and "magnified itself" in defiant blasphemies against God (cf. Gen. 25; Amos 1:11; the Book of Obadiah). Its mountains of strength will be reduced to desolation.

In contrast, the mountains of Israel will be unshaken and will serve as the blessed habitation of God's people as He promised (36:1–15). His word to Israel is sure: "Behold, I am for you" (v. 9). Israel's exile will end, and she will be brought back to her inheritance. But just as Edom is the symbol of perpetual opposition to God, so Israel is the type of all God's children and the promises to her include in prophetic perspective the blessings of all who "lift up their eyes to the hills from whence their help comes" (Ps. 121:1). Ezekiel's words look forward to the rehabilitation of a people of God not limited by geographic boundaries. Purged and redeemed from the power and the condemnation of sin, this people will be free to "worship the Father in spirit and in truth" and not only "on this mountain nor in Jerusalem" (cf. Jn. 4:20–24).

Restoration of a Heart of Flesh (36:16–38). Israel's restoration as God's chosen people, however, is not for its own sake, but for the sake of God's holy name. On her own record, Israel does not deserve to be restored. Unholy and unclean, she could no longer serve the holy purposes of God's name, and therefore God poured His wrath upon her. By their victory over Israel, the heathen nations were led to believe that the God of Israel was weaker than their idols and unable to carry out the purpose of His holy name in the face of their opposition (36:16–20).

But "the heathen shall know that I am the Lord" when for His "holy name's sake" God gathers Israel out of all countries and brings her into her own land (36:21–24). His forgiving grace will wash her clean from the filthiness of her evil and loathesome ways; He will put His spirit within her and thus remove the stony hardness of disobedience and give her a pliant "heart of flesh" that yields itself to God's will (vv. 25–27). When Israel is again God's people and He is their God, the blessings on this relationship will have no limits. It will be a paradise regained (vv. 28–38).

God kept these promises, first of all, by bringing a chastened, penitent, and forgiven Israel from captivity to "build the ruined places and plant that that was desolate" (36:26). But rehabilitated Israel will serve again as God's instrument in His plan of restoring all men to fellowship with Him that they may hallow His name. By the power of God's Spirit and by "the sprinkling of the blood of Jesus Christ" (I Pet. 1:2), the hearts of all men in all nations become God's dwelling place and receive the power to yield themselves to His will.

Restoration to Life (37:1–14). Pride and despair appear to be opposite extremes of man's reaction to a given situation, but in God's analysis of man's fearfully wicked heart, they are but the reverse sides of the same coin, unbelief. After Ezekiel has deflated the pride of Israel and made it clear that restoration will not come "for their own sakes," he turns to silence the voices that say, "Our hope is lost; we are clean cut off." In one of the most impressive visions of the book, God lets Ezekiel demonstrate that Israel's despair grows out of unbelief in His unlimited power to fulfil His promises.

True, Israel's hopes for the future appeared dead and buried forever in the Exile. Her prospects of revival were like a vast array of dead men's bones, lying dismembered and dry as dust in a great plain. Shall they live again? Yes, says God, by the power of His creative word. When Ezekiel speaks it at God's command, the power of death vanishes. The bones arrange themselves according to their proper functions and are covered with sinews and flesh. "Breath came into them and they lived, and stood upon their feet, an exceeding great army" (37:10).

By this vision Ezekiel was to remind Israel that God's word of promise has not become weaker since He "formed man of dust from the ground and breathed into his nostrils the breath of life and man became a living soul" (Gen. 2:7). Let not Israel doubt His power when the same God now says: "I will open your graves, and cause you to come up out of your graves, and bring you into the land of Israel" (37:12).

But this demonstration of God's life-giving power contains assurances beyond the revival of Israel as a nation. The vision of the future, that God gives Ezekiel again and again, begins at that point, but it does not end there. A revived Israel is that earthly clay out of which God will call into being the people of His eternal Kingdom. It will become the Kingdom of Heaven in its full and most final sense when the resurrection words are spoken over those "that sleep in the dust of the earth" (Dan. 12:2) by Him Who is the Resurrection and the Life (Jn. 11:25; 5:25–29; I Thess. 4:16) and all the Israel of God will be gathered into the heavenly Canaan.

Restoration to Unity (37:15–28). Ezekiel at God's direction had at various times "acted out" the judgment of God. In the same way, he now performs a symbolic act to describe another phase of Israel's restoration. What he does is very simple. On one piece of wood is inscribed the name of Judah and his companions, and on another piece of wood the name of Joseph and his companions. These represent the two parts of the nation since the division of the kingdom after Solomon. Now Ezekiel puts the two sticks together and holds them in his hand as a unit (37:16–19).

In explaining what he has done, Ezekiel begins with the simple assurance that in its restoration the previous divisions among the people will cease. Again this promise is phrased in terms of the Old Covenant as in 34:11–31 and 36:22–30, but it includes all the blessings of the everlasting covenant of peace. The unification of Israel involves more than the consolidation of national interests. The ties that bind God's people together are the result of the fulfilment of His plan of salvation for all men. We acknowledge this unity of God's people in the New Covenant when we confess: I believe in One Holy Christian and Apostolic Church.

Restoration to Safety from All Evil (38:1—39:29). Will there be no enemies to trouble this united and peaceful kingdom? What if it is attacked? Will it endure? It is to questions such as these that the prophecy against Gog gives a graphic answer.

Yes, restored Israel will have enemies. To the very end, they will combine their demonic forces to undo what God has established. But when "the kings of the earth set themselves and the rulers take counsel together . . . [God] will speak to them in his wrath and terrify them in his fury and dash them in pieces like a potter's vessel" (Ps. 2).

In assuring His people that the restoration of Israel will not be thwarted, Ezekiel foretold the destruction of seven foreign nations in the immediate vicinity of Palestine (25:1—32:32). As a guarantee for the continued and unending protection of God's people to the end of time, he now describes the defeat of enemies more remote from Israel. Dwelling on the very borders of its world, they have not been among those who molested Israel in the past. But they will come "in the latter years." Yet, like the seven nations of the past, their doom is also sealed in a sevenfold "thus says the Lord God" (38:3, 10, 14, 17; 39:1, 17, 25).

The ringleader of this confederacy of evil is "Gog of the land of Magog." His name does not occur anywhere else in the Old Testament as the leader of hostile forces. His base of operations can only be identified in a general way. Magog, Meschech, Tubal, Gomer, and Bethgormah are mentioned as sons and descendants of Japheth in Genesis 10:2, 3 and denote people in the extreme north. Allied with them is Persia in the east, Cush and Put (Egypt) in the south.

God Himself misleads this ferocious and well-armed horde ("I will turn you about," 38:4) to an attack on the restored land of Israel (vv. 1–9). God will thus give free reign to Gog's unholy desire for spoil and plunder (cf. II Sam. 24:1 and I Chron. 31:1). The gratification of Gog's lust seems to be within very easy reach; there should be little resistance from a quiet people dwelling in unwalled cities (vv. 10–13). But his might notwithstanding, the devices of Gog will end in the vindication of God's holiness (vv. 14–16). This campaign is no sneak attack; God has known about it in advance and His prophets have spoken of it in former days. The terrors of the Day of the Lord, which these prophets had already portrayed, will also fall upon Gog (vv. 17–28).

Once more the advance of Gog is briefly described in order to dwell more fully on his complete annihilation (39:1–16). It will overtake him even in the homeland of Magog and its coastlands. Gog will leave behind in the land of Israel so many weapons that the people will be supplied with firewood for seven years. Another measure of the catastrophic defeat of Gog is that only sustained and organized efforts will make it possible to dispose of the corpses. These will be so many that they will fill a whole valley, which will be known as the Valley of the Multitude of Gog (v. 11). In addition the birds of prey, already mentioned in verse 4, will do their part to clear the land of this uncleanness (Is. 34:6; Jer. 46:10). So in the face of the most severe onslaught against His Kingdom, God's holy name will be glorified among men (vv. 17–24).

But these promises of His protection after the restoration of Israel apply as well to the immediate situation to which the prophet now returns (39:25–29). Israel's deliverance from the Exile will vindicate

His holiness in the sight of many nations. As a part of God's ultimate purposes for man's salvation, it cannot fail to come to pass.

Gog also appears in New Testament prophecy (Rev. 20), and the setting is the same. His attack comes after the Kingdom of God has been established. In both accounts, the alliance of evil against the Kingdom of God ends disastrously. The very gates of hell shall not prevail against it. All attempts to interpret the highly figurative language of Ezekiel and Revelation that go beyond this general assurance of God's unfailing and unending protection of His people against all enemies are beset by uncertainties, to say the least, and run the danger of ignoring other clear Scripture regarding the course of God's Kingdom to the end of time.

4. The Vision of Restoration (40:1—48:35)

As Moses was given a glimpse of Canaan from Mount Nebo, so from "a very high mountain," the Lord lets Ezekiel see the Promised Land of the New Covenant. Ezekiel's eyes scan a scene of activity: the fulfilment of God's promises of salvation to Israel, a salvation which through His chosen nation extend to all people.

From the very beginning God had made clear that Israel was to play a part in His eternal decree of restoring man to fellowship with His Creator. God chose Israel when she was a wretched aggregation of slaves and made Israel a people of His promise. As His people they were to be holy, for He the Lord God is holy. The covenant that He made with Israel made provisions by which she could serve His holy purposes. Prophet after prophet proclaimed the sad fact that Israel had broken this covenant, and thereby destroyed herself as the instrument of salvation. But God's mercies are greater than Israel's sin. She again will play a prominent part in God's program of bringing salvation to all men. In effect, God will begin all over again and do for Israel what He did at the time of the Exodus from Egypt: "I will take you for my people and I will be your God" (Ex. 6, 7). Ezekiel now says it in similar words: "My dwelling place shall be with them; and I will be their God, and they shall be my people" (37:27).

Israel's liberation from the Exile and her restoration to her own land will be like a second Exodus. But as Israel in the beginning was unworthy of God's choice as His people, so her revival will not be for her own sake, but for the glory of His holy name. His name will be hallowed first of all when Israel accepts the forgiving mercy for her unholiness and by the help of His Spirit lives in holy communion with Him. God will be glorified above all when, in and through a cleansed Israel, He restores all men to a holy fellowship with Him. All of this Ezekiel had been privileged to promise in the preceding chapters.

Now in the closing chapters of his book, Ezekiel is given a vision of God's ultimate purposes for mankind fully and perfectly realized. He presents a picture on a grand scale with bewildering masses of detail, but the basic motif is unmistakably clear: God's people are in possession of the blessings of the promised New Covenant, with the aid of His Holy Spirit, and they respond to it with a new heart of obedience and in full fellowship with God.

Because Ezekiel is to relate what he sees to his contemporaries, this picture of the future quite naturally has the framework and the patterns of the Old Covenant. Under its provision, a returned and penitent Israel again becomes the instrument of God's mercy. But Ezekiel is permitted to look beyond to the time when all that the Old Covenant foreshadowed in the purposes of God becomes the completed salvation of the New Covenant.

Thus out of the forms and patterns of the Old Covenant—its temple, its ritual, its theocratic ordering of all phases of life, the Land of Promise itself and the holy city—there emerges a panorama of the established communion of God with man. The barrier between Holy God and unholy man has been removed. There is access to God, fellowship with God, acceptable worship of God, and daily pardon from God.

As under the Old Covenant, every area of man's life is affected when he comes under the sway of God's Kingdom. Furthermore, man remains forever in full possession of these inalienable blessings of the Kingdom of God, for it is the Kingdom of Heaven.

We who live under the New Covenant and enjoy its blessings cannot fail to understand what Ezekiel promises and describes in the picture language of the Old Covenant. Through the blood of the New Covenant, shed by the Lamb of God to take away the sins of the world, the symbolism of the Old Testament has become a reality. Cleansed by that blood, our hearts become a temple of the Holy God. By the indwelling of His Spirit, we are enabled to dedicate our thoughts, words, and deeds to Him in the worship of praise and obedience. Day by day we can come to the throne of grace for pardon and renewal. But like Ezekiel and the people of the Old Covenant, we also live by faith and not by sight. There are still greater things to come. John, the seer of the New Covenant, promises them like Ezekiel in the terms of the Old Covenant, and he directs our gaze to the undying glories of the Canaan above and of the heavenly Jerusalem (Rev. 21:1—22:21).

We sketch only the main features of Ezekiel's grand vision. He presents the promised future not only in terms familiar to his hearers, but also with the same precision and profusion of detail that characterize the provisions of the Old Covenant.

Temple of the Restored People (40:1—42:20). What Ezekiel sees is directly opposite to the conditions prevailing in the Israel of his time (40:1–4). To undₑᵣscore this fact, he tells us that the vision came to him when he had spent twenty-five years in captivity; Jerusalem and the temple had lain in ruins for fourteen years. In such a hopeless situation there could be hope for the future only in visions of God.

In these visions Ezekiel is brought to the site of the destroyed city of Jerusalem which, no longer in ruins, is now occupied by a new temple. No human builders are involved; it stands completed and ready for Ezekiel to see. From its detailed description, we recognize it as similar to Solomon's temple in many respects, thus indicating its continuity as the dwelling place of God among His people. The new features that appear serve mainly to emphasize its chief characteristic: absolute holiness. There is nothing here any longer to defile the place where God resides (40:4—42:20).

The Glory of the Lord Enters the Temple (43:1–12). It is significant that Ezekiel, who had seen the glory of God depart from the old desecrated temple (11:23), should now see it returning to a holy habitation as "the place of my throne and the place of the soles of my feet."

Worship of the Restored People (43:13—46:24). In this temple God does not dwell in isolated and unapproachable holiness, for this is a place of fellowship where a cleansed and renewed people has access to His holy presence in holy worship. The regulations for this worship are also patterned after the provisions of the former temple; there are sacrifices performed by a faithful priesthood for a people living under a perfect rule of God.

But there are also noticeable differences from the pattern of the Old Covenant. Perhaps the most significant and revealing are the absence of a high priest and the elimination of the Day of Atonement, just as in the description of the Holy of Holies there is no mention of a mercy seat on which the high priest sprinkled the sacrificial blood on that annual day. By virtue of an accomplished atonement, the people can draw near to receive forgiveness from a reconciled God and bring the offerings of their devotion and praise (cf. Heb. 9:11–14).

Living Waters and the Promised Land of Inheritance (47:1—48:35). God dwells among His people and blessings stream forth from this restored and holy relationship (47:1–12). They are like a river whose waters transform bitter stagnation into abundant fruitfulness. The river Ezekiel sees flows from below the door of the temple eastward and becomes a deep flowing body of water, capable of transforming a desert into a fertile field and sweetening the water of the Dead Sea. It flows perennially and grows in its course without tributaries. So will flow the spiritual waters of God's grace and salvation that purify, nourish, and change the dry and dreary lives of men.

Ezekiel's vision ends with a view of the Land of Promise apportioned for inheritance among all twelve tribes of Israel and clustered about a New Jerusalem (47:13—48:35). As the temple stands built and ready for the worship of God by His people, so the land is God's to give without campaigns by conquering armies of men. At its center is the dwelling place of God from which emanate the waters of life. No one is excluded from partaking of the blessings of the land; there is room in the Kingdom of God for a people composed of all of the tribes of men. Though their numbers be as the sand of the sea, all have the assurance of an imperishable inheritance which the King has in readiness for them, for "The Lord is there."

Daniel

G. DOUGLAS YOUNG

THE BOOK OF DANIEL is one of the most remarkable books of prophetic vision ever written. The only book to which it is at all comparable is the Book of the Revelation in the New Testament. Written during the Babylonian exile, it shows in a remarkable way the march of empire; all nations are under the sovereignty of God. Interestingly enough, it is Nebuchadrezzar (spelled according to the Babylonian pronunciation), the pagan conqueror, who confesses the sovereignty of Israel's God: "Now I Nebuchadrezzar praise and extol and honour the King of heaven, all whose works are truth, and his ways judgment: and those that walk in pride he is able to abase" (4:37; cf. 2:47; 6:26).

The great themes of prophecy in Daniel are of vital concern to the children of God today: the apostasy of God's people; the revelation of the man of sin; the tribulation; the Second Coming, the Millennium, and the Day of Judgment. The preview of the last days given to Daniel six centuries before Christ is still, nearly twenty-six centuries later, our own preview, save that we are nearer the Last Judgment.

But before we consider the prophetic panorama of history the visions of Daniel portray, let us dispose of the question of authorship. Historically, both Judaism and Christendom have received Daniel into the Canon as a genuine work of the period of which it alleges to speak, the sixth century B.C., its author, Daniel. Many scholars believe that the Book of Daniel, as we have it, comes from the times of the Maccabees, approximately 165 B.C., author(s) unknown. They believe it was issued to strengthen the faith of the people in those days of persecution under a pseudonym, the author(s) creating the impression that a sixth century Jew, Daniel, was the real author. But there is no evidence that the Jews ever issued under a pseudonym a book claiming to be a revelation from God, dating it centuries earlier than the time of public presentation. In the absence of convincing historic and scientific evidence, there is no need to depart from the accepted Judeo-Christian tradition of a sixth century B.C. date and authorship by Daniel.

I. Miscellaneous Babylon Experiences (1:1—6:28)

1. Captivity and Preparation for Court Service (1:1–21)

The Book of Daniel opens with the dateline firmly fixed, 607 B.C., the third year of the reign of Jehoikim. We are at once ushered into a scene with which we are unfortunately well acquainted today: the occupation of a country and the seizure of its inhabitants and their forced labor at the will of the conquerors. The day of the Gentiles has dawned under Nebuchadrezzar who plans to use the flower of Jewish youth in service at his court in Babylon (1:3, 4).

Daniel and three of his friends were among those selected from the king's seed and from the princes of Judah. These physically fit young men were assigned to a three-year course of indoctrination which involved every aspect of their lives (1:5). During this time they were to be fed on royal fare, and since this included both wine and other foods forbidden the Jews, these four young men demonstrated their faith by requesting permission to make substitutions (v. 8).

The prince of the eunuchs was reluctant to grant permission, but Daniel persuaded him to permit a trial of ten days to test the effects of a simple diet (1:12–14). Once its value was exhibited, full permission was granted to abstain from the king's meats and drinks for the remainder of the three years (vv. 15, 16).

Not only had they honored God in their refusal to depart from what He had prescribed for them, but their preferred food proved far more wholesome than that which they refused. It was noticeable that God had blessed them, for at the end of the three years they excelled in matters of wisdom and understanding, and Daniel's God-given power of interpreting dreams was marked (1:17). The king found none like them among all the young men being trained for royal service (vv. 18–20).

2. Nebuchadrezzar's Fourfold Image (2:1–49)

The Forgotten Dream (2:1–13). Daniel's power to interpret dreams was dramatically demontrated by his revelation of the meaning of Nebuchadrezzar's dream. Apparently afflicted by insomnia prompted by the fear engendered in his heart by a dream, Nebuchadrezzar was desperate for tranquility. In history, he is one of the early seekers of peace of mind, but not the last. He turns to his magicians, astrologers, soothsayers and Chaldeans for help in interpreting his dream. Apparently to test them, Nebuchadrezzar insists that he has forgotten the dream and that the wise men must first reconstruct it themselves (v. 9).

The Chaldeans (or wise men) insist that the king asks the impossible (2:10, 11). The stubborn ruler, however, has vowed that all the wise men in his kingdom shall be slain if they cannot interpret the dream, and he is ready to carry out his threat (vv. 12, 13).

Prayer for Wisdom (2:14–23). When Daniel learns what is planned, he immediately gathers together his three friends and addresses God in fervent prayer for a key to the "secret." The revelation of the dream is given Daniel, and his prayer of thanksgiving is one of the most beautiful and lyrical expressions of the wisdom of God in Holy Writ (vv. 20–23).

Daniel hastens to Arioch, the one whom the king has ordered to destroy all the wise men, and tells him, "Destroy not the wise men of Babylon; bring me in before the king, and I will shew unto the king the interpretation" (2:24). In full recognition of the urgency of the request and realizing that no time must be lost when so tyrannical a king is involved, Arioch at once brings Daniel before the king (v. 25).

Daniel tells Nebuchadrezzar that the dream which he calls "the secret" has been revealed to him by the "God in heaven that revealeth secrets" (2:28). The absolute humility of a true man of God is displayed in Daniel's insistence that no wisdom of his own enables him to set forth the dream of the king.

The Vision Described (2:31–35). Daniel then describes one of the great apocalyptic visions. He tells Nebuchadrezzar what he saw in the dream: a colossus, the parts of which were made of different materials, symbolizes four successive kingdoms. But the revealed image is not only one of imperial power; there is action: "and the stone that smote the image became a great mountain, and filled the earth" (v. 35).

The Dream Interpreted (2:36–45). Daniel embarks at once upon the interpretation of the dream. Babylonia is the first great world empire: "Thou art this head of gold" (vv. 36–38). In identifying the empires which are to follow upon Nebuchadrezzar's, scholars have been at variance. Some would interpret the order of empire as Babylon (vv. 37, 38), Medo-Persia, Alexander's Empire (v. 39) and the successors of Alexander (vv. 40–43). But the traditional conservative view—and the only one that fits verse 44—holds that the colossus of Nebuchadrezzar's dream typifies Babylon (604–538 B.C.), Medo-Persia (539–333 B.C.), Greece (490–146 B.C.), and the Roman Empire (27 B.C.–A.D. 455).

One distinguished commentator has pointed out that gold properly represents the absolute autocracy of Nebuchadrezzar; silver, the monarchial oligarchy of Medo-Persia, in which the nobles were equal to the king in all but office; brass, the aristocracy which was characteristic of Greece; and iron, the democratic imperialism of Rome. The two legs of the image represent the separation of the Roman Empire into the eastern and western divisions. The feet and toes of iron and clay suggest the fragile combination that results when the iron of Rome is mixed with the clay of popular will.

"The stone cut without hands" (2:33–35) represents the messianic kingdom and the victory of the coming King whose rule shall "encompass the whole earth." Some regard this fifth kingdom as the Church (vv. 44, 45); others see in this kingdom the organization that will be set up in the Millennium, the period of one thousand years spoken of in Revelation 20. Since it is declared to be a kingdom which shall never be destroyed, it is hard to limit it simply to a period of one thousand years. Inasmuch as it is a kingdom which destroys four literal earthly kingdoms, it appears not to be a spiritual kingdom only, such as the Church would be. Therefore it seems reasonable to suggest that the Church which is being called out from the nations of the earth will constitute the spiritual aspect of the fifth kingdom; and the actual coronation of Jesus, son of David, on David's throne will be the regal affirmation of God's power in terms of an earthly kingdom. This certainly would appear to be verified by the statement that "the kingdom and dominion and greatness of the kingdom under the whole heaven shall be given to the people of the saints of the most High, whose kingdom is an everlasting kingdom, and all dominions shall serve and obey him" (7:27).

Nebuchadrezzar's Confession and Daniel's Advancement (2:46–49). Nebuchadrezzar, enchanted by the assurance of his power and convinced of the truth of Daniel's revelation, at once appoints Daniel to a high position, prostrates himself before Daniel and makes his confession to the power of Daniel's God. But even then it is not a recognition of one God, for Nebuchadrezzar speaks of Him as "God of gods"—that is, head of multiple deities. That is all the pagan tyrant is willing to affirm. In Daniel's rise to power, he takes with him to seats of authority his three friends, Shadrach, Meshach and Abednego.

3. The Image of Gold: Three Friends Tested by Fire (3:1–30)

One of the unforgettable passages in Daniel and one that is clearly relevant to our day is the account given of Nebuchadrezzar's erecting an image of himself, plated with gold, and demanding that all men bow down at a given signal. Failure to do so would mean death. The dramatic account of the fiery furnace has become the symbol of the tyranny of despots on the one hand and the valiant endurance of their victims on the other.

One interesting aspect of this moment in history is its tragic repetition. Adolph Hitler demanded an idolatry of his people in terms of devotion to himself which his Nazis enforced by sword, and millions of Jews perished, some of them in fiery furnaces. Whereas Nebuchadrezzar in the sixth century put up a statue of gold, Hitler in the twentieth century raised his picture on huge placards over the countryside and splashed millions of swastikas in every corner of Germany. The demand was the same whether the tyrant said, "Fall down and worship" or "Heil Hitler!"

Nebuchadrezzar's image of gold was set up and, on signal, worship was to be made to the Babylonian tyrant (3:1–7). The failure of Shadrach, Meshach and Abednego to obey the edict was duly reported (vv. 8–12), and the men were ordered to appear before the king.

When Nebuchadrezzar asked them if it were true that they would not bow the knee before the image of gold (3:13–15), the three Jews made an answer that rings down through the ages: "We have no need to answer you in this matter. If it be so, our God whom we serve is able to deliver us from the burning fiery furnace; and he will deliver us out of your hand, O king. But if not, be it known to you, O king, that we will not serve your gods or worship the golden image which you have set up" (vv. 16–18).

These words of valor spoken long ago by young men dedicated to God proclaim a truth still valid in our day. Paganism can be challenged only by men willing to be martyrs.

The full fury of Nebuchadrezzar demanded that the men be bound and placed in the flames (3:19–23). Now the king might have, at that point, put the matter in the back of his mind as finished business, but this was not to be. Drawn to the scene of the crime, the despot sees, not three, but four men in the furnace (v. 24). Some grain of conscience still left, Nebuchadrezzar correctly interprets the fourth to be like the Son of God (v. 25) and orders the youths released. They walk out of the furnace unscathed (vv. 26, 27).

The testimony of the young Jews' faithfulness causes the king to decree reverence toward their God and to promote Shadrach, Meshach and Abednego to places of power. In Nebuchadrezzar's affirmation, "there is no other God that can deliver after this sort" (3:29), we note recognition of God, but no lasting conversion. While God does not promise to exempt His children from persecution, He does assure them He will walk with them through the fire of persecution and the deep waters of adversity.

The great lesson of the fiery furnace highlights the loyalty of three men, the sovereignty of God, and the working out of the Lord's redemptive power. The fiery furnace is also a symbol of the great deliverance of the Jews that lies ahead in the last days. In the fiery furnace of that persecution, the Messiah will again deliver, coming in power and glory to save His people.

4. Tree Vision and the King's Madness (4:1–37)

Nebuchadrezzar's Dream (4:1–18). This section of Daniel opens with a doxology. The influence of the Jewish youths and Daniel may have brought Nebuchadrezzar a new appreciation of the great power of the Lord (vv. 1–3), but he still fails to recognize his obligation to God.

Nebuchadrezzar describes his dream of a great tree, lofty and flourishing (4:10–12). Suddenly it is cut down at the order of a heavenly watcher. Its fruit is scattered, its branches are no longer a shelter for birds and beasts, but its stump is left. Then in verse 15, after the manner of dreams, the tree takes the part of a man whose heart is to be changed into that of a beast. Upon concluding his account of the dream, Nebuchadrezzar asked Daniel (here called by his Babylonian name, Belteshazzar) to interpret its meaning.

Interpretation of the Dream and its Fulfilment (4:19–37). Daniel explains that the tree is Nebuchadrezzar, that its abundance symbolizes Nebuchadrezzar's wealth and power, that its being cut down indicates a break in his power and a period of madness. Daniel holds out the hope that the period will be shortened (a "lengthening of tranquility," v. 27) if the king repents his iniquities.

The blow did not fall at once, but twelve months later as the king walked in pride, certain of his own power, disaster struck. When the blow fell, the king had just completed this boast: "Is not this great Babylon, that I have built for the house of the kingdom by the might of my power, and for the honour of my majesty?" (4:30). Even as he vaunted his pride, he was stricken with the mania that is called "lycanthropy." In the grip of this lunacy, the victim imagines himself an animal and acts like one (vv. 32, 33).

After a season, the king's mind was restored. Again he honored God, this time in a way that showed he was at last coming to understand the true meaning of God's power (4:34). In Daniel 2:47, Nebuchadrezzar reveres Him as a God of gods (one of many) and "a revealer of secrets"; in 3:28, 29, Nebuchadrezzar sees Him as one who responds to faith, but still a Hebrew deity; but in this third affirmation of Nebuchadrezzar (4:34), God is "the most High," the one "whose dominion is an everlasting dominion." Nebuchadrezzar has learned the lesson of humility: "those that walk in pride he is able to abase" (v. 37).

The wholehearted praise of the Lord by Nebuchadrezzar, a man whose arrogance and wickedness made reform seem remote, testifies to the power of God and indicates that judgment in this life is essential discipline. With lunacy gone and sanity restored, Nebuchadrezzar returns to the throne. The figure of the stump which had indicated his later return to power is thereby fulfilled.

5. The Handwriting on the Wall (5:1–31)

But the lesson learned by one man is still to be learned by another. Learning the hard way at the School of Experience where the tuition is always high and, in human estimate, often exorbitant, was as prevalent in the sixth century B.C. as it is today. Nebuchadrezzar's successor, Belshazzar, exemplifies one scholar's view: "All we learn from history is that we do not learn from history."

Belshazzar's Feast (5:1–4). Belshazzar's day of reckoning arrives at night after an evening of drinking and licentious revelry. From the house of God at Jerusalem, the golden vessels had been taken, and it is from these sacred cups the Babylonian lords drink.

In a scene dramatic, sudden, and strange, a hand appears and writes on the plaster of the wall of the king's palace certain words (5:5). Belshazzar, pale and shaken by this event, called at once for every wise man in the kingdom. Not one of them could interpret the words.

The queen in this crisis recalled that there was a man in the kingdom whom Nebuchadrezzar had found gifted in the interpretation of dreams, and she at once recommended that Daniel (Belteshazzar) be brought before the king (5:10–13). Upon Daniel's arrival, the king explains that he has heard of him and asks if Daniel can read the writing on the wall. Great gifts would be Daniel's if he is able to do this: rich clothing, jewelry and power.

Daniel answers, "Let the gifts be to thyself and the reward to another," then opens his interpretation with a lesson in history. What Daniel tries to impress on Belshazzar needs to be taught in each generation: there is sin, judgment, and redemption. Daniel points out the power and glory Nebuchadrezzar had, the despotic control he exercised over his subjects; yet there came upon him a madness that caused him to be like a beast, and thus was he humbled.

Daniel drives the lesson home: "And thou his son, O Belshazzar, hast not humbled thine heart, though thou knewest all this" (5:22). In detail, Daniel outlines Belshazzar's sin: dishonoring God in using the vessels of the Lord's house, licentiousness, drunkenness, and dreadful idolatry. Daniel sums up Belshazzar's failure in one great statement, "And the God in whose hand thy breath is, and whose are all thy ways, hast thou not glorified" (v. 23).

After this powerful introduction, Daniel goes on without pause. It is the God Whom Belshazzar has not honored Who speaks to him now: "Then was the part of the hand sent from him; and this writing was written" (5:24). In short, Daniel is saying, "These are God's words to you."

The words on the wall were MENE, MENE, TEKEL, UPHARSIN. Now these were weights, the last being the smallest. Furthermore, the last word had more than one form and could be interpreted as not only a measure, but a word for Persians. Daniel translates this inspired acrostic: "Mene: God hath numbered thy kingdom, and finished it. Tekel: Thou art weighed in the balance and art found wanting. Peres: Thy kingdom is divided, and given to the Medes and Persians" (5:26–28). The rule of Belshazzar is over, and the kingdom is gone. That very night, not long after Belshazzar had clothed Daniel in royal garments, given him a gold chain and proclaimed him third ruler in the kingdom, Belshazzar, king of the Chaldeans, was slain. Darius, the conqueror, took over.

Thus another world power had struggled to the top, become profligate, was judged by God, destroyed and replaced. Were we to put the successive kingdoms of this world on a graph, we would see again and again parallel lines representing early energy, mounting prosperity, crest of power and the downward plunge to oblivion. Years or centuries may be involved in the process so often repeated in history. Sometimes the downward descent is swift, as in the case of Belshazzar; sometimes slow, involving centuries of decline, as in the case of the Roman Empire, but the direction and end are the same.

6. *Darius, Daniel and the Lions' Den (6:1–28)*

Daniel's High Estate (6:1–3). When the Babylonian empire came to an end with the death of Belshazzar, Cyrus was head of the Medes and the Persians. As conqueror of Babylon, he placed that city in charge of one of his assistants, Darius, the Mede. Secular historical sources are silent concerning this Darius, but the fact that it has not yet been possible to identify him from sources outside the Bible neither proves that he did not live nor that his mention indicates a confused tradition.

During this short reign of Darius occurred one of the most important incidents in the life of Daniel. Darius set up a council of 120 princes and over them were placed three presidents, one of them Daniel. Apparently Daniel's gifts as an administrator were so highly regarded and his tasks performed so well that Darius had in mind to set him over the entire realm (6:3).

The Plot against Daniel (6:4–9). This immediately excited the jealousy of the other two presidents and the princes. Since they knew that no charge could be made against Daniel, they endeavored to trick the king into destroying him. Craftily they devised a plan to involve Daniel in such a way that his very integrity would be bound to guarantee his destruction. It is a testimony to the godly witness of Daniel that these evil conspirators knew that Daniel's obedience to his God would be first and that he would accept martyrdom under Darius in preference to disloyalty to God. Darius, at the request of the instigators, made a decree that anyone who made a petition to any god or man for thirty days, save to Darius, should be cast into the lions' den. Furthermore, this decree was declared irrevocable, which a law of the Medes and Perisans was traditionally understood to be (vv. 7–9).

Daniel Cast into the Lions' Den (6:10–17). The decree did not cause Daniel to change his course. He went as he always did to the the throne of grace, and three times daily he opened the windows of his dwelling as he knelt facing the direction of Jerusalem (v. 10). The plotters, rejoicing in their success, hastened to Darius to demand Daniel's punishment. Only their insistence drove Darius to carry out the decree. Despite Darius' deep reluctance to have Daniel punished, Daniel was placed in the lions' den (vv. 16, 17).

Daniel's Deliverance (6:18–24). Unhappy, sleepless, Darius held out the night, but early the next morning he hastened to the den. He called out to find if Daniel's God had delivered him and rejoiced when Daniel told him that the mouths of the lions had been stopped. Darius then had "those men which had accused Daniel," together with their families, sent to their deaths in the den. The punishment of the evil men was in line with the Persian custom of the time which caused the families to suffer the same fate as the evildoers.

Darius' Decree (6:25–28). Darius immediately wrote another decree extolling the God of Daniel, "the living God." In his praise of God, he declares that "his kingdom . . . shall not be destroyed, and his dominion shall be even unto the end" (v. 26). In the mouth of a pagan potentate is put a prophecy that will surely be fulfilled.

Daniel's faithfulness was rewarded by his great prosperity in the reigns of Cyrus and Darius (6:28). Certainly the biography of Daniel is not a long one, but enough of the story of his life is given to make his name a synonym for courage and faithfulness. His heroic character was formed in his constant walk with God. No greater testimony could be given to the power of prayer than his safety in the lions' den. In the hour of Daniel's affliction, God was with him and brought him safely through the terror and the danger.

One of the songs so popular with children and young people appropriately extols Daniel:

> Dare to be a Daniel,
> Dare to stand alone;
> Dare to have a purpose firm,
> And dare to make it known!

The kind of daring that characterizes Daniel only comes by utter and abiding faithfulness to Daniel's God Who is "the same yesterday, today and forever."

II. Visions of Four Empires and a Fifth (7:1—8:27)

In the visions in this section, the symbolism of Nebuchadrezzar's dream described in chapter 2 is extensively developed. The fourfold image which the monarch beheld portrayed, according to Daniel, four great kingdoms. These have been interpreted to be Nebuchadrezzar's, the Medo-Persian, Greek and Roman empires. A fifth kingdom, the Kingdom of God, was prophetically typified in the stone that struck the image and filled the whole earth.

Study of the Book of Daniel is simplified if we recognize that the great theme of its visions and prophecies is the march of empire and the final triumph of the messianic Kingdom. Whatever the kingdom of this earth—in each case the identity of the kingdom is not so important as the principle of history under which it operates—its rule and end are part of the great plan of God. Chapters 7 and 8 amplify the great prophetic dream Daniel interpreted for Nebuchadrezzar (2:1-49).

1. Daniel's Four-Beast Vision and the Ancient of Days (7:1-28)

The Four Beasts (7:1-8). One night during the reign of Belshazzar, Daniel saw the winds of heaven upon the sea. Out of this sea—the symbol of humanity—came four beasts, regarded, in general, as analogous to the great empires in Nebuchadrezzar's vision.

The first was a beast like a lion which had an eagle's wings (7:4). These wings were plucked, and the lion was lifted up and made to stand like a man, and a man's heart was given it. Certainly this would seem to identify the kingdom as Nebuchadrezzar's, for it depicts action parallel to the story of the king who in his madness imagined himself for a season to be a beast (4:16, 34).

The second beast was like a bear, and this beast was directed to devour much flesh (7:5). This is appropriate to the Medo-Persian Empire which quickly dominated Babylonia, Libya, and Egypt.

The third beast described as being like a leopard is usually identified as Alexander's empire (Greece) which struck swiftly and engulfed the known world with astonishing and unforgettable rapidity (7:6).

The fourth beast was simply a great beast, terrible and strong, adorned with ten horns (7:7, 8). Among them was a little horn that arose and pulled out three of the original ten horns by the roots. In this little horn were "eyes like the eyes of man, and a mouth speaking great things," phrases which suggest tremendous arrogance and presumption. This last great beast has usually been identified as the Roman Empire.

Some, however, have identified the four kingdoms as Babylon, Media, Persia, and Greece. But this identification seems to offer more problems than it solves, and we prefer the classic interpretation of the four as Babylon, Medo-Persia, Greece and Rome. It appears to be true to history in terms of symbolic interpretation. Again the scholar is to be reminded that the vision is giving a principle of world empire, rather than a detailed account of every occurrence.

The Ancient of Days (7:9–14) In verses 9 and 10, we enter into a scene symbolic of God on the throne of judgment. The white garment worn by the Ancient of days, His white hair, the throne of flame, and the ministry of multitudes suggest the majesty of God Himself. Solemnly the judgment is announced with the opening of the book. The end of the kingdoms immediately follows (vv. 11, 12).

The Son of Man is seen coming in power and glory. He draws near to the Ancient of days to receive dominion, glory and power. To Him is given a Kingdom that shall include all people, nations and languages, all of whom shall serve Him. His Kingdom is sure, eternal and indestructible (7:13, 14). This memorable scene is re-enacted almost identically in the vision of John (Rev. 5:6–10).

The Vision Interpreted (7:15–28). Daniel, puzzled by the scene he has witnessed, seeks an interpretation. He is told that the great beasts are four kings "who shall arise out of the earth" (v. 17). These kings, Daniel's guide points out, shall be defeated by "the saints of the most High" (v. 18).

The fourth kingdom (7:23–25) is given special attention and its description parallels that already given in verses 7 and 8. A salient characteristic of the victorious little horn is arrogance. It is prophesied that he shall do certain things, all actions now familiar to us as the marks of our twentieth-century dictators (v. 25).

He shall speak great words against the most High.

He shall wear out the saints of the most High.

He shall think to change times and laws.

Arrogance, dictatorship, and ruthless ordering of laws without constitutional safeguards are prophesied. Do we have such kingdoms today? We do, and two of them openly avow atheism, oppose any allegiance to the Christian faith and set their own rules. What despotism will fill the final role of the little horn we do not know, but certainly the character of the Antichrist has been delineated.

So also has his power. He shall rule until "a time and times and the dividing of time." The Antichrist will flourish, but not forever. Some have interpreted "time" to mean a year, "times" to be two years, and the "dividing of time" as half a year, or a total of three and a half years. Whatever may be the length of time—and this is bound to be indefinite—the end of the little horn is certain. When his dominion is taken away (7:26), Gentile power ends, and the way opens for the fifth kingdom, the Kingdom of Heaven (v. 27).

2. *Daniel's Ram, He Goat and Little Horn Vision (8:1–27)*

In the visions in this chapter, likewise received during the reign of Belshazzar, a close-up of the second and third kingdoms is presented. The two-horned ram pushes westward, northward and southward, and no beasts can withstand him. As Daniel studies the vision, he sees a goat coming from the west. The goat strikes the ram, breaks his two horns and becomes, in turn, the unconquered one. Now the goat had a notable horn, and out of this horn come four smaller horns.

Daniel is informed that the two-horned ram is the Medo-Persian Empire, and the rough goat is Greece. The four horns are interpreted as the division of the Greek Empire assigned to four of Alexander's generals upon his death: Macedonia, Thrace, Syria and Egypt.

One of the generals held Syria, and founded the line of kings known as the Seleucids. In 175–170 B.C., one of these kings, Antiochus Epiphanes, became powerful and persecuted the Jews and desecrated the temple of God. The passage describing the little horn in his role as tyrant and desecrater of the temple has generally been interpreted by evangelical scholars as having been fulfilled in Antiochus Epiphanes. But it is also held to be a picture of the latter days in which a world-wide Antichrist holds sway. This certainly seems reasonable in the light of verses 22 through 27 when the interpreter sums up the tremendous might of the tyrant.

III. The Vision for Daniel's People and City (9:1—12:13)

1. *Daniel's Confession, Intercession, Prayer for Restoration (9:1–19)*

Daniel was deeply concerned about a prophecy God gave Jeremiah concerning the seventy years of Jerusalem's desolation ("And this whole land shall be a desolation, and an astonishment; and these nations shall serve the king of Babylon seventy years. And it shall come to pass, when seventy years are accomplished, that I will punish the king of Babylon, and that nation, saith the Lord, for their iniquity, and the land of the Chaldeans, and will make it perpetual desolations"—Jer. 25:11, 12). In one of the great intercessory prayers of the Bible, Daniel pours out his soul to the Lord in behalf of his people. He fully acknowledges Israel's guilt (9:4–14), and begs for the forgiveness of Israel, not "on the ground of our righteousness, but on the ground of thy great mercy" (v. 18). The prayer fits Israel's need today and the power of God still operates in history to bring about the events symbolically represented to the prophet Daniel.

2. The Prophecy of the Seventy "Weeks" (9:20–27)

As Daniel prays, God sends an angelic representative to give understanding. God answers the cry of Daniel's heart for the end of the desolation by giving, through Gabriel, a brief survey of the entire future of His relationship with the Jewish people.

The prophecy given makes clear that there is a definite period of desolation, "seventy weeks of years" (9:24, RSV). Now the word rendered "weeks" simply means a period divided into seven. Thus it is definitely misleading if we try to study this Scripture with conventional methods of measuring time. We do better to think in terms of seventy periods of time, each of which is divided into seven parts.

In this period of seventy sevens, God has a sixfold program for the salvation of Israel and her holy city:

To finish the transgression. The great transgression has been the apostasy of Israel, and it has brought deep affliction.

To put an end to sin. Ezekiel's words illuminate this part of the program: "Neither shall they defile themselves any more with their idols nor with their detestable things, nor with any of their transgressions" (Ezek. 37:23).

To atone for iniquity. An essential sacrifice is to be offered for the atonement of sin.

To bring in everlasting righteousness. This righteousness is to be brought into effect by God Himself through the Messiah.

To seal both vision and prophecy (prophet). The visions and prophecies of all the great men of God beginning with Moses, once complete, will establish their authenticity. The Old Testament prepared the way for the New, and once the Messiah comes, the Old Testament dispensation is closed.

To anoint a most holy place. This seems to refer to the enduement of the Holy Sprit, or, as another has suggested, the establishment of a great millennial temple of God.

Daniel has been given an outline of the program God proposes to carry out. Daniel is informed of the date for the inauguration of this long range plan: the going forth of the word to restore and build Jerusalem (9:25). This word, God's own command, operates in history when Cyrus in approximately 537 B.C. permits the Jews to return to their land. The "seventy sevens" begin with one of the several returns, the one decreed by Cyrus or one of the returns thereafter (cf. Ezra 7:11–26).

From this beginning to the cutting off of the Messiah (Christ on the cross) are to be seven sevens and sixty-two sevens or sixty-nine periods of the seventy prophesied. Some Bible scholars have interpreted seven sevens to cover the period from the first return from exile under Zerubbabel to the completion of the work of Ezra and Nehemiah and sixty-two sevens for the period between that time and Christ's first coming. Others regard the crucifixion as the closing of the sixty-nine weeks, and 9:26 would seem to substantiate this point of view.

In verse 26, two great events are predicted: The Messiah (the anointed one) shall be cut off, "but not for himself," and the destruction of the city (Jerusalem) and the sanctuary (temple). It is generally agreed that the destruction of the temple and Jerusalem by Titus in A.D. 68, some thirty-five years after the crucifixion of Christ, fulfilled this prophecy.

Verse 27 opens with a statement of great importance: "And he shall confirm the covenant with many for one week." There is no general agreement as to the interpretation of this verse. Some consider this prophecy concerning the seventieth week as having already been fulfilled in and around the times of the Messiah, Jesus Christ. The one who causes the covenant to prevail is taken by some to mean the Messiah Himself. Others believe that the prophecy has not yet been fulfilled and interpret the one making a covenant as the Antichrist who first aids, then persecutes, regathered Israel. He it is who declares their new temple and makes the sacrifice to cease. This abomination that desolates (Mt. 24:15) is also described in the twelfth chapter of Revelation.

This is not the end of the matter in Daniel's prophecy, for he returns to this theme after a double interlude in which he describes a vision of the glory of God and gives additional details concerning the coming kingdoms of Medo-Persia and Greece.

3. Daniel's Vision of the Glory of God (10:1–19)

In the third year of Cyrus, Daniel had another great vision. Why Daniel did not return with the children of Israel who had been permitted to go to Jerusalem in the first year of Cyrus' reign is not stated. What in the King James Version is rendered "the time appointed was long" is better rendered "a great conflict" (RSV, 10:1).

In the preceding chapter, God had given Daniel a great vision which drove him to continued prayer and fasting. At this point, Daniel is given a vision of the glory of God which is much like the one given to John (Rev. 1:13–15).

When the man of the vision speaks to him, Daniel is overcome, but he is assured by the words of the messenger that he is well beloved by God. The messenger assures Daniel that his prayers have been heard and therefore has he come (10:11–19).

4. Prophecies Concerning Persia and Greece: Antiochus (10:20—11:35)

The Great Conflict (10:20, 21). Daniel is given some additional information about the holy city and his people. The heavenly messenger indicates that a spiritual struggle is taking place behind the scenes, the great warfare of verse 1. As the messenger struggles with the spiritual power behind Persia, he is assisted by the spiritual power behind Israel, namely, Michael. In verse 20, he indicates that the time of Persia is short because he is now returning to fight with the power behind Persia. When Persia ceases to be, Greece will come on the scene.

Greece, then Antiochus (11:1–20). The period of Persian domination will include three kings after Cyrus—Cambyses, Smerdis, Darius Hystaspis. Then Greece will become the dominant power on the world scene: "a mighty king [Alexander the Great] shall stand up" (v. 3).

In turn, this kingdom shall break up into four divisions (11:4). The struggle between two of Alexander's successors is described in detail. The king of the south (with respect to Palestine) is the one who reigned over Egypt and North Africa, Ptolemy Soter, 322–305 B.C. The king of the north (of Palestine) is Seleucid whose capital was Damascus. The historical relationship of the Ptolemies and the Seleucids during a period extending approximately from 325 to 165 B.C. is accurately predicted.

Antiochus and the Antichrist (11:21–35). A "vile contemptible [RSV] person" is the prophetic introduction to Antiochus Epiphanes. Cunning, treacherous, diabolical, a soul without honor, he makes covenants and alliances which he honors only as long as he wishes. In history, Antiochus fully lived up to the prophecies about him. He was often called Epimanes, "madman," instead of Epiphanes, "illustrious," the title he assumed. In this section we have described a series of conquests and betrayals, capped finally by the pollution of the sanctuary and widespread persecution of the Jews.

5. The King at the End (11:36–45)

With verse 36 of chapter 11, there comes a change in personnel. Some deny this and insist that the passage continues to speak about Antiochus Epiphanes. One well known commentator, however, who sees the difficulty in making the description fit Antiochus, says, "How far the events here described correspond to the reality is a very doubtful point." This problem is resolved when the language is accepted as that of prophecy, not history. Thus it is neither of the time of Daniel nor of the time of the Maccabees in which Antiochus lived, but still further in the future. Almost all evangelical scholars regard the language as prophetic and apply it either to the Romans or the Antichrist. The latter view was advocated by Jerome and has been traditionally the interpretation of the Church.

As in the days toward the end of the Seleucid empire, a wicked king desecrated the temple in Jerusalem and persecuted the Jewish people, so in the end of this age, a wicked ruler will once again desecrate the sanctuary and persecute the people of God. It is this event, still in the future, that is predicted in the prophetic language at the end of chapter 11. Some feel that this is the one who makes the convenant with the Jews and breaks it in the middle of the seventieth "week" (9:27), the abomination of Daniel 12:11 and Matthew 25:15. These see additional details of the picture in Revelation 12 and in the beast out of the sea of Revelation 13.

In the end of this age, there will be one who magnifies himself and turns against the people of God with great persecution. His period of blasphemies and power is allowed to continue, according to some scholars, three and a half years (Rev. 13:5). This is the one who is destroyed in the 19th chapter of Revelation just before the great events of the thousand years commence in Revelation 20.

6. *Michael and the Resurrections (12:1–3)*

The spiritual power behind Israel, Michael, stands up to deliver Daniel's people. In verse 1 of chapter 12 he speaks of this time of trouble as one "such as there never was since there was a nation." In the Olivet Discourse, Jesus seems to be talking of the same time of trouble when He says that unless those days were shortened, no flesh should survive (Mt. 24:21, 22). But they, "children of thy people," that is, Daniel's people Israel, are to be delivered out of the trouble, "some to everlasting life and some to everlasting contempt." Some see the first deliverance as the one pictured by Paul in I Thessalonians, chapter 4, the rapture of the Church. These see the second as that pictured in Revelation 20 which takes place at the end of the thousand years. Still other scholars view the resurrections as one general resurrection of the righteous and the wicked together at the end of this age.

7. *Events at the End (12:4–13)*

Daniel, in still another vision, sees two men standing on either side of a river: one clothed in linen was standing upon the water of the river. The one standing upon (or over) the river asks the one clothed in linen, "How long to the end of these wonders?" The answer is brief: "It will be for a time, times, and a half." When the Antichrist has practically destroyed the people of God, then he himself will come to an end (12:7). In view of the fact that there is another view of the entire passage, we again observe that while some have interpreted this as meaning three and one half years of persecution of the Lord's people, others regard it as an appointed time—the exact period of which is known only to God—during which persecution will take place.

Daniel asks the question already asked, "O Lord, what shall be the end?" God's answer is that the words are sealed until the time of the end. God wishes some of His predictions to be understood in part; others are to remain concealed until the full period of the complete revelation comes. When the time comes that these words are needed, they will be understood. God does give a general answer, however. He says that during the period while the fulfilment is still in the future, many will be purified, but the wicked will continue to do wickedly. In this period, the wicked will not be able to understand, but the righteous will understand (12:10).

One striking bit of prophecy is made. The daily sacrifice is to be taken away, the abomination set up, and there are to be 1290 days (12:11). These words are interpreted symbolically by some. They refer to the persecution under Antiochus; but in a much deeper sense, in the broad history of the world, they describe the times of the Antichrist. The persecution under Antiochus lasted ten days longer than three years. In like manner, there will be a generally extended period at the end of this age in which events analogous to the times of Antiochus take place.

The other view is that Daniel 12:11, Matthew 24:15, and Revelation chapters, 11, 12, and 13:5 refer to the seven years of the seventieth "week" of Daniel's prophecy which come at the end of this age. In this last age, God again deals with the Jewish people. There will be a temple and sacrifices. When the temple is again desecrated and an abomination set up, then the end is near.

Hosea

KYLE M. YATES, SR.

LOOK AWAY to Palestine, in the last half of the eighth century (750–700 B.C.)

I. The Setting

Jeroboam II is the king in Samaria, the capital of the northern kingdom. Uzziah reigns in Jerusalem, the capital of the southern kingdom. These kings extended the boundaries, set up stable governments, put down border disturbances, and gave the people of all the land a welcome era of peace and prosperity. Amos came to Jeroboam's kingdom with a message of doom. Tragic judgment loomed immediately ahead.

Hosea, a native of the northern kingdom, came on a few years later to drive home the Lord's pronouncements of judgment and disaster and destruction. Sin would bring certain doom. The setting of his messages was beset with problems (4:1, 2, 6, 8, 10–14, 17; 5:4;

663

6:9, 10; 7:8–16; 8:1, 7, 8; 9:1, 9, 10; 13:2, 3, 6, 16). All through his long ministry he waded through anarchy, revolt, bloodshed, feuds, immoral behavior, broken homes, class hatreds, corrupt courts, extravagance, drunkenness, slavery, and shallow religious observance. Idolatry and ignorance and godless indulgence combined to make an intolerable situation. Priests had failed and were lined up with bandits and racket bands. Worship was formal, professional, and meaningless. It was a pathetic situation. How could God look with favor on such people? How could a spiritual prophet hope to do anything with such godless people? Kings and priests and princes were all against him. He had no help from his own home. Sin and selfishness and greed and paganism mocked him at every turn. His was a hopeless task.

Amos preached in Israel about 760 B.C. Isaiah and Micah delivered God's messages in Judah, the southern kingdom, about 740 B.C. These four mighty men of God (Amos, Hosea, Isaiah, and Micah) made up the quartet known as the eighth century prophets. It would be exceedingly difficult to exaggerate the contribution of the big four. They were God's immortal challenge to sin and immortality and idolatry and paganism. They brought His deathless word of warning and denunciation and doom. With that stern word, they pronounced the divine promise of hope and salvation and victory.

II. The Man

Hosea grew up in the northern kingdom about the time Amos came to preach his terrific series of messages. The young man was powerfully moved. He was clean, keen, tenderhearted, exceedingly sensitive, strangely poetic, deeply spiritual, strongly evangelistic, genuinely in love with God, unusually bold and courageous, and fiercely infuriated because of the immorality, the insincerity and the callous indifference of those who had been commissioned to teach true religion. Some one has said that "lightning flashed from his tear-dimmed eyes." With strange insight he was able to understand the true nature of sin, the certainty of deserved judgment, the love of the Lord, the need for repentance, and the way of salvation. He was essentially a lover. Even his unfaithful wife, though unworthy, was loved with unquenchable devotion. He came to see and understand God's love for His faithless people. With flaming heart and impassioned tongue, he went among the people with the burning, evangelistic challenge to tell of the amazing grace of God. He was God's anointed herald to a sinful people with the true message of full salvation.

III. The Interpretation of the Marriage

Hosea married Gomer, the daughter of Diablaim. How is this experience in his life to be interpreted? Some claim that the story is an allegory, a nice little parable, and therefore not the account of an actual historical event. According to this view, Gomer was an imaginary character invented to illustrate God's love for sinning men. Others take the narrative to be strictly literal, declaring that Gomer was an unchaste woman, a prostitute, an actual adulteress at the time of the marriage. The most sensible theory takes it to mean that Hosea married Gomer, who was, at that time, not an actual adulteress but one who became unclean and unfaithful after her marriage. Hosea suffered untold agony in that experience.

IV. The Book

The preaching of God's highly endowed prophet was pointed, personal, pungent, penetrating, powerful, and persuasive. It is a poignant appeal spoken over and over, through uncontrolled sobs, to a hardened people urging them to come home to God. He sobs his great heart out as he calls them to repentance and confession and to a new life with God. All the way through, the anguished cry is heard above the din and the turmoil and the sordid manifestations of selfish seeking. Clearly he reveals a picture of God's hatred of sin, of the tragic consequences of wilful sinning, of God's inevitable coming in severe judgment on sin, and of God's unquenchable love that burns on in spite of every sinful manifestation until repentance brings healing and salvation and victory. Nothing equals it in all literature. We find ourselves swept by its rushing torrent of eloquence until we weep our way through its amazing lines to see the great heart of love winning the ultimate victory. It is difficult to find the outline but no distinct disappointment is felt because it defies a logical arrangement. It is the heart cry of a champion human lover representing the champion Lover of all times seeking His own.

V. The Outline

Hosea's heartbreaking home life brought on by Gomer's infidelity illustrates Israel's unfaithfulness to the Lord (chs. 1—3). The nation Israel, unfaithful and unrepentant, is challenged by the preacher to come home to the faithful God who loves and will save (chs. 4—14). A holy God suffers as He sees the foul sin of Israel; sin is intolerable in the presence of holiness (chs. 4—7). A just God must bring severe judgment. The divine visitation is imminent. (chs. 8—10). A loving God will provide restoration, healing, forgiveness and full salvation. Love will have the victory (chs. 11—14).

1. Sin (4:1, 2, 10–13; 5:4; 7:9, 10, 13; 8:1, 7, 8; 9:9, 10; 10:13; 13:2, 6, 12)

Hosea clearly presents the divine hatred of sin. It is infinitely ugly in God's sight; it is unspeakably horrible. He cannot endure it; it breaks His heart. It is a breach of faith, a betrayal of love, spiritual adultery, unfaithfulness. The three words: *pesha, awon,* and *hattath,* represent the three areas of sin. They are wilful rebellion, warped or twisted or depraved condition of the heart, and a tragic missing the mark. These people were in sacred covenant relationship (marriage). They had ceased to love the Lord and had turned wilfully to the gods of the land. Hosea said: "They have transgressed." "They have rebelled against me" (7:13). "They have left off heeding the Lord" (4:10).

What does sin do? It saps the vital juices—physical, mental, and spiritual—until a mere shell is left. The radiance, the winsomeness, and the attractiveness are gone. Decay is gradual, imperceptible, fatal. It works secretly, silently, stealthily, to bring ruin, to separate from God, to leave ugly scars, to contaminate, to degrade, to destroy. It brings poverty, drabness, futility, frustration, and death. It robs the individual of the power to make moral and spiritual distinctions. "It cuts the optic nerve of the soul." It hurts the holy heart of God, the supreme Lover. Spiritual adultery stabs at the heart of the Lord. Hosea felt the hurt in God's heart.

2. The Sure Judgment (4:6, 9; 5:10, 12, 14; 6:11; 8:7, 14; 9:17; 12:11, 14; 13:7–9, 12, 16)

Love spurned called for judgment. Deliberate breaking away from the covenant vows made retribution inevitable. In stern language he speaks: "They shall reap the whirlwind." "For thee a harvest is prepared." Judgment is certain, automatic, determined. God's full recompense is inescapable. The character of God makes it impossible for Him to let Israel's sin go unpunished. The dark picture of judgment is painted against the glowing picture of the Lord's pure love for His own chosen ones. He loves. He must bring judgment. "O Israel, thou hast destroyed thyself." Because of her unprecedented unfaithfulness, Israel's punishment is to be exceedingly severe. Sin against love is the worst of all. A holy God brings, through His dedicated prophet, the sure word of doom. Sin must receive its punishment. The full penalty must be borne.

3. Lack of Knowledge (2:8; 4:1, 6, 11; 5:4; 6:6; 11:3)

Israel had been chosen, called, and commissioned to be a powerful missionary to the nations. What a challenging opportunity! What a wonderful privilege! What a terrific responsibility! How pitifully Israel had failed! Instead of being a teacher of truth, she had become so utterly ignorant that she was only fit to be despised. She was stupid, brainless, insensible, untaught, unable to teach others about the Lord. She did not know Him. He was an utter stranger to her. How could she minister to others? How could she witness of the love and grace and mercy of God? Israel did not know Him any more than Gomer knew Hosea. He had chosen Israel, led her, taught her, loved her. She did not know Him. She had no understanding of Him and His love and grace. Because of this ignorance of God, communion with Him was impossible. The priests who had been anointed to teach the people and to unveil the character and love of God had failed miserably in their sacred task.

Hosea cries out: "My people perish for lack of knowledge" (4:6). "They knew not that it was I who healed them" (11:3). "There is no truth, nor love, nor knowledge of God in the land" (4:1). How pathetic! The pain of being misunderstood was one that had torn the heart of Hosea. He declares that God's heart writhes under the sting of that same truth. Lack of knowledge lies at the heart of the rebellion, the infidelity, the spiritual adultery that was evident on every hand. The Lord's love was rejected. His purpose neglected, His patience mistaken, His mercy unappreciated, because of the stupid ignorance of the very people who were God's chosen missionary. It would be difficult today to estimate the terrible drain that ignorance of God makes on the program set up to witness to His wondrous love and grace. When we know Him, we love Him. When we know and love Him, we gladly witness to His saving grace in our hearts.

4. The Love of God (2:14, 19, 20; 6:4-6; 9:10; 11:1, 3, 8; 14:4)

Not until we get to John 3:16 do we find anything comparable to Hosea's tremendous pictures of the marvelous love of God for His people. The prophet has been a walking sermon on love. Leander who swam the Hellespont, Romeo and Juliet, Robert Browning and Elizabeth Barrett—all give us beautiful pictures of love for the chosen lover, but not one of these famous lovers can stand by the side of the majestic Hosea who loved the sinful, adulterous, unfaithful woman even when she had become so foul and unattractive that the men of the market place could see no good thing in her. It was Hosea who brought the full price of a slave and paid the ransom demanded by the slave owner to buy back the one who had been so exceedingly sinful. He did all this because he loved her with a love that was stronger than anything else in the world. She did not deserve such treatment. She had sinned away every right to his love. She was not fit for his home and his heart and his love, but his love was so strong, so pure, and so unselfish that he was drawn on to the deed that culminated in her full ransom. That was the love that shone through all his sermons and now shines on through his deathless messages in his book for us.

In this book we are constantly brought face to face with the matchless love of God. It is the distinctive, the dominant note. "I will love them freely" (14:4) is God's triumphant word concerning His sinful people who are on the verge of turning back to the divine Lover in sincere repentance. That love is true, deep, tender, forgiving, unchangeable, eternal. It has survived all the tragic experiences, the sinful unfaithfulness, the disloyalty, the callous indifference of the bitter years. It has been resisted, outraged, wounded, grieved, disappointed. God's ever recurring refrain has in it such words as: "I will betroth . . ." (2:19), "I will heal . . . I will love them freely . . ." (14:4). His love never lets go, never loses heart, never grows cold. It always moves forward, singing the glad song of victory. It is strangely hopeful. It is strongly certain of itself. It is truly forgiving, even to the uttermost. It reaches out loving arms into the depths of sin and shame and depravity and degradation. It goes on out for the sinners to the brink of utter destruction where their wilfulness has dragged them. Even though their sin is against the pure love of the Redeemer, it cannot blunt nor destroy nor cool the strange ardor of the divine love.

Our Lord's picture of the father in the story of the prodigal son (Lk. 15) seems to find a sweet harmonious note in this old book of the Old Testament. In a measure, Hosea was allowed to enter the holy of holies of divine mysteries and fathom some of the matchless secrets revealed in Jesus' parable concerning the father of the prodigal. It is amazing to find the old prophet in possession of so many of the richer hues in that immortal picture of the Father. He sensed the Father's hatred of sin and His undying love for the sinner. Such a love would find a way to redeem and save the slave of sin.

5. *Genuine Repentance* (5:15; 6:1; 10:12; 11:9; 12:6; 14:1, 2)

Hosea is beautifully prepared to emphasize the necessity for a literal turning back to God. For years his lonely heart had cried out to Gomer, begging her to come back home to the true lover who had a right to her love and who yearned for her return. Love still called to her. In this deeper and larger realm the prophet made his unceasing appeal to God's wandering people. "O Israel, return unto the Lord, thy God" (14:1) was his text. We must remember that Hosea is essentially an evangelist. It is his way of preaching. His call is personal. He pleads. He seeks always to persuade. He begs for decisive action. The appeal takes into account the miserable state, the helpless condition, the wasted years, the sin-ruined hearts, the inadequacy of ritual, the amazing love of the heavenly Lover, the only way home, the divine forgiveness, and the full salvation to be available for a repentant soul.

The word *shuv* ("turn," "return") is at the heart of repentance. It has in it the essential elements of the New Testament word *metanoia*. The deepest thing fallen men can offer God is not character nor holiness nor goodness, but contrition. Joel has said: ". . . rend your heart and not your garments" (Joel 2:13). Jesus made repentance and faith the keynote of His preaching. The Hebrew word and the Greek word carry much more than the idea of Godly sorrow and even more than "change of mind." They involve the whole orientation of the heart and will and affection until the individual is a new creature.

The pleading evangelist reminded the people that their ugly sins cried out for repentance and confession. How could they continue in sin? "You have plowed wickedness. You have reaped iniquity" (10:13). The very character of God made a strong demand for repentance. Hosea seemed always to say: "If you only knew Him— His character, His heart, His love—you would come back to Him." The very fact that the divine love was so pure, so intense, so powerful, made it obligatory that sinners come home to God. He loves them. He wants them. They belong to Him. The welcome will be hearty. The forgiveness will be complete. Hosea reminds the people that repentance involves a consciousness of personal sin, a sense of the call of God and a full-hearted turning to Him in confession and commitment.

"Break up your fallow ground. It is time to seek the Lord" (10:12). What a challenge! Israel is the unfaithful wife; Israel, the prodigal. Hosea presents the basic lines in the picture made eternally famous by our Lord in Luke 15. The prodigal came home to the loving father who yearned and waited and loved and welcomed the sinning boy to his arms and to his home. Throughout this prophecy, Hosea seeks to make sinful Israel say: "I will arise and go to my father" (Lk. 15:18). That, at least, was the verdict so diligently sought in his fervent preaching.

6. The Sure Salvation (2:14, 19, 20, 23; 3:2; 6:1, 2; 11:8, 9; 14:4)

The name Hosea means "salvation." Each time that name is spoken, assurance is given. In his most thrilling deliverance, the prophet represents God as saying: "I will heal . . . I will love them freely" (14:4). The grace of God is to have its way in making victory possible. God is in love with His bride. Sin has brought ruin and misery and tragedy and judgment. The divine Lover will not be turned aside. He will seek and find and woo her and bring her back to His heart and to His home. The full ransom price will be paid. Atonement will provide new creatures with new loyalties, new natures, and a new life. The God of grace promises to restore. He is the great refresher and beautifier of life. He provides full healing. It is the triumph of love in grace. New hope, new joy, new life, and a restoration to her former place as God's missionary to the peoples of the earth, are all guaranteed. Our Lord came in the fulness of time to make atonement on Calvary's hill and to give full demonstration of God's love in action. It was through His atoning death that salvation came.

7. *Full Forgiveness (2:14, 19, 20; 3:2, 3)*

What is more precious than divine forgiveness? It is man's greatest need and heaven's greatest gift. Hosea learned from God the secret of forgiveness. He was taught the secret by seeing God forgive and redeem the people. Right before his eyes the prophet caught sight of the grace of God bringing to men the treasure that we speak of as forgiveness. He sensed the sacredness of that divine gift, full and free and flowing, eternal in its effectiveness. Infinite love pulls and hopes and constrains until unfaithful sinners come home.

8. *A Final Word*

Let us remember that we are the bride of Christ and we ought to be devoted to Him alone. Our bodies, our minds, our hearts, our purest love, are all His. His love calls strongly to us to come back to Him with genuine love and undying devotion. How can we be unclean or disloyal or untrue to Him? May we never forget His deathless love for us and His purpose to bring all men back to His great heart.

Joel

JOHN B. GRAYBILL

JOEL THE PROPHET lived in days like our own. Calamity had struck the Hebrew nation. One senses fright and despair in the description of the locust plague that swept the land and which, unless quickly removed, would jeopardize the nation's survival.

Locust plagues are a frequent threat in the Middle East. Swarms come quickly, darkening the sun; every green thing is devoured, until the trees stand, white and bare, stripped even of their bark. One swarm is estimated to have numbered 24,420 billions of locusts! *The National Geographic Magazine* (Volume XXVIII) December, 1915, contains the description of a severe locust plague which occurred in Jerusalem in 1915.

I. The Locust Plague and its Removal (1:1—2:27)

It seems evident that a devastation by locusts and not an attack by hostile human armies is here described. The prophet actually uses figurative speech to describe the locusts. They are called a "powerful people" (2:2), an "army" (v. 5), "warriors" and "soldiers" (v. 7);

even horses and chariots are mentioned (vv. 4, 5). But always "like" or "as" gives the key to these references. The locusts are *as* terrifying as a war horse and *like* a devastating human army, which lives off the land. Such figurative language is common in the Old Testament.

1. The Plague of Locusts (1:1–20)

Joel opens his book by asserting that he speaks the word of the Lord (1:1). He has been sent by God to interpret to the people the meaning of the devastation he describes. So complete is its destruction that even old men, prone to exaggerate memories of remote experiences, cannot find a parallel to it. Four kinds of locusts are mentioned (v. 4). It is difficult to identify these with species now known. Some believe that four stages of locust life are here meant; others, that successive waves of the locust invasion are described.

Even the grain and drink offerings which would be the first part of each harvest, brought to the temple as a sacrifice, are lost. Thus the priests are left hungry (1:9). As leaders of the people they are implored to call a solemn fast (vv. 13, 14).

This calamity is called "the day of the Lord" (1:15). Some commentators regard this term, whenever it occurs in the Bible, as eschatological—describing the future troubles which are to usher in the messianic day, or referring to that great day itself. There is no doubt that the phrase usually carries this reference. But there is no reason why it always must. Context determines meaning, and it seems clear here that Joel refers to the locust visitation as a Day of the Lord and (a parallel expression) as destruction from the Almighty.

The mention of fire and flame (1:19) and of waterworks dried up (v. 20), probably means that, as often is the case, the visitation of the locusts was accompanied by severe drought. "Pastures of the wilderness" (vv. 19, 20) are the great stretches of unfenced and uncultivated grazing land where the Bedouin or tent dwellers roam. Even these remote areas are stripped. Not only the prophet, but even the wild animals cry to God (2:20) in their extremity—a vivid use of personification (cf. Jer. 14:5, 6).

2. The People Urged to Repent (2:1–17)

The idea of a day of national repentance has already been suggested (1:13, 14). Now it is further developed, with additional mention of the calamity which makes it necessary. Again this destruction is called the Day of the Lord (2:1), that is, a day of God's judgment upon the people for their sin, a "day of visitation" (Is. 10:3). That God is the commander of this army (2:11) is the prophet's interpretation of the terrible event. Yet there may be more in this mention of the Day of the Lord than the divinely inspired commentary on the judgment of the locust plague. Possibly Joel is seeking to say that this visitation is but a foretaste or type of the future Day of the Lord, of which he clearly speaks in chapter 3.

The language here, though vivid, is not exaggerated. Those who have observed such an attack of locusts say that the clouds, darkness, and gloom of verse 2 are literally true. The onward march of the destroying insects is vividly described; it proceeds as an army of men (2:4–9). Even earthquake and darkness (v. 10) are terms used to describe such a plague by men who have experienced one (cf. *The National Geographic Magazine* referred to above). The verbs throughout this section (vv. 1–11) are properly rendered in the present tense (RSV) for the prophet is describing an event which takes place in his own time.

Yet there may still be hope—if only the people will now repent in sincerity, (2:12, 13). The ancients had an involved ceremony for mourning which easily degenerated into hypocrisy. Jesus often criticized it (Mk. 5:38–40). Rent *hearts,* not garments, will stop the calamity. Joel knows God's merciful nature. The word translated "merciful" (v. 13) comes from a Hebrew root meaning "womb" and denotes God's compassion for His own offspring. "Kindness" (v. 13) is well translated by the Revised Standard Version as "steadfast love"—God's faithfulness to His covenant promises, motivated by love. God is repenting; that is, He is ready to change His attitude and action toward His people when they repent. The use of the word "repent" does not imply fickleness on the part of the Almighty. God is not a man that He should repent—He does not blow hot and cold—yet He does *relent* when His people turn to Him, and this action of relenting is called repentance.

The people—all of them—should turn to God. The old and young, even the newly wed (2:16) who were normally exempt from many duties (Deut. 20:7; Lk. 14:20) must assemble and, led by the priests, pray for God's forgiveness and sparing. They shall appeal to God to defend the honor of His good name (2:17). Then Israel will not come to be "a byword among the nations" (2:17, RSV; not "that the heathen should rule over them," KJV), nor will God's name be disgraced.

3. God Pities and Promises Relief (2:18–27)

Evidently the people responded to Joel's message, for this section is full of comfort as the renewal of nature is promised. "I will restore unto you the years that the locust hath eaten" (2:25) can well be called a summary of the prophet's message to the pious of his own day. In this section, it is very important to observe the tenses of the verbs in the Revised Standard Version; they are translated more accurately than in the King James Version.

Verse 18 is narration, not prediction. God "became jealous for his land and had pity on his people," and promised immediate relief. Jealousy to the Hebrew mind was almost synonymous with love (Song 8:6). His jealousy prompted Him to promise relief. The locusts will be removed, driven into the Dead Sea and the Mediterranean (2:20) as the locusts of the Egyptian plagues were driven by a wind into the Red Sea (Ex. 10:19). Jerome and other ancients testify to such a dispersion of a Palestinian locust plague in their days.

The use of the term "northerner"—accurately translated by the Revised Standard Version (2:20)—for this army has caused some discussion. Locust plagues do not ordinarily come from the north; rather, they originate in the Arabian Desert to the south and east of Palestine. However, invasions from the north are not unknown, the latest having occurred in 1915. Scholars agree that the references to the eastern and western seas are literal, so that it seems best to understand "northerner" not as referring to some end-time foe from the north, but rather to the locusts which came in Joel's time from that direction.

God then promises to restore prosperity to the land (2:19, 22–27). The early and the latter rains are to be restored (v. 23). In Palestine the early rains come in October and November, breaking the long summer drought. Then the farmer plows the land and sows the seed. The latter rains, which occur in March and April, are much desired, for they guarantee a rich harvest. The early rain will come "moderately" (KJV) or "for your vindication" (2:23, RSV). The Hebrew text thus translated is both interesting and difficult. Literally it says, "For he has given you the early rain for righteousness." The ancient Jews and early Christians understood the word translated "early rain" ("former rain," KJV) to mean "teacher," and so saw in the expression "teacher of righteousness" a reference to Messiah. Modern commentators reject this interpretation as forced and are about equally divided between the rendering of the King James Version—that the rains will come down "moderately," that is, not so fast that they will run off and do no good, and the Revised Standard Version interpretation—that the rains will come "for your vindication," that is, to vindicate God's people before the heathen (2:17, 19). In Isaiah 40–66 the word "righteousness" is used in the sense of "vindication" or "salvation" (for example, Is. 45:8).

With the return of the rains will come good crops and the prosperity they bring to an agricultural community. "Grain, wine, and oil" (2:19, 24) are the necessities of the good mentioned in the famous ancient statement in Psalm 104:15. And the great goal of all prophetic preaching will be attained when the people know "that I am the Lord" (2:27; Jer. 24:7; Hos. 2:20).

The Future Day of the Lord (2:28—3:21)

The Old Testament prophet characteristically brought two messages, one for his own day and the other for the remote future. To his contemporaries, he declared God's judgment in the events of the present day, but he did not stop there. Sooner or later his thought was projected ahead to the messianic age. True, neither the prophet nor his hearers were able to distinguish clearly between these two messages, but to the Christian living in this gospel age, the distinction is a valid and necessary one. Having interpreted the locust plague to his contemporaries, Joel is now enabled under the guidance of the Holy Spirit to look ahead and predict the judgment of the great and last Day of the Lord (of which the locusts were a preview) and other events of the messianic age.

The rest of the Book of Joel (2:28—3:21) develops this theme. After an announcement of the outpouring of God's Spirit, the two principal subjects of prophetic preaching concerning the last days are presented: (1) a time of great trouble, climaxed by a battle of the nations, in which God will destroy world powers and vindicate Israel; (2) the messianic age of peace and prosperity which follows.

This pattern of thought is frequently found in the prophets: for example, Isaiah 24–27, Jeremiah 30, Ezekiel 38, 39, and Zechariah 12–14. This apocalyptic message is taken up in the New Testament

Apocalypse, for much of the Revelation is concerned with these topics, and the Revelation builds upon the foundation already laid by the Old Testament prophets. The great climax of the time of trouble is described in Revelation 19, where a rider on a white horse comes to vanquish the rebellious nations and reign. Just as opinions have differed as to the meaning of the visions in the Revelation, so there has been no unanimity about the meaning of the oracles of Joel and the other prophets.

Some expositors believe these visions figuratively predict Christ's conquest of the forces of evil in His atoning death, resurrection and the building of His Church on earth. Others look for a more literal fulfilment of these prophecies at the end of time. Among the latter group there are many differences in detail. Possibly elements of both views are right, and no one yet fully understands the magnitude of the victory over evil for which the whole creation waits (Rom. 8:18–25).

1. *The Spirit of the Lord to be Poured Out (2:28–32)*

These verses constitute chapter 3 in the Hebrew Bible, while our chapter 3 is considered chapter 4 by the Jews. The Hebrew division points up the great change of theme at 2:28 more forcefully than does the arrangement in the Christian Bible.

"After these things" other events will take place. After *what* things? The prophet seems to mean that just as the plague and drought were signs of God's displeasure with His people, and as the restoration of the fertility of the land indicated His renewed favor, so there will take place an even greater indication that God is pleased with men (cf. Lk. 2:14, RSV): He will pour out His Spirit upon them (2:28). The effects here ascribed to the effusion of God's Spirit are amazing and terrifying beyond those of the locusts' descent. Peter rightly sees in the Pentecostal experience a fulfilment of these words (Acts 2:16–21). In a way the fulfilment in the book of Acts exceeds what the prophecy promised. Joel foresees the Spirit poured out on all classes of Hebrews, but beginning with the conversion of Cornelius (Acts 10), it became evident that participation in the New Covenant was an experience into which all men might enter.

Yet the thoughtful student of Joel is moved to ask whether Joel's whole prophecy has been fulfilled with the inauguration of the new dispensation. Were the wonders in the heavens mentioned in 2:31

seen at Pentecost? What of the events predicted in Joel 3? Perhaps the Apostle John gives the key when he writes, "Children, it is the last hour; and as you have heard that antichrist is coming, so now many antichrists have come; therefore we know that it is the last hour" (I Jn. 2:18, RSV). That is to say, Christ at His first coming brought His Kingdom to earth; the last days are here. But the last days have not completely come; there are now many Antichrists, but Antichrist is still to come. Men still await the consummation of all things (Acts 3:21). It is the belief of many that some of Joel's predictions await fulfilment in the events connected with the Second Coming.

Joel says that God's Spirit will be given to "all flesh" (2:28). The context indicates that by this he meant all kinds of people—young and old, slave and free, of the Hebrew race. The rest of men—the Gentiles—will be destroyed (3:2, 4, 8, 11, 12, 17, 19). But Mount Zion and Jerusalem shall have some escapees (2:32). It was not every Old Testament prophet who was given to see what Isaiah saw, that "Gentiles shall come to thy light, and kings to the brightness of thy rising" (Is. 60:3).

The Holy Spirit came upon men during Old Testament times to enable them to serve God acceptably (Judg. 6:34; I Sam. 16: 13, 14). Certainly He was in the world and dwelling in the saints then also, although they sometimes had little consciousness of this fact. But in a special way, the new age was to be one of the Spirit (Is. 32:15; Zech. 12:10; Jn. 7:39). All of God's people would now be priests and prophets, for the idea, stated when the law was given but never achieved, would now become actual (Ex. 19:5, 6; I Pet. 2:9, 10). The verb "pour" indicates the abundance of this spiritual gift. Thus Joel's prophecy is fulfilled not only on the day of Pentecost, but throughout the new age that day inaugurated (Acts 2:39).

This pouring out of the Spirit is connected with apocalyptic portents of terrifying nature (2:30, 31), and then shall follow the Day of the Lord. But from the judgments which will accompany this final day (3:2, 4, 12, 16) those who call upon God will be delivered (2:32). Not all of the Hebrews, but only those who call upon God's name shall be "those that escape" (RSV), also called the "remnant" (KJV) or "survivors." This should be compared with Paul's doctrine of the remnant (Rom. 11).

Concerning the fulfilment of this prophecy of terrifying portents, opinions differ. Some refer it to the unusual signs seen at the crucifixion (Mt. 27:51–53); others to the events connected with the destruction of Jerusalem in A.D. 70, and still others to the times of the Tribulation believed by many to precede the Second Coming. The second and third groups both appeal to the Olivet discourse (Mt. 24, Lk. 21) in support of their views.

2. *The Judgment of the Nations (3:1–17)*

The Hebrew prophets preached in a day when the people of God were a small minority in a hostile world, their independence constantly threatened by their more powerful neighbors. A part of the prophetic message was the proclamation that those pagan neighbors would in time engulf and destroy the Hebrews. Still there was hope, for in the last days Israel would be restored and blessed, and the Gentiles punished (Is. 10:5—11:16; Amos 9:11, 12). Joel here expresses this expectation. The events of chapter 3 fit into the framework stated in 2:30–32. These judgments on the nations will prepare the way for the deliverance of Jerusalem and God's dwelling there.

At this time God will gather the nations to the valley of Jehoshaphat and there judge them (3:2). Whether a definite place is meant by "valley of Jehoshaphat" is not known. The tradition that this is the Kidron valley, east of Jerusalem, has no real basis. The language of Zechariah 14:4–11, often referred to in this connection, is extremely figurative and of doubtful connection with Joel's prophecy. We know of no valley called by the name of Jehoshaphat. Joel probably chose this designation, which means "The Lord has judged," as symbolic of the event. "The valley of decision" (3:14), a synonymous expression, lends support to this idea. The nations will be judged because they have persecuted and scattered Israel. Captives of war were often sold as slaves, and healthy children commanded good prices (3:3). The Phoenician cities of Tyre and Sidon, great trading centers of the Old Testament world, are especially singled out for condemnation, as are also the ancient enemies of Israel, the Philistines (the "coasts of Palestine," 3:4, KJV). Our word "Palestine" is derived from the name "Philistine."

It is said that the nations have sold the people of Judah and Jerusalem to the Greeks (3:6). The Hebrew expression is "sons of Yavan" (spelled "Javan" in the English Bible), our Ionians. Some have contended that a mention of the Greeks is unlikely in a pre-Exilic book, and thus Joel must be writing in a later period but this argument is not convincing. *Yavan* occurs elsewhere in pre-Exilic books and in other ancient Semitic languages of pre-Exilic times. Our knowledge of the Greeks is being pushed back by recent discoveries, making it increasingly unlikely that the Hebrews in the eighth century B.C. could have been ignorant of the sons of *Yavan,* or that Hebrew slaves could not have been sold to them. Ezekiel (27:13) mentions Phoenicians trading with *Yavan.*

Under God's judgment, the children of the Phoenicians and Philistines will themselves be sold (3:8). This prediction was fulfilled when the Sidonians were sold into slavery by Artaxerxes III in 345 B.C.; and the Tyrians and people of Gaza in Philistia, by Alexander the Great in 332 B.C. The Sabeans were a famous trading people (I Kings 10:1, 2; Ezek. 27:22, 23) from Sheba in southern Arabia. No doubt Jews were among the buyers of these slaves from the seascoast of Palestine, some of whom were finally resold to the Sabeans.

After this prose statement of God's judgment upon the nations follows a poetical version of the same theme (3:9–17). In figurative language the nations are called together for war and judgment. Synonymous parallelism predominates, the second line of the pair repeating (in different words) what the first line has stated. Exactly what it is (beside God's command) which causes these nations to gather, we are not told. Mobilization for war is clearly described; plowshares into swords, pruning hooks into spears (v. 10; Is. 2:4; Mic. 4:3). But this battle will take a strange turn. God's mighty ones—the heavenly armies—will come down to fight (v.11, cf. Rev. 19:14), and God will sit to judge the nations as when one puts the sickle to the ripe grain (Is. 17:5; Mt. 13:39), or treads the grapes in the wine press (v. 13; Is. 63:1–6; Rev. 14:14–20). The battleground will become a valley of decision; God will decide against (or judge, v. 2) the Gentiles. The terrifying character of that day is emphasized when the sun and the moon are darkened (v. 15), God roars like a lion (Amos 1:2; Jer. 25:30), and the universe shakes (v. 16). This is the great Day of the Lord, of which the locust plague was but a faint forecast.

Yet the same God Who is the terror of the heathen is the hope of His people. They will be defended—had the nations come down to fight against them?—and delivered (3:16). All Israel will know certainly that God is dwelling with His people in Jerusalem, which will be forever cleansed from the ceremonial defilement of the Gentiles.

3. *Blessing upon Israel after the Judgment (3:18-21)*

Joel concludes his oracle with a vision of the exaltation and prosperity of the Hebrew people. The land will become extremely fertile: sweet wine, milk and water will be abundant. From the very temple shall come a stream watering the dryest, most desolate parts of Palestine (3:18). The "stream beds" (ASV; "rivers," KJV) of Judah are the *wadis*, which are dry river beds most of the year. Now they shall be perennially full. The "valley of Shittim" or acacia trees (for that is what the Hebrew word *shittim* means) shall be watered by a stream flowing from the temple itself. This valley is probably the Wadi en-Nar, the name given to the Kidron valley as it extends through the Judean desert to the Dead Sea. Lower parts of this valley are full of acacia trees. The picture of a stream from the temple probably derives from the spring Gihon, which was situated under the hill of the temple, the water of which was used to irrigate the Kidron valley for a short distance.

Ezekiel's vision of the healing waters from the temple is strikingly similar (47:1-12). The water will transform those barren wastes, so that "the desert shall rejoice and blossom as the rose" (Is. 35:1). These visions form the background for John's "river of the water of life" which makes glad the new Jerusalem (Rev. 22:1, 2).

But in contrast to Judah's fertility, Egypt and Edom, her ancient persecutors, the shedders of innocent blood shall be desolate (3:19; Ezek. 29, 35), while Jerusalem shall be the eternal city of God.

Authorities differ in their interpretation of Joel's last verse. The King James Version represents one school of thought: "I will cleanse their blood guiltiness." According to this view, the wondrous age just described will be founded upon a new disposition of the hearts of God's people. Their blood-guiltiness will be cleansed, a new covenant made with them, and God's law written upon their hearts (Jer. 31:31-34).

The other interpretation of this verse is expressed by the Revised Standard Version: "I will avenge their blood, and will not clear the guilty." According to this, the prophet maintains that the innocent blood of Judeans (3:19) will be avenged by God and those guilty of these violent crimes will not go unpunished. Neither of these interpretations is without difficulty, for the Hebrew text is not clear, but the King James Version provides the more fitting conclusion to the book.

Joel's final sight of glorified Zion fully accounts for the amazing scene of verses 18–21: "for the Lord dwells in Zion." In Old Testament times, God manifested His presence in Jerusalem by the cloudy and fiery pillar over the temple. Ezekiel saw this manifestation, called by the Hebrews *Shekinah* ("dwelling token"), depart from the city before it fell (Ezek. 11:22–24). But he saw it return to glorified Zion (Ezek. 43:1–5) and ends his vision with the statement that the new city shall be called *Jahweh Shammah*—"the Lord is there" (Ezek. 48:35). So too John sees that in the new Jerusalem "God himself shall be with them, and be their God" (Rev. 21:3). Thus the great purpose of the incarnation is finally fulfilled; Paradise is regained, and again God walks with His people as He did in Eden.

Amos

ARNOLD C. SCHULTZ

THE TONE of Amos' message is set by the great proclamation at the beginning of his prophecy. From Zion the Lord's voice, like the roar of a lion, will be heard in judgment.

I. Prophecies Against the Nations (1:1—2:16)

1. Superscription and Proclamation (1:1, 2)

The superscription and the proclamation are in some ways closely related. The reference to Jeroboam II points up the fact that Amos labored in one of the most difficult times of the prophetic period. The statement, "two years before the earthquake," indicates more precisely the time of his ministry because it refers to an earthquake which, it appears, was accompanied by a total eclipse (5:8; Zech. 14:5, 6). Such a phenomenon took place in 763 B.C. It would appear, then, that approximately 760 B.C., or the last half of Jeroboam's reign, when the evil forces set in motion by the king were bearing their rotten fruit, is the time of Amos' great career. He is, consequently, one of the earliest of the writing prophets. While this period marked the most brilliant age of the northern kingdom, it was also the most corrupt. The superscription (1:1) thus provides the reason for the proclamation (v. 2), which is an announcement of judgment. The proclamation provides the text, or the essence, of the message of the prophecy. God will come to punish sin.

2. Indictment of Neighboring Nations (1:3—2:3)

While Amos was commissioned to minister specifically to Israel, his preaching was not limited to the northern kingdom. The first part of his book—an indictment of the neighboring nations—indicates the breadth of his vision. God deals with sin wherever it is found and by whomever it is committed. To indict the foreign nations in the beginning of his prophecy enabled Amos, no doubt, to gain the attention and good will of his immediate audience. More significantly, Amos' message declares the universal sovereignty of God. The Lord is the supreme ruler of the universe, and inseparably connected with this doctrine is the idea of the moral responsibility of all people. Nation after nation—Damascus, Philistia, Tyre, Edom, Ammon, Moab—is summoned by the Lord to judgment, in each instance with the striking expression, "For three transgressions . . . and for four I will not turn back the judgment" (1:3, 6, 9, 11, 13; 2:1). The prophet is saying that transgression after transgression, without limitation, has made punishment necessary. Repetition of the same expression gives terrible emphasis to the prophet's words.

The root meaning of the Hebrew word *transgression* is *rebellion* against authority; in the case of the nations, against the sovereignty of God. The Lord has the moral right and the power to bring them to justice. The basic sin of which nations are guilty is their inhumanity, their violation of those natural laws which are written in the heart and conscience of men everywhere. The seriousness of their transgression consists in rebellion against the God-given knowledge of the right which they possessed, not necessarily that they had violated Israel.

Damascus is condemned for her barbarous treatment of prostrate Gilead (1:3); Philistia, for giving herself in utter abandon to the slave traffic (v. 6); Tyre, not only for her slave traffic but for turning her back upon a covenant held sacred (v. 9); Edom, for his unbridled hatred of his own brother (v. 11); Ammon, for savage brutality against Gilead (v. 13); Moab, for inhuman violation of natural respect for the dead (2:1). These peoples had ignored their moral responsibility to God.

3. Indictment of Judah and Israel (2:4–16)

The prophet now turns his attention to Judah and Israel. If the neighboring nations cannot escape judgment, much less shall the chosen people, for they have enjoyed a position of privilege. The Judeans shall be brought to judgment for rejecting the revelation that God had entrusted to them (2:4) and for their idolatry. The words, "their lies" (v. 4), refer to their idols, the Baalim and Ashtaroth, who had no real existence and therefore were actually deceiving them. Israel is condemned, too, for her forgetfulness of the Lord, which has been demonstrated in constant debauchery. The sins of Israel are set against the historical background of God's special care and concern for His people (vv. 9–12).

II. Three Discourses Against Israel (3:1—6:14)

Amos was sent especially to Israel and he now unleashes upon these chosen people the full fury of his moral indignation. His attack takes the form of three addresses which develop the idea of the text of his prophecy (1:2). Each address begins with the formula, "Hear this word" (3:1; 4:1; 5:1).

1. A Declaration of Judgment (3:1–15)

The first of these addresses emphasizes the necessity of judgment. The election of Israel, far from protecting Israel from punishment, made judgment inevitable (3:1, 2), since the greater the privilege is, the greater the responsibility. By a series of questions the prophet illustrates the law of cause and effect to show that he has come up to Bethel by the command of the Lord to warn Israel of danger (vv. 3–8). When God speaks, the prophet must prophesy. Even heathen Egypt and Philistia (v. 9) will be astonished at the destruction of the luxurious living in the palaces of Samaria which unrighteous accumulation of wealth had made possible.

2. *The Depravity of Israel (4:1–13)*

Amos proceeds in his second address to describe Israel's utter depravity. The society women of Samaria, well-fed, pampered creatures, are compared to cows grown fat and ferocious through feeding in the rich pastures of Bashan (4:1). Amos in this strikingly appropriate figure (Deut. 32:14; Ps. 22:12; Ezek. 39:18) charges the women with contributing to the decay of Israel. They make demands upon their husbands to satisfy their continual craving for pleasure, and consequently are a party to the brutal oppression of the poor. When judgment falls, the women like stampeding cattle will run for the breaches in the walls of the city in an attempt to escape (v. 3).

The prophet now turns his attention to the multiplied and corrupted religious rituals attended by the Israelites at such famous shrines as Bethel and Gilgal. Ironically, since to go to Bethel was synonymous with transgression, Amos invites the Israelites to multiply their pilgrimages to their altars (4:4). These journeys to the shrines not only failed to win the favor of God, but the more enthusiastically they were observed, the farther the people were separated from Him. This was because such ritualism was a substitute for godly living. This principle is as true today as it was in Amos' time. Wherever and whenever mere form and ceremony are permitted to replace moral obedience and true fellowship with God, our worship will be rejected and our altars will fall as did the ancient high places.

The ceremonial sins of Israel were merely an evidence of a more serious problem. The prophet goes to the root of the matter as he analyzes the condition of the people's will and heart and their attitude toward the Lord. Again and again the Lord says, "You did not return to me" (4:6, 8–11, RSV). Worship, offered by hands stained with sin, coming from hearts completely indifferent to the Lord's expectations, was unacceptable. Amos did not substitute morality for religion; rather, he was saying that righteousness in relation to one's fellow men is evidence of a right relation to God.

3. A Lamentation for Israel's Sin and Doom (5:1—6:14)

As the prophet begins his third address, he sings a dirge (5:2, RSV) over the nation as though it were already dead:

> Fallen, no more to rise,
>   is the virgin Israel;
> forsaken on her land,
>   with none to raise her up.

Toward the close of this address, Amos shows how completely the Israelites have given themselves over to sensual gratification, confident that no judgment could reach them. In spite of their moral depravity and failure to recognize the Lord's moral character, they believed themselves assured of a claim to His favor. The requirements of the Lord were few: "Seek good and not evil . . . Hate evil, and love good, and establish justice in the gate. . . . let judgment roll down like waters, and righteousness like an ever-flowing stream" (vv. 14, 15, 24, RSV). Simple though the requirements were, they were high in that they necessitated the uprooting of the deeply rooted selfishness of the human heart. To comply with God's demands would mean a revolution in their way of life.

III. Five Symbolical Visions of Israel's Condition (7:1—9:10)

The third part of the prophecy of Amos contains five symbolical visions of Israel's condition. They were perhaps delivered in Bethel. Even though it is quite impossible to determine how the visions came to the prophet, whether in an experience of ecstasy or in a dream, they are real visions. In his account, Amos clearly distinguishes between the visions and the historical experiences of his encounter with Amaziah, the priest of Bethel (7:10–17). The imagery of the visions is drawn from the rural life of his home.

1. Devouring Locusts (7:1–3)

The first vision is that of the plague of devouring locusts. Amos had already referred to the Lord's use of locusts in an act of mercy, to bring Israel to see her sin (4:9). Now the prophet again refers to locusts, pointing out that they are being used by God to punish Israel for her rebellion against Him. But the prophet's prayer for mercy identifies him with his people, and God's mercy is made clear in the withdrawal of the locusts before they had completely destroyed the vegetation of the land.

2. Flaming Fire (7:4–6)

The second vision, a flaming fire, shows God in open controversy with His people. What Amos saw was a severe drought, which in Palestine might well be described as flaming fire. The prophet saw and felt the heat of the sun as a consuming conflagration. It seemed to him that under the blazing heat of the sun even the "great deep," the source of the life-giving waters of spring and rain, had been consumed. The land seemed on the verge of destruction as vegetation withered. But again Amos pleads for his people, and ultimate destruction is averted.

The first and second visions parallel the chastenings enumerated earlier (4:6–11). They are given as typical of all the attempts which God had made to bring Israel to repentance. The vision of the flaming fire was perhaps designed to present a more terrifying judgment than that of the plague of locusts. These first two visions reveal an insight into the meaning of the actual plagues with which the people were familiar. The prophet habitually dealt with real facts, and his prophecy had already indicated that by plagues God had sought to awaken the people.

Amos' analysis of Israel's condition was thoroughly objective. He had been a shepherd in the semi-wilderness of Judah, but he was familiar with the great cities of the country and their famous sanctuaries. He knew Samaria and Bethel, and because of his background, he could view them with the objective detachment of an outsider. But a real prophet is not made only by his objective analysis of a particular situation and the application of the objective word of God to that situation. A true prophet is one who has agonized with his people in the condemnation he proclaims and in the prayers he has offered. There has never been a prophet who was not first a man of prayer. The prayers of Amos, "O Lord God, forgive, I beseech thee!" (7:2, 4), are a true index of his character and gave him the moral right to pronounce the message of God.

3. *The Plumb Line (7:7–9)*

In the third vision, God holds in His hand a plumb line to measure Israel. The first two visions are based upon catastrophes in the world of nature. The third vision is based upon Israel's national life. With the plumb line, the Lord proves to the prophet the intolerable deviations of Israel from God's righteous requirements. Amos is made to understand that Israel has been found wanting and that judgment is now inevitable. The words, "I will never again pass by them" (7:8, RSV), are spoken with such terrible finality that the prophet realizes the utter hopelessness of continued intercession. But because the Lord has spoken, Amos must prophesy (cf. 3:8). He bows silently before the inevitability of God's judgment, and the vision closes without a prayer.

4. *A Priest's Interruption (7:10–17)*

When Amos proclaims the message of the Lord, "I will rise against the house of Jeroboam with the sword" (7:9), his preaching is interrupted by the sycophant priest, Amaziah, who has sold himself to the king (v. 12). This is the crisis toward which the prophet has been moving. The report that the priest gave to Jeroboam, king of Israel, was, of course, exaggerated; Amos had not actually said that the king himself should be killed. Amaziah's charge that Amos had conspired against the king (v. 10) was a deliberate distortion of the facts, for the prophet was a lone voice announcing in a spiritual wilderness that God was going to bring the nation to judgment.

There is more here, however, than a local conflict in Israel, for the situation represents the struggle that takes place in every age, the struggle between the priest and the prophet, the priest as the tool of the king, and the prophet as the messenger of God. It symbolizes the attempt of any state church to stamp out by law religious freedom.

With the power of the government behind him, Amaziah orders Amos to leave the country. The unspiritual character of the priest stands in sharp contrast with the prophet of God. Amos' response to the priest pulsates with spiritual vitality. He was not a professional prophet in the ordinary sense. His denial of membership in the prophetic guilds was a denial of the priest's charge that he was engaged in a plot against the king (7:14). However, he was a prophet in the true sense of the term because he had been called directly by God.

The call came to him as he was following his flock (7:15). When Amos says that he was also a dresser of sycamore trees (v. 14), he refers to his seasonal occupation of piercing the low grade figlike fruit of the sycamore in order to get rid of the insects that infest it. A piercer of sycamore fruit was among the lowest in rank and, together with Amos' work as a shepherd, reflected the humble origins of the prophet. From this common life Amos was suddenly called by God. He was called by the Lord out of his ordinary occupation to be God's messenger. This commission had nothing to do with any profession, before or after the call, nor with his talents. Amos was a prophet in the best meaning of the word. But more than that, the account of the struggle between Amos and Amaziah reveals that an important step forward has been taken in the progressive revelation of God to man.

The prophet now pronounces the final doom of the land. The responsibility for the severity of the punishment must not be placed upon the shoulders of Amos. The message of God was in line with the ordinary consequences of defeat in war in ancient times. The prophecy was fulfilled when Samaria was destroyed by the Assyrians in 722 B.C.

5. The Basket of Ripe Fruit (8:1–14)

The persistent prophet continues his interrupted preaching with a fourth vision, that of the basket of ripe fruit. Israel is represented as late summer fruit, overripe, and ready for judgment. In this vision the same element of finality that appears in the vision of the plumb line serves to emphasize the seriousness of Israel's position. The discourse that follows (8:4–14) reveals Amos as the outstanding champion of social justice in the Old Testament. He denounces the greed of the Israelites, their enslaving of the poor, their sale of the worthless quality of wheat, and their constant dishonesty. The cost to them will be earthquakes, darkness, and destruction.

6. The Lord at the Altar Inflicting Chastisement (9:1–10)

The fifth and last vision is one of destruction followed by a vivid description of the inescapable results of judgment. Amos now departs from the symbolic method and describes the Lord Himself at the altar of the shrine at Bethel. Just as Isaiah saw the Lord, so Amos experiences a theophany (a visible manifestation of God). The sovereignty of God demonstrated in nature and in history is again proclaimed (9:5, 6). Rebellion against God could only result in destruction by a succession of catastrophes. The destruction begins in the shrine, the center of Israel's false worship, and spreads throughout the nation. Although frantic attempts are made to escape, no hiding place, in hell or in heaven, can save the wicked when the sovereign power of God decrees judgment.

IV. Promises of Israel's Restoration (9:11–15)

The promises of Israel's restoration constitute a message of hope, for although judgment on Israel is not averted, the nation is not completely destroyed (9:8). Amos offers a beautiful picture of the restoration of Israel as a result of her purification. The Lord promises, "I will raise again the fallen hut of David. . . . I will build it up as in the days of old" (v. 11). As the hand of their God was seen in the disaster that led to the reduction of Israel to a remnant, so His hand will ultimately vindicate His righteousness and sovereignty in the restoration of the chosen people.

God governs the course of history in both the fall and the restoration of the nation. His sovereignty is described as conquering the heathen and they are now his possession. (James, in Acts 15:15–17, uses Amos 9:11, 12, as an illustration of the fact that the Gospel has universal implications spreading to all peoples.) God is the sovereign of nature, and the soil produces its crops in marvelous abundance. The scattered people return from captivity to rebuild the ruined cities and reconstruct the land from which "they shall never again be plucked up" (9:15).

The eschatology of Amos, or his doctrine of last things, is thus quite simple and clear. While he makes no prediction of a personal Messiah, it is significant that he relates the restoration of the reunited nation to the house of David (9:11).

Obadiah

DONALD W. B. ROBINSON

An Oracle of the Lord Against Edom vv. 1–4
The Awful Fulfilment vv. 5–9
Esau's Sin Against His Brother Jacob vv. 10–14
The Wider Context: The Day of the Lord vv. 15–18
House of Jacob to "Possess Their Possessions" vv. 19–21

THE SHORTEST BOOK in the Old Testament claims a true prophetic character ("the vision") and is authenticated by giving the name of its author. The title, "the vision of Obadiah," belongs to the whole book and declares its God-given character. Whoever Obadiah was—the name is not uncommon in the Old Testament—his book is first of all instructive to us on account of an incidental feature in its composition. Obadiah appears to quote an earlier prophetic utterance concerning Edom, taking it, we might say, as his text. (The same utterance occurs in the course of Jeremiah's Edom prophecy in 49:7–22.) That Obadiah is quoting, is suggested by his manner of introducing the passage. The words, "We have heard tidings from the Lord and a messenger has been sent among the nations," are the words of human reporters; yet they are introduced by the rubric "Thus says the Lord God." We have here the conception of the inspiration not merely of men but of Scripture. Not only the direct statements of God, as in verse 4, but the narrative and literary "scenery" incidental to the divine pronouncements, as in verse 16, are taken by the prophet as issuing from the mouth of God.

692

I. An Oracle of the Lord against Edom (vv. 1–4)

Who was Edom and why did it incur the wrath of God? "Esau," says Genesis 36:9, is "the father of the Edomites in Mount Seir:" or as verse 8 puts it, "Esau is Edom."

When Esau left his father Isaac's home, he made his dwelling in the mountainous country south of the Dead Sea and east of the Arabah (the wadi linking the Dead Sea with the Gulf of Aqabah; it runs south southwest for a hundred miles). Mount Seir is the usual Biblical name for this area, and God gave it to Esau for a possession, as He reminded the Israelites when they had to journey round it on their way from Egypt to Canaan (Deut. 2:1–8). The area is about one hundred miles by twenty and is extremely rugged. Some of the valleys, such as that in which the ruins of Petra may still be seen, are of spectacular beauty, surrounded by rose-red sandstone cliffs. In Obadiah, the country is called Mount Esau, and once Teman, although the latter is strictly a place within Edom, possibly near Petra. Bozrah, some twenty-five miles from the southern tip of the Dead Sea, was one of Edom's cities and perhaps its capital in the days of the earlier prophets.

But the most remarkable locality was that called "the rock" in the King James Version (v. 3) and by its Hebrew name Sela in the Revised Standard Version. This was fifty miles south of the Dead Sea: a valley plateau, accessible only through a narrow ravine nearly a mile long and dominated at the further end by an enormous bluff. In this stronghold, the Edomites believed themselves invulnerable, the more so as in the event of an attack they could retire to the top of "the rock" itself. Later known as Petra (which means "rock" in Greek as Sela does in Hebrew), it became the capital of the Nabatean kingdom, whose ruined tombs and temples, cut in the living sandstone of the red cliffs, are still a source of wonderment to visitors.

But Edom's supposed impregnability was nothing to God. From the eagle's nest of the Sela itself, God would bring Edom down (v. 4). For it belongs to God to "cast down strongholds, and every high thing that exalteth itself against the knowledge of God" (II Cor. 10:4, 5). Obadiah echoes the thought of Amos (9:2) and Habakkuk (2:9).

The pride of man is frequently represented in Scripture as the ambition to climb aloft and occupy the seat of God (Is. 14:13, 14). Such pride is often the fruit of human wisdom—the conceit that man knows better than God—and it is conspicuous that Edom and Tyre, both of whom were renowned among men for their wisdom, exalted themselves against God (Ezek. 28:2–4). In this they typify all the fallen sons of Adam. For man first sinned when he withdrew his confidence in God Who made him and yielded to the insinuation, "Ye shall be as gods, knowing good and evil" (Gen. 3:5). The pride of man's heart deceived him (v. 3) and, by God's decree, slew him (cf. Rom. 7:11).

But how did God bring Edom to the ground? Not by some celestial visitation, but by the hands of surrounding nations. This is a normal phenomenon of God's working. "Shall there be evil in a city, and the Lord hath not done it?" (Amos 3:6). The word of God had declared that when the nations conspired to war against Edom, they were in effect acting at the instigation of an ambassador of heaven. The Assyrian was the rod of God's anger against Jerusalem (Is. 10:5); and so are all nations the instruments of His will.

This short oracle is the same as appears in Jeremiah 49:14–16. The relation of the two passages has naturally been the subject of minute literary study. The details of this do not concern us. No solution is decisive, but it is not improbable that the oracle was in circulation (whether framed in the first place by Obadiah or not) prior to the writing of this book. Certainly the prophets did not speak only once and fall silent; nor did they write in complete ignorance of one another.

II. The Awful Fulfilment (vv. 5–9)

This section, while containing two or three points of contact with the Edom prophecy of Jeremiah 49 (cf. Jer. 49:9 with Obad. 5), is not simply reproducing an earlier oracle. It introduces a new theme: a terrible disaster has befallen Edom. Edom's own allies have unexpectedly turned against him, devastated him and driven him from his territory (v. 7). This is seen as the fulfilment of God's Word that Edom should be made small among the nations and utterly despised (v. 2).

Two figures of speech illustrate the appalling completeness of Edom's ruin. Was Edom the victim of some hit-and-run raid, the work of marauding adventurers (v. 5), so common in Old Testament days? Far from it. Such "robbers by night" would leave plenty behind them. But Obadiah, as he recalls the prophecy of a more than ordinary attack, breaks off to interject: "How you have been destroyed!" (v. 5). For Edom has been ransacked, thoroughly pillaged: more thoroughly than vines are stripped in a grape harvest, for the harvesters at least leave gleaning behind them. One can visualize the systematic search into caves and rock-hewn buildings as Edom's "treasures" are "sought out" (v. 6).

This characteristic picture of the judgment of God illustrates the truth that "there is nothing covered that shall not be revealed; and hid that shall not be known" (Mt. 10:26). An important commentary occurs in I Corinthians 3:18 to 4:5: "The Lord . . . will both bring to light the hidden things of darkness, and will make manifest the counsels of the heart."

We know too little of the situation to say who Edom's allies were who broke their league and drove Edom from his territory. (An apparent turning of Moab and Ammon against their ally Edom is described in II Chron. 20:22, 23, but the incident is too early to be the one in question.) But we know that by 312 B.C., the Nabateans were in secure possession of Mount Seir, and it may be that Obadiah witnessed the beginnings of a Nabatean invasion in the sixth century. The Nabateans were an Arab people racially related to the Edomites. It is worth noting that the prophet Malachi speaks of a devastation of Edom which presumably took place in the fifth century B.C., and those who refer the standpoint of Isaiah 56—66 (actual or prophetic) to the days of the restoration of Judah can see in Isaiah 63:1–5 a vivid allusion to Edom's defeat at the Lord's hand in that period ("Who is this that cometh from Edom . . . ?"). But whatever the details, Scripture bears witness to the certainty of God's declaration made in Isaiah 34:5: "My sword . . . shall come down upon Idumaea [Edom] and upon the people of my curse, to judgment."

III. Edom's Sin against his Brother Jacob (vv. 10–14)

Many nations are condemned in the Bible for pride and self-sufficiency. Against Edom is an additional and a more painful reproach: "Was not Esau Jacob's brother?" (Mal. 1:2). Upon Israel had been laid the charge, "Thou shalt not abhor an Edomite; for he is thy brother" (Deut. 23:7). The unnatural hostility which Edom bore to Israel reached its peak in the events following the fall of Jerusalem in 586 B.C., here depicted, but it was strangely foreshadowed in the divine ordering from old time. "Two nations are in thy womb," God told Rebecca when the children struggled together within her (Gen. 25:22–26), "and the elder shall serve the younger." This, says Paul, was "that the purpose of God according to election might stand, not of works, but of him that calleth" (Rom. 9:11). In the estimation of Isaac, Esau should have been the inheritor of the promises to the seed of Abraham; and Isaac acted in this confidence when he proceeded (as he thought) to bless Esau before he died (Gen. 27:4). But Rebecca, for all her duplicity, knew otherwise. And in any event Esau, notwithstanding his natural endowments and his formal covenant status certified by circumcision, sold his birthright "for one morsel of meat" (Heb. 12:16).

There is room for pity in the spectacle of Esau, "profane person" though he was (insensitive, that is, to spiritual realities), who "afterward, when he desired to inherit the blessing . . . was rejected" (RSV). Here is no unenlightened heathen or deluded idolator. Here is a grandson of Abraham, not by the bondwoman but by the free woman, a recipient of the seal of faith in circumcision. But he knew not the time of his visitation. And with his pitiful course in view, the writer to the Hebrews warns professing Christians to look "diligently lest any man fail of the grace of God: lest any root of bitterness springing up trouble you, and thereby many be defiled" (Heb. 12:15–17).

At a number of stages in the Old Testament, the hostility of Esau's tribe to Jacob's is evident, notably when Moses wanted to lead the Israelites along "the king's highway" from Ezion-Geber through Edomite territory. The story of Edom's sharp refusal is in Numbers 20:14–21 (cf. Deut. 2:1–8). David found it necessary to subjugate the Edomites and put garrisons throughout their land (II Sam. 8:14). Amaziah had war with Edom during which he captured Sela (II Kings 14:7) and hurled ten thousand captives from its height (II Chron. 25:12). Judah was invaded by Edom and seriously weakened in the days of Ahaz (II Chron. 28:17). The prophet Amos in the eighth century denounced Edom "because he did pursue his brother with the sword, and did cast off all pity, and his anger did tear perpetually, and he kept his wrath for ever" (Amos 1:11).

But the crowning breach of the brotherly relationship came when

Jerusalem and Judah lay prostrate and broken at the feet of the Babylonian army in 586 B.C. The central charge of Obadiah's accusation (vv. 10–14) has a close parallel in Ezekiel's parable against Mount Seir in Ezekiel 35: "Because you cherished perpetual enmity, and gave over the children of Israel to the power of the sword, at the time of their calamity, at the time of their final punishment" (v. 5, RSV; cf. vv. 12 and 15). In Lamentations 4:22, Edom is also mentioned for her iniquity in relation to the fall of Jerusalem. Most poignant of all is the cry that was wrung from the lips of those who wept when, by the waters of Babylon, they remembered Zion: "Remember, O Lord, against the children of Edom the day of Jerusalem; who said, Rase it, rase it, even to the foundation thereof" (Ps. 137:7).

All this is given its most detailed expression in Obadiah (vv. 10–14) where the enormity of Edom's guilt mounts as reproach follows reproach. Not only did the Edomites render no help; they actively participated in the sack of the city, in looting and in cutting off the refugees; and they exulted as they did so.

IV. The Day of the Lord (vv. 15–18)

One of the most remarkable features of the Old Testament prophets is the relation they so often establish between a particular event of their own day and "the day of the Lord" in which all the purposes of God are consummated. This interpretation of events not only gives a more than passing significance to the prophetic words; it shows that every generation is in a sense equidistant from "the day of the Lord" and that all our times must be viewed in its light.

The judgment of Edom now becomes a facet of the great judgment of God on all the nations. Moreover, the principle of that judgment —just retribution—is exemplified in the case of Edom: "As thou hast done, it shall be done unto thee" (v. 15). There is one code for Edom and for Babylon (Jer. 50:29; Ps. 137:7, 8). Ezekiel has already declared, "As thou didst rejoice at the inheritance of the house of Israel, because it was desolate, so will I do unto thee: thou shalt be desolate, O Mount Seir, and all Edom" (Ezek. 35:15). The righteousness of God has this unyielding element: "Just and true as thy ways, O King of the ages!" (Rev. 15:3). He judges every man according to his works.

"The day of the Lord" is the establishment of the eternal sovereignty of God in the earth over all resistance to His will. It is, in its fullest sense, the consummation of the age which God inaugurated with the creation. To say that "the kingdom shall be the Lord's" (v. 21) is to say that God will reign and that every knee will bow to Him. Moreover, "the day of the Lord" is regarded as "near." This is an important statement. While the Old Testament never loses sight of the ultimate consummation, it recognizes that the victory of God is seen in particular visitations of judgment and salvation in every age. In this way, the Kingdom of God drew near even in Obadiah's time.

The doom of the heathen is pictured in the ironical sketch of verse 16. The cup of drunken festivity of which the nations partook in celebrating their victory over Jerusalem is turned for them into "the cup of the wine of this fury" (Jer. 25:15) which God forces the nations to swallow.

Against this dark background, the salvation of God's own people appears the brighter. Mount Zion, despite its having been the scene of so much sorrow and desolation, is the haven of the escaped remnant of the house of Jacob. The prophet Joel, in the famous passage that formed the text of Peter's sermon at Pentecost, quotes this identical prophecy (perhaps from Obadiah himself): "for in Mount Zion and Jerusalem there shall be those that escape, *as the Lord hath said.*" The "holiness" of Mount Zion in this context means its freedom from the violation of heathen invaders and from any "abomination of desolation." These truths find their final Biblical expression in Revelation 21:27: "And there shall in no wise enter into [new Jerusalem] any thing that defileth, neither whatsoever worketh abomination, or maketh a lie."

The purpose of this sanctification of Jerusalem is that the whole of the inheritance of Jacob may be rehabilitated. Full possession of the Promised Land was historically never more than a fleeting experience for Israel. Perhaps under David it found a momentary realization; but mostly it was a hope to be enacted in the day of the Lord. Since the Edomites are in the forefront of the ranks of Jacob's dispossessors, in the Book of Obadiah their subjugation is mentioned first. They are not merely to be driven from Mount Seir—an achievement Obadiah perhaps saw with his own eyes—they shall be punished as stubble before the flame (v. 18) in the day of Jacob's ascendancy. The whole nation, including the northern tribes, "the house of Joseph," will engage in the extermination of Esau.

V. Israel Possesses Her Possessions (vv. 19–21)

A graphic picture now follows of the way in which the house of Jacob will "possess their possessions" (v. 17). Despite some uncertainty in the Hebrew text as to the correct syntax of this passage, the main lines are clear enough. It is notably those parts of Israel's inheritance historically most susceptible to invasion that we are assured will revert to Israel's hands: the Negeb (south from Hebron), the Shephelah (the plains of Judah towards the sea), Gilead (Transjordan) and Phoenicia in the north.

Two groups of exiled Israelites are mentioned among those who will share in the recovery of Israel's possessions. "The captivity of this host of the children of Israel" ("the exiles in Halah who are of the people of Israel"—RSV) which will occupy Phoenicia is probably a reference to exiles from the northern kingdom captured by the Assyrians in the eighth century; and "the captivity of Jerusalem which is in Sepharad" is some part of the Babylonian Captivity of the early sixth century. Sepharad is unlocated, but see Gen. 10:30.) By this means is envisaged the gathering of the outcasts of Israel, another promised achievements of the reign of God (Is. 11:12; Ps. 147:2; Mk. 13:27; Jn. 11:52).

The whole description recalls the first attempt of Israel in the days of Joshua to enter into her possessions. But where the first attempt failed, through disobedience, the second will succeed. In the final glorious theocracy, judges ("saviours," as in Judg. 2:16–18) will again be raised up to keep the land in subjection, and in the ruling of Mount Esau from Jerusalem we discern that "the kingdom of the world is become the kingdom of our Lord and of his Christ: and he shall reign for ever and ever" (Rev. 11:15).

Jonah

CLAUDE A. RIES

THE BOOK OF JONAH differs from other works of the Minor Prophets in that it is almost wholly biographical, rather than a book of prophecy. It is largely the story of a man, a storm, and the living God. The man is God-called but disobedient, then obedient but embittered; the storm, God-appointed and God-controlled. Over both is God, all-observant, just, and full of pity.

To some this book seems simply a fable or allegory. The Bible portrays Jonah as an actual historical person, as attested by the writer of II Kings 14:25 and by Jesus (as recorded in Mt. 12:39–42; 16:4; Luke 11:29–32). He is mentioned, moreover, in the apocryphal books of Tobit (14:4, 8, written about 200 B.C.) and II Maccabees (6:8, written about 100 B.C.).

700

The book deals with incidental and essential facts. Strangely enough, the incidentals are more often thought of than the essentials. The incidentals are the storm, the big fish, the gourd and the worm. The essentials are persons—Jonah, the sailors, the Ninevites and God. Here is Jonah, a strong patriot, bigoted and perverse; Nineveh, wicked, repentant, forgiven; God, righteous and just but withal full of love and pity for the wicked.

I. The Rebellious Prophet (1:1–17)

1. The Lord Calls, Jonah Rebels (1:1–3)

Jonah was called of God to be a foreign missionary to heathen Nineveh "Arise, go . . . cry. . . !" Every word is full of urgency. The righteous and all-seeing God of all mankind was not unaware of Nineveh's high-handed wickedness. This wickedness, this "breaking up of all that is good and desirable," marked the awful disintegration of Nineveh's life. No man knew this better than Jonah, who was also aware of the merciful and compassionate heart of God (4:2). Torn between these realities—Nineveh's sin unto death, God's life-giving mercy—Jonah decided to run away from God—just as far as he could. He "rose to flee to Tarshish," the ancient commercial city in southern Spain. Jonah was called to be a street preacher in a big city, but preferred to be a quiet tourist enjoying the bracing sea air. The experience is one of seemingly endless declension: he goes down to Joppa (modern Jaffa), down into the ship, and down into the depths of the sea.

2. The Lord Interposes a Storm (1:4–6)

The narration next introduces a series of God-appointed agencies thrown in Jonah's path to bend him back to the way of obedience. "But the Lord hurled a great wind into the sea." It was sent by the One to Whom Jonah had vowed allegiance. God is in the lashing storm as well as in the still small voice, in whichever is needful for man's good.

What a strange contrast develops! The heathen mariners praying and busily working, the God-commissioned prophet not only prayerless but asleep! The captain (literally, "the chief of the ropes") exhorted the runaway prophet to awake and pray for their mutual safety.

3. The Sailors Intervene (1:7–16)

The mariners seek to discover who and what is the reason for the terrific storm that imperils them. They propose to find out by lot. When the lot falls on Jonah, he does not deny the accusation. The sailors continue to interrogate him concerning his country, occupation and people. Jonah makes no clean breast of the matter, though he reveals his identity and his waywardness, causing the considerate mariners much anxiety. The heathen sailors made Jonah conscious of the great gulf between his creed and his conduct. "The men were exceedingly afraid." They show respect to Jonah even though he is the cause of their trouble. They hesitate to cast him into the sea, but at the critical hour Jonah is cast forth, and the sea becomes calm. The effect upon the seamen is sobering. They too fear the Lord exceedingly, offer sacrifices and make vows.

4. The Lord Interposes a Big Fish (1:17)

Another God-appointed agency in Jonah's behalf and for God's glory is introduced in a manner anticipating similar passages (4:6, the gourd; 4:7, the worm; 4:8, the wind). The belly of the fish becomes Jonah's habitat for three days, significantly the same length of time that Jesus was to be in "the heart of the earth" (Mt. 12:40).

But the story does not end here, although many people know little about Jonah other than his experience in the leviathan. The Book of Jonah, it has been said, comprises five greats: a great refusal, a great fish, a great city, a great jealousy, and a great God. Unfortunately, Jonah was not a great prophet!

II. The Reinstated Prophet (2:1—3:10)

1. Jonah Prays (2:1–9)

"Then Jonah prayed to the Lord his God." Remarkably, this prayer is one of thanksgiving, not of petition. Jonah is thankful his life has been spared. He had been passing through one crisis after another, and in each crisis the prophet must have learned to call upon his God with new fervor. "I called out of my distress and he answered me" (2:2). When the sailors detected him, when the lot fell on him, when he was cast into the sea, when he was going down into the depths of the sea, Jonah had occasion to petition God in view of his disobedience. The grand summary is given in 2:9: "What I have vowed, I will pay" and "Deliverance belongs to the Lord." So Jonah now prays to the Lord, the covenant-keeping God Who is his God (2:1), voicing praise and thankfulness. He has abandoned his disobedient flight "from the presence of the Lord," recognizing anew that the Lord is his God.

Doubtless Jonah's prayer is not recorded in its entirety, but what we have is made up largely of quotations (though not literally) from different psalms. The general tone of the prayer is the same as that of Psalms 28, 116, and 130. The similarity with these psalms can be seen if Psalm 120:1 is compared with Jonah 2:2, Psalm 42:7 with Jonah 2:3, Psalm 31:22 with Jonah 2:4, Psalm 142:4 and 5 with Jonah 2:7, Psalm 31:6 with Jonah 2:8, and Psalm 3:8 with Jonah 2:9. The prayer is beautiful in its progression from danger to deliverance and on to faith and praise.

The vivid descriptions of his sad plight in the belly of the big fish are many, as it plunges through the deep waters carrying its cargo of human flesh, a disciplined and chastened prophet of the Lord "Out of the belly . . . of Sheol I cried and thou didst hear my voice" (2:2b). Confined in the stomach of the big fish, he seemed already numbered among the dead, recalling the words of the psalmist, "The cords of Sheol were round about me. . . . In my distress I called upon the Lord . . . he heard my voice . . ." (Ps. 18:5, 6.) Note also verse 6b, "yet thou didst bring up my life from the pit," the place of corruption.

The consequent transformation in Jonah's life becomes apparent. "But I with the voice of thanksgiving will sacrifice to thee" (2:9). The phrase "but I" reflects an "I" far different from that of the man of 1:30; the I's of Galatians 2:20 are anticipated. When one of Augustine's former paramours called to him as he passed by after his conversion, he paid no attention to her. Then she said, "It is I, Augustine." To which Augustine replied, "But it is not I," meaning the "I" she knew. The climax to the whole prayer is found in the closing words, "Deliverance belongs to the Lord."

The whole gruelling ordeal since he "fled from the presence of the Lord" had accomplished its purpose. The Lord delivers Jonah. "And the Lord spoke to the fish and it vomited out Jonah upon the dry land" (2:10). The detour Jonah took proved to be the roughest distance between two points.

3. Jonah Obeys God's Call (3:1–4)

The third chapter begins as does the first chapter. "The word of the Lord came to Jonah." This expression or one similar to it occurs six times in the book (1:1; 3:1, 3; 4:4, 9, 10). Jonah's commission is renewed, "Arise, go . . . proclaim. . . !" Jonah's response is swift obedience; he no longer arises to flee from the presence of the Lord. "So Jonah arose and went to Nineveh according to the word of the Lord."

God purposed to save Nineveh. Everything is done with dispatch. "Arise, go . . . cry. . . !" was the terse commission. Jonah leaves the country quickly, has a short boat ride, a short whale ride, a short message to Nineveh, a short experience with the gourd, a short question from God. God sought to save Nineveh and perhaps other cities.

Nineveh is described as "that great city" (1:2; 3:2; 4:11), "an exceeding great city" (3:3). In the eyes of God it was a great city as the Hebrew phrasing of 3:3 brings out, "a city great to God," freely translated "an exceedingly great city." Frequently an ancient city included large tracts, as grazing plots and fields for cultivation. Hence the reference to "much" cattle in 4:11.

Since a day's journey equalled about twenty miles, we are given some idea of Nineveh's size in the phrase, "three days' journey in breadth" (3:3). The literal reading is "a walk three days." Is this descriptive of the circumference or the diameter, of the city, or does it imply rather that three days were required to see the principal points of interest? The Revised Standard Version places the emphasis on the diameter.

Some scholars who had long regarded Nineveh only as a myth-city were startled by the discovery in 1847 by Sir Austen Layard of Nineveh (modern Kuyunjik). Nineveh, as known to the Hebrews, included not only Nineveh proper but also a number of adjacent towns, among them Calah, eighteen miles south (Gen. 10:11, 12).

"Yet forty days and Nineveh shall be overthrown" (3:4). Whether these simple words, five words in the Hebrew, were of themselves repeated over and over as Jonah traversed the city, constituting his whole message, or whether these words form the epitome of his message, is difficult to say. There is no promise here in these words of mercy or pardon and yet there was a calling on God for mercy by all of Nineveh. The word "destroyed" or "overthrown" is the one used for the overthrow of Sodom and Gomorrah (Gen. 19:25, 29). To Jonah at least, the emphasis was on the destruction of Nineveh which seemed to be his main drive from his first call to the time of the rebuke by God for his bigoted and ungodlike attitude.

The cryptic words of Jonah remind one of other terse words seen in the Book of Daniel, in the banqueting hall of Belshazzar, *Mene, Mene, Tekal, Upharsin.* But what a difference in the sequels in the two cases! Nineveh repents and God mercifully spares. Belshazzar did not repent and judgment immediately followed.

4. King and Ninevites Repent (3:5–9)

"So the people of Nineveh believed God . . ." (3:5). Indeed a refreshing statement to be recorded of one of the most vile people that the world has ever seen! The king, greatly stirred, sends out a decree for everyone to turn from his evil way and implore God for mercy. People and king alike bring forth "fruit that befits repentance," for "the people proclaimed a fast and put on sackcloth" and "the king removed his robe and covered himself with sackcloth and sat in ashes." All these portray a sincere spirit of repentance. This is attested by the word of Jesus (Mt. 12:41).

Nineveh had her four thousand-plus gods, some great, some small. Her strength was believed to be in the vast number of them, and now as a result of one sermon they turn from all these so-called deities and embrace the God of the Hebrews, the Lord. The preacher from a despised people gives a message of judgment resulting in a whole city being turned to the Lord. They turn from their evil ways which spells repentance and to God which means faith. Jesus used the same formula, "Repent and believe the gospel" (Mk. 1:15).

His overwhelming success transcending the visible results of Noah, prophets and Jesus, however, saddened the prophet.

5. The Lord Withholds Judgment (3:10)

"God saw . . . and repented." The Hebrew word for repent (*naham*) means to sigh, grieve, groan; it implies no relationship to sin. Rather, God's heart is convulsed at man's iniquity in view of the terrible judgments following man's pursuit of sin. If man truly repents, that is, turns from sin, God shows mercy and forgives. If man continues in rebellion against God, ignoring God's "repentant" heart, then God sends judgment as he did at the time of the flood. "It repented the Lord . . . and grieved him at his heart" (Gen. 6:6). The people of Noah's time did not turn from sin to God; judgment was inevitable. But the Ninevites did "turn from their evil way," so "God repented of the evil which he said he would do to them and he did not do it."

Was Nineveh overthrown? Yes, but not as Jonah had so greatly hoped. Nineveh was cast down indeed, but cast down in repentance and utter humility. God's program for man is primarily one of construction, not destruction. Here in Nineveh, God's word had "accomplished . . . and prospered in the thing for which he [God] sent it" (cf. Is. 55:11). "The power of God's irresistible Spirit had destroyed the wicked city spiritually, so it did not need to be destroyed physically."

III. The Retired Prophet (4:1–11)

1. The Lord Displeases Jonah (4:1–5)

"But it displeased Jonah exceedingly and he was very angry" (4:1). The Hebrew is vivid: *It was evil to Jonah, a great evil, it became hot to him.* This word "evil" is a crushing, an infliction of injury. Here is seen the true feeling of Jonah. What God did to or for the Ninevites in sparing them when He said He would destroy them, was "a crushing" to Jonah. Jonah felt that God had inflicted on him a great injury. As a result of apparent double-facedness of God, Jonah loses all patience with God and "becomes hot," that is, hot tempered.

Characteristic of the whole Book of Jonah is the first word of this fourth chapter, "but." It expresses "opposition, contradiction, discrepancy." The whole atmosphere and spirit of the book are colored by this little word, "but." We have in 1:3, "but" in opposition; in 1:4, "but" in answer to opposition; in 1:5, "but" in contradiction to the prevailing incident; in 1:13, "but" in contradiction (God's power in the tempest thwarted their headway); in 2:9, "but" contrary to the situation (Jonah gives thanks to God); in 3:8 "but" joins and completes the preceding phrases; in 4:1 "but" in opposition (a "but" of despondence); in 4:7, "but" in teaching a lesson of love in opposition to other "buts." Though a small word, "but" frequently carries a great cargo of opposition to the will of God as seen in the life of Jonah.

Paradoxes abound in the Book of Jonah. "It displeased Jonah, he was angry,—and he prayed to the Lord" (4:1, 2). Jonah, angered beyond expression with the God Who called him, prays to this God. At least he did not run away as formerly. In 2:1-9 his prayer was thanksgiving, here it is complaint.

He prays, "I knew that thou art a gracious God. . . ." He realizes God's judgment and mercy are not narrowed to one nation, as was his "my country" (4:2). Compare Exodus 34:6, Numbers 14:18, Psalms 103:8, 145:8, and Joel 2:13. But Jonah was not willing to go on a mission of mercy. "The Ninevites deserve no mercy," reasoned Jonah. God thought otherwise. God had shown mercy on the renegade prophet, but this forgiven renegade was angry when God showed mercy on people who had no previous knowledge of the Lord.

"Therefore," that is, because you are this kind of a God in the face of the awful wickedness of the Ninevites, "take my life from me. I prefer death to life in this kind of an ordered world." He is echoing Elijah's cry of despondency (I Kings 19:4) but he is without Elijah's reason for it.

The Lord replies with a simple but pointed question "Do you do well to be angry?" He asks why Jonah is so heated in temper when He is doing this. Jonah clearly shows his lack of confidence in God's judgment and lack of faith in God's true character.

Jonah not only expresses his disgust with God but acts upon it (4:5). On a hillside just outside of the city, he constructs a booth of twigs and branches as did the ancient Jews for the Feast of Tabernacles (they to worship and praise God, Lev. 23:42; but Jonah to pout and criticize God) "till he should see what would become of the city" (v. 5b).

Jonah was a man of many contradictions, God-fearing but disobedient, patriotic but inhumane, divinely-called but humanly-willed, commissioned to feel compassion for cities but sensitive only to gourds.

2. Jonah Displeases God (4:6–10)

The Lord graciously orders a broad-leafed plant to grow up over the booth, shielding Jonah from the hot sun. The shade it gave and the fact that God was beginning to do something pleasant for Jonah greatly pleased the prophet. "He rejoiced with great rejoicing upon the gourd." The sparing of wicked Nineveh by God "displeased Jonah exceedingly." The giving to him of this fleeting temporal blessing, however, caused him to be "exceedingly glad" (cf. vv. 10, 11).

God caused a worm to attack the plant, "so that it withered." Jonah retired from the line of battle and became engrossed with the trivia of a perishing world. God took note and sent a worm. But Jonah failed to realize that his grief was but the shadow of God's hand reaching out after him. Opposite was the reaction of the patriarch Job when, deprived of his vast temporal possessions, he said, "The Lord gave, and the Lord has taken away; blessed be the name of the Lord" (Job 1:21). Jonah lacked that vital commitment.

The God whom Jonah thought was working in his behalf now seems to have turned against him through the devouring worm and now through the hot sultry east wind. So shaken is his confidence in Israel's God that he again asks to die. All this because of the character of God as he believes that character to be!

"But God. . . ." How opposite to Jonah is the character introduced by that "but!" Again God asks Jonah as to the justification of his anger, to which Jonah replies emphatically in the affirmative. Compare Christ in the Garden of Gethsemane "sorrowful even unto death" (Mt. 26:38).

The outstanding message of the book is found in the last two verses of this chapter (4:10, 11). It is based on a fundamental principle: *The measure of our regard for anything is seen in our expenditure of self for it.* Jonah had not put forth a single effort to tend the gourd and advance its growth. He had not planted it, nor watered it, yet he pitied it and mourned because of its passing with parental tenderness, though it was a thing "which came up in a night and perished in a night."

3. *The Lord Shows Great Pity (4:11)*

One of the high-water marks of the Old Testament is found in the words by God "And should I not pity Nineveh. . . ?" (4:11, RSV). "Should I not spare Nineveh?" (KJV). The Hebrew word for pity has the force of compassion. Compare Ezekiel 16:5: "None eye pitied thee, to do any of these [things] unto thee, to have compassion upon thee. . . ." Suffering is the acid test of all true ministry at home or abroad. "Should I not look with compassion on Nineveh, with its teeming thousands whom I've created and worked for, as well as so many helpless dumb beasts?"

All through the narrative of Jonah, God's attitude has been one of pity, patience and power toward Jonah. Divine compassion and pity have been God's attitude toward the sailors, and toward Nineveh with its 120,000 children and other inhabitants.

The great message of the book is that the compassion of God for man is the soul of vital salvation and the dynamic of all missionary endeavor. For all men, even Israel's most cruel oppressors, are God's creation, capable of responding to God and are regarded by Him with tender compassion.

The prophet Amos portrayed God as sovereign over the nations. "For three transgressions and for four I will not turn away the punishment," and with each fresh indictment he called a nation from the roster of nations. The prophet Obadiah portrayed God as the God of justice. "As thou hast done, it shall be done unto thee" (Obad. v. 15). But in Jonah, God is portrayed as the God of mercy and pity, "Shall I not have pity?"

Jonah's success, like that of Elijah, was not in the noise, the fire and the tempest, but in obedience to the still small voice. Like Elijah, Jonah looked for the earthquake, the political overthrow, the destruction of the city. Instead, Jonah heard the voice of repentance, enlivened by faith in the hearts of the Ninevites. The change wrought by the refining fire of the love of a gracious God in the hearts of men transcends physical catastrophe producing only waste and destruction. In the case of the Ninevites Jonah could not see this. Jonah's jerky unrhythmical gait, leaping forward here, falling back there, so characteristic of self-willed people of God, fails to glorify God now as well as then.

Jonah, the first foreign missionary of Israel, failed miserably to grasp the true significance of his great mission. As far as we know, he became a retired missionary prophet, useless to God in this role, and a clogged channel in bringing the riches of grace to needy peoples outside his own immediate country.

Does not Francis Thompson epitomize Jonah's hectic days?

> I fled Him, down the nights and down the days;
> I fled Him, down the arches of the years;
> I fled Him, down the labyrinthine ways
> Of my own mind. . . .
>
> Adown Titanic glooms of chasm'd fears
> From those strong Feet that followed, followed after. . . .
>
> Is my gloom, after all
> Shade of His hand, outstretched caressingly?
>
> Ah, fondest, blindest, weakest,
> I am He whom thou seekest.

Micah

ROSS E. PRICE

THE WRITER of this beautiful and moving little volume of classical Hebrew poetry refers to himself as Micah, the Morasthite (1:1),
who preached in the days of the three kings, Jotham, Ahaz, and
Hezekiah. His home was the little village of Moresheth, near Gath
in northern Philistia, about twenty miles southwest of Jerusalem,
not far from the famous Lachish, and close to the international highway that ran from Mesopotamia to Egypt.

He was a contemporary of the eloquent Isaiah. Micah from the
country and Isaiah in the chief city called upon the two Hebrew
nations to repent and return to the Lord as their only safeguard
against the Syrian invasions from the north and the menace of the
armies of the Assyrian colossus to the east.

The fact that his father's name is not mentioned, as in the case of
some of the other prophets, leads us to believe that his family was

711

of insignificant and humble status. His major concern is with the injustices of the wealthy land-grabbers of the city who defrauded and oppressed the peasant population of the day.

Micah's main activity as a prophet seems to have been from 738 to 698 B.C. According to Jeremiah (26:18) he was active during the reign of Hezekiah. The opening prophecy of his book is against Samaria before the siege and fall of that city in 721 B.C. Probably he, as well as Isaiah, met death in the early years of the reign of the wicked king Manasseh (II Kings 21:16). Thus he was also a younger contemporary of Hosea, and he may even have known Amos.

He must have been a man of strong convictions, great courage, and striking personality. According to his own testimony, he was filled with the Spirit of the Lord (3:8). As a true prophet, he uncovered sin and pointed the way to forgiveness. Though a fierce prophet of doom he was also a winning evangelist, a yearning, tender pleader with men. He seems to have had Amos' passion for justice and Hosea's heart of love. Sincerity was one of his chief virtues. Unsophisticated and rustic, he was nevertheless an artist in language, deftly using figures, similes, and descriptions that carried weight.

I. The Reproof of Samaria and Judah (1:2—3:12)

1. Appearance of the Lord in Judgment (1:2—2:13)

The Indictment (1:2–7). Micah calls upon the earth and all its inhabitants to hear the word of the Lord as He speaks from the very temple in Jerusalem where His holiness has been disregarded. The Lord is about to leave His place in the heavens and descend in judgment upon the strongholds of earth. Especially is He concerned with the sins of the two nations descended from Jacob. Samaria will be razed to the ground, and her instruments of idolatry burned in the fire. That which she has gained through her harlotry shall become the plunder of faithless foes. The fulfilment came at the time of Sargon's siege of Samaria which ended in the city's destruction, January, 721 B.C. The enemies were careful to smash all the idols of the city.

Lamentation over Samaria and Judah (1:8–16). Stripped of his clothing, the prophet now laments the certain judgment that is to come upon these nations of Palestine. The invading Assyrian army in

701 B.C., in fact, took all the walled cities of Palestine and laid siege to Jerusalem itself. The poetry of Micah in verses 10 to 14 of this chapter makes a unique and interesting play on words. Lachish, one of the strongest of those walled cities and one of the first to accept idol worship after the death of Solomon, according to II Kings 18:14, comes in for most severe judgment. The prophet names, in all, twelve cities that shall thus suffer desolation. He then turns to their mother, Israel, who must see her children dragged into captivity and urges her to shave her head bald like that of the vulture as a token of her grief and mourning.

Woe to the Oppressor (2:1–5). This passage pronounces woe upon the greedy rich who lie awake nights to dream up ways in which to defraud the poor of their hereditary farms. The prophet tells them that the time is at hand when they shall lose all such ill-gotten lands to the invading Assyrians and themselves be stripped of their wealth.

Preaching only Promotes Plundering (2:6–11). But these greedy ones not only plunder the poor, but reject all correction from the true prophets of God. They seek to listen only to the false prophets who promise them times of drinking and ease. It is not that God's patience is short or that His word is ineffective, but rather that the covenant people have rejected His prophets for those of their own liking.

The Lord's Little Flock (2:12, 13). Verses 12 and 13 come as an interlude promising that the true believers will be led back from the Captivity by their divine King as a flock of precious Bozrah sheep.

2. The Lord's Denunciation of the Rulers, False Prophets, and Priests of Israel (3:1–12)

Oppression of the Poor (3:1–4). An indictment is addressed to rulers of the land who in their ruthless and cannibalistic oppression of the poor have cut themselves off from any possibility of the Lord's hearing their cry for help in the day of calamity when their government is overthrown by the invader.

False Prophets (3:5–8). Micah's accusing finger now turns toward false prophets who, though preaching peace and future well-being, are actually devouring the people. Because of their false leadership, the Lord promises them only consternation, darkness of understanding, and lack of vision and insight. They who are supposed to have God's message for the people will have no answer from God. Micah hastens to assure them that in himself alone abides the fulness of the Spirit of the Lord which is manifest in his faithful declaration of the sin of his nation (3:8).

Mercenary Priests (3:9–12). He does not cease this castigation of leaders until he has included the mercenary priests in his indictment. They who offer false comfort to the people are no better than those who build the city with the blood of the oppressed, or those who take bribes which pervert justice, or those who prophesy falsehoods for pay. The climax of it all involves a time when their beloved Zion shall be plowed as a field (3:12), and Jerusalem shall become a heap, even as Samaria. (The Massoretes, a famous group of ninth century Hebrew scholars, mark this verse as the exact center of the book of the Twelve Prophets.) To this day Mount Zion is neglected and covered with trees and shrubs, unlike Mount Moriah where now sits the Moslem "Dome of the Rock." Better that it be thus uncultivated than to be cultivated in the service of sin.

II. The Comforting Hope of a Redemptive Future (4:1—5:15)

1. The Issue of Days to Come (4:1—5:1)

Establishment of the Lord's House (4:1-5). As he looks at the future with its promise of the ultimate triumph of the grace of God, Micah finds hope. He sees a time when the Lord's house will be established upon the mountains of enduring peace. Zion will be the center of true worship. From it will issue the divine law, and, by reason of the righteous judgments of the Lord issuing from it, weapons of war will no longer be needed for the settlement of international difficulties.

Reassembling of the Remnant (4:6-8). The remnant of the kingdom of Zion shall be reassembled. God's magnificent minority is to be composed of that which was lame and cast off—rehabilitated into a kingdom over which the Lord Himself shall reign. So often God's people are a company of redeemed harlots, criminals, sinners and offcasts of the earth. Here are redemptive condescension and uplifting grace.

Promised Rescue (4:9—5:1). Micah sees the promise of rescue from the Captivity in Babylon with triumph for Zion. Though many nations are now gathered against Zion and the judgment of exile in Babylon is certain, out of it all will come a gracious deliverance and a true God-fearing government. The Lord will make the wrath of man to serve His purpose for the deliverance of His people and the destruction of the wicked.

2. Rise of the Deliverer and the Victories of His Righteous Remnant (5:2–15)

Rise of the Deliverer from Bethlehem (5:2–5a). A Deliverer will arise from Bethlehem. Micah sees in this Deliverer of village birth, one Who is Himself the pre-existent God, standing in the midst of His little flock to feed and strengthen them, a true man of peace.

Victories of the Remnant (5:5b–9). His next vision is that of the victory of the seven shepherds and eight princes over the land of Assyria. Thus does Micah's God choose the weak to confound the mighty. The outcome will assure the supremacy of the remnant of Jacob among the nations (vv. 7–9). Victory is thus to be achieved over all adversaries.

A Purged Land (5:10–15). But the Lord must surely purge the land of its trust in carnal weapons, its sorceries, and its idolatry. Only then can true vengeance overtake the nations that disobey His will.

III. The Lord's Great Lawsuit with Israel (6:1—7:20)

1. The Lord's Plea and Indictment (6:1–16)

The scene changes. Micah has preached of judgment and pointed out the only source of hope and comfort—the Deliverer from Bethlehem. He now proceeds to set forth the way of salvation. This third section opens with a great court scene. The Lord is in a great lawsuit with His people Israel. As divine plaintiff He makes His plea and indictment of the accused (6:1–16).

Message to the People (6:1–5). The whole of creation constitutes the jury; the Lord addresses His message to Israel in the presence of the hills and mountains of the earth. Israel is reminded of God's deliverance of them from Egyptian bondage, and His later frustrations of the opponents of His people, even Balak and his hireling prophet, Balaam. The plague was stayed at Shittim, and the army had been circumcised at Gilgal. Let Israel make its reply in the presence of the same landscape that witnessed the Lord's deliverances.

True and Acceptable Worship (6:6–8). True religion, moreover, is the only acceptable worship. True repentance is not evidenced simply by burnt offerings or a multiplicity of sacrifices, or even rivers of sacred oil. The sacrifice of the precious first-born, the fruit of one's body, cannot atone for the sin of the soul. What the Lord requires is justice, loving-kindness (loyalty), and a sweet readiness to accept divine guidance. The divine plan of forgiveness of sins on the ground of Christ's atonement is intended to bind our hearts to God's holy decrees, not to free us for wickedness. Micah should not be misconstrued here as teaching salvation by works. Our righteousness is the result of forgiveness, not its procurement.

Justice *(mishpat)* was Amos' favorite term (Amos 5:24). Loyalty *(chesed)*—steadfast love, kindness, mercy—was Hosea's theme (Hos. 6:6). And Isaiah emphasized a ready obedience to the Lord (Is. 2:9–19; 6:5). Micah thus sums up comprehensively in these three phrases the cardinal teachings of the true Hebrew religion. Practice justice, love kindness, and walk humbly with your God! True worship involves fairness, magnanimity, and a lowly heart. The first two are conditioned upon a surrendered readiness to walk with God.

Message to the Wicked City (6:9–16). Then follows the Lord's message to the wicked city. He deplores its treasures of wickedness (6:9–12)—the short bushel, the overweighted balance, violence, falsehood, and double-talk. God promises deceivers the frustration that arises from futility (vv. 13–16)—eating unsatisfied, gnawing hunger, sowing but not reaping, hoarding but not saving, working the oil and the wine presses to no avail. The sins of Omri and Ahab beget nothing but hissing and reproach.

2. Israel's Confession of Guilt and Prayer for Forgiveness and Favor (7:1–17)

Israel Bewails her Corruption (7:1–6). The only true way to repent toward God is to plead guilty. Then God can have mercy. So Israel bewails her own moral corruption. "Woe is me!" she cries. Lack of spiritual fruitage, lack of uprightness, wickedness in high places, confidences betrayed until a man's foes are the members of his own household—these are the sins she confesses.

Israel's Message to the Lord (7:7–13). But true repentance begets hope, and hope sings its song to the Lord. "The Lord will hear, He will not allow my enemies to rejoice over me. He alone is salvation and light. Meekly will I accept His chastisements for He alone can really plead my cause and accomplish my deliverance. Those who today ask 'Where is your God?' shall seek me out tomorrow, when the world lies desolate for its pagan ways."

Israel's Prayer (7:14–17). Israel prays for the restoring discipline of her Shepherd. This longing of the soul for the spiritual pastures of its homeland recalls the days of close fellowship between the Shepherd and His sheep, and the rod of God's deliverance from bondage. Confident of the Lord's return to her defense, she sees the nations coming with fear and trembling to God lest His judgments overthrow them.

3. The Final Verdict (7:18–20)

Micah cannot conclude his prophecy without a play upon the meaning of his own name: "Who is like unto the Lord?" God's is the final verdict. No other God pardons iniquity, graciously regards the misdeeds of His people, tempers His anger with steadfast love, in pity washes away our sins, casting them into the sea of His forgetfulness, and faithfully keeps His covenant oath with our fathers. Micah would have his auditors see the folly of forsaking such a God only to incur the judgments of His chastisements or the frustration of their own selfish and sinful follies.

Some Great Themes

Great themes in the theology of Micah would include the following:

1. His Teaching about the Nature of the Lord. He is a great judge, concerned about ethical righteousness, seeking to convert the world through Zion, loving peace and offering great hope and promise to those who serve Him. Every unsocial act is an insult to Micah's God. God is not indifferent to world situations, nor has He forgotten how to be gracious to the penitent. God identifies Himself with the poor and promises judgment upon those who live selfish, luxurious lives, while sucking the life-blood of the poor. Their costly sacrifices cannot appease His wrath.

2. The Nature of the Lord's True Minority or the Remnant. They are as precious to God as the most superior breed of sheep to a shepherd. Made up of society's outcasts, the remnant is valuable to the Lord. When Messiah appears, He will gather them and make them a blessing in the earth.

3. The Person and Work of the Messiah of Lowly Birth. God's true Man will come from the humble sphere—not from the wealth of Jerusalem, but from tiny Bethlehem. He will be a great Redeemer. And as pre-existent God, He loves peace and imparts strength to His people.

4. True Religion. Justice, kindness, and humble obedience to the will of God are the marks of true religion.

5. Redemption. Zion and Jerusalem, though destined for anguish, suffering, punishment, exile and captivity, will return to the Lord and become a kingdom of redeemed souls through which the evangelization of the nations may be realized.

6. Righteousness and Social Ethics. Social injustices reveal basically a people that hate the good and love the evil. Religion and ethics are inseparable. Whereas Amos attacked the *liquor* problem, Micah attacks the *land* problem.

7. Our Blessed Future Hope. Micah joins Isaiah in the vision of a time of future universal peace and righteousness. The weapons of war are to become instruments of production as love becomes the new social dynamic. But this will be realized only through the Prince of Peace.

Nahum

CLARENCE B. BASS

THOUGH NAHUM is called, by popular generalization, a "minor prophet" (because of the brevity of his writing), the Book of Nahum is far from being of minor importance in Hebrew literature. It has been cited, in fact, as one of the finest examples of the literary style of its culture.

Its literary style is both poetic and prophetic, combining the imagery of pictorial liveliness with the blunt directness of prophetic utterance. These two characteristics are fused throughout the book, giving a vitality of expression which carries the reader from one

719

swift movement of thought to the next as he is caught up in the emotion of the author. In both poetic fire and sublimity, it approaches the best of Hebrew literature. With a skilfully artistic handling of the theme, it exudes a vividness of energy, a grandeur of power, a brilliance in description, and a richness in metaphor and analogy. Its style animates the action, boldly capturing the imagination as if the author were painting with firm brush strokes, each imagery adding to the picture until the final portrait unfolds.

As prophetic literature it moves with deliberate directness, yet with vehement passion. Nahum presents no abstract prophetic declaration, for he is caught up emotionally by personal involvement in his pronouncements. His strikingly single-minded prophecy has one theme: God's sovereignty vindicated in vengeance against the enemy of His people. He moves with boldness to this theme at the very beginning, and restates it throughout with such clarity that historical developments later demonstrate its fulfilment almost to the exact letter.

Little is known of Nahum apart from this brief book. He is not referred to elsewhere in the Scripture except possibly in the genealogical table of Luke. All that we know about him is that he lived in Judah, probably at Elkosh, the location of which cannot be determined with certainty; and that he was a contemporary of Jeremiah. The name "Nahum" means "consolation," "full of comfort."

The date of the book is based upon internal evidence and known historical facts. Since Nahum refers to the capture of Thebes (No-Amon, 3:8) and forecasts the fall of Nineveh, the book must have been written between these two fixed dates. Thebes fell to the Assyrians in 661 B.C., and the subsequent fall of Nineveh took place in 612 B.C. (604, alternate date). The best estimate places the writing of the book about 620 B.C.

Nahum's message, though prophetic in character, was written to meet a particular situation existing in his time and to bring comfort to his own people. Nahum contrasts the powerful imperialism of a despotic, vicious, pagan nation and the ultimate triumph of God's justice and sovereignty.

Assyria, whose capital was Nineveh, had dominated the destinies of Judah and its neighboring lands through a succession of warrior-rulers. Great battles between Assyria and Egypt had engulfed Judah as the tides had swept back and forth through its land. Sargon had taken the ten tribes of the northern kingdom into captivity in

722 B.C. When Hezekiah, king of Judah, revolted against Assyrian tyranny, Sargon's successor, Sennacherib, plundered and pillaged the villages of Judah and took more than two hundred thousand prisoners.

During the time of Nahum, the Assyrians, a ferocious, barbarous people, had an exceptionally cruel king, Assurbanipal. The atrocities and violence committed during his reign were ruthlessly carried out without regard to human decency. Small wonder that Nahum epitomizes this despotic characteristic by calling Assyria the "harlot of nations" and the tribute exacted "the harlot's hire."

There was no hope in Judah. Seemingly, the endless succession of tyranny would continue to hold Judah helpless in the grasp of its cruel enemy (1:15—2:2), since Nineveh was at a peak of ascendancy in power and glory (3:16, 17). Judah was forced to pay tribute to satisfy the rapacious thirst of a pagan people who flaunted their heathen gods before the world. Forlorn men could see no diminishing of the power of Assyria as its military might continued to engulf and dominate its foes.

The natural question arose, "Has God abandoned us? If God is sovereign, why does our enemy who worships pagan gods prosper, while we suffer under his tyranny? Where is the justice of God?" Theoretical doubt turned to practical despair. Judah ignored the pleading of Isaiah and other prophets, turned from trust in God to alliances with other nations, and depended upon miltary pacts rather than the sufficiency of God to deliver them.

Suddenly Nahum bursts upon the scene. As if in derision against the might and power of Assyria, he blatantly announces, "The Lord is a jealous God and avenging . . . the Lord takes vengeance on his adversaries" (1:2). He blasts his message—received in prophetic vision—Nineveh will fall! His message is unbelievable in the light of the ascending might of that wanton city, reveling in its power and glory. Nevertheless, thunders Nahum, God will humble this proud and haughty people and ultimately vindicate His promises to His own people.

Nahum's message is, therefore, a dual one, addressed to Nineveh and to Judah. Nahum predicts for Nineveh destruction, desolation, and oblivion: "No more shall your name be prepetuated; from the house of your gods I will cut off the graven image and the molten image. I will make your grave, for you are vile" (1:14). The prophet offers the hope and consolation of a future under the sovereign

reign of God: "Keep your feasts, O Judah, fulfil your vows, for never again shall the wicked come against you; he is utterly cut off" (1:15).

Three odes, distinct yet interrelated, develop the message. Structurally, verses 2 through 10 of chapter 1 form a psalm rather than a prophecy, and constitute the prelude to the book. The theme of the prelude is the greatness of God as "jealous and avenging" against iniquity and injustice, similar in nature to Psalms 46, 48, 93, and 97. Verse 11, addressed specifically to Nineveh, reflects a transition from the psalm to the prophecy and, with verses 12 and 14, supplies the preface to chapter 2. Verses 13 and 15, with verse 2 of chapter 2, are assurances of comfort to Judah and do not form a part of the prophecy. Chapter 2 constitutes the *prophetic theme,* while chapter 3 projects the *prophetic realization* as being actual.

I. The Prelude (1:1–10)

1. Introduction (1:1)

Acknowledging his "burden" to concern Nineveh, Nahum nevertheless addresses both Judah and Nineveh, sometimes collectively (1:1–8); sometimes individually, as Nineveh (vv. 11, 14) and Judah (vv. 12, 13, 15).

2. The Nature of God (1:2–6)

His Character in the Administration of Justice (1:2, 3). God's nature is boldly defined: He is "jealous" and "revenging" (v. 2). His jealousy denotes His zealousness for full and complete fidelity by man. The two parallels are developed: God jealously demands obedience and will wrathfully avenge disobedience. Three times His avenging nature is mentioned, each time with the accompanying concept that He has "reserved," "stored-up," wrath for those who are disobedient (v. 2). He is slow to anger, but when provoked, His wrath (fury), arising out of His holy nature (not as an unreasonable temper), will wreak its vengeance (v. 3).

His Character Illustrated in Nature (1:4–6). The extensiveness of this wrath is demonstrated in nature where the very elements are broken asunder. What mere man can stand against it (v. 6)?

3. *God's Administration of Justice (1:7–10)*

Refuge for the Faithful (1:7). In the middle of this startlingly bold and abrupt declaration of the vengeful wrath of God, Nahum asserts, almost with tenderness, "The Lord is good" (v. 7). For the obedient, He is in loving-kindness a refuge and a stronghold in the day of trouble.

Vengeance upon the Evil (1:8–10). Again with an abrupt reversal, the prophet returns to his theme. "But" is the connective that places God's wrath parallel to His loving-kindness, "he will make a full end of his adversaries" (v. 8).

The implications of Nahum's message are self-evident: as for Nineveh, God's wrath will be extended in vengeance to her utter destruction because of her sin; as for Judah, God's destruction of Nineveh will vindicate His sovereignty in the affairs of men. But the implication goes beyond that. "What do you imagine [plot] against the Lord" (1:8) means literally, "Who do you think God is?" Addressing both Nineveh and Judah, Nahum is virtually saying: Do you Assyrians think that you can resist God without enduring the consequences? Do you Judeans think that you can protect yourself with alliances and military pacts? God will make a full end (v. 9) to *all* who perversely follow their own ways. Heed the warning!

II. Nineveh's Destruction Announced as Part of God's Plan (1:11–15; 2:2)

1. *Deliverance of Judah (1:12, 13, 15; 2:2)*

God's plan has two facets: A chastisement of Assyria because of her iniquities, and a lesson to Judah of God's sovereign provisions for her. "Though I have afflicted you" (1:12) suggests that God has used Assyria as a rod of correction against Judah's infidelity in order to bring Judah back to Himself. Now at last the yoke is to be broken—good tidings of peace are to come (vv. 13, 15). "The Lord is restoring the majesty of Jacob" (2:2). His promises are being kept; His sovereignty is vindicated! Nahum challenges, "Keep your feasts,

O Judah, fulfil your vows, for never again shall the wicked come against you" (v. 15).

2. *Judgment against Assyria (1:11, 14)*

The whole evil of Assyria seems to be represented by one person whose name is to be destroyed, that is, his line will cease and his family be no more. His idols will be destroyed and death shall be his end.

III. *Nineveh's Destruction to Be Complete (2:1, 3–13)*

1. *Successful Siege (2:1, 3–9)*

The prophet vividly describes the siege and capture of Nineveh. A shatterer, one who would "dash into pieces," has come up against the city (2:1). Against his work there is no defense. "Man the ramparts," "watch the road," "gird your loins," "collect all your strength"—it will come to nothing. Chariots will rage in the streets; soldiers will stumble as they rush to battle stations; rivers will flood the city; destruction, utter destruction, shall abound (vv. 3–6). The people of Nineveh shall flee with faint hearts while the invading horde pillages and plunders the riches of the city. Though leaders of the city will call to the fleeing populace, none shall turn back (vv. 7–9). Nahum sees the raging devastation of the city reach such a peak that immediately its crescendo reverberates, there comes an ominous quiet amid the ruins.

2. *Despair of the People (2:10–13)*

Desolation before Judgment (2:10–12). Desolation and ruin! The city is empty, void, a waste; the people are filled with anguish and fear. The hand of God's wrath is felt (v. 10). Where is the mighty Nineveh, the den from which has come the roaring lion to devour her enemies (2:11)? The invincible city, filled with the plunder of other cities, itself lies plundered.

Judgment against People as a Nation (2:13). As if to sound the final death-knell, the prophetic voice of God, through the prophet Nahum, thunders in wrathful vengeance, "Behold, I am *against* thee." No more shall Nineveh rule in barbaric paganism. Her chariots are to be burned, her young men are to be killed, her preying upon other nations will cease, the voice of her ambassadors will be silenced, for she will become a forgotten city, buried under the avenging wrath of the "jealous" God.

In a more subdued tone, the prophet begins the final phase of his prophecy. Having described the utter destruction of the city with passionate vehemence, he turns to a reasoned, logical explanation of its necessity.

IV. Nineveh's Destruction Caused By Her Sin (3:1–18)

1. Inevitability of Judgment (3:1–4)

Nineveh's sin is her crime against other nations. The carnage she had inflicted on them has made it appropriate to describe her as the "bloody city, full of lies and robbery." In her rape of other nations, she has become a harlot, graceful and charming, yet deadly in treachery and deceit. Multitudes have been slain, corpse has been heaped upon corpse, as a result of her cunning whoredom.

2. National Annihilation (3:5–18)

This harlot, Nineveh, has failed to consider the Lord Who is "jealous and avengeth" (1:2). She has despised, rejected, resisted, and wilfully disobeyed Him. Now "Behold, I am against thee, saith the Lord of hosts" (3:5). The wrath of avenged righteousness will be felt; Nineveh is to be exposed before the world and ultimately annihilated. Other nations will see her plight, but none shall mourn her. There will be no comforters (vv. 6, 7).

As if not to leave Judah in comfort about the plight of Nineveh, Nahum draws a parallel between Thebes (No or No-Amon), which Nineveh had conquered, and Nineveh itself. Though addressed to Nineveh, the message to Judah is obvious. Are you better than Thebes? Nahum asks. Thebes was fortified by a natural location by the sea and by an alliance with Ethiopia and Egypt, "an infinite strength," yet Thebes was defeated. So shall Nineveh be (3:8–14)! As if by an aside, so shall Judah be, if she relies on alliances with others, and does not trust God!

The extent of the judgment against Nineveh is summarized and defined (3:13–18). Though the city may prepare for the siege, its doom is sealed. The armies will be destroyed; Nineveh's national leaders are to be defeated—all because of the sin of the nation.

V. Postlude (3:19)

As if to add to the woes of Nineveh, Nahum pointedly asserts again the inevitability of its destruction. "There is no healing thy bruises; thy wound is grievous" (3:19). When such destruction does come, all who hear will clap their hands in hilarity at Nineveh's plight.

Though the prophecy arose out of the particular situation occurring in Nahum's day and was intended primarily for the people of that time, its message is contemporary in its relevance to all ages. The judgment which Nineveh suffered will be the inevitable judgment of all men who proudly and arrogantly resist God and do not humble themselves before Him.

Habakkuk

DAVID A. HUBBARD

THE TITLE of the Book of Habakkuk (1:1) serves merely to identify the author who, along with Haggai and Zechariah, is called *the prophet* (cf. 3:1). This may be a technical title, denoting an official position in the religious community, or it may merely indicate that this writing was considered worthy of the prophetic tradition. The prophet is said to have seen an "oracle" or "utterance" ("burden" in KJV), the implication being that what the prophets saw they spoke by the command of God.

I. Problem: God Has not Judged the Moral Depravity of Judah (1:2–4)

Without further introduction, the prophet plunges immediately into his message. He does not direct his indictment against the people, but rather against God. His prophecy, in contrast to those of most of his fellows, is a dramatic dialogue between the Lord and himself. Whereas his great contemporary, Jeremiah, was primarily concerned with the awfulness of sin and the need for repentance on the part of the people, Habakkuk was primarily concerned with the awfulness of sin and the need for judgment on God's part. He could not reconcile the sordid situation in Jerusalem and Judah with God's hatred of sin and His righteous nature.

A more detailed account of the violence, strife, and lawlessness, which Habakkuk mentions without elaboration, may be found in Jeremiah. Disregard of the Mosaic law (Jer. 5:5; 7:8, 9), violence and oppression (Jer. 7:5, 6), treachery and injustice (Jer. 5:25–28) were all part of the pattern of Judah's conduct. The moral fiber of the nation was so weak that the reform of Josiah in 621 B.C. produced no lasting effect. The tragic death of the good king during a battle with the army of the Egyptian Pharaoh Nechoh about 609 B.C. wiped out the last, best hope of Judah for a genuine conversion to righteousness (II Kings 23:29).

To Habakkuk it seemed that the people of Judah and Jerusalem had passed the point of no return. Repentance and revival were impossible: the Ethiopian cannot change his skin, nor the leopard his spots (Jer. 13:23). God's drastic judgment was the only alternative. Habakkuk, who was theologian and philosopher as well as prophet, plead passionately with the judge of all the earth, firmly convinced that this delay in judgment was a blot on His righteousness.

II. God's Solution: The Chaldeans Will Judge Judah (1:5–11)

God's answer to Habakkuk's complaint was not long in coming. However, God replied in the plural as though His response were intended for a larger audience than the prophet. Possibly the answer is directed to the sinful people themselves, for the word translated "among the nations" (1:5) may originally have been the very similar Hebrew word for "scoffers" or "traitors," as the Greek translation indicates. Paul quotes this verse in Acts 13:41 in a form closely related to the Greek translation and uses the word "scoffers" (KJV, "despisers") rather than "among the nations." If this response was addressed to the treacherous Israelites, the statement that they would not believe if told (v. 5) is readily understood. One of their fatal flaws was that the citizens of Judah presumed upon the grace of God and lulled themselves into a false sense of security and peace (Jer. 8:11). They did not believe that the God of the Covenant would deal harshly with them.

But judgment must and will come. God, the sovereign of the nations, will bring the judgment in the form of the Chaldean (Babylonian) army (1:6). The description of this army with its swift cavalry (v. 8) suggests a date for the writing after the capture of the Assyrian capital Nineveh in 612 B.C. and in all probability after Nebuchadrezzar's defeat of the Egyptian hosts at Carchemish in 605 B.C. Apparently, at the time Habakkuk wrote, the Babylonian army held full sway in the Near East and had no worthy rival. The judgment predicted took place in 597 B.C. when Jehoiakim (himself a shocking example of Judah's unrighteousness) revolted against Nebuchadrezzar, who sacked Jerusalem in reprisal (II Kings 24:1, 2). The date of the book, then, may be fixed with considerable certainty between 605 and 597 B.C.

This description of the power-thirsty Babylonians and their ruthlessness in battle has been substantiated by the verdict of history and by their own inscriptions. Their practice of building earthen, inclined planes in order to storm a fortress or city wall is accurately pictured in 1:10. Neither religion nor regard for human life curbed their ventures. The only god they recognized was their own might (v. 11). In this awful panorama of the enemy who was being brought to judge Judah, God gave His answer to Habakkuk's first problem.

III. Problem: Why Are Wicked Chaldeans Used to Punish the More Righteous (1:12–17)?

God's response to the first problem brought no final satisfaction to Habakkuk. Instead of lifting the prophet's burden, God added to it. The answer to the previous puzzle left Habakkuk with a thornier one. He realized that God was using the Babylonians for chastisement and correction, and he even seemed to sense that in the midst of this judgment God would honor his Covenant by sparing some of the people (1:12). But his basic problem (v. 13) was how God could justify the use of wicked instruments to scourge the more righteous inhabitants of Judah.

The exact identity of the righteous is not made clear. Habakkuk may have used the term in a relative manner to denote that his people, though deserving of judgment, were much more righteous than the inhuman, godless Babylonians. More probably the term "righteous" refers to a godly remnant within Judah, which, the prophet feared, was destined to suffer along with more wicked countrymen.

The reports of the savagery of the Babylonians had reached Jerusalem, and horror gripped the prophet's heart as he envisaged Jerusalem sharing the fate of Nineveh. To appreciate the destructive power of the Babylonians, one need only recall that the vast metropolitan area of Nineveh, which, according to Jonah 4:11, sheltered 120,000 children, was so thoroughly razed that within a century or so of its siege it became a grazing site for sheep and was destined to lie buried for almost twenty-five hundred years.

With a vivid imagery born of his desperation, Habakkuk described the ruthless inhumanity, the unbridled vandalism of the forces of the imminent conquerors. Like a fisherman armed with rod and net, the Babylonian sits beside a stream which God has stocked lavishly with human fish (1:14, 15). He brings up catch after catch, and when he has dined sumptuously, he continues to fish. The surplus of his catch he dumps out on the shore to die (v. 17). Appalled by this outrageous waste of human life and especially by the thought that his kinsmen might be the next to feel the tug of the hook and the snare of the net, Habakkuk asked God how long this brutality would go on unchecked by His righteous intervention (v. 17).

IV. God's Solution (2:1–20)

1. The Righteous Remnant will be Preserved (2:1–5)

Though overwhelmed, Habakkuk was not hopeless. He was an honest seeker, not a dabbler in divine affairs, so he waited for God's answer, which he knew would be forthcoming. Wisely he withdrew to his "watchtower," that place of solitude and silence where the voice of God could break in upon his listening soul without the distraction of the multitudes (2:1). God, Who looks upon the heart, read his sincerity and honesty and replied accordingly. The answer came in the form of a vision which the prophet was to inscribe on tablets (like the law at Sinai) with large and clear-cut letters that could be read on the run (v. 2). Following a promise that the vision was trustworthy and sure to come (v. 3), God proceeded with a threefold reply to Habakkuk's second problem.

The exact translation of verses 4 and 5 is highly problematic, but the English versions have certainly preserved the basic idea—the marked contrast between the righteous who trust God and are faithful to Him and the proud, debauched, bloodthirsty Babylonians. The latter are treacherous and fail; the former are righteous and live. The self-centered pagans are contrasted with the trusting and trustworthy righteous remnant. Hababbuk had feared that the righteous would be swallowed up in the wave of judgment (1:13), but God assured him that the righteous would be saved because they were faithful. The word translated "faith" in 2:4 carries with it the idea of faithfulness and dependability. The righteous depend on God and, in turn, can be depended upon by Him. They need not fear the ravages of enemy attack, because God has guaranteed their survival. As God revealed to Ezekiel (Ezek. 9:3, 4) that those who grieved over the abominations in Jerusalem would be singled out for survival by a mark on the forehead, so He promised that Habakkuk's righteous compatriots would be granted asylum in the citadel of His care.

The importance of this passage for New Testament thought can scarcely be exaggerated. It plays a pivotal part in the arguments of Romans 1:17, Galatians 3:11, and Hebrews 10:38, 39. The prophet's assurance of the rescue of the faithful righteous from the wrath of the Babylonians helped to shape the apostle's conviction that only those deemed righteous *by faith* would escape the wrath of God. The Old Testament promise of escape from physical destruction became the seed-plot for the New Testament doctrine of justification by faith.

2. The Chaldeans' Doom is Assured (2:6–19)

As the righteous remnant will be preserved, so the haughty oppressor will be destroyed. This fate is announced graphically in the form of a taunting proverb pronounced by the nations which the Babylonians have victimized. Five *woes* punctuate this passage, tolling their direful knell to drive their awful message home.

Certainty of Retribution (2:6–8, 15–17). The first and fourth stanzas of this taunt-song affirm the certainty of retribution. God will see to it that the Babylonians are repaid for their heinous crimes measure for measure. They will be plundered as they have plundered others (2:8) and will be made to drink of the cup of God's wrath as they have forced others to drink to the bitter dregs (vv. 15, 16). They will pay dearly for the violence done to Lebanon, when they stripped her forests to build their palaces and massacred her animals to entertain their nobles (v. 17). God is not mocked, and the Babylonians were not exempt from the law of sowing and reaping (Gal. 6:7).

Folly of Plundering (2:9–11). The second woe stresses the folly of plundering. The Babylonian king fortified himself in a fabulous palace whose hanging gardens were one of the seven wonders of the ancient world. But this citadel had been built with the spoils of conquest, not with the fruit of honest toil. No edifice constructed with such evil means could long endure. The royal fortress became a source of shame instead of glory (2:10). In a burst of poetic irony, the stones and beams are said to cry out in protest against those who build their houses with stolen goods, felling timber and quarrying stone which are not their own. History confirmed the verdict of this stanza, for the fortress-palace in Babylon provided no refuge for the king and his nobles when the forces of the Persians took the city in 539 B.C. (Dan. 5:30).

Emptiness of Tyranny (2:12–14). The mocking chant of the nations continues with the third woe which proclaims the emptiness of tyranny. Not only did the Babylonian tyrant build his palace with looted materials; he constructed and strengthened cities with transported slave labor. But all this was in vain; the frenzied effort, the arduous toil led only to emptiness when these cities were destroyed by the invading Persians. The fruit of their toil went up in smoke. Jeremiah applied this passage to the destruction of Babylon which he foresaw in 51:58. The last verse of this woe (2:14; cf. Is. 11:9) is a reminder that God's will is not finally fulfilled in earthly empires but in the spreading of the knowledge of His glory (sovereign majesty) throughout the earth. The empire-builders of this world are doomed to failure, in spite of any apparent success, because God's final program has room for only one universal sovereign—Himself.

Vanity of Idolatry (2:18, 19). The succession of woes climaxes with

an announcement of the vanity of idolatry. This is the final indictment. No nation can long succeed whose trust is not in the Lord of
hosts. Though the army of the Babylonians was strong, their trust
was misplaced. By worshiping idols they humiliated themselves, paying homage to something that had to be inferior to them, for it was
their own creation (2:18). Furthermore, this creation could not sustain in time of need because it could give them neither aid nor instruction (v. 19). As the righteous cannot help but triumph, because
they are linked to a conquering God, so the wicked are doomed to
failure because the gods they serve are worthless.

3. *The Sovereign Lord is Ruling (2:20)*

The third part of God's reply to Habakkuk is both encouragement
and rebuke. The prophet need not fear, for the sovereign God is on
His throne; yet the prophet need not protest too much about God's
program, for he is included in "all the earth" which must keep a
reverent silence before Him. There is a ring of finality in this verse.
The furious clamor of the Babylonians, the growing panic of Judah,
the passionate questioning of the prophet—all these must yield in
silence to the sovereign will of God. The righteous judge of all the
earth will do right. Faithfulness to Him will have its reward, and
rebellion against Him carries with it its own awful destiny. A moral
God governs a moral universe; the Babylonians broke the law of God
only to be broken by it.

V. The Prophet's Response to God's Solution (3:1–19)

As Job, whose problems were not unlike Habakkuk's, begged for
an opportunity to lay his case before God (Job 23:1–7) and then
could only repent when God revealed Himself (42:5, 6), so Habakkuk responded, not with rebuttal but with prayer and praise. He had
met the God of righteousness and power, and he could but yield to
Him.

1. *A Prayer for God to Work as in Days of Old (3:1, 2)*

The imminent crisis recalled to the prophet the glory of the
Exodus, the finest hour in Israel's history. His prayer asked for a
repetition of that grand redemption. He had heard the report of

God's mighty acts in the wilderness, and undoubtedly he looked forward, as did many of his fellow prophets, to a great and final Day of the Lord; but his plea was that God would renew His work of deliverance in his day, between these two splendid times. In the midst of the wrathful judgment, he asks that God be merciful to His own.

2. A Description of the Revelation of God (3:3–15)

In this poetic description, past and present seem to merge. In his mind's eye, the prophet recalled the Exodus and wilderness experiences and saw their glorious pattern repeated in the midst of his own circumstances. God revealed Himself from Teman and Mount Paran (cf. Deut. 33:2, Judg. 5:4), in the southern desert, just as He had once revealed Himself in the desert at Sinai. The awesome majesty of this theophany (manifestation) shook the everlasting hills and struck terror to the hearts of the desert tribes, Cushan and Midian (3:4–7).

The prophet, as he reflected upon this striking scene, asked whether the Lord was angry with the rivers or the sea, so great was the impact of His appearing (3:8). This verse and those that follow form a mosaic of allusions to the intervention of God when the Israelites crossed the Red Sea (Ex. 14:21–29) and the Jordan River (Josh. 3:14–17) and when the sun stood still at Gibeon (cf. Hab. 3:11 and with Josh. 10:12–14). In 3:13 the question is answered: God was not angry with river or sea, but marched forth for the salvation of His anointed people.

3. A Confession of Complete Confidence in God (3:16–19)

Habakkuk was both overwhelmed and encouraged as he relived the victories of the past (3:16). The thought of God's fearsome judgment struck terror in the prophet's heart, yet he knew that when God had scourged the people of Judah with the Babylonian whip, He would break the whip and cast it into the fire of His judgment. His questions answered, Habakkuk waited quietly for the day of trouble, knowing that the day of trouble would also mean the vindication of God's righteousness, which the prophet had sought desperately to safeguard.

Invasion may mean devastation and deprivation (3:17). A besieged nation must recruit farmers to be soldiers; an attacking army must live off the produce of their victims. Crops and flocks must necessarily suffer under such circumstances, but faith in God may remain staunch. Habakkuk knew full well that he stood to lose all that he had and to see his country ravaged; but he also knew that neither peril, famine, nor sword could separate him from the love of God. This confidence was his joy and strength. Like Paul, he knew the warmth of divine contentment in any state (Phil. 4:11). He had met the living God; he had looked into the eyes of eternity. Nothing could erase the reality of that indelible vision.

This psalm, one of the finest pieces of poetry in the Old Testament, concludes with Habakkuk's testimony to the wonder of God's strengthening grace (3:19). He had been imbued with a fresh vitality which could only be compared with the swiftness of a deer, and he affirmed that God would lead him forth in victory. The reference to treading upon high places is reminiscent of Deuteronomy 32:13, 33:29, II Samuel 22:34, and Psalm 18:33. All these passages suggest triumph over and possession of a land. Habakkuk was one of a train of believers who have learned to be more than conquerors through Him who loved them. The notations of tune and accompaniment (3:1, 19) seem to indicate that Habakkuk's prayer struck a responsive chord in the hearts of the believing community and gained a place in public worship.

This little book testifies clearly to the conquest of doubt by faith. Habakkuk made the journey from questioning and skepticism to trust. He began by upbraiding God, and he ended by worshiping Him. The lessons he learned—the assurance that God will rescue those who trust Him, the certainty that sin will be punished, and the confidence that the sovereign Lord is ruling the affairs of men and the universe—have a striking relevance for today. The God of Habakkuk stands ready to instruct in a similar fashion all who will take His yoke and learn of Him.

Zephaniah

EDWARD J. YOUNG

ZEPHANIAH, a true prophet of the Lord, faced a corrupt and godless nation, Judah. Such a nation, even though it was believed to be the chosen people, could not endure, for the Lord is a just God Who is no respecter of persons. Far to the northeast was the mighty Assyria which was to be used of the Lord as His instrument to bring about the destruction of Judah. This destruction would be a day in which the righteousness of the Lord would be vindicated. It would truly be a Day of the Lord.

Zephaniah rightly seeks to inspire fear of that day in his hearers. He appeals for repentance and points out that only through such a judgment can mercy come to those whom God truly intends to deliver. The pure remnant which has been delivered will one day sing the praises of the just Lord, Who dwells in her midst.

736

Prophecy of God's Judgments (1:1—2:3)

1. Ancestry and Identity of the Prophet (1:1)

Unlike that of other prophets, the ancestry of Zephaniah is traced back through four individuals. Hezekiah is probably mentioned because he was a man of prominence, and hence may have been the great king of that name. Zephaniah, therefore, would have been of royal stock, and hence his denunciations of the royal house assume particular interest.

Josiah reigned from 639 to 609 B.C. Not only was Assyria still standing, but it would also seem (2:2—3:8) that Zephaniah uttered his prophecies before the reformation of Josiah.

The message of the prophecy is not a product of Zephaniah's own heart, but is a word, that is, a revelation, which the Lord gave to him. A true prophet, he uttered what had come to him by divine revelation.

2. Announcement of Certain Judgment (1:2–6)

The prophet launches immediately into his main theme. His first words may be rendered literally, "destroying, I shall make an end," that is, "I shall utterly bring to destruction." This destruction is to include everything. This universal judgment is first announced in general terms (1:2), and then in detail—men and beasts, birds and fish, the stumbling blocks (that is, works of wickedness through which men fall), and finally, the wicked ones. To emphasize the universality of the judgment, the prophet uses language taken from the account of the flood in Genesis ("from the face of the earth"; cf. Gen. 6:7). The coming judgment is to be as severe as was the flood.

Announcement of a general judgment serves as an introduction to a specific judgment upon Judah and Jerusalem. If the world is not to be spared because it is wicked, can Judah have reason to expect deliverance? God is no respecter of persons, and, although the inhabitants of Judah were the chosen people, they were also sinners.

The sin of Judah appeared primarily in idolatry, and the judgment was to involve a destruction of the various forms in which idolatry had manifested itself. This idolatry was Canaanitish in nature, and central in it was the service of Baal. On the roofs of the houses, altars had been erected for the worship of stars. Some of the people had completely turned their backs on the Lord, but others evidently sought to worship both the Lord and Malcham (Milcom or Molech).

3. Announcement of the Day of the Lord (1:7–9)

Reflecting upon Habakkuk 2:20, Zephaniah commands all to be silent, that is, to submit in humility to God. He speaks of God as the Lord God and uses a Hebrew word which signifies God as all-powerful and sovereign. The passage is reminiscent of Isaiah's language. Indeed, the prophecy of Zephaniah is a little mosaic of Isaianic thought and language.

Men are commanded to be silent because the Day of the Lord is near. Although all days belong to God, nevertheless this is a day in which His sovereignty will be particularly manifested in a work of judgment, and so in a peculiar sense, it is said to be His. There have already been such days (cf. Joel 1:15), but this is a day in which strong judgment will strike Judah.

On this day there is to be a sacrifice, namely, Judah herself, and the invited guests are the nations. They have been consecrated, or set apart, for this particular task of consuming Judah. Isaiah (cf. Is. 13:3) had similarly described them as God's "holy ones." Thus, following Isaiah, Zephaniah explains the downfall of Judah as a punishment of God for her sins, and holds that the nations who brought about that downfall were simply God's instruments.

This judgment will fall with equal severity upon men of all ranks and classes. The king Josiah is not mentioned, for he was to die before the judgment came. The princes and king's sons, however, would not escape, nor would those who, through wearing foreign dress, showed that their inward disposition was far from God. Likewise, those servants who violently entered houses to steal would feel the wrath of the Day of the Lord.

4. The Day of the Lord a Day of Woe (1:10–13)

In order to show that no class of the inhabitants of Jerusalem will escape the judgment, the prophet pictures the cries that arise from all parts of the city. The exact location of the Fish Gate is not known, but it may have been in the northern wall. That it was a prominent place is clear from its being mentioned. The Second Quarter was probably the lower city (cf. II Kings 22:14), and the hills mentioned were in that part of the city. The Maktesh (that is, mortar) was a valley. The first reason for wailing is that the Jewish merchants are destroyed. The ordinary business of the city, which had caused it to flourish, now ceases completely.

There will be no escape from divine punishment. The phrase "to search with lamps" (RSV) or lights suggests a minute and detailed search for those who seek to escape from God (cf. Luke 15:8). This minute search will result in punishment for those who do not believe that God will do anything. The figure of their settling (coagulating or congealing) upon their lees seems to be taken from wine, which is left upon its dregs and is not drawn off. Such men are practical atheists, for they pay no attention to the workings of God.

They will be compelled, however, to recognize God's sovereignty, for He will bring the judgment upon them. Their gods will be plundered, and they will thus come to learn that God is in control even of their own lives.

5. Judgment is not to be Delayed (1:14–18)

In order to arouse sinners from their indolence and to bring them to repentance, Zephaniah describes the terrors of the day of the Lord. He uses the medium of fear, as he must, for unless the people are convinced of the terrible nature of judgment, they will continue in their apathetic condition. "Near," calls out the prophet, "is the day of the Lord," and it is the thought of nearness that is most emphatic in his message. The day is also called a great day, for its effects are great, so that the mighty man must cry bitterly, for despite all his efforts, he cannot deliver himself.

The prophet then employs many different words to depict the terribleness of the day. On that day, the wrath of God is manifested, and consequently, it is a day of distress and anguish. Men will walk as though they were blind, that is, they will grope about for an escape, and will find none. Their blood will be counted as worthless as the dust, and they will not be able to purchase deliverance through silver or gold. Human sin is responsible for such a judgment.

6. *Exhortation to Repentance (2:1–3)*

Judah is commanded to gather itself together, that is, to take spiritual stock of its condition, for it is now a nation white with shame. If it does not do this, the judgment is near at hand, and Judah will perish, as the chaff is driven away by the wind. The pious, who show their humility in obedience to the commands of the Lord, are enjoined to practice a deeper search for humility and righteousness that they may be delivered.

God's Judgments of Nations (2:4—3:8)

1. *Destruction of Philistia Announced (2:4–7)*

The admonition to repent is further strengthened by the statement that the Philistines, the ancient enemy of Judah, will also perish. At the same time, the fourth verse, with its mention of four of the Philistine cities, also serves to introduce the announcement of judgment upon Philistia. The Philistines are mentioned as a representative of the heathen nations about Judah, and not until later are other heathen nations brought in.

In announcing the destruction, Zephaniah makes use of a play on words: *azza* (that is, Gaza) will be *azubah* (forsaken), and *eqron* (that is, Ekron) will be *teaqer* (pronounced tay-ah-kehr; destroyed). We do not know why Zephaniah omits mention of Gath, the remaining Philistine city. A woe is pronounced upon the entire nation, which is called a nation of the Cherethites (that is, the Cretans). This designation contains a play upon the word *karath* (to cut off, exterminate). It is as though the prophet had addressed the nation as ready for extermination.

In this announcement, the first gleam of hope appears. The land of Philistia, in its entirety, will be made a desolation, for the Word of God is against the Philistines, but there will be a remnant of Judah, those who come safely through the judgment to live in and enjoy the land of Philistia.

2. *Moab and Ammon to be Destroyed (2:8–11)*

The Moabites and Ammonites, as descendants from Lot, were blood relations to Judah. Nevertheless, on every possible occasion they manifested an attitude of hostility and enmity. They rejoiced at Judah's misfortunes, and they also made boasts (literally, did great things) against Judah. This latter probably refers to attempts to invade Judah and to steal its land.

Moab and Ammon, therefore, will perish as did Sodom and Gomorrah. This terrible announcement simply means that they will be completely destroyed. The remnant of God's people, who themselves have been delivered, will take Moab and Ammon as their own possession. This would mean that the heathen nations themselves will one day become the very servants of the people of God and will thus become incorporated into the Kingdom of God.

That this conversion will be of a spiritual nature is shown by the statement that God will make lean (famish), and so, make to vanish (that is, destroy) all the gods of the nations. He will thus manifest His own superiority not only over peoples, but also over the systems of idolatry.

3. *Universality of the Judgment (2:12–15)*

Zephaniah now turns his attention to the south and mentions, not the Edomites, who were close neighbors, but the Ethiopians, the most remote people known to Judah in the south. They are directly addressed, as though to point out that, although living at such a distance from Judah, nevertheless, they too will be included in the judgment. To describe the judgment, terms are taken from the field of war. The sword which will slay the Ethiopians is from God.

Suddenly the prophet begins to use the third person and makes a direct announcement concerning the destruction of Assyria. He does this by means of a wish, and his words may be rendered literally, "And may he stretch out his hand against the north, and may he destroy Assyria." At that time Assyria was the great power which was seeking the destruction of Judah. Actually Assyria lay more to the northeast than to the north, but inasmuch as its armies had to invade Palestine from the north, it was to that direction that Judah had to look for its enemy. Zephaniah reflects upon the language of Isaiah

13 as he describes the desolated capital city of Assyria, Nineveh. Far from being a great and prosperous city, Nineveh is to become a desert, the habitation of the beasts and birds of a desert region. Those who pass by will hiss and shake their fists as a sign of scorn, as though the place were not worthy of consideration. The destruction of the city did actually occur in 612 B.C. at the hands of the Babylonians and Medes.

4. The Corrupt City, Jerusalem (3:1–8)

Jerusalem must be brought to repentance, and so the prophet again turns his attention to her. If the corrupt condition of Jerusalem be brought before the eyes of his hearers, they may repent and turn unto the Lord. Such a city can only be an object of woe, for she is an oppressive city, that is, one in which men are oppressed. Such a condition leads to pride, and Jerusalem will not hear a voice of warning, when spoken by the prophets of God. Sin deafens the ears, so that men do not hear words of warning. The voice of God was found both in the written law (the Pentateuch) and in the words of the prophets. These, however, were ignored by the city, for her sins precluded her from listening to them. Had she trusted in God, she would have drawn near to Him in hearkening to the words of His revelation.

When the officials are corrupt, the citizenry itself is likely to be corrupt. The princes in Jerusalem (3:3) were as hungry for prey as roaring lions, and the judges could only be compared in rapaciousness with the wolves that roamed in the evening. At such a time there should have been faithful messengers of God, but instead, the prophets were faithless who proclaimed as the word of God the thoughts of their own hearts, thoughts which the people wished to hear and which would encourage them in their wickedness. Men like Zephaniah and Jeremiah stood out as notable exceptions. Even the priests, who should have taken the lead in the worship of God, perverted the law. They treated holy things as though they were profane, and hence, made the true worship of God practically impossible.

This truly tragic condition of things continued (3:8) even though the Lord Himself was present in the city and constantly manifested His righteousness. He caused His righteous law and truth daily to be proclaimed, not by the mouths of false prophets, but by prophets such as Zephaniah himself, and thus He called attention to His own righteousness. There was therefore no excuse for continued sin.

To substantiate the claim that He has been righteous, the Lord is introduced (3:6) as speaking. He reminds the citizens of Jerusalem that He has already laid other nations waste through judgment, and hence, can do the same thing to Jerusalem itself. These judgments have been brought about because of the sinfulness of the nations in question and, hence, are righteous. By means of a short summary (vv. 7, 8) the prophet brings to a close his statement concerning judgment and the need for repentance. Making it clear that He desired repentance, God had expressed a confidence that the nation would obey. God does not desire the death of the wicked, and in sending prophets to a rebellious nation, His loving-kindness is manifested. The nation, however, was not ready to listen to His word, and instead of repenting, showed itself more zealous in the performance of wicked deeds. Zephaniah employs a forceful idiom: "They rose up early, they corrupted all their doings." Their zeal to do evil was so great that they are pictured as rising up early in the morning to begin the practice of evil.

Consequently, the Lord calls upon His people, the humble of the land, to wait for Him, for He will appear in judgment as for prey, that is, for the taking of prey. This prey consisted in those who would be rescued from the judgment and would truly be a spoil which belonged to the Lord (cf. Is. 53:12). This prey will be gathered when the Lord carries out His purposes, namely, the gathering together of the nations so that He can pour out upon them His anger and wrath to consume them.

Promised Blessings (3:9–20)

1. Salvation and Deliverance (3:9–13)

The promise enunciated in the remaining verses is connected with the judgment. Believers are commanded to wait for the Lord in judgment, for by means of this judgment, redemption itself will be brought to them. The fruits of this redemption are the cleansed lips of the people. When the heart is impure, the lips speak impure things. When they are pure, the heart also is pure. The prophet is simply teaching the truth that the hearts of wicked people will be purified, and consequently this people will speak with purified lips. As a result they will truly call upon the Lord, and serve Him with one shoulder. The figure is taken from the bearing of a burden equally with both shoulders, hence, with one accord. Thus the purpose of the deliverance is that men may call upon God in worship.

Reflecting upon the language of Isaiah 66:20, Zephaniah names the most remote heathen nations to show that all the nations will one day come to God to worship Him. This does not mean that all men will be converted, but rather that from all lands there will be true worshipers.

The redemption is to be accomplished by God alone, and is therefore seen to be wholly of grace and not at all of human merit. It is explicitly stated that at the time of the redemption (3:11) the deeds by means of which the people had transgressed against God will not cause them shame, for the pride which had lain at the base of their sins will be removed by God Himself. In beautiful, flowing language, the prophet depicts the character of those that will be redeemed. They will be a humble people and lowly, for they will have been conquered by the sovereign grace of God.

2. Salvation Demands Praise (3:14-20)

The closing verses constitute a command to the redeemed to praise the Lord in song for the wondrous redemption which He has accomplished. The enemies of the people will be removed, and also the judgments which stood to condemn them. Instead, the people are accepted of the Lord Who, as a mighty warrior to defend them, is in their midst. Therefore they need never fear. This gracious message of the prophet thus closes on a note of deliverance and of exaltation of the conquering grace of God. It is a deliverance which was not brought about by human effort but by divine grace, when the mighty warrior, Jesus Christ, by the shedding of His own blood, delivered those who were His.

Haggai

GEOFFREY W. BROMILEY

Sᴉxᴛᴇᴇɴ YEARS before the prophecy of Haggai, the capture of Babylon by Cyrus and the new policy of the Persian ruler had made it possible for a group of exiled Jews to return to Jerusalem under the leadership of Sheshbazzar (Ezra 1:1–11). In the first flush of enthusiasm, they had cleared the site of the temple, set up an altar, made preparations for rebuilding and even laid the new foundations (Ezra 3:1–13). But owing to opposition and intrigues, the work was suspended; and since the affairs of the post-Exilic community did not prosper, the project was continually postponed and seemed impossible of fulfilment. With all the tasks and difficulties of reconstruction, the provision of a temple seemed to have no great claim to priority of interest or effort. It was against this background of failure and apathy, accompanied by economic hardship, that Haggai and his fellow-prophet Zechariah were raised up early in the reign of Darius (520 B.C.) to call the people to a fresh assessment of the situation and a new attempt at rebuilding.

I. Call to Examination (1:1–6)

Having carefully dated his prophecy, and claiming to speak with divine authority, Haggai summons the community to a consideration of its position. Is it really fulfilling the purpose of restoration? Is it not preoccupied with material concerns and neglectful of its true function? Is it not guilty of a wrong sense of proposition, and suffering the inevitable consequence? Has not the time come to take seriously the fact that the house of God is still in ruins? The appeal takes two forms which are closely related; the first is a direct summons to the rulers, and the second, a general address to the people.

1. Opening Call to the Rulers (1:1, 2)

The civil and religious rulers—Zerubbabel who had succeeded Sheshbazzar as governor under the Persian overlordship, and Joshua the high priest—are first confronted with the apathy and excuses of the people. In their kingly and priestly functions, they are to be significantly associated with the prophet in initiating the building of the temple. As leaders, moreover, they are responsible for the attitude of the returned exiles. It is to them, therefore, that the appeal of the prophet is primarily addressed.

2. General Call to the People (1:3–6)

While the prophet still seems to be speaking directly to the rulers, his words have a wider application to all the people. They are much concerned in building fine houses for themselves, but have little sense of responsibility for the ruined house of God. Yet their preoccupation with material well-being has brought them little reward. Their harvests are poor; their clothing is inadequate; their wages cannot keep pace with inflation. Obviously the time has come, not for a reapplication to material qeustions, but for a radical reappraisal of their whole scale of priorities.

II. Declaration of Divine Judgment (1:7–11)

What the rulers and people have to see is that the service of God, as expressed in the rebuilding of the temple, must be regarded as the first essential in the reconstitution of the life of the nation. It may not seem sensible to devote to a temple energies and materials which are urgently needed for other purposes, but there can be no solution of other problems—even the material and economic—unless priority is given to the work and worship of God. Hence the prophet issues an urgent summons to rebuild and explains that the intractable political and especially economic problems are an inevitable judgment upon their failure in discernment and discipleship.

1. Summons to Build (1:7, 8)

The time has come to take stock and to take action. Possibly some are arguing that only the very best will do for God, and therefore cedar must first be bought and transported from Lebanon. Ideally, this is no doubt true. But what God now wants is action. There is wood on the mountains, and if this is the best to be had, it will suffice if only the people will show an interest and really do the work. What gives God pleasure is the zealous doing of what can be done rather than the pious willing of what is impossible. The main essential now is to build. In terse, simple language, the prophet calls the rulers and people to glorify God by consecrated action.

2. Explanation of Economic Difficulties (1:9–11)

But he also shows them why it is that life has been so hard and disappointing in post-Exilic Judah. It is not due merely to local or wider economic factors. It is because they are under the judgment of God for their failure to give Him and His work and worship the first place in the life of reconstituted Israel. They have not honored Him, and therefore He has not honored them, and all their efforts at material prosperity have brought them disappointment and disaster. To seek material above all other ends is not merely to miss spiritual rewards; it is to condemn oneself to frustration even in that which is sought. This is the lesson of bitter experience which the prophet brings before rulers and people, and it gives point and urgency to his demand for a prompt and drastic reorientation.

III. Response of the People (1:12–15)

Unlike the majority of his pre-Exilic predecessors, Haggai meets with a ready response on the part of both leaders and people. He is thus able to give to the nation a second message, not of rebuke and challenge, but of encouragement and promise. That which they are prepared to do at the command and under the inspiration of God will enjoy the divine blessing, and therefore they can give themselves to it with every prospect of a successful issue.

1. Movement of Obedience (1:12)

Led by Zerubbabel and Joshua, the returned exiles accept the call of Haggai as a summons from God. In a proper attitude of reverence and humility, they realize that their attitude and conduct in relation to the temple have been mistaken; and they are ready to undertake at once the neglected work of reconstruction as Haggai has commanded.

2. Promise of Divine Help (1:13)

They are conscious, however, that their resources are weak and that there may be attempted interference of the kind which stopped the original project (cf. Ezra 5:3–5). In answer to the natural consciousness of human insufficiency, Haggai is commissioned to give them the assurance that God Himself is with them in this undertaking. They can thus give themselves to it with complete confidence that, in spite of the apparent impracticability of the task, they will not be frustrated so long as they are prepared to obey.

3. Work Begun (1:14, 15)

With this word of encouragement, and moved by God Himself (as is the case in all genuine obedience), the rulers and people make a definite beginning on the temple site only three weeks after the prophetic word had first come to them. Their response does not evaporate in a mere act of repentance and rededication. It issues in specific action in accordance with the reassessment to which Haggai has called them. The rebuilding of the temple has now become the first and most urgent of all the tasks in national reconstruction, and all efforts are concentrated upon this primary goal.

IV. Message of Encouragement (2:1–9)

As is always the case in any enterprise, it is not long before a mood of skepticism and criticism and futility establishes itself among at least some of the people. After all, it is good no doubt to build the house of God, but what an unworthy and insignificant structure it is! And is there any real hope that it will ever be properly completed? Almost a month after the start of rebuilding, therefore, Haggai delivers a further message of encouragement and promise in which he answers the doubters, gives a fresh assurance of the divine assistance, and promises that God Himself will make this new house a place of glory and peace.

1. Human Disparagement (2:1–3)

As is only natural, there are those who are disappointed at the lowly scale of the enterprise. A few still remember the glories of Solomon's temple (cf. Ezra 3:12), and they cannot resist pointing out how much better things used to be when they were young, and how mean and paltry are the plans and achievements of the present. In these circumstances, there is the danger that the first enthusiasm will be checked by the spread of a critical and pessimistic spirit; and Haggai is commissioned by God to give the divine answer to a wrong human estimation.

2. The Divine Presence (2:4, 5)

In the first place, he assures Zerubbabel and Joshua and the people that, small though the work may be from the human standpoint, it may be done with vigor and courage because God is with them, fulfilling the promise given when He redeemed Israel out of Egypt and again out of Babylon (cf. Ex. 29:45, 46 and Is. 43:2). On the strength of the divine presence, there need be no reason for fear or despondency in spite of the apparent insignificance of the work.

3. Glory of the New House (2:6–9)

Secondly, he promises in the name of God that in and through the turmoil of history, the new temple will grow from small beginnings to be a place of glory, surpassing that of the first house, and also a place of peace. God Himself will see to this, for it is He Who is the true temple-builder. While we need not doubt a certain temporal fulfilment of this prophecy, the message here has a wider reference to God's restoration of the shattered temple of the body of Christ and His building of the temple of the Church as the new Israel. There is thus a deeper and messianic significance in Haggai's enjoining of a humdrum religious task, especially in the promise that God will endow with greater glory that which is mean and despicable in the eyes of men.

V. Promise of Blessing (2:10–19)

The divine promise is not restricted, however, to the act of divine service undertaken in obedience to the call of God. Once the foundation of the new temple is laid, three months after the work began, Haggai gives to the people the further encouragement that they will now see a turn for the better in their temporal affairs. So long as the land stood under the desecration of a ruined and abandoned temple, everything was made unclean. But now that the work is going forward, Haggai is bold to give definite assurance that material needs will be amply met.

1. A Ritual Comparison (2:10–14)

The prophet illustrates the situation from the law of cleanness and uncleanness (Lev. 10:10, 11). While one holy thing does not sanctify others, that which is unclean has a contagious quality by which it corrupts everything it touches. In the case of Israel, the ruined and neglected temple has been the canker which has affected every other aspect of national reconstruction, frustrating even the most sincere and strenuous efforts in other directions.

2. Solution of Economic Problems (2:15–19)

The prophet proves his thesis by reference to the economic difficulties experienced by the people so long as the temple was left in ruins. Now that they have begun to build, however, he gives them the assurance that they will see the end of material problems. Indeed, he challenges them to take note of the date in order that there should be no doubt as to the interconnection betwen the obedient honoring of God and the resulting divine provision for temporal needs.

VI. Confirmation of Zerubbabel (2:20–23)

The prophecy concludes with a special message to the governor, Zerubbabel, who has taken the lead in response to the prophetic summons. At a time of confusion and change among the nations, he will be confirmed in his position as the divinely elected leader of the people, thus typifying the messianic King Who, as the Elect of God, summoned to build a temple not made with hands, will remain when all earthly kingdoms and governments are shaken and destroyed.

1. Shaking of the Nation (2:20–22)

With the general promise to the people, a particular assurance is given to Zerubbabel, who had been first summoned to undertake this work and who had led the response of the people. He is told that the time of instability so marked at the outset of the reign of Darius will continue. Neither political nor military security is to be expected among the nations, for God Himself is at work to overrule and judge.

2. The Promised Ruler (2:23)

But Zerubbabel is not to fear, even though his position may seem to be weak by human reckoning, for he has been chosen and established by God Himself. In obedient dependence upon divine grace, he can count on it that his rule will continue in spite of the flux and hostility of the external world.

The upshot of the prophecy is that political, no less than economic, well-being depends ultimately upon a primary readiness to do the will of God and to seek His kingdom and glory. Where individuals or nations set themselves to attain material security as a first objective, they condemn themselves to inevitable loss and disappointment. But where they are prepared for a first loyalty to God and His cause, they can depend upon the gracious provision of God for material needs (Mt. 6:31–34).

With the final message to Zerubbabel, as in the promise of 2:6–9, the prophecy is given a messianic range and depth which make it more than the mere illustration of an important truth. As the ruler called by God to rebuild the temple, Zerubbabel foreshadows the Builder of the eternal and spiritual house Who is prepared for absolute obedience to the divine will even to the point of death, Who is thus enabled to build a temple of surpassing peace and glory, and Who is established in a Kingdom which endures when all the dominions of earth are broken in the final judgment.

Zechariah

MARTEN H. WOUDSTRA

ZECHARIAH, a younger contemporary of the prophet Haggai, addressed himself to the same task as Haggai, that of inducing the people to rebuild the temple. His written message forms a significant link between the earlier prophets to whose ministry he makes reference (1:6) and the later phases of God's redemptive work to which his book bears such eloquent testimony. Thus he helps us to look forward to the day when the completed Kingdom of God will be established and to fill our joyful expectation regarding that day with rich scriptural content.

753

I. Call to Conversion (1:1–6)

All is not yet well with the returned exiles. Initial repentance, caused by the grim fulfilment of earlier prophecy (1:6), must be followed by continued conversion (v. 3). Only thus will God's wrath, so real before the Exile (v. 2), be removed and fellowship be restored between God and His people.

II. Visionary Disclosure of God's Purposes (1:7—6:15)

1. Vision One: Appearances Deceive (1:7–17)

A troop of horsemen, their leader in front, patrols the earth and reports it to be at rest (1:8–11). It looks as if God is not moved by compassion for His languishing people (v. 12) who are waiting for the great upheaval of the messianic age (cf. Hag. 2:21, 22). But the prophet is informed by an angel that this is not really so. God's loving and intense interest ("zeal") is in His chosen people (vv. 14, 16, 17); His displeasure is turned against the arrogant nations who delight in being instruments in Israel's downfall (v. 15).

2. Vision Two: The Destroyers Destroyed (1:18–21)

Israel's enemies, represented by a fourfold symbol of power, the horn, will find their perfect match in the four smiths, instruments of divine power for the redemption of God's people. The number four, probably denoting the four quarters of heaven, suggests the world-wide character of the forces which oppress Israel, a view common to other prophecies as well (cf. Dan. 8:8; Hag. 2:6.)

3. Vision Three: Perfect Safety of an Open City (2:1–13)

A young man with a line ready to take the measurements of Jerusalem (2:1, 2) is told that the city's boundaries will not be measurable, since its population will spill over into the country (v. 4). The safety of this open city will consist in the divine protection without and the divine indwelling within (v. 5). Let everyone hasten to return to this city whose safety and sanctity are in God alone (vv. 6–13).

4. Vision Four: Satan Silenced (3:1–10)

The filthy garments of the high priest symbolize his people's sins and his own (c. Is. 4:4, 64:5). Satan's accusation is not accepted because of God's immutable choice (3:2). Instead, removal of sin is guaranteed (v. 4) and promise of still greater glory through the Branch, that is, the Messiah, is made (v. 8). In His time the subjective removal of sin will also be accomplished objectively (v. 9).

5. Vision Five: The Temple Rebuilt by the Spirit Alone (4:1–14)

A seven-branched candlestick, flanked by two olive trees 4:1–3), represents the restored temple (vv. 6–10; cf. Ex. 25:31–40; I Kings 7:49). As this lamp is fed with oil, not by man's hand, so the temple will be restored by the Spirit of God alone. The reality of the new temple will be the Spirit. All obstacles in building it will be removed by the Lord under Whose supervision it stands (vv. 7–10). The inexhaustible sources of oil assure the future temple's spiritual abundance (vv. 11–14).

6. Vision Six: The Curse Destroys Sin (5:1–4)

A giant scroll, flying through the air, represents God's curse against sin. This curse will affect all sinners, those who sin against the first table of the law (perjury) and those who sin against the second table (theft).

7. Vision Seven: Personified Sin Banished (5:5–11)

The woman in the measure is wickedness personified. Her attempted escape is prevented by means of a heavy leaden lid. She is carried away, ephah and all, as far as two women with stork-like wings can carry her. Thus God banishes sin from Israel.

8. Vision Eight: Four Chariots (6:1–8)

From between the heavenly pillars proceed four chariots to the four winds of heaven. They receive their orders from the Lord of heaven and earth, and fulfil their mission. The north country (cf. 5:11) will experience the Spirit's activity in terms of judgment and in preparation of Messiah's coming (cf. 2:7; 1:11; 6:15).

9. Coronation Scene (6:9–15)

In a coronation scene, a crown upon the high priest's head speaks of a future Person Who will be Priest and King, Messiah and Branch. Royal rule and priestly atonement will be united in Him.

III. A Prophetic Message to the People (7:1—8:23)

A delegation from Bethel inquires about the need for further fasting (7:1–7). Although no direct answer is given, general principles are laid down. Only such fasting pleases God as is wholly dedicated to Him and is accompanied by the doing of His will. Questions about form lose their significance when the essence of religion is ignored. A summary of the teachings of the former prophets shows that the hearkening to God's voice is the prerequisite of God's hearkening to our voice (vv. 13, 14). The rejection of God's words had previously brought the divine wrath (v. 12). Concern about religious observances, in themselves legitimate and even required, must not obscure the real issue. Desolation follows when true mercy and compassion for others are neglected (v. 14).

The question of fasting is not abandoned (cf. 8:19) but lifted to a higher plane. God's redemptive and punitive "zeal" (vv. 1, 2) will make Jerusalem the scene of peaceful old age and joyous youth (vv. 3–5). Enduring life, in which God's saving righteousness and blessed communion with Him are the experience of His redeemed people, is the Old Testament view of life eternal (vv. 7, 8; cf. Is. 65:20).

With the beginning of "these days" (8:9), circumstances will be radically different. The state of disorder will give way to a condition of universal peace and well-being. There is every reason for vigorous and cheerful occupation (vv. 9–13).

If the people wish to enjoy God's goodness permanently they shall have to observe His moral demands (8:14–17).

The original question concerning fasting (cf. 7:3) is now answered indirectly. That solemn fasts will become cheerful feasts is another way of repeating the promises made earlier. Again these promises are linked with the observance of truth and peace (8:18, 19). So attractive will be true service to God (cf. 2:11; Is. 2:2, 3) that the singular privilege of the Jews in having "God with them" will incite the holy jealousy of all nations and tongues (v. 23).

IV. The Emerging Kingdom (9:1—14:21)

1. The King and His Kingdom (9:1—11:3)

With chapter 9 the second part of Zechariah opens with the prophecy of God's judgment over the nations dwelling in the general territory assigned to Israel by divine promise (9:1-7; cf. Gen. 15:18). This leads to and prepares for the messianic promise of 9:9, 10, verse 8 forming the transition between the prophecies of judgment and verse 9. The future Messiah is pictured in His saving qualities as He rides triumphantly to His city (cf. Mt. 21:1-7; Is. 45:21; Ps. 72). The King's glory will reside in the King's God, but royal attributes as commonly understood He will not have.

The establishment of His realm is described (9:11-17). Released from captivity, Israel will unitedly conquer her foes in the power of the Lord (vv. 11-14). The prophet vividly describes the definitive triumph of Israel in which there shall be no more room for mercy upon God's enemies (v. 15).

Temporal and eternal judgments coincide in the prophetic perspective as God's saving acts result in prosperity for the restored community (9:16, 17). The prosperity of Israel will be rooted in her dependence upon Him Who gives these blessings (10:1). As long as the people trust idols, they wander about without a shepherd (v. 2); but God will have mercy upon His flock (vv. 3-12). They will gain victory over their enemies because the Lord is with them (vv. 3-5).

Judah and Joseph, the two parts of the covenant nation, will be fully restored to God's favor (10:6); joy and numerical gain will be theirs (vv. 7, 8). That the restoration described transcends the limits of Israel's national existence is evident from the mention of world powers which had ceased to exist in the prophet's time; for example, Assyria (v. 10, although cf. Ezra 6:22; Lam. 5:6). God's power over world empires is thus vividly portrayed (v. 11), so that the returned Israelites will triumph in His name (v. 12).

The lament which opens chapter 11 is over the dread judgments of the nations previously described. The end of stately trees symbolizes the downfall of worldly rulers (vv. 1-3).

2. The Two Shepherds (11:4–17)

A very enigmatic passage follows. In a vision the prophet must symbolically act out the part of a good shepherd and of a foolish one. The former, of necessity a divine person (cf. 11:10, 13), refers to the Messiah. The theme of verses 4–14 is the laying down of his office on the part of the good shepherd (vv. 9–11). Previous to this, God shows the activities of the good shepherd (vv. 7, 8a) and contrasts them with the desperate condition of the flock (a "flock of slaughter," v. 4) when the flock is not properly cared for (vv. 5, 6).

This prophecy involves not only a broad and universal aspect which finds expression in verses 6 and 10, but also a narrow and particularistic aspect as verse 14 clearly reveals (vv. 15–17). Israel's rejection is thus viewed within the context of her solidarity with all the world's inhabitants. The good shepherd's activity among the flock of slaughter serves ultimately the purpose of their abandonment to themselves and their destructive tendencies (v. 9), a result brought about by their own guilt (vv. 12–14). The leaders show only contempt for the work of the good shepherd. His place is then filled by the foolish shepherd (vv. 15–17).

It is not necessary to interpret this vision as involving two consecutive stages in history, although there is a possible allusion to the Roman destruction of Jerusalem. The total fulfilment of the entire prophecy, in view of its universal application, must lie at the end of time. In this vision, the past and the future, the Last Days, go hand in hand.

3. Jerusalem Attacked and Delivered (12:1–9)

The nations will assemble against Jerusalem (12:2, 3), but Jerusalem's strength will be in the Lord's protection over her, more particularly in One Who will be a representative of the royal house (cf. 3:8; 6:12).

4. Inward Blessings Promised (12:10–14)

God's Spirit will be poured out. A genuine lament over the One Who first was pierced (12:10) will take place as the house of David mourns the rejection of the Son and Lord of David, but the prophet sees this only dimly (cf. II Pet. 1:1–12). The reference to Hadadrimmon is obscure (cf. II Kings 23:29 and II Chron. 35:25). The entire population, its families and subdivisions, will participate in the national lament (vv. 12–14; cf. Jn. 19:37; Acts 2:37–41).

5. *Threefold Purification (13:1–6)*

People and royal house will be cleansed from sin through water from a fountain (cf. 3:9; Mic. 7:19; Is. 4:4; Ezek. 36:25). Two concrete sins will be purged, idolatry and false prophecy, represented by images and false prophets (13:2–6). The deception otherwise resorted to by the latter will come to an end. Scars left upon their bodies from self-inflicted wounds (cf. I Kings 18:28) will call for a lame excuse (v. 6).

6. *Death of the Shepherd (13:7–9)*

In Old Testament language this prophecy describes a difficult period of God's people, caused by their shepherd's death and their own dispersion. Its ultimate reference is to Christ (Mt. 26:31), but this does not exclude earlier fulfilment or later repetition. The sword comes at God's behest (13:7), a universal calamity prevails among the people, but a remnant remains. It too will suffer affliction but the Lord will hear its cry and call it His people.

7. *The Day of the Lord (14:1–21)*

This is "a grand apocalyptic vision of judgment and redemption." Cosmic changes will accompany the Day of the Lord (Joel 2:10, 11). Jerusalem is besieged and plundered (14:1, 2). The Lord fights against the nations (vv. 3–5). Ominous changes in nature in general and in Judah and Jerusalem in particular will take place (vv. 6–11). Enemies will be punished with fearful plagues (vv. 12–15), but those who remain will observe the annual feasts in Jerusalem (vv. 16–19). The sacred precincts of the *cultus* (worship or rites) will have widened and become co-extensive with daily life and common pursuits, thus sanctifying all of life and making it a part of temple worship (cf. Ezek. 37:26, 27; Jer. 3:16, 17; Rev. 7:15; 21:22).

From the mixed character of the imagery employed, referring now to cataclysmic upheavals, now to regular pilgrimages to Jerusalem, it seems to this writer that no such literal interpretation of the passages is intended. The prophecy has in view various aspects of the gospel age with particular emphasis on its conclusion. Premillennial writers find in Zechariah's final chapter a summary of events at the return of the Lord in glory.

Zechariah's prophecy, though at times obscure and difficult to interpret, possesses a grandeur of scope and a wealth of spiritual wisdom. At once profound and spectacular, the Book of Zechariah should bring to the Christian not only new insights but also sure comforts in the midst of a bewildered generation.

Malachi

BURTON L. GODDARD

THE TIDE OF Old Testament prophecy was fast ebbing. Many voices had spoken. Only one more, that of Malachi, remained to be heard. Then divine revelation would cease for the space of four hundred years. What would God now say through His prophet?

Indeed, what *could* Malachi say in the light of the conditions which prevailed about him? The northern kingdom of Israel had fallen to the Assyrians in 721 B.C. A century and a half later, the southern kingdom had succumbed in the face of the Babylonian invasion. The land had been despoiled. The most able of the Jews had been taken captive to Central Asia. A half century later a pitiful remnant had returned and after discouragements and setbacks, spurred on by the prophetic ministry of Haggai and Zechariah, had constructed a poor substitute for the glorious temple of Solomon. Then God had been pleased to send a man of faith and action, Nehemiah, to lead the people in the rebuilding of the walls and the restoring of the old way of life, centered in the covenant relation between Himself and His chosen people. Ezra, also, a faithful scribe, had brought before the people once more the Word of God and stressed its importance for their daily living. But the response had left much to be desired. Defilement of the temple, neglect of observances commanded by Moses, withholding tithes, presenting of unlawful and despicable offerings on God's altar, carelessness in the observance of the Sabbath and intermarriage with idolatrous peoples characterized the times.

What *could* Malachi be expected to say, except to call attention to the just and demanding requirements of the sovereign God, to warn and rebuke and tell of the certainty of coming judgment? Yet throughout his message holds the promise of untold blessing awaiting the righteous and the entreaty to sinners, expressed or implied, to turn again and do the will of God and enjoy His blessing.

I. Undeniable Love: God's Love for Israel (1:1–5)

The drama of love, mentioned by the beloved disciple when he said, "Herein is love, not that we loved God, but that he loved us . . ." (I Jn. 4:10), had been unfolded centuries before, when the God of heaven chose for Himself a people, set His affection upon them and entered into a covenant with them. The covenant had promises, obligations and conditions, a sign and a seal, but at the heart and core of it, binding it together and making it possible, was the love of God for His people. Their own love had failed. They had been untrue to their obligations and untrue to their God, but His love through the years had been constant, warm, abiding (cf. Deut. 7:8; Jer. 31:3, and so forth).

In Malachi's day, ungrateful hearts were rehearsing this theme against the covenant head: "Wherein hast thou loved us?" (1:2). It was a question that must be answered if God was to charge Malachi's contemporaries with filial disobedience (1:6) and covenant neglect (2:8). The Almighty could have picked evidence at random, but He chose rather to base His case upon a single, pivotal illustration, namely, His treatment of two brothers, Jacob and Esau, and their posterity (1:2–4). Jacob had been preferred above his brother in the sovereign good pleasure of the Lord (Rom. 9:10, 11). On the other hand, not only was Esau's seed (Edom) stranger to the covenants of promise, but his children had reaped the judgment of God because of their sin (1:3, 4; cf. for example, Obad.). The voice of the Lord had never affirmed with reference to the line of Esau, "I have loved you," and the contrast suggested in God's dealings with Israel as over against His treatment of Edom was evident to all. Only wilful blindness, or stubborn refusal to consider the evidence, or base ingratitude could produce the charge that God's love had not rested upon Jacob. The Lord *did* love Israel. The covenant of grace was not just a legal agreement consisting of cold phrases and letters of stone. No, it was vibrant with divine love, the unchanging love of a changeless God for an unworthy people.

Against the background of this affirmation the words of God now pour from the lips of His prophet.

II. *Unacceptable Sacrifices: Corrupt Offerings by Corrupt Priests (1:6–14)*

It was in the light of the Old Testament sacrificial system that John the Baptist said, "Behold the Lamb of God, which taketh away the sin of the world" (Jn. 1:29). If the Mosaic sacrifices were to be a proper vehicle for worship and serve as types pointing to Christ, the antitype, they must be carried out according to the pattern revealed to Moses on Sinai.

The post-Exilic priests, however, had little regard for revealed patterns; they were a law unto themselves. They cared not whether the Lord be "father" or "master" (1:6) or "a great king" (v. 14). The law said of the offerer, "Let him offer a male without blemish" (Lev. 1:3), but the priests received from his hands the blind and the lame and the sick and the torn (1:8, 13) and were party to his transgression. Do you not know, thunders the Lord, that under such circumstances "I have no pleasure in you . . . neither will I accept an offering at your hand" (v. 10).

On His part, God could say, "I have loved you," but the *priestly* record was one of unfaithfulness, from the kindling of strange fire by the sons of Aaron (Lev. 10:1), to the transgression of the sons of Eli (I Sam. 2:12, 13), to the profaning of the Lord's table by the post-Exilic priests (1:7, 12). These priests had a form of godliness, but only an empty form.

Actually, the people had not said, "Wherein hast thou loved us?" nor had the priests boasted, "The table of the Lord is contemptible" (1:7) nor "The fruit thereof, *even* his meat, is contemptible" (v. 12), but that was what they thought in their hearts, and their actions betrayed their thoughts. God therefore speaks through His prophet that He might prick the conscience of His people. It is as though we hear His words as recorded by another prophet, "Come now, and let us reason together" (Is. 1:18), for the *heavenly* Sovereign seeks to awaken them to the absurdity of the thought that they would so treat even an *earthly* governor (1:8). Their conduct has been reprehensible, yet they seem not to have realized it.

III. Unkept Obligations: The Priests' Neglect of the Covenant (2:1-9)

For the priests to obscure God's truth for Old Testament worshipers by the acceptance of corrupt offerings was a sin of great moment, and it was clearly symptomatic of the apostate condition of the priesthood. Intended as mediators in the covenant set-up, they apparently had no regard for the covenant. Although it was their responsibility to teach God's law to the people, they had failed in this function. They had not even tried. As judges, they had accepted bribes (2:9). Because they were not men of integrity, they had been a stumbling block to the people (v. 8). The common people, expecting the priests to set standards of conduct by their example, had fallen. Well could Nehemiah say, "They have defiled the priesthood, and the covenant of the priesthood" (Neh. 13:29).

The priestly line had descended from Levi (cf. 2:4, 5). In this fact may be observed the amazing grace of God, for Simeon and Levi in vengeance had so conducted themselves as to cause the name of Jacob "to stink among the inhabitants of the land" (Gen. 34:30), and upon his deathbed their father had this to say of them, ". . . instruments of cruelty are in their habitations. . . . I will . . . scatter them in Israel" (Gen. 49:5-7). Yet God had committed to Levi the sacred priestly office, honoring the tribe with signal honor. If any should have known firsthand the truth of God's assertion, "I have loved you," it was the priest. But no, recipients of the grace of God though they were, the priests had denied Him and forsaken the covenant.

Of all people, the priests should have partaken of the blessings of the covenant, but God could not bless religious leaders who were themselves apostate. Instead, His curse must rest upon them (2:2), and they must be visited with ignominy (v. 3).

IV. Untrue Husbands: Rebuke for Idolatry and Divorce (2:10–16)

Like priests, like people! It was ever thus. A corrupt leadership results in a corrupt populace. The *priests* had neglected the Levitical covenant; the *people* had neglected the stipulations of the law. This, according to the Word, the people had done in two ways, two ways which were in reality one: They had divorced their Jewish wives (2:13, 14) that they might take to themselves wives from among non-Jewish, idolatrous peoples (v. 11).

The law of Moses prohibited intermarriage with the inhabitants of the land, for they were worshipers of other gods (Deut. 7:3), and such marriages would inevitably lead to heathen practices of worship (Ex. 34:16) and work counter to the Lord's desire for a godly seed and a holy nation dedicated to the one true God.

Experience had proved the wisdom of the commandment. No sooner had the Israelites left Sinai than the subtlety of Balaam employed this type of infiltration in a last, desperate attempt to thwart the divine purpose for the chosen people to prevail over the Moabites and enter the promised land (Num. 25:1, 2; 31:16). Later, so dedicated a leader as King Solomon fell prey to temptation of this kind and lost his usefulness in the covenant program (I Kings 11:1–11). Ezra rent his garments upon hearing of the widespread sin of similar type among the post-Exilic Jews (Ezra 9:1, 2), when even the priests and Levites were transgressors (Ezra 9:1), and one in the priestly line was so bold as to become son-in-law to Sanballat the Horonite (Neh. 13:28).

The good pleasure of God could not rest upon such covenant breakers. God's will could only be that they be cut off from His people (2:12), for not only were the precepts of the Lord of hosts disregarded, but in the process, as a necessary accompaniment, the guilty parties were traitor (v. 10) to those who were bound together with them in the close relationship of children of God, covenant participants, namely their own wives, whom they put away in order to join themselves to idolaters (vv. 13, 14).

In such a situation, God could only condemn severely what was taking place. Yet there was more to the story, for the Lord God hates divorce in and of itself (2:16).

There was good reason for God's attitude toward divorce. To put away a wife was to transgress against a spouse with whom had been shared the tender, warm ties of early marriage and to treat lightly the vows, actual or implied, taken before God in consummation of the marriage (2:14). If indeed the Mosaic dispensation provided for a "bill of divorcement," it was only a temporary accommodation because of Israel's hardness of heart (Mt. 19:7, 8), and the position of God from the beginning (Mt. 19:4, 5) is well expressed in that "he hateth putting away" (2:16). Certainly in the situation dealt with by Malachi, the divorcing of the wife was, as is clear from the original Hebrew, a sinful act.

V. Unexpected Judgment: The Coming of the Lord (2:17—3:6)

When men sin again and again and are not brought into judgment by God, they tend to become confirmed in their disregard for the Almighty and conduct their lives as though the world were without moral government. So it was with the sinners of Malachi's time, and the careless, impudent words which were attributed to their imaginations, "Where is the God of judgment?" were apt indeed.

God had something to say in reply. He would come, and when He came, He would come swiftly and in judgment (3:1–5). The way would be prepared before Him by His messenger (v. 1). As one reads the prophecy of Isaiah and the Book of Matthew, he watches the pieces of the picture fall together in a perfect mosaic. Isaiah had spoken of "The voice of him that crieth in the wilderness, Prepare ye the way of the Lord" (Is. 40:3), and as John the Baptist entered upon his ministry, Matthew identified him as the one foretold by Isaiah (Mt. 3:3). Yet if God was coming and John was to prepare the way before Him, the Lord Who would come suddenly to judge and to purify, the "messenger [or angel] of the covenant" (3:1), could be none other than the incarnate Son of God. Of His coming in judgment, John the Baptist cried out: "Now also the axe is laid unto the root of the trees" (Mt. 3:10). He added, "He will thoroughly purge his floor, and . . . will burn up the chaff with unquenchable fire" (Mt. 3:12).

Matthew records elsewhere, in vivid language, how the Lord Who came entered the temple and purged it of uncleanness (Mt. 21:12), and how the divine messenger pronounced judgment again and again as He spoke these words of denunciation, "Woe unto you, scribes and Pharisees, hypocrites" (Mt. 23:13, and so forth). Surely the coming of the Righteous One drove the dividing wedge deeper and deeper, made the issues clearer than ever, and prepared the way for the Great Assize and the day of doom for impenitent transgressors.

VI. Unmeasured Blessing: God's Promise if Tithes are Forthcoming (3:7–12)

A new subject is introduced by these words, "Will a man rob God? Yet ye have robbed me" (3:8). With this startling pronouncement and accusation, God returns to the charge of failure on the part of Israel to carry out the precepts of worship outlined by His servant Moses. This time it is the people, not the priests, who are addressed. The rebuke was that appointed tithes (see Lev. 27:30, 31; Num. 18:20, 21; Deut. 14:22, 23) and offerings (the word is variously used for free will gifts, the half-shekel tax for the sanctuary, first-fruits, portions of sacrifices reserved for the priests, and so forth) have been withheld. In consequence, a curse rested upon the people, and they were deprived of blessing.

But again the God of judgment was also a God of grace. Let the people turn from their wicked ways and render obedience to the revealed will of their covenant God, and He would open the sluice gates of heaven and flood them with blessing (3:10). Indeed, so great would be the blessing that field and orchard would be no more prey to the natural enemies of harvest but would produce fruit (v. 11), so much so that the eyes of the nations would be opened wide in recognition of the abundant fruitage which would be forthcoming.

VII. Unwarranted Assertions: The Sure Meting Out of Justice (3:13—4:3)

Yet the same hearts which framed the question, "Where is the God of judgment?" kept on devising complaints against their Sovereign: there was no profit in serving Him. Those who openly repudiated His prescribed way of life were said to gain rather than to suffer and to be free from a hand of correction from above (3:14, 15).

But because there was a faithful remnant in the land, there were lips which were not party to such folly. God always has His own. There are always seven thousand who have not bowed the knee to

Baal. The majority might utter hard speeches against their Maker, but the minority, the little flock, testified to one another of the justice and righteousness and love and mercy of God (3:16). The day of the Lord's coming with its portioning out of justice and the sparing of the righteous ones would vindicate their faith, even as the repeated judgments of history had borne unmistakable witness in the past (cf. RSV translation of v. 18).

God's critics were wrong. Justice *would* prevail and the wicked *would* be punished. The God of heaven was not oblivious to what was happening; records were being kept. There was a "book of remembrance" (3:16; cf. Ps. 69:28, Rev. 20:12, and so forth), and the day would come when those whose names were written in it would be owned of the Judge and spared the doom of the ungodly.

One cannot read the opening verses of the final chapter without calling to mind the words of Zephaniah, "The day of the Lord . . . is a day of wrath, a day of trouble and distress, a day of wasteness and desolation" (Zeph. 1:14, 15) or the words of Joel, "The day of the Lord is great and very terrible; and who can abide it?" (Joel 2:11).

Surely judgment will come, sinners be destroyed, and the godly have final triumph over their foes. Even as the sun pushes above the horizon and its advancing rays bring warmth and joy, so after the dark night of sin and sorrow and injustice another sun, even perfect righteousness, shall flood the world with cleansing, healing touch, and for the first time since the Fall, all will be made right. In that day, gone will be the questions: "Wherein hast thou loved us?" (1:2); "Where is the God of judgment?" (2:17); "Wherein have we robbed thee?" (3:8); and "What profit is it that we have kept his ordinance . . . ?" (3:14). Gone will be hypocritical worship, covenant breaking, idolatry, divorce, and stewardship failure. In the fullest sense, that day will be the Day of the Lord, and as it comes it will bring unmeasured blessing to those whose names are written in the Lamb's book of life (cf. Rev. 21:27).

VIII. Unforgettable Farewell: An Admonition, a Promise, a Threat (4:4–6)

As one comes to the Book of Malachi, he scarcely hears the voice of the prophet, is scarcely aware that a human personality is involved. It is God Who speaks. Perhaps more than in any other book in Scripture, the words are the very words of God.

But God is not to speak again for a long, long time. Four hundred years and more are to elapse before a prophet is again to arise in Israel. The closing words of the book are thus in a very real sense God's Old Testament farewell. They are significant. They begin with admonition; they end with a threat. But in between, as all through the prophets, the God of loving-kindness shows Himself in a gracious promise. In fact, the threat is only the negative side of the promise.

The *admonition* is to remember the law of Moses (4:4), the law both priests and people had forgotten or despised. It has always been and ever shall be that the way of obedience is the way of blessing. God has spoken; we can but carry out His will.

The *promise* is that Elijah will come before the Day of the Lord to turn wayward covenant children back to the faith of their fathers (4:5, 6). For four hundred years this hope and expectation remained in the hearts of faithful Israelites until one came in the spirit and power of Elijah, of whom it was said, "Many of the children of Israel shall he turn to the Lord their God. And he shall . . . turn the hearts of the fathers to the children" (Lk. 1:16, 17). Of this same John the Baptist, Jesus said, "And if ye will receive it, this is Elias, which was for to come" (Mt. 11:14).

Perhaps it is to be expected that the Old Testament should come to a close with blended warning and hope, culminating in the veiled threat of a *curse* (4:6). Jerusalem had killed the prophets and stoned those whom God had sent unto her, so that her house was left desolate (Mt. 23:37, 38). But outside the city wall on Mount Calvary, a transaction was to take place which would change the night into day and make possible the New Jerusalem where sin would reign no more. The covenant is still in force; the sons of Jacob have still not been consumed (3:6). The godly still speak to one another of the sovereign God (3:16) Who is a God of judgment and a God of grace and salvation. The Day of the Lord will yet be consummated, and the *New* Testament, in contrast to the *Old*, well ends, "Even so, come, Lord Jesus. The grace of our Lord Jesus Christ be with you all. Amen" (Rev. 22:20, 21).

Between the Testaments

Between the Testaments

DAVID H. WALLACE

THE PERIOD "between the Testaments" technically commences with the close of the Old Testament Canon.

I. History

For purposes of historical reconstruction, however, it is preferable to consider the entire Persian period which reaches back into late Old Testament times. This era may be dated from the rise of its first figure of prominence, Cyrus, in 538 B.C., to its close after the death of Artaxerxes in 424 B.C. Cyrus was known to the Greeks as well as to the Old Testament writers; II Chronicles, Ezra, Isaiah, and Daniel all allude to him. His fame rests upon his conquest of Babylon in 538 B.C., which established him as the leading ruler of the ancient world of his day. In Jewish history, Cyrus is important because of his lenient policy toward the Jews, for he allowed them to return to Palestine to rebuild their ruined civilization. All the sacred vessels plundered by Nebuchadrezzar were restored to the Jews with Cyrus' blessing for the resumption of the temple services.

During the Captivity, the Jews' houses and lands had fallen into decay so that much reconstruction was necessary. First their homes and then the temple were rebuilt. Reconstruction was begun in 536 B.C. and completed some twenty years later. But during this interval much opposition came from the Samaritans to the north, and from neighboring marauding tribes and passing armies.

Quite different from his father was Cambyses, the son of Cyrus, for he was stupid, arrogant and cruel. Darius supplanted him in

773

522 B.C., and proceeded to organize his kingdom into twenty "satrapies" or states. The Jews prospered under Darius' government, but national stamina had waned, and the prophetic ministries of Haggai and Zechariah were needed to rekindle national zeal. Ezra 6:15 describes the people's joy at the completion of the temple, but their jubilation was restrained by recollection of the grandeur of Solomon's temple as compared to the restored edifice. Darius died in 486 B.C., having met defeat in one of the decisive battles of human history: the Battle of Marathon where Miltiades' armies conquered the Persian forces.

Darius' eldest son, Xerxes, referred to in the Old Testament as Ahasuerus, mounted the throne in 485 B.C. and was assassinated twenty years later. His son, Artaxerxes, became king, and was influenced by Ezra to permit the remaining Jews in Babylon to return to Palestine. Ezra and Nehemiah rebuilt and governed Jerusalem, and at this time national attention was turned again to the Mosaic law. With Malachi the prophets passed from the scene until the time of John the Baptist. Religion eventually became externalized, its spirit dried up, lost in ritual and form. Artaxerxes died in 424 B.C. after a peaceful reign of forty years. After his death the Persian empire began to disintegrate, for moral and political decay had set in.

The Greek period takes its rise from Alexander the Great who confirmed his dominion over Greece and Asia Minor by defeating the Persian armies at the Battle of Arbela in 331 B.C. Indoctrinated with Greek language and culture because of his studies under Aristotle, Alexander sought to disseminate these beneficent influences throughout his domain. This effort is referred to as "Hellenization." Not satisfied with ruling Greece, Asia Minor, and Egypt, Alexander attempted to take India, but his troops refused to advance further. Not long afterward he died in a drunken stupor at the age of thirty-three.

Alexander's policy was twofold: conquest and fusion. Despite his vigor in military affairs, he seems to have been, like Cyrus, a humane and lenient ruler of subject nations. His outstanding significance for Jewish history is that he is responsible for two great movements which prepared the way for the coming of the Gospel: the Jewish Dispersion, and the spread of Greek culture among the peoples of the ancient Near East.

Upon his death, Alexander's empire was divided among his five generals, or *diadochoi*. Seleucus received Babylon, Ptolemy Lagi was given Egypt, Antigonus took Phrygia, Lysimachus inherited Thrace and Bythinia, and Cassander assumed control of Greece and Macedonia. The last three are of only minor importance for Biblical history. Seleucus added Syria and Phoenicia to his domain, and Ptolemy Lagi annexed Palestine to Egypt. So little Judah, lying between the countries of these two powerful generals, was often the battleground over which they fought.

Although Ptolemy Lagi was a warrior, his interests included cultural pursuits also. He is chiefly responsible for founding the great ancient library at Alexandria, which was completed by his son, Ptolemy Philadelphus. In this period at Alexandria, Jewish and Greek cultures came into sustained peaceful contact, and the results of this union pervaded both cultures for centuries. Ptolemy III was a warrior, not a patron of the arts, but like his predecessors he was kindly disposed towards the Jews both in Egypt and Palestine. The century under the first three Ptolemies was a golden age for the Jews, for it was an era of general peace, prosperity, and advance.

The Seleucids in Syria grew envious of the Ptolemies' control over Palestine and in 198 B.C., after a series of contrary circumstances, the Ptolemaic dynasty lost Palestine to the Seleucids. Thus Palestine came under the power of Antiochus the Great, and in doing so was plunged into one of the most oppressive periods in all Jewish history. Seleucid sovereignty was short-lived because the great power of the west, Rome, brought pressure against the Seleucids. At the battle of Thermopylae the Roman legions defeated the Syrians, and again at Magnesia in 190 B.C. Antiochus was forced to pay a crushing war indemnity to the Romans, and to finance this he seized the treasuries of Jewish temples.

In 175 B.C. the Seleucid throne was assumed by Antiochus IV, a son of Antiochus the Great. Antiochus IV, who bestowed upon himself the title Epiphanes ("Illustrious"), is responsible for the most vile outrages ever perpetrated upon the Jews up to this time. Sometimes erratic, sometimes eccentric, he was uniformly wanton and brutal to the Jews, upon whom he tried to force a universal acceptance of Greek culture and religion. Prior to his reign the Jews had co-existed successfully with their conquerors, but when Antiochus attempted to coerce the mto accept Greek religion, the great majority resisted, at first passively, and later actively.

In 168 B.C. the Jewish war of independence, or the Maccabaean revolt, broke out when a godly priest, Mattathias, withdrew to

Modein with his five sons to avoid the persecutions of Antiochus. He was pursued even to this little town twenty miles west of Jerusalem where the Hellenizers tried to force him to perform profane rites. He refused and, in a fit of rage, killed the Hellenizer and a traitorous Jew. So the war began. They fled from Modein into the countryside to arouse loyal Jews to do battle against Antiochus and to pillage centers of Jewish disloyalty. Soon after the revolt began, Mattathias died, and leadership was taken up by his third son, Judas Maccabaeus. "Maccabee," probably meaning "Hammerer," is the name given to the revolt.

At the outset under the generalship of Judas, the rebellion, now enlarged to a full scale war, met with solid success. He defeated the Syrians at Emmaus, and again between Hebron and Jerusalem in the mountains to the east. Jerusalem itself was taken, and the temple was cleansed and rededicated in 165 B.C. The next year saw the death of Antiochus, at whose passing all Palestine rejoiced. An abortive attempt to make a conditional peace with Judas Maccabaeus was ventured by Lysias, Antiochus' successor in the field, but Judas rejected the offer, vowing to secure complete liberty for the Jews. At the Battle of Adasa in 160 B.C., Judas was slain.

At this point the history of the movement becomes confused. Jonathan, another son of Mattathias, was appointed to succeed Judas. But through court intrigue and treachery, both of which were progressively to characterize the Maccabaean revolt, he was captured. Simon, yet another son, was given the mantle of leadership. He declared Jewish independence in 142 B.C. and confirmed it by terminating Syrian influence in Palestine. In 135 B.C. Simon was assassinated by his son-in-law who sought the throne. To Simon goes the credit for securing Jewish independence as an accomplished fact.

The period of Jewish independence dates from the time of Simon, and concludes with the entry of Pompey into Palestine in 63 B.C. At the death of Simon, John Hyrcanus, the third son of Simon, assumed the office of high priest and took over as well civil and military control. In order to secure political independence of Judah, Hyrcanus sought a treaty of alliance with Rome, but Rome was at this time under the Gracchi and preoccupied with internal affairs, and so refused. At the death of Hyrcanus the dynasty began to degenerate rapidly. After this time the Pharisees and Sadducees came into power, and played off one side of the royal house against the other in attempts to secure positions of dominance.

Jannaeus, son of Hyrcanus, because of his rage against the Pharisees, enlisted the help of foreign troops to kill six thousand Jews. This precipitated a civil war in Judah which was to last six years and cost fifty thousand lives. Not only the nation but also the royal family was ruptured by mutual strife, slaughter, conspiracy, and partisanship. Eventually both factions appealed to Pompey to arbitrate the dispute. He did so by entering Jerusalem and killing twelve thousand Jews. Thus fell the Hasmonaean dynasty; the fiery spirit of Judas Maccabaeus was dead, Jewish independence was abolished, and Judea was reduced to a tributary of Rome and occupied by foreign military garrisons. Palestine was to remain in bondage for two millenniums.

II. Literature

The literature of the period "between the Testaments" falls into two classes commonly called the "Apocrypha" and "Pseudepigrapha." The Apocrypha (the hidden things), dealing mostly with the history of the Maccabaean rebellion and with certain fictitious stories emerging from this period, have existed under an ambiguous and clouded status. These books were accepted by the Early Church because they were included in the Greek version of the Old Testament, but they were rejected as non-canonical by the Jews, who referred to them as the "outside books." On the other hand, the Pseudepigrapha (false writings) were never given canonicity by any group. This class of writings is concerned with prophecies of the end of the world allegedly written by outstanding figures of the Old Testament, such as Enoch, Moses, and Ezra, but in fact written long after their time. The problem of the relation between the Apocrypha and the Pseudepigrapha is compounded by the fact that some of the Apocrypha are pseudepigraphical, and some of the Pseudepigrapha are not pseudonymous. Obviously, therefore, this is not a realistic classification.

In the fourth century, Jerome and Cyril of Jerusalem used the term "apocrypha" to denote all Jewish religious books which were extra-canonical. Sometimes the word takes on a disparaging meaning, especially when used of the "apocryphal" gospels; this is to say they are spurious or heterodoxical. However, as time passed the old distinction between Apocrypha and Pseudepigrapha came into use, but confusion resulted. The English scholar, R. H. Charles, broke the accepted pattern by including III Maccabees in the Apocrypha, and II Esdras, formerly in the Apocrypha, was shifted to the Pseudepigrapha. In recent years, scholars have attempted to restore the usage of Cyril and Jerome, which designates the entire corpus of extracanonical literature as Apocrypha. Henceforth, the use of the term Pseudepigrapha is a concession to an unhappy practice.

In the more restricted sense, the Apocrypha include thirteen books which have been included in the English Bible, but are denied equal rank with the canonical Scriptures. These books are: I Esdras, II Esdras, Tobit, Judith, The Rest of the Book of Esther, Wisdom of Solomon, Ecclesiasticus, Baruch, Letter of Jeremiah, Additions to Daniel, The Prayer of Manasses and I and II Maccabees.

How did these books find their way into many of our present Bibles? To seek the answer, one must go back to the early stages of manuscript transmission and translation. The first Latin Bibles were translated in the second century A.D. from Greek documents which included the Apocrypha. In A.D. 391 Jerome initiated an original translation from the Hebrew and Greek Bibles. He designated the twenty-four Old Testament books as canonical, and all others, apart from the New Testament, he set apart as "apocryphal." Later, at the urging of friends, he included hasty translations of Tobit and Judith. At the Council of Carthage in 397, it was decided to include the Apocrypha as suitable for reading, and as a result the Apocrypha came to be regarded as on a parity with Jerome's Canon.

More than a millennium later, at the Council of Trent in 1546, the Roman Catholic Church, in reaction to the question raised by the Reformers about the limits of the Canon, decided that the Apocrypha were of equal standing with the undisputed canonical books of the Old Testament. Further, whoever questioned the canonical status of the Apocrypha and the decision to include them in the Canon was anathemetized. This stand was reaffirmed by the Vatican Council of 1870. The Protestant Reformers opposed this inclusion on the ground that intrinsic evidence showed the Apocrypha unworthy to be classed with the canonical books. Luther acknowledged that the Apocrypha were "useful and good to be read," and accordingly included the Apocrypha (excluding I and II Esdras) at the end of his translation of the canonical books. The Church of England took the position in the Thirty Nine Articles (1562) that the Apocrypha were profitable to read, but were not to be determinative in matters of doctrine. Eventually the Apocrypha were set apart in a secondary class. The Wycliffe Bible omitted them, the Coverdale Bible included them, and the King James Version reversed itself, having excluded them quite uniformly after the nineteenth century.

Following these ecclesiastical rejections of the Apocrypha, popular and scholarly interest in these books declined, but in the nineteenth century, concern for the background of the Gospel was quickened. The period between the Testaments came to be recognized as crucial for an understanding of New Testament events—the movements within Judaism, the impact of Hellenistic culture, and the ebb and flow of world politics. Attention was turned again to the Apocrypha as a source of light on this crucial period, and a renewed appreciation was directed also to the religious quality of this literature. Although there is no serious modern Protestant attempt to include the Apocrypha in the Canon, regard for them is augmented by the fact that most of the pre-Nicene Church Fathers put them on an equality with the canonical Scriptures.

The Apocrypha contain many characteristic forms of literature: popular hero stories, religious history, religious philosophy, moralism, poetic and didactic lyrics, proverbial Jewish wisdom, and that odd genre called apocalyptic. A few safe generalizations may be made about the dates and place of origin of these books. Most of them were composed in Palestine, written in either Hebrew or Aramaic, although a few were originally written in Greek. Roughly, the dates of composition are from around 300 B.C. to A.D. 100. While quite uniformly the Apocrypha reflect the Jewish mind, these books came to be repudiated by the Jews after A.D. 70 when Titus razed Jerusalem. The result was a return by many Jews to the Torah (the five books of Moses), and the natural consequence was a rejection of all nonsacred writings. No other books must be allowed to compete with the Scriptures. An additional supporting factor which compounded this rejection of non-canonical writings was the appearance of some of the books of the Christian "sect." Gamaliel is said to have decreed in A.D. 80 that any Jew who read the Christian writings was under an anathema. To enforce this decision, there was executed a systematic destruction of these apocryphal books, especially the Semitic originals. This Jewish campaign was successful to the extent that no more books of this sort were written, but this did not prevent Christians from preserving these writings, nor did it prevent the Jews from committing extensive portions to memory, a feat of which the Semitic mind is entirely capable.

First Esdras begins abruptly with the account of Josiah's celebration of the Passover in Jerusalem. This book is a compilation of parts of II Chronicles, Ezra, and Nehemiah; it contains all of Ezra except a few verses. But the order of chapters is not the same, for Ezra 4:7–24 follows Ezra 1 in the arrangement of I Esdras. Also the non-canonical story of the three guardsmen has been added. Second Esdras, also called IV Ezra, has in common with I Esdras only the name; the contents are entirely different. It is an apocalypse which alleges to be a prophecy by Ezra about the end of time.

Tobit is a morality story whose title is the name of the chief figure. The purpose of the story is to oppose apostasy in Judah and to glorify the law and religion of the Lord. Judith is the story of a Jewish heroine who, by bravery and devotion to God, delivered Judah from peril. Clearly a fiction, it was written to encourage the nation to resist the foes of their religion and country. The Rest of Esther is a collection of some 107 verses originally interpolated throughout canonical Esther.

The Wisdom of Solomon is a pseudepigraph although it is part of the Apocrypha. Typical of Jewish wisdom literature, it treats such issues as the problem of evil, the way of salvation through wisdom, the nature of God, and the weaknesses of Gentile religion. Ecclesiasticus, also called the Book of Sirach, is the only book in the Apocrypha whose author is known. Like the Wisdom of Solomon, it is classed as wisdom literature, and as such contains parables, fables and aphorisms in defense of Judaism. Baruch stands midway between apocalyptic and wisdom literature, and in addition it is full of prayers and exhortations.

The Letter of Jeremiah is misnamed, for it is not a letter and it was not sent by Jeremiah. Rather, it is an anonymous summons to the Jews to preserve the religion of their fathers against the sin of idolatry and foreign worship. The additions to Daniel are a collection of fanciful stories of which only one relates to canonical Daniel. An excellent example of devotional writing is found in the Prayer of Manasses which evinces a lofty penitential and reverent spirit.

Of special interest to students of the history of the Maccabaean revolt are the two books of the same name, I and II Maccabees, though written by two authors. First Maccabees covers a span of about forty years from 175–135 B.C. Both the literary and historical quality of this book are very high. Second Maccabees describes the events of the Maccabees from 176–161 B.C. It is filled with thaumaturgic elements, or feats of magic, and is therefore much less dependable history than I Maccabees.

The books of the Pseudepigrapha include Ethiopic Enoch, Slavonic Enoch, the Assumption of Moses, Psalms of Solomon, II and III Baruch, IV Maccabees, and a few others. Since these books have never been accorded canonical standing by any religious group, they are of lesser importance, but still they are highly significant for discerning movements of Jewish religious thought in this period.

Of predominant concern to modern Biblical scholars has been the discovery of the now-famed Dead Sea Scrolls in a cave at the northwest of the Dead Sea in 1947. Placed in ceramic jars inside these caves over two thousand years ago, these scrolls are significant for at least two reasons: they include two copies of Isaiah in the Hebrew text which antedate the earliest previous text of Isaiah by hundreds of years and serve to confirm the accuracy of the later text; secondly, the accompanying scrolls are the literary remains of a hermit-like society of men who had withdrawn from the wider circles of Judaism in attempt to revive the ancient religion of their fathers. This society, if not actually a segment of the Essenes, was very much like them in life and doctrine. The dates of the rise and eclipse of the Dead Sea community are difficult to fix, but if the period of occupation of their monastery is indicative, they were an organized group from about 140 B.C. to A.D. 68.

Some scholars and journalists have noted certain doctrinal resemblances between the Dead Sea community and the New Testament, and have concluded that the Christian Church is but an extension of certain religious ideas first advocated by this group. However, a critical analysis of the teachings of the Dead Sea community and of the New Testament reveals the true distinctiveness and uniqueness of the life and doctrine of Christ. The abiding significance of the Dead Sea Scrolls lies in the light they shed upon a previously little-known group of Jews who had, by their withdrawal, implied a rejection of the excesses in life and religion in Judaism as a whole.

III. Institutions

Several new institutions made their appearance in Judaism between the time of the Exile of the Jews and the coming of Christ. The temple was rebuilt by Herod, but this cannot be said to be an innovation. However, the emergence of the synagogue, the Sanhedrin and the religio-political parties sounds a new note in Judaism, and these institutions play a meaningful role in the events recorded in the New Testament.

To trace the development of the synagogue, one must go back to the time of the Exile in the sixth century B.C. Enforced separation from the temple gave rise to the need for a local house of worship and religious instruction, and so the synagogue came into existence. Worship in the synagogue did not include sacrifice, for this was done only in the temple, but the service was devoted to reading of the Law and the Prophets. The liturgy included prayers, songs, and occasionally a homily. In each synagogue a scroll of the law was preserved in an "ark" or small closet. No worship service could take place in a synagogue unless at least ten men were present, and every congregation had its ranks of officers, each of whom was charged with a given duty. By the time of the return of the Jews to Palestine, the synagogue had become so firmly lodged in Jewish life as a local house of worship that the reconstructed temple did not completely displace it, and this acceptance continues to the present.

The origin of the Sanhedrin is clouded, but it is known to have functioned in Judaism in early Roman times. "Sanhedrin" is a Hebrew form of a Greek word which means "council." In the widest sense it designated simply a court of justice, but in the technical sense it referred to the body of seventy-one men in Jerusalem who constituted the highest Jewish tribunal, or supreme court. Its members were drawn from the aristocracy, the priesthood, elders, and from the scribes, Pharisees and Sadducees; Matthew 26:3, 57 and other passages indicate that the acting high priest was the head and ruling official. During the Roman period in Palestine, the Sanhedrin reached the peak of its influence, for it was almost completely in control of the internal affairs of the Jews. It was empowered to pass judgment in respect to religious, civil, and criminal law, and in strictly religious affairs its authority extended to all Jews of the Dispersion. That it had the right to try certain capital offenses is clear from the Synoptic Gospels which record that the death of Christ was ordered by the Sanhedrin. This tribunal passed out of existence after A.D. 70, and the seat of authority was moved north to Tiberias.

Of the plethora of parties, groups, divisions, and cliques within Judaism at the time of our Lord, only three are important: the scribes,

Pharisees, and Sadducees. After the fall of the monarchy in Israel, the priests became the chief officers of the nation, and it was under Ezra that the scribes probably originated. With renewed interest in the Torah, there developed a concern for the application of the Torah to various situations in life. It became the task of the scribes to search the law to determine its requirements and applications. In time the scribes came to be acknowledged as professional students and defenders of the Jewish law. Out of this intense concern for the application of the law, there arose a body of oral tradition which was eventually elevated to a position of authority equal to the Scriptures themselves. The practical result of their efforts was to impose a stifling set of religious restrictions upon the Jews, and it was against this corrupting influence that Jesus inveighed (Mt. 23). Scribal tradition finally reduced the vital religion of the Old Testament to sterile, codified rabbinism.

Although it is not established with certainty, it is probable that the Pharisees emerged from that group of orthodox Jews, called the "pious ones," who resisted Greek influences in the time of Antiochus Epiphanes. The name "Pharisee" is from a Semitic word meaning "separated ones," a title originally given them by their enemies in pre-Christian times. Their separation was from the Hellenizing tendencies of their day, and was therefore thought to be pleasing to God. Closely allied with the scribes, they upheld the strictest forms of Jewish worship, revered the Torah and the rabbinic tradition which encrusted it, and generally acted as religious spokesmen for and to the common people. The doctrinal beliefs which distinguished the Pharisees as a party included resurrection, divine punishment upon the wicked and bliss for the righteous, the existence of angels, divine sovereignty over history, and the supremacy of the Torah. Divergence of doctrinal opinion existed within the Pharisaic party, but it was over marginal issues. Early in his public ministry, Jesus came under their attack because He was thought to have broken Jewish law. They in turn became the object of His wrath for their external concept of righteousness. Because of an inner, though debased, vitality the Pharisees survived the destruction of Jerusalem in A.D. 70, but their influence was weakened by the times.

A casual reading of the Gospels might lead to the conclusion that the Pharisees and Sadducees were largely in harmony, but in fact they were usually inimical to each other, and it was only their common hostility to the life and ministry of our Lord that brought them temporarily together. In the latter days of the Maccabaean dynasty, they opposed each other violently, the Sadducees in power under Jannaeus, and the Pharisees in the ascendancy under Alexandra. The name "Sadducee" is probably taken from Zadok, the high priest of II Samuel 8:17. As in the case of the Pharisees, the origin of the Sadducees is shrouded; scholars incline to assign their appearance to Maccabaean times. Whereas the Pharisees shared the interests of the common people, the Sadducees tended to associate themselves with the aristocracy and ruling classes. They were more concerned with political than religious affairs, but what religious tenets they held constituted chiefly a negation of the creeds of the Pharisees. It is noteworthy that, in common with Christ and the apostles, they rejected the authority of the oral tradition and recognized only the Torah as religiously authoritative. They opposed Jesus, not primarily for religious reasons, but because His claims and His following among the common people tended to jeopardize the political status of Palestine, and with it their vested interests and fortunes. Because they were so closely knit to the political structure of their times, they were eclipsed when that structure was obliterated by Titus in A.D. 70.

New
Testament
Backgrounds

New Testament Backgrounds

JULIUS ROBERT MANTEY

ALEXANDER THE GREAT began the Greek invasion of the Near East in 334 B.C.; that same year he defeated the Persian army at Granicus in Asia Minor, and again the following year at Issus. In 332 B.C. he reached the Phoenician coast (Lebanon) and captured Sidon and Tyre after a long siege. Proceeding south, he was welcomed in Jerusalem without resistance and with regal reception. The Jewish priests were in ceremonial costumes and the citizens were dressed in white garments (Josephus, *Antiquities*, Book XI, VIII, 5). This friendly demonstration influenced Alexander to offer the Jews generous terms. No one was taken into slavery; they were permitted free enjoyment of their laws and religious liberties; they were exempted in sabbatical years from paying taxes. Thousands of young Jews enlisted in Alexander's army and marched south to help him conquer Egypt, and then helped subdue what remained of the Persian army in the Near East.

Seventy cities were colonized and settled by people friendly to Alexander and became centers of Greek culture, including Antioch, Jerusalem and Alexandria. Greek sports became so popular that Jewish priests were accused of neglecting duties to participate in them. Greek philosophy and culture were generally received and entered into dynamic competition with Jewish concepts and culture. Polytheism especially became a snare to the Jews. But when Antiochus Epiphanes, a Syrian ruler, sought to force polytheism upon the Jews, the Maccabean revolt ensued in 167 B.C. After twenty-five years of guerrilla wars, bloody struggles and costly sacrifices, the Jews won independence, first religious and then political, and they maintained it until 63 B.C. Then the Romans marched in and took over.

I. Benefits Derived from the Greeks

An outstanding and providential benefit of Greek culture to the Jews was the Greek language. For three and one-third centuries prior to Christ's birth the Jews had been exposed to it. Since it was advantageous to them to learn to speak and to read Greek, they became a bilingual people.

Ptolemy Philadelphus, who became king over Egypt in 283 B.C., is credited with having invited the Jews to send able scholars to Alexandria in Egypt to translate the Hebrew Old Testament into Greek (Josephus, *Antiquities*, XII, 2). This translation is called the Septuagint and is abbreviated LXX, meaning seventy. Well-received and widely read, this translation became a notable factor in popularizing the use of Greek in services of worship and in furnishing a religious vocabulary for Christians. Most of the quotations in the New Testament come from the Septuagint.

Of all ancient languages, the Greek language was the best medium for accuracy of expression. And in New Testament times it was better in this respect than it is now. It had eight cases which, with the use of prepositions, facilitated stating truth unambiguously. And its tense system exceeded that of all the other ancient languages in making unmistakably clear what a writer had in mind. In addition to the tenses which we have in English, the Greeks had an *aorist* tense, the chief function of which was to state the single occurrence of an act or event, whereas the *present* tense was used to express continuous or repeated action. The fact that the *aorist* tense occurs in I John 2:1 in the verb "sin" makes clear that John was urging Christians to abstain from all sin: "These things I write unto you that you not sin at all." But in I John 3:9, where the verb "sin" occurs in the *present* tense, the correct translation is, "He that is born of God does not continue sinning." The use of the Greek *present* tense in I John 3:8 makes clear that to the Apostle John habitual indulgence in sin was proof that one was not a Christian: "He that continues practicing sin is of the devil."

Not only through its complex and adequate verb system, but also because of its extensive philosophical, ethical and religious vocabulary, the Greek language was the best vehicle for the record of

God's glorious revelation in Christ given in the New Testament. Modern Romance languages, and the English language, have deep roots in Greek. So much of the Greek has been assimilated into the English, that of the approximately five thousand words in the Greek New Testament about one-fifth of them have been transliterated into the English language, as a whole or in part. Many times only a syllable, such as a prefix or a suffix, has passed into the language, but frequently whole words from the Greek have become a part of our English vocabulary: paradox, paradise, planet, plastic, plethora, pleurisy, pneumatic, pneumonia, poem, police, polygamy, polyglot, polygon, and many others.

II. The Jews under Roman Domination

When the Roman general, Pompey, invaded Judea and captured Jerusalem in 63 B.C., Jewish independence came to an end. Like Alexander the Great, Pompey followed the Roman governmental custom of not interfering with religious customs. He permitted Hyrcanus, the high priest, to exercise full liberty in matters of worship. Pompey started back to Rome soon afterwards with the Jewish king, Aristobulus, and his wife and four children, in order to have them as a part of his exhibit of conquered rulers and their families for his triumphal procession in the city of Rome.

To understand what follows we need to go back in history. In 129 B.C., the Idumeans, descendants of Esau, who lived between Judea and Egypt, were conquered by the Jews and given a choice: either leave their country empty-handed, or accept the Jewish religion, outwardly at least, by submitting to circumcision. They chose the latter.

Herod the Great was an Idumean. Although not a real Jew at heart, he became king of the Jews. Herod's father, Antipater, had become a general in the Jewish army. Not many years after the Romans invaded Palestine, they appointed Antipater as chief civil ruler over the Jews. He appointed his son Herod over the territory of Galilee, where Herod distinguished himself and won favor from the Romans. Herod was a very astute politician and a man of forceful character. He managed time after time to ingratiate himself with those over him in government. With high taxes collected from the Jews, he bribed governors and emperors, and so gained political favor that in 42 B.C. he was appointed tetrarch of Judea. In 40 B.C., when soliciting help in Rome after the Parthians had invaded Judea, he was given the title of king by the Roman senate, and was subsequently aided by a Roman army in driving out the Parthians.

The Parthians had helped Antigonus, a son of Aristobulus, deposed by Pompey in 63 B.C., to become king of Judea. The Jews preferred Antigonus to Herod, since Antigonus was a descendant of the famous Maccabean kings. So they had sided with the Parthians in fighting against Herod and the Romans. But Herod, the unwanted Idumean, regained dominion and was reinstated as ruler in 37 B.C.

Herod took immediate steps to destroy more than 100 outstanding Jewish citizens, including all but two members of the Sanhedrin, on the ground that they had supported Antigonus.

Herod had at least ten wives. Most favored of these was the beautiful Mariamne who was of royal Jewish descent. But Herod's sister, Salome, was jealous of her and by insidious innuendo and slander created suspicion in Herod's mind as to Mariamne's loyalty.

Owing to pressure from the Jews, Herod appointed Aristobulus, brother of his wife Mariamne, as high priest. So popular was this appointment that Herod feared for his own position and had his brother-in-law drowned. Within a few years Herod had executed one relative of his after another. Some of these were his mother-in-law, Alexandra, and her father Hyrcanus, a high priest; his uncle, Joseph; and his favorite wife, Mariamne. And in 6 B.C. he had two of his sons executed, Alexander and Aristobulus, sons of Mariamne.

It was within a few months of this time that Herod sent out the brutal order to slay all the children in Bethlehem two years old and under, since he had learned from the wise men that a child destined to become king had been born there.

At the age of seventy, a few days before his death in 4 B.C., on the ground that his son Antipater had plotted to succeed him in office, Herod had him killed. Herod's will specified that three of his sons should reign over his dominion: Archelaus over Judea and Samaria; Antipas over Galilee and Perea; Herod Philip over Auranitis, Trachonitis and Batanea, which were situated north and east of Lake Galilee. Fearing that people would not mourn when he died, Herod gave orders to arrest hundreds of eminent Jews and to have them slain on the same day that he died. However, after his death, the members of his family refused to acquiesce in such brutality.

Archelaus was unpopular as a ruler from the very beginning. A delegation was sent to Rome to protest against his confirmation as ruler by the emperor Augustus, but their mission failed. His rule was full of injustice, gross cruelty, and wanton slaughter of Jewish citizens. He was unable to establish and maintain order. Consequently, in A.D. 6 he was deposed and banished to Gaul and his property was confiscated.

He was succeeded by Coponius, a Roman, who had the title of procurator. Several Romans served in this capacity between A.D. 6 and 26, when Pontius Pilate was appointed. On one occasion Pilate took temple funds (corban, Mk. 7:11) to pay for an aqueduct which channeled water into Jerusalem. When thousands of Jews demanded the return of these funds, Pilate had a large number of them wounded and killed (Lk. 13:1). Pilate met with growing opposition and was deposed after ten years in office.

Such acts of misrule alienated the Jews more and more and tended to bring on the revolt of A.D. 66 that lasted four years and culminated in the destruction of the temple and Jerusalem in A.D. 70.

III. New Light from the Dead Sea Scrolls

While the Dead Sea Scrolls, some of which were first discovered in 1947, throw light mostly on Old Testament books, they nevertheless contribute considerably to a better understanding of the New Testament. They give us a vivid picture of the religious and cultural customs that were prevalent when John the Baptist and Jesus of Nazareth challenged their contemporaries. Many affinities of thought and language are common to both the New Testament and the Scrolls. Such terms as "the elect," "light and darkness," "sons of light," "the two ways," "lake (river) of fire," occur in both. There are both similarities and differences in ideas and practice. Both held that the rite of induction into the order by immersion in water had no saving benefits. Communal fellowship was compulsory among the Covenanters (Essenes) but optional with the Christians (Acts 4:32–37).

Whether John the Baptist was influenced by the Essenes is doubtful, but there is no question about his agreement with them on the necessity of genuine repentance as a prerequisite to baptism (Lk. 3:7–17). Josephus (*Antiquities*, Book XVIII, 5.2) confirms the emphasis on the need of repentance before baptism: "John commanded the Jews to exercise virtue both as to righteousness towards one another and piety toward God and so to come to baptism; that baptism would be acceptable to him, if they made use of it, *not in order to the putting away of some sins,* but for the purification of the body; supposing that *the soul was thoroughly purified beforehand by righteousness*" (italics mine). Translators of the New Testament into modern speech, such as Weymouth, Goodspeed and Williams, therefore render Matthew 3:11 in this way, "I indeed baptize you in water because of repentance."

IV. How The New Testament Canon Developed

After the ascension of Christ, as churches were formed and Christianity expanded, no New Testament books existed as authoritative sources for preaching the Gospel. The Old Testament was regarded as inspired both by Jews and Christians, and parts of it were read regularly and expounded in synagogue and church worship services. Christians made effective use of messianic passages to show Jesus of Nazareth as fulfillment of them.

Believers were dependent upon the testimony of people who knew and had heard what the Saviour said and did. Hence the witness of the apostles became the chief authoritative source for establishing and confirming the reliability of all information pertaining to Christ.

While the apostles were alive and their testimony was available, and the preaching of the Gospel was limited to Palestine and contiguous areas, the need for written records was not urgent. But after the death of the apostles, and others who had seen and heard the Lord Jesus, the situation changed. If the events of our Saviour's life and his teachings had not been written, we would be dependent merely upon hearsay and tradition.

Fortunately, through God's providence and the impulsion of the Holy Spirit, some of the apostles, and other intimate associates who saw and heard them frequently, have given us written, authoritative and historical records of their knowledge of the most important fact in history as well as the unequaled and divine message which we have in Christ. Luke definitely states that many "eyewitnesses" had committed to writing certain facts and teachings pertaining to Christ, and that he himself, after careful research, was writing to confirm the certainty of such vital truths (Lk. 1:1–3). It is likely that some of these records to which Luke refers were made before the Saviour was crucified. Some no doubt were brief accounts, possibly letters to relatives or friends, of particular events, such as a miracle or description of the reaction of friends or foes to what Jesus had said or done. Such eyewitness accounts Luke and the other gospel writers had access to, to a certain extent at least, when they gave the world these tremendously treasured writings. Of course, they also knew and interviewed many people who had seen and heard Christ.

The first of the Pauline epistles, many believe, is Galatians, written around A.D. 48, before the Jerusalem conference recorded in Acts 15. If the conference had preceded the writing of it, the Apostle Paul would surely have made mention of its conclusions, for doing so would have been a clinching argument against Gentile believers' having to submit to circumcision.

V. Recent Confirmatory Evidence from the Papyri

It is rather ironic that the earliest New Testament fragment discovered among the papyri affirms the existence of the last and latest Gospel. This fragment, found in Egypt, consists of John 18:31–33, 37, 38, and was published by C. H. Roberts in 1935 (*An Unpublished Fragment of the Fourth Gospel*). It is a copy made close to A.D. 100, possibly from the manuscript which John himself had written. It furnishes unassailable and reliable proof of the dependability and preservation of the Gospel of John as we have it in Greek today; for the text of the fragment agrees word for word with the Nestle Greek New Testament text which is in popular use at present. Here we have proof positive that the autograph copies of the New Testament have not been miscopied and that their words have been transcribed accurately and preserved generation after generation.

Other extraordinary confirmatory evidence that the books of the New Testament were written in the first century and that they were treasured as precious and authoritative is the discovery of *Egerton Papyrus 2*. It was purchased from a dealer in 1934 in a collection of papyri and consists of four fragmentary pages of sayings of Christ. It is evidently part of an unknown gospel, paraphrasing ideas expressed in our four Gospels. This phenomenal discovery is explored in Bell and Skeat's *Fragments of an Unknown Gospel and Other Early Christian Papyri*, 1935. It paraphrases the thought of no less than 21 verses occurring in the four Gospels. Just when it was written is uncertain. Perhaps its greatest historical value lies in the fact that it furnishes new and convincing evidence that all the Gospels were written before A.D. 100 and that the Fourth Gospel could have been written by the Apostle John.

The oldest manuscript we have of the Gospel of John, except the fragmentary parts just mentioned, is the *Bodmer Papyrus II,* dated around A.D. 200. It was found in Egypt in 1955 and contains the first 14 chapters of the Fourth Gospel, plus several fragments of other chapters in it. It is valuable and noteworthy as our oldest witness (by about 150 years) for clearing up difficult readings in two verses concerning which there has been considerable uncertainty. In John 7:8 we read, "I go *not yet* up to the feast," instead of "I go *not* up to the feast." The manuscripts are almost equally divided on these readings, so much so that the Nestle Greek text in one edition has one and then in another the other reading. Now the scales are tipped decisively in favor of the words *not yet.* And in John 7:52 *Bodmer Papyrus II* has inserted the Greek article before the word *prophet:* "See that *the* (not *a*) prophet does not rise out of Galilee." None of our translations inserts the article *the* here. However, the context definitely implies that the Messiah was being discussed. Other prophets had come from Galilee.

A flood of light has come upon the text of the New Testament through comparative study of thousands of ancient manuscripts as well as from the papyri. The *Beatty Papyri* of the third century, which contain large sections of the New Testament, have proved very helpful. The science of textual criticism reveals that the copying of manuscripts has been so accurate that there is uncertainty about only one-thousandth part of the New Testament, and that no teaching of it now stands in jeopardy.

Before the end of the first century, every book of the New Testament was written and highly treasured, but these books had not yet been assembled in one volume. As churches learned that another church or churches had copies of a book which they did not have, they arranged to acquire a copy for themselves. Thus gradually all the New Testament books were assembled. This process was almost complete at the end of the second century.

From the ascension of Christ onward, the teachings and authority of Jesus had full recognition in all the churches. The chief work of the apostles and the other preachers was to so proclaim Christ and His teachings that their hearers would accept Him as Saviour and Lord. His life and teaching illuminated, fulfilled and outranked much of the Old Testament.

In worship services, parts of both the Old and New Testaments were customarily read. Both before and after the death of the apostles, their writings were highly treasured. Their oral and written testimony was regarded as the best and final authority as to what Christ had said and done. After their death, their writings more than ever were considered indispensable as well as trustworthy and authoritative in all the churches.

As early as A.D. 95, Clement of Rome quoted freely from Matthew, Luke, Hebrews, Romans, Corinthians, and so forth, in his long letter to the Christians in Corinth. *The Epistles of Ignatius* (A.D. 115) have scores of quotations from the Gospels and the Pauline epistles (Eph. 5; Rom. 6, 7). *The Epistle of Polycarp* to the Philippians (A.D. 120) makes extensive use of verses in Philippians and also cites nine of the other Pauline epistles as well as ten of the other New Testament books. Not only have these and other contemporary writers quoted New Testament books as authoritative and inspired, but they have also given evidence that their whole philosophy of life was governed by the truths set forth in the New Testament (cf. *The Didache,* about A.D. 120; *The Shepherd of Hermas,* A.D. 130; *The Epistle of Barnabas,* A.D. 130). To the authors of such writings, the teachings of Christ and the apostles were authoritative and absolutely dependable in all matters of faith and Christian conduct. In *The Epistle of Barnabas* we first find the phrase "it is written," referring to a New Testament book (IV. 14).

By A.D. 170 most, if not all, of the books of the New Testament were very likely being read on a par with Old Testament books. Their inherent quality of inspiration and authority, originated and motivated as they were by the Holy Spirit, led to their acceptance and acknowledgment. However, in some churches a few "apocryphal" books, written in the second century, were also read at times. Certain heresies, such as Gnosticism, challenged the authority of the New Testament message and questioned the authenticity of some New Testament books. Such disagreement and conflicting views motivated Christian leaders to come to an understanding as to what books were to be regarded as most worthy and useful in the preservation and proclamation of Christianity. In *The Muratorian Fragment,* dated in the late second century, all the New Testament books are listed except III John, James, Hebrews, I and II Peter. Complete unanimity evidently had not yet been attained in the matter of the New Testament Canon.

In the fourth century, a few general epistles, especially II Peter, were still questioned by some, as well as the book of Revelation. In one of his pastoral letters, Athanasius (A.D. 296–373) included all 27 books we now recognize. He wrote: "These are the wells of salvation so that he who thirsts may be satisfied with the sayings in these. Let no one add to these. Let nothing be taken away." And in the Council of Carthage in 397, well attended by delegates from many churches, this declaration was made: "Aside from the canonical Scriptures, nothing is to be read in church under the name of divine Scriptures." The 27 books in our New Testament were acknowledged as the only ones qualified to belong to the New Testament Canon.

Back of the choices made as to what books should receive this high recognition is this noteworthy fact: Whenever it was certain that an apostle had written a book, that book was deemed indispensable and was considered worthy to be a part of the Canon. The apostles had firsthand knowledge of what they wrote; they had had personal contact with Jesus of Nazareth. The next most authoritative writers would naturally be men who knew the apostles well and had often heard them give their testimonies. They were in an ideal and unique historical relationship to give reliable information as to the message and the interpretations given by the apostles.

The
Gospels

The Gospels

F. F. BRUCE

FOR SOME THIRTY years after the death and resurrection of Christ, the necessity for a written account of His ministry was not greatly felt. So long as eyewitnesses of the saving events were alive who could speak with confidence of what they had seen and heard, the living voice sufficed by way of testimony. Even when the good news was told by men and women who had not had direct contact with Christ in the days of His flesh, they could always appeal to the authority of those who spoke with first-hand knowledge. And this attitude of mind was long in dying out. As late as A.D. 130, Papias, bishop of a church in Phrygia, tells us how eagerly he used to interview those who knew the apostles and ask them what the apostles really said, for he felt that in this way he was in much closer touch with the original gospel facts than he could ever be by reading a written record.

But, as these thirty years began to come to an end, there were many who began to realize the need for something more than the spoken testimony of the eyewitnesses. The eyewitnesses were growing old, and if the Second Coming of Jesus did not take place very soon, the eyewitnesses would shortly die. Their testimony could not be allowed to die with them, nor could it be left to the uncertain chances of preservation by word of mouth. It is not surprising that it is around this time (A.D. 60) that we find the first beginnings of gospel writing.

Our information about the circumstances in which the Four Gospels came into being is derived partly from the evidence of the Gospels themselves, and partly from statements made by reliable Christian writers of the early post-apostolic age. By combining the information

799

supplied by these two sources, we can come to the following conclusions about the writing of our Gospels.

I. Mark's Gospel: First of the Four?

By common (though not universal) consent nowadays, the earliest of our four Gospels to be written was Mark's. Mark, the evangelist, is almost certainly to be identified with John Mark, the son of Mary of Jerusalem, who is first mentioned in Acts 12:12. At an early date in his Christian career, he accompanied Paul and Barnabas on their first missionary journey; later, when Paul and Barnabas separated on the eve of their second journey, he accompanied Barnabas to Cyprus; later still he appears as a companion of Paul in Rome, and the last reference to him in the New Testament indicates that he was a companion of Peter in the same city. For some years, we gather, between A.D. 54 and 64, he served the apostle as interpreter and aide-de-camp. It may be that Peter never completely lost the Galilaean accent, and found the services of an interpreter useful when he embarked on more widespread journeys in the Mediterranean world. Among the places which Peter and Mark visited together was Rome, and it was in Rome, we are told, that the leaders of the Church approached Mark and asked him to set down in writing the story of Jesus as Peter so often told it. Mark complied with their request, and this is the origin of our earliest Gospel—at any rate in its first form.

The internal evidence of Mark's Gospel agrees well enough with this account. While there are certain sections in it which probably did not come from Peter, it seems probable that, for the most part, this is the gospel story as Peter presented it. In Mark's Gospel there is not much of reverential awe displayed towards the Twelve Apostles, and least of all towards Peter. There are several places in this Gospel where the written narrative in the third person can very easily be turned back into a spoken narrative in the first person, as it came from Peter's own lips. And the scope of Mark's Gospel coincides exactly with the scope of the gospel story as Peter is known to have told it in the early days of the Church's history. For example, in Acts 10:36–43 we have a summary of the Gospel as Peter preached it in the house of Cornelius at Caesarea—the first occasion on which the Gospel was preached to non-Jews. This summary represents the good news as something which "began from Galilee, after the baptism which John preached" and continued until Christ's rising from the dead. But this is exactly how Mark views the story: for him "the beginning of the gospel of Jesus Christ, the Son of God" (Mk. 1:1) is the ministry of John the Baptist, and the culmination of the Gospel is the discovery of the empty tomb and the announcement "he is risen" (Mk. 16:6).

In fact, Mark's Gospel can be shown to be constructed around a framework which corresponds remarkably with the summaries of primitive gospel preaching by Peter and other apostles which are reproduced in Acts and can also be traced in various places in the New Testament epistles. Not only Mark's Gospel, but the other three too, may to a large extent be envisaged as written transcripts of the witness of the apostles to Christ. The Gospels are not biographies; we should regard a biography as strangely defective if it recorded practically nothing of the hero's course of life before he reached the age of thirty. The four evangelists did not write with a biographical intention; they were concerned rather to communicate to their readers the revelatory act of God in Christ, which was expressed in His works and teaching, His death and resurrection.

II. Luke's Gospel: A Book of Beauty

Luke's Gospel has been thought to reflect more of a biographical interest than the other three, but even Luke's biographical interest is strictly subordinated to the main purpose of his writing. What that main purpose was he tells us himself, in the first four verses of his Gospel. It was that a member of the Roman middle class, whom he styles the "most excellent Theophilus," should be more accurately informed about the beginnings of Christianity than he had been previously.

Christianity had been established in Rome for quite a long time before Luke wrote his Gospel. But it had been confined, in the main, to the Jewish community of the city and to immigrants from the eastern Mediterranean shores. If the official classes of Roman society took cognizance of it at all, they thought of it as an obscure and disreputable oriental cult. About A.D. 60, however, something happened which obliged some people at least in official circles at Rome to take an interest in Christianity. The best-known Christian in the world, a Roman citizen named Paul, who was being tried by the Roman governor of Judea on charges arising out of his activity as a Christian apostle, appealed to have his case transferred from the provincial governor's court to the jurisdiction of the emperor in Rome. His appeal was allowed, and Paul was sent to Rome. It was necessary for certain members of the imperial court to investigate the situation, and this gave rise to a more intelligent interest in Christianity on the part of such people than they had entertained before. But where could they get a reliable account of the rise and progress of Christianity? Such information as they could obtain was fragmentary and not too trustworthy. Theophilus was probably a representative of this circle, and it was to supply him and others like him with an authoritative account of the matter that Luke composed his work—which consisted not only of his Gospel, but also of the sequel to his Gospel, the Acts of the Apostles. In this twofold work, Luke traces the origin and development of Christianity from the events immediately preceding the birth of Christ down to Paul's arrival in Rome.

Luke, as a conscientious historian, went to the best sources of information for material for his narrative. By the time that he wrote, there were in existence many works which attempted to give an account of the life and work of Christ. Of these by far the best was Mark's Gospel, which probably appeared at a time when Luke's own gospel-composition was already well advanced. There was also a collection of the sayings of Jesus, arranged according to subject-matter and set in a narrative framework, of which it is widely held that both Luke's Gospel and Matthew's made use. It is, however, lost, as is every other piece of gospel-writing which existed before Luke wrote (apart from Mark's Gospel); and our present concern is with the Gospels which have come down to us as part of the New Testament.

Luke, a Gentile by birth and a doctor by profession, was a friend and fellow-traveler of the Apostle Paul. He was probably a member of the first Gentile church that was founded, the church of Antioch in Syria, and both there and in his various journeys with Paul, he had ample opportunity to meet and interrogate people who could give him first-hand information about the events which he wished to narrate. Although he himself was not a companion of Jesus in the days of His ministry, he tells us that his authorities were people who "from the beginning were eyewitnesses, and ministers of the word" (Luke 1:2). He had opportunity to meet Peter and other apostles, James, the brother of Jesus, and other members of the Holy Family, Philip, the evangelist, and his four prophesying daughters, and others who could tell him what they had seen and heard during the lifetime of Jesus and the earlier days of the Church's history. And he certainly made good use of the opportunities which came his way.

Something of the debt which we owe him may be realized if we consider how many of the most familiar and best loved gospel stories are found in his Gospel alone. But for Luke, we should never have known the parables of the good Samaritan and the prodigal son. It is he who tells us of the pharisee and the publican, of the rich man and Lazarus, of the rich fool, the unjust steward, and the importunate widow. It is to him that we owe our knowledge of the incidents of the grateful Samaritan leper, the restoration to life of the widow's son of Nain, the grace shown to the penitent woman who washed Jesus' feet with her tears, and Martha's complaint about her sister's failure to help her with the housework. It is he alone who has preserved the accounts of Jesus' appearance before Herod, the ruler of Galilee, of His prayer for God's forgiveness upon those who crucified Him, of His assuring reply to the plea of the repentant robber who was crucified alongside Him, and of His companionship in resurrection with the two disciples on the Emmaus road, as He "expounded unto them in all the scriptures the things concerning himself" (Lk. 24:27).

Some of those parables and incidents which are peculiar to Luke's narrative remind us of one of the outstanding traits of his character —a special sympathy with women and other despised and underprivileged groups, such as Samaritans and social outcasts and victims of the economic and political situation of the day. Of course, this sympathy was shown by Jesus Himself, but it was an aspect of the ministry of Jesus which Luke evidently found very congenial, and he has emphasized it in his record. In this Gospel preeminently Jesus is revealed as the Friend of sinners. And Luke portrays Him in this role with such grace and charm that his Gospel has often been acclaimed as the most beautiful book in the world.

III. Matthew's Gospel: The Rightful King

Matthew's Gospel, which stands at the beginning of the New Testament in the order with which we are best acquainted, was probably not the earliest Gospel to be written, but there is no book of the New Testament which could so fittingly occupy this introductory position. For Matthew's first chapter begins with a genealogical tree whose roots go down deep into Old Testament history, showing how Jesus is the descendant of Abraham and the heir to King David's throne. But if in the first chapter He is presented as the fulfilment of the hope of Israel, Matthew's second chapter presents Him as the fulfilment of Gentile aspirations, for the wise men from the east who come to worship Him represent the first coming to pass of the promise: "Gentiles shall come to thy light, and kings to the brightness of thy rising" (Is. 60:3).

Matthew's Gospel probably made its first appearance in the region of Syria and Palestine, and represents the outlook of Jewish-Christian communities—not, however, those Jewish-Christian communities which were zealots for the Law and looked with grave suspicion on the Gentile mission, for the Gospel closes by emphasizing that the proclamation of the Gospel to *all nations* was the last charge laid by the risen Lord upon His disciples.

This evangelist may well be described as a "scribe which is instructed unto the kingdom of heaven . . . which bringeth forth out of his treasure things new and old" (Mt. 13:52). Like Luke, he has derived his material from a variety of sources, but he arranges it so as to make his work primarily a digest of the teaching of Jesus. The nativity narratives of chapters 1 and 2 serve as a prologue to this Gospel, and the passion and resurrection narratives of chapters 26–28 serve as an epilogue, but the account of the ministry of Jesus which occupies chapters 3–25 is organized around five great discourses, in each of which the evangelist has brought together the teaching of Jesus concerning a particular aspect of the Kingdom of Heaven (which was, of course, the great theme of His teaching). The first of these discourses, usually known as the Sermon on the Mount (chs. 5–7), sets forth the law of the Kingdom; the second (ch. 10) lays down the procedure for the proclamation of the Kingdom; the third (ch. 13) illustrates by means of seven parables the growth of the Kingdom; the fourth (ch. 18) contains instruction about the fellowship of the Kingdom; the fifth (chs. 24, 25) records the eschatological discourse on Olivet followed by three parables which describe the consummation of the Kingdom. The narrative material of chapters 3–25 is arranged in such a way that each block of narrative leads up naturally to the subject of the discourse which follows it. Consequently, it is usually rather easy to remember exactly where in Matthew's Gospel a given passage is to be found.

Matthew's Gospel was probably written around A.D. 70, the year in which the city and temple of Jerusalem were destroyed. There are one or two places in the Gospel which suggest that the author knew that this event, which Jesus had foretold, had actually taken place by the time of writing.

The three Gospels which we have discussed thus far are called the Synoptic Gospels, because they contain so much material in common that they can be set out in parallel columns synoptically, that is to say, in a form in which all three records can be seen together. Yet each Gospel has its distinctive quality: Matthew presents Jesus as the rightful King, Mark as the obedient Servant of the Lord, Luke as the sympathizing Son of Man.

IV. John's Gospel: The Incarnate Word

The Fourth Gospel has a quality which sets it apart from the others in a category all its own. It is traditionally ascribed to the last survivor of those who were companions of Jesus, and the internal evidence confirms the view that this Gospel is the work of an eyewitness. John, the beloved disciple, we are told, gave this "spiritual Gospel" to the churches before his death, which took place around A.D. 100. He had reflected long on the significance of the life and work of Jesus; his memories of those early days became clearer rather than dimmer with the passing of the years; and he experienced in a full degree the fulfilment of Jesus' promise that He would send His Spirit to make His teaching plain to His disciples. Much that he and his fellow-disciples had failed to understand at first became clear to him as time went on. No doubt, as he grew older, many of his younger friends would come to him to hear about those wonderful days when he had walked and talked with Jesus, and he, for his part, never tired of telling them what they wanted to hear. It would indeed be a tragedy if he should die without putting his reminiscences on permanent record. At last he did record them, and in consequence we have John's Gospel in our New Testament.

When we read one of the earlier Gospels, we sometimes get the impression that in the story which we are reading there is more than meets the eye, something beneath the surface, which if we only could grasp it would give fuller meaning to the record. This is especially true of Mark's Gospel. But when we come to John's record, he brings this deeper truth to the surface, so that what was formerly implicit now becomes explicit: the ministry of Jesus was the activity of the eternal Word of God, who had become incarnate as man for the world's salvation. The mighty works of Jesus were "signs" through which those who had eyes to see might behold the glory of God dwelling among men in the person of His Son. In Him every other revelation which God had ever given of Himself reached its fulfilment and culmination: to see Christ was to see the Father; He was the way, the truth and the life, apart from Whom none could come to God. John thus supplies the key to the undrestanding of the gospel story told by the other evangelists.

Out of his vast store of reminiscences, John selected a few significant works and words of Christ for his record. He tells us the purpose for which he selected these, and this purpose is as much that of the other Gospels (and indeed of the whole Bible) as it is that of the Gospel of John: "these are written, that ye might believe that Jesus is the Christ, the Son of God; and that believing ye might have life through his name" (Jn. 20:31).

Matthew

GEORGE ELDON LADD

THE PURPOSE OF Matthew's Gospel is to witness that Jesus was the Messiah of Old Testament promise and that His messianic mission was to bring the Kingdom of God to men. These two themes —Jesus' Messiahship and the presence of the Kingdom of God—are inseparably linked together, and each embodies a "mystery"—a new disclosure of the divine, redemptive purpose (see Rom. 16:25, 26).

The mystery of the *messianic mission* is that before Messiah comes as the heavenly Son of Man with the clouds of heaven to establish the Kingdom over all the earth, He must first come in humility among men as the suffering Servant to die. This was unheard-of to the first century Jew. To the Christian today Isaiah 53 clearly predicts the sufferings of Messiah. However, Messiah is not named in this passage, and the context (Is. 48:20; 49:3) specifically names Israel as God's servant. It is not surprising therefore, to learn that the Jews did not understand that Isaiah 53 referred to Messiah. They looked for a Messiah who would come in power and victory, and the Old Testament does indeed promise such a Messiah.

The Son of David is a divine King Who will rule in the messianic Kingdom (Is. 9, 11; Jer. 33), when all sin and evil will be taken away and peace and righteousness will prevail. The Son of Man is a heavenly being to Whom the rule over all nations and kingdoms of the earth is to be committed. The Old Testament does not indicate how these two prophetic concepts of the Davidic King and the heavenly Son of Man are related to each other, or how either of them can be identified with the suffering Servant of Isaiah 53. Therefore, first century Jews looked for a conquering Davidic Messiah or a heavenly Son of Man, not for a humble Servant of the Lord Who would suffer and die. The messianic mystery—the new disclosure of the divine purpose—is that the heavenly Son of Man must first suffer and die in fulfilment of His redemptive messianic mission as the suffering Servant before He comes in power and glory.

Birth and Infancy of Messiah (1:1—2:23)

1. Genealogy (1:1-17)

Matthew opens his Gospel by tracing the lineage of Jesus through David to Abraham to show that Jesus is the Son of David. This genealogy gives the ancestry of Joseph while the different genealogy in Luke's Gospel probably gives that of Mary. The wording of verse 16 carefully indicates that Joseph is not the father of Jesus. The variant texts appearing in the margin of the Revised Standard Version embody an old, but distinctly inferior, textual tradition.

2. Birth Narratives (1:18—2:18)

In Jewish practice, an engagement was held in much higher significance than it is today, and unfaithfulness after an engagement was equivalent to adultery and the breaking of the marriage vow. After the engagement of Mary and Joseph but before their wedding, Mary was found to be pregnant; Joseph assumed that she had been unfaithful. The law permitted Joseph two courses of action: He might expose Mary by bringing her before the court or he might divorce her privately, for a Jewish engagement could be broken only by a divorce. Joseph was inclined to the kinder choice when an angel appeared in a dream telling him that conception had taken place in Mary's body by a creative act of the Spirit of God and that she would bear a son who should be called Jesus, meaning "the Lord saves." Here Matthew strikes the keynote of the character of Jesus' messianic mission. He is not to come as a King to reign in glory, but He is to save His people from their sins. This Virgin Birth of Messiah is the fulfilment of the true meaning of the prophecy in Isaiah 7:14, and the coming of Messiah is to mean that God has come to His people. Joseph was obedient to this dream, and the marriage was not consummated with Mary until after the birth of her Son.

The fact that Herod the Great had been made king of the Jews by the Roman Senate in 40 B.C. and reigned until his death in 4 B.C., enables us to date approximately the time of Jesus' birth. Joseph and Mary had journeyed from Nazareth to Bethlehem because of the taxation imposed by Rome (Lk. 2:4). While they were still in Bethlehem, wise men, similar to those in Daniel 2:2, came to Palestine, probably from Mesopotamia, guided by an unusual heavenly phenomenon. Whether this was an unusual astronomical event or a supernatural appearance cannot be determined. They came first to Jerusalem, where Jewish scholars referred them to the prophecy in Micah 5:2 that the ruler of Israel should be born in Bethlehem. The wise men found the infant Jesus in Bethlehem and worshipped Him, presenting rich gifts.

When King Herod heard that a new king had been born, he was disturbed and determined to destroy any possible rival. He first tried to locate the new king through the wise men; but when he was frustrated in this objective, he took the drastic means of murdering all baby boys in Bethlehem under two years of age. This inconceivably brutal act is in character with what we know of Herod the Great from our historical sources. He was a ruthless murderer of any who frustrated his desires.

3. Removal to Nazareth (2:19–23)

Jesus' life was saved only when an angel warned Joseph in a dream to flee Bethlehem and find refuge in Egypt. Doubtless the journey and stay in Egypt were financed by the gifts of the wise men. Joseph remained in Egypt until he heard that Herod the Great had died. In 4 B.C., Herod's son Archelaus succeeded to the rule of Judea and Samaria. Galilee and the Transjordan area of Perea were given to another son, Herod Antipas. Joseph returned from Egypt to Nazareth in Galilee; and here Jesus lived until the time for His messianic ministry.

Prelude to the Messianic Ministry (3:1—4:25)

1. Preparatory Ministry of John the Baptist (3:1–12)

Jesus' public ministry was prepared and introduced by John the Baptist. For many years no prophet had appeared to Israel to announce the will of God. Suddenly a new prophet appeared in the person of John the Baptist announcing that the Kingdom of Heaven was at hand and that men should repent in preparation for it. John's garb of camel's hair and the leather girdle recalled the apparel of Elijah (2 Kings 1:8). His proclamation of the Kingdom of Heaven was nothing less than an affirmation that the Old Testament promises of the coming of God's Kingdom were about to be fulfilled.

The Kingdom of God means two things: salvation and judgment. This twofold work was to be carried out by the Messiah Who would baptize with the Holy Spirit those who responded favorably, as prophesied in Joel 2, but He would baptize those who rejected His ministry with the fire of judgment. John set forth this twofold baptism by the illustration, still a familiar sight in the Near East, of the threshing operation. The farmer throws the beat-out grain into the air with the winnowing fork that the wind may separate the wheat from the chaff. That the baptism of fire refers to judgment is shown by the phrase, "the chaff he will burn with unquenchable fire" (3:12).

The preparation demanded by the coming of God's Kingdom was repentance. This idea of repentance is derived from the Hebrew word which literally means "to turn around." The repentance demanded by John meant a right-about-face, a turning to God. John proclaimed that all men, even the Jewish people, required this repentance. Many Jews of this time claimed that the mere fact of their Jewish descent assured them a place in the future Kingdom. This claim John flatly denies with the assertion that God can raise up new children to Abraham and does not depend upon the Jewish race to provide a people for His Kingdom. The sons of Abraham as well as other men must show the fruits of repentance. Apart from repentance, they will suffer the judgment which the Messiah is to bring (3:10).

The outward sign of this repentance was baptism in water. Ceremonial washings were common among the Jewish people. Furthermore, when a Gentile became an adherent of the Jewish religion, he was required among other things to submit to a ceremonial bath or baptism. John now requires all men, including Jews, to submit to a new baptism in confession of their sins.

2. Baptism of Jesus (3:13–17)

We do not know how long John's ministry continued. Even though the reports in our Gospels are quite brief, we may infer from John 3:5, which sketches the wide influence of his ministry, that his preaching and baptizing continued for some time. In the midst of it Jesus appeared from Galilee requesting baptism. As John talked with Him, it became evident that Jesus had no sins which required either confession or repentance. In His presence, John was conscious of his own sinfulness and confessed that he, John, should be baptized by Jesus. Jesus, however, replied that John should baptize Him that He might fulfil His messianic ministry. By His baptism, Jesus, although not Himself a sinner, identified Himself with sinful men and took His place with them. This act of self-humiliation and identification with sinners was a manifestation of God's righteousness.

The descent of the Holy Spirit upon Jesus and the voice from heaven signified the formal divine endowment for His messianic mission of bringing the Kingdom of God to men. Verse 17 may well be paraphrased "This is my beloved Son Whom I have chosen to accomplish my purpose among men." It indicates that Jesus is more than Messiah, and that His mission as Messiah is grounded in the fact that He is God's Son.

3. Temptation of Jesus (4:1–11)

Jesus' temptation is closely associated with the baptism and the inauguration of His messianic ministry. The phrase "Son of God" carries messianic significance; it refers not only to His relationship to God, but also to the position He is to fulfil (Ps. 2:7). The various temptations have one element in common, the temptation to use messianic powers in a way which is not conformable to the will of God. Jesus is tempted to use His power to satisfy His own physical need by turning stones into bread; to attract the admiration of the people through a meaningless display of power by jumping from a pinnacle of the temple without injury; or to achieve His messianic mission of a rule over the world other than by conformity to the will and purposes of God. Throughout these temptations, Jesus shows that, as the veritable Son of God, He has come to do the will of His Father and to be completely submissive to His Father's will.

4. Summary of Galilean Ministry (4:12–25)

Matthew now sketches in a few strokes the ministry of Jesus. After the arrest of John the Baptist, described in Matthew 14:3-4, Jesus went to the city of Capernaum on the Sea of Galilee and entered upon His messianic work. Matthew describes His message (4:17), the call of the first disciples (vv. 18–22) and the character of the ministry (vv. 23–25). The time involved in these last verses is obviously of considerable duration, for Jesus went throughout all Galilee preaching the good news of the Kingdom of God and healing all kinds of sicknesses as a manifestation of the power of the Kingdom of God among men. The fame of Jesus spread throughout all the Palestinian area (v. 25).

Discourse I: The Righteousness of the Kingdom *(5:1—7:29)*

Matthew has constructed his Gospel around five great discourses, interspersing them with narrative sections. Each discourse ends with a similar formula (see 5:28; 11:1; 13:53; 19:1; 26:1). The first discourse deals with the righteousness associated with the Kingdom of God. A righteousness greater than that of the scribes and Pharisees is required to enter into the Kingdom of Heaven (5:20). The scribes were the professional scholars of the Old Testament law; and the Pharisees were the laymen who observed . . . with the utmost care the teachings . . . of the scribes. "Scribal righteousness" consisted of the proper observance of a great minutiae of interpretation of the Mosaic law, covering every area of life and conduct. Sometimes this legal observance was associated with deep religious and ethical feeling; at other times it became mere formalism and casuistry. The righteousness of the Kingdom is the righteousness which meets the standards of the Law and the Prophets (5:17)—a phrase which refers to the entire Old Testament. By His teaching, Jesus will bring to fulfilment the true objective of the entire Old Testament.

1. The Beatitudes (5:1–16)

The Beatitudes have to do primarily with the relationship of men to God and the Kingdom of God or God's rule. The word "blessed" includes the idea of happiness. These Beatitudes picture the man who has submitted himself in complete obedience to the rule of God. These "sons of the Kingdom" enjoy a present happiness and are assured a greater blessing in the future Kingdom. Their blessedness or happiness comes from God and is not destroyed by persecution (5:11–12). They are to exercise a salutary influence in the world comparable to salt and light (vv. 13–16).

2. The Character of Kingdom Righteousness (5:17–48)

The righteousness required by the Kingdom of God is a righteousness of the heart. It demands perfection, even the righteousness of God Himself (5:48). Not only is murder an act of sin; anger and abusive language bring men under divine condemnation (vv. 21, 22). A man cannot truly worship God while he is guilty of an unforgiven offense against a brother (vv. 23, 24). Men must therefore give attention to their human relationships lest they eventually fall under the divine judgment (vv. 25, 26).

The sin involved in adultery consists not only of the outward act, but also of the thought in the mind and intent in the heart (5:27, 28). A man should go to any extreme to solve the problem of lust. A particular manifestation of lust is unjustifiable divorce (vv. 31, 32).

Kingdom righteousness must manifest itself in complete honesty. No oath of any kind should be necessary to assure the truthfulness of words which come from a righteous heart (5:33–37).

Kingdom righteousness must also be free from a spirit of revenge of personal wrongs. A son of the Kingdom is always ready to suffer for righteousness, whether it involves physical abuse or the loss of personal goods (5:38–42).

Kingdom righteousness is summed up in one word: love. God bestows His gifts upon all men, both good and evil; and those who would be the sons of God must follow the divine example of love toward both friends and enemies (5:43–48). Such righteousness, demanded by the Kingdom of God, can be only the gift of God; it is of such a character that no man of himself can attain to it.

3. The Practice of Kingdom Righteousness (6:1—7:12)

The righteousness of the Kingdom has to do primarily with a man's relationship toward God. Only a false righteousness parades itself before men (6:1). Kingdom righteousness manifests itself in the giving of money to the poor in such a way that the gift is not known by other men, only by God (vv. 2–4). The true measure of prayer is what a man does in secret, not in public (vv. 5–8). It is concerned first of all with the glory of God and the coming of His Kingdom on earth. The prayer for personal needs is important, but secondary to spiritual concerns. At the heart of prayers is forgiveness; divine forgiveness cannot be separated from human forgiveness (v. 12). The parable in Matthew 18:23–25 shows that human forgiveness is grounded upon and is a reflection of divine forgiveness (6:14, 15). Fasting should be a secret spiritual discipline (vv. 16–18).

Kingdom righteousness involves not only a proper relationship to God, but also a proper attitude toward material possessions. These must always be subordinate to and in the service of the Kingdom of God (6:19–21). The "evil eye," which looks with envy and greed upon material possessions, fills the whole body with darkness (v. 23). Kingdom righteousness requires complete devotion to God; it tolerates no division of loyalty between God and material possessions (v. 24). The sons of the Kingdom should therefore live in complete trust that God will supply the necessary provisions for the physical life; they are not to be pressed by anxiety and worry for these things. Ambition is to be directed toward the Kingdom of God and God's righteousness, rather than toward the acquisition of wealth (vv. 25–34).

Kingdom righteousness manifests itself in a generous attitude toward other men. It is hypocrisy to condemn others and to be unconscious of greater faults in one's own life (7:1–5). This, however, does not mean a lack of discrimination. Wicked people cannot be permitted to profane holy things (v. 6).

The gifts of God's Kingdom are freely available to men. It is the mission of Jesus to bring them. One need only ask to receive, or knock to have the door opened. More than an earthly father, the Father in heaven is willing to give good gifts to His children (7:7–

11). God's generosity should evoke a similar generosity on the part of the sons of the Kingdom (v. 12).

4. The Choice of the Kingdom (7:13–27)

The offer of the righteousness of the Kingdom sets before men two gates: a narrow gate leading to life and a broad gate leading to destruction. The narrow gate is the way of complete submission to the will and the reign of God; only a few are willing thus to submit themselves. The wide gate is the way of self-assertion, however expressed—whether in terms of external righteousness, human recognition, or the pursuit of material goods. Many pursue this easy way (7:13, 14). False prophets will appear, knowing nothing of the Kingdom of righteousness (vv. 15–20). It is not enough to profess discipleship to Jesus; there must be an experience of the righteousness of the Kingdom which means the realization of the will of God (vv. 21–23). The destiny of men depends upon whether they accept and practice the righteousness of God's Kingdom (vv. 24–27).

5. The Manner of Jesus' Teaching (7:28, 29)

The impact Jesus' teachings made upon the people was not alone due to the content of His teaching, but to the way in which He taught. His teaching created astonishment, "for he taught as one who had authority, and not as the scribes" (7:29). The scribes, professional students of the law of Moses, had accumulated a great mass of oral interpretation by which they applied the law to every conceivable situation in daily life. Since all conduct must be brought under the control of the law, it was therefore imperative for a teacher of the law to be intimately familiar with the Scripture itself and also with the accumulated oral interpretation. Scribal teaching consisted, in large part, of recalling what the scribes had taught and of applying existing law to the present situation. This type of teaching stands in direct contrast to the prophets of the Old Testament who came to the people with the announcement, "Thus saith the Lord." The prophet announced the message which came direct from God; for the scribe the entirety of the will of God was embodied in the written law and in the scribal interpretation.

In contrast to both prophet and scribe, Jesus employed a different method in His teaching. He spoke not as a prophet proclaiming the word which came from God; He was not a scribe bringing a new interpretation of the authoritative law. In contrast to both prophet and scribe, He spoke in His own name and authority. He spoke as a new interpreter of the law. "You have heard that it was said to the men of old. . . . But I say unto you." His Word was its own authority. His teaching set forth the righteousness of the Kingdom of God and expounded the true meaning, that is, the fulfilment of the righteousness of the law of Moses.

Narrative I: The Mighty Deeds of the Kingdom (8:1—9:38)

1. A Series of Miracles (8:1—9:8)

Matthew follows the discourse on the righteousness of the Kingdom with a collection of the deeds or the wonderful works of the Kingdom of God. In chapters 8 and 9 he collects a series of mighty works or miracles, the purpose of which is to illustrate the working and power of the Kingdom among men in the person of Jesus. These incidents are not arranged chronologically. Tied together with few specific references of time and sequence, they are to be taken as a topical grouping of events on different occasions, arranged by Matthew to illustrate the mighty works of the Kingdom of God through Jesus.

Contact with a person afflicted with leprosy caused ceremonial uncleanness, but when Jesus touched a leper, his leprosy was immediately cleansed. Jesus' answer to the leper's question, "I will; be clean," (8:3) reflects the same authority embodied in His words, "I say unto you." They show His authority over disease and physical evil. The sacrifice which Jesus commanded the healed man to make is a witness to the priests rather than to the people. The Greek in verse 4 reads, "for a proof to them," and may refer either to the priests or the people; probably it refers to the priests. Jesus commanded the leper not to publicize his healing among the people. This prohibition is associated with the "messianic secret" and the hidden Messiahship of Jesus.

The incident with the centurion (8:5–13) illustrates the power of Jesus' word, the character of true faith and the tragedy of unbelief. This centurion, a commander of a hundred men in the Roman military, was a Gentile soldier who apparently came from one of the many Graeco-Roman cities scattered throughout Palestine, especially in Galilee. As an officer he knew what it meant to exercise authority, and he recognized a far greater authority in the word of Jesus, an authority before which disease fled. In this Gentile, Jesus found a faith manifested by few Israelites.

Faith is the recognition of the true character of the mighty acts of God. The Jews, looking either for a Davidic king or a heavenly Son of Man, stumbled when the Kingdom of God appeared among them in the humble form of a carpenter from Nazareth. Such spiritual dullness carried tragic eternal consequences. In the day of the consummation of the Kingdom of Heaven, warns Jesus, many Gentiles will enter into the Kingdom and enjoy fellowship with the patriarchs, while "the sons of the kingdom"—the Jews who because of their history and tradition were the proper heirs of the Kingdom —will be excluded and suffer divine judgment.

The occasion of the healing of Peter's mother-in-law (8:14–17) serves to illustrate the fact that Jesus' messianic mission fulfils the Servant prophecy of Isaiah 53:4. Here is the messianic secret: that the Messiah must appear among men as the suffering Servant before He comes in glory and power as the heavenly Son of Man.

Jesus is indeed the Son of Man, but the Son of Man fulfilling an utterly unforeseen role of humility and suffering. Jesus tells a scribe enthusiastically offering himself for discipleship that to follow the Son of Man, he must be ready to renounce all worldly securities (8:20). He must fully weigh the implications of discipleship before he breaks with the past. To another prospective disciple, reluctantly offering to follow Jesus after he had discharged certain family responsibilities (v. 21), Jesus makes a seemingly harsh reply: "Let the [spiritually] dead bury the [physically] dead." That is, the demands of the Kingdom of God must have priority over all other claims upon a man's life; and discipleship must be willing to pay this price.

The stilling of the storm (8:23–27) again illustrates the authority and the power of Jesus' word, this time over the forces of nature. The "little faith" of the disciples is seen in their slowness to realize that such authority was actually present in Jesus' word. It is now beginning to dawn upon the disciples that the ordinary categories of human experience are inadequate to describe the power residing in Jesus (v. 27).

Gadara, where the demon-possessed men emerged from the tombs, is a city some eight miles southeast of the Sea of Galilee in Gentile country. The demons recognized in the person of Jesus the Son of God Who will one day be their judge (8:29). This unheard-of power brought fear rather than faith to the people of this city, and they begged Jesus to leave their country.

Jesus returned to Capernaum—His own city—where a paralytic was brought to Him (9:1, 2). Instead of healing him, Jesus forgave his sins. Forgiveness of sins is a divine prerogative (Is. 43:25), and the scribes considered Jesus guilty of blasphemy, that is, of claiming divine powers. Subsequent healing of the paralytic substantiates Jesus' claim: that the Son of Man from heaven is now a man among men with divine authority to forgive sins (v. 6). The people therefore glorified God because such authority was being exercised among men (v. 8).

2. The Kingdom and the Old Order (9:9–17)

Matthew was a Jew who collected taxes for his fellow Jews and turned them over to the representatives of the Roman government. The "tax collectors" were therefore a symbol of the hated Gentile rule over Israel; and "good" Jews considered tax collectors, immoral people, and also Jews who did not observe the scribal traditions, to be equally "sinners." The Pharisees considered all such persons to have surrendered their place within the true Israel or the people of God, but instead of trying to win them back, they held aloof and despised them. The Pharisees viewed righteousness as an entirely human work. God had given man the Ten Commandments, and it was man's responsibility to conform to the law to win the favor of God. By seeking out neglected and despised people, Jesus shocked the Pharisees. In terms of Pharisaic standards, it would be impossible to engage in table fellowship with these "sinners" and yet keep the law of ceremonial purity, because the sinners did not observe the laws of pure foods. Therefore, from the Pharisees' point of view, Jesus was breaking the law of Moses by eating with tax collectors and "sinners" (8:10). Jesus' answer is that these people are sick and need a physician. In the Kingdom of God, God is no longer waiting for men to turn to Him, but is in fact seeking out the lost. Jesus' purpose is not to rescue those who consider themselves righteous but to bring salvation to those who know they are sinners (9:12–13).

Many who had received John's baptism continued to follow John rather than becoming disciples of Jesus. In answer to their question of why Jesus and His disciples do not observe the usual semi-weekly fast (9:14), Jesus replied in terms of the Old Testament messianic expectation of the marriage between God and His people (Hos. 2:19, 20). Since the messianic bridegroom is present, joy rather than fasting is the order of the hour. Jesus hints, however, that because of the "taking away" or death of the bridegroom, there will come a time of sorrow.

The presence of the Kingdom of God and the messianic salvation requires a new external order. That the Old Testament institutions are to give way to something new is illustrated by the parables of the old garment and the old wineskin (9:16, 17).

3. More Miracles (9:18–38)

This section concludes with four more messianic deeds: the healing of the woman with a chronic hemorrhage, Jesus' mastery over death, the healing of two blind men, and the exorcism of a demon (9:18–34). The phrase "son of David" (v. 27) is synonymous with "Messiah." Jesus' messianic mission is not to be king over Israel, but to bring deliverance and salvation to those afflicted by evil and sin. The healing of the dumb demoniac is a manifestation of amazing power. Even the Pharisees recognized supernatural power in Jesus but attributed it to demonic sources, thereby revealing their own spiritual blindness.

Matthew concludes the section of messianic works with a summary (9:35–38). The incidents related in chapters 8 and 9 are selected from a wide and extensive ministry reaching throughout all the cities and villages of Galilee. The ministry consisted of *preaching* the good news about the Kingdom, and *healing* all sorts of diseases. The Kingdom is present in word and in deed.

This passage also introduces the next section in which Jesus entrusts the twelve disciples with an extension of His own messianic ministry.

Discourse II: The Proclamation of the Kingdom (10:1–42)

1. The Preachers and their Mission (10:1–15)

This chapter contains Jesus' charge to the twelve for their present and future ministry. It is in fact the commission for the preaching of the Gospel of the Kingdom throughout the entire area until the return of Christ. This is indicated by a comparison of verses 5 and 18. The immediate mission of the twelve is to be limited to Israel. They are to go neither to the Gentiles nor among the Samaritans, but only to "the sons of the kingdom" (8:12) in an endeavor to save the lost sheep. The future ministry of the disciples and their successors is to go beyond Israel; for they will be dragged before governors and kings and will bear a witness before the Gentiles (10:18).

The ministry of the disciples, like that of their Master, is twofold: the word of the Kingdom and the works of the Kingdom (10:7, 8). They are to announce the presence of the Kingdom of Heaven, and they are to perform the works of the Kingdom in delivering men from the power of evil, thus demonstrating the Kingdom's presence. They are to throw themselves entirely upon the hospitality of the people to whom they minister. Those who receive these emissaries of the Kingdom of Heaven will experience the benediction of peace, but those who reject the emissaries, and therefore their message, invite terrible doom on the Day of Judgment (vv. 9–15).

2. The Response to be Expected (10:16–42)

In verse 16, Jesus looks beyond the immediate mission of the twelve to the mission of the Kingdom of Heaven throughout the course of this age. His disciples can expect opposition and persecution by Gentile governors and kings. They are assured, however, that the Spirit of God will speak through them in the hour of need. The preaching of the Gospel of the Kingdom will divide members of families against each other and will even bring violence to the point of death, but those who remain steadfast to the end of their lives have the assurance of salvation (10:22). The fact that many Jewish cities will reject the message of the Kingdom (vv. 14,15), and the consequent extension of the preaching of the Kingdom to the Gentiles (vv. 17, 18), does not mean that God will abandon Israel. God's mission to Israel will not be complete until the Second Coming of Christ (10:23). The Gospel still must go "to the Jew first."

The disciples of Jesus are to expect the same kind of treatment He experienced (10:24, 25). But they are not to fear this hostile treatment. Rather, they are to proclaim publicly what Jesus has taught them privately (vv. 26, 27). Loss of physical life is of little consequence in contrast to the salvation of the soul (v. 28). If death comes to Jesus' disciples, it does not mean that the Heavenly Father has abandoned them (vv. 29–31). Whatever the cost, one must confess Christ among men, for He will be acknowledged before the Father who is in heaven. Denial of Christ on earth means denial in heaven (vv. 32, 33). The decision demanded by the claims of Christ will cut squarely across family ties. Therefore when there is a clash of loyalties, loyalty to family must give way before loyalty to Christ (v. 37). In fact, loyalty to the Kingdom of God must mean a readiness for death itself. The cross of which Jesus speaks in verse 38 is an instrument of death, and it does not refer to the bearing of burdens, but to a willingness to suffer anything, including the loss of life. He who saves his life will eventually lose his life; but he who loses his life for Christ's sake will preserve it in the life to come (v. 39).

As men receive the emissaries of Jesus, they receive Jesus Himself; and in doing so they receive God (10:40). The "little ones" in verse 42 refer not to children but to disciples of Jesus, who in terms of social status are humble and insignificant. The least consideration shown to such a humble person because he is a disciple will receive everlasting recognition (v. 42).

Narrative II: The Presence of the Kingdom (11:1—12:50)

Matthew now groups a number of events whose primary purpose is to illustrate that the Kingdom of God is a present reality in the person and works of Christ. There is no temporal connection between 11:1 and 11:2; 11:1 provides a summary statement of an extensive teaching and preaching mission throughout the cities of Galilee, whereas a number of selected incidents are related in the following verses.

1. The Kingdom and John the Baptist (11:1–15)

In the first, John the Baptist sends emissaries with a question. John had been imprisoned for rebuking the immoral conduct of Herod Antipas. In prison John heard about the deeds which Jesus was performing as the Messiah, but these deeds were not what John had expected. John had announced the coming of one who would baptize men with the Holy Spirit and with the fire of divine judgment. John expected Jesus to inaugurate the eschatological Kingdom of power and glory and establish the Kingdom of God upon the earth in a form that would grind all human kingdoms before it and fill all the earth. Instead of such world-shaking events, the Messiah was giving sight to the blind, healing the lame, cleansing lepers, restoring hearing to the deaf, occasionally raising the dead, and preaching good news to the poor. Therefore John sent disciples to Jesus to ask if He was indeed Messiah or if another should be expected (11:2, 3).

Jesus' answer is, in effect, a quotation from the messianic promise in Isaiah 35:5, 6. By thus quoting the prophet, Jesus asserts, "The fulfilment of the messianic age is taking place." Yet He adds the strange words, "Blessed is he who takes no offense at me" (11:6). There is something about Jesus' ministry which could easily cause offense. He is the Messiah; but He has not appeared to fulfil the role commonly expected of the Messiah. His ministry is one of healing and saving power rather than that of bringing the final judgment and establishing the Kingdom in glory upon the earth. This is the messianic secret.

When the disciples return to John, Jesus attempts to allay any doubt in the mind of the crowds by asserting that John the Baptist was indeed the fulfilment of the prophecy of Malachi 3:1 concerning the forerunner of the Messiah. In 11:14 He flatly asserts that John fulfilled the prophecy about the return of Elijah. John was the last figure of the age of the prophets (v. 13). He was indeed the greatest of the prophets; but since the days of John until the present, a new event has been taking place. Verse 12 is best translated, "From the days of John the Baptist until now the kingdom of heaven has exercised its power, and violent men lay hold of it by force" (see RSV margin). The Kingdom of God is first of all the redemptive act of God in the person of Christ overcoming the enemies of God and His rule. Jesus here asserts that since the days of John the Baptist, the redemptive rule of God has broken into history and has exercised its power in the acts of healing and redemptive blessing performed by Jesus. The reaction of men has been an eager one. They have seized upon the blessings of the Kingdom with an eagerness which amounts to violence. The parallel saying in Luke 16:16 bears out this interpretation of the passage.

2. *The Challenge to the Present Generation (11:16-30)*

Jesus then utters a fearful condemnation upon the present generation, because it has refused to recognize the presence of the Kingdom in His person and acts of power (11:16–24). They are like stubborn, sullen children playing a game of mimic. They will neither play wedding and dance, nor play funeral and mourn. This stubborn generation of Israel rejected both the semi-ascetic appearance of John the Baptist and the non-ascetic ministry of the Son of Man. This generation is condemned because the wisdom of God, which was revealed both in John and in Jesus, is vindicated and illustrated by deeds which should be recognized by all who are responsive to God as the works of God Himself (v. 19). Chorazin and Bethsaida, cities of Galilee in which Jesus had performed unrecorded mighty works, will suffer fearful condemnation because they did not recognize the wisdom of God and repent of their unbelief (vv. 20–22). Proud Capernaum will suffer destruction as did Sodom, and in the Day of Judgment, the citizens of Capernaum will suffer an even more fearful penalty (vv. 23, 24).

While this generation has rejected the Messiah, some have responded to His message (11:25–30). The "wise and understanding," that is, the religious leaders and doctors of the law in Judaism, had refused to receive the new revelation in Christ, but those who are called "babes" by Jesus, the humble and the meek of the land, have responded to divine revelation. Jesus then asserts that He and He alone is the revealer of God. The Father and the Son share a direct unmediated, intuitive mutual knowledge; the Son knows the Father in the same way that the Father knows the Son. However, other men may enter in to a knowledge of God only as it is mediated through Jesus. Here is a claim to a unique knowledge of God which sets Jesus apart from all other men. He is indeed not only a man; he is "the Son" and possesses a knowledge of the Father which only deity itself could possess. The mediated knowledge of God is available for all who labor and are heavy laden. They are invited to come to Jesus and find rest by taking His yoke upon them in exchange for the heavy yoke of the traditions of the scribal teachings.

3. Opposition to the Kingdom (12:1–45)

Matthew now relates several incidents to illustrate the antagonism of the Pharisees to Jesus. They condemned Jesus and His disciples for plucking grain on the Sabbath and rubbing the husks of the kernels in their hands in order to eat the grain (12:1, 2). From the scribal point of view such an act constituted work, in violation of the Sabbath regulations. Jesus answers that the Old Testament itself contains occasions when strict interpretation of the law had been violated without guilt, and that formal observance of the law without a merciful concern for the needs of men is meaningless in the eyes of God (v. 7). The Son of Man is Lord of the Sabbath (v. 8) and therefore has authority to set aside scribal legalism with reference to its observance.

Before healing the lame man on the Sabbath in one of the synagogues (12:9–15), Jesus reminds the Pharisees that they themselves will rescue a sheep which has fallen into a pit on the Sabbath, and yet feel that they have not broken the law. It is therefore proper to perform acts of mercy on the Sabbath. Jesus thereupon restored the man's withered hand, incurring thereby the settled hostility of the Pharisees who now determined to destroy Him.

A third incident is the healing of a blind and dumb man through the exorcism of the demon (12:22–29). The people were amazed and began to feel that Jesus might well be the Messiah, the Son of David; but the Pharisees accused Him of employing a supernatural but demonic power received from the prince of demons. Jesus answers that this is utterly impossible. To cast out demons by demonic power would mean civil war in the satanic kingdom. The power by which He casts out demons is the Spirit of God; and it is the evidence of the activity and presence of the Kingdom of God in their midst (v. 28).

In the parable of the strong man, Jesus teaches that He has invaded the realm of Satan (the strong man's house) to rescue men and women from satanic domination (plundered his goods); and this deliverance of demon-possessed men and women has occurred only because He, Jesus, has first bound the strong man (12:29). Verses 28 and 29 are among the most important in the Gospel for an understanding of the Kingdom of God. The Kingdom of God is the power of God active in Jesus through the Holy Spirit by Whom Satan is defeated and men delivered from satanic rule. The "binding" of the strong man is a figure of speech, and is not intended to mean that Satan is now completely defeated and put out of action. It merely means that his power is broken and his activity is curbed. No longer may he exercise his influence over men as formerly, because the power of God's reign has invaded his realm for the purpose of defeating him and rescuing men from his sway.

Jesus now convicts the Pharisees of hopeless blindness (12:30–32). He says that all sorts of blasphemy will be forgiven—even blasphemy against the Son of Man. But when blindness to spiritual realities is so perverse that a man cannot distinguish the power of the Spirit of God from demonic power, his enslavement to darkness is such that he can never find forgiveness.

The Pharisees spoke evil words against the Spirit of God because they were evil at heart (12:33–37). An evil heart reflects itself in evil words. In the Day of Judgment, men will be either convicted or acquitted by their unguarded words which reflect the character of the inner man. These words of blasphemy against the Holy Spirit will condemn the Pharisees.

The Pharisees now ask that Jesus, if indeed He is the Messiah, demonstrate this fact by a supernatural sign (12:38–45). Since they have already refused to recognize the signs of the Kingdom of God in His miracles, Jesus answers that no other sign will be given them except the sign of the resurrection. In the Jewish designation of time, any part of the day can be called a day; "three days and three nights" may mean the whole or any part of a three-day period. Jesus' generation is less responsive to God's message than former generations. The Ninevites repented at the preaching of Jonah; the Queen of Sheba (I Kings 10:1–10) was eager to hear human wisdom; but the present generation is deaf to the proclamation of the Kingdom of God. The parable of the unclean spirit (vv. 43–45) indicates that although Israel had been purified from idolatry after the Babylonian Captivity, their refusal to receive a positive blessing, that is, the Messiah, leaves them more susceptible than ever to relapse into a worse spiritual condition.

4. Fellowship in the Kingdom (12:46–50)

The question of Jesus' mother and brothers (12:46–50) brings out the fact that fellowship in the Kingdom of God does not follow the line of family ties, but of obedience to the will of God. The Old Covenant had been administered primarily in terms of the family; the New Covenant will be administered in terms of individual obedience.

Discourse III: The Mystery of the Kingdom (13:1–58)

The parables in chapter 13 illustrate the presence of the Kingdom of God to those who have eyes to see, but veil it from those whose heart is heavy in unbelief. The parables have both revelatory and judicial purpose. Those who have already accepted Jesus and His ministry and have recognized the power and the presence of the Kingdom in His person will find in the parables a further illumination of that which they have already understood. Those whose hearts are dull, whose ears heavy and whose eyes are closed will find in the parables only that which confuses them (13:10-16). However, the parables illustrate the fulfilment of that which many prophets and righteous men longed to see (v. 17), nothing less than the presence of the Kingdom of God.

All of these parables illustrate the mystery of the Kingdom of God (Mk. 4:11) or the several facets which belong to this mystery (Mt. 13:11). A "mystery" is a technical concept having to do with divine revelation. It does not refer to something which is mysterious or difficult; it designates a purpose hidden in the heart of God until the proper time for its revelation to men (Rom. 16:25, 26). The mystery of the Kingdom is this: before the Kingdom of God is established on earth in power and glory, it has entered into history in the person of Christ to work silently and secretly among men in advance of its full disclosure. The former revelation of the coming of the Kingdom is set forth in Daniel 2; and some variation of this expectation is found in different circles of contemporary Judaism: the Kingdom will come in power to destroy the pagan nations, grind them to powder and then fill all the earth with righteousness. The new revelation of the divine purpose is that this eschatological Kingdom of glory has already come among men in the "meek and lowly Jesus" (Mt. 11:29) to bring men rest for their souls rather than to implement final judgment upon the wicked.

1. The Parable of the Sower (13:1–9)

Interpreting the parables requires an understanding of the literary form of parable. A parable is not allegory. An allegory is an imaginative story freely created, so that all details might convey meaning. A parable is an illustration drawn from daily experience designed to set forth a single basic truth; the details may or may not carry meaning. Thus in the parable of the four soils, the truth conveyed does not depend on the fact that there are *four* soils; there might have been three or five with no modification of the essential message. The element of growth in several parables is not an element of Kingdom truth, but only the life setting of the stories. Such details should not be pressed in interpretation. The facts that the treasure was hidden, that the pearl must be purchased, that leaven gradually and slowly permeates the dough, and that the seed produces a growth which later dies, convey no theological truth about the Kingdom, but belong only to the local color of the parabolic method.

2. The Parabolic Method Explained (13:10–23)

Each parable illustrates a different aspect of this new redemptive purpose; and therefore Matthew speaks of the "mysteries of the Kingdom." The Kingdom of God is like a sower who scatters seed which falls upon all kinds of soils: upon hard packed ground where the birds can devour the seed, upon rocky, shallow ground where there can be no permanent growth, upon thorny soil where the growth is choked out. Only a part of the seed falls upon good ground and brings forth a harvest (13:3–9). Thus it is with the Kingdom of God which is now being proclaimed among men. It will not have uniform success. Some will appear to receive the message of the Kingdom, but the evil one will snatch it away from them. Others will seem to receive it and will manifest apparent life; but because they are shallow, they will not be able to withstand persecution but will fall away as soon as tribulation is experienced. Others receive the word of the Kingdom only to see it become choked in their lives, because of the cares of the world and the desire for wealth. Only a few of those who hear the word of the Kingdom will produce fruit unto everlasting life (vv. 18–23). In other words, the Kingdom of God in its present activity in Christ must be cordially and heartily received by men or it will produce no fruit within them.

This was indeed something unheard of among the Jews. How could the Kingdom of God be dependent upon the human response for its fruitfulness? How could one conceive of the Kingdom of *God* experiencing only partial success among those who receive it? This was contrary to the Jewish expectation of the Kingdom and apparently not in accord with the Old Testament prophecies. However, the new truth is that the Kingdom of God is now working among men, but it is not sweeping away the wicked; in fact, the word which falls upon their ears may lie like seed upon the path and never take root. The Kingdom as it has now come among men does not force itself upon them; it must be received by willing hearts. But wherever such soil is found, the Word of the Kingdom brings forth abundant fruit.

3. Other Parables (13:24–52)

The parable of the wheat and the tares illustrates another facet of the revelation of the Kingdom of God (13:24–30). According to the Old Testament expectation, the Kingdom of God would mean judgment for the wicked and salvation for the righteous. The parable of the wheat and the weeds teaches that before the Day of Judgment and Salvation when the separation of the righteous and the wicked will take place, the Kingdom of God has come among men; but the sons of the Kingdom and the sons of the evil one are to live intermingled until the day of harvest. It is important to note in the application (v. 38) that Jesus Himself says that the field is the world. The Old Testament expectation sees the Kingdom producing a society of righteousness and peace undisturbed by evil. Jesus said that the Kingdom of God has come; but society is to continue in a mixed condition until a final separation at the Day of Judgment.

The parables of the mustard seed and the leaven further illustrate the fact that the present manifestation of the Kingdom of God is in an unexpected and unimpressive form (13:31–33). However, the day is certain to come when the Kingdom of God will fill all the earth. The Kingdom is now like a grain of mustard seed which is the smallest of all seeds; but in the day of consummation, it will become a great shrub which will fill all the earth. The element of growth or of gradual development from the seed to the plant is not a part of the truth illustrated by the parable. In I Corinthians 15:37, 38, the illustration of growth is used to describe that which is entirely supernatural—the resurrection from the dead. In the parable of the seed, the means by which the seed becomes a tree is not a part of the message of the parable. It is clear from our Lord's teaching that the Kingdom will come in power only with His personal return in glory and power. Then, and then only, the Kingdom will fill all the earth. The one point of this parable is that, unforeseen by the Old Testament revelation, a new stage in the redemptive purpose is to take place: before the Kingdom comes in glory, it has entered into the world like a grain of mustard seed in a small and despised form.

This same truth is illustrated by the leaven. In its present manifestation, the Kingdom of Heaven is like a bit of leaven which cannot be detected in a bowl of meal. But the day will come when all of the bowl will be filled with leaven, that is, when the earth will be filled with the Kingdom of God. The process of gradual leavening is not a part of the parable. Furthermore, we are not required to think of leaven as a symbol of evil. Leaven is expressly commanded in the celebration of the Feast of Weeks (Lev. 23:17), where it is a symbol of the daily bread which God had given for the sustenance of human life. Again, unleavened bread was commanded to be eaten at the time of the Exodus as a symbol of the haste required for the flight from Egypt, because there was no time to make leavened bread (Ex. 12:11, 34, 39; Deut. 16:3). In this parable, leaven as a common element in daily experience provided a vivid illustration of the contrast between the two stages of the Kingdom; in the present as small and insignificant, but in the future as all-enveloping.

The parables of the hidden treasure and the pearl of great price (13:44–46) teach that although the present manifestation of the Kingdom of God has assumed an unexpected and insignificant form, it *is* nevertheless the Kingdom of God and is therefore of superlative value. No cost, however great, should stand in the way of its possession. The fact that the treasure and the pearl are purchased is not of the essence of the parable, but only local color. The one great truth is the infinite value of the Kingdom of God in this unexpected form of its appearance among men.

The parable of the dragnet (13:47–50) again looks into the future and contrasts the consummation of the Kingdom with the present movement which it has set up among men. The present work of the Kingdom of God is like a net which gathers up all sorts of fish. Jesus' ministry and teaching brought into existence a new group of men who were His disciples. Among them, however, was a Judas who betrayed Him. In His retinue were those who turned away when they understood the true character of His ministry (Jn. 6:66). Jesus Himself foretold that false prophets would arise from the circle of His followers (Mt. 24:11). Many who bore the name of Jesus and professed to teach and minister in His name were not true disciples (Mt. 7:21–23). Could such a mixed movement really be the work of the Kingdom of God? The parable of the net teaches that the Kingdom of God in its present manifestation among men brings within its influence men who are both good and bad. There will, however, be a separation when the evil will be taken away in the Day of Judgment.

The purpose of Jesus' teachings is that His disciples might themselves become teachers, that is, scribes who have been trained for the Kingdom of Heaven. The treasury of their teaching contains things both new and old: they are to bring out the true meaning of the Old Testament teaching, and they are to set forth the new revelation which Jesus has brought to men (13:51, 52).

4. The Response to Jesus Parables (13:53–58)

Jesus visited Nazareth where He had lived until He entered His public ministry. His neighbors had known Him as the son of the carpenter; His four brothers and His sisters were still living in this town. The background of familiarity led the people to conclude He could not be the Messiah; and their unbelief made it impossible for Him to manifest the powers of the Kingdom of God in their midst.

Narrative III: The Crisis of the Kingdom (14:1—17:27)

Matthew now groups a number of events which show the crisis of opposition by the leaders of the Jews, and a crisis of understanding on the part of His disciples.

1. Crisis of Opposition (14:1—15:20)

The circumstances pertaining to the death of John the Baptist are related (14:1–12). Upon the death of Herod the Great in 4 B.C. (2:19), Palestine was divided among three of his sons. Herod Antipas be-

came tetrarch of Galilee and the Transjordan area of Perea. A fourth
brother by the name of Philip who lived in Rome was married to
Herodias. Herod Antipas had fallen in love with his brother Philip's
wife; and he persuaded Herodias to forsake Philip while he, Antipas,
divorced his first wife that he might marry Herodias in violation of
Leviticus 20:21. John the Baptist by rebuking this illicit relationship
had incurred the hatred of Herodias. Herod had therefore imprisoned John in Machaerus, a fortress near the Dead Sea. Salome,
the daughter of Herodias and Philip, was able to bring about the
death of John the Baptist. Now Herod was led to believe that Jesus
was really John the Baptist arisen from the dead.

When Jesus heard of the death of John the Baptist, He withdrew
to a place where He might be alone (14:13). However, the crowds
followed Him, and His compassion was such that He could not ignore
them. When the day slipped away and there was no way to provide
food for the crowd, Jesus took five small rolls and two fish and
fed the multitude (vv. 14–21). This is the only miracle recorded in
all four Gospels. The discourse on the bread of life in John 6:27–59
shows that the miracle was not an end in itself, but symbolized the
spiritual food which Christ has come to provide for hungry men.

Still desiring to be alone, Jesus dismissed the crowd (14:22) and
sent His disciples in a boat toward the east side of the sea while He
remained alone to pray. A sudden storm descended upon the boat,
and sometime between three and six A.M., Jesus came to them walking on the water. The disciples thought that they beheld only an ap-
parition, but Jesus' reply, "It is I" is the language of deity (Ex. 3:14).

The incident of Peter's walking on the water and the stilling of
the storm brought forth from the disciples the confession, "Truly you
are the Son of God" (14:34). This phrase does not yet have its full
theological significance; but the disciples, contrary to Jesus' neighbors in Nazareth, have the growing realization that Jesus is more
than a man, and more even than Messiah; He is indeed a divine
being, the Son of God.

Matthew now relates a controversy over the question of purity
(15:1–20). Most of our Lord's ministry was devoted to Galilee. The
Gospel of John indicates that on several occasions He journeyed to
Jerusalem and taught there; but most of the time He was preaching
in Galilee. The doctors of the law and their disciples, the Pharisees,
sent a delegation from Jerusalem to Galilee to investigate the character of His ministry. They were dissatisfied when they found that

He transgressed the tradition of the elders. The scribes and Pharisees believed that in addition to the written law, Moses received on Mount Sinai from God a body of oral law which had been passed on by word of mouth through the centuries. This oral tradition covered many matters not mentioned in the written law of the books of Moses, particularly those having to do with ceremonial purity. This cleansing had nothing to do with sanitation, but only with ritual or ceremonial purity. They believed, for instance, that water should be poured on the hands before eating; but they found that Jesus neglected to observe this tradition of the oral law.

In reply to their criticism (15:2), Jesus accused the doctors of the law of transgressing the written Word of God by their oral tradition. As an illustration, He cited the method by which the commandment to honor one's parents was circumvented by the oral tradition (vv. 4-6). To honor father and mother means to provide for their physical needs when they are in want. This was a proper filial duty. However, the scribal tradition permitted one formally to present such money as an offering to the temple rather than giving it to his parents; yet this dedication was only a legal fiction, for the son was free to use the money for his own desires. By this tradition, the scribes nullified the Word of God.

Jesus then swept aside the entire rabbinic structure of ceremonial cleanliness by asserting that holiness is a matter of the heart and not of alleged clean or unclean foods (15:11). He condemned the Pharisaic teaching of externalism by calling it a spurious growth which will be uprooted (v. 13) and by affirming that such teachers are blind guides who with their followers will fall into a pit (v. 14). In response to a question by Peter, Jesus explained at greater length that foods cannot make one unclean in the sight of God, because they enter the stomach only to be evacuated from the body. That which defiles is that which comes from the heart. Not foods, but such things as evil thoughts, murder, adultery, and the like, defile a man and make him unclean before God (vv. 19, 20).

2. *Withdrawal to the North (15:21–39)*

Jesus journeyed north from Galilee to the district of Tyre and Sidon where a Gentile woman of Canaanite descent called upon Him to heal her daughter (15:21, 22). Jesus replied that His ministry was directed primarily to Israel. This is, in fact, the only known occasion when Jesus journeyed outside of Palestine. The Jews were by preparation and tradition the heirs of the Kingdom of God (8:12), and Jesus addressed Himself almost exclusively to them. When the woman persisted, Jesus answered her in very brusque language of Jewish idiom by referring to the Jews as children and the Gentiles as dogs (v. 26). The woman, undiscouraged by the apparent rebuff, turned Jesus' very sayings into a plea for help. Jesus then responded to her unswerving faith and her daughter was healed (v. 28).

Jesus returned to the neighborhood of the Sea of Galilee and continued His healing ministry which led the people to glorify the God of Israel (15:29–31). The feeding of the four thousand (vv. 32–39) is an entirely separate incident from the earlier feeding of the five thousand, although some scholars insist they are two versions of one event. The word for basket in verse 37 is a different word from that used in 14:20. The latter refers to a small basket carried on the arm, while the word in 15:37 refers to a much larger container. After this miracle, Jesus went to the region of Magadan (late manuscripts read Magdala). We do not know its location.

3. Further Conflict (16:1–12)

The Pharisees and Sadducees now unite in their opposition to Jesus (16:1–12). They represent two different parties in Judaism who generally were vigorously opposed to one another. The Pharisees were a legalistic party who followed the oral traditions of the scribes; the Sadducees were a priestly party who rejected the entire oral tradition of the scribes and were quite open to Gentile influences. Their common opposition to Jesus led them to join forces and test Him by asking for a sign from heaven. They were not sincere in this request; they desired only to trap Him and to prove that He was not the Messiah. Their request was in line with the temptation that Jesus cast Himself down from the temple to prove that He was the Messiah (4:5, 6). Jesus replied that He will not give them the kind of sign they requested, for they were blind to the signs which were already evident in their presence. There will, however, be one great sign given to this evil and faithless generation: the sign of Jonah, that is, Jesus' resurrection from the dead (12:39–41).

Jesus used the disciples' failure to bring bread as an occasion to warn them of the leaven of the Pharisees and the Sadducees (16:5–12). They did not understand and assumed at first that He referred to some particular type of bread which the Jews considered to be unclean. Jesus rebuked them for their spiritual blindness and explained that He referred to the corrupting teaching of the Pharisees and Sadducees. There is an important contrast here between the Jews and the disciples. Both were perplexed by our Lord's teachings. For the Jews whose problem was that of spiritual blindness and hardness of heart, Jesus had only condemnation. For His disciples whose problem was not of the heart, but of an understanding of His messianic disclosure, He has great patience.

4. Crisis of Faith (16:13–20)

The confession at Caesarea Philippi is the turning point in our Lord's messianic revelation. He has come to be the Messiah, but He is not the kind of Messiah looked for by either the Jews or the disciples. They were looking for a ruling king; but He has come to be the suffering Saviour. Furthermore, Judaism had never understood, nor had the Old Testament revealed, that the Messiah would be the incarnate Son of God. Jesus now knew that the time had come to lead His disciples a step further in their understanding of His mission and person.

When they came into the area of Caesarea Philippi in the very northern regions of Palestine above the Sea of Galilee, Jesus asked the disciples what opinions men held about Himself, the Son of Man. By calling Himself the Son of Man, Jesus indicated that He was an heavenly being who is to come with glory to establish the Kingdom of God upon the earth. However, the appearance of the Son of Man on earth as a man among men before His coming in glory was utterly unexpected and bewildering to the Jewish mind. The disciples' answer to Jesus' question was that men regarded Him as fulfilling the highest human role possible to conceive. Some held that He was John the Baptist, apparently risen from the dead; others thought that He was Elijah fulfilling the prophecy of Malachi 4:5; still others thought that he was a re-embodiment of Jeremiah or one of the prophets. In answer to Jesus' persistent question, Peter replied that Jesus is indeed the Messiah and yet more than the Messiah; He is the Son of the living God. Peter, speaking for the other disciples, recognizes that Jesus is more than a man; He is in fact a divine being. Jesus replied that this is indeed a truth which can be known only by divine revelation.

Now that the disciples have realized that Jesus is the divine Messiah although appearing in a form largely unforeseen in the Old Testament, He reveals to them that as the Messiah, He has a two-fold purpose which was not clearly revealed in the Old Testament. The first of these was to bring into existence the Church. The much disputed meaning of 16:18 must go back to the Aramaic language of our Lord's original teaching. The Aramaic for "Peter" and for "rock" is the same word: *kepha.* "You are *kepha,* and on this *kepha* I will build my church." The simplest meaning of the passage is that Peter as the representative of the Twelve Apostles is, together with them, to be the foundation of the Church (see Eph. 2:20; Rev. 21:14).

This interpretation is by no means a concession to the Roman view that Jesus imparted to Peter an official authority which he may transmit to his successors. The more generally accepted Protestant interpretations are that either Peter's faith in Jesus as the divine Messiah, or the object of Peter's faith, the Lord Himself, is the rock upon whom the Church is to be built. The word "church" (*ekklesia*) does not refer to an organization or a building, but to the people of God. *Ekklesia* was used in the Greek Old Testament to refer to Israel as the people of God, and Jesus' use of the word indicates that He purposes to create the new people of God as successors to Israel. The Church will do battle against its mortal enemy, Hades or death; but the Church will be stronger than death, and the gates of death will be forced open and men will be rescued from its power and brought into the realm of life (16:18).

Jesus will entrust to His Church the keys of the Kingdom (16:19). These keys are spiritual knowledge (Lk. 11:52) by which the doors into the Kingdom of Heaven are opened that lost men may enter into the realm of life. Binding and loosing refer to the power to admit or to exclude men from the realm of the Kingdom of God. These words describe no official arbitrary authority; but it remains true today that men in the grip of death are loosed from its bondage and brought into the blessings of the Kingdom of God only through the human agency of those who constitute the Church of Jesus Christ.

5. Preparation of Jesus' Disciples for His Death (16:21—17:27)

A further amazing revelation to the disciples is that Messiah must suffer and die and be raised again from the dead (16:21). We must constantly be reminded that first century Jews did not understand

Isaiah 53 and were not looking for a suffering Messiah. Therefore when Peter rebuked Jesus, telling Him that this should never happen to Him, he was sure that he had the Word of God as his authority; for Messiah was to be a conquering king, not a suffering, dying servant. Jesus, however, rebuked Peter for his spiritual blindness. The disciples have not yet understood the full purpose of God in the coming and mission of Messiah.

Jesus then lays down a new principle of life for the people of God (16:24–27). According to the Old Testament revelation, when Messiah brings His Kingdom, the people of God would enter into the full enjoyment of life and peace. Jesus says that although the Messiah has come and although the Kingdom of God has come into the world in His person, the principle of suffering and death remains part of the experience of God's people; in fact, Messiah's disciples must always be ready to die for the sake of their Master. The Son of Man is yet to come in the glory of His Father, and in that day the disciples of Messiah who have been ready to suffer and die for His sake will enter into life. However, the experience of Jesus' disciples during this age is not to be one of unrelieved suffering. Before all of His disciples have experienced death, they will behold a great manifestation of the Son of Man in His Kingdom (v. 28). This may be a reference to the Transfiguration; but more likely it is a reference to the resurrection and ascension of our Lord, or to Pentecost and the rise of the Christian Church and the destruction of the Jewish state. Jesus had pronounced historical judgment upon cities which rejected the message of the Kingdom of God (11:20–24). The Kingdom of God was to be taken away from Israel and given to a new people (21:43). The Kingdom of God is primarily the redemptive rule of God manifesting itself in history; and the destruction of Jerusalem and the rise of the Christian Church are a visitation of God's Kingdom.

The disciples have now begun to appreciate that Jesus is a divine being; and the Transfiguration serves to deepen this conviction and enlarge their understanding (17:1–13). We do not know the site of this experience; tradition places it either on Mount Hermon, which is in the neighborhood of Caesarea Philippi, or Mount Tabor, southwest of the Sea of Galilee. Jesus' appearance was so changed that His face and garments shone with radiance, the shining of His incarnate deity. Moses and Elijah represent the Law and the Prophets which find their fulfilment in the person of Christ. The bright cloud which overshadowed them is the Shekinah glory of God's presence (Ex. 24:15–18); and the voice is, of course, God's voice. Small wonder that the disciples were struck to the ground with awe!

As they descended from the mountain (17:9), Jesus commanded the disciples to keep this knowledge secret lest the public proclamation of Jesus as the heavenly Messiah start a popular uprising among the people which would frustrate the redemptive purpose of the cross. Only when He has been raised from the dead and the full character of His Messiahship understood can it be publicly proclaimed. The disciples, however, still have problems. Jesus is indeed the Messiah; but where is the fulfilment of the scribal teaching that Elijah must appear to prepare the way for Messiah in fulfilment of Malachi 4:5, 6? Jesus answers that Elijah has already come and that the prophecy of Malachi was fulfilled in John the Baptist. He has, however, been put to death, and the Son of Man will also suffer a similar fate.

Jesus' first act after the Transfiguration was a miracle manifesting the power of God's Kingdom (17:14–18; see 12:28). This power is nothing which works magically, for the disciples had been impotent to effect the healing (17:19). The works of the Kingdom are evident only when there is perfect faith in God. Such faith can move any obstacles which stand in the way of the accomplishment of the divine redemptive purposes. Verse 21 of The King James Version is not found in our oldest Greek Bibles, but was copied into the later texts from Mark 9:29.

During the days following the Transfiguration, Jesus renewed the note of suffering and death to be followed by His resurrection. This continued to cause acute distress to the disciples (17:22,23).

The temple tax (17:24–27), a tax of a half shekel (about 32 cents) was levied upon all Jews for the support of the temple in Jerusalem. It was Jesus' custom to pay this tax; but in this saying to Peter, He made it clear that He did so only by way of concession. As the Lord and owner of the temple (v. 25), Jesus was not required by God to pay the tax, but lest He bring offense to the Jews, He directed Peter to fulfil this obligation.

Discourse IV: The Fellowship of the Kingdom (18:1–35)

The fourth of the great discourses in Matthew's Gospel has to do with the life and fellowship created by the Kingdom of God working among men. Two virtues characterize the fellowship of the Kingdom: humility and forgiveness.

1. Humility (18:1–20)

Humility is illustrated by a little child. The disciples were arguing the question as to who was greatest in the Kingdom of Heaven. Jesus insisted that such self-seeking was alien to the Kingdom of God. The disciples of the Kingdom must change their disposition and habits to begin a new life of complete humility and dependence upon God (18:3, 4). In verses 5 and 6, little children represent humble believers in Jesus.

Verses 7 to 9, an interlude in the discussion of humility, refer to occasions of stumbling in personal life. The character of this age is such that temptations are inevitable; but one should take any measures, however drastic, to avoid occasions for stumbling.

The theme of humility is resumed in verse 10 where children are again representative of humble believers. God has a special concern for children and directs angels to care for them (Heb. 1:14). Verse 11 in the King James Version is beautiful, but it is not found in the earliest Greek Bibles. In verses 12 through 14, Jesus speaks of the shepherd's concern for wandering sheep to illustrate God's desire that these little ones should not perish.

Humility does not mean, however, that one is to submit passively to ill treatment (18:15–20). In the fellowship of the Kingdom, that is, in the life of the Church, discipline is essential. The offended party is first to go to the offender alone and try to rectify the evil; if unsuccessful, he is to take two others as witnesses and attempt a reconciliation. If the offender is recalcitrant, the case is to be brought before the fellowship of the local church. If this action is futile, the offender is to be excluded from the fellowship of the church. The authority of the Church to deal with sin given in 16:19 is repeated (v. 18); and such action is to be conducted in the spirit of prayer (v. 19). This promise of the great power of prayer has to do specifically in this context with matters of church discipline where two or three are gathered together in the name of Christ with His presence in their midst (v. 20).

2. Forgiveness (18:21–35)

Forgiveness is a second manifestation of the fellowship of the Kingdom. Jesus had placed forgiveness at the heart of the Lord's prayer, teaching His disciples to pray for the forgiveness of sins as they forgave others (6:12). Forgiveness is one of the most important manifestations of the life of the Kingdom. When Peter asked if forgiveness is required seven successive times, Jesus replied that it is required seventy times seven. The meaning of this forgiveness is illustrated by the parable of the king and the debtor who owed the king a debt of ten million dollars—an utterly crushing debt (18:23–35). Although the king completely forgave him his debt, the servant was unwilling in turn to forgive a fellow servant of an obligation of a mere twenty dollars. With inflexible justice untempered with grace, he demanded complete payment. When the king heard of this unmerciful conduct, he rescinded his forgiveness and demanded full payment. This is a parable; and its details cannot be pressed to embody any teaching about whether God will first forgive sins and then retract His forgiveness. The parable embodies a simple and clear truth: When a man professes to have been forgiven an incalculable debt of sin, but is utterly unwilling in turn to forgive the minor offense of another, his profession is a mockery and void of reality. God's forgiveness precedes and provides the basis for the forgiveness of brother with brother, and it is such forgiveness that must characterize Christian fellowship.

Narrative IV : The Conflict Caused by the Kingdom (19:1—23:39)

1. Teachings on the Way to Jerusalem (19:1—20:28)

The next four chapters consist largely of incidents illustrating the conflict between the Jews and Jesus. The Pharisees tried to trap Jesus by a question about divorce (19:3). Behind their question was a debate between the two wings of the sect of the Pharisees, one of which believed that divorce was allowed only in the case of unfaithfulness, while the other believed that divorce could be permitted for all sorts of reasons. The question put to Jesus in effect asks, Which school of the Pharisees was correct? Instead of answering directly, Jesus appealed to the creation ordinance saying that marriage is fundamentally indissoluble, for the two partners in marriage become one (vv. 5, 6). Divorce which was permitted in the law of Moses was a concession to the sinfulness of men and not the ideal (vv. 7, 8). Therefore, the marriage bond can be broken only by infidelity.

The disciples respond that if marriage is in effect indissoluble, a man would be safe not to join himself to a woman lest it turn out to be an unhappy relationship. Jesus replied that sexual continence is a gift which only a few can practice. Some men practice such continence as a result of physical emasculation (19:12), while others practice sexual continence and have deprived themselves of all family relationships for the sake of the Kingdom of God; but this is a course of conduct which only a few can follow. The use of the word "eunuchs" had a double meaning and is not to be taken literally in verse 12. Our Lord did not glorify celibacy or asceticism as such. The normal relationship for man is that of the family life; those who forego this natural relationship to serve the Kingdom of God are the exception rather than the rule.

The children who were brought to Jesus (19:13–15) appear not to be infants, but children old enough to come to Jesus. It is still true that it is easy to lead children to love Jesus; and such child-like responsiveness is necessary to any man if he is to receive the Kingdom of Heaven.

A rich young ruler came to Jesus with a question about eternal life (19:16–30). His question has reference to life in the age to come (Jn. 12:25; Mt. 25:46), not a present spiritual experience. The oldest text is correctly translated in the Revised Standard Version, while the reading of the King James Version follows the wording of Mark and Luke. This young man had conscientiously observed the law from his youth. However, one obstacle stood in his way, and this was his attachment to his wealth. Therefore Jesus told him to do something He had never commanded another: to dispose of his goods and follow Jesus in discipleship (19:22). The young man on hearing this turned away, for he was not ready to pay that price.

Then Jesus said to His disciples that it was easier for a camel to go through the eye of a needle than for a rich man to enter the Kingdom of God. This statement is hyperbole for that which is humanly impossible; and the disciples correctly understood it when they asked "who then can be saved?" (19:25). Jesus agreed with them, asserting that it was only the supernatural grace of God which can free a rich man from his bondage to wealth that he may become the disciple of God's Kingdom. It should be noted from verses 23 and 24 that the two phrases, "the Kingdom of Heaven" and "the Kingdom of God" are interchangeable and synonymous. The former is the Aramaic; the latter, the Greek form of expression.

Peter, remembering Jesus' word to the young man that he would have treasure in heaven if he abandoned his riches, reminds Jesus that the disciples have left everything to follow Him; and he asks about the treasure which they will receive (19:27). Jesus replies that in the age to come when the world will be transformed after the Son of Man comes in glory, the disciples will share His rule in the coming Kingdom. Sacrifice of possessions in this life assures one of a hundred fold reward as well as eternal life (v. 29). However, this reward cannot be interpreted strictly as a matter of merit, for there is another principle at work, the principle of God's grace. This gracious principle will upset the legalistic principle of merit and desert, so that many who seem to deserve a first place will be last, while those who seem to be last will be first (19:30).

This principle of grace Jesus illustrates by a parable of a householder who employed laborers at different times through the day to work in his vineyard (20:1-16). He hired men at six in the morning, at nine, at twelve and at three P.M. At five P.M. he found others who had been idle all day, and they too went to his vineyard for a very brief period. When the day's work was ended, all workers were given the same pay whether they had worked one hour or twelve. Those who worked twelve hours received what they were promised: a day's pay. Those who had worked less than a day received as a gracious gift a day's pay which they did not deserve. Such is God's generosity (v. 15) that the Kingdom of Heaven is God's gift to those who do not deserve it.

As Jesus approached Jerusalem for the last time, He repeated His warning that the Son of Man is to be delivered to death, even to the hands of the Gentiles, but that He will be raised on the third day (20:17-19).

Although Jesus had lived an example of humility and had taught that humility was one of the most important virtues in the life of the Kingdom, the disciples were still filled with ambition and a hunger for position and power. The mother of James and John, no doubt at their urging, asked Jesus to give her sons the places of honor in His future Kingdom (20:20, 21). When they insisted that they were prepared to share the cup of Jesus' sufferings, Jesus replied that the disposition of the future Kingdom was in the hands of His Father. When the other apostles heard of this request for a favor, they were angry with James and John (v. 24).

Jesus used this incident as the occasion to teach the way of true greatness. The human measure of greatness is the exercise of authority and rule over other men. Men love power. In the fellowship of the Kingdom, the measure of greatness is found in service. Jesus, the Son of Man, has not come seeking a position of power and influence over men, but to sacrifice His life as a ransom for many. His disciples should follow His example; the truly great man is the one who is willing to serve and set aside questions of rank and position.

2. Healing at Jericho (20:29–34)

As Jesus left for Jericho for His last journey to Jerusalem, a great throng of people followed Him. Two blind men who had apparently heard of Jesus' healing powers called out to Him, "Have mercy on us, O Lord, thou son of David." When in answer to Jesus' question, they asked that they might see, the Great Physician in all compassion gave them sight.

3. Events in Jerusalem (21:1–22)

Realizing that the time of crisis had come, Jesus deliberately fulfilled the messianic prophecy of Zechariah 9:9 by entering Jerusalem riding upon an ass (21:1–11). On His journey to Jerusalem, He was accompanied by crowds of people coming to the city for the feast of the Passover; and as He entered Jerusalem, the prophetic symbolism of His entry was recognized, and He was hailed as the Messiah. It was quite proper for a royal person who makes a peaceable visit to ride upon such an animal and by this means, Jesus indicated that His Messiahship was not one of political conquests nor military victory. Yet, it is an overt claim to Messiahship which the people recognized and interpreted in their own way. Their cry "Hosanna" literally means "save now" (Ps. 118:25), but the term had probably become a general expression of praise. The title, "Son of David" (21:9), is synonymous with "Messiah."

Jesus' first act after His triumphal entry was quite unmessianic measured by the popular expectation (21:12–17). The Jews looked for a conquering king who would exalt the Jewish nation, magnify the temple, and overthrow the political enemies of Israel. Instead of this, Jesus challenged the conduct of the religious leaders of the nation. In the court of the Gentiles, the priests had established tables to change money because the temple tax of a half shekel had to be paid in proper Jewish coinage. The priests had also established shops to sell animals for sacrifice. Jewish literature indicates that the priesthood practiced extortion in the sale of these sacrificial animals. Jesus challenged this misconduct of the priesthood by driving out the merchants and overturning the tables of the moneychangers. Such a course of conduct, coupled with the healing of the blind and the lame, must have perplexed the people; and it, of course, angered the religious leaders. The children, however, continued to cry "Hosanna to the Son of David" (v. 15). Jesus returned to Bethany, a village located a mile and a half southeast of Jerusalem on the slopes of the Mount of Olives (v. 17).

Early in the spring before the leaves opened, the Palestinian fig tree produced a green fruit which was eaten by the peasants. If there were no green figs on a tree when the leaves appeared in the spring, there would be no harvest in the late summer. Returning to Jerusalem, Jesus sought these green figs on a tree by the wayside, but found only leaves (21:18–22). Jesus cursed the barren tree and it withered away. This was quite certainly a prophetic act and parable. The fig tree represented the Jewish nation which abounded in the leaves of religious profession, but was barren of real fruit. That this barrenness was particularly evident in the Jews' rejection of Jesus as the Messiah is explicitly taught in verse 43.

4. Controversies with the Jews (21:23—22:46)

Representatives of the Sanhedrin, the Jewish supreme court, challenged Jesus' authority to teach because He was not an accredited rabbi (21:23). Because their challenge was insincere, Jesus said He would answer their question only if they answered one of his: "The baptism of John, whence was it? From heaven or from men." Knowing of no answer which would not reveal their hypocrisy or anger the people, they said, "We do not know." And Jesus refused to declare his authority (vv. 24–27). He then took the initiative in the controversy and insisted that obedience is found not in lip service and profession, but in conduct (vv. 28–32). Jesus has offered to the Jewish people the Kingdom of God. The religious leaders, scribes and priests have refused to enter the Kingdom; but the unorthodox tax collectors and sinful women had accepted His message and therefore have entered into the Kingdom.

Jesus then uttered a parable which clearly set forth the character of His mission (21:33–46). The farmers to whom is entrusted the vineyard are Israel and their leaders. The servants whom the householder sent from time to time represent the prophets. The son, who is finally sent to receive the produce of the vineyard, represents Jesus Himself. Because Israel rejected the prophets and finally God's own Son, the vineyard will be taken from them and given to other farmers who will be faithful. Verse 43 is of oustanding importance. Jesus had offered Israel the Kingdom of God. Because they have rejected it, this same Kingdom will be taken from them and given to another people. Here is a clear teaching that the Christian Church is to succeed the nation of Israel as the custodian of the Kingdom of God. The priests and the Pharisees, recognizing the force of the parable, determine to seize Jesus. (Verse 44 of the King James Version is not found in the oldest Greek texts).

The parable of the wedding garment (22:1–14 again teaches that the Jews who have rejected the Messiah are to be themselves rejected from the messianic feast, while Gentiles are brought in to take their place. The Jewish nation which was invited to the blessings of the Kingdom of Heaven scorned the invitation; and as a result, God's judgment will fall upon them. In their stead, the wedding room is to be filled with an unexpected assembly of people gathered up from the streets; these represent the Gentiles. However, this salvation of the Gentiles is not to be a universal experience (vv. 11–14). One of the guests was not properly arrayed, so he was cast out. A place at the messianic feast of the Kingdom of God can be enjoyed only when one is properly arrayed in the wedding garment which God Himself must provide. Many hear the call of invitation, but only a few will finally be chosen to enjoy its blessings (v. 14).

The Herodians were Jews who favored the ruling Herodian family and full cooperation with the Roman masters. The question about paying taxes to Rome (22:15,16) was designed to trap Jesus. If He approved, He could be accused to the Jews of being a traitor; if He disapproved, He could be accused to the Romans of disloyalty. Jesus' answer avoided the trap. His answer does not mean that life is to be divided into two spheres: the political and the spiritual. While the divine Lordship over all of life is not denied, it is recognized that the state has a legitimate claim upon a man's loyalty if this claim does not interfere with the claims of God (v. 21). There is here no limitation of the sphere of divine sovereignty.

The insincerity of the question of the Sadducees about the resurrection (22:23–28) is shown by the fact that they did not believe in any form of resurrection. Jesus asserted that the resurrection of the dead is grounded in the fact that God is the living God, and therefore those who belong to Him must share His life. Likeness to the angels in the resurrection (v. 30) means only full participation in immortality which will make the institution of marriage no longer necessary for the propagation of the race (Lk. 20:36).

The question of the Pharisee about the greatest commandment (22:36) brings the answer that perfect love for God and for one's neighbor will fulfil the entire law. Jesus' question to the Pharisees implies that they should recognize from the Old Testament itself that Messiah is more than the Son of David, that He is in fact David's exalted Lord (vv. 41–46). Jesus thus used in the 110th Psalm to point out the blindness of the Pharisees in failing to recognize the greatness of His person and His exalted Messiahship.

5. Denunciations of the Scribes and Pharisees (23:1–39)

Jesus denounced the Pharisees for being concerned only with the fulfilment of the law, not with its spirit. From Jewish literature we know there were Pharisees who were deeply concerned about the spirit and true meaning of the law; but the predominant group in our Lord's day were the extreme legalists concerned with external matters. The Word of God can never be an end in itself, but must lead men to a true heart relationship toward God; otherwise Scripture is misused. Furthermore, the Pharisees were enamored of pride of position and religious leadership, whereas the way of God's Kingdom is the way of self-forgetful ministry (23:10–12). The practice of the Pharisees prevented their followers from accepting the message of Jesus and therefore closed the door of the Kingdom of Heaven to those who otherwise might enter in (v. 13). Verse 14 is not found in the oldest Greek testaments. The oral tradition of the Pharisees, which they considered as binding as the written law of Moses, nullified the true meaning of the law (vv. 16–24).

Verse 24, incorrectly translated in the King James Version, pictures the ludicrous character of the Pharisees' conduct in their fussiness about legal details in contrast to their total neglect of the great principles of spiritual life.

Jesus then uttered a series of severe judgments upon the Pharisees (23:25–36) and concluded the denunciation by announcing the destruction of Jerusalem because the holy city had rejected its Messiah. However, this rejection is not final and ultimate; the day will come when Israel will say, "Blessed be he who comes in the name of the Lord" (vv. 37–39). The Kingdom of God is not taken from the Jews that they might be forever abandoned; "all Israel" is yet to be saved and brought within the redemptive purpose of God.

Discourse V: The Future of the Kingdom (24:1—25:46)

1. Prophecy of the Coming of the Kingdom (24:1–36)

Jesus told His disciples privately, as well as announced publicly, that Jerusalem would be destroyed and the temple utterly devastated. This led the disciples to ask a twofold question: "When will the temple be destroyed, and what will be the sign of Christ's return and the close of the age?" (24:3). These two events are related, since the destruction of Jerusalem as well as the Second Coming of Christ are divine manifestations of God's kingly reign or Kingdom. Matthew is clearly more concerned with the second question than with the first. He reports our Lord's words, under the inspiration of the Spirit, in such a way that he describes the course of the age and its consummation, but says little about the destruction of Jerusalem. Verses 4 through 14 describe the character of the age to its consummation. The interval between Christ's earthly ministry and His Second Coming will be marked by the appearance of false christs and false prophets who will lead men astray by wars, by various calamities, by tribulation, by apostasy and by wickedness.

It is not the mission of Jesus' disciples to convert the world and transform it into the Kingdom of God. In fact, until Christ comes again, men must be ready to endure suffering to the point of death (24:13). However, they have a mission. Throughout this age, the good news about the Kingdom of God, which Christ had offered to Israel and which the Jews had rejected, is to be given to a new people, the Church (21:43). When this mission has been accomplished and the Gospel has been proclaimed throughout the entire world, the end of the age will take place (24:14).

Verses 15 to 31 describe in detail the events of the end of the age, particularly two: the Great Tribulation and the coming of the Son of Man. The evil and hostility to God's people which will characterize this age will manifest itself in the last days in a period of particular intensity. The abomination of desolation, the Antichrist, prophesied by Daniel (Dan. 9:27) will inflict fearful persecution upon the Church. The persecution of the Great Tribulation and that experienced throughout the course of the age differ in degree, not in kind. To prevent a complete martyrdom of the Church, God will shorten the time of this persecution (24:22).

The Second Coming of Christ is to be no secret event recognizable only by a few, but, like a flash of lightning, evident to all. It will be attended by a shaking of the present physical order of the universe (24:29). The Son of Man will appear with power and great glory, and His appearing will be the signal for gathering His elect, the Church, from the four winds, from one end of heaven to the other. The Apostle Paul speaks of this event as the rapture or the catching up of the elect to meet Christ in the air (I Thess. 4:17).

The question the disciples had asked Jesus about the time of the destruction of Jerusalem (24:3) is answered in verses 32 to 35. The destruction of Jerusalem, described in Luke 21, is a type of the Great Tribulation detailed in Matthew 24. Therefore, while Matthew 24:15–22 refers primarily to the eschatological Antichrist, there is a secondary reference to the siege of Jerusalem by the Roman armies in A.D. 66 to 70. This is implicit in Matthew, but explicit in Luke. This event will occur within a generation; and there will be signs which will show that this historical event is about to take place.

2. Warnings to Readiness (24:37—25:30)

Jesus concludes the Olivet Discourse by emphasizing the unknown time of the end and the necessity to watch. No one knows the day nor the hour of the coming of the Son of Man, neither the angels of heaven nor the Son, but the Father only (24:36). In view of the uncertainty of the time, men are called upon to watch (24:42–44; 25:13). The Greek word which is translated "watch" does not mean to look for something, but to be awake; thus, since the time of

Christ's coming is not known, men must always be awake and prepared for it.

The meaning of watching or wakefulness is illustrated in the paragraphs which follow. To watch means not to be immersed in eating, drinking, marrying and giving in marriage as in the days of Noah (24:37–39), but to be awake to the reality and the importance of the things of God. Christ's coming will mean a separation of men: those who are awake will be saved and those who are asleep will suffer judgment (vv. 40, 41). Those who are not awake will not look for Christ's coming and will therefore fight with their fellow servants and pursue an evil course of conduct (vv. 48, 49). The coming of Christ will catch such faithless servants utterly unawares and bring them to judgment (vv. 50, 51).

The parable of the ten virgins (25:1–13) further illustrates the meaning of watching for Christ's return (v. 13). In the Christian Church, those who wear the externals of the Christian life will not be really prepared to stand in Christ's presence. They will be like foolish virgins who are invited to be bridesmaids, but whose folly causes them to be unprepared. Such will be excluded from the wedding feast at the coming of Christ. Watching therefore means to be alert and awake to one's own spiritual condition.

The parable of the talents further illustrates the meaning of watching for Christ's return (25:14–30); it means to be awake to one's opportunities to serve the Master. Christ has given to His servants various gifts, and His return will test the faithfulness of His servants in the use of their gifts. Their rewards are based not on actual accomplishment, but upon faithfulness. The man who gained two talents received the same reward as the man who gained five talents because he had exercised the same measure of faithfulness. The man who bears the name of a servant but proves faithless demonstrates he is no servant at all; for him there is only judgment.

3. The Judgment of the Nations (25:31–46)

Jesus concluded the Olivet Discourse with a vivid picture of judgment. This picture cannot be interpreted as a single event and fitted into a prophetic program of the future. It is rather a dramatic picture illustrating the single great truth of what the coming of the Son of Man will mean in terms of the ultimate separation of men. The basis of this separation of men is their treatment of the disciples of Jesus. Jesus will send His disciples, whom He calls His brethren (25:40; see also 12:50, where Jesus' brethren are those who do the will of His Father), into the world with the Gospel of the Kingdom of God. Those who receive the representatives of Jesus and their message and treat them kindly thereby receive Christ Himself (10:40); those who reject the disciples reject their Master. This parable of judgment does not advocate teaching of salvation by good works. The basis of salvation is the attitude of men toward the Master Who identifies Himself with His brethren. Eternal punishment on the one hand and eternal life on the other are the final issue of this judgment (25:46).

Passion of the King (26:1—27:66)

1. The Plot to Betray Jesus (26:1-16)

Jesus knew that His death lay immediately ahead and again warned His disciples of this impending event (26:1, 2). Meanwhile, the Sanhedrin, plotting in the palace of the high priest how they might destroy Jesus, feared to take action during the time of the Passover lest there be a popular uprising against them (vv. 3–5). A tender event occurs in Bethany in the house of Simon, one whom Jesus had healed of leprosy (vv. 6–13). Simon was probably the father of Mary, Martha and Lazarus. Mary (Jn. 12:3) anointed Jesus' body with a flask of very expensive ointment whose value was equal to a year's earnings of a working man. The disciples protested this as a waste of money; but Jesus saw in it a symbolic act in anticipation of His death and burial. Furthermore, since it was customary for a Jewish king to be anointed to his office—and the word "Messiah" means "anointed one"—this act may perhaps be taken as Jesus' anointing before His messianic death.

Meanwhile, one of the disciples, Judas Iscariot, was plotting with the priests and arranging a time and place where they might seize Jesus without causing an uprising among the people (26:14–16). We are not told why Judas stooped to this nefarious act. Perhaps he was one who, like the Jews at large, looked for a Messiah who would be a conquering king and warrior to exalt the Jews over their enemies. When Jesus refused to accept this role, Judas may have decided that He could not be the Messiah and was only an impostor, and therefore he determined to turn Him over to His enemies. In any case, the priests gave Judas thirty silver shekels for his cooperation, a sum equal to nearly twenty dollars.

2. The Last Supper (26:17–29)

At the beginning of the eight-day Feast of the Passover, Jesus assembled with His disciples to observe it and instituted what has come to be called the Last Supper (26:17–30). Jesus indicates to Judas that He realized Judas was about to betray Him. During the meal, Jesus took bread and a cup and gave them to His disciples as symbols of the covenant which had been foretold in Jeremiah 31:31. Although the word "new" does not occur in the oldest Greek texts of our Gospels, this meaning is clear from I Corinthians 11:25. The word "covenant" means not an agreement between equals, but one between a benefactor and his inferior; God has graciously bestowed His gifts upon those who do not deserve them. Jesus now establishes the New Covenant in His shed blood to fulfil the meaning implicit in the Old Testament sacrificial system. Through the pouring out of His blood, men are to receive the forgiveness of their sins. This act of sacrifice commemorated in the Lord's Supper looks forward to the day of Christ's coming when it will be celebrated in the Kingdom of God (26:29).

3. Events in Gethsemane (26:30–56)

After singing a psalm, Jesus and the disciples left Jerusalem and went out toward the Mount of Olives to an olive grove called Gethsemane. After telling His unbelieving disciples that they would soon abandon Him (26:31–35), Jesus took His three closest disciples and went ahead into Gethsemane to pray. Although He had come into the world for the specific purpose of bearing the sins of men the awfulness of this experience began to engulf Jesus. He shrank from its terror. In deep distress and in need of the support of His dearest friends, He asked them to watch with Him while He went on to pray alone. His prayer that, if it were possible, God might take away the cup of His suffering for the sins of men depicts in tragic colors the reality of His agony. But it is something far more terrible than physical death that looms ahead; He sees the darkness of the doom entailed by the sins of the world which He is about to bear. His disciples are insensitive to the agony He is experiencing, and He finds that they have failed Him and left Him utterly alone in His hour of testing. They have gone to sleep. In His words is no complaint (v. 40), only the heartbreak of loneliness.

Suddenly Judas and some of the Jewish rulers with a band of the temple guard break into the garden, and in the darkness, Judas identifies Jesus to the Jews by kissing Him (26:47–49). Peter (Jn. 18:10) drew a sword and was prepared to take his stand and fight to the death. Jesus rebuked him, indicating that God's purposes are not to be accomplished by physical force. When He surrendered to the temple guard, the disciples forsook Him and fled.

4. The Trials (26:57—27:26)

Jesus was now brought to the house of Caiaphas, the high priest, where members of the Sanhedrin, the Jewish supreme court, had gathered to conduct a hearing (26:57–68). After some time, when His accusers were unable to produce any legitimate cause for condemnation, the high priest put Jesus under oath and challenged Him flatly to assert whether or not He was the Christ, the Son of God (v. 63). Throughout His ministry, Jesus has not publicly proclaimed that He was the Messiah. For the Jews, Messiah meant a Davidic king who would lead the Jews in battle against their enemies, and such a proclamation would have stirred up widespread rebellion against Rome (cf. Jn. 6:15). Jesus had called Himself the Son of Man, a title which designates a heavenly supernatural being who is to come in the clouds to conduct the Last Judgment and to inaugurate the Kingdom of God in glory (Dan. 7:13,14). However, it was unheard of that the Son of Man should first appear on earth as a man among men, especially to suffer and die. In the mouth of the high priest, the phrase "Son of God" probably is to be understood as synonymous with the Messiah; for in a Jewish context it can bear this meaning.

Jesus' answer was clear: He asserted He was the Messiah; furthermore, the Sanhedrin would hereafter behold Him as the heavenly Son of Man sitting on the right hand of God and coming in the clouds of heaven (26:64). By this utterance, Jesus claimed to be more than Messiah; He claimed to be a divine being Who would sit at the right hand of God. Now as He was being judged by the Sanhedrin, He asserted that in the future they would stand before Him in judgment and He will act as God in judgment. Such a claim to divine prerogatives was, in the eyes of the Sanhedrin, blasphemy; and Jesus was immediately condemned to death.

In the meantime, Peter has followed at a distance (26:58) to see what would happen. Accused by a maid of being a follower of Jesus, Peter three times denied it with an oath (vv. 69–75).

In these days when Judea and Samaria constituted a Roman province governed by the procurator Pontius Pilate, the Jewish Sanhedrin was permitted a large measure of authority over the internal affairs of the Jews; but they were not permitted to execute the death penalty without the approval of the Roman governor. The Sanhedrin therefore took Jesus to Pilate to receive his approval of their sentence of Jesus (27:1, 2).

Meanwhile, Judas was seized with remorse for his treachery. Perhaps Jesus was not Messiah, but Judas knew He was innocent of any crime worthy of death. When he saw Jesus condemned, he attempted to return the money and then committed suicide (27:3–10). Apparently his attempt to hang himself was not altogether as he designed it, for Luke tells us that he fell headlong and was killed (Acts 1:18).

When Pilate conducted a hearing of Jesus (27:11–14) and listened to the accusations of the priests, he recognized that Jesus was no ordinary culprit, but the innocent victim of Jewish intrigue (v. 18). Having a sense of justice, he attempted to effect Jesus' release. The populace who a few days before had hailed Jesus at the triumphal entry as their Messiah are now disillusioned, for He has not performed the messianic acts of political and national deliverance expected of Messiah. When Jesus, a beaten, bound prisoner, was shown to the crowd, they were convinced that His offer of a few days ago as Messiah was the act of an impostor; for Messiah was to be a royal ruler, not a broken victim of the Roman soldiers. It was therefore easy for the leaders of the Sanhedrin to stir up the crowd to demand Jesus' death. Pilate attempted to substitute for Jesus a notorious criminal by the name of Barabbas; but the crowd would have none of it. Pilate had the authority to release Jesus; but the recent history of Palestine had been marked by a series of bloody revolts against Rome, and Pilate's greatest aim was to keep the people reasonably contented. One human life more or less was not important; so Pilate shrugged his shoulders over the entire matter, washed his hands

before the crowd and told them that they could have their way
(vv. 24–26).

5. Crucifixion (27:27–56)

Before the execution, the soldiers made sport of Jesus, mocking
Him as a pretended king (27:27–31). The pavement (Jn. 19:13)
where this occurred may be seen in Jerusalem today.

Jesus was led forth to a small eminence outside the city wall to be
crucified. This place was called "the place of a skull" (Aramaic, *Golgotha*; Latin, *Calvary*); the reason for this name is not known.
Offered an opiate to dull the pain, Jesus refused to drink it. He was
crucified with two bandits who may have been revolutionaries
against Rome. It was a Roman custom to indicate by a placard the
crime for which one was condemned; and the charge in this case
was that of high treason (27:37). The placard showed what Rome
would do with any man who claimed to be the king of the Jews or
their Messiah.

The Jews mocked Him saying that if He were the Son of God, He
should come down from the cross (27:42). But because He *was* the
Son of God, He remained on the cross to accomplish the atonement for sin. They said that if He came down from the cross, they
would believe on Him, but it is only because He stayed on the cross
that we today believe on Him as our Saviour.

A supernatural darkness fell over the land at twelve o'clock, lasting until three (27:45). At this time, Jesus cried out in the Aramaic
tongue, "My God, my God, why hast thou forsaken me?" The penalty
for sin is death—separation from God and the divine blessings—and
in this moment, Jesus experienced death. We may reverently say
that He stepped into hell in our stead. That He bore both our sins
and the doom entailed by our sins is the heart of the atonement.
Having accomplished this atonement, He cried with a loud voice and
gave His spirit to His Father (v. 50).

In this moment, an earthquake shook the land; and the veil of
the temple which excluded the people from the holy of holies where
the Shekinah presence of God dwelt was rent in two from top to
bottom (27:51), thus signifying that because of the death of the
Son of God, all men in His name may now enter into the immediate
presence of God with no need of coming to the temple. Verses 52
and 53 show that Jesus' death conquered death; this resurrection

of some of the Old Testament saints is a sign and a guarantee that at His Second Coming, all of the saints will be raised up into everlasting life.

The events which attended Jesus' death and His own conduct made a remarkable impression upon the Roman officer; he was compelled to confess, "Here is a supernatural person" (27:54).

6. Burial (27:57–66)

Jesus' body was taken from the cross with the permission of Pilate by Joseph of Arimathea and embalmed according to the Jewish custom and placed in a small cave cut out of the rock somewhere outside of the city (27:57–61). The priests and the Pharisees, desiring to prevent the possible theft of His body by His disciples, sent a guard before tomb and sealed the stone (vv. 62–66).

The Resurrection (28:1–20)

1. The Women and the Angel (28:1–10)

The crucifixion occurred on Friday. Saturday was the Sabbath, and at dawn on Sunday morning, the first day of the week, Mary Magdalene and Mary, the mother of James and Joseph, came to the tomb bringing fresh ointments. But they found the stone rolled away from the tomb and the tomb itself empty. An earthquake had occurred and an angel had rolled back the stone, striking terror into the hearts of the guards before the tomb. This act of the angels in removing the stone was not to permit Jesus to come forth, but to let the women enter and discover Jesus' body was no longer there. The angel met the women and told them that Jesus had risen from the dead and that they should tell His disciples that He would meet them in Galilee. This, however, does not exclude appearances of Jesus in Jerusalem. As the women went to tell the disciples, Jesus met them. That they held Him by the feet and worshipped Him (28:9) indicates a bodily resurrection.

2. False Witness of the Guards (28:11–15)

Meanwhile the guards at the tomb told the priests all that had happened, and the priests bribed the guards to spread the story that they had fallen asleep at their watch and that the disciples had stolen the body of Jesus during the night while they were sleeping.

3. The Ascension (28:16–20)

Matthew brings the Gospel very abruptly to an end without relating the many resurrection appearances of our Lord; he records only one other incident. The eleven went to Galilee as Jesus had commanded them. Here Jesus met them and gave them "the great commission." Because all authority in heaven and on earth had been given to the resurrected Lord, His disciples have a fourfold mission: They are to go into all the world; they are to make disciples of all nations; they are to baptize disciples in the name of the Father and of the Son and of the Holy Spirit; they are to teach the disciples to observe all that Jesus had commanded. As they fulfil this commission, Jesus promised to be with them even to the consummation of the age. This remains the divinely appointed privilege and responsibility of the Church until Jesus comes again in glory.

Mark

RALPH EARLE

THE GOSPEL OF MARK gives a brief resume of Jesus' public ministry. Unlike Matthew and Luke, it makes no refernce to the birth or childhood of Christ. It has no genealogy of Jesus. Matthew has 76 verses of introduction before beginning his account of the public ministry of the Master. Luke has 183. In contrast, Mark has only 13. After the title (1:1), the ministry of John the Baptist (vv. 2–8), the baptism (vv. 9–11) and the temptation (vv. 12, 13), Mark plunges immediately into his recital of the public ministry.

It will thus be seen that this Gospel is concerned primarily with the Man rather than His message. Mark presents Christ in action, rather than quietly teaching. His is "the Gospel of the strenuous life," yet he describes five withdrawals of Jesus. The busier one is, the more does he need times of retirement. The Master was balanced as well as busy. He knew the value of fellowship with the Father. In His humanity He needed, as we do, rest and recreation.

Mark presents Jesus as "the Servant of the Lord" (cf. Is. 52:13—53:12). He is both the *conquering* Servant and the *suffering* Servant. He stands, as the ox, between the plow and the altar, ready for service or sacrifice. In Jesus' case it was both—first service, then sacrifice. In these two ways He "gave" Himself for humanity.

I. The Period of Preparation (1:1–13)

The first verse probably constitutes the title of the Gospel, although some hold that it is simply the heading for John the Baptist's ministry. The Greek word for "Gospel" means "good news," so this verse might be translated: "The beginning of the glad tidings about Jesus Christ, the Son of God." That summarizes the significance of this Gospel.

It has been common in the past to assume that Mark's interest was historical, rather than theological. But today it is being increasingly recognized that his Gospel has a strong emphasis on theology. That fact is highlighted in the last clause of verse one. Jesus is both the Jewish Messiah and the eternal Son of God. Mark's Gospel reflects just as definite a belief in the deity of Jesus as does John's. This doctrine did not have its rise in the second century. It was the foundation on which the first generation believers built their faith. There is still no other support for Christianity (I Cor. 3:11).

1. The Ministry of John (1:2-8)

"It is written"—this phrase underscores the importance of the Old Testament. The perfect tense in the Greek means, "It has been written and still stands written." That is, this expression found so often in the New Testament emphasizes the irrevocable, unchanging character of God's Word. Mark quotes Malachi and Isaiah who foretold the coming of John the Baptist as the forerunner of Jesus.

John, the baptizer, was a rugged individual, as befitted his wilderness environment and pioneer work. The striking description of his dress and food—camel's hair (sackcloth) and leather belt; locusts and wild honey—probably reflects Peter's vivid preaching. People flocked all the way from Jerusalem down to the Jordan—twenty miles away and four thousand feet lower—in spite of the rugged return trip. John was having what today we call a stirring revival.

But John's function was only to prepare the way for Jesus. He baptized with water; the Coming One would baptize with the Holy Spirit.

2. The Baptism of Jesus (1:9-11)

As the representative Man, Jesus submitted to John's baptism, although with Him there was no confession of sins (cf. 1:5). But the main significance of the event lies in the coming of the Holy Spirit upon Him for His ministry and the voice from heaven, which declared: "Thou art my beloved Son; in thee I am well pleased" (ASV). At the baptism of Jesus, the three members of the Trinity were for the first time distinctly revealed. As Jesus came up out of the water, the Spirit descended on Him as a dove, and at the same time the Father's voice called from heaven: "Thou art my Son." It was a high moment in history. The deity of Jesus was definitely affirmed by a divine disclosure at the very beginning of His ministry.

3. The Temptation of Jesus (1:12,13)

Matthew and Luke record the details of Jesus' threefold temptation by Satan. Mark gives only a brief, general account. But he has several distinctive items. He emphasizes the fact that the temptation followed the baptism "immediately"—*euthus*—which occurs over forty times in his Gospel and nine times in this first chapter. It highlights the rapid action of Jesus' busy life.

Typically, Mark uses a stronger verb than Matthew and Luke when he writes: "The Spirit *drives* him out into the wilderness" (literal translation). He alone mentions the "wild beasts" as companions of Jesus. Their melancholy howls at night added to the weirdness of the lonely wilderness. But Jesus' public inauguration (at His baptism) must be followed by a private initiation into the ministry.

II. The Galilean Ministry (1:14—9:50)

While John majors on the Judean ministry of Jesus, all three Synoptic Gospels record mainly His activities in Galilee. Here was where He apparently spent the bulk of His time.

The Galilean ministry may be divided into three periods. The first began with the arrest of John the Baptist; the second, with the appointment of the Twelve Apostles; the third, with Jesus' retirement to the region of Tyre and Sidon. In the first, He was gathering His disciples. In the second, He was ministering to the multitudes. In the third, He was turning His attention to the private instruction of His disciples.

1. The First Period (1:14—3:12)

Jesus' great Galilean ministry began with the arrest and imprisonment of John. When John's preaching was silenced, a greater Preacher appeared.

The opening declaration of Jesus is fraught with theological significance. He said: "The time [not *chronos*, time in general, but *chairos*, "the appointed time, right season, opportune moment"] is fulfilled." God's clock was striking the hour. It was the great moment of opportunity for the Jewish nation. The Messiah had come. The Kingdom of God was at hand. Repentance and believing the Gospel—these were the two requirements for receiving the Kingdom. But the Jews rejected the call, and the Church of Jesus Christ replaced the Jewish theocracy.

The First Four Disciples (1:16–20). The first incident in this period was the call of the four fishermen as disciples. Simon and Andrew, James and John—these two pairs of brothers were given the honor of sharing in Jesus' public ministry. Himself a carpenter, the Master chose busy workingmen to work with Him. The Kingdom of God is no place for laggards or dullards.

A Busy Day in Jesus' Life (1:21–34). It all happened in Capernaum, at the northwest corner of the Sea of Galilee, where Jesus made His headquarters. On the Sabbath day (Saturday), he attended the worship service at the synagogue. Known as a Jewish teacher, He was invited to speak. The listeners were amazed at His tone of divine authority, in contrast to the rabbinical habit of quoting human authorities.

Suddenly the sermon was interrupted by a demon-possessed man shrieking that this Jesus of Nazareth was "the Holy One of God," or Messiah. Jesus silenced "the unclean spirit"—Mark's favorite expression (ten times) for demon—and cast it out. He did not wish testimony from that quarter, nor did He apparently want His Messiahship proclaimed publicly at this time. The people were "amazed"—a strong verb used only by Mark.

After curing the demoniac in the synagogue (1:21–28), Jesus went home with Peter for dinner. They found Peter's mother-in-law lying prostrate with a fever. Jesus healed her (vv. 29–31) and she served the meal.

The one topic of conversation that day in Capernaum was what had happened in the synagogue. Since it was forbidden to bear burdens on the Sabbath—which lasted from sunset Friday night until sunset Saturday night—the people had to wait. But that evening there took place a sunset healing service (1:32–34), at which "the whole city was gathered together at the door" (v. 33).

Though worn out with His heavy day, Jesus rose early the next morning for a sunrise prayer meeting (1:35–39). In fact, Mark uses three adverbs in the Greek to emphasize that it was "very early in the morning, while it was still night" that Jesus rose to pray. Though divine He was also human, and He needed fellowship with His

Father to get guidance for His next moves. When the tardy disciples found Him in the solitary place of prayer He announced that He must move on to new towns. His primary mission was preaching (v. 38), not healing.

The first chapter closes with the cleansing of the leper (1:40–45). Jesus showed that His compassion was equal to His power.

The Healing of the Paralytic (2:1–12). This miracle is described in all three Synoptic Gospels, but it is described most vividly by Mark. He alone mentions the fact that the helpless man was borne on his pallet by four men. When they could not reach Jesus because of the tightly-packed crowd, these persevering friends carried the paralytic on his padded quilt up the outside stairs to the flat roof. There they literally "unroofed the roof" above Jesus and lowered the pallet into His presence. Realizing that the man's first need was forgiveness of sins, Christ first assured him of this—much to the indignation of the scribes. Jesus then healed the man's body as proof that He could heal his soul.

For the first time we find here the expression "Son of man." It occurs fourteen times in Mark and eighty-one times altogether in the Gospels. In every instance, it is applied by Jesus to Himself. In the non-canonical book of Enoch, the title indicates the pre-existent, personal Messiah. The book of Daniel (7:13) probably furnishes the background for Jesus' use of "Son of man."

The Call of Levi (2:13–17). The calling of Levi, or Matthew, is the second incident in which Jesus came into conflict with the Pharisees. In the former it was because He dared to assume the divine prerogative of forgiving sins (vv. 6-11). Here it was occasioned by His eating with "publicans and sinners" (v. 16). Since these tax collectors were working for the Roman government and had considerable contact with Gentiles, they were considered "unclean" by the strict Pharisees. But Jesus made Himself friendly to sinners in order to save them.

The Roman method of collecting taxes was to "farm out" the required revenue to wealthy *publicani*. They sublet the contract to others and these, in turn, sublet to the actual tax collectors mentioned in the Gospels. Hence the translation "publicans" (KJV, ASV) is incorrect. Because of their greed and graft, they were despised and hated throughout the Roman Empire, especially by the Jews.

In answer to the Pharisees' objection, Jesus replied: "I came not to call the righteous, but sinners to repentance" (2:17). Both "righteous" and "sinners" should be put in quotation marks, for Christ was using the terms in the sense the Pharisees used them. Actually these religious leaders, with all their formal, legal righteousness, were but sinners in God's sight.

The third clash with the Pharisees came over the question of fasting (2:18–22). John's disciples and the Pharisees "were fasting," as the Greek says. But on this fast day Jesus' disciples were eating. When objection was made, Jesus defended His followers by asserting that while the bridegroom (Christ) was with them, it would be unfitting to fast.

Then Jesus gave two brief parabolic statements—about sewing a patch of undressed cloth on an old garment and pouring new wine into old wineskins (not "bottles," KJV), which could stretch no farther as the fermenting wine expanded.

The law prescribed only one fast a year, the Day of Atonement (Lev. 23:27); but at this time the Pharisees prided themselves on fasting twice a week (Lk. 18:12). The second century *Didache* says that Christians fasted on Wednesday and Friday, while the Jews fasted on Tuesday and Thursday. But asceticism is of pagan, not Christian, origin. It is based on the false teaching that all matter is evil.

Sabbath Controversy (2:23—3:12). The fourth and fifth clashes with the Pharisees arose over the question of Sabbath observance. The fourth had to do with plucking grain on the Sabbath day (2:23–28). The disciples were passing through grainfields and plucked the heads of wheat or barley—not "corn" (KJV), a term which in England is used for wheat, but which in the United States means something far different.

There was nothing wrong about the disciples helping themselves to all the grain they wanted to eat (Deut. 23:25). But to pluck the heads of wheat and rub off the husks in their hands—that was harvesting and threshing! This is a typical example of harsh legalism which makes mountains out of molehills. Jesus came to cleanse the motives of men, so that they would be activated by love.

The fifth and final clash with the Pharisees recorded in this section (2:1—3:6) had to do with healing on the Sabbath—specifically the man with the withered hand (3:1–6). The Pharisees in the synagogue literally "kept watching him closely," with the narrowed eyes of cruel criticism, to see whether He would heal the man on the Sabbath. Jesus put His critics on the spot by asking a loaded question: "Is it lawful to do good on the Sabbath days, or to do evil? to save life, or to kill?" Their only answer was sullen silence. But the Pharisees went out of the synagogue to plot murder with the Herodians. Was this keeping the Sabbath?

Some people are shocked by the idea that Jesus would be angry (only here in the Gospels). But we should notice carefully the wording: "And when He had looked around about on them with anger, being grieved for the hardness of their hearts" (3:5). Only anger that is mixed with compassionate grief is Christian. Furthermore, the verb "looked" is aorist, whereas "grieved" is the continuous present. This suggests that the anger was a momentary flash of indignation against their selfish, unreasonable attitude, while the grief was an abiding feeling of compassion. Love must not be reduced to mere immoral or even amoral sentiment. Without hatred of evil, there is no true love of good. Anger at sin is the necessary sign of a moral conscience.

Jesus' popularity is strikingly described in 3:7–12. He was followed by a great multitude not only from Galilee, but also from Judea and particularly Jerusalem, from Idumea—south of Judea, mentioned only here in the New Testament—and Perea ("across the Jordan"), and even from the far off region of Tyre and Sidon. His fame as a healer drew the crowds.

2. The Second Period (3:13—7:23)

Friends and Foes (3:13–35). The second period of Jesus' ministry began with the appointment of the Twelve Apostles (vv. 13–19). These were called for two specific purposes: (*1*) "that they should be with him"; and (*2*) "that He might send them forth to preach" (v. 14). A call to preach always implies a call to prepare.

Lists of the apostles appear in all three Synoptic Gospels, as well as the first chapter of Acts (cf. Mt. 10:1–4; Lk. 6:12–16; Acts 1:13). Peter's name always comes first. All the lists divide naturally into three groups. In every case the first group comprises the four fishermen. The second group always begins with Philip, and the third, with James the son of Alphaeus.

"Simon" is a very common Jewish name. "Peter" is from the Greek *petros,* meaning "a stone." Why Jesus called James and John "sons of thunder" is not certainly known (cf. Lk. 9:54). For "Thaddaeus," Luke has "Judas the brother of James," probably a variant name for the same individual. "Simon the Canaanite" (KJV) should be

"Simon the Cananaean"; Luke calls him *Zelotes,* "the zealot." In the revolt against Rome in A.D. 66-70, the nationalistic party was called "the Zealots." But the term may here simply indicate that Simon was a zealous person. "Judas Iscariot, who also betrayed him" is always the final sad note.

Jesus received opposition from both friends and foes (3:20–27). "He comes home" (v. 19b), that is, to Capernaum. The crowds thronged Him until He did not even have time to eat. His family said, "He is out of his mind." The scribes from Jerusalem had another explanation: "He has Beelzebub and by the ruler of the demons he casts out demons" (v. 22, literally). Christ pointed up the absurdity of their position (vv. 23–27).

Jesus went on to warn against the unpardonable sin (3:28–30), which He identified as blasphemy against the Holy Spirit. Apparently the scribes were guilty of this inexcusable moral confusion when they deliberately and wilfully labeled the work of the Holy Spirit the work of Satan. It should be obvious that most of those who in modern times have feared that they had committed the unpardonable sin have been guilty of no such thing. Usually it is just another trick of Satan to keep people from believing in Jesus Christ for their salvation.

The true family of God (3:31–35) consists of those who do the will of God. The question has often been raised as to who the "brothers" of Jesus were. Some have said they were His cousins; others, children of Joseph by a previous marriage. But the simplest conclusion is that they were the children of Joseph and Mary. Jesus was Mary's "firstborn son" (Lk. 2:7), implying that she had others.

Mark's Gospel is the Gospel of *action.* So it has only four of the full-fledged parables of Jesus. Three of them are recorded in the fourth chapter.

Teaching in Parables (4:1–34). The first is the parable of the sower (vv. 1–20). It might better be called the "parable of the soils," for the distinction in kinds of soil is the whole point of emphasis. This is one of the few parables of which the explanation is furnished by Jesus, and it is given at length in all three Synoptic Gospels.

"Stony ground" (4:5, KJV) is better rendered "rocky ground" (ASV, RSV). It does not mean ground covered with stones, but a thin layer of earth over a ledge of rock. This would cause the seed to come up quickly because of the added heat, but would also dry out rapidly.

The lessons of the four soils are exceedingly pertinent. Hard hearts, beaten down by the traffic of life, do not actually accept the Gospel. Shallow hearts react emotionally, but there is no genuine repentance for sin. Strangled hearts are the real danger for most Christians in our crowded modern life. Even in the good hearts, there are degrees of fruitfulness (4:20).

In between the parable and the explanation there is a brief statement of the reason for teaching in parables (4:10–12). On the surface it seems that Jesus claimed He taught in parables so that people would not understand Him. But there is another side to it. Truth is only hidden (in parables) in order that it may be revealed (vv. 21–25). Literally Jesus said: "The lamp does not come in order that it may be placed under the peck measure or under the couch, does it? Is it not that it may be placed on the lampstand?" (v. 21). In Jesus' day they used tiny clay lamps with olive oil in them, not "candles" (KJV). In a further statement, Jesus enunciated this important principle of life: "The measure you give will be the measure you get" (v. 24, RSV).

Of the four parables found in Mark, one is given only by him—the parable of the seed growing secretly (4:26–29). This is related to the parable of the sower. The point emphasized here is that the seed grows "of itself" (*automate*, automatically). It is an encouragement to the Christian worker to sow the seed of the Word faithfully, knowing that God will give the increase.

The parable of the mustard seed (4:30–32) is found in all three Synoptics. The traditional interpretation is that in spite of its small beginning the Kingdom of God will become a great power in the earth, giving comfort to multitudes of people. Certainly the Kingdom of God cannot be identified, as some have maintained, with an apostate visible church.

This section concludes with the statement that Jesus spoke to the crowds only in parables, but that privately He explained all things to His own disciples (4:34, 35).

The First Withdrawal (4:35—5:20). The first of five withdrawals of Jesus was to the east side of the Sea of Galilee. On the way across occurred the stilling of the storm (vv. 35–41). Jesus was so worn out with His constant ministry to the multitudes that He quickly fell asleep on the cushion in the stern of the fishing boat. So deep was His slumber that He did not hear the rising gale. With the waves crashing over the bow and the boat already "filling" (not "full," KJV), the disciples in terror wakened Him. The Master spoke two words. The wind ceased its raging and the waves sank to a quiet slumber. The same Master can still the storm in the human heart.

The Gerasene demoniac (5:1–20) shattered the silence of the solitude on the eastern shore of the lake. But Jesus stilled the storm within this raging, raving maniac by casting out the legion of "demons," very different, is a plural word.)

The picture of the Gerasene demoniac is a striking portrait of sin. Sin is suicide (5:3), insanity (v. 4) and self-destruction (v. 5). But just as the Gerasenes preferred to have the murderous maniac threatening their lives rather than Jesus threatening their business, so many today hug to their bosoms the serpent of sin and turn away the Saviour.

The cured demoniac, on the other hand, wanted to stay close to Jesus (5:18), but the Master had an assignment for him—witnessing at home (v. 19). The ardent evangelist was soon evangelizing "the Decapolis" (v. 20), a league of ten cities, as the name indicates, stretching from Damascus in the north to Philadelphia (modern Amman) in the south. These cities were marked by a strong Hellenistic culture. The preaching of the former notorious demonaic doubtless paved the way for a more cordial reception of Jesus on His next visit to the Decapolis (7:31).

Raising of Jairus' Daughter (5:21–43). This miracle and the healing of the woman with a hemorrhage form a very interesting, intertwined story. When Jesus returned to Capernaum (cf. Mt. 9:1 "his own city"), He found a great crowd awaiting Him. But one man had a pressing need that claimed priority. Jairus, a synagogue ruler, begged the Master to come and heal his dying daughter. As Jesus was on the way to Jairus' house, a woman who had been afflicted with a flowing of blood for twelve years touched His garment and was instantly healed. Pale and timid as she was, she sought to escape unobserved. But Jesus compelled her to testify openly (vv. 30–34), not out of cruelty, but out of compassion. He had a spiritual blessing to add to her physical benefit.

Meanwhile, Jairus was doubtless beside himself with anxiety because of the lengthening delay. How could Jesus stand there talking to a woman when his daughter was dying? The climax came when a messenger informed him that his child was now gone. But Jesus, "ignoring" (RSV) the report, quietly said to Jairus: "Stop being afraid; just keep on believing" (5:36, literally).

Taking Peter, James and John, Jesus accompanied the stricken father to his home. There He ordered the wailing friends and professional mourners out of the room. Taking the child by the hand, He said in Aramaic, *"Talitha cumi."* Perhaps these were the very words with which the girl's mother usually wakened her in the morning. The same Living Word that spoke worlds into being restored life to the little girl's body. Jesus commanded the parents to give her something to eat. It was their responsibility to care for her now.

The Rejection at Nazareth (6:1–6). This must have been one of the saddest days in Jesus' public ministry. He left Capernaum and walked a day's journey (about twenty miles) over the hills to Nazareth, His home town. In spite of His amazing teaching in the synagogue, His old friends and neighbors turned a cynical eye on Him. Their attitude effectually prevented His working miracles. Only twice is it recorded that Jesus marveled—here at the unbelief of His fellow townsmen and elsewhere at the faith of a Roman centurion (Mt. 8:10; Lk. 7:9).

Mission of the Twelve (6:7–13). One of the high points of Jesus' ministry was the mission of the twelve. "Send forth" is *apostello,* which means "send on a mission." The noun *apostolos* gives us our word "apostle." Jesus sent the Twelve Apostles on a brief missionary tour of Galilee, since He Himself could not reach all the hundreds of towns and villages.

He sent them out "two by two" (RSV). They were to travel light —"no bread, no bag, no money in their belts; but to wear sandals and not put on two tunics" (6:8,9, RSV). The "bag" ("scrip," KJV) was evidently a pouch for carrying food. For this quick trip they were to depend entirely on the hospitality of the people.

Death of John the Baptist (6:14–29). The sordid story is recorded at this point because Herod thought that Jesus was John risen from the dead. Herod Antipas, tetrarch of Galilee and Perea (4 B.C.–A.D. 39), was a son of Herod the Great (37–4 B.C.). While entertained in the home of his brother at Rome, Antipas had become infatuated with his brother's wife, Herodias, and married her, divorcing his own wife. The holy prophet from the wilderness sternly denounced the whole immoral business. For his preaching he was put in prison. Herodias "had it in for him" (6:19, literally). But Herod feared John and "kept him safe" (v. 20, RSV). When he heard the prophet speak, he was "much perplexed" (RSV; not "did many things," KJV). But Herodias concocted a clever scheme. She was so enraged at John that she stooped to making her own daughter, Salome, a common dancing girl, entice the drunken Herod. The result was the head of

John the Baptist brought on a "platter" (RSV) and presented to the offended Herodias. Human hate was satiated with this sacrifice.

Jesus' Second Withdrawal (6:30–44). This withdrawal was apparently to the northeast corner of the sea, where He fed the five thousand (6:30–44). The Master sought solitude with His disciples. But when He found a crowd awaiting Him, He taught them until evening and then gave them a free supper.

The disciples learned an important lesson at this point. Worried with the big crowd, they urged Jesus to "send them away" (6:36). The Master replied, "Give ye them to eat"—the "ye" is emphatic in the Greek. The disciples protested that if they had two hundred denarii—a denarius was a day's wage, about 20 cents—they could not feed the multitude. Yet when they brought the little lunch to Jesus and let Him bless and multiply it, they actually did feed the vast crowd. It took only five small barley loaves—about as large as a tiny pancake—and two sardine-sized fish to feed five thousand men, plus a few hundred women and children who ate separately from the men (Mt. 14:21).

This is the only miracle of Jesus recorded in all Four Gospels, but Mark's account is the most vivid. His word for "companies" is *symposia* (cf. "symposium") and for "ranks" *prasiai*, which means "flower beds." To Peter the people in their bright oriental garments on the green hillside looked like beautiful flower beds. Incidentally, Mark's mention of the green grass (6:39) is an interesting confirmation of John's statement that this miracle took place near the Passover season (March-April), for only in the spring is the grass green in Palestine.

The story of Jesus walking on the water (6:45–52) is omitted only by Luke. Because of the danger of a political revolution (cf. Jn. 6:15), Jesus ordered His disciples to embark in the boat while He dismissed the crowd. Then He spent most of the night on the mountain top in prayer. From there He saw the disciples struggling against a northeast wind which kept them from reaching Bethsaida, near the entrance of the Jordan River into the Sea of Galilee. This was "the other side" (v. 45) of a small bay north of the place where he fed the five thousand. In the fourth watch of the night (3:00–6:00 A.M.) Jesus came to them, walking on the waves. When He entered the boat, the wind ceased (6:51). Thus by a double miracle He again demonstrated that He was Master of the elements. Amazed, the disciples were yet slow to understand and believe (v. 52).

The northeast wind had driven the boat toward the west side of the lake. So they landed at Gennesaret, a small plain about three miles long and a mile wide. Here Jesus carried on a healing ministry (6:53–56).

Controversy over Cleansing (7:1–23). Again Jesus came into conflict with the Pharisees, this time over the matter of ceremonial cleansings. Some scribes from Jerusalem joined the local Pharisees in criticizing the disciples for eating "with hands defiled, that is, unwashed" (v. 2, RSV). Since Mark was writing for Romans, he goes on to explain the Jewish custom. Before a Pharisee would eat he must wash his hands "oft" (v. 3). So says the King James Version. But the Greek is *pygme*, "with a fist." Dozens of explanations have been given as to what this might mean. Probably "diligently" (ERV, ASV) conveys the general idea correctly. The translators of the Revised Standard Version finally left the word untranslated.

The "tradition of the elders" was a body of oral regulations handed down from the great rabbis of the past and later reduced to writing. The phrase is found only here (7:3, 5) and in Matthew 15:2. The rabbis sought to protect the law of Moses by putting a "fence" around it. This consisted of detailed instructions for daily living and made religion a burden to the people (cf. Acts 15:10).

Added to washing hands ceremonially before every meal was the "baptism" of cups, pitchers, and copper vessels (7:4); "tables" (more accurately "couches") is not in the oldest manuscripts. It is significant that in the Jewish Mishna, no less than thirty chapters are devoted to the cleansing of vessels! No wonder Jesus scored the Pharisees for their undue emphasis on externals. He called them "hypocrites" (v. 6).

It was a very serious charge that Christ brought against these religious leaders. He accused them of rejecting the commandment of God in order to keep the tradition of men (7:8, 9). As an example He cited the case of corban. A man could free himself from obligation to care for his parents by declaring that his money was devoted to God. Thus the divine command, "Honor thy father and thy mother," was made void (vv. 10–13).

Then Jesus pointed out the real source of defilement as not anything from without, but only that which came from within (7:15). With their background of distinction between clean and unclean foods, the disciples could not understand this revolutionary statement. When they privately requested an explanation, Jesus asserted that only what comes out of the heart can defile a person (vv. 17–

23). The expression "purging all meats" (v. 19) is probably an added explanatory note by the evangelist (cf. "This he said, making all meats clean," ASV; "Thus he declared all foods clean," RSV).

3. The Third Period (7:24—9:50)

Third Withdrawal (7:24-30). This phase of Jesus' Galilean ministry began with His third withdrawal, to the region of Tyre and Sidon. Once more He sought solitude with His disciples, but His presence was discovered by a Gentile woman, a native "Syrophoenician." Mark, writing in Rome, uses this term so that his readers would not confuse it with Libyo-Phoenicia in North Africa. Syrian Phoenicia is what is now called Lebanon.

In desperation because of her daughter's demon possession, this woman begged Jesus for help. His reply, "It is not right to take the children's bread and throw it to the dogs" (7:27, RSV), sounds harsh on the surface. But the Master probably had two purposes in mind: *(1)* to test the woman's faith and *(2)* to reprove the disciples for their attitude (cf. Mt. 15:23). They shared the common Jewish idea that all Gentiles were dogs. Apparently the woman sensed Jesus' real attitude. Her keen, quick, courageous retort obviously pleased the Master and He granted her request.

Healing of the Deaf Mute (7:31-37). Returning from Phoenicia, Jesus avoided the territory of the unfriendly Herod Antipas (cf. Lk. 13:31) and went instead to the east side of the Sea of Galilee, into the region of the Decapolis. Here He healed a deaf mute. Apparently this man was not entirely dumb, for when healed he spoke "plain" (7:35). This miracle, recorded only by Mark, was performed privately (v. 33) to avoid publicity. But it was impossible to hide such happenings. The significant verdict of the people was, "He hath done all things well" (v. 37).

Fourth Withdrawal: The feeding of the four thousand (8:1-10) is recorded only by Mark and Matthew. Many scholars have held that this is just a variant account of the feeding of the five thousand. But the differences outweigh the similarities. In the earlier miracle, the disciples spoke first; here Jesus took the initiative. There the crowd had been with Him one day, here for three days. There is also a difference in the size of the crowd, the amount of food—here seven loaves and a few small fish—and in the number of baskets filled. Also a different word for baskets is used. There it was the twelve lunch baskets of the apostles. Here it was seven large hampers, such as the basket in which Paul was let down from the wall in Damascus (Acts 9:25).

Teaching and Healing (8:11–26). When Jesus returned to the west side of the Sea of Galilee (v. 10), the Pharisees demanded from Him "a sign from heaven" (vv. 11–13). The Jews expected the Messiah to attest His coming by a spectacular light in the sky. In reaction Jesus "sighed deeply." The Greek word, found only here in the New Testament, is an intensive compound indicating strong feeling. With a statement that no sign—of the kind they asked (cf. Mt. 16:4; Lk. 11:29)—would be given that generation, Jesus left His questioners, embarked in the boat, and crossed again to the east side of Galilee.

On the way across, the Master warned His disciples against the leaven of the Pharisees and the leaven of Herod (8:14–21). The former was hypocrisy, pride, a legalistic spirit; the latter, worldliness and a desire for political power.

This passage is of significance in supporting the fact of two feedings. In the allusion here (8:19,20) to the miracles, the distinction between the two kinds of baskets is observed. In all six references to the feeding of the five thousand (Mt. 14:20; 16:9; Mk. 6:43; 8:19; Lk. 9:17; Jn. 6:13) the word is *kophinos*, which suggests "lunch basket." In all four references to the feeding of the four thousand (Mt. 15:37; 16:10; Mk. 8:8, 20), the word *spuris* may be translated "hamper." Such complete consistency is strong evidence for careful accounts of two separate feedings.

When they reached the northeastern shore of the Sea of Galilee, there occurred the healing of the blind man of Bethsaida (8:22–26). This and the healing of the deaf mute in the Decapolis (7:31–37) are the only two miracles recorded by Mark alone. They have much in common. In both cases Jesus took the victim aside from the crowds, used spittle, and touched the afflicted part of the body. But this one is unique in being the only recorded miracle of Jesus which took place in two stages. Twice He touched the blinded eyes before the man could see clearly. It has been suggested that this was a symbol of the fact that it took two miracles (feedings) to open the blind eyes of the disciples.

Fifth Withdrawal (8:27–30). At Caesarea Philippi, Peter's great confession took place. Jesus asked His disciples how people were identifying Him. After various answers had been given, He turned the question squarely on them: "But you, who do you say me to be?" (8:29, literally). Peter rose to the occasion with the momentous declaration: "Thou art the Christ!"

Caesarea Philippi—so called to distinguish it from the Caesarea on the Mediterranean—was named after Philip, son of Herod the Great. It was located at the foot of snow-capped Mount Hermon, near the main source of the Jordan River. Its former name, Paneas, was due to the ancient worship here of the Roman god, Pan—the Greek word for "all." It was in the ancient place of the worship of the all-god that Peter confessed: "Thou art the Messiah."

Jesus' command that they should tell no one may seem strange. But He did not want a public proclamation of His Messiahship at this time, lest the people's erroneous ideas about a political Messiah cause a revolt against Rome.

This incident (8:27–30) is the midpoint of Mark's Gospel and marked the turning point in Jesus' ministry. Heretofore He had been ministering to the multitudes. Hereafter He would devote most of His time to instructing His disciples. They had confessed Him as Messiah. Now He must show them that the Messiah is to suffer and die. His coming death at Jerusalem becomes the main topic of conversation with them.

So here we find the first prediction of the Passion (8:31–33). The word "began" (v. 31) suggests a new beginning in His teaching. The climax of Jesus' ministry would, of course, be His death and resurrection. Because the disciples shared the erroneous Jewish ideas of an earthly messianic kingdom, Jesus had to begin a period of indoctrinating them in the concept of a suffering Messiah. This was necessary if their faith was not to be completely shaken by the coming events at Jerusalem.

But the disciples must suffer as well as their Master—and so the discourse on the cost of discipleship (8:34—9:1). Here Jesus uttered one of His most important sayings: "Whosoever will come after me, let him deny himself, and take up his cross, and follow me" (v. 34). This cuts right across the world's philosophy of life. Instead of self-assertion, Jesus taught self-denial. Every one enters the Kingdom of God through the door of self-humiliation. Then there is the further step of taking up one's cross, or complete submission to the will of God. "Deny" and "take up" are both in the aorist tense, suggesting crises of self-denial and self-surrender. But "follow" is in the continuous present; it is a lifelong assignment.

The first verse of the ninth chapter belongs with the eighth chapter. The inconsistency of some of the chapter divisions—made in the thirteenth century—is shown by the fact that in Matthew the dividing point is after this saying, not before, as in Mark.

Probably Mark 9:1 is not a prediction of the Transfiguration; its language implies more. What Jesus must have meant was that some of His apostles would witness the rapid spread of the Gospel after the coming of the Holy Spirit to empower the Church. Pentecost and its mighty postlude, as described in Acts, seem to fulfil this promise.

The Transfiguration (9:2–8). The Transfiguration occurred a week after what is previously recorded. Probably the event took place on one of the southern spurs of Mount Hermon, rather than at the traditional side on Mount Tabor. The latter is too low (one thousand feet) and seems to have had a fortress on it at the time.

As the Master was praying (cf. Lk. 9:29), His divine nature burst through the bonds of flesh, and the disciples glimpsed the glory of God in the face of Jesus Christ. Even His garments glistened. Moses and Elijah, representing the Law and the Prophets (Old Testament), appeared on the scene. Peter wanted to make three booths, one each for Jesus and His visitors. But a voice from heaven rebuked this implied equality and silenced Peter's ill-considered speech. Said the Father: "This is my beloved Son; hear him" (9:7). When the cloud—betokening the Shekinah of God's presence (Ex. 40:34)—lifted, the disciples found themselves alone with Jesus.

During the descent from the mount (9:9–13), Jesus commanded the three apostles not to tell what they had seen, until after His resurrection. Perplexed at the role Jesus was playing as the Messiah, they asked: "How is that the scribes say that Elijah must first come?" (v. 11, ASV). Jesus' reply was that Elijah had already come. Matthew (17:13) adds that the apostles understood this to refer to John the Baptist. The latter was like Elijah in his dress (II Kings 1:8), in his bold denunciation of the king's sin, and in the fact that in each case, it was the wicked king's wife who sought the prophet's death. In other words, the ministry of John the Baptist as the forerunner of Jesus fulfilled the prophecy of Malachi 4:5 as far as Christ's first coming was concerned. What further fulfilment there may be in connection with the Second Coming, time will tell.

The Transfiguration was followed by the healing of the epileptic boy (9:14–29). No doubt Jesus would have enjoyed staying on the mount in the heavenly fellowship, but He had left the glory above to come down into a world of sordidness, suffering and sin. The descent from the mount was a parable of His whole ministry. In the valley below was a boy writhing on the ground in epileptic fits, wallowing in his foam, helpless and hopeless—a symbol of the world in its sin. Matthew specifically states the boy was an epileptic. The Greek word means "moonstruck" (Mt. 17:15).

When the boy was brought to Jesus, the demon took out its spite on its victim (9:20). In anguish the father pleaded with Christ: "If thou canst do anything, have compassion on us, and help us" (v. 22). Jesus threw back the man's phrase, "If thou canst!" (ASV). The limitation was not in His ability, but in the man's faith. Earnestly, yet humbly, the father replied: "I believe; help thou mine unbelief." Quickly the Master commanded the demon: "Come out of him, and enter no more into him" (v. 25). What comfort those last words must have brought to the poor father's distraught heart!

The disciples who had stayed at the foot of the mount wanted to know why they had been unable to exorcise this demon, especially since they had cast out many demons before (6:13). Jesus answered that He cured only by prayer (9:29). The added phrase "and fasting" (KJV) is not found in the oldest manuscripts.

As Jesus and His disciples were making another tour of Galilee, He gave a second prediction of His Passion (9:30–32). Again He emphasized both His death and resurrection.

Teaching on Humility (9:30–50). Appropriately, this is followed by a section of teaching on humility (9:33–41). When the party returned to Capernaum, Jesus asked an embarrassing question: "What is it that ye disputed among yourselves by the way?" (v. 33). They were ashamed to answer, for they had been arguing about who should be the greatest. This may have been occasioned by the Master's choice of the three to accompany Him on the mount of Transfiguration. In any case, it was a sad commentary on the selfishness and smallness of the disciples. Jesus proceeded to give them a lesson in humility. He set a little child in their midst and declared that kindness was a sign of real greatness.

To John, the son of Zebedee, Jesus had to give a warning against sectarianism (9:38–41). The disciples were not to restrain the ministry of those who "followed not us" (v. 38). Said the Master: "He that is not against us is for us" (v. 40). Christians should appreciate all those who are ministering in the name of Jesus, whatever their denominational badge.

Following on the heels of this, Jesus issued a solemn warning against giving offense (9:42–50). For one who would cause a child or young convert to stumble, it would be better if a large millstone drawn by a donkey—so the Greek indicates—were hung around his neck and he be cast into the sea. If a person's "right hand"—his closest friend, or fondest occupation—causes him to stumble, he had better cut off the friendship than to lose his soul forever.

The word for "hell" here is Gehenna, which means a place of fiery torment. It is a very significant fact that the strongest teaching on hell in the New Testament is found in the so-called "simple teachings" of the gentle Galilean. It was He who described hell as a place "where their worm dieth not, and the fire is not quenched" (9:48; verses 44 and 46 are not in the oldest manuscripts). To such solemn warning sounded by the One Who knows how awful hell is, careful heed should be given. Gehenna is not simply a place of death (Hades), but of torment.

III. The Perean Ministry (10:1–52)

The first verse of the tenth chapter, which marks the beginning of a new stage in Jesus' ministry, records His final departure from Galilee. From now on His labors will be in Judea and Perea ("beyond the Jordan"). The best Greek text reads "Judea and beyond the Jordan" (RSV), which means that He spent these last months of His ministry partly in Judea and partly in Perea.

1. Teaching on Divorce (10:1–16)

Here Jesus dealt with an important issue, the question of divorce (10:2–12). Some Pharisees asked Him if it was lawful for a man to put away his wife. Their motive was to get Jesus into trouble. Herod Antipas was ruler of Galilee and Perea. If Jesus condemned divorce, He might expect to suffer the same fate as John the Baptist. If He condoned it, the strict religious groups—John's disciples and some Pharisees—would lose confidence in Him. How was He then to escape the two horns of the dilemma?

Very wisely Jesus countered with the question: "What did Moses command you?" For the Jews, Moses was the highest authority. The Pharisees replied that Moses permitted a legal divorce (Deut. 24:1). Jesus explained that Moses made this concession because of the "hardness of your heart" (10:5). Divorce was already taking place among the Israelites. Moses sought to discourage this by requiring that a man must have a scribe make out a certificate of divorce which would set forth the reasons for the separation. This would tend to limit divorce and at the same time protect the rights of the wife.

Jesus went on to say, however, that God's original plan was that marriage should be permanent. One man and one woman united for life—that was the divine purpose. This requires that a man "leave his father and mother"—which some fail to do—and "cleave" (literally, "be glued to") his wife. Modern marriage needs more glue! "Joined together," which is literally "yoked together," suggests equal partnership.

When the disciples asked Him in the house for further light on the subject, Jesus solemnly asserted that divorce and remarriage constitute legalized adultery. In a parallel account, Matthew 19:9 says that Jesus made one exception: "except for fornication." But Mark is recording the divine principle, as Jesus gave it *privately* to His disciples. According to Matthew, the question of the Pharisees was: "Is it lawful for a man to put away his wife for every cause?" Jesus answered them *publicly:* "No, not for every cause; only for fornication." With the Pharisees, Jesus treated the legal aspect of the question, in keeping with current rabbinical discussion. In doing so, He endorsed the strictest interpretation of Deuteronomy 24:1.

Mark has one other significant difference from Matthew. He quotes Jesus as saying that if a wife divorces her husband and remarries, she commits adultery. Matthew, writing for Jews, omits this, since a Jewish woman had no such legal rights. But among the Romans a wife could divorce her husband; so Mark includes the admonition for his Roman readers. In any case, easy divorce is absolutely condemned by Scripture.

Appropriately, this teaching on divorce is followed by the blessing of little children (10:13-16). They are the saddest displaced persons of modern civilization. One often wonders why parents do not love their children enough to stay together for their sake.

When the disciples scolded mothers for bothering the busy Master with their little children, Jesus was "indignant" (10:14, RSV). This is a strong word in the Greek, used only here of Christ. The care of children is one of the important responsibilities of the Church.

What did Jesus mean when He said, "of such is the kingdom of God"? (10:14). It may be translated, "to such belongeth the kingdom of God" (ASV; cf. RSV). Moffatt and Goodspeed support this rendering, as do many of the best commentators. But the statement may also mean that the Kingdom of God is composed of those who have the childlike characteristics of dependence and trust. Verse 15 would seem to favor the latter interpretation.

Mark gives more attention to the gestures of Jesus than do the other evangelists. So here he relates: "And he took them up in his arms, put his hands upon them, and blessed them" (10:16). The strong compound Greek verb—found only here in the New Testament—may well be rendered "was fervently blessing."

2. Riches and Ambition (10:17–45)

The story of the rich young ruler (10:17–22) is found in all three Synoptic Gospels (cf. Mt. 19:16–22; Lk. 18:18–23). It evidently made a great impression on the disciples. Mark alone records that the young man came running to Jesus and that he fell on his knees. He was eager and earnest to know the way of eternal life.

Christ's reply—"Why callest thou me good? there is none good but one, that is, God"—has sometimes been taken as evidence that He disclaimed sinlessness and deity. But probably what He meant was: "Don't call me good unless you are willing to accept me as the Messiah, the Son of God."

Jesus then cited the sixth, seventh, eighth, ninth, and fifth of the Ten Commandments. He omitted the first four, which have to do with duties to God, and concentrated on duties to man. In place of the tenth commandment, He added a substitute: "Do not defraud." This may have been a special warning to the rich young man.

When the seeker testified that he had kept all these from his youth, the Master looked at him with tender love. Knowing the only key that would fully open this person's heart, He commanded him to dispose of his riches. The man did not meet the test. He left in sorrow, defeated and disappointed.

Immediately following the young ruler's departure, Jesus sounded a warning against riches (10:23–31). When He stated that it was hard for a rich man to enter the Kingdom of God, the disciples were astonished, for in Old Testament times, material prosperity was considered an evidence of divine blessing. But Jesus challenged them with a still more blunt declaration. According to the best Greek text he said: "Children, how hard it is to enter the kingdom of God!" (v. 24).

Then Jesus made a striking statement about a camel going through the eye of a needle (10:25). Some have talked about a needle's-eye gate in Jerusalem, big enough for pedestrians but too small for camels. Scholars are agreed that this is only wishful thinking. Others have claimed that the root of "camel"—which comes from the Greek —may mean "rope." But there is no need of enlarging the needle's eye nor reducing the camel. Jesus' listeners would understand and appreciate the typical oriental hyperbole. To express an utter impossibility, the Jewish Talmud speaks of an elephant going through a needle's eye. Jesus declared that salvation is humanly impossible but divinely possible (v. 27).

Peter took advantage of the opportunity to offer a plaintive observation: "Lo, we have left all, and have followed thee" (10:28). They had not been like the rich young ruler. Jesus replied that they would receive an abundant reward here and hereafter (vv. 29, 30).

Then comes the third and last prediction of the Passion (10:32–34). Jesus walked courageously at the head of His followers toward Jerusalem. Sensing impending doom, the disciples feared as they followed. The Master then gave the most detailed description thus far of His coming betrayal, condemnation, Roman trial, mockery, death, and resurrection.

But what a sad sequel! The request of James and John that they might occupy the most honored seats on either side of Jesus in His glory (10:35–40). Matthew 20:20 indicates that their mother accompanied them in their petition.

Jesus replied that they did not know what they were asking. Could they drink His cup and be baptized with His baptism; that is, share His sufferings? With amazing and deplorable complacency, they answered, "We are able"—just as many sing that song today. Actually, no one is able to drink His cup of infinite agony.

As a lesson to all the disciples, Jesus enunciated the law of true greatness (10:41–45). The rulers of the Gentiles "lord it over them" (v. 42, ASV, RSV), but it is not to be thus among Christ's followers. Humble service is the real sign of greatness (vv. 43, 44). Jesus taught this not only by precept, but also by example (v. 45).

Mark 10:45 is one of the outstanding theological passages in this book. The Son of Man came to earth to give his life "a ransom for many." The Greek preposition "for" literally means "instead of" or "in place of." Thus this verse declares the doctrine of a substitution-ary atonement. Furthermore, the Greek word for "ransom" was com-monly used in the first century for the redemption money paid for the freeing of a slave. In the New Testament, the term occurs only here and in the parallel passage in Matthew 20:28. One can rejoice in the great truth that Christ paid the ransom for our redemption, to free us from the slavery of sin, without idly speculating as to whom the ransom was paid. The central truth abides: God's people are a redeemed people.

3. Blind Bartimaeus (10:46–52)

The healing of Bartimaeus is Mark's closing incident in Jesus' last journey to Jerusalem and occurred near Jericho. The blind man ap-pealed to Him as the "son of David"; that is, the Messiah. His per-sistence and faith were rewarded with healing, and he became a grateful follower of Jesus.

IV. Passion Week (11:1—15:47)

It is certainly not without significance that one-third of the Gospel of Mark (chs. 11–15) is taken up with the happenings of Passion Week. In this short period was concentrated the focus of Jesus' earthly ministry. His primary mission in the world was to procure man's salvation by His death on the cross. Here is the heart of Christianity.

1. Sunday: the Triumphal Entry (11:1–11)

Jesus presented Himself to the Jewish nation as her Messiah. The crowd of Galilean pilgrims accompanied Him down the western slope of the Mount of Olives, spreading garments and leaves as a carpet for the donkey on which He rode. Their shouts of praise (11:9,10) showed that they expected Him to enter the holy city in triumph and set up His messianic Kingdom on earth. But we learn from the other Gospels that the Jewish leaders rejected Him; and so the "triumphal entry" ended in tears (Lk. 19:41). This was Israel's last opportunity to accept Jesus of Nazareth as her Messiah. Nearly two thousand years of tragic history have followed the fateful deci-sion of that first Palm Sunday. The central event of the ages was the incarnation. All history is now dated "Before Christ" or "In the Year of Our Lord." But the Jewish leaders were blind to the Light of the World.

2. Monday: (11:12–19)

The two events of Monday were the cursing of the barren fig tree and the cleansing of the temple.

Cursing of the Fig Tree (11:12–14). On the way into Jerusalem from Bethany, Jesus saw a fig tree with leaves on it. Since this species normally has fruit before leaves, He naturally expected to find some ripe figs waiting for Him. When He found no fruit, He cursed it. Some have criticized the Master for this. But certainly the destruction of a fig tree beside the road (Mt. 21:19)—and hence no one's private property—was justified as an object lesson to the disciples that they would never forget. God's abhorrence of hypocrisy was shown by the cursing of this fig tree which boasted of having fruit that was not there, as it was later by the sudden death of Ananias and Sapphira (Acts 5:1–11).

Cleansing of the Temple (11:15–19). This seems to have been one of the main incidents which precipitated Jesus' death. Hitherto most of the opposition had come from the Pharisees; but when Jesus threatened the power, prestige and pocketbook of the priestly Sadducees, they became enraged at Him and sought His destruction.

The priests were carrying on a very lucrative business in the outer court of the Gentiles. They required that the annual temple tax be paid with the Phoenician silver half shekel, and then charged a handsome fee for making the exchange from Roman money. They also sold approved animals for sacrifice—at exorbitant prices. Jesus declared they had made God's house of prayer a den of robbers (11:17). Commercialism often becomes the curse of religion.

John's Gospel places a cleansing of the temple at the beginning of Jesus' ministry (Jn. 2:13–17). This has often been pointed out as a contradiction to the Synoptic account. But anyone acquainted with the rapid retrogression of religion will not have any difficulty in believing that Jesus would have to cleanse the temple twice in three years. This was the second messianic act of Jesus in Passion Week (cf. the triumphal entry). It was a fulfilment of the prophecy in Malachi 3:1–3.

3. *Tuesday (11:20—14:11)*

Faith and Fear (11:20–33). For Jesus this was the big, busy day of Passion Week. Some thirteen items are recorded by Mark. It was the last day of His public ministry.

The first incident was the lesson of the withered fig tree (11:20–26). On the way back into Jerusalem on Tuesday morning, Peter called attention to the fact that the fig tree, cursed the previous day, had withered. He was evidently surprised. Jesus used the incident to teach a second lesson, that of faith. No matter what mountains of difficulty may block the progress of Christian life or service, they can all be removed by believing prayer (v. 23). But one must always have a forgiving spirit if his prayers are to be answered (v. 25).

The second event was the challenge to Jesus' authority (11:27–33). As He was walking in the temple the members of the Sanhedrin —the chief priests, scribes and elders—confronted Him, demanding to know who gave Him authority to cleanse the temple. Very cleverly Jesus countered with another question, offering to answer theirs if they would answer His. Where did John get his authority? Obviously the answer to both questions was the same; but the Jewish leaders refused to commit themselves. They *dared* not say it was human, and they *would* not say it was divine. They were not concerned with truth, but only with the consequences of their answer (vv. 31, 32). When they dishonestly replied, "We cannot tell," Jesus refused to answer their question. The wilfulness of moral blindness is here seen in its awful reality.

Parable and Controversy (12:1–44). The parable of the wicked husbandmen follows (12:1–12). The vineyard was the Jewish nation (cf. Is. 5:1–7). The husbandmen were the leaders of that nation; they had beaten, stoned and killed the prophets God sent them. Now they were about to slay His Son. So obvious was the point of the parable that the members of the Sanhedrin sought to arrest Him (v. 12), but they feared the crowd.

Jesus had publicly silenced the Jewish leaders. Now they tried a different tactic, that of slyly asking Him questions in the hope of incriminating Him before the crowd. Three questions were thrown at Him. After answering all of them, He asked one that the Jews could not answer.

The first was the question of paying taxes (12:13–17). Very

cleverly, as they thought, the leaders sent representatives of two opposing parties—the Pharisees who hated Roman rule and the Herodians who supported it. Seeking to put Jesus off His guard, they flatteringly said they knew He always told the truth and didn't care who objected (v. 14). Then they closed in with their question: Should they pay taxes to Caesar or not? If He said, "Yes," the nationalistic Pharisees would have said to the crowds: "See, he is no prophet of God, for he is not loyal to our nation." If He said, "No," the Herodians would immediately have reported Him to the governmental authorities as a dangerous revolutionary who advocated rebellion against Roman rule. Whichever way He answered, He would be caught on one horn of the dilemma.

But Jesus was more than a match for their duplicity. He asked for a denarius. Looking at it, He inquired: "Whose is this image and superscription?" When they answered, "Caesar's," He confounded them by suggesting that if the tax money carried Caesar's name and picture it obviously belonged to him and should be given to him: "Render to Caesar the things that are Caesar's." Then for good measure He added: "and to God the things that are God's." Actually if they had paid their dues to God in faithful obedience, they would not have been subject to Caesar.

The second question was about the resurrection (12:18–27). This time it was the Sadducees, mentioned only here in Mark. They did not believe in any resurrection. So they concocted a hyperbolical, hypothetical case of a woman who had seven brothers as husbands (cf. Deut. 25:5). Now, whose wife would she be in the resurrection? Jesus, in reply, accused them of not knowing the Scriptures or the power of God (12:24). Then He explained that there will be no marriage in the next life. This does not mean, however, that there will be no recognition of our loved ones in heaven. Personal immortality would seem to imply that we shall know each other. As a crowning argument Jesus quoted the words of God to Moses at the burning bush, where He declared that He was the God of Abraham. Therefore Abraham still lives.

The third question came from a scribe and had to do with the first commandment (12:28–34). Literally his query was: "Of what kind is the principal commandment of all?" There was considerable debate among the rabbis about this, and apparently the scribe wanted help.

In reply Jesus referred him to the Shema (Deut. 6:4,5), which every pious Pharisee recited twice a day. The basic requirement of the law is a supreme love for God, which is the total response of our whole being to Him. For good measure Jesus defined the second commandment as enjoining genuine love of one's neighbor. Christianity is not complete without both. Neither passive piety nor social activity alone is adequate.

Before the crowd left, Jesus posed a question (12:35–37; cf. Ps. 110:1). How can the Messiah be both David's son and David's Lord? No one could answer (Mt. 22:46). But to us the solution is clear in the combined humanity and deity of Jesus (Rom. 1:3, 4).

Christ then sounded a warning against the scribes (12:38–40). They were proud, loving to promenade in public places. They were also greedy and dishonest. Pious prayers failed to cover their sin.

This chapter closes with the interesting incident of the poor widow's two mites (12:41–44). The treasury was located in the court of the women in the temple. Here Jesus saw a widow cast in two tiny copper coins, together worth about half an American penny. Jesus said she had cast in more than all the wealthy people with their offerings of silver and gold. Giving is measured not so much by what is given as by what is left. It is also measured by the spirit of loving devotion.

The Olivet Discourse (13:1–37). The only long discourse in Mark's Gospel is found in all three Synoptics (cf. Mt. 24, Lk. 21). Significantly, it has to do, at least in part, with Christ's Second Coming and the end of this age.

As Jesus was leaving the temple, one of His disciples called His attention to the big stones and beautiful buildings. Josephus tells us that the temple was built of white stones about thirty-seven feet long, twelve feet high and eighteen feet wide. The sanctuary is thought to have been about 150 feet high—the same as the Jerusalem Y.M.C.A. tower today. It was built of white marble, its roof gilded with gold. Probably it was one of the most beautiful buildings of that day, but Jesus predicted it would be utterly destroyed.

Later, as they were sitting on the Mount of Olives, the four fishermen-disciples asked the Master what He meant. He warned them of terrible sufferings ahead (13:3–8). He told them they would need patience under persecution (vv. 9–13). Then He predicted the time when the abomination of desolation would be set up in the temple, precipitating the worst tribulation the world has ever seen (vv. 14–23). Whether this refers to the destruction of Jerusalem in A.D. 70, with the attending horrors of the preceding siege, or to the so-called Great Tribulation at the end of this age is a matter of debate. Some would refer the description thus far in the chapter to the first century and begin the reference to the end of the age at verse 24. But premillennialists usually interpret the first part of the chapter as referring to the Great Tribulation which will precede the Second Coming. Both agree in referring the latter part (vv. 24–37) to the coming of Christ (v. 26). The terminology of verses 24 and 25 is usually interpreted as figurative apocalyptic language. But the events of the past two decades have made us less certain that this language cannot be literal. At least, we are faced with the possibility of greater cataclysmic catastrophies in the material realm than the world has ever dreamed of before.

The lesson of the fig tree (13:28–31) has taken on fresh significance with the establishment of the new nation of Israel on May 14, 1948, and its subsequent phenomenal growth. This adds greater emphasis to the climactic admonition to watch (vv. 32–37). The word "watch" is underscored three times by Jesus (vv. 33, 35, 37). This is where Christ put the supreme emphasis. We may not understand all the signs, but we can and must "watch."

Chapter 14 opens with the plot against Jesus (vv. 1, 2). The chief priests (Sadducees) and scribes (Pharisees) united in this.

The Anointing at Bethany (14:3–9). This anointing is probably the same as that described in Matthew 26:6–13 and John 12:2–8, but certainly different from that in Luke 7:36–50. John places it on the Saturday evening before Palm Sunday, which seems the better chronology. Mark and Matthew put it here as related to the events of Passion Week. It is a perfumed picture of spontaneous, wholehearted love and devotion. Note the Master's appraisal: "She has done a beautiful thing to me" (14:6, RSV).

The treachery of Judas (14:10, 11) was precipitated by his anger at the "waste" of the costly perfume. His greed for money got the best of him.

4. Thursday: The Last Supper (14:12–25)

It is generally held that Jesus spent Wednesday in retirement. Some, however, would put the last three incidents above on Wednesday afternoon and evening.

The preparation of the Passover (14:12–16) took place on Thursday afternoon. Jesus sent two disciples into Jerusalem to get the provisions for the Passover meal and have everything ready for eating it between sunset and midnight.

The Last Supper (14:17–21) was a solemn occasion. Jesus first predicted that one of His own apostles would betray Him (v. 18). It was even one who dipped in the same dish with Him (v. 20). According to oriental custom, one could not harm a person with whom he had just eaten. This made the crime of Judas doubly diabolical.

The institution of the Lord's Supper (14:22–25) took place at the close of the Last Supper, probably after Judas left the room (cf. Jn. 13:30). Jesus explained to the disciples that the broken bread symbolized His body, and the cup His blood of the Covenant. The first Lord's Supper ended with the singing of a hymn, probably the last part of the Great Hallel—Psalms 115–118.

When Jesus warned that His disciples would be scattered that night, Peter expressed himself with great self-confidence (14:26–31). Then Jesus definitely predicted Peter's denials.

5. Friday (14:26—15:20)

Jesus in Gethsemane (14:26–52). Probably right after midnight— and so, early Friday morning—Jesus' agony in Gethsemane took place. Leaving eight apostles at the gate of the garden, He took the inner circle of three into the grove of olive trees. Finally He left them, "went forward a little" (14:35), fell on the ground and prayed in anguish of spirit. His petition (v. 36) was that, if possible, He might be saved from drinking "this cup"—separation from His Father's face, as He Who knew no sin was made sin for us (II Cor. 5:21). But then He bowed His head in humble submission and prayed: "Nevertheless not what I will, but what thou wilt." That is the greatest prayer anyone can pray.

Three times Jesus prayed, and three times He returned to find the trio of apostles sleeping. Probably the middle part of verse 41 should be translated as a question: "Are you still sleeping and taking your rest?" (RSV). That fits the context much better.

The arrest of Jesus (14:43–52) followed quickly. Judas "kissed him fervently" (v. 45, literally), again revealing the depths of his depravity. Peter (cf. Jn. 18:10) tried to defend his Master. But when the disciples saw that Jesus was actually arrested, they all forsook Him and fled (14:50). The young man present (vv. 51, 52) was probably John Mark, the writer of the Gospel. No other reason can be given for the insertion of this minor incident.

The Jewish Trials (14:53–72). Jesus' first trial was before Caiaphas, the high priest (14:53–65), who apparently summoned an emergency meeting of the Sanhedrin—"all the chief priests and the elders and the scribes." They had difficulty getting false witnesses to agree. But finally when the high priest demanded that Jesus tell whether He was the Messiah, and He declared He was, Christ was charged with blasphemy and condemned to death (vv. 61–64). He was then spit upon and mocked (v. 65).

Peter's denials (14:66–72) form a sad story and underscore his need of Pentecost for power to witness (Acts 1:8). Thrice he denied his Lord before the cock crowed twice.

The Roman Trial (15:1–20). The trial before Pilate differed from the Jewish trial in that the Roman governor was eager to release Jesus. But the Jewish leaders would have none of that; they demanded the release of Barabbas and the crucifixion of Christ (vv. 11–14). Pilate stands condemned because he was aware of Jesus' innocence and the reason for His arrest (vv. 10, 14). Yet he scourged Jesus—a heartless piece of cruelty—and delivered Him over for crucifixion (v. 15).

The soldiers' mockery of Jesus (15:16–20) is a sordid story indeed. They dressed Him up like a king and jeered at Him. In Christ's Passion, God's holiness and love stood out in terrific contrast to man's sin and hate.

The Crucifixion and Burial (15:21–47). The crucifixion, is the central event of the redemption story. The account is given in remarkably restrained language. It was nine o'clock in the morning when they hanged Him on the cross (v. 25). The passersby mocked and jeered (vv. 29–32). From noon until three in the afternoon, the sun refused to shine on its Creator writhing in agony of body and deeper anguish of soul. The cry of dereliction (v. 34) gives us a minute glimpse of the depth of His despair. His Father had forsaken Him.

At Jesus' death, the inner veil of the sanctuary was rent in two from the top to the bottom (15:38). The significance of this is indicated in Hebrews 9:1–15 and 10:19–22; it symbolized the fact that the way was now opened into the very presence of God. In this age every true believer can enter the Holy of Holies of sanctified fellowship with the Holy One Himself.

The faithful women (15:40, 41) were last at the cross and first at the empty tomb. Prominent among them was Mary Magdalene, mentioned here for the first time in Mark's Gospel.

The burial of Jesus (15:42–47) was taken care of by Joseph of Arimathea, a member of the Sanhedrin. Lovingly he laid the body in a new tomb which had been hewn in the rocky cliff.

V. The Resurrection (16:1–8)

The resurrection is the climax of the Gospels. Without it the crucifixion would have been in vain (cf. Rom. 4:25). Mark tells of the women, including Mary Magdalene, who came first to the tomb on Sunday morning. There they were told by angels that Christ was risen.

Mark 16:9–20 is not found in the two oldest Greek manuscripts, Vaticanus and Sinaiticus of the fourth century. It seems probable that it was not originally a part of this Gospel.

Luke

J. NORVAL GELDENHUYS

IN THE BEGINNING of the Christian era the Christians pinned their faith to the living word as it was expounded to them by the apostles and other witnesses who had both seen and heard the incidents recorded in the Gospel. As the Church, however, expanded and as the apostles disappeared one by one from the scene, the need for an authoritative account in writing of the facts upon which the Christian faith is founded became more and more urgent, and Luke with his mature and farseeing mind became acutely aware of this need. It was for this reason that he undertook this task.

I. The Gospel's Preface (1:1-4)

Luke points to the fact that many other people had already undertaken to write the story of the things "which have been accomplished among us." Luke nevertheless emphasizes (v. 3) that his work exhibits its own peculiar characteristics. In the first place, his inquiry into the actual sequence of events had led him to the incidents which took place at the very beginning of the gospel story. Thus we find that he does not commence his Gospel, as did Mark, with the first public appearance of Jesus, but with the announcement of the birth of His forerunner, John the Baptist.

Secondly, he investigated "all things." He thus purposefully examined all the data to hand in order to reproduce the facts as fully as might be necessary. This does not mean that he includes *everything* in his Gospel. Though he examined *all* the data, nevertheless, in compiling his Gospel under the guidance of the Holy Spirit, he selected only those facts which he reckoned to be most important. That Luke strove to give the essential details is shown by the fact that his Gospel is the most detailed and comprehensive of the four. Many of the most beautiful acts, parables and sayings of Jesus known to us today appear only in Luke's narrative.

Thirdly, he examined everything "closely." His investigation was, therefore, neither superficial nor hurried. For long periods (during his journeys with Paul and at other times), he conducted thorough research regarding the gospel history until he was qualified to narrate the actual course of events.

In the fourth instance, he declares that it was his aim to give "an orderly account" of the gospel happenings—not just a conglomeration of facts. He does not mean that he intended to present a strictly chronological arrangement of his subject-matter, but rather that he intended his story to form a coherent whole.

Luke's Gospel is addressed to Theophilus, a seeker after established truth, and through him to all those who desire to learn the good tidings in full assurance of faith.

II. Preparation for the Saviour's Mission (1:5—4:13)

1. The Saviour's Forerunner (1:5-80)

Birth of the Saviour's Forerunner Announced (1:5-25). Although Luke begins his Gospel with the annunciation of the birth of John the Baptist, in this incident, as indeed throughout the whole narrative, he is really busy delineating Christ, that is, in everything he tells he shows clearly Who Christ is. The history of John is told simply because it leads to Christ. The expression "in the days of Herod" (v. 5) points to a dark and disastrous period in the history of the Jewish people. Against this dark background, Luke paints the story of the dawn of a new day in the life of mankind—the coming of Christ for which preparation is made by John the Baptist.

The son whom Elizabeth should bear to Zechariah—so the angel stipulated (1:13)—was to be called John. This name, according to Hebrew etymology, means "the Lord is merciful" or "the (free) gift of God." It alludes thus to the grace of God which was to descend on the nation. It was characteristic of God's dealings with Israel that to those chosen for special tasks He often gave names appropriate to these tasks. The name of John's father (v. 5) meant "God remembers his covenant" and that of his mother (v. 5) "God is the absolutely faithful One." The three names together indicate that the mercy of God, which was shortly to be revealed in the Saviour for whose coming John was to "make straight the way," was the result and outcome of God's remembrance of His covenant and of His absolute faithfulness.

Birth of the Saviour Announced (1:26-38). The angel hailed Mary and called her "favoured one" (v. 28). By this he did not mean, as Roman Catholic doctrine teaches, that she was able to show grace because in herself she was full of grace. No, he meant that she had received grace. God bestowed His unmerited, gracious favor upon her to an exceptional degree in choosing her to be the mother of His Son. Naturally, then, Mary was overwhelmed by the words of the angel.

Gabriel, the celestial bearer of joyful tidings, reassured Mary again with the same words, "Do not be afraid," with which he had brought reassurance to Zechariah (1:13). He named the reason she should not be afraid: she had found favor with God. In other words, God had looked upon her with favor and bestowed favor on her. Her humble station in life and her own sense of unworthiness need cause no fear. God had favored her by choosing her to bear a son who should be called Jesus. The Hebrew interpretation of this name is "the Lord saves." The son was to be that One through Whom God would accomplish the "salvation and preservation of His people." Like John, Jesus also would be "great" but His "greatness" would be completely different from that of John. Of John it was foretold: "he shall be great before the Lord" (v. 15), but of Jesus it was said: "He shall be great and will be called the Son of the Highest" (v. 32). His greatness would therefore exceed all other greatness. To Him would be given the royal power and dominion ascribed in the Old Testament to the messianic King who should arise out of David's line (Ps. 2:7; II Sam. 7:14; Ps. 89:26, 27). His Kingdom would be, however, not a mere transient, earthly kingdom, but spiritual and eternal, consisting not of an earth-born nation, but of the spiritual Israel.

First Song in Honor of the Saviour (1:39–45). At the end of the day when dusk is falling, and again at the beginning of a new day when the first rays of the sun begin to appear, one hears the lovely songs of birds as they wing their way through the air. We are therefore not surprised to discover in the dusk of the Old Testament and the dawn of the New Testament dispensations how various people, favored by God, burst into song. When Elizabeth greeted and blessed Mary, she was so inspired in her utterances that we cannot but regard them as a song. She was thus the first singer at the dawn of the new era.

Elizabeth nobly and voluntarily retires into the background. She unreservedly and joyfully acknowledges that far greater honor had been done to her youthful kinswoman than to herself. When they meet she is in no way envious of or unsympathetic towards Mary on whom an even greater gift has been bestowed. She humbles herself and breaks into song about Mary's great privilege, the greatest indeed which could fall to the lot of womankind, namely, to be the mother of her Lord. Only because she was filled with the Holy Spirit could Elizabeth attain these heights of magnanimity and spiritual insight.

Mary Praises God Who Gave His Son to be Saviour of the World (1:46–56). Mary's reaction to the words of Elizabeth is a spontaneous breaking into song. Her Magnificat was more elevated than Elizabeth's song, but at the same time more controlled. There is a majestic quality about her hymn of praise. It is remarkable that she makes not a single direct reference to the Son Who had been promised her. Yet throughout this hymn she acts on the assumption that He really has been promised to her, and this fact supplies the inspiration of her whole song. In her hymn of praise, Mary lauds the all-excelling perfection of God—His divine power (vv. 49, 51), His holiness (v. 49), His mercy (v. 50), and His faithfulness (vv. 54, 55). She sees all these attributes of God mirrored in full perfection in the fact that He was engaged in fulfilling His promises regarding the Messiah Who was to be both King and Saviour. And still today, only in and through the incarnation of Jesus, do we learn to know God with full certainty as the Almighty, the Holy, the Merciful and the Faithful One.

Forerunner of the Saviour is Born (1:57–61). "He shall be called John" are the crucial words in this section. Throughout the history of God's revelation to man as told in Holy Scripture, we see the great importance God attaches to the names given to people. The various names of God Himself (for example, "I am that I am") in marvelous manner indicate His divine virtues and perfection. God changed Abram's name to Abraham, Jacob's to Israel, and so forth, because He wanted them to have names appropriate to their tasks. It is therefore natural that when the new era was just about to begin, the chief characters should be known by names bearing a particular meaning.

Zechariah Praises God for His Grace and Redemption through the Divine Saviour of Whom His Son is to be the Forerunner (1:67–80). Zechariah combined, as it were, in his hymn of praise all the echoes of Old Testament times in a joyous outpouring of hope and faith. There is a close relationship between the name of his son and the theme of his song. On the writing-tablet for which he asked, he wrote: "He shall be called John." John means "God is merciful," and Zechariah's whole song celebrates God's wonderful acts of mercy which spring from the fact that the essence of His being is mercy.

2. Birth and Childhood of the Saviour of the World (2:1–52)

The Saviour Born in Bethlehem (2:1–7). The preparatory revelation of the Old Testament was long since completed. Christ's forerunner, John, had already been born; the "fulness of time" had come. At last was born the promised Saviour Whose coming had been so earnestly longed for. In a few verses—simply, clearly and naturally written— Luke records this stupendous fact. The extreme simplicity of the narrative forms a striking contrast to the incomparable importance of the recorded events. The eternal Son of God had left the glory He shared with the Father and had humbled Himself to be born as a human child in the very poorest of circumstances: He was laid in a manger.

The Saviour's Birth Announced to Shepherds (2:8–20). The hope of the ages was ultimately realized. For that reason the glad tidings brought by the angel are a cause of great joy to the shepherds and the whole nation—to all who were awaiting His coming, to every true member of the people of God. He Who was born was "the Saviour," that is, the One Who saves from every ill, need, sin, punishment and death, Who safeguards us from disaster and ruin and grants us salvation in the richest sense of the word. But He was also "Christ, the Lord," that is, the Anointed, the Messiah Who was Himself also God. The name "Christ" points to Him as the fulfilment of the promises of God and the One Who was anointed in perfect manner by God Himself to be the great Prophet, Priest and King— the Divine Saviour. As such He is Himself also "the Lord."

The Saviour Subjected to the Requirements of the Law and His Suffering Predicted (2:21–39). "When the fulness of the time was come, God sent forth His Son, made of a woman, *made under the law,* to redeem them that were under the law" (Gal. 4:4, 5). That is why He Who was without sin or guilt and had been begotten by the Holy Spirit also had to meet nevertheless all the requirements of the law and by so doing fulfil all righteousness (Mt. 3:15). The ceremonies of circumcision and of purification after childbirth indicated that every human being was born in sin which could only be cleansed by the shedding of blood and by sacrifices. Thus when

Jesus, the spotless and Holy One, subjected Himself to these requirements, it was not for His own sake, but to show that He was voluntarily placing Himself under the law and fulfilling the obligations laid upon His people in order to bring about their salvation. The name "Jesus" (Saviour), which was given to Him on the occasion of His circumcision in obedience to God's command, is a strong indication of this fact.

Simeon had been told to wait for the coming of the "Sun of righteousness" (Mal. 4:2), the star of the House of Jacob. As he stood with the child in his arms, he saw at last in the person of Jesus the salvation of God and understood that he was free to depart in peace, for he had now been exonerated from the task of looking for the Messiah. In Simeon's song of praise, the strife and the suffering which lay ahead of Jesus were referred to for the first time in the Gospel. Jesus was to be, so he said, as it were, a stone over which many would stumble and fall and go to eternal doom, but which would cause others to rise and be eternally saved. Those who thought too highly of themselves and trusted in their own merits and strength would in the end come to a sad downfall, because their pride and arrogance prevented them from perceiving their lost and needy state and from taking refuge in Jesus. But the humble and lowly, bowing at His feet in confession of sin and believing in Him, would be raised up to life eternal by His mighty arm.

The Saviour as Child (2:40). The intellectual, moral and spiritual development of the child Jesus was as real as His physical growth. He was completely subject to the ordinary laws of bodily and mental development, except that in His case there was no question of sin and weakness exerting an evil influence on Him. Both in soul and body He grew with a perfection unknown before or since. He was true man indeed, but He was perfect man, even as a little child, and throughout the years of growth and development, of increase in true wisdom and stature, the grace of God and the love of God were His guide, His protection and His support.

The Saviour in His Father's House (2:41–52). It is striking that the first words of Jesus to be recorded in the Gospel are those found in verse 49 in which He so clearly pointed out His divine Sonship and His divine calling, namely, the necessity to be about His Father's business and to glorify Him in everything. The Greek word which we translate as "must" indicates a divine necessity. Jesus *must,* that is, He could not but be engaged in glorifying His Father.

It was not a case of compulsion from without; His whole being yearned to serve and obey the Father voluntarily. This divine calling was to such an extent the most important thing in His life that even His tenderest human ties had to take second place. To the child Jesus, the supreme importance of His calling was so natural a fact and such a matter of course that He expressed astonishment that Joseph and Mary had not perceived it. Yet, when they came to fetch Him, He went with them, voluntarily and without demur, back to Nazareth, where He was subject to them, for that also was the will of His Heavenly Father.

Just as Luke in 2:40 sums up in one pregnant sentence the life, growth and development of Jesus from His birth to His twelfth year, so he gives in verse 52 an exquisite summary of the next eighteen (approximately) years of His life, up to the time when He began His public ministry. He underwent a process of development which was natural and yet absolutely perfect both mentally ("increased in wisdom") and physically ("and in stature"). At each stage of His life He was perfect, but between the perfection of a child and that of a grown man there is a vast difference—the difference between perfect innocence and perfect holiness. Therefore we are told that Jesus *increased* in wisdom and stature and also in favor with God and man. There was thus growth and development in His human nature and being, but in such a manner that His life and thought were constantly in full accord with the will of God. For the first time, God's ideal at the creation was completely realized; Jesus was Perfect Man in both soul and body. Adam and Eve had also been perfect at creation, but their spiritual perfection before the Fall was the perfection of innocence. In order to attain to adult spiritual perfection, they should have voluntarily and deliberately chosen good and rejected evil. Alas, this they failed to do. But Jesus did not fail. Without external coercion, He chose to serve the Father voluntarily and absolutely and to resist the wiles of the evil one. That is why God could explicitly show Him favor and indicate that with Him He was well-pleased.

Moreover, because He lived among the people of Nazareth and other parts of Palestine as an absolutely perfect human being both spiritually and physically, it was impossible for them (at least, for all such as were not completely degenerate) not to feel drawn towards Him. His body had never been marred by sin and was, in the best sense of the word, beautiful and attractive. His gaze was pure and lofty, the mirror of the untainted nobility of His soul. Because His whole being was without spot or blemish or weakness of any kind, He was Perfect Man and could not but be in favor with every right-thinking individual. This explains Luke's statement that He increased in favor *with man* also. In proportion as His mind and body developed into full, adult maturity, He was more and more loved and respected by all.

This state of affairs continued throughout the years before He began His public ministry. Then came the inevitable crises of which Simeon had spoken, for then the promised Messiah, the Son of God, publicly exposed the rottenness of the nation's spiritual life and began to fulfil His calling as Messiah and Saviour in a way which could not be misinterpreted. The result was that people took sides, either for or against Him. Those who loved darkness better than light opposed Him and His divine claims. Consequently, He was no longer in favor with the people as a whole and soon the words of Isaiah 53 were to be fulfilled.

3. The Saviour's Way Prepared by the Forerunner (3:1–20)

In verses 3 through 14, Luke shows how John, by means of an earnest and urgent call to sincere conversion, was engaged in preparing the nation for the advent of the Messiah. In verses 15 and 16, he narrates how, when the people began to wonder whether he was himself the Messiah, John deliberately retired into the background and uncompromisingly pointed them to Christ, the One Who was coming, as the promised Saviour. He could administer only an outward baptism, but Jesus would effect inner purification and regeneration. Just as fire consumes whatever is destructible and so acts as a purifying agent, so would the Messiah through the Holy Spirit destroy sin and those sinners who deliberately clung to their evil-doing. Consequently, all who persisted in sin would be destroyed, but whosoever humbly confessed his sin and took refuge in Jesus would be saved, cleansed from sin and freed from the punishment and power of sin.

4. The Saviour's Baptism, Genealogy and Temptation (3:21— 4:13)

The Saviour Baptized (3:21, 22). Because the baptism of Jesus meant to Him the final assumption of His work as Saviour—a work which was to be perfected through suffering and death—it was an event of supreme importance to Him. For that reason we find Him engaged in prayer just after His baptism, in the same way as He was so often found later in His public ministry, either before or after some important occasion. While He was in prayerful communion with God after His baptism, "the heaven was open." Here is one of those many instances in Holy Scripture where we are faced with a divine act which is unfathomable and incomprehensible to our human intellect. But even if we cannot grasp just how "the heaven was opened," the fact remains that, after Jesus had offered Himself—completely and voluntarily as man's substitute and Saviour, God vouchsafed to His human consciousness a perfect revelation, not only of the majesty and glory of His Father, but also of the truth that He was indeed His Son. What God revealed by the opening of the heavens and the descent of the Spirit, He confirmed and amplified by means of a voice from heaven which said: "Thou art my beloved Son; in thee I am well pleased" (3:22).

The Saviour Related to the Whole of Humanity (3:23–38). Luke is now about to relate our Lord's public acts. All lesser personalities are relegated to the background, and henceforth Jesus, the chief figure in the divine drama, will rightly occupy the center of the stage. That is why Luke apparently considers this the appropriate time to give the Saviour's genealogy. Throughout his Gospel, Luke bears in mind the all-embracing meaning Jesus has for the whole world. He therefore emphasizes the fact that Christ as man is related through Adam to the whole human race. As the Second Adam, made of a woman but conceived of the Holy Spirit, His advent and activities have universal meaning—not only for Israel, but for the whole world.

Satan Defeated under Most Difficult Circumstances (4:1–13). Because He was true man, Jesus was also actually able to be tempted and, from His childhood until the end of His life, He was exposed to all the temptations which men must contend against, except those which come from within and proceed from original sin or are the result of earlier deeds of sin. The temptations which befell Him in the wilderness were, however, special temptations. They were aimed not only at tempting Him as man, but at attacking Him as the Messiah engaged in carrying out His messianic calling. This is apparent from the fact that these temptations came to Him immediately after His baptism when He finally undertook His life's work as Saviour and when God not only expressed His approval of His decision and conduct by means of a voice from heaven, but also equipped Him for carrying out that calling by the public bestowal of the Holy Spirit upon Him in all His fulness.

When the Son of Man had reached the limits of spiritual and physical endurance, then only did the battle against the evil one approach its climax. Because Christ successfully resisted him in spite of the fact that the devil came with his most cruel temptations at the very moment when His circumstances could not have been more unfavorable, He proved that He had completely triumphed over Satan. What a striking contrast to Adam who so easily succumbed to temptation under extremely favorable circumstances!

In the history of the temptation of Christ, as in other episodes narrated in the Gospel, we perceive Christ's recognition of the absolute authority of the Word of God and the manner in which He used it as the guiding principle of His life as man. That which was written in the Scriptures gave Him the final and conclusive reply to anything and everything the devil might put forward. He did not argue with him, but dismissed him unreservedly each time with one single pronouncement out of the Word of God.

III. Galilean Ministry of Jesus (4:14—9:50)

1. Jesus' Declaration that He is the Saviour Sent by God (4:14–32)

In this passage Jesus unequivocally declared that He was the One anointed by God with the Holy Spirit to preach good news to the poor, especially the poor in a spiritual sense (4:18–21). God had sent Him to heal those who were brokenhearted and living in a state of spiritual poverty, to proclaim release to those who were captive and bound fast in the power of sin and spiritual misery, to open the eyes of those who were spiritually blind, to raise up again and lead forward to victory those who were cast down and spiritually broken and, in this way, "to proclaim the acceptable year of the Lord," that is, the messianic era, that period of time introduced by His ministry during which God would grant free salvation to all who sought refuge with Him.

2. Revelation of His Divine Authority (4:33—5:26)

His Power over Evil Spirits (4:33–37). After the Saviour had in the wilderness so decidedly resisted the temptations of the devil, the evil one directed the full force of his hellish fury against Christ and tried in every way to prevent the establishment of His kingdom. One of the weapons of which Satan made use in the struggle was causing people to be possessed of devils. Jesus accepted this challenge too and, in order to prove Himself the true Saviour, He revealed His power over evil spirits, signifying that He had truly conquered the power of Satan.

He Reveals His Power over Physical Ills (4:38–44). Thus far Luke has portrayed Jesus as the One who was anointed with the Holy Spirit as the Son of God and the Messiah (at His baptism), as victor over the temptations of the devil (in the wilderness), as the One Who spoke with the ultimate authority vested in His own divinity (at Nazareth and Capernaum), and as He Who had power to drive out devils (in the synagogue at Capernaum). Now he shows us how Jesus has power also to free people from physical ills. Because Jesus came to deliver man as man; He came to save his body as well as his soul. Thus throughout the Gospel, we see Him acting as the great healer, not only of spiritual ills, but also of bodily illness.

He Reveals His Authority over the Fish of the Sea (5:1–11). Luke continues to reveal the universal character of Christ's power. He shows that Jesus was also the all-powerful ruler of the fish of the sea. He was also becoming recognized and followed by His disciples as a unique personality. When Peter, as the result of this revelation of His power, began to see Jesus in His divine majesty, it immediately and instinctively gave him a sense of his own sinfulness. The first natural reaction of a man placed in such circumstances is to feel unworthy of continuing to exist in the sight of the Holy One. Peter impulsively exclaimed: "Depart from me, for I am a sinful man, O Lord." Jesus understood Peter's feelings and therefore instantly gave a reassuring reply: "Do not be afraid; henceforth you will be catching men." Instead of allowing his despair and fear to exclude him from discipleship, the Saviour assured him that he would in the future be a successful follower of His.

He Heals Even an Incurable Disease (5:12–16). It was, however, not only as the all-powerful ruler over even the fish of the sea that Jesus revealed Himself. He also proved that He was the omnipotent physician who could cure even a disease like leprosy which was, humanly speaking, incurable.

His Divine Authority to Forgive Sin (5:17–26). Jesus not only governed the forces of nature and effected cures, but in this passage

He revealed also His right and His power to forgive sin. Because this right and this power belong exclusively to God, Jesus thus unequivocally proclaimed His oneness with God. It is comparatively easy to say: "Your sins are forgiven you," for no one can prove the contrary. But when a paralyzed man is bidden, "Rise and walk!" actual healing must be seen to follow, otherwise it becomes clear to all that the words are valueless. Commanding the paralyzed man to get up and go home, Jesus dramatically proved by His might over things visible His power over things invisible.

3. Jesus' Role as the Saviour of Sinners (5:27–32)

In the preceding passage, we saw that Jesus had divine authority and power even to forgive sins. In this one, we discover that He came for the express purpose of calling sinners to repentance and of so reshaping their lives that they would become His disciples.

4. Inauguration of a New Order by the Saviour (5:33—6:49)

Luke has already pointed out the unique authority and power of Jesus and the inimitable way in which He acted towards the outcasts of Jewish society, seeking them in love and bringing them to repentance. Now he shows that Jesus Himself expressly taught that the form of worship which He preached and was instituting differed completely from that of the followers of John and of the Pharisees (5:33–39).

The Saviour is Lord also of the Sabbath (6:1–11). Luke continues steadily to carry out his purpose of letting us see Jesus more and more clearly as the One Who reveals Himself as the Messiah, the Saviour of the world. In the latter portion of the fifth chapter, we find Jesus proclaiming that He had ushered in a completely new way of worship. Now He pointed out that it even affected the observance of the Sabbath. He declared unequivocally that He as the Messiah, the Son of Man, had the authority to determine the spirit and the manner in which the Sabbath was to be observed. After His ascension, He even taught His Church, through the inspiration of the Holy Spirit, to change the day on which the Sabbath-rest was observed (the seventh day of the week) to the first day of the week, the day on which He arose from the dead, in order to symbolize the fact that the Old Covenant of works had yielded place to the

New Covenant of faith and freedom. He brought into being a new, spiritual observance of the Sabbath instead of the old observance which held rigidly to the letter of the law. Since the spiritual purpose of the original laws governing the Sabbath was realized in and through Him, it is fitting that Christians should always devote the first day of each week to Him.

While, in the first few verses of this passage, Jesus as Lord of the Sabbath showed that the observance of the Sabbath was not a matter of hairsplitting and a strict adherence to the letter of the law, in verses 6 through 11 He taught positively what can and must be done on the Sabbath, namely, helping people who are in need when God calls us to do so.

The Saviour Appoints His Apostles (6:12–16). The ancient chosen people of God had steadfastly refused to acknowledge Jesus as their promised Saviour. It became necessary, therefore, to call into being the new people of God from among the faithful "remnant" of Jewry, and so we find Luke describing how Jesus chose the Twelve Apostles to be the founders of His Church.

He Proclaims the Laws of His Kingdom (6:17–49). In the Sermon on the Mount, the revelation of Jesus as the Messiah unfolds more rapidly, for in this sermon He announced the "laws of the kingdom" with absolute authority. He did not quote some other authority or use the words of the Old Testament prophets, "Thus saith the Lord," but spoke on the basis of His own, final, divine authority as no man had ever yet spoken. Because He is One with the Father, He stated that the weal or woe of each individual life depends in the very first place on the attitude which that person adopts towards Him and His words (particularly vv. 22, 46–49).

5. Revelation of His Unlimited Power (7:1—8:56)

He Reveals His Power to Heal (7:1–10). In this passage Luke is still engaged in describing Jesus as He increasingly reveals Himself. Here he gives an example of how the Saviour, by means of His divine power, healed from a distance someone who was at the point of death. The centurion of Capernaum exhibited to a striking degree the two requirements which are indispensable if one desires to receive blessing, namely, an humble heart and absolute faith in Christ.

The Saviour is Lord also over Death (7:11–17). Not only could Jesus heal a dying man from a distance, but He even had power to raise men from the dead. In this striking example of this power revealed in Christ, Luke wonderfully reveals the Saviour's sympathy with those who mourn and His absolute and divine power over the invisible spirit world. We see Him here as the loving Comforter, the conqueror of death and the uniter of people with loved ones parted from them by death.

Jesus Claims to be the Promised Divine Saviour (7:18–35). Jesus proclaimed that a man's attitude towards Him is the absolute test of true greatness and that He, the greatest of all, is the messenger of the covenant spoken of in the third chapter of Malachi and is therefore Himself God (vv. 23–28). Since in Malachi 3 the "messenger of the covenant" is also named "the Lord," He has every right to apply these words to Himself.

The Saviour Forgives a Woman Her Sins (7:36–50). Luke emphasizes the fact that Jesus came to seek and to save those who were lost. The touching homage showed by the woman to Jesus was the result of the forgiveness and salvation she had found through Him. The love which poured from her heart was consequently not the cause, but the result, of her being forgiven and the proof that she had received forgiveness for her many sins.

The Saviour Served by Redeemed Women (8:1–3). After Jesus had left the carpenter's shop and was giving His whole time and attention to His public ministry as the Christ and Saviour, He was poor and possessed nothing whatever, for He had left all for Mary and her children. Furthermore, He never used His divine power to perform miracles by which He might obtain the necessities of life Himself. Though He was the Son of God, He humbled Himself to the extent of being willing to accept from a little group of women whom He had healed the material means to sustain life.

The Saviour Teaches Crowds in Parables (8:4–18). In Galilee, the Saviour's preaching and the miracles of healing and raising the dead caused a great stir among the people, for they flocked together and followed Him wherever He went. In spite of all He had done and said and revealed to them, however, the crowds were wilfully blind and deaf to the real meaning of His doctrine and His acts. Of the earth earthy, they refused to be taught of Him in the true sense of the word. Therefore, He resolved that in the short period still remaining to be spent with them, He would usually address them in parables. They brought this punishment upon themselves by reason of their reluctance to open their hearts to His spiritual lessons.

In the future the opportunity to learn the inner meaning of His doctrine would be vouchsafed only to those who earnestly sought the truth. In the presence of those who were unwilling to seek Him in earnest, He would no longer speak in clear and definite terms about the Kingdom of God. His disciples and other believing followers whose understanding had been enlightened would, however, because of these parables, be even more thoroughly equipped to be the future founders of His Kingdom.

In the parable of the sower, the Saviour stressed the fact that the fruitfulness of faithful hearers of the Word will be unusually great. As a rule, wheat-seed does not show a hundred per cent increase. The seed, the Word of God, possesses in itself a living power and is so pure and good that wherever the ground is prepared for it in human hearts by faith in and obedience to Him, the harvest will be immeasurably abundant, beyond all human expectation.

Although Jesus spoke in parables, His final purpose was nevertheless that the light of the Gospel should be shed abroad in its full brilliance (8:16, 17). He initiated His followers into the true knowledge of the mysteries of His Kingdom, not in order that they might keep it a secret, but that they might freely proclaim it to all with whom they came in contact. Even if circumstances forced Him, as it were, to whisper the truth in their ears, yet they would shortly be required to go out into the world and openly proclaim the Gospel, that is, make known what was hidden and bring to the light that which was concealed.

The Saviour's True "Family" (8:19–21). In His attitude towards His Father in heaven and in the revelation of His messianic calling as the Son of God, the demands made by human relationships had no place. Although He was faithful and devoted to His mother and His family circle throughout all the years of His life, He rebuked them in no uncertain manner when, actuated by false and defective human considerations, they attempted to restrict His activities and re-order His life as *they* thought best.

The Saviour Reveals His Power over Nature (8:22–25). It is certain that the powers of evil, permitted thereto by God, attempted by means of a fierce storm to wreck the boat containing Him and His disciples, as Jesus lay sleeping the sleep of extreme physical exhaustion. In this way they hoped to overthrow God's whole plan of salvation. Jesus knew that Satan was responsible for the storm and for that reason, we are told, He "rebuked the wind and the sea."

It was not that He regarded them as evil spirits, but that He saw in this particular storm the machinations of the devil. In rebuking them He really rebuked the ministers of Satan who were at that moment making use of them.

The "earth and the fulness thereof" belong to the Lord, and He rules the path of wind and storm; yet sometimes God allows the evil one temporarily and in a limited way to control the forces of nature. Not only did Jesus calm the fury of the wind, He also brought the pounding waves to instant rest and quiet. A moment before, the wind was raging and the waves roaring, but at His word of command, immediate calm prevailed and the surface of the water became as smooth as glass. What a mighty revelation of the omnipotence of Him through Whom the Father created all things, including the earth and the forces of nature!

Demons Forced to Acknowledge the Authority of the Saviour (8:26–39). All the indications are that after the incarnation of the Word, the Son of God, Satan also sought incarnation in human beings in order to oppose Christ as Man and Saviour of the world. The devil wished, as it were, also to become man. It was for this reason that so many instances of possession of the people by devils characterized the period of Christ's public ministry on earth. This passage gives a striking description of the triumph of Jesus over the power of evil.

The Saviour is Lord Over Life and Death (8:40–56). As a further revelation of Jesus' divine power, He healed a woman who for years had suffered from an incurable disease (that is, incurable by human means) and raised a little girl from the dead. He thus proved Himself Lord over both life and death.

6. Continued Revelation of His Divine Authority (9:1–27)

The Saviour Clothes His Apostles with His Power and Authority (9:1–6). Jesus was able not only to perform wonderful miracles Himself, but could give to His disciples the power, the ability and the right to go and do in a wider sphere what He Himself had done and was doing. An ordinary human leader, however illustrious, cannot endow his followers with bodily or mental powers which will enable them to emulate him; but Jesus could, and in so doing, He gave a fresh revelation of His divine greatness, His mercy and His love.

Even Herod's Attention Focuses on the Saviour (9:7–9). The acts of the twelve disciples turned the attention of the populace and even of the tetrarch Herod in the direction of Jesus. The most important requirement in all preaching and in all philanthropic work is that it should result in everyone's speaking of *Him*. Those who proclaim His Word and those who serve Him, even His Church, should always remain in the background and let Him be the central figure.

The Saviour Miraculously Feeds the Multitude (9:10–17). This miracle is an important highlight in our Lord's public ministry. By means of this wonderful act, He established beyond all doubt that He is the omnipotent Saviour Who is able to make provision for all the needs of mankind.

The Saviour Acknowledged by His Apostles as the Christ of God (9:18–22). The preparatory work and teaching of the Lord Jesus now ultimately bore fruit and His prayers were answered. The disciples had at last, through the influence of the Holy Spirit, learned to see Him as the Christ, the Son of God, and without hesitation to confess Him as such. Now Jesus (v. 22) began to prepare their minds for the terrible shock which lay ahead of them. He, the Messiah of God, was to suffer and be rejected, even put to death at the hands of men, namely, the spiritual and secular leaders of the chosen people. But He promised them He would rise from the dead on the third day.

The Followers of the Saviour Challenged to Bear His Cross (9:23–27). After He had prophesied the *via dolorosa* for Himself in the near future, Jesus also spoke about the cross which His disciples would need to bear if they wished to be true followers of His. A believer's "cross" does not consist in ordinary human ills and griefs, such as disappointments, sickness, death and poverty, but in those things which we must either suffer or forfeit in the service of Christ —abuse, persecution and suffering even to the point of death on the one hand, and self-denial on the other. These things overtake us as the result of our faith in Him and our obedience to Him.

7. The Saviour's Divine Glory Revealed (9:28–50)

Before Jesus deliberately and of set purpose chose to follow the road to Jerusalem where He was to be taken prisoner, tortured and crucified, it was vouchsafed to three of His most intimate followers to behold Him for a few moments in all His divine glory (9:28–36). This was the miraculous climax of the gradual revelation of Himself before He finally set foot upon the path of suffering and death. Because Jesus had come to fulfil both the Law and the Prophets, God purposely allowed Moses, through whom in particular He had given the Law to us, and Elijah, a typical representative of the Prophets through whom God had spoken and prepared the way for the coming of Christ, to come to Him and appear to the disciples. Once more God spoke with a voice from the cloud which over-shadowed them in witness of the fact that He was well-pleased in Jesus and exhorted the world to listen to Him with attention and in faith and obedience, for this was truly His Beloved Son (v. 35).

The Saviour Heals Where His Apostles Failed (9:37–45). The con-dition of the lunatic child was utterly hopeless and critical; even the disciples of Jesus could do nothing to save him. But the moment Christ appeared on the scene, victory ensued. At His command even this most obstinate demon was forced to yield.

The Saviour Teaches His Disciples to be Humble and Forbearing (9:46–50). By calling a little child to His side, Jesus gave the disciples an object lesson, namely, that he who would be great must first of all learn to be truly the least (vv. 46–48). The zeal with which the dis-ciples tried to promote the honor of their Master was a mistaken one, possibly inspired by pride and selfishness. Jesus taught them (vv. 49, 50) to be more magnanimous and more tolerant.

IV. Journey from Galilee to Jerusalem (9:51—19:44)

1. *The Saviour's Mission of Redemption (9:51–56)*

The Saviour's revelation of Himself had already reached a glorious climax on the Mount of Transfiguration a week after the disciples had confessed that He was the Christ of God (9:20). He Himself had elected to follow the way of humiliation, suffering and death in order to carry out the divine plan of salvation, and He had already more than once pointed out to the disciples what lay before Him. Although He knew only too well everything that was appointed to befall Him, He unswervingly followed the road that led to Jerusalem. In answer to the question raised by James and John, the sons of thunder: "Lord, do you want us to bid fire come down from heaven and consume them?" (that is, those who would not receive Him), the Saviour once more urged them to be tolerant. They were to be magnanimous toward all who served Him even if their methods were different (v. 50), and tolerant toward those who were inimical toward Him and His disciples, for He had come not to destroy people by means of His divine power but to save them.

The High Cost of Following the Saviour (9:57–62). The road Jesus was following led to the cross, and those who wished to follow Him must pay the highest possible price. It is, therefore, particularly fitting that Luke should give an account of the three men who desired to follow Jesus. The privilege and the importance of following Jesus are so tremendous that there can be no place for excuses or cowardice or compromise with the world.

The Saviour Proves that He has Defeated Satan (10:1–20). In decisively rejecting the temptations of Satan (4:1–13), Jesus established in principle the fact that He had gained victory over him. During His public ministry, this victory was repeatedly revealed when He released those who were possessed of devils. The campaign of the seventy disciples against the powers of darkness proved that Satan's strength was already crippled. He was a conquered foe, and whenever he was challenged to battle in the name of Jesus, a glorious victory over him ensued.

The Saviour is One with God the Father (10:21–24). Jesus was not drawing a comparison between intellectual and non-intellectual people, but between those who nurse the wrong attitude toward Him and those of a right, childlike disposition. By word and deed, Jesus had already revealed himself as the Son of God, and now (v. 22) He declared in no uncertain terms that He was One with the Father. All things had been delivered to Him by His Father, He alone had full and perfect knowledge of the Father, and only through Him could anyone come to know the Father. Not only did He know the Father, but He was able to reveal Him to others. It followed inevitably, therefore, that He was absolutely One with the Father.

The New Commandment of the Saviour (10:25–37). The lawyer was posing a purely academic question when he asked, "And who is my neighbor?" But Jesus' reply, in the form of parable, answered the highly practical question "Whose neighbor am I?" or "Do I act the neighbor toward those who need my love and my help?" According to the Jewish way of thinking in those days, loving one's neighbor involved only members of one's own race (namely, Jews of unmixed origin and therefore not Samaritans or heathen). In His parable of the Good Samaritan, Jesus very definitely taught the truth that neither nationality nor any other consideration ought to limit one in loving and helping his neighbor.

2. The Saviour's Instructions on Service and Prayer (10:38—11:13)

How to Serve the Saviour (10:38–42). This story about the two sisters, Mary and Martha, should not be taken to mean that Jesus considered a life of quiet worship and contemplation the best way of exercising one's religion and that He disapproved of an active Christian way of living. His purpose was not to contrast the two, but to show that we should not be troubled and flustered in our active service of Him. We should also not be impatient and dissatisfied with our fellow Christians or with our Lord and be so busy with external things that we neglect the most important of all —worship of God in spirit and in truth.

The Saviour Gives a Model Prayer (11:1–4). The Saviour, it is true, had already in the Sermon on the Mount taught His disciples how to pray, that is, what principles to honor in prayer. Afterward He gave the "Our Father" as an example of a prayer which meets all the requirements of true prayer (Mt. 6:9). But at this point, one of His disciples became so acutely conscious of his own inability and that of his fellow disciples really to pray as Jesus prayed that he begged the Lord to teach them a model prayer. Jesus consented and gave the "Our Father."

The Saviour Teaches that Prayer should be Accompanied by Faith (11:5–13). In the previous passage we found Jesus complying with the disciple's request, "Lord, teach us to pray." Now He proceeded to teach them by means of two parables to pray with firm assurance that their prayer would be answered.

3. Christ's Warnings to Enemies and Followers (11:14—14:35)

The Saviour Accused and Acclaimed (11:14–28). Once again Jesus revealed His divine power by expelling a demon from a dumb man. This striking miracle caused bystanders to marvel. Some were inclined to consider it proof that this man of Nazareth really was the Messiah (cf. Mt. 12:23). Others refused to acknowledge Him to be the Christ and yet could not deny that He had performed a miracle, so they blasphemously declared that He had done so through

"Beelzebub, the prince of demons." Jesus, "knowing their thoughts," exposed the hollowness and falsehood of their accusation by pointing out that, since Satan accomplished his work by means of demons subordinate to him, it was illogical to suppose that he would oppose his own ministers and release their human victims from their accursed sway, since to destroy the work of his satellites would be to undermine his own power. By means of the parable contained in verses 21 and 22, our Lord showed He had power to expel these demons because previously (especially during the period of His temptation in the wilderness) He had vanquished Satan and deprived him of all his power. For that reason, He was able to undo the devil's evil work and command the demons to come out of their victims.

The Saviour is Greater than Solomon and Jonah (11:29–32). Jonah was a sign to the men of Nineveh, because he came to them as one sent by God and was most wonderfully rescued from the fish's belly. He was, so to speak, raised from the dead as a proof that he really had been sent by God. In the same way, Jesus would, by His resurrection, give irrefutable proof that He had been sent by God as the Christ, the promised Saviour.

The Saviour Warns against Wilful Blindness (11:33–36). Jesus uttered a solemn warning that the understanding of the man who refused to accept God's revelation of the way of salvation with a believing heart would become more and more hardened and darkened. No one can wilfully keep the light of the Gospel out of his heart without doing violence to his own Spirit.

The Saviour Accuses the Scribes and Pharisees (11:37–54). Although Jesus by word and deed gave a clear revelation of Himself as the promised Messiah, the Pharisees persisted in their unbelief, and the conflict between Him and them became ever more acute. In this passage, Jesus pointed out that the religion of the scribes and Pharisees had become a mere matter of fulfilling external duties and obligations; it did not proceed from the heart and was not the practical expression of their love of God or their fellowmen (v. 42). They were also blameworthy because their motives were not pure (v. 43). More often than not they were zealous as religious leaders, not for the glory of God but in order to seek honor for themselves.

The Saviour said further that, because the attitude of the Jewish nation and their leaders was still unchanged, God had, in His inscrutable wisdom, determined, if they again rejected those whom He sent (namely, the Saviour, John the Baptist and after them the apostles and the first Christians), to bring final judgment upon the nation which was responsible for rejecting the ambassadors of God and even putting some of them to death. The Jews of an earlier epoch who had caused the prophets and ministers of God to be murdered had already paid dearly for their evil deeds with banishment and national disaster. But the Jews living in the time of Jesus and of the founding of the Christian Church were guilty without any extenuating circumstances because they had rejected the Son of God Himself and crucified Him. After that they had persecuted His followers to the uttermost, putting many of them to death in the years preceding the Jewish-Roman war. During this war which began a few decades after the crucifixion of Jesus (A.D. 67–71), the words contained in verses 49 through 51 proved terribly true.

The Saviour Warns against Hypocrisy (12:1–12). Jesus taught that hypocrisy in one's religion is not only a despicable sin, but also a vain attempt to conceal the true state of affairs. Truth will always out—to some extent in this life, and completely at the end of the world. It is therefore useless to dissimulate. His disciples were not to yield to the temptation to be hypocritical through fear of men, for men could kill their body only, not their soul. God alone was to be feared and honored (vv. 4, 5), for to Him belongs all power forever and ever to destroy and to punish.

The Saviour Warns against Covetousness (12:13–21). The central thought in this parable is that it is not only a heinous sin to make worldly riches and pleasure one's chief aim in life, but that it is also a foolish and fatal mistake.

The Saviour Warns against Anxiety (12:22–34). The Saviour's exhortation to His disciples to rid themselves of anxiety about material things is connected with His earlier warning against covetousness. The best remedy for cupidity and a feverish clinging to one's earthly possessions is the development of true faith in the Heavenly Father's care. When one's riches consist in earthly treasures, whether great or small, his heart will be earthbound, but when one is rich in God and in things eternal, he will be heavenly-minded, whether he has material possessions or not. It is not the mere fact of *possessing* this world's goods that makes one materially-minded or worldly, but one's attitude toward them, nor will lack of possessions automatically make one heavenly-minded. Only freedom within oneself from selfishness and covetousness, combined with true devotion to the Lord, can produce that effect.

Believers Must be Faithful until the Saviour Returns (12:35–48).
The words of our Saviour recorded in this passage are closely associated with the above exhortation not to be worldly- but heavenly-
minded. His disciples were to be so bound to Him by ties of love
and loyalty that the anticipation of His Second Coming would be
the greatest passion of their lives as they went about day by day
faithfully fulfilling their mission. Such behavior on their part was to
be proof that their treasure was truly "laid up in heaven" and that
they were indeed heavenly-minded. At the same time Jesus urged
them not to let the fact that He was coming again at some time in
the future induce in them as believers and, above all, as spiritual
leaders an attitude of passive expectation. Rather, it was to inspire
and challenge them to the utmost activity in supplying the needs
of those for whose spiritual welfare they were responsible (vv. 43–
46).

The Saviour Brings Division (12:49–53). Fire has a double action:
it destroys what is impermanent; it purifies and refines what is indestructible. The Saviour in these few verses expressed the earnest
desire and yearning of His heart that His life's work of bringing
salvation to the world might be completed in order that His grace
might, through the power of the Holy Spirit, enter the hearts of
men in full measure, to effect the downfall and destruction of evildoers and bring purification and refinement to believers.

Peace with the Saviour must be Made in Time (12:54–59). Since
Jesus came "to cast fire upon the earth" (v. 49), each individual
should realize how serious matters are and take care to set his house
in order while time and opportunity yet remain. All men, according
to verses 57 through 59, are fellow-travelers on the road to God, the
Eternal Judge, and each one must take pains to reconcile himself
with his fellowmen while opportunity still remains. Above all, each
one must make sure that he has the right relationship with Christ
while the day of grace still obtains.

The Saviour Rejects a False Belief (13:1–5). At that time, the belief
was commonly held that persons who were overtaken by disaster
were particularly great sinners and were, for that reason, caused by
God to suffer calamity. Jesus rejected this false premise and warned
the Jews who brought Him the report of the murder of certain
Galileans that they themselves would perish unless they repented
in time. Those Galileans were no greater sinners than themselves.

The Saviour Utters a Solemn Warning (13:6–9). This parable (cf.

Hos. 9:10 and Joel 1:7) obviously refers to Israel. God had given them every opportunity to bear fruit, but they were still unfruitful as their rejection of Him, the promised Christ, only too clearly proved. Yet, as the result of Christ's pleading on their behalf, God would give them a final chance. If they persisted in their unbelief and sin, they would be irretrievably cut down from their privileged and protected position as the chosen people of God.

After the crucifixion of Jesus, God continued to make every effort to call the Jews to repentance—by the resurrection and ascension of Jesus, by the miracle of Pentecost, and by the subsequent preaching of the apostles and the rise of His Church. The majority, however, refused to repent and punishment inevitably overtook them in the form of the Roman-Jewish war of A.D. 67–71.

A secondary meaning symbolized in the fate of the unfruitful fig tree is the warning that the same dire end will befall every individual who wilfully elects to remain unconverted.

The Saviour Heals on the Sabbath (13:10–17). The Saviour never failed to notice individual cases of exceptional misery among the crowds around Him. Now His eyes fell upon the woman who "was bent over and could not fully straighten herself." He immediately called her to His side and healed her of the "spirit of infirmity," that is, a spirit which had been the cause of her illness for eighteen years. The ruler of the synagogue was indignant because this work of healing was done on the Sabbath, but the words and action of Jesus so mercilessly exposed the falsity of His enemies' point of view that they were utterly confounded, while "the people rejoiced at all the glorious things that were done by him."

The Saviour Claims Complete Ultimate Victory (13:18–21). By means of these two parables, Jesus taught that the Kingdom of which He was the founder and representative would reach full maturity in spite of its inauspicious beginning and the strong opposition constantly offered to it. Nothing could impede its growth and complete development. Our Lord gave no indication at this point as to how and when it would reach completion, but in the light of other pronouncements made by Him, it is clear that the final establishment of His Kingdom will take place only after His Second Coming.

Saviour Utters Another Solemn Warning (13:22–30). No matter how gloriously and completely the Kingdom might continue to expand, there was a real danger (so Jesus warned them) that even those who had repeatedly seen and heard Him might nevertheless be excluded from it. The doorway leading to eternal life is exceedingly narrow, and only those who strive with all their might to enter in by it will be saved. When once the door has been shut and the time of grace is past, many will endeavor to obtain entry but in vain, for it will then be eternally too late. The "householder," that is, the Lord, will have shut the door and those who failed to enter during the "acceptable year of the Lord," when the door of grace still stood wide open, will then be unable to enter.

Even His Enemies will Ultimately Acknowledge the Saviour (13:13–35). In the region east of the Jordan where Jesus was apparently moving about at that time, the Jewish authorities had little power. So the enraged Pharisees tried to frighten Jesus into fleeing into Judea where He would be completely in the power of the Jewish Sanhedrin, by reporting to Him that Herod, who was ruler over Galilee and the land east of the Jordan, was seeking to kill Him. But He would not allow Himself to be intimidated. On the contrary, He ordered them to tell "that fox" (for Herod, though a weak ruler, was exceedingly cunning) that, in spite of all his threats, He would continue to release people from their physical and spiritual misery until His work in that region was completed. In verse 35, Jesus meant that those who do not accept Him during the time of grace will, at His Second Coming, recognize Him with pain and grief as the Christ of God, for it will then be too late to find salvation through Him.

The Saviour Exposes the Hypocrisy of His Enemies (14:1–6). The question which Jesus put to His persecutors proved that He was fully aware of their desire to trap Him. Moreover, His question placed them in an awkward position. If they answered that He was justified in performing acts of healing on the Sabbath, it would set Him free to continue doing so. On the other hand, they could not say it was unlawful to heal on the Sabbath day in view of the obvious misery of this dropsical man. The Saviour's words exposed the hypocrisy of His enemies so clearly that not one of them was able to utter a single word in reply.

The Saviour Warns against Pride (14:7–14). Jesus was not, by means of this parable, recommending the exercise of false humility, but He was pointing out that God's righteous judgment, and not man's self-esteem or the arrogant presumption of so many of the Pharisees, is the sole measure of "greatness" in the Kingdom of Heaven. The best seats at a wedding feast are assigned according to the host's own judgment and are not to be snatched by presumptuous guests.

The Fatal Foolishness of Refusing the Saviour's Invitation (14:15–24). By means of this parable, Jesus issued a warning that there will be many who will have no share in the blessings of His Kingdom. Only those who accept His invitation will "taste his banquet" (v. 24). Those who refuse the Lord's invitation which He offers in and through Jesus will be inexorably turned away when they seek entrance at the end of the world when His Kingdom will be gloriously revealed in all its fulness. Because they chose of their own free will to let the day of grace slip by unheeded, they will have only themselves to blame for their exclusion from the Kingdom. In verse 24 we note how Jesus associates Himself with the "master" of the parable and makes reference to His own messianic wedding feast.

The High Cost of Following the Saviour (14:25–35). Jesus wished to discourage superficial discipleship, so He turned to the multitude and told them very firmly the absolute demands He made of anyone desiring to be a true follower of His (v. 26). He who would follow Him as Lord and guide was to do so unreservedly and unconditionally. All other loyalties were to be subordinate to the loyalty and affection He demanded. Only that man could be His disciple who, in order to serve and glorify Him, was willing to deny himself and to renounce all ambition and self-interest and even to die for His sake (v. 27). He who was unwilling to renounce and sacrifice everything for Christ's sake was just as worthless as a disciple as salt which had lost its taste and had consequently been thrown away as unfit for "the land or the dunghill" (vv. 34, 35).

4. The Saviour of the Lost (15:1–32)

The Saviour Teaches Why He Gives so much Attention to the Lost (15:1–10). Instead of the Pharisees being glad that someone had at last come to call the lost sheep of Israel to true repentance, they took it amiss of Him that He should minister to the spiritual needs of the people. To prove to them how unfounded their criticism of Him was, Jesus used three parables. The first two showed in a striking way how right, natural, and necessary it was that He should turn His attention to the outcasts of Jewish society and how wrong was the attitude of His critics.

The Saviour Sheds Light on the Human and Divine Aspects of Conversion (15:11–32). This third parable is closely connected with the foregoing pair but, whereas in the latter the emphasis is laid on the seeking love of God and the divine aspect of conversion,

Christ in this parable clearly reveals the human side of the matter, namely, that a life of sin and backsliding is due essentially to a rebellious breaking away from God. When a man has wasted his life in the service of the idols of pleasure and selfishness in that "far country" of sin, he is, in the end, rudely awakened to the fact that that land has nothing to offer by way of compensation for the precious treasures he has squandered there. He is left poverty-stricken and unsatisfied in the depths of his being. The first step towards conversion takes place when he becomes aware of his wretched plight in that "far country" of sin and realizes his spiritual poverty and dire disgrace. So inexpressibly wonderful is the love of God that He not only forgives the repentant sinner, but goes to meet him halfway and embraces him in love and pardon. The Heavenly Father does not upbraid and punish the returned prodigal and demote him to the position of slave or servant, but accepts him in Christ as His beloved child and bestows upon him all the privileges and the full status of sonship.

The attitude of the elder brother trenchantly illustrates the outlook of the Pharisees. They were spiritually estranged from God and their religion had degenerated into slavish observance of duties on the one hand, and into self-glorification on the other. Though they were themselves without spiritual fervor and far removed from God, they despised and shunned people like the publicans and other sinners whom they considered unworthy of inclusion in the true Israel.

5. The Saviour's Commands to His Followers (16:1—17:10)

Jesus taught the disciples to be so free from avarice and so full of unselfish love that they would readily share their worldly goods with those who were in need, whenever God prompted them to deeds of kindness (16:1-9). In this way, they would lay up for themselves indestructible treasure in heaven, for in the hereafter those who had been assisted and succored by them in this life by means of a proper use of their material possessions would, as it were, welcome them and give evidence in their favor. How sharp is the contrast between this welcome in the eternal dwelling place of God and the lot of the unjust steward who was received into the homes of his fellow miscreants only because of their guilty consciences and, at that, for a short while only, before death forever claimed him!

The Saviour Exposes the Pharisees (16:14–18). The Lord knew the hearts of the Pharisees and exactly what their motives were in exercising charity before men. Jesus pointed out to them that being honored by the people for their riches and show of piety was not what mattered, but whether God had a good opinion of them.

The ministry of John the Baptist formed the bridge between the Old and New Testament dispensations. He began, and Jesus and His disciples continued, to preach that the Kingdom of God was at hand —in and through Christ (16:16). Everyone who, like many publicans and sinners, listened to Him in faith strove with the greatest zeal, self-sacrifice and determination to force his way, as it were, with spiritual violence into the Kingdom—the sphere in which the supreme authority of God is revealed. Such a man did his best to enter by the narrow door, but the Pharisees reviled Jesus and refused to believe in Him, thus shutting themselves out of the Kingdom.

The Saviour Declares by what Standard God Judges People (16:19–31). This parable of our Lord illustrates clearly the truth contained in verse 15b: "What is exalted among men is an abomination in the sight of God." During his lifetime the rich man was an outstanding example of a person held in high esteem by men, but his frightful misery after death proved that, although he had been highly thought of by men, yet, because of his heartless selfishness, he was an abomination in the sight of God, the Righteous Judge, Who knows the human heart.

It was not our Lord's intention to use this parable to satisfy our curiosity about life after death. He was providing a striking object lesson to impress upon us the seriousness of *this* life, since the choice which we make in this world decides our eternal weal or woe. The parable does not imply that the mere possession of material wealth will lead to our eternal damnation or that a life of poverty and privation is all that is necessary to insure our eternal salvation. Our *attitude* towards riches and poverty is the important thing—whether we believe in God and serve Him with a penitent heart, irrespective of our circumstances, or whether we reject Him, a thing we can equally well do whether we are fabulously rich or desperately poor.

The Saviour Warns against Being a Stumbling Block (17:1–10). In verses 1 and 2, Jesus stated that the punishment meted out to anyone who causes someone else to sin will be so terrible that it would be better for him to die a violent death before he was able to play the role of tempter. By dying he would not only avoid committing this great sin, but he would also escape the resulting penalty which will be worse than being cast into the sea to drown. On the other hand (vv. 3, 4), He taught that it was just as important that His disciples should forgive those who sin against them (that is, place stumbling blocks in their way) as that they should refrain from being a stumbling block to others. But forgiveness was not to be misinterpreted as weakness. No, the erring brother was first to be rebuked and shown the error of his way and then to be forgiven if he showed signs of repentance.

6. Ingratitude of Nine Lepers Healed by the Saviour (17:11–19)

The Saviour's command to the lepers, "Go and show yourselves to the priests," was given at the same time as the word of power whereby they were healed. Healing took place while they were, in obedience to His command, in the very act of making their way to the various priests who were set in authority over them. To the Samaritan who was the only one to turn back when he saw that he was cured, Jesus gave the order, "Rise and go your way; your faith has made you well" (v. 19); that is, He assured the man that it was his *faith* which had saved him and that he was not only cured of physical disease, but was saved in every sense of the word because he truly believed in Jesus and had come into close, personal contact with Him. Although the other nine had also been granted healing of the body, their superficial faith had only flared up for the moment because of this miracle. This fact, coupled with their ingratitude, kept them from entering into the intimate, personal contact with Him which the Samaritan had established.

7. Suddenness of His Return Predicted (17:20—18:14)

Jesus taught in this passage that the coming of the Kingdom of God will not take place in such a way that people can, by a close study of signs, establish precisely when it is to happen. They will not be able to say: "Lo here!" or "Lo, there [comes the Messiah]." The reason for this is twofold: In the first place, the Kingdom of God on earth has already come in and through Jesus, to save and to judge the Jewish nation. It has saved those who have acknowledged and obeyed Him as the Messiah, and it has judged those who have rejected Him. Secondly, the final coming of the Kingdom will take place so suddenly and unexpectedly that no one can foretell with any degree of accuracy the actual time of His Second Coming (vv. 22–37).

From other utterances of our Lord (cf. Mt. 24) it is clear, however, that He did teach that there will be certain perceptible signs of His Second Coming, though there will be only general indications of the approaching end of this dispensation. The exact year, day or hour, however, cannot be foretold. Christ's coming will be sudden and unexpected and those who are not prepared for it will be forever lost.

The Saviour Teaches Believers Never to be Discouraged (18:1– 8). Furthermore, Jesus taught that if His Second Coming seems to be unduly delayed, believers are not to be discouraged but are to continue in prayer. The Saviour will come in due season and answer their prayers by destroying the power of Satan and causing His chosen ones to triumph.

This parable has a secondary and more general meaning, namely, that at all times we are to persevere in prayer without becoming despondent if the answer is long in coming.

The Saviour Warns against a Lack of Humility (18:9–14). The previous parable stressed the importance of persevering, believing prayer; this one indicates the right attitude of mind for the individual believer to adopt in making his daily petitions. The Saviour pointed out that it was not the Pharisee whom God considered justified, even though he had every appearance of righteousness. His religion was a matter of form and was spoiled by conceit and an unloving contempt of other people. It was the tax collector who was granted forgiveness by God when he took refuge with Him in his spiritual need. Conscious of his guilt, he humbly pleaded for mercy and it was he who went away justified rather than the Pharisee. It was not that he had *earned* forgiveness by the humility of his prayer. But because of his self-contempt and confession of sin, he was freely granted that forgiveness which God in His mercy extends to all who truly repent.

8. *Jesus, Little Children, and the Rich Young Man (18:15–30)*

Because the attitude of Jesus towards little children was completely different from that of the disciples, He called the mothers to come to Him with their little ones. At the same time, He admonished the disciples not to prevent little children from coming to Him, for "to such," said He, "belongs the kingdom of God." By "such" He meant all those who have the receptive minds of little children and exhibit the humility and complete trustfulness natural to them.

The Saviour and the Rich Young Man (18:18–30). The rich young man had never yet succeeded in freeing his soul from the bondage of his great wealth and had never yet chosen to serve God only. He was still trying to serve God *and* mammon. If he seriously wished to inherit eternal life, it was essential to get rid of that one great stumbling block in his life. Humanly speaking, it is just as impossible for a rich man to enter the Kingdom of God as it is for a camel to go through the eye of a needle. No one can, in his own strength, conquer the temptations which come in the train of great wealth. As long as he tries in his own strength to extricate himself from the devilish toils of overweening love of earthly possessions, he will always fail. Human endeavor can save no one; it is only through the grace of God that the rich, as well as the poor, obtain salvation (v. 27).

9. Toward the End of the Journey (18:31—19:44)

The Saviour again Announces His Approaching Death (18:31–34). For the fourth time, Jesus in these verses foretold that He was to be delivered to His enemies, to suffer and to die (9:22, 44; 13:33). From then onward, His whole life was to be overshadowed by the cross until the full light of victory blazed forth at His empty grave.

The Saviour Reveals His Power over Blindness (18:35–43). At the Saviour's word of command, the blind beggar who believed in Him was immediately healed of his blindness. From that very moment, he followed Jesus, glorifying God for restoring his sight through the Messiah. The multitude who were present, and who at that time cherished great expectations of Jesus, could not do otherwise than acknowledge that God was doing wonderful and mighty acts through the medium of this man of Nazareth. Had not their own eyes just witnessed this miraculous recovery of sight?

The Redeeming Grace of God Triumphing through the Saviour (19:1–10). This incident, which took place only a few days before the crucifixion, is a beautiful example of how the redeeming grace of God was seen to triumph through the actions of Jesus. The

Saviour's words to the redeemed tax collector Zaccheus, "the Son of man came to seek and to save the lost," epitomizes the story of the Passion of our Lord which followed shortly after this episode.

The Saviour Instructs His Followers and Warns His Enemies (19:11-28). By means of this parable, Jesus taught (*1*) that the final revelation of the Kingdom of God will not take place immediately, (*2*) that a great responsibility rests upon the shoulders of each individual follower of His to labor faithfully until He comes, (*3*) that the coming of the Kingdom of God in full perfection will not mean political triumph for the Jews but the Last Judgment, for then those who have been faithful to Him will be rewarded and those who have been unfaithful and hostile will be punished. In this way Jesus was also once more preparing His disciples for what was shortly to happen to Him and making another appeal to the Jews to repent. It was at this juncture that Jesus finally and purposefully set His face to go to Jerusalem (v. 28).

The Saviour Weeps over Jerusalem (19:29-44). In the words quoted in verse 42, Jesus gave expression to the yearning of His soul that the Jewish nation should accept, even at this eleventh hour, the salvation which God was offering to them in and through the Saviour. Alas, He realized only too well that it was already too late. Because they persisted in their ungodly unbelief, they were wilfully blind to the opportunities for obtaining salvation which were still given to them. By their own fault the way to salvation was hidden from their eyes, and for that reason fearful punishment would overtake them. God would ordain that a mighty foe (the Romans, naturally, since they were at that time the only worldly power strong enough to play that role) would come and besiege Jerusalem and destroy it utterly and massacre its inhabitants in the most frightful way (vv. 43, 44). For this reason, Jesus wept.

V. The Last Days of the Saviour in Jerusalem, His Crucifixion and Burial (19:45—23:56)

1. Second Cleansing of the Temple, Silencing His Enemies (19:45—21:4)

At the beginning of His public ministry, Jesus entered the temple and cleared it drastically (cf. Jn. 2:13-25). The religious leaders of the Jews, however, opposed Him and soon all the old malpractices in the temple were again the order of the day. It follows as a matter of course that when Jesus entered the temple shortly before His crucifixion, He should once more exhibit His aversion and inexorable opposition to all those unholy practices.

The Saviour Exposes the Insincerity of His Persecutors (20:1–8). From their attitude toward Jesus, it was only too evident that the Jewish rulers arrogantly and in a spirit of criticism denied the authority of John the Baptist who had so clearly pointed to Him as the Messiah (Jn. 1:29). Nevertheless, from fear of the people, they never openly denied that John was a prophet and even went to such lengths of hypocrisy as to be baptized by him (cf. Mt. 3:7). Because they would not give an honest reply to Christ's pertinent question, our Lord, in turn, refused to answer theirs. In this way He exposed their insincerity and the fact that they were no longer qualified to be the spiritual leaders of the nation.

The Saviour again Claims Absolute, Divine Authority (20:9–18) By means of His triumphal entry into Jerusalem and the purging of the temple, Christ had clearly and powerfully proclaimed that He was the Messiah. Now again, by means of this parable, He reaffirmed it and informed His enemies that He was well aware of their murderous designs. He warned them also that if they persisted in carrying them out, a tragic fate would befall them. Furthermore, this parable was Christ's answer to the question they asked Him (v. 2), namely, that He did these things by the authority of the Father Who had sent Him.

The Saviour and Secular Authority (20:19–26). In the reply Jesus made to His persecutors' question, we see no attempt at evasion. On the contrary, He clearly and unambiguously declared that it behooved them to "render to Caesar the things that are Caesar's," namely, taxes and everything else due him as their secular ruler. God had ordained that the Jews should come under Roman domination, and in their free use of the emperor's coinage they factually acknowledged him as their earthly ruler. Therefore, they were obliged to pay tribute to him as long as he continued to be their emperor. Jesus did not specify in detail all the things which were due to Caesar; He was no doubt referring more particularly to the taxes. From other utterances of His (cf. Jn. 19:11) and especially from His whole attitude towards the Roman government, it is, however, clear that our Lord was also referring to the honor, submission and obedience which everyone owes to secular authority insofar as it does not clash with his higher loyalty towards God. For Jesus the relationship of the individual to God outweighed all other considerations. He therefore added immediately, "and to God the things that are God's." His whole life and all His utterances show that He meant by this nothing less than the unconditional surrender and devotion of man to his Creator. From this it follows that, though it is necessary to "render to Caesar the things that are Caesar's," that injunction is subject to the more important corollary, "and to God the things that are God's." Thus, in final instance, "to render to Caesar the things that are Caesar's" is only a part of the all-embracing rendering "to God the things that are God's." Because God commands us to obey earthly authority except when it violates His laws, we show obedience to God, the King of kings and Lord of lords, when by His command we submit ourselves to secular authority.

The Sadducees Silenced by the Saviour (20:27–40). After Jesus had proved to the Sadducees that their question was based on erroneous premises, He pointed out to them that even Moses (who, according to them, did not believe in the resurrection) had implied immortality (and therefore resurrection, since the two concepts are inseparable) by calling God "the God of Abraham and the God of Isaac and the God of Jacob" so many years after the death of the patriarchs (cf. Ex. 3:6). If the latter were not immortal, God would not have been called their God, for He is not the God of the dead, but of the living. His covenant with the patriarchs was not only eternal, but personal. Therefore, it followed that though they had died, they were still alive and will also at the consummation of the age receive the resurrection life. True life, according to the Bible, is life for both soul and body, therefore immortality includes also the idea of resurrection; that is, the reunion of the soul with the risen, glorified, celestial body.

The Saviour is More than a Mere Human Messiah (20:41–44). After Jesus' question (v. 41) had silenced His audience and forced them to begin to think, He pointed out that the Old Testament itself expressly taught that the Messiah was much more than a mere Son of David. For (so He declared) David himself in one of his psalms (Ps. 110) called the Messiah his "Lord." Although He was, humanly speaking, a descendant of David (as foretold in the Old Testament; for example, II Sam. 7:8–29; Is. 9:6, 7; Mic. 5:2, and as appears from a wealth of data in the New Testament), He was much more than a mere human ruler of the dynasty of David. Jesus' claim that because He was the Messiah, He was also the Son of God was in complete agreement with Old Testament prophecies (cf. Ps. 2:7, 12).

The Saviour Warns against False Leaders (20:45–47). Although Jesus knew that by so doing, He would fan the flame of the murderous hatred of Him which His enemies cherished, He did not hesitate to speak the truth and unequivocally warned His disciples against the sin of which so many of the Jewish leaders were guilty.

The Saviour Praises the Gift of the Widow (21:1–4). The contributions made by many of the wealthy did not impress Jesus at all, for He knew that they represented no sacrifice. What they gave was very little in comparison with what they possessed. But because this widow, in spite of her dire poverty, gave all she had to live on, her gift, small as it was, counted for far more in His sight than all the donations of the others.

2. Coming Destruction of Jerusalem Announced (21:5–24)

Long before the coming of Jesus to the earth, God had already announced that He, the Angel of the Covenant, the divine Messiah, would come to the temple to purge and to punish (Mal. 3:1–5). Luke previously described how the Saviour not only came to the Jewish nation, but how He had entered the temple in the capacity of Messiah and Christ and had drastically cleansed it of all the evil practices prevalent there. He also described how He repeatedly preached to the multitude, rebuked the obdurate Jewish leaders and powerfully proclaimed that He was the Messiah. His persecutors, however, persisted in their rejection of Him and thereby sealed the fate of themselves, the temple and the city. Thus, when the disciples commented on the beauty of the temple, Jesus specifically foretold that before long that lovely building would be devastated. One who was "greater than the temple" had come (Mt. 12:6) but, because the people had rejected Him and made a mere building (the temple) the center of their decadent worship according to their own inclinations and ideas, God permitted it to be razed to the ground to punish this unbelieving nation. After Jesus had warned the disciples (vv. 7–9) not to be misled by people or events, He told them all that would first take place before the destruction of Jerusalem and the temple (vv. 10–19).

Jesus revealed to them (21:20) what the sign would be of the coming devastation of Jerusalem. It was not to be confused with His own Second Coming, for the destruction of the city and temple would not be preceded by the revelation of Himself as the Messiah in all His messianic glory. But when believers saw the city surrounded by earthly armies, they then would know that the hour of its destruction had struck. The approach of these forces was to be the signal for all believers to flee immediately, not only out of the city, but also from its environs and from the whole province, and to take refuge on the mountains of Gilead beyond the Jordan and outside Judea (v. 21). We learn from history that the believers obeyed this injunction, for when the first reports came that Jerusalem was about to be encompassed by the Roman armies, virtually all the Christians fled across the Jordan to the little city of Pella, east of Jordan, known today as Kherbit-el-Fahil, where they remained until after the destruction of Jerusalem.

In verses 23 and 24 Jesus prophesied specifically that Jerusalem would fall into heathen hands and be ruled over by the heathen "until the times of the Gentiles are fulfilled," that is, until the end of the present dispensation when He will come again in divine majesty and power to establish His eternal Kingdom on the new earth (vv. 25–33), once the final judgment day is past. The first part of this prophecy was literally fulfilled in A.D. 70 when Jerusalem was utterly destroyed. After a siege lasting about five months, the celebrated Roman general, Titus, son of the Emperor Vespasian, overran the city with his mighty army, destroyed and plundered the temple, and slew the Jews—men, women and children—by tens of thousands. When their lust for blood had been sated, the Romans carried off into captivity all the able-bodied remnant of the Jews (for they had done away with all the weaklings and the aged), so that not a single Jew was left alive in the city. For many years after the destruction of Jerusalem, no Jew was allowed in the city or its vicinity. Only on one day in the year—the day of remembrance of the destruction of the temple—were they allowed to mourn over the city from neighboring hilltops.

The first Jews to be allowed to re-enter and inhabit a part of Jerusalem were the Christians of Jewish descent who had fled to Pella and who were permitted, some time after the Jewish-Roman war had ended, to occupy a certain part of the ravaged city. Today the old, original Jerusalem is mainly in the possession of heathen, and a Mohammedan mosque occupies the hill on which the temple formerly stood. Never since the destruction of Jerusalem in A.D. 70 has the old Jerusalem proper been in the hands of the Jews. Although modern Israel has quite a big population, the majority of the Jews are still scattered over the face of the earth. The Saviour's striking prophecy, down to the last detail, has thus been literally fulfilled.

3. His Return to be in Glory and Majesty (21:25–36)

After Jesus had explained (21:24) when "the times of the Gentiles" would be fulfilled and the end of this dispensation would occur, He went on (v. 25) to make prophecies concerning the signs which will appear just before and at the time of His Second Coming. Before the fall of Jerusalem there would be isolated instances of disaster "in various places" (cf. v. 11), but before the end of the world, the whole of mankind will be involved in a mighty turmoil. There will be "signs in sun and moon and stars" and the life of the nations of the earth will be totally disrupted by reason of the fear and anxiety which will seize their minds and plunge them into despair (vv. 25, 26).

In the midst of all this unbounded misery, the Son of Man, the glorified Christ in all His divine might and majesty, will come again and in such manner that every eye will behold Him (v. 27). When the trees begin to sprout, we know that spring is at hand; similarly will believers know, when they see these prophecies being fulfilled, that His Second Coming is near and God's dominion is about to be openly and completely revealed (vv. 29–31). He will come like a thief in the night, it is true (Lk. 12:40), and no one can foretell precisely when His advent will take place. But while unbelievers will continue to be wrapped up in their earth-bound business, taking no notice of the signs of His coming, believers will recognize in the events here prophesied a definite sign that His coming is near. That day will not overtake them suddenly and unexpectedly (v. 34).

After making these awe-inspiring pronouncements, Jesus proclaimed the absolute certainty that all these prophecies will be fulfilled (v. 33). The Saviour, unlike the prophets and other men of God, did not say: "God has spoken through me and therefore it will come to pass." No, He spoke with personal and absolute authority, because He was and is God, one with the Father and the Holy Ghost. No one had ever before had the right to dare to speak thus, but *He* could do so, because He could not only foretell historical events but also was Himself, in unison with the Father and the Holy Spirit, the all-powerful controller of those events.

The Saviour's prophecies concerning the end of the world were not intended to satisfy human curiosity about the program of the ages or to give His disciples grounds for gloating over the final destruction of the wicked. No, He always stressed the importance of the challenge presented by coming events. They were a call to true repentance and constant watchfulness (vv. 34–36).

4. Judas' Arrangement to Betray the Saviour (21:37—22:6)

The Jewish leaders, determined to kill Jesus, were planning how to accomplish their base ends without causing an uproar among the people. They finally decided not to kill Him until after the Feast of the Passover, since it was clear that the multitude (and, in all probability, especially those who had come to Jerusalem from Galilee and the land east of the Jordan) would not tolerate His being harmed (Mk. 14:2). They intended to wait until the crowds had again dispersed and there was accordingly no danger of an uprising among the people before getting rid of Him by some means or other, but God willed it otherwise. Because it was His will that Jesus, the Lamb of God, should die on the great day of the Passover as the perfect, atoning sacrifice, He overruled the decisions of the Jewish authorities. The unexpected action of Judas cancelled the decision of the Jewish rulers not to have Jesus captured during the festive season, since Judas' treachery enabled them to seize Him at a time and place when the people could not demonstrate in protest against their action.

5. Institution of the Holy Communion (22:7–38)

Jesus was well aware of Judas' devilish plans and the murderous determination of His persecutors to destroy Him. But there was still a great deal which He wished to teach His disciples on that evening of the Passover, and He particularly wished to partake of it with His disciples for the last time and to institute His own Supper in place of the Old Testament Passover, that rite which, symbolizing His perfect work of redemption, had been a preparation for the Lord's Supper. Because His hour was not yet, and Judas could not be permitted to succeed in betraying Him to His enemies until everything was in readiness, Jesus kept the place where He and His disciples were to eat the Passover a secret as long as necessary (cf. vv. 9–13). He always chose to frustrate the evil designs of His enemies by natural precautions, rather than by miracles. As a result of these precautions, Judas found no opportunity beforehand to go and tell the Jewish authorities where our Lord intended to eat the Passover, and the Saviour could accordingly sit down in peace with His disciples to eat the Last Supper. Jesus passionately desired to celebrate the Passover with His disciples because His institution of the Lord's Supper at the celebration of that last Passover was a sign that everything was now in readiness for the completion of His work of redemption. The preparatory, Old Testament dispensation was now to yield place to the New.

On the eve of His crucifixion, Jesus knew that His life of self-sacrifice and humiliation on this earth was ending. He also knew that the day would dawn when He would come back in triumph and lead His followers into their wonderful inheritance of perfect redemption and salvation. The idea of a messianic feast is often used to symbolize the state of full salvation which will be ushered in at the end of the world. For that reason the Saviour referred (vv. 16–18) to the celebration of a feast after God's dominion has been completely revealed and redemption through the grace of God, as symbolized in the rites of the Passover, has become a reality.

Humility is to be Characteristic of the Followers of the Saviour (22:24–30). It is quite probable that it was the disciples' squabbling among themselves which precipitated Jesus' action of washing their feet (cf. Jn. 13). When—so we picture the scene—He noticed how ambitious and self-seeking His disciples were in spite of all His teaching, He got up without a word, girded Himself with a towel, and began to wash their feet. When He had finished and they were all again peacefully sitting around the table, He uttered the words of special admonition (vv. 25–30). With what force they must have struck the hearts and minds of the disciples in those circumstances! They were to seek not earthly glory and worldly power as their reward, but heavenly joy and a holy calling in His eternal Kingdom. Verses 28, 29 and 30 strikingly illustrate the fact that, even on the eve of His crucifixion, Jesus was fully aware of His divine sonship.

The Saviour Prays for and Warns Peter (22:31–34). Jesus stated that by means of the events which were at hand—the capture and crucifixion of the Saviour—Satan would make a last desperate attempt to break up the ranks of His followers and to scatter them like chaff before the wind. The devil passionately desired to sift them like wheat and to see them blown away like chaff as Judas had allowed himself to be blown away. But the Saviour had prayed for His faithful disciples, especially for Peter who had played and was still to play a leading role, that their faith might not fail. While Satan acted the cunning adversary, Jesus acted as intercessor and advocate, pleading for His disciples and especially for the one whom He had previously appointed to be their leader. The Saviour assured Peter, therefore, that His faith would not utterly and permanently fail because He was interceding for him. Peter would suffer a temporary lapse of faith. But after he had again been restored, through the power of God, to true belief and faithfulness, he was to strengthen the other disciples in their faith and loyalty to Christ after they too had stumbled and temporarily succumbed to the severe temptations to which they had been subjected.

The Saviour Warns His Disciples to be Prepared for Difficult Times (22:35–38). From then on, Jesus said, He would no longer be with His disciples in human guise nor would they any longer be, as before, honored and feted as the disciples of a revered and beloved Master. He had already been rejected by the Jewish authorities, and soon He would be killed and regarded by virtually the whole nation as a hateful criminal. The immediate result would be that they, as the followers of the Crucified One, would become despised outcasts, persecuted by everyone. They would no longer be able to depend for their means of subsistence on the generous gifts of the populace, but would in the future have to make their own way through an inimical world, depending upon their own effort and industry for a livelihood. Therefore, in a striking metaphor, the Saviour told them that they would need to be just such determined and single-minded followers of Him in the battle of life as the soldier who sacrifies everything, even his mantle, in order to buy a sword and keep on fighting. The disciples were, however, still blind regarding the spiritual nature of His work and Kingdom. They continued to hope that He would establish His messianic Kingdom through external force. Accordingly, they understood His words in connection with the buying of a sword literally and did not grasp their real meaning (cf. v. 38).

6. Christ's Atonement for the Sin of the World (22:39—23:56)

Jesus taught that the holy and righteous wrath of God against sin must needs overtake Him to the uttermost because He had offered Himself without reservation as the substitute for doomed humanity. The wages of sin is death in an absolute sense—the death of both soul and body. Spiritual death entails the complete abandonment of a man by God. How frightful it must thus have seemed to Jesus, Who had always lived in the closest and most uninterrupted intimacy with God, that He must suffer all these things! How terrible to know that He Who had never committed sin of any kind was to die on the accursed cross as a condemned criminal, laden with the sins of the whole world, because He was the Lamb of God destined to be sacrificed! No human mind can ever plumb the depths of His suffering there in Gethsemane when the full realization of all He was to suffer in soul and body came over Him, the Sinless One.

Yet, although His whole being flinched from all that awaited Him, and although the devil used all his power and all his cunning at that eleventh hour to drive Him away from the road to the Cross, Jesus was never for one moment guilty of the least sinfulness or of unwillingness to complete the task He had undertaken. It was only natural and right that, goaded by circumstances, He should pray: "Father, if thou art willing, remove this cup from me" (v. 42), but, He immediately added: "Nevertheless, not my will, but thine, be done," and He offered Himself anew, freely and unconditionally, in obedience to the will of God as revealed in the prophecies of the Old Testament, to drain the cup of suffering and death to the very last dregs.

The Divine Authority of the Saviour Revealed, even on the Eve of His Death (22:47-53). In Gethsemane Jesus bowed low in deep submission to His Father, but during the last stages of the way of humiliation, suffering and death, even as in the earlier part of His public ministry, He never once exhibited the least sign of weakness or fear of His human persecutors and judges. The history of His capture strikingly reveals that the Perfect Man was a far greater personage than were all His enemies, even when He appeared to be their impotent prey. The Saviour faced His betrayer and His persecutors with such obvious calmness and lack of fear, and with such regal dignity (Jn. 18:6), that they were at first too nonplused to lay hands on Him. In the silence that fell upon them after He had healed the slave's ear, Jesus turned to the Jewish leaders who had come with the soldiery to be present at His capture and declared to them that they were able to carry out their evil designs, not because they came under shelter of the natural darkness of the night, but because in that hour Satan and his satellites, both human and spiritual, were being permitted by God to overpower the Son of the Most High and to subject Him to humiliation, suffering and death. He added that He had been captured by His persecutors, not because He was powerless to prevent them from taking Him, but because He was surrendering Himself of His own free will to be sacrificed in order to obtain salvation for guilt-laden humanity.

The Saviour Denied by Peter (22:54–62). Judas betrayed the Saviour because his heart was evil. When the full realization of what he had done came upon him, he lapsed into a state of spiritual despair and agony of mind and hurled his soul into eternal darkness by taking his own life. Peter, on the contrary, denied his Lord only through weakness. It was not that he did not love Him or believe in Him, but his courage was not strong enough to withstand the tremendous temptation to deny Jesus three times during that disastrous night. When he realized that he had denied his Lord, he was overwhelmed with bitter grief at his faithlessness. True repentance on his part paved the way to forgiveness for him by Jesus.

The Saviour Claims Divine Sonship (22:63–71). We learn from this passage that it was not only in the days when He was admired by the multitudes or only while He was alone with His disciples that Jesus claimed to be the Son of God in the full meaning of the word, but also when He was surrounded by His enemies, with perhaps only John, the beloved disciple, lurking near (Jn. 18:16). Even though He knew that to make such a claim in the presence of His enemies would be to provide them with the final evidence against Him which they needed to persuade the people to have Him put to death, He stated unequivocally that He was the divine Messiah and none other than the Son of God (vv. 70, 71).

The Saviour Falsely Accused and Sentenced to be Crucified (23:1–25). Jesus was charged before the Sanhedrin with having blasphemed against God in that He had called Himself the Son of God. Such an indictment, however, involving as it did the religious sentiments of the Jews, would have carried no weight with the Roman governor, Pontius Pilate, so before him His persecutors accused Jesus of totally different crimes. Had Pilate been convinced that these charges were true, he would not have hesitated for one moment to condemn Him to death. Probably, however, his suspicions were almost immediately aroused that these accusations were false and, after he had interviewed Jesus in his palace (cf. Jn. 18:33–38), he became firmly convinced that the Saviour was completely innocent of any treachery toward or rebellion against the Roman government. Jesus admitted, it is true, that He was the King of the Jews, when Pilate questioned Him on that point, but He so clearly convinced Pilate that His Kingdom was a spiritual, not a temporal one (Jn. 18:36), that the Roman judge could not fail to perceive that it was *envy* which had motivated the Jewish authorities in handing Him over to judgment (Mt. 27:18; Mk. 15:10). Pilate's position was a thorny one. He knew very well that the accused was innocent and he pronounced Him innocent, but at the same time he realized that the fanatical Jewish leaders were determined to procure a death sentence for Him. Pilate was therefore glad to evade responsibility by sending Jesus to Herod on the pretext that He belonged to Herod's jurisdiction, seeing that He was a Galilean. No matter what Herod's verdict might be, Pilate would then be absolved of all responsibility in the matter.

At an earlier period of his life, Herod had shown signs of spiritual interest and hunger. We are told that he listened with joy to the words of John the Baptist, but in course of time he deteriorated spiritually and morally (Lk. 3:19, 20) and even went so far as to put John the Baptist to death without cause. Now, because he had abandoned himself completely to spiritual blindness and moral decay and wished to see Jesus out of curiosity only, the latter answered him never a word. Herod had failed to make use of his chance to repent when John the Baptist rebuked him about his sinful life, and now he was so deeply sunk in sin that even Jesus had no word for him.

Pilate had, earlier that morning, clearly and expressly pronounced Jesus innocent. At the same time, with equal clarity, he had shown his own weak, vacillating character when he, in spite of his conviction, dispatched this innocent man to be tried by Herod, just because he feared the fanaticism of the Jews. When Herod sent Him back, Pilate continued to vacillate. Finally, he abused his high calling as judge and, having stifled the demands of his conscience to dispense justice and righteousness, gave way to selfish considerations involving his own honor, safety and interest. In this way he finally became a mere instrument in the hands of the bloodthirsty persecutors of the Innocent One.

The Saviour Addresses the Weeping Women (23:26–32). Because Jesus knew what a fearful judgment was shortly to overtake the Jewish people, He uttered these words (vv. 28–30) expressing His infinite compassion for that doomed nation. It was right and fitting that these women would still find place in their hearts to pity one who was, to all intents and purposes, a condemned criminal. But their perspective was wrong: they failed to realize what lay ahead of them and of the Jewish nation as a whole, if they persisted in their unbelief. Far rather should they bewail themselves and their children, for *His* Passion, however excruciating, would be but the doorway to eternal bliss, while theirs would lead to the destruction of the nation and to the eternal woe of every individual Jew who continued wilfully to reject Him. When we read the history of the Roman-Jewish nation and of Palestine, we see Jesus' prophetic words translated into stark reality. What a revelation we find in the episode with the weeping women of the Saviour's absolute lack of self-pity and His unwavering conviction that the eternal weal or woe of each individual is dependent on the attitude of that person towards Him!

The Saviour Sacrificed as the Lamb of God (23:33–49). God's ideal of creation was fully realized in the person of Jesus. He was the Perfect Man in body and in soul. When He began His public ministry, it became clearer and clearer that He was to be sacrificed as the Lamb of God and would die in circumstances of the most intense pain and humiliation. Now, at length, on Golgotha, the words uttered by the prophet Isaiah hundreds of years previously were fulfilled: "He is despised and rejected of men; a man of sorrows, and acquainted with grief: and we hid as it were our faces from him; he was despised, and we esteemed him not. . . . But he was wounded for our transgressions, he was bruised for our iniquities: the chastisement of our peace was upon him; and with his stripes we are healed" (Is. 53:3–5).

Only Luke records the prayer of the Crucified One for His enemies (v. 34), doubtless because, throughout his Gospel, he focuses attention on the boundlessness of the Saviour's love for sinners and the forgiving heart of God. After he records this prayer, Luke mentions the fact that the soldiers divided His garments among themselves by casting lots for them. How poignantly he brings home to us the fact that Jesus was now completely denuded of everything—His honor,

His disciples, His life (for already He was beginning to suffer His death throes) and now finally His clothes, the last remnant of His earthly possessions! Thus, for our sakes, He became poor in the absolute sense of the word, so that we might be made rich in and through Him.

There is no doubt that Jesus' prayer to the Father to forgive His enemies made a deep impression on the mind of one of the two criminals who were being crucified at the same time as He. When he perceived from Jesus' behavior and character that He was no ordinary man but the *Holy One,* faith was born in his heart and he believed that this man was not only the Messiah, but the One Who could in mercy save him. No matter how weak and faltering his faith, it was nevertheless sincere as he pleaded with Christ to have pity on him. Because he still saw Jesus as the Messiah Who would one day return in all His messianic glory to establish His Kingdom on earth, he begged Him to think of him at that time. And because there was in this prayer of his, however mistaken his premises might be, a looking up in faith to Jesus, the Saviour assured him that He would not only remember him *one day* at His Second Coming, but that he would *that very day* be with Jesus in Paradise as a redeemed soul partaking of the joys of heaven (v. 43).

In Gethsemane, Jesus made His final decision to take upon Himself the sins of mankind. Because the wages of sin is eternal death, it was necessary that Jesus should experience on the cross utter abandonment by God and the pains of hell. The Son of God had to undergo a period of utter spiritual darkness in His capacity of substitute for a guilty world. For that reason it was impossible for nature, the creation of God through the Son (Jn. 1:3), to remain unaffected on that day. Accordingly, complete darkness fell over the land from twelve o'clock until three, followed by an earthquake which rent the rocks in the vicinity (Mt. 27:51). Simultaneously, the veil of the temple which separated the "Holy" part from the "Holy of Holies" (where God had in Old Testament times so often in a very special way revealed Himself) was torn in two. This was a sign that by the perfect sacrifice of the Lamb of God the way had been opened to every believer to enter into the most intimate communion with God, without the necessity for further sacrifices. It was also a sign that the temple and the old ceremonial form of worship were no longer needed. The old dispensation which had served a preparatory function had now yielded place to the new dispensation founded on the all-sufficient redemptive work of the Son of God. The words of Jesus in verse 46 teach us that, when the hours of darkness and desertion by God had passed, a calmness descended again upon the Saviour's soul and He was once more conscious of the closest communion with God. The words also show that, after the physical and spiritual suffering He had endured, Jesus again revealed that He Who was dying there was the Lord of life and death. He had not been forced to die, but had of set purpose voluntarily laid down His life to become the Perfect Sacrifice.

The Saviour Buried by Loving Hands (23:50–56). By His utter humiliation and the pains of hell and death He had endured, Jesus had already completed the work of reconciling man with God. For that reason God allowed Him to be buried by His own faithful and beloved circle of worshippers, so that the prophecy was fulfilled which said that although He would be crucified as a condemned criminal and thus be given a "grave with the wicked," yet He would be "with the rich in his death" (Is. 53:9). Never again would He, the Lamb of God, be the object of man's mockery, insult and torture. He had finished His work (Jn. 19:30) and the honorable burial in a rock-hewn tomb, belonging to the noble Joseph of Arimathea and never yet used as a grave, presaged His ascension to glory.

VI. Resurrection and Appearances of the Risen Lord and His Ascension (24:1–53)

1. The Saviour's Triumph over Death (24:1–12)

Angels announced the glad tidings of the Saviour's birth, and angelic beings from the world invisible were used of God to tell the women at the grave that He had risen from the dead. The fetters of death and hell could not hold Him. His triumphal resurrection from the grave, after He had brought about full reconciliation between God and man through His Passion and sacrificial death, was the spontaneous expression of what He was—Perfect Man and the Son of God. Heavenly heralds proclaimed the wonderful tidings that Jesus was no longer there in the grave where they had laid His crucified body, but that He had risen from the dead and was alive.

The Risen Saviour Opens Blind Eyes (24:13–34). In the outburst of the two disciples who were going to Emmaus, we see clearly the

struggle raging in their hearts between hope and despair. All the
other disappointed and bewildered followers of Him Who had been
crucified were in like case. Jesus allowed these two first to relieve
their feelings before He expressed His sorrow at their attitude and
rebuked them for having so little spiritual insight and understanding
as not to believe *everything* the prophets had foretold. If they really
knew the Scriptures and truly believed in the Living God, they
would know also that God had, through the prophets, revealed that
He must needs suffer and die *before* He could, as the Messiah, enjoy
the glories of victory ascribed to Him in the Old Testament. Thereupon Jesus, Who knew the Old Testament Scriptures perfectly because He and the Father and the Holy Spirit were the joint authors,
expounded to them, from the first book of the Old Testament
to the last, all the passages relating to Himself. But it was only
when He sat down to table with them and took bread, blessed and
broke it and gave it to them, that the eyes of these two disciples
at Emmaus were opened, and they suddenly realized that their
guest was none other than Jesus Himself. As soon as they had come
to this realization, Jesus disappeared, satisfied that He had accomplished His purpose of letting them know that He had indeed arisen.
He also wished to teach them that His visible presence would now
no longer remain with them. In the future they would have to hold
communion with Him no longer as a man but as their Risen Lord
Who was shortly afterward also to be their ascended, glorified Lord.

In spite of the fact that Jesus had vanished from their sight so
soon after they had recognized Him, the two disciples no longer
doubted. They knew for a certainty that He had risen from the dead
and was alive as the Messiah, the promised Saviour.

2. Doubts of His Followers Dispelled (24:36–49)

It took the Risen Saviour Himself to convince His bewildered followers that He had indeed arisen from the dead. The combined
testimony of the women at the grave, of Peter and of the two disciples at Emmaus, could not bring complete reassurance to the
minds of the others, even if it did now and then succeed in making
the flame of their faith burn a little more brightly (v. 35). But they
were not completely convinced until the Risen Lord Himself appeared to them and dispelled their doubts. On the day of the resurrection, Jesus expounded to the two disciples at Emmaus the hidden

meaning of the Old Testament (vv. 25–27), and now again, on this later occasion (vv. 45–47), He "opened the minds" of the eleven disciples and enabled them to discern the spiritual truths contained in the Holy Scriptures. He again pointed out how the Scriptures recorded that it was necessary for Him to suffer as the Christ and to rise again from the dead on the third day, in order that the glad tidings of repentance and forgiveness of sins might be proclaimed in His name on the grounds of His work of reconciliation and His power to save. This message was to be proclaimed first in Jerusalem to the Jews, but afterwards to the whole world. On those who had been witnesses of His death and resurrection rested the tremendous responsibility to broadcast these tidings. They, and all believers after them, would have to go out into all the world and tell what they had seen and heard and experienced. If they trusted in their own strength, they would be unable to carry out this mandate, but Jesus Himself as the resurrected King of His Church would, after His ascension, send "the promise of the Father" upon them, that is, the Holy Spirit Who is the greatest of all gifts and in Whom and through Whom all good gifts are bestowed (v. 49).

3. The Saviour's Return in Triumph to the Father (24:50–53)

The Saviour had already on Easter Sunday arisen in His glorified, celestial body, but now He was to be finally restored to divine power and glory with the Father in heaven. He therefore led His disciples, when forty days had elapsed since His resurrection, to a place on the Mount of Olives near Bethany (Acts 1:12) where He took farewell of them. Then, in the capacity of eternal High Priest, He lifted His hands and blessed them as the high priest usually did when he emerged from the temple at important festivals (cf. Ps. 110 and Heb. 7–9). His arms were still outstretched in blessing when He was removed from their sight as they gazed up at Him with receptive and worshipful hearts.

He Who from the beginning had dwelt in divine glory with the Father now returned to Him in His human form, though that form was now a resurrected and celestial body (cf. Acts 1:11).

Through His Spirit He is and remains, however, forever with His followers and His Church on earth (Mt. 28:20). To the disciples, His ascension to divine glory was the final proof that He was indeed the Christ, the Son of God, and at the same time Himself the

Almighty God, Who had power to fulfil His promises. Moreover, the angel (Acts 1:11) repeated the same glorious assurance which Jesus Himself had so often given them (for example, Jn. 14), namely, that He would come again in person. This time, however, He would come, not to suffer again, but to establish God's royal dominion completely and eternally and to set up His heavenly Kingdom in all its perfection.

Because of all these various circumstances and because of their glorious expectations, the disciples were full of joy as they returned to Jerusalem even though they had just taken farewell of their Lord in visible, bodily presence. While they were waiting for the promise concerning the coming of the Holy Spirit to be fulfilled, they continued with one accord in prayer and supplication and praise to God (Acts 1:13, 14).

John

CARL F. H. HENRY

LIKE THE SYNOPTIC ACCOUNTS, John's Gospel proclaims Jesus of Nazareth as the promised Redeemer of a lost race. Its scope, content and arrangement, however, stress the great fact of Christ's deity. The purpose of the book (given in what is usually cited as the key verse, 20:31) is to convince the reader that "Jesus is the Christ" (the Messiah of Old Testament prophecy) and "the Son of God" (God come in flesh) so that, moved to repentance and trust, he may "have life" through or in His name.

Whereas Mark's record begins with the public ministry of Jesus, and Matthew and Luke with His birth of a virgin (and the Old Testament line of promise), John sketches the person and activity of Christ from eternity. A lofty prologue (1:1–18) introduces the Gospel. In majestic prose, this initial portion presents Jesus of Nazareth as the eternal Logos become flesh (v. 14), uniquely manifesting deity in human nature (v. 18). Creation (v. 3), history (vv. 5–16), and conscience (vv. 4, 9) find their meaning and unity in the Divine Redeemer (v. 17). Linking the destiny of the whole creation to the resurrection of the incarnate and crucified Logos, the Gospel thus sweeps from eternity to eternity.

I. The Revelation of the Word in Eternity (1:1, 2)

The One who "became flesh" (v. 14) was in eternity past not simply an idea, but a person alive and at work in the divine society of the Godhead. This central figure of the Gospels existed "in the beginning" (1:1, 2); existed "with" or "face to face" with God (vv. 1, 2), that is, in personal relationship and fellowship. In this pre-incarnate state, He was not inferior to Deity, for the Word was very

God (v. 1). From the outset of John's exposition, therefore, the reader is driven to his knees to worship the God of the incarnation.

II. The Revelation of the Word in Creation (1:3, 4, 9)

In stressing the eternal activity of the Logos, John's Gospel also illuminates the record of creation in Genesis. In the Mosaic account, the Word of God likewise creates ("God said . . . and it was so") the universe and life. The Fourth Gospel identifies that *Word* by "which" God created as the eternal, personal Word; the Logos Himself was the divine agent in the creation of all things. The material world, therefore, has not begotten the mental and the moral and the personal; rather, "things" and the world of creatures owe their existence to the Living God.

John, the evangelist, however, does not list the graded forms of creature life found in Genesis. Instead, he moves at once to "the crown of creation," to man as the unique bearer of God's image (cf. Gen. 1:27; 2:7). Being "lighted" by the Logos (1:4) is what distinguishes man among the creatures. Man's distinctiveness is not simply a comparative superiority over the animals in respect to physical or mental complexity; rather, he is different in kind. The human species by creation is specially endowed for spiritual fellowship with God (v. 9), and therefore holds the unique prospect of a destiny in eternity.

Man and the universe, history and science, morality and reason, have their integrating source and meaning, therefore, in the eternal Word. This Word is revealed throughout the finite creation, but especially in the spiritual nature of man (cf. Rom. 1:20; 2:15).

III. The Revelation of the Word in Redemption (1:5—21:25)

The term "darkness" ("the light is shining in the darkness; and the darkness is unable to put it out," 1:5) is the first hint of the awesome conflict between light and darkness permeating this Gospel. It is a stark reminder that the created world is now a fallen world, that mankind is now snared in sin. Despite creation in God's image, man is spiritually and morally disqualified from divine fellowship and needs supernatural restoration to sonship (v. 12). In Genesis, cosmic darkness supplies the setting for the Creator's "Let there be light!"

In John's Gospel, the gloom of a fallen moral world is the background against which the Redeemer lights the hearts of men otherwise doomed in sin. Like the Old Testament, therefore, the Fourth Gospel presents the human race lost in sin, powerless to save itself, and God Himself providing His promised salvation as an act of unmerited grace.

1. The Sweeping Witness of the Prologue (1:9–14, 16–18)

The majestic opening of John's Gospel announces that the Word stooped from the eternal world into the sphere of time and flesh to redeem sinners. The Light Himself—Who by creation had illuminated mankind—stepped into the created order (1:9; cf. v. 13). He "was made flesh" (v. 14). Adding human nature to what He "was" eternally, that is, Deity, He became what He "was not," that is, the God-man. (Using a singular rather than plural pronoun, some early Church Fathers infer the Virgin Birth from John 1:13: "*Who was* born, not of blood, nor of the will of the flesh, nor of the will of man, but of God"). He dwelled, or "tabernacled," as God-man among men. Although Moses had given men the law in God's name, yet that great lawgiver was hardly law incarnate. Jesus Christ, however, was grace and truth come in flesh (v. 17). Two climactic affirmations of the prologue reveal the incomparable superiority of Hebrew-Christian religion over the pagan religions: (*1*) the *spirituality* of God and (*2*) the divine *incarnation* once-for-all in Christ (v. 18). (The oldest manuscripts read not simply "the only begotten Son," but "God only begotten.")

The prologue anticipates the great struggle between belief and unbelief that shadows the Gospel. Although the incarnate Word came to "his own," that is, His created world and creatures to whom redemption had been promised, He was nonetheless rejected (1:11, 12). Only those who "received" Him, who "believed on his name," He authenticated as children of God (v. 12). The disciples rejoiced as included participants of His grace (v. 16).

2. The Crowning Witness of the Old Dispensation (1:5–8, 15, 19–28)

The appearance of Jesus of Nazareth was not a sudden, unexpected development in the history of mankind. Especially through the Old Testament revelation, the world was divinely prepared for the coming of the Messiah. Prior to the coming of the Light of the World, the lamp of prophetic witness had shone steadily in the long night of sin. Four centuries of silence followed the last inspired Old Testament prophecies until John the Baptist announced the Messiah's imminent presence (1:6–8). John resists every effort of the curious Jewish religious leaders to attach finality to his own ministry (vv. 19–23). In contrast to the coming Messiah's baptism of regenerating and sanctifying power (vv. 24–26), John's baptism of water simply expressed confession of sin and need of forgiveness. John looks for the grand climax of the Old Testament in the coming Messiah, Who eclipses every prefigurement of Him (v. 15). The great fulfilment is now at hand (v. 23).

3. The Opening Witness of the New Dispensation (1:29–51)

The Baptist's bold identification of Jesus as the promised sin-bearer, "the Lamb of God" Who bears the world's sin (1:29), is on the basis of special supernatural revelation (vv. 31–34). The Redeemer is distinguished by the fact that the Spirit abides on Him, and that He baptizes men into the Spirit (v. 33). He is the veritable Son of God (v. 34).

Jesus' public ministry begins unspectacularly when two of the Baptist's disciples, Andrew (Simon Peter's brother) and presumably John, the writer of the Fourth Gospel, follow the newly-identified Messiah and are invited to dwell with Him. These circumstances are spiritually symbolic, since "following and abiding" become the great pattern for all Christ's disciples.

Acknowledgement of Jesus as the Messiah of prophecy (1:41) opens the New Testament era. Personal evangelism expands the company of disciples to include not only Andrew and John, but Peter, Philip and Nathaniel as well (vv. 41–49). While spiritual insight is slight and their knowledge inadequate (v. 45), their elementary faith is genuine. The chapter closes with Jesus' mention of signs to come. Recalling Jacob's vision of the ladder, Jesus speaks of Himself, the Son of Man, as the unique bridge between heaven and earth, the special locus of God's disclosure (v. 51).

4. The Great Signs and Public Discourses (2:1—12:11)

Previously we noted that John's Gospel differs from the others not only in scope, but also in substance and structure. Its scope reaches from eternity to eternity—from eternity past to the incarnation and crucifixion, then through the resurrection to the heavenly head of a new humanity Who will return for His own (21:22). In substance John neither contradicts the other Gospels nor adds any wholly novel assertion about Jesus of Nazareth. Nonetheless, he more fully expounds God's self-disclosure in the incarnate Christ, by emphasizing the deity of the God-man. The purpose of the Gospel, namely to promote worship of Jesus Christ as the supreme revelation of the Father, is apparent also in the structure or arrangement of content.

The prologue stresses Christ's entrance into the created world and into the historical order from outside the sphere of time; His true home is in the eternities (1:1–18; cf. 3:13). This same theme colors even the concluding devotional postscript: the finite world cannot exhaust what might be said about the God-man (21:25). Following the prologue, John the Baptist appears on the threshold of Jesus' public ministry to herald the Lamb of God promised in the Old Testament. The Baptist brings his own adherents to the Messiah, yielding prominence to Jesus and His disciples (1:19–51). The Jews who accept Jesus as promised Messiah become forerunners of Samaritans who in turn acclaim Him as "the Saviour of the world" (4:39, 42) and of Greeks in search of Jesus (12:21); the crucified Son of Man will draw to Himself also the Gentiles (12:32).

Anyone who follows Jesus' public ministry in John after reading the earlier Gospels immediately senses striking differences in content and arrangement of material. The Synoptic Gospels (so-called because they reflect more fully than the Gospel of John the earthly or human aspect of Christ's life and the chronological order of events) certainly, like John's Gospel, present Jesus Christ not simply as a man, but as supernatural in His being and work. Nevertheless, the Fourth Gospel radiates a special individuality because of its marked concentration on our Lord's deity, and because of its peculiar choice and arrangement of content to reinforce that emphasis.

Particular inclusions and omissions of material illustrate this interest in Christ's deity. Absent from John's Gospel are the genealogies of Matthew and Luke; any reference to Christ's birth is incidental (cf. 1:13). Missing also from John are the Transfiguration, the agony of Gethsemane, the cry of forsaking on the cross. Surely John does not obscure the humanity of Christ, for he notes such details as Jesus' weariness, thirst (4:6, 7) and weeping (11:35). Actually, John presupposes the Synoptic narratives. Under divine impetus, however, he supplements what is already known to highlight a particular perspective.

To one aware of the proportions of the Fourth Gospel, this perspective is obvious at once. John pictures only twenty days out of the three-year public ministry of Jesus Christ. He selects only eight miracles as sufficient for his purpose. The discourses are not much greater in number, although some are found only in the Gospel of John. The subject of Passion Week comprises two-fifths of the entire Gospel. The swift tempo of the Logos' sudden manifestation to assume human nature for the ministry of redemption, related in the opening chapters, slows up noticeably for the events of Passion Week (12:12—19:42), and for the Risen Christ's commissioning of followers joined to Him in the awesome task of human rescue (20:1—21:25).

Both selection and arrangement of content reflect Jesus Christ not as a divine envoy or delegate merely, but as God Himself come into the world for man's salvation. Both the works and words of Jesus underscore this overwhelming truth. Almost half of the Gospel prior to Passion Week emphasizes Jesus' great signs and public discourses (2:1—12:11), progressively enlarging the truth of Christ's Messiahship. The recurring similarity of arrangement (alternation of miracles, discourses, and attendance at the national religious feasts), and the subsequent interdependence of these three elements to reflect God's disclosure of Himself in Christ, show a literary arrangement designed to enforce this theological truth.

This important segment of the Gospel covers Jesus' public ministry in the following general pattern: two miracles (sometimes one), followed by a discourse or two, the whole punctuated three times by the Messiah's sudden visit to the holy city and His presence in the temple at the sacred feasts. This triple movement of miracles, discourses and deeds centers in Jesus Christ Himself. For John, the miracles are not merely external works of power, but are *signs*, a translation the Revised Standard Version carefully preserves. The discourses of Jesus converge around the eight "I am's." The blending of prophecy and fulfilment in feast-attendance finds its great consummation during Passion Week, when observance of the Passover merges into the Lord's Supper (13:1–30).

The Gospel of John therefore demonstrates the disciples' growing faith in Jesus as the Divine Redeemer of Old Testament promise. But it portrays also later traces of post-resurrection comprehension to show the reader what the disciples themselves had been slow to understand. Apparently speaking in retrospect after the actual event, the author almost at the beginning of the Gospel explains that he sometimes reports data not obvious to the followers of Jesus at the time (2:22; cf. 12:16). Throughout the Gospel, John carefully guards whatever links the life, words and deeds of Jesus of Nazareth to prophecy and to the eternal background of redemption's unfolding history. The book of John is therefore more than an "objective historical" report. John observes that Jesus performed "many other signs" unspecified in the Gospel (2:23; 20:30); to report these "many other things" would have been an impossible task (21:25). The signs and discourses selected for this Gospel, these revelations of God in Christ, are authentic and adequate to acknowledge firmly Jesus of Nazareth as the Messiah of prophecy, the true Son of God.

John records the following of Jesus' *signs:* (1) changing of water to wine (2:1–12), (2) cleansing the temple (2:13–22), (3) healing the nobleman's son at a distance (4:43–54), (4) healing the helpless cripple at the pool of Bethesda on the Sabbath (5:2–16), (5) feeding the five thousand (6:1–15), (6) walking on the waters of Galilee (6:16–21), (7) healing the man born blind (9:1–41) and (8) raising Lazarus (11:1–47). The accompanying discourses reveal that these marvels were intended to be far more than mere acts of wonder.

The First Sign: Water and Wine (2:1–12). The sign of Cana, which opens Jesus' public ministry (simultaneously detaching Mary His mother from any right to command Jesus in His redemptive office, v. 4), displays not only Jesus' remarkable power, but unveils Him as Messiah and Son of God: "This beginning of miracles (signs) did Jesus in Cana of Galilee, and manifested forth his glory; and his disciples believed on (in) him" (v. 11). The other signs similarly trace this pattern of God's dynamic self-disclosure in Christ.

The miracle of Cana discloses Jesus not merely as a worker of mighty wonders but as the Christ, the promised Redeemer. The meaning of this event at Cana, like most of the signs in John's Gospel, has a definite correlation with the Old Testament. John carefully observes that the waterpots used at the wedding feast in Cana were in accordance with the Hebrew rites of purification (2:6). That the six waterpots each contained "two or three firkins apiece," or a total of 120 to 180 gallons, reveals the extent of the ritual observances. When an embarrassing lack of wine occurs, Jesus requests that these waterpots be filled to the brim with water. He thereby dramatizes the inadequacy of the waterpots, long associated with the Old Testament ritual of cleansing, to meet the present need. In these same waterpots, Jesus turns the water into wine, which elsewhere in Christian teaching symbolizes the blood of Christ. At the time, the disciples probably did not fully comprehend this symbolism. But John's comment is significant, namely, that in this first sign Jesus manifested "his glory" (v. 11; cf. 1:14).

Without the accompanying explanatory discourse, however, the specific truth about Jesus' person and work dramatized by each sign is neither obvious, nor even discernible. The miracles reveal Jesus Christ in action; the discourses reveal Him in speech. Revelation in historical acts is inadequate; necessary to define the meaning of events is revelation in word.

The Second Sign: Cleansing of the Temple (2:13–22). Illustrative of this fact is the sign at the Jerusalem Passover. Driving out the money-changers, sheep and oxen with a warning against commercializing the temple (vv. 15, 16) was no miracle in the usual sense. The disciples, in view of the Old Testament, inferred from the event only a godly zeal for the integrity of the temple as a house of worship and sacrifice (cf. Ps. 69). Jesus' sign meant far more, however. In answer to the Jews, Jesus fixed its specific meaning: "Destroy this temple, and in three days I will raise it up" (2:18, 19). The evangelist indicates that Jesus referred not merely to the destruction of the temple, but to the resurrection of His body (vv. 20, 21). His cleansing of the temple, therefore, dramatically signifies that Jesus' very body is the place where God is propitiated. Without this atonement, all the temple sacrifices become empty; with it, they become superfluous. As John notes, this truth was not apparent to the disciples until after Christ's resurrection. Once the resurrection had occurred, however, the relationship of the temple sacrifices to Christ's self-sacrifice shone from both the Old Testament and Christ's teaching (v. 22). The King James Version somewhat obscures Jesus' activity in this situation: "Jesus . . . found in the temple those that sold oxen and sheep and doves, and the changers of money sitting: and when he had made a scourge of small cords, *he drove them all out of the temple, and the sheep, and the oxen . . .*" (vv. 13, 14). This translation unfortunately stresses Jesus' dealings with the money-changers. The Revised Standard Version only slightly strengthens the textual emphasis on the sacrifices: "In the temple he found those who were selling oxen and sheep and pigeons, and the money-changers at their business. And making a whip of cords, *he drove them all, with the sheep and oxen,* out of the temple. . . ." Among the gospel writers, only John calls pointed attention to the expulsion of the animals.

John uses the discourses that follow the signs to unlock and release the inner meaning of Christ's works. A case in point is the conversation with Nicodemus after Jesus' miracles at the feast in Jerusalem (3:2; cf. 2:23). Nicodemus' visit is notable for several reasons. The very fact of the visit holds an element of surprise: he was "of the Pharisees" (3:1), that dominant Jewish sect so often flayed by Jesus for its mere formalism and externalism in spiritual matters; he belonged to the Sanhedrin ("a ruler of the Jews," v. 1), responsible for the spiritual destiny of the Hebrews. Of the many disturbed or at least curious observers (cf. "we know," v. 2), he alone came to Jesus. Nicodemus reveals, moreover, his relatively high view of Jesus: he calls him "rabbi," a term usually reserved for those trained in recognized official schools, concedes a divine origin for Christ's mission ("come from God"), and traces Christ's marvelous works to the fact that God is "with him" (v. 2).

Nonetheless, Jesus has much to forgive about Nicodemus' visit. In the first place, despite his religious interests and concerns, Nicodemus had come "by night" (3:2). Interestingly enough, Jesus closes the interview by noting that men love darkness as a cover for evil or shame (v. 19). His "relatively high" view of Jesus, moreover, is far from adequate. Jesus is more than "a teacher" come from God, more even than the greatest of the prophets. It is not enough to say that God is "with him" (v. 2). Jesus therefore confronts Nicodemus with the great fact of His divine incarnation (v. 13), of His absolute uniqueness (cf. "only begotten Son," v. 16). Furthermore, those who do not believe in the name of this "only begotten Son of God" already stand condemned before God (v. 18). The climax, however, is the disclosure that, although professing that he was driven to Jesus by the "signs," Nicodemus has no understanding of their meaning. He does not see that Jesus Christ, man's Redeemer, is God come in the flesh, and that even a Hebrew rabbi like himself needs to be born anew (v. 3). Inadequate are the waterpots of purification; only the best wine, now available, can meet the need. Inadequate are the temple sacrifices; final conquest and judgment of sin are only in the flesh of the Messiah. Baptizing into the Spirit is the Messiah's picture of spiritual regeneration.

In talking with Nicodemus, Jesus states the great pivot-points of

Biblical theology: *(1)* the indispensability of repentance and *(2)* the necessity of the new birth (3:5). He shows that sinful man can be born again because of *(3)* the incarnation (v. 13) and *(4)* atonement for sin by Christ (v. 14), and stresses that *(5)* divine justification is the only alternative to condemnation (vv. 16–18), and *(6)* sanctification the only alternative to human depravity (v. 21).

The Gospel adds another important contrast. Inadequate as water is in contrast to wine, inadequate as animal sacrifice is in contrast to the Messiah, so John the Baptist's baptism is inadequate in relation to that of Jesus (3:22–28) whose Spirit is without measure (v. 34; cf. 1:26, 33).

The discourse with the Samaritan woman (4:5–42) is an example of superb personal evangelism. Conversation begins with the known and proceeds to the unknown; it bares a life's moral failure and need; it offers the means of redemptive healing; it enlists a ransomed soul to reach others. This demonstration of the Lord's passion for the lost (v. 32) contrasts tellingly with the disciples' concern only for physical food (v. 8). The discourse means more, however. Following John's familiar pattern of sign and discourse, this narrative contrasts running water with living water (v. 10). To the Samaritan woman, the promise of satisfying all future thirst (v. 15) is as incredible as the notion of spiritual birth in contrast to physical birth was to Nicodemus. Despite all its value as preparation for the new dispensation, the old dispensation becomes an obstacle by overestimating itself (v. 12) and by its contamination through the Samaritans (vv. 20, 22). Jesus, who had turned water into wine at Cana in Galilee, here speaks to the Samaritan woman of living water as the symbol of everlasting life (v. 14) and discloses Himself to be the Messiah (v. 26).

The important point for what is just ahead, however, is the spirituality of God. The Samaritans had regarded Mount Gerizim as the divinely-approved place of worship while the Jews insisted upon Jerusalem. Both were soon to yield to a greater fact: not any given location, but the Messiah Himself would be the new place of access to the Father: "The hour is coming when neither in this mountain nor yet at Jerusalem shall men worship the Father. . . . The hour cometh, and now is, when the true worshippers shall worship the Father in spirit and in truth. . . . (I know that Messiah cometh). . . . I that speak unto thee am he" (4:21–26). That God is spirit (invisible, cf. 1:18, 14:9; and immaterial, cf. 4:21) logically anticipates recognition of Christ as "the Saviour of the world" (4:42; cf. 1:29). No longer need men journey to one divinely appointed place to worship Him. The fate of the temple in Jerusalem and the fate of the God-man are indeed closely related; it is Christ, the giver of spiritual life, who now fits men unfailingly for their eternal destiny (4:14).

This arrangement (the sequence of two signs and discourses, the whole punctuated by the Messiah's presence in the temple at feast-time) is now to be repeated in the Gospel. As in the earlier pattern, one miracle occurs in Cana of Galilee (4:46), the other in Jerusalem (5:2).

The Third Sign: Healing at a Distance (4:43–54). Something more than Jesus' conquest of dread disease marks the third sign, the healing of the nobleman's son. It repeats and strengthens the fact, just asserted in Samaria, that the universal power and presence of God is unveiled in the person of Jesus Christ. The nobleman's plea that he "come down (to Capernaum) ere my child die" (v. 49) assumes that Jesus must be physically and visibly present to manifest His power in human life. Jesus' healing of the nobleman's son at a distance demonstrates His lordship over space (v. 51). Jesus rebukes the nobleman (v. 48) for stipulating belief on visible results instead of taking Jesus simply at His word. Accordingly, when the nobleman believes on the authority of Christ's word, the healing takes place (vv. 50–53). The Gospel will enlarge this point to stress that faith in Christ's spoken word is sufficient and final in matters of eternal destiny (5:25) and gives assurance in all affairs of this life as well (14:19).

The Fourth Sign: Healing the Impotent Man (5:2–16). This miracle took place shortly after Jesus' arrival in Jerusalem at feast-time (v. 1). His association with the Passover moves toward and climaxes finally in His own death and Resurrection (13:1—19:42) as fulfilment of the Passover. John's fourth recorded miracle, the healing of the infirm man, occurs near the sheep market. Here animals were presumably gathered for sacrifice. Here, too, the afflicted who waited expectantly at the pool for healing expressed their hopes in superstitious legends (5:4). The narrative teaches no doctrine of general faith healing, for among "a great multitude of impotent folk, of blind, halt, withered" (v. 3), Jesus singled out but one (v. 6), and that one surely not because of his faith (v. 7). Once again a *sign* communicates and propels the divine revelation in Christ. The healing takes place on the Sabbath (v. 9). It is effected at Christ's command apparently without the infirm man's expressed will (v. 7). Healing of the nobleman's son bespoke Christ's lordship over space; the healing at Bethesda expresses His lordship over time. Invoked originally for man's observance, the Sabbath is intended for man's good. But it is also the Son of Man's right to supersede the Sabbath as the agent and revelation of the Father. "My Father worketh hitherto, and I work" (v. 17). So He asserts the prerogative of Deity to justify the healing at the pool of Bethesda on the Sabbath day. Already seeking His life on the ground of Sabbath violation (v. 16), the Jews now determine to kill Jesus as a blasphemer, since they disbelieved His claim that God was His unique Father (v. 18).

Additionally noteworthy in this sign at Bethesda is the absence of personal volition by the one who hears Christ's command. While this feature was present also in the healing of the nobleman's son, in this fourth sign it gains special and growing importance. The plea for Christ's intervention "ere my child die" (4:49) implies the nobleman's belief that death removes the human personality forever from Christ's power. The miracle of Bethesda suggests Christ's power over human life even in the absence of an expressed personal desire for His ministry. The key to this emphasis comes in the succeeding discourse: "the Son quickeneth whom he will" (5:21). This refers to the future resurrection of the dead, a fact that the raising of Lazarus (anticipated in v. 20) will dramatize to announce that death does not remove human personality outside or beyond the Messiah's call. Restoration of the infirm man anticipates future resurrection of the dead at Christ's bidding: "Marvel not at this: for the hour is coming, in the which all that are in the graves shall hear his voice, and shall come forth; they that have done good, unto the resurrection of life; and they that have done evil, unto the resurrection of damnation" (v. 29). Jesus Christ is Lord over the human personality forever.

Christ's discourse to the Jews fully asserts (5:19–29) and substantiates (vv. 30–47) His claim to deity. The titles "the Son of God" (v. 25) and "the Son of man" (v. 27) majestically sweep into repeated use of the personal pronoun. Jesus' messianic self-consciousness in the last half of the discourse is crowned with the great declarations: "I am come in my Father's name . . . ye will not come unto me . . ." (vv. 43, 40). He affirms a unique relation to the Father (vv. 19–23) and to mankind (vv. 24–29).

The Son does not act in rivalry to nor independently of the Father. Constantly aware of the Father's plan and work, He fulfils them identically with the Father (5:19). The Son has continual access to the secrets of Deity. At the same time, the Father continually loves the Son, who as in the recent miracles manifests the Father's purposes. Christ's claim to divine access and intimacy enlarges to include other prerogatives of Deity. Like the Father, the Son will raise and quicken the dead, and is entrusted with judgment of the human race. The Son is to be honored even as the Father; refusal to honor the Son dishonors the Father also (v. 23).

Stripped from the Jews, therefore, is any reliance on their notion that to reject Jesus is to honor God. Their decision against Jesus is a decision against God Himself, for Father and Son are not to be isolated in their work. The God of Judaism is none other than the Father who promised the Messiah, or in Jesus' words, "the Father which hath sent" the Son (5:24). To reject Jesus is to rob the promise of its fulfilment, and means being driven to an alien god with no promise of redemptive intervention. Judaism's rejection of Christ explains its discomfort in the presence of the Old Testament promises, and its swift deterioration to liberal forms that have no messianic hope. Growing emphasis on the "sending" Father ("him that sent me," 5:24, 30, 36, 37), as well as on Jesus "the sent one" (v. 38) finally climaxes in the miracle of the blind man healed in the pool of Siloam "which is by interpretation, Sent" (9:7).

Not only in relationship to the Father as sender (5:19–23) but also in relation to mankind under condemnation and death, the Son plays a special role (vv. 24–29). Simply to hear and to believe His word lifts men out of future condemnation into present spiritual life (v. 24). Refusal to hear His present invitation to rise from spiritual death to life means answering His voice in a future resurrection summons to damnation (vv. 25–29). "The Son of God" will judge mankind precisely "because he is the Son of man" (vv. 25, 27), because as God in the flesh He confronts man with His divine claim upon human nature.

Transition from the objective and impersonal "the Son" to the personal pronoun "I" openly fixes Jesus' claim as the incarnate Son (5:30), and anticipates the great series of "I am's" as well as the coming emphasis on His own distinctive perfections ("my name," 14:26; "my peace," 14:27; "my love," 15:9; "my joy," 15:11; "my glory," 17:22).

The present concern, however, is the manner in which Jesus contradicts the charge of blasphemy. After reasserting His manifestation of (and not opposition to) the Father's will and judgment (5:30), Jesus produces the "witnesses" that show and support His claim to deity. These witnesses are: *(1)* John the Baptist, the promised forerunner, whom the Jews themselves had already interrogated (vv. 32-35); *(2)* the Father's revelation in His works (cf. 5:17, 19; 14:10, 11), a revelation now in process but as yet incomplete (cf. 5:20, 36); and *(3)* the Father's spoken revelation in Old Testament prophecy (vv. 37-47). Jesus' enemies did not recognize Him because they rejected the scriptural testimony to the promised Redeemer. Even apart from the Baptist's witness and that of Jesus' works, the witness of Moses (the law, the sacrifices, the prophecies) is sufficient to condemn their unbelief (5:45-57). The supreme witness, however, is Christ Himself, although this evidence is by no means isolated and independent of other confirmations (v. 31). Yet Jesus does not rest His claim exclusively on the Baptist's testimony, which itself comes from a superior source (5:34; cf. v. 41). Jesus disparages neither His own authority nor the authority of Scripture, on which He insists (cf. "and they are they which testify of me," v. 39). Yet above all, the messianic self-consciousness retains priority (cf. "I know . . . ," v. 32; "I receive . . . I say," v. 34; "I have," v. 36). Those who charge Jesus with grandiose self-assertion (v. 18) are themselves guilty of mutual self-inflation (v. 44). For this reason they welcome only false messiahs, not the divinely sent One (vv. 42, 43). They prefer honoring each other to divine honor (v. 44) which results from honoring the Son equally with the Father (cf. v. 23). Thus they deprive themselves of eternal life (v. 40; cf. v. 26).

The Fifth Sign: Feeding the Five Thousand (6:1-15). The pattern of two signs followed by discourses repeats itself in chapter 6. Although the approaching Passover is noted in introducing the signs (v. 4), the Messiah in this case is not reported in attendance at the feast. Feeding the five thousand (vv. 1-15) and walking on the water (vv. 16-21) precede the discourses on Christ, the bread of life (vv. 22-59), and on Christ, the life-giving Spirit (vv. 60-71). The Messiah's attendance at the Feast of Tabernacles (7:1-52) in turn supplies the framework for further discourses on Christ, the Light of the World (8:12-30) and Christ, the fount of freedom (8:31-59). None can recognize this swift sequence of miracle, discourse and feast-activity without sensing that Jesus increasingly takes priority over all else as the unveiled Messiah and Son of God. "I am the bread of life" (6:35); "I am the light of the world" (8:12); "I am . . . before Abraham was" (8:58); "I am the door" (10:7); "I am the good shepherd" (10:11); "I am the resurrection and the life" (11:25); "I am the way, the truth and the life" (14:6); "I am the true vine" (15:1, 5)—this is the disclosure of God in Christ toward which point all the deeds, words and signs, until at last Peter and John (and every disciple thereafter) with full heart respond to the "follow me" (21:19, 22) of One whose voice is no longer merely that of a teacher (cf. 1:38) but that of the Risen Redeemer and Lord.

The feeding of the multitudes and the walking on the sea are more than mighty dramatic works; they are a commentary on the person and mission of Jesus of Nazareth. Significantly also, in the course of His self-disclosure to the Jews (cf. 2:1; 4:46), these miracles maintain continuity of the Messiah's ministry among the Gentiles in Galilee. Even the disciples, however, are slow to appropriate the signs' primary teaching, namely, the Lord's own sufficiency in the face of the inadequacy of all other resources (6:7; cf. 2:3; 4:11; 5:7). Jesus did not hesitate to bless natural means as far as they went. He consecrates the five loaves and two fishes with thanks. Miraculously, more than enough food appears for all the hungry whom Jesus commissions the twelve disciples to supply (6:11). The multitudes readily infer that Jesus is "that prophet that should come into the world" (v. 14; cf. 1:21). But more significantly, the sign unveils Him as "that bread of life" (v. 48) that forever satisfies the soul's spiritual hunger, the bread symbolized in Moses' day by the manna (vv. 31–35).

The throngs saw in Jesus simply the meeting of their physical needs, and plotted, accordingly, to make Him king of an immediately re-established earthly kingdom. Jesus therefore withdrew alone to the privacy of the mountains (6:15). Whispering only of a new prophet (v. 14) and king (v. 15) in their midst, the multitudes miss Jesus' priestly significance completely, and hence fail to understand His entire mission. Later, on the other side of the Sea of Galilee, the people hear that to receive life fit for eternity offered by the Son of Man (vv. 26, 27), they must comprehend Jesus' miracles spiritually. To eat the bread of which He speaks is to believe on Jesus Christ Himself (6:29, 35, 36, 47, 53–58). This bread is a divine provision, is "sent" (v. 29) "from heaven" (vv. 31, 32, 50), is "he which cometh down from heaven" (v. 33; cf. v. 41).

The Sixth Sign: Walking on the Water (6:16–21). The sign to the multitudes is accompanied by an equally dramatic sign to the disciples, the Lord's walking on the water. Crossing the Sea of Galilee by night, the disciples were frustrated midway by a violent contrary wind. Jesus appears from nowhere, as it were, walking on the sea. When the disciples receive Him into the ship, they reach their destination swiftly. Whether the Gospel intends an additional miracle by the words "and immediately the ship was at the land . . ." (v. 21) is unsure. Some expositors find here only the emphasis that time and space appear short in the company of love; others suggest that in contrast to their long delay, the disciples now completed their journey speedily. If a miracle is intended, it must not be detached from the already disclosed manifestation of Christ's lordship over wind and sea. This is clear from the sign-value of this miracle. If the multiplied loaves speak of the incarnate bread come down from above, the miracle on the sea displays resurrection life, human nature lifted to new spiritual capacities.

The key is in our Lord's emphasis on spiritual life and resurrection, and in intimations of His ascension, concepts which seemingly defy all that we know of nature's operations. In the private conversation with His disciples (6:60–71) Jesus asks: "What and if ye shall see the Son of man ascend up where he was before? It is the spirit that quickeneth; the flesh profiteth nothing: the words that I speak unto you, they are spirit and they are life" (vv. 62, 63). The miracle of walking on the sea has its meaning in the Living Flesh, as does the miracle of the multiplied loaves in the Living Bread. This word *living* bears great significance: it speaks of an incarnate, ascended Redeemer who lifts to a spiritual destiny in eternity all who put their trust in Him (cf. 4:14). This eternal world where Christ must also be encountered as Lord gains increasing consideration in John's Gospel. In fact, this is the theme, already intimated through the multiplied bread and the walking the waves, which underlies the last of the eight great signs, namely, the raising of Lazarus. A connection is maintained between feeding on Christ and the resurrection (6:54). Even the uneaten fragments are carefully preserved (v. 13). Whoever partakes is assured not only of eternal life but of a resurrection fit for eternity (vv. 39, 40).

The professed followers of Jesus recognize more and more that belief in Christ involves decision of an ultimate character. Some find His teaching offensive (6:60), many fall away (v. 66), and apostasy is present even in the circle of the twelve disciples (v. 71). The confidence of true followers, however, is voiced by Simon Peter; Jesus of Nazareth is God come in the flesh and speaks the words of eternal life (v. 69). Provoked by His claim to deity (cf. 5:18; 8:58; 10:30), determination to kill Jesus grows among unbelieving Jews (7:1). Unbelief strikes even among His own brethren (7:3–5).

The Messiah's visit to the temple for the Feast of Tabernacles (7: 1–52) precedes the great discourses on Christ, the Light of the World, and on Christ, the fount of freedom. The lengthy treatment of Jesus' activity at the feast indicates the growing importance of His ministry in the temple at feast-time, and prepares the way for the final fulfilment of the Hebrew Passover in the Lord's Passion. The Gospel records the murmuring of Jesus' brethren when the feast was "at hand" (v. 2), and His insistence that His time had "not yet fully come" (vv. 6, 8). Jesus attends "not openly, but as it were in secret" (v. 10).

Even so, He was the object of a manhunt by Jews—was Nicodemus perchance among them?—who debated whether He was a deceiver or a good man (7:12). Since either verdict is objectionable, Jesus—teaching openly in the temple "about the midst of the feast" (v. 14)—renews the debate over His divinity (vv. 16–18; cf. 5:19–47) that began after the Sabbath healing at the pool of Bethesda. He now reminds the Jews that Hebrew law did not exclude circumcision on the Sabbath (cf. Lev. 12:3, the eighth day), that by making a man "every whit whole" He fulfilled the Sabbath's intention to further the ultimate good of man (7:23).

The unbelieving Jews' rejection of His authority and Messiahship then centers in the fact of His coming into their midst from Bethlehem and Nazareth (7:27) and not by some sudden supernatural appearance. This turn of affairs provokes Jesus' exclamation (a moment of unforgettable solemnity that John records decades later) that they know full well Who and whence He is (vv. 28, 29). While many of the people are disposed in His favor (v. 31), the Pharisees and chief priests seek His arrest (v. 32). Jesus asserts cryptically that His crucifixion will mean their separation from God, but His restoration to the Father (vv. 33–36).

On the last and great day of the feast, Jesus "stood and cried, saying, If any man thirst, let him come unto me, and drink. He that believeth on me, as the scripture hath said, out of his belly shall flow rivers of living water" (7:37, 38). In this promise of the gift of the Holy Spirit, fulfilled at Pentecost (v. 39; cf. 1:33), Jesus applies to Himself the Mosaic account of the water from the rock (Deut. 8:15) just as previously He had interpreted the manna. The people however, are divided among themselves, and through ignorance concerning His birth some seek to disqualify Him by reference to the prophets (7:40–44). The arresting officers return empty-handed, however. Nicodemus reminds the angered Pharisees that Hebrew law establishes guilt only after a hearing and trial of the accused (vv. 48–53). Their reply, that no prophet arises in Galilee, discloses ignorance both of the prophets (cf. Jonah) and of their own law. It reveals, likewise, a growing determination to kill Jesus.

As Bible students are aware, just before the discourses in the temple, the King James Version includes the story of the woman taken in adultery (7:53—8:11). (The Revised Standard Version excludes this account from the main text because most ancient authorities either omit the passage, or insert it—with textual variations—at this point, or at the end of John's Gospel, or after Luke 21:38. While the passage bears all the marks of reliable tradition, the present manuscript support for its inclusion is weak.) Although Jesus overrules the Old Testament punishment of adultery by stoning, He does not minimize the woman's physical transgression ("do not sin again," 8:11). He considers more serious the spiritual sins of the scribes and Pharisees ("Let him who is without sin . . . cast the first stone," v. 7). As the sinless one, He himself determines the judgment, and forgives rather that condemns (v. 11).

Jesus' proclamation of Himself as the Light of the World and as the fount of freedom constitutes His most extended statement to the Jews (8:12–59). The former discourse is spoken in the treasury (v. 20), presumably with the brilliant temple candelabra in the background. The exposition turns in part on the meaning of the Feast of Tabernacles which commemorates the divine cloud by day and the pillar of fire by night of the wilderness journey: "I am the light of the world: he that followeth me shall not walk in darkness, but shall have the light of life" (v. 12). In the ensuing controversy, Jesus speaks even more bluntly about the Jews' unbelief. In view of the resurrection to follow, Jesus alludes to His coming crucifixion as a decisive answer to whether or not He was in rivalry with the Father (vv. 28, 29).

Christ, presented as the fount of freedom (8:31–59), continues the remarks made at the feast. This discourse, however, is to the Jews who believed His claim (vv. 30, 31). It teaches that loyalty to the Son of God preserves men from tyranny, particularly from the tyranny of sin (v. 36). When the Jews claim freedom from bondage through their physical descent from Abraham, Jesus stresses that anyone who practices sin is enslaved. Since spiritual kinship to Abraham requires a similarity of character (vv. 33–43), their intention to murder Jesus marks them as the children not of Abraham, but of Satan (v. 44). Thereupon the Jews charge Jesus with demon-possession (vv. 48–52). The break is now open and complete, the Jews' unbelief cold and crude. In the temple itself, they take up stones in an unsuccessful attempt to kill Jesus (vv. 56–59).

The Seventh Sign: Healing of the Man Born Blind (9:1–41). As already indicated, John records the signs not merely to manifest recurring works of power; he uses them as a commentary on Jesus Himself, whose presence and ministry during the feast days become increasingly important in the Gospel. The signs (revelation in act), furthermore, support His authoritative teaching (revelation in word). Belief in the Messiah rests on the authority of His word (4:50); this word remains valid even apart from the signs (13:19; 14:29). The healing of the man born blind (9:1–41) underscores the significance of the revealed word and relates specifically to Jesus' previous discourse ("As long as I am in the world, I am the light of the world. When he had thus spoken . . ." 9:5, 6). The blind man's predicament indicated no special wickedness on his or his parents' part; rather it provides a providential occasion to manifest the Messiah in deed as well as in word (vv. 2, 3). The Messiah must work "the works of him that sent me" (v. 4) and once again on the Sabbath day (v. 14).

The dramatic healing occurs by obediently washing in the pool of Siloam, meaning Sent (9:7, 11). Noting only the broken Sabbath, unbelieving Jews accuse Jesus of being a sinner (v. 16), and in keeping with previous decisions concerning any who confess Jesus as Christ (v. 22), expel the healed man from the synagogue (v. 34). The blind man grows in comprehension: first, "a man . . . called Jesus" (v. 11); then, "a prophet" (v. 17), possibly free from sin (vv. 25, 31); one worthy of disciples (vv. 27, 28); on speaking terms with God (v. 31); "from God" (v. 33). Jesus raises the confession even higher to belief in Himself as the Son of Man (RSV 9:35; many ancient manuscripts read "Son of God", cf. KJV), whereupon the healed man worships Him (v. 38).

The healing manifests more than Christ the Messiah; it portrays also the predicament of the Jews' unbelief. The phrases "blind from birth" (9:1) and "born blind" (vv. 2, 19, 20, 32) have cumulative force. To this reference to blindness, the Pharisees themselves unwittingly are the key. Their dismissal of the healed man not simply as born blind, but as "altogether born in sins" (v. 34) prompts Jesus' emphasis that hostility to the true light means Judaism's permanent blindness (v. 39). Indeed, the absence of a sense of need already betrays that permanent blindness (v. 41).

Failure of the Jews to understand Jesus' parable of the good shepherd (10:1–18) likewise verifies their lack of discernment (10:6). He discredits the Pharisees as reliable guides (vv. 1, 8, 10, 12, 13). He himself is the authentic shepherd (vv. 2–5, 7, 9, 11, 14, 15). The true shepherd's willingness to die for his sheep (v. 11), and to do so voluntarily (vv. 15, 17, 18), emphasizes the Messiah's world mission (v. 16). The parable relates His death to a specific divine purpose that also includes His triumph over death (vv. 17, 18). Confused even more by these claims (v. 19), His listeners argue as to whether or not Jesus is demon-possessed (vv. 19–21).

The Messiah now goes to Jerusalem for the feast of dedication (10:22–43). People still doubt His authority (v. 24) despite His works (v. 25). Their continuing unbelief promises only doom (v. 26). His own sheep, on the other hand, brought within the orbit of the Father's protection (vv. 27–29), are forever secure (cf. 6:39, 54). Jesus' assertion of unique unity with the Father (10:30) incites the Jews to another attempt to stone him (vv. 31, 32) for blasphemy (v. 33). Jesus' reference to the Old Testament magistrates as "gods" (Ps. 82:6) is really no evasion of His own unique claim. Rather, He reminds the Jews that, since the Old Testament (its authority unbreakable) designated as "gods" even men *"to whom* the word of God *came,"* no basis exists to charge with blasphemy the Son of God "whom the Father consecrated and *sent into the world"* (and Who defines "the word of God." 10:36). If they still disbelieve His words (note the implied superiority of faith resting in the authority of His word), Jesus invites their belief for His works' sake. Another attempt on His life follows His claim that "the Father is in me, and I in him" (v. 38), a claim that will soon have larger significance (cf. 14:20). Darkness and the prospect of death shadow His witness that He is the light as well as the life of men. Jesus retreats to the Jordan where John the Baptist first identified Him as Messiah (vv. 40, 41). There many believe (v. 42).

The Eighth Sign: Raising Lazarus (11:1–47). The eighth and final sign, the raising of Lazarus, crowns the Messiah's ministry of miracles. It furnishes supreme evidence that Jesus is "the resurrection and the life" (v. 25), that His power extends beyond death. Men's souls can never escape His command; like Lazarus, every man is within Jesus' reach. To trust Christ gives an abiding recognition of the true shepherd's voice (vv. 25, 26, 43). The fellowship that Lazarus knew with Jesus in Bethany (11:1–5) held prospect of resumption in eternity (cf. 14:2, 3). Martha indeed had clung to the doctrine (accepted by the Pharisees as against the Sadducees) of the future resurrection of the dead (11:24), had even acknowledged Jesus as the promised Messiah and Son of God (v. 27). Mary likewise worshipped Him as Lord (v. 32). Both sisters suggest, however, that death even for the believer is a tragedy over which Jesus Himself has no power (vv. 32, 39). Nevertheless, the raising of Lazarus represents the believers' restoration to fellowship with Christ beyond the grave and demonstrates the relationship of regeneration to resurrection unto eternal life without judgment (5:24, 29).

In Bethany, therefore, Jesus gives a momentous sign of His lordship over death (11:43–45). He Himself for three days and three nights will taste death, yet without corruption, for He is greater than Lazarus. Indeed, Lazarus is a commentary on Jesus Who, in His forthcoming death, resurrection, and ascension, is supremely God's sign of God's Kingdom among men.

After the raising of Lazarus, the shadow of death clings more frequently to Jesus' name and ministry. While many believe on Him, others inform the Pharisees concerning Him (11:46). Together the chief priests and Pharisees plot His destruction (v. 47). Caiaphas unwittingly reflects their blindness by asserting the expediency of Christ's death to spare the nation (vv. 51, 52). Jesus retreats to the wilderness country near Jordan and, with His disciples (v. 54), awaits the Passover when the religious leaders plan to capture Him (vv. 55–57).

The scenes that follow preface our Lord's Passion. Anointing in Bethany by Mary, with Lazarus and Martha present (12:1, 2), precedes His entrance into Jerusalem. Despite Judas' protests over the "waste" of the costly ointment (vv. 4–6), Jesus vindicates the act as one of devotion. At the same time it betokens embalming, a timely significance in view of His approaching death (vv. 7, 8). Besides Jesus, the Jews' hostility now includes Lazarus, who is marked for death because his restoration to life has attracted wide confidence in Jesus' claim (12:9–11).

5. The Climactic Passion Week (12:12—19:42)

Triumphal Entry (12:12–19). Jesus' Sunday entrance into Jerusalem inaugurates the events of Passion Week, the climax of John's Gospel. Jesus comes in meekness rather than in majesty, doubtless in protest to erroneous expectations of an earthly ruler. Even the disciples, however, fail to recognize His arrival as entry upon the way to the cross (v. 16) and with the throngs hail Him as king (v. 13).

The Gentiles Seek for Jesus (12:20–36). The Gentiles at the feast are important to His mission. As any discerning reader of the Old Testament knows, seeking of the Messiah by the Gentiles presupposes two developments: the Jews' complete rejection (hence the crucifixion) of Jesus, and instead of the Jews, the response of the Gentiles. When therefore His disciples announce the approach of the Gentiles, Jesus forsakes earlier assertions that His hour had not yet fully come and proclaims: "The hour is come that the Son of man should be glorified" (v. 23; cf. 12:35; 13:1, 31; 14:31, and so on). Life through death becomes His theme (12:24–26). His own death is more than an example, however, since it bears upon the sinner's redemption (v. 27). He will be crucified, but because of the universal significance of His death (vv. 32, 33), He will draw even the Gentiles to Him. This lifting up of the Son of Man is the very crisis of human history itself and seals the doom of Satan (v. 31).

The Jews Reject Jesus (12:37–50). The unbelief of the Jews remains, however, and fulfilled is Isaiah's prophecy that their stubborn unbelief invites the penalty of blindness. Many of the chief rulers believe, however (cf. 3:1), but lack courage to confess (12:42, 43). Jesus reiterates that faith in God and faith in Himself are one and the same act; likewise, rejection of Him is a simultaneous rejection of the Father (12:44–50).

Passover and the Lord's Supper (13:1–30). His imminent death marks Jesus' return to the eternal order from which He came into the world (vv. 1, 3). Bearing human nature on high, He will inaugurate new but undefined relationships with His disciples on earth. The occasion of washing the disciples' feet (vv. 2–16) introduces the distinction between Jesus' present and impending future relationship to His followers ("What I do thou knowest not *now;* but thou shalt know *hereafter,*" v. 7) and gives instruction in Christian service and humility (vv. 12–17). Christ is the pattern as well as the Redeemer of life; His disciples are to be sent into the world to fulfil the mission He has inaugurated (v. 20). Thus the meaning of *sent* is enlarged, and the concept of "apostle" (a sent one) comes into view.

When Peter startles at the Messiah's approach to him with towel and basin (13:5, 6), Jesus emphasizes the necessity of both once-for-all regeneration and the daily experience of sanctification ("If I wash thee not, thou hast no part with me," v. 8; "He that is washed needeth not save to wash his feet," v. 10).

The footwashing (nowhere in the New Testament regarded as an ordinance enjoined for perpetual observance) also calls attention to Judas' deceit (13:10, 11; cf. 12:4–6). But Jesus explains His inclusion of Judas in the twelve in view of the prophecy of Psalm 41:9 (13:18). He now speaks openly of the coming betrayal (13:21). He makes one last high appeal to Judas (v. 26) who responds with an unchangeable, final decision (vv. 27–30). The events of this chapter precede the Passover Feast (vv. 1, 29), but usually the private gathering of Jesus and the disciples is considered the occasion of instituting the Lord's Supper recorded in the other Gospels.

Discourses in Parting (13:31—16:33). Marked tenderness now colors Jesus' words to the closed company of His true disciples. They are about to be bereaved (13:33) and they will be tempted to consider themselves orphans (cf. 14:1, 18). Instead, however, the ties of mutual love will be deepened (13:34, 35). The only one aware that Jesus speaks of His imminent death (vv. 31, 32) is Peter who volunteers for martyrdom (v. 37). Jesus foretells his denial (v. 38), which occurs at Peter's next appearance in this Gospel (18:10–18).

Jesus' now defines a new coming relationship with His followers (note the contrast between *now* and *afterwards*, 13:36). Likewise, He exhorts them to express His love (13:34, 35) as He had expressed the Father's love for them. Until His betrayal and arrest, the Gospel therefore focuses attention on Jesus' parting discourses to His disciples (14:1—16:33), and on His prayer of intercession (17:1–26).

The disciples now sense, even if obscurely, that Jesus is to be separated from them; they will be left in a hostile world (14:1; cf. v. 27). Succinctly stated, the answer to their troubled hearts is faith in the living God who has revealed Himself in Jesus Christ (14:1), the only way to the Father (vv. 4–7). The words and works of Jesus are the Father's words and works (vv. 9, 10); they are adequate evidence that "I am in the Father and the Father in me" (v. 11).

Jesus elaborates the remarkable legacy He bequeaths to His disciples. His physical absence will be no disadvantage, but will actually fulfil a specific plan (cf. "because I go unto my Father," 14:12, 28). His assurances provide: *(1)* the prospect of a blessed immortality involving personal reunion with Him in abiding-places He is preparing for them (vv. 2, 3); *(2)* a specific task of evangelism and missions whose success will exceed even His own (v. 12); *(3)* experience of the power of prayer in His name, through which He will continue to work in their midst (vv. 13, 14); *(4)* the gift of the Holy Spirit to indwell them permanently (vv. 16, 17); *(5)* the comfort of His resurrection appearances to them (vv. 18, 19); *(6)* the Holy Spirit's quickening of His words to preserve their vitality despite His absence (v. 25, 26); *(7)* the peace which Jesus Himself experienced on the way to Calvary (v. 27). The discourses that follow elaborate the Spirit's future teaching ministry (16:13), the fulfilment of which the Church historically identified with the inspired New Testament writings. These assurances conclude Jesus' private discourses with His disciples (v. 33).

His instructions anticipate a decisive transition in relationship with His followers. It is this transition which carries the message of the Fourth Gospel beyond that of the earlier Gospels, and foresees Pentecost in the Acts of the Apostles, where the Risen Christ participates in the life of His radiant Church. This transition rests in a strategic development of the terms "abiding" and "abiding place." The abiding place of the Logos is in eternity in abiding fellowship with the Father (1:1, 2; 17:5). Divine redemptive love moved Him to this earth (3:13, 17), however, to "tabernacle" or to abide in human nature (1:14), to indwell those He is to redeem, those for whom He will prepare abiding places in heaven (14:2).

Christ's follower's are not to yearn for those heavenly mansions, however, because of spiritual emptiness and frustration in this life. John's Gospel moves beyond the work accomplished in history by Jesus of Nazareth *for* sinners to an anticipated work *in* their lives by the Risen Christ. Long before reunion in a blessed future immortality, believers are to be linked with Him in an intimate spiritual union. This union already lifts them above divine judgment to present participation in a life fit and pledged for eternity (5:24). In His post-resurrection physical absence, He is spiritually present in the lives of His followers, hearing and even energizing their prayers (14:13–15). The believer's union with Him, in fact, will be no less vital than that between the Father and the incarnate Son: "In that day you will know that I am in my Father, and you in me, and I in you" (v. 20). "Abide in me, and I in you . . . apart from me ye can do nothing" (15:4, 5). But precisely this union with Christ will bring persecution to the disciples, because this relationship is foreign to fallen mankind (15:21; 16:1–3). As the climax of Jesus' life and death, His ascension to the Father will vindicate His righteousness and represent a great moral triumph. Indeed, it is the prerequisite for sending the Holy Spirit by whose dynamic enablement the disciples will triumph. The coming of the Spirit will inaugurate the new epoch in which Christ will be glorified in their hearts and lives (16:13, 14).

Chapters 15 and 16 are really not one unified discourse, for they develop many themes. After His resurrection, however, Jesus integrates these pre-crucifixion instructions with the words: "Receive ye the Holy Ghost" (20:22). Our Lord's transition from the ministry of teaching to that of prayer (cf. Heb. 7:25) comes in chapter 17:1–26. Christ had previously intimated a new prayer relationship that the disciples themselves would practice (14:13; 16:26). Now He provides them also with the memory of this great intercessory prayer.

It is Jesus' most specific statement on unity, one far different from some modern pleas for ecclesiastical unity in disregard of apostolic beliefs (17:20,21). In this prayer throb the great facts of the unity of the Son and the disciples with the Father; of the unity of future believers with the disciples and apostles; and beyond this, of the unity of all future believers. Unity in love is to persuade the world that Jesus is sent by the Father (vv. 21,23,25). Yet Jesus balances this emphasis on God's love with corresponding emphasis on God's righteousness ("Holy Father," v. 11; "O righteous Father," v. 25). Unity (vv. 11, 21, 23, 26), truth (vv. 8, 14, 17, 19, 20), righteousness (vv. 11, 25), and love (vv. 23, 24, 26) all resound in this high-priestly prayer.

Betrayal and Arrest in the Garden of Gethsemane (18:1–12). The betrayal and arrest introduce the beginning of the end. As the "I am" reveals His identity (vv. 5, 6, 8), those who come to seize Jesus are momentarily repulsed. Jesus then surrenders Himself to His captors. Then Peter, rebuked for resorting to force (v. 11), soon stands with the arresting officers in denial (18:18), just as Judas had stood in betrayal of the Lord (v. 5). The irregularities of Jesus' arrest, preliminary hearing and trial are obvious in the narrative. Most prominent, however, is the real reason for the Jews' insistence on His crucifixion, namely, Jesus' claim to be the Son of God (19:7). Jesus reminds Pilate that, as one who bears authority under God (v. 11), it is he who stands at the bar of judgment. Jesus claims kingship, but not of an earthly empire (18:36, 37). When charged by Jesus' enemies with tolerating sedition (19:12), the Roman governor yields to the pressures of the mob (vv. 13–16) and delivers Jesus to be crucified. Pilate's superscription on the cross, Jesus of Nazareth the King of the Jews (vv. 19, 21, 22), offends the chief priests. Its trilingual wording (Hebrew, Greek, Latin) actually declares that Christ's universal mission included the Gentiles also (v. 20).

Crucifixion and Burial (19:16–42). During His suffering on the cross, a highly symbolic development occurs: the establishment of *a new family on the basis of redemption.* Deeper than the blood of human ties runs the blood of unity in the cross. Jesus commends John to Mary: "Woman, behold thy son" (19:26), and Mary He commends to John: "Behold thy mother" (19:26). Moment by moment prophetic Scriptures are fulfilled on the cross (vv. 24, 28, 36, 37). The last cry, "It is finished" (v. 30), comes from Jesus' lips as He partakes of voluntary death (v. 33). The "finished work" of Jesus (cf. 5:36) has become a victorious reality. Pilate's relinquishing of the body of Jesus to Joseph of Arimathea (19:38) is the last time Jesus' body is subject to any earthly ruler. Drawn from secret into open devotion by the cross (v. 40), Joseph, together with Nicodemus, prepares the body for burial.

6. The Risen Lord and His Redeemed Family (20:1—21:25)

The Empty Tomb (20:1–18). Tidings of resurrection (vv. 1–8) break upon the first day of the week, and the swift-moving historical events outpace the disciples' comprehension of related Scripture (19:9; cf. I Cor. 15:4). While the resurrection appearances serve to show Jesus Christ alive after His Passion (20:11—21:23), they also supplement His teaching ministry (cf. Acts 1:3). To Mary Magdalene, who first supposed Him to be the gardener, Jesus reiterates the necessarily new relationship that the resurrection and ascension establish between Him and His disciples (20:17).

Other Resurrection Appearances (20:19—21:2). To the disciples cringing behind locked doors in fear of the Jews, He comes with the assurance of peace (cf. 14:27). He shows them His pierced hands and side, reminds them they are to carry forward His mission of redemption, and in a preliminary way endows them with the Holy Spirit (20:19–23). Permitted a reassuring touch ("reach hither thy finger . . . and reach hither thy hand," v. 27), even unbelieving Thomas acknowledges his resurrected Lord and God. In the era inaugurated by Christ's resurrection and exaltation, however, a new basis of faith is necessary: "Blessed are they that have not seen, and yet have believed" (21:29).

Instructions to His Disciples (21:3–23). The Christian churches owe their fullest glimpse of the Risen Lord's ministry between the resurrection and ascension to the closing pages of John's Gospel. The last chapter especially illumines those intriguing days, and indicates how, while bequeathing to His followers a lively expectation of His return (cf. "till I come," 21:22, 23), Jesus challenges them with their responsibility to evangelize a lost world and to cull out a fellowship of redemptive love. In the familiar pattern of miracle and discourse that reappears in this chapter, the draught of fishes caught by obedience to the Risen Lord, rather than by self-assertion, may suggest the cosmopolitan and universal nature of the Church (the number 153 is assertedly the number of species of fish in the Sea of Galilee; cf. v. 11). The feast in the narrative is one to which the Risen Lord gathers His followers (v. 12). He feeds the disciples, but they in turn are to feed His sheep (vv. 13, 15–17). Both for the Lord and for the redeemed, a life of love and devotion enters into soul-winning. Christ's final communication, therefore, concerns not only the universality of His Church, but its spirit as well. The spirit of service is to be that of loving the Lord Himself. It does not involve for everyone the predicted martyrdom of Peter in his old age (vv. 18,19). For all authentic disciples, however, it does involve the daily self-crucifixion of abiding in His will and of following in His steps (v. 22).

Acts

JOHN H. GERSTNER

THE GREAT THEME of the Acts of the Apostles is the coming of Christian power and its demonstration in the building of the Church. How Christ's great commission begins to be realized through the action of the Holy Spirit in the dedicated lives of the apostles and the enthusiasm of their converts is the dramatic history Luke, inspired by the Holy Spirit, gives us in this letter to Theophilus.

The book is a special history of the extension of the Church, to the Jews first and then to the Gentiles, as centers of faith are established at strategic points in the Roman Empire. Luke so arranges the historical material that the progress of the Gospel is immediately evident. The Book of the Acts is distinctly a schematic history designed to edify no less than to narrate. We may therefore view the Acts as a historical sermon on Christian power, its source and its effects.

In speaking of the "former treatise," Luke is not referring to a distinct work, but views his Gospel as "a first installment" of the narrative that is continued in the present book (1:1). Thus the unity of "Luke-Acts" is intimated in the very opening words of this second part of the one volume. This intimation is so fully substantiated in its pages that the common authorship of these two works is one of the most generally accepted critical opinions.

Common authorship is further suggested by the name of the person to whom Acts is written. Who Theophilus was is not certain, but the name is identical with the person to whom Luke's Gospel is written. It has been conjectured that this "excellent" person is some Christian of rank, perhaps Flavius Clemens.

Whether the announced content of the book, "all Jesus *began* both to do and teach," further stresses the continuity of Luke-Acts is a moot question (1:1). Certainly from the English version, we would judge that the author is implying that Luke was a record of what Jesus *began* to do and teach while Acts was the record of what Jesus *continued* to do and teach.

In the third verse, stress is placed on *how* Christ appeared, rather than on *why* He appeared or *what* He said. "He showed himself alive," that is, manifested Himself clearly so that they saw Him living and fully recognized Him. Emphasis is on the objective factuality (as if to anticipate future skeptics who would account for the resurrection story in terms of wishful thinking). Luke says that faith in the resurrection rests not on *fallible* hopes but on *infallible* proofs; not on pious expectations but on demonstrative evidence. Plato and Aristotle employ the same Greek word to denote "the strongest proof of which a subject is susceptible." Probably no fact in the Lord's life was more clearly attested than His resurrection. The record makes clear that not only by night but by day, not only one person but many, not only women but men, not only separately but together, the followers of Christ saw Him, talked with Him, touched Him, and listened to Him. This experience gave them certainty of the resurrection and instilled in the early Church its great message, "He is risen!"

But still there is a difference in the way Jesus "was seen of them" before the resurrection and after it. The words "was seen" here intimate the evanescent character of Christ's appearance. We know from the Gospels that He appeared and disappeared with equal suddenness and that His presence, though recognizable, was altered. The fleeting quality of His appearances made it clear to His disciples that this was a period of transition. Though He was no longer with them continually as He had been, neither had He left them completely as He was about to do.

I. Waiting for Christian Power (1:1–26)

After ordering them to remain where they were, in Jerusalem, Christ proceeds to explain the necessity for His strict command (1:4). Christ has absolute authority over His subjects and need never give reasons for His directions, but, in sweet condescension, He does so, even adding the consoling fact that they would not have to wait many days. The reason for His order is disclosed in the fact that they were about to be baptized with the Holy Spirit, a baptism different from the water baptism of John the Baptist (v. 5).

What is this baptism with the Holy Spirit? Obviously, the reference is not to the regenerating work of the Holy Spirit, for that gift had already been given. Christ explicitly said to Nicodemus that "except a man be born of water and of the Spirit, he cannot enter into the kingdom of God" (Jn. 3:5); that is, that water baptism lacks value apart from Spirit baptism, or regeneration. The Old Testament had long made it clear that a new heart and a heart of flesh, which God alone could give, would bring a person to God. The disciples, to whom Christ said, "You shall be baptized with the Holy Spirit," had already been regenerated by the Spirit; what, therefore, was this baptism of the Holy Spirit? In the Acts, the baptism by the Holy Spirit seems to be a provision of the Holy Spirit by which the recipient receives the supernatural power necessary for initiating the world expansion of the faith (1:5; 2:4, 17; 8:17–19; 9:31; 10:38, 44, 45; 11:15, 16, 28; 13:2, 4; 19:2, 6).

The apostles could not conceivably have known what Christ meant by the imminent baptism with the Holy Spirit, for they did not, at that point, know as we do what lay ahead of them. They did, however, sense rightly that the announcement was momentous and that something epochal was about to happen. Thinking of the Messiah Who was saying this, and the one really big thing in their expectations, the restoration of Israel, they put two and two together (1:6) and asked "Lord, will you at this time restore the kingdom to Israel?" Christ neither denied their conception nor confirmed it. Since their question, after all, dealt with the time element, "at this time," Christ ruled their query as out of order. In the spirit of Calvin's remark that hell was made for the overly curious, He rebuked them: "It is not for you to know times or seasons which the Father has fixed by his own authority" (v. 7).

Like the great teacher He was, our Lord, having told His disciples what not to ask—questions about times and seasons—proceeded then to fill the vacuum with positive directives: "But you shall receive power when the Holy Spirit has come upon you; and you shall be my witnesses in Jerusalem and in all Judea and Samaria and to the end of the earth" (1:8). The apostles, who had expected to be rulers in the Kingdom about to be restored, are appointed to be witnesses. Not the power to dominate others, but the power to win them for Christ is to be theirs. Earthly power could make kings; only heavenly power could produce witnesses. Thirteen times, in this book, the word "witness" is used.

Verse 8, the key text for the Book of Acts, outlines the early witnesses' theater of operations. They were to witness first in Jerusalem (2:14—8:3), next in all Judea (9:32—11:18), then in Samaria

(8:4–40) and finally, unto the end of the earth (11:19—28:31). It might be well here to point out that *"unto* does not fully represent the Greek preposition *(heōs)*, which can only be expressed in English by such strengthened forms as *out to, even to, as far as,* all suggesting the idea of great distance."

While He was speaking, Christ was taken up and a cloud received Him out of their sight before their gazing and incredulous eyes. They could not turn their eyes away, as the conviction came that their Lord was leaving them for a long, long time. As the bereaved disciples watched, two men (were they Moses and Elijah, who having earlier spoken of His departure were now present to behold it?) chided their inactivity while graciously assuring them that He would some day return again "in the same way" (1:11). Many agree with Dwight L. Moody that the phrase means that Christ's return will therefore be personal, visible and in the clouds.

In willing obedience to their Lord, these early Christians returned at once to the upper room to await the baptism with fire (1:13). Among the 120 charter members of the Christian Church, the brethren of Jesus are conspicuous by their presence; Judas Iscariot is conspicuous by his absence. The other children of Mary who doubted their brother during His life were persuaded to believe in His Messiahship after His death and resurrection. Like Thomas, they were prepared now to acknowledge Him as their Lord and their God. Reflecting upon this in the light of Jesus' stretching out His hand toward His disciples and saying: "Here are my mother and my brothers! For whosoever does the will of my Father in heaven is my brother, and sister, and mother" (Mt. 12:48, 49), we realize now that in recognizing Jesus as more than a brother, they really became His brethren.

In relating Judas' betrayal, Peter (1:16–20), in the spirit of "there but for the grace of God, go I," refrains from any personal censure, and merely gives the facts of Judas' treachery and dreadful end. The description of his death, however, differs from the account in Matthew (Mt. 27:3–10). Some find irreconcilable discrepancies in the two accounts, as if Judas were destined to cause tragedy in death no less than in life—to destroy the written Word as he had sought to destroy the incarnate Word. He is, however, no more successful in the former than in the latter. The salient points are not in question, and where there appear to be areas of difference, these may be brought about by our imperfect knowledge of the entire matter. That Judas committed suicide, that a field was purchased with thirty pieces of silver, and that it was known thereafter as the field of blood are the certain, grim facts of the tragedy.

The account of Judas' betrayal and end is preliminary to choosing another "to be a witness with us of his resurrection." The decision is that the successor shall be chosen by lot. The lot falls upon Matthias who thereupon becomes an apostle (1:23–26).

II. The Coming of Christian Power (2:1–47)

1. The Source of Christian Power: The Holy Spirit (2:1–13)

The founding miracle of Christianity was the great outpouring of the Holy Spirit. Some one has truly said, "That the system of the world is, proves there was once a miracle; that the Church of Christ is, proves that it was established by a miracle." This miracle took place at Pentecost, the celebration of the Feast of Weeks, (cf. Lev. 23:15–22). Tradition has it that the giving of the law also took place at Pentecost. As Christ fulfilled the Passover by becoming the paschal lamb, so now the ancient giving of the Sinaitic law at Pentecost was fulfilled by inscribing it on the hearts of all those to whom the Holy Spirit came (cf. Jer. 31:31–35).

Thus, as the disciples waited in Jerusalem, according to the Lord's command, they were baptized with the Holy Spirit (2:2, 3). A rushing wind was heard, tongues descended, and one rested on each of them and all began to speak. On the day of Pentecost, people from the entire Dispersion scattered all around the Mediterranean area were present. To these different language-speaking groups the Christians began to speak. In one such group, standing near Thomas perhaps, several different native dialects were spoken, none of which Thomas knew. But as he spoke, some of these people realized that he was speaking in their language even though he had never learned it. Those who understood Thomas were amazed to hear him speaking in their own languages; others in the group may have thought he was speaking some kind of gibberish. Meanwhile, Philip was speaking in another area, and the same thing was happening. Some understood him speaking in their own language; others thought he was mad or drunk (2:4–13).

That which Pentecost prophetically symbolized has been fulfilled in our era. At the beginning of the nineteenth century the Word of God had been translated into some seventy languages; today it has found its way into well over a thousand. Witnesses now speak the wonderful things of God, so that almost every man on the face of the earth can hear the message in his own tongue. Pentecost was the reverse of Babel with its confusion of tongues, an intensification of the original Pentecost. No one has put it more brilliantly than Moody: "When God set forth His fiery Law (Deut. 33:2) He proclaimed it in one tongue, but the story of grace was told in the language of every nation under heaven."

2. *Pentecostal Witness to the Dispersion (2:14–47)*

The sermon which Peter delivered to the Dispersion Jews and the consequences that followed upon it run the gamut of Christian truth:

1. In Peter's quoting Joel 2:28–32, the Church takes its stand on the Old Testament. The Christian apologetic is rooted in prophecy, a fact illustrated by the quotation from Joel, which is now fulfilled in the events at Pentecost and in the miracles of Christ (2:16–21).
2. A new and final era, characterized by the outpouring of the Holy Spirit, is recognized (vv. 17, 18).
3. By typical prophetic foreshortening, the present and the future are viewed together—the visitation of divine grace occurring at Pentecost and the signs of the end of the age (vv. 19, 20).
4. The great theme of Peter's address, "Jesus is Lord and Christ," is vividly stressed as Peter presents Jesus of Nazareth as one approved of God, Whose "miracles, wonders and signs" attest His deity. As Suffering Servant, Risen Lord, David's Royal Son, Peter presents Him as both Lord and Christ (vv. 22–31).
5. Predestination in its most extreme and most sublime form— the crucifixion of Christ—is linked at once with free will and man's inescapable responsibility (v. 23).
6. The atonement is implied in the deliverance by God (v. 24) of His Son, and its great corollary, the remission of sin, is explicitly announced (v. 38).
7. The total depravity of man is implied in the fact that Christ, "attested by God," is crucified by "lawless men" (vv. 22, 23; cf. v. 40).

8. The doctrine of repentance is succinctly stated (v. 38).
9. Baptism in the name of Jesus Christ is enjoined (v. 38).
10. The indwelling Holy Spirit is promised to all believers (v. 38).
11. The inclusiveness of Christianity is stressed as Peter points out that the promise of the Holy Spirit is to you (Jews) and others (Gentiles) who are described as "far off" (v. 39).
12. The covenant relationship, now fulfilled in Christ, is extended to "everyone whom the Lord our God calls to him" (v. 39).

Thereupon follows the living testimony of the truth of the New Covenant. Out of the life and instruction of the Twelve Apostles grew the fellowship of believers. The cardinal points of the way are given (2:42–47):

1. The authority of the apostles is recognized (v. 42).
2. Communion is celebrated (v. 42).
3. Prayers are regularly offered (v. 42).
4. Miracles continue so that the promise of "greater things than I do shall ye do" is being fulfilled.
5. The early Christian community practices sharing of material goods (vv. 44, 45).
6. The joy of the new life finds expression in continued blessing and evangelistic success (vv. 41, 46, 47).

In summary, the sermon inaugurated a new day and produced eight distinct results on the part of those who heard it: conviction, curiosity, obedience, perseverance, fear, unselfishness, worship and growth.

When the people asked what they should do, Peter said: "Repent, and be baptized every one of you in the name of Jesus Christ for the forgiveness of your sins; and you shall receive the gift of the Holy Spirit" (2:38). "Repent" means "change your mind," and this inward change is to be followed by the outward sign, water baptism. This gift of the Holy Spirit could not be the initial one, because it follows repentance, faith and baptism, and these are the result of the initial, regenerating gift of the Holy Spirit. "Except a man be born of the Spirit, he cannot enter into the kingdom of God" (Jn. 3:5). Therefore this reference (2:38) most likely alludes to the special endowment of the Holy Spirit.

Three thousand were added as a result of Peter's address (2:41). We recall the classic observation that "the first time the law was preached three thousand were killed (Ex. 32:28); the first time grace was preached three thousand were saved." Since we are not told to what they were added, we must presume that they were added to the Church, because the subsequent description shows them to be a worshiping community within the larger Jewish community. The early saints are described as devoting themselves "to the apostles' teaching and fellowship . . ." (2:42); older versions state they "persevered" in these things. We are reminded of Christ's words: "If you continue in my word, you are truly my disciples" (Jn. 8:31). A true characteristic of a disciple is his adherence to the truth. I have, said Paul, kept the faith. He numbered heresy among the works of the flesh (Gal. 5: 19, 20). That the Holy Spirit is the conservator of orthodoxy is clear, for where the Spirit of truth is, there will be sound doctrine. Indifference to apostolic doctrine would surely differentiate any group from the apostolic community.

They were also steadfast in fellowship (2:42). Hardly less conspicuous than their love for their risen Lord was their love for each other. They had, in truth, "one body, one faith, one baptism, one hope, one Lord, one God and Father of all" (Eph. 4:5).

Undoubtedly their "breaking of bread" (v. 46) was an expression of this fellowship. The term itself may refer to the eating of ordinary meals; or it may mean the Lord's Supper.

Prayer, likewise, may refer to something more than ordinary prayers. Possibly the Christians were in the habit of observing regular hours of prayer. The canonical hours, which grew out of early Christian tradition, come mainly from the Acts: *tierce,* "For these men are not drunk, as you suppose, since it is only the third hour" (2:15); *sext,* "The next day, as they were on their journey and coming near the city, Peter went up on the housetop, about the sixth hour" (10:9); *none,* "Now Peter and John were going up to the temple at the hour of prayer, the ninth hour" (3:1).

The multitude probably sensed the presence of God in the fellowship of Christians. We are told that those outside the fellowship knew "fear," which may mean awe or terror; probably the two were combined. No doubt the people recognized in the Christians' joy and harmony sure signs of God's presence with them; hence, reverence. They would necessarily be filled with terror at the same time; for these joyous people were believers in the Christ whom Israel had crucified, and if they had the blessing of God, how must God feel toward the crucifiers? The association of the people's feelings with the miracles of the apostles suggests that the Israelites must have felt as Nicodemus: "No one can do these signs that you do, unless God is with him" (Jn. 3:2).

The fellowship of these early Christians extended to everything, for they had all things in common. That they shared their property no less than their faith and love was apparently a spontaneous expression of Christian affection.

This "Christian communism" was totally unlike Marxist communism. It is ironic and tragic that one point of similarity often leads people to overlook the many differences:

(1) The impulse is love, rather than planning.

(2) Sharing grew out of faith in God, rather than a denial of His existence.

(3) It was voluntary, rather than obligatory.

(4) The people who engaged in it were the Church rather than enemies of it.

The continual growth of the Church—"And the Lord added to their number day by day those who were being saved" (2:47)—was a divine work. In many places *today, men* are adding *baptized heathen* to the *roll*. In the *early days,* the *Lord* added to the *Church* those who were being *saved.*

III. Early Days of the Church (3:1—12:25)

1. In Jerusalem (3:1—7:60)

Healing the Lame Man and Consequences (3:1–26). The miracle performed in the name and by the power of Jesus of Nazareth took place at the ninth hour when Peter and John went up to the temple to pray (3:1–11). The apostles had no power of their own and claimed none, in contrast to their Lord Who never hesitated to act in His own name and receive adoration Himself.

The miracle was a convincing one. The people, who through more than forty years (4:22) had seen the lame man at the gate of the temple begging, were filled with wonder and amazement. In an instant the one who had no power of his own rested in faith upon the living Christ and leaped up, stood and walked. Like the man whose blindness Christ had cured, this man's deliverance from lameness showed forth "the works of God" (Jn. 9:2, 3).

This miracle also illustrates God's "*over* answers to prayer." Expecting mere alms, the beggar looked up hopefully; but God gave him above anything he could ask or think. There is a parallel in the account of the woman of Samaria who asked for information about a detail, the location of the proper place of worship. In answer, she was shown the object of worship Himself.

Once the healing of the lame man attracted the attention of Jerusalem, Peter quickly seized the opportunity to preach Christ. As one scholar has pointed out, "The miracle broke up the hard ground, and these faithful watchers were ready to run in and cast the living seed into the open furrow."

The character of Acts as a book of the witnesses is in sight here. Immediately Peter disavowed his own power to perform the miracle. He pointed to Christ. As John the Baptist had said, "He must increase and I must decrease," and as Paul echoed later, "We preach not ourselves but Christ," so Peter says now, "And his name, by faith in his name, has made this man strong . . ." (3:16). Although Peter attributes "ignorance" (v. 17) to the Jews in crucifying Jesus, he does not exonerate them for their crime; he calls them to repentance "that your sins may be blotted out" (v. 19).

Although the crime of the Jews cannot be denied, it can be forgiven; Christ has returned to them through His witnesses, so that they may be saved. He will not return again until the Jews repent. Only then will come the refreshing and the restoration of all things. Paul says, in Romans 11:25, 26, that "a hardening has come upon part of Israel, until the full number of the Gentiles come in, and so all Israel will be saved."

Peter and John Before the Sanhedrin (4:1–22). "And as they were speaking to the people, the priests and the captain of the temple and the Sadducees came upon them . . ." (v. 1). The religious leaders were "grieved" at the preaching of the Messiah. What priests were they who would be pained rather than delighted with the story of the resurrection? The Sadducees were the professional religionists who were in it for what they could get out of it—and they got out plenty! Having killed the Prince of Life Himself, these custodians of the carnal status quo intended to make short shrift of His witnesses. Thus, while the apostles were in the act of speaking, the priests, captain of the temple and the Sadducees put them in custody until the next morning. By suppressing the truth which they themselves should have been preaching, they illustrated the charge of Jesus that they would neither enter in themselves nor allow others to do so (Lk. 11:52). But in spite of them, some five thousand others had entered in (v. 4).

The next morning when the two prisoners were placed in the center of the semicircle of officials facing the president, they once again testified to Jesus Christ. In the later speech of Stephen (ch. 7), his censure of the Israelites for rejecting their Messiah, as their fathers had rejected the prophets sent to them, brought on martyrdom. The charge Stephen made was not new; it had already been made and now Peter was making it: ". . . by the name of Jesus Christ of Nazareth, whom you crucified . . . This is the stone which was rejected by you builders . . ." (4:10, 11).

Peter's mention of the rejected cornerstone referred to Psalm 118:22. Its immediate application at the time it was written was to those of David's day who had rejected him, but its pre-eminent application was to the rejection of the Messiah Himself. In a lesser sense, the rejected apostles, on whom Christ was building His Church, illustrated the same truth.

Nothing so offends worldly people as to be told that they must be saved (4:12). Having no true righteousness, they delude themselves into thinking they do have it. Those who really possess true righteousness always recognize that it is of grace. They rejoice in the only name under heaven whereby one must be saved and rely entirely on Christ. But not the Sadducees! They must have been particularly incensed at these words about the necessity of salvation, for in the next verse it is written: "Now when they saw the boldness of Peter and John, and perceived that they were uneducated, common men, they wondered; and they recognized that they had been with Jesus" (v. 13).

The question as to what must we do to be saved never occurred to the Sadducees as it did to the Philippian jailer on a later occasion. Their question was simply: What must we do to save our faces and our jobs? If these fanatics continued to preach the guilt of the rulers in the crucifixion of their despised Messiah and the abominable doctrine of the resurrection of Jesus—after all, these Nazarenes are worse than the Pharisees who at least had the grace to put off the resurrection to the future—the standing of Sadducees was doomed. These men had to be stopped, but how? The most effective way would be to put them to death as blasphemers, but unfortunately, there was a cured cripple standing in plain sight and about five thousand new believers. A less drastic measure was called for at this moment. A threat—that was it! That would silence them and not endanger us. After all, we do not care too much what they think—there have always been some Galilean visionaries around—as long as they don't talk too loudly or persuade too many people.

Once again hirelings tried to silence the shepherds. "So they called them and charged them not to speak or teach at all in the name of Jesus" (4:18). The inevitable answer came: "Whether it is right in the sight of God to listen to you rather than to God, you must judge; for we cannot but speak of what we have seen and heard" (vv. 19, 20).

The Disciples among Themselves (4:23–37). "Prosperity has often been fatal to the Church, persecution never." Christ had said: "A servant is not greater than his lord. If they have persecuted me, they will also persecute you" (Jn. 15:20). The servants were seeing this truth underlined by events. Christ had said: "Blessed are you when men revile you and persecute you and utter all kinds of evil against you falsely on my account. Rejoice and be glad, for your reward is great in heaven" (Mt. 5:11, 12). His disciples were seeing the reviling and feeling the blessing. They were leaping for joy, and they had no desire whatever for this joy to cease; therefore they had no desire for the persecution to end. All they asked was strength to endure (4:29). This has been called "a second Pentecost."

Part of the secret of the early disciples' holy boldness is found in Acts 4:28, where it is said that these evil actions of men were in accordance with the plan God "had predestined to take place." This is paralleled in the statement: Jesus was "delivered up according to the definite plan and foreknowledge of God" (2:23). The certainty that these terrible threatenings of men were actually the predestined purpose of God and would work together for good strengthened the early Church.

An outer proof of inner power was given the disciples: "And when they had prayed, the place in which they were gathered together was shaken . . ." (4:31; cf. 19:18 and Ps. 68:8).

Again we see the church at Jerusalem (4:32–37) as a happy Christian community, holding all things in common and united in prayer, apostolic doctrine, faithful worship, love to one another and noble living toward those without. Barnabas was especially noted for his generosity, implying that such was not an obligation and, perhaps, even uncommon. And Barnabas was a Levite who did not pass by on the other side of the road. Christ was making Levites into Good Samaritans!

Trouble from Within: Ananias and Sapphira (5:1–16). Turning from the persecution of the church from without, we find trouble from within. Of this internal trouble there are two kinds: One is fatally serious and requires drastic measures—we might call it "mortal" sin; the other is serious but not fatal, and requires corrective measures—we might call this "venial" sin. In the early church was a case of deliberate falsehood and hypocrisy, and the only solution was utter removal of the offenders. This is the story of Ananias and Sapphira. The second involved the murmuring of the Hellenists against the maladministration of the benevolences; the solution was a more effective machinery for handling temporal matters. Thus was the first diaconate formed.

Nowhere is the optional character of the generosity of the early Christian community more sharply delineated than in the story of Ananias and Sapphira. These persons wanted to appear to give everything while holding back some of it. Peter rebuked their hypocrisy, explaining that they did not have to give anything, but to pretend to give was intolerable in a Christian community. Upon Peter's pointing out that Ananias had lied not unto men but to God, Ananias died. Shortly afterwards, the situation was repeated with Sapphira. Death was also her penalty (5:5–10).

The desired effect was produced: "Great fear came upon the whole church" (5:11). So at the very outset of the history of the Christian Church, God showed conclusively how He felt about lying and hypocrisy. "By this act, the Holy Spirit shows for all time what He thinks of such hypocrisy, and He thinks no better of it that He now delays its punishment."

This whole episode is all the more remarkable because it is not really characteristic of the New Testament. We have already noticed that at Pentecost people were gathered together, rather than dispersed as in the Babel incident. But, lest there be any misunderstanding, God shows that His holiness is still inviolable.

One other detail of this story deserves comment. "The young men rose and wrapped him up and carried him out and buried him" (5:6; also v. 10). Were these "young men" officers or perhaps deacons? If so, it makes the first molding of the disciples into a well-knit organization separate from the synagogue.

Another description of the prosperity of the early church follows the tragedy of Ananias and Sapphira. Healing is especially mentioned. Even the shadow of Peter effects cures. The apostles were now, in Christ's absence, successful in curing demoniacs, as in

Christ's presence they had not been (Mt. 17:14–21; Mk. 9:18, 19; Lk. 9:40, 41). It seems apparent that through their developed faith, Christ was nearer to them now than He was when visibly in their midst. One difference between the Biblical healer and the modern counterpart is manifest in the statement concerning the apostles that they healed *all*.

The rhythmic pattern running through these chapters is best described by Dr. K. S. Latourette's expression, "Advance Through Storm." After the storm of opposition from the Sanhedrin (4:13–22), there is the advance (4:23–37). Then the storm occasioned by the defection of Ananias and Sapphira (5:1–11) is followed by another advance (vv. 12–16). This, in turn, rouses another storm of opposition from the authorities (vv. 17–39), which only serves again to advance the cause (vv. 40–42).

In the last-mentioned storm, the Pharisees appear on the scene. This sect had arisen during the conflict of the Jews with Antiochus Epiphanes on the side of the Maccabees. Thereafter the Pharisees stayed out of the political struggles and cultivated their detailed conception of religion. Whatever the origin of the word "Pharisee," which means "Separatist," they accepted it and lived up to it.

It was a Pharisee, Gamaliel, whose counsel shielded the Christians from the still more hostile Sadducees. His view—that if this movement were not of God, it would come to naught, and if it were, naught could be done against it—shows the religious character of pharisaic thinking (5:34–39). This not only distinguished the Pharisees from the utterly worldly Sadducees, but also made them bitter opponents.

That the antagonism between Sadducee and Pharisee should work together for good to the Church is a dramatic instance of God's making the wrath of men to praise Him. This deliverance of the early Christian community has been likened to the deliverance of Israel from Egypt. Later there was to be a similar deliverance of the early Church of the Roman Empire when the leniency of one emperor would cancel out the severity of another and allow the Church to march to triumph. Still later the Church of the Reformation arose and developed while the Holy Roman Empire and Roman Imperial Church cancelled out each other's effort to destroy the rising Church in her infancy.

The reference to Theudas (5:36) has posed for some a question of Biblical accuracy, because a "Theudas" mentioned by Josephus lived later than this, not earlier. There is, however, no proof that the two Theudases are the same; nor, if they are, that it is Luke, rather than Josephus who errs.

Trouble from Within: Murmuring about Charities (6:1-7). The next internal problem to face the early church was maladministration: "The Hellenists murmured against the Hebrews because their widows were neglected in the daily distribution" (v. 1). As one critic has observed, "It is remarkable that both the internal disorders —the hypocrisy recorded in Chapter 5, and the murmurings recorded in Chapter 6—sprang from the open-handed charity exercised towards the poor. . . . One root of bitterness grew in the givers, and another in the receivers." Instead, apparently, of being grateful for what was given, the recipients could only complain of what they did not receive.

Although the grievance may have been niggardly, it did reveal an inequity. Administrative changes were in order like the change made in Israel when Moses, discovering he could not handle all the problems of Israel, appointed seventy helpers—elders. Here the apostles, only twelve in number, do not have time to meet the increasing needs of the growing church without sacrificing time for their principal mission—leaders in word and life. Virtually every minister since that time has, sooner or later, discovered he cannot do everything.

The men appointed were deacons in everything but name. That two of these, Philip and Stephen, were also authorized to preach and baptize does not indicate that they were not deacons, but merely that they were something more than deacons. Their role as evangelists should not be confused with the office of the deacon. At the same time, we must bear in mind that deacons, as such, are not evangelists or pastors. To carry out their function of ministering to the material needs of Christians, the deacons must be "full of the Holy Spirit and wisdom" (6:3).

Trouble from Without: Martyrdom of Stephen (6:8—7:60). No sooner had the storm of dissension produced an advance, the establishment of the diaconate, than another storm arose in which one of its members, Stephen, was the center. Apparently, the fact that he was a Hellenist prejudiced the Jews of the synagogue against him. As so often happens, men who do not have worthy aims in the first place are not scrupulous in the means they take to reach them. They set themselves against Stephen and accused him of the crime of blasphemy: "We have heard him speak blasphemous words against Moses and God" (6:11). The fact that Ananias and Sapphira had paid with their lives for their false witness did not deter these nationalistic brethren.

In Stephen's arraignment there is a striking similarity to Jesus' indictment before the same people in Matthew 23. Stephen's majestic response to the Sanhedrin remains to this day one of the greatest statements of the creed of the Church (7:2–53). This first martyr of Christianity was the only one, save the Lord Himself, to refer to Christ as the Son of Man, and the first to receive a vision of Him in His exaltation. In the midst of the glowering faces of his outraged enemies, at the very time they were accusing him of blasphemy, Stephen's face shone.

Despite a painful, violent death, his martyrdom was so triumphant that the sacred writer, without impropriety, describes his end by the phrase, "fell asleep." Probably most important of all was the testimony of Stephen's prayer of forgiveness and his joyful acceptance of death. The impact of that witness must have profoundly affected Saul who stood by "consenting to his death," that same Saul who later was to become, like Stephen, a believer and a martyr.

2. Samaria: The Samaritan Pentecost (8:1–25)

The martyrdom of Stephen inaugurated a great persecution which scattered the Church "throughout the region of Judea and Samaria, except the apostles" (8:1), and marked the beginning of the Christian Dispersion, which would, in turn, bring the Gospel to the Jewish Dispersion and involve the Gentile world.

Philip went down to Samaria—Jews were beginning to have dealings with the loathed Samaritans—where his ministry was blessed by miracles. "For unclean spirits came out of many who were possessed, crying with a loud voice; and many who were paralyzed or lame were healed" (8:7). At this point, Simon "who had previously practiced magic in the city and amazed the nation of Samaria, saying that he himself was something great" (v. 9) entered upon the scene. When this "great man" saw the miracles of the Holy Spirit done through Peter, who had followed Philip, he recognized the real thing. The term "simony" grew out of his foolish and wicked attempt to buy these spiritual gifts with money. When Peter answered him in no uncertain terms, "Thy money perish with thee!" (v. 20) and warned him to repent, Simon begged that their prayers might be made for him (v. 24).

The coming of Jewish Christians to Samaria was marked by three noteworthy facts:

1. There is evidence of a transformed spirit, for the Jews usually had no dealings with the Samaritans. John, who once thought of calling down the fire of destruction upon the Samaritans (Lk. 9:54), now prays for the pentecostal fire of blessing (8:15).

2. The coming of the apostles shows that church order, no less than evangelism, is a concern of early Christians.

3. The extension of the enduement of the Holy Spirit in pentecostal power is associated with the apostles. In Philip's ministry there were notable conversions and he himself wrought miracles, but the special gift of the Holy Spirit came only when Peter and John arrived.

3. The Ends of the Earth: Philip and the Ethiopian (8:26–40)

After his very successful evangelism in Samaria, Philip was taken away suddenly to devote himself to the salvation of one person in the desert. This "desert place" of Gaza probably refers to the old city which was destroyed by Alexander the Great and at this time was only a deserted ruin (8:26). Near here the treasurer of one of the Candaces, a dynasty of queens of Merowe in Ethiopia and North Sudan, was riding in his chariot and reading Isaiah 53, wondering about its meaning. When Philip preached Christ as the predicted sufferer, this man believed and was immediately baptized (v. 38). No one knows certainly what happened to the Ethiopian after his conversion, but tradition holds that he returned to his country and introduced Christianity there.

4. The Conversion of Paul and His Preparation (9:1–31)

This first account of the conversion of Saul of Tarsus will be related in great detail two other times in the Acts (22:1–21; 26:2–23), not to mention a number of casual and incidental allusions. The sheer space devoted to Paul's conversion indicates its tremendous importance. For example, more verses are given to it than to Pentecost, the conversion of Cornelius and the Jerusalem Council, all events of the first magnitude; indeed, more than to any other subject in Acts.

Paul was a man of massive native ability. It is easy to believe the statement that had he been a philosopher, he would have surpassed Plato. Coleridge regarded his Epistle to the Romans as the most profound book ever written, and others feel the same way about Ephesians. Luther, describing the impact of Paul's writing, said, "Paul's words have feet and hands; they run after, they seize." Yet with all his profound scholarship and brilliancy in presenting truth, he was one of the most active men who ever lived. Gifted as a savant, his life was not lived in an ivory tower but centered in the arena of milling men.

But however far Paul may tower over his fellows, he falls immeasurably below Jesus, and no one knew this better than Paul himself. Recognizing Jesus as Lord and Master, Paul entirely subjected himself to Him. Thirteen times in his epistles he speaks of the "unsearchable riches of Christ." The power only Christ could give explains what happened to Paul on the Damascus road. That Paul's experience could have been simply an epileptic seizure, or sunstroke blindness, or any such natural phenomenon, seems out of the question in the light of sober criticism. If epilepsy could do this to men, it would be regarded not as a disease, but as man's greatest boon. Some one has said, "If Paul had a fit on the road to Damascus, it is the only known fit followed by such mighty historical consequences."

The circumstances of Paul's conversion while "breathing out threatenings and slaughter against the disciples of the Lord" (9:1) prompted Chrysostom, an early church father, to write, "Christ, like a skilful physician, healed him when his fever was at the worst." At the very moment when the divine power threw him to the ground, and caused him perhaps to fear judgment, came the merciful query, "Saul, Saul, why do you persecute me?" (v. 4). By not avenging His persecutor, Christ destroyed Paul as persecutor. He overcame his enmity by making him a friend.

The similarity between the preparation of Ananias (9:10) to bring sight and the Holy Spirit to Paul and the preparation of Peter to perform a like service for Cornelius is striking. The precision with which God plans indicates that He cares as much for the means as the ends.

In the account of the conversion, certain matters are significant. The word "saints" is first used in verse 13. Paul openly and immediately professed his new faith (vv. 14, 15). Verse 17 is highly significant for an understanding of the transmission of divinely given powers. Since Ananias was neither an apostle nor, apparently, an evangelist, perhaps "the gift was so peculiarly divine, that the external medium was comparatively unimportant." We note also that here, as in other endowments of the Holy Spirit after conversion, the reference is to an enduement for special work, and not a regenerating function of the Holy Spirit, which presumably had already been performed.

Then once again we have the advance after the storm—in this instance, in the storm: "When after many days had passed, the Jews plotted to kill him [Paul]" (v. 23).

5. *Judea: Peter in Lydda, Joppa and Caesarea (9:32—11:18)*

Lydda and Joppa (9:32–43). As "Peter went here and there," he came to Lydda, where he miraculously healed a palsied man, Aeneas. Christianity was now spreading into the regions beyond Jerusalem (9:32–35). In other words, Peter's visit here, as to Samaria and Antioch, shows a progressive approval of the spread of Christianity by the apostles from Jerusalem.

Nothing is mentioned in relation to Aeneas except his sickness; but it is different with Dorcas of Joppa, a woman "full of good works, and acts of charity" (9:36). Dorcas, says Luccock, "was founder of an International Ladies Garment Workers' Union, one of the greatest labor unions of all time, with branches in all lands." Full of good works herself, her example has provoked multitudes to the same good works; she has probably put more sewing circles in business than any other person in history.

Certain disciples, probably beneficiaries of Dorcas' good works, sent for Peter. Just as a widow once sent for Elijah on behalf of her son who had died, so in this instance the sons sent for Peter on behalf of the mother saint who had died. Like Elijah (I Kings 17:17; cf. II Kings 4:32), Peter brought the dead person back to life by kneeling down and praying (9:40). But in all probability Peter was thinking not of Elijah, but of Christ Who in the house of Jairus had excluded all but three disciples, Peter, James and John, before healing Jairus' daughter.

Caesarea (10:1–48). The Gentile centurions of the New Testament commonly appear in a good light. Of one Christ said He had not seen such faith, no, not in all Israel. The centurion who beheld

Christ die was moved. In Acts also the centurions appear in good circumstances, and Cornelius fits this pattern. Rough Roman soldier that he was, he was still a man of religious refinement. Busy with his many secular duties, he observed with military regularity the traditional hours of prayer, for though he was a Gentile and a foreigner, he was thoroughly Jewish in his faith. Furthermore, his life was marked by a sincere devotion to God (10:4). Now he was to be given through the gracious providence of God a deep understanding of the New Covenant, for God was not going to leave Cornelius unacquainted with new truth. But to grant Cornelius a particular revelation of *deeper* fellowship, God had first to give to another man, namely Peter, a revelation of *inclusive* fellowship.

The preparation of Peter involved significantly Peter's sojourn in Joppa at the home of Simon, a tanner. Old prejudices were beginning to give way, for Simon as a curer of pigs' hides was, from a Jewish standpoint, engaged in an illegitimate business.

In this very house Peter had a vision that was to be one of the decisive experiences of his life. It occurred during the sixth hour of prayer (noon). Three times God showed him a sheet let down from heaven, which contained clean and unclean animals, those allowed and those forbidden. When asked to eat, Peter "was not hungry enough, even in a trance, to forget his Jewish regulations and scruples. . . ." Orthodoxy forbade his eating unclean food; in obedience to the Lord, he could not obey the Lord. Illustrating the possibility of learning to do something that God had commanded (abstain from certain foods) without doing so *because* God commanded it, the impulsive apostle once again uttered that hopeless contradiction in terms, "No, Lord" (cf. Mt. 16:22).

Christ is gentler with His servant this time than when he had tried to prevent Him from going to the cross, so twice He repeated the vision to teach Peter the great lesson: the difference between clean and unclean was forever over, because the same Lord who once made the distinction had obliterated it. Indeed, He had made the distinction in the first place, so that ultimately He could obliterate it: "In thee and in thy seed shall all the nations of the earth be blessed" (cf. Gen. 12:1–3).

The crucial character of this encounter comes into focus with these words: "And on the following day they [Peter and friends] entered Caesarea" (10:24). Cornelius was expecting them and had called together his kinsmen and close friends. Peter's entering Cornelius' house was a radical departure in the light of Jewish prejudice against Gentiles. To the Jew "the Gentile was an abomination; his touch defiled, his customs were abhorrent, his religion was a blasphemy." Now a Jew was entering the very house of, and mingling fully with, a dog of a Gentile. Cornelius, though no doubt proud of his Roman lineage and his office as a centurion, realized the condescension of Peter in coming into his house and was even prepared to worship him (vv. 25, 26). Peter instantly refused such homage on the grounds that he himself was merely a man.

In opening his sermon in Cornelius' house, Peter made a pronouncement that is often misinterpreted. When he said, "Of a truth I perceive that God is no respecter of persons: but in every nation he that feareth him, and worketh righteousness, is accepted with him" (10:34, 35), he was using a technical term, "respect of persons," which refers only to discrimination on unjust grounds. This was certainly forbidden in the Old and New Testaments. God, however, "respects" persons, but not on unjust grounds. He accepts some on the basis of their representative, Christ, and rejects others on the basis of their sin. The righteous person has a right to God's favor, and the unrighteous has earned His disfavor; for God to reject the righteous or to accept the unrighteous would be to make a mockery of both justice and logic.

Not only were Cornelius and his household converted, but the Holy Spirit came immediately upon them. It is important to note that not only did the Holy Spirit come upon them, but He did so without the laying on of the hands of the apostles or of anyone. In Samaria, the Spirit's coming waited on Peter and John's laying on of hands, but here the Spirit comes first and the baptism follows. One scholar surmises: "In this case the gift of the Holy Spirit preceded baptism, to convince Peter and the rest clearly that they were accepted of God." Still another theologian declares, "The lesson is obvious; the work of the Holy Spirit is independent of confession or baptism or the imposition of apostolic hands; nor need there be an interval of time between the acceptance of Christ and the reception of his Spirit in all the fulness of his power."

Aftermath (11:1–18). Those who called in question Peter's action in eating with an uncircumcised Gentile were not evil in their attitudes, only bewildered. When first they hear of the event, they are as perplexed as Peter himself was when the Lord in a vision commanded him to eat unclean animals. The action was not only unheard of but it also violated their basic principles. No wonder they demanded an explanation of Peter (v. 3). Once he gave it, they accepted it as readily as had Peter, once he understood the vision.

Peter's defense rested on two points: First, God had appeared to him in a vision setting aside the old law of separation; the "wall of partition" was broken down. Second, the Holy Spirit had actually been sent upon the Gentiles by God before they had been circumcised or baptized. "If then God gave the same gift to them as he gave to us when we believed on the Lord Jesus Christ, who was I that I could withstand God?" (11:17). The vision had been afforded to Peter alone and everyone else had to trust his integrity. It was therefore gracious of God to give this corroborative evidence which all could see—the pouring out of the Spirit which produced supernatural gifts. One commentator suggests that Peter with deliberate shrewdness had brought some Jewish brethren with him to Cornelius' house to see for themselves, and thus be able to testify afterwards what happened.

The implicit teaching of the evangelical principle versus the sacramental is clearly demonstrated, for here the Gentiles were made Christians first and baptized afterwards. The work of grace preceded the sign of it. The fact that these persons became members of the invisible Church before being joined to the visible church proves beyond question that the sacrament of baptism is an evangelical, rather than absolute, necessity.

6. The Ends of the Earth (Continued) (11:19—12:25)

Antioch (11:19–30). After the settlement of this initial controversy occasioned by the baptism of the Gentiles without circumcision, Luke resumes the narrative of the spread of the faith. Since the death of Stephen he has noted the extension of the faith into Samaria, Ethiopia, Caesarea, Joppa, and so on. Now he reports its spread as far as Phoenicia and Cyprus and Antioch (11:19). He then goes into detail concerning the Gospel in Antioch (vv. 22–30).

At Antioch the disciples were first called Christians (11:26). Just as Cornelius was the first individual Gentile whom the Church evangelized, so Antioch the Golden was the first city in which the transition was made from the Jewish to Gentile Christianity. The persecuted and scattered disciples preached the word to none except Jews (v. 19). "But there were some of them, men of Cyprus and

Cyrene, who on coming to Antioch spoke to the Greeks also, preaching the Lord Jesus" (v. 20). These Greeks were probably the "God-fearing ones," who participated in certain Jewish practices without ever becoming full Jewish "proselytes." One might say that at Antioch a Pauline Christianity was to develop before Paul. Was Paul's later sojourn here the occasion of his realizing that Gentiles may become Christians without first becoming Jews?

Paul, Barnabas, Simeon of Niger, Lucius of Cyrene, and Manean were among the early missionaries to the city which was later to become the operational base for the Apostle Paul. These Antioch missionaries "founded the first Gentile church." The very use of the word "Christians" implied that these were heathen converts, for that term not only was not used for Jewish Christians but was used to distinguish other Christians from them. The Antiochians may have felt distinct from the Jewish Christians but they did not feel separate from them. When Agabus predicted a coming famine, the Gentile church at Antioch took up an offering for Judea which they sent by Barnabas and Paul, thus becoming the first church to support another in distress (vv. 28, 29).

This new center of Christianity needed an adequate leader. Just as Andrew had brought his brother, Peter, the greater person, to the Lord and His work; just as Farel persuaded Calvin to do the great work at Geneva which Farel had begun but could not finish; so Barnabas went to Tarsus to "look up" Saul. He was just the man Antioch needed, and Barnabas was intelligent enough to see it and humble enough to admit it.

Persecution and Spread of the Jerusalem Church by Herod (12: 1–25). The death of James, the Church's second martyr, showed the solidity of the Christian community and the growing cleavage with Israel at this time. James was not only a Jew himself, but also a strict observer of Jewish tradition; yet he stood with Peter in urging that Gentiles be admitted without circumcision. This made him so obnoxious to the Jews that when Herod murdered James in Jerusalem, the act was applauded. Thus encouraged, Herod proceeded further and the state took over the role of persecution from the ecclesiastical authorities who had initiated the practice.

By Herod's order Peter went to prison a second time. No doubt because officials knew of his previous escape, the government took extra precautions and installed a round-the-clock guard. Four sets of four soldiers watched him for six hours each; a couple of them were actually chained to him. Meanwhile, a prayer meeting was asking for Peter's release; but when the prayer was answered they thought the girl was crazy who had brought the word that Peter was at the door, having been delivered from his incarceration by a miracle.

Now Herod, a New Testament Pharoah, met his apparent judgment. According to the account in Josephus, Herod on this occasion saw an owl, which was an omen to him of his imminent death, and he died in agony a few days later.

IV. Paul's First Missionary Journey (13:1—14:28)

1. Cyprus (13:1-12)

Like Moses, Paul began his recorded public ministery in combat with a false magician. But where Moses confined his miraculous activity to external nature, the apostle turned on Elymas himself, smiting him with blindness.

2. Pisidian Antioch (13:13-52)

At Perga, Paul and Barnabas lost one of their fellow-warriors, John Mark, who may have been frightened by the dangerous, robber-infested territory that lay before them, or disappointed because they did not more extensively cultivate Cyprus. The two apostles began a successful invasion of the Asia Minor mainland, wielding only the sword of the Holy Spirit. The magnitude of this power is evident to the Christian who reflects on the fact that this evangelism succeeded where later the military might of the Crusades found the same territory impossible to conquer.

Paul rose in Antioch in Pisidia and delivered a strictly historical sermon, relating the salient features of the past history of salvation. The climax of the sermon and the history was in John the Baptist, the witness, and Jesus, the Messiah (13:16-41). The coming of the Messiah was a direct fulfilment of prophecy, specifically the prediction in Psalm 2:7, "Thou art my Son."

While he spoke primarily to the Jews, Paul kept the Gentile proselytes before him also, and in the end it was these, not the Jews, who were saved. Paul may have sensed the unbelief of his fellow-countrymen before the outward expression of it appeared. "Beware, therefore, lest there come upon you what is said in the prophets: 'Behold, you scoffers, and wonder, and perish; for I do a deed in your days, a deed you will never believe, if one declares it to you'" (vv. 40, 41). The actual expression of rejection seemed to be precipitated by the acceptance on the part of the Gentiles. They would not enter into the Kingdom nor permit others to do so. This seems to be a characteristic of evil from the beginning for Cain not only would not himself worship God acceptably, but slew his brother Abel because he did.

The turning to the Gentiles, Paul said, was the fulfilment of prophecy and predestination. "And Paul and Barnabas spoke out boldly, saying, 'It was necessary that the word of God should be spoken first to you. Since you thrust it from you, and judge yourselves unworthy of eternal life, behold, we turn to the Gentiles.'"

3. Iconium (14:1-7)

The Antioch ministry ended in persecution by the unbelieving Jews. Yet the missionaries were jubilant and moved on in full triumph. "It is not enough to say that they were joyful although they were persecuted; for they were joyful because they were persecuted." Nor were they hardy soldiers of the Cross only at Antioch but their courage went with them to Iconium—and everywhere. No one has paid them more perfect tribute than Calvin: "Now whithersoever they fly, they carry with them the same courage still; whereby it appeareth that they were not only furnished for one combat, but even for continual warfare; which Luke doth now prosecute. He saith first, that they came to Iconium, and therewithal he showeth that they sought not there some haven where they might rest quietly, but they entered the synagogue as if they had suffered no hurt at all."

Iconium is known today as Konia or Konya, once famous as the point of origin of the modern power of the Turks. Very few remains remind one of its apostolic past, but beautiful mosques mark this agricultural community of some hundred thousand souls. When Paul and Barnabas came to Iconium, the synagogue leader, in traditional fashion, asked them if they had a word of exhortation. We are reminded that our Lord had, under similar conditions, been invited to speak, and this custom of inviting visiting Jews to speak persists even to this day.

Since Luke gave us Paul's missionary message in detail at Antioch, he concentrates his attention on the effects of the preaching at Iconium. Paul's speaking was so effective that "a great multitude of the Jews and also of the Greeks believed" (14:1). But the preaching of Christ also had another profound effect; it stirred up the Jews against the Gentiles. Christ had said that He brought not peace but a sword, and where the truth is preached there are bound to be consequences.

Action generates reaction, and this is true in the spiritual world. A multitude believed, others disbelieved, and the latter group poisoned the minds of the others (perhaps the undecided) against the brethren (14:2). To this reaction there was, according to Scripture, another and greater reaction in the opposite direction: the apostles continued to speak boldly for the Lord (v. 3).

But the struggle between the "mind-poisoners" and the apostles became so irreconcilable that schism was inevitable. "But the people of the city were divided (*eschisthe*); some sided with the Jews, and some with the apostles" (v. 4). This is the first time the word "schism" has occurred in the Acts. It seems possible that the occasion was actually the first clear-cut schism in the history of the early Church. Tension between the Christian Jews and the non-Christian Jews had existed from the beginning of Acts. Peter called on them to repent and be saved. At the same time, the Christian community remained a part of Israel. Stephen was martyred, Peter and John imprisoned and all the apostles forced to flee during the Herodian persecutions, but, apparently, the unbelieving Jews had not yet separated from the believing Jews and Gentiles. That seems to be what happened at Iconium. The unbelief of the Jews at Iconium was so active that they separated the multitude and so "the forwardness of men causeth that the gospel, which ought to be the bond of unity, is (so soon as it cometh abroad) the occasion of tumults."

Thus the preaching of Paul at Iconium brought about exceptional faith on the part of many, the first schism recorded in Acts, and desperate persecution which forced the apostles to flee (14:5, 6). This is a common outcome in the Acts.

4. Lystra, Derbe and Return to Syrian Antioch (14:8–28)

The garrison town of Lystra, a center of Roman culture, seems to have had no synagogue. At least, Paul and Barnabas appear to be dealing entirely with pagan Gentiles.

The abysmal darkness of the Lystrians is shown with dramatic luminosity by the two actions attributed to them: When Paul miraculously healed a cripple, the people attempted to worship Barnabas and Paul as Zeus and Hermes; and when the apostles refused to be worshipped, the Lystrians tried to murder at least one of them.

After a visit to Derbe, Paul and Barnabas engaged in "follow-up work." Retracing their steps they further established the work at Lystra, Iconium, Antioch in Pisidia, and Perga. Principally they ordained elders, probably after the people had selected them by vote (14:23). Fasting was observed in connection with these solemn installation services, probably in acknowledgment of unworthiness, and in preparation for the fervent prayer of the occasion. At this point, the two missionaries went home to Syrian Antioch on furlough from their fruitful foreign service. It is interesting to reflect that their itinerary, short as it was in miles, represented a more difficult and time-consuming travel than the modern missionary who traverses half the globe to reach his station.

V. The Jerusalem Council (15:1–29)

The Jerusalem Council represents, probably, the first "creative controversy" in the history of the Christian Church. It was convened to debate and settle a fundamental theological question and was no mere "rubber stamp" administrative assembly. It interrupted the missionary work of the Church in order to settle and clarify the missionary message. It was time well spent, for had time from actual work not been taken to settle a matter of faith, the work would have lost its faith, and having lost its faith, the work itself would have died.

The controversy concerned the necessity of circumcision and other Old Testament rites for salvation. Some of the sect of the Pharisees at Antioch thought these essential, and they were highly displeased with Paul and Barnabas, who were receiving Gentiles into the Christian faith without these rites. They were apparently so incensed that they would not even permit Paul and Barnabas to speak, at first, in the assembly (15:12). Peter and James also testified that God was actually saving the Gentiles without circumcision and had predicted that in the last days He would restore the residue of men (vv. 15–17). It is difficult to see what bearing that verse had on the precise point of the controversy, which was not whether Gentiles would be saved, but whether they would be saved without the Jewish rites. At any rate, it was the consensus of the assembly that God's will was with Paul and not the Pharisaic Jewish Christians.

Still, the Council had respect for the law of Moses. It realized that the law was universally recognized and practiced among the Jews and should be treated with deference though no longer with a sense of obligation to it. Hence the decree: "Therefore my judgment is that we should not trouble those of the Gentiles who turn to God, but should write to them to abstain from the pollutions of idols and from unchastity and from what is strangled and from blood" (vv. 19, 20).

The question as to why fornication is listed along with obviously ritualistic, or morally indifferent, matters, has been answered in various ways. Differing explanations view fornication here as: (1) concubinage, (2) impurity because associated with idolatry, (3) deuterogamy, (4) unlawful marriage, or (5) promiscuous sexuality. Every one of these explanations is less than satisfying. Concubinage was strictly ruled out by Christ, as was, of course, deuterogamy. Impurity associated with idolatrous practices only makes the "fornication" double evil. Promiscuous sexuality could not so much as be mentioned among the children of God and its wrongness would be taken for granted. Unlawful marriages (within degrees, for example) seems to us least unsatisfactory, though the concubinage theory is mildly feasible because of the example of Abraham, David and others.

A couple of incidental details in the Council are worth noting in passing. Verse 11 shows that salvation was by grace in the Jewish dispensation no less than in the Christian. "But we believe that we shall be saved through the grace of the Lord Jesus, just as they will" (v. 11); that is, the Jews, accustomed to the yoke of the law, as the Gentiles were not, still expected to be saved only by grace. Another interesting sidelight is that James, the cousin of Jesus, was presiding over the Council of which the first "pope," Peter, was but a subordinate member (15:13).

VI. Paul's Second Missionary Journey (15:36—18:22)

1. Antioch to Troas (15:36—16:10)

With the controversy settled by the Council, Paul and Barnabas were free to resume their missionary ministry; but they were blocked by an unfortunate disagreement. They differed in their opinion as to the suitability of John Mark (who had previously left them in the lurch at Perga and returned home) as an associate in the new mission journey. Barnabas seems to have regarded Mark's repentance as reason enough to reinstate him in service. Paul, who no doubt accepted the genuineness of Mark's repentance and its restoration of him to fellowship, did not think that it made him worthy as a missionary worker. No reconciliation was possible and the two friends parted, with Barnabas and Mark leaving for Cyprus, where they must have faced some embarrassing questions about the whereabouts of their former traveling companion. Paul went out with Silas, apparently enjoying the endorsement of the Antioch congregation (15:39, 40).

Great pioneer missionary that he was, Paul constantly revisited his churches. He may not have built again on other men's foundations, but he built again and again on his own. This persistent, unremitting pastoral care is an outworking of his unceasing prayer for the people in his churches (Eph. 3:14–19). John Wesley is a modern example of an evangelist who covered vast tracts of territory but cultivated every inch of it. Like Paul, he deserved the epithet, "the world was his parish."

Paul took a new companion for his travels, Timothy, who was half Jewish and half Greek. "Paul wanted Timothy to accompany him; and he took him and circumcised him because of the Jews that were in those places, for they all knew that his father was a Greek" (16:3). The Jewish practice in administering their rite of circumcision, the ancient equivalent of baptism, lies between Protestant and Roman Catholic practice. While the Protestant permits only ordained ministers to baptize and the Roman Church allows even an unbeliever, in emergencies, to do it, the Jews permitted *any Jew* to perform their initiatory rite. So we cannot tell whether Paul, on this occasion, did it himself, or had it done.

There is no inconsistency in Paul's circumcising Timothy while refusing adamantly to have Titus circumcised (Gal. 2:3). He had no objection to Jewish rites as such. Only when they were regarded as necessary to salvation did he and the other apostles object. Against such Judaizing, Paul was opposed with all the integrity and intensity of his being. In the case of Titus, the matter was crucial. Those who wanted him circumcised insisted that it was necessary to his salvation. Paul would not grant that supposition for a moment, and, therefore, refused to tolerate the rite for Titus.

In the case of Timothy, however, no such issue was at stake. We cannot imagine that the church of Lystra from which Timothy came, and which was one of Paul's own, could have any doubts about the status of Old Testament rites. So nothing stood in the way of Timothy's circumcision, and there was something to be said in favor of it. The Jews to whom Paul would be going, not yet familiar with the new teaching, would be unnecessarily offended, and, indeed, would not permit Timothy to come with Paul into Jewish privileges. So without violation of principle, Paul would become all things to all men that he might by all means win some, just as his Lord, before him, had paid the temple tax when it was not necessary, for the same reason.

After his follow-up work, Paul looked for new worlds to conquer for Christ. But at first he was hindered by the Spirit, probably to show him—and us—that God guides us away from some places as well as to others; or, away from some in order to come to others which have priority in the divine plan. "The stops, as well as the steps, of a good man are ordered by the Lord."

One of the areas from which Paul was deflected seems to be North Galatia, since he went through South Galatia. "And he went through the region of Phrygia and Galatia, having been forbidden by the Holy Spirit to speak the word in Asia" (16:6). This poses the famous North versus South Galatian problem. Without entering into the controversy, we will simply assume the Southern theory, agreeing with Ramsay that "the phrase which Luke employs correctly describes that part of the Galatian province in which Antioch and Iconium were situated, and there is no ground whatever for inserting at this point a visit to North Galatia, which would have taken the travellers entirely out of their way."

In any case, Paul arrived at Troas, near ancient Troy, which itself proved to be only a point of departure. There he received the call to Macedonia in a vision and went on to Europe in spiritual victory.

2. *Troas to Athens (16:11—17:15)*

In obedience to the heavenly vision, Paul came to Philippi in answer to the call of the man of Macedonia, who, as someone has remarked, "turned out to be a woman." This happens again and again. Luccock points out that "the young preacher goes out from the theological seminary as Paul went into Europe. He has heard a call from a world of need. But when he arrives at the first landing place, he usually finds just what Paul found—a few women."

We have mentioned earlier that the picture at Lystra was of a thoroughly degraded paganism. The light of God in Judaism had, with all the weakness of Judaism, illumined the dark places of the earth. This is seen again in Lydia, a seller of purple of Philippi, at the place of prayer. She listened eagerly to Paul and became the first convert in Europe.

We now meet one of the degraded women who were victims of benighted heathenism, a ventriloquist used by evil men to make money by her gift. She was possessed by the devil and then by men, his instruments. Though she plagued Paul for several days, only gradually was he provoked to drive out the devil. Why did he wait? Perhaps he did not know until then that he was given the grace to release the girl. This seems reasonable.

Though the girl was responsible for her enslavement, there is a difference between such a relatively passive victim and positively evil persons. To this latter class belonged her exploiters who, instead of seeing the power of God through Paul and repenting, notice only their financial loss and determine to take vengeance. When the demon *went out*, the men's hope of gain *went out*. Exactly the same form of verb is used in verses 18 and 19.

Once again a man (Paul) was placed in prison for his good works. Apparently the two things most likely to lead to jail are excessively bad works or excessively good ones. Paul is placed in stocks because he has liberated a possessed girl and broken up an illegitimate business.

Like the lark when it is disturbed, so the early missionaries, when made to suffer, began to sing. From this hold the prisoners were set free, not by angels who delivered Peter and John, but by an earthquake of the Lord, Who makes the wrath of nature, no less than that of man, to praise Him. The familiar story of the Philippian jailer's terror, near-suicide, conversion and baptism, together with all his household in the course of the evening, is a dramatic study in religious experience.

3. Athens (17:16–34)

After their ministry in Philippi, which naturally turned that city upside down, the missionaries pushed southwest about a hundred miles to Thessalonica and then fifty miles farther along the same road to Berea. "His stay in the former city intimates how the gospel should be preached, his experience in Berea, how it should be received" (Erdman).

After the Thessalonican critics had driven Paul from the responsive Bereans, he came to Athens. At this time she was the cultural and religious capital of the world, although in Paul's day, past the peak of her intellectual achievement. It has been said of this period that it was easier to find a god in Athens than a man. A breakdown of genuine intellectuality opens the gates for the crassest of superstitions, and so it is in our day in the cults, such as Theosophy or Christian Science, no less than in ancient Greece.

Paul begins his great sermon on Mars Hill, overwhelmed by this overpowering religiosity of the Athenians. "Men of Athens, I perceive that in every way you are very religious. For as I passed along, and observed the objects of your worship, I found also an altar with this inscription, 'To an unknown god.' What therefore you worship as unknown, this I proclaim to you" (17:22, 23).

So Paul finds his point of contact in the Athenian altar to an unknown god; the God they do not know, he would declare to them. Reasoning from natural revelation, which Paul and the Athenians both recognized, Paul came to the affirmations of Scripture with which his preaching to the Bereans, who accepted the authority of the Word of God, began. If only a few Athenians believed, that cannot be blamed on Paul's procedure here. Certainly we agree with the statement that "the preaching comparatively failed at Athens, not because of the preachers method, but in spite of it." This is comparable to a modern quip: "The play was a success, but the audience was a failure." Remember that in Berea, as well as elsewhere, Paul had preached in a synagogue where, presumably, there were true believers to begin with, who showed the state of their hearts by immediately embracing Jesus Christ as He was offered in the Gospel.

Some think that Paul's statement to the Corinthians, to whom he came after his visit to Athens, "I determined to know nothing among you save Christ and him crucified," reflects a disillusionment with his approach to the Athenians. This is an uncalled-for assumption. Surely the sermon on Mars Hill reflects nothing but a burning zeal to bring the Athenians to Christ. Paul's very effort to become an intellectual to the intellectuals that he might win them proves his zeal for Christ. Furthermore, while success is never measured by the number of converts, there were a good number of converts in virgin territory (17:34).

Verse 26 should read: "And he made from one every nation of men to live on all the face of the earth, having determined allotted periods and the boundaries of their habitation." The old reading, "hath made of one blood all nations," is based on a weak text, a western reading which is usually an inferior, inflated text. "Blood" is omitted in the best manuscripts. The meaning of the verse would be that men have one creation, rather than one blood, though the truth of the latter may be implicit in the former.

The Revised Standard Version translates verse 30 in this way: "The times of ignorance God overlooked, but now he commands all men everywhere to repent." "God winked at" of the older versions is unacceptable. The meaning of the statement is that God did not enter into judgment with men at this time of ignorance, that is, He did not visit his (full) wrath on them. He did not declare (so clearly) His disapprobation; for *that* He has appointed a Day of Judgment.

4. Corinth and Return (18:1–22)

When Paul left Athens to go to Corinth, he did something comparable to leaving Edinburgth for Glasgow. One is the literary, cultural and religious center of the country; the other, the commercial capital. The two key cities were relatively close together.

In spite of the fact that Corinth was a commercial center, noted the world over for its gross licentiousness, the witness was there and the synagogue existed. Here Paul came, but his work was largely among the Gentiles. At the time of his epistles to Corinth, three congregations of Christians existed in the city. One of these was at the house of Aquila and Priscilla (18:2,3), Jews of Pontus, who had been driven out of Rome, presumably by the decree of Claudius.

The character of Gallio is one of the most debated matters, but the date of his office is one of the most widely accepted in New Testament chronology. The generally accepted date of Gallio's proconsulship is A.D. 52. An inscription was found at Delphi mentioning Gallio as consul—it also contained a reference to Claudius, and can be dated August of A.D. 52. With the date of the consulship approximately fixed, Paul's first visit to Corinth and thus the writing of I Thessalonians can be determined.

The character of Gallio is diversely estimated. Scottish seceders and traditional conservatives generally have regarded him as the symbol of moral indifferentism in high political places. Calvin castigates his hands-off policy: "But nothing is more absurd than to leave the worship of God to men's choice. Wherefore, it was not without cause that God commanded by Moses that the king should cause a book of the law to be written out for himself, (Deut. 17:18) to wit, that being well instructed, and certain of his faith, he might with more courage take in hand to maintain that which he knew certainly was right." Over against this, liberals have always admired the attitude and policy of Gallio, regarding him as "a man of high character and philosophical disposition." This view of Gallio has come to be shared by conservative scholars also since the general adoption of the separation of Church and State. One critic represents this point of view in these words: " 'Sweet Gallio' as he was called, the brother of Seneca, the famous philosopher, was a man of most genial and attractive character; and here he stands forth as one who vindicated the majesty of law and of justice; he insisted that no man should be tried as a criminal because of his religious beliefs. Gallio is really a noble example of religious tolerance."

Paul's Third Missionary Journey (18:23—21:16)

1. The Ephesian Pentecost (18:23—19:41)

Paul revisited his churches in Galatia and Phrygia en route to Ephesus, the center of his third missionary tour. Apollos had been there before him. Apollos is represented as a gifted preacher who knew only the baptism of John the Baptist (18:24–28).

Again in Acts 19:1–12, the allusion to the disciples in Ephesus who knew only the baptism of John may be to a group of Apollos' disciples. Following, as it does, a reference in the preceding chapter to the limitations of Apollos during his ministry in Ephesus, this seems feasible. Moreover, chapter 19 begins with an otherwise unnecessary reference to Apollos' presence in Corinth. And the basic similarity of the views of these Ephesian disciples and of Apollos suggests a relationship of teacher with students getting basic instruction.

The crucial question concerning these Ephesian disciples is the meaning of Paul's question to them, "Did you receive the Holy Spirit when you believed?" (19:2). That this question does not refer to their possession of the Holy Spirit seems clear. First, John the Baptist's ministry was a saving one; it brought people to repentance and remission of sins. He baptized with water, to be sure, and this was somehow inferior to the baptism with fire. Nevertheless, it was a true baptism, the symbol of the washing away of sins—the washing of regeneration which is a work of the Holy Spirit. Second, these disciples were believers in the Christ John preached. As belief is wrought by the Holy Spirit, they must have possessed the Spirit to that degree. Christ had said, "Except a man be born from above," that is, by the Spirit, he could not "see" nor "enter" the Kingdom (Jn. 3:3, 5). But these men had seen and had entered and so must have been born again by the Spirit. Third, the present reference to the reception of the Holy Spirit is to a post-belief reception. The English Revision reads: "Have you received the Holy Ghost *since you believed?*" The Revised Standard Version is more ambiguous: "Did you receive the Holy Spirit *when* you believed?" The tense (aorist) indicates past time—after or since you believed. If this is correct, Paul is asking about a reception of the Holy Spirit after belief, and this could *not* be a query about His regenerating work which is *before* belief. Furthermore, the whole context of Acts suggests that this is, as it has been called, the Ephesian Pentecost. Each of these Pentecosts has marked not a regenerating but an endowing coming of the Spirit. Lastly, the immediate context implies this: "And when Paul had laid his hands on them, the Holy Spirit came on them; and they spoke with tongues and prophesied" (v. 6). Hence we find ourselves persuaded that this is another instance of the Holy Spirit's endowing the believer with special gifts rather than a normal regenerating activity.

At Ephesus, Paul taught for three months in the synagogue until opposition forced him to "argue daily" for two years in the hall of Tyrannus, probably a believer. At Rome, Paul used his own lodging as a meeting place (Acts 28:30); at Ephesus, he used the school of Tyrannus (Acts 19:9); and at Corinth, the house he used was next to the synagogue. We have already noted Paul's separation from the Jews at Iconium, possibly the first schism of Israel from the Christian Church. Now "when some were stubborn and disbelieved, speaking evil of the way before the congregation, he withdrew from them, taking the disciples with him . . ." (19:9). Calvin praises Paul's action with these words: "Now, Luke saith that Paul departed from them, and did separate the brethren, by which example we are taught, that when we have experience of desperate and incurable stubbornness, we must lose our labour no longer. Therefore, Paul admonished Titus to avoid a man that is an heretic, after one or two admonitions (Tit. 3:10). For the word of God is unjustly blasphemed, if it be cast to dogs and swine."

Just as Paul had trouble with the owners of the possessed girl of Philippi because, in delivering her, he had brought an end to their nefarious profits through her, so now that he delivers some out of the kingdom of Diana into the Kingdom of God, he incurs the wrath of Diana's silversmiths. Diana was a great goddess and the center of Ephesian life. In Ephesus, the religion of the community was dominated by the worship of Diana, the Great Artemis. The temple dedicated to Diana was one of the Seven Wonders of the World. She was not Artemis, the Greek huntress and virgin sister of Apollo, but Artemis, the mountain goddess, mistress of the soil of Ephesus when the Greeks took possession in early times. Though the colonists gave her a Greek name and a Greek temple, Diana remained thoroughly Asiatic. Obscene and degraded rites were part of the cult of Diana.

The worship of Diana was a lucrative business to the profiteers who cynically sold idols. Because they wanted to continue their money-making activities, they had no intention of letting Paul continue his mission in Ephesus. They therefore sang praises to their goddess and appealed to provincial patriotism at the same time with their cry, "Great is Diana of the Ephesians." Only the cool-headed fairness of the town clerk checked the tempestuous crowd and restored order.

The Sceva incident (19:13–17), like the Elymas episode, demonstrates the difference between the power of God and the power of magic. The incantations and exhortations of Sceva and his sons are futile against the very demons who obey the true servants of God. Modernism has reached a new level of futility; it exorcises the devils by denying their existence. By comparison, Sceva and his sons look good.

2. Macedonia, Achaia and Return (20:1—21:16)

After his long ministry at Ephesus, Paul again engaged in follow-up work by going to Greece for the three winter months before going on to Jerusalem in the summer. Eight men from six different cities accompanied him: Sopater of Berea, Aristarchus and Secundus from Thessalonica, Luke from Philippi, Gaius from Derbe (a different man from Paul's host in Corinth), Timothy from Lystra, and Tychicus and Trophimus from Ephesus. Paul had not only made converts and organized congregations, but he had also recruited and trained workers. This illustrates the personal and practical genius of the apostle, who, as the saying goes, could not only do the work of ten men, but could also get ten men to work.

Returning from Greece to Troas where he had first had his vision of the need to evangelize Europe, Paul held a long farewell meeting with the faithful. Apparently the service continued far into the night, for Eutychus, who had found a seat only on the window sill, was overcome by sleep and fell to the ground. While many lesser men than Paul, in less time, have been able to put their Eutychuses to sleep, they have not always so successfully roused them. Paul revived Eutychus from the death which his three-story fall had caused.

The company then proceeded down the coast of Asia Minor. "But going ahead to the ship, we set sail for Assos, intending to take Paul aboard there; for so he had arranged, intending himself to go by land. And when he met us at Assos, we took him on board and came to Mitylene. And sailing from there we came the following day opposite Chios; the next day we touched at Samos; and the next day after that we came to Miletus" (20:13–15). To this final meeting point the elders of Ephesus are summoned to meet their apostle. In verse 17 the men are called "presbyters"; in verse 28, "overseers" or "bishops." The identity of the two offices, thus incidentally taught, seems inescapable (cf. Tit. 1:5, 7).

To these elders Paul gives one of the most touching, personal addresses of his life: He is rendering an account of his ministry to them as they must in time render account of theirs (20:20-35). In this farewell testimony, he stresses his faithfulness to his complete duty: "I did not shrink from declaring to you anything that was profitable, and teaching you in public and from house to house . . . Therefore I testify to you this day that I am innocent of the blood of all of you, for I did not shrink from declaring to you the whole counsel of God. . . . In all things I have shown you that by so toiling one must help the weak, remembering the words of the Lord Jesus, how he said, 'It is more blessed to give than to receive'" (vv. 20, 26, 27, 35). Paul not only preached the full-orbed Christian message, but he did not feel himself free from the blood of men until he had done so.

Paul also reminded the elders of his personal ministry; he had gone from "house to house." His teaching was not restricted to public instruction, but was also given privately and specifically. This phase of the pastoral work is often more delicate, difficult and avoidable, for while people like to see the pastor, they do not always like to hear his message, "Thou art the man." What Calvin said is true to this very day: "For they be rather bears than sheep, who do not vouchsafe to hear the voice of their pastor, unless he be in the pulpit; and cannot abide to be admonished and reproved at home, yea, do furiously refuse that necessary duty."

Sadder than the actual parting with Paul was his sad prediction, "I know that after my departure fierce wolves will come in among you, not sparing the flock; and from among your own selves will arise men speaking perverse things, to draw away the disciples after them" (20:29, 30). The Galatians had been, even during Paul's active contact, bewitched. The Ephesians were to become the prey of wolves, which would rise out of their leadership after his departure. The "fierce wolves," whose coming Paul predicted, did come and tried to devour the Ephesian flock, and John was called perhaps to defend it. Under his leadership, Ephesus became the center of the Church, as Antioch had been under Paul, and Jerusalem under Peter. There are many legends concerning these later Ephesian years of John, but of reliable data there is a scarcity.

We learn from the Apocalypse that John was exiled to Patmos (Rev. 1:9), and that he had probably had close contact with the seven churches of Asia to which the letters are addressed (Rev. 2:3). Irenaeus cites Polycarp as authority for the famous story of John, who, going to bathe at Ephesus, and perceiving Cerinthus within, rushed out of the bathhouse without bathing, exclaiming, "Let us fly, lest even the bathhouse fall down, because Cerinthus, the enemy of truth, is within." The internal evidence is stronger than the external for the lovely report Jerome gave: When the Apostle John was too old to serve, he would be borne into the church and, mustering all his remaining strength, say, "Little children, love one another." Tradition is very strong for John's death during the early years of Trajan after he had been released from Patmos under Nerva.

The literature shedding most light on the actual religious conditions in the Ephesian area during this period is the Epistles of John and the letters to the seven churches. From these we learn that Paul's "fierce wolves" took the form of Docetists who repudiated the incarnation, saying that the physical life of Jesus was not real, but a mere appearance.

Paul's farewell sermon concludes with an appeal for stewardship. Pointing to his own labor, which enabled him to give to and not take from the needy, he urged the elders to follow his example. He eloquently points to an unrecorded saying of Jesus Himself, "It is more blessed to give than to receive" (20:35).

Paul en Route to and in Rome (21:17—28:15)

1. In Jerusalem (21:17—23:35)

Just as our Lord had to set his face as a flint to go to Jerusalem, so Paul knew his little *via dolorosa* stretched before him and he was reminded of it at each step: Miletus (20:65), Tyre (21:4), and Caesarea (21:11, 12).

In Jerusalem it became very quickly evident that the fears of his friends were no idle ones; only the Roman police were able to save Paul from the Jewish mob. They listened, however, as he addressed them in their own language. He reminded them that he was a Jew, that he had been reared in a strict tradition, and that he had originally been as opposed to Christianity—and more so—than they were now. But when he concluded his message with the declaration that God Himself had changed his mind by a miraculous conversion, followed by a commission to proclaim the Gospel to the Gentiles, his audience found these words unendurable. The chief captain had to save Paul's life from his frenzied fellow-countrymen. He was taken to Caesarea for safekeeping.

2. In Caesarea (24:1—26:32)

Before Felix (24:1–27). Five days later Paul was accused before Felix, the governor, by the lawyer for the Jews, Tertullus. He attempted to show that Paul was the enemy of the Romans because he preached sedition; the enemy of the Pharisees because he taught heresy; and the enemy of the Sadducees because he desecrated the temple. Although the accused easily disposed of these charges, Felix, who was more interested in being popular with the Jews than ascertaining the truth, postponed decision—for two years.

Before Festus (25:1–22). When Festus succeeded Felix, he heard Paul's case. He, too, could find no fault in him, but he also was afraid of the Jews and wanted peace at any price. Paul, who was capable of indignation when his patience was sufficiently imposed upon, made an end to the subterfuge of trial by appealing to Caesar. Festus, no more desirous of currying the ill will of the emperor, by submitting to him a criminal who had committed no crimes, than he was to touch off a Jewish insurrection by not finding Paul guilty, "passed the buck" to Herod Agrippa II, who happened to be visiting in his province.

Before Agrippa (25:23—26:32). Agrippa, better versed in the practices of the Jews although no more concerned about them than Felix or Festus, heard Paul, showed some concern, but after a while left in spite of the apostle's most tender appeal which almost persuaded him to become a Christian.

3. Voyage to Rome (27:1—28:15)

Thus Agrippa gave the trouble-maker, Paul, back to the governor. Festus, although not happy about sending him to Caesar, had no choice, so Paul was soon on a ship bound for Rome. But the sea was as tumultuous as the Jews had been. Indeed, only Paul was at peace. By a divine revelation to him that all would be saved from an impending shipwreck he, the prisoner, was able to console all the men. Impressed with Paul during the shipwreck, the stranded travelers were still more amazed to see him, while preparing a fire on the mainland, calmly shake off a deadly viper. When the ship resumed sailing after the winter, kind friends on the island saw Paul off, and when he arrived in Puteoli, about 150 miles from Rome, friends met him there and still others came out to greet him all along the way. While the animosity of men sent the Apostle Paul on this long journey, the love and affection of many friends made it a blessed one. "On seeing them Paul thanked God and took courage."

4. Ministry at Rome (28:16–31)

When the great prisoner arrived at his appointed jail, he was received with deference; for, while the Jews would have killed him, the Romans were so impressed by Paul that they gave him every possible liberty consistent with his status. Indeed, they gave him their heart. Many of the Praetorian Guard and others who came into contact with the evangelist in chains were brought by him into bondage to Christ. What had happened to him "has really served to advance the gospel" he told the Philippians in one of the several important letters that he wrote from Rome (Phil. 1:12). He referred not only to the converts made by him but to the greater courage and zeal which other Christians as well, emboldened by his example, displayed in their witnessing.

The Book of Acts closes with Paul still preaching Christ to Jews and Gentiles. It is probable that he was released from this trial and permitted to visit Spain which was so much on his heart. Later the Apostle to the Gentiles, who was to make the church of Rome the greatest of the ancient world, was to die in this very city, the capital of the Gentile world. The planting of the flag of Christ alongside the banners of Caesar constituted the taking of the major beachhead of the world and made way for the subjugation of mankind, a work which still goes forward. The apostles are gone, but not the Acts of God's Spirit. These shall go on until Christ Himself comes to reign in glory.

In Acts we are shown how the Christians witnessed in Jerusalem, in Judea, in Samaria and to the ends of the earth. As this witness was ventured, more and more Jews disbelieved while more and more Gentiles believed. Thus God began to graft the wild olive branches into His olive plant.

The Epistles

The Epistles

EVERETT F. HARRISON

THE WORD "epistle" means something written, or instruction conveyed in written form. During the first Christian century, in which the epistles of the New Testament were being penned, people in the Greco-Roman world were writing letters. Some of these bear a certain similarity to those in the New Testament, but the differences are significant.

I. The Epistles as a Literary Form

Ordinarily a letter states the identity of the writer and gives the name of the person or persons addressed, conveys a few words of greeting, states the business of the communication, then concludes with appropriate words of farewell. In general, this scheme is followed in the New Testament epistles, but conventional terms of greeting are usually replaced by others freighted with spiritual import, such as grace and peace. Furthermore, the thought moves along more exalted lines. There is no place for trivial matters in documents which concern themselves with eternal truths. These differences emphasize the fact that the letters of Scripture were not addressed to a general public, but were written for Christians by Christians. Nor were they essays striving to attain a wide circulation by literary excellence, but messages of urgency calculated to meet the pressing needs of the saints.

Use has sometimes been made of the circumstantial character of these writings to make it appear that the documents in question are not necessarily authoritative for future generations of Christians,

1011

since the writers produced them with no such use in mind, but only to meet immediate situations in the lives of believers. Even if it were true that the writers had no awareness that their letters would survive their own time, this does not rule out the purpose and providence of God by which their written deposit should become the standard for the Church throughout the centuries. Occasionally the epistles themselves reflect the desire of the writers to have their works circulated so that other believers may profit from them. This provision for circulation of the writings (Col. 4:16; Rev. 2:17) at least hints at the prospect of preservation of such letters in order that they may be made available to others.

It was a natural step from this situation to the gathering together of the letters into a collection. Peter knew of such a collection of Paul's letters (II Pet. 3:15, 16). While it is not necessary to suppose that he had personal acquaintance with all the letters of Paul in the New Testament, Peter's language at least points to a process which reached its culmination in the acknowledgment by the various churches that certain writings by apostolic men possessed unique value and deserved to be treasured for Christians in the future.

New Testament writers often followed the custom of dictating their message to scribes who did the actual penmanship. This raises the interesting question of the relation between the two men involved in the production of the letter. Did the author expect the secretary to take down his statements word for word, or did he grant him a measure of freedom in shaping the language in the interest of correct phrasing and attractive styling? For one thing, it ought to be remembered that these scribes were not public secretaries hired for the purpose, men who were selling their services for a price, but rather believers performing a service (Rom. 16:22). They were therefore presumably specially careful to present the thought of the writer. Probably the writer looked over the finished product in order to check it before it was sent out. Certainly it is possible to speak of a somewhat typical Pauline style, which would hardly be possible if the various scribes who served the apostle were permitted extensive liberty in transcribing what they heard. There were times when the writer took the pen himself to impart a personal touch to the letter or to impress a truth by this more immediate contact (Gal. 6:11). Paul seems to have developed the habit of affixing his name in his own handwriting as an unmistakable mark of genuineness (II Thess. 3:17).

It may be well to raise the question as to the quality of the New Testament epistles from the standpoint of literary excellence. As a rule, they manifest a better command of language than the secular letters belonging to everyday life of the period. On the other hand, there is no straining for artistic effect. Whatever greatness attaches to these writings as literature is due not to the education or conscious striving of the writers, but to the greatness of the theme into which these men entered with whole-souled abandon. Language was a poor vehicle for the truths of redemption, but the grandeur of those truths brought the statement of them to great heights at times. Romans 8 and I Corinthians 13 are examples of sections which, because of their beauty and power, have commanded universal admiration.

In structure the epistles usually present a foundation of doctrinal truth upon which practical application and exhortation are built. In some of them the division is marked, as in Ephesians, where the transition (4:1) is clearly perceptible. But it is unwise to conclude that every epistle should rigidly conform to this pattern; often teaching and appeal are intermingled through much of the text. The writer to the Hebrews even refers to his whole composition as a word of exhortation (13:22).

II. Classification of the Epistles

The epistles fall naturally into two groups: the Pauline and the General (sometimes called Catholic). The latter group seldom indicates the location of the people addressed. No greetings to individuals appear. Another classification may be made: letters intended for churches and those addressed to individuals. The Pastoral Epistles belong in this latter category. Philemon was written to an individual, but the church in Philemon's house is included. Most of the letters written to churches were sent to a single congregation, such as the Epistles to the Thessalonians and I Corinthians, but in the case of Galatians, several churches in a given area are addressed.

Paul's letters, which constitute the most important unit in this literature, fall into four groups: *(1)* The Eschatological Epistles, so called because they deal considerably with the last things, the things of the future, are I and II Thessalonians. *(2)* The Soteriological Epistles, so designated because they deal with salvation, include

Galatians, I and II Corinthians and Romans. *(3)* The Prison Epistles, so called because Paul was a prisoner when he composed them, include Ephesians, Colossians, Philemon, Philippians. They are sometimes described as the Ecclesiological Epistles because of their emphasis on ecclesiology or the doctrine of the Church. *(4)* The Pastoral Epistles are I and II Timothy and Titus. The first and third of these are especially concerned with counsel to Paul's younger fellow-workers about the organization and care of the churches. Second Timothy is more personal than pastoral.

It is not feasible to divide the epistles according to the background of the people receiving them; in other words, to label some of the epistles Gentile and others Jewish. Most of the congregations were predominantly Gentile, with some Jewish believers among them. However, Hebrews and James seem to have been directed to groups made up almost entirely of Hebrew Christians.

III. Origin of the Epistles

Why were the epistles written at all? Since they were addressed to believers, they were not intended to be evangelistic, even though the Gospel is often stated in them and they furnish many texts for evangelistic sermons. The letters presuppose the reception of the Gospel. In general, they are a substitute for verbal instruction; distance compelled the writers to resort to this means of contact. Occasionally the epistles were called into being by letters of inquiry from the churches about questions of Christian life or procedure in the assemblies (I Cor. 7:1).

Paul was a great founder of churches, but he was a pastor also. He needed to keep in touch with his converts, and letters made this possible. The Epistle to the Romans prepared the way for his coming to a church which he did not personally establish. The Second Epistle to the Corinthians prepared the way for the apostle's return to a congregation which had given him considerable trouble. Enemies charged Paul with preferring to write letters rather than to appear in person because his letters were more effective than his presence or speech (II Cor. 10:10). But it is well to remember that such charges came from detractors. Paul could speak effectively as well as write with vigor.

Special reasons dictated the writing of some of the epistles. Philippians, for instance, was called forth by the generous gift of this church to Paul the prisoner. Writing primarily to thank them, he touched on other things as well. Sometimes Paul made use of the letter to reveal his own circumstances; this is especially true of the Prison Epistles. Paul's condition and prospects were of grave concern to his friends. Sometimes a letter was devoted in great measure to a defense of his apostolic office or conduct. This emphasis, dominant in the early part of Galatians, is a notable strain in II Corinthians. Again, heresy needs combatting, and this accounts for Galatians, in which the doctrine of grace is passionately defended against legalism. Colossians, too, was called forth largely by the need to counsel that church against certain men in error who had perverted the truth and detracted from the glory of Christ.

Young churches often bristled with problems induced by the high ethical demands of the new faith. Several such problems are treated in I Corinthians. Because Christians were a minority in a godless society, their very piety widened the gulf between them and their neighbors. A rising resentment against them sometimes led to persecution, and for this reason I Peter was needed to give believers comfort and assurance in the midst of trial. Warning against false teachers largely accounts for the writing of II Peter and Jude. The lack of adequate leadership in the congregations made the writing of the Pastoral Epistles a necessity.

But beyond all these and other special factors was the compelling desire of the writers to build up the saints in their faith by means of instruction. Converts must grow in grace, increase in love and good works, and understand the implications of Christian teaching for their daily lives. They must share the mind of Christ, seek to be pleasing to Him, live the heavenly life here on earth, and thus exhibit the genius and power of the Christian faith before the world.

IV. The Epistles in Relation to the Book of Acts

Luke's record in Acts gives the historical background of the spread of the Gospel from Jerusalem to Rome. In it we learn how the many churches addressed in the epistles were founded. The epistles, on the other hand, depict the inward growth of converts. In the Acts we have a record of preaching to the unsaved. The great redemptive acts of the Son of God are given as the burden of the apostolic message. We learn that Christ died and rose again. We need the epistles, however, to tell us why Christ died and what is the significance of His rising from the dead. There is far more interpretation in the epistles than in Acts. Both portions agree, however, in picturing a Church of Christ which is both imperfect and supernatural. It makes mistakes, yet nothing short of the grace and power of God can account for the transformations which characterize its life.

V. *The Epistles in Relation to the Gospels*

References to the events of the life of Christ are relatively scanty in the epistles, but the same Figure who dominates the Gospels is central to the epistles. The interest shifts to His present position as Lord and Head of the Church. Matters relating to the life of Christ on earth were certainly of interest to believers, but such things were probably covered in the oral instruction of new converts. Incidentally, this instruction helped to determine the content of our Gospels, which were written later than most of the epistles. Since believers had learned the facts of Jesus' life by oral teaching, such things did not require repetition in the epistles. In the Gospels, Christ is the principal speaker; in the epistles, He is the principal one spoken of.

With reference to the Gospels, the epistles occupy a position comparable to that which the Prophets hold with respect to the law. They are the stronghold of interpretation and application. In the Gospels lie the seed truths developed in the epistles. For example, in His teaching in the upper room, Jesus hints that the new position of believers, as being in Him, is a deep and abiding experience, which compensates them for losing Him by His withdrawal into heaven. But only in the epistles do we have a full statement of the meaning of this relationship; *in Christ* is Paul's key phrase.

In the realm of ethical teaching, the two sections clearly harmonize. The demand for sacrificial living is found in both the Acts and the epistles, and so is the cruciality of love. The writings of the apostles prove these men had sat at Jesus' feet.

Jesus' teaching presents the ideal for the child of God. We learn the divine standard for thought, attitude, and conduct which glorifies the Father in heaven, but there is very little information which would give us an answer to the question: How can these things be realized? For this, we must turn to the epistles where the divine provision in the Word and the Spirit is unfolded in all its glorious sufficiency.

VI. The Epistles in Relation to the Old Testament

When the epistolary writers handle the gospel message, they are not satisfied to root it in the events of the earthly life of Jesus of Nazareth. Instead, they carry it back to the divine purpose and show that it is grounded in the ancient promises made by God through the prophets and set down in the Holy Scriptures (Rom. 1:2). Practically every topic dealt with in the epistles is shown to be anticipated, supported or illustrated in some way by the Word of God, for that Word is quoted to enforce the teaching. This habit may well be due to the influence of our Lord Himself upon the disciples, especially in the teaching which He gave them between the resurrection and the ascension.

VII. Principal Themes

As an irreducible minimum, three broad areas stand out: the Lord, the Church, the world. Without the Lord there would have been no Church. It is to the Lord that the Church owes its difference from the world. At the same time, because of the Lord, the Church has an obligation to the world, and this is to make known to it the saving mercy of God in Christ.

Jesus Christ is the foundation upon which believers are built up in faith and life (I Cor. 3:11). There is no other. The saints are acceptable to God because they have been reconciled to Him by Christ (II Cor. 5:18–21). They must put on Christ to find victory over the flesh (Rom. 13:14). Even their prayers depend for acceptance upon being offered in His name (Eph. 2:18; Heb. 13:15). They grow up into Him in all things as the perfect Man (Eph. 4:15). Christ is their Lord, their great High Priest, their Intercessor.

Though the Church is mentioned twice in the Gospels (Mt. 16:18; 18:17) and its growth is sketched in Acts, only the epistles present any great amount of teaching concerning it. Here we learn of the divine purpose which takes Jews and Gentiles with different backgrounds, antagonisms, and prejudices; molds them together into one new man in Christ; and creates the Church as the body of Christ. As Head of the Church, Christ fills it with His risen life and directs its activities by His Spirit. This pilgrim Church, once it has completed its ministry on earth, will be gathered home to the Lord as His bride in glory. Meanwhile it is charged with nurturing the saints and shining as a light of testimony before the world.

The world is represented as lying in spiritual darkness, held in the grip of Satan, walking in the lusts of the flesh, bound for perdition; yet it is the object of the love of God. Christians are to beseech men to be reconciled to God, and by their manner of life create on the part of sinners a desire to be saved, so that "those without" may be brought into the warm circle of Christian fellowship.

VII. Unity of Teaching

Do the writers of the epistles have the same message, or do they each have their own version of what Christianity is? Each makes his own distinctive emphasis, but the underlying harmony throughout is in agreement with the apostolic tradition. The author of the Epistle to the Hebrews conceives of Jesus as the great High Priest. John presents Him as the incarnate Word. Peter thinks of Him as the perfect Sufferer and as the Lamb of God. Paul declares Him the Head of the Church, the last Adam, the universal Lord. In the sphere of ethical obligation, John magnifies the need of righteousness and love. James pictures Christian conduct as the product of a higher wisdom and of obedience to a superior law. Peter insists on holiness, sobriety, submissiveness, and perseverance amid the trials of life. Paul bases everything on the primacy of faith which flowers into love and hope. Liberty, to be wholesome, demands charity. So in everything, the believer must realize that he is to give account to his Lord. All this serves to emphasize the richness of Christian truth. All is not given to one man to expound; the contribution of each one is needed if believers are to have a well-rounded conception of what is involved in our Christian profession: obedience to one Lord and adherence to a common faith underlie everything.

VIII. Permanent Value

The epistles fulfil the pledge of Jesus that the Spirit would guide His disciples into all truth. Things not clearly perceived in His own teaching are here spelled out and illuminated. These letters not only tell us what manner of men we ought to be as Christians; but they also show us how the truths of the Gospel transformed and shaped the writers themselves, Paul especially. We look in vain to find in them meticulous regulations for conduct. We find instead the exposition of principles sufficient under the Spirit's guidance for every generation of believers. To assess the contribution of the epistles is impossible. We have only to imagine a New Testament without them to appreciate how much they mean to our faith and life.

Romans

GORDON H. CLARK

THE EPISTLE to the Romans, the longest, the most systematic, and the most profound of all the epistles, and perhaps the most important book in the Bible, was written by the Apostle Paul (1:1, 5). He was in Corinth at the time (15:26; 16:1, 2). The careful

composition of the letter suggests that after some tempestuous experience there he had a period of leisure before he took relief money
to the saints in Jerusalem. This puts the date early in A.D. 58. Unlike
the other epistles, Romans was written to a church he had never
visited (1:10, 11, 15). All the ingenuity of destructive criticism has
never been able to impugn the authenticity of the epistle. Therefore,
without further ado, we turn from the questions of criticism to a
study of its message.

I. Introduction and Theme (1:1–17)

Because Paul had never visited Rome, although several of his
friends and converts had gone there to live, he opened his letter with
a longer salutation than ordinary. It would have been odd for a
private person to address such an important congregation, and
utterly out of place to impose upon them such a treatise on fundamental doctrine. Therefore, Paul begins by stressing his apostolic
calling (1:1, 5).

Incidental allusions show the scope of Paul's mind and furnish a
wealth of material for topical study. Although this article can
spare no room for detours from the main subject, one paragraph may
be used to give a few examples.

The doctrine of election is hinted at, in that Paul was *called* to be
an apostle (1:1), and the Roman Christians were also *called* by
Jesus Christ. These Christians were called to be *saints*. Paul never
suggests that only some Christians, officially canonized, are saints.
And as the epistle is addressed to *all* of them (1:7), Paul evidently
expected them all to read it. This is the Protestant principle of an
open Bible. Then, too, the unity of the Old Testament and the New
Testament, to which later reference will be made, is asserted (1:2).
The deity of Christ is emphasized (1:3, 4, 7). The occurrence of
this idea here is significant because in A.D. 58 there were still many
living who had seen Jesus. The deity of Christ therefore is not a
legend that took centuries to develop, perhaps under Greek influence, but was commonly accepted from the very first. Again, when
Paul calls himself the *slave* of Christ Jesus (1:1; cf. 7: 6, 25; 12:11;
14:18; 16:18) and *worships* God (1:9; 9:4), he allows for no distinction between two acts of worship, the one *(doulia)* to be paid
to deceased saints and the other *(latria)* to God alone—much less a
third form *(hyperdoulia,* or superslavery) to be paid to the Virgin
Mary.

After the salutation (1:1–7), Paul expresses thanks for the remarkable faith of the Romans. He assures them of his desire to visit them and to preach the Gospel in Rome also, "for it is the power of God unto salvation to every one that believeth;" and then he introduces the theme of the epistle, *justification by faith* (1:17).

Here two points are to be especially noted. First, as was mentioned above, the message of the Old Testament is essentially the same as the message of the New Testament. Just as the promises which God made by the prophets are themselves the Gospel (1:2, 3; cf. Gal. 3:8), and as Jesus began at Moses to expound what *all* the Old Testament taught of him (Lk. 24:27), so justification by faith is an Old Testament doctrine. Paul takes his theme from Habakkuk 2:4. Second, the fact that the first four books of the New Testament are called Gospels produces the impression that Romans is not the Gospel. A distinction is sometimes drawn between the Gospel to be preached at evangelistic services and something else, perhaps called doctrine or theology, that is dismissed as not so important. But here (1:15–17) Paul emphatically identifies the doctrine of justification by faith with the Gospel. The verse from Habakkuk confirms that the Gospel is the power of God because in it is revealed a righteousness that comes from God by faith. What this means is the burden of the epistle.

II. The Need of the Gospel (1:18—3:20)

1. Condemnation of the Gentiles (1:18–32)

The need of the Gospel, that is, the need of justification by faith, is based on God's wrath against the sin of mankind. This sin may be divided into impiety (1:19–23) and iniquity (vv. 24–32). Wrath, guilt, and liability to punishment are appropriate because men know the truth and yet suppress it. What is known of God has been made clear to them (Acts 14:17). The eternal attributes of omnipotence and deity, though invisible, are clearly seen in the created universe, rendering it inexcusable for a man not to worship God. The race, refusing to glorify and thank God, became stupid, so stupid as to fall to the level of idolatry. They worshipped birds, beasts, and even reptiles.

Because of this impiety, God gave them over to iniquity and to vile passions. This abandoning of man to his lusts is not a passive permission, but is the active and effective wrath of verse 18. One terrible result was sexual perversion which was so vicious that the Apostle Paul does not refer to men and women, as the translations have it, but simply to males and females.

Since they thus reprobated God, God gave them up to a reprobate mind. All sorts of evils followed: maliciousness, murder, deceit, backbiting, cruelty, and so forth. Yet, though they wished to exclude all knowledge of God from their minds, they could not altogether succeed. They still knew the just judgment of God, namely, that people who practice such things are worthy of death; nonetheless they continued in their wicked way and entirely approved of those who did such things.

2. Condemnation of the Jews (2:1—3:8)

The Jews were only too willing to admit that the Gentiles were as evil as Paul had said. But in the very act of judging the Gentiles, the Jews condemned themselves, for they were doing essentially the same thing, namely, breaking the law of God. Despising thus the riches of God's goodness, the Jews were treasuring up wrath for themselves because God's judgment is based on strict justice. God rewards each man according to his works. To those who are patient in well doing, God will give eternal life; to those who obey not the truth, He will give tribulation and anguish. And this applies to the Jew as well as to the Gentile. God is no respecter of persons. The Gentiles sinned without the Mosaic law—they shall perish without it; the Jews sinned under the law—they shall be judged by it. For having or hearing the law does not justify; only the doers of the law shall be justified. (In a sense the Gentiles too have the law of God, not the Mosaic law to be sure, but from their creation in the image of God they have the moral law written on their hearts.) If God's wrath were the last word, strict justice would be satisfied, but no one would be saved. But before the righteousness that is given to man through faith can be explained, more emphasis must be put on human sin.

The Jews had many spiritual privileges. They knew more about God than the Gentiles did. Unfortunately, this made them proud, conceited, and Pharisaical. The contrast between their profession and their conduct caused the Gentiles to blaspheme. Those privileges increased, not decreased, their responsibility. Circumcision and the ritual are privileges, but to profit from them one must keep the law. The true child of God is not one who makes an outward profession by receiving the sacraments; he is a Jew who is one inwardly, one in whom the outward sacramental sign truly represents an inward spiritual reality.

To have the sacraments and the oracles of God is a great privilege, even if some misuse them. Man's lack of faith does not nullify God's promises. God will be true, even though every man is a liar. Some Jews try to argue that their unfaithfulness contrasts so sharply with God's faithfulness that God's goodness is put in a much clearer light. But to emphasize God's goodness is to glorify Him. Therefore God ought not punish them for their unfaithfulness. Nonsense! By that argument God could not even punish the Gentiles. It would always be proper to do evil that good might come. But it is never right to do wrong. There is never an excuse for disobeying God's commands. Those who adopt this wicked principle are most justly condemned.

3. Condemnation of All Men (3:9–20)

To those who by patience in well doing seek for glory and incorruption, God will give eternal life. But there are no such persons. All are under sin. There is none righteous, no, not one; there is none that seeketh after God. Whatever "religion" may be, Christianity is not man's search for God nor is the Bible a record of such a search; Christianity is God's search for rebellious man and the Bible is His message of redemption. Men need redemption, for their throat is an open sepulchre, their feet are swift to shed blood, and there is no fear of God before their eyes.

The law was given that every mouth should be stopped and that the whole world should be guilty before God. For by the works of the law no one shall ever be justified in God's sight.

Surely there is a deep need of some good news.

III. Brief Statement of Justification by Faith (3:21–31)

If Romans is the most important book of the Bible, this section is the most important section in Romans. With full realization of the beauty of the Psalms, the majesty of Isaiah, and the popularity of John 3:16, one has good reason to judge that Romans 3:25, 26 contains more of the Gospel than any other sentence in the Bible. Let us study the section with great care.

The question is, If all are guilty and deserving of God's wrath, how can anyone be saved?

The answer is, God demands righteousness, but He has Himself furnished the righteousness He demands. It is a righteousness that is not based on our obedience to the law. To be sure, the Law and the Prophets have taught this righteousness and have made it clear ever since the fall of Adam. It is a righteousness of God, not of man; but man receives it by faith in Jesus Christ. The faith referred to is not some vague general religious faith. Currently there are voices in the public press exhorting the people to have faith; sometimes the object of this faith is said to be man, sometimes God, and sometimes the object is left unidentified. In contrast, the faith of which Paul speaks is definitely faith in Jesus Christ.

This faith is not itself the righteousness that God gives, nor is it the basis of the righteousness; rather, it is the means of obtaining it.

This plan of redemption is suitable to all, for all men are in the same state; they are all guilty; they have all sinned.

Now comes the main statement on justification. But first, it is extremely important to know what the term justification means. This is discovered by observing how it is used by Paul and by other New Testament writers.

In Romans 2:13 it is said, "The doers of the law shall be justified." Since doers of the law would not be sinners, yet they would be justified, it follows that justification does not mean pardon. Doers of the law cannot be pardoned. The remark applies also to Romans 3:4, for God is never pardoned; and to Romans 3:20.

Since justification is connected with righteousness, could "justify" mean to make righteous? Once again, Romans 3:4 shows that it cannot, for no one makes God righteous. When too in Luke 7:29 "the publicans justified God," they did not make God righteous. (Cf. Lk. 7:35; 10:29).

Key to the meaning is seen in the way justification is contrasted with condemnation. "By thy words thou shalt be justified and by thy words thou shalt be condemned" (Mt. 12:37; cf. Rom. 5:16; 8:33, 34).

To condemn a man is not to make him unrighteous; when a judge condemns a prisoner, he does not make him a criminal. The condemnation is not a moral change in the person at all. To condemn is to declare a man's guilt. The accused has already committed the crime, he is already an evil character; the judge merely declares publicly that he is guilty. Since justification is the opposite of condemnation, it is God's judicial sentence that the accused is not guilty. Justification therefore means acquittal.

The accused, however, is guilty. He is a sinner. How then is justification or acquittal possible? Obviously it cannot be merited. Sinners do not merit God's favor. Justification therefore is a free gift, entirely gratuitous, a matter of grace. Still, this does not explain how a just God can justly declare a guilty sinner to be innocent.

This seemingly impossible result was accomplished through the redemption that is in Christ Jesus.

God sent Christ to die as a propitiatory sacrifice. To propitiate means to appease an injured party, to turn aside his wrath, to make him favorable to the offender. This is what Christ's blood accomplished.

If it seemed unrighteous for God to acquit the guilty, Christ's death satisfied the requirements of righteousness, so that God could justify the sinner and at the same time remain just Himself. Christ's death, therefore, was a sacrifice to satisfy divine justice and as a consequence to reconcile us to God.

Of course, not all sinners are acquitted. The benefit is restricted to those who have faith in Christ. Faith is the means by which the benefits of Christ's death are applied. The basis, as distinguished from the means, of justification is Christ Himself, or more particularly, Christ's personal righteousness.

Thus justification excludes all human boasting in the deeds of the law. Christ has satisfied God's requirements for us.

IV. Abraham, a Confirmation of Justification (4:1–25)

That justification by faith is the only method of salvation, and has been the only method since the fall of Adam, is seen in the example of Abraham. Abraham was justified by faith, not by works, for he had no works of which to boast. Scripture is clear on this point (Gen. 15:6).

The wording here, if detached from the main material of Romans 3:25, 26, might give the impression that faith itself is the basis of justification. But Paul allows himself some abbreviation of language in view of the fact that he had spoken so explicitly in the verses above. He had already spoken of faith in Christ and of being justified by faith in His blood. When God acquits a sinner, He does so on the ground of a righteousness that He gives to the sinner. The righteousness comes to the sinner by faith; but from the beginning (1:17) Paul has indicated that it is the righteousness and not the faith which God regards when He says, Not guilty. One should never forget that it is the object of the faith, and not the faith itself, that produces the result.

The imputation of righteousness, and this is grace, shows that redemption is not something that God owes us for our works. David made that clear (Ps. 32:1, 2). God counts us righteous, not because of what we have done, but because He puts Christ's righteousness to our account.

The principle of grace excludes even circumcision (and baptism and the Lord's Supper as well) as a basis of acquittal. Abraham was justified first and circumcised afterward. Hence Abraham could be the father of believing Gentiles as well as of believing Jews.

Similarly, the nature both of the promises and of the law supports justification by faith. God's promises are ours for merely believing them; their fulfilment does not depend on our keeping the law. The law specifies penalties for disobedience, and if we depended on the law for God's blessing, faith would be useless, and the promises would be useless too. Not only that, but since we are never sure that we shall obey the law, assurance of salvation must depend on faith, promise, and grace. Only in this way can we be sure.

Abraham is an excellent illustration, for the promise God gave him was hard to believe. Yet he did not stagger at it. Now the book of Genesis is not just so much ancient history. It explains the only plan of redemption that God has ever offered to mankind. Imputation applies to us today as much as it did to Abraham, provided, of course, that we believe on Christ Who was crucified for our sins and was raised again for our justification.

V. Results of Justification (5:1–21)

Although the results of justification continue through chapters 6, 7, and 8, these three form a special section, so that chapter 5 must be treated as a single unit.

The first mentioned result of justification is peace with God. Previously we had been enemies of God. But through Jesus Christ we receive peace, grace, and hope. Even our tribulations are now a blessing because they produce patience, experience, and a hope that shall not be disappointed. All this depends on the work of Christ, Who died for us even while we were yet sinners and enemies. Now that we have been reconciled to God by the death of His Son, and are no longer enemies, it is all the more certain that He will save us from the wrath to come.

Christ's death is the effective factor; and before further results of justification are given in the next three chapters, it is necessary to explain more in detail just how Christ's death accomplishes its purpose.

Romans 5:12–21 are about the most difficult verses in the epistle. To understand them it is best to fix in mind, first, how they are introduced. The design of the paragraph is to explain justification. From 3:21 on, the merit of Christ's sacrifice has been prominent, and the immediately preceding verses stress that merit. The work of Christ is now to be explained by a comparison with the work of Adam. Any interpretation that destroys the comparison must be incorrect. Of course, the work of Adam and the work of Christ are antithetical in some important particulars; these differences are carefully mentioned and set aside in 5:15–17. But there is also a most important point of similarity; correct interpretation must discover what it is.

The difficulty of the passage is aggravated by its complicated grammatical structure. Verse 12 begins the comparison between Adam and Christ, but it breaks off half way through. The comparison is resumed in verses 18 and 19. Verses 13 and 14 are a sort of parenthetical remark attached to the end of verse 12, and verses 15, 16, and 17 form another parenthesis attached to the end of verse 14. The main thought therefore is found in verses 12, 18, and 19.

The analogy of these verses is this: Christ is the cause of our righteousness and justification in the same way that Adam is the cause of our sin and condemnation. How then did Adam cause our sin?

Did Adam bring sin and death upon all men by reason of the fact that all men followed his example and, themselves, committed voluntary transgressions?

This interpretation must be rejected for four reasons. First, the phrase "all sinned" uses a tense which in Greek refers to a single act in past time and not to many acts in the present. Second, the purpose of these verses (and this is certainly made especially clear in verses 16 and 17) is to show that Adam's one sin, not our many sins, is the cause of death. Third, the idea of imitating Adam's example is explicitly ruled out in verse 14. And fourth, if we die because we imitate Adam's example, then, to maintain the comparison between Adam and Christ, justification would have to be the result of imitating Christ.

Perhaps then, when it says "all sinned," it means "all became corrupt"; that is, Adam's sin caused him to deteriorate physically and spiritually, and since we naturally inherit his depraved nature, we sin and die.

This interpretation also must be rejected. It is true, of course, that we inherit a depraved nature from Adam; but such is not the sense of this passage. First, "all became corrupt" is an impossible translation. The text says, "all sinned." Second, it ruins the comparison between Adam and Christ. If we become sinners and die because of a moral change for the worse, it would follow that we are justified because of a moral change for the better. Such an idea is essentially a justification by works, or at best, it is the Roman Catholic position of justification by faith plus works. Luther and Calvin, however, have made it forever clear that justification is by faith alone—without works, lest Abraham should boast. Third, verses 15–19 emphasize the *one* sin of Adam as the ground of our condemnation. Neither our depravity nor our sinfulness is said to be this ground.

None of this denies that we are in fact depraved, nor that we commit sins, nor indeed, as we shall see in the following three chapters, that justification is followed by a moral change and good works. It does deny that any of these things is the basis on which God acquits the sinner.

The only interpretation that does justice to the text is that Adam was our substitute or representative. He acted in our stead. Therefore when he sinned and died, we all sinned and we all died. His representative act, his one sin—not his many sins that he committed in later life—is the ground upon which God condemned us. His one act made us all guilty.

This view of how Adam's sin is the cause of our guilt preserves the comparison between Adam and Christ, for the whole scriptual description of our relation to Christ is permeated with the concept of representation. We die with Christ; we are crucified with Christ; we rose with Him; and we sit with Him in heavenly places. These phrases cannot be true of us personally, for we had not been born when Christ was crucified. These expressions are true representatively. When Christ died, He paid the penalty of sin in our stead. He took our place. He was our substitute or representative. Therefore as the guilt of the one man Adam was imputed to us for condemnation, so the righteousness of the one man Jesus Christ was imputed to us for our justification.

It is sometimes claimed that this interpretation is the result of theological prejudice. Quite the contrary! The natural mind, which wants to boast, would never have invented this doctrine. The men of the Reformation maintained it because the Bible itself forced it on them. To the self-righteous justification, by means of faith, on the ground of Christ's imputed righteousness, is the scandal of the Cross.

VI. Reply to First Objection: Justification Promotes Sin (6:1—8:39)

1. Justification Produces Sanctification (6:1–23)

The magnitude of God's grace is seen more clearly when contrasted with the extent of sin. Therefore Paul had just said, "Where sin abounded, grace did much more abound." From this just sentiment, however, the sinful mind has a natural tendency to draw fallacious inferences. Hence Paul introduces an objection to his doctrine by the question, "Shall we continue in sin that grace may abound?"

Recall (3:7, 8) that the unbelieving Jews had inconsistently and slanderously accused Paul of teaching "Let us do evil that good may come." It is necessary, therefore, to defend justification against the charge that it encourages sin. This defense is the doctrine of sanctification.

Justification and sanctification are sometimes misunderstood by being too sharply separated and contrasted. The adversitive *but* is put between them: We are justified by faith, *but*, for some mysterious reason, we must now do good works. Other Christians avoid the sharp antithesis, but leave the two as somewhat unrelated facts. Instead of using the *but*, they use *and*: We are justified by faith, *and*, to change the subject, we are sanctified by works.

Paul, however, connects them closely. Not *but*, not *and*, but *therefore*. We are justified by faith, *therefore* we should not sin.

Sanctification is the purpose of justification. And so surely does justification produce its result that Paul is able to say, "Sin shall not have dominion over you" (6:14). To borrow other scriptural expressions, one might say, justification is the straight gate and sanctification is the narrow way that leads to glory.

In answer to the question, "Shall we continue in sin that grace may abound?" the main point of the first fourteen verses is briefly this: No one who comes to Christ for salvation from both the guilt and power of sin can possibly want to continue sinning. Christ's work on the cross was an expiation of sin. The sinner who trusts in Christ's shed blood knows that his "old man is crucified with him, that the body of sin might be destroyed" (6:6); and considers himself "dead with Christ" (v. 8). If a man does not thus identify himself with Christ's purpose to destroy sin, and if, instead of grief and hatred of sin, he cherishes the notion that he may continue in sin that grace may abound, the conclusion is inevitable that this man knows nothing of Christ and has not been justified. To speak plainly, it is psychologically impossible to trust Christ's redeeming blood and to want to continue in sin. Sanctification is not merely the purpose of justification, as if the purpose might fail; but rather sanctification is the inevitable result.

There is a progression of thought in chapter 6. The first fourteen verses consider the question, Shall we sin in order that grace may abound? This envisages a wicked calculation of habitual sinning. Verse 15 asks a different question: Shall we sin because we are under grace? This envisages not the wicked calculation of habitual sin, but the lazy indifference of an occasional sin. Verse 1 asks, Shall we sin *in order that?* Verse 15 asks, Shall we sin *because?*

Lazy indifference may not be so heinous as wicked calculation, but it is equally excluded. With the illustration from slavery that Christ Himself used, Paul constructs an easily understood syllogism: No man can serve two masters; we are no longer servants of sin but slaves of God; therefore it is God Whom we should obey.

2. Law and Grace (7:1–25)

In some ways this chapter is perhaps even more difficult than 5:12–21. Yet the Protestant reformers were well agreed as to its meaning. The difficulty is to determine whether Paul is speaking of a regenerate or an unregenerate person. Most of the expressions in verses 7–13 can easily be taken as referring to the unregenerate, especially since the verbs are in the past tense. But can verses 14–25, in the present tense, refer to the unregenerate? Or is Paul describing the normal experience of a Christian?

To answer this question one should observe the position of chapter 7 as a whole. The plan of the epistle makes sanctification the topic of chapters 6 to 8. To expect anything but an incidental reference to the unregenerate state would be to break the continuity of the argument.

Then too, the wider context of all of Paul's epistles, and indeed the whole Bible, teaches that the Christian experiences a conflict with sin, whereas the unregenerate man is at ease in sin. Perhaps the unregenerate may have some twinges of conscience (1:32; 2:15), but since there is no spiritual life, no new strength, the conflict is extremely superficial (Ps. 73:4–12; 119:70; Mt. 13:13–15; Rom. 3:9–18).

Now the person spoken of in this chapter is inwardly inclined to good. Nearly every one of the last twelve verses emphasizes this in sharp contrast to the four references just listed. Here the person hates the evil he does, he wants to do good, he delights in the law of God after the inward man, and he thanks God for deliverence through Jesus Christ. These things are not true of the unregenerate.

The experience described, therefore, is the normal experience of a devout Christian. The more sincere he is and the more faithfully he tries to please God, the more conscious is he of the struggle. Thus the very occurrence of the struggle is evidence of his regeneration. (Cf. Ps. 38:4; 40:12; Is. 6:5; Mt. 26:41; I Cor. 3:1–4).

The present chapter therefore enforces the teaching of the previous chapter (6:12, 13, 16) that sanctification is not, like justification, an instantaneous act. Sanctification is the life process of growing in holiness. And this requires effort (Gal. 5:17; Jas. 4:7; I Pet. 2:11). Verse 24 therefore is not to be understood as a doomed man's cry of despair, but as the introduction to the thanksgiving evoked by the answer to the question.

These general remarks do not solve all the incidental difficulties of particular verses. There are still a number in the first half of the chapter. But the main idea is not now left in doubt. The law of God is good, it is spiritual, it should be an object of delight. Nevertheless, as the law could not justify the sinner, neither can it of itself sanctify the Christian. The law may indeed show what God requires, but it cannot give the life, inclination, or strength to do good. Grace is needed. But is this grace sufficient? The next chapter answers this question.

3. *Assurance of Salvation (8:1–39)*

This section of three chapters (6:1—8:39) teaches, as we have seen, that justification by faith, far from encouraging sin, produces sanctification. The present chapter, the last of the three, considers assurance of salvation. This assurance is a stage in the process of sanctification.

The break between the chapters, which, of course, is not of Paul's doing, is an unfortunate medieval blunder, for it obscures the fact that 8:1 is the conclusion of the thought in 7:25. *Because* God has delivered me from this death of sin, *because* He has given me the strength to struggle, *therefore* there is no condemnation to them that are in Christ Jesus. This assurance is supported in seven short paragraphs.

(1) We are freed from the law (8:1–4). The law could not justify the sinner; it can only condemn him. But Christ did what the law could not do; and therefore its condemnation does not reach the believer.

(2) Salvation is actually begun in regeneration, justification, and sanctification (8:5–11). The Spirit of God dwells in the believer. Therefore, instead of being carnally minded, and at enmity with God, the believer is interested in the things of the Spirit. The work of the indwelling Spirit extends even to the resurrection of the mortal body.

(3) We are children and heirs of God (8:12–17). The indwelling Spirit makes us children and enables us to address God as father. When we think of God as father, the Holy Spirit is witnessing *with* (not *to*) our spirit that we are God's children; and if children, then we must be heirs of God and joint heirs with Christ.

(4) Affliction does not refute this (8:18–28). Christ was the Son of God, and He suffered; if we suffer with Him, it confirms rather than refutes our sonship. These sufferings are not restricted to what people ordinarily call persecution. They include all our earthly limitations and weaknesses, all our trials and burdens, and our subjection to physical death. In these sufferings we may groan and not know what to pray for; but the same indwelling Spirit "maketh

intercession for the saints according to the will of God. And we know all things work together for good to them that love God."

(5) We have been predestinated to eternal life (8:28–30). Reasons for assurance have been building up toward a climax. They converge on the eternal purpose of God. The transition from the previous paragraph is the phrase, "who are called according to his purpose." God has a plan or purpose for history; this plan includes not only the grand scheme of things but also every detail, for God works *all things* together; according to this divine purpose God has called or chosen them who now love Him. For those persons whom He foreknew or chose, He also predestinated to live a Christ-like life; and those whom He thus predestinated, He called; since they were effectually called, He justified them; and those whom He justified, He will also glorify. There is in this progression no point at which an individual can drop out. Every one of each preceding class is included in each succeeding class. All the predestinated are justified; all the justified shall be glorified. Since this process from beginning to end is controlled by God, and does not depend on our working all things, the doctrine of predestination is a most important ground of assurance of salvation.

(6) God is for us (8:31–34). He was so interested in our salvation that He did not spare His own Son; it cannot be supposed that God would give His Son and hold back the lesser gifts of sanctification and glorification. God is in control. It is He Who has justified us; and that settles the matter.

(7) God's love is immutable (8:35–39). This final paragraph adds no further grounds of assurance, but rather summarizes them and enforces their application. A series of factors are mentioned, famine, peril, sword, angels, powers, things to come, that sometimes becloud a Christian's assurance; but none of them is omnipotent, and God is. He has chosen to love us. Therefore nothing can separate us from the love of God which is in Christ Jesus our Lord.

VII. Reply to Second Objection: It Annuls God's Promises (9:1—11:36)

1. God's Sovereign Choice (9:1–33)

Paul naturally yearned for the salvation of his own race; and he saw that rejection of Christ by the Jews and the justification of

Gentiles by faith produced the illusion that the Word of God was of no effect. Had not the promises been given to the Israelites?

No, they had not. At least the promises were not given to the physical descendants of Abraham as such. Ishmael was excluded in favor of Isaac. Esau also was excluded in favor of Jacob. These exclusions are inherent in the promise itself; that is, the choice is God's.

Note well that the choice was made before the children had been born and before either of them had done any good or evil. This was to show that the determining factor is God's purpose. Election does not depend on our works, but on Him that calleth.

Was God then unjust to choose Jacob, and not Esau, before they were born and apart from their works? Not at all. In the first place, it is not a question of justice, as if Jacob and Esau had some claim on God, but of mercy and compassion. Furthermore, it was God's prerogative also to harden Pharaoh's heart for the purpose of displaying His power in him.

Is then God unjust in punishing the wicked, seeing that no one can possibly resist God's will? Not at all. No one has any right to find fault with God. God is like a potter. Out of the very same lump of clay He makes one vessel for honor and another for dishonor. It is ridiculous to suppose that the clay can dictate to the potter.

God therefore fitted out certain vessels for destruction in order to make known the riches of His glory on the vessels of mercy which He prepared unto glory. And these vessels of mercy include some Gentiles and exclude some Jews.

The distinguishing factor between the two groups is faith in Christ. Some Gentiles have faith; but some Jews, in fact the majority, trusting in their own works, find Christ to be a stone of stumbling and a rock of offense.

2. Jewish Zeal and Disobedience (10:1–21)

Nevertheless, Paul naturally desires the salvation of the Jews. Unfortunately, they are ignorant of the incarnation and the resurrection, though Moses prophesied of the Messiah, and their zeal is centered in multitudinous works. The righteousness of faith, on the other hand, comes more easily, simply by the acceptance of the Gospel.

Now, the Gospel briefly is this: If thou shalt confess that Jesus is Lord, Adonai, the Jehovah of the Old Testament, and sincerely believe in His resurrection from the dead, thou shalt be saved. And this applies to Jew and Gentile alike.

But faith or belief in this Gospel depends on hearing it; and this presupposes preaching; and this requires the dispatch of missionaries and evangelists to all nations. Now, the Jews have indeed heard, but they did not believe our report; therefore God is provoking and angering them by choosing the Gentiles.

3. The Future of Israel (11:1–36)

Hath God then cast away His people forever? Not at all. First, His people, in the sense of those individuals whom He foreknew, God has not cast away. This does not mean all the Jews. For as it was in the time of Elijah, so now the elect are a remnant. Election is of grace, not of works, so that while the remnant obtained grace, the rest were blinded. God gave them the spirit of slumber and caused them to stumble in order to bring salvation to the Gentiles.

Of course, no one would suppose that God would cast away the remnant elected by grace. But there is also another sense in which God will not cast off His people. The Jews as a race still figure in God's plan and they will have a glorious future. For if the impoverishment of the Jews in the first century enriched the Gentiles, the return of the Jews in the future will produce much greater blessings. It will be like life from the dead.

The history of the Church can be illustrated by an olive tree. Some of its original and natural branches were broken off so that branches from a wild olive tree could be grafted in. This, of course, is no compliment or ground of boasting for the Gentiles. And if God did not spare the natural branches because of their unbelief, the Gentiles should take heed lest God spare not them also. Furthermore, if God has grafted in wild branches, is it not all the more certain that He will graft back the natural branches at some future date?

The blindness of the Jews is to continue until "the fulness of the Gentiles" be come in. This fulness may indicate a time when the great majority of Gentiles then living shall have been converted. Virtually the whole world will be Christian. Such an interpretation makes a proper contrast with "all Israel" in the next verse. Or "the fulness of the Gentiles" might possibly refer to a time when all the Gentiles whom God has chosen for salvation, even though not a majority, have been saved and God will save no more of them. At any rate, when this fulness occurs, then the great majority of the Jews shall be saved also. This ultimate conversion of the Jews was prophesied in the Old Testament.

"O the depth of the riches both of the wisdom and knowledge of God! How unsearchable are his judgments and his ways past finding out! . . . For of him, and through him, and to him are all things: to whom be glory forever. Amen" (11:33, 36).

VIII. Practical Exhortations (12:1—16:27)

1. Service in the Church (12:1–21)

With the main exposition of doctrine completed, Paul here turns to a series of directions for everyday living. There are some coherent paragraphs in these five chapters, but there are many passages which are merely lists of successive items.

First comes a general exhortation to present ourselves as living sacrifices to God (12:1, 2). Such service is intelligent worship. Then Paul passes on to the idea that each person has his particular function in the Church. There are many members of the one body and God has given them different measures of faith. Some are called to prophesy, others are called to minister, to teach, to exhort, or to rule. Each should perform his office with simplicity, diligence, and cheerfulness, remembering that they are all members of the one body.

The virtues which are to be exemplified in this service, some of which indeed apply beyond the strict confines of the church organization, are love, zeal, hope, patience, and hospitality. Humility should replace conceit. Peace should be sought rather than vengeance. "Be not overcome of evil, but overcome evil with good."

2. Political Duties (13:1–14)

Goverment is not merely a human invention; it is ordained of God for the good of the governed; and therefore a Christian is obliged to obey the laws, not only from fear of civil penalties, but chiefly for conscience toward God. The employment of the sword and the collection of taxes are, briefly, the two chief functions of the State. By the term "sword," Paul means the penalties of disobedience, obviously including capital punishment, and doubtless war as well.

From this passage James I of England and other absolute monarchs have argued for the divine right of kings, and some theologians have concurred that subjects must invariably submit. John Calvin and John Knox, on the contrary, pointed out that rulers also have obligations, and when they fail to discharge their obligations, they may be disobeyed and even replaced. Peter (Acts 5:29) said, "We ought to obey God rather than men." The midwives of Egypt also (Ex. 1:17) and Moses' parents (Ex. 2:3) disobeyed Pharaoh. If then government is ordained of God, it would seem reasonable that it has no authority contrary to God's commands.

But in all ordinary cases, and this is most of the time, a Christian should obey the law.

He should, of course, obey the law of God—the Ten Commandments which specify the contents of love. The light of the Gospel has dawned, heaven is nearer than it was, so therefore "let us put on the armour of light."

3. Personal Responsibility (14:1–23)

Some people are weak in the faith. Instead of limiting their scruples to the precepts of God's Word, they are conscientiously opposed to eating pork and are strict in the observance of feast and fast days.

Such persons should be received into church membership and should not be despised. But they are not to be received for the purpose of disputing matters in doubt; that is, the weak and superstitious Christian who eateth not is not to set the standards for Christian conduct. It is not their prerogative but God's to judge the actions of the more mature Christian. Both groups are trying to serve the Lord, and all shall stand before the judgment seat of Christ. Each individual therefore must personally assume his responsibilities as he sees them.

Although it is the weaker group that is apt to be censorious and cause friction, it devolves chiefly upon those who are stronger in the faith to diminish the friction by a policy of accommodation. Eating pork and drinking wine are not sins, they are matters of indifference; but precisely because they are indifferent they do not constitute the Kingdom of God. The Kingdom consists of righteousness, peace, and joy in the Holy Ghost. Therefore if any form of indifferent conduct is likely to cause a weaker Christian to violate his conscience, the stronger Christian, though he may allow himself these things on other occasions, is obliged to forego them in such circumstances. For violation of conscience, the doing of what one believes wrong, is a sin that God condemns. No one should lead a weaker Christian into this sin.

4. Paul's Missionary Ambitions (15:1–33)

The opening verses of this chapter confirm and enforce the duties just enjoined partly by an appeal to the example of Christ. We should try to please our neighbor, when it is to his good, for Christ pleased not Himself. Christ also received us, and therefore we too should receive the weak in faith.

The work of Christ brings to Paul's mind the calling of the Gentiles, and this introduces Paul's missionary ambitions. He has been particularly anxious to preach the Gospel in places where Christ has not been named. This aim of starting new churches in unevangelized territory is the reason why Paul has not been able to visit Rome. Fortunately, at present his work in Greece is about finished and he can think of taking the Gospel to Spain. This will give him the oft desired opportunity of visiting the imperial city. First, however, he must deliver to the poverty stricken saints in Jerusalem the relief money that the Greeks have so generously contributed. Then he plans to sail for Spain. He asks the Roman Christians to pray for his safety during his stay at Jerusalem, for there is always the danger that the Pharisees might arrest him and have him executed.

5. Personal Greetings (16:1–27)

In his travels, Paul had met multitudes of people. A number of his converts, for one reason or another, had gone to Rome. Therefore Paul sends greetings to more than two dozen saints by name. Phebe, who apparently is to carry the letter, he commends to the Romans for her faithful service. Priscilla and Aquila, who have hazarded their lives for Paul, now put their house in Rome at the disposal of the Roman church for one of its particular congregations, and so on.

In conclusion, Paul warns the Romans to avoid those who deviate from the doctrine that has been taught. They may be fair of speech, but they serve not our Lord Jesus Christ.

Then after including some salutations from his associates, Paul ends the epistle with a benediction and a doxology.

I Corinthians

PHILIP E. HUGHES

THIS IMPORTANT LETTER was written by the Apostle Paul from Ephesus (cf. 16:8) some time between the years A.D. 55 to 57, during the period of his third missionary journey. It is the first of two letters sent by him to the Corinthians which are still extant. But that there had been at least one earlier letter, now lost, is apparent from what he says in 5:9, "I wrote unto you in an epistle not to company with fornicators." First Corinthians is remarkable for its wealth of content and for the light it throws on the condition of a young church, with its great gifts and serious problems, in a pagan setting during the first generation of the age of the apostles.

It was while engaged on his second missionary journey that Paul first set foot on the soil of Greece, under the impulse of the vision in Troas (Acts 16:9, 10). After traveling southward through Macedonia and preaching in Athens, he arrived in Corinth where he met Aquila and his wife Priscilla, who had recently come to the city and in whose home he stayed. In Corinth he preached the Gospel to both Jews and Gentiles, earning his daily bread meanwhile by working at his craft of tentmaking, which was also Aquila's trade (Acts 18:1–4).

The city of Corinth, a seaport strategically situated on the isthmus which joined the Greek mainland to the southernmost "island" known as the Peloponnesus, was one of the great commercial centers of the ancient world. Not only was it a populous cosmopolitan center, but it was notorious as a place of vice and immorality in which the idolatries of heathenism and their accompanying licentiousness flourished. It was in this setting that Paul, on his first visit, spent no less than eighteen months proclaiming the message of salvation and founding a church (Acts 18:11). To this church some three years later he wrote the letter now known as I Corinthians.

I. Greetings and Thanksgiving (1:1–9)

1. Salutation (1:1–3)

Paul makes it clear in the opening sentence of the epistle that he is writing in his capacity as an apostle, literally as one "sent forth." What he says, therefore, comes with the full force of his apostolic authority. Sosthenes, who was evidently with him in Ephesus at the time, and who had become chief ruler of the synagogue in Corinth during Paul's original visit to Corinth (Acts 18:17), is coupled with the apostle in this introductory salutation. He is now spoken of as "the brother," that is, the fellow-Christian well-known to the Corinthian believers; and it is probable that he had been converted, like Crispus, his predecessor as chief ruler of the synagogue at Corinth, through the ministry of Paul.

This opening salutation, considered in the light of the contents of the epistle, affords valuable information concerning Paul's doctrine of the Church. This letter shows the Christian community at Corinth as split apart into factions, puffed up with self-esteem, guilty of lack of discipline, immorality and libidinousness, careless in the conduct of public worship, and caught in grave doctrinal error in so crucial a tenet as that of the resurrection of the dead. Yet the Apostle Paul does not forbear to assign to it the title of *church* and to describe its members as "sanctified in Christ Jesus," "called" (of God), and "saints." It is clearly evident, then, that he was no perfectionist in his doctrine of the Church as it exists in this present world. The Church's perfection and sanctity reside not in itself, but "in Christ Jesus" (cf. 1:30). Its errors and imperfections, blameworthy indeed, are the marks of the fierce assaults of enemies from within and from without whose object is to destroy the flock of Christ (cf. Acts 20:29, 30). But the very fact that the church should have been brought into existence at all in so dark and wicked a place can be attributed only to the power of Almighty God (cf. 1:18–31), not to the ability of Paul or his fellow-laborers (cf. 3:5–8); and because it is the work of *God,* not of man, Paul knows that it is a work for eternity which no power of evil can possibly frustrate (cf. 1:8, 9; Phil. 1:6).

The salutation is, in general, similar in form to those which introduce all of Paul's epistles.

2. Thanksgiving for Spiritual Riches of the Corinthian Church (1:4–9)

The blessings enjoyed by the Corinthian church, for which Paul gives thanks, had displayed themselves in many ways, particularly in the spiritual or charismatic gifts that had been granted to them. These gifts, listed in 12:8–10, were evidence of the powerful working of the Holy Spirit in and through their community. The enjoyment of these gifts stands in startling contrast to the serious faults and abuses which had been permitted to gain a footing in the Corinthian congregation. From this state of affairs we may learn that, however great our enrichment in spiritual blessings may be, we are always in danger of falling into sin and error, especially through the temptation to spiritual pride. Consequently, the apostolic warning, "Let him that thinketh he standeth take heed lest he fall." (10:12) should be kept constantly in mind. The root trouble with the Corinthian church was that its members had inexcusably become puffed up with pride and selfishness because of their enrichment with spiritual gifts; and this had inevitably led to the misuse of these gifts and the dishonoring of God who had given them. In this connection, "puffed up" is a key expression in the epistle (see 4:6, 18, 19; 5:2; 8:1; 13:4; and the idea of leaven, even a little of which puffs up the whole lump, 5:6, 7).

Paul, it should be noticed, does not allow the heartbreaking disappointment, which the abuses and disorders within the church at Corinth must have occasioned him, to cause him to doubt the reality of the work of God in that place. All along it is *in God* that he trusts and *to God* that he looks. Man may be unfaithful, but *God is faithful,* and those whom God has called cannot be called in vain. In the day of our Lord Jesus Christ, it will be seen that the Word of God and the work of God cannot fail (vv. 8, 9).

II. Serious Failings Reproved (1:10—6:20)

1. Divisions and Factions (1:10—4:21)

Christ is Not Divided (1:10–17). The Apostle Paul exhorts his readers to display that perfect unity which should be characteristic of all who are brethren in Christ. (Note the significant way in which he addresses them as brethren in vv. 10, 11). This exhortation was necessary because of the report he had received of the quarrels which had split them into factions. There appear to have been four rival parties: (*1*) those who professed to follow Paul; (*2*) those who professed to follow Apollos; (*3*) those who professed to follow Peter (Cephas); and (*4*) those who professed to follow Christ. To what special advantages the last mentioned party laid claim is uncertain, but it may be that its leaders attempted to make capital of the fact that they had known and followed Christ during His earthly ministry ("according to the flesh") and were therefore supposedly superior to Paul, who had not known Christ in this way. (Note the implications of what Paul says in II Cor. 5:15; 10:7; 11:23.) Christians, however, together form one body in Christ, and Christ is not divided (cf. 12:12). In view of these divisions, Paul is even thankful that so few in Corinth were baptized by him with the result that it could not be suggested that he had by baptizing gone out of his way to get a following for himself.

The Preaching of the Cross (1:18–31). The proclamation of the Gospel was the activity on which Paul had concentrated in Corinth; and the message of Christ crucified, stumblingblock though it was to the Jews with their traditionalism, and foolishness to the Greeks with their love of philosophy, had proved to be the power of God and the wisdom of God to every believer, transforming lives and personalities and rescuing them from the degradation of their surroundings. Nor, for the most part, were those chosen by God persons whom the world would regard as wise or powerful or of high birth. In everything, therefore, the wisdom, the power, and the glory belong to God; all that the Corinthian believers are they owe to Christ. Thus it is in the Lord alone, not in self or party or in supposed human ability, that any Christian ought to glory.

Paul's Preaching in Corinth (2:1–5). The apostle adds a moving appeal to the knowledge of his Corinthian brethren that he had shunned the arts of rhetoric and philosophy when he came to them, that he had preached not himself but the crucified Saviour to them, and that his ministry among them had been marked by human weakness and fear and much trembling. There could be no question, then, of their faith standing in the wisdom of men. The power they had experienced through faith in Christ was none other than the power of God. He had, in fact, given them no excuse whatever for the formation of a Paul party.

True Wisdom (2:6–16). Not that Paul deprecated wisdom—on the contrary, the message he proclaimed was precisely the essential and only true wisdom; for it was the wisdom *of God,* not the groping speculation of fallen man. It is a wisdom from which fallen man has cut himself off because of his sin. Indeed, the vanity of his reasoning is such that this divine wisdom appears as foolishness to him. Apart from the operation of God's grace, he cannot know it. Only by the revelation and teaching of the Holy Spirit is it possible for him to receive it. The redemption which God has in Christ extends to the whole man—to the intellect as well as to the soul and the body. Nor is this divine wisdom the possession only of a select few, as was the case with the teaching of the current "wisdom" religion of Gnosticism, but of every single believer, however humble his gifts or his education. It is summed up in the expression "the mind of Christ" (2:16), for, as Paul has previously reminded his readers, it is "Christ Jesus who of God is made unto us wisdom" and all things else (1:30).

Divisions a Sign of Unspirituality (3:1–4). There is, as Paul so frequently emphasizes, a constant warfare in progress between the Spirit and the flesh (cf. Gal. 5:17; Rom. 7:14—8:13), and this warfare continues at the center of the life of the Christian throughout his earthly pilgrimage. The factions which had destroyed the unity of the church in Corinth were an indication that the Christians there were not walking by the Spirit but were allowing the flesh, the downward pull of the old unregenerate life, to gain an ascendancy. They were behaving as though they were still fallen men with no experience of the uplifting power of the Spirit. This was a contradiction of their Christian profession.

Proper Conception of Christian Ministers (3:5–9). Paul and Apollos were both men of exceptional capacities: the former was remarkable for his intellectual brilliance, dynamic personality, and energy of purpose; the latter for his eloquence, his spiritual fervor, and his diligence as a teacher of Christian truth (cf. Acts 18:24, 25). Both were learned in the Scriptures. Two men of this caliber could not have failed to make a strong impression in Corinth as they boldly proclaimed the message of Christ; but the last thing they had intended was for their names to become the banners of rival factions in the church. Paul accordingly finds it necessary to instruct his readers concerning the true nature of Christian ministers. They are *servants* in God's employ, not masters and demagogues; they are fellow-laborers for God, not for self. In the light of the fact that it is the work *of God* to which they have been called, and that it is God, not man, who gives the increase to their sowing and watering of the good seed of eternal life, they are in themselves of no importance. All things are of God (II Cor. 5:18) and to glorify the names of Paul and Apollos as party leaders was to ignore this truth. Moreover, Paul who planted and Apollos who watered are *one*, united in Christ, the one Saviour; and the Corinthians who had been converted and built up through their ministry had not been won to Paul or to Apollos, but to Christ. They were the husbandry and building *of God*, not of Paul or of Apollos or of any other man whom they might profess to follow.

Building on the One Foundation (3:10–15). The mention of building causes Paul now to leave the metaphor of farming. He had laid the foundation (planted, v. 6), and upon this foundation Apollos had built (watered, v. 6); but that foundation, which is indeed the *only* foundation—all else is a quicksand—is Jesus Christ (not Paul). Though Apollos, from the ministerial point of view, built upon the foundation laid by Paul, yet the believer must not forget that he also has the responsibility of constructing a life upon the one foundation of Jesus Christ. Six different materials with which to build are mentioned, and these naturally fall into two groups of three each: (1) gold, silver, precious stones; (2) wood, hay, stubble. Paul pictures the building which the Corinthians are constructing upon the one foundation as being tested by fire. If the structure is of gold, silver, or precious stones, then it will abide, for these cannot be consumed but are only purified by the flames, and he who has built with these materials will be rewarded; but if it is of wood, hay or stubble, then it will be consumed and the one who has used these materials will suffer loss—although, because he is placed upon the one foundation, he himself will be saved.

The fire of which the apostle speaks is metaphorical, not literal, and is explained by the reference to "the day" (v. 13), that is, the day when Christ appears in glory and the flame of His presence will test and make apparent the work of all men (cf. 4:5). This teaching, together with the doctrine of reward and loss which is found both here and throughout the New Testament, gives great emphasis to the responsibility of every Christian to live worthily before God. Factions in the church, not to mention the other serious aberrations which come to light in the course of this epistle, indicated that, in general, the Corinthian Christians were building on the foundation of Jesus Christ with wood, hay, and stubble.

The Temple of God (3:16, 17). The admonition of the previous verses is enforced by the reminder to the Christians at Corinth that they are the temple of God. Paul uses the interrogatory "Know ye not," "Surely you know," to remind his readers of a truth concerning which they could not plead ignorance (cf. 5:6; 6:2, 3, 9, 15, 16, 19). This is true of believers both corporately (Eph. 2:20–22) and individually (6:19). It is the obligation of all to keep that temple holy and free from defilement. Paul's language here is illuminating because, although he does not develop the idea, it clearly indicates that the temple at Jerusalem is no longer the place of God's abode, but the hearts of those who are regenerated through faith in Christ (cf. 6:19; II Cor. 6:16; I Pet. 2:5; Acts 7:48). In Christ every one of the promises of God's covenant of grace is fulfilled; those who are Christ's are God's chosen people; and it is in the midst of them, as His temple, that He dwells forevermore (cf. Lev. 26:11, 12; Jer. 32:38–41; Ezek. 37:26, 27; Rev. 21:3). The significance of Paul's terminology here, then, is far-reaching, more particularly to the Jew who boasted of his physical descent and of his material temple (cf. Jn. 8:33–45; Rom. 2:28, 29; Gal. 3:16, 26–29).

Proper Conception of Christian Ministers Resumed (3:18—4:17). In 3:18–23 Paul draws together some of the threads of these first three chapters. What the fallen, self-complacent world praises as wisdom God counts as foolishness and vanity. (The classic analysis of this state of affairs is found in Rom. 1:18–32.) But the Christian should never glory in men, even though those men be apostles, for it is to Christ that he belongs, and all things find their meaning and their consummation in the Almighty Creator, not in any creature.

Those who, like himself and Apollos and Peter, are occupied in the work of the Gospel should be thought of, Paul repeats (cf. 3:5), as ministers (servants) and also, he adds, as stewards of God's mysteries. The steward is answerable to his master, and it is required of him, not that he should become a master himself with a following, but that he should prove himself faithful in fulfilling the duties entrusted to him by his master. If persons other than his master pass judgment on him, that is beside the point; indeed, it is not even legitimate for him to judge himself; for it is by his master and by him alone, that he is judged. So it is with Paul, Christ's servant and steward. Adherents of rival factions in the Corinthian Church had spoken censoriously of Paul and his ministry (4:3); but Paul's concern was not to be swayed by such judgments of men, but to be faithful in the prosecution of his divinely-given stewardship, until the coming of his Lord, Who alone has the right to pass judgment on his work. For the Corinthians to engage in party-strife and to be puffed up, one against another, was entirely without justification. They were passing judgment where they had no right to pass judgment, and they were glorying in men and living by the standards of the flesh. There was nothing for them to glory in except that which they had received *from God* (v. 7).

Paul then paints a starkly realistic word-picture of what it had meant to him and others to be an apostle (4:9–13). It is a portrait entirely devoid of all the glamor with which the world is accustomed to invest its leaders and favorites. The call of Christ had led the apostles to a life which this world, with its love of ease and popularity, abhors as miserable and unenviable. The apostles are like those abject captives appointed to a painful death who used to bring up the rear of a Roman triumphal procession; they are accounted fools, they are despised, hungry, thirsty, miserably clad, buffeted, homeless, toiling, reviled and persecuted, treated by the world as worthless refuse. Yet Paul, who is the apostle to the Corinthians, is their father in the faith—the one who in Christ Jesus had begotten them through the Gospel (v. 15). Through the faithfulness of his ministry, God had transformed their lives. Paul was no leader of a faction, but they, as his spiritual sons, should imitate him in the renunciation of wordly wisdom and pride and in single-minded devotion to Christ, their only master. Timothy, also, whom he had sent to them, and who, together with Silas, had joined Paul in Corinth during his original visit to that city (Acts 18:5), was also one of Paul's converts (v. 17; cf. I Tim. 1:2; II Tim. 1:2; Acts 16:1).

A Warning to Those who are "Puffed Up" (4:18–21). Some in Corinth who were puffed up with arrogance were saying that Paul would not come to them, insinuating that he was lacking in authority and too weak-willed to impose discipline on recalcitrant members. This, they no doubt asserted, was why he had sent Timothy instead of coming himself. Paul, however, affirms his intention to come to them in the near future, and then it will be seen whose words are empty and who has the real power of authority. It depends on the nature of their response to this letter whether he comes to them "with a rod" to enforce discipline, as a father is entitled to come to his disobedient children, or with the love and gentleness which are called forth by a family whose members are at harmony with each other.

III. Paul Replies to a Letter the Corinthians Had Sent Him (7:1—14:40)

1. Questions concerning Marriage (7:1–40)

The opening words of this chapter show that the Corinthians had written a letter to Paul in which they had sought his advice and instruction on certain matters. The recurrence of the formula "now concerning . . ." at 8:1, 12:1 and 16:1 indicates that he is dealing in turn with the points they had raised, though it is probable that other matters dealt with in the latter half of this epistle had been mentioned by the Corinthians in the same letter. The present chapter contains Paul's counsel concerning various queries in connection with marriage and the home; these were occasioned by the situation of a young church in a pagan setting. Ought a Christian to marry? Should a wife who has been converted leave her unconverted husband? Should a converted husband put away his unconverted wife? What about the children in a home where one parent is converted? Is marriage a handicap to the Christian? Should a father who has a daughter of marriageable age give her in marriage?

2. Limitations of Christian Liberty (8:1—11:1)

Problem of Meat Which had been Offered to Idols (8:1–13). It would seem that the Corinthians had claimed in their letter to have knowledge of the true situation concerning meat which had been offered to idols; but Paul gently reminds them that knowledge apart from love "puffs up" and is unedifying (8:1, cf. 13:2), and that the important thing is, through love, to be *known* of God (v. 3). It is indeed a fact, as the Christian well knows, that there is but *one* God and that all the other so-called gods and idols which men worship are, in fact, no-gods and, literally, non-entities. Meat, therefore, which has been sacrificed to idols and then offered for sale in the market is no cause of concern to him who has this knowledge. But there are some Christians who have not a strong grasp of this knowledge and who still think that the gods of heathendom are a reality in the world. To them the eating of such meat can be a "stumbling-block to them that are weak and wounding to their conscience" (v.

9). Hence Paul's emphatic admonition (vv. 9–13) to those who have knowledge not to sin against Christ by using their liberty in such a way as to cause offense to those who, though weak in knowledge, are nonetheless their brethren in Christ. In a word, knowledge must never be divorced from love.

Necessity of Forbearance and Self-Discipline (9:1–27). Paul now affirms the liberty and the rights which are his as an apostle, but reminds his readers of the way in which he has restricted his liberty and foregone his rights so that the Gospel might not be hindered. They must not imagine, however, that he claims anything meritorious for such conduct; for he finds himself under necessity to preach the Gospel; it is the great compulsion of his apostolic calling and the consuming purpose of his ministry. Though free from all men, he makes himself the servant of all so that he may win the more. His liberty is brought under the discipline of love. Like an athlete running with a single objective, he practices self-control and brings his body into subjection, for the sake of the Gospel.

Warning Example of the Children of Israel (10:1–15). There is a grave danger lest the Corinthians, puffed up by their superior knowledge, consider themselves immune to contamination from idolatry. Let them take warning from the history of "their fathers" in the Old Testament. Led and blessed by the one true God though they had been, enjoying spiritual benefits and the manifold blessings the Lord bestowed, they had lusted after evil things, they had lapsed into the idolatry of the people that surrounded them, they had committed fornication, they had tried and provoked the Lord, and had murmured and rebelled against Him. Their history is highly relevant to the situation in which Christians are placed, and what is written about them is written not merely for our interest, but for our admonition. The lesson is pointedly stated in verse 12. But Paul immediately adds the assurance that there is no question of the fall of God's people being inevitable; with every temptation that overtakes the believer, God, if we will but look to Him, provides a way of victory and escape. If the Corinthian believers are wise, then, they will heed Paul's warning, and, far from treating idolatry as a light thing, will flee from it.

The Table of the Lord and Pagan Altars Incompatible (10:16–22). At the sacrament of the Lord's Supper, the partaking of the one loaf and of the one cup is not an empty act; it is significant of the communion, the oneness of believers with Christ and with each other.

Although idols are non-entities and there are no rivals to the one true God, yet there is a reality, a power, which lies behind pagan worship and sacrifice—the power, namely, of demons, which are real enough. Participation in pagan sacrifice signifies communion with these demon powers. A Christian must never treat idols and heathen sacrifice as so insignificant that he is careless of his association with them. The distinction between demons and the Lord is a real distinction, for demons are entities. And so participation at the table of demons is completely incompatible with participation at the table of the Lord. The misapplication of Christian knowledge and the misuse of Christian liberty in this respect contributed a serious threat to the integrity of the Corinthian church. That it continued to be a menace seems to be implied by the strong admonition which Paul felt it necessary to write in a later letter (II Cor. 6:14–18).

Practical Advice Respecting this Particular Problem (10:23—11:1). This section of the letter is concluded with the statement of a number of principles which should govern the Christian's conduct: (*1*) It is not only what is legitimate that matters, but what is helpful and edifying. (*2*) The good of one's fellowman should be sought before one's own good. (*3*) It is unnecessary to make scrupulous inquiries as to whether the food bought in the meat market or set before one when dining in the home of a pagan friend has been previously offered to idols. (*4*) If, however, one is told that it is meat that has been offered in sacrifice to idols, then one should abstain from eating it—for the sake of him who told you, for otherwise he will imagine that one makes no difference between partaking of idol sacrifices and partaking of the Lord's Supper. (*5*) All that one does should be done to the glory of God with the salvation of others in view.

Though the problem of meats offered to idols may no longer be a problem of our age, nonetheless the principles enumerated by the Apostle Paul are valid and relevant to the situation of the Christian in society today and in every generation, however much external circumstances may alter.

3. *Veiling of Women in Public Worship (11:2–16)*

Paul instructs the Corinthians that women should have their heads covered during attendance at public worship, and that the reason for this is grounded in the very nature of things as God has ordained them. There is indeed a fundamental order in the constitution of the world which the Christian must recognize and respect. Man was created first, not woman. Woman was created for man, not man for woman. Man by creation is the image and glory of God, while woman is the glory of man. The head of woman is man, the head of man is Christ, and the head of Christ (in His mediatorial office) is God. For man to worship with his head covered is to dishonor his head (Christ) and the divine image in which he has been made. For woman to worship with her head uncovered is to dishonor her head (man) to whom by creation she is subject. Man worshipping with his head uncovered and woman with her head covered is a reflection of the order of creation. That is why it is natural for a woman to have long hair—it is part of her glory—whereas for a man to have long hair is a shame to him. This is the consensus of mankind in general and also of the churches of God. At the same time, however, the fact of this graded order of creation does not clash with the fact that *in the Lord*, that is, in the scheme of redemption, man and woman enjoy an equality (cf. Gal. 3:28), and in this world are mutually indispensable to each other. The important point in this passage is that the orderliness which belongs to the very structure and fabric of creation is the proper basis of all other orderliness in this world, whether in public worship or in the life of the family or of the nation.

4. *Disorderly and Uncharitable Behavior at the Lord's Supper (11:17–34)*

What greater contradiction could there be than that the Lord's Supper should have been the scene of the divisions which split Corinthians asunder (v. 18) and of gluttony, drunkenness and selfishness (v. 21), whereas this sacrament should, above all else, have been the expression of their unity and fellowship of love in Christ (cf. 10:16, 17)? Behavior so alien to the spirit and example of Christ could not be said to be *in remembrance of Him* (11:24–26). In fact, whatever their gathering was intended to be, it was certainly not *the Lord's Supper* (v. 20). To partake of this sacrament unworthily and profanely, as they had been doing, was to eat and drink their own condemnation and was also, indeed, the reason why some of them had been overtaken by illness and even death (vv. 27–29).

The account given in this passage of the institution of the Lord's Supper gives the facts as the apostle had received them from the

Lord Himself (on what occasion or under what circumstances we do not now know) and as he had handed them on to the Corinthian believers (11:23; cf. v. 2; also 15:3). It is in essential agreement with the accounts which are given in the first three Gospels, as a comparison of the texts will show. It is wrongheaded to treat such differences as are apparent as discrepancies or as due to the later development of church tradition; for, on the contrary, they echo the fuller explanation of the significance of this sacrament which our Lord must have given at the time of its institution during the long discourse that night in the upper room, of which John has given us a portion (Jn. 13–16).

5. Concerning Spiritual Gifts (12:1—14:40)

Diversities of Gifts Flowing from the One Spirit (12:1–30). As the opening words suggest, Paul is now turning to another point which had been raised in the Corinthians' letter to him. Prior to their conversion, Paul reminds them, they had been led astray to dumb idols quite incapable of conferring any gifts upon them. But in turning to the one true God, they had been enriched with a variety of spiritual gifts (cf. 1:4–11). Paul's purpose here is to emphasize that the diversity of these gifts, distributed to different persons, could in no sense be pleaded as an excuse for division and discord among the believers, since all these gifts come from one and the same Spirit. The intention of the one God is that in the Church there should be diversity in unity, or unity in diversity; for God, being one, cannot be the author of division and strife. This the apostle illustrates by drawing their attention to the human body, which is compounded of many members differing widely from each other in appearance and function. Yet together they form a completely harmonious whole. Indeed, they are indispensable to each other if the proper functioning and well-being of the body are to be maintained, so much so that, if one member suffers, all the rest suffer with it and the whole body is affected. This should also be true of those who by faith and grace together constitute one body in Christ, however much they may differ from each other in spiritual gifts (vv. 8–10) or in their respective functions (vv. 28–30).

An Encomium of Love, the Best Gift of All (12:31—13:13). The gifts of which Paul has been speaking had, scandalously, led to pride and rivalry in the Corinthian Church. Those to whom they had been granted had allowed the impressive external manifestations of these gifts to puff them up with self-importance, as though they were *their gifts*. They had neglected the best and most vital gift of all, the hidden, inward, unspectacular gift of love, by which all other gifts must be animated and informed, if they are to be of any worth at all. In this famous passage, Paul reminds the Corinthians of the more excellent way of love. This is really the very heart of our epistle, for the root-cause of every failing and inconsistency for which the apostle has had to rebuke them was precisely *lack of love*. Chapter 13 is, in its negative aspect, a picture of the deplorable state of affairs that had arisen in the church at Corinth—enjoying spiritual gifts, but using them without love: impatient, unkind, jealous, boastful, arrogant, rude, irritable, resentful, unjust, intolerant, malevolent.

In its positive aspect, the chapter is a perfect picture of the character of Christ, the example for all who follow Him. Besides, the spectacular gifts, by which the Corinthians set so much store, were passing and impermanent; whereas love never fails, but abides forever. Again, every Christian must remember that, however great and spectacular the gifts granted to him, his perception and knowledge are only partial, that it is God alone who knows all things fully, and that it is only when at last he sees his Master's face, that he will know even as also he is known (cf. I Jn. 3:2). And so to love, he must add —and this means he must preserve a humble view of himself—faith and hope, until the day of Christ's appearing dawns when faith will give way to sight and hope to fulfilment. But love abides forever.

The Right Use of Spiritual Gifts (14:1–40). The Corinthians had been guilty of a failure in love. They had also been deficient, where spiritual gifts were concerned, in their estimate of priorities. Thus they had rated the gift of speaking in an unintelligible tongue higher than the gift of prophesying. The former impressed their immature minds as more wonderful and spectacular, and therefore more desirable. But Paul points out that the latter should be more highly prized. It is evident that by prophesying Paul means the gift of proclaiming and expounding the truth of God rather than predicting the course of future events, "forthtelling" rather than "foretelling." Prophesying is to be preferred because it is comprehensible to all and leads to the edification, encouragement, and comfort of the whole congregation; whereas speaking in tongues is unintelligible and therefore unedifying except to him who has that gift. Spiritual gifts are not granted to be used in a selfish manner; in their use the edifying of the church must always be kept in the forefront (v. 12). Worship must be with the understanding; otherwise, it degenerates into vain and meaningless superstition. Accordingly, there should be no speaking in tongues at public worship unless at the same time there is an interpretation of what has been said (vv. 5, 13–28). Five words spoken with the understanding are better than ten thousand unintelligible words (v. 19). The first great principle of public worship, then, is that all things should be done with the purpose of edifying (v. 26).

The second great principle of public worship is that all things should be done decently and in order (14:40). Disorderliness had become a mark of congregational gatherings at Corinth; men speaking in tongues without interpretations; several prophesying at once, instead of one after another; and women speaking and asking questions when they should have remained silent. Had there been more love and more humility, these things would not have been.

IV. The Resurrection of the Body (15:1–58)

1. Christ's Resurrection a Central Fact of the Faith (15:1–20)

The core of the Gospel, which Paul had preached to the Corinthians, was that for our sins Christ had died, been buried, and risen again in accordance with the Scriptures (cf. Lk. 24:26, 27, 44–47). The risen Saviour, moreover, had been seen by many witnesses, and last of all, in a special manner, by Paul himself. This was the Gospel they had believed. Its dynamic power had transformed their lives in a way which would have been unlikely had it been no better than a myth or a falsehood.

Some among them, however, were denying that there was such a thing as resurrection from the dead. If they were correct, then it followed that Christ had not risen, but was still dead and buried, and that Paul and his fellow evangelists were false witnesses. It meant, further, that faith in Christ was a vain thing, for it is obviously absurd to repose one's faith in a *dead* person—a dead Saviour is a contradiction in terms—that the Corinthian converts were still in their sins, and that those who had died trusting in Christ had perished. The resurrection of Christ, however, is a *fact*—a fact which they know not only by Paul's testimony, but also by the reality of their own experience (cf. 1:18)—a fact which has significance for all eternity, for Christ's resurrection guarantees the resurrection from the grave of all who trust in Him. He by His rising from the dead is the first fruits, and therefore also the pledge, of a great harvest of all believers.

2. Sequence of Events (15:21–28)

What Paul has just said he now links with the incarnation. Death came into the world through the sin of the first man, Adam; resurrection, the conquest of death, has come through the righteousness of the second Man, Christ (cf. vv. 45, 47; Rom. 5:12–14). It is precisely because Christ's resurrection was a *human* resurrection that it has vital significance for the whole human race. But, as the figure of the firstfruits suggests, there is a proper order of events. Christ is raised first, thereby becoming the pioneer and guarantor of our resurrection; then, at His coming, those who are Christ's are to be raised. Then, too, every enemy, including the last enemy which is death, will have been subdued by Him and He will deliver the Kingdom over to His Father, and God will be all in all. All this, together with the subjection of the Son Himself to the Father, is to be understood of Christ in His office as mediator; for His work of salvation will then have been completed and the sovereign purposes of God established for all eternity. The everlasting unity in essence and dignity of the First and Second Persons of the Godhead is not in question in this passage.

3. The Resurrection and Christian Suffering (15:29–34)

What possible point can there be in the perils, the hardships, the persecutions, the "daily dying" which Paul endures for Christ's sake if there is no resurrection and no life to come? It would be far more logical to adopt the creed of the hedonist, "Let us eat and drink, for tomorrow we die!" The willing endurance of so many sufferings is possible only because of the sure hope of resurrection.

4. The Present Body and the Resurrection Body (15:35–49)

It is the same body that is raised; that is, there is real continuity. But there will also be a great difference—just as, though there is indubitable oneness and continuity, a seed that is sown differs immensely from the plant that springs up from the ground. The beauty and glory of that which springs up are immeasurably greater than of that which was sown. So the resurrection body of man, in startling contrast to his present body, will be imperishable, glorious, powerful, spiritual, and everlastingly stamped with the image of our Heavenly Saviour.

5. The Complete Victory over Death (15:50–58)

Those who die in the faith of Jesus Christ are like sleepers awaiting the reveille of that trumpet which shall sound at Christ's coming. Then, in a split second, they will be roused and raised and clothed with incorruption and immortality. Then at last the prophetic saying, "Death is engulfed in victory" (Is. 25:8), will be fulfilled. This means that, for the Christian, death has lost its sting, which is sin and which Christ the sin-bearer has removed, and its strength, which is the law whereby sin is judged and punished. This being so, the Christian's logic ("therefore," v. 58) is to continue unmoved and immovable in the work of the Lord, no matter what sufferings it may involve, knowing that in the Lord it is leading to an everlasting, heavenly harvest.

V. Conclusion (16:1–24)

1. Collection for the Poor Christians at Jerusalem (16:1–4)

This would seem to be another matter concerning which the Corinthians had requested counsel in their letter to Paul (see the opening formula of the chapter). The Christians in Jerusalem were, as a result of their confession of Christ, poverty-stricken to a calamitous degree. Paul was organizing a fund in the various churches, so that when he returned to Jerusalem, he could take money with him for the relief of the need there. He advises his readers to put by something for this purpose every first day of the week according to the degree of their prosperity—and the Corinthians were certainly not wealthy! It is a subject to which the apostle returns at greater length in II Corinthians (chs. 8 and 9).

2. Paul's Plans for Visiting Corinth (16:5–9)

Evidently Paul had originally intended to cross over from Ephesus and pay the Corinthians a brief visit (v. 7) en route northwards to Macedonia and then to return to them from Macedonia. Now, however, he declares that it is his purpose to go straight to Macedonia in the late spring (v. 8), without first crossing to Greece, and then subsequently to come south to them for a prolonged visit, perhaps even spending the whole winter with them.

3. Exhortations, Directions and Salutations (16:10–24)

Paul commends Timothy to the Corinthians in rather careful terms, for he feared that, should his young friend and fellow worker come to them, they might despise him—probably because of his youth (cf. I Tim. 4:12); and he tells them that Apollos, whom he would also have liked to come to them, would visit them later on. Who "the brethren" mentioned in verses 11 and 12 were we do not know, though it seems likely that one of them was called Erastus (Acts 19:22). The unwillingness of Apollos to visit them at this juncture may well have been connected with the party strife at Corinth, which might have been aggravated by his presence (cf. 1:12; 3:4–8).

The joining of "Maranatha" to "Anathema" in the King James Version of verse 22 is due to a misunderstanding of the former term. "Anathema" is a Greek term meaning "an accursed thing," while "Maranatha" is an Aramaic expression which means "Our Lord is coming" or "Our Lord, come!" (cf. Rev. 22:20). It was no doubt a common greeting or motto among Christians in the Apostolic Church. The proper division and sense of the verse are given in the Revised Standard Version, "If any one has no love for the Lord, let him be accursed. Our Lord, come!"

II Corinthians

PHILIP E. HUGHES

THIS LETTER WAS written by the Apostle Paul from Macedonia (cf. 2:13; 7:5–7; 8:1; 9.2) probably some six months after the composition of I Corinthians. Its chief purpose is to vindicate the authenticity of Paul's apostleship and to prepare the way for his impending visit to Corinth. In comparison with I Corinthians and others of Paul's epistles it has unjustly suffered a measure of neglect, for in it the rich depths of the affection, faith, and devotion of the

1063

apostle's heart are revealed in a manner unsurpassed elsewhere in the New Testament. Certain false apostles had invaded the Corinthian church and by their erroneous teaching were seeking to lead the people astray and to usurp the apostolic authority that belonged properly to Paul. They had also cast serious slurs on his character. Anxious for news of the reaction of the Corinthians to his earlier letter, he had moved north from Ephesus to Troas, hoping there to meet Titus, who had carried that letter, and to hear what he had to report. As Titus did not arrive, however, Paul traveled by the northern route into Macedonia, where at last he found Titus and was overjoyed at the favorable news he brought from Corinth. Thereupon he wrote our present letter and sent Titus, together with two brethren, with it to Corinth (8:16, 18, 19, 22–24).

I. Special Greetings (1:1–11)

1. Salutation (1:1, 2)

The opening greeting is similar in form to that of I Corinthians and the rest of the Pauline epistles. But, in view of the contents of this epistle, Paul's description of himself as "an apostle of Christ Jesus by the will of God" gains added significance, for this was a claim which the rival fake apostles who had invaded the Corinthian church could not honestly make. The salutation, in which Paul associates Timothy with himself, indicates that Timothy, who with Silas had assisted Paul in the work of evangelism during his first visit to Corinth (1:19), was with him in Macedonia when this letter was being written. The letter is addressed not only to the Corinthian Christians, but also to all the saints in Achaia—that is, to small scattered groups of believers in the Roman province of Achaia, which comprised all the territory south of Macedonia.

2. Expression of Thanksgiving and Trust (1:3–11)

This passage reflects the gratitude and relief with which Paul sat down to write this letter after receiving from Titus the reassuring report of the response which his earlier letter to Corinth had evoked (cf. 7:6). He blesses God for the mercies and the comfort which He unfailingly gives. All the sufferings, oppositions, and tribulations endured in the prosecution of his ministry are more than counterbalanced by the grace and consolation supplied from above. The magnitude of Paul's sufferings from the Gospel becomes particularly apparent in this epistle (cf. 4:8–11; 6:4, 8–10; 7:5; 11:23–28; 12:-7–10). Indeed, the keynote of the epistle is that human weakness is matched and overcome by divine grace. Thus here Paul speaks of a crushing affliction which overtook him and threatened his very life when he was in Asia, but from which God delivered him, raising him as it were from the dead (cf. also 2:14; 4:7, 16; 12:9, 10).

II. Paul's Answer to his Critics (1:12—7:16)

1. Variation of his Plan for Visiting Corinth (1:12—2:4)

Paul's original intention had been to cross the sea from Ephesus to Corinth and to pay the church there a short visit before proceeding northward to Macedonia; and then, on his return from Macedonia, to visit them again so that they might have the pleasure of his company a second time in the course of this one journey (1:-15, 16). But subsequently, as he told them in the earlier letter, he altered this plan and decided not to cross to Corinth, but to travel up from Ephesus and around to Macedonia, and then to come down to them in Corinth for a prolonged stay, perhaps for the whole winter (I Cor. 16:5–8). So far as the Corinthians were concerned, the only difference was that he now proposed to pay them one long visit instead of two short ones. His enemies in Corinth, however, had seized on this perfectly legitimate change of intention as an opportunity for charging him with insincerity and unreliability. Hence the Apostle Paul's protestation of his complete sincerity and his appeal to the Corinthians' personal knowledge of him as one the veracity of whose word could be relied on. He is not one to say "Yes" and "No" in the one breath. His character is bound up with the Gospel he so faithfully preached to them, which they had proved for themselves to be one great affirmative. They had found all the promises of God to be "Yes" in the Christ Whom he had proclaimed. How could a fickle and untrustworthy man have been the minister of such a message?

They should, moreover, have known him well enough to realize that there must have been a good reason for his change of plan.

It was not, as his opponents had been whispering, unconcern for their welfare, but loving considerateness that had prompted the revision of his itinerary; it was to spare them and to give them an opportunity of mending their attitude to him. Indeed, so devoted to them was he that he had written "out of much affliction and anguish of heart and with many tears" (1:23; 2:4).

2. Punishment and Forgiveness of the Serious Offender (2:5–11)

Until modern times the offender in question here was all but universally identified with the incestuous Corinthian mentioned in the earlier letter (I Cor. 5). But many modern commentators have put forward the opinion that Paul is referring here to some other person who had offered an affront to him personally or to someone who was his representative in Corinth. Whoever the man was—and the writer accepts the traditional view—it is plain that the congregation at Corinth had imposed discipline of a severe nature upon him (probably excommunication) and that the offender had shown genuine grief and repentance. Paul therefore counsels them to forgive him and publicly to receive him back into their fellowship with love. The important lesson to be learned is that ecclesiastical discipline is necessary and should be applied in certain cases, but that its aim should ever be the restoration of the fallen brother. There must always be room for repentance and forgiveness. The inexorable zeal of the rigorist has no sanction in the New Testament, for the exclusion of the possibility of grace and mercy is a denial of the central principle of the New Testament, so much so that for a brother-in-Christ to be overwhelmed with an excess of sorrow and hopelessness is for Satan to win an advantage—and that means a setback to the Church of Christ.

3. Paul's Disappointment at Titus' Absence in Troas (2:12–16)

Paul's main task in Troas, as everywhere, was the preaching of the Gospel, and he found a real responsiveness to the message of Christ in that city. But so great was his concern for the welfare of the Corinthian church that he was restless until he received the news which he was expecting Titus to bring. He had indeed hoped to encounter Titus in Troas, but being disappointed of this hope, he hurried on to Macedonia, so that he might find Titus with the minimum of delay. So much for the critics who were asking the Corinthians to believe that he had no consideration for them!

In characteristic fashion Paul at this point breaks off into a digression—but a digression so prolonged that the account of his meeting with Titus in Macedonia is resumed only in 7:5. It is a digression, however, only so far as the account of his journey from Ephesus to Macedonia is concerned, for otherwise it is thoroughly and richly appropriate to the great theme of the epistle, which is the magnification of God's grace in and through human frailty. It must not be thought that Paul's impatience for news of Corinth prevented him from seizing the opportunity of the "open door" he found at Traos. On the contrary, what he says implies not only that he faithfully proclaimed the Gospel, but also that there were converts there (from whom he took leave), with the result that he cannot forbear to thank God Who in Christ always leads him to triumph wherever he goes and whatever his circumstances. It is this spontaneous thanksgiving that sparks off the prolonged digression.

4. Paul's Letters of Commendation (2:17—3:5)

Once again Paul affirms his sincerity and disavows any connection with so many—and in particular, in this context, with those false apostles who had imposed themselves on the Corinthians—who are no better than hawkers of the Word of God, that is, whose main concern is their own material benefit without any true concern for the benefit, spiritual or material, of those to whom they profess to minister. Such persons would arrive with pretentious letters of commendation and, when they judged the time was ripe for them to depart, would demand similar testimonials from those on whom they had been battening. Paul, however, their genuine apostle, has no need of such credentials. The believers in Corinth are themselves his letter of commendation: the miraculous transformation achieved by the Gospel in their lives is something for all to read and acknowledge. They are a letter *of Christ,* not written with perishable ink, but with the Spirit of the living God, not engraved on stone tablets, but on the pulsating tablets of the heart. All this is of God in Christ; and so there is no suggestion of self-commendation or self-sufficiency on Paul's part. But for the almighty power of God, none of this would have taken place.

5. *Comparison between the Old and New Covenants (3:6–18)*

The distinction just made between tablets of stone and tablets that are human hearts is in fact an echo of Ezekiel 11:19 and leads on to an explanation of the difference between the law and the Gospel. Under the old dispensation the law, given to Moses on Sinai, was written on tablets of stone. It was an external ordinance standing over against the sinner and condemning him, as a breaker of God's commandments, to death. Hence Paul speaks of it as the letter which kills. But it would be a serious mistake to infer from this that the law is evil; on the contrary, as Paul writes elsewhere, it is holy and just and good (Rom. 7:12) and love is the fulfilling of the law (Rom. 13:10). It is because *man* is evil that Paul speaks of it as the ministration of condemnation and death. It is because *God* is its author that Paul speaks of it as glorious. But it is far surpassed in glory by the ministration of the Spirit whereby, in accordance with the promises associated with the New Covenant (cf. Jer. 31:33; Ezek. 11:19; 36:26), God places His law—the *same* law —within the hearts of His people. This New Covenant comes to fulfilment in Jesus Christ, the *only* law-keeper, Whose perfect obedience is applied to every believing heart by the vital and regenerating operation of the Holy Spirit, so that the law of God is no longer an external and accusing ordinance but an inward principle which, through the power of Christ, the believer is now at last able to keep, and delights to do so.

Just as the Israelites of old had been unable, because of their rebellious spirit, to look on the glory radiating from Moses' face after he had received the law from God, and Moses had placed a veil over his face to hide that glory from their eyes (Ex. 34:29–35), so that veil still shuts them off from a true understanding of the Old Covenant, and it is removed only when they turn in faith to Christ, who is the key to the Scriptures (cf. 1:20; Jn. 5:46, 47). To behold the glory of the Lord is to be transformed progressively into the image of His likeness. Paul is not speaking theoretically, but from the depth of his own experience and knowledge; for he was of the stock of Israel and prior to his conversion had been a Hebrew of the Hebrews (Phil. 3:5). Only by closure with Christ had the veil been removed from his heart so that he beheld His surpassing glory.

6. Character of Paul's Ministry (4:1–6)

Paul affirms yet again the absolute integrity and sincerity of his ministry before both man and God. The first half of verse 2 may be taken together with verse 5 to portray the character of the false apostles whose presence in Corinth was such a menace to the church there—underhanded, crafty, distorters of the Word of God, and preachers of themselves rather than of Christ. Verse 3 probably indicates that they had criticized the Gospel preached by Paul as unacceptable; but Paul retorts that if his Gospel is veiled, it is veiled to those who are perishing—to those, namely, who have a veil of unbelief over their heart (cf. 3:15). The resulting darkness can be dispelled, as he so well knows, only by the shining of the sovereign God in the heart; just as the Israelites beheld the divine glory beaming from Moses' face, the sinner by turning to Christ may in His face behold the unfading splendor of that light which the knowledge of the glory of God produces (cf. 3:16).

7. Paul's Confidence in the Face of Affliction (4:7—5:10)

In a passage of great power and beauty, Paul shows that in the service of the Gospel the frailty of the human frame is such that perseverance and victory in the face of unremitting affliction and persecution can be attributed only to the strength of God and not of man. Like the pitchers of Gideon's army which were smashed so that the lamps within them might shine out into the surrounding darkness, the fragile earthern vessel of the Apostle Paul's body was continually, as it were, being broken, so that the light of Christ's life within might be displayed. The eternal glory ahead immeasurably exceeds the temporary affliction of this present life. Besides, the Christian knows that the frail tent of this present body which we now have on earth is to be superseded by the permanent dwelling with which we shall be endued at Christ's appearing. Thus, the complete man, body as well as soul, will be saved and glorified. For a Christian to die before the appearing of Christ means, it is true, an intermediate period of "nakedness," a disembodied state; but it is nonetheless a period of being present with the Lord, and therefore a state of bliss and satisfaction which will ultimately be crowned by the experience of being clothed with the eternal and heavenly body. The Christian, accordingly, regards his body with seriousness and remembers that he must stand before the judgment seat of Christ to give an account of the things done in this body on earth.

8. *The Ministry of Reconciliation (5:11—6:10)*

The true background of the grace of God is the wrath of God. In the solemn light of the Day of Judgment, man's greatest need is for reconciliation with God and the message of the Gospel is precisely this, that in Christ, Who died and rose again for the sinner, God was reconciling the world to Himself. Christ bore our sins on the cross in order that we, through faith in Him, might bear His righteousness. A man in Christ is, therefore, a new creation; he is reborn the man God intended him to be in creation; and the relationship of harmony and love between man and his Maker which was destroyed by sin is restored in Christ. But it is important to notice that *all* is of God: from beginning to end, reconciliation is *God's* act of grace on behalf of His fallen and helpless creatures (5:18).

The awful responsibility of the ministry of this message, which brings men face to face with the ultimate issues of eternity, causes Paul to reaffirm his sincerity and genuineness, under every circumstance, as a minister of the Gospel of reconciliation (6:1–10). In this moving passage, the utter devotion and selflessness of the apostle shine through so clearly that those who had permitted themselves to entertain doubts of him must have been put to shame when they read these words, and they could hardly have failed to notice how great in reality was the contrast between their own true apostle and those self-seeking false apostles who had invaded their church.

9. *Paul's Appeal to the Corinthians (6:11—7:4)*

The depth of Paul's feeling for the Corinthians is now manifested by a direct declaration of his openhearted love for them. If there was any narrowness of affection, it was in themselves, not in him; and so he touchingly appeals to them, as a father to his children, to respond with a like warmth and breadth of love. Then, still speaking as a father to his children, he admonishes them not to enter into alliance with unbelievers. No yoke could be more unequal than this, for the ultimate separation of mankind is into believers on the one hand and unbelievers on the other. He reminds them that they are the temple of the living God (cf. I Cor. 3:16; 6:19) and that the great promises of God's covenant of grace apply to them as God's people (6:16–18; see Lev. 26:12; Jer. 31:33; Ezek. 37:26, 27). To be the beneficiaries of these promises carries with it the obligation of separation from all that would defile flesh or spirit and of dedication in holiness to God (7:1). Paul then assures the Corinthians once again of his undying affection for them, in contrast to the false apostles, by whom they have been wronged, corrupted, and defrauded (7:2, 3). He is, moreover, despite his afflictions, filled to overflowing with joy and comfort because of them. The reason for this appears in the next section.

10. Meeting with Titus in Macedonia (7:5–16)

The narrative of his movements which was broken off at 2:13 is now resumed. There he explained that not having found Titus at Troas, he journeyed on into Macedonia. Here he alludes to severe tribulations which he encountered on reaching Macedonia, but tells how God comforted him by the arrival of Titus with the news that his letter had produced in the Corinthians that godly sorrow which leads to repentance. In accordance with his injunctions they had obediently put right what was amiss. Titus, too, had been well and suitably received and the confidence in the Corinthians which Paul had expressed to him had been amply justified. All this made Paul rejoice. The mention here (7:6, 7) of the great comfort he had received should be linked with the thanksgiving for comfort in the opening portion of the epistle (1:3–11).

Until recent times the letter to which he refers in this passage (cf. also 2:3, 4) was universally identified with our present I Corinthians. A number of modern commentators have maintained, however, that Paul is referring to a severe "intermediate" letter, supposedly written and sent during the time between the composition of our two canonical epistles. It has been postulated that the last four chapters of II Corinthians do not belong there, but are a major portion of the severe "intermediate" letter which somehow became mistakenly attached to the end of our epistle. In our judgment, however, the unanimous traditional view is much to be preferred, especially as the modern theory is unsupported by external evidence of any kind.

III. Collection for Needy Christians at Jerusalem
(8:1—9:15)

Jerusalem was the Mother Church of Christianity. Paul's collection for the Christians there was prompted by the state of extreme poverty in which, for a variety of reasons, they found themselves. But other considerations no doubt reinforced his decision to initiate this charitable work. Gifts coming from "Gentile" churches to the "Jewish" church in Jerusalem might be expected to give a powerful impulse to the unity of the Christian Church, as a practical demonstration of the truth that in Christ Jesus there is neither Jew nor Gentile, but all are one (Gal. 3:28). It might almost seem like a Christian counterpart to the temple levy which the Jews of the Dispersion, so conscious of their national identity, remitted year by year to Jerusalem. There was also a certain logical rightness about the project: the Gentiles are indebted for spiritual things to the church in Jerusalem, from which the blessings of the Gospel had radiated forth, and so they have a duty to minister to the material needs of their brethren there (Rom. 15:26, 27).

It would seem that the Corinthians had been slow in their response to Paul's appeal—for Titus had started the collection in Corinth during the previous year (8:6, 10). Paul, therefore, gently incites them by bringing to their attention the example of the Macedonian Christians who, though themselves extremely poor and passing through a testing time of affliction, had contributed willingly and joyfully and beyond their means (vv. 1–5). Above all, of course, there is the example of our Lord Jesus Christ, through Whose poverty they had been eternally enriched (v. 9). Paul does not wish to impose a burden on the Corinthians, but he does want them to match their intention by their performance (vv. 11–15) thereby showing that they who abound in so many other things abound also in the grace of Christian generosity (8:7; 9:6–8). A liberal response will mean blessing to the whole Church, uniting them in love with their distant brethren in Jerusalem who will be stirred to thanksgiving and prayer on their behalf (9:12–15). This whole matter must be seen in the light of God's inexpressible gift to them, and to all believers. Thus, in the ultimate issue, they should not view themselves as givers, but as receivers (v. 15).

Paul advises them that he is sending Titus and two unnamed brothers, whom he warmly commends to them, to prosecute this project in Corinth, so that the collection may be completed and ready by the time that he himself arrives (8:16—9:5).

IV. Paul Affirms his Apostolic Authority (10:1—13:14)

1. Accusations of Cowardice and Weakness Answered (10:1–11)

Paul now turns to deal still more explicitly than previously (see 1:12–17) with the charges made against him by his opponents in Corinth. It was being said that he was bold from a distance when writing letters, but weak and unimpressive when present in person. Such critics, however, are judging him by their own standards, which are those of the flesh. But he is coming to Corinth shortly and then they will find out for themselves that, unless they show obedience to his apostolic authority, he is just as bold in deed when present as he is by letter when absent. To their cost they will then see the strong position they have tried to build up for themselves cast down.

2. Invasion of his Territory by Impostors (10:12–18)

These self-opinioned impostors who had been endeavoring to turn to their own advantage the work of Paul in Corinth were illegitimately invading a territory which God had never measured out for them. Paul is no such invader. He is the Corinthians' true apostle who had followed the course marked out for him by Christ in bringing the Gospel to them, and who is hopeful that in the future this course will extend beyond them to more distant lands as yet unreached by the Gospel. He is God's commended apostle, not needing, like the false apostles, to fall back on self-commendation.

3. Authenticity of his Apostleship Vindicated (11:1—12:18)

Throughout this epistle, it is apparent that Paul is embarrassed at having to say so much about himself. It has, however, become necessary that he should establish his apostolic authority beyond dispute because of the serious threat to the church in Corinth presented by the advent of the false apostles. He, the spiritual father of the Corinthian believers, is jealous over them, as a father who has espoused his daughter as a pure virgin to one husband. They are in grave danger of being seduced away from Christ, to Whom they have been pledged, by these men who are preaching another Jesus and a different Gospel from that which they had received from Paul (11:1–4).

In contrast to Paul, who had consistently refused any remuneration when ministering the Gospel in Corinth, so that there might be no suggestion that he was doing so from mercenary motives (see I Cor. 9:11–18), the false apostles had been living like parasites on the Corinthian Christians. These invaders, in an attempt to find some cover for their own covetousness, had invented the cruel calumny, first, that had Paul's message not been worthless he would have accepted some payment for it, and, second, that had he really loved the Corinthians, he would not have turned away from the gifts that they had offered him for his bodily needs. Both these slanders, when leveled against a man like Paul, were fantastic. But the Corinthian believers were inexperienced, and the false apostles were very cunning and persuasive. Paul therefore denounces the latter in the plainest terms: their deceits are of a kind with those of their master, Satan, who is accustomed to disguise himself as an angel of light (11:5–15).

Paul then embarks on the famous account of the incessant and terrible sufferings he had endured as an apostle of Jesus Christ. Against this amazing catalogue, those who had set themselves up in Corinth as his rivals could claim no possible comparison, for their conduct was governed by self-interest and the desire for physical ease. The list which he gives, prolonged though it is, is not exhaustive, as a comparison with the Acts will show. There are also many incidents mentioned here which are not recorded in the Acts. And, as we know from those chapters of the Acts which tell of Paul's subsequent experiences, there were still many and severe afflictions for the apostle to undergo before his testimony was sealed with a martyr's death. These considerations remind us that the object of Holy Scripture is not biographical, to glorify man, but evangelical, to make man wise unto salvation (11:16–33).

There was also another remarkable way in which Paul's apostleship had been attested. With great delicacy and humility, he tells us how fourteen years previously he had been caught up into paradise and there had heard things which he was not permitted to divulge. To keep him from being over-elated at these great revelations he was given a "thorn in the flesh"—some unwelcome affliction, the nature of which is not disclosed, but which was like a messenger of Satan buffeting him. The Lord's answer to his thrice repeated prayer for deliverance was, "My grace is sufficient for you, for my power is made perfect in weakness." This is indeed both the keynote and the climax of the whole epistle: God's power triumphing over and through human weakness, so that a Christian may learn to welcome infirmities and persecutions as opportunities for the manifestation of the transcendent power of God (12:1–10).

No, Paul has nothing to fear from comparison with these (in their own eyes) "super-apostles" (12:11; cf. 11:5). But in reminding the Corinthians that the signs of the true apostle were performed in their midst when he was with them, and in advising them of his impending visit to them, a further calumny whispered against him by his enemies comes to light—namely, that he was making a profitable business, "lining his own pocket," out of the collection which he had sent Titus to organize. It is sufficient for Paul, in rebutting this calumny, to appeal to the Corinthians firsthand knowledge of his own integrity and to remind them that his sending of "the brother" with Titus on this mission was for the purpose of removing any possible grounds for slander of this kind (12:11–18).

4. Warnings to Any Who Continue to Oppose his Authority (12:19—13:10)

Paul leaves no doubt in the minds of his readers that he is really on the point of coming to them, and that, on his arrival, he is prepared to adopt firm measures to enforce discipline and obedience, holding, if necessary, an apostolic court at which witnesses will be called to testify against those who have been causing trouble. However great his weakness, the power of God will be displayed through him as Christ's apostle. He exhorts them, therefore, to examine and test themselves and to array themselves on the side of truth. The interval between the receipt of this letter and his arrival will give them an opportunity for doing this and for putting things in order.

5. An Exhortation and Salutation (13:11–14)

Paul brings the letter to a close with (1) an exhortation to the Corinthians to show forth the harmony, love, and peace that should characterize a fellowship of Christian brethren; (2) a salutation from all the saints, and (3) a benediction in which the doctrine of the Trinity is naturally and clearly implied.

Galatians

JAMES I. PACKER

THE identity of the Galatians to whom Paul wrote, the date of his letter, and the relation between the events described in 1:15—2:10 and the parallel record in Acts, are teasing problems of scholarship which need not concern us here. All that we need to know to understand the epistle is the information about the Galatians which Paul himself provides. They were among his own Gentile converts. They had at first welcomed him and his message with great enthusiasm (4:13–15); they had believed, been baptized (3:27), received the Holy Spirit (3:5), and for a time "run well" (5:7). Now, however, Paul has learned that they were in danger of losing hold of his Gospel and "turning to a different gospel—not that there is another gospel, but there are some who . . . want to pervert the gospel of Christ" (1:6, 7, RSV). This letter expresses Paul's reaction to the news.

The trouble-makers at Galatia were apparently Jewish Christians, who wished to convince Paul's converts that they would have to be circumcised (5:2–4; 6:12–15) and keep the ritual law (4:10)—become Jewish proselytes, in fact—if they were to be saved. "They make much of you, but for no good purpose; they want to shut you out"—from the "Israel of God" (6:16)—"that you may make much of them," by accepting their directions as to how you should become members (4:17). The Judaizers seem to have taught that, while faith in Christ was a good start, it was not of itself enough to save Gentiles; Gentile believers needed to be circumcised, for only the circumcised would inherit the promises which God made to Abraham. It is this view which Paul attacks.

The Judaizers also criticized Paul personally, as we can see from his elaborate self-defense. Paul (they must have said) was not an apostle in the full sense (cf. 1:1), but was dependent on the Jerusalem leaders, the original apostles, both for his Gospel (cf. 1:11, 12) and for his commission to preach (cf. 2:7–9). He was, however—so their misrepresentation of Paul continued—a disloyal subordinate, for the Jerusalem policy was to circumcise all Gentile converts (cf. 2:3 ff.), and this he would not do. Among Jews, he still affirmed the need of circumcision for salvation (cf. 5:11), but in other company he suppressed this requirement of the Gospel, simply to avoid unpopularity (cf. 1:10). That was why the Galatians had never heard him mention it. But—so the Judaizers claimed—what Paul had told them could not save them unless they were circumcised.

It is no wonder that Paul's letter shows signs of violent agitation. The Judaizers' position was a challenge, not merely to his own personal integrity, but to the whole theology of the Gospel for which he had long contended. Was the keeping of the Mosaic law, in whole or in part, a necessary ground of salvation, alongside the cross of Christ? Was the message of faith in Christ crucified alone an incomplete Gospel? Was Christ the Saviour of the circumcised only? Did He live and die to bolster up the legalism of the Pharisees? Was the Christian Church just a Jewish sect, and did Gentiles have to become Jews in order to be Christians?

Paul wrote to the Galatians to vindicate his own thunderous "no" to these questions against the Judaisers' equally emphatic "yes," and his letter is the most violent piece of polemical writing in the New Testament. Here is Paul, the Apostle, fighting for "the truth of the gospel" (2:5) and the survival of Christianity; battling for grace and faith against works and merit, for salvation through Christ against salvation through law, for freedom from law against bondage to it, for Christ's Christianity against a new form of Judaism. Here is Paul, the ex-Pharisee, fighting to save others from the depths of bitterness and despair into which, as he had proved, works-religion plunges all its honest devotees. Here is Paul, the pastor, fighting for the souls of his sheep; for he saw that the Judaizers were actually taking from his Gospel that very saving power which they claimed to add to it, and that acceptance of circumcision would mean severance from Christ (5:4). Here, finally, is Paul, the Christian, fighting for the honor of his Saviour and the right to glory in Christ's cross alone (6:14). And he fights with the devoted energy and noble passion which alone could be proper to the defense of so great a cause.

I. Introduction (1:1–9)

1. Paul's Greeting to the Galatians (1:1–5)

Paul's salutation is no mere formality, but sets the stage for what is to come by introducing some of the epistle's basic themes. First, Paul takes occasion to announce himself as "an apostle"—not a delegate of the Jerusalem leaders but an apostle in his own right— "not from men" (as if he were just acting as spokesman for a party), "nor through man" (as if he owed his position to such a party), "but through Jesus Christ and God the Father" (1:1, RSV). My authority and commission, says Paul—he will develop the thought later—have come to me directly from the God I serve. Then for a moment he dwells on the saving work of Christ, a proper grasp of which cuts at the root of the Judaizing position. "Grace to you and peace from . . . our Lord Jesus Christ, who gave himself for our sins to deliver us"—strictly, *rescue,* a very vigorous word—"from this present evil age"—the order of unredeemed things, to which all legalistic religion belongs (cf. 4:1–5; 1:3, 4, RSV). Christ atones, and Christ rescues; Christ wins redemption for His people, and Christ bestows it on them; salvation, from first to last, is all Christ's work, and Christ's salvation lifts man out of the realm of legalism altogether. Paul here gives advance notice that he will have no truck with views which represent salvation as partly man's achievement, and not wholly the gift of Christ's grace.

2. Occasion for Writing: their Lapse from the Gospel (1:6–9)

Then Paul states what has prompted his letter. He is amazed, he says, that the Galatians could so soon lapse from God, who through the Gospel "called you in the grace of Christ." To think that already you are rejecting God's word, God's grace and God's Son in favor of a barren, legalistic "gospel," which, indeed, is not the Gospel, but a ruinous perversion of it! Those who preach any other gospel than that which you heard from me, whoever they are, says Paul, can only do you harm. May God's curse fall on them all! This is strong language, but not too strong, for the Judaizers' teaching really had jeopardized both the truth of the Gospel and the souls of the Galatians. The violence of Paul's language (and compare the even rougher words in 5:12, RSV) is simply the measure of the burden of responsibility which he felt for both (cf. 2:5; 4:19). The speaker here is Paul, the pastor, unable to contain the savagery of his grief as he thinks of the wolves tearing God's flock (cf. Acts 20:29). Small-hearted men who do not feel strong love for divine truth and human souls will do well not to censure the overflow of such titanic passions.

II. Paul's Authority and the Authenticity of His Message (1:10—2:21)

Verse 10 is flung out as a comment on the preceding verses, and forms an abrupt transition to what follows. The Revised Standard Version makes the meaning clear. "Am I now [in what I have just said] seeking the favor of men [by unprincipled compromise], or of God [by unflinching loyalty to His truth]? Do I talk like a man-pleaser? Were I still the man-pleaser I was in my Pharisaic days, when I sought the applause of Jewry by my zeal for the oral law (cf. 1:14), I should not be Christ's bondslave today. But his bondslave I am; and it is by unswerving adherence to the gospel, committed to me, that I serve him." This is the claim implicit in this rather elliptical verse. Having made it, Paul spends the rest of this section quoting facts (cf. 1:20) to prove it.

1. Paul's Gospel Revealed to Him by Christ (1:10–24)

In 1:11–24, he tells us that the content of his Gospel, and his conviction of its truth, was not the result of human teaching, either before or after his conversion, but of the revelation to him of the glorified Christ on the Damascus road (vv. 12, 16). (In verse 15, the Revised Standard Version's "had called" is wrong. God's act of calling Paul to faith did not precede the revelation; rather, the revelation itself was the means of the calling.) God is the author of my convictions, says Paul, not man; certainly not the Jerusalem apostles nor any Judean teacher, for I had virtually no contact with Christianity in Judea for years after my conversion (vv. 18–22). Thus Paul refutes the charge that he depended on others for his knowledge of the Gospel.

2. Paul's Gospel Acknowledged by Other Apostles (2:1–10)

Next, Paul tells us how, when he visited Jerusalem "fourteen years after," he made a point of discussing his Gospel fully and frankly with the "pillars" there, in order to insure that no theological disharmony between Antioch and Jerusalem should arise to threaten his Gentile work (2:2). During his visit, "false brethren" (Christian-ized Pharisees?) pressed for the circumcision of Titus, his Greek companion; but Paul would not allow this, lest he should seem to be surrendering the vital principle that Gentiles need not become Jews in order to be Christians (vv. 3 ff.; cf. 3:28). Meanwhile, the "pillars," Peter, James, and John, had approved Paul's Gospel without addition or alteration, recognized his calling as the apostle to the Gentiles, and formally welcomed him and Barnabas as fellow-laborers (vv. 6–10). These facts are Paul's answer to those who spoke of him as a subordinate of the Jerusalem apostles and as the preacher of a Gospel which those leaders could never approve.

3. Paul's Gospel Vindicated against Compromise (2:11–21)

Now Paul proceeds to turn the tables on those who accused him of inconsistency by relating an incident in which Peter was the compromiser and Paul the champion of a consistent application of gospel truth. "Certain . . . from James" once persuaded Peter to withdraw from table-fellowship with Gentile Christians at Antioch; Paul, seeing this behavior to be a contradiction of the Gospel, publicly rebuked him for it (2:11–14). In verses 15–21 Paul explains why. The Christian Jew, who confesses that he cannot be justified through the law (because he has broken it), but only through faith in Christ, thereby admits that in the sight of God he is no different from, nor better than, "sinners of the Gentiles." This does not mean that Christ has made him a sinner (of course not!); what Christ has done, rather, is to make him see himself for the sinner he always was. But if the Christian Jew now reverts to acting as if, after all, Jews can gain righteousness by exact observance of the law, he becomes a transgressor in a new sense. He sins against grace; for his attitude is an implicit denial both of his need of Christ's atoning death (v. 21) and of his representative participation in it (vv. 19, 20). For trusting Christ means accepting identification with Him in His death, and thereby "dying to the law." So far as believing sinners are concerned, the law is now satisfied, and they have done with it; neither its promises (3:12) nor its threats (3:10) concern them any more; henceforth, Christ lives in them, and they live by faith in Him. For them to behave as if they were still "under law," therefore, shows at least misunderstanding, and at worst contempt, of the saving grace of Christ.

III. The Way of Salvation (3:1—4:31)

1. Salvation in Christ is by Faith, not Works (3:1–14)

Paul has shown that the justification of the Jew in Christ brings him down as low as the Gentile; now he shows us that the justification of the Gentile in Christ lifts him up as high as the Jew. The argument of this section is designed to show, not merely that faith is the only way of salvation, but that faith is the way of full salvation.

Without faith, man has nothing; having faith, he possesses everything; and in neither case can works of law gain him anything. As far as salvation is concerned, works of law are as useless as they are needless.

The apostle opens his argument with a set of shattering questions. Fools! Who bewitched you away from Christ? Tell me your experience: did you receive the Spirit, and did you see miracles wrought, by works or by faith? Have all your experiences (3:4, RSV) taught you nothing? Can you be so stupid as to believe that the road ahead for you is to return to the way of works? *Think!*, says Paul; as you value your souls, think out what your own past experience proves! (vv. 1–5).

Having thus, as he hopes, jerked his readers' minds into action, Paul rushes on to prove that salvation is by faith and not by works (3:6–14). First, he shows from Old Testament statements about Abraham that justification is always by faith (vv. 6–9). Then he argues the converse, that justification is never by works of law (vv. 10–12). How could it be? he asks. The Old Testament says that "the just" (he whom God accepts as righteous) "shall live" (in enjoyment of God's favor) "by faith" (Hab. 2:4, quoted in 3:11; follow here the KJV wording). "But the law does not rest on faith" (v. 12, RSV). All that the law does is to command perfection and curse sin. Had we been left to the mercy of the law, we should all have perished. But—Paul races on—Christ has redeemed us from its curse! Now, in Him, Gentiles possess "the blessing of Abraham" (justification, full and free), and Jew and Gentile together receive "the promise of the Spirit" (a reference probably to Joel 2:28, 29; see Acts 2:16–21). None of this, however, is through works; it is all by faith 3:13, 14).

2. Salvation in Christ is through Promise, not Law (3:15–22)

Paul now buttresses his case by showing that the Old Testament depicts "the blessing of Abraham" as a covenant gift, a promise to be received by faith, and never as conditional upon law-keeping (3:15–22). His argument runs thus: (*1*) Even on the human level, a unilateral deed of gift (this is the meaning, whether one translates "covenant," KJV, or "will," RSV) has permanent validity once it has been made; later arrangements do not supersede it (v. 15). (*2*) It was by such a deed of gift that God made over salvation to

Abraham and his seed (v. 16). (Note that singular, Paul adds; it is a reminder that the promise had Christ specifically in view, as the "seed" in Whom the rest of Abraham's sons should find their inheritance, vv. 19, 22). (3) The Mosaic law, given four centuries later, does not therefore cancel the covenant, nor put the gift of salvation on a new footing. Chronologically and theologically, the covenant has priority over the law (vv. 17, 18). *(4)* The law's sole purpose was to subserve the covenant by exposing sin (vv. 19, 22) and so driving men to Christ (v. 24). Its connection with God's saving purpose was only external and indirect, and the manner of its promulgation showed as much; for, as it came to man, it was doubly remote from God, being given by angels via a human mediator. It was not given by direct divine utterance, as was the promise to Abraham (vv. 18–21). Thus it appears that the heart of God's saving revelation is the covenant, not the law; and the response which the covenant requires is not works, but faith.

3. Those who Trust in Christ are Sons, not Slaves (3:23—4:7)

Paul now moves on to contrast what he and his readers had become through faith with what they had been before (3:23—4:7). No longer were they slaves under law; in Christ they were sons and heirs both of Abraham and of God (3:29; 4:7). Once they had served "the elemental spirits of the universe" (an astrological name for the angels who ruled the stars, here applied to Satan's hosts, 4:3; cf. 4:9, RSV). Those days, however, were now past; Christ had redeemed them from servitude for sonship and the presence of His Spirit in their hearts prompting them to call on God as their Father proved them to have become sons indeed (4:6, 7).

4. Expostulation (4:8–20)

At this point, Paul pauses to expostulate with his readers. God brought you out from idolatrous superstition and the dominion of demons (4:8, 9; cf. I Cor. 10:20) into the knowledge of Himself. How can you bear to revert to your former servile state?—as you surely will if you lapse into legalism (vv. 8, 9). Paul notes sorrowfully that they had already taken the first steps in that direction (v. 10), and breaks into a moving appeal to his "little children" (v. 19) to follow where he led (v. 12) and resist the blandishments of the Judaizers (vv. 17, 18). Once you welcomed me and my message; how is it that now you turn against me (vv. 15, 16)?

5. *Those who Trust in the Law are Slaves, not Sons (4:21–31)*

This leads Paul back to the main track of his argument: having shown that those who rely on Christ for salvation are sons and heirs of God, not slaves, he now proceeds to demonstrate the converse—that those who rely on the law are slaves and not sons, and so cannot inherit. He finds in the story of Abraham's two sons, children of two mothers, one "born after the flesh" (v. 23; cf. Gen. 16:1 ff.) through unblessed human effort, one born "after the Spirit," "by promise" (vv. 29, 23; cf. Gen. 21:1 ff.), through supernatural divine action, a pattern and a principle directly applicable to the matter in hand. It is this that he means when he calls the story an allegory (v. 24). The pattern is of two rival claimants for Abraham's inheritance, one having the status of a slave, the other of a free man. The principle is that the inheritance goes to the latter, the child of grace and promise, and not to the former (v. 30, quoting Gen. 21:10).

IV. *The Path of Freedom (5:1—6:10)*

The allegory ends with the thought that the Christian's status before God is not that of a slave, but of a free man. Taking up this thought, Paul now reminds his readers (5:1) that their filial freedom from the tyranny of legalistic religion is Christ's own gift to them, and must be valued, safeguarded against loss and abuse, and expressed by a responsible exercise of love.

1. *Freedom Must not be Lost Through Legalism (5:1–12)*

Paul's first point in this section, emphatically stated, is that Christian liberty must not be surrendered by reverting to a legalistic system. The significance of circumcision, as the Judaizers preached it, was that it marked a return to the principle of law-keeping for salvation, and consequently an abandonment of the principle of salvation by faith in Christ only. A religion that is not wholly a faith-religion is not a faith-religion at all, but a works-religion; and if the Galatians were to revert to a works-religion by receiving circumcision, they would sever themselves altogther from Christ and grace (5:2–4). Those who seek all from Christ, and wait for "the hope of righteousness" (the blessedness promised to the righteous) by faith only, need not expect to receive anything from Christ, for only the faith which renounces all trust in works can enter into a saving relationship with Christ (vv. 5, 6). At this point, Paul appeals once more to his converts to reject Judaizing and hold fast to Gospel truth (vv. 7–12).

2. Freedom Must not be Abused through License (5:13–26)

Equally, however, Paul continues, they must safeguard their freedom against license. Freedom from the need to earn salvation through law-keeping was not given them in order that they might not keep the law at all, but as an occasion for free and loving service of their fellows—which is, in fact, the true fulfilment of the law (5:13, 14). Only trouble can follow if they fail here (v. 15). Therefore, "walk by the Spirit, and do not gratify the desires of "the flesh" (v. 16, RSV). It is true that the Spirit and the flesh are at war within you, so that you find in yourself resistance and opposition to everything you would do (v. 17); if, however, you are being led by the Spirit into a life of victorious contention against sin and spontaneous uprightness and love, the very quality of your law-keeping proves that you are not "under the law" (v. 18). For this "fruit of the Spirit" only appears in the lives of those who have been "born of the Spirit" (4:29) and "live by the Spirit" (5:25, RSV) in penitent, self-denying faith towards Jesus Christ (vv. 22–26), and such have been decisively delivered from the sphere of law.

3. Freedom Must be Expressed through Service (6:1–10)

Do not let sin set you at each other's throats (5:26), but fulfil the "law of Christ" by mutual love, care and forbearance, remembering your own susceptibility to sin and the solemn account of your life that you must one day give (6:1–5). Incidentally, see that you pay your ministers a proper salary (v. 6). (Paul is a practical man!) Remember, you live under the eye of a just Judge; do not be so stupid and irreverent as to suppose that you will lose nothing by sinning, nor so faithless and fainthearted as to doubt that if you give yourself tirelessly to welldoing in his service you will be duly rewarded (vv. 7–10).

V. Postcript: Sacrificial Living in Contrast to Legalism (6:11–18)

Here Paul takes the pen from his amanuensis and scrawls a few last words in his own writing. "See with what large letters I am writing to you with my own hand" (6:11, RSV; KJV misunderstands the verse). The issue between himself and the Judaizers, he writes, boils down to this: a radically different attitude to the Redeemer's cross. The Judaizers are ashamed of the cross; they want to glory in human achievement; hence they compromise the Gospel in order to escape the reproach of the cross from their fellow-Jews, and to gain applause by winning scalps for the Judaism which the cross condemns (vv. 12, 13). "But God forbid that I should glory, save in the cross of our Lord Jesus Christ"—which has severed the connection between me and all the objects of profit, pleasure and pride which once enslaved me, and lifted me out of "the present evil age" (1:4) into the realm of new creation and new life (6:14, 15). God bless all the true Israel, who hold fast to this principle of glorying in the cross alone (v. 15)! For this, and this alone, is the way of liberty and of life.

Ephesians

WILBER T. DAYTON

EPHESIANS has been called the "grandest of all the Pauline letters." Its loftiness, dignity, and serenity of expression are surpassed only by its sublime truths. It leaves ceremony and controversy behind as it soars into the heavenlies and views life in the light of eternity. The idea which dominates the whole epistle in different forms is the unity of Christians as a single society with Christ as its invisible head. First, the apostle exults in the gracious, all-inclusive purpose of God for the saints; then he bows in humble petition for the personal fulfilment of the divine purpose in human life. The remainder of the doctrinal section (through chapter 3) sketches this unity in transformed lives, broken barriers, and the incorporation of both Jews and Gentiles into one body. Appropriately, discourse blends into prayer and prayer into doxology. The last half of the epistle is generally called hortatory, because it exhorts Christians to the new life. It treats of the Christian walk and warfare that fitly follow such gracious divine provision for the saints.

I. Salutation (1:1, 2)

In the salutation Paul sets the pattern of the epistle by pushing the human into the background and focusing attention on Deity. In two verses, reference is made five times to Christ and to God the Father. Paul's own importance is found not in his human qualifications, but in his divine commission. And the honor of his readers is not based on their illustrious background, but on their relationship to the Lord Jesus Christ. Accordingly, even his greeting is an evangelical adaptation of both the Greek and Hebrew custom. He can wish them nothing better than the loving favor of God and the peace that flows from it.

II. Thanksgiving for the Plan of Salvation (1:3–14)

The apostle breaks out in praise to God at the thought of Who God is and what He has done for man. As Father of our Lord Jesus Christ, He is the fountainhead of all the benefits that have come through redemption. It is He Who knew us from eternity, made room for us in redemption, and revealed His gracious purpose for us in Christ.

1. God's Purpose for the Church is Holiness, Grace and Glory (1:4–6)

Since these qualities are of God's essence (I Pet. 1:16; I Jn. 4:8), the goal of redeeming grace is a people restored to the image and likeness of the Maker. For the present order, this gracious plan includes blamelessness (1:4; I Thess. 5:23), and for the eternal ages, it provides faultlessness (Jude 24). But for both time and eternity, the good pleasure of His will is that we be established as sons of God, so bearing the family resemblance, through grace, that our lives will bring praise to Him as He reveals what He is through us. Thus, to acceptance with God through Christ is added the manifestation of God through redeemed human personality.

2. Christ's Redemption, Uniting All in Him (1:7–12)

In the whole plan of salvation, Christ, the Beloved, is central, and redemption is His role (1:7). Applied to man, this means, first, forgiveness of sins—the removal of the barrier that separated man from God. But forgiveness, measured in terms of the bounty of grace, is not just a negative thing—a rescue from destruction—it is access to an abundance of wisely planned and generous benefits (v. 8). To draw near to God is to move into a progressive unfolding of matchless riches of His provision for the saints (v. 9). God's ultimate purpose includes, but goes beyond, individual perfection (Col. 1:28). It is His plan to gather together in Christ all the redeemed of earth with the hosts of heaven in one glorious, everlasting society. To a place in this blessed and eternal order, God has foreordained us. When grace has its perfect work, sinful man is so transformed that he does credit to and enhances the glory of God (v. 12).

3. The Holy Spirit's Seal, Sample and Pledge of Inheritance (1:13, 14)

Lest there be any mistake, Paul specifically includes the Gentile Ephesians to whom he is writing. They also had heard the Gospel, had become believers, and had received the promised Holy Spirit (cf. Acts 19:1–6). To them also the Holy Spirit was the seal of divine ownership and protection as well as the earnest of their inheritance—the sample and surety of heaven.

III. Prayer That Christian Life May Correspond to Divine Provision (1:15–23)

Thanksgiving for grace already bestowed is mingled with petition for enlargement of capacity through the work of the Spirit. Paul prays that increased spiritual insight may make real the great hope to which we are called, the measureless glory of God's achievement in the saints, and the matchless power which the Father of glory makes available to His saints.

In verse 19, Paul uses four words that suggest dynamics, energy, strength, and ability, to describe the power of God in Christian experience. These words stir memories of the divine triumph already accomplished by this power in Christ and the assurance of the Christian's victory. Power that raised the Saviour from death and the grave, that exalted Him to the right hand of the Father, that gave Him supremacy over every present and future dominion, that put all things under His feet, and that made Him the head and fulness of the Church—such power is sufficient for every need.

IV. The Unity of All Believers in Christ (2:1—3:21)

1. Release from Death and Sin to Union with Christ (2:1–10)

Release from spiritual death and from sin is essential to Christian unity. The patterns of sin, as followed by the disobedient ones of this world, are spiritual death. Yet Paul acknowledges that we also were involved at one time and were all subject to the wrath of God. But God, out of His abundant mercy and love, changed all this. He made us alive together, raised us up together, and made us sit together in the heavenlies in Christ (2:5, 6). As we were lost in sin together, so we are joined in Christ and with Christ. The purpose of God is an eternal one—to demonstrate in us through future ages what grace can do (v. 7).

But salvation is no cause for pride, though it does occasion rejoicing; we did not save ourselves. Works could not avail. Grace did it—the gift of God. We are His workmanship, and the glory belongs to Him. Yet human decision is still required. Salvation is in response to our faith (2:8), and it falls short of its goal until it issues in good works, which God has planned from the beginning (v. 10). Through them God's glory is revealed in man.

2. Privileges of the Gospel Shared by the Gentiles (2:11–22)

Paul reminds the Gentiles that a double benefit is theirs. By long-established heathen traditions and practices, a wall had separated them from the privileges of God's people (2:11, 12). But God not only made a way for them; He also broke down the dividing wall that separated Jew and Gentile. Once the Jew and Gentile are in Christ, they are both on the same basis and are united in one great commonwealth. The blood of Christ accomplishes this. By it all are brought near, and the enmity is gone (vv. 13–17). Spiritually, Jews and Gentiles no longer exist. In Christ there is only the new man— the Christian. Regardless of race, sex, or background, there is access by one Spirit to God (v. 18). God has but one citizenry, one household, and one holy temple. Upon the one foundation of the apostles and prophets, with the one cornerstone of Christ, all have their place (vv. 19–22).

3. *Mystery of the Union of All Saints in Christ (3:1–13)*

In the beginning of chapter 3, Paul prepares to bow the knee in worship at the thought of such matchless grace of God. But that we might bow with him, he digresses until verse 14 to explain more fully how this grace was revealed. Paul says it was a mystery (v. 3), something that could not be reasoned or guessed in previous ages. Paul knew it by the only possible means, revelation through the Spirit (vv. 4, 5). By remarkable direction, the Holy Spirit had led Paul again and again to minister to other nations until he recognized that he was indeed God's minister to the Gentiles and that through him God's Spirit was offering the unsearchable riches to those who had not formerly been evangelized. At last to all earth and heaven is manifest the mystery that it is the eternal purpose of God to offer grace to all equally through Jesus Christ.

4. *Prayer that this Reality be Fully Experienced (3:14–19)*

Finally, in reverent humility, Paul prays that such marvelous provision of grace may be met by human appropriation. No unaided reason could fathom such grace, but God, through His Spirit, can grant an abundant empowerment in the inner man, measured only by the fabulous wealth of divine glory (God's ability to reveal Himself). Through this, Christ can so richly dwell in the heart by faith that one's roots may deeply penetrate the rich soil of divine love until a comprehension takes hold of the tremendous proportions of Christian privileges in grace. Though the love of Christ exceeds the reach of human knowledge, one can imbibe until he is filled with divine love. And that is to be filled with God, for God is love (3:17–19). This is Paul's prayer for his readers.

5. Doxology to God for Abundant Grace (3:20, 21)

Doxology is the fitting close to such a confident prayer. God is able to do what is asked. Indeed, He can do exceeding abundantly above all that we ask or think—not by some power as yet unrevealed, but according to that power which He has already set to work in us (3:20). To Him be glory forever in the Church through the Lord Jesus Christ, Who furnished such redemption (v. 21).

V. Exhortation to Walk as Christians (4:1—6:9)

On the basis of the great doctrinal truths of the first three chapters, Paul presents urgent practical exhortations. Though the practical is never absent from the doctrinal section, nor the doctrinal from the practical, the emphasis in the remaining chapters is heavily weighted toward the type of conduct that should be reasonably expected in view of the abundant grace through Jesus Christ our Lord.

1. A Walk in Unity of the Spirit (4:1–16)

Central in this walk is unity. Nothing less is fitting in the light of God's great concern as expressed on Calvary (2:15), in the work of the Spirit (4:3, 4), and in all the provisions for the Christian life (vv. 4–6). But unity of the Spirit is not automatic. It must be promoted by a humble attitude, a patient spirit, a willingness to over-look irritations, and an active cultivation of those things which preserve peace (vv. 2, 3). God's provision for unity is perfect. There is only one true body of believers, one Holy Spirit administering its affairs, one common hope set before all, one Lord and giver of life, one approach by faith, one basic sign of admission to this body, and one God and Father supervising, directing, and indwelling all.

In this unity, diversity must also be recognized. But as in a human body, unity is enhanced, not destroyed, by the differences that exist— if only all parts are responsive to a central control. So the triumphant Christ bestows a variety of gifts to different individuals for the benefit of the whole group (4:7, 11). The purpose is unity, not divi-sion. Apostles, prophets, evangelists, pastors, and teachers are not engaged in a contest of greatness, but rather in a cooperative enterprise of fitting all saints into a perfectly functioning, mature man, capable of resisting error and championing the truth by word and deed (v. 12). And this figure is complete only as the head is Christ and as each part is knit together in vital contact, each contributing through love to the life and growth of the whole (vv. 15, 16).

2. A Walk in Newness of Life (4:17–32)

This is not as Gentiles walked apart from God's grace (4:17–19). Lacking content in their thinking, having their understanding darkened, being alienated from the source of life by their ignorance and blindness, and having lost the sensitivity that would correct them, they plunged into all excesses, greed, and filth.

But now Christ is known, and with Him there is a whole new life (4:20–24). To become a Christian involved a negative human act, a positive divine act, and a positive human act. The old man, with his corrupt practices, is put off. God makes new the spirit of the mind and grants life. The new man, thus created after the pattern of the righteous and holy God, takes the place of the old. This is God's blueprint for making Christians.

As truly as there is the creation of a new spiritual life, so there must also be a new pattern of daily living (4:25–32). Instead of lying, truth must prevail (v. 25). Anger must be purged of its sinful and malicious elements (v. 26). The devil must be excluded from his former advantage over thought and conduct (v. 27). Industry and generosity must displace stealing (v. 28). Worthless speech must give way to that which encourages fellowmen and improves their lives (v. 29). In short, whatever would displease the Holy Spirit must cease, lest He be grieved, since it is He Who seals us unto the great consummation of redemption at the end of the age (v. 30). This certainly excludes all negative, unkind, and malicious conduct toward others (v. 31). The safe rule is to follow the example of God Who for Christ's sake forgave us. In like manner we should be sensitive to the feelings of others, treat them kindly, and forgive their offenses (v. 32).

3. A Walk in Love (5:1–21)

In fact, the whole requirement of Christian ethics is to imitate God as children who endear themselves to their father by idealizing and imitating Him (5:1); and this is to walk in love, imitating

Christ's redemptive love for us (v. 2). This excludes trifling with matters of purity and the rights of others. Such is abhorrent to saints (v. 3). Even cheap and suggestive talk, ribald humor, and unseemly conversation are repulsive to those who walk in love. They prefer to give thanks (v. 4). The vile and questionable things add up to idolatry—putting something else in God's place—and exclude one from any part in Christ and God (v. 5). Let there be no confusion along this line. These things of the old life occasion the wrath of God. One must stay far from them, since he is now a child of light (vv. 6–8).

The walk of love is a life in which the Spirit brings forth fruit after His kind. Therefore the pattern is goodness, righteousness and truth, and the motive is to please the Lord (5:9, 10). So far from sharing in the worthless and senseless conduct from which one was saved, the Christian must now oppose and reprove evil as the light of God shows it in its true nature (vv. 11–13). God calls to something better. This is no time to sleep or lie dead in sin. Christ is giving light. There is not time for folly. One must walk carefully, jealously guarding the passing of time lest an evil age rob him of his opportunity of loving service to God (vv. 14–16).

Times like these demand discernment. One must understand the will of the Lord. Instead of indulging in experiences of debauchery, one needs the fulness of the Spirit (5:17, 18) and must act accordingly. His heart and lips should overflow with praise and edifying meditation, giving thanks always to God and conducting himself humbly toward others as those who reverence God (vv. 19–21).

4. A Walk of Humility and Justice in Human Relations (5:22—6:9)

The walk of love is also a walk of humility and justice in human relations. Wives find their happiness and usefulness in loving devotion to the good of husband and home, as God ordained (5:22–24). There cannot be two heads, and strife violates love. Husbands, likewise, must forsake selfish interests and return the love and devotion that makes the home a balanced society (v. 25). Christ again is the example. As He loved the Church, gave Himself for it, and sought its purity, glory, and holiness, so man owes his wholehearted love and devotion to wife and home, forsaking all others for the fulfilment and perfection of marriage (vv. 26–33). Here the Church becomes an illuminating analogy for marriage counselling, and earth's sweetest union becomes a symbol of heaven's best.

Children also have a part in the Christian walk; they owe reverent obedience to parents (6:1). This is both a divine commandment and a provision for their own welfare (vv. 2, 3). In return, parents owe children reasonable discipline and Christian nurture (v. 4). Employees serve both Christ and the employer. Thus due service is doubly required and twice rewarded (vv. 5–8). Likewise, human authority is tempered and made reasonable by reverence toward God (v. 9).

VI. Exhortation to Be Strong in the Lord (6:10–18)

1. Firm Stand against the Enemy (6:10–13)

As a final word, Paul exhorts all, as brethren, to be fully equipped and strong in the Lord and in the mighty power that He has made available to man (6:10, 11). Human valor is not adequate for spiritual conflict, for it is not mere men that we face. Only God's armor can prevail against the principalities, authorities, world rulers of this darkness, and the spiritual hosts of wickedness that attack the human spirit even in the sacred realm of contemplation of heavenly things and communion with God (vv. 12, 13).

2. Full Equipment for Defense and Offense (6:14–17)

To stand in this conflict requires that one's strength be supported by truth, that his vitals be protected by righteousness, that his progress be in God's message of peace, that his moving defense be faith, that his intelligence be safeguarded by a saving knowledge of God, and that his weapon be none other than God's own Word. Only as one uses the full armor given by the conquering Christ can he overcome the enemy. But with it, victory is sure. Christ has already overcome the same foe (1:20–22).

VII. Exhortation to Pray: Benedictory Remarks (6:18–24)

Making full use of these weapons of spiritual warfare, man still has one more great resource for security and achievement. One must pray always with alertness and persistence—for himself, for others, and for the success of the work of God and for all of God's workers (6:18–20). To do less is to miss life's great privilege and to fail in carrying out a tremendous responsibility.

With the emphasis on prayer, Paul is content to close his discourse and to turn his attention to introducing Tychicus, the messenger (6:21, 22). In keeping with the message of the book, he wishes for all saints God's greatest blessings of peace—love, faith, and grace—from God the Father of our Lord Jesus Christ.

Philippians

RALPH A. GWINN

THE EPISTLE to the Philippians is one of Paul's most personal letters. Writing to a group of personal friends whom he loved dearly, the apostle expresses deep appreciation of their devotion to him. He writes to them not so much as the apostle who established the church in Philippi as their father in Christ.

The dominant note of this short letter is joy. Its radiant quality is the more remarkable in view of the fact that Paul was writing from prison.

1097

I. Salutation (1:1, 2)

Paul begins his letter with his customary salutation. Unlike his usual opening, however, he refers here to himself and Timothy as slaves of Christ Jesus. His more frequent opening is "Paul, an apostle. . . ." His readers are addressed as "saints," Paul applies the term "saints" to all believers (even when writing to the Corinthians who had many grievous faults). The word might be rendered "holy ones." The same word is used of the third person of the Trinity, the *Holy* Spirit.

II. Thanksgiving and Prayer for the Philippians (1:3–11)

An introductory thanksgiving is the rule in Paul's letters (Galatians is a notable exception). His thanksgiving is not merely formal. It is sincere. These Philippians held a special place in Paul's heart. His prayers for them are always mingled with joy. He is especially grateful for their partnership in the Gospel.

Verse 6, one of the great New Testament texts, rings with the certainty of a settled conviction. Paul uses the perfect tense here: "I stand persuaded that. . . ." The good work of which Paul speaks in this verse is probably best understood as a reference to the new life in Christ. As far as the construction is concerned, verse 6 should be connected with verse 3. The English might be read thus: "I, standing persuaded that he who began a good work in you will accomplish it at the day of Christ Jesus, thank my God. . . ." This would indicate that Paul's statement in verse 7 ("to think this of you") connects more properly with verses 4 and 5, not with verse 6 as the English text would suggest.

Paul calls God to witness—perhaps because the thing he says might appear surprising in view of his rather short personal acquaintance with these people. Nevertheless, they had worked themselves deeply into his heart. He yearns for them with the affection of Christ Jesus, and this goes deep!

Because of his love for them, his prayer is that their love may also grow. Obviously then this love (and life) of Christ does not spring full-bloomed in the life of the Christian. This is perhaps nowhere more apparent than in this letter to the Philippians. Christ has some difficult ground to traverse in the life of the Christian, ground which has long been under the control of sin, ground which was not present in His own life.

Though the prayer for increased love might be anticipated, the specific area in which love is to grow does come as a surprise (1:9). Love is to abound increasingly in the sphere of knowledge and all discernment. We find in Paul then this rather startling blending: we are to love in knowledge and discernment, and we are to believe in our hearts (Rom. 10:9, 10).

This prayer for increased love in knowledge and discernment has a specific purpose—and it is a purpose clause, not a result clause, that is used here. The goal in view is that the Philippian Christians may approve what is excellent and that they may be pure and blameless for the day of Christ, standing filled (the perfect tense signifies action completed in past time whose effect continues into the present) with the fruit of righteousness which comes through Christ. The fruit of righteousness then is not the result of a directionless love, but the product of an increasingly intelligent love. For Paul the final end is always the same—the glory of God (cf. Rom. 11:36).

III. For Paul to Live is Christ (1:12—4:1)

1. The Gospel is Carried Wherever Paul Goes (1:12, 13)

Perhaps verse 12 is an application of Romans 8:28. Certainly it is a remarkable statement coming from a man who has been some little time a prisoner. Paul indicates that his imprisonment has had a twofold blessing. First, the whole praetorium, the emperor's guard, has learned the real reason for his captivity. It was not because of any wrongdoing, but because of Christ. Paul uses the simple phrase "in Christ"—"it has become evident that my bonds are in Christ." Probably he is using the phrase "in Christ" in his usual manner: "It has become obvious throughout the whole prateorium that in reality I am Christ's prisoner, and only incidentally Rome's prisoner" (1:13). He does say as much in II Corinthians 2:14 (RSV).

2. Believers in Rome are Encouraged (1:14)

The second blessing which has accompanied Paul's imprisonment is the encouragement to other Christians to witness without fear.

Paul says that most of the brethren have been made confident. There were some in his day, as well as in ours, reluctant to speak for Christ.

3. *Paul's Attitude Reflects Christ (1:15–18)*

On the other hand, there were some, as there still are today, who proclaimed Christ from an altogether wrong motive. Those who disagreed rather sharply with Paul thought they now had an open door. Not only that, they understood so little of the love of Christ that they took delight in the thought that Paul would be further troubled by their freedom to do and teach as they pleased. Paul's response to their attitude is one of the most magnificent indications of the closeness of his walk with Jesus Christ. He simply says that regardless of their motives, Christ is being preached, and in that he rejoices. There may be many things that accompany such preaching that he does not like; nevertheless, the fact that Christ is being preached is ground for rejoicing. The central core of teaching about Christ must be right (the letters to the Romans and the Galatians would positively rule out any other standpoint), and granted that, Paul can rejoice in the proclamation of that truth even though there may be much else he would rather have changed.

4. *A Difficult Decision: to Live Here Below for Christ or to be with Christ (1:19–26)*

Paul looks forward to release, yet at the same time he is realistic about Roman political expediency. The alternative of death is also faced. If for him to live means Christ, then to die is even more desirable, for that means life in the very presence of Christ. This is *far* better. No longer would he see dimly, but face to face. While this would be his personal preference, the desire to continue to serve Christ in this life is also great. If the choice were his to make, Paul would find it very difficult to decide between the two.

5. *The Meaning of "To Live is Christ" (1:27—2:30)*

The Manner of Life is to be Worthy of the Gospel (1:27–30). Without attempting to impose upon Paul an arbitrary outline, one can certainly detect in what follows an unfolding of what is meant by "to me to live is Christ." The Christian is to conduct himself in a manner that befits his high calling. "Let your manner of life be" is in the imperative. This is a command which deals not only with overt behavior, but reaches down into the inner recesses of the life. The motivation of the Christian is not to spring from selfishness. Rather, his mind-set should be that of Christ Himself. We find here something that occurs more than once in Paul's writings—a great doctrinal statement not merely to give instruction in theology, but for the effect it should have on life (cf. his well-reasoned conclusion of I Cor. 15). "Truth is in order to goodness." The point is sometimes missed in this passage. Christ is not held up just as an example for our outward imitation. Rather, we are to have the same attitude, the same disposition as Christ "who, though he was in the form of God . . . humbled himself." "To me to live is Christ" means that the very life of Christ will be seen in us.

Another point should be observed here. To Paul, as to any Jew, "the name which is above every name" could refer only to the Jews' sacred name for God, the sacred tetragrammaton, *YHWH*. This is the term which is consistently rendered as Lord in the King James Version and in the Revised Standard Version, and as *Jehovah* in the American Revised Version. Quite simply, Paul says that this name belongs to Jesus.

The Attitude of Christ is to be Ours (2:1–18). If one indeed has the mind of Christ, Paul suggests further directions in which this will be manifest in life. One would not then be constantly grumbling (2:14) —whether aloud or in the heart. Surely a continuous grumbling about people and circumstances does not reflect the life of Him "who, when he was reviled, reviled not again." One will have the same genuine concern for others that was so evident in Him Who stooped to the cross for us (cf. Mt. 20:26–28). Paul sees this kind of love in Timothy (2:20, 21) and in Epaphroditus (vv. 25–30).

6. Surpassing Worth of Knowing Christ (3:1–11)

Before Paul met Christ on the Damascus road, he had good reason for confidence. His background and his attainments as he lists them are imposing (3:5, 6). It is very easy for us to read such a list without appreciating what these things meant to Paul; they were his whole life. One's pedigree and his status with reference to the law were the measure of his standing. In another place (Gal. 1:14) he mentions that he outdid many of his contemporaries in his attainments. Then suddenly he was arrested by Christ. When he grasped the surpassing excellence of Christ, everything else faded into the background; indeed, those other things could only be regarded as rubbish. In view of his own experience it is little wonder that he could write: "If any one is in Christ, a new creation! The old things are gone; look, new things have come" (II Cor. 5:17).

Paul is saying another thing here that is important: it is *either* the old way *or* Christ's way, not *both . . . and*. The righteousness that comes from God through faith in Christ is radically different from the former legal righteousness (3:9). It is Paul's great desire that he might know Christ in all His fulness, that he might know the power of His resurrection (cf. Eph. 1:19, 20; 2:5), that he might know the fellowship of His sufferings, that he might even share the experience of His death, if possibly he might attain to the resurrection from the dead (vv. 10, 11). This last expression seems strange with its apparent lack of certainty. That Paul is really expressing doubt as to his participation in an ultimate resurrection is very difficult to accept in the light of I Thessalonians 4:13 and following; Romans 8:11, 23, 38, 39; I Corinthians 15.

7. *Necessity of Growth (3:12–16)*

Paul continues by declaring that he has not reached the goal which he desires. Still he presses on toward the goal—he can do nothing else in view of the fact that he has been seized by Christ. Apparent in these few verses is one of the great truths emphasized frequently by Paul. The Christian life cannot be static, it is a life of constant growth. The babe in Christ (I Cor. 3:1, 2) is to grow up in every way to mature manhood (Eph. 4:11–16). This concept of growth is of great importance with reference to our judgments of others. Normally we judge others in relation to our own level of attainment; somewhat less often we judge with reference to Christ; very rarely indeed do we form our judgments with reference to the progress an individual has made since he became a Christian.

The writer recalls an illustration he read or heard somewhere that was helpful to him. The parents of a baby are delighted when the little one begins to walk. Perhaps he takes only a step or two and falls, but the news goes to all the relatives and friends: "Our baby is beginning to walk." If, however, ten years later that same child can take only a step or two and falls, there is no elation on the part of the parents. So it is with God. Our heavenly Father is delighted when our new life is manifesting itself in growth. The level of attainment is far short of what He desires, of what it will eventually be, but He is pleased with each evidence of progress toward the desired goal of full conformity to His Son. The goal is high, so high that it cannot be reached until "we shall see him as he is." But there is no doubt in Paul's mind as to its actual attainment.

8. Contrast between the Enemies of the Cross and the Friends of the Cross (3:17—4:1)

At present, to be sure, we live as aliens in a foreign land, for our citizenship is in heaven from which we await the coming of Him Who shall change our bodies of humiliation so that they will be like His glorious body (3:20, 21). Such a task is not difficult for Him Who has the power to subject all things to Himself. We cannot wonder then at the supreme confidence of the apostle: He Who began a good work in you will accomplish it at the day of Christ Jesus (1:6). The writer to the Hebrews has the same confidence: "Looking unto Jesus the author and finisher of our faith" (Heb. 12:2).

What a sharp contrast is this picture with that of those who are enemies of the cross of Christ: their end is destruction, their god is their stomach, their glory is their own shame, they think only of earthly things (3:17–19). For such Paul weeps. And he exhorts his beloved readers to stand fast in the Lord (4:1).

IV. Some Final Exhortations (4:2–23)

1. Plea for Unity and Peace (4:2–9)

The apostle has a special word of exhortation for two women of the church in Philippi who have been particularly helpful in the work of the Gospel. Paul uses a term here which occurs frequently in this epistle. The word *phroneō* appears in 1:7; 2:2 (twice); 2:5; 3:15 (twice); 3:16; 4:2; 4:10 (twice). One needs only to glance at the passages to realize that the word means more than simply "to think." It takes in the disposition, the pervading spirit, and involves a sympathetic interest. Our common saying "Put your heart in it," carries the same connotation. Thus Paul is asking that Euodia and Syntyche not only think the same thing, but also that they let this oneness of mind reach into the deeper recesses, into motivation and attitude. Would not Paul address the same appeal to many churches today?

The words of 4:4–7 are often read rather lightly. We need to remind ourselves that Paul was writing this little letter with its note of deep and abiding joy and thankfulness from prison. Paul wears the externals of life very casually. To judge from what Paul wrote just after this (vv. 11–13), he was not always so unconcerned about these externals. He states that he has *learned* to be content regardless of the circumstances. This same education is possible for all children of God because the same Lord who lived in Paul dwells in them. One could almost say that 4:13 is a brief summary of Galatians 2:20.

It would be an interesting project to study Paul's references to the life of thought. The matter comes up frequently in this letter. We have already had occasion to note the frequency of the term *phroneō*. Now he speaks (4:7) of the peace of God which surpasses all understanding (a word having to do with the mind). This peace at the same time guards Christian hearts and minds. He immediately follows this with an exhortation to fill the thought life with the consideration of things that are true, worthy of respect, and so forth.

2. Concluding Testimony and Repeated Thanks (4:10–20)

Paul closes his letter by graciously thanking the Philippians for their generosity toward him. In doing so he points out that their gifts to him constituted a partnership with him in the Lord's work. As God had supplied his need through the generosity of the Philippians, so God would supply their needs. The wonderful thing that Paul indicates here is the abundance of God's provision. He does not just barely meet the need; rather, He provides according to His riches in glory in Christ Jesus. To such a God and Father be all glory.

3. Greetings and Benediction (4:21–23)

The salutation concludes the letter. Here too there is a reminder of the greatness of Paul. He sends to the Philippians his own greeting together with those who are in Rome with him, and especially the Christians of Caesar's household. Because Paul was a prisoner in Rome, it would be easy for those who loved him dearly, as did the Philippians, to have a special antipathy against the Roman emperor. He would stand as the epitome of the power holding Paul in prison. That same antipathy could easily spread to the entire household of Caesar. But among these there are those who are Christians. In a touch of true thoughtfulness, Paul sends their particular greetings to his friends in Philippi.

Colossians

LEON MORRIS

LETTERS IN ANTIQUITY usually began, as here, with the name of the writer(s), then those of the addressee(s), followed by a thanksgiving and perhaps a prayer.

I. Greeting (1:1, 2)

Paul uses the conventional form, but makes it definitely Christian. Notice that he reminds his readers that his apostolate came "by the will of God." It was not of human origin. He characterizes the church at Colosse as "saints [that is, men set apart for God] and faithful brethren."

II. Thanksgiving (1:3–8)

Paul is thankful for the continuing growth of the Colossian believers in the faith. He mentions their faith and hope and love (cf. I Cor. 13:13, and elsewhere; it was an early Christian habit to join these three together, not always in the same order). Faith in Christ is the basic Christian attitude. There can be no Christianity without that. Love is the necessary outreach towards others of a living faith. A true faith will always work by love (Gal. 5:6).

Here special stress is laid on hope. The early Christians were for the most part members of the depressed classes. The ordinary conditions of life gave them but little hope, and the gospel message transformed life for them. It gave them hope in this life and in that to come. This hope is solidly based, being "laid up for you in heaven" and thus beyond all earthly attack. The Colossians heard of this hope in the gospel message which, Paul says, is spreading throughout the world and bringing forth fruit. The Colossians had known this from the first time they had heard the Gospel, and Epaphras (who himself was a Colossian, 4:12) had also taught them the same thing. It was this man who had brought Paul news about the Colossians, and particularly about their "love in the Spirit."

III. Prayer (1:9–12)

Paul has already spoken of his continual prayer for them, and he repeats this, adding something of the content of his prayer. He prays that they may know more of the will of God, that they may live fruitful lives, that they may be strengthened with the divine power, and that they may have a right attitude of thankfulness.

IV. God's Work in Christ (1:13-23)

1. Redemption (1:13, 14)

Paul loses no time in coming to the great truths of the faith. The previous verse has made the point that God has transformed the lives of believers, and the thought is continued with the idea of deliverance from "the power of darkness." The Holy Scripture is certain of the power of the evil one, but it is even more certain that God has delivered from every foe those who trust Him. "Translated" (KJV) means "removed" or transferred" (as in the RSV). The imagery is that of a people taken captive by the foe, but now brought back from the land of the enemy into their rightful kingdom. This is further explained as *redemption*, the process whereby those in bondage or under sentence of death were released from their plight by the payment of a price. The price is the death of the Lord. (The words, "through his blood," in KJV are lacking in the best manuscripts, and the meaning is clear without them.)

2. The Excellence of Christ (1:15-19)

From the work of the Saviour, Paul passes to His person. When he says that Christ is the image of God, he means that we see God exactly in Him. "The firstborn of every creature" does not put Him among created beings, but indicates that he stands in the same relation to all creation as the heir, the firstborn, does to a father's property. Paul sees this as eminently reasonable, since the Son was responsible for all creation. "Thrones," and so forth, are spiritual powers; all such are subject to Christ. He is superior to all things, and indeed all things hold together ("consist," KJV) only by Him. Not only is He supreme over creation, He is supreme over the Church. The unity of Christians one with another and their subordination to Christ are both in mind when the Church is spoken of as the body of which He is the Head. Christ is given the titles "the beginning" and "the firstborn from the dead." He is pre-eminent above all. The Gnostics thought of a number of divine spiritual beings who together made up "the fulness." Paul brings out the greatness of Christ by pointing out that "all fulness" (or "all the fulness," RSV) dwells in Him.

3. Reconciliation (1:20–23)

One effect of sin is to make men the enemies of God. Retrieving this situation is one aspect of the work of Christ. So Paul speaks of Him as "making peace," and as reconciling everything to God. He does not say merely "all men" but "all things," and specifically includes everything in heaven as well as on earth. This statement cannot be fully understood here and now, but at least we can say that Christ's atoning work has effects far beyond our imaginings, so that nothing at all remains unaffected by it. Notice that Paul stresses the place of the death of Christ. Reconciliation is effected not by good works, nor by knowledge, but by the death of the Mediator.

V. Paul's Ministry (1:24—2:3)

Paul has described himself as a minister (that is, servant) of the Gospel. This involves him in suffering, but he rejoices in it. It is his privilege in this way to complete what Christ began in His Passion. This does not mean that Paul's sufferings are in any way atoning; Christ's sufferings are never described by the word used here of Paul. But Christ suffered to bring men salvation, and Paul is allowed to suffer that men may hear the Gospel and come to salvation. Paul likens his work to a "dispensation" (KJV) or "office" (RSV), the word denoting the oversight of a large estate exercised by a trusted slave. It includes an important commission, a measure of freedom in discharging it, and responsibility to the owner. The "mystery" (revealed secret) of how men are saved was never known before, but Christians are now able to proclaim it. The Gospel being what it is, Paul labors incessantly to bring it before men, with the divine power working in him. He mentions particularly people like those to whom he is writing, whom he has never seen. He has a "conflict" (KJV; the word is that from which we derive "agony") for them, so passionately does he desire to bring Christ before them. He cannot forbear to speak once more of the excellency of Christ. "All the treasures of wisdom and knowledge" are in Him.

VI. False Teaching Denounced (2:4–23)

1. Walking in Christ (2:4–7)

Paul is about to give a serious warning. Characteristically, he prefaces it with a word of praise. He has never been to Colosse, but he knows of the steadfastness of the faith of the Christians there. He urges them to "walk" (the metaphor implies steady, if unspectacular, progress) in Christ.

2. The Completeness of Christ's Work (2:8–15)

He warns the Colossians against being led astray by philosophy (the ancient equivalent of science in our day). It is too easy to trust in human traditions. "The rudiments of the world" (KJV) may refer to spirit beings, "the elemental spirits of the universe" (as RSV puts it). These were widely held in antiquity to interfere in the affairs of men; the Colossians would have been in subjection to them by their ritual observances. It seems likely that Paul is still speaking of what men might do, and warning the Colossians against proceeding according to human rules of procedure instead of according to Christ.

As before in this epistle, when he mentions the name of his Lord, Paul expresses in a few words something of His marvelous preeminence. Once again he employs the Gnostic concept of the "fulness" to show that Christ is divine in the fullest sense. The "fulness" is not spread over a mulitude of divine beings. "All the fulness of the Godhead" dwells bodily in Him. From this it is but a step to the completeness of the work wrought by Christ in believers. They should not look to man, for they are "complete" in Christ ("come to fulness of life in him," RSV).

The reference to circumcision is probably symbolical, the meaning being that baptism is a symbolical sharing of Christ's death ("the sins of the," in KJV, should be omitted as in RSV with the better manuscripts; the putting off of "the body of flesh" probably has a two-fold reference: (1) to Christ's putting off the body in death, and (2) the believers' death to the old man.) The symbolism of baptism is then used to remind them of the new life they have in Christ, a new life that is owing to Christ. Back Paul comes to the cross, ever central for him. This time he sees it as a doing away with bills of accusation that might be written against believers. Christ has blotted out the handwriting. He has nailed it to the cross at Calvary. Thus Paul brings out the point that we have nothing to fear. Christ has triumphed over all opposition.

3. An Exhortation against Specious Ritual (2:16–23)

The Colossians were being tempted to embrace a form of religion which put great stress on the externals (and some had succumbed, 2:20). It included an apparent humility in worshipping angels, but this submission is really a self-assertion, a parading of piety, a satisfaction in their vaunted insight into spiritual things ("not" before "seen" in v. 18 should be omitted with the better manuscripts). There is "a shew of wisdom" in what the Colossians are doing, but there is nothing more.

Throughout this epistle, Paul has been dwelling on the surpassing excellence of Christ and on the completeness of the work of salvation He wrought on the cross. Paul's complaint against the heresy of the Colossians is that it does not do justice to what they know of God. Those who hold to it are "not holding fast to the Head," and it is the Head from which all receive the full supply of their spiritual needs.

Becoming a Christian is such a transforming experience that those who have undergone it are "dead" to the old relationships. This means that they should not act as though they were merely worldly people. Their conduct is determined by their relationship to Christ, not by what is worldly-wise. This brings out the folly of the Colossian heretics. They have submitted themselves to regulations which in the last resort are "the commandments and doctrines of men." Their deeds may have the appearance of wisdom and humility, but they have no more. Basically, they proceed from an effort of the will, that is, an act of self-assertion.

VII. The Christian Life (3:1—4:6)

1. The New and the Old (3:1–11)

Paul has already reminded his readers that they have "died" with Christ (2:20). He returns to the metaphor, pointing out that it is not merely negative, but positive. Christians have "been raised with

Christ." In Him they have entered into a new life. This will involve certain negations, but primarily it is a joyous and positive affair. So Paul turns his readers' attention to the place of Christ at God's right hand (notice the implications of this for "the finished work of Christ"), and urges them to base their conduct on that. They should seek only those things that are appropriate to one who belongs to the exalted Lord. Their life even now is in the closest connection with Christ (3:3) and, when He comes again, they are to appear with Him. It is obvious that their conduct day by day should reflect these great facts. So Paul calls upon them to kill ("mortify," KJV) everything in them that belongs to the old way of life.

The fact that in writing to a Christian church he finds it necessary to issue warnings against the kind of sin mentioned (3:5) shows not only the background that some of the converts had, but also the tremendous difficulty they must have had in breaking completely with their past. It is always in season to remind Christians that their standards must come from Christ, not from their pre-regenerate days. Paul does not minimize the consequence of accepting low standards. "The wrath of God" (v. 6) is often overlooked in modern theology, but in the Bible it is very real. It is provoked always and only by sin. So Paul urges them to turn away from these sins and, after reminding them of their past, he goes on to catalogue further evils to be avoided (v. 8). He wants there to be no doubt that Christian standards are of the highest. In verses 9 and 10 he exchanges the metaphor of dying and rising again for that of putting off the old and putting on the new. But the thrust is the same. Christians have a new life and must not be as those without the power of God within them. Paul completes this section with a reminder of the oneness in Christ which removes all divisions.

2. Exercise of Christian Virtues (3:12–17)

We come to the positive virtues demanded of believers. The verb "put on" is that for putting on clothing—so naturally should Christians array themselves in these qualities. Notice that the virtues Paul selects are the self-effacing virtues, those which stress care for others. In the thought of the day the important qualities were courage, manliness and the like; meekness was thought of as practically equivalent to "mean-spirited." But Christianity did not draw its standards from the world. It was, and always is, something radically new. The primary concern of the believer is not that he should stand well in the eyes of the world, but that he should serve others in serving his Master. Especially does Paul urge to the exercise of love (v. 14, "charity," KJV).

Self-giving love is the characteristic Christian attitude. It is continually insisted upon throughout the New Testament, and its importance cannot be overestimated. Where it is the dominant sentiment, all of life is bound together in one harmonious whole. The Christian should also so live that the peace of God is supreme in his heart. Paul reminds us that we were called "in one body" (that is, the Church) to that end. The Christian life is joyful. The consequence of having "the word of Christ" dwell within is joyful song coupled with loving admonition of one another. This duty of Christians is often insisted upon in the New Testament. Here the note of censoriousness is excluded by the note of holy joy. Paul gathers all together with the strong exhortation to do everything in Christ's name. Bearing in mind the significance of the "name" in antiquity, this means all should be in harmony with what Christ stands for. All should be done with an eye to the glory of God.

3. Family and Social Relationships (3:18—4:1)

Paul now turns to the principal social relationships and urges his readers to live out their faith in the circumstances in which God has set them. We can always live our lives as service to God. He begins with wives and husbands. He counsels submission of wives, but not the total submission common in the ancient world, only such as "is fitting in the Lord." This is balanced by the call to husbands to love their wives and to refrain from acts of bitterness towards them. Children must obey their parents, and this not by way of conforming to some abstract concept of duty, but, as throughout this epistle, because that is the conduct that the Lord expects of His people. Most people in antiquity thought of a father's rights over his children as very nearly absolute, but Paul reminds fathers that they too have duties. He urges them not to provoke their children, for they may easily discourage them.

His longest exhortation is for the slaves. When such became Christians and came to look on barriers as done away in Christ, they must have found it difficult to perform the duties appropriate to their station. Paul reminds them (and us) that Christianity, while it infuses a new spirit into social relationships, does not abolish a man's station in life. Eventually the Christian spirit must abolish slavery. But Christianity is not primarily a movement for social reform and, while slavery lasted, Christian slaves must be model slaves. They must do their service to their earthly masters as part of their service to Christ. It is to Him and not to them that they must look for their reward. Masters are reminded that they have a Master in heaven. Let them bear this in mind and treat their slaves with fairness.

4. Exhortation to Prayer and to Walking in Wisdom (4:2–6)

Paul has a few more exhortations. First he urges continuance in prayer and, in accordance with the note struck earlier, reminds them of the place of thanksgiving. He asks prayer for himself, not for release from prison or for comfort or the like, but that he may make the Gospel clearly known. In one sense, believers should never care how outsiders regard them. Their Master is Christ, not the world. But in another sense, they must live carefully before outsiders, making the most of every opportunity, for it is thus that they commend Christ to those that do not believe. Their speech must have that convincing quality that comes from association with Christ.

VIII. Conclusion (4:7–18)

1. The Mission of Tychicus 4:7–9)

This letter has been taken up with weighty and practical affairs. Paul has been concerned with great spiritual truths and their application to the situation at Colosse. He has said little about personal concerns, but he realizes that the Colossians will want to know about these. He accordingly sends to them Tychicus (evidently the carrier of the epistle) for the twofold purpose of bearing all the personal news and of giving the Colossians encouragement. With him Paul has sent Onesimus (see the Epistle to Philemon).

2. Greetings (4:10–17)

When he is writing to a church he knows, Paul does not usually send many greetings (which may create ill will); but when, as here, he writes to a church he has not visited, he not uncommonly sends a number of greetings. He begins with greetings from people near him to the church (4:10–14), from which we see that not many Jews were working with Paul (v. 11). He follows with greetings to certain people, and the suggestion that the Colossians interchange letters with the Laodiceans. The personal message to Archippus— very unusual in Paul's letters—is of interest (v. 17).

3. Signature (4:18)

It was Paul's custom to write a few words in his own handwriting at the end of an epistle. This authenticated it and showed to all that the letter was genuine. So here Paul takes the pen and writes his greeting. He calls on his friends to remember his fetters and concludes, as is his custom, with a prayer that grace be with them.

I Thessalonians

J. DWIGHT PENTECOST

PAUL AND HIS two companions in the ministry at Thessalonica, Silas (Acts 15:22; 17:4) and Timothy (Acts 18:5; I Thess. 3:2), join in the salutation to the church. While they are a local assembly ("of the Thessalonians"), they are in vital union with God the Father and the Son ("in God . . .").

1116

I. Relation of Paul to the Thessalonian Church (1:1—3:13)

The first movement of the book is devoted to recounting the historical and personal relationship between Paul and the church in Thessalonica. There is thanksgiving for their faithfulness, a recounting of the character of Paul's ministry, and a statement of Paul's present relationship to them.

1. Response of the Thessalonians to the Gospel (1:2–10)

The reception of the Gospel by the Thessalonians (Acts 17:4) had produced a character of life that evidenced the genuineness of their new birth. Paul is looking at them positionally, that is, in view of their righteousness in Christ, else he could not give unqualified thanks for all of them (1:2).

Prayer of Thanksgiving (1:2–4). Paul begins with a prayer of thanksgiving. In the frequent intervals in which Paul prayed for them, their reception of the Gospel supplied the occasion of his prayer (v. 3): the work engendered by their faith, the toil performed by their love, and the endurance inspired by hope. But the ultimate cause of his thanksgiving was their election (v. 4).

Proofs of Election (1:5–10). After his prayer the author states two proofs of their election. The first is their reception of the Gospel by the ministry of the Holy Spirit (v. 5); the second is the reproduction of the Gospel in their lives (vv. 6, 7). They welcomed the word of God, even as Paul had, with the result that they trumpeted forth the word of the Lord (v. 7). This is seen in the extensive dissemination of the word through them (vv. 8–10). It is significant that the "sounding forth" was not only in their words, but in their lives. A transformed life was their best testimony (v. 9).

2. Recounting the Character of Paul's Ministry (2:1–12)

Soon after the founding of the Thessalonian church, there arose antagonism to the Gospel (Acts 17:5–9). Paul's motives and life were impugned; in order to discredit his ministry, they discredited the minister. It became necessary for Paul to deliver a vindication, for if Paul were not God's messenger they had not received God's message.

Purity of his Motives (2:1–6). Paul's apostolicity is demonstrated first by the purity of his motives. Paul here uses the method of contrast (cf. "for" in vv. 1, 3, 5, 6, and "but" in vv. 2, 4, 7–12). He moves from the negative to the positive. The fact that the preaching of the Gospel was accompanied by suffering demonstrated it was not done from selfish motives (vv. 1, 2). That he sought to please God, not men (vv. 3–6), showed he was not motivated by selfishness.

Purity of his Emotions (2:7, 8). The second demonstration lies in the purity of his emotions. Instead of being moved by self-love, Paul had been impelled by love for the Thessalonians in spite of all opposition. As a nurse he had cared for them, fed them, and guarded them.

Purity of his Life (2:9–12). The third demonstration is in the purity of his life (vv. 9, 10). The proof is then given. The genuineness of his love was attested by his labor, which was both difficult and exhausting. His life toward God ("holily"), toward others ("righteously"), and inwardly ("unblamably") was beyond reproach. To supplement his work as a nurse (v. 7) ministering to them in their immaturity, he had dealt with them also as a father to instruct and discipline them (v. 11) and bring them into God's Kingdom.

3. Reception by the Thessalonians (2:13–16)

The genuineness of Paul's apostleship is best proved by the results of his ministry among them. He emphasizes two facts. First, they accepted his message as the word of God, objectively receiving it as the truth and subjectively welcoming it. Secondly, even in the face of the same persecution suffered by believers in Judea, they endured the persecution and their faith had not failed.

4. Relation of Paul to the Thessalonians (2:17—3:13)

Those seeking to discredit him before the church had evidently made the accusation that Paul cared little for his converts.

Intention of Paul (2:17–20). Paul first states his intention to visit them. This intention arises from his great desire to see them, and is based on what they mean to him (vv. 19, 20). To be absent from them was to Paul a bereavement closely akin to the loss of a loved one. Paul's desire to see them led to his sending Timothy from Athens to visit them and to bring him word in Corinth. Thus the mission of Timothy was the second refutation to the accusation.

Mission of Timothy (3:1–10). Timothy was sent to do three things: primarily to establish the church (v. 2); second, to comfort them in their faith (v. 2); and third, to bring Paul word concerning their faithfulness (v. 3). The report of Timothy brought comfort to Paul (vv. 6–10). After expressing his fears (v. 5), Paul writes of the favorable effect of this report. Comfort came to Paul, first, from the fact that they shared the same desire to see him that he did for them (v. 6), and, second, from their faithfulness despite the severe persecutions they were enduring (vv. 7–10). So deep was Paul's concern that the report of Timothy was a "gospel" or good news to him. The report both satisfied Paul concerning their present experience and created a deeper desire both for further personal fellowship with them and for their maturity (v. 10).

Prayer for Reunion (3:11–13). The lifting of such a burden through the mission of Timothy could only conclude in prayer. The first petition expresses the wish to return to Thessalonica (v. 11). In the second (vv. 12, 13), Paul prays they might experience the work of God which would produce in them a love for one another and for all men. The ultimate purpose of the petition (v. 13) was that they might be established in holiness when they appear at the judgment seat of Christ (I Cor. 3:12–15; II Cor. 5:9, 10) to be examined for rewards.

II. Exhortations of Paul to the Thessalonian Church (4:1—5:24)

The shortcomings of the Thessalonians referred to in 3:10 naturally led to exhortations from the apostle. Paul is continuing as the nurse who cherishes (2:7) and the father who admonishes (2:11). The words in 4:1, 9, 13, and 5:1 suggest that the church had written for information on certain questions which Paul is now answering.

1. Concerning the Conduct of the Believer (4:1–12)

Laxity in Morals (4:1–8). In introducing the exhortations to the believers, Paul is not pleading for a new kind of life but rather a progression in the life they had been taught would please God. The exhortations were not to correct, but rather to prevent failures. The first concerned laxity in morals (vv. 3–8). The church was surrounded by the low moral standards of Gentile heathenism which practiced sexual looseness. Paul states that God requires complete separation unto Himself (v. 3) and then shows what that separation entails (vv. 4–8). This is stated negatively (v. 3) and then positively (vv. 4, 5). The answer to immorality is marriage. Yet even marriage is safeguarded, for the wife is not to be taken solely for the satisfaction of physical desire (v. 5). The Lord is the avenger, not only of the one guilty of immorality outside the marriage relationship, but also of the one who misuses the marriage relationship itself. Three reasons are given for heeding the exhortation: God is a judge (v. 6b); He has called us to holiness (v. 7); the one who fails to keep this exhortation is not ignoring the command of man, but the command of God (v. 8).

Love of the Brethren (4:9–12). The second exhortation concerns love of the brethren. Paul again is concerned not so much with correction of a deficiency as with encouraging Christian virtue. In both the Old and New Testaments the obligation to love is clearly stated. Paul encourages the brethren to fulfil what is their known obligation. Their manifestation of God's love should produce a desire to live quietly and to labor diligently (v. 11). This exhortation seems to deal with idleness caused by an expectation of the Lord's return (cf. II Thess. 3:6–15) which led to meddling in others' affairs. The peace of the church was jeopardized within and its testimony nullified without. Such actions were violations of love for the brethren. The purpose of the exhortation (v. 12) is that they might bear a consistent testimony before the world and provide fully for the needs of the members within the assembly.

2. Concerning the Consolation of the Believers (4:13—5:11)

Two perplexing problems faced the Thessalonians. The first was the relation of dead saints to the living saints in the future translation of believers at the *parousia* (presence). The second was whether living saints could be subjected to the judgments of the Day of the Lord which would follow the *parousia,* Paul proceeds to answer these questions for their comfort (4:18; 5:11).

The Rapture of the Saints (4:13–18). These believers so lived in the light of the hope of the imminent return of Christ that they were disheartened and perplexed when some of their number died before the promised translation. This raised a problem (v. 13) which Paul answers (vv. 14–18). Their question was not whether the departed believers would participate in the resurrection, since they were assured of the resurrection of the body; but what would be the relation, they asked, between resurrected saints and saints living on earth at the *parousia?* This problem was very real to the Thessalonians, for their loved ones were dying. Comfort had given way to consternation.

In answering this problem, Paul teaches that dead believers will participate in the translation along with the living (4:15). They were not to sorrow; the Lord at His appearance will include the sleeping ones. The resurrection of Jesus from the dead guarantees both His coming for the living saints and the inclusion of the dead believers. That the resurrection here in view includes believers only is seen from the fact that this teaching is addressed to "brethren" (v. 13) and to those who believe (v. 14), and further, from its restriction only to those who are "in Christ" (v. 16). The word "sleep" is used only for the death of a believer, and suggests rest from labor, continuation of life, and a future awakening from that state.

After stating the great truth, Paul now proceeds to outline the program of this translation (4:15–17). First, the dead will rise (v. 16); next, the living will be caught up (v. 17); then, the two groups will be united together (v. 17); finally, as one group they will meet the Lord in the air to be with Him forever (v. 17). The signal which heralds this great event is a shout or cry, such as was used to summon a gathering, even as might be authoritatively given by an archangel sounding a trumpet in the service of God. The sphere in which all this takes place is "in the clouds." "With the Lord" expresses intimate association (cf. Jn. 14:3). The result of this instruction (v. 18) was clarification of their ignorance (cf. v. 13) and comfort in their bereavement.

The Day of the Lord (5:1–11). The second problem is now considered by Paul. Some interpreters hold that he continues his teaching on the translation of the Church here. However, it seems that Paul is raising a new subject. The discussion begins with words which introduce something new ("But of," KJV; "But as to," RSV). The phrase "times and seasons" has to do with the setting up of the Kingdom on earth (Acts 1:7). The term "day of the Lord" in the New Testament refers to the future judgment on Israel and the nations on the earth (cf. II Thess. 2:2; Acts 2:20; II Pet. 3:10; Amos 5:18; Is. 2:12; Joel 2:31; Zeph. 1:14–18; Mal. 4:5). The change in pronouns (v. 3) looks to those left on the earth after the translation of the Church, who will undergo the wrath of the Day of the Lord.

Paul emphasizes two facts concerning the Day of the Lord. The first is the suddenness and uncertainty of its arrival (5:1–3). Instruction concerning times and seasons was unnecessary because it was a well-known fact from Scripture that the judgment might be expected imminently. This fact is stressed (v. 2; cf. Mt. 24:43, 44; Lk. 12:39, 40; II Pet. 3:10). The explanation is given (v. 3) to emphasize the suddenness of the coming as well as the inescapable consequences for those upon whom judgment falls.

The second fact stressed by the author is presented in the great contrast begun in verse 4. Believers of the present age have no part in the judgments of the Day of the Lord. The prophets (Joel 2:2; Zeph. 1:15; Amos 5:18–20) had emphasized that the Day of the Lord is to be characterized by darkness. The apostle emphasizes the fact that believers are no longer in darkness, but are in the light (5:4, 5, 9). For this reason they will not be subjected to the judgments of the Day of the Lord. They are not only in the light, but of the light (v. 5; cf. Eph. 5:8, 9; Jn. 8:12).

These two facts lead Paul to an exhortation to the believers (5:6–10). They should be characterized by watchfulness and purity in life as the result of this teaching. Negatively, they are warned against indifference and recklessness, and positively, they are exhorted to watchfulness and soberness. One reason for watchfulness (v. 7) is that the sons of darkness are marked by lethargy and indifference, and believers should not share in the unfruitful works of darkness. Another reason is that believers are of the day, that is, they have the nature of light (v. 8). The third reason is that they have been born again (v. 8). Here the tense of the verb ("putting on," KJV, "put on," RSV) refers to the once-for-all action which took place when the individual received Christ as personal Saviour. At that time he put on the breastplate, which guarded the heart, and the helmet, which guarded the head. Thus, since he has put on the armor of God, he should continually be living as a child of light. An explanation follows (v. 9).

Our destiny is not wrath but deliverance. This wrath in the context can be none other than the wrath of the Day of the Lord. The deliverance is the deliverance promised to the saints by translation (4:16, 17). Ultimate salvation from the very sphere of sin is in view here. The certainty of this deliverance rests on the Deliverer,

Whose work is the basis of our hope (5:10). His work is given in the words "who died for us"—"for us" emphasizing redemption through death. The ultimate purpose of the work is that we might live with Him, enjoying the fulness of His fellowship forever.

The conclusion is stated (5:11). The truth about last things was designed to comfort those who were troubled. The word translated "comfort" (KJV) or "encourage" (RSV) is the same word used in 4:18 and points up the fact that the truth of the Lord's coming was designed to produce not only watchfulness and purity but comfort as well.

3. *Concerning Conduct in the Church (5:12–22)*

The Apostle Paul now turns to concluding exhortations. First, he has a word concerning the relation of the assembly to the elders who are over them (5:12, 13). From the plural "them," it is evident that there were a number of elders in the Thessalonian church. Their labor is explained by the words "are over you," which refer to leadership and management of all kinds (cf. I Tim. 3:4, 5, 12; 5:17; Rom. 12:8), and was not official but informal. The words "admonish you" show that the elders did the work of teaching and reveal the major part of their task. They were to be esteemed, not because of their official position, but because of their work. Their relation was a spiritual one, as the phrase "in the Lord" shows.

In the next place, Paul gives a word concerning the whole assembly (5:14–22). Instruction is given concerning those who were out of step (v. 14). This is followed with an admonition concerning their relation to one another (v. 15), and another concerning their relation to God (vv. 16–18). He concludes with a command concerning the relation of believers to the life of the assembly (vv. 19–22). The warning about quenching has to do with the manifestations of the Spirit in the local church. While unbelievers may resist the Spirit (Acts 7:51) and individual believers may grieve the Spirit by sin (Eph. 4:30), the assembly may prevent the manifestation of the Spirit through them (v. 19). The danger of this development is stressed (v. 20). Prophesying was the Spirit's method of teaching truth before the Scriptures were complete (Eph. 4:11; I Cor. 12:28) and if the Spirit was prevented from doing so in the assembly there would be ignorance. Yet a safeguard is given (v. 21). They are not to receive teaching indiscriminately but are to make certain that the instruction is from the Spirit. They are to receive that which is intrinsically good and hold themselves aloof from every kind of evil.

4. *Concluding Prayer (5:23, 24)*

The hortatory section of the epistle (4:1—5:24) has made great demands upon the readers. An appeal for mere human effort is in vain. Thus Paul turns in prayer to God Who can prosper these exhortations. Sanctification here is viewed as a process to be brought to conclusion in a final act. Progressive sanctification will ultimately be completed at the coming of the Lord Jesus Christ. This assurance rests upon the faithfulness of God (v. 24). Our complete conformity to Christ does not depend upon self-effort, but upon the work of God Who began the process at our salvation and Who will complete it at the coming of the Lord Jesus Christ when we enter into the fulness of eternal salvation.

5. *Final Requests (5:25–28)*

In the concluding words, Paul's exhortation to prayer on his behalf (5:25) may be designed to allay the objection that he had lost interest in them (2:17–20). The injunction to the elders to manifest love to the brethren (v. 26) may be designed to win back those who were rebellious (vv. 12, 13). The command to read the epistle may have been made in order to attract those who rejected Paul's apostolic authority (2:1–12) to hear the word and be instructed by it. The epistle concludes with the familiar Pauline benediction of grace upon all the church at Thessalonica.

II Thessalonians

J. DWIGHT PENTECOST

BEFORE PROCEEDING to problems raised by the report of affairs in Thessalonica, Paul is moved by the deep feeling existing between himself and the Thessalonians to an extended prayer of thanksgiving and intercession on their behalf.

I. Introduction (1:1–12)

1. Salutation (1:1, 2)

Paul, Silas, and Timothy again join in greetings to the believers in Thessalonica. Except for several brief additions, the salutation is

1125

identical with that prefixed to the first epistle. The pronoun "our," following Father, emphasizes that God is the Father of believers as well as the Father of the Lord Jesus Christ. The words "from God the Father and the Lord Jesus Christ" stress the source of the grace and peace experienced by the Thessalonians. Paul is emphasizing the privileged spiritual position of these saints; while they resided in Thessalonica, they were positionally in God and in Christ (cf. Jn. 14:20).

2. Thanksgiving (1:3–10)

In the former letter the author had used words of praise concerning these believers (I Thess. 1:2–10) which they evidently disclaimed as though unworthy of such praise. Paul shows them that his former commendation was justly deserved. He is under obligation ("we are bound") to give such thanks; that is, he would consider it a failure to discharge a moral obligation to God if such thanksgiving were not expressed. He cites two grounds for this thanksgiving. First, it is deserved because their faith has increased. The word used for "groweth" (KJV) or "is growing" (RSV) signifies an internal organic growth. It is proof that they possess eternal life. The concern previously expressed about their faith (I Thess. 3:10) now gives way to approbation. Second, it is deserved because their love to one another has increased. The word "aboundeth" (KJV) or "increasing" (RSV) emphasizes a wide diffusion, and was used of a flood or prairie fire spread over a wide area. Paul had prayed for this very thing (I Thess. 3:12). Since these virtues were produced by God and not by men, Paul is obligated to thank Him for these remarkable answers to prayer in such a short time.

The consequences follow (1:4). Those who had ministered in Thessalonica could point with pride to what God had done in the church there. The emphasis on "we ourselves" seems to indicate that, while the apostle normally did not point to any church by way of example, their growth had been so phenomenal that the Thessalonians were made an example to other churches. To safeguard against their glorying in their own work, Paul bases his glorying on their steadfastness and faithfulness as witnessed by patient endurance in testings. Their "persecutions" refer to what they suffered because they were believers, and the "afflictions" (RSV) or "tribulations" (KJV) to what they endured because they lived in a hostile world.

Paul shows the Thessalonians the Godward aspect of their steadfastness and faithfulness (1:5, 6). While some might feel God is unjust to permit His saints to suffer, their attitude demonstrated that God is righteous. Paul proves the righteousness of God in all His dealings, first, by showing the purpose of the suffering (v. 5): that they might be made worthy of the Kingdom of God. The word translated "counted worthy" (KJV) or "made worthy" (RSV) literally means "to declare or reckon worthy." They were not granted a place in the Kingdom because of their sufferings, but their position in the Kingdom was the result of their attitude in the sufferings (Rom. 8:17). Through their sufferings, God was perfecting the saints.

Paul further upholds the righteousness of God by noting that eventually He will deal in judgment with all the unrighteous from whom the persecutions come (1:6). Concerning this, Paul observes first, that for God to punish the wicked is an act of divine justice. Further, at the time of judgment God will bring the saints into their rest (v. 7). "Rest" here signifies the slackening of a taut bowstring; hence, it implies the loosing of the strain imposed by continued threat of persecutions. Again, Paul gives the time when the sinners will be recompensed with judgment and the saints rewarded with rest. It will be at the second advent of Christ. Paul does not refer to the rapture as the time of the rewarding of the saints (I Thess. 4:13–17), but rather to the second advent (cf. Rev. 19:11–16; Mt. 25:31), for he is dealing mainly with what awaits the persecutors and they will not be judged until the return of Christ to the earth. The saints will receive their rewards in heaven following the translation of the Church.

Finally, Paul summarizes the judgment and its results for unbelievers. The Lord will inflict vengeance. This judgment is meted out to two groups: those who do not know God, evidently Gentiles who reject the light given them; and those that obey not the Gospel, evidently Jews and Gentiles who had heard the true Gospel proclaimed. The punishment is clearly defined as eternal separation from the Lord (1:9). Since the word rendered "punish" (KJV) or "suffer punishment" (RSV) is from the same root as "righteousness," God is not vindictive, but rather just and righteous in the judgment. "Destruction" does not mean annihilation, but rather "ruination, the loss of all that gives worth to existence." As all who die in Adam experience the first death, separation from God (Rom. 5:12), so in this judgment all sinners will experience the second death, eternal separation from God (Rev. 20:14). They will be separated from

His presence, the source of light, and from His power, through which men are brought to life. Those who had felt the power of men will behold the power of the Lord at His coming.

Paul relates Christ's coming to the saints in two ways (1:10). First, He is coming to be glorified in the saints. The redeemed host will be, as it were, a polished mirror to reflect and diffuse the light of the glory of the Lord. Secondly, he will be "admired" or "wondered at" in all who believe. Since the preposition "in" is repeated here, Paul is not speaking of the wonder experienced by glorified believers, but of the breath-taking amazement that grips those on earth at the time of the Lord's return, when they behold His glory in the saints. Since unbelievers are unable to receive the resplendent glory, they must be banished from the Kingdom, so that His glory may be fully revealed (Mt. 25:31). The works of the Thessalonians (1:3) prove the genuineness of their faith and guarantee their participation in the coming manifestation of His glory.

3. Intercession (1:11, 12)

Paul has just shown that the revelation of Jesus Christ will bring judgment on the unsaved, rest for the saved, and glory for the Lord in His saints. He is now constrained to offer a prayer of intercession for the Thessalonians because of their bright prospect. First, he prays that they may be worthy of God's call. They have been called to salvation (cf. II Tim. 1:9; Eph. 4:1) and they are also called into His Kingdom and glory (I Thess. 2:12). Consequently, they are now to live in such a manner that when that day comes, they will be counted worthy to have been called. Secondly, Paul prays that the Thessalonians may carry to fruition every resolution prompted by goodness and every work produced by faith. This again stresses a course of conduct in accord with their call. The ultimate purpose is stated in conclusion (1:12). It is that the Lord Jesus Christ, Who will be glorified at His revelation (v. 10), may be glorified now by the lives of the believers.

II. Instruction of the Thessalonian Believers (2:1–17)

Paul next deals with the important doctrinal problem raised by the report from Thessalonica. Certain false teachers, in view of present persecutions, were teaching that the Church's translation had already passed and that the Thessalonians were already in the Day of the Lord. Paul had to correct these misinterpretations.

1. Correction of a Misconception (2:1, 2)

The chapter introduces a new subject with the word "now." Having dealt with the second advent, Paul comes specifically to that phase of the subject which had been misconstrued. He is writing to defend the truth he had previously taught them (2:5; cf. I Thess. 4:13—5:11), that believers will not remain for the Day of the Lord. He begins with a request addressed to the believers ("brethren"). Paul is not requesting them "by" (KJV) the coming of Christ, but rather "concerning" (RSV) the coming of Christ. The two aspects of the translation are given. "The coming of our Lord Jesus Christ" points to the divine side in which Christ will be present (I Thess. 4:16). "Our gathering together" (KJV) or "our assembling to meet him" (RSV) emphasizes the human side in which believers will be translated into His presence (I Thess. 4:17). This word is used elsewhere (Heb. 10:25) to signify the gathering of believers for worship.

Paul states his request that they not be upset (2:2). "Shaken" suggests the figure of a ship tossed by the waves because it is insecurely moored or has slipped its moorings. "Soon" (KJV) or "quickly" (RSV) implies sudden shock that would produce a settled state of agitation ("troubled," KJV; "excited," RSV). This state comes "from the mind," that is, as a result of an apparently reasonable presentation by false teachers. That which suddenly shocked their minds, producing agitation as well as persistent unrest, was the report that the Day of the Lord was already present. This teaching was purported to have originated with Paul ("from us") and to have come to them by special revelation ("by spirit"), or by a report of the apostles' teaching ("by word"), or by a forged letter ("by letter").

The translation "is at hand" (KJV) is clearly wrong. The word does not signify nearness but actual presence, and should be rendered "is already here" or "has come" (RSV). The better manuscripts have "day of the Lord" (RSV) rather than "day of Christ" (KJV). In seeking to dispel the confusion created by this error, Paul proceeds to prove that, severe though these were, the persecutions they were enduring could not be those of the Day of the Lord.

2. *Revelation of the Man of Sin (2:3–10)*

The request of Paul (2:1) now issues in a command. They were not to entertain the deception, no matter how it was purported to have originated with him.

The Thessalonians need not be shipwrecked in their hope and restless in their hearts. For one thing, the Day of the Lord could not be present without the appearance of a specific rebellion against God, about which Paul had taught them previously. The King James Version here is misleading, for it omits the definite article and translates the noun "a falling away." The word here signifies a military or political rebellion, and in the Old Testament was used specifically of rebellion against God. Paul thus calls to their attention what had been taught them previously, that the Day of the Lord would begin with "the rebellion" against God (cf. Dan. 7:24, 25; 8:10–14; 9:26, 27; Rev. 12:7–17). Since this specific rebellion had not yet come, they could not be in that Day.

Character of the Man of Sin (2:3–5). The second reason they need not be deceived is that the Day of the Lord could not be present until the "man of sin" or the "man of lawlessness" had been revealed. This one is described many places elsewhere in Scripture (cf. Dan. 7:8; 8:23; 9:26, 27; 11:36; Zech. 11:16, 17; Mt. 24:15; Rev. 13:1–10; 17:12, 13; 19:19, 20).

Out of the great body of truth concerning the person here mentioned Paul summarizes only certain major facts. He is called the lawless one (2:3), that is, the one in whom lawlessness is embodied and through whom lawlessness reaches its peak of development. Controlled by Satan, whose character is lawlessness, this one cannot be other than lawless. Again, he is called the "son of perdition" (v. 3), in view of his destiny (Rev. 19:19, 20). Paul next describes his conduct. He is called the "opposer" or "adversary." Since this one is controlled by Satan, it is significant that he should bear the name of Satan, which in Hebrew means "adversary." In addition he is also known as the "exalter." The two notions are inseparably united in Paul's thought. Instead of exalting God, he exalts himself and in so doing the "exalter" becomes the "adversary." The result of this opposition and exaltation is that he goes through the act of being officially seated ("sitteth," KJV; "takes his seat," RSV) in the temple as god (cf. Dan. 11:41, 45; 12:11; Mt. 24:15; Rev. 13:5, 6). Paul makes no effort to be exhaustive, for they had been taught already (2:5).

Restrainer of the Man of Sin (2:6, 7). Having described the character and conduct of the man of sin (2:3–5), Paul shows them why the man of sin had not yet been revealed. A restraint had been placed upon the program of Satan which sought to produce the man of sin and present him to the world as its god (vv. 6, 7). Many explanations have been given as to who or what the restrainer is. Some have held that it is government. However, governments will continue after the coming of the man of sin; while governments may control civil lawlessness, they could not control spiritual lawlessness. Others have held that it is the principle of law. However, law never curbs, but only defines, lawlessness. Still others hold that Satan is the restrainer, restraining until at last he is ready to present his lawless one. If so, Satan would be working against himself throughout the present age. It would seem that the only one able to restrain the working of Satan is God Himself. Hence, many interpreters emphasize that the Holy Spirit, residing in the Church, which is His temple, does the work of restraining sin and Satan until the Church is translated, after which the man of sin will be revealed. Although He will still be operative in the world, as He was in the Old Testament before His permanent indwelling of believers, the Spirit will not restrain after the translation of the Church.

This restraint is for one purpose (v. 6): to withhold the revelation of the man of sin until the appointed time set by God. Paul saw a lawless system at work in his day (v. 7), even as John did (I Jn. 2:18; 4:3), yet the restrainer has done His work so that the full revelation of lawlessness in the lawless one is yet future. "Taken out of the way" (KJV) or "is out of the way" (RSV) should read "shall get out of the way," and evidently refers to the cessation of the restrainer's ministry.

The Ministry of the Man of Sin (2:8–10). The counterfeit nature of this lawless one is stressed by Paul. The man of sin has a "coming" as Christ will have. He possesses power over men and the earth as Christ will have. He works signs and wonders (Rev. 13:4) even as Christ did. He has a great following as Christ will have. However, he is the deceiver and Christ is the way, the truth, and the life. Those who follow the man of sin possess neither eternal life nor the love of the truth.

3. Judgment of Unbelievers (2:11, 12)

Their rejected love of the truth sets a divine law in operation. Absence of truth produces active promotion of evil. "Strong delusion" does not refer to a passive consent to wrongdoing, but rather to an active participation in the plan of Satan. This condition is imposed by God in accordance with His law that light rejected brings greater darkness. The inevitable result is condemnation. By the term "the lie," Paul summarizes the whole plan and purpose of Satan as it culminates in the manifestation of the man of sin.

4. Thanksgiving and Prayer (2:13–17)

Although some are destined to condemnation, Paul is moved to thanksgiving because of those who are destined to salvation (2:13–15). The purpose of God in election is to bring believers ultimately to complete salvation. The method God uses to accomplish this is stated in the phrases "through sanctification" and "belief of the truth." That which was rejected by the followers of "the lie" is the very basis of the believer's salvation. The channel of truth is "through our gospel," and the final goal is "that you may obtain the glory of our Lord Jesus Christ." From such a great purpose and destiny issues the appeal that they "stand fast" and "hold to the traditions" which Paul had delivered, and not be swayed by false reports that robbed them of their hope. A prayer for their inward encouragement and outward establishment in word and work concludes the section.

III. Injunctions to the Thessalonian Believers (3:1–16)

As Paul draws the epistle to a close, he takes up the practical consequences of his teaching concerning the coming of the Day of the Lord. The fourfold repetition of "command" (3:4, 6, 10, 12) sets the theme.

1. Call to Prayer (3:1–5)

In coming to the conclusion of his message ("finally"), Paul first of all requests their support in prayer. He desires prayer for the active ministry of the word of the Lord. "Have free course" (KJV) or "speed on" (RSV) literally means "to run without any hindrances or obstacles to impede the path." He also desires prayer for the preservation of the ministers in their ministry. The request is made because they are engaged in a battle against the prince of the power of the air, Satan himself. Paul is confident that the Lord will deliver them from all their enemies because He is faithful. This faithfulness will be manifested as God puts them on a sound foundation ("stablish," KJV; "strengthen," RSV) and preserves them by actively guarding them ("keep," KJV; "guard," RSV). The "evil" (3:3) from which they will be guarded probably refers to the evil one. God's faithfulness will cause the Thessalonians to receive Paul's correction so they will be conformed to His love and the patience of Christ.

2. Commands concerning Discipline in the Assembly (3:6–15)

Paul proceeds to show the practical effect of his teaching about the Lord's return. Whereas some in the assembly were in idleness (cf. I Thess. 5:14), the brethren were not to continue such an one in fellowship. Paul points to himself as an example of industry (3:7–10). Lest he set a bad example by letting others support him, Paul surrendered the rightful support which an apostle might expect (v. 9) and worked to support himself. To set a good example he had the right to forego a right. The danger of such idleness was that it produced idleness in others (v. 11). Consequently the believers were to separate such ones from their assembly. Apostolic authority is now brought to bear on the question. Paul issues a command, as from a general to a soldier out of step, that the indolent are to become industrious (v. 12).

Paul anticipates that some may be so firmly entrenched in their indolence and false interpretations that they will not heed his commands and corrections. He thus instructs the believers to separate themselves from those disobedient to his teaching (3:4). Such an one is not to be treated as an enemy, nor cut off from the possibility of future fellowship, but treated as an erring brother, so that he may be brought to obedience and restored to fellowship (v. 15). All relationships are to be aimed at restoration of the offender. Paul concludes the commands with a prayer that the Lord will grant peace in the assembly.

IV. Farewell (3:17, 18)

Perhaps because of the circulation of false letters purporting to be from Paul (2:2), the apostle adds a few words in his own distinctive handwriting, which would certify the genuineness of this epistle. The epistle closes with the familiar apostolic farewell.

I Timothy

WALTER W. WESSEL

THE PASTORAL EPISTLES differ from the other letters of Paul in that they are addressed to individuals who are concerned with church organization (Titus) and administration (Timothy). If the theology of these letters does not often reach the heights of Paul's other epistles, their practical nature compensates for that lack. This is particularly true of I Timothy which gives instructions concerning conduct in public worship (with special reference to women), lays great stress on high qualifications for Christian leadership, underscores the necessity of dealing positively with false teaching, provides much information about various groups in the church and what is to be the minister's relation to them and, above all, emphasizes the importance of godliness in carrying out the work of the Christian ministry. Although written in the first century to help an inexperienced pastor to cope with a local church situation, this letter contains much that is of contemporary significance and value.

I. The Opening Salutation (1:1, 2)

First Timothy is a letter and thus opens with a standard epistolary address. Paul, the writer, is an apostle of Jesus Christ "under orders" (1:1). His apostleship gives authority to what he is about to write and indicates that this is more than a private letter from one friend to another. It is an epistle with authority! Timothy, the recipient, is Paul's spiritual son (1:2) and thus is addressed, "my true child in the faith" (RSV; cf. II Tim. 1:2; Phil. 2:22). A triad of blessings finding their source in God and Christ is pronounced (1:2), and Paul is then ready to turn to the business at hand.

II. The Situation at Ephesus (1:3–17)

Paul had left Timothy at Ephesus in charge of the church there. Before leaving for Macedonia, he had given Timothy instructions relative to certain persons who were teaching false doctrines. Paul repeats those instructions here. Timothy is to charge the false teachers not to spread their teaching in the church. Whatever precisely this teaching was, Paul's objection was that it promoted speculations rather than "godly edifying" or perhaps better rendered, "divine stewardship." The false teaching fostered an idle curiosity rather than a resolve to serve God faithfully. Paul's practical approach to the Gospel and his insistence on its relevance to life could not tolerate these perversions. Such teaching completely misconstrued the very goal of Christian living, namely, love which springs from a pure heart, a good conscience and genuine faith (1:5).

Now some persons in the Ephesian church had forgotten this. They had become self-styled teachers of the law without even knowing its real function. Thus Paul, in this passage, points out that the divinely appointed purpose of the law is not to be a kind of plaything—a means of engendering worthless speculations—but rather God's standard which is to reveal sin and thus place man under God's condemnation. This truth is in complete accord with the "good news" of God's provision for the remission of sins through Jesus Christ. And this glorious "good news" has been entrusted to Paul!

The mention of Paul's great privilege in being a herald of the Gospel causes him to break into a song of thanksgiving to God. These lyrical passages in Paul are like smoldering volcanoes ready to erupt at any time! He thinks of his pre-Christian life and of his activities as persecutor of the Church. How black Paul's sins looked to him! The law certainly performed its God-given function in his life. But in the midst of his rebellion against God, there came mercy and super-abounding grace. Christ Jesus had come into the world to save sinners and Paul knew himself to be just that—a sinner, indeed, the foremost of sinners! In saving him Christ demonstrated that no man is outside the reach of His super-abounding grace and mercy. This great truth sets Paul's heart to singing again in verse 17.

III. The Charge to Timothy (1:18–20)

At this point Paul returns to the basic concern of his letter. Since Timothy needs to have his confidence bolstered and to be encouraged in his work, Paul issues his charge to him in accordance with the (favorable) predictions which had been made about Timothy even before he became a minister. Paul uses the symbol of warfare (a favorite of his) to describe the work of the ministry. The two pieces of fighting equipment are faith (certainly here more than right belief!) and a good conscience. Three times in I Timothy Paul conjoins "faith" and "a good conscience." Faith and morals are inseparable. Alexander and Hymenaeus, of whom we know nothing apart from this reference, had failed to combine these two. Their deliverance unto Satan is probably to be understood as ostracism from the church (the world was considered Satan's domain). Note that the purpose of Paul's action was remedial ("that they may learn not to blaspheme"), not punitive (cf. I Cor. 5:5).

IV. Instructions Concerning Public Worship (2:1–15)

1. *Prayers (2:1–8)*

The prayers under discussion are *public* prayers which, Paul says, are to be offered for all men. Men in positions of authority are particularly to be included. One reason for this instruction is probably to be found in Paul's desire to indicate the Christian attitude toward the State. In the first Christian century, pagans commonly believed that the Church was a secret society with sinister political ends. Paul saw in public prayers for those in authority a means to allay such fears. Even more important than this, Christ Jesus had come into the world to save sinners, and this included men in authority. Since God would "have all men to be saved and to come unto the knowledge of the truth," Christians are to pray to that end.

Another motive for such prayers is mentioned in verse 2. Some have taken this statement to mean "Pray for those in authority that you may be left alone to live comfortably." But verses 2 through 4 seem to suggest that the Christian's desire for a quiet and peaceful life is in order to practice godliness and that full opportunity may be given to propagate the Gospel. In verses 5 and 6, the content of the Gospel, which in verse 4 is referred to as "the truth" and which God desires all men to know, is given. Here there is an affirmation of monotheism ("there is one God"), a proclamation of a mediator ("one mediator between God and man, the man Christ Jesus") and a statement of the mediator's work ("who gave himself a ransom for all"). These great affirmations constitute the "good news" which Paul was appointed to preach. He reiterates in verse 8 his instructions concerning prayers, adding that they must be offered by men of pure actions and motives.

2. *Conduct of Women (2:9–15)*

It must be kept in mind that Paul is thinking primarily about public worship. He first lays down certain requirements for women's dress: they are to dress modestly and sensibly (not shabbily!), that is, they are not to go beyond the limits of womanly reserve. Paul rules against coiffures and flashy ornamentation, because he fears that such things are liable to distract the thoughts of Christians at public worship. The Christian woman's adornment is rather to be an inward one of good deeds. In verse 11 Paul turns to the part which a woman is to have in the public worship of the church. He says flatly hers is to be a silent role! She is to be a follower, not a leader. She is neither to teach publicly nor to assume authority over men. The reasons given are: (1) the priority of man's creation ("Adam was first formed, then Eve"); (2) woman, apparently, is more easily led astray ("the woman being deceived was in the transgression"). Now lest this rather severe censure of woman in relation to the public worship of the church should overly discourage her, Paul adds in verse 15 that she is preserved for a contribution to the Christian cause through her divinely appointed function as a child-bearer (and rearer), a function to be accompanied by a godly life.

V. Qualifications of Church Officers (3:1–13)

1. Bishops (3:1–7)

Paul now turns his attention to the officers of the church. The office of bishop was apparently the same as elder (cf. Tit. 1:5–7, where "bishop" and "elder" are used interchangeably), the former word emphasizing the function of the office and the latter its title. When the pastoral epistles were written, the word bishop did not have its modern meaning, but simply indicated an overseer in the local church. To aspire to such an office is a good thing, but the qualifications are high. The list that follows reveals no special order but certainly is all-inclusive. Such things as the bishop's relationship to his wife, his children and to the world outside are included along with both positive virtues and denials of excesses. In addition, the bishop is not to be a recent convert, since his position demands mature spiritual discernment. One cannot help but wonder how many of the Ephesian Christians who had been aspiring to this office changed their minds after hearing this list of qualifications! The standard is high, but so is the office, and thus the qualifications dare not be lowered.

2. Deacons (3:8–13)

The first reference in the New Testament to deacons is found in Acts 6. The high qualifications listed in that passage are "a good reputation, full of the Spirit and of wisdom" (Acts 6:3). Philip, one of the first deacons, was a man "full of faith and of the Holy Spirit" (Acts 6:5). In the passage before us the qualifications for this office are given in more detail. A close look at the list reveals that the office demands almost the same qualifications as that of bishop. It is difficult to know whether the women mentioned in verse 11 were deaconesses, deacons' wives (KJV) or deacons' helpers. Whoever they were, they too had to meet high spiritual qualifications.

VI. Purpose of the Charge (3:14–16)

The instructions in this letter are written to Timothy because Paul, although he hoped to rejoin his son in the faith shortly, feared he would be detained. He writes that Timothy might "know how to behave in the household of God" which probably refers to the discharge of his duties as a minister. The household (better "house") of God is the Church of the living God which supports ("pillar") and protects ("bulwark," RSV) the truth. A mystery in the New Testament is not something mysterious, but rather a revealed secret. The "mystery of our religion" (RSV) is none other than Jesus Christ, as the six phrases of the credal hymn-fragment of verse 16 reveal. "Manifested in the flesh" refers to His incarnation; "justified in the Spirit," to the establishment of His claims by the Holy Spirit; "seen of angels," in all probability to the witness of angels to His resurrection; "preached unto the Gentiles," to the world-wide proclamation of the Gospel (although this occurred after the ascension); "believed on in the world," to the success of that proclamation; and "received up into glory," to His ascension. This is obviously a credal hymn-fragment since it mentions nothing of the central events of apostolic preaching, Christ's death and resurrection.

VII. Instructions Concerning Apostasy (4:1–16)

1. Apostasy Described (4:1–5)

The Christian Church early discovered that wherever the truth about Christ was proclaimed, error soon crept in. False teaching had already come to the church at Ephesus. The "latter times" of verse 1 does not refer to some remotely future age, but to the time impinging on Timothy's ministry. Otherwise, the instructions which follow would be irrelevant for Timothy's situation. Consistent with his strong beliefs in the reality and power of the spirit world (cf. Eph. 6:12), Paul attributes to demonic spirits the ultimate cause of error in the Church. The agents, however, of these evil spirits are people, more specifically, liars with numbed consciences. The main elements of their false teaching are: (*1*) they forbid people to marry; (*2*) they enjoin abstinence from certain food. There can be little doubt that this false teaching reveals an incipient Gnosticism with its false view that matter is evil. Paul recognized the implications of such teaching and here declares that God created these foods, and what God creates is good and to be enjoyed by all men. Certainly Christians who believe and know the truth are not excluded from enjoying what God has created. Indeed, nothing is to be "tabooed" (Moffatt) if it is received with thanksgiving. This probably refers to "grace" before meals as verse 5 seems to indicate. If this is the correct interpretation, "the word of God" in this verse refers to the reading of Scripture (Old Testament) at meals which was accompanied by prayer.

2. Methods of Dealing with Apostasy (4:6–16)

The approach is gentle, positive and constructive. Timothy is to inform his congregation. He is not to demand but to remind. By so doing he will prove himself to be a man of sound doctrine. The positive approach is again revealed by Paul's instruction to avoid "godless and silly myths" (RSV), in all probability a reference to the "fables and endless genealogies" of 1:4. Timothy is also to keep himself "spiritually fit" (Phillips). One must not interpret Paul as depreciating the value of physical fitness (cf. I Cor. 9:24–27) as such. He is here making a comparison. Physical fitness is of the order of time; spiritual fitness, of eternity. Paul's conviction of the value of godliness inspires him to labor and toil. His hope, which is fixed on the living God, is buttressed by the fact that although God's benevolence and mercy are extended to all men (cf. Mt. 5:45), He has in a special way (through personal salvation) revealed His delivering power to those who believe.

Now Timothy is to command and teach these positive truths. By exemplary living, he is to overcome the handicap of being so young. Public reading of the Scriptures, preaching and teaching are also enjoined, together with an exhortation to use to the full his special divine endowment received at the time of ordination. This is an indication that the Holy Spirit's gifts are liable to be lost or at least atrophied if not used. Concentration and practice are necessary to spiritual maturity. Timothy's ministry can only be fulfilled by giving continuous attention both to his personal life and to his teaching. The reference to saving himself in verse 16 refers either to working out his own salvation (cf. Phil. 2:12) or to preserving his effectiveness in the ministry.

VIII. Instructions Concerning Groups and Individuals in the Church (5:1—6:21)

In this section dealing primarily with groups, it is remarkable that Paul devotes so much space to the problem of widows. However, the sixth chapter of Acts indicates that the problem was an early and pressing one in the church.

1. Older and Younger Men and Women (5:1, 2)

The church is like a family and Timothy is to treat the various age groups as corresponding close relatives. In connection with younger women, Paul adds the admonition "with all purity" because of the inherent moral danger in that relationship.

2. Widows (5:3–16)

This section deals with both the responsibility of the church to widows and their responsibility to the church. A real widow is one who has not only lost her husband, but has no one to look after her. Such a widow is to be "honoured," that is, given financial aid. Of course, if a widow has children or grandchildren they are to look after her. A real widow is contrasted with a loose-living widow in that she puts her hope in God. The church has no obligation to the loose-living widow because she has no living connection ("dead while she liveth") with the church. Timothy is exhorted to "lay down these rules" (Moffatt) concerning widows, and a further word is added to the effect that any Christian who refuses to provide for his own relatives has (1) denied the faith, (2) is himself worse than an infidel, for even unbelievers in that day took care of their own.

In the next section beginning with verse 9, Paul passes from a discussion of ordinary widows to a consideration of those who are employed by the church as Christian workers. In order to be so enrolled, a number of qualifications had to be met. The age requirement (not under 60 years) indicates that these widows were not the only ones aided by the church, because most often young widows with children would be the most destitute. The qualities mentioned in verse 10 would make such a widow a valuable asset to the work of the church.

Younger widows are to remarry. The reasons listed here seem to indicate disappointing experiences with young widows. Paul discourages their entering the service of the church because they become restless and remarry anyway, thus breaking their pledge. Then, too, the very nature of the work of a widow, that of visiting in the homes of the congregation, causes young widows to become gadabouts and gossips. So it is deemed best for these young women to remarry and raise a family and thus avoid the dangers inherent in being placed on the list as a serving widow.

3. *Elders and Prospective Elders (5:17–25)*

Attention now is again turned to the elders in the church (cf. 3:1–7). "Double honour" is prescribed for elders who do their work well, especially those who preach and teach. "Double" is here probably best taken as "ample," and "honour," whatever else it means, certainly includes the idea of remuneration as is clear from the quotations that follow. The first of these is from Deuteronomy 25:4 (cf. its use in I Cor. 9:9), and the second is parallel to Luke 10:7. The quotation from Luke has no bearing on the dating of I Timothy, since sayings of Jesus were circulated in the church long before any of the Gospels were written. Not only does an elder's remuneration come under discussion in this passage, but also his accusation. In order to protect him from malicious intent, no accusation is to be accepted unless there are two or three witnesses. On the other hand, sinning elders must not be spared. Strict discipline is to be meted out to the guilty for its salutary effects upon all.

Verse 22 clearly refers to ordination. If one ordains a man prematurely he is held responsible for the sins of the unworthy man. One scholar has paraphrased the last clause of verse 22 in this way: "Make sure you appoint 'pure' men and keep yourself 'pure' in the process." How important purity in the ministry must have seemed to Paul is revealed by the emphasis he places upon it in the Pastorals. Verse 23 seems to have little connection with what precedes. Apparently Timothy was in delicate health, and here he is admonished not to be a water drinker exclusively, but for the sake of his health to use a little wine. Impure water probably contributed to indigestion. The connection of verses 24 and 25 with verse 22 is more apparent. First impressions must not always be followed in considering men for the ministry. A continuous acquaintance is to be preferred, because while some men's sins are immediately evident, others do not appear until later. The same is true of good deeds. Usually they are immediately revealed. However, if they are not, ultimately they appear.

4. Slaves (6:1, 2)

The principles of the Gospel were in conflict with the institution of slavery. However, since any open protest would have been futile, Paul adapted himself to existing conditions. He knew that the Gospel itself strikes at the very heart of the system. Thus he instructs Christian slaves, who because of their new-found inward liberty might be tempted to look down upon their masters, to honor them. Masters who had disrespectful slaves would have nothing but contempt for their religion. Also if a Christian slave had a Christian master, he was not to take advantage of him. Indeed, the slave in such circumstances had an even greater responsibility, because his master had the same faith and love as he.

5. False Teachers (6:3–10)

This is the final blast in the epistle against false teaching and closely parallels 1:3–5. Heresy is here specifically defined as teaching not corresponding to the words of Christ nor to doctrine which accords with godliness ("Christlike living," Phillips). The description of the false teacher and the results of his teaching climaxes with the statement "supposing that gain is godliness" (v. 5). The RSV correctly translates the phrase, "imagining that godliness is a means of gain." As one scholar observes, "The false teachers are to all appearance religious, but behind their religion there is a sordid and earthly motive. . . . A reputation for high religious character has always been an asset for the man who aims at worldly power and success." The godly man will be content with his earthly lot, while snares await the covetous man. A well-known proverb is quoted to support Paul's contention in verse 9 that riches bring ruin to the greedy man. Because no article is found before the word "root" (v. 10), it is supposed that Paul is saying that the love of money is only one of many roots of evil. This is not likely, because he has extreme cases in mind. It is the *love* of money, and not money per se, that is the root of all evil.

6. Timothy (6:11–21)

Here Timothy is again addressed directly. He is to shun a desire for worldly gain and to pursue virtues which will lead to positive action ("fight the good fight of faith," 6:12). The "profession before many witnesses" of verse 12 probably refers to Timothy's baptism. Paul's charge is made before awesome witnesses, namely, the life-giving God and the confessing Christ. The doxology of verse 15 appears to be a spontaneous outburst at the mention of God's sovereign ordering of events and not a quotation from a hymn or an adapted synagogue doxology.

Paul is not yet through with the subject of wealth. Here he addresses through Timothy not those who aspired to be rich (as in 6:5–10) but those who already had attained abundance. His admonition is twofold: (1) put your trust in God, not riches; (2) do good and use your wealth to that end.

The final plea to Timothy that he should guard his commission includes one last word against the false teachers (Gnostics?) with a concluding brief benediction.

II Timothy

WALTER W. WESSEL

IF I TIMOTHY reveals the kind of church every pastor would like to have, II Timothy discloses the kind of pastor every church would like to have. No other book of the New Testament more clearly sets forth the varied responsibilities and high qualifications of the minister of the Gospel. These are brought to a fitting climax in II Timothy by the challenging statements of 4:1–5, a passage which

1146

every pastor would do well to study. The pleas of the letter take on a deeper significance when we remember that Paul, at the time of writing, is a prisoner at Rome, and the time of his "departure" is at hand. Because his life's work is just about ended and he is anxious that the Lord's work be perpetuated by faithful men who would pass on the received faith, Paul writes down numerous charges in the letter. He also desires that Timothy join him before winter and that he bring with him John Mark, the coat he left at Troas, and the books and parchments. Paul wanted to pass from this life surrounded by his friends and his books! History does not record whether this desire was fulfilled.

I. Introduction (1:1–5)

1. Salutation (1:1, 2)

Paul is Christ's apostle by the will of God and is entrusted with the message that life is promised in Christ Jesus. He writes to his "dearly beloved son," Timothy.

2. Thanksgiving (1:3–5)

As in all his letters except Galatians, Paul recognizes the commendable qualities of his fellow Christians and thanks God because of them. His prayers for his "beloved son" rise to God day and night. Although eager to see Timothy, he is even more eager that Timothy fulfil his ministry. Paul thus recalls the godly stock from which Timothy came and expresses confidence that the same faith exists in him.

II. First Charge (1:6–18)

1. Rekindle your Gift (1:6, 7)

It was not that Timothy needed a new gift; he needed to keep the gift he had glowing brightly. Even the gifts of the Holy Spirit atrophy unless used. Apparently one of Timothy's special weaknesses was timidity.

2. Be Willing to Suffer (1:8–10)

This was included in the rekindling of his gift. There was a stigma attached to bearing witness to the Gospel in the first century as in the twentieth. In suffering for Christ's sake, Timothy is not left to his own resources. Available to him is the very power of God. The mention of the name of God leads Paul into a statement of His saving and calling activity in the lives of Christians. We are here reminded that the activity of God in our behalf was not because of our works, but because of His own eternal "purpose and grace," which was brought to fulfilment in the appearing of Christ Jesus. The work of Christ in this passage is described in terms of the abolishment of death and the granting of immortality.

3. Paul's Example (1:11, 12)

Paul was appointed a preacher, apostle and teacher (cf. I Tim. 2:7) in order to propagate this "good news." In fulfilling these offices, suffering is entailed, but he is not ashamed (cf. Rom. 1:16). He is confident that "what has been entrusted" (RSV) to him (sound doctrine), or perhaps as the KJV rendering suggests, what he has committed to God (his life and all else), God is able to guard until the Day.

4. Guard the Truth (1:13, 14)

Paul's example is the basis of his exhortation to Timothy to follow the "form" of sound words. The word translated "form" ("pattern," RSV) means a rough draft or outline sketch and suggests that Timothy was free to fill out Paul's basic teachings. The manner in which Timothy is to guard the truth is by faith and love. No rancor could arise out of such a defense of the faith.

5. Paul's Present Situation (1:15–18)

The rejection of Paul by "all they which are in Asia" is best understood as not a general defection but, as one commentator suggests, "indifference and coldness from friends who ought to have stood by him." Paul already has expressed concern lest Timothy should be ashamed of him (II Tim. 1:8), and here he shows that such a fear had grounds. Phygelus and Hermogenes, of whom we know nothing more, had deserted him. Onesiphorus, on the other hand, refused to be ashamed of Paul, the prisoner, and the fact that when he arrived at Rome he sought out Paul and "braced [him] up" (Phillips) is given special commendation. At Ephesus too, before he went to Rome, Onesiphorus was a great help.

III. Second Charge (2:1–13)

1. Be Strong (2:1)

The "therefore" of verse 1 indicates a connection with the preceding passage, and the emphatic personal pronoun strikes a contrast. In contrast to the weak Asian brethren, Timothy is to "be strong in the grace that is in Christ Jesus."

2. Pass on the Message to Faithful Men (2:2)

The importance of Christian education is underscored by this charge to entrust the received faith to reliable teachers who in turn will teach others.

3. Examples of Soldier, Athlete, and Farmer (2:3–7)

Three illustrations of this passage stress the complete loyalty and devotion of the Christian minister. As a soldier, he must endure hardships and be a man of a single purpose; as an athlete, he must keep strict discipline; and as a farmer, he must work hard.

4. Jesus Christ, the Inspiration for Steadfastness (2:8–13)

In the difficult ministry to which Timothy is called, he is urged to keep looking unto Jesus Who is here described as "of the seed of David" and "raised from the dead." Because of the proclamation of the Gospel of the incarnation and resurrection, Paul is now a prisoner, but he is willing to suffer for the salvation of the elect. Again Paul cites part of a Christian hymn (cf. I Tim. 3:16), the main purpose of which is to exhort ("if we believe not, yet he abideth faithful") in the face of hardships in serving Jesus Christ. He is the inspiration for steadfastness in the ministry.

IV. Third Charge (2:14—3:17)

The main concern in this passage is the false teaching already present and yet to come into the Ephesian church. The apostle here as in I Timothy 4:6–16 suggests ways of dealing with heresy.

1. Avoid Vain Disputings and Senseless Controversies (2:14–26)

Timothy's approach is to be twofold. He is to keep his congregation informed and is to give diligent attention to his ministry. He is to be a workman, not a disputer. This involves "rightly handling" (RSV) the word of truth, which in this context would include the shunning of inconsequentials. The insidious spread of false teaching is likened to gangrene, a repulsive disease which rapidly brings death. Two of the false teachers are referred to by name, Hymenaeus, whom we know from I Timothy 1:20, and Philetus, who is mentioned only here. They taught a spiritual (past) resurrection, but denied a future (physical) one. For those who regarded matter as intrinsically evil, a future physical resurrection was particularly difficult, but Paul insists (cf. I Cor. 15) that it is a basic precept of the Christian faith. In contrast to the uncertainties of the false teaching, "the foundation of God standeth sure." If this is a reference to the true Church, the Old Testament quotations that follow constitute a double attestation to the genuineness of its membership: (1) God knows His own (Num. 16:5) and (2) His own separate themselves from iniquity (Num. 16:26 or Is. 52:11). The latter would seem to exclude Hymenaeus and Philetus, since they had refused to depart from iniquity.

In verses 20 and 21, Paul retains the figure of a building for the church. As in a building there are various kinds of vessels, so the church contains various kinds of people. In order to be a vessel unto honor, a man must "purge himself from these" (Hymenaeus and Philetus, or perhaps as the RSV renders it, "from what is ignoble").

In the final verses of chapter 2, the conduct of the servant of the Lord is set forth. The stress is on shunning heresy of both doctrine and life and on teaching those in error with gentleness, patience, and meekness. History has proved that this is the best way to bring men in error to repentance and truth. There is some doubt about the rendering of the last part of verse 26 owing to the uncertainty of the antecedents of the pronouns "him" and "his." Phillips' paraphrase clarifies the meaning: "They may come to their senses and be rescued from the power of the devil by the servant of the Lord and set to work for God's purposes."

2. *Warnings of Approaching Apostasy (3:1–9)*

Apostasy, though present at Ephesus, is to become worse as the end approaches. The phrase "last days" refers to the time immediately preceding the consummation. That this final period is primarily in mind is indicated by the use of the future tense in verses 1 and 2, but the conditions described are not wholly unrelated to Timothy's day as revealed by the use of the present tense from verse 6 on. The catalogue of vices (3:2–4) shows some similarity to the list in Romans 1:28–32. The mention of women as particularly susceptible to the deceit of these false teachers is consistent with I Timothy 2:14. Jannes and Jambres (v. 8) are not found by name in the Old Testament, but occur in an ancient commentary on Exodus 7:11, 8:7, and 9:11 as the names of the two magicians who withstood Moses. Apparently their opposition to Moses was widely known. There will be a limit to how far the apostasy will go, because eventually men will recognize the folly of the false teachers as they did that of Jannes and Jambres.

3. *Continue in the Faith (3:10–17)*

The prospect of difficult times makes it imperative that Timothy continue in sound doctrine. Paul calls attention to his own example of suffering for the faith. Out of much experience he has come to realize that "all that will live godly in Christ Jesus will suffer" (cf. I Pet. 4:12, 13). This is particularly true in view of the growing evil in the world. Timothy is to look to Paul's teaching and to the Scriptures. They are the source of salvation while the instrument is faith in Jesus Christ. Verse 17, which clearly teaches the inspiration of Scripture, has as its main point their profitableness. The profitableness of Scripture, however, arises out of the fact that it is "God-breathed." The purpose of Scripture is to make the minister a spiritually mature man, "equipped for every good work" (RSV).

V. Fourth Charge (4:1–8)

1. Preach the Word (4:1–5)

This charge is based on what Paul has just said about the use of Holy Scripture, and it is given in view of the account that Timothy must some day give to Jesus Christ, the judge. The judgment spoken of here is both universal ("the quick and the dead") and eschatological. The five imperatives which follow constitute the substance of the charge. Paul again stresses a positive approach to the crisis at hand. The primary duty of Timothy is to preach the Word of God. He must be at this task constantly, in season and out of season. His preaching will necessarily involve reproof, exhortation, and rebuke, but always in a gentle spirit and with adequate teaching. The urgency of the faithful yet gentle preaching of the Word is enjoined in view of the time soon to come when men will not tolerate sound teaching. Men will have "itching ears," that is, they will only listen to what they want to hear. In view of such conditions, Timothy is exhorted to "make full proof of [his] ministry."

2. Paul's Triumphant Confession (4:6–8)

Paul has now come to the end of his ministry. He is at the point of being executed, but has yet one great confession to make. In the language of the arena (cf. I Cor. 9:24, 25), he summarizes his life's work: "I have fought . . . I have finished . . . I have kept." The apostle had a divine sense of having fulfilled his ministry. The reward for having completed his divinely appointed task is a "crown of righteousness" which Paul does not explain or define. He only adds that it will not be awarded until the Day, and it will not be restricted to him alone but granted to all that love Christ's complete triumph ("his appearing").

VI. Personal Instructions and Information (4:9–19)

Since all had either left or forsaken Paul with the exception of Luke, he is anxious for Timothy's visit. The fact that Paul had sent several of his closest associates away on missions when, at this time especially, he would have enjoyed their presence and comfort reveals his complete commitment to the work of the Gospel. Tychicus was probably sent to Ephesus in order to make it possible for Timothy to come to Rome. The genuineness of this letter is strongly indicated by the almost passing reference to the cloak left at Troas and the desired books and parchments. These apparently were greatly valued by Paul.

In his first defense, Paul, though forsaken by all, was successful. This afforded him opportunity for witness. However, from the sentiment of verses 6–8, the situation had deteriorated and, when Paul wrote this letter, he was expecting soon to die. Yet Paul can triumphantly say, "The Lord shall deliver me from every evil work," a statement which must be taken spiritually as the following words, "and will preserve me unto his heavenly kingdom," indicate. This glorious thought prompts the doxology of verse 18.

VII. Concluding Greetings and Benedictions (4:19–22)

Prisca (Priscilla) and Aquila were close associates of Paul (cf. Acts 18:2, 18, 26; Rom. 16:3; I Cor. 16:19). He wants to be remembered to them and to the household of Onesiphorus whom Paul already singled out for special praise in 1:16–18. The Erastus mentioned here is probably the associate of Timothy mentioned in Acts 19:22. Trophimus is known to us from Acts 20:4.

The appeal of verse 9 is repeated with the added words "before winter," that is, before shipping ceased for the season. Furthermore, Paul needed his coat before the cold weather set in!

The letter closes with the conveyance of several personal greetings and a benediction.

Titus

RICHARD MUNN SUFFERN

IN ALL OF HIS epistles, Paul exercises toward young churches the authority of one "not a whit behind the very chiefest apostles." But in those to Timothy and Titus, he displays this apostolic consciousness and responsibility in a unique and intimate way with trusted friends and delegates on high business of the Lord. From these few documents we can fully appreciate the infinite care Paul used in working with junior assistants in pushing forward the tremendous missionary program of the rapidly growing Church of Jesus Christ. Therefore, in studying the content of the Epistle to Titus, let us observe the comprehensive grasp that Paul has of the spiritual problems of the primitive church on the island of Crete and the sympathetic yet forceful way in which he encourages Titus to take them in hand.

I. Salutation (1:1–4)

The opening words of greeting to Titus are arresting. Paul usually calls himself a "slave of Jesus Christ" (Rom. 1:1; Gal. 1:10; Phil. 1:1). But here he uses the rarer term "slave of God" (cf. Acts 16:17), adding the more usual title "apostle of Jesus Christ" with two qualifying phrases expressing the purpose of his apostleship as the spreading of "the faith of God's elect and the [experiential] knowledge of divine [reverential] truth founded upon a hope of eternal life" (1:1, 2). That life, says Paul, was promised before all eternity by "God who never lies," and was revealed as His Word in the preaching with which Paul "has been entrusted at the command of God our Saviour" (vv. 2, 3).

Paul salutes Titus as his "true son in respect to [their] common faith" (1:4), in much the same way as he addresses Timothy, his other close co-laborer, in his first epistle to him (I Tim. 1:2). No higher tribute can he pay them than to declare that faith in Christ has made them as father and sons. To be noted is the fact that the best texts omit the word "mercy" in the usual formula of greeting, and Christ is called "Saviour" rather than as more frequently "Lord" (1:4). So "God our Saviour" and "Christ Jesus our Saviour" named in such close sequence express well his great concern for the salvation of the Cretans, for which purpose he is writing this letter. Thus the salutation sets both the spirit and the theme of the epistle.

II. General Instructions for Reforming Church Life in Crete (1:5–16)

In 1:5 Paul refers to his having left Titus in Crete. Paul must have visited Crete with Titus. A well-known commentator states that "the various attempts to bring this circumstance within the time included in the Acts of the Apostles seem all unsatisfactory." Modern scholarship has also generally conceded that this visit must have been among the apostle's activities after release from four years of imprisonment (that is, the two years at Caesarea, A.D. 60-61, and the two years at Rome, A.D. 62-63). Probably Paul went to Spain as he so desired (Rom. 15:24, 28) and then on his return voyage east to

Asia Minor, which we know he visited after his release, stopped at Crete, leaving Titus to follow up as apostolic delegate the important work of bringing a weak, corrupt church under stricter Christian discipline. There had been a church there very early (Acts 2:11); but apparently Judaizing influences had hindered seriously the progress of the Gospel. Titus is to instal good leadership (1:5–9), and secondly, root out Jewish legalism which is sapping the spiritual life of the Cretan Christians (1:10–16).

1. Qualifications for Elder Leadership (1:5–9)

Paul urges "complete reform of all that is lacking" (1:5). The verb for "reform" denotes anything from reorganization to new policies and regulations (cf. Acts 24:2). This will involve more competent evangelical leadership. Titus is to select, ordain, and instal fit elders in each city parish of Crete, much as we find Paul and Barnabas doing for the Galatian churches in Acts 14:23.

A brief word should be said about the "presbyters" or "elders." In 1:7 Paul also calls them "episcopoi" or "overseers," "bishops." These titles were interchangeably used in the early apostolic period for the ruling and preaching leadership of local churches, at least as late as A.D. 70 (cf. Acts 20:17, 28; Phil. 1:1; I Tim. 3:1–7; 5:17–19; I Pet. 5:1, 2). One term denoted eligibility of those of age and experience as it was customarily used in the Jewish synagogue; the other term, the responsibilities of this office for supervision. Early in the second century, such leaders as Ignatius and Polycarp distinguished in their use of the two titles as if they were two separate orders in the church. J. B. Lightfoot makes this clear in his well-known study on the Christian ministry in his commentary on the Epistle to the Philippians. He says that this development of an episcopal order in a diocese of churches was made necessary by the tensions which existed between Gentile and Judaizing Christians, by the emergence of the heresy of Gnosticism, and not least by the martyrdom and death of the original apostles. Already in these early pastoral epistles of Paul to Titus and Timothy, one can see apostolic authority being applied to parish tensions and problems of heresy in the churches of Crete and of Ephesus. This is what one would expect to find in the early Church, and such exercise of apostolic authority cannot be construed as evidence of the late post-Pauline composition of these pastoral epistles as modern criticism often supposes. Later the term "episcopoi" was taken from the local parish eldership and given to those church leaders who succeeded to such overseeing responsibilities of the apostles. Only centuries later during the Protestant Reformation did the Calvinists return to the primitive pattern of the parity of the ministry, eliminating the episcopacy and placing apostolic authority in the decisions of a presbytery of elders.

The qualifications for the "episcopal eldership" (1:6–9) are parallel to what Paul outlines for Timothy in even fuller detail (I Tim. 3:1–7). Some qualities should hardly have required mention, but they were apparently sadly lacking even in the leadership of such Christian communities as Ephesus and Crete. The elder is to be a Christian family man, of character beyond reproach. Both traits to be overcome and traits to be cultivated are listed by Paul: not self-willed, not quick-tempered, not given to drinking, nor violent, nor avaricious, but friendly, virtuous, and temperate. Paul then concludes with distinctly Christian characteristics, just, holy, self-controlled, and holding fast to the "faithful word [of the Gospel] as taught to him" (cf. also I Tim. 4:3), so that he can be a strong exhorter and defender of the faith with "healthy teaching" in the church (1:9). Paul uses the word "healthy" repeatedly in these pastoral epistles to describe the saving, healing work of the gospel message in contrast to the unhealthy, sickening influences of Jewish legalism upon Christian faith and life (cf. 1:13; 2:1, 2, 8; I Tim. 1:10; 6:3; II Tim. 1:13; 4:3).

2. *Special Warnings against Judaizing Influences (1:10–16)*

One can read in any good Church history text the story of the great heresies which attacked the early Christian Church during the first three centuries and later. None was more devastating than the earliest —that known as Judaizing Christianity. We learn early of the "party of the circumcision" in Acts 15, in the Epistle to the Galatians, and from many other brief Pauline references. This epistle to Titus shows that this "party" is disrupting the Cretan church (1:10). It is likewise mentioned with grave concern in I Timothy 1:3–11 and II Timothy 4:1–5, referring to similar distressing conditions in the churches where Timothy is serving.

Judaistic Christianity sought to shackle faith in Jesus Christ as personal Saviour to the faithful observance of old Pharisaic legalism. Is was natural for Jewish converts to Christianity to try to reconcile their new-found faith in Christ with the requirements of Talmudic law in which they had been reared. This might involve the Jewish dietary laws regulating clean and unclean foods, or the sacred rite of circumcision, or the keeping of the many festivals of the Jewish year. It might be easy to become confused about these matters because, after all, Jesus was a Jew and He had spoken in the Sermon on the Mount: "Till heaven and earth pass, one jot or one tittle shall in no wise pass from the law, till all be fulfilled" (Mt. 5:18). Jesus' meaning of this "fulfilment" was not at once apparent, not even to the apostles. Only slowly did Peter come to understand freedom from "kosher" rules as a Christian (Acts 10:9–16), and Christ's will to have Gentile believers baptized (Acts 10:34–48). It took a tremendous experience of conversion on the Damascus road to break the persecuting spell of the Mosaic law upon Paul's life (Acts 9:1–22). It was easy to cling to old liturgical customs with their sacred taboos and superstitions controlling almost every aspect of Jewish family life and to allow these things to cramp a free life of love and good will toward all mankind.

Titus had considerable experience with this legalism, for he as a Greek had become a Christian in the great Gentile mission church of Antioch in Syria of which the Apostles Barnabas and Paul were pastors (Acts 11:19–26; 13:1–3). It was in that church that a great controversy between Jewish and Greek members had broken out over the question of the necessity of requiring circumcision for all Gentile Christian converts, so that finally Paul and Barnabas had to take the issue before the apostles in Jerusalem around A.D. 48 (Acts 15:1–21). There Paul, Barnabas, Peter, James and the others conferred, arguing the case carefully. Finally they decided to permit a large amount of liberty from the ceremonial practices of Judaism. According to Galatians 2, Titus as a prominent Gentile leader in the Antioch church figured as a test case for the evangelical cause, and Paul writes that he was not forced to be circumcised "in order that the truth of the gospel might remain unto you" (Gal. 2:5).

So Paul has some very hard things to say about these Cretan Judaizers, much as Jesus had to say about the Pharisees in such passages of the Gospels as Matthew 23. Paul is reminded of a stinging verse from the pen of one of their own Cretan poets, Epimenides: "The Cretans are always liars, evil beasts, and lazy stomachs!" (1:12). Misleading, uncontrolled disturbers of the peace of the church, these false Christians must be "muzzled" (v. 11), so that they do not continue "upsetting" whole households for the sake of personal gain. This sounds rather like the plaguing activities of some modern cults that are rampant today. Paul wants Titus to take these ancient cultists in hand firmly that they may, if possible, be restored to spiritual "health" through faith in Christ (v. 13). Paul does not hesitate to say that this will mean breaking with all "Jewish myths and commandments of those [rabbis] who reject the truth" (v. 14).

To appreciate what Paul is speaking about one needs only to read a little in Louis Ginzberg's *The Legends of the Bible* (Simon and Schuster, 1956), or in some collection of the apocryphal Old Testament books and pseudepigraphical writings, that is, spurious works purporting to emanate from Biblical characters (cf. Charles C. Torrey, *The Apocryphal Literature, A Brief Introduction*, Yale University Press, 1945, p. 118 on II Esdras), or even in some edition of the Dead Sea Scrolls (cf. Millar Burrows, *The Dead Sea Scrolls*, Viking Press, 1955, pp. 365-370 on the Habakkuk Commentary). Since the days of the Exile, the Jewish religious imagination had run wild in the interpretation of sacred history. Joseph Gaer, a modern Jewish authority, writes about these Jewish Midrashic and Talmudic legends as follows:

In interpreting the Law, teachers used anecdotes, stories, parables, fables, and every other conceivable device which could elucidate a general principle or moral concept to a people uprooted, transplanted and held in captivity. In their nostalgic recollection of Biblical times, preachers often went far beyond anything implied in Scriptural narrative. And the more romanticized the stories, the better the people liked them. This narrative lore, used originally as exposition, grew rapidly into a body of learning known as Haggadah, meaning "legends." The Law and the ritual, firmly fixed upon Mosaic Law, became more rigid with the passing of time (*The Lore of the Old Testament*, Little Brown and Co., 1951, p. 7).*

Now Paul was set against the importation of any of this legend (the "haggadah" of the Midrashim) or of any of the rabbinical ritualistic prescriptions (the "halakah" of the Talmud) into Christianity. (We can also well imagine what Paul would say about modern form-criticism of the Gospels which tries to reduce the lives of Christ to various genres of ancient religious folk tales!) As a former rabbi, Paul knew the pitfalls of legend and ritual only too well. He knew that they could not help one to know the saving love of God in Christ. He was concerned only about Old Testament history and

---

* By permission.

the facts of Christ's advent into history and atonement for sin. Ceremonial purity was not the important thing, but only purity of heart (cf. Mt. 15:11). These Judaizing Christians needed desperately an evangelical faith in Christ Who could set them free spiritually from sin and externalities. As it was, "nothing is pure to them who are defiled and unbelieving, for both their minds and their consciences are defiled" (1:15)—an accurate description of the hopeless neurotic state of frustrated legalists who can never quite achieve purity! "They profess to know God but by their actions they deny him"; they are complete frauds ("reprobate," ASV) in their own field of specialization, namely works-righteousness (v. 16). This is the ironical bankruptcy of self-appointed saints! (Note what Jesus says in Matthew 7:15–29.)

III. Specific Instructions for Preaching (2:1–15)

Paul now proceeds to outline the "healthy teaching" which he believes Titus must impart in his preaching and pastoral mission among the Cretans (2:1). This consists of points of Christian ethics which must be carefully observed by each age group and class, free and slave (vv. 2–10). To this Paul adds a brief summary of the Gospel to show how the Christian life will grow out of a genuine experience of salvation (vv. 11–15).

1. Moral Responsibilities of Christians (2:2–10)

The older men are to be urged to be temperate, dignified, and self-controlled, and not only that, but "healthy in faith, love and patience," a triad of peculiarly Christian virtues to which Paul was wont to refer (cf. Thess. 1:3; I Tim. 6:11, 12; II Tim. 3:10).

The older women likewise are to be exhorted to live as "consecrated" Christians, so that they will be good teachers of virtue to the younger girls who will some day become chaste, dutiful wives, good housekeepers, and loving mothers in Christian homes "where God's word will not be blasphemed" (2:3–5).

As for the behavior of young men, Titus must be a good example in their midst, both through his deeds and his teaching which will be "sincere and dignified, healthy and beyond reproach," so that there can be no grounds for criticism (2:6–8).

Finally, Christian slaves are to obey their masters, aiming to please, to be cooperative and honest, so that thereby the doctrine of God the Saviour may be shown forth in all its adornment (2:9, 10).

2. Relationship of Salvation to Personal Ethics (2:11–15)

The mention of "adorning the doctrine of God our Saviour" leads Paul to compose one of those remarkable summaries of the Gospel of the saving grace of God with which his epistles abound. This one is a devotional meditation upon the theological foundations of all Christian ethics. It is as if he grows weary talking about the importance of being and doing good and forthwith launches out into the deep of God's grace which is the source of power for the Christian life. God's grace has been revealed to all men in the incarnation of His Son to teach man how he must "deny irreverence and worldly [material] lusts" (2:11, 12). Paul uses the same verb "deny" that Jesus uses in Matthew 16:24–26: "If any man will come after me, let him deny himself, and take up his cross, and follow me." One should observe that the word "lusts" is not an adequate translation of the word which Paul uses to denote all the desires and drives of the human will. In Galatians 5:24, Paul speaks of this self-denial as a "crucifixion of the flesh with the passions and desires [lusts]." Thereby, Paul tells Titus, one can live "justly and reverently before God, looking forward to the blessed hope of the second coming of the great God and Saviour Christ Jesus who gave his life to ransom man from lawlessness and to purify for himself a people eager to do good" (2:11–14). Christ is here called boldly "God," that is to say, "divine," according to the most obvious interpretation of Paul's words (cf. also in I Jn. 5:20). This is the good news which Titus must preach (v. 15). There is no true Christian faith without good works of personal self-denial and love.

IV. Concluding Instruction for Christians in the World (3:1–15)

Paul wants Titus to keep before the Cretan church their responsibilities as Christian citizens, if the church is to make the strong impact upon the world that it should (3:1, 2). To this he adds a personal testimony to God's power to save all sinners however evil they may be and a warning against arguing with legalists (vv. 3–11).

1. Civil and Social Responsibilities of Christians (3:1, 2)

The Cretans had been a little more than 125 years under Roman rule. Before this the famous Greek historian Polybius had written that the Cretans lived under a democracy but were very lawless. Paul must have observed this on his visit and felt that the Christians must strive to support law and order (cf. Rom. 13:1-7). The Cretan culture was very ancient, going back to the great Minoan period of 1500 B.C. As a maritime power, Crete had controlled the whole eastern Mediterranean world, but now it was a decadent province in the Roman Empire. Only the Christian community could build a better state through a wholesome, friendly society to which the Christians could contribute a spirit of gentleness and humility in place of the prevailing spirit of unfair criticism and contention (3:2).

2. God's Power to Save any Sinner through Christ (3:3-7)

Lest Titus lose heart and faith in God's power to save even the basest Cretan sinner who repents and believes, Paul takes a glance back into his, and Titus', and all Christians' black sinful past, and on behalf of all testifies to the saving power of God through the "washing" (3:5) of the Holy Spirit who is "shed" (v. 6; cf. Acts 2:33) upon believers in Jesus Christ "our Saviour" (v. 6) for the "regeneration" (v. 5; cf. rebirth in Jn. 3:3-6) and "renewing" (v. 5; cf. "new creature" in II Cor. 5:17) of personal spiritual life. The Gospel of God the Saviour and Christ the Saviour, it will be recalled, was the burden of Paul's opening salutation to Titus (1:1-4). This salvation will not come by man's futile efforts to be good through works of righteousness and ceremony, whether pagan or Jewish, but only through forgiveness of sin ("justification," 3:7) by the "kindness and love" (v. 4), "mercy" (v. 5) and "grace" (v. 7) of God in Christ. This grace saved Paul. It can save any Cretan who comes to Christ for forgiveness.

3. Advice to Preach the Gospel, Not to Argue (3:8-11)

This "faithful word" Titus must preach in order that believing Christian Cretans may "be outstanding in good works" (3:8). All arguments with legalists about the minutiae of law or about the "genealogies" (for example, of the patriarchs) are utterly "foolish" and should be avoided (vv. 9–11)—good advice to remember when dealing with any form of modern cult, such as Mormonism or Jehovah's Witnesses! If they persist, they must be shunned.

4. Closing Personal Requests (3:12–15)

From the place where he was writing this epistle to Titus, probably Ephesus, Paul was planning to go to Macedonia. While in prison in Rome, he had promised to visit the Philippians, and he wanted also to preach up in Epirus at Nicopolis. So he asks Titus to plan on meeting him there as soon as he sends either Artemas or Tychicus to take his place on the Cretan field. Artemas must have gone, as we read in II Timothy 4:10–12 of Titus' going to Dalmatia further up the coast and Tychicus' going to Ephesus. Apparently Zenas and Apollos are on the way to Alexandria (cf. Acts 18:24), and Paul wants Titus to entertain them on their stopover in Crete (3:13, 14). They are probably carrying this letter to Titus. Paul extends to Titus greetings from all those with him and in turn greets the Cretan church with God's grace (v. 15). God's grace is, after all, sufficient to heal and to bless even this afflicted fellowship in Christ.

Philemon

JAC. J. MÜLLER

THE BACKGROUND of this very short letter by the Apostle Paul is briefly as follows: Onesimus, a slave and a Colossian (cf. Col. 4:9, "one of yourselves"), belonging to Philemon, a wealthy Christian slave-owner, ran away from his master at Colossae, after having apparently committed theft (cf. vv. 15, 16, 18, 19). He found his way to the metropolis Rome, where he came in contact with Paul in some way or other, and was converted under his influence and ministry (v. 10). Paul thereupon sent him back to his owner (v. 11), with this letter of recommendation in his favor, to be delivered to Philemon. Therein he pleaded with Philemon to receive back the penitent (and meanwhile converted) slave with good will, and to forgive and rehabilitate him because he would no longer be only a slave to him, but "more than a slave . . . a beloved brother in the Lord" (RSV).

I. Title and Salutation (vv. 1–3)

In the salutation Paul styles himself "a prisoner of Jesus Christ" (or, "for Christ Jesus," RSV). Instead of the usual reference to his

1164

apostleship, he introduces himself as one who finds himself in captivity for the sake of Christ and His cause (cf. also v. 13). From the prison in Rome, he is writing Philemon this very personal letter as from heart to heart.

Philemon of Colossae, to whom the letter is directed, seems to have been a slave-owner (vv. 15, 16), who offered his house as a place of gathering for believers. He was well acquainted with Paul, as the tone of the whole letter indicates, and apparently came to conversion under his ministry at Ephesus (v. 19; cf. Acts 9:10, 26), and could rightly be called a "dearly beloved fellow-labourer" on account of his fervent love for the saints (vv. 5, 7), and the fact that he put his house at the disposal of the believers as a meeting-place, and possibly took part himself in preaching the Gospel. The letter is furthermore addressed to Philemon's wife, Apphia, a beloved sister in the faith, and to his son, Archippus, called "our fellow-soldier" in the cause of the Gospel (cf. Col. 4:17)—and also to the "church in your house" (v. 2). Of such "house churches" mention is also made in Romans 16:5, I Corinthians 16:19, and Colossians 4:15.

The family circle and attendant slaves formed a small community who were spiritually ministered to in the home, especially so where in the newly established churches no suitable places of assembly were available for the whole congregation. In the first instance, however, after the adoption of the Christian faith, the "church in the house" would have consisted of the believer's family, the members of his household in a wider sense, together with the slaves or servants belonging to it. Commenting on this praiseworthy phenomenon of "house churches," Calvin makes the following deduction: "A rule is here laid down as to what it becomes all Christian households to be—that they be so many little churches. Let every one, therefore, know that this charge is laid upon him—that he is to train his house in the fear of the Lord, to keep it under holy discipline, and, in fine, to form it in the likeness of a Church" (*Commentary on Colossians* 4:15). A householder should thus regulate his family in spiritual matters, that he discharges also the duty of prophet and priest within the walls of his dwelling. In the home, children get their first impressions of the Christian religion, and the foundation is there laid for their subsequent confession of faith in Jesus Christ and for a saintly character and virtuous Christian life. There the householder holds forth the Word of God to the whole family as they gather around the sacred book; there he offers prayer and supplication to the Lord on behalf of all; there the family is bound together by ties of spiritual communion, and is trained to take its place in the Church as a whole as a living member of the large household of God on earth.

If Paul, furthermore, ends his salutation with a prayer for grace and peace to them (v. 3), he recalls thereby all that is real and indispensable in the Christian religion. There is no grace unless God bestows it, and there is no real peace unless it flows forth from God's conciliation with sinful man. All this is only experienced by the believer as a gift of God through Jesus Christ, the fount of all spiritual blessings.

II. Thanksgiving for Philemon's Love and Faith (vv. 4–7)

Supplication and thanksgiving go hand in hand; the one is not complete without the other in prayer life. There must be thanksgiving not only for blessings personally received, but also for gifts of grace bestowed on our brethren, wherewith they could further the interests of the Kingdom of God. To such thanksgiving, intercession is linked as an essential part of the communion of the saints, and in such prayer, churches as well as individuals can be remembered by name before the Lord. In this the prayers of the apostle serve as an example to us.

The thanksgiving to God is based on Philemon's faith toward the Lord Jesus, and—as fruit thereof—his love towards the believers or saints, that is, those set apart for God and devoted to His service (vv. 5, 7). This includes the whole perfection of a Christian man, for to faith and love all the actions and all the duties of our life relate, and they properly describe faith-in-action, and the sum of all godliness in mind and deed, profession and practice.

To the thanksgiving is added the petition that Philemon's fellowship or participation in the faith may become effectual in the full knowledge ("may promote the knowledge," RSV) of all the good which is to be found in believers in Christ and tending to His glory. A sharing of the faith must not be something static, but dynamic, must function effectually and reveal the full activity of a life of faith and goodness.

III. Plea for Onesimus (vv. 8–12)

With an appeal to the fact that he was an aged man (or "ambassador," RSV) and a prisoner of Christ (v. 9), Paul begins his entreaty on behalf of the runaway slave Onesimus, whose name he now mentions for the first time. "I beseech thee for my child, whom I have begotten in my bonds, Onesimus" (v. 10), or "I appeal to you for my child, Onesimus, whose father I have become in my imprisonment" (RSV). The runaway slave got in touch with Paul in Rome—in what way we know not, whether in needy circumstances or in genuine desire of salvation—and the apostle during his own captivity became a spiritual father to him, leading him to faith in Christ and to conversion.

Owing to this personal experience of the saving grace of Christ, Onesimus (meaning in Greek "useful" or "profitable") indeed became very useful as a regenerated man both to Philemon and to Paul, although in his former state he was useless or unserviceable (v. 11). Christ made the whole difference. And this gave Paul confidence to plead with Philemon to receive Onesimus back, to whom he had become attached as to his "very heart" (v. 12).

IV. Paul's Consideration in Sending Back Onesimus (vv. 13–16)

Though Onesimus would perform many services to Paul in his captivity, and he would have retained him, yet he could not keep him without the approval of his lawful owner, whose mastership over him had to be fully acknowledged, because the bond of slavery was not to be severed in a revolutionary way. At that time Christianity took account of the fact that slavery existed as an old and established social and economic institution. The liberation of Onesimus had to be the result of voluntary action on the part of Philemon, and was not to happen under pressure from outside as if under compulsion (v. 14). Philemon, being a Christian, would of his own free will begin to judge matters according to the norms of the Gospel, and receive the returning and meanwhile converted slave lovingly into his household circle again, and then possibly grant him his freedom willingly. Paul does not definitely prescribe such a liberation, but gently suggests such a voluntary act of good will.

In the adventures of Onesimus, a providential act of God could also be discerned. Man proposes; God disposes. Onesimus' flight is ultimately seen in a new light. It became the means of his conversion, and the issue gives the right to speak here of a deed and purpose which reached farther than what Onesimus had in mind with his flight. God had overruled everything for his good. He could now return to Philemon as a "brother," spiritually never again to be parted from him (vv. 15, 16). For in Christ a new relation between master and servant comes into existence. Henceforth Philemon will own Onesimus "no longer as a servant, but more than a servant, a brother beloved . . . in the flesh and in the Lord" (v. 16). Although the former relation of master towards slave is maintained, a new spirit and disposition will henceforth govern that relation. Onesimus would still be a slave, but no longer be regarded as a "thing," a tool or mere instrument in the service of his master, but he would now also be regarded and treated as a "beloved brother." A new relation of brotherhood in the Lord between master and slave had been added since the conversion of Onesimus. Both master and slave are now "in Christ." A double bond of union now began to exist: in the natural sense Onesimus would be a "brother in the flesh" because they were fellow-countrymen (cf. Col. 4:19) or perhaps even members of the same family; and in a spiritual sense he would be "brother in the Lord" by their common faith in Jesus Christ.

Here we see the master-servant relation as it is sanctified by the influence of Christianity and conversion. Its significance lies in the example which Paul offers of the practical application of his sentiment expressed elsewhere regarding the problem of slaves, namely, that Christianity does not deny or abolish differences in culture and position, but introduces a new spirit in those relationships, that is, the mind and disposition of Christ. On the one hand, the slave must remain in the state in which he is called (I Cor. 7:20-22), and is expected to obey his earthly master (Col. 3:22; I Tim. 6:1, 2); on the other hand, however, in the new Christian relation of life there is no slave or freeman, but Christ is all and in all (Col. 3:11; Gal. 3:28). Paul does not in so many words preach the emancipation of slaves in the name of Christendom, but he knows that the Christian faith creates a new inner relation between men which binds them together as brothers beyond and notwithstanding social differences. The condition of old-time slavery as well as modern relations between master and servant could be sanctified by the Christian faith, and each could find and recognize a brother in the other, whom he could love for Christ's sake.

V. *Appeal to Philemon to Receive Onesimus (vv. 17–21)*

Paul ends his request by appealing to Philemon to accept Onesimus in Christian friendship and fellowship just as he would Paul himself, seeing that they are partners who share Christ and their mutual love with one another and are of the same disposition (v. 17). Every obstacle in the way of a friendly reception had to be removed. If Onesimus had wronged his master and caused him loss or robbed him before he ran away, Paul would make it good. Philemon could put down the amount owing to Paul's account. The apostle was ready not only to ask forgiveness for Onesimus, but also to offer compensation for the wrong done. He would repay everything, and was willing to guarantee it with the signature of his own hand (vv. 18, 19)—although Philemon could at the same time be reminded of his own debt to Paul, that he had to thank Paul not only for something, but for himself, as he was indebted to him for his own conversion (v. 19). Paul wishes to remind Philemon of the pardon he himself received, to make him understand how grace freely received calls to remission of debt, when a fellow sinner also comes to conversion.

Thus the appeal to Philemon ends in an expression of confidence in Philemon's obedience to Paul's wish and to his duty as a Christian. Philemon could not refuse his request nor deny the claim of Christian brotherhood. Yes, Philemon would even do more than Paul had said, would go farther than he was expressly asked to do (v. 21). Probably this indefinite expression was a suggestion of the eventual liberation of Onesimus from slavery by his owner; in any case, it would set Philemon thinking about what the Lord really asked of him. He would as a Christian believer do everything that Christian love and Christian duty urged upon him. In the end, these very principles of Christianity would make it impossible for the Christian conscience to tolerate slavery in its bosom any longer.

VI. Personal Matters: Greetings (vv. 22–25)

Apart from personal greetings and the usual benediction, the letter ends with the expectation of the apostle's own release from captivity in answer to their prayers. All his hope was placed in God Who hears prayer (v. 22). In this matter Paul and all believers could rely on precious promises contained in God's Word (for example, Mt. 6:6; 7:7; 18:19, 20; Jn. 14:13, 14; 15:16; Lk. 18:7), and also be encouraged by striking testimonies in the early Church in connection with answered prayer, such as recorded in Acts 4:24–31 and 12:5, 11, 12.

Living churches consist of praying congregations, and the God of the Church is the God Who answers prayer.

A very striking analogy exists between the history of Onesimus and the gospel story. In the mediatory efforts of Paul for the spiritual and social reinstatement of Onesimus, we have a touching picture of the redemption of a sinner through Jesus Christ. The sinner is God's property, but has repudiated His right of ownership, and turned his back upon God. After dreary and hope-forlorn wanderings in sin, he eventually flees to Jesus for refuge and help. In Him he is not only born anew, but in Him he also finds a substitute to whose account all his debt is put, and an intercessor who pleads his cause before God, and induces the Father to accept him to His grace for Christ's sake.

The necessity of restitution, the way of substitutionary satisfaction, the possibility of forgiveness, the mind of a peacemaker, and the claim to obedience are all put forward in this grand picture of a sinner's redemption and his return to God.

Hebrews

A. BERKELEY MICKELSEN

THIS LETTER DEALS with the person of Jesus Christ, His work as the priest of God, and the response which the Christian should make to such a person and such a work. Because the language of the letter is replete with references to the priestly ritual of the Old Testament tabernacle, many fail to see the profundity and magnificence of this book.

The epistle was written to a local Christian church, probably in or about Rome. The original readers were Jewish Christians who spoke and wrote Greek; their Old Testament was a Greek translation called the Septuagint. So the writer, in his teaching about Christ, makes use of Old Testament language and ideas with which his readers were already acquainted. He knew them well (cf. 5:11–14; 6:9–12; 10:32–36; 13:22). There must have been a mutual love between the writer and his readers, for he makes clear how much he is counting on their prayers (13:18). In this letter he is giving them advanced Christian teaching to be placed on the foundation of the Old Testament which they already have (6:1–3).

I. Prologue: Course and Climax of Divine Revelation (1:1–3)

The Christian faith was not "something new with no background." By the prophets God had spoken to the people. How? By dreams, visions, and direct speech, God made Himself known. Yet these disclosures of God were often hundreds of years apart. Moses and Malachi were separated in time by a thousand years. Hence, revelation in the Old Testament is viewed as being fragmentary in character. But in the last of these days, that is, in the climax of God's plan of redemption, God spoke no longer simply by prophets but by His own Son. Who is He? Not only is He heir of all things and the agent through Whom God made the universe, but He Himself is God. He is the radiance or outflowing of God's essential glory, the exact representation of God's substantial nature (1:3). These are the strongest statements in the New Testament for the full deity of Jesus Christ. He maintains the universe by His mighty word; in Him is God's supreme revelation. Yet revelation without redemption would be meaningless. To tell men about health without enabling them to become healthy would not be good news. But the third verse ends on a note of good news. The One Who is the heir of all things, Who was active in creation, Who possesses the essential being of God, and Who maintains creation, is the One Who redeemed man. His ascension proves that He completed the work. Not only is history summarized here, but life has meaning and history has purpose. As in the prologue of John's Gospel, so here the reader is awed by the splendor of deity. Christ is before history, in history, and above history.

II. The Pre-eminence of Christ Himself (1:4—4:13)

The first major section of Hebrews shows why Christ has such an exalted character, why He must be fully man as well as fully God. The truths are so essential that the writer immediately applies them to his readers.

1. Superiority of Christ to Angels (1:4–14)

In Daniel and Zechariah, as well as in many books coming from the period between the Old Testament and the New Testament, angels play a prominent role in God's dealings with mankind; yet their tasks show their subordinate position. They are spirits in holy service sent forth to aid believers who are about to inherit salvation (1:14). Of seven quotations from the Old Testament (vv. 5–13), five show the superior dignity and position of the Son.

Of the five quotations applied to Jesus, four are good examples of typology. Typology takes what is said of an Old Testament person, event, experience, or institution, and applies it to a New Testament person, event, experience or institution. Although some of the passages quoted from the Old Testament by the writer of Hebrews are interpreted literally, most of them are interpreted typologically. Psalm 2:7 historically was spoken to an Israelite king either on the day of his ascension to the throne or on the anniversary of the occasion (1:5a), but the exalted language applies to Jesus. The words in II Samuel 7:14 were spoken to Solomon, but in a far greater way they are true of Jesus (v. 5b). The "him" of Deuteronomy 32:43 (Septuagint) originally was God, but what is said is equally true of Jesus (v. 6). Psalm 45 was written in celebration of a king's marriage, but again, the exalted language is more appropriate to Jesus than to a human ruler (vv. 8, 9). Psalm 102:26–28 is said of God in the Old Testament, but in verses 10 and 11 the words are applied to Christ.

In contrast to the angels, Jesus is a Son and God is His Father. The angels are to worship Him when He returns a second time (1:6). His throne is the throne of God, and in a way true of no man, He loves righteousness and hates iniquity (vv. 8, 9). He laid the foundations of the earth, and creation is the outcome of His effort (vv. 10–12). In contrast to the temporal creation, He abides forever (v. 12).

Angels were never told to sit at God's right hand until God should subdue their enemies (1:13; Ps. 110:1). Christ stands exalted; angels stand to serve.

2. *Warning: Peril of Indifference to these Truths (2:1–4)*

Because Christ is superior to angels, His good tidings must not be disregarded. The writer urges his readers to pay attention lest the currents of life carry them far from the truths that Jesus proclaimed. Other Biblical writers or translators associate angels with the giving of the law: Stephen (Acts 7:38, 53); Paul (Gal. 3:19); the Septuagint translation of Deuteronomy (33:2), and the writer of Hebrews (2:2). This message of the angels is declared valid. Penalities were inflicted for disobedience. If this is true of that which angels helped to initiate, how much more should the readers be attentive to what Jesus initiated, since He is superior to them.

The proof that Jesus' message is superior to the Mosaic law is seen in that God confirmed the preaching of the apostles by signs and wonders, miraculous powers, and distributions of the Holy Spirit upon the early Christians as recorded in the Book of Acts. This phenomenon of the first years of the Christian Church testified to the supernatural character of the Christian faith and the oneness of all who believed, whether Jews or Gentiles, in Jerusalem, Samaria, or in Ephesus (cf. Acts 2:2–4; 8:17; 10:44–45; 11:15; 19:6).

3. *The Reason Christ Became Human (2:5–18)*

The phrase "the world to come" or "the world which is about to be" (2:5) would be puzzling did not the next clause—"concerning which we are speaking"—help to explain it. The writer has just spoken of the "so great salvation" (v. 3). Therefore, the "world which is about to be" must be the future extension of what we already have. Our salvation concerns not only our internal spiritual life, but also all aspects of life—the external world, nature, the political and social spheres of existence. The whole realm of man's existence is to be in subjection not to angels, but to man himself (Ps. 8:4–6). Although this may be man's destiny, man does not now find an harmonious world of nature or of human beings around him. How will the promise of the psalmist be realized? The writer of Hebrews says it is in Jesus Himself. He, Who now is being crowned with glory and honor because He tasted death for every person, will bring into reality this promise for mankind.

This tasting of death meant suffering for Jesus, suffering which brought Him to a state of completion or perfection. This does not mean that He had been defective. It means that His experience had been incomplete. Both Jesus, the sanctifier, and the people who are sanctified are from God (2:11). This is true of Jesus because He has the same nature as God (1:3), and it is true of Christians because God created them and renewed them.

Jesus and believers are close to each other because Jesus voluntarily became man. As man He suffered, and by His death He destroyed Satan. Satan, because he brought death with its terrors into the experience of man, is said to have "the power of death." Satan is said to be "destroyed," because his doom has been sealed by the redemptive work of Jesus. By His death Jesus released those who, because of their fear of death, were subjects in slavery (v. 15).

The fact that Jesus was made like His brothers in all respects (save in the matter of sin, cf. 4:15) is the basis for His High Priesthood (2:17b and chapter 7) and His ability to make expiation for the sins of the people (2:17c and 8:1—10:18). To cover over sin does not mean to cover it up. Jesus' atoning death brings a change in the sinner who trusts Him and blots out the iniquity for which punishment is due.

4. *Christ's Position is Greater than That of Moses (3:1–6)*

Readers are characterized as "holy brothers" who are sharers in a heavenly call. They are called to consider Jesus, the one of Whom their confession speaks. He is compared and contrasted with Moses. Moses and Christ are both faithful in God's house. Moses is faithful in his role as servant *in* the house. Christ is pictured as a son *over*

God's house, that is, as one having authority over the house. The word "house" describes the people of God in both the Old Testament and the New. Christ's supremacy over Moses, the great Old Testament lawgiver, shows His person is unique and His position incomparable.

5. Warning: Unbelief Brings Temporal and Eternal Effects (3:7—4:13)

How men respond to Christ is supremely important. A quotation from Psalm 95:7–11 warns of the danger of hardening hearts. Note the emphasis in the psalm upon the speaking of the Holy Spirit. It is not simply that He spoke, but rather that He *is speaking*. The psalm in its historic setting refers to the generation in the wilderness who angered God by refusing to go forward into the Promised Land.

The cause of defeat in the past or in the present is regarded as the same—an evil heart of unbelief. Immediately after the quotation comes the urgent appeal to "watch out lest this kind of heart be in you." Unbelief—a lack of trust—brings withdrawal from the living God and separation is inevitable. Daily exhortation is the preventive against being hardened by the deceitfulness of sin. Verse 14 gives the answer to a very difficult question: How do *we* know that a man has become a sharer of Christ? The answer is very clear: He has become a sharer of Christ if he keeps his original confidence firm until the end of his life. This total life picture is the criterion. The wilderness generation did not keep their confidence firm, but became disobedient and turned back. Unbelief caused the disobedience and the exclusion from the land.

The first eleven verses of chapter 4 explain the nature of God's rest and the tragedy of the believer's failure to enter into it. Both the writer and the readers have had good tidings preached to them, just as did the wilderness generation, but lack of faith brought defeat to that generation. However, believers now are entering that rest. What is that rest? It is not the land of Canaan. It is primarily a future state of blessedness where the believer walks with God in harmony and peace. The believer is now entering that state but he does not possess it. This real rest, for which the Sabbath stood as a symbol, still awaits the people of God (v. 9). Those who have fully entered this rest have ceased from their earthly works (the tasks and activities that God has assigned) just as God rested from His works of creation (v. 10). We are exhorted to make every effort to enter into this rest and warned not to fail because of disobedience (v. 11).

In the familiar passage of 4:12 we see the Word of God, the Christian Gospel in all the breadth and scope of its teaching, pictured as the examiner of the reflections and thoughts of the heart. Not only does this Word of God judge the heart, but God Himself judges (v. 13). Nothing is hidden from His eyes. This should make the Christian alert to the serious dangers of unbelief and inspire him to keep on in the Christian life until he reaches God's eternal rest.

III. The Priesthood of Jesus Christ (4:14—10:18)

This section deals with the *work* of Christ, Whose exalted position is described in the first section. It answers the question: What meaning do the death and resurrection of Jesus have for the believer, and what meaning do they have in the program of God?

1. Importance of His Priesthood for Personal Conduct (4:14–16)

Note the importance of Christ's ascension. As great High Priest, Jesus has ascended through the heavens. In the light of this fact, the believer is constantly to hold fast his profession. Jesus can sympathize with us in our weaknesses because He personally was put to the test in all respects and in a similar manner to us "yet without sin." Does this mean simply "without a sinful nature or condition" or "without committing any sin?" The former would mean that Christ was put to the test in every way we are, except that no temptation came to Him from a nature that was inclined away from God. The latter would mean that Christ was put to the test in every way we are without surrendering to these pressures and sinning. Most authorities favor the latter because it stresses Christ's victory. Such an high priest gives us confidence to come before God in prayer to receive mercy and find grace.

2. Qualifications of a High Priest (5:1–10)

The writer begins by discussing the priesthood of Aaron (5:1–4) and lists the characteristics essential for Levitical priests. An important one was the ability to deal with sinners—those who were ignorant and wandering astray—because the priest himself was beset by such weaknesses. Since the priest had to be physically perfect, such weakness was not of a physical nature, but rather moral and spiritual. Because of such defects, the priest offered sacrifice both for himself and for the people.

The writer then sets forth the characteristics of Christ as our High Priest. He, like the Levitical priests, was appointed to His office. A clause from Psalm 2:7, "Today have I begotten thee," is applied to Jesus with the meaning, "This day I have appointed you to the office of a priest." Although Christ was a priest in one sense when He was upon earth, He really began His priestly service at His ascension. Jesus in the days of His flesh was a priest forever.

Like Melchizedek, Jesus went through soul-searching experiences in the process of sacrifice. His manner of praying indicates the pressure of life's experiences. He prayed with loud crying and tears to the One Who was able to bring Him safely through the experience of death (5:7). This is the meaning of the phrase "to save from death." The fact that Jesus is said "to learn obedience" and "to be made perfect" does not mean He was disobedient before or morally imperfect at an earlier time. Rather, He learned to obey in the sphere of man, in which He had never lived before. In doing this He became complete. He directly experienced what it is to live as a man.

3. Warning: Immaturity and Apostasy are Conquered only by Faith, Longsuffering, and Hope (5:11—6:20a)

At this point in the epistle, we see the readers clearly. We view their weaknesses and their strengths. Their weaknesses can become worse; their virtues can be strengthened. The readers are urged to awake out of lethargy and to respond alertly.

Condition of the Readers (5:11–14). The writer has much to say about Christ being designated a high priest like Melchizedek. However, it is difficult for him to expound this theme because of the condition of his readers (vv. 10, 11). Instead of being mature so that they could teach others, they themselves need to be taught elementary principles. These principles are found in the sum total of God's revealing self-disclosures and dealings with His people. The readers need milk—the elementary principles—rather than solid food—the more advanced teaching. Spiritual diet is determined by the use of the Christian's spiritual faculties. Constantly exercised, they develop sharp discernment between good and evil.

Call for Advance on the Part of the Readers (6:1–3). The opening words of chapter 6 are majestic: "Wherefore having left the elementary teaching about Christ, let us move ourselves on towards maturity." The believer must be constantly moving toward this goal of maturity. The foundation has been laid, so there is no need to re-lay it.

The foundation consists of six teachings grouped in three pairs. The first two—repentance and faith—go together. Repentance represents the negative side of conversion—the turning away from dead works or legalism. Faith represents the positive side of conversion—a trust in God. This is one of the few places in the New Testament where "repentance" has a purely negative note. Almost always it implies a change of mind that constitutes the beginning of a new religious and moral life (cf. Lk. 24:27; Heb. 6:6; II Pet. 3:9).

The next pair are "baptisms" and "laying on of hands." "Baptisms" (ablutions, RSV) is plural since at the inauguration of the Christian faith there were three kinds of baptism: Jewish proselyte baptism, the baptism of John, and Christian baptism. The laying on of hands was a solemn practice of the Church during its early days. Perhaps this teaching focuses upon the bestowal of the Holy Spirit (cf. Acts 8:15, 18; 19:5).

The last two foundational elements are the resurrection and eternal judgment.

In verse 3 we see the writer's dependence upon God. We will move ourselves toward maturity, if God permits. Were God to call some of the readers to His presence, they would come as immature rather than mature Christians.

Condition of Others who Fell Away (6:4–8). In contrast to those who are going on to maturity are others known to the writer who fell away from their experiences of divine grace. None of the readers were in this group (v. 9), but the writer tells about these as a warning so that none of these readers would thus depart. The latest Greek lexicon (Bauer) translates the word "taste" as "come to know." Thus before these fell away they had: (*1*) received a once-for-all enlightenment (cf. Eph. 1:18; 3:9); (*2*) come to know the heavenly gift (on the word "gift" see Jn. 4:10; Rom. 5:15, 17); (*3*) become sharers of the Holy Spirit (on the word "sharer," see Heb. 2:14; 3:1, 14; 12:8); (*4*) come to know the nobility of the Gospel; (*5*) come to know the miracles of the age to come; and (*6*) experienced renewal (v. 6). The phrase "to renew again" states clearly that these were once re-

Melchizedek's Life and Personality in the Old Testament (6:20b—7:3). The life of Melchizedek is summarized in Genesis 14:17–20. He was a Canaanite, yet he feared God. The city which later became Jerusalem was his capital. He was both a priest and a king. His superiority to Abraham is shown in that Abraham paid tithes to him. When Abraham obeyed God's call and traveled from Ur of Chaldees to Canaan, he did not know that he would find a fellow believer in God Who made the heavens and the earth. Nothing is said in the Old Testament record about Melchizedek's birth or death. No genealogy is mentioned, not even his parents. So far as the Old Testament record is concerned, Melchizedek has constancy and permanence, and thus bears strong resemblance to the Son of God.

Melchizedek's Superiority to the Levitical Priesthood (7:4–10). The writer of Hebrews defends this superiority of Melchizedek to the priesthood of Levi on the ground that Levi and his posterity were descendants of Abraham. Abraham paid tithes to Melchizedek and received a blessing from Melchizedek. Melchizedek is pictured in the Old Testament record as one who lives. Levi, because his great grandfather paid tithes to Melchizedek, is regarded as himself paying tithes. This concept of family solidarity is hard for us to understand. Levi, though not individually present when Abraham paid tithes to Melchizedek, was potentially the offspring of Abraham, and the family traits were already in evidence and functioning. Because of this concept of family solidarity, Levi is looked upon as paying tithes.

Christ's Superiority to the Levitical Priesthood (7:11–28). The Levitical priesthood brought no perfection. If it had, there would have been no need for Jesus to arise from other than Aaron's descendants. But the coming of Jesus as a priest meant a change in the law. Jesus was from the tribe of Judah—not from the tribe of Levi. The law said nothing about the tribe of Judah in connection with the priesthood. A human commandment brought about the consecration of a priest in the Levitical priesthood. Jesus became a priest because of His indestructible life and His inherent nature.

The Levitical priesthood was abolished (7:18) because the law, which put this priesthood into operation, did not bring perfection. But the better hope, which took the place of the Levitical law, does bring perfection. The solemn oath of God by which Jesus was initiated into the priesthood made Jesus a priest forever. An eternal priesthood, of course, means an eternal covenant. Jesus is the guarantee of the validity of this covenant. Death cut off the ministry of the Levitical priests. Because Jesus abides forever, His priesthood is permanent.

What can He do as a priest, and what kind of a priest is He? He can save for all time those who come to God through Him (7:25). The present tense of the participle "coming" shows that those whom Jesus saves for all time are those who constantly come to God through Him. Christians who are not in the process of drawing near to God at all times act as if their allegiance and interest were to someone else or something else. Jesus' holiness as a priest is described in verse 26. The uniqueness of His sacrifice is stressed in verse 27; by offering Himself once for all, He dealt with sin. This work brought Him to a state of being perfect or complete, a state He will have forever.

5. The Heavenly Sanctuary and the New Covenant (8:1–13)

Where does Jesus carry on His priestly ministry? What covenant does He administer?

The writer of Hebrews, in summarizing chapter 7, says that the kind of high priest we have is one Who has taken His seat at the right hand of God's throne in the heavens. He is the minister of the true tent or tabernacle that the Lord set up. The earthly tabernacle is said to have the heavenly or true tabernacle as its model. Moses constructed the earthly tabernacle according to the plan that would best set forth the holiness of God. Heaven is a real place, but it is not an earthly place. God, though omnipresent, chooses to reveal Himself in a particular heavenly place. There Christ carries on His ministry. But since the nature of heaven and its glories are quite beyond our comprehension, we must not think of the earthly tabernacle as being a replica of the heavenly reality. It was the best that could be done to convey God's holiness. But our own future experience will show how dimly upon earth we grasped the majesty of God and the heavenly sphere which is the proper background for that majesty.

The covenant that Christ administers is one that had been known for a long time. God announced it to Jeremiah during the Exile (Jer. 31:31–34). In Hebrews 8:8, 10, this New Covenant, which Jeremiah described as being made with the house of Israel and the house of Judah (8:8), is announced in verse 10 as being with the house of Israel. The terms "Israel" (name of northern kingdom), "Judah" (name of southern kingdom), and "Israel" (name of a united kingdom) are terms by which Jeremiah describes the people of God in the Old Testament. In the fulfilment of this prophecy and in the inauguration of the New Covenant, the people of God are seen to be Jews *and* Gentiles who have believed in Jesus as Lord and Saviour —Christians. In Hebrews 10:15, Jeremiah 31:33 is again quoted with the explanation that the Holy Spirit is testifying to *us* in these words of Jeremiah. The New Covenant is the covenant of the Christian Church of which Christ is the head, and His shed blood guarantees its eternal validity. This New Covenant, says the writer of Hebrews (8:13) has made the Old Covenant obsolete, and that which is becoming obsolete is near destruction.

6. Priestly Service under the Old and New Covenants (9:1–28)

Chapter 9 explains what is involved in priestly service and what its results are.

Setting of the Priest's Ministry under the Old Covenant (9:1–10). In the opening verse, the stress is upon the earthly sanctuary. This is in contrast to where Christ serves (8:1–5). The writer then enumerates the furniture in the holy place and the most holy place. In verse 4, the most holy place is said to have the golden altar of incense. (Golden "censer" of King James is unfortunate since such an article is not mentioned in either the holy or most holy place by the Old Testament.) Although the golden altar of incense was located in the holy place, its function and purpose involved the presence of God in the most holy place. Hence, in a general way the most holy place had the service of this item of ritual furniture.

Continual service in the holy place is contrasted with the yearly service in the most holy place. This yearly service carries a great lesson. The Holy Spirit was showing that the way into the most holy place was not opened while the division between the holy and the most holy place prevailed. Here is a discerning observation; a barrier can testify as well as an opening. In the holy place, ceremonial cleansing was achieved, but never the perfecting of the worshipper's conscience. When a man's conscience testifies to God's broken standard, something needs to be done for the man or he will be engulfed by his sins. This relief was not brought by the gifts and sacrifices of the Old Testament.

Importance of Blood under Both Covenants (9:11–22). Now Christ has appeared. His High Priesthood is on the basis of good things that have come to be, namely, His atoning death. By means of the heavenly sanctuary and His own blood, He has obtained eternal redemption. Ceremonial rites brought ceremonial cleansing (v. 13). How much more does the blood of Christ bring the genuine cleansing that satisfies the conscience! As mediator of the New Covenant, Christ's death provided redemption from sins committed under the First Covenant. For a will to be in force, the testator must die. Christ, the mediator of the New Covenant, by His death put it into operation. The First Covenant was initiated and consecrated by blood. The writer of Hebrews adds some details about the inauguration of the First Covenant that are not found in the Old Testament (for example, the water, scarlet wool, and hyssop; the sprinkling of the tabernacle and all of the vessels of service with blood—cf. Ex. 24:1–6). These details emphasize the solemnity of the dedication of the First Covenant.

Setting of Christ's Ministry under the New Covenant (9:23–28). The heavenly realities where Christ now ministers as a priest are consecrated by Christ's sacrifice. Furthermore, He appears before the presence of God for us. He is there (v. 24) because He was manifested once upon earth at the consummation of the ages to annul or remove sin through His own sacrifice (v. 26). Christ was offered once for all (v. 28). His death can never be repeated. There can be no second dying for Christ, but there is a Second Coming of this one Who is both priest and sacrifice. When He comes again, it will not be to atone for sin. That ministry was completed the first time. Chapter 9 extends from the ritual of the First Covenant to the return of Christ to consummate salvation. Hence the setting of Christ's priestly ministry is both upon earth and in heaven. The basis was laid upon earth; the results are applied in heaven. Those results are consummated by the coming of Christ to those who are eagerly awaiting Him and the deliverance He will accomplish.

7. *Inadequacy of the Sacrifices under the Law Contrasted with the Efficacy and Finality of Christ's Sacrifice (10:1–18)*

The basic question here is: What sacrifices or sacrifice can take away sins?

The Old Testament sacrifices are looked upon as a shadow never ble to perfect those who come to present their offerings. Constant offering, argues the writer of Hebrews, indicates a lack of finality of result. To be in a cleansed state would remove the consciousness of unatoned-for sin. But the continual consciousness of this kind of sin brought the repeated offering of sacrifice. Here is remembrance of sin without removal.

What is the New Testament sacrifice and why is it effective? (10:5–18). Psalm 40:6–8 stresses two elements: (1) "a body thou hast prepared for me"; (2) the will of God. The English translations of Psalm 40:6 are from the Hebrew text, which may be translated "thou hast given me an open ear" (RSV) or "mine ears thou hast opened" (KJV). The writer of Hebrews follows the Septuagint, or Greek version of the Old Testament, that has the word body in place of ears. In this version, the psalmist shows his obedience by dedicating his body. In the Hebrew text of the Psalms, he shows his obedience by using his opened ears, that is, by listening. In a typical manner these words of the psalmist are looked upon as being spoken by Jesus when He comes into the world. God prepared a body for Jesus. This was God's will. Since the "prepared body" was part of God's will, God took away the sacrifices to establish His will—the offering of the body of Jesus Christ once for all (vv. 9, 10). The sacrifice is effective because it is final; Christ as a priest has taken His seat at the right hand of God. The standing position of the Levitical priests indicated the incompleteness of their work. By one offering God has brought to a position of completeness those who are being sanctified or consecrated. The New Testament sacrifice brings about the remission of sins so that they are no longer remembered. Hence this section on the priesthood of Christ ends with an exalted priest (vv. 12, 13), an effective offering (v. 14), a New Covenant in operation (vv. 15, 16), and a pardoned people— sins and iniquities forgiven (vv. 17, 18).

IV. The Perseverance of Christians (10:19—12:29)

How does the writer want his readers to respond to the truths he has set forth? This he carefully treats in the remainder of chapter 10, and in chapters 11 and 12.

1. Attitudes to be Sought; Attitudes to be Shunned (10:19–38)

This section deals with the responses of the readers. The writer praises those responses that make the readers stronger Christians.

Those that weaken or defeat are solemnly set forth with their possible consequences.

First, the reader is urged to act (10:19–25). The entrance into the sanctuary has been consecrated by the blood of Jesus. This new and living way was made possible by the humanity of Jesus Who is now our great High Priest. This means that the believer may come near or approach God with a true heart, full assurance, and purified within and without. He is to hold fast his profession and encourage his fellow believers. Since this can be done only in gatherings of believers, a Christian who isolates himself from fellow Christians jeopardizes his spiritual growth.

Next we face more warning similar to that in chapter 6 about the tragedy of apostasy (10:26–31). Two further experiences of divine grace on the part of the apostate are listed in this section: (1) He is said to have a knowledge of the truth. The Greek word could also be translated "full knowledge." (For the use of this word in the Pastoral Epistles, see I Tim. 2:4; II Tim. 2:24–26, especially v. 25; II Tim. 3:7; Tit. 1:1.) (2) He is said to have been sanctified. This is a positional sanctification (cf. I Cor. 6:11). The nature of the rebellion is further amplified: (a) "If we constantly sin deliberately" are words that describe a complete awareness of what is being done; (b) The apostate is pictured as having trampled under foot the Son of God—complete disdain; (c) He has come to consider the blood of Christ by which he was sanctified to be unclean; (d) last and worst of all, he has insulted the Spirit of grace. To thus insult the Holy Spirit in spite of all the experiences of divine grace certainly puts the sin here in the same category as the blasphemy against the Spirit on the part of the Pharisees (Mt. 12:31, 32; Mk. 3:28, 29). Mark describes the sin of the Pharisees as an eternal sin that could not be forgiven (Mk. 3:29). The writer of Hebrews says that for this kind of deliberate, wilful sinning, there is no more sacrifice for sin (no atonement), but rather a frightful expectation of judgment and a fury of fire that will devour such opponents (10:26, 27).

Note that these apostates or retractors do not satisfy the definition of the writer of Hebrews as to what it means to be a sharer of Christ. One has become a sharer of Christ, according to the writer of Hebrews, if he keeps his original confidence firm until the end of his life (3:14). So, although these retractors are said in chapter 6 to have become sharers or partakers of the Holy Spirit, they are never said to have had a lifelong allegiance to Christ. They did not abide or continue (cf. Jn. 15:2, 6; Rom. 11:22). In contrast, those who have a lifelong allegiance are constantly bringing forth fruit, listening to the voice of Jesus, and following Him (Jn. 15:5; 10:27). By making every effort to confirm or make certain their election (II Pet. 1:10) they demonstrate they are the elect of God.

After this solemn warning, the writer appeals to his readers to exhibit steadfast endurance (10:32–39). Such endurance was theirs through the trials that came to them immediately after their conversion. They are, therefore, not to throw away their confidence. Faith, not timidity, will bring them to their goal—a safekeeping of their soul.

2. Faith in Action—Illustrious Examples from the Past (11:1–40)

Faith is the confident assurance or title deed of what we hope for —a conviction about things that are not seen. Faith or trust in God is a reality that believing men exhibit in their earthly walk. This confident assurance is about things that, although not seen, are real. Faith is no leap into the dark. It is an affirmation that God has spoken, that God is, that God will do what He has promised.

The writer now takes up concrete examples of faith. The first group of men lived in the period from creation to Noah (11:4–7): Abel, Enoch, and Noah. The emphasis is on their faith and what they did. Abel's faith is seen in his sacrifice; Enoch's faith, in his pleasing life and his translation; Noah's faith, in the building of the ark. This pattern is followed throughout the chapter. This is the kind of faith that James and Paul talk about—a faith that works.

The second period, extending from Abraham to Joseph (11:8–22), stresses the importance of faith among the partriarchs. In the lives of Abraham, Isaac, and Jacob, the founding fathers of the Jewish theocracy, another important characteristic of faith comes to light. Not only does faith work, but it has the capacity to look beyond the present. This affects life in the present. Abraham was expecting a city whose designer and craftsman was God (v. 10). Abraham, Sarah, Isaac, and Jacob did not receive the promise, but in the light of the promise they confessed that they were strangers and sojourners upon the earth. Their awareness of another realm affected their earthly life.

The next period deals with only one man—the place of faith in the life of Moses (11:23–29). Several phases of his life are mentioned:

his birth, his voluntary identification with his own people after being reared and educated by the daughter of Pharaoh, the intervention of God in connection with the first Passover and the crossing of the Red Sea. There is paradox involved in true faith. This was certainly true of Moses who endured as seeing the One Who is invisible (v. 27). With such perception, Moses courageously brought the Israelites from Egypt to Palestine on the east of Jordan.

The last period covers twelve or thirteen centuries, extending from the Exodus to Maccabean times (11:29–38). The unnamed heroes of faith are as important as the named ones. Believers from the times of the Maccabean struggles are recognized. (For the necessary historical background to understand 11:35b, see the apocryphal work, II Maccabees 6:18–31 and 7:1–42.) A trust in God and basic conviction about the hereafter and life on this earth certainly characterize these men and women. They lived in great physical deprivation, but they had committed themselves to God without reservation and therefore they had the essential for life in time and eternity.

In the last two verses of the chapter (11:39, 40) the writer of Hebrews shows that men of faith of all ages are bound together. The saints of the Old Covenant would not have been made perfect (11:40; cf. 9:15) without God's action in Christ many years later.

3. *Incentives for Action in the Present and in the Future (12:1–29)*

The last verse of chapter 11 has the phrase "without us" or "apart from us." This brings the writer back to his present readers.

The record he has reviewed provides a great host of witnesses. This example is to give incentive for the readers to run the race with perseverance. Another incentive is the example of Jesus. Consideration of Jesus and His earthly life should dispel any weariness on the part of believers. Still another incentive is the discipline of God because it shows that God is treating us as sons. He wants us to share His holiness. The "afterward" of chastening for the Christian is the peaceful fruit that righteousness bears.

The Christian is not to be a cripple, but is to march straight forward, striving for peace and sanctification. We are to strive earnestly for sanctification in the strength that God provides. Passivity has no place in the believer's character. He must not allow anything to embitter him because he remembers the downward track of Esau. In contrast to Mount Sinai, the believer comes to Mount Zion, that is, the heavenly Jerusalem. He comes to hosts of angels in festal assembly. He comes to a collective group—the Church of firstborn ones having been enrolled in heaven. He comes to God, the judge of all. He comes to individual believers—the spirits of just men having been made perfect. He comes to Jesus, the mediator of the New Covenant. He comes to an atonement—the blood of Jesus that far surpasses the sacrificial blood that Abel poured out. Having such a prospect and belonging to a kingdom (the reign and rule of God) that cannot be shaken, the believer serves God in awe and reverence.

V. Postscript: Exhortations, Personal Concerns, Benediction (13:1–25)

The last chapter shows the loving relationship that existed between the author and his readers. They must exercise hospitality. Marriage must be kept holy both by conduct before marriage and in marriage. The imperative should certainly be supplied in verse 4: "Let marriage be honorable . . . let the marriage bed be undefiled because. . . ." Contentment, not covetousness, is to characterize Christians. They are to remember their former spiritual leaders—their message and manner of life (13:7).

Devotion to the unchanging Christ is the guide for conduct. The "yesterday" of verse 8 goes back to the incarnation, the "today" represents the time of writing, and the "forever" includes eternity future. Jesus will be the God-man forever. He was not the God-man for eternity past. Therefore, when God's Son became man, it was the climax of revelation, and it is only right that we should count time from this event. The altar of verse 10 is the cross, the sacrifice was Jesus Himself (v. 12). Knowing the meaning of this sacrifice, we should gladly bear Christ's reproach. Doing good and showing generosity are "the offerings" that the Christian provides as he seeks to be well-pleasing to God. Obedience to their present spiritual leaders is urged. Finally, the writer asks prayer for himself.

The doxology of verses 20 and 21 is now very famous. The stress is upon the resurrection. The writer emphasizes that the blood of the New Covenant is the blood of an Eternal Covenant. The wish that God may work in the readers is beautifully expressed.

The writer describes his whole epistle (13:22) as a word of exhortation. With Timothy, he plans to visit the readers. The fact that the letter includes greetings of those from Italy favors the view that the writer was outside of Italy. If we were writing from the United States, it would be strange to say, "Those from the United States send greetings." But if we were writing from Borneo, the phrase, "Those from the United States send greetings" would make good sense since the number would be so few.

Throughout the centuries, as men have read Hebrews, they have known that the grace of God has reached not only the original readers, but all who have since reflected upon its profound message.

James

STEPHEN WM. PAINE

THE EPISTLE DECLARES itself to be the writing of James. Three persons of this name are mentioned in the New Testament. However, James the son of Joseph and Mary, half brother of our Lord, is accredited historically by the Christian Church as the author of this epistle.

Reared in the same godly Jewish family with Jesus, James in his teaching presents a striking resemblance to our Lord. A comparison of this epistle with the Sermon on the Mount quickly reveals at least a dozen clear parallelisms. Chosen as the moderator of the Jerusalem church subsequent to Pentecost, James gave to his epistle a note of unassuming authority. Devoid of all apology, its 108 verses contain fifty-four commands.

Clearly Christian in its acknowledgment of the claims of Christ (1:1; 2:1, 7), and in its reference to the Second Coming (1:12; 5:7, 8), and to personal regeneration through faith (1:18, 21), the epistle is reminiscent of the teaching in the so-called "wisdom literature" of the Old Testament as seen in Job, in some of the Psalms, and in Proverbs and Ecclesiastes. It places the good and the evil in juxtaposition, and speaks on the fundamental theme of "pure" religion.

The author has in view the faithful believers who are an example of pure religion under test and trial. These he encourages. James also has in view the more fleshly and self-seeking, whose conduct shows them as failing the test of pure religion. These he rebukes. But throughout the epistle, true heart-religion, whether as *tested* in the lives of the faithful or as *testing* and judging the lives of the carnal, is the theme of this book.

James makes repeated use of paradox as he asserts the superiority of the spiritual values so commonly unrealized. Thus James tells of two kinds of faith, two kinds of wisdom, two kinds of temptation, two kinds of confidence, two kinds of self. These will be noted as they occur in the development of the theme. James is practical and nontheological in emphasis. His first chapter, which speaks of God's program of actual sanctification in the believer, sets forth in minature the topics to be treated more fully in the remaining chapters.

I. God's Purpose, the Believer's Advancement in Pure Religion (1:1–27)

1. Temptation that Builds: Helpful and Harmful Testing (1:1–12)

The apostolic greeting, addressed "to the twelve tribes of the dispersion," indicates that this general epistle has especially in mind the Jewish Christians who had been dispersed from Jerusalem as a result of the persecutions of the early Church (cf. Acts 8:1, 4).

James refers to the sufferings of these Christian refugees, declaring the paradox that these are cause for rejoicing (1:2; cf. Mt. 5:11, 12). He calls them "testings" and goes on to say that they are equivalent to a "proving" of their faith, which is "meticulously working out" the end result of *patience* or *endurance* in them (v. 3).

The believers are to hold steady under the process (1:4), letting this patience come to its completion, imparting to them a wholeness and maturity of character with no qualitative spiritual deficiency (cf. Rom. 5:3–5).

This obedient and patient submission to testing, and to God Who purposefully permits it, implies a certain wisdom of the Spirit (1:5) —quite foreign to worldly wisdom—a wisdom imparted only by God in response to the believer's petition, that petition couched in terms of a faith (v. 6) which is not marred by indecision or inner quibbling and mixed ambition (true wisdom and false).

The one who, contrary to the above injunction, oscillates between self-concern and spiritual aspiration is likened to the wave which, with no motive power of its own, reaches sharply for the shore only to recede in futility. Such seeking will get nothing from God (1:7). It only points to a certain duality of the spiritual personality amounting to civil war in the heart. Such a one is a "two-souled man" (v. 8) and an "unsettled" Christian in every respect (the fleshly and the spiritual self).

Still on the topic of personal holiness through testing (cf. Heb. 12:9, 10), James notes (1:9) that the "brother of low degree," the Christian of humble circumstances is, contrary to common thought, in a much more advantageous position for spiritual advancement ("exaltation"). He may almost boast (a closer translation than *rejoice*) in his poor station. The wealthy, too (vv. 10, 11), if he is spiritually discerning, will find grounds for glorying in the humiliating characteristics of his station, namely, the fleeting quality of wealth, yes, of life itself. And James recalls the Old Testament symbol for the shortness of human tenure, the verdant grass (cf. Ps. 90:5, 6; Is. 40:6, 7). Thus James inserts another of his key thoughts, that of true confidence and false.

He closes his homily upon the temptation that builds with the use of a beatitude (1:12) declaring that he who has patiently endured the temptation, that is, the trial or test, having shown himself approved (better than *tried*), shall receive the "crown of life." And meaningful indeed is the addendum that this crown is advertised for those who love God with divine love, or *agape*.

2. Temptation that Destroys: Helpful and Harmful Testing (1:13–16)

Now passing to temptation in the sense of incitement to evil (1:13), he declares that this kind of temptation is not to be attributed to God, but rather (v. 14) to the seducing (*drawing, dragging*) power of strong natural desire. Here again is the intimation of conflict in one's "drives," of spiritual duality. This self-centered desire is present at birth (v. 15), and sin "when full grown" (cf. the "full grown" work of patience, v. 4) begets death. And the apostle adds with emphasis, "Make no mistake about it" (v. 16).

3. God Himself the Believer's Chief Good: True and False Confidence (1:17, 18)

The thought of enrichment, advancement, is strong in this chapter. The word "to receive" occurs several times; the word "to lack," as well. The matter of earthly wealth is adduced as a negative example. There is a warning against "strong natural desire" as making temptation lethal instead of edifying.

Now James summarizes this doctrine with the declaration (1:17) that God is the believer's chief good, and that every good endowment and gift is from Him Who is called the "Father of lights" and of Whom it is said that He changes not.

4. *Consequent Exhortation to Personal Holiness (1:19–27)*

In the light of the lessons learned in the school of adversity, James now enjoins a spirit of obedience which shall be keen to hear, to sense the will of God (1:19), moderate in self assertion through speech, restrained in wrath—so damaging to the Christian's testimony (v. 20). In fact, he proceeds to the root of the matter, urging them to put away (v. 21) the spiritual uncleanness of self-will, thus becoming capable of receiving in humility the implanted life-giving word (true and false wisdom).

This probity of heart will, if genuine, issue in practical righteousness (true and false faith). James warns his readers against a rationalizing spectatorship of divine truth (v. 22). He wants them to be doers of the Word (*poets of the word,* Greek). He adduces the simile of the man who idly glances at his face in a mirror with no real purpose (vv. 23, 24). He clarifies his earlier reference to "the word" by identifying it now with the law, which he calls "the perfect law of liberty" (v. 25).

James closes this initial chapter, a survey of pure religion, with the assertion that this pure religion is not an appearance of piety (vv. 26, 27), but the ability to be restrained in speech and compassionate to the needy. It involves as well a separation from the defilement of the world's point of view.

III. Tests of Pure Religion (2:1—5:20)

1. *Test of Self-seeking Partiality: True and False Confidence; Fleshly and Spiritual Self (2:1–13)*

James now attacks a problem which he has noted in the churches and which he feels demonstrates a breach of pure religion. This is the practice of ingratiating deference to persons of wealth or rank. The cause for such partiality would be some form of self-seeking (fleshly and spiritual self, 2:4), some hope for advantage (true and false confidence).

James' appeal to the "royal law" (2:8), as also to the "law of liberty," seems to be a reference to divine love as the heart of the law, the law *par excellence.* Compare Jesus' epitome (Mt. 22:36–40; Jn.

13:34) and that of Paul (Rom. 13:9, 10; Gal. 5:14). This "royal law" of divine love, he avers, is the only basis of social conduct which does not yield condemnation (v. 9), and this law of love abhors partiality (cf. Mt. 5:44–48). Their defection from this law of love is not to be excused lightly on any basis of "general average" of righteousness (vv. 10, 11) for it is an index of obedience. The believer must adopt a standard of complete probity as judged by the "law of liberty," the law of love (v. 12). He who defects from loving mercy must be judged by unyielding law (v. 13).

2. Test of Faith Operative through Love: True and False Faith (2:14–26)

James is still testing pure religion by the law of love as he turns to the area of faith, declaring that mere religious confidence, mere intellectual assent is devoid of saving power (2:14).

He cites as an example of such "faith" the idle good wishes of the man whose heart does not stir him to loving provision for a needy brother (2:15–17), or the futile and ethically meaningless assent of eternally committed evil spirits, as to the existence of God (v. 19). With the challenge to his readers, "Do you wish to know?" that is, "Are you considering the cost to yourself of such knowledge?" he refers to the positive examples of Abraham (vv. 21–24) and of Rahab (v. 25) who demonstrated the heart-quality of their faith by appropriate deeds.

3. Test of Love as an Approach to Life: True and False Wisdom (3:1–18)

James now approaches the matter of pure heart religion from another angle as he brings into juxtaposition and contrast the two basic methods for success, first that of fleshly self-seeking, then that of spiritual self-giving. He opens with a warning against assumed superiority of wisdom, "Don't all of you be teachers, lest this be an occasion for inner condemnation" (3:1). He then proceeds at once to the point of the Christian's speech, his tongue, as an index of his spirituality.

The man of restrained speech is seen as spiritually mature (3:2). The controlling power of bit and bridle with a horse (v. 3), or of a ship's rudder (v. 4), or the cruciality of a small incipient fire in a great pile of wood (v. 5) is compared with the cardinal importance of the tongue. The tongue is rightly pointed out as an apt avenue for Satan's inroads, an accurate index of carnality of spirit (v. 6). Nor is there human deliverance from this scourge (v. 7). Despite the fact that every *nature* (more accurate than *kind*) of beasts, birds, serpents and sea animals has been subjugated by *human nature,* here is a demonstration of that human nature which itself defies man's power of subjugation, poisonous to self and to others (v. 8).

The matter of duality, of inner conflict, is again suggested (fleshly and spiritual self). Here is an individual capable of benediction, of benignity and love, yet at times guilty of contradictory and nullifying passions (3:10). This sad and undesirable situation betokens a lack of that unity of identity shown in nature by the fountain which always produces one kind of water or by the fig tree and the vine which can always be depended upon for their characteristic fruit (vv. 11, 12).

The direct appeal is now made for a true wisdom of "beautiful behavior" (good conversation) and meekness (3:13), rather than that "bitter self-seeking zeal" as a heart characteristic which in confusion nullifies good works by evil (vv. 14–16). Here is no cause for preening oneself on getting his own way, nor for covering over one's spiritual need, for such is an "earthly, natural, demonic" rationale or kind of wisdom.

In all this James parallels very closely the Old Testament teachings which depict wisdom as unrelated to temporal success (Prov. 17:16), as evading the scornful (Prov. 14:6), the self-confident (Prov. 28:26), the wrathful (Prov. 14:29), and as depending upon their fulfilment in Christ.

Like a dish of beautiful, luscious fruit, James sets forth the contrastingly pure heavenly wisdom (3:17, 18) with its integrating unity of divine love. Compare the fruit of the Spirit described in Galatians 5:22, or the qualities of divine *agape* delineated in I Corinthians 13. Here is none other than personal permeation by the Holy Ghost, the indwelling Christ, "who of God is made unto us wisdom" (I Cor. 1:30).

4. Test of Selfish Faction: Fleshly and Spiritual Self (4:1–12)

Like a storm breaking out from an ugly black cloud, the spectacle of shameful self-seeking and faction now bursts upon the reader.

The controlling hues are eager, rapacious desire accompanied by the paradox of poverty and barrenness (4:1, 2). Here too is absence of prayer, the spiritual means of enrichment, and the blight of prayer unanswered because of self-condemning carnality (v. 3; cf. I Cor. 3:1–3).

Here too is the corollary of kinship with the world (4:4), a secret yearning for its smile which amounts to nothing less than unfaithfulness, coolness of heart, toward the heavenly Bridegroom—a treacherous duality of spirit. James' reproachful epithet "unfaithful spouses" occurs in the feminine only, perhaps a token that the unfaithfulness is against Christ, the Church's divine husband.

Verse 5 is a passage of great difficulty. Some careful Biblical scholars do not believe this was intended as an Old Testament reference, for the quotation appears nowhere in Scripture. We incline to follow this point of view, which would conclude the discussion of spiritual unfaithfulness in verse 4 with the challenge, "Do you think that the scripture speaks to no effect?" Undoubtedly James is thinking of such Old Testament references to spiritual adultery as the often repeated formula "Israel went awhoring" and the parables of Jeremiah 13:27, Ezekiel 23, Hosea 2, and elsewhere.

Verse 5 then continues, "Does the Spirit which he made to dwell in us earnestly yearn to envy?" The implied answer is a negative, and James continues, "But he [the Spirit] gives more grace." Then follows the quotation from Proverbs 3:34, reflecting the Septuagint translation, "The Lord resisteth the proud; but he granteth favour to the humble."

To this humility before God and resistance to Satan (4:7), he now calls his readers. Let them with resolution address themselves to God (v. 8) Who will meet their seeking more than halfway. Let them confess their misdeeds and open up their carnally divided hearts to the cleansing of the Holy Spirit (cf. Ps. 24:3–5). As they thus yield themselves to God (cf. Rom. 12:1, 2), they may expect a melting of spirit, a holy yearning and hunger (v. 9), which through humbling will dissolve in great spiritual exaltation.

This, then, will be the divine solution for "the strife of tongues." And against the background of this spiritual cleansing, James re-iterates the caution against evil speaking and judging one another (4:10), equating such to a disregard of, an assumption of superiority to, the law of love (v. 11), a usurpation of the prerogative of God (v. 12) Who alone is able to judge with complete wisdom, and Who holds all human life in His loving hand.

5. *Test of Self-Willed Life Direction: True and False Confidence (4:13–17)*

James next addresses himself to another manifestation of fleshliness, the impudence of those presuming to make plans without deference to the will of God, governed only by a preoccupation for personal gain (4:13). He reminds them of the tentativeness of life itself (v. 14), in view of which all plans should be related to the will of God (v. 15), apart from which the making of plans is to "boast in your buffoonery" (v. 16; "rejoice in your boastings," KJV), this being a form of wickedness. Those who have this knowledge but who fail to heed it are guilty of sin (v. 17).

6. *Test of Charity in the Acquisition and Stewardship of Wealth: True and False Confidence (5:1–6)*

James now addresses those whose preoccupation has been the laying up of earthly riches even to the point of sharp dealing and fraud. He calls them to bewail the paradox of lost investment (5:1–3). Their treasures have proved perishable (v. 2; cf. Mt. 6:19, 20; Lk. 6:24, 25); and even worse, the rust of their hoarded wealth will be a destructive witness against them (v. 3).

They laid up treasure in the last days, in the very shadow of approaching judgment, and that by defrauding their employees (5:4), whose cries of injustice have already reached the ears of the judge, none other than the Lord of hosts. In contrast with the suffering and want of their workers, they themselves have been pampered and have lived in luxury (v. 5). They have also had a share in persecuting the Gospel, even to the extent of the death sentence (cf. 2:6, 7).

7. *Test of Patience under Oppression: Helpful and Harmful Testing (5:7–11)*

The writer turns from the false confidence of the unjustly wealthy to the true confidence of those who hold steady under unjust trial, encouraged by the thought of Christ's Second Coming (5:7). He reminds them of the slowness—and certainty—of the maturing harvest (vv. 8, 9,). The very thought of harvest, and of the imminence of judgment, should deter them from grumbling and evil speaking.

James mentions the prophets of old as examples of discipline under hardness (5:10), those whom men nowadays beatify (v. 11), and he cites Job particularly, who so aptly illustrates God's basic tenderness and purposefulness in testing,

8. Test of Restraint in Commitments: True and False Confidence (5:12)

The warning against the use of oaths in stating what one will or will not do seems kindred to the teaching in 4:13–17. Who can be certain enough about the future to make grand and sweeping commitments? Recall Jesus' warning in the Sermon on the Mount (Mt. 5:34–37). Both heaven and earth and the city of Jerusalem (a frequent reference in oaths), yes, even the hairs of their own heads (also mentioned in oaths) lay in the province of God's discretion. To ignore this would involve inner condemnation.

9. Test of Prevailing Prayer: True and False Confidence (5:13–20)

James closes his epistle on the note of divine love demonstrating itself in prevailing prayer. The one who suffers ill should betake himself to prayer (5:13); the one who is of good spirits should raise a psalm of praise. The Christian afflicted with illness should place full confidence in God (v. 14) and should also draw upon the faith of those in whose godliness he has confidence (recall Jesus' words, "Where two of you shall agree . . . ," Mt. 18:19). The act of anointing gives point to faith. The promise of forgiveness as well as healing bespeaks the condition of tenderness and openness on the part of the afflicted, as does also the added injunction to mutual prayer and confession of faults as a prelude to answered prayer (v. 16). Here again is the tender atmosphere of *agape*, selfless divine love. The well-known mighty answers to prayer obtained by Elijah, so truly human, are adduced as an encouragement to faith (vv. 17, 18).

The theme of the prevailing prayer of divine love seems to extend finally to verses 19 and 20, where the intercessor is seen as bringing about the winning of the backslider with its eternal gain of a saved soul and sins forgiven. Here then is the beautiful climax of James' inspired discussion of "pure religion," the religion of outflowing, Spirit-implanted (cf. Rom. 5:5) divine love.

I Peter

ROBERT PAUL ROTH

THIS BEAUTIFUL LETTER was written to Christians in Asia Minor to stimulate in them a joyful hope in the face of coming persecution.

I. Peter's Greeting to His Readers (1:1, 2)

In this remarkable introductory greeting Peter follows the sensible, ancient custom of first introducing himself and then naming his

1201

readers. As an apostle, that is, one sent out with power and authority to represent the One Who has commissioned him, the Lord Jesus Christ, he is writing to the "exiles of the dispersion." Peter applied this technical Jewish phrase to Christians generally with new meaning. Just as the Jews outside Palestine considered themselves in exile, since they perpetually found their hope and destiny in the Promised Land, so now Christians in a deeper sense consider themselves exiles and strangers in this world, since their hope and destiny is in the Kingdom of Heaven which Christ bought with His blood. Not only are they strangers in this world, but they are also scattered in various places for a specific purpose in God's predestined plan.

For this Kingdom they must wait in hope, but in the meantime they have been chosen and predestined by God for "obedience to Jesus Christ and for sprinkling of his blood." Predestination involves neither fatalism nor philosophical determinism. It is the work of God by which He chooses, calls, and gathers us into a holy band for the purpose of bringing salvation to the world. God calls us to witness of Christ before we even think of coming to Him. Predestination therefore involves a holy task in which we are consecrated by the Spirit to share in the saving work of Christ by the sacrament of His blood. That this alludes to the ratification of the Covenant at Sinai (Ex. 24:7) is obvious to Peter's readers. After Moses received the promise of the people to be obedient to the Covenant of God which he had read to them, he sprinkled the blood of the sacrificial oxen on the altar, thus binding the people irrevocably to God in the Covenant of His Word. So now in the blood shed on Calvary, Christians are irrevocably bound to Christ so that they may abundantly receive His grace and peace.

II. The Trinitarian Doxology (1:3–12)

As Paul did in the Epistle to the Ephesians (Eph. 1:3–14), Peter opens this letter with a doxology that extols the magnificence of the entire Godhead. For each special gift from each person of the Trinity, we are admonished to give a special response.

The Father offers providential *care* (1:3–5). By His mercy and power we are kept for an inheritance "imperishable, undefiled, and unfading." A condition of this inheritance is that we are born anew according to the principle Jesus announced to Nicodemus, "Unless one is born of water and the Spirit, he cannot enter the kingdom of God" (Jn. 3:5). Because of this merciful care, we remain *hopeful* in the midst of the fiery trials that beset us.

The gift of the Son Jesus Christ is always wrapped in the paradox of *suffering* (1:6–9). The only begotten Son came into the world to suffer rejection and death, and the very hour of humiliation was His hour of greatest *glory* (Jn. 17:1). Far from seeking to escape pain and oppression, Christians must accept suffering joyfully knowing that through such discipline their faith is made sure and the outcome is the certain salvation of their souls. This too is the Christian's glory. As Paul says: "Now I rejoice in my sufferings for your sake" (Col. 1:24).

The Holy Spirit *reveals* the Word of God to us in a paradox. Christ's glory, hidden in humiliation, is received by us with great *rejoicing* (1:10–12). Indeed, the Christian can sing in his sadness and laugh through his tears because he knows that victory will be his at the last day. The Christian neither mourns the past nor fears the future, because the presence of the Spirit tells him that the past is resurrected in the first coming of Jesus Christ and the future is sealed in the second. Although the Spirit's revelation rests on eyewitness testimony, yet faith is not in things seen but in the inner witness which recognizes that certain great promises of God have been fulfilled in Jesus of Nazareth (cf. II Pet. 1:19). While our modern critical scholars customarily look for that which is new and unique in the Christian message—and indeed the Christian Gospel is ever fresh and new to an aged and dying world—it is significant that the earliest Christians authenticated their message by declaring Jesus to be the fulfilment of that which was old. The same Spirit that guided the ancient children of Abraham now comforts Christians.

III. Our Relation to God (1:13—2:10)

1. Be Holy in All Your Conduct, for He is Holy (1:13–16)

Christian conduct ("conversation" in KJV is obsolete) never precedes but always follows the speech of God. After the great doxology comes the "therefore" of Peter's exhortation to holiness. Because God is holy and has spoken to us in His holiness, we can be exhorted to holiness; that is, the indicative of God's sanctifying act precedes the imperative of human conduct. This is the reverse of human thinking about our behavior. Emerson, for example, says: "When duty whispers low, 'Thou must!' the youth replies, 'I can.'" But the Gospel says: "God, who is holy, has made you holy; therefore you must be what you are!" Everything we are exhorted to do rests upon what God has done in Christ, both in Calvary's redemption of the past and in the coming grace of the last day. We love God because He first loved us (I Jn. 4:19); therefore, be not conformed to this world and its lusts, but be transformed according to the holiness of Christ (Rom. 12:2). This world is headed for decay and death. If we cling to it, drawn by its compelling temptations, we shall go down with it. But the holy God is coming. Set your hope firmly in Him and act according to that hope, for it is alive and will never die.

2. *Conduct Yourselves with Fear, for You Were Ransomed with Blood (1:17-21)*

When men demand a god whom they need not fear, they get an idol which they cannot respect. This point is brought home in the fable of the frogs who asked Jupiter for a king. When a log dropped into their pond, they leaped for shelter. Soon they hopped closer and closer to this dead thing, and finally they jumped all over it and sat upon it with comfortable familiarity. While God is above, loving and merciful, He is never familiar in the sense that He can be taken for granted.

God is our Father, but those who in the Spirit call Him Father will conduct themselves in awe and respect for His judgments. He is no respecter of persons; He is utterly impartial. In the original Greek, the words suggest a metaphor taken from the theatre in which the characters of a play—the *dramatis personae*—come out with various masks. God is the critic who judges us not by the masks we wear in our play-acting, but rather by the holiness which is bestowed upon us through the resurrected Christ. Those who walk in Christ have the marks of Christ upon them, and they are recognized by God as His children by the works they do. They are known by God Who sees beneath the paint and powder of this world's theatrics. Indeed, the faces we wear to the world are only Halloween horrors before God. Hidden to the world but revealed to God is the true person who has been separated from sin and raised to living communion with Christ. Such a person will do the works of Christ because he, like Christ, is a child of God.

There is no contradiction in this teaching of judgment by works and the Pauline teaching of justification by faith. Paul, Peter, John, James, and the author of Hebrews, all present Jesus' teaching that those who have done good will be raised to the resurrection of life and those who have done evil, to the resurrection of judgment (Jn. 5:29; II Cor. 11:15; I Pet. 1:17; Rev. 20:13; Jas. 1:25; Heb. 13:21). But those good works have been exchanged for the old futile ways by the prior work of Christ, the author of our faith, Who was destined for this purpose from before the foundation of the world. The fruits of our faith are always the works of Christ constraining us in love, "For God is at work in you, both to will and to work for his good pleasure" (Phil. 2:13). And Christ's work is not a work of this world which is in bondage to decay, nor even of silver or gold, but rather His work is the giving of His life and His very self for us. Thus Luther has used this passage in explaining the second article of the Creed: "I believe that Jesus Christ . . . has bought and won me . . . not with silver and gold, but with his holy and precious blood, his innocent suffering and death."

3. *Love One Another Earnestly, for You have Tasted the Kindness of the Lord (1:22—2:3)*

Peter's chief concern in this letter is to instil hope in the hearts of his readers. This hope is grounded on nothing less than the ransom paid by Christ in the offering of His blood. Christ's redeeming work issues in holiness and fear and love in the lives of those who belong to the Lord. Since they have been born anew by this spiritual work, they are now nourished by the living and abiding Word which is not perishable as the grass of the field (Is. 40:6–9). The food of this world issues in corruption and death, but the spiritual food of Christ is the "sincere milk of the word." The rendering of the King James Version is both closer to the Greek and truer to the meaning than that of the Revised Standard Version, since the context demands a reference to the *living Word*. This Word which was before the world, which lived and worked in Abraham and the prophets, which was made manifest in Jesus in these latter times, is now bringing spiritual nourishment which enables Christians to grow in grace. Christians are exhorted to be as greedy for this food as a newborn child is for milk!

4. *Come to that Living Stone and Be Built into a Spiritual House, for You are a Chosen Race (2:4–10)*

To Simon, the apostle whom Jesus named Peter (Rock), the metaphor of the living stone must have been startlingly real. It was not novel, for the prophets and the psalmists often called God a rock (Ps. 18, 28, 31, 42, 62, 71, 78, 89, 92, 94, 95; II Sam. 22:2; Is. 8:14; 17:10). But in Christ two new aspects are added to the concept: Jesus Christ is called a rock, both a cornerstone and a stone of stumbling, and Peter himself together with the members of the Church are called building stones. When Jesus said: "You are Peter, and on this rock I will build my church" (Mt. 16:18), He was using the same metaphor Peter uses (2:6), and Peter was the first stone or building block which Christ the builder used. The apostle became a living stone in the erection of Christ's Church, and he, together with all Christians, may be called a rock in this profound sense, because as members of Christ's Church they share in the life of this holy temple. Other metaphors which describe the same unity are Jesus' symbol of the vine and branches and Paul's figure of the Church as the body of Christ.

Membership in this holy house comes only by the election of God. We do not make Christ the king by our election of Him. On the contrary, He makes us members of His elect assembly by His choice of us. And this comes to us mysteriously when we are no people at all, miserable exiles and refugees. So it was with Abraham wandering from Ur of the Chaldees; so it is with the Gentiles outside the Covenant. Thus Hosea had seen the wisdom of God in giving mercy to people who had no mercy (Hos. 2:23).

IV. *Our Relation to Men (2:11—3:12)*

1. *Believers, Be Subject to Every Human Institution (2:11–17)*

Love for one another stems from our love to God, and this, in turn, issues from the love and kindness God has shown us. Our conduct is always developed in relation to the two supreme acts of God, the ransom of the cross and the coming "day of visitation." Because of the mercy shown in the first advent, it is possible for men to stand in the judgment of the second. Therefore Peter exhorts his readers to abstain from contaminating attachments to the things of this world and conduct themselves before the Gentiles wholly in accord with the righteousness of God. Because this involves a life of obedience to all the powers that are ordained by God, it will affect every station and order of life from servant to king.

Peter, like Paul (Rom. 13:1), accepts government as divinely ordered, but this does not mean any particular governmental structure has a divine right to existence. Anything from tyranny to anarchy might well be justified on this basis. It simply means that law as such has been instituted by God for the protection of the weak and the furtherance of the common weal. Law has authority not because it has the weight of traditional precedent or the strength of established practice or the consent of the majority or the justification of any philosophical or sociological ideal, but simply because it is the will of God! Christians are exhorted to obey the law and serve the governing powers only for the sake of the Lord, so that their works may glorify Him at the last day.

2. Servants, Be Submissive to Your Masters (2:18-25)

For the same reason, servants are admonished to serve their masters with all respect, not for the sake of the master, though he may be truly blessed by it, but for the sake of the Lord. Peter therefore asks the servants to be submissive both to gentle and overbearing masters. Human justice would seem to require refusal to serve an unfair employer, but Peter insists that such service, if accepted patiently, has God's approval. But for the revelation of the Cross, this would make no sense at all; hence Peter's reference to it to explain his meaning.

When Christians have been called to suffer, their martyrdom has inevitably been a witness to Christ. Just as Jesus suffered cruel death on a tree although He committed no sin, so Christians must willingly and cheerfully follow in His steps. All of this recently remembered history Peter tells his readers in the language of the prophet Isaiah, indicating once more that what happened in Jesus of Nazareth was neither a surprise nor a matter of private interpretation, but a fulfilment of the prophetic plan of God. Peter did not mean, however, that by imitating Christ we gain merit for salvation, for Christ is no second Moses giving us a new law to follow. He is rather the Saviour

Who "himself bore our sins in his body on the tree" (2:24). No conduct on our part can save us from sin, but patient obedience in the name of Christ will bear witness to the world that our strength is in Him Who died that we might live.

3. Wives, Be Submissive to Your Husbands (3:1–6)

Just as the state and the economic order are based on obedience and service, so also is the family. Certainly the emancipation of women is one of the blessings the Christian Gospel has given to the culture of this world, but this freedom is not won by delivering the wife from the lordship of her husband. In the family, as in every other order, there can be only one master. If this master is subject to the Lord Jesus Christ, the family will be at peace in communion with God, but if the husband is an unbeliever, he must be won for Christ through the patient example of a loving wife. This behavior must not be the deceptive seduction of painted prettiness, but the sincere and abiding love of sacrifice and service.

4. Husbands, Live Considerately with Your Wives (3:7)

Peter parallels Paul's Epistle to the Ephesians in this series of exhortations. Paul says, "Husbands, love your wives, as Christ loved the church and gave himself up for her . . ." (Eph. 5:25). Indeed, the admonitions to the weaker in the series (subjects, servants, wives) would be totally misunderstood as a special pleading for quietistic submission to authoritarianism were it not for the obligation of the strong to humble themselves for the weak as Christ humbled Himself before the world. This is the essence of Christian humility, not abject groveling of the weak before the strong, but the sacrificial service of the strong for the weak. To exhort wives to submit to their husbands without also exhorting husbands to be like Christ in their treatment of their wives is to condone tyranny. However, to admonish both to serve as the Lord Himself served is to forge a bond of perfect peace in the unity of the Spirit.

5. All of You, Have Unity of Spirit (3:8–12)

Finally, Peter concludes and crowns his series of exhortations with a general statement to all classes and types of people and a quotation from Psalm 34.

V. Blessings for Righteousness' Sake (3:13—5:11)

1. Keep Your Conscience Clear when You Suffer for Wrong (3:13–17)

Peter now applies Jesus' teaching in the Beatitudes (Mt. 5:10) to a specific situation of suffering which confronts his readers. Jesus had warned His disciples that they would be dragged before rulers and authorities, but He said they should not be anxious, "for the Holy Spirit will teach you in that very hour what you ought to say" (Lk. 12:11, 12). The fact that Christians are now faced with the real probability that they will be persecuted for doing the very things God had commanded them to do is not accidental or arbitrary. It is the will of God that they should suffer, just as God had sent His Son into the world to endure the pain of sin. Peter never says that one Christian can vicariously suffer for another—only Christ can do this—but the suffering of the Christian does bring a blessing upon himself. Certainly this does not mean that he should seek suffering to gain a blessing, but that if suffering should be thrust upon him, he is to accept it and understand it as God's way of salvation.

2. As Christ Died for Sins, so Baptism is a Sign of Our Death to Sin (3:18—4:6)

In a teaching identical to that of Paul (Rom. 6:1–13) and the author of Hebrews (Heb. 7), Peter shows that the meaning of redemption is made plain in Christian baptism. Because of sin there is suffering in the world, but through the death of Christ, deliverance is promised and made possible. Every sacrifice of the Old Covenant to cover sin was tainted with the corruption of this world, but Christ, the perfect sacrifice, fulfilled once and for all the law, defeated Satan and all his powers, and pleased God.

Since sin brought death into the world, nothing less than death itself would overcome sin. Death is not extinction, but separation from God. It is manifest in three ways: (1) the spiritual separation from God whereby we walk in the course of this world, (2) the physical cessation of bodily functions whereby we take a further step of separation from God and our fellows, and (3) the final separation of eternal death which is experienced by the damned. That the horror of death was thus experienced by Jesus when He suffered on the cross is revealed in His words: "My God, my God, why hast thou forsaken me?" In this death He went to the place of the dead, as does every man, only He went in both humiliation and victory. By enduring our condemnation, He also proclaimed God's triumph over sin, death, and the devil.

Water symbolizes this purgation and victory, because water is used both to kill and to cleanse. As in the days of the flood, so it is now in Christian baptism. In baptism we symbolize our death to sin and our rising again to walk with Christ in newness of life. St. Paul also speaks of baptism as a dying to sin and a rising to life: "We were buried therefore with him by baptism into death, so that as Christ was raised from the dead by the glory of the Father, we too might walk in newness of life" (Rom. 6:4). Interpretations on baptism vary. Many regard baptism as the very symbol for the individual believer of what God did in Christ. Baptism then expresses our conversion as "a good conscience toward God." The Lutheran view, which this expositor shares, is that baptism is the sacrament by which God brings His elect into the body of Christ which is the Church. According to this position baptism in its deepest sense is not something we do in response to God's mercy; it is something that happens to us; it is a holy suffering. We choose to be born again in baptism as little as we chose to be born in the flesh. Peter says: "Baptism . . . now saves you, not as a removal of dirt from the body but as an appeal to God for a clear conscience."

It should be realized that Christians generally agree that the new birth is God's gift. When we are born again by the Holy Spirit we accept the Lord as our Saviour, for "no one can say 'Jesus is Lord' except by the Holy Spirit" (I Cor. 12:3). And since Christ has through His sufferings offered us this gift of new life, we must arm ourselves to do battle seriously against the powers of sin from which we have been freed.

Some interpreters say that I Peter 4:6, together with Ephesians 4:9 and others, indicates that Christ preached in the realm of the dead to those who had not heard the Word in their previous existence in the flesh. This would not give credence either to a purgatory or to a second-chance salvation, nor would it militate against the missionary urgency of the Gospel for us, but it would help us understand how God's mercy could be extended to those whom we have failed to reach.

3. Since the End is at Hand, Hold Unfailing Love (4:7–19)

Far from encouraging moral lassitude, the urgency of the coming end infinitely increases the Christian's ethical concern. The Thessalonians so misunderstood the significance of the new and final age that they stopped working, and Paul had to tell them: "If any one will not work, let him not eat" (II Thess. 3:10). So Peter now exhorts his readers to use the gifts and talents God has bestowed with unfailing love upon them. The practice of Christian love in the community builds the holy temple, the Church. The function of the Church in the dying age is to cover the multitude of sins with love, to speak the Word of God in love and to render services of mercy in love.

4. Elders, Be Examples; Members, Be Humble Under God (5: 1–11)

Having brought his reader to consider his conduct under oppression as a member of the Church, Peter now closes his letter with an exhortation to both elders and members. Conduct in the order of the Church is no different from conduct in any other order of society; the same imperatives apply. The elders who have the responsibility of oversight must not rule for selfish gain, but for the welfare of the members, and the younger members must humble themselves "under the mighty hand of God." Note that the humbling is not under the elders but under God. Everything must be seen in the light of the antagonism between God and His adversary Satan. This conflict personally involves every man, since he is the prey the devil seeks. Yet the Christian can be confident because he knows he belongs to a fellowship that bears the marks of Christ's pain, so that no matter how much suffering he is called upon to endure, he will survive in eternal glory with Christ.

VI. Salutation (5:12–14)

Peter sends personal greetings in rather cryptic language. Sylvanus is mentioned as his scribe. "She who is at Babylon" could refer to his wife, but more probably refers figuratively to the church in Rome where Mark was serving as Peter's special assistant.

II Peter

ROBERT PAUL ROTH

THE EPISTLE OF II Peter is very different from I Peter. While I Peter is a letter of joyful hope in the face of suffering, II Peter is an epistle of faithful truth in the face of falsehood.

I. Peter's Greeting to His Readers (1:1, 2)

While Peter greets his readers in the same manner as he does in I Peter, he fails to identify them specifically. He does describe them in a significant way, however. He is a servant and an apostle of Jesus Christ, but they "have obtained a faith of equal standing" in the righteousness of God. James Moffatt translates this passage: "Those who have been allotted a faith of equal privilege with ours," and comments that "*allotted* implies the free favor and goodness of God, and the equity of our God points to the divine freedom from favoritism."

Faith is never obtained by right or merit but comes as a gift which God gives equally to Christians of all generations. This is the solution to the unequal distribution of the gifts of this world. How can we be equally thankful when some are rich and some are poor, some are wise and some are foolish, some are strong and some are weak? The answer is that by faith we have not just a gift, but the Giver. In faith God gives us Himself and His righteousness. When we have the Giver, we no longer need be anxious about this gift or that, for we have the one thing needful throughout eternity. Again, God gives Himself in faith to everyone, to the Jews first and now to the Gentiles. While God chose the Jews as His elect people, so that they might cradle Christ, He has now elected the Gentiles too, and this election extends down through the centuries so that the contemporaneous disciple has no advantage over the subsequent one.

John Henry Jowett called this greeting the clarion call of the Christian to liberty, equality, and fraternity—not mere economic or political freedom, but spiritual freedom which paradoxically finds its fruition only in complete bondage to Christ. As Luther says, the Christian man is the most free lord of all and at the same time he is the most dutiful servant of all. Man does not have the absolute option to be free or not to be free; he is free only to serve God or the devil.

Likewise, equality and fraternity are not the sociological egalitarianism and brotherhood so popular today, but are rather the oneness and communion we have in Christ Who is the source of faith and hope and life. Only in this love which flows from the knowing heart of God can there be a growth of grace and peace among men. Out of the misguided concern for justice, men will try to force equality and brotherhood upon society with plans and programs, but in faith human inequities become opportunities for service and witness to Christ.

II. The Knowledge of the Word (1:3–21)

1. Become Partakers of the Divine Nature and so Confirm Your Election (1:3–11)

Peter's thought at this point is remarkably close to that of Paul who writes to the Corinthians: "And we all, with unveiled face, beholding the glory of the Lord, are being changed into his likeness from one degree of glory to another; for this comes from the Lord who is the Spirit" (II Cor. 3:18). Peter states this good news as a simple declarative, because it is a fact that God "has granted to us all things that pertain to life and godliness." But then, as does Paul, Peter changes his mood to an imperative of extreme urgency. Because God has made us partakers of His divine nature, "for this very reason make every effort to supplement your faith with virtue. . . ."

First, we must consider the tremendous weight of meaning in the announcement that we have become partakers of the divine nature. When Christ dwells in us, we become separated from our sin, dead to this world, and filled with the mighty fulness of God! Freed from the corruption of this world with its passions of lust, ambition and greed, the Christian becomes yoked to Christ in godly discipline. By sharing in the life of Christ, Peter means nothing less than the glorious participation in the perfection of God.

Secondly, we must notice that although this participation is a free gift, the Christian life is characterized by earnest discipline. Grace is given at the cost of Jesus' blood and is received only in the response of our total self-surrender. This return of ourselves to God is expressed in spiritual fruitfulness: virtue, knowledge, self-control, steadfastness, godliness, brotherly affection, and love. While the Christian man has none of the profligacy of the prodigal son, neither does he have the passive legalism of the Pharisee. Gratefully and diligently he is working out his faith through love.

Finally, Peter cautions his readers that the lack of such diligence brings the terrible risk of losing election. The history of salvation is always played out on the stage of freedom, so that although it is God Who predestines us and not we ourselves, this divine election can be freely lost if we choose. Hence Peter exhorts his readers to confirm their election and make sure their entrance into the everlasting Kingdom.

2. Remember God's Word for We were Eyewitnesses (1:12-18)

In this passage and in the one immediately following, we have two tenets of the Gospel that must always be kept together: eyewitness facts and the testimony of faith. In this passage and the next, Peter refers to the historical facts of the two reports, that of eyewitnesses concerning Jesus of Nazareth and that of the prophets of previous generations. In both cases, however, a second factor is necessary to our understanding: the testimony of faith given to us by the power of the Spirit.

Peter's manner of speaking intimates that he expects to die soon. Perhaps he is in prison under the persecution of Nero. This departure does not worry him, but he is careful to provide for the instruction and leadership of his flock before he leaves. In all probability, Peter made arrangements with Mark to record his Gospel after he was gone. We have both the Gospel of Mark and the tradition concerning its Petrine source as evidence that this was so. The necessity of this record of an eyewitness cannot be minimized. John rests his Gospel on it: "And the Word became flesh and dwelt among us, full of grace and truth; we have beheld his glory . . ." (Jn. 1:14). Paul reminds both the Galatians and the Romans that Jesus was born of a woman under the law. The evangelists Matthew and Luke take great pains to trace Jesus' genealogy through the families of both Mary and Joseph. This is indeed no cunningly devised myth; it is remembered history which can be checked and verified in the most acceptable scientific and legal fashion! Peter himself was with Jesus on the holy mountain when Jesus was transfigured and he heard the voice from heaven "borne to him by the Majestic Glory" (1:17).

At this point, however, fact and faith are united, for it is the objective witness of faith that distinguishes Peter's vision from the realm of subjective hallucinations. A subjective vision is a private matter which cannot be communicated from one person to another. If a person claims to have had such a vision, we can believe him or disbelieve him but we cannot obtain a similar experience for ourselves. The experience of Peter, on the contrary, is the experience of every Christian, for faith tells us all, as the voice told Peter, that Jesus is God's beloved Son!

The empirical facts concerning Jesus are not sufficient by themselves; they must be coupled with the faith-fact which is borne to us by the majestic glory of the Holy Spirit. It would be a grave mistake to think that one could know Christ simply by looking into His face and hearing His words; it would be an equally serious blunder to suppose that one could have Christ simply by receiving an idea, a teaching, a message, or a dogma about Him. Christ was a particular person Who died under Pontius Pilate, but Who also rose from the dead so that His fellowship can be experienced by all who believe in Him. The experience of Christ must always unite the hard facts of history and the harder facts of faith. Pilate had before him in his praetorium the facts of history, but Judas had in addition the facts of faith. This is the reason Jesus could say to Pilate, "He who delivered me to you has the greater sin" (Jn. 19:11). This is also why He said the sin against the Son of Man could be forgiven, but the sin against the Holy Spirit is unforgivable. The voice of the Spirit is absolute in its authority, objectivity, and majesty.

3. We Have the Prophetic Word Made More Sure (1:19–21)

In addition to the witness of contemporaries, we have the historical witness of the prophets who lived in earlier generations. On the basis of the covenant God made with Abraham, the prophets repeatedly and consistently foretold of the coming of One Who would redeem Israel and be a saviour to the world. Sometimes this promise was expressed in the metaphor of kingship: the coming One would be God's anointed, the Messiah-King. Sometimes the prophets used the poetic imagery of the Son of Man Who would come in a divine cataclysm with the shaking of the heavens and the melting of the earth. At still other times, the prophets used the figure of a suffering Servant Who would be despised and rejected by men. By the richness and variety of their figures, the prophets embellished the great theme of prophecy: God was coming to save the world He had made.

This promise has now been fulfilled in Jesus of Nazareth. Figure and reality are one. So Peter preached in Jerusalem on the day of Pentecost: David "being therefore a prophet, and knowing that God had sworn with an oath to him that God would set one of his descendants upon his throne, he foresaw and spoke of the resurrection of Christ, that he was not abandoned to Hades, nor did his flesh see corruption" (Acts 2:30, 31). Not only were the apostles witnesses of the resurrection of a man from His grave, but they were witnesses that God does not lie, that His promise was surely fulfilled. To the New Testament writers, this latter fact is more authoritative than any other argument or evidence than can be marshaled on behalf of their message.

While modern man looks for scientific certitude or the kind of evidence that will stand up in a court of law, the apostles and early Christians found a higher authority, and if we are to have the same truth that set them free, we must appeal to the same authority. Scientific or legal testimony may not be privately prejudiced or subjective, but it is still human. Scripture is neither private nor merely human. When the prophets spoke, they were not speaking for themselves nor for humanity; they were speaking for God under the impulse of the Holy Spirit Whose authority is absolute! We do not know *how* the Spirit inspired the prophets—indeed, to quarrel over the method is as meaningless as it is fruitless—but we do know they were inspired, for we have the written Word and the faithful agreement of thousands of witnesses.

III. False Teachers (2:1–22)

1. As There were False Prophets, There will be False Teachers (2:1–3)

The close affinity between this chapter and the Epistle of Jude has led many interpreters to believe that there was borrowing one way or another. Although this is doubtful, it is certain that the problem both authors faced was the same. This chapter is distinctive from the writings of Peter in its message of doom. We are not walking through a merry meadow with soft sunlight here. We are in a dark forest with giant pines shouting in their silence of the power and holiness of God.

The single theme that runs through the chapter is that false teaching leads to false conduct. The idea is father of the deed. The particular heresy which concerns Peter in this letter is Antinomian Gnosticism (which held that under gospel dispensation, the moral law is of no use, faith being the only necessity for salvation). Gnosticism was the popular spirit which ruled over the ancient world, a spirit which was contrary to the Gospel and which therefore fought bitterly for the defeat of Christianity. Weary of the frustrations and anxieties of this world, the Gnostics looked with nostalgia to another world which they conceived as the original source of life and light from which their spirits had somehow strayed. This other world, in the Gnostic view, is the true world of the spirit whereas the present world in which we find ourselves is a false world of matter. Since the material world of the senses imprisons our spirits, according to the Gnostics, some of them thought they could escape the fetters of the flesh by leading lives of ascetic abstemiousness. Others felt they could indulge in sensual experiences without regard to law or discipline, since these material things are false and unreal anyway. This latter doctrine and practice Peter calls a damnable heresy.

While the mood of our age has not been cast in the direction of another world, in recent times, owing probably to two wars and the great depression, men have been shaken from their materialistic optimism and faith in the evolutionary progress of this world. As a result a new spirit seems to be dawning upon the horizons of history, a spirit which is heavy with fatigue and fraught with pessimism. Once more this false teaching will spawn monstrous conduct, and the letter of Peter will again speak with fresh power and pertinence.

2. God, Who did not Spare the Wicked of Old, Will Now Keep the Unrighteous under Punishment but Will Rescue the Godly from Trial (2:4–10a)

The Gospel cannot be described in such simple terms as optimism or pessimism. The Gospel permits neither an easy compromise with the sensual passions of this world nor a laborious escape from the material world of our senses. Instead, the Gospel brings the two-edged sword of death to the flesh and resurrection to the body. Far from escaping the body and floating into a mystic realm of the heavens, the Christian knows his salvation to be a transformation of the body, so that what was formerly ruled by the satanic power of the flesh is now in Christ ruled by the life-giving power of the Spirit. That which is under the flesh is destined for destruction. God did not spare any of His creatures, neither angels that sinned nor the ancient world nor Sodom and Gomorrah; all were condemned to wait in punishment until the Last Judgment. But as God preserved Noah and Lot, so He will preserve the righteous from trial. This does not mean that Christians are exempt from suffering the pain and death pervading this world. It does mean that Christians, free from the chains of the nether world, rest in the consolation of paradise until the last day.

3. *The Nether Gloom of Darkness has been Reserved for the Wicked (2:10b–22)*

These wicked, presumptuous and overbold creatures dare to blaspheme against God's glories, whereas even the angels who share these glories do not speak a critical word before the Lord. In consequence, these people have become like stupid brutes. They are "born to be caught and killed." Like dogs chasing their tails, they have been driven by their lusts into a mad whirl with the result that they devour themselves. They have been worse than animals because, like Balaam, they have tried to prostitute their evil-doing. (*Beor*, RSV, is a textual correction of *Bosor*, KJV, a town in Gilead.)

It would have been better for these monstrous creatures if they had never known the way of righteousness than to have fallen from grace by despising God's will. To exist in this world in ignorant separation from God is punishment indeed, but to exist eternally with the knowledge of God but without hope of fellowship is the horror of hell. "The nether gloom of darkness" is obviously figurative language. While no other language can be used to express a reality which is beyond the categories of this visible world, hell is no less real because our spatial and temporal categories are inadequate. Hell is low and dark compared to heaven which is high and bright. Certainly hell is more than a psychological state of mind or a delusion of unreality. Hell is plainly the state where the wicked are abandoned completely to themselves and their insatiable passions.

Rather than indicating that heaven and hell are non-spatial and non-temporal, the Biblical writers do not hesitate to use these categories, plainly showing that in heaven God is specially present and in hell God is specially inaccessible. This does not mean that heaven is just another place like the earth, only better, nor does it mean that heaven is no specific place at all; it means that heaven is a place where God is present with his infinite glory and where the redeemed will rejoice everlastingly in that glory.

IV. The Coming of the Lord (3:1–18)

1. Scoffers Will Come in the Last Days Questioning the Lord's Coming (3:1–4)

Peter says this is the second letter he has written to his readers. It should not be supposed, however, that our canonical I Peter was the previous letter to these Christians, for this letter has been lost. I Peter was sent to the churches of Asia Minor while II Peter was sent to an unknown destination.

The coming of the Lord is one of the most crucial issues of the Christian faith. Throughout the New Testament two things are repeatedly announced: the Son of Man is coming in the future and the hour of His coming is known only to the Father. Jesus had been asked by the Pharisees when the Kingdom of God would come, and He told them it would not come with signs to be observed (Lk. 17: 20). Just before the ascension, the disciples asked Jesus if this were the time He would restore the kingdom to Israel, and He said, "It is not for you to know the times or the seasons" (Acts 1:7). Yet Jesus also said to His disciples on their mission to Galilee that they would not go through all the towns of Israel before the Son of Man would come (Mt. 10:23). This has led many people to believe either that Jesus was a mistaken apocalyptic visionary or that He spoke in a symbolism which meant that the Son of Man would come not in a literal future, but "spiritually" in an eternal present.

But when Jesus spoke to His disciples in Galilee of the coming of the Son of Man, He was referring to His first advent. This is proved because He sent the disciples only to Israel, not to the Gentiles or the Samaritans (Mt. 10:5). Only when the Son of Man was rejected by Israel does He turn to the Gentiles, but His first coming was sealed when Peter confessed Jesus to be the Christ. This occurred before the disciples had canvassed all the towns of Israel.

Jesus was neither mistaken nor misleading when He said the Son of Man would return. He warned His disciples against those, on the one hand, who would anticipate the coming by saying, "The time is at hand" (Lk. 21:8) and those, on the other hand, who would deny the coming by saying, "My master is delayed" (Mt. 24:48). We must always be ready, for He will surely come, but at what hour no one knows except the Father, for He will come as a thief in the night (II Pet. 3:10; Mt. 24:43; I Thess. 5:2; Rev. 3:3; 16:15).

Peter now warns his readers in the same manner against cynical scoffers who impatiently reject the Christian hope in the return of Christ. Since the fathers (either the patriarchs or the previous generation, but not the apostles) have died, they say, things have continued as they were from the beginning of creation. Paul had to deal with the same impatience and skepticism among the Thessalonians. Today we are continually confronted with the same problem.

2. *The Word which Created by Water will Destroy by Fire (3:5–10)*

These scoffers should realize that to deny the Second Coming of Christ and the final judgment is also to deny the creation as well as the Word Who made us in the beginning and Who will judge us in the end. They should also recognize the fact that God looks upon the passing of time from a perspective different from ours. Especially in view of His mercy, He delays the judgment to allow time for the wicked to repent, not wishing that any should perish. When the time is right, when God's purposes have been fulfilled, He will bring an end to the course of this world. He will do it with the same voice with which He brought it into being. He will do it in a flash, in the twinkling of an eye, with cataclysmic fire. No one can predict this moment, for He will come as a thief, yet in the midst of this temporal uncertainty, every Christian knows the absolute surety of His coming.

3. *Since All will be Dissolved, Hasten the Lord's Coming with Lives of Holiness (3:11–18)*

Finally, this message of the final outcome is crowned with an ethical injunction. This is logical, for the Christian ethic grows out of the Gospel which is the message concerning God's Son, His coming to die and His coming in glory. Because Jesus conquered death, we *can* lead lives of holiness; because He will come again in life, we *must* do so! Since the Lord is forbearing, the only thing which delays the final judgment is the persistent wickedness of the world. Therefore the Christian can hasten the coming of the Lord by ridding himself and the world of every spot and blemish of wickedness. This has been Paul's earnest plea too, says Peter, even though some perverse people try to twist his writings to mean something else, just as they do with other Scriptures (perhaps both the Old Testament and other writings of the apostles). Many have tried to make Paul advocate some kind of Antinomianism (lawlessness) because of his emphatic proclamation of the free grace of redemption, but both Paul and Peter agree, together with Jesus and the apostles, that sturdy discipline must be born of steadfast love. The Christian life springs from grace that is free, but never cheap.

I John

FRED L. FISHER

THE FIRST EPISTLE OF JOHN was written to a Christian community of the first century primarily to encourage its members to live the kind of life consistent with fellowship with God and His Christ. It deals with such vital themes as righteousness, love, truth and assured knowledge. The author does not consider these themes merely as ethical requirements, but as religious realities based upon the Christian revelation of God and His Son, the Lord Jesus Christ. Therefore, Christian doctrine lies at the root of the book, and one is tempted, at times, to think of it as a doctrinal exposition of the reality of the incarnation of God in Christ. If we are to follow the mind of the writer, however, we must avoid this temptation, since he is primarily concerned with the quality of the Christian life of his readers.

The letter, as also II John and the Gospel of John, is written to combat the errors of Gnosticism which in its early stages of development invaded the Christian communities of Asia Minor in the latter part of the first century. This heresy, starting from belief in the evil of all material substance, denied that a righteous God could have any essential relation to matter. This led to the rejection of the reality of the incarnation and to the denial that Jesus of Nazareth is in reality the Son of God (I Jn. 4:1–6). Faith in Christ, according to this speculation, was the first step in a process of salvation which was to be completed by progressive knowing (hence the name, Gnostics) of the spiritual realities that led to God. Since, to the Gnostics, the body, being material, was evil and beyond redemption, the actions of man in the flesh had no spiritual meaning or significance. As a result, they taught that Christians need not struggle against temptations of the flesh, but may yield to any desire; such submission assertedly would have no bearing on fellowship with God. Since they acknowledged no spiritual restraint on the Christian's actions, these Gnostics were known as Antinomian (that is, against law).

Authorship of these epistles has traditionally been ascribed to John, the Apostle, the son of Zebedee. All the external evidence favors this tradition, and, though it has been challenged by some scholars, the evidence does not warrant the rejection of tradition. However, the value and inspiration of the writings do not depend wholly on this tradition, since the writer does not identify himself except by the title "the elder," which he uses in II and III John.

The date of the epistles must be placed in the second half of the first century, between A.D. 85 and 100. First John, probably written last, may have been appended originally to the Gospel of John as a sequel to that great Christian document.

The plan of the book does not follow a logical order. The writer thinks and writes intuitively with constant repetition of recurring themes. The book defies outlining and one must be satisfied to follow the course of the author's thoughts as he deals with the great cluster of ideas which, to him, constitute the essence of the Christian life.

I. The Basis of the Christian Life (1:1–5)

Two related strands of thought are presented. First, the reality of the incarnation of God in Jesus of Nazareth is stressed (1:1–4). Notice how John emphasizes the fleshliness of the historical manifestation of the eternal Word of Life. He wants us to understand that all of God was present in the earthly life of Jesus of Nazareth and that the incarnation has ultimate meaning for human life because it brings an eternal quality into the life of the believer and makes possible his fellowship with God. No progressive knowing of other spiritual realities is required; Christ is not just the first step in the process of salvation, He is the whole of salvation. Second, John emphasizes that God is light (v. 5), a description that teaches God's absolute righteousness which dispels the darkness of sin, falsehood, sorrow, hatred, peril and death. John makes perfectly clear that the character of God is the foundation of all religion. Since God is light, we must walk in light (vv. 6, 7); since God is spirit, we must worship in spirit and in truth (Jn. 4:24); since God is love, love is the one indispensable sign of sonship (4:7, 8, 16).

II. Meaning of Walking in the Light (1:6—2:2)

Certain necessities are emphasized. We must have an ideal of perfection (2:1a). "Sin" is used absolutely in this clause; our ideal is never to sin. However, John recognizes that, though we should constantly strive for this goal, we must ever fail to reach it; hence, we must recognize our sins and failures (1:8, 10). Self-righteousness is a delusion which points to lack of real spirituality. We may rely on God's forgiveness and cleansing power (1:7, 9; 2:1b, 2). If we habitually walk in the light (1:7) and confess our sins as they occur (v. 9), we may claim the provision for our forgiveness made through the cross of Christ (2:2). God promises to forgive, to restore the Christian to His fellowship (1:9), and to cleanse us of all unrighteousness (vv. 7–9), thus enabling us to overcome our sins.

III. Accompaniments of Fellowship with the Father (2:3–28)

1. Obedience (2:3–5)

We are to make a practice of obeying the will of God. The word "keep" in this passage means to be on the watch to find and fulfil every wish of God.

2. Christlikeness (2:6)

We are to make a practice of imitating Christ in His life of positive righteousness.

3. Love (2:7–11)

We are to make a practice of loving our brethren. Love in this epistle means an unselfish devotion to the welfare of the brother. It is a positive quality of life, not primarily emotional but spiritual. It confers on us the responsibility of helping our brethren become what they should be in their Christian life. This is the true meaning of the principle of the priesthood of believers. Opposed to love is hatred, which involves an attempt to use others for our own ends and thus to destroy their true personality.

4. Separation (2:12–17)

We are to reject the world and its ways. In John's thought, "the world" signifies unredeemed humanity in opposition to God. Since we have overcome the world through our redemption (2:12–15), we are to reject worldly things as valid principles of life (v. 16) because they do not have their source in the Father and are transitory in character, being already in the process of passing away (v. 17).

5. Orthodoxy (2:18–28)

We must adhere to the truth, that is, the gospel truth. Truth is opposed on the religious level by those who have the nature of "antichrist" (2: 18, 19). This term in John's thought means not only those who are opposed to Christ, but those who would substitute something else (knowledge, in the case of the Gnostics) as the center of our spiritual quest. Truth is important in the Christian life; our beliefs determine our actions. The validity of Christian belief is based on the testimony of the Holy Spirit (vv. 20–23) and the testimony of Christian experience (vv. 24–26). Gospel truth is the basis of all other truth (v. 27) and loyalty to it is the basis of our confidence when Christ appears at the end of time (v. 28).

IV. Righteousness, the Mark of Sonship (2:29—3:24)

1. The Reality of Sonship (2:29—3:3)

The key verse of this section (2:29) makes righteousness, moral likeness to God, the evidence of the reality of sonship to God.

Chapter 3, verses 1 to 3, sets forth the glorious reality of our sonship to God. It is a present reality, not just a future hope (v. 1a); it makes us strangers whose true nature cannot be understood by the world (v. 1b). Glorious as the present reality is, the future is even more wonderful (v. 2). Such hope inspires us to continue the struggle to achieve real purity of life (v. 3).

2. The Possibility of Purity (3:4–10)

Purity of life is possible for the Christian. The nature of sin is spiritual lawlessness (3:4); this is the meaning of the phrase, "transgression of the law." Because the power of sin has been broken in the Christian's life (v. 5), the real Christian is distinguished by his habit of living righteously (vv. 6–10). In this passage, the verbs are in the present tense to indicate a course of life, rather than particular acts which may not be in character with our real nature. The Christian gives up spiritual lawlessness (cf. v. 4) when he surrenders to Christ in faith. Though he may commit isolated acts of sin, this experience guarantees that he will not live a life of sinfulness (v. 9). The contrast is made between the children of God and the children of the devil. The children of God practice righteousness (v. 6) and are really righteous (v. 7) just as "that one," Jesus Christ, is righteous (v. 7). The children of the devil, or unredeemed humanity, practice sin (v. 8) and are of the devil, that is, their spiritual lawlessness has its source in yielding to his influence (v. 8). This is to be expected because Satan has practiced lawlessness from the beginning of his career as the devil.

3. *The Essence of Righteousness (3:11–18)*

That the essence of righteousness is love is a common New Testament emphasis found in the teachings of Jesus (Mk. 12:29–31), the writings of Paul (Rom. 13:8) and the Epistle of James (2:8). Love, the desire to seek the welfare of others, is contrasted with hatred, the desire to destroy others (3:12). Love is the one indispensable sign of the reality of conversion (vv. 13–15). That love is not primarily emotional, but an active spiritual principle, is seen in its supreme manifestation in the sacrifice of Christ (v. 16) and in the fact that it leads one to share actively in the needs of others even to the extent of sacrificing our possessions (v. 17). The Christian must guard himself against the temptation to superficial love (v. 18).

4. *The Results of Righteousness (3:19–24)*

The fruit of love is growth in the spiritual life. Love leads to obedience and gives confidence before God. Sincere love assures the heart of the reality of sonship to God and gives confidence that our life is pleasing to God (3:22) and that our prayers will be answered. Continued obedience to God in all areas of life is the proper outcome of faith in Jesus Christ (v. 23) and brings us to such vital union with Christ that the presence of the Holy Spirit is a conscious reality (v. 24). This gives us such assurance that we know that Christ is abiding in union with us.

V. *Need for the Practice of Spiritual Discrimination (4:1–6)*

John points out that many spirits (that is, prophets who speak of spiritual things) have gone out into the world (4:1). It is therefore necessary that the Christian make a practice of testing preachers to see whether they come from God or not. The test to be applied is given in verses 2 and 3. The true preacher confesses the reality of the incarnation; he centers his message in Christ Who came in the flesh of Jesus of Nazareth. This is always the test of the true preacher: he makes the center of his religion and his message rest in Jesus.

In contrast, the false prophet in John's day centered his message in knowledge of supposed mysteries that transcended the revelation of God in Christ. The modern false prophet may find another center, but his subordination of Christ to something else as truly partakes of the spirit of Antichrist as did the Gnostic of John's day. Antichrist does not refer here to some political ruler, but to the spirit of evil which leads men to set up a religion rivaling the true religion.

Test of a man's spiritual character lies, John says (4:4–6), in his recognition of the truth. The children of God have conquered the spirits of false prophets because of the greatness of God Who dwells in union with them (v. 4). The false prophets belong to this world system, a system that sets a premium on those things that exalt the pride of man in himself. Because of this, their message gains a hearing that is sometimes wider than the hearing granted to the true message of the incarnation (v. 5). It remains true, however, that those who have their source in God listen to "us" (the true preachers) and the refusal of others to listen reveals that they belong to the spirit of error (v. 6).

VI. Love, The Proof of Sonship (4:7–21)

1. Source (4:7, 8)

Love is possible only for those who have been spiritually begotten of God and have a personal knowledge of God. Lack of love is a sure sign that one has never come to know God. This follows from the fact that God is love (4:8). This is the third of John's great descriptions of God. He points out that God is spirit (Jn. 4:24), that God is light (I Jn. 1:5), and that God is love. Spirit describes God's mode of existence; light, His character; but love, His essence. It is the deepest thing that the New Testament has to say about God.

2. Meaning (4:9, 10)

What does it mean to love? John tells us in verses 9 and 10. God's love was manifested in His gift of His only Son that He might be a propitiation for our sins, a way by which our sins might be removed as a barrier of fellowship with God. The true essence of love is not found in the fact that we love God, for our love for Him is a response to His grace and is merited by the object of it. The true essence of love is found in God's love for us, sinners who did not merit His love, and in the sacrifice that He made for our sins. The love of God is the pattern for human love—intelligent, righteous and self-giving.

3. Inspiration (4:11–16a)

John points out the inspiration of love. We are under obligation to love one another, since God loves us (4:11). Love does what physical sight cannot do; it makes God real to us. Our union with Him brings our love to its perfection (v. 12). Love also is the basis of our assurance that God does actually dwell in us (v. 13). John turns aside in verses 14 and 15, as he often does, to reiterate a point made previously. In this case, he re-emphasizes the thought of the first verses of the letter—the reality of eyewitness testimony to the incarnation. In verse 16a he returns to his theme of love, and asserts that he has experienced and believed the love that God has for us.

4. Activity (4:16b–21)

The man who lives in the sphere of love finds an abiding fellowship with God and a firm confidence in his own salvation which makes him unafraid of the Judgment Day and sustains him in a life in the world which is like the life that Jesus lived (4:16b–17). Fear is cast out by the power of love and those who live in the realm of love do not experience fear (v. 18). We have the ability to love because He first loved us (v. 19). It is not "we love him," as in the King James Version, but simply "we love." All our love is rooted in an experience of God's love for us. The obligation to love our brother in Christ is emphasized (vv. 20, 21); John finds it impossible to believe that one who does not love his brother can really love God. To John, the first commandment of God, the most important one, is that we love our brother. John is probably thinking of the Christian brother, though this would surely not exclude the wider commandment of Christ that we should love our neighbor as ourselves. John's particular interest is in the Christian fellowship, so he does not bring the obligation to love the world into focus at this point.

VII. *Great Assurances of the Christian (5:1–20)*

John has already presented in other connections the truths he now restates, expands, and emphasizes in this passage.

1. *Victory over the World (5:1–4)*

The first verse tells us that everyone who believes that the man of Nazareth, Jesus, is really the eternal Messiah of God has experienced a new birth. This experience generates a love in our heart for the true and righteous God, which, in turn, generates a love for those who are begotten of Him. This verse reminds us that the brotherhood of man is only a fancy until it becomes a Christian brotherhood. Verse 2 points out that we are sure of our love for others when we practice our love for God—habitual obedience to His commandments. Verse 3 emphasizes that habitual obedience to God is what love for God amounts to in actual practice. Love for God is not an emotion so much as it is a great guiding principle of life. Verse 4 amplifies the statement in verse 3 that the commandments of God are not burdensome, since the child of God continually conquers this world system through his faith in God. Faith in God gives us a new set of values by which we are able to carry out the kind of life that sets its values in God.

2. *The Finality of Jesus Christ (5:5–12)*

The Christian assurance in the finality and absoluteness of Jesus Christ is restated. The theological basis of faith in God is the belief that what God does in the world for the redemption of man reached its finality and completeness in the life of Jesus Christ (5:5). The witness to the finality of Christ is said to be the water, the blood and the Holy Spirit (vv. 6–8). Verse 7, containing the trinitarian formula, is not in the best Greek texts of I John and should not be insisted upon as a proof of the Trinity, though nothing in it is contrary to the spirit of the epistle.

To understand what John means by the water, the blood and the Spirit as witnesses to the reality of the incarnation, we must remember that the Gnostics taught that the eternal Spirit came upon an ordinary man named Jesus at the time of his baptism and abode with him until Gethsemane; the eternal Christ did not die or suffer. John, however, insists that not only does His baptism give witness to the incarnation of God in Christ, but the cross is equally such a testimony. The Holy Spirit was connected with the earthly work of Christ at both ends; He descended upon the incarnate Son of God at His baptism to endue Him with power for His work of redemption; He descended in fulness upon the disciples at Pentecost as a testimony to the completeness of Christ's work. Peter, in his speech at Pentecost, recognized the coming of the Spirit as a sign that the new age had begun. All this is considered the testimony of God which we should receive, since we are in the habit of receiving the testimony of men (v. 9). When we receive it and have faith in God, we have a spiritual experience which confirms the truth of God's witness which He has testified concerning His Son (v. 10). The one who does not believe is guilty of making God a liar. The essence of God's testimony is that eternal life is found through union with Christ, so that he who has the Son has life and he who does not have the Son is devoid of life (vv. 11, 12).

3. Reality of Salvation (5:13)

One purpose of the letter was that Christians might know of a certainty that they have eternal life. The Gnostics were saying that faith in Christ is but an initial step in a process which might bring salvation in the end. As in many systems of religion today, Gnosticism lacked real assurance of salvation. John states that real assurance is possible to the Christian. On the basis of what he has written, confirmed by their own spiritual experience, they may know that they are saved.

4. Answered Prayer (5:14–17)

The child of God has assurance of answers to prayer. The only limitation on his request is that it should be "according to his will" (5:14). For the child of God, this is not so much a limitation as a safeguard. God's children desire nothing contrary to the will of the Heavenly Father. When we seek and find God's will and make that our prayer, we know that God hears and grants to us what we ask of Him. This we know (v. 15). The difficult-to-understand verses which follow (vv. 16, 17) must be interpreted in the light of this necessity of praying and asking what we believe to be the will of God. We are, in the will of God, to pray for our brethren when they sin—this is a Christian obligation. However, such prayer must be offered with faith that it is the will of God that the brother be restored. There are cases when the Christian who prays is convinced that the erring brother is "beyond hope" (that is, is sinning unto death). This opinion of the praying Christian may or may not reflect the actual state of the sinning brother's spiritual condition. However, as long as it is the opinion of the praying Christian that the sinning brother is beyond hope, he cannot pray for him with confidence; therefore, John does not command that he should pray for him at all. The Revised Standard Version translation of these verses is in error. John is not distinguishing a certain kind of sin which is "mortal" from other kinds of sin which are less serious. He is speaking of a course of life, a life which is so confirmed in the course of sin that one is beyond the touch of God's grace and power. This is indeed possible, but not all those in sin are so confirmed in sin (v. 17). The thought of the verses centers in the opinion of the praying Christian about the spiritual state of the brother who is sinning. Only God *knows* the truth in this matter. However, the Christian may have an opinion which makes it impossible for him to pray for the brother involved.

5. *Truth of the Gospel (5:18-20)*

A series of assertions, beginning with the words "we know," is concerned with the truth of our spiritual convictions. Verse 18 insists that our knowledge of the saving power of God is truth. This power is such that it delivers the Christian from the power of sin and Satan and brings him into a vital fellowship with God that makes it impossible for him to continue to live a life of sin. Verse 19 insists that the Christian division of all the world into two spiritual camps —those who are of God and those who are under the power of Satan —is a true distinction. Verse 20 insists that the Christian's conviction that Jesus Christ is the eternal Son of God has its source in the spiritual experience of the child of God and is true. Therefore, we are not to doubt that the theological basis of our faith is true.

VIII. Admonition to Guard Against Idolatry (5:21)

Though our spiritual climate is different today, John's closing admonition against idolatry has enduring significance. An idol is any *thing* that comes between the individual and God. Our conception of idolatry must be enlarged to include many things that people of our day idolize. It is the Christian's enduring necessity to be on guard against the encroachment of *things* upon his devotion to the living God known in Jesus Christ.

II John

FRED L. FISHER

THE EVIDENCE INDICATES that the author of II John is the same as the author of the Gospel and I John, though this has not been universally accepted.

The letter is addressed to "an elect lady," which probably is exactly what is meant, though many interpreters take this as a figurative expression designating a church. The evidence for the latter use is weak, and the reason to expect it here is obscure. The epistle seems to be a private note to some Christian woman of John's acquaintance, probably a widow, and was occasioned by his meeting some of her children whom he found to be true to the faith of Christ (cf. 4).

This letter warns this Christian woman against indiscriminate fellowship with unbelievers (vv. 7-11).

The leading ideas of the epistle are love, truth and obedience, which partly involve and partly supplement one another. Obedience without love is servile; love without obedience is unreal; neither of them can flourish outside the realm of truth.

1235

I. The Walk in Truth and Love (vv. 1–6)

1. Address and Greeting (vv. 1–3)

John addresses his friend in the spirit of Christian love, commending her good reputation among Christians, "those who have come to know the truth." He asks for her the threefold blessing of grace, mercy and peace from "God the Father" and from "Jesus Christ." The repetition of the preposition "from" indicates the separate personality of Father and Son, while the titles used indicate their unity.

2. Past Loyalty Commended (v. 4)

The lady has been true to God and had reared her children in the realm of truth. For this John commends her.

3. Love and Obedience Enjoined (vv. 5, 6)

John emphasizes again the essential commandment of love among Christians, one "that we have had from the beginning." This stress on the fellowship of believers is prelude to what he is going to have to say later about a Christian's relationship to those who are not Christian. While he wishes to emphasize the principle of love as vital and valid in Christian experience, John does not want to invalidate the principle of Christian separation. Love is not to be interpreted merely as good will toward men, but as a moral principle that leads us to walk according to the commandments of God.

II. Unscriptural Ways Contrasted (vv. 7–11)

1. Deceivers in the World (vv. 7–9)

John points out that many deceivers have gone out into the world, for example, Gnostic preachers who denied the reality of the incarnation (v. 7). These men, deceivers and Antichrists, do not abide in the doctrine of Christ or have God as their father (vv. 7, 9). The Christian must therefore guard himself against being led astray lest he lose what he has already accomplished in Christ and fail to receive the full reward of his faithfulness (v. 8).

2. *Wisdom in Discriminating Fellowship (vv. 10, 11)*

A false preacher is not to be received into one's house; he is not worthy of the hospitality offered to real Christians. In the day in which John writes, itinerant preachers made their way from place to place, living by the hospitality of Christians. Thus, to offer such hospitality was really to participate in the work of the preachers.

The admonition to give him no greeting is clear when we understand that the word "greeting" means more than "hello." It involves wishing him Godspeed in his work. Obviously to do this in relation to false preachers puts one in the position of approving the message preached. The abiding principle of these verses is that Christians must be careful that the cause to which they give their money, their time, their influence is consistent with the gospel truth.

III. Conclusion (vv. 12, 13)

John ends the letter with a promise that he will soon visit the friend and speak many things directly to her, and with a greeting from her "elect sister." This last seems to agree best with the interpretation that takes the "elect lady" to be an individual Christian.

III John

FRED L. FISHER

THERE IS NO REASON to doubt that John, the apostle, was the author of this epistle if his authorship is accepted for the Gospel and the other two epistles which bear his name.

The letter is addressed to "Gaius . . . whom I love in truth" (note the parallel with II Jn. 1). From the letter it would seem that Gaius was a loyal and active layman with considerable property, a man of prominence in his church. John seems to have met some of the brethren from the church who spoke well of him and informed John of some internal trouble in the church that involved Gaius and Diotrephes.

The purpose of the letter is to commend Gaius for his Christian hospitality in entertaining itinerant Christian preachers and helping them on their way, thus participating in their missionary work.

I. Greetings to Gaius and Commendation (vv. 1–8)

1. Salutation (vv. 1, 2)

John identifies the recipient of the letter, assures him of his personal love, and wishes for him material and physical prosperity in proportion to his spiritual prosperity.

2. His Ministry to Brethren (vv. 3–8)

John expresses the joy that is his because of the report that Gaius is walking in the truth (v. 3). He states that his greatest joy in the ministry—in this all true ministers share—is to find that his spiritual children are making a habit of walking in the truth of the Gospel.

He commends Gaius heartily for his extension of the hospitality of his home to those who are brethren, even though they were strangers to Gaius (v. 5). These men were Christian missionaries who went out because of the "Name," that is the name of Jesus Christ, and took nothing from the Gentiles, that is, pagans. Thus they were dependent on the help of Christians along the way to sustain them in their ministry (v. 7). John says that Gaius does well when he entertains them and brings them "forward on their journey" (v. 7, "send them on," RSV). This expression means to pay the expenses of their travel. This is to be done in a manner that is "worthy of God." Though our modern method of supporting missionaries has changed, it should still be done in a manner worthy of God. The motive which John gives for such help to Christian missionaries is that we may become fellow-workers with them for the truth of the Gospel (v. 8).

II. Leaders Contrasted (vv. 9–12)

1. Apostate Diotrephes (vv. 9–11)

John explains that he had written the church, probably about missionary support, but Diotrephes, described as one who loves the pre-eminence in the church, refused to receive John (v. 9). John promises to recall the works of Diotrephes to the church when he comes and remind them that Diotrephes had not only talked against John and refused to receive the Christian missionaries into his home, but had cast out of the church (perhaps Gaius was one victim) those who did receive them (v. 10). Gaius is admonished not to imitate the evil worker but the good, knowing that the man who does good is from God but the man who does evil has never seen God (v. 11).

2. Good Demetrius (v. 12)

Demetrius is approved as one of those who does good and has the testimony of the brethren, as well as of John, to his Christian character and zeal.

III. Conclusion (vv. 13, 14)

John speaks of many other things he wishes to say but does not wish to write down (v. 13), and expresses a hope that he will soon be able to visit Gaius (v. 14). He prays that Gaius may have the Christian blessing of peace, sends salutations from the friends of Gaius and asks him to greet John's friends by name for him (v. 14).

Jude

E. EARLE ELLIS

IN AN OBSCURE corner of the New Testament is the letter called Jude, known more for its brevity than its content. Jude's theme of judgment is never popular in a comfortable church. Yet in this capsule of Scripture is a divine message which is ever relevant for the Church of God. And perhaps it has never been more relevant than it is today.

I. Greeting and Purpose (vv. 1–4)

Jude calls himself Jesus Christ's "slave," a term frequently used by New Testament writers (II Pet. 1:1; Tit. 1:1; Rom. 1:1). This term stands in capital letters over all that Jude writes, and emphasizes the brand-mark common to all true Christians.

Jude does have a claim to fame, however; he is the brother of James. A number of men called James appear in the New Testament. One of these, a brother of Jesus and leader in the Jerusalem church, was also brother to one named Judas, or Jude. There is, in addition, an apostle called Judas "the brother" (or son) of James

1241

(Lk. 6:16). Since Jude distinguishes himself from the apostles, the former suggestion is the more probable. It serves to identify Jude as one who, although not an apostle, knows the apostolic doctrine and can, therefore, speak with authority.

In keeping with Paul's practice (Rom. 1:6; I Cor. 1:2), Jude speaks of believers as "called ones," and adds to the usual Jewish greeting, "peace," the distinctively Christian virtues, "grace" and "love."

While Jude had intended to write them on a common evangelical theme, certain serious developments within the church impelled him to change his mind (vv. 3, 4). His letter is an exhortation to the "saints," that is, Christian believers (cf. Acts 9:13), to put up a real fight for the faith" (cf. vv. 17 ff., Phillips). "Faith" means here a body of apostolic doctrine (cf. Gal. 1:23; Phil. 1:27) including intellectual and moral truths—truths which are endangered by certain quislings in their midst. Long before, the apostles had prophesied there would come such counterfeits, and Jude intends to apply their predictions in no uncertain terms. These men, who have eased themselves into the Christian fellowship, are without genuine piety. They have (1) perverted the wonderful truth of the "grace of God" into a license for sinful behavior and (2) denied the authority and lordship of Jesus Christ.

Jude is here concerned with a heresy later known as Antinomian Gnosticism. Its champions pretended to possess a "secret clue to knowledge" and used Christian freedom as an excuse to sin. While it was most fully developed in the second century, the error begins right in the New Testament churches (cf. Rom. 6:1 ff.; I Cor. 5:1 ff.; Rev. 2:14, 20). Second Peter, written to Jude's readers, predicts this very evil (II Pet. 2:1–22). It has now reached such alarming proportions in the church that Jude devotes the whole of his correspondence to it. The importance of having a "New Testament church" is rightly stressed today. Jude's letter raises an important question: "What kind of New Testament church?"

II. God's Past Judgments upon Evil Persons (vv. 5–11)

Jude proceeds to apply former divine judgments to the present situation. Of these the first three—judgments upon the unbelieving Israelites, the fallen angels, Sodom and Gomorrah—form the substance of the section; the last three—Cain, Balaam, Korah—compare the present false teachers to three sly Old Testament characters.

Israel in the wilderness is used elsewhere in the New Testament as a prototype of the Church in the present age (cf. Heb. 3:10 ff.; I Cor. 10:1–15). It is an especially appropriate warning here since these men, like unbelievers in the Exodus, associated themselves with the people of God and then betrayed their faith. Church membership is no sure sign of salvation; the faithful "wheat" and the unfaithful "weeds" (Mt. 13:24–30) grow together, but in His own time, God will pull up the "weeds" and destroy them.

The sin of the angels is that they "failed in their high duties and abandoned their proper sphere" (Phillips). This depicts a disobedience or rebellion of some undisclosed nature. The reference doubtless relates to II Peter 2:4, and the source of the thought may lie in interpretations given in Jewish tradition to two Old Testament passages. In Genesis 6:1 ff., the "sons of God" were viewed as angels who lusted after the "daughters of men." In another interpretation the sin of the fallen angels was a usurpation of authority. These traditions are present in the apocryphal Book of Enoch which Jude seems to have known. Jude does not elaborate but merely alludes to the tradition mentioned in II Peter to illustrate the truth he desires to convey: even angels, God's highest order of creation, who sinned, were brought under divine judgment. How then can sinful men expect to escape God's wrath?

The sin of Sodom stressed here is sexual perversion, both fornication and homosexuality. If the phrase, "even as" (v. 7), refers to the sin of the angels, it draws a close parallel between their sin and that of Sodom. In Sodom's case, at least, the emphasis is placed upon the type of sin which brought God's judgment. It is not unlike a judgment brought against our age by a contemporary French writer who predicts that when future historians write of modern man, a sentence will suffice: "He fornicated and read the papers." For this sin, Sodom and Gomorrah "are now before us as a specimen of the fire of the ages in the punishment which they are undergoing" (Weymouth). Unlike the first two, Sodom's judgment remains visible to all in the "continually smoking wasteland" at the southern end of the Dead Sea. The fire of God's judgment is eternal in its effect, consuming utterly and offering no possibility of restoration (cf. Mt. 3:12; 18:8; Mk. 9:43).

These men, Jude continues, are guilty of these very sins (vv. 8–10;

cf. II Pet. 2:10, 11). They use their so-called "dreams" or "revelations" (*1*) for immorality (as Sodom), (*2*) to reject authority (as the fallen angels), and (*3*) to blaspheme the "heavenly glories" (Phillips). Their "blasphemy" may have been a skeptical or mocking attitude toward the supernatural world, a sin not unknown in our own time. More likely their sin is a defaming of or sitting in judgment upon the supernatural realm, thereby usurping the authority of God. Thus, the dispute of Michael and Satan serves to emphasize the point: even the archangel would not usurp God's prerogative of judgment upon the most evil of the angelic "dignities." Not so these men. Against things of which they are spiritually ignorant, they blaspheme; things which they naturally comprehend, they pervert.

The Old Testament comparisons conclude with three further examples (v. 11). As if to emphasize the gravity of his condemnation, Jude precedes these with a "woe" that is reminiscent of Jesus' judgment upon the Pharisees (Mt. 23). As the first three, these illustrations may represent the particular kinds of wickedness characteristic of the false teachers. Cain is known for his hatred of the righteous (I Jn. 3:12) and for his lack of faith (Heb. 11:4); Balaam led Israel into immorality and idolatry (Num. 31:16; Rev. 2:14); Korah rebelled against God's appointed authorities (Num. 16). In like manner these Antinomian Gnostics tempted Christians to idolatry (through the eating of meat offered to idols?), encouraged immorality in the name of "Christian liberty," and rebelled against the authority of the apostles and of the leaders of the Church.

III. Indictment of the False Christians (vv. 12–16)

The letter continues with a twelvefold indictment describing the character of these false teachers. In the apostolic church, the Lord's Supper was preceded by a meal called "*agape*" or "love feast." The first two criticisms of the false teachers are leveled at their conduct at these gatherings. They evidently gathered apart from the other Christians, cared only for themselves, and ignored the proper significance of the meal (cf. I Cor. 11:20–22). Indeed, the sum total of their actions is nothing but a barren and chaotic expression of their true spiritual condition. Jude depicts this by means of four natural phenomena—clouds, trees, waves, stars. Instability and purposelessness are the dominating theme in the descriptions: clouds which give promise of moisture but actually are without substance, being dispersed and wafted by the winds; trees which are "twice dead," not only unfruitful in autumn but uprooted from the ground; aimless waves which produce only the foam of their wild thrashing; stars which have deserted their proper orbit and whose fate is to be engulfed in the trackless wastes of darkness forever. In first century traditions, stars sometimes symbolized angelic beings, and the last example may be an allusion to the fallen angels spoken of earlier in the letter (cf. v. 6; Is. 14:12; II Pet. 2:4, 17; Rev. 1:20; Enoch 80:6).

The last six characteristics begin with a quotation which is not in the Old Testament but in the Book of Enoch (1:9), a composition of the first or second century before Christ. This writing was probably known to Jude's readers although there is no evidence that it was regarded as Scripture. Because of Jude's citation, some church fathers thought it inspired, but this estimate was never generally accepted. Jude does not quote it as Scripture, and the context suggests that he cites the "prophecy" simply as a well-known judgment which finds appropriate fulfilment in the false teachers. It concisely summarizes this aspect of II Peter 3 and underscores the "ungodly" character and practices of these men. The five remaining characteristics (v. 16) concern not their attitude toward God, but their relationship to other men. These evil workers make great claims and complain or flatter as the occasion requires, but underneath they are motivated only by one factor: *self*.

IV. Contrast between the False and Genuine Christians (vv. 17–23)

In closing, Jude gives an exhortation to the true believers. He recalls that their apostles kept telling them that scoffers would arise who had a "lust for ungodliness" (Acts 20:29; I Tim. 4:1; II Tim. 3:1-9; II Pet. 3:2 ff.). These things, therefore, are quite within the providence and control of God; they need not be an occasion for despair or reprisal. Rather, true Christians must demonstrate their qualitative difference from the "fifth column." As they cause destructive divisions, so you must "build up;" as they are worldly, without the spirit and limited to the natural realm, so you must pray in the power of the Holy Spirit. By doing this, believers will "keep themselves" (cf. vv. 1, 24; Phil. 2:12, 13) in the love of God, the true foundation from which to "contend for the faith" (cf. v. 3).

This "love of God" will mold their attitude even toward false Christians. For as they remember the mercy of Jesus Christ in granting them eternal life, they will in turn show mercy to those who remain under the power of sin (vv. 21–23). Earnest discussion may turn some from the road to ruin they are on; convinced apostates one may only "pity in fear." Their sin may be compared to a leper's flesh-spotted tunic—something to be avoided at all costs.

V. Doxology (vv. 24–25)

In this well-known benediction, Jude rests his case. The final and secure hope for Christians in temptation is God Himself. He is able to keep them from falling; He is able to cause them to stand—faultless and with the exceeding joy of victory (cf. Rom. 14:4; Col. 1:22). The latter picture is of the sons of God in the resurrection, before "the presence of his glory." At this note of final consummation and full deliverance, the focus of the doxology turns toward God. Perhaps in answer to some of the errors against which he has written, Jude stresses that God alone is God; He alone is Saviour. Many manuscripts add here "through Jesus Christ our Lord." The ascriptions of praise—glory and majesty, dominion and power—are attributes which characterize God from eternity to eternity. Man cannot "give" them to Him; he can only recognize them and adore.

Revelation

MERRILL C. TENNEY

EPILOGUE: CHRIST'S CALL 22:6–21
   Call to Obedience 22:6–11
   Call to Labor 22:12–15
   Call to Love 22:16–20
   Benediction 22:21

To MANY READERS of the Bible the Book of Revelation is an absolute mystery, an insoluble puzzle. They never read it because they are sure that it cannot be adequately interpreted, least of all by them. By taking such an attitude, however, they miss a great part of God's truth, for the book was written to help the Church, not to mystify it, and a special blessing is promised to those who accord it a hearing (1:3).

It should be fairly obvious that the book never would have been written at all if the writer did not expect that his readers and hearers would profit by it. Its meaning must have been sufficiently plain to them to warrant their reading it and using it. Not everything in it is immediately clear, but a great deal of its content can be interpreted and applied by the prayerful student.

Introduction (1:1–8)

One of the main keys to the book is its introduction, which comprises the opening verses of the first chapter. They are like the title page of a book which tells the reader what the content is, who the author is, what its purpose and destination are, and what the theme of action will be.

The real title is not the one at the heading of the page, which was supplied by the copyist of the original manuscript, but the title in the text: "The Revelation of Jesus Christ" (1:1). It may have two meanings: either (1) the revelation of which Christ is the subject, so that the revelation *is* Christ, or (2) a disclosure of truth which Christ possesses and which He imparts to us. The latter is probably correct because of the wording: "The Revelation . . . which God gave unto him" (1:1). Christ had disclaimed knowledge of the future when He was on earth (Mt. 24:36) by saying that it rested wholly in the hands of His Father. Now the Father has given to Him the vision of the future which He can unfold to His servants.

The other interpretation is possible and fitting, for the Revelation is indeed a disclosure of the person of Christ. In its four successive visions, it presents four different portraits of Him and gathers its prophecy around the manifestations of His person. The first, in Revelation 1:12–20, is the picture of Christ in the churches, as He administers their affairs. The second is Christ before the throne, as He takes the authority over the world and the commission to finish His redemptive work (5:1–14). The third is Christ in judgment, coming to destroy the hostile kingdoms of earth and to assert His right to rule (19:11–16). The last is Christ in eternity, the joy of His people (21:22–27). Even if the statements of the text are not always plain, these pictures are understandable by everybody. One should expect the book to give a full presentation of the person of Christ as He deals with His Church down through the years.

The *purpose* of the book is declared also: "to shew unto his servants things which must shortly come to pass" (1:1). Revelation is definitely predictive. Of course, not everything in it is predictive, but much of it is. It tells in advance what the perils of the Church are, what the general trends of world politics, world religion, and world society will be, and what will be the outcome at the end.

The *method* of this disclosure is indicated by the word *signify*, that is, to make known by signs or symbols. Just as signs on the road tell the motorist when stops and railroad crossings are ahead, so the "signs" in Revelation tell the reader what he may expect on the road of history that stretches out before him. Some of these symbols are explained; many are taken for granted; and in some cases we have lost their full meaning. Nevertheless, they had value for the audience of John's day, and they have value now. The Lord expected them to be understood by His servants, for whom John was the chosen recipient and transmitter of the Revelation.

The *time* of the fulfilment of these predictions is not stated exactly. Their beginning was to come shortly, for the text says, "the time is at hand" (1:3). The culmination of them will be the final judgment of the world and the establishment of the City of God, which have obviously not yet taken place. Certain aspects of the book have already been fulfilled; others are trends that are always visible in the world; still others are shadows of action not yet complete.

The *destination* of the book is the Seven Churches of Asia named later in the first vision. The writer was well known to them. These churches were situated in a rough circle, starting with Ephesus, and moving north to Pergamos, then southeast to Sardis, Philadelphia, and Laodicea, then northwest again to Ephesus. A messenger carrying this document could reach each of them in turn by traveling along the connecting highways. There were other churches in the province, but these were selected because they were the most prominent or the most representative of the group. Their varied characteristics made them a cross section not only of the churches of Asia, but of the churches of all time. The warnings and promises directed to them are intended for us as well.

The *greeting* of the book (1:4, 5a) is from God the Father, and God the Spirit, and God the Son. The eternity of God the Father, the vigilance of God the Spirit, like lamps of fire before the throne, and the resurrected person of God the Son give the book its stamp of authority.

The *dedication* is given also: "Unto him that loved [loveth] us, and washed [loosed] us from our sins in his own blood, and hath made us kings [to be a kingdom] and priests unto God and his Father: to him be glory, and dominion for ever and ever. Amen" (1:5b, 6). These three acts of Christ constitute our salvation: "He loveth us"—the motive; "He loosed us"—the act; "He made us to be a kingdom and priests"—the destiny. These are the reasons why the book is dedicated to Him, and why we offer grateful worship.

The *motto* of the book is in verse 7: "Behold, he cometh with clouds: and every eye shall see him." This is the main burden of Revelation from the beginning to the end. In the first vision, His coming is promised to the Church. In the second vision, His coming becomes the climax of God's process in dealing with the world. In the third vision, His coming is the catastrophic culmination of the conflict between God and Satan which has been going on since Eden. In the last vision, the effect of His coming is the introduction of the eternal state.

Last of all is the *signature* on the book: "I am Alpha and Omega, the beginning and the ending, saith the Lord" (1:8). As a book bears the name of its publisher to show that it is sponsored by a reputable firm, so the Revelation has a signature that shows the divine sponsorship. The eternal God, almighty in power, without beginning and without end, is the executor of the plans related here, and will carry them through without failure.

I. First Vision: Christ and the Church (1:9—3:22)

The structure of Revelation develops naturally into four visions of unequal length and of differing content. All of them, however, are introduced in the same manner and with almost identical phraseology. Each mentions the seer personally, to show that the things which he recounted were a part of his personal experience. Each begins with the phrase, "I was in the Spirit," (1:10; 4:2; 17:3; 21:10) which implies that he was under the power of the Holy Spirit in a state different from ordinary physical existence. He was transferred to a different scene of action where he saw things that were not ordinarily given to mortal sight. Each occurrence of this phrase refers to a different place. The first vision states that he was in Patmos, which was doubtlessly physically true in relation to all of them (1:9), but the context of the vision indicates that he was carried into the presence of Christ Who was walking in the midst of the lampstands (1:13). The second located the seer in heaven (4:1, 2); the third, in a wilderness (17:3); and the fourth, in a mountain (21:10). This kind of organization makes the book an orderly unit, arranged to develop a definite theme, and shows that a careful survey of it may aid in interpreting its mysteries.

1. Portrait of the Priestly Presence (1:9–20)

Obviously this portrait is not a photograph. It is an idealized representation which brings out the character of Christ as He deals with His Church in the progress of the present age. He is human in form, and still wears the body of the incarnation. The white hair indicates eternity and dignity. The eyes as a flame of fire are able to pierce all hypocrisy to discern the Church as it really is. The feet like burnished brass mark the tread of impending judgment. The voice like the sound of many waters dominates the babel of other distractions. The sharp sword slays all falsehood by His truth.

2. Letters to the Seven Churches (2:1—3:22)

The messages to the churches are uniform in structure, though the proportions of the component elements differ. Each has a salutation to the "angel" of the church, who is its guardian and leader.

Perhaps the word "angel" should here be interpreted in its original sense of "messenger," rather than in its technical sense of a heavenly being. Each letter begins with an identification of Christ taken from the initial portrait. For each church there is a word of commendation if it is deserved, the condemnation of its specific sins, and a challenge to repentance. Finally, a special promise is given to the individual members who rise above the temptations that beset their particular group.

Ephesus (2:1–7) was the church that was endangered by its own success. It was orthodox, industrious, and faithful; but its love was cooling, and the Lord called it sharply to repentance.

Smyrna (2:8–11) had been a suffering church. Poverty and the hatred of the Jewish population of the city had brought great hardship to them. The Lord offered no adverse criticism of this church; He had only encouragement as it faced tribulation.

Pergamos (2:12–17) was situated at the very center of heathen worship by the great altar of Zeus. Perhaps that is why the phrase, "where Satan's seat is" (v. 13), occurs here. Already one of its members had suffered martyrdom for his faith. The influence of this heathenism had penetrated the church. The "doctrine of Balaam" refers to the teaching of a heathen prophet who succeeded in corrupting the people of Israel by introducing immoral types of worship among them (Num. 25). The church of Pergamos needed to purify itself, and to expel these persons.

Thyatira (2:18–29) had much the same problem. It must have been a more active church than Pergamos, for the Lord spoke of its "love, service, faith, patience, and works" (v. 19). Idolatry and immorality were taught in the church by some woman called Jezebel, the name of the heathen wife of Ahab, who brought these sins into Israel (I Kings 16:31–33).

For the church of Sardis (3:1–6) the Lord had little to say that was good, except that there were a few who "had not defiled their garments" (v. 4). He warned them to strengthen the few remaining virtues they possessed.

The church of Philadelphia (3:7–13) gained the most unqualified commendation. Despite the fact that it was the weakest of the seven, the Lord promised to give it full opportunity for service and to vindicate it in the presence of its enemies.

Laodicea (3:14–22) is distinguished by having the worst record and the greatest promise. Outwardly prosperous and powerful, it was completely proud and complacent, feeling no need of anything that the Lord could offer. He threatened to reject it utterly, yet pictured himself standing at its threshold, knocking and waiting for admittance.

In all seven letters, the final challenge to the overcomer is addressed not to the group, but to the individual. The action of the church begins with the response of each single member. All of these exhortations are spoken in the light of the Lord's coming, which becomes more urgent as the letters progress, until he says, "I stand at the door . . ." (3:20).

II. Second Vision: Christ and the World (4:1—16:21)

Having given the divine view of the churches, the revelator moves on to the second main vision. The voice that summoned the seer to this new vision said: "I will shew thee the things which must be hereafter" (4:1). This is a fulfilment of the initial promise of the book (1:10, 19). From this point on to the end, it is understood that Revelation is speaking of the future, but what is the "future"?

Four different principles or schools of interpretation try to answer this question. The *Preterist,* who believes that the prophecies of the Book of Revelation have already been fulfilled, says that the language of this verse is simply the conventional usage of all such literature, which puts under the guise of prediction what is happening in the present. Revelation, according to this viewpoint, is only a symbolic description of the historical circumstances in which the Church of the first century was involved, and really contains no prophecy.

The *Historicist* has another view. He contends that Revelation gives a symbolic panorama of all history down to the end of time. The overthrow of Rome, the Saracen invasions, the Reformation and the struggle with the Papacy have been identified by expositors. This view takes the element of predictive prophecy more seriously, though its advocates are by no means agreed on the details of interpretation they set forth.

The *Futurist* school holds that the entire content of Revelation beginning with the fourth chapter is confined to the consummation of the age. The Futurist interpretation has the advantage of greater definiteness than the others, though one wonders how the readers could "read, hear, and keep" things that would never take place in their lifetime.

The *Idealist* says that Revelation was never intended to describe actual history, but that it is the symbolic picture of the moral and spiritual conflict between good and evil. This view emphasizes the spiritual and ethical quality of Revelation.

All these views have something of value to contribute. The Preterist reminds us that the roots of Revelation are in history, and that it must be interpreted at least partially in contemporary terms. The Historicist recognizes its historical span from the first century to eternity. The Futurist tries to do justice to the predictive quality of Revelation. The Idealist reminds us that the study of this book is intended to strengthen the moral and spiritual fibers of a living church.

1. Commission of the Lamb (4:1—5:14)

The two opening chapters of this vision provide the setting for all subsequent action in the book. The scene is in heaven, centered on the throne of God. Around it are ranged various orders of beings: the four "beasts," or better, "living creatures," which seem to represent animate creation; the elders, who represent redeemed humanity, twelve for Israel and twelve for the Church; and the innumerable host of angels ranged around the throne in concentric circles. In the hand of Deity lies a small scroll, sealed with seven seals. Its significance is not stated, but deduction from its importance gives the impression that it contains the commission to execute God's redemptive purpose for the world.

As the seer gazes on the scene, a strong angel issues this challenge "Who is worthy to open the book, and to loose the seals thereof?" (5:2). When no volunteers appeared, the seer "wept much" (v. 4). Was it possible that the redemption of creation should go by default? The angel told him not to weep, for the Lion of the tribe of Judah, the Root of David, had proved Himself worthy to undertake the task. These titles of Christ connect His work directly with the prophecy of the Old Testament. As the Lion of the tribe of Judah, He is the heir of the patriarchal promises to Abraham, Isaac, and Jacob (Gen. 49:9, 10). As the Root of David, He is the scion of the royal house Who is entitled to the throne which has been long vacant (Lk. 1:32). From patriarchs and kings He has inherited the rights of God's covenants which enable Him to take the scroll and to unfold the purpose of God.

Nevertheless He is not introduced as a king, but as "a Lamb as it had been slain" (5:6). Not by his royal rights, but by his sacrificial death has He prevailed over His enemy. "Slain" is a mild translation of the word used here; it really means "slaughtered." Christ died a sacrifice to pay the penalty of sin. Judgment has fallen on Him, and by Him the forfeited rights of humanity have been restored. As He opens the seals, He is carrying forward the work of redemption which was begun at Calvary.

2. Breaking of the Seven Seals (6:1–17; 8:1–5)

The breaking of the seven seals introduces a series of judgments which may not be totally new in character, but which are invested with a new significance by the purpose for which they are exercised and by their connection with the prospect of the coming of Christ. The first four are closely related in kind and in sequence. Their imagery is uniform, and each one is logically the result of the one preceding.

The first seal brings a rider on a white horse, armed for battle and crowned for conquest, like a Roman general setting out on a campaign. He seems to represent *imperialism*, the desire of man for power.

The second horse is flame-red, and its rider is empowered to take peace from the earth. Conquest means war; and the second judgment is war that devastates and subjugates the lands over which it rides.

The third horse is black, the color of famine. The scales carried by the rider signify scarcity of food that must be rationed by weight. "A quart of wheat for a denarius" (RSV) means that the ordinary day's wage of a laboring man would buy only enough grain to sustain him, with nothing left to clothe or shelter him, or to support his family. War always brings economic scarcity in its wake, with an imbalance of luxury goods. In this judgment, oil and wine are still abundant, but the staple grains are scarce.

The fourth horse, called "pale," is literally "green," the sickly, greenish-gray color of death. "Death" may mean disease or pestilence, and Hades, the personified unseen world of the dead, follows along with it. Epidemics accompany famine as one of the results of war.

These four judgments are not novelties, nor can we say that they will appear only in the future. The point of this account is that God will make them the means of preparing the way for Christ's coming.

The fifth seal introduces a new force: the prayers of the martyrs.

The souls of those who lost their lives for Christ cry out from under the altar. They demand vindication, because their persecutors have prospered, while they have suffered torture and death. God is not unmindful of their need, and will act in due time.

The sixth seal implies that cosmic forces will be loosed to bring judgment. Earthquakes, the obscuring of the light of the sun and moon, a hail of falling stars, and atmospheric disturbances that make the sky appear to be rolled up like a scroll will bring terror on the earth. With the seventh seal (8:1) there comes a new set of judgments which will be treated more fully farther on.

The seals are all general in character. They represent forces which lead up to the final judgments. The first four are in a sense abstractions: force, war, famine, death. These, with the dissension of nations, the suffering of martyrs, and the elements of nature, will all work toward the end of bringing the climax of God's redemptive purpose.

3. Parenthesis (7:1–17)

The Sealing of the 144,000 (7:1–8). The seventh chapter is a parenthesis in the seals between the sixth and the seventh. God's judgments are suspended while He places a protective seal on the foreheads of His servants. This group belongs to Israel, and there seems to be no very good reason for not taking the statement literally. Twelve tribes are mentioned, although Dan is omitted from the list, and Manasseh and Joseph really duplicate each other.

The Unnumbered Multitude (7:9–17). The second half of the parenthesis is devoted to another group who are quite different. The first group contained a fixed number; the second, "a great multitude, which no man could number." The 144,000 were taken from the children of Israel; the unnumbered multitude were composed of "all nations, and kindreds, and people, and tongues." The 144,000 were upon the earth; the multitude were before the throne in heaven. They seem to be the great miscellaneous body of the saved, who have been lifted into heaven.

4. The Seven Trumpets (8:6—11:19)

The seventh seal brings a change in the method of judgment. All of the preceding seals deal with forces that are currently operative in the earth, and that are simply adapted for the purpose of judgment. At the seventh seal, a censer, filled with coals from the altar, is flung into the earth. In the great vision of Isaiah (Is. 6) one coal was used to purge Isaiah's lips. In this passage, a full censer is used to purge the earth.

Trumpets were used to call assemblies together or to convey orders in battle (Num. 10:1–10). These trumpets announce the judgments of God on the material earth. Unlike the seals, they are not abstract, but concrete.

Sounding of the Trumpets (8:7—9:21; 11:15–19) The first trumpet brings a rain of hail and fire upon the earth mingled with blood (8:7). It sounds like some kind of chemical warfare. It would leave one-third of the earth a scorched, slimy, smelly landscape.

The second trumpet sends a huge, jagged mass of material plunging into the sea. The resulting chemical change in the water makes it seem like blood. One-third of the fishing and one-third of the shipping are ruined.

At the third trumpet, a star falls from heaven, and poisons one-third of the springs of water, with fatal effects for many men.

The fourth trumpet extinguishes one-third of the light of sun, moon, and stars.

These first four affect chiefly the physical resources of the earth. The last three trumpets affect the personal life of man.

The fifth trumpet reveals a "star" falling from heaven to earth. Because a personal pronoun is applied to it (9:2), we are justified in interpreting it as representing some being, probably an angel (1:20). It may refer to Satan, who was driven from heaven, and who is now permitted to bring forth upon the earth a horde of demons who torment men for five months. They are likened to locusts who can inflict a painful sting with their tails, as scorpions do. Since they cannot be exterminated, they will make life unbearable for men.

The sixth trumpet will be similar in character (9:14). "The four angels which are bound at the river Euphrates" seem to be a quartet of specially malignant beings, who will command an army of 200,000,000 horsemen. One-third of the earth will be decimated by this plague.

The important note at this point is that under these plagues "men repented not" (9:20). Having refused to serve God, they are given a taste of what the devil can do. Logically one would expect that they would turn to God, but instead they cling obstinately to their idolatries, murders, occult arts, lust, and theft.

Parenthesis: the Little Book (10:1–11). At the end of the sixth trumpet, as at the end of the sixth seal, there is an interlude of thought which brings in three episodes: the angel with the little book, the measuring of the temple, and the two witnesses.

The angel with the book is a person of great authority, though he is not named. Some expositors think that he is Christ; others, that he is simply one of the most prominent of the angelic order. The little book in his hand may be the same scroll described in chapter 5, now open for all to see. He declared that there will be no further delay, but that when the seventh trumpet shall sound, the mystery of God will be finished (10:6, 7). This "mystery of God" is the purpose which God had declared through the prophets, and which would be brought to its conclusion by the opening of all the seals.

The eating of the book means simply that the seer was to absorb all that was in the scroll that he might be able to declare God's message. Ezekiel was commanded to eat a scroll which was written on both sides, and then to go to speak to the house of Israel (Ezek. 2:8—3:4). Jeremiah used a similar metaphor: "Thy words were found, and I did eat them: and thy word was unto me the joy and rejoicing of mine heart" (Jer. 15:26).

The Measuring of the Temple (11:1, 2). The measuring of the temple is indicative of preservation and protection. The passage seems to imply that a temple will be built which will be under Gentile control for three and one-half years.

The Two Witnesses (11:3–14). Coupled with the fate of the temple, and prophesying for the same period of time (v. 3) are the "two witnesses." There is little unanimity among expositors as to who they are. They bear a strong resemblance to Elijah, who closed the heavens in the days of Ahab (I Kings 17:1), and Moses, who brought plagues upon Egypt. These two men appeared with Jesus in the Mount of Transfiguration (Mt. 17:3), where they talked with Him about His coming death (Lk. 9:31). Perhaps they will reappear in the last days as messengers of God (Mal. 4:5, 6).

The seventh trumpet evoked an announcement: "The kingdoms of this world are become the kingdoms of our Lord, and of his Christ: and he shall reign for ever and ever" (11:15). This proclamation makes clear that the consummation has come.

5. The Signs (12:1—14:20)

Beginning with the twelfth chapter there is a section giving greater detail about the consummation of the age in the form of "signs." The word "wonder" in 12:1 (KJV) or "portent" (RSV) means the same thing as "sign." A sign is an object which stands for or directs attention to something else. Signs on the road point the way to a distant town; signs on store-fronts tell what firm occupies the building and what it sells. These signs depict the various forces in conflict with one another as the struggle between God and Satan for the rule of the world comes to its climax.

The Woman (12:1, 2, 5, 6, 14–16). The first sign is the woman, clothed with the sun, who is about to bear a man child. Many explanations have been offered, but perhaps the broadest interpretation would be that the woman is the historic people of God, Jew or Christian, in its long continuity, and that the man child is the promised seed, which should ultimately overcome Satan. This accords well with the prediction of God at the dawn of history (Gen. 3:15), and it identifies the man child with that seed which God preserved and which found its headship in Christ (Gal. 3:16). In the last days, the people of God will be in travail through persecution and suffering, and they will produce a seed bearing the image of Christ who will be caught up to the throne.

The Dragon (12:3, 4, 7–13, 15–17). The sign of the dragon is explicitly identified as Satan (v. 9). The seven heads and ten horns are symbolic of his power. The "third part of the stars of heaven" (v. 4) may refer to the angelic host, some of whom must have rebelled against God with him, and who were therefore expelled from the divine presence (v. 9). His persecution of the woman (v. 13) is caused by his failure to conquer heaven, and by the reaction from defeat.

The most important verse in this twelfth chapter is the eleventh: "And they overcame him by the blood of the Lamb, and by the word of their testimony, and they loved not their lives unto the death." Victory over Satan in public or in private is founded on the sacrifice of Christ, which has cut the ground from under his accusations (Rom. 8:33), because by the blood of Christ men are freed from the guilt and penalty of sin (Rom. 5:9). The testimony of the saved refutes Satan's lies, and their willingness to sacrifice their lives for

Christ is the exact opposite of Satan's philosophy of self-will. These things he cannot gainsay or resist.

The Man Child (12:5). The man child can be identified both with Christ and His Church. The prophecy of Psalm 2:9 is applied to both (Rev. 2:27). Christ and His Church are one, and the privileges that He possesses are shared by His followers.

Michael, the Archangel (12:7). His name means "like God." He is mentioned by Daniel as one of the "chief princes" (Dan. 10:13). In Jewish tradition he was one of the seven great angels that served God, each with a different function. He was the champion of God's holiness and the defender of His people.

The Beast from the Sea (13:1–10). The beast out of the sea is a composite figure taken from the four beasts of Daniel's vision (Dan. 7:1–7). The lion represented Babylon; the bear, Medo-Persia; the leopard, the Greek empire of Alexander the Great; and the fourth, with its iron teeth, Rome. Here the combination is given in reverse order to show that the last empire of earth would combine all the powers of its predecessors. It rises from the "sea" which is the type of the restless people (17:15). The description seems to indicate that empire and its head are united in the one figure, and that the beast is a personage who will become the head of the world. He is the emblem of a godless, totalitarian state.

The Beast from the Earth (13:11–18). Along with the beast from the sea comes the beast from the earth. His authority is religious, rather than political, but both work hand in hand. He possesses a mild and persuasive manner, but a diabolical authority (v. 11). He has at his disposal all the political authority of the first beast, which he uses to promote the worship of that beast, and to compel all men to bow to him. He can perform miracles, even to making the image of the first beast speak (v. 15). This worship he compels by economic pressure, since everyone must have on him "the mark of the beast" to be able to buy or sell. Those who resist will be reduced to starvation or slavery.

Perhaps the Roman state was the immediate example of this tendency when Revelation was written. Its emperor, Domitian, demanded that he be called "Lord and God." His worship was promoted by the religious authorities of Asia, and the imperial seal had to be placed on business documents to make them legal.

While these conditions did illustrate the principles discussed here, the prophecy seems to speak of a time yet to come. Totalitarianism is alive today in forms stronger than that of Rome. The "forty-two months" (13:5) ties the reign of the beast to the time of the end.

The "mark of the beast" (13:18) has been a standing puzzle for centuries. Basically it is built on the usage of the letters of the alphabet as numbers. The Greeks used the first letter of the alphabet as 1, the second letter as 2, and so on through to the end of the series. By adding together the values of the individual letters in any person's name, a number could be obtained which would be the "number" of his name. Since many combinations can add up to the same number, 666 is still indeterminate. Many guesses have been made, but no solution is certain. The most recent is that it stood for the sum of the initials on one of the coins of Domitian.

The Lamb on Mount Zion and His Followers (14:1–5). The last personage in this list is Christ, who again appears as the Lamb. Mount Zion is not the geographical site in Jerusalem, but the celestial Zion, "the city of the living God, the heavenly Jerusalem" (Heb. 12:22). The 144,000 with him are probably identical with the group mentioned in chapter 7. The number is the same; they have the Father's name written in their foreheads (v. 1); and they have been redeemed from the earth (v. 3). If the two groups are the same, then both the redeemed Jews and the redeemed Gentiles are translated into the presence of God as the final judgments of earth begin.

Parenthesis: The Angelic Announcements (14:6–20). In Greek drama, deaths, battles, and other events were not usually enacted, but were announced by messengers, so that the situation could be explained without making the performance too complicated. The announcements of Revelation 14 serve a somewhat similar purpose. They tie together the rest of the book with the seventh trumpet, and show how all these things can be related to it.

The first announcement is the preaching of the everlasting Gospel (14:6, 7). The retributive aspect is stressed; nevertheless, even judgment demands a return to God. It is the last call to men to accept God's generous provision of forgiveness and salvation.

The second is the declaration of the fall of Babylon. A detailed account is given in the third vision of Revelation; here it is only mentioned to set the chronology straight.

The third announcement (14:9–11) is the converse of the first; not mercy, but punishment is stressed. Between the worship of God and the worship of Satan's emissary, there can be no compromise. The doom of eternal destruction hangs over those who succumb to the pressure of evil.

The fourth angel speaks of the final harvest of the wheat of the earth as Christ, the Son of Man, reaps it (14:14–16). The harvest is ripe or overripe, and must be cut. The same figure appears in the Gospels, where a double crop of tares and wheat is predicted (Mt. 13:33–49).

The fifth announcement (14:17–20) changes the metaphor slightly from wheat to grapes. "The vine of the earth" is the growth of evil, the opposite of the "true vine" of John 15. The wicked are thrown into the winepress of God's wrath, where like grapes they are trodden under foot. The "winepress" is a preview of the last great battle between Christ and Antichrist (Rev. 19:11–21).

6. Seven Vials or Bowls (15:1—16:21)

By rights the seven vials or bowls (RSV) should be classed as one of the signs, for they are so listed (15:1). They are a separate series of seven following along after the seventh trumpet, and they occupy so much space in the narrative that they deserve to be treated separately. They are the intensification and conclusion of the physical judgments on the earth which began with the seals and continued with the trumpets. They seem to be confined to the last short period of time which is called by some expositors "the great tribulation," since the first bowl affects those who "had the mark of the beast" (16:2).

Singing Saints (15:1–4). Prior to the outpouring of these bowls there is a contrasting scene in heaven. All those who "had gotten the victory over the beast, and over his image, and over his mark, and over the number of his name" stand on the sea of glass before the throne and join in a triumphant song (v. 2). The song implies that they may include both the 144,000 of Israel and the great Gentile multitude mentioned in chapter 7. The theme is "the song of Moses and the Lamb," which recalls the triumphal chant of Exodus 15, in which Moses celebrated the overthrow of Pharaoh in the Red Sea, and the worthiness of Christ, Who delivered them from the beast and his image.

Judgments (15:5—16:21). From within the sanctuary in heaven emerges a procession of seven angels, clothed in the garments of judgment (15:6). In their hands are placed seven bowls filled with the wrath of God, which they pour into the earth. The bowls are much like the trumpet-judgments, but are more intense. The first, like the plague of boils on Egypt (Ex. 9:8–12) causes festering sores. The second (16:3) turns the sea into blood. Navigation ceases; commerce dies; fishing is impossible. The third (16:4–6) affects the inland waters in the same way. The fourth increases the heat of the sun, bringing unendurable heat and dangerous radiation. The fifth bowl (16:10, 11), after the searing heat, brings impenetrable darkness. Such a sequence would be totally unnerving, since the darkness comes without warning and continues without intermission. The sixth bowl causes the drying up of the Euphrates River, the boundary between East and West, allowing the hordes of the "kings of the east" to invade the West at their pleasure.

To add to this "war of nerves" caused by the final plagues, the dragon, beast, and false prophet begin a campaign of demonic propaganda to draw all nations to the last great battle. The center will be Armageddon, or, as the Hebrew word means, the "mountain of Megiddo" (16:13–16). Megiddo was an ancient city located on the edge of the plain of Esdraelon which had been a battlefield for centuries. It lies just south of the junction of the coastal road in Palestine which runs north and south, and of the road from east to west, which is the caravan route to India and the East. As the meeting point of three continents, it is a strategic spot for attack.

The bowl of the seventh angel (16:17, 18, 21) was not poured out upon the earth, but upon the air. The concluding cataclysm brings the announcement, "It is done," or, freely, "It's all over!" Earthquake and a destructive hail follow, the hailstones weighing one hundred pounds.

The three series of the seals, the trumpets, and the bowls, whether successive, simultaneous, or overlapping, bring the reader down to the end of the age when the contending forces of God and Satan must have their final contest. This crisis is discussed in more detail in the next section.

III. Third Vision: Christ and Victory (17:1—21:8)

The third vision of Revelation deals with separate phases of the crisis: the downfall of Babylon (17:1—18:24) which depicts in symbolic form the collapse of the present world-system; the response of heaven (19:1–10) or the heavenly view of the collapse;

the victory over the beasts (19:11–21) which presents Christ as the final victor; the millennial Kingdom (20:1–6) in which He reorganizes and administers the affairs of the world; the last rebellion and the judgment of the white throne (20:7–15); and the new heavens and the new earth (21:1–8). The portrait of Christ connected with this section is to be found in Revelation 19:11–15. He is the triumphant victor, riding on the white horse, invincible in power, and ready to overthrow his enemies.

1. Fall of Babylon (17:1—18:24)

Two entire chapters are devoted to this subject. Babylon was the original city on the Euphrates, founded almost immediately after the flood (Gen. 11:19). Nebuchadrezzar made it the most prosperous city of the ancient world. Its gates were covered with colored tile; in its hanging gardens grew the fruits and flowers of all the Orient; its fortified walls seemed proof against attack; its commerce brought all the goods of the world to its doors. It was the center of heathenism. Long after it had ceased to be a political power, the priests of Babylon were famed for their learning and for the rites they celebrated in honor of the gods.

Babylon thus became the emblem of the height of godless culture. Pictured in this chapter as a harlot whose favors intoxicate the spirits of all those connected with her, she becomes the symbol of the abandoned civilization that is supported by anti-Christian force.

The seventeenth chapter gives the divine view of Babylon. Seated on the hideous beast which holds all political power, she lolls at ease, decked in the most expensive purple and scarlet robes, and wantonly offering a cup of indulgences to any who will drink. John may have identified her with Rome, which for him would be "that great city, which reigneth over the kings of the earth" (17:18). The name might apply equally well to Paris, London, or New York, or to any city that sums up the corrupt power of the present time.

The heads of the beast are interpreted in this passage. Because they are called "seven mountains on which the woman sitteth" (17:9) they have been identified with the seven hills of Rome. "Mountain," however, can in prophetic language be a term for a kingdom (Is. 2:2). The next verse (17:10) says that there are seven kings, which tends to confirm the idea that the heads are kingdoms. The ten horns represent the ten contemporaneous kings who revolt against Babylon, the harlot, and destroy her (v. 16). Babylon is the social, economic, and religious civilization of the last days, embodied in a city that dominates the earth.

The eighteenth chapter gives the earthly view of Babylon's fall. The first eight verses are taken up with an angelic announcement: "Babylon the great is fallen, is fallen." As the source of moral corruption, God has judged her, and she is utterly desolate. He summons his people to leave her, lest they share in her sins and plagues.

Three classes of people mourn her overthrow. The kings of the earth (18:9) have lost their social center, and feel keenly the fall of Babylon's court and prestige. The merchants (v. 11) have lost their best market, where luxury wares of all kinds were exchanged. The mariners (v. 17) mourn the loss of the port where they sold their cargoes at a profit and found the pleasures that delighted them.

The doom of Babylon is pronounced finally by a mighty angel, who declares that it shall sink into the sea of forgetfulness as a millstone, never to rise again.

2. *The Response in Heaven (19:1–10)*

Babylon's fall brings a response of joy before the throne of God. The four Alleluias (19:1, 3, 4, 6) express the gratitude of the worshippers for the removal of the debasing influence and for the avenging of the martyrs. There is a sharp contrast here in the fall of the harlot and the marriage of the Lamb. The "bride," or "wife," is a figure of the Church. The same metaphor occurs in Ephesians where the comparison is drawn between the two in the injunction: "Husbands, love your wives, even as Christ loved the church, and gave himself for it" (Eph. 5:25). The "fine linen" which she wears is the righteousness the believers have wrought. As Babylon was clothed in the gaudy robes of display, the bride of Christ will be adorned by the simplicity of holiness.

3. *Victory over the Beasts (19:11–21)*

A new aspect of Christ is now revealed in His conquest. Equipped for war, He and the heavenly armies descend to meet the armies of the Antichrist in the last battle. His titles, Faithful and True (19:11), the Word of God (v. 13), King of Kings and Lord of Lords (v. 16) describe His character and His power. No description of battle is given, but the victory is complete.

4. *The Millennial Kingdom (20:1-6)*

There are three main interpretations of this passage. The post-millennial view looks upon the Millennium as a period closing the conquest of the world by the preaching of the Gospel. After a long gradual process with many apparent reverses, the majority of men are won to Christ and His Kingdom comes. At the end of an indefinite period of peace and righteousness, He will return to judge the living and the dead, and the ages of eternity will begin.

The amillennial view treats the thousand years as wholly figurative, either as representing the reign of the saints with Christ in heaven, or else considers them to be the present age in which the Gospel is preached freely and in which Satan is restrained. There will be no outward and visible reign of Christ on earth until after the judgment.

The premillenarian view holds that Christ will return to earth to abolish all outward opposition, that He will establish here an outward visible Kingdom lasting one thousand years more or less, and that a short final conflict with Satan shall end in his complete defeat, the judgment of the wicked, and the coming of the city of God. The premillennial interpretation is generally more literal than the other two.

Without insisting on any one of these views, it seems that the millennial reign is placed in chronological order after the conquest of earth by Christ and before the judgment of the white throne. It seems to be an interim in which Christ gives the earth a sample government such as it has never had before. It may be that this reign is the era of peace and righteousness predicted in Isaiah 11:9: "They shall not hurt nor destroy in all my holy mountain: for the earth shall be full of the knowledge of the Lord as the waters cover the sea."

5. *Final Conflict and Judgment (Rev. 20:7-15)*

Even a perfect government cannot make a perfect people. When Satan is released from his imprisonment, there will still be some who will rebel. But the attack on the saints meets sudden destruction (20:9), and Satan will be cast into the lake of fire with the beast and false prophet.

The judgment of the throne is the final assize for the world. There are gathered the dead, presumably the wicked, since the righteous have been raised and are reigning with Christ. They will be judged by "the books" which contain the records of their deeds, and by "the book of life," which is the register of the citizens of the Kingdom of Heaven. There will be no errors in the records, and the decisions will be irreversible.

6. The New Heavens and the New Earth (21:1–8)

The concluding part of the third vision reveals the eternal state of the saved in a new heaven and new earth. The new Jerusalem, only mentioned here but in the next vision described in more detail, is the gift of heaven rather than the invention of earth, the supreme expression of redemptive power.

IV. Fourth Vision: Christ in Eternity (21:9—22:5)

The third and fourth visions of Revelation are designed as a contrasting pair. Both are introduced by one of the angels who had the bowls; and in both the summons to the seer are identical: "Come hither, I will show thee . . ." (17:1; 21:9). Both deal with women, but one is a harlot, and the other a bride. The third vision occurred in a wilderness; the fourth in a mountain. The third ends with the overthrow of earth and all that is in it; the fourth presents a renewed earth and the eternal state of glory. The third revealed a corrupt city, Babylon; the fourth discloses a pure city, the new Jerusalem.

1. The New Jerusalem (21:9–21)

Again the vexing problem of literality appears. Is this city a solid cube, with a wall 216 feet high, having streets of metallic gold, gates of oyster pearl, and foundations of mineral jewels? Perhaps the best answer is that the seer was endeavoring to describe glories that could only be likened to the most gorgeous jewels he knew, and that the immense size and the dazzling colors of this city overwhelmed him. He saw it as he had seen the other cities of his own day, walled as a defense against enemies, built with gates open to all quarters of the compass for access by everybody, and beautiful beyond description.

The city is described by seven negatives, as if the seer could not find words for positive description, but could only say how it was different from the cities of earth.

It had *no temple* (21:22). Every city of John's day was filled with shrines, but in this city God dwelt directly with His people, and no building was needed.

It had *no sun or moon* (21:23). God's presence illumined it, so that there was no fluctuation between day and night.

Its gates were *never shut* (21:25). Walled cities usually closed their gates at night to keep out robbers and marauders. In this city there was nothing to fear.

Nothing that defiles can enter (21:27). Most of the eastern cities reeked with filth, and their streets were used as garbage dumps and sewers. In this city there will be neither physical nor moral uncleanness.

"And there shall be *no more curse*" (22:3). The first paradise of God was ruined by sin. God placed a curse on the ground that compelled man to wring his living from it by wearisome toil. In this city there will be work, but no frustration.

No night will ever fall on the city (22:5). In the Oriental cities few people went out at night. Thieves and footpads abounded, and travel was dangerous. In the new Jerusalem, the perils of darkness will never occur, because there will be no night.

No lamp will be used (22:5). The presence of God will make artificial light unnecessary.

2. *New Life with God and the Lamb* (21:22—22:5)

What will the positive activity of this life be? Heaven will not be a place of gilded dullness, nor of everlasting boredom. There will be numerous activities for its inhabitants.

There will be *perfect worship*. God and Christ will be the temple, and personal adoration will be the spontaneous outflow of every heart (21:22).

There will be *perfect enjoyment*. The nations and the kings shall come to the city to exhibit their works and to bring it their glories (22:24, 26).

There will be *perfect service*. "His servants shall serve him" (22:3). The inhabitants of that city will find their highest pleasure in carrying out the assignments that God gives them.

There will be *perfect victory.* "They shall reign for ever and ever" (22:5). The defeats of this life will be unknown. Every act will be a success, and eternal life will be an unending triumph.

Epilogue: Christ's Call (22:6–21)

The last sixteen verses of Revelation constitute an epilogue or summary for the entire book. The four great visions, presenting four stages in the drama of redemption, have closed. What do they mean? How can this symbolic, imaginative, apocalyptic work provide anything concrete for modern believers? Must we dismiss it as a piece of ancient writing which could be understood only by men of its own time, or by scholars who have the time and the interest to wrestle with its obscurities?

Note that the angel who talked with the seer and who showed him the last vision told him not to seal up the prophecy of the book (22:10). It was not to be hidden, but was to be used for the benefit of all comers. In consideration of the fact that it showed "Things which must shortly be done" (22:6), there is one message that it stresses: "Behold, I come quickly."

1. Call to Obedience (22:6–11)

This last quoted phrase occurs at three points in the Epilogue and summarizes its practical message. It occurs first in 22:7, where it makes an appeal to obedience. In this book are numerous challenges and commands, such as the one to come out of Babylon. If the reader believes that the Lord is really coming, he will obey His commands that he may not be found disobedient at His return.

2. Call to Labor (22:12–15)

The second use of this phrase is an appeal to labor. "And behold, I come quickly, and my reward is with me, to give every man according as his work shall be." We are saved by grace, but rewarded according to works. An expectant attitude will make men want to be as productive as possible, so that when the Lord judges their works He may find some permanent results that He can commend.

3. *Call to Love (22:16–20)*

The last appeal is to the emotions. The last promise of the Bible is "Surely I come quickly" (22:20), and with full heart the seer answers, "Even so, come, Lord Jesus" (22:20). Obedience and labor are both the product of love; and the crowning declaration of personal feeling which closes the book is the seer's intense desire to see Christ, "whom not having seen, we love" (I Pet. 1:7, 8), and Whom we shall see at His appearing.

4. *Benediction (22:21)*

Beautiful and brief is the benediction with which John closes the Revelation. With words of blessing, the Bible is brought to its gracious conclusion: "The grace of our Lord Jesus Christ be with you all. Amen."

Contributors

Allis, Oswald T. *The Five Books of Moses*

B.D., University of Pennsylvania; M.A., Princeton University; Ph.D., University of Berlin; D.D., Hampden-Sydney College. Instructor in Semitic Philology, Princeton Theological Seminary, 1910-1922; Assistant Professor, 1922-1929; Professor of Old Testament History and Exegesis, Westminster Theological Seminary, 1929-1930; Professor of Old Testament, 1930-1936; Payton Lecturer, Fuller Theological Seminary, 1952. Moderator, Presbytery of Philadelphia, 1934. Author of *The Five Books of Moses* and *Prophecy and the Church*.

Andersen, Francis I. *The Historical Books*

Th.L., Australian College of Theology; M.A., Johns Hopkins University, 1958 and candidate for Ph.D., 1959. Senior Tutor, Ridley Theological College, Australia, 1953-. Fulbright and Gilman Scholar, Johns Hopkins University, 1957-1958.

Archer, Gleason L., Jr. *Isaiah*

B.A. and Ph.D., Harvard University; B.D., Princeton Theological Seminary. Professor of Biblical Languages, Fuller Theological Seminary, 1948-. Author of *In the Shadow of the Cross* and *The Study Manual of the Epistle to the Hebrews*.

Bass, Clarence B. *Nahum*

B.A., Wheaton College; M.A., Wheaton Graduate School of Theology; Ph.D., University of Edinburgh; Post-Doctoral Studies, University of Zurich. Professor of Systematic Theology, Bethel Theological Seminary, 1955-. Author of *Survey of the Old Testament* and *The Writings and Writers of the New Testament*.

Blackwood, Andrew W. *The Poetical Books*

B.A., Harvard University; Th.B., Xenia Theological Seminary; D.D., University of South Carolina. Emeritus Professor of Homiletics and Chairman of the Practical Department, Princeton Theological Seminary. Author of twenty books (nine Pulpit Book Club selections) including *Leading in Public Prayer, Pastoral Leadership,* and *The Preparation of Sermons*.

Bromiley, Geoffrey W. *Haggai*

M.A., Cambridge University; Ph.D. and D. Litt., University of Edinburgh. Former Vice-Principal, Tyndale Hall, Bristol. Professor of Church History and Historical Theology, Fuller Theological Seminary, 1958-. His writings include *Reasonable Service, Baptism and the Anglican Reformers, Thomas Cranmer, Theologian,* and *Sacramental Teaching and Practice of the Reformation Churches*.

1271

Broomall, Wick
Esther

Th.B. and Th.M., Princeton Theological Seminary; M.A., Princeton University; Pastor, Westminster Presbyterian Church, Augusta, Georgia, 1958-. Former Professor of Systematic Theology and Hebrew, Erskine Theological Seminary. First Dean of Southeastern Bible College. Author of *The Holy Spirit* and *Biblical Criticism.*

Brown, W. Gordon
Ecclesiastes

A.B., McMaster University; M.A., University of Toronto. Pastor, Runnymede Baptist Church, Toronto, 1946-; Dean, Central Baptist Seminary, Toronto. Summer lecturer, Eastern Baptist Seminary and Gordon Divinity School. Executive Council of Fellowship of Evangelical Baptist Churches of Canada. Author of *Pagan Christianity.*

Bruce, F. F.
The Gospels

B.A., Cambridge University; M.A. and D.D., Aberdeen University. Rylands Professor of Biblical Criticism and Exegesis at the University of Manchester, England, 1959-. Formerly Lecturer in Greek at the Universities of Edinburgh and of Leeds, and Professor of Biblical History and Literature at the University of Sheffield. President, Victoria Institute, London. Editor, *The Evangelical Quarterly,* and *The Palestine Exploration Quarterly.* His published works include *The Books and the Parchments, The Spreading Flame, The Book of the Acts,* and *Second Thoughts on the Dead Sea Scrolls.*

Clark, Gordon H.
Romans

B.A. and Ph.D., University of Pennsylvania. Instructor in Philosophy, University of Pennsylvania, 1924-1937; Professor of Philosophy, Wheaton College, 1937-1943; Professor of Philosophy, Butler University, 1945-. Author of *Readings in Ethics, A Christian Philosophy of Education, A Christian View of Men and Things,* and *Thales to Dewey.*

Dayton, Wilber T.
Ephesians

B.A. and B.D., Houghton College; M.R.E. and Th.D., Northern Baptist Theological Seminary. Professor of Theology and Greek, Marion College, 1943-1957. Associate Professor of New Testament Greek, Asbury Theological Seminary, 1957-. Chairman, Seminary Division, Education Commission of National Association of Evangelicals.

Earle, Ralph
Mark

B.A., Eastern Nazarene College; B.D. and Th.D., Gordon Divinity School. Post-doctoral studies, Harvard and Edinburgh. Professor of New Testament, Nazarene Theological Seminary, 1945-. Author of *The Story of the New Testament, Meet the Minor Prophets,* and *Meet the Apostles.*

Ellis, E. Earle
Jude

B.D. and M.A., Wheaton College Graduate School; Ph.D., University of Edinburgh. Assistant Professor of New Testament Interpretation, Southern Baptist Theological Seminary. Author of *Paul's Use of the Old Testament.*

Fisher, Fred L.
I, II, and III John

B.A., Oklahoma Baptist University; Th.M. and Th.D., Southwestern Baptist Theological Seminary. Professor of New Testament, Northern Baptist Seminary, 1945-1946, and Hardin-Simmons University, 1946-1952. Professor of New Testament Interpretation, Golden Gate Baptist Seminary 1952-. Holland Foundation Lecturer, Southwestern Seminary, 1957. Writer of Adult Sunday School Lessons, 1958-1959, Sunday School Board of the Southern Baptist Convention. Author of *A Composite Gospel* and *Christianity is Personal.*

Geldenhuys, J. Norval   *Luke*

B.A. and B.D., Pretoria University, South Africa; Th.M., Princeton Theological Seminary. Elsie Ballot scholar, University of Cambridge and Princeton University. Director of Publications, Dutch Reformed Church, and of the United Protestant Publishers, South Africa; General Editor of Afrikaans Bible. Author of *Commentary on the Gospel of St. Luke, Supreme Authority, The Intimate Life,* and also a number of religious books in Afrikaans.

Gerstner, John H.   *Acts*

B.Th. and M.Th., Westminster Theological Seminary; Ph.D., Harvard University; D.D., Tarkio College. Jackson Scholarship, Harvard Divinity School. Professor of Church History and Government, Pittsburgh-Xenia Theological Seminary, 1950-. Author of *Ephesians, American Calvinism,* and *Gospel According to Rome.*

Goddard, Burton L.   *Malachi*

Th.B., Westminster Theological Seminary; S.T.M. and Th.D., Harvard University. Dean, Gordon Divinity School and Professor of Old Testament, 1943-. President, Deerwander Bible Conference Association. Regular contributor to *Daily Manna Calendar.*

Graybill, John B.   *Joel*

B.A., Wheaton College; B.D., Faith Theological Seminary; Ph.D., Brandeis University. Director, Department of Bible and Theology, Providence-Barrington Bible College. Contributor of *Jeremiah* to *Wycliffe Commentary.*

Grider, J. Kenneth   *The Prophetic Books*

Th.B. and B.A., Olivet Nazarene College; B.D. and M.A., Drew Theological Seminary; Ph.D., Glasgow University. Holder of Hamilton and Dundonald grants for study in Scotland, 1950-1952. Associate Professor of Theology, Nazarene Theological Seminary, 1953-.

Gwinn, Ralph A.   *Philippians*

B.A., Seattle Pacific College; B.D., Fuller Theological Seminary; Ph.D., Edinburgh University. Associate Professor of Religion, Knoxville College, 1957-. Contributing editor, *The Theological Wordbook.*

Harris, R. Laird   *Psalms*

Th.B. and Th.M., Westminster Theological Seminary; M.A., University of Pennsylvania; Ph.D., Dropsie College. Professor of Bible Exegesis, Faith Theological Seminary, 1937-1956; Visiting Professor of Bible, Wheaton College, 1957-1958; Professor of Old Testament, Covenant College and Seminary, 1956-. Moderator, Bible Presbyterian Church, 1956; Secretary, Evangelical Theological Society, 1949-1954. Author of *Introductory Hebrew Grammar, Inspiration and Canonicity of the Bible,* and *Inspiration and Interpretation.*

Harrison, Everett F. *The Epistles*

Th.B. and M.A., Princeton Theological Seminary; Th.D., Dallas Theological Seminary; Ph.D., University of Pennsylvania. Professor of New Testament, Fuller Theological Seminary, 1947-. Griffith Thomas Lecturer, Dallas Theological Seminary, 1958. Author of *The Son of God Among the Sons of Men;* reviser of *Alford's Greek Testament;* editor of *A Dictionary of Theology.*

Henry, Carl F. H. *John*

B.A. and M.A., Wheaton College; B.D. and Th.D., Northern Baptist Seminary; Ph.D., Boston University. Professor of Philosophy of Religion, Northern Baptist Theological Seminary, 1942-1947; Professor of Systematic Theology and Christian Philosophy, Fuller Theological Seminary, 1947-1956. Editor of *Christianity Today,* 1956-. Author of *Remaking the Modern Mind, Christian Personal Ethics,* and other works. Editor of *Contemporary Evangelical Thought* and *Revelation and the Bible.* Consulting editor, *The Biblical Expositor.*

Hubbard, David A. *Habakkuk*

B.D. and Th.M., Fuller Theological Seminary; Ph.D., University of St. Andrews. Assistant in Hebrew, Fuller Theological Seminary, 1950-1954; Lecturer in Hebrew and Old Testament, St. Andrews University, 1955-1956; Assistant Professor of Biblical Studies, Westmont College, 1957-.

Hughes, Philip Edgcumbe *I and II Corinthians*

B.D., University of London; M.A. and D. Litt., University of Capetown. Secretary of Church Society, London; Member, Studiorum Novi Testamenti Societas. Lecturer of Mortlake Parish, London, 1957-. Editor of *The Churchman,* of *The International Reformed Bulletin* and of *Scripture Union Notes.* Author of *Scripture and Myth* and *The Divine Plan for Jew and Gentile.*

Kerr, David W. *Numbers*

B.D. and Th.M., Westminster Theological Seminary; candidate, Th.D., Harvard University. Member, Committee on Articles of Faith, General Assembly of Presbyterian Church in Canada, 1950-1953. Professor of Old Testament, Gordon Divinity School, 1953-.

Kitchen, Kenneth A. *Proverbs*

B.A., University of Liverpool (School of Archaeology and Oriental Studies). Tyndale Lecture in Biblical Archaeology, 1957. Assistant Lecturer in Egyptian and Coptic, University of Liverpool, 1957-.

Kuhn, Harold B. *Deuteronomy*

S.T.B., S.T.M., Ph.D., Harvard University. Refugee ministry in Germany; Supply Preacher and Missioner, United States Army and Air Force in Europe. Professor of Philosophy of Religion, Asbury Theological Seminary, 1944-.

Ladd, George E. *Matthew*

Th.B., Gordon College; B.D., Gordon Divinity School; Ph.D., Harvard University. Olson Memorial Lectures, Bethel Theological Seminary, 1956. Professor of Biblical Theology, Fuller Theological Seminary, 1950-. Author of *The Blessed Hope* and *Crucial Questions About the Kingdom of God.*

Laurin, Robert B.   *Job*

B.D., and ThM., Fuller Theological Seminary; Ph.D., University of St. Andrews. Teaching fellow (Hebrew), Fuller Theological Seminary, 1953-1954; Associate Professor of Old Testament, California Baptist Theological Seminary, 1956-.

Leupold, H. C.   *Genesis*

B.D., Chicago Lutheran Seminary; D.D., Capital University. Professor of Historical Theology, Martin Luther Seminary, 1922-1929; Professor of Old Testament, Evangelical Lutheran Theological Seminary 1929-. Secretary, Committee on the Revision of the Liturgy. Author of *Exposition of Genesis, Exposition of Daniel, Exposition of Zechariah,* and *Exposition of Ecclesiastes.*

Mantey, Julius Robert   *New Testament Backgrounds*

Th.D. and Ph.D., Southern Baptist Theological Seminary; D.D., Union University. President, American Research Society. Professor of New Testament, Northern Baptist Theological Seminary, 1925-. Author of *A Manual Grammar of the Greek New Testament, A Hellenistic Greek Reader,* and *Was Peter a Pope?*

Martin, William J.   *I and II Samuel*

Th.B., Princeton Theological Seminary, B.A. and M.A., Trinity College, Dublin; Ph.D., University of Leipzig. Rankin Lecturer in Semitic Languages, Department of Archaeology and Oriental Studies, University of Liverpool, England. Author of *Stylistic Criteria and the Analysis of the Pentateuch* and *Dead Sea Scroll of Isaiah.*

Mickelsen, A. Berkeley   *Hebrews*

B.A., M.A., and B.D., Wheaton College; Ph.D., University of Chicago. Associate Professor of Bible, Wheaton Graduate School, 1951-.

Morris, Leon   *Colossians*

B.D. and M.Th., University of London; Ph.D., Cambridge University. Vice Principal, Ridley College, Melbourne, 1945-. Author of *The Wages of Sin, The Story of the Cross,* and *The Lord from Heaven.*

Müller, Jac. J.   *Philemon*

B.A. and M.A., University of Stellenbosch; Th.D., Free University of Amsterdam; D.D., University of South Africa. Former Scriba and Assessor, Dutch Reformed Church (South Africa); National Chairman, Students' Christian Association of South Africa, 1954-. Professor of New Testament, Theological Seminary, Stellenbosch, 1946-. Author of *When Christ Comes Again, The Essence of Christian Sectarianism,* and *Grace to You* (a commentary on six epistles of Paul).

Packer, James I.   *Galatians*

B.A., M.A., and Ph.D., Corpus Christi College, Oxford. Senior Tutor, Tyndale Hall, Bristol, 1954-. Author of *Fundamentalism and the Word of God,* and a new translation of Luther's *Bondage of the Will.*

Paine, Stephen W.   *James*

B.A., Wheaton College; M.A. and Ph.D., University of Illinois. President, National Association of Evangelicals, 1949, 1950. Lay Vice President, Wesleyan Methodist Church,

1947-. Professor of Greek and President, Houghton College, 1937-. Author of *Toward the Mark, Studies in the Book of James,* and *The Christian and the Movies.*

Payne, J. Barton   *Leviticus*

B.A. and M.A., University of California; B.D., San Francisco Theological Seminary; Th.M. and Th.D., Princeton Theological Seminary. National Secretary, Evangelical Theological Society, 1955-. Professor of Old Testament, Wheaton Graduate School, 1954-. Author of *An Outline of Hebrew History, Hebrew Vocabularies,* and *Theology of the Old Testament.*

Pentecost, J. Dwight   *I and II Thessalonians*

B.A., Hampden-Sydney College; Th.M. and Th.D., Dallas Theological Seminary. Professor of Bible and Doctrine, Philadelphia College of Bible, 1948-1955; Assistant Professor of New Testament Literature and Exegesis, 1955-1958, and Acting Professor, 1958-, Dallas Theological Seminary. Author of *Things to Come.*

Pfeiffer, Charles F.   *Joshua*

B. A., Temple University; B.D., Theological Seminary of the Reformed Episcopal Church; Ph.D., Dropsie College. Moderator, General Synod of the Reformed Presbyterian Church, 1947-1948, 1958-1959. Lancaster School of the Bible 1950-1954; King's College, 1953-1955; Professor of Old Testament, Moody Bible Institute, 1955-1959; Associate Professor of Old Testament, Gordon Divinity School, 1959-. Author of *The Dead Sea Scrolls, The Book of Leviticus, The Book of Genesis,* and *Between the Testaments.*

Price, Ross E.   *Micah*

B.D., M.A. and D.D. (hon.), Pasadena College; M.Th., McCormick Theological Seminary. Dean, Division of Graduate Studies in Religion, Pasadena College, 1948-. Author of *Youth and Worship, John Wesley on Pulpit Oratory,* and *Crisis Experiences in the Greek New Testament* (co-author).

Renwick, A. M.   *I and II Chronicles*

B.D., M.A., and D.D., University of Edinburgh; D. Litt., Lima University, Peru. Moderator, Free Church of Scotland, 1930; Head, St. Andrew's College, Lima, 1926-1943; Head, Instituto-Chileno-Britanico, 1943-1944; Professor of Church History, Free Church College, Edinburgh, 1944-. Author of *The Story of the Church.*

Ries, Claude A.   *Jonah*

B.D., Winona Lake School of Theology; M.A., Syracuse University; Th.D., Northern Baptist Theological Seminary. Chairman, Division of Theology and Christian Education, 1952-, Vice President, 1955-, Houghton College.

Robinson, Donald W. B.   *Obadiah*

B.A., University of Sydney; B.A. and M.A., Cambridge University. Senior Lecturer, Moore Theological College, New South Wales, 1952-, and Vice Principal, 1959-. Author of *Josiah's Reform and the Book of the Law.*

Roehrs, Walter R.   *Ezekiel*

B.A., Concordia College; M.A., Concordia Seminary, St. Louis; Ph.D., University of Chicago. Dean of Religion, Concordia Teachers College, 1941-1944. Professor of Old Testament, Concordia Seminary, 1944-. Editor, *Concordia Theological Monthly,* 1952-.

Roth, Robert Paul   *I and II Peter*

B.D., Northwestern Lutheran Seminary; M.A., University of Illinois; Ph.D., University of Chicago. Professor of New Testament and Dean of Graduate School, Lutheran Theological Southern Seminary, 1953-.

Schultz, Arnold C.   *Amos*

B.A. and M.A., University of Chicago; B.D. and Th.D., Northern Baptist Theological Seminary. Professor of Bible, Bluffton College, 1937-1944. Professor of Old Testament, Northern Baptist Theological Seminary, 1944-. President of Middle District of General Conference of Mennonites, 1943-1944.

Smith, Wilbur M.   *The Book and the Books*

D.D., Evangelical Theological College, Dallas, Texas, 1932. Professor of English Bible, Moody Bible Institute, 1937-47, and Fuller Theological Seminary, 1947-. Editor, *Peloubet's Select Notes on the International Sunday School Lessons*. Author of more than a dozen books, including *Therefore Stand, This Atomic Age and the Word of God*, and *Chats from a Minister's Library*.

Steele, Francis Rue   *The Old Testament*

B.A., Cornell University; M.A. and Ph.D., University of Pennsylvania. Assistant Professor of Assyriology, University of Pennsylvania, 1948-1953. Annual Professor, American Schools of Oriental Research, Baghdad, 1949-1950, 1951-1952. Presently Home Secretary for North America of the North Africa Mission.

Suffern, Richard Munn   *Titus*

B.A., Haverford College; B.D., New Brunswick Theological Seminary; Ph.D., Johns Hopkins University. Professor, New Testament Greek and Church History, Biblical Seminary in New York, 1944-.

Tenney, Merrill C.   *Revelation*

Th.B., Gordon College; M.A., Boston College; Ph.D., Harvard University. Professor of New Testament, Wheaton College, 1943, and Dean of Graduate School, 1947-. President, Evangelical Theological Society, 1951. Author of *Resurrection Realities, John: The Gospel of Belief, Galatians: the Charter of Christian Liberty, The Genius of the Gospels*, and *Interpreting Revelation*.

Thompson, J. A.   *I and II Kings*

M.Sc., B. A. and B.Ed., University of Queensland; B.D. and M.A., University of Melbourne. Director, Australian Institute of Archaeology, 1946-1956; Lecturer in Semitics, Melbourne University, 1950-1956; Lecturer, Old Testament Studies, Baptist Theological College, Sydney, 1957-. Author of *Archaeology and the Old Testament* (in two parts).

Thomson, J. G. S. S.   *Jeremiah and Lamentations*

B.A., Oxford University; B.D., M.A. and Ph.D., University of Edinburgh. Lecturer, Department of Hebrew and Semitic Languages, University of Edinburgh, 1950-1956; Professor of Old Testament, Columbia Theological Seminary, 1956-1959. Author of *The Praying Christ*.

Unger, Merrill F.   *Exodus*

B.A. and Ph.D., The Johns Hopkins University; Th.M. and Th.D., Dallas Theological Seminary. Professor of Greek, Gordon College, 1947-1948; Lecturer in Archaeology,

Gordon Divinity School, 1947-1948; Professor of Old Testament and Chairman, Old Testament and Semitics, Dallas Theological Seminary, 1948-. Author of *Introductory Guide to the Old Testament, Archaeology and the Old Testament, Biblical Demonology, Israel and the Aramaeans of Damascus,* and *Unger's Bible Dictionary.*

Verhoef, P. A. *Ruth*

M.A., University of South Africa; M.Th., Theological Seminary, Stellenbosch; Th.D., Free University, Amsterdam. Professor of Old Testament, Stellenbosch, 1950-. Author of *What about the Jews, The Apocrypha* (a translation), and *A Study on the Prophecies of Nahum and Habakkuk.*

Vos, Johannes G. *Song of Solomon*

B.A., Princeton University; Th.B., Princeton Theological Seminary; Th.M., Westminster Theological Seminary. Chairman, Department of Biblical Literature, Religious Education and Philosophy, Geneva College, Beaver Falls, 1954-. Author of *The Scottish Covenanters: Their Origins, History and Distinctive Doctrines.*

Wallace, David H. *Between the Testaments*

B.A., University of Southern California; B.D. and Th.M., Fuller Theological Seminary; Ph.D., University of Edinburgh. Graduate study, University of Basel. Instructor, California Baptist Theological Seminary, 1956-1957; Fuller Theological Seminary, 1957-1958. Associate Professor of Biblical Theology, California Baptist Theological Seminary, 1959-.

Wessel, Walter W. *I and II Timothy*

B.A. and M.A., University of California (Los Angeles); Ph.D., University of Edinburgh. Western Baptist Seminary, 1953-1956; Professor of Bible, North American Baptist Seminary, 1956-.

Woudstra, Marten H. *Zechariah*

B.D., Th.M. and candidate for Th.D., Westminster Theological Seminary. Graduate work, Free Reformed University, Amsterdam, and Dropsie College. Associate Professor of Old Testament, Calvin Theological Seminary, 1955-.

Wright, J. Stafford *Ezra and Nehemiah*

B.A. and M. A., Cambridge University. Vice-Principal, Tyndale Hall, Bristol, 1930-1945 and Principal, 1951-. Senior Tutor, Oak Hill College, London, 1945-1951. Author of *Man in the Process of Time.*

Yates, Kyle M., Sr. *Hosea*

B.A. and M.A., Wake Forest College; Th.M. and Th.D., Southern Baptist Theological Seminary; Ph.D., University of Edinburgh; D.D., Mercer University. Member, Committee on Revision of the American Revised Edition of the Bible (R.S.V.), 1938-. Professor of Old Testament and Hebrew, Southern Baptist Theological Seminary, 1922-1942; Professor of Bible, Baylor University, 1956-. Author of *Solomon to Malachi, Essentials of Biblical Hebrew,* and *Preaching from Great Bible Chapters.*

Young, Edward J. *Zephaniah*

B.A., Leland Stanford Junior University; B.D. and Th.M., Wesminster Theological Seminary; Ph.D., Dropsie College. Professor of Old Testament, Westminster Theological Seminary, 1946-. Moderator, Orthodox Presbyterian Church, 1956. Editor, Tyndale Old Testament commentaries. Author of *Introduction to the Old Testament, The Prophecy of Daniel, Studies in Isaiah,* and *Arabic for Beginners.*

Young, Fred E. *Judges*

B.A., Wm. Jewell College; B.D., Crozer Seminary; Ph.D., Dropsie College. Graduate study, University of Pennsylvania, New York University and Brandeis University. Professor of Biblical Philology, Central Baptist Theological Seminary, 1955-.

Young, G. Douglas *Daniel*

B.Sc., Acadia University; B.D. and S.T.M., Faith Theological Seminary; Ph.D., Dropsie College. Professor of Old Testament Literature and Dean of Trinity Seminary (Evangelical Free Church of America), 1957-. Moderator, General Assembly of Bible Presbyterian Churches. Director of Israel-American Institute of Bible Studies. Author of *A Grammar of the Hebrew Language* and *Ugaritic Concordance.*

Index by Bible Books